BIOGRAPHICAL DICTIONARIES

SECOND
SUPPLEMENT

ROBERT B. SLOCUM

BIOGRAPHICAL DICTIONARIES

AND

RELATED WORKS

An International Bibliography of Collective Biographies,
Bio-bibliographies, Collections of Epitaphs, Selected
Genealogical Works, Dictionaries of Anonyms and Pseudonyms,
Historical and Specialized Dictionaries, Biographical
Materials in Government Manuals, Bibliographies of Biography,
Biographical Indexes, and Selected Portrait Catalogs

SECOND SUPPLEMENT

GALE RESEARCH COMPANY • THE BOOK TOWER • DETROIT, MICHIGAN 48226

Library of Congress Cataloging in Publication Data

Slocum, Robert B
  Biographical dictionaries and related works.

  1. Biography--Bibliography. I. Title.
Z53.1.S55 Suppl.   016.92   67-27789
ISBN 0-8103-0973-4 (v. 1)
ISBN 0-8103-0974-2 (v. 2)

Printed in the United States of America

CONTENTS

CONTENTS

CONTENTS

CONTENTS

CONTENTS

PREFACE

The second supplement to *Biographical Dictionaries and Related Works* (1967; first supplement, 1972) contains approximately 3,800 entries. Taken together the three volumes now include well over 12,000 entries.

The arrangement of the bibliography follows that of the first two volumes (the user should consult the prefaces of these volumes for detailed statements on the arrangement of material, alphabetization, etc.); numbering of items picks up where the first supplement left off. One change in the second supplement has been the moving of dictionaries of anonyms/pseudonyms from National or Area Biography to a more logical position—the section on Language and Literature of the Biography by Vocation division.

In a few places in the present supplement you will note that certain numbers in the normal sequence of successively numbered items have not been used. Such omissions occur because the final editing revealed (too late for renumbering) out-of-place items. They were carried over to their proper positions; the maneuver resulted in the use of letters *a, b,* etc. at the end of some whole numbers.

Whatever other imperfections may be found in this supplement are, of course, the responsibility of the compiler. Perhaps too the latter should apologize for the fact that the user must use indexes in the three volumes to arrive at a complete picture of the material under particular countries, subjects, etc. A combined set of indexes at the end of the second supplement was seriously considered, but the pressure of time and other projects led the compiler to postpone this rather sizeable task to a possible future, entirely revised multi-volume edition.

I am indebted to and grateful for the expert assistance of Paul P.W. Cheng, East Asia Librarian, Cornell University Libraries, in matters bibliographical concerning the Far East. My colleagues, Ved P. Kayastha and Anthony Niseteo have continued their early interest in this bibliography and have made me aware of

PREFACE

useful works in their respective fields of concentration—South and Western Asia and the Romance and Slavic worlds. Other people in the Cornell community have been helpful on various points. And Mrs. Betty Rush, typist (and husband William) have been with this project from its start 10 years ago and have performed nobly on its behalf. Robert C. Thomas and Annie M. Brewer of the Gale Research Company staff have kept me from foundering on editorial and technical shoals. To the named and unnamed above and to my patient wife, Christine, my sincerest thanks.

BIBLIOGRAPHICAL NOTE

Below are listed works that were useful in the compilation of the second supplement to *Biographical Dictionaries and Related Works*. They, of course, extend the lists found in the main volume (1967) and the first supplement (1972):

American reference books annual. 1970- . Littleton, Colo., Libraries Unlimited.

Andersen, Axel. *Introduktion til håndbogslitteraturen.* [bind] 2: p. 159-447. København, Bibliotekscentralen, 1968.

Arnott, James Fullerton. *English theatrical literature, 1559-1900; a bibliography incorporating Robert W. Lowe's A bibliographical account of English theatrical literature published in 1888,* by James Fullarton Arnott and John William Robinson. London, Society for Theatre Research, 1970.

Bako, Elemer. *Guide to Hungarian studies.* Stanford, Calif., Hoover Institution Press, 1973. 2v.

Berlin. Preussische Staatsbibliothek. Orientalische Abteilung. *Katalog der Handbibliothek der Orientalischen Abteilung.* Leipzig, O. Harrassowitz, 1929.

Bibliografia dell'età del Risorgimento. In onore di Alberto M. Ghisalberti. Vol. 1. Firenze, L.S. Olschki, 1971.

Bibliographie der Wörterbucher erschienen in der Deutschen Demokratischen Republik, Sozialistischen Republik Rumänien, Tschechoslowakischen Sozialistischen Republik, Ungarischen Volkrepublik, Union der Sozialistischen Sowjetrepubliken, Volkrepublik Bulgarien, Volksrepublik Polen ... 1945-1961—1971-197 . Warszawa, Wydawn. Naukowo-Techniczne, 1965-197 . (6v. as of 1974).

Biographisches Lexikon der hervorragended Ärtze aller Zeiten und Völker ... Hrsg. von August Hirsch. 2 Aufl. ... 1. Bd. (p. [xi]-xxxvii: *Verzeichniss biographischer und bibliographischer Sammelwerke und Schriften).* Berlin, Wein, Urban & Schwarzenburg, 1929.

BIBLIOGRAPHICAL NOTE

Blake, John B. *Medical reference works, 1679-1966; a selected bibliography.* John B. Blake and Charles Roos, editors. Chicago, American Library Association, 1967.

Bosa, Réal. *Les ouvrages de référence du Québec; bibliographie analytique compilée sous la direction de Réal Bosa.* Quebec, Ministère des affaires culturelles du Québec, 1969.

Craig, Hardin. *A bibliography of encyclopedias and dictionaries dealing with military, naval and maritime affairs, 1577-1971.* 4th ed. rev. and corr. Houston, Tex., Dept. of History, Rice University, 1971.

Czerny, Robert. *Einführung in die tschechoslowakische Bibliographie bis 1918; praktische Übersicht der Informationsquellen.* Baden-Baden, V. Koerner, 1971.

Douai, France. Bibliothèque communale. *Catalogue méthodique des imprimés de la Bibliothèque communale de Douai,* par Benjamin Rivière. Douai, Impr. E. Linez, 1897-1911. 5v. (See especially: v.4, p. 21-32, "Biographie française").

Duignan, Peter. *Guide to research and reference works on Sub-Saharan Africa.* Edited by Peter Duignan. Compiled by Helen F. Conover and Peter Duignan with the assistance of Evelyn Boyce, Leselotte Hofmann, Karen Fung. Stanford, Calif., Hoover Institution Press, Stanford University [1971 or 2].

Eller, Povl. *Historisk ikonografi.* København, Dansk historisk faellesforening, 1964.

Enciclopedia de orientación bibliográfica. Director: Tomás Zamarriego. Barcelona, J. Flors, 1964-65. 4v.

Fairbank, John King. *Japanese studies of modern China; a bibliographical guide to historical and social-science research on the 19th and 20th centuries,* by John King Fairbank, Masataka Banno and Sumiko Yamamoto. Cambridge, Mass., Harvard University Press, 1971. (1971 reissue; first published in 1955).

France, Armée. État-major. Service historique. *Guide bibliographique sommaire d'histoire militaire et coloniale française.* Sous la direction de René Couret. Paris, Impr. nationale, 1969.

Geoghegan, Abel Rodolfo. *Obras de referencia de América Latine; repertorio selectivo y anotado de enciclopedias, diccionarios, bibliografías, repertorios biográficos, catálogos, guías, anuarios, índices, etc.* Buenos Aires, Impr. Crisol, 1965.

BIBLIOGRAPHICAL NOTE

Gillett, Theresa. *Catalog of Luso-Brazilian material in the University of New Mexico Libraries.* Compiled by Theresa Gillett and Helen McIntyre. Metuchen, N.J., Scarecrow Press, 1970.

Goonetileke, H.A.I. *A bibliography of Ceylon; a systematic guide to the literature on the land, people, history and culture published in Western languages from the sixteenth century to the present day ...* Zug, Switzerland, Inter Documentation Co., 1970. 2 v.

Hancock, P.D. *A bibliography of works relating to Scotland, 1916-1950.* Edinburgh, University Press, 1959-60. 2v.

Harvard University. Library. *Canadian history and literature; classification schedule, classified listing by call number, alphabetical listing by author or title, chronological listing.* Cambridge, Mass., Published by the Harvard University Library; distributed by the Harvard University Press, 1968.

Harvard University. Library. *Reference collections shelved in the Reading Room and Acquisitions Department. Classification schedule, classified listing by call number, author and title listing.* Cambridge, Mass. Published by the Harvard University Library; distributed by the Harvard University Press, 1970.

Hoppe, Hermann. *Katalog der wichtigeren, hervorragenden und besseren Schriften deutscher Literatur welche in den Jahren 1801 bis Ende 1868 erschienen sind.* St. Petersburg, Verlag von Hermann Hoppe, 1871.

Instituto Nacional del Libro Espanol. *Libros españoles; catálogo ISBN.* Madrid, I. N. L. E. y Agencia Española del International Standard Book Number (ISBN), 1973.

Jackson, Richard. *United States music; sources of bibliography and collective biography.* Brooklyn, Institute for Studies in American Music, Dept. of Music, Brooklyn College of the City University of New York, c1973.

Johnsen, Arne Odd. *Norsk militaerhistorisk bibliografi.* Redaktører: Arne Odd Johnsen, Gunnar Christie Wasberg. Medarbeider: Tom Arbo Høeg. Utgitt av Forsvarets krigshistoriske avdeling. Oslo, Gyldendal Norsk forlag, 1969.

Lenox Hill Publishing (Burt Franklin). *Bibliographies and reference works; bibliographies, bio-bibliographical repertoires, catalogues of libraries and special collections, inventories of archives, palaeography, diplomatics, historiography, encyclopedias, literary histories, concordances, author lexicons.* New York, 1972.

BIBLIOGRAPHICAL NOTE

Mailloux, Pierre. *Bibliographie annotée des ouvrages de réference en usage au Bureau de la bibliographie rétrospective*. Montreal, Bibliothèque nationale du Québec, Ministère des affaires culturelles, 1973.

McCabe, James Patick. *Critical guide to Catholic reference books.* Littleton, Colo., Libraries Unlimited, 1971.

Michaux,. Monique. *Iconographie militaire française. Bibliographie.* Chateau de Vincennes, 1971- . At head of title: Ministère d'État chargé de la défense nationale. État-major de l'Armée de terre. Service historique.

Mitchell, Sir Arthur. *A contribution to the bibliography of Scottish topography*, by the late Sir Arthur Mitchell and C.G. Cash. Vol. II. Edinburgh, Printed at the University Press by T. and A. Constable for the Scottish Historical Society, 1917.

Newberry Library, Chicago. *Catalogue of the Greenlee Collection, the Newberry Library, Chicago.* Compiled by Frederick Holden Hall. Boston, G.K. Hall Co., 1970. 2v.

Nunn, Godfrey Raymond. *Asia; a selected and annotated guide to reference works.* Cambridge, Mass., M.I.T. Press, 1971.

Pagel, Julius Leopold. *Historisch-medicinische Bibliographie für die Jahre 1875-1896.* Berlin, S. Karger, 1898. (In: Mann, Gunter, comp. *Internationale Bibliographie zur Geschichte der Medizin, 1875-1901.* Hildesheim, New, York, G. Olms, 1970. p. [1]-386).

Paris, Bibliothèque nationale. Département des périodiques. *Répertoire national des annuaires français, 1958-1968 et supplément signalant les annuaires reçus en 1969.* par Monique Lambert, conservateur au Département des périodiques. Paris, Bibliothèque nationale, 1970.

Pauly, Alphonse. *Bibliographie des sciences médicales.* London, D. Verschoyle, 1954. (See especially columns 47-87).

Perales Ojeda, Alicia. *Las obras de consulta (reseña histórico-crítica).* México, Universidad Nacional Autónoma de México, Facultad de Filosofía y Letras, Seminario de Consulta y Bibliografía, 1962.

Pohler, Johann. *Bibliotheca historico-militaris; systematische Übersicht der Erscheinungen aller Sprachen auf dem Gebiete der Kriege und Kriegswissenschaft seit Erfindung der Buchdruckerkunst bis zum Schluss des Jahres 1880.* New York, Burt Franklin, 1961. 4v. (Reprint of the 1887-1899 (Cassel, Ger. ed.) Vol. 4:

Lebensbeschreibungen, Denkwürdigkeiten und Breifwechsel: Sam melwerke (p. 1-71).

Riedlová, Marie. *Biografické slovníky. Soupis publikací z fondů Státní vědecké knihovny v Olomouci.* V Olomouci, Státní vědecka Knihovna, 1969.

Royal Commonwealth Society. Library. *Subject catalogue of the Library of the Royal Empire Society, formerly Royal Colonial Institute.* By Evans Lewin. London, 1930-37. 4v.

Royal Commonwealth Society. Library. *Subject catalogue of the Royal Commonwealth Society, London.* Boston, Mass., G.K. Hall Co., 1971. 7v. (Supplements the *Subject Catalogue of the Library of the Royal Empire Society* and the *Biography catalogue of the Library of the Royal Commonwealth Society*).

Saffroy, Gaston. *Bibliographie des almanachs et annuaires administratifs, ecclésiastiques et militaires français de l'Ancien Régime et des almanachs et annuaires généalogiques et nobiliaires du XVIe siècle à nos jours.* Paris, Librairie Gaston Saffroy, 1959.

Saffroy, Gaston, *Bibliographie généalogique, héraldique et nobiliaire de la France des origines à nos jours, imprimés et manuscrits.* Tome I: *Généralitiés ...* Paris, Librarie Gaston Saffroy, 1968.

Sharma, Hari Dev. *Indian reference sources; an annotated guide to Indian reference books,* by H.D. Sharma, S.P. Mukherji, L.M.P. Singh. Varanasi, Indian Bibliographic Centre, 1972.

Sheahan, Eileen. *Moving pictures; a bibliography of selected reference books for the study of the film with emphasis on holdings in the Libraries of the Yale University.* New Haven, Yale University Library, 1973.

Smith, Sam B. *Tennessee history, a bibliography.* Sam B. Smith, editor and compiler. Luke H. Banker, assistant editor. Knoxville, University of Tennessee Press, 1974.

Stein, Henri. *Manual de bibliographie générale (Bibliotheca bibliographica nova).* Paris, A. Picard, 1897.

Stock, Karl Franz. *Bibliographien, Sammelbiographien und andere bibliographische Hilfsmittell der Steiermark. Arbeit aus der Universitätsbibliothek Graz.* Bad Godesberg, Bundesforschungsanstalt fur Landeskunde und Raumordnung, 1969.

Stock, Karl Franz. *Personalbibliographien österreichischer Dichter und Schriftsteller von den Anfängen bis zur Gegenwart. Mit Auswahl ein-*

BIBLIOGRAPHICAL NOTE

schlägiger Bibliographien, Nachschlagewerke, Sammelbiographien, Literaturgeschichten und Anthologien. Von Karl F. Stock, Rudolf Heilinger, Maryiène Stock. Pullach bei München, Verlag Dokumentation, 1972.

Têng, Ssŭ-yü. *An annotated bibliography of selected Chinese reference works.* Compiled by Ssŭ-yü Têng and Knight Biggerstaff. 3d. ed. Cambridge, Mass., Harvard University Press, 1971.

Totok, Wilhelm. *Handbuch der bibliographischen Nachschlagwerke.* Hrsg. von Wilhelm Totok, Karl-Heinz Weimann and Rudolf Weitzel. 4., erw., völlig neu bearb. Aufl. Frankfurt a. M. Klostermann, 1972.

Walford, Albert John. *Guide to reference material.* 3d ed. London, Library Association, 1973- . (Vol. 1: *Science & Technology.--*)

Watson, Gayle Hudgens. *Columbia, Ecuador and Venezuela; an annotated guide to reference materials in the humanities and social sciences.* Metuchen, N.J., Scarecrow Press, 1971.

Wernigg, Ferdinand. *Quellen zur Wiener Biographie. Versuch einer praktischen Einleitung.* (In *Festscrift zum hundertjährigen Bestehen der Wiener Stadtbibliothek 1856-1956.* Wien, 1956. p. 125-153).

UNIVERSAL BIOGRAPHY

UNIVERSAL BIOGRAPHY

BIBLIOGRAPHY, INDEXES, PORTRAIT CATALOGS

8272 ADLERBERTH, ROLAND
Människan i blickpunkten: memoarer och biografier; ett
urval. Lund, Bibliotekstjänst, 1965. 54 p. 21cm. (Biblio-
tekstjänsts bokurval, nr. 51) 'People in the limelight'; memoirs and biographies, a selection. A bibliography of prominent personalities of the world.

8273 BEUGHEM, CORNELIUS À, fl. 1678-1710.
Bibliographia historica, chronologica & geographica novissima, perpetuo continuanda, sive, Conspectus primus catalogi
librorum historicorum, chronologicorum, & geographicorum;
tam sacrorum quam profanorum &c. ... Accedit ejusdem Museum seu Syllabus iconum sive imaginum illustrium à saeculo
hominum, quae in ejus Musaeo spectantur. Amstelaedami,
Apud Janssonio-Waesbergios, 1685. 788 p. 14 x 8cm. Beughem's (bookseller's) catalog of European books to the year 1651
contains an index of portraits of European celebrities, including
263 physicians.

8274 BIBLIOTHECA BIOGRAPHICA; reichhaltige Sammlung von
Monographien zur Geschichte einzelner Personen und
Familien ... Aus dem antiquarischen Bücherlager von Paul
Neubauer in Köln am Rhein. [Köln, 1889?] 341 p. Biographical
library; a bibliography of monographs on the history of individ-
uals and families (primarily European) held by the bookseller
Paul Neubauer in Cologne.

8275 BIOGRAFISKE AVISARTIKLER 1940-55. København, Bibliotekscentralen, 1974. 141 p. 21cm. "Faellesregister til
biografiske artikler i Avis-kronik-index 1940-55." An index to
biographical articles (universal in coverage) in Danish newspapers.

8276 BIOGRAPHICAL DICTIONARIES MASTER INDEX; a guide to
more than 725,000 listings in over fifty current who's whos
and other works of collective biography. Dennis La Beau [and]
Gary C. Tarbert, editors. 1st ed., 1975-1976. Detroit, Gale

Research Co. [1975]   3 v.   29cm.   Indexes primarily contemporary American and Canadian biographical dictionaries,
with a few of international scope added.

8277   BROWN, WILLIAM GARROTT, 1868-1913.
A list of portraits in the various buildings of Harvard University.   Prepared under the direction of the late Justin Winsor.
Cambridge, Mass., Library of Harvard University, 1898. 52 p.
25cm. (Harvard University. Library. Bibliographical contributions, no. 53) Cover title. Serves also as a biographical dictionary (ca. 400 brief notes) of famous world figures and scholars.

8278   CHICOREL INDEX TO BIOGRAPHIES. Edited by Marietta
Chicorel. 1st ed. New York, Chicorel Library Pub. Corp.,
1974. 2 v. 26cm. (Chicorel index series, v. 15-15A) A bibliography of individual biographies and autobiographies in subject
index form (persons and professions or activities, A-Z).

8279   CONSTABLE, WILLIAM GEORGE, 1887-
Collections of historical portraits and other forms of iconography in Great Britain. London, Published for the Historical
Association by G. Bell, 1934. 23 p. 22cm. (Historical Association leaflet no. 96) A guide to the portrait collections of museums, libraries, etc. in Great Britain.

8280   CONTEE, CLARENCE GARNER, 1929-
A Pan-African index to Current biography, 1940-1970 [by]
Clarence G. Contee with the assistance of Sharon Harley.
Monticello, Ill., Council of Planning Librarians, 1976. 20 p.
28cm. (Exchange bibliography, 951) An index to biographies of
Black notables in the volumes of Current biography.

8281   DRUGULIN, W., Leipzig.
Verzeichniss von sechstausend Portraits von Aerzten,
Naturforschern, Mathematikern, Reisenden und Entdeckern,
welche zu den beigesetzten Preisen von dem Leipziger Kunst-
Comptoir (W. Drugulin) zu beziehen sind. Wiesbaden, M. Sändig, 1973. 175 p. 21cm. Reprint of the Leipzig, 1863 ed. List
of 6,000 portraits of physicians, scientists, methematicians,
travelers and discoverers; a bookseller's sales catalog and bibliography of portraits.

8282   FALK, BYRON A
Personal name index to the New York times index, 1851-1974
[by] Byron A. Falk, Jr. [and] Valerie R. Falk. Succasunna, N.
J., Roxbury Data Interface [1976-   v. 26cm. Contents: v. 1. A.
An index to an index. When complete this index will present
about 3,000,000 name entries. Vol. 1 contains ca. 90,000 name
citations.

8283   GAETANI, PIER ANTONIO, conte
        Museum Mazzuchellianum; seu, Numismata virorum doc-
trine praestantium quae apud J. M. Comitem Mazzuchellum
Brixiae servantur, a P. A. de Comitibus Gaetanis ... edita
atque illustrata. Accedit versio Italica studio Equitis C. Mei
elaborata. Venetiis, A. Zatta, 1761-63. 2 v. illus. folio.
The numismatic collection of Count G. M. Mazzuchelli which
features portraits of various scholars, humanists, etc. of early
modern Europe.

8284   [GAY, JULES] 1807-187-?
        Iconographie des estampes à sujets galants et des portraits
de femmes célèbres par leur beauté, indiquant les sujets, les
peintres, les graveurs de ces estampes, leur valeur et leur
prix dans les ventes, les condamnations et prohibitions dont
certaines d'entre elles ont été l'objet. Par M. le c. d'I ***.
Genève, J. Gay et fils [etc.] 1868. 791 columns. 23cm. A catalog of engravings, including portraits of women famous for
their beauty and a dictionary of the engravers represented in
the catalog.

8285   INDEX BIO-BIBLIOGRAPHICUS NOTORUM HOMINUM. Edidit
        Jean-Pierre Lobies. François-Pierre Lobies adjuvante.
Cooperaverunt Marianne Seydoux [et al.] cum plurimus redac-
toribus. Osnabrück, Biblio Verlag, 1972-   v. 26cm. Issued in fascicles. Bio-bibliographical index of famous people;
part B (v. 1) is a bibliography of bio-bibliographical dictionaries,
collections, etc.; pt. C (Corpus alphabeticum)--5 vols. as of
1976--is the index itself.

8286   IRELAND, NORMA (OLIN) 1907-
        Index to women of the world from ancient to modern times;
biographies and portraits. Westwood, Mass., F. W. Faxon Co.,
1970. xxcviii, 573 p. 24cm. (Useful reference series, no. 97)
945 collective biographies (published in Great Britain and the
United States) analyzed to yield an index to the biographies and,
in some instances, portraits of ca. 13,000 women.

8287   KERR, LAURA J   1916-
        Who's where in books: an index to biographical material.
Ann Arbor, Michigan Association of School Librarians, 1971.
vi, 313 p. 23cm. Indexes 4,060 names from 551 collective biographies. Designed primarily for the school library.

8288   LEYDEN. RIJKSUNIVERSITEIT.
        Icones Leidenses; de portretverzameling van de Rijksuni-
versiteit te Leiden. Leiden, Universitaire Pers Leiden, 1973.
304 p. ports. 27cm. "Samengesteld in opdracht van de Stich-
ting Historische Commissie voor de Leidse Universiteit." With
a summary in English. A volume of portraits and accompanying
biographical notes (for lesser known figures) in chronological

arrangement of the collections of Leyden University. As more
modern times are approached (17th-20th centuries) the portraits
and the data are predominantly for Dutch nationals (especially
scholars, and professors at the University). Alphabetical approach thru' index.

8289   MARQUIS-WHO'S WHO, INC.
       Marquis who's who publications: index to all books, 1975.
Chicago, Marquis Who's Who, inc., 1975. 500+ p. A combined
index to the over 200,000 biographies in the current editions of
Who's who in America, Who was who in America, the various
regional who's who for the United States, Who's who in finance
and industry, Who's who in the world, Who's who in government
and Who's who of American women. An earlier edition (488 p.)
appeared in 1974?

8290   NOHRSTRÖM, KYLLIKKI
       Elämäkertoja ja muistelmia; kirjaluettelo. Helsinki,
Suomen Kirjastoseura, 1964. 151 p. 21cm. A bibliography
of biography and memoirs; international.

8291   ORSINI, FULVIO, 1529-1600.
       Imagines et elogia virorum illustrium et eruditorum, ex
antiquis lapidibus et nomismatibus expressa, cum annotationi-
bus ex bibliotheca Fulvii Ursini. Romae, A. Lafrerii Formeis,
1570. 110 p. illus. folio. Portraits and praise of famous and
learned men expressed in the medallions, etc. held in the library of Fulvio Orsini.

8292   OVERSEAS DIRECTORIES, who's who, press guides, year
       books and overseas periodical subscriptions. London,
Publishing and Distributing Co.   v. illus. 22cm. Began ca.
1960? A bibliography of directories, who's who volumes, etc.

8293   PARIS. BIBLIOTHÈQUE NATIONALE. DÉPARTEMENT DES
       ESTAMPES.
       Catalogue de la collection des portraits français et étrang-
ers conservée au Département des estampes de la Bibliothèque
nationale. Paris, G. Rapilly, 1896-1911. 5 v. in 3. 26cm.
"Commencé par Georges Duplessis, continué par Georges Riat
[P. A. Lemoisne, Jean Laran]" Catalog of the collection of
French and foreign portraits kept in the Dept. of Prints and Engravings of the National Library in Paris. H. Stein (Manuel de
bibliographie générale) considers the work of only mediocre
value, since it actually contains only a partial listing of the portraits (the Dept. of Prints and Engravings possesses only a portion of the portraits in the Library). An alphabetical listing
(which stops at Louise-Mauron?--continuation and supplement
on slips?).

8294   PARIS. BIBLIOTHÈQUE NATIONALE. DÉPARTEMENT DES ESTAMPES.
Inventaire de la collection Lallement de Betz. Rédigé par Auguste Flandrin. Augmenté d'un table alphabétique et d'une notice par Joseph Guibert. Paris, J. Dumoulin, 1903. ix, 788 p. 26cm. Inventory-catalog of the topographical pieces and portraits in the Lallement de Betz Collection of the Dept. of Prints and Engravings, French National Library.

8295   PARIS. BIBLIOTHÈQUE NATIONALE. DÉPARTEMENT DES ESTAMPES.
Les portraits aux crayons des XVIe et XVIIe siècles conservés à la Bibliothèque nationale (1525-1646) Notice, catalogue et appendice, par Henri Bouchot. Paris, H. Oudin, 1884. 412 p. 2 ports. 27cm. Portrait sketches of the 16th-17th centuries (1525-1646) conserved in the Dept. of Engravings of the French National Library; a catalog.

8296   PORTRAITS OF WOMEN LOAN EXHIBITION FOR THE BENEFIT OF ST. JOHN'S GUILD AND THE ORTHOPAEDIC HOSPITAL, from the 1st to the 24th of Nov., 1894, National Academy of Design, New York. [New York, Knickerbocker Press, 1894] 106 p. 20cm. A catalog of portraits of famous women.

8297   PRAGUE. MĚSTSKÁ KNIHOVNA.
Postavy a osobnosti (seznam životopisů a osobních monografié) sestavil Zdeněk Gintl. Praha, Tiskem a nákladem Melantricha, 1936. 836 p. 26cm. (Spisy Knihovny hlav. mésta Prahy. Řidi dr. Jan Thon. čis. 20) Completed and edited after Gintl's death by Miroslav Herman. Preface and epilogue in Czech and French. A bibliography of biographies of famous figures and personalities in world civilization.

8298   ROYAL COMMONWEALTH SOCIETY. LIBRARY.
Subject catalogue of the Royal Commonwealth Society, London. Boston, G. K. Hall, 1971. 7 v. 37cm. Supplements the Subject catalogue of the Library of the Royal Empire Society and the Biography catalogue of the Library of the Royal Commonwealth Society. Bibliography of biography (collective and individual) will be found in vol. 7, p. 1-177. Material obtained before 1959-60 will also be found in the Biographical catalogue of the Royal Commonwealth Society, 1961 (q. v.)

8299   SASKATCHEWAN. PROVINCIAL LIBRARY. BIBLIOGRAPHIC SERVICE DIVISION.
People in books; a bibliography. Regina, 1972. 206 p. 28cm. Cover title. A catalog of biographical and autobiographical works held by the Library.

8300 SILVERMAN, JUDITH, 1933-
  Index to young readers' collective biographies: elementary and junior high school level. 2d ed. New York, R. R. Bowker, 1975. xxv, 332 p. 27cm. Helps locate biographical data about 5,890 individuals in ca. 500 collective biographies. 1st ed. appeared in 1970.

8301 SOROK LET ZhZL; izd., vyshedshie v izd-ve "Mol. gvardiia: katalog, 1933-1973. Otv. red.-sost. S. N. Semanov; pre-disl. G. Pomerantsevoi, S. Semanova. 2. dop. i ispr. izd. Moskva, Mol. Gvardiia, 1974. 284 p. illus. 21cm. (Zhizn' zamechatel'nykh liudei; seriia biografii, vyp. 14 (546)) A bibliography of the over 500 biographies of world-famous figures of the past (chiefly) which have appeared in the Soviet series: Zhizn' zamechatel'nykh liudei; seriia biografii. The first ed. of this catalog (q. v.), covering the years 1933-1963, appeared in 1963 and was entered under: Zhizn' zamechatel'nykh liudei: seriia biografii. (Indexes).

8302 STANFORD UNIVERSITY. LIBRARIES. DIVISION OF SPECIAL COLLECTIONS.
  Portraits; a catalog of the engravings, etchings, mezzotints, and lithographs presented to the Stanford University Library by Dr. and Mrs. Leon Kolb. Compiled by Susan V. Lenkey. [Stanford, Calif.] Stanford University, 1972. 373 p. port. 28cm. A catalog-bibliography of 1,647 portrait prints useful as a resource for general historical studies; identification of the subjects of the portraits was established from the Library of Congress Catalog of Printed Books and H. W. Singer's Allgemeiner Bildniskatalog.

8303 STANIUS, ELLEN J
  Index to short biographies: for elementary and junior high grades. Metuchen, N. J., Scarecrow Press, 1971. 368 p. 22cm. Analyzes under biographee the contents of 455 collective biographies, 295 of them published since 1960.

8304 [YOUNG, HENRY]
  A list of bibliographies of authors (literary and scientific) London, Printed by Hazell, Watson & Viney [1932] 8 numb. 1. 21cm. Includes bibliographies of bio-bibliographies of individual writers (largely British)

DICTIONARIES, BIO-BIBLIOGRAPHIES, ETC.

General (All Periods)

8305 ADAMS, RUSSELL L.
  Great Negroes, past and present. Illustrated by Eugene Winslow. Edited by David P. Ross. 3d ed. Chicago, Afro-

Am Pub. Co., 1969. ix, 212 p. illus., ports. 29cm. Over 175 brief one or two-page biographies of important Negroes from ancient to modern times and from many professions. Aimed at the juvenile audience.

8306   [ALBRECHT, ERDMANN HANNIBAL]
Gallerie der Menschen nach alphabetischer Ordnung; oder, Bilderbuch für die Jugend. Leipzig, 1798. 1 v. illus., ports. An illustrated dictionary of biography for young people.

8307   ALBUQUERQUE, ARCY TENÓRIO CAVALCANTE DE, 1899-
Cem benfeitores da humanidade, por A. Tenorio d'Albuquerque. Belo Horizone [Brazil] Grande Loja de Minas Gerais, 1969. 3 v. illus., ports. 23cm. 100 benefactors of mankind from Hippocrates to Albert Schweitzer. Collective biography; no definite arrangement. Written from a Masonic point of view.

8308   ARIEL, AHARON
Lekhsikon historii. Tel-Aviv, 1964. 2 v. (1380 columns) 24 plates. 27cm. Edited by A. Ariel and Joshua Prawer. A dictionary of history (in Hebrew) that includes many biographical sketches.

8309   BARBIER, ANTOINE ALEXANDRE, 1765-1825.
Examen critique et complément des dictionnaires historiques les plus répandus, depuis le Dictionnaire de Moréri, jusqu'à la Biographie universelle inclusivement. Genève, Slatkine Reprints, 1970. iv, vii, 493 p. 23cm. Reprint of the Paris edition of 1820. Vol. 1 only (A-J) was prepared and published. A complement to the historical dictionaries from Moréri's La grand dictionnaire historique to the Biographie universelle (Michaud) with chiefly biographical entries.

8310   BARRÉ, LOUIS, 1799-1857.
Nouvelle biographie classique, contenant, jusqu'à l'année 1840, la liste des principaux personnages de tous les pays, ainsi que leurs actions et leurs ouvrages les plus remarquables. 2. éd. Paris, Firmin. Didot frères, 1844. 555 p. 12.⁰ A 3d (unpaged) ed. was issued in 1845. A biographical dictionary covering personalities of all countries and times to the year 1840.

8311   BASKIN, WADE
Dictionary of Black culture, by Wade Baskin and Richard N. Runes. New York, Philosophical Library, 1973. 493 p. 22cm. Includes biographical sketches, more than 160 of them being of Black women.

8312   BILDNISSE DER BERÜHMTESTEN MENSCHEN ALLER VÖLKER
UND ZEITEN. Ein Supplement-Kupferband zu jedem bio-
graphischen Wörterbuche, besonders zu dem Conversations-
Lexicon. Zwickau, Schumann, 1819-32. 7 v. (chiefly ports.)
4.º An earlier edition, comprising 420 portraits, issued in 35
"suites" (or fascicles), appeared in Saarbrucken (18--?-1822)
Portraits of the most famous individuals of all nations and periods; a supplement to biographical dictionaries, especially the
Conversations-Lexicon.

8313   BIOGRAFIA UNIVERSAL; galeria de hombres célebres. Cua-
dros basquejados por varios autores. 2. ed. Barcelona,
B. Bastinos, 1880. viii, 504 p. 160 illus. 8.º Universal biography; gallery of famous men, with biographical sketches by
various authors.

8314   BLANCHARD, PIERRE, 1772-1856.
Neuer Plutarch; oder, Kurze Lebensbeschreibung der
berühmtesten Männer und Frauen aller Nationen von den alt-
esten bis auf unsere Zeiten. Nach dem Franzosischen des
Peter Blanchard neu hrsg., verm. und fortsegetzt von Friedrich Kraft. Pesth, C. A. Hartleben, 1815. 6 v. in 3. ports.
16.º The new Plutarch; or, Brief biographies of the most famous men and women of all nations from the most ancient times
to the present.

8315   CHAMBER'S BIOGRAPHICAL DICTIONARY. Edited by J. O.
Thorne. Rev. ed. New York, St. Martin's Press, 1969,
c1968. vii, 1432 p. 25cm. The first ed. appeared in 1962
(v, 1432 p.)

8316   CHESNEL DE LA CHARBOUCLAIS, LOUIS PIERRE FRANÇOIS
ADOLPHE, marquis de, 1791-1862.
Dictionnaire des armées de terre et de mer; encyclopédie
militaire et maritime ... Contenant dans le texte plus de 1700
eaux-fortes ... par Jules Duvaux. 3. éd. Paris, A. Le Chevalier, 1865. 2 v. illus. 26cm. 1st ed. issued in 1862-64
(2 v.: 1320 p.) A general military and naval dictionary which
does include biographical sketches.

8317   COLLINS DICTIONARY OF PEOPLE AND PLACES. [Editors:
James Mallory and others] London, Collins, 1975. 383 p.
illus. 21cm. On spine: Dictionary of people and places. A
gazetteer/biographical dictionary.

8318   COLLINS GEM DICTIONARY OF BIOGRAPHY. Edited by James
Mallory. London, Collins, 1971. 511 p. 12cm.

8319 DANTÈS, ALFRED LANGUE, 1830-1891.
Tables biographiques et bibliographiques des sciences, des
lettres et des arts, indiquant les oeuvres principales des
hommes les plus connus en tous pays et à toutes les époques,
avec mention des éditions les plus estimées. Paris, Delaroque
frères, 1866. vii, 646 p. 22cm. A bio-bibliography; biographical and bibliographical tables of the world's great scientists,
litterateurs and artists.

8320 DICCIONARIO BIOGRÁFICO DE HOMBRES ILUSTRES.
Madrid, Blass, 1920. 1 v. 32.º A general biographical
dictionary of famous people in history; listed in Mansell but not
in Palau y Dulcet.

8321 DICCIONARIO UNIVERSAL DE HISTORIA Y DE GEOGRAFÍA,
por Francis de Paula Mellado [et al.] Madrid, Mellado,
1846-50. 8 v. 26cm. Vol. 8: Supplement. Universal dictionary of history and geography; with biographical entries.

8322 DICCIONARIO UNIVERSAL DE HISTORIA Y DE GEOGRAFÍA.
Contiene: primero. --Historia, propiamente dicha.--se-
gundo. --Biografía universale.--tercero. --Mitología. --cuar-
to. --Geografía antigua y moderna. Obra dada a luz en España
por una sociedad de literatos distinguidos, y refundida y aum.
considerablemente para su publicación en México con noticias
históricas, geográficas, estadísticas, y biografías sobre las
Américas en general, y especialmente sobre la República Mexicana, por Lucas Alaman [et al.] México, Tip. de Rafael, 1853-
55. 7 v.

---- ----Appendice. Coleccion de artículos relativos a la República Mexicana, por José María Andrade [et al.] México,
Impr. de J. M. Andrade y F. Escalante, 1855-56. 3 v. A universal dictionary of history and geography. Part 2 is a dictionary of biography. An expansion of the Spanish edition of the
same title (Madrid, 1846-50) with biography of the Americas and
Mexico.

8323 DICTIONARY OF WORLD HISTORY. General editor: G. M. D.
Howat. Advisory editor: A. J. P. Taylor. London, Nelson, 1973. xxvii, 1720 p. 28cm. Includes 8,000 biographical
entries.

8324 DICTIONNAIRE UNIVERSEL ET CLASSIQUE D'HISTOIRE ET
DE GÉOGRAPHIE, comprenant l'histoire proprement dite,
la biographie universelle, la mythologie, la géographie ancienne
et la géographie moderne. Sur le plan du dictionnaire de
Bouillet, d'après les écrivains les plus estimés et les ouvrages
les plus accredités de toutes les époques et de toutes les nations. Et mis en ordre par un société de professeurs. Nouv.
éd. Bruxelles, Parent, 1853-54. 4 v. Universal and classical

dictionary of history and geography, comprising ... universal biography, mythology, etc.

8325 DIPLOMATICHESKIĬ SLOVAR'. Glavnaia red.: A. A. Gromyko [i dr. Pererab. i dop. izd.] Moskva, Izd-vo politicheskoi lit-ry, 1971-73. 3 v. 22cm. Dictionary of diplomacy (world politics) Includes biographies of leading diplomats of all countries and periods. Contents. --t. 1. A-L. --t. 2. --K-P. --t. 3. R-IA.

8326 DIZIONARIO BIOGRAFICO. Complemento di ogni dizionario. A cura di Antonio Bollani [et al.] Milano, Ceschina, 1973. 559 p. 36 plates. 24cm. A universal biographical dictionary; brief data--three to ca. 70 lines; three columns to a page.

8327 DUFOUR, ANTOINE, d. 1509 Les vies des femmes célèbres. Texte établi, annoté, et commenté par G. Jeanneau. Genève, Droz, 1970. lxi, 214 p. plates. 18cm. (Textes littéraires français, 168) A compilation of some 94 short biographies of women famous in antiquity in the Bible and in medieval times.

8328 DUPINEY DE VOREPIERRE, JEAN FRANÇOIS MARIE BERTET, 1811-1879. Dictionnaire de noms propres; ou, Encyclopédie illustrée de biographie, de géographie, d'histoire et de mythologie. Paris, M. Lévy, 1876-1893. 2 v. (800 p.) illus. 4.º Issued in parts; no more published. Covers A-Maupas, with supplement which covers A-Fuster. A dictionary of proper names: biography, geography, history & mythology.

8329 DURIVAGE, FRANCIS ALEXANDER, 1814-1881. A popular cyclopedia of history, ancient and modern, forming a copious historical dictionary of celebrated institutions, persons, places, and things; with notices of the present state of the principal cities, countries and kingdoms of the known world to which is added a chronological view of memorable events ... Hartford, Conn., Case, Tiffany & Burnham, 1841. 717 p. illus. 24cm.

8330 ENCICLOPEDIA BIOGRÁFICA DE LA MUJER. Barcelona, Ediciones Garriga, 1967-68. 2 v. illus., ports. 26cm. Contents. --1. A-H. --2. I-Z. Biographical encyclopedia of women.

8331 ENCICLOPEDIA MILITARE; arte, biografia, geografia, storia, tecnica militare. Milano, Il Popolo d'Italia, 1927-33. 6 v. illus., ports. 30cm. "Direttore: Alberto Malatesta." A dictionary of military science that includes military biography. Emphasis is on Italy.

men ... Done from the best authors, and very useful for schools
... 2d ed.: to which is added a supplement. London, Printed
for H. Rhodes [etc.] 1708. [378] p. 16cm.

8346   THE HUNDRED GREATEST MEN; portraits of the one hundred
           greatest men of history, reproduced from fine and rare en-
        gravings. London, S. Low, Marston, Searle, and Rivington,
        1879-80. 8 v. in 4. ports. 37cm. Biographical sketches ac-
        company the 100 portraits. Contents.--v. 1-2. Poetry and art.
        --v. 3-4. Religion and philosophy.--v. 5-6. History and sci-
        ences.--v. 7-8. Politics and industry.

8347   JAVORSKY, FRIEDRICH
           Lexikon der Wiener Strassennamen. Wien, Verlag für
        Jugend und Volk [1964] 281 p. 20cm. Dictionary of Viennese
        street-names with explanation of the names or accompanying bio-
        graphical sketches of persons after whom streets are named.

8348   JOHNSON, SELBY
           Who are they? A biographical reference book. 2d rev. ed.
        Exeter [Eng.] Wheaton, 1965. v, 271 p. 20cm. A juvenile ref-
        erence work containing ca. 1,000 entries; universal biography.
        1st ed. (1945) mistakenly entered under: Johnson, Stanley Currie
        by LC (1948 supplement)?

8349   JOUBERT, LÉO, b. 1826, ed.
           Dictionnaire de biographie générale, depuis les temps les
        plus anciens jusqu'en 1870. Publié sous la direction de Léo Jou-
        bert. Paris, Firmin Didot frères, 1870. 3, 748 p. 20cm. A
        dictionary of general biography from ancient times to 1870.

8350   KYOTO KYŌIKU DAIGAKU. FUZOKU MOMOYAMA CHŪGAKKŌ.
           Poketto Nihon sekai jimmei jiten. Kyoto, 46 (1971) 643,
        23, 26 p. port. 15cm. Cover title: Nihon sekai jimmei jiten.
        Edited by Takeshi Nakamura. A universal Japanese biographi-
        cal pocket dictionary.

8351   [LACROIX, JEAN FRANÇOIS DE] 18th cent.
           Dictionnaire portatif des femmes célèbres, contenant l'his-
        toire des femmes savantes, des actrices, & généralement des
        dames qui se sont rendues fameuses dans tous les siècles, par
        leurs aventures, les talens, l'esprit & le courage. Nouv. éd.,
        rev. & considérablement augm. Paris, Belin [etc.] 1788. 2 v.
        18cm. First published in 1769 under title: Dictionnaire histor-
        ique portatif des femmes célèbres. "Pocket" dictionary of fa-
        mous women.

8352   LANGE, WILHELM, 1875-1950.
           Genie, Irrsinn und Ruhm. Genie-Mythus und Pathographie
        des Genies [von] Wilhelm Lange-Eichbaum [und] Wolfram Kurth.

6., völlig umgearb. und weitere 800 Quellen verm. Aufl. München, E. Reinhardt, 1967. 764 p. 24cm. Genius, madness and fame. "Pathographien" (p. [303]-559) includes 558 biographical sketches ("pathographies") of persons of varying fame, especially their pathological histories.

8353   LEVATI, AMBROGIO, 1788-1841.
Dizionario biografico cronologico, diviso per classi, degli uomini illustri de tutti i tempi e di tutte le nazioni. [Classe V: Donne illustri] Milano, N. Bettoni, 1821. 3 v. in 1. 22cm. Each vol. has also separate t.p. Chronological biographical dictionary divided by classes, of the famous people of all times and countries. Class 5: Women.

8354   LE LIVRE D'OR DES PEUPLES. Plutarque universel, biographies des célébrités de tous les pays et de tous les siècles, par l'élite des écrivains français sous la direction de Pierre Lefranc. Paris [1865-74] 6 v. illus., ports. 30cm. 'The book of gold of the peoples.' The universal Plutarch; a collection of short biographies of the famous of all countries and eras.

8355   LÓPEZ MUÑIZ, GREGORIO, 1899-
Diccionario enciclopédico de la guerra. Director: Gregorio López Muñiz. Madrid, [Editorial Gloria, 1954-[67?] 13 v. illus., ports. 27cm. Vols. 2-13 have imprint: Madrid, Editorial Gesta. An encyclopedic dictionary of military science which includes biography.

8356   LÜHE, HANS EGGERT WILLIBALD VON DER, b. 1800, ed.
Militair-Conversations-Lexikon. Bearb. von mehreren deutschen Officieren. Leipzig, C. Brüggemann und O. Wigand, 1833-41. 8 v. 22cm. Vols. 5-8 have imprint: Leipzig, Adorf. A biographical and historical encyclopedia of military affairs. Danish ed. issued in 1837-1843 under title: Militair conversationslexicon.

8357   THE McGRAW-HILL ENCYCLOPEDIA OF WORLD BIOGRAPHY; an international reference work. New York, McGraw-Hill [1973] 12 v. illus. 29cm. 5,000 biographies of persons famous in world civilization are included.

8358   MACKEY, ALBERT GALLATIN, 1807-1881.
Encyclopedia of Freemasonry. Rev. and enl. by Robert I. Clegg. With illus. and descriptive index. With supplemental vol. by H. L. Haywood. [In three vols. including Freemasonry and similar rites from ancient times to after World War II] Chicago, Masonic History Co., 1946. 3 v. illus., ports. 26cm. Contents.--v. 1. A-Lyons, Congress of.--v. 2. M-Zurthose.-- v. 3 (supplemental) A-Zuni Indians. First ed. issued in 1874-78. Includes biographies. Cover title: Mackey's revised encyclopedia of Freemasonry.

8359   MAUNDER, SAMUEL, 1785-1849.
        The biographical treasury; a dictionary of universal biog-
        raphy. 13th ed., reconstructed, thoroughly rev. and partly re-
        written with above 1000 additional memoirs and notices, by Wil-
        liam L. R. Cates. London, Longmans, Green, Reader, and
        Dyer, 1866. 1154 p. 18cm. Contains ca. 10,000 biographies.
        A later ed. was issued in 1873?

8360   MILLOR, ALEC
        Dictionnaire de la Franc-maçonnerie et des Franc-maçons.
        Paris, P. Belfond, 1971. 323 p. illus. 22cm. (Collection
        "Sciences secrètes") Dictionary of Freemasonry and of Free-
        masons. Masonic biographies (A-Z): p. 227-321.

8361   MELZI, GIAN BATTISTA, 1844-1911.
        Il novissimo Melzi; dizionario enciclopedico italiano in due
        parti: I. Linguistica. II. Scientifica. 35. ed. rev. e aggiornata.
        Milano, Vallardi, 1963. 2 v. illus., ports. 21cm. Part 2 of
        this Italian encyclopedic dictionary includes biographical sketches
        (accompanied for the most part by portraits) of world-famous
        persons.

8362   NEUER PLUTARCH; oder, Biographien und Bildnisse der
        berühmtesten Manner und Frauen aller Nationen und Stände
        von den älteren bis auf unsere Zeiten. 4. Aufl. Mit Verwendung
        der Beiträge des Freiherrn E. von Feuchtersleben, neu bearb.
        von Aug. Diezmann. Wien, Hartleben, 1858. 4 v. ports. The
        new Plutarch; or, Biographies and portraits of the most famous
        men and women of all nations and classes from the older times
        to the present. The first edition appeared in 1853 in Pest (5
        vols., each of which contained 120 portraits).

8363   NISENSON, SAMUEL
        Illustrated minute biographies; 150 fascinating life-stories of
        famous people from the dawn of civilization to the present day,
        dramatized with portraits and scenes from their lives. Designed
        and illustrated by Samuel Nisenson. Text by William A. DeWitt.
        [Rev. ed.] New York, Grosset & Dunlap [1970] 160 p. illus.,
        ports. 28cm. (Illustrated true books) One-page biographies of
        150 well-known musicians, scientists, philosophers, writers,
        artists, soldiers, and political leaders from ancient to present
        times, in biographical dictionary arrangement.

8364   PALM, GEORG FRIEDRICH, d. 1798.
        Lebensbeschreibungen und Charakterschilderungen berühm-
        ter Männer. Hannover, Hahn [1796?]-98. 3 v. Issued also un-
        der title: Gallerie merkwürdiger Männer aus der älteren und
        neueren Geschichte, in a 5-vol. ed. (Hannover, Hahn, 1794-98)
        Lives and character sketches of famous men of all epochs and
        nations.

8365   PEETERS, JULIEN GUILLAUME, b. 1828.
        Petit biographie universelle. Anvers, Ve. Lamot-Jacobs,
        1858. 112 p. 16.° A small dictionary of universal biography.

8366   POMORSKA ENCIKLOPEDIJA. [Redakcija: direktor: Miroslav
            Krleža. Glav. redaktor: Mate Ujević] Zagreb, Izd. i nakl.
        Leksikografskog zavoda FNRJ, 1954-64. 8 v. illus., ports.
        30cm. Tinted celluloid spectacles for steroscopic viewing in
        pocket of vol. 1. A nautical encyclopedia in Serbo-Croatian
        which has many of the features of a general encyclopedia, but
        which, of course, concentrates on things naval. In this regard
        it contains many biographical sketches of world-renowned men
        of the sea: navigators, naval officers, marine scientists, etc.

8367   POPP, GEORG, ed.
            Die Mächtigen der Erde; Herrscher, Staatsmänner, Bürger
        und Abenteurer, die den Lauf der Geschichte mitbestimmten.
        Hrsg. von Georg Popp. [3. Aufl.] Wurzburg, Arena-Verlag
        [1959] 474 p. 8.° (Das Grosse Arena-Buch) The mighty of
        the earth, brief biographical sketches of rulers, statesmen,
        citizens and adventurers who decided the course of history.

8368   PRIGENT, SIMONE
            Qui est-ce? Par Simone Prigent et Georges Simoni. Illus.
        de Philippe Daure et Jacques Poirier. [Paris] Hachette [1971]
        185 p. col. illus., ports. 29cm. (Les Beaux livres Hachette)
        A juvenile biographical and picture-dictionary; universal cover-
        age.

8369   RIVERAIN, JEAN, 1907-
            Dictionnaire des marins célèbres des temps lointains à
        nos jours. Paris, Larousse, 1967. 157 p. illus. 24cm. Dic-
        tionary of famous naval figures from ancient times to the pres-
        ent.

8370   ROBINSON, HERBERT SPENCER
            The dictionary of biography [by] Herbert Spencer Robinson
        and a staff of editors. Rev. and enl. ed. Totowa, N. J., Row-
        man and Littlefield, 1975. xii, 530 p. 21cm. Includes 4000
        paragraph-length biographies of world figures, 125 more than
        the 1st ed. (Garden City, N. Y., Doubleday, 1966—xii, 500 p.)

8371   ROGERS, JOEL AUGUSTUS, 1880-1966.
            World's great men of color. Edited with an introd., com-
        mentary, and new bibliographical notes by John Henrik Clarke.
        New York, Macmillan [1972, c1946-47] 2 v. ports. 22cm.
        Includes 200 biographies of great men of the Negro race: 116
        (chronologically arranged) fairly extensive biographies in the
        main text, 84 brief sketches on pages 538-563 of vol. 2 ("Great
        men of color in brief").

8372   ROHDEN, PETER RICHARD, 1891-1942, ed.
        Menschen, die Geschichte nachten; viertausend Jahre Welt-
geschichte in Zeit- und Lebensbilder. 2. verm. Aufl. Hrsg.
von Peter Richard Rohden. Wien, L. W. Seidel, 1933. 2 v.
plates, ports. 23cm. 1st ed., 1931, edited in 3 v. by Rohden
and Georg Ostrogorsky. Men who made history; 4,000 years of
world history in biography.

8373   SANDBERGER, FRANK, 1941-
        Prosopographie zur Geschichte des Pyrrhos. Stuttgart
[Druck: Universität Stuttgart] 1970. v, 216 p. 21cm. Inaug.-
Diss. —Ludwig-Maximillans-Universität, Munich. A biographi-
cal dictionary (85 names) of contemporaries of Pyrrhus, King of
Epirus: his friends, associates, enemies, etc., many of whom
are prominent in Greek history from ca. 320 to 270 B. C.

8374   SEDEÑO, JUAN
        Suma de varones ilustres. En la qual se contienen muchas
sentencias y grandes hazañas y cosas memorables de 224 em-
peradores, reyes y capitanos que ha havido de todas tiempos,
per orden del A. B. C. y las fundaciones de muchos reynos y
provincias. Toledo, J. Rodriguez, 1590. 360 l. 28cm. Compendium of famous men; containing the opinions and great exploits of 224 emperors, kings and captains of all epochs. First
published in 1551.

8375   SEGOVIA, ANGEL MARÍA
        Figuras y figurones. Biografías de los hombres que más
figuran actualmente en España, historia, vida y milagros de
cada uno de ellos, con una relación exacta de las virtudes,
méritos, vicios, apostasías, casualidades que más contribuyeron
á su elevación. Madrid, 1877-78. 2 v. ports. folio. 'Figures
and pretentious characters.' Biographies of men who achieved
prominence in Spain, in history and an account of how they a-
chieved their station.

8376   SEGYE INMYŎNG TAESAJŎN. The world biographical diction-
        ary. Seoul [1973] [8], 2214 p. 27cm. In Korean. Edited
by Kim Mong-p'il.

8377   SHINSHŪ SEKAI JIMMEI JITEN. Tokyo, Fuji Shobo, 48 [1973]
        430 p. 19cm. A Japanese universal biographical diction-
ary. Edited by Kenji Yanai.

8378   SIDDONS, JOACHIM HAYWARD, 1801?-1885.
        The military encyclopedia; a technical, biographical, and
historical dictionary, referring exclusively to the military
sciences, the memoirs of distinguished soldiers, and the narratives of remarkable battles, by J. H. Stocqueler [pseud.]
London, W. H. Allen, 1853. vi, 362 p. 23cm.

8379 GLI STATI E LE CIVILTÀ. [Enciclopedia monografica della
      storia] Bologna, N. Zanichelli [1961] 760 p. illus., ports.
      24cm. (AZ panorama) An encyclopedia of world history that
      includes a biographical dictionary of historical personages on
      pages [545]-753.

8380 THEATRUM PONTIFICUM, IMPERATORUM, REGUM, DUCUM,
      PRINCIPUM, pace et bello illustrium. Antwerpiae, Apud
      Petr. de Jode, 1651. 1 v. 170 ports. 4.º 'The theater of
      Popes, emperors, kings, dukes, princes, famed in peace and
      war.' A universal biographical collection with 170 portraits.

8381 VICENS VIVES, JAIME
      Mil figuras de la historia. Hombres ilustres. Vidas famo-
      sas. Documentos iconográficos seleccionadas en los archivos
      del Instituto Gallach. Semblanzas biográficas originales de ,
      Jaime Vicens Vives. Barcelona, Instituto Gallach de Librería y
      Ediciones [1944] 2 v. illus., 1,000 ports. 31cm. One thousand
      figures of history; a collection of portraits and brief biographies.
      Vol. 1: From the origins of history to the Renaissance. Vol. 2:
      From the Spanish Empire to the 20th century.

8382 VINCENT, BENJAMIN, 1818-1899.
      A dictionary of biography, past and present, containing the
      chief events in the lives of eminent persons of all ages and na-
      tions, preceded by the biographies and genealogies of the chief
      representatives of the royal houses of the world. Edited by
      Benjamin Vincent. Detroit, Gale Research Co., 1974. 641 p.
      geneal. tables. 23cm. Reprint of the 1877 ed. (London, Ward,
      Lock) which was a revision of Haydn's Universal index of biog-
      raphy, published in 1870 in series: The Haydn series.

8383 VITE E RITRATTI DEGLI UOMINI PIÙ CELEBRI DI TUTTI I
      TEMPI E DI TUTTE LE NAZIONI. Compilazione diretta da
      Salvatore Muzzi. Bologna, Ajudi, 1864. 1 v. 4.º Lives and
      portraits of the most famous men of all times and nations.

8384 VOJNA ENCIKLOPEDIJA. Glavni urednik: Nikola Gaževič.
      Glavni redaktori: Ilič Predrag [i dr.] Redaktor za ilustra-
      cije: Miroslav Petrović. Pero crteži: Franjić Adalbert. Kolor-
      dijapozitivi: Cikota Bogoljub, Đorđević Miodrag, Koman Mitja.
      Fotografije: Matić Natalija. Kartografija: Mardešić Petar [i
      dr.] 2. izd. Beograd, Redakcija Vojne enciklopedije, 1970-75.
      10 v. illus., ports. 30cm. A dictionary of military science in
      Serbo-Croatian that includes a large number of biographies of
      military figures in world history. First edition issued beginning
      in 1958.

8385 WEBSTER'S BIOGRAPHICAL DICTIONARY. Springfield,
      Mass., G. & C. Merriam Co. [1972] xxxvi, 1697 p. 26cm.

"A Merriam Webster." Latest edition. A dictionary of names of noteworthy persons, with pronunciations and concise biographies. First published in 1943 (?)

8386 WHO DID WHAT. The Mitchell Beazley illustrated biographical dictionary. 5000 men and women who have shaped the world's destiny. [General editor: Gerald Howat] Rev. ed. London, M. Beazley, 1975. 387 p. illus., ports. 26cm. With over 1,000 portraits, photographs, etc. American edition (New York, Crown Publishers, 1974 — 1st ed. ?) issued under title: Who did what; the lives and achievements of the 5,000 men and women — leaders of nations, saints and sinners, artists and scientists — who shaped our world (383 p.).

8387 [WICHMANN, CHRISTIAN AUGUST] d. 1807.
Geschichte berühmter Frauenzimmer nach alphabetischer Ordnung ... zusammengetragen. Leipzig, Cnobloch, 1772-75. 3 v. Covers A-L (or M?) only. No more published. British Museum lists alphabet as Aban's Gemahlin to Lydia, die Heilige. A dictionary of famous women in world history.

8388 WILHELM, THOMAS A
A military and naval encyclopaedia, comprising ancient and modern military and naval technical terms, biographical sketches of distinguished officers, and historical accounts of all North American Indians, as well as ancient warlike tribes; also the military and naval battles, from the earliest period to the present time. Compiled from the best authorities of all nations, with an appendix containing the Articles of war. By Thomas Wilhelm. [San Francisco?] Headquarters, Eighth Infantry, U. S. Army, 1879. 1386 p. 17cm. The 2d ed. (1881) does not include the biographical sketches.

8389 WITTSTOCK, ALBERT
Autodidakten-Lexikon. Lebensskizzen derjenigen Personen aller Zeiten und Völker, welche auf aussergewöhnlichem Bildungs- und Entwicklungsgange sich zu einer hervorragenden Bedeutung in Kunst and Wissenschaft emporgearbeitet haben. 1.-4. Lieferung. Hrsg. unter Mitwirkung von mehreren Fachgelehrten von Albert Wittstock. Leipzig, Mentzel, 1874-75. xv, 230 p. 8.° No more published? Biographical sketches of those persons of all times and nations who attained special prominence in art and science through their unusual training and development.

8390 WOODWARD, BERNARD BOLINGBROKE, 1816-1869.
Encyclopedia of chronology, historical and biographical, by B. B. Woodward and William L. R. Cates. London, Longmans, Green, 1872. viii, 1487 p. 23cm. A dictionary of universal history and biography.

8391 YI, SŎNG-HO
  Segye inmyŏng taesajŏn. Seoul, 1960-   v.
  27cm. A general biographical dictionary (in Korean).

Classical World

8392 ANTHON, CHARLES, 1797-1867
  A classical dictionary: containing an account of the principal proper names mentioned in ancient authors and intended to
elucidate all the important points connected with the geography,
history, biography, mythology, and fine arts of the Greeks and
Romans. Together with an account of coins, weights, and
measures, with tabular values of the same. New York, Harper
& Bros., 1857. xv, 1451 p. 26cm.

8393 ENCYKLOPEDIE ANTIKY. Zprac. kol. za ved. Ludvíka
  Svobody. 1. vyd. Praha, Academia, 1973. 741 p. illus.
25cm. Encyclopedia of the ancient world; includes biographical
sketches of classical personalities.

8394 ERRANDONEA, IGNACIO, ed.
  Diccionario del mundo clásico. Barcelona, Editorial
Labor, 1954. 2 v. (xix, 1810 p.) illus. 23cm. Contents.--t. 1.
A-I.--t. 2. J-Z. Dictionary of the classical world, including
many biographical sketches.

8395 FUCHS, JOHAN WILHELMUS
  Classics illustrated dictionary. Translated from the Dutch
by Livia Visser-Fuchs. General English editing and adaptations by Kathleen Bolton. New York, Oxford University Press
[1974] 200 p. illus. 22cm. Translation of Klassiek vademecum.
Includes brief biographical entries of figures in Greco-Roman
and early Christian civilization.

8396 LAMER, HANS, 1873-1939.
  Wörterbuch der Antike, mit Berücksichtigung ihres Fort-
wirkens, in Verbindung mit Ernst Bux and Wilhelm Schöne verfasst von Hans Lamer. 6., völlig neu bearb. Aufl. Stuttgart, A.
Kröner [c1963] xii, 639 p. 18cm. (Kröners Taschenausgabe, Bd.
96) A dictionary of antiquity that includes biographical entries.

8397 LEMPRIERE, JOHN, 1765?-1824.
  Bibliotheca classica; or, A dictionary of all the principal
names and terms relating to the geography, topography, history,
literature, and mythology of antiquity and of the ancients; with a
chronological table. By J. Lempriere. Rev. and corr. and divided ... into three parts. By Lorenzo L. Da Ponte and J. D.
Ogilby. 10th American ed., greatly enl. in the historical department, by L. L. Da Ponte. New-York, W. E. Dean, 1838. 803 p.
24cm. At head of title: Dean's sterotype edition. First published in 1788. Part II: History, antiquities, &c. (p. 320-667) in-

cludes numerous biographical sketches. Later published (1949) under title: Classical dictionary of proper names mentioned in ancient authors (q.v.).

8398   LEMPRIERE, JOHN, 1765?-1824.
      Classical dictionary of proper names mentioned in ancient authors, with a chronological table. New ed. rev. with additions, and a short notice of J. Lempriere by F. A. Wright. New York, E. P. Dutton, 1949. xxviii, 675 p. 20cm. First published in 1788 under title: Bibliotheca classica. In large part a biographical dictionary.

8399   LÜBKER, FRIEDRICH HEINRICH CHRISTIAN, 1811-1867.
      Reallexikon des klassischen Altertums. 8. vollständig umgearb. Aufl., hrsg. von J. Geffcken und E. Ziebarth in Verbindung mit B. A. Müller, unter mitwirkung von W. Liebenam [et al.] Leipzig, B. G. Teubner, 1914. xii, 1152 p. plans. 26cm. Dictionary of classical antiquity, with biographical sketches included.

8400   MAŁY SŁOWNIK KULTURY ANTYCZNEJ. Grecja, Rzym. Pod red. Lidii Winniczuk. [Wyd. 2.] Warszawa, Wiedza Powszechna, 1968. 445 p. illus. 21cm. (Wydawnictwa popularno-encyklopedyczne) Dictionary of classical antiquities and culture: Greece & Rome. 1,900 entries, including biographies.

8401   OLSHAUSEN, ECKART
      Prosopographie der hellenistischen Königsgesandten. Lovanii, 1974-   v. 24cm. (Studia Hellenistica, 19

Contents.--T. 1. Von Triparadeisos bis Pydna.

The royal functionaries of Hellenistic rulers (from Macedonia to Egypt) from 321 B. C. forward. Biographical sketches are arranged alphabetically under ruler.

8402   THE OXFORD CLASSICAL DICTIONARY. Edited by N. G. L. Hammond & H. H. Scullard. 2d ed. Oxford, Clarendon Press, 1970. xxii, 1176 p. 26cm. Includes many biographical sketches.

8403   SEYFFERT, OSKAR, 1841-1906.
      A dictionary of classical antiquities: mythology, religion, literature, art. Rev. and edited by Henry Nettleship and J. E. Sandys. New York, Meridian Books [1956] vi, 716 p. illus. 21cm. (The Meridian library, ML 2) First published in 1891. Translation of Lexikon der klassischen Altertumskunde (Leipzig, 1882) Includes biographical sketches.

8404   SEYFFERT, OSKAR, 1841-1906.
       Lexikon der klassischen Altertumskunde. Kulturgeschichte
       der Griechen und Römer. Mythologie und Religion, Litteratur,
       Kunst und Altertümer des Staats- und Privatlebens. Leipzig,
       Bibliographisches Institut, 1882. viii, 732 p. 8.° (Meyers
       Fach-Lexika) A dictionary of classical antiquities; includes bio-
       graphical sketches for persons famous in antiquity.

8405   SLOVNÍK ANTICKÉ KULTURY. Praha, Svoboda, 1974. 717 p.
       illus., [47] plates. 29cm. (Členska knižnice) A dictionary
       of classical culture and biography.

8406   SMITH, Sir WILLIAM, 1813-1893.
       A smaller classical dictionary. Edited by E. H. Blakeney.
       London, J. M. Dent; New York, E. P. Dutton [1910] xvi, 607 p.
       illus. 18cm. (Everyman's library [no. 495]) Includes biogra-
       phical sketches of famous persons of antiquity.

8407   WARRINGTON, JOHN
       Everyman's classical dictionary: 800 B. C. -A. D. 337.
       London, Dent; New York, Dutton [1961] xxxvii, 537 p. geneal.
       tables. 20cm. (Everyman's reference library) Includes bio-
       graphical entries.

8408   WOODCOCK, PERCIVAL GEORGE
       Concise dictionary of ancient history. New York, Philo-
       sophical Library [1955] 465 p. 21cm. (Mid-century reference
       library) Biographical sketches of notable figures of antiquity are
       included.

Middle Ages

8409   AULT-DUMESNIL, ÉDOUARD D', b. 1796.
       Dictionnaire historique, géographique et biographique des
       croisades, embrassant tout la lutte du christianisme et de l'is-
       lamisme depuis son origine jusqu'à la prise d'Alger par les
       armes français. Paris, J. -P. Migné, 1852. cxcvi, 1042 col-
       umns. 28cm. (Encyclopédie théologique, t. 68) (Nouvelle
       encyclopédie théologique, t. 18) Historical, geographical and
       biographical dictionary of the Crusades—the conflict between
       Christianity and Islam from its beginnings to the conquest of
       Algeria by the French.

8410   FINES, JOHN
       Who's who in the Middle Ages. New York, Stein & Day,
       1971. xii, 218 p. 24cm. Some 100 biographies of persons who
       lived between the end of the Roman Empire and the 15th century.

8411   SELLE-HOSBACH, KARIN, 1939-
       Prosopographie merowingischer Amsträger in der Zeit von

511 bis 613. Bonn, Selle-Hosbach, 1974. 184 p. 21cm.
Thesis--Bonn. A prosopography of 217 Merovingian officials in
biographical dictionary format.

Modern World

8412 AGAN, PATRICK
Is that who I think it is? New York, Ace Books, 1975-
v. ports. 18cm. Each vol. is a biographical dictionary of
present-day world-wide celebrities who have more or less
receded from public view; vol. 1 has 100 biographies with 200
accompanying portraits (2 portraits for each biographee, past
& the present).

8413 ANNUAIRE BIOGRAPHIQUE; ou, Supplément annuel et continuation de toutes les biographies ou dictionnaires historiques,
contenant la vie de tous les hommes célèbres ... morts dans le
cours de chaque année. Par M. R. A. Henrion. Années 1830-
1834. Paris, Lagny, 1834. 2 v. 8.º No more published?
Biographical annual of famous men who died in the course of
each year (years covered: 1830-1834)

8414 ANNUAIRE HISTORIQUE ET BIOGRAPHIQUE DES SOUVER-
AINS, des chefs et membres des maisons princières, des
familles nobles ou distinguées, et principalement des hommes
d'état, de guerre ... Paris, Direction des archives historiques,
1844-45. 2 v. 8.º Compiler: Aimé-Antoine de Birague? No
more published; only v. 1 and v. 2 (3 fascicles) appeared? A
yearbook of historical and biographical data for Europe's royal
families, nobility, statesmen, military leaders, distinguished
families.

8416 ATLANTIC BRIEF LIVES: a biographical companion to the
arts. Edited by Louis Kronenberger. Associate editor:
Emily Morison Beck. Boston, Little, Brown, 1971. xxii, 900 p.
25cm. "An Atlantic Monthly Press book." 1081 short biographies of persons (chiefly deceased) in various fields of cultural
endeavor: theater, fine arts, literature, etc.; world-wide
coverage.

8417 BALLESTER ESCALAS, RAFAEL
Los forjadores del siglo XX. Revisión religiosa por R.
Castelltort. Barcelona, De Gassó Hnos. 1960. 418 p. illus.
20cm. (Enciclopedias De Gassó) Collection of over 150 biographies of statesmen, soldiers, writers, religious figures,
etc., of the 20th century (and some 19th century notables who
were "forgers of the 20th").

8418 BAUR, SAMUEL, 1768-1832.
Interessante Lebensgemälde der denkwürdigsten Personen
des achtzehnten Jahrhunderts. Leipzig, Voss, 1803-21. 7 v.

18cm. **Vol.** 7 has added t.p.: Biographische Schilderungen aus-
gezeichneter Menschen unseres Zeitalters, 1. Bd. (no more
published?) 'Interesting' portrayals of the most memorable
persons of the 18th century.

8419   BERGER, THEODOR, 1683-1773.
Die durchläuchtige Welt; oder, Kurtzgefasste genealogische,
historische und politische Beschreibung aller ietzlebenden
durchläuchtigen hohen Personen, sonderlich in Europa. In
Vorstellung dero Namen, Geburts-Zeit, Regierung, mit Bey-
fügung der berühmtesten Alten und neueren Scribenten eines
jeden Staats. Zum dritten mahl aufgeleget. Hamburg, J. C.
Kissner, 1730-31. 5 v. illus.

---- ----Beytrag zu den vier Theilen der Durchl. Welt, von
Zeit der letzteren Ausgabe 1730, bis ietzo 1735. Hamburg, J.
C. Kissner [1735] 344 p. A large biographical compendium devoted primarily to European nobility living at the time of the
work's compilation. A later ed. in 6 vols. (including supplement) was issued in 1739 (Breslau, J. J. Korn)? An earlier ed.
in 4 vols. was issued in 1710-11 and was compiled by S. H.
Schmidt (Hamburg)

8420   BILDER VOM INTERNATIONALEN FRAUEN-KONGRESS, 1904.
Im Auftrage des Berliner Lokal-Komitees redigiert von
Eliza Ichenhaeuser. Berlin, A. Scherl, 1904. 48 p. ports.
15 x 24cm. Portraits from the International Congress of Wom-
en, Berlin, 1904, with biographical sketches. On cover: Hrsg.
von der "Woche" ...

8421   BILDNISSE DES 16. JAHRHUNDERTS. Wien, W. Frick, 1947.
12 p., 85 plates (part col.) 26cm. Portraits of 16th century personalities.

8422   BIOGRAPHIE UNIVERSELLE DES CONTEMPORAINS. Rédact.-
gérant: B. Lunel. Paris, 1849. 1 v. Universal biography
of contemporaries (1st half of the 19th century) Intended as an
annual, but only 1849 vol. was issued (?)

8423   BIOGRAPHY NEWS. v. 1-   Jan. 1974-   Detroit, Gale Research Co.   v. illus. 28cm. monthly. Vol. 1-
Jan. 1974-   : edited by Frank Bair and Barbara Nykoruk.
Clips and reproduces articles of biographical interest from
more than 50 U. S. daily newspapers; contemporary personalities of general interest and national scope in all fields are featured. Each issue contains nearly 100 alphabetical entries with
accompanying photos.

8424   THE BLUE BOOK; leaders of the English-speaking world.
1970-   Chicago, St. James Press.   v. 26cm. annual.

An annual listing of living persons "in the United Kingdom, Ireland, Australia, New Zealand, Canada and the United States of America who have achieved distinction in the arts and sciences, business or the professions." It is a successor to The Royal blue book (1968-69) 1975 (4th) ed. latest as of 1976.

8425   BOBER, JURAJ
        Laureáti Nobelovy ceny. Vyd. 1. Bratislava,
Obsor, 1971. 380 p. 24cm. Laureates of the Nobel Prize; 330 winners of the Prize in the various fields of endeavor.

8426   BRANTÔME, PIERRE DE BOURDEILLE, seigneur de, d. 1614.
       Vies des hommes illustres et grands capitaines, français et étrangers, du seizième siècle. Augmentées de notes et d'observations historiques et anecdotiques des éditeurs. Paris, Desmarest, 1810. 3 v. [Collection universelle des mémoires particuliers relatifs à l'histoire de France, t. 67-68] Lives of illustrious and great soldiers, French and foreign, of the 16th century. Includes 199 biographies.

8427   CANNING, JOHN, 1920-   ed.
       100 great modern lives; makers of the world to-day, from Faraday to Kennedy. London, Oldhams Books, 1965. 649 p. illus., ports. 23cm. A collection of biographies by various writers; scientists, artists, statesmen, etc. of the 19th and 20th centuries, beginning with Michael Faraday & concluding with the astronauts Yuri Gagarin and John Glen.

8428   CELEBRITY REGISTER. 1959-   New York, Harper & Row
       [etc.]   v. ports. 27cm. Title varies: 1959, International celebrity register. U. S. ed. Editor: 1959-   C. Amory. 1963 ed. has subtitle: An irreverent compendium of American quotable notables. 1959 & 1963 editions only were published? Concerns largely contemporary Americans but is also world wide in coverage.

8429   COMPÈRE-MOREL, ADÉODAT CONSTANT ADOLPHE, 1872-
       Grand dictionnaire socialiste du mouvement politique et économique national et international. Paris, Publications sociales, 1924. 1057 p. 32cm. A dictionary of socialism that includes biography.

8430   CUMBERLAND'S PORTRAIT GALLERY; being a collection of
       portraits of celebrated persons. Engraved by eminent artists from authentic pictures. To which are prefixed original memoirs. London, J. Cumberland, 1832. nos. ports. 8.º Issued in various numbers, of which the British Museum, e.g., has nos. 3-4, 6-9.

8431   DARET, PIERRE
        Tableaux historiques ou sont gravés les illustres François
et éstrangers de l'un et de l'autre sexe ... avec les éloges
sommaires. Par Pierre Daret et Louis Boissevin. Paris,
Chez L. Boisseuin [1664?] 5 l., 197 ports. 30cm. A collection
of 197 portraits of famous persons of the 16th and 17th centuries;
engravings by Daret, Boissevin and Moncornet.

8432   DICTIONNAIRE D'HISTOIRE CONTEMPORAINE, 1776-1969.
        Ouvrage publié sous les auspices de la Commission inter-
nationale pour l'enseignement de l'histoire et sous la direction
de Émile Lousse et Jacques de Launay. Préf. de Maurice Bau-
mont. [Lausanne] Éditions Rencontre, 1969. 469 p. 19cm.
[Le Rayon de l'histoire] A biographical dictionary of modern
history, 1776-1969.

8433   DOLLINGER, HANS
        Lexikon aktueller Persönlichkeiten; Namen die Schlag-
zeilen nachten. München, Heyne, 1972. 159 p. ports. 18cm.
(Heyne-Buch, Nr. 973) A dictionary of the world's outstanding
personalities of the 20th century.

8434   DREUX DU RADIER, JEAN FRANÇOIS, 1714-1780.
        L'Europe illustre, contenant l'histoire abregée des souve-
rains, des princes, des prélats, des ministres, des grands
capitaines, des magistrats, des savans, des artistes, & des
dames célèbres en Europe dans le XVe siècle compris, jusqu'à
présent. Ouvrage enrichi des portraits gravés par les seins de
Sieur Odieuvre. Paris, Odieuvre et Le Breton, 1755-65. 6 v.
ports. 4.º A collection of biography and ca. 600 portraits of
celebrated men and women in Europe from the 15th century to
the mid 1700's.

8435   EISENSTAEDT, ALFRED, 1898-
        People. New York, Viking Press, 1973. 259 p. illus.,
ports. 34cm. Includes photographs of more than 300 well-
known people of the 20th century (celebrities, actors, politicians, writers, etc.) with an alphabetical index to the portraits
at end of volume.

8436   ENCYCLOPÉDIE ANARCHISTE. Paris, La Librairie interna-
        tionale [193-?-34] 4 v. 32cm. Edited by Sébastien Faure.
Encyclopedia of anarchism and anarchists.

8437   FAMOUS LIVES; a magazine of biographies. v. 1, no. 2-3.
        Apr.-June 1929. New York, Magazine Publishers. 2 nos.
in 1 v. illus. 29cm. bimonthly. Editor: Harold Hersey. Vol.
1, no. 1 never published.

8438   FENDT, TOBIAS, 16th cent.
        Monumenta sepulcrorum cum epigraphis, ingenio et doc-
trina excellentium virorum: aliorumque tam prisci quam nostri
seculi, memorabilium hominum, de archetypis expressa, ex
liberalitate nob. & Clariss. viri, D. Sigfridi Rybisch & Cae-
sarei Consiliarii pictorem & civem Vratislaviensem in aes incisa & edita. [Vratislaviae] 1574. 6 l., 125 plates. 32cm. Republished in Frankfurt, 1575: Monumenta illustrium virorum per
Italiam & Galliam. 3d ed.: Monumenta clarorum doctrina
praecipue toto orbi terrarum virorum collecta, passim in aes
incisa sumptus et studio Siegfr. Rybisch. Frankfurt, 1589.
The same 125 pictures made by Fendt were later published with
some added eulogies and an index under title: Marci Zuerii
Boxhornii Monumenta illustrium virorum & elogia. Amsterdam,
1638. Epitaphs, portraits, & sepulchral monuments (with biographical data therefrom) of learned Europeans of the Renaissance and early modern period.

8439   GALSKÝ, DESIDER
        Kdo je kdo ve 20. století. Desider Galský, Richard Žá-
kovský. [Vyd. 1] Praha, Svoboda, 1967. 473 p. 17cm. A
who's who of the 20th century. In Czech.

8440   HISTOIRE GÉNÉRALE DES HOMMES VIVANTS ET DES
        HOMMES MORTS DANS LE XIXe SIÈCLE. Par des
écrivains de diverses nations. Genève, 1860-74. 5 v. folio.
General history of men living and men who have died during the
19th century; a collection of universal biography by authors of
several nations.

8441   HUMM, FELIX
        Handschriften von europäischen Persönlichkeiten aus dem
16.-19. Jahrhundert. Katalog der Ausstellung im Kunsthaus
Chur, 6. Juni-14. Juli 1969. [Auswahl aus der Autographen-
sammlung des Rätischen Museums Chur. Chur, Rätisches Mu-
seum] 1969. xvi, 108 p. facsims. 23cm. (Schriftenreihe des
Rätischen Museums Chur, Heft 6) This catalog of an exhibition
of manuscripts of European personalities (chiefly people instrumental in the cultural and political life of the 16th-19th centuries)
serves for the most part also as a biographical dictionary; pages
1-102 are arranged in biographical dictionary format with brief
biographical notes and description of manuscripts (letters, etc.)
written in the hand of the biographee.

8442   HYAMS, EDWARD S
        A dictionary of modern revolution. [New York] Taplinger
Pub. Co., 1973. 322 p. 21cm. Includes biographies of men
and women who "have transformed the economic, political and
social structures of a great part of mankind during the past century."

8443   LES ILLUSTRES MODERNES; ou, Tableau de la vie privée des
       principaux personnages des deux sexes, qui, depuis la
       renaissance des lettres, ont acquis de la célébrité en Europe,
       tant en politique ou dans les armées, que dans les arts, les
       sciences & la vie contemplative. Paris, Leroy, 1788. 2 v. in
       10 pts. ports. folio. Famous moderns; men and women of
       Europe who acquired notoriety in various fields of endeavor from
       the Renaissance to the latter part of the 18th century.

8444   INTERNATIONAL PORTRAIT GALLERY. Detroit, Gale Re-
       search Co., 1968-74. Over 2300 portraits of authors,
       statesmen, military men, civic leaders, and others. In 5 series,
       each with 350 to 750 plates with tabbed file folders and master
       index including an alphabetical list, list by vocation, chronologi-
       cal list of birth and death dates and day by day calendar of an-
       niversaries. There is also a master index for the entire set.
       Size: 8 1/2 x 11". Contents. —no. 1. Basic collection of portraits
       of famous persons from early times to the present.--no. 2. A
       supplemental collection of portraits of famous persons from
       early times to the present. Black collection: Portraits of Ne-
       groes important from early times to the present. Selection and
       biographical notes by Daniel T. Williams.--no. 3. Second gen-
       eral supplement.--no. 4. Literary figures supplement.--no. 5.
       Juvenile authors supplement.

8445   KLIMESCH, KARL, RITTER VON
       Köpfe der Politik, Wirtschaft, Wissenschaft und Kunst.
       Augsburg, J. W. Naumann, 1953. 2 v. ports. 28cm. Con-
       tents.--[1] A-K.--[2] L-Z. Famous figures in politics, econom-
       ics, scholarship and art; alphabetical arrangement.

8446   LAQUEUR, WALTER ZE'EV, 1921-
       A dictionary of politics. Edited by Walter Laqueur, with the
       assistance of Evelyn Anderson [and others] London, Weidenfeld
       and Nicolson, 1971. [7], 593 p. 25cm. Includes biographies of
       important figures in world politics of the 20th century.

8447   LAUNAY, ANDRÉ JOSEPH
       Dictionary of contemporaries. Compiled by A. J. Launay.
       [New York] Philosophical Library [1967] 368 p. 23cm. An his-
       torical chronology which contains brief biographical sketches of
       persons especially identified with particular eras in world his-
       tory.

8448   LAZIĆ, BRANKO M
       Biographical dictionary of the Comintern, by Branko Lazitch
       in collaboration with Milorad M. Drachkovitch. Stanford, Calif.,
       Hoover Institution Press, Stanford University, 1973. xxxii,
       458 p. 24cm. (Hoover Institution publications, 121) Includes
       716 biographies of Communist International (1919-1943) personnel.

8450   LIGOU, DANIEL
        Dictionnaire universel de la franc-maçomnerie: hommes il-
        lustres, pays, rites, symboles. Sous la direction de Daniel
        Ligou. Conception et réalisation: Daniel Beresniak et Myriam
        Psachin. Paris, Editions de Navarre, 1974. 2 v. (1398, [40] p.,
        [20] leaves of plates) illus. 28cm. A universal dictionary of
        Freemasonry; a prime element in this alphabetically arranged
        dictionary are the biographical sketches of prominent Masons of
        the past.

8451   MANSCH, ANTON
        Intellectual world; gallery of contemporaries. Author: Dr.
        Anton Mansch. Berlin-Charlottenburg, A. Eckstein [191-] [196]p.
        ports. 48cm. Each portrait, except one, is accompanied by a
        biographical sketch in English, German, French, or Swedish, ac-
        cording to the nationality of the subject.

8452   MARTELL, PAUL
        World military leaders. Paul Martell and Grace P. Hayes,
        editors. Trevor N. Dupuy, executive editor. New York, R. R.
        Bowker Co.: Dunn Loring, Va., T. N. Dupuy Associates [1974]
        268 p. 29cm. A biographical directory of military and civilian
        personnel in senior positions in military establishments in all na-
        tions of the world (some 114 countries are covered).

8453   MEN OF ACHIEVEMENT. v. 1-   1974-   Cambridge,
        Eng., Melrose Press.   v. ports. 26cm. The 1st volume
        (1974) of this projected annual contains some 6,000 biographies
        (with portraits) of living persons (international coverage). Edi-
        tor: 1974-   Ernest Kay.

8454   MIRECOURT, EUGÈNE DE, 1812-1880.
        Histoire contemporaine. Portraits et silhouettes au XIXe
        siècle. Paris, 1867-71. 140 nos. 16.° Mirecourt's collection
        of brief biographies of European personalities (chiefly French)
        of the 19th century. Each no. contained ca. 64 to 100 pages and
        treated one biographee generally (some deal with 2 or 3) Issued
        in various editions.

8455   MUSÉE BIOGRAPHIQUE. Illustrations [des] célébrités et
        notabilités du dix-neuvième siècle. t. I, livraison 1-3.
        1 v. ports. 8.° No more published? The museum of biogra-
        phy. Illustrations of the celebrities and notables of the 19th
        century.

8456   THE NEW YORK TIMES BIOGRAPHICAL EDITION; a compila-
        tion of current biographical information of general interest.
        v. 1-   Jan. 1, 1970-   [New York, New York times &
        Arno Press]   v. (loose-leaf) ports. 30cm. weekly. Con-
        tains ca. 20 to 50 articles per week of biographical interest (a-
        bout one half are obituaries) reprinted in their entirety from the
        Times.

8457   PAN'GONG TODŎK KYOYUK YŎN'GUHOE.
        Pan'gong todŏk kyoyuk sajŏn. Seoul [1970] 902 p. 22cm.
    A dictionary of communism and ethics which includes short bi-
    ographies of world figures past and present prominent in those
    areas or whose activities relate to them.

8458   PANTHÉON DE LA GUERRE; panorama of the World War and
        its heroes, the largest painting in the world, 402 feet long--
    45 feet high, painted by twenty-eight famous French artists, as-
    sisted by more than one hundred other artists under the direc-
    tion of Pierre Carrier-Belleuse and Auguste-François Gorguet
    and containing six thousand life-size portraits of World War he-
    roes and leaders representing all the Allied Nations. With a
    correct landscape of the battlefields of France and Belgium as
    they appeared in 1914-1918 ... New York, Stockbridge Press,
    1932. 15 p. illus., ports. 29cm. Text on verso of folded
    plate.

8459   THE PANTHEON OF THE AGE; or, Memoirs of 300 contempo-
        rary public characters, British and foreign, of all ranks
    and professions. 2d ed. London, Printed for G. B. Whittaker,
    1825. 3 v. ports. 17cm. Caption title: Public men of all
    countries.

8460   PÉREZ EMBID, FLORENTINO
        Forjadores del mundo contemporáneo; colección de biografías
    dirigida por Florentino Pérez-Embid con la colaboración de Pab-
    lo Tiján. [2. ed.] Barcelona, Editorial Planeta [c1962-63] 4 v.
    illus. 24cm. Forgers of the contemporary world; a collection
    of 244 biographies of men of the Western world (Great Britain
    and Germany dominate the scene) from the French Revolution to
    the near present.

8461   REILLY, ROBIN
        Wedgwood: the portrait medallions [by] Robin Reilly and
    George Savage. London, Barrie & Jenkins [1973] 379 p. ports.
    31cm. A 'biographical dictionary' in that the portrait medal-
    lions and cameos are arranged alphabetically and are accom-
    panied by biographical notes. Main emphasis is on 'heads of
    illustrious moderns from Chaucer to the present time.'

8462   REILLY, ROBIN
        Wedgwood portrait medallions; an introduction. London,
    Barrie & Jenkins [1973] [49] p. ports. 22cm. "A fully illus-
    trated record of the exhibition held at the National Portrait Gal-
    lery, London, from 3rd October 1973 until 5th January 1974."
    Includes portraits and brief biographies of 102 historical per-
    sonalities in Europe (17th-18th centuries). In biographical dic-
    tionary arrangement. See also the same author's Wedgwood:
    the portrait medallions.

8463   ROOKE, PATRICK J
Famous people of the 19th century. London, Hart-Davis,
1973. xii, 116 p. 21cm. A biographical dictionary of figures
of world importance in the 19th century.

8464   SANDERS, LLOYD CHARLES, 1857-
Celebrities of the century; being a dictionary of men and
women of the nineteenth century. Edited by Lloyd C. Sanders.
Ann Arbor, Mich., Gryphon Books, 1971. 2 v. (vi, 1077 p.)
22cm. Reprint of the 1887 one-volume ed. (London, Cassell)

8465   SARAKĀRA, NIKHILA
Namabhūmikaya. Calcutta, Bak-Sahitya, 1965. 558 p.
23cm. In Bengali. A biographical dictionary of ca. 282 persons
of the 20th century (world-wide) in the news at the time of
publication of the volume. Issued under the author's pseudonym: Sripanatha.

8466   SCHANG, F   C
Visiting cards of celebrities often illustrated by memorial
postage stamps, together with photographs, drawings and other
material from the collection of F. C. Schang. Paris, F. Hazan
[1971] 271 p. illus., ports. 21 x 25cm. 19th and 20th century
celebrities; with biographical data, portraits, memorabilia and
an alphabetical name index.

8467   SERIE DI VITE E RITRATTI DE' FAMOSI PERSONAGGI DEGLI
ULTIMI TEMPI. Milano, 1815-18. 3 v. ports. 4.º
Compiled by the 'Editore de' poemi inglesi di Gray recati in
verso italiano.' A series of lives and portraits of famous persons of recent times, chiefly European figures of the 18th century.

8468   SETH, RONALD
Encyclopedia of espionage. London, New English Library,
1972. 683 p. 22cm. Consists primarily of biographical sketches of persons involved in intelligence work—from Delilah (Biblical character) to Richard Helms.

8469   TABLETTES BIOGRAPHIQUES. Mémorial universel des
hommes du temps, publié par une société des gens de lettres sous la direction de A. Berthon [et al.] Paris, 1876-83.
8 v. 8.º A collection of universal biography; men of the times
(19th century)

8470   THE TIMES, LONDON.
Obituaries from The Times, 1961-1970, including an index
to all obituaries and tributes appearing in The Times during the
years 1961-1970. Compiler: Frank C. Roberts. Reading, Eng.,

Newspaper Archives Developments Ltd. [1975] 952 p. 32cm.
For the most part "a biographical record of 1,500 men and women whose life stories helped to shape the world we know." 600
of the entries are for people of countries other than Great Britain.

8471   TUNNEY, CHRISTOPHER, 1924-
        A biographical dictionary of World War II. London, Dent,
1972. viii, 216 p. 23cm.

8472   TWO THOUSAND WOMEN OF ACHIEVEMENT; a biographical
        record of most distinguished achievement, circulating
throughout the world. 1st-4th ed. (?); 1969-1972 (?) London,
Melrose Press. 4 v. ports. 26cm. Edited by Ernest Kay.
Superseded by The World who's who of women, 1973-
American women of achievement comprise the vast majority of
the entries.

8473   VALKO, WILLIAM G
        The illustrated who's who in reigning royalty; a history of
contemporary monarchial systems. Philadelphia, Community
Press, 1969. 263 p. ports. 18cm. "A Vasilikon publication."
Royalty from more than 100 nations is covered.

8474   WAITE, ARTHUR EDWARD, 1857-1942.
        A new encyclopaedia of Freemasonry (Ars magna latomorum)
and of cognate instituted mysteries: their rites, literature, and
history. New introd. by Emmett McLoughlin. New and rev.
ed. New Hyde Park, N. Y., University Books [1970] 2 v. illus.,
ports. 24cm. Includes biographical sketches in its alphabetical
arrangement, as well as sections like "Lesser Masonic personalities" (p. 13-31, v. 2).

8475   WEBER, EMIL
        Pioniere der Freiheit; hundert Lebensbilder bedeutsamer
Vorkämpfer für Freiheit, Recht und Kultur. Bern, J. Lukas
[1943] 192 p. ports. 22cm. Pioneers of freedom; 100 biographical sketches of important champions of freedom, law and
civilization in Europe especially and Switzerland in particular.

8476   WHO'S WHO IN THE UNITED NATIONS AND RELATED
        AGENCIES. [1st ed.] New York, Arno Press, a New York
Times Company, 1975. xxxiii, 785 p. 24cm. (Arno Press
who's who series)

8477   WHO'S WHO IN THE WORLD. 1st-   ed.; 1971/72-
        Chicago, Marquis Who's Who, inc.   v. 31cm.

8478   THE WORLD WHO'S WHO OF WOMEN. v. 1-   1973-
      ed. Cambridge, Eng., Melrose Press.   v. illus.
26cm. Supersedes Two thousand women of achievement (1969-
1972).

8479   WURZBACH, ALFRED WOLFGANG, Ritter von Tannenberg,
      1879-1957.
      Katalog meiner Autographen-Sammlung. Wien, W. Krieg.,
1954. 144 p. 22cm. 1196 autographs with 'biograms' of various contemporaries of the author.

NATIONAL OR AREA BIOGRAPHY

NATIONAL OR AREA BIOGRAPHY

AFGHANISTAN

8480　ADAMEC, LUDWIG W
　　　　Historical and political who's who of Afghanistan. Graz,
Akademische Druck- u. Verlagsanstalt, 1975. ix, 385 p., [60]
leaves. geneal. tables. 28cm. On spine: Who's who of Afghanistan. Personal names in English and Arabic. Biography
& genealogy of Afghanistan past & present.

8481　HANIFI, MOHAMMED JAMIL
　　　　Historical and cultural dictionary of Afghanistan. Metuchen,
N. J., Scarecrow Press, 1976. viii, 141 p. 23cm. (Historical
and cultural dictionaries of Asia, no. 5) Includes biographical
sketches (although not a great many) of native and foreign personages who have been influential in the historical and cultural
development of Afghanistan.

AFRICA

Bibliography, Indexes, Portrait Catalogs

8482　FUNG, KAREN
　　　　Index to 'Portraits' in West Africa, 1948-1966. (In African
studies bulletin, Stanford, Calif., Hoover Institution, Stanford
University v. 9 no. 3, Dec. 1966, p. 103-120) An index to por-
traits of West African political leaders in the periodical West
Africa.

General Works

8483　AFRICA SOUTH OF THE SAHARA. 1st-　　ed. ; 1971-
　　　　London, Europa Publications.　　v. illus. 26cm. The
fourth section, "Other reference materials," includes a "Who's
who in Africa south of the Sahara" (e. g. , 1972 vol. , p. 943-
1024)

8484　ANNUAIRE DES ÉTATS D'AFRIQUE NOIRE: gouvernements
　　　　et cabinets ministeriels, partis politiques. 2. éd. Paris,

ÉDIAFRIC, 1962. 443 p. illus., ports. 24cm. 1st ed. appeared in June 1961. Who's who of politics in 14 French-speaking African states. Bulk of the text (p. 121-403) contains brief
biographies of leading government officials, country by country, and of inter-African organizations.

8484a   ANNUAIRE PARLEMENTAIRE DES ÉTATS D'AFRIQUE NOIRE:
         Députés et conseillers économiques des républiques d'ex-
         pression française, 1962. Paris, Annuaire Afrique, 1962.
         332 p. illus., ports. Advertising matter interspersed. In-
         cludes 1,100 brief biographies of the political personnel and ad-
         ministrative service officers of 14 French-speaking African
         republics.

8485   DICKIE, JOHN, 1923-
         Who's who in Africa: the political, military, and business
         leaders of Africa, by John Dickie and Alan Rake. London, Af-
         rican Development, 1973. 602 p. illus., maps. 22cm.

8486   DICTIONARY OF AFRICAN BIOGRAPHY. 1st-   ed.
         1970-   London, Melrose Press.   v. ports. 25cm.
         annual. Concerned with living Africans. Edited by Ernest Kay.

8487   LES ÉLITES AFRICAINES: Cameroun, RCA, Congo, Côte-
         d'Ivoire, Dahomey, Gabon, Haute-Volta, Mali, Mauritanie,
         Niger, Sénégal, Tchad, Togo. 3. ed. Paris, Ediafric-Ser-
         vice, 1974. 490 p. 27cm. Cover title. "Numéro spécial du
         Bulletin de l'Afrique noire." A biographical dictionary of poli-
         tical leaders of the nations of French-speaking West and Equa-
         torial Africa; the biographical data is, in many cases, rather
         slim. 2d ed., 1972.

8488   FRIEDRICH-EBERT-STIFTUNG. FORSCHUNGSINSTITUT.
         African biographies. [Bad Godesberg] Verlag Neue Gesell-
         schaft [1971-   c1967   v. (loose-leaf) ports. 23cm. Trans-
         lation and revision of biographies of African statesmen of today
         (German edition, 1967-1970: Afrika Biographien). Issued in
         parts. Fascicules coming out currently. As of 1976 there were
         4+ volumes issued.

8489   LA POLITIQUE AFRICAINE EN 1969: Cameroun, RCA, Congo,
         Côte d'Ivoire, Dahomey, Gabon, Haute-Volta, Mali, Mau-
         ritanie, Niger, Sénégal, Tchad, Togo. 2. ed. Paris, EDIAFRIC,
         La Documentation africaine [1969] 333 p. 27cm. Cover title.
         "Numéro spéciale du Bulletin de l'Afrique noire." Covers former
         French Africa (excepting the Malagasy Republic). Biographies
         of political leaders, including mayors, are provided.

8490   STANDARD ENCYCLOPEDIA OF SOUTHERN AFRICA. [1st
         ed. Cape town] Nasou [1970-   v. illus., ports.

27cm. Includes biographical sketches and portraits of historical and cultural figures, past and present, of Southern Africa.
Vol. 10 (1974, covering: Sle-Tun) latest vol. issued.

8491   TABLER, EDWARD C
        Pioneers of South West Africa and Ngamiland, 1738-1880.
Cape Town, A. A. Balkema, 1973 [c1972] ix, 142 p. 26cm.
(South African biographical and historical studies, 19) A biographical dictionary with biographies of 333 adult male foreigners who travelled and settled in South West Africa and Ngamiland: traders, missionaries, hunters, explorers, miners and
concession-seekers.

AMERICA

(Including North America)

8492   ASSINIWI, BERNARD
        Lexique des noms indiens en Amérique. Montréal, Leméac,
1973. 2 v. 20cm. (Collection Ni-t'chawama/Mon ami, mon
frère) Contents. --1. Noms géographiques. --2. Personnages
historiques. A dictionary of Indian names in North America;
vol. 2 is a biographical dictionary of Indians prominent in history.

8493   DICCIONARIO ENCICLOPÉDICO DE LAS AMÉRICAS; geografía,
        historia, economía, política, literatura, arte, música, de-
porte, cine, teatro, etnografía, fauna, flora, ciencias genera-
les. 1. ed. Buenos Aires, Editorial Futuro, 1947. 711 p. 24cm.
Encyclopedic dictionary of the Americas; includes brief biographical entries.

8494   VIZOSO GOROSTIAGA, MANUEL DE
        Diccionario y cronología histórica americana. Buenos
Aires, Editorial Ayacucho [1947] 539 p. 24cm. Dictionary and
chronology of the history of the Americas; biography included.

ARGENTINE REPUBLIC

Bibliography, Indexes, Portrait Catalogs

8495   SABOR, JOSEFA EMILIA
        Las fuentes biográficas para la República Argentina. (In
Bibliotecología, revista del Centro de Estudios Bibliotecológicos,
Buenos Aires. v. 3, no. 1, sep. 1955, p. 3-12) Biographical
sources for the Argentine Republic; analyzes 29 works published
between 1857-1955.

General Works

8496   BIDONDO, JORGE A
Notas para la historia de los gobernadores de Jujuy. Jujuy,
Dirección Provincial de Cultura, 1971. 165 p. 27cm. Biographical sketches of the governors of the Province of Jujuy, 1835
to the present. Chronological arrangement with alphabetical
listing at end.

8497   BIEDMA, JOSÉ JUAN, 1864-1933.
Iconografía de próceres argentinos; información biográfica.
Buenos Aires, Club de Gimnasis y Esgrima, 1932. 181 p. ports
19cm. Iconography (portraits) of leaders of the Argentine Independence movement, with biographical data.

8498   CAFFARO ROSSI, JOSÉ MARÍA
50 [i. e. Cincuenta] semblanzas argentinas. [Con dibujos
de A. Rodríguez Mendoza] Buenos Aires, G. Kraft, 1954. 218 p.
ports. 21cm. 50 portraits with biographies of famous Argentines.

8499   CARAFFA, PEDRO ISIDRO, b. 1868.
Celebrità argentine dell' epoca dell' indipendenza nazionale;
brevi cenni biografici; con ritratti ed annotazioni. Ravenna, E.
Lavagna, 1921. xii, 256 p. ports. 23cm. Brief biographical
sketches of famous Argentines of the era of the national independence movement, with portraits.

8500   CARAFFA, PEDRO ISIDRO, b. 1868.
Hombres notables de Cuyo. La Plata, Talleres Sesé, Lar-
rañaga, 1908-10. 2 v. ports. 19cm. At head of title, v. 1:
Museo Histórico Nacional. Vol. 2 published by J. Sese. A 2d
ed. in 1 v. (315 p.) appeared in 1912. Notable men of the Province of Cuyo (Argentine Republic)

8501   CORDOBA, ARGENTINE REPUBLIC. UNIVERSIDAD
NACIONAL.
Universitarios de Córdoba. Por Pablo Cabrera. Córdoba,
1916-   v. 29cm. (Biblioteca del tercer centenario de
la Universidad Nacional de Córdoba) Alumni or former students
at the National University of Cordoba who achieved prominence
in Argentina or the Province of Cordoba. Only one vol. (v. 1)
was ever issued?

8502   DICCIONARIO BIOGRÁFICO. Buenos Aires, "C" Signo Editorial Argentino, 1954.   v. 23cm. Contents. --1. Provincia de Buenos Aires. No more published. A biographical dictionary of the Argentine Republic. Vol. 1 covers the Province
of Buenos Aires.

8503   DIZIONARIO BIOGRAFICO DEGLI ITALIANI AL PLATA. Com-
           pilato per cura degli editori-proprietari Barozzi, Baldis-
        sini & Cia. 1. ed. Buenos Aires, "Argos," 1899. 363 p. 18cm.
        A biographical dictionary of Italians in the River Plate region of
        the Argentine Republic during the 19th century.

8504   FERNÁNDEZ, JUAN RÓMULO, 1884-
           Hombres de acción (cien biografías sintéticas de personas
        que contribuyeron a la independencia, organización y afianza-
        miento de la República Argentina) Buenos Aires, Librería del
        Colegio [1940] 215 p. ports. 21cm. 'Men of action'; 100 biogra-
        phies of persons who contributed towards the independence, or-
        ganization and security of the Argentine Republic.

8505   FONTENLA FACAL, PEDRO A   189-=
           Primer diccionario biográfico [argentino] contemporáneo
        ilustrado; contiene más de tres mil biografías y dos mil graba-
        dos. Buenos Aires [19--] 244 p. 2000 plates. 'First' biogra-
        phical dictionary of contemporary Argentina; containing more
        than 3,000 biographies and 2,000 engravings. This work is
        listed by Palau y Dulcet and Geohagan.

8506   GUERRA, JUAN NÉSTOR, 1904-
           Mar del Plata, sus calles, plazas y monumentos. Mar del
        Plata, Ediciones Apolo, 1967. 122 p. illus. 23cm. The
        streets, plazas and monuments of the City of Mar del Plata, Ar-
        gentine Republic (population over 100,000); in large part a biogra-
        phical dictionary of Argentine personages (as well as famous
        figures in world history and culture) since many of the entries
        consist of personal names of those after whom streets, etc. were
        names.

8507   HOGG, RICARDO
           Guía biográfica. Buenos Aires, Impr. de Peuser, 1904.
        250 p. illus. Cover title: Guía biográfica argentina. Biogra-
        phical guide to Argentina.

8508   INSTITUTO ARGENTINO DE CIENCIAS GENEALÓGICAS.
           Genealogía [de los] hombres de Mayo. Buenos Aires, Re-
        vista del Instituto Argentino de Ciencias Genealógicas, 1961.
        ciii, 383 p. illus. 23cm. Introductory essay on the Cabildo de
        Mayo by Roberto H. Marfany. A genealogical-biographical dic-
        tionary of leading figures in the Argentine's War of Independence,
        1810-1817.

8509   LULIO, ORESTES DI
           Antecedentes biográficos santiagueños. Santiago del Estero,
        1948. 297 p. 28cm. Biography of persons born in the 16th-18th
        centuries in the Argentine province of Santiago del Estero.

8510   QUIÉN ES QUIÉN EN EL RÍO DE LA PLATA; histórico.
           [Buenos Aires, 1958-   v. illus., ports. 24cm.
           Editor: 1958-   F. Monte Domecq. Who's who in the River
           Plate region, Argentine Republic; a biographical dictionary.
           1958 vol. only one published?

ARMENIA

8511   ALPOYACHIAN, ARSHAK, 1879-1962.
           Patmowt'iwn hay Kesarioy. Gahire (Cairo), W. Phaphaz-
           ean, 1937. 2 v. (34, 2479 p.) illus. 25cm. History of Ar-
           menians in the Province of Kayseri, Turkey. With many bio-
           graphical sketches at end of various sections of the work ar-
           ranged alphabetically. With 2 indexes to Armenian names:
           Armenian characters (p. 2321-2461) Latin characters (p. 2461-
           2469)

8512   ANASYAN, HAKOB SEDRAK'I
           Haykakan matenagitowt'yown, 5.-18. dd. Erevan, Haykakan
           SSRh G. A. Hratkch., 1959-   v. 27cm. Contents.--1. A-
           Arhakel, Salatsoretsi. Armenian bio-bibliography of the 5th to
           the 18th century. Entry by forename.

8513   ANMORHATS' DEMK'ER. Erevan, Hayastan, 1965. 294 p.
           ports. 21cm. Prepared for the alumni organization Ner-
           sisyants'ineri Avandakan Handipowmner Kazmakerpogh
           Handznazhoghov. Cf. p. 5. Edited by Daniel D'znowni. "Un-
           forgettable personalities'; the former students of the Nersissian
           School. Arranged alphabetically by activity (entries under fore-
           names) Alphabetical summary by activity (p. 292-295).

8514   ÇARK, Y   G
           Türk devleti hizmetinde Ermeniler, 1453-1953. Istanbul,
           Yeni Matbaa, 1953. xvi, 302 p. ports. 20cm. Armenians in
           Turkish Government service; biographies arranged chronolo-
           gically within each chapter. Alphabetical index of names: p.
           295-302.

8515   EREMIAN, ARAM, 1898-
           T'iflisi haykakan pant'ēonnerowm. [Vienna] Mechitarian,
           1940. 8, 110 p. 18cm. (Azgayin matenadaran, h. 148) Added
           t. p.: Das armenische Pantheon zu Tiflis. The Armenian
           Pantheon in the cemeteries of Tiflis; 68 biographies arranged by
           date of birth.

8516   GIRK' HEROSNERI MASIN. Erevan, Haykakan SSRh G. A.
           Hratakch., 1964. 455 p. illus., ports. 27cm. In Armen-
           ian. Added t. p.: Kniga o geroiākh. The book of Armenian he-
           roes of World War II; Heroes of the Soviet Union. Edited by
           Ervand Khaleyan.

8517   MALKHASYAN, ARMO
        Sovetakan Banaki hay gorisich'nerĕ. Erevan, Hayakakan
        SSRh Petakan Hratakch., 1963. 498 p. illus., ports. 23cm.
        Added t. p.: Armo Malkhasian. Armiane deiateli Sovetskoi
        armii. Biography of Armenians active in the Soviet Army, 1917-
        1963.

8518   PETROSYAN, HOVHANNES, 1892-1961.
        Hay gitnakanner, hraparakakhosner, zhowrhnalistner ...
        Erevan, Hayakakan SSRh Petakrapalan, 1960-   v.
        27cm. Added t. p.: Armianskie uchennye, publitsisty, zhurnal-
        isty; s biobibliograficheskimi primechaniiami, sostavil Ov.
        Petrosian. Armenian scholars, orators and journalists; a bio-
        bibliographical work, with a preface by Bishop Garegin. Ar-
        ranged chronologically, with alphabetical index (v. 1, p. 537-
        539). Vol. 1 (539 p.) only one published?

ASIA

8519   AJIA MONDAI KŌZA. [Tokyo?] Sōgensha [1939-40]
        12 v. illus. 20cm. Asian problems; vol. 12 contains a
        'who's who' of Asia.

8520   AJIA REKISHI JITEN. Tokyo, Heibonsha, 1959-62. 10 v.
        illus., ports. 27cm. An historical dictionary of Asia that
        includes biographies of important figures of Asian history; with
        romanized index of names and an index of Chinese characters.

8521   THE FAR EAST AND AUSTRALASIA, 1971; a survey and direc-
        tory of Asia and the Pacific. [3d annual ed.] London,
        Europa Publications [1971] xix, 1376 p. illus., maps. 26cm.
        "Who's who in the Far East and Australasia": p. 1191-1352. An
        annual publication. 1st ed., 1969; 2d ed., 1970.

8522   JAPAN. GAIMUSHŌ, CHŌSAKYOKU.
        Gendai Tōa jimmei kan—Shōwa 25 nemban. Tokyo, Tōhō
        Kenkyūkai, 1950. 197 p. Who's who in East Asia, covering
        Korea, China and Southeast Asia. Index.

8523   LOUIS-FRÉDÉRIC, pseud.
        A dictionary of Asia: archaeology, art, ethnology, geog-
        raphy, history, languages, literature, music, mythology, re-
        ligion, science, sports, technology, theater, etc. from the
        earliest times to the present [by] Louis Frederic. Foreword by
        Jeannine Auboyer. [Villecresnes, France] Louis Frederic
        Publisher [foreword 1975-   v. illus. 24cm. Bio-
        graphical entries are a significant part of the dictionary. Ex-
        pected to be complete in 5 vols. Contents: v. 1. A-F.

8524   THE ORIENT YEAR BOOK. 1934-   Tokyo, Asia Statis-
            tics Co. [etc.] 1933-   v. illus. 24-26cm.
        Formed by the union of the Japan yearbook (1905-31) and the
        Japan times year book (1933) Title varies: 1934-40, The Japan-
        Manchoukuo year book; 1941, Far East year book; 1942-
        The Orient year book. Vols. for 1934-41 published by the Ja-
        pan-Manchoukuo Year Book Co. Includes a who's who section
        (e. g., 1942 ed., p. [1112]-1271) Ceased with 1942 ed.

8525   SEKAI JIMMEI JITEN. Tōyōhen. Tokyo, Tokyodo, 1973.
            4, 476 p. 19cm. Approximately 5,100 Asian personalities,
        (excluding Japan) with emphasis on Chinese. Arranged in Japa-
        nese syllabic order. Edited by Toshio Kawabe and Tadashi
        Nakamura.

8526   THOMPSON, VIRGINIA Mc LEAN, 1903-
            Who's who in Southeast Asia (August 1945-Dec. 1950) Com-
        piled by Virginia Thompson and Richard Adloff. Washington, D.
        C., Library of Congress Photoduplication Service, 1950-
            reels. 35mm. Microfilm & photostatic copy of typewritten
        cards held by the Library of Congress. Countries covered: Thai-
        land, Burma (6 reels of microfilm) and Indonesia (ca. 600 sheets
        36 x 22cm.) Includes biographical sketches of Europeans promi-
        nent in Southeast Asian affairs.

AUSTRALIA

Bibliography, Indexes, Portrait Catalogs

8527   GIBBNEY, HERBERT JAMES
            A biographers' index of parliamentary returns (New South
        Wales, Queensland & Victoria) 1850-1889, compiled by H. J.
        Gibbney & N. Burns. Canberra, Dept. of History (Australian
        Dictionary of Biography) Institute of Advanced Studies, Austra-
        lian National University, 1969. xiii, 180 p. 26cm. An index to
        biographical references or materials to be found in the printed
        papers of the legislative assemblies of New South Wales, Vic-
        toria and Queensland.

General Works

8528   BARNES, A   R
            A dictionary of Australian history [by] A. R. Barnes [and]
        J. C. Horner. Melbourne, Cassell Australia, 1970. 184 p.
        19cm. Circa half of the volume is devoted to biographical ma-
        terial.

8529   BLAIR, DAVID, 1820-1899.
            Cyclopaedia of Australia; or, Dictionary of facts, events,
        dates, persons and places connected with the discovery, explo-
        ration, and progress of the British dominions in the south, from

the earliest dawn of discovery in the Southern Ocean to the year
1881. Melbourne, Ferguson and Moore, 1881. xii, 780, xv p.
29cm.

8530   BURGESS, HENRY THOMAS, 1839-1923.
        The cyclopedia of South Australia. An historical and com-
mercial review. Descriptive and biographical, facts, figures,
and illustrations. An epitome of progress. Adelaide, Cyclopedia Co. (A. G. Selway) 1907-09. 2 v. illus., ports.

8531   DE BRUNE, AIDAN
        Fifty years of progress in Australia, 1878-1928. Edited by
Aidan de Brune. Waterloo, Australia, Halstead Print. Co.,
1929. xi, 310, [6] p. illus., ports. 22cm. Pages 201-259 contain biographical details of well-known citizens of the period.

8532   THE HISTORY OF QUEENSLAND: its people and industries.
        In three volumes. Brisbane, States Pub. Co., 1919-
        v. illus. 28cm. Includes biographical sections. Vol. 1
only issued or available?

8533   [HUMPHREYS, HENRY R   MORIN]
        Men of the time in Australia: Victorian series. 2d ed.
Melbourne, 1882. clxxxi, 274 p. 1st ed., 1878.

8534   LEADING PERSONALITIES OF WESTERN AUSTRALIA.
        Perth, Paterson Brokensha, 1950. 342 p. ports. 26cm.

8535   LEARMONTH, ANDREW THOMAS AMOS, 1916-
        Encyclopaedia of Australia. 2d ed. Compiled by Andrew
and Nancy Learmonth. London, New York, F. Warne [1973]
viii, 606 p. illus. 23cm. 1st ed. appeared in 1968. An alphabetically arranged work that includes biographical entries.

8536   LEAVITT, THADDEUS W   H
        Australian representative men. 1st ed. Melbourne, Wells
and Leavitt, 1887. [607] p. incl. 123 ports. 29cm.

8537   LEVEY, GEORGE COLLINS
        Hutchinson's Australasia encyclopaedia, comprising a de-
scription of all places in the Australian colonies, an account of
the events which have taken place in Australasia, and the biographies of distinguished early colonists. London, Hutchinson,
1892. [5], 437 p. map. 8.°

8538   LOYAU, GEORGE F
        The representative men of South Australia. Adelaide, G.
Howell, 1883. ii, 264 p. front., port. 19cm.

8539   MARTIN, ALLAN WILLIAM
          Members of the Legislative Assembly of New South Wales,
          1856-1901. Biographical notes [by] A. W. Martin and P. Wardle.
          Canberra, Australian National University, 1959. xii, 249 p.
          21cm. (Australian National University, Canberra. Social science
          monograph 16) A biographical dictionary.

8540   MATTERS, E   Mrs.
          Australasians who count in London & Who counts in Western
          Australia. [n.p.] 1913. 246 p.

8541   MENDHAM, ROY, 1890-
          The dictionary of Australian bushrangers. Melbourne, Haw-
          thorn Press, 1975. 179 p. illus. 23cm. A biographical dic-
          tionary of Australian outlaws whose activities were generally
          confined to the 'outback,' the countryside or isolated areas.

8542   MORRISON, W   FREDERIC
          The Aldine centennial history of New South Wales, embrac-
          ing sketches and portraits of her noted people; the rise and prog-
          ress of her varied enterprises; and illustrations of her boundless
          wealth, together with maps of latest survey. Sydney, Aldine
          Pub. Co., 1888. 2 v. illus., ports. 29cm.

8543   MORRISON, W   FREDERIC
          The Aldine history of Queensland, illustrated, embracing
          sketches & portraits of her noted people, the rise & progress of
          her varied enterprises, & illustrations of her boundless wealth,
          together with maps of the latest survey. Sydney, Aldine Pub.
          Co., 1888. 2 v. illus., ports. 29cm. Vol. 2 contains biogra-
          phical sketches of leading Queensland citizens.

8544   NAN KIVELL, REX DE C
          Portraits of people connected with Australia, New Zealand
          and the South Seas from 1579 to 1960 (with a few additions from
          public collections) in the Rex de C. Nan Kivell Collection.
          [n. p.] 1962. 284 p. Draft of text; mimeographed.

8545   PARLIAMENTARY HANDBOOK OF THE COMMONWEALTH OF
          AUSTRALIA. 1st-   ed.; 1901-15--   Canberra.
          v. 24cm. Title varies: 1901-15--1932, Biographical hand-
          book and record of elections; 19   Parliamentary handbook
          and record [of elections] 1901-15--   issues published by
          Commonwealth National Library (1960-   called National Li-
          brary of Australia) Prepared by Commonwealth Parliament Li-
          brary. The most recent issues contain portraits and biographi-
          cal sketches of all those currently serving in the Australian
          Parliament.

8546   PASCOE, J   J
        History of Adelaide and vicinity with a general sketch of the
        province of South Australia and biographies of representative
        men. Edited by J. J. Pascoe. Adelaide, Hussey & Gillingham,
        1901. [Adelaide, Austraprint, 1972] xviii, 691 p. illus., ports.
        25cm. Biographies on p. 225-589, with a biographical index on
        p. 690-691. Many portraits of members of the then Australian
        Parliament are included (1901).

8547   RYDON, JOAN
        A biographical register of the Commonwealth Parliament,
        1901-1972. Canberra, Australian National University Press,
        1975. xvii, 229 p. 30cm. (Australian parliaments: biographi-
        cal notes, 5)

8548   THOMSON, KATHLEEN
        A biographical register of the Victorian Legislature, 1851-
        1900 [by] Kathleen Thomson and Geoffrey Serle. Canberra,
        Australian National University Press, 1972. xxiv, 238 p. 29cm.
        (Australian Parliaments: biographical notes, 4) Correct title
        from erratum slip; erroneously printed on t. p. and cover: A
        biographical register of the Victoria Parliament, 1859-1900. A
        biographical dictionary.

8549   WATERSON, DUNCAN BRUCE
        A biographical register of the Queensland Parliament, 1860-
        1929. Canberra, Australian National University Press, 1972.
        xvii, 205 p. 29cm. (Australian parliaments. Biographical
        notes, 3) A biographical dictionary.

8550   WHITINGTON, DON
        Inside Canberra; a guide to Australian federal politics [by]
        Don Whitington and Rob Chalmers. [Adelaide] Rigby [1971]
        296 p. 25cm. A dictionary of contemporary Australian politics
        which includes biographical entries.

AUSTRIA

8551   ANDERSKY, ED
        Militärisches Pantheon der hohen Generalität und Staabsof-
        fiziere der K. K. oesterreichischen Armee von 1800 bis auf
        die neueste Zeit. Mit Nachtrag. Wien, 1846-48. 2 v. 8.⁰
        Military pantheon of the generals and staff officers of the Aus-
        trian Army from 1800 to 1848 (ca.)

8552   BIOGRAPHISCHE BEITRÄGE ZUR WIENER ZEITGESCHICHTE.
        Herausgeber: Franz Planer. Wien, Verlag Franz Planer,
        1929. 2 v. in 1 (708 p.) 4.⁰ (Wiener Gesellschaft. Jahrbuch
        1-2, 1928-1929) Biographical contributions to the contempo-
        rary history of Vienna; some 4500 biographical sketches are
        included.

8553   COECKELBERGHE-DÜTZELE, GERHARD ROBERT WALTHER
        VON, 1786-1857.
            Curiösitaten- und Memorabilien-Lexicon von Wien. Ein
        belehrendes und interhaltendes Nachschlag- und Lesebuch in
        anekdotischer, artistischer, biographischer, legendarischer,
        pittoresker, romantischer und topographischer Beziehung. Von
        Realis [pseud.] Hrsg. von Anton Köhler. Wien, 1846. 2 v.
        illus. A dictionary of the curiosities and memorabilia of Vienna;
        included among the entries are biographical sketches and anec-
        dotes about people involved in Viennese culture and affairs.

8554   ECKSTEIN, ADOLF, ed.
            Das Parlament. Die politischen Persönlichkeiten Öster-
        reich-Ungarns in Wort und Bild. Wien, A. Eckstein, 1879-81
        [v. 3, 1880] 3 v. ports. 42cm. The Austrian Parliament ca.
        1880; the political personalities of Austria-Hungary in words
        and portraits.

8555   DIE GEISTIGE ELITE ÖSTERREICHS; ein Handbuch der
            Führenden in Kultur und Wirtschaft. [Gesamtredaktion:
        Marcell Klang] Wien, C. Barth, 1936. 1026 p. 24cm. The in-
        tellectual elite of Austria; a biographical dictionary of more than
        1,000 of Austria's leading intellectuals and creative artists of the
        1st half of the 20th century, especially the 1930's.

8556   HAMMER-PURGSTALL, JOSEPH, Freiherr von, 1774-1856.
            Porträtgallerie des steiermärkischen Adels aus der Hälfte
        des XVIII. Jahrhunderts. Wien, 1856. 20 p. 50 ports. 50
        portraits and biographical notes of Styrian nobility from the last
        half of the 18th century; alphabetical arrangement, Althann to
        Zehentner.

8557   HAMMERLE, ALOIS JOSEPH
            Skizzen und Beiträge für ein allgemeines salzburgisches
        biographisches Lexikon. Salzburg, 1879-80. 192 p. 8.º Issued
        in fascicles, of which only 4 were published (Abelzhauser to
        Barmherzige Schwestern). Sketches and contributions for a gen-
        eral biographical dictionary of Salzburg, Austria.

8558   KNAUER, OSWALD
            Das österreichische Parlament von 1848-1966. Wien,
        Bergland Verlag [1969] 316 p. 19cm. (Österreich-Reihe, Bd.
        358/361) Primarily a register of the members of the Austrian
        Bundesrat and Nationalrat (Parliament) from 1848 to 1966; how-
        ever, the lists do include birth and birth/death dates and a
        phrase describing the parliamentarian's chief profession or ac-
        tivity.

8559   KOLLER, LUDWIG, Father
            Geistliche Schriftsteller, Künstler und Forscher Öster-

reichs. [Göttweig, N. Ö: Stiftsbibliothek, 1952] 140 p. 29cm.
Religious writers, artists and scholars of Austria; an alphabetical list with the authors' dates of birth/death—covers all periods.

8560   OESTERREICHISCHE NATIONAL-ENCYKLOPÄDIE; oder,
        Alphabetische Darlegung der wissenswürdigsten Eigenthüm-
lichkeiten des Oesterreichisches Kaiserthumes, in Rücksicht
auf Natur, Leben und Institutionen, Industrie und Commerz,
öffentliche und Privat-Anstalten, Bildung und Wissenschaft,
Literatur und Kunst, Geographie und Statistik, Geschichte,
Genealogie und Biographie, so wie auf alle Hauptgegenstände
seiner Civilisations-Verhältnisse. Wien, I. Klang, 1834-38.
6 v. illus., ports. The Austrian encyclopedia; alphabetical
representation of [among other subjects] biographies of famous
Austrians. A volume of portraits contained in the Encyclopedia
was issued separately (in 2 parts?) in 1837-38 (?)

8561   PEMMER, HANS, 1886-
        Der Döblinger Friedhof. Seine Toten, seine Denkmäler
[von] Hans Pemmer und Ninni Lackner. Wien, 1848. 66 p.
illus. The Döblinger Cemetery in Vienna; 313 tombs are noted,
with biographical material from epitaphs.

8562   PEMMER, HANS, 1886-
        Der Friedhof zu St. Marx in Wien. Seine Toten, seine
Grabdenkmäler. [Wien] Amt für Kultur und Volksbildung, Re-
ferat Heimatpflege, 1951. 96 p. illus. 8.º The cemetery at
St. Marx in Vienna. Bio-bibliographical remarks on 300 grave-
sites (taken largely from the epitaphs).

8563   PEMMER, HANS, 1886-
        Der Wiener Zentral-Friedhof. Seine Geschichte und seine
Denkmäler. Wien, Österreichischer Bundesverlag, 1924. 184 p.
illus. 8.º Vienna's Central Cemetery; its history and monuments, with biographical data therefrom.

8564   PROMINENTEN-ALMANACH. 1.-   Bd.; 1930-
        Wien-Leipzig.   v. ports. Edited by Oscar Friedmann.
No more published? An almanach of prominent Austrians; includes brief biographies with bibliographies and sources. The
portraits are especially noteworthy.

8565   RECHNITZ, STEFAN
        Grabstätten berühmter Männer und Frauen. Ein Rundgang
durch die Wiener Vorstadtfriedhöfe. Mit einer Zusammen-
fassung der auf dem Wiener Zentralfriedhof befindlichen Ehren-
gaben berühmter Persönlichkeiten. Wien, Gerlach & Wiedling,
1948. 223 p. 8.º The graves of famous men and women; a
tour through Vienna's suburban cemeteries. With brief biographical notes of 1800 persons and descriptions of their tombs.

8566   RECHNITZ, STEFAN
        Die Grazer Friedhöfe. Eine Auslese Grabstätten berühm-
ter und denkwürdiger Personen. Zum 170jährigen Bestand
des Steinfeld- (1787-1957), 150jährigen Bestand des St. Peter-
(1807-1957) und zum 140jährigen Bestand des St. Leonhard-
Friedhofes (1817-1957) Wien, 1957. 1 v.

        ---- ----Nachtrag 1 [und Gesamt- und Einzelregister und
Fortsetzung] Wien, 1957/58-60.   v. The cemeteries of
Graz; a selection of the burial places of famous and memorable
persons. Contains numerous brief biographies.

8567   RIGLER, RUDOLF RICHARD
        Grabschriften aller Friedhöfe von Grätz. Gesammelt und
nach der Zeitfolge geordnet. Als Fortsetzung der Wanderungen
zu den Gottesäckern in den Umgebungen der Stadt Gratz von J.
C. Kautzner. St. Peter Friedhof. Grätz, 1836. viii, 160 p.
775 inscriptions on the tombstones of cemeteries of Graz arranged chronologically (by death date); with biographical data.

8568   SCHEIBERT, JUSTUS, 1831-1904.
        Illustrirtes Militär-Lexikon für die K. und K. Österreichisch-
ungarische und deutsche Armee, von J. Scheibert und W. Porth
... unter Mitwirkung der Generale z. d. Wille (Bearbeitung der
Militär-Litteratur) sowie anderer hervorragender Fachmänner.
Mit ca. 600 Abbildungen und einem Anhange: Militär-Litteratur.
Berlin, W. Pauli's Nachf. (H. Jerosch) 1897. 840, 39 p. illus.
28cm. An illustrated military dictionary for the Austro-Hungarian and German Armies which includes biographical sketches
of leading military figures.

8569   STRACK, JOSEPH
        Die Generale der österreichischen Armee. Nach K. K.
Feldacten und andern gedruckten Quellen. Wien, Keck & Sohn,
1850. iv, 320 p. 8.º   The generals of the Austrian Army.

8570   WERNICKE, RUDOLF
        Vierundsechszig Porträtzeichnungen. Mit einer Einleitung
von Wilhelm Jenny. Linz, Institut für Landeskunde von Oberösterreich, 1959. 64 p. ports. 8.º (Schriftenreihe zur bio-
graphischen Lexikon von Oberösterreich, 1) 64 portraits of
prominent figures from Upper Austria.

8571   WILHELM, ARTHUR
        Die Reichsrats-Abgeordneten des allgemeinen Wahlrechtes.
Ausführliche Biographien. Wien, M. Perles, 1907. 119 p.
front. (3 ports.) 28cm. The delegates to the Austrian Parliament's Legislative Assembly; biographical particulars.

8572   WINKLERN, JOHANN BAPTIST VON, v. 1768.
        Biographien denkwürdiger Steiermärker. (In Steier-
        märkische Zeitschrift, neue Folge. Graz. Bd. 6, I (1840) p.
        82-139; 6, II (1841) p. 27-80; 7, I (1842) p. 52-114) Biographies
        of 168 famous Styrians from Ulrich von Liechtenstein to the end
        of the 18th century; lacks any definite arrangement and without
        index.

8573   WURZBACH, ALFRED WOLFGANG, Ritter von Tannenberg,
        1879-1957.
        Joseph Kriehuber und die Wiener Gesellschaft seiner Zeit.
        Katalog der Portratlithographien Kriehubers mit ausführlichen
        Angaben über die von ihm dargestellten Personen, in vier Bänd-
        en. [2. verm. und vollständig neu bearb. Ausg.] Wien, W.
        Krieg, 1955-57. 2 v. in 3. 24cm. Joseph Kriehuber and the
        Viennese society of his age; a catalog. Vol. 2 (in 2 parts) com-
        prises a biographical dictionary of Viennese personalities litho-
        graphed by Joseph Kriehuber (pt. 1: A-Engelhartt; pt. 2: En-
        nöckl-Hye) No more vols. were published?

BALTIC STATES

8574   DEUTSCHBALTISCHES BIOGRAPHISCHES LEXIKON 1710-1960.
        Im Auftrag der Baltischen Historischen Kommission begon-
        nen von Olaf Welding und unter Mitarbeit von Erik Amburger und
        Georg von Krusenstjern hrsg. von Wilhelm Lenz. Köln, Böhlau
        Verlag, 1970. xiii, 930 p. 26cm. A biographical dictionary of
        Germans in the Baltic States, 1710-1960.

8575   PANTZER, GERHARD VON, 1913-1966.
        Personen- und familienkundliche Literatur in baltischen
        Zeitschriften, 1948-1960. Köln [Isabella v. Pantzer] 1970. 52 p.
        21cm. (Baltische Ahnen- und Stammtafeln. Sonderheft Nr. 10)
        Bibliography of persons and familites in the Baltic States in peri-
        odicals issued in those States, 1948-1960.

BARBARY STATES

8576   AL-QĀDIRI, MUHAMMAD IBN AL-TAYYIB, d. 1773.
        Nachr al-mathani de Mouhammad al-Qâdiri. Traduite par
        A. Graulle. Nendeln, Liechtenstein, Kraus Reprint, 1974. 2 v.
        23cm. (Archives marocaines; publication de la Mission scien-
        tifique du Maroc, v. 21, 24) Caption title. Vol. 2 translated by
        P. Maillard. Reprint of the Paris (E. Leroux) 1913-1917 ed.
        Biographical sketches of eminent personages of the Barbary
        States who flourished from the year 1001 to 1100 (Moslem calen-
        dar--1592-1689 in the Christian calendar) Arrangement is
        chronological (year by year); there is, unfortunately, no index
        of names.

BELGIUM

(See also FLANDERS)

8577   ASSOCIATION ROYALE DES DEMEURES HISTORIQUES DE
BELGIQUE.
Catalogus van de tentoonstelling gewijd aan het Belgisch
portret van de XVe tot de XVIIIe eeuw, behorend tot Belgische
privé verzamellingen. Kasteel Laarne, september-november
1970. Catalogue de l'exposition: le portrait belge du XVe au
XVIIIe siècle, de collection privées belges. Château de Laarne,
septembre-novembre 1970. Brussels, 1970. 118 p. ports.
24cm. In Flemish and French. At head of title: Koninklijke
Vereniging der Historische Woonsteden van België. Ca. 59
portraits of Belgian men and women (15th-18th century) with biographical comments on the sitters and the painters; some of
the sitters and painters are unknown, however. Chronological
arrangement; there is no index or table of contents.

8578   BERNIER, THÉODORE ANTOINE, 1843-1893.
Dictionnaire géographique, historique, archéologique,
biographique & bibliographique du Hainaut, par Théodore Bernier. Mons, H. Manceaux, 1879. xxvii, 640 p. geneal. tables.
19cm. Geographical, historical, archeological, biographical
and bibliographical dictionary of the province of Hainaut,
Belgium.

8579   LA CHAMBRE DES REPRÉSENTANTS IN 1894-1895.
Bruxelles, Société belge du librairie, 1896. 470 p. ports.
8.° Portraits and biographical sketches of the Chamber of
Representatives of the Belgian Parliament, 1894-1895.

8580   DEL VAUX DE FOURON, HENRI JOSEPH BARTHÉLEMI,
1796-1858.
Dictionnaire biographique de la province de Liège avec des
chronologies des princes qui ont dominé dans les différents pays
formant la province. Liège, Typ. de F. Oudart, 1845. vii,
147 p. 22cm. Biographical dictionary of the province of Liege
. . .

8580a   JANSEN, EVERMODE JOSEPH, 1871-
Bio-bibliografisch naamboek der voormannen en voorname
familiën der Kempen. Brecht, Druk L. Braeckmans, 1925.
108 p. 25cm. Bio-bibliographical 'book of names' of the leading personalities and eminent families of the Campines (Kempen) district of Belgium.

8581   MOLLE, PAUL VAN, 1897-
Het Belgische Parlement 1894-1972. Le Parlement Belge
1894-1972. Antwerpen, Standaard Wetenschappelijke Uitgeverij,

1972. 445 p. ports. 26cm. A bio-bibliographical dictionary
of members of the Belgian Parliament from 1894 to 1972.

BOHEMIA

(See CZECHOSLOVAKIA)

BOLIVIA

8582   COSTA DE LA TORRE, ARTURO
        Catálogo de la bibliografía boliviana; libros y folletos, 1900-
        1963. La Paz, 1966 [i.e. 1968-   v. 24cm. Catalog of
        Bolivian bibliography, 1900-1963; actually this work is bio-bib-
        liographical in nature. Some of the biographical sketches are
        fairly substantial. 1st vol. only available as of 1976.

8583   DÍAZ ARGUEDAS, JULIO, 1889-
        Paceños célebres: esbozos biográficos. 1. ed. La Paz
        [Bolivia] Ediciones Isla, 1974. 224 p. 20cm. Biographies of
        60 distinguished, deceased citizens of La Paz; arranged in no
        particular order.

8584   DÍAZ ARGUEDAS, JULIO, 1889-
        Sintesis biográfica, histórica y geográfica de los nombres
        de las calles, avenidas, plazas y parques de la ciudad de La
        Paz. La Paz, 1951. 111 p. fold. plan. 19cm. A biographical,
        historical and geographical synthesis of the names of the streets,
        plazas and parks of the City of La Paz, Bolivia.

8585   HEATH, DWIGHT B
        Historical dictionary of Bolivia. Metuchen, N. J., Scare-
        crow Press, 1972. vi, 324 p. 22cm. (Latin American histori-
        cal dictionaries, no. 4) Includes brief biographies of important
        historical figures of Bolivia.

8586   SANABRIA G   , FLOREN
        Bolivia, ciudadanos notables. La Paz, Producciones In-
        formativas [1974?] 240 p. illus. 28cm. Bolivia and notable
        citizens of Bolivia. Biographical dictionary of living Bolivians
        on pages 155-237 (3 columns to a page). Presidents of the Re-
        public; 48 biographies (p. 63-81).

BOTSWANA

8587   STEVENS, RICHARD P   1931-
        Historical dictionary of the Republic of Botswana. Metu-
        chen, N. J., Scarecrow Press, 1975. 189 p. map. 23cm.
        (African historical dictionaries, no. 5) Includes biographical

entries: natives and foreigners involved in the historical development of Botswana.

BRAZIL

8588   ASLAN, NICOLA
        Pequenas biografias de grandes maçons brasileiros. Rio de Janeiro, Editora Maçônica, 1973. 422 p. 24cm. A biographical dictionary of 66 famous Brazilian Freemasons.

8589   BARRETO, JOÃO PAULO DE MELLO, 1891-
        Frases célebres brasileiras. Série 1-   Rio de Janeiro, Irmãos Pongetti, 1947-   v. illus. 22cm. Brazilian quotations followed by biographies of their authors, and histories of the phrase quoted. Série 1 only published?

8590   BERGER, PAULO
        Dicionário histórico das ruas do Rio de Janeiro, I e II regiões administrativas (centro). Rio de Janeiro, Olímpica Editora, 1974. 145 p. illus. 25cm. An historical dictionary of the streets of Rio de Janeiro. Includes biographical sketches of the persons after whom streets are named (primarily distinguished Brazilians and Portuguese, with a number of world figures); entries are generally under surnames where people are involved and thus the work serves as a type of biographical dictionary.

8591   BITTENCOURT, AGNELLO, 1876-
        Dicionário amazonense de biografias. Rio de Janeiro, Conquista, 1973. 517 p. 21cm. (Edições Academia Amazonense, 4) A biographical dictionary of Amazonas, Brazil; entry by forename.

8592   BOUTIN, LEONIDAS
        Diccionário biográfico brasileiro. Curitiba, Composto e impresso na Papelaria Max Roesner, 1971. 127 p. 21cm. Biographical dictionary of Brazil.

8593   BRAZIL. CONGRESSO. CÂMARA DOS DEPUTADOS. BIBLIO-
        TECA.
        Deputados brasileiros; repertorio biográfico dos membros da Câmara dos Deputados, Sétima Legislatura, 1971-1975. Brasilia, 1971. 630 p. ports. 22cm.

        ---- ----Supplemento. Brasilia, 1974. 34 p. ports. 22cm.
        A biographical dictionary of members of the Chamber of Deputies, Brazilian Congress, for 1971-1975 (the 7th Legislative session).

8594   BRAZIL. MINISTÉRIO DA FAZENDA.
         Ministros da Fazenda, 1822-1972. Rio de Janeiro, 1972.
         223, [15] p. illus. 23cm. Brazilian ministers of the Treasury,
         1822-1972; 120 biographical sketches in chronological order, with
         alphabetical index (by forename) at end.

8595   BRAZIL. MINISTÉRIO DA VIAÇÃO E OBRAS PÚBLICAS.
         Dados biográficos dos ministros. Rio de Janeiro. Serviço
         de Documentação [pref. 1961] 164 p. 23cm. Biographies of
         84 ministers of federal transportation and public works, Brazil,
         1861 to 1961; chronological arrangement.

8596   BRAZIL. MINISTÉRIO DOS TRANSPORTES. SERVIÇO DE
         DOCUMENTAÇÃO.
         Dados biográficos dos ministros. 2. ed. Rio de Janeiro,
         1968. 171 p. 24cm. First ed. issued in 1961 by the Ministerio
         da Viação e Obras Públicas (Serviço de Documentação) Biogra-
         phical sketches (in chronological arrangement, i. e., dates of
         service) of Brazilian officials who served as ministers of agri-
         culture, commerce and public works, industry, transport, etc.
         from March 1861 to 1968.

8597   CAMPO BELLO, HENRIQUE LEITE PEREIRA DE PAIVA DE
         FARIA TAVORA E CERNACHE, conde de, 1904-
         Governadores gerais e vice-reis do Brasil. Pref. do
         Exmo. Sr. A. G. de Araujo Jorge. Edição oficial e comem-
         orativa. Pôrto, Delegação Executiva do Brasil as Comemo-
         rações Centenárias de Portugal, 1940. 135 p. 26cm. At head
         of title: Conde de Campo Bello (D. Henrique) Biographical
         sketches of the 49 governors and viceroys of Brazil under Por-
         tuguese rule (1549-1808); chronologically arranged.

8598   DICIONÁRIO DE HISTÓRIA DO BRASIL: moral e civismo.
         Organização geral: Departamento Editorial das Edições
         Melhoramentos. Redação de temas e biografias: Brasil Bandec-
         chi [et al.] Colaboração: Hélio Vianna [et al.] 4. ed. São Paulo,
         Edições Melhoramentos, 1976 (c1973) vii, 618 p. 27cm. A
         dictionary of Brazilian history; biography is a major part of the
         dictionary.

8599   FOSSARI, DOMINGOS
         Assim os viejo ... homens do meu tempo. [Florianópolis,
         Distribuidor: Lunardelli Representações] 1973. 1 v. (chiefly
         ports.) 26cm. Contemporary prominent personages of the
         State of Santa Catarina, Brazil; 107 portraits (in cartoon format)
         with accompanying characterizing phrases.

8600   FREITAS, GASPAR DE
         Paulistas na Universidade do Coimbra. Coimbra, 1958.
         218 p. illus., ports. 26cm. "Supplemento de 'Brasilia.'" Bra-

zilians (especially those from Sao Paulo) at the University of
Coimbra, Portugal.

8601   INSTITUTO HISTORICO E GEOGRAPHICO BRASILEIRO, RIO
        DE JANEIRO.
        Diccionario historico, geographico e ethnographico do
        Brazil ... Introducção geral. Rio de Janeiro, Imprensa Na-
        cional, 1922-   v. illus., ports. 30cm. Historical, geogra-
        phical and ethnographical dictionary of Brazil. Each chapter of
        vol. 2 deals with a different State. At the end of each chapter is
        a biographical dictionary (by forename) of notable persons of the
        particular State.

8602   LEÃO, ERMELINO AGOSTINHO DE
        Contribuições historicas e geographicas para o diccionario
        do Paraná. Curityba, Empresa Graphica Paranaense, 1926-
             v. 27cm. Cover title: Diccionario historico e geographico
        do Paraná. Historical and geographical contributions for the
        dictionary of Parana. Includes many biographical entries (under
        forenames!) Only 4 fascicles (604 p., A-Faisqueira) published?

8603   MELO, VERÍSSIMO DE
        Patronos e acadèmicos; Academia Norte-Riograndense de
        Letras (antologia e biografia) Rio de Janeiro, Editoria Pongetti,
        1972-   v. 22cm. An anthology with biographical bio-
        bibliographical sketches of patrons and members of the Academia
        Norte-Riograndense de Letras (State of Rio Grande do Norte,
        Brazil) There are 40 bio-bibliographies in vol. 1.

8604   MENDONÇA, RUBENS DE
        Dicionario biográfico mato-grossense. Com um pref. de
        Francisco de Aquino Corréa. 2. ed. [Gioânia, Editora Rio
        Bonito] 1971. 165 p. 22cm. Biographical dictionary of Mato
        Grosso.

8605   NOGUEIRA, OCTACIANO
        Parlamentares do Império (obra comemorativa do sesqui-
        centenario da instituição parlamentar no Brasil) [por] Octaciano
        Nogueira e João Sereno Firmo. Brasilia, Centro Gráfico do
        Senado Federal, 1973. 2 v. (686 p.) ports. 21cm. Vol. 1 is
        an alphabetical list of Brazilian legislators, 1823 to 1899, with
        birth and death dates, characterizing phrase, dates of service
        in the Imperial Legislature, and references to biobibliographi-
        cal sources.

8606   NÔVO DICIONÁRIO DE HISTORIA DO BRASIL, ILUSTRADO.
        Redação dos temas e biografias: Brasil Bandecchi, Leo-
        nardo Arroyo, Ubiratan Rosa. Colaboradores: Myriam Ellis
        [et al.] 2. ed., rev. [São Paulo, Edições Melhoramentos,
        [1971] 645 p. illus. (part col.) 24cm. New illustrated diction-

ary of the history of Brazil. Biographies are included. First edition (617 p.) was published in 1970.

8607   OLIVEIRA, CAROLINA RENNO RIBEIRO DE
Biografias de personalidades célebres; para uso do aluno nos diversos níveis do ensino e dos estudiosos da historia do Brasil. 11. ed. ampliada, atualizada e melhorada: nova orto-grafia. [São Paulo] Editora do Mestre [apresentação 1972] 369 p. ports. 21cm. An extensive compilation of biographies (over 400—each page is in 2 columns) of persons prominent in the history and civilization of Brazil. Arrangement is by topic: e.g., discoverers of Brazil, pioneers of aviation, painters, musicians, popular figures, etc. Alphabetical approach (by forename) thru' name index at end of volume.

8608   RIVERA, BUENO DE
Pioneiros e exponentes de Minas Gerais. Redator e editor responsável: Bueno de Rivera. Belo Horizonte, Edições Guia Rivera, 1970/71. 243 p. ports. 33cm. A biographical dic-tionary of distinguished figures in Minas Gerais' present and past history and civilization. Alphabetical arrangement by fore-name.

8609   RODRIGUES, OLAO
Veja santos! [Santos, Brazil] Prefeitura Municipal de Santos, Administração General Clovis Bandeira Brasil [1973?] 650, [64] p. ports. 23cm. A dictionary of streets in the City of Santos, Brazil, with biographical sketches of persons after whom many of the streets are named (largely famous Brazilians and Portuguese, although figures of other nationalities are in-cluded).

8610   SILVA, HUGO VICTOR GRIMARÃES E
Deputados provinciais e estaduais do Ceará. Assembléias legislativas: 1835-1947. Fortaleza, Editora Jurídica [1951] 544 p. Provincial legislative members and statesmen of the State of Ceará, Brazil.

8611   SOUZA, ANTONIO LOUREIRO DE
Baianos ilustres, 1564-1925. 2. ed. rev. e aumentada. [Salvador, Brazil] 1973. 347 p. illus. 27cm. 151 biographies of famous natives or residents of the State of Bahia, Brazil from 1564 to 1925. Arranged chronologically. No alphabetical name index.

8612   SPALDING, WALTER, 1901-
Construtores do Rio Grande. Porto Alegre, Livraria Sulina Editora, 1969-   v. illus., ports. 24cm. (Co-leção Biografias, no. 4
A bio-bibliographical dictionary of prominent personalities in

the history of the State of Rio Grande do Sul, Brazil; alphabetical by forename. Surname index for vols. 1-2 at end of v. 2.

8613   TORIYAMA, TOYOYASU
        A vida dos imigrantes japoneses pioneiros do Brasil. [São Paulo, Brazil, Empresa Jornalística Agrícola Noguiyo Shimbun [1972] 210 p. illus. 24cm. (Vejam o passado dos pioneiros, 6) Circa 150 biographies of Japanese immigrants who attained distinction in Brazil: most of the sketches are of people still living. In Portuguese and Japanese.

8614   VASCONCELLOS, JOSÉ MARCELLINO PEREIRA DE, 1812-1874.
        Selecta brasiliense; ou, Noticias, descobertas, observacões, factos e curiosidades em relação aos homens, á historia e cousas do Brasil. Rio de Janeiro, Typ. Universal de Laemmert, 1868. 276 p. 19cm. A kind of encyclopedia or dictionary of things Brazilian; part I (p. 1-179) is a biographical 'dictionary' (alphabetical by forename[s]) of 114 famous historical personages.

8615   VILLAS-BÔAS, PEDRO
        Notas de bibliografia sul-rio-grandense: autores. Porto Alegre, A. Nação em co-edição com o Instituto Estadual do Livro, 1974. 615 p. 23cm. A bio-bibliographical dictionary of the Brazilian state of Rio Grande do Sul.

BULGARIA

8616   BELEZHITI BŬLGARI. [Sŭstaviteli: Boris Cholpanov, Vasil Giŭzelev. Redaktsionna kolegiiâ: Simeon Mitev i dr.] Sofiiâ, Dŭrzh. voenno izd-vo, 1968-   v. illus. 25cm. Each vol. has also special t. p. Contents.--1. 681-1396.--2-3. 1396-1878. Famous Bulgarians through the centuries.

8617   DANCHOV, NIKOLA GEORGIEV, 1878-
        Bulgarska entsiklopediiâ. Sofiiâ, Kn-vo St. Atanasov, 1936. 1720 p. illus., ports. 21cm. At head of title: N. G. Danchov i I. G. Danchov. An encyclopedia of Bulgaria still useful for its many short biographies of Bulgarian personalities.

8618   KRATKA BŬLGARSKA ENTSIKLOPEDIÂ. [Glaven redaktor Vladimir Georgiev. Sofiiâ] Bŭlgarska akademiiâ na naukite [1963-69] 5 v. illus. 29cm. At head of title: Bŭlgarska akademiiâ na naukite. Bŭlgarska entsiklopediiâ. A general Bulgarian encyclopedia which stands as one of the best sources for Bulgarian biography.

8619   OBORISHTENTSI. Sbornik ot istoricheski ochertsi za narodnite
        predstaviteli na oborishte prez 1876 godina. [Red. i sŭstav.
        Khristo M. Ionkov] Sofiiā, Dŭrzhavno voenno izd-vo, 1972.
        296 p. ports. 22cm. Biographies of 69 Bulgarian revolution-
        ists, natives of the Oborishte region, instrumental in the Up-
        rising of 1876 in Bulgaria. Alphabetically arranged.

8620   POD ZNAMETO, CHERVENOTO; album na zaginalite v borbata
        protiv kapitalizma i fashizma ot Varnenski okrŭg, 1904-
        1945. [Sŭstaviteli: Nikola Chakŭrov i dr. Redaktor: Petŭr
        Terziiski] Sofiiā, Partizdat, 1973. 191 p. illus. ports. 32cm.
        At head of title: Okrŭzhen komitet na BKP. Okrŭzhen komitet na
        bortsite protiv fashizma i kapitalizma. Okrŭzhen partien
        arkhiv. Okrŭzhen istoricheski muzei, Varna. Includes 196
        short biographies (generally accompanied by portraits) of Bul-
        garian patriots from the district of Varna, especially those of
        socialist or communist orientation. The period covered is 1904
        to the end of World War II.

8621   SEPTEMVRIĬSKOTO VŬSTANIE 1923; entsiklopediiā. Sŭstaviteli
        Georgi Mishkov [i. dr.] Pod red. na Georgi Mishkov i
        Ekaterina Peovska. Sofiiā, Partizdat, 1973. 312 p. illus.,
        ports. 21cm. A dictionary of persons and events during the
        September Uprising of 1923 in Bulgaria.

8622   TE VECHNO SHTE ZHIVEIĀT. [Sŭstaviteli: Vasil Lesichki,
        Stoio Lesev] Sofiiā, Izd-vo na BKP, 1972. 191 p. illus.,
        ports. 32cm. On page preceding t. p. : Okrŭzhen komitet na
        BKP—Kyustendil. Contains over 3000 biographical sketches and
        portraits of Bulgarian communists, arranged chronologically
        (3 periods: 1919-1925, 1926-1940, 1941-1944) with an alphabeti-
        cal name index.

8623   V IMETO NA SVOBODATA, 1923-1944. [Biogr. danni i snimki
        na] Zaginali v borbata protiv kapitalizma i fashizma v Per-
        nishki okrŭg. [Sŭstaviteli: Boris Gotev i dr. Redaktor: Sveto-
        zara Atanasova] Sofiiā, Partizdat, 1972. 172 p. illus., ports.
        30cm. At head of title: Okrŭzhen komitet na BKP. Okrŭzhen
        istoricheski muzei—Pernik. Biographies (and, in most instan-
        ces) portraits) of 209 Bulgarian Communists active from 1923
        to 1944, and chiefly natives of Pernik Okrug (district) with an
        alphabetical name index at end of vol.

8624   ZVEZDI VŬV VEKOVETE. [Biograf. danni i snaimki na] zagi-
        nali revoliutsionni bortsy protiv kapitalizma i fashizma, 9
        iuni 1929-9 septemvri 1944. [Red. Stoiān Stoimenov, Vasil
        Mikhailov. S predg. ot Stoiān Stoimenov] Sofiiā, Izd-vo na
        Bŭlgarskata komunisticheska partiiā, 1972. 796 p. ports. 33cm.
        At head of title: Muzei na revoliutsionnoto dvizhenie v Bŭlgariiā.
        A huge collection of biographical sketches and portraits of Bul-
        garian Communists and patriots active from June 1923 to Sep-
        tember 1944.

BURMA

8625   BURMA
        History of services of gazetted and other officers serving
under the Government of Burma (corrected up to 1st July, 1936).
Compiled in the Office of the Accountant-General, Burma. Rangoon, Supdt. , Govt. Print. and Stationary, 1936-   v.
24cm. Contents: v. 1.
                    pt. 2. Officers of Public Works Dept.
Contains useful biographical data for native and British-born officials of the British-controlled government of Burma prior to
the 2d World War. An index of names at the end of each vol.
yields an alphabetical approach.

8626   MARING, JOEL M
        Historical and cultural dictionary of Burma, by Joel M.
Maring and Ester G. Maring. Metuchen, N. J. , Scarecrow
Press, 1973. vi, 290 p. 23cm. (Historical and cultural dictionaries of Asia, no. 4) Includes biographical sketches, although not in great number.

8627   SEIN MYINT, U
        Hnit hna-ya Myanma naing-gan thamaing abidan. [Rangoon,
1969] 616, [8] p. 18cm. A dictionary of Burmese history; includes biographical entries. In Burmese.

8628   WHO'S WHO IN BURMA; a biographical record of prominent
        residents of Burma with photographs & illustrations. Com-
piled and published by the Indo-Burma Publishing Agency, Calcutta & Rangoon. Culcutta, Printed at the Calcutta Fine Art
Cottage [1927?] 262 p. illus., ports. 26cm. "[Issued] under
the patronage of H. E. Sir Harcourt Butler, Governor of Burma. " A predecessor (?) of the triennial Who's who in Burma
which began publication in 1961.

CAMEROONS

8629   CAMEROONS, SOUTHERN. PARLIAMENT. HOUSE OF
        ASSEMBLY.
        Southern Cameroons House of Assembly: Who's who. Il-
lustrated biographies. Lagos, Govt. Press, 1954. 16 p.
ports.

CANADA

Bibliography, Indexes, Portrait Catalogs

8630   JAIN, SUSHIL KUMAR
        A classified guide to Canadian biographical sources. Wind-
sor, Ont. , 1967. 17 l.

8631   McGILL UNIVERSITY, MONTREAL. LIBRARY. REFERENCE
        DEPT.
        Canadian biography; a student's guide to reference sources.
        Montreal, McLennan Library, McGill University, Reference
        Dept., 1973. 13 p. 28cm.

General Works

8632   ACADIA UNIVERSITY, Wolfville, N. S.
        Records of the graduates, 1843-1926. Arranged by classes.
        Rev. and enl. by A. C. Chute. Wolfville, Associated Alumni
        of Acadia University, 1926. 296 p. port. 23cm. A biographi-
        cal register. Revision and extension of the 1909 ed. which
        covered the years 1843-1908.

8633   ALBUM OF CANADIAN MAYORS, prepared from photographs
        and biographical data gathered by the Canadian Press Syn-
        dicate. Montreal, 1902. 1 v. ports.

8634   BANNERMAN, JEAN MACKAY
        Leading ladies, Canada, 1639-1967. Dundas, Ont., Carrs-
        wood [c1967] xxiii, 332 p. ports. 24cm. Canadian women of
        British ancestry prominent in various fields of endeavor.

8635   BROWN, PETER LAURIE, 1882-   ed.
        The Conservative blue book. Toronto, 1932. 187 p. ports.
        21cm. Biographical sketches and portraits of leaders of the
        Conservative Party of Canada.

8636   BURNHAM, HAMPDEN, 1860-1940.
        Canadians in the imperial naval and military service a-
        broad. Toronto, Williamson, 1891. 240 p. illus. 19cm.

8637   CAMPEAU, FABIEN RENÉ ÉDOUARD, 1844-
        Illustrated guide to the House of Commons and Senate of
        Canada, containing the portraits and autographs of the governor
        general, the members of the cabinet and the members and offi-
        cers of the Senate and House of Commons, with a biographical
        sketch of members of both houses. [vols. 1-3] Ottawa, F. R.
        E. Campeau, 1875-85. 3 v. ports. 20-23cm. Ceased with
        1885 volume? Vols. for 1875, 1879, 1885 were published (only?)

8638   CANADA. PUBLIC ARCHIVES.
        The Canadian directory of Parliament, 1867-1967. Edited
        by J. K. Johnson. Ottawa, Queen's Printer, 1968. viii, 731 p.
        24cm. Biographies of legislators after the formation of the
        Confederation.

8639   THE CANADIAN PARLIAMENTARY COMPANION. 1862-1897.
            Ottawa, J. Durie. 25 v. 17cm. annual. Includes biogra-
        phical sketches of Federal and provincial legislators, members
        of legislative council in Quebec, governors, lieutenant-gover-
        nors. Succeded by the Canadian parliamentary guide, q. v.
        Some editions have title: The Canadian parliamentary compan-
        ion and annual register.

8640   COOPER, JOHN ALEXANDER, 1868-   ed.
            Men of Canada; a portrait gallery of men whose energy, a-
        bility, enterprise and public spirit are responsible for the ad-
        vancement of Canada, the premier colony of Great Britain.
        Edited by John A. Cooper. Montreal, Canadian Historical Co.,
        1901-02. xviii p., 296 p. of ports. 25cm. About 1200 persons
        are represented.

8641   DEROME, LOUIS JOSEPH AMÉDÉE, 1841-1922.
            Galerie nationale des gouverneurs généraux du Canada,
        1608-1921. [n. p.] 1921. 1 v. ports. 24.° Cover title: 50 bio-
        graphical sketches and portraits.

8642   DRUMMOND, GRACE JULIA
            Women of Canada. Montreal, Women of Canada Pub. Co.,
        c1930. 241 p. Ca. 200 Canadian women (including French Ca-
        nadians) are represented.

8643   DUMAS, SILVIO
            Les Filles du Roi en Nouvelle-France; étude historique
        avec répertoire biographique. Québec, Société historique de
        Québec, 1972. xv, 382 p. illus. 23cm. (Cahiers d'histoire,
        no. 24)
        On pages [169]-349 is a biographical dictionary of Frenchwomen
        who migrated to New France (Canada) in the 17th century to
        serve as wives to the colonists there.

8644   ENCYCLOPEDIA CANADIANA. Toronto, Grolier of Canada,
            1975. 10 v. illus., ports. 26cm. In addition to the many
        biographical sketches (over 3500) of Canadians of the past (and
        present) there is a section: "Contemporary biographies" in vol.
        10 of the set. Much of the biographical material is reproduced
        from the Dictionary of Canadian biography (q. v.). First pub-
        lished in 1957. Copyrighted at least 11 times to 1975.

8645   AN ENCYCLOPEDIA OF CANADIAN BIOGRAPHY CONTAINING
            SKETCHES AND STEEL ENGRAVINGS OF CANADA'S
        PROMINENT MEN. Montreal, Canadian Press Syndicate, 1904-
        05. 3 v. plates. Figures prominent at the turn of the 20th cen-
        tury; a single biography on each page with facing portrait. An-
        other edition (or reprint) issued in 1907?

8646   FAUTEUX, AEGIDIUS, 1876-1941
            Patriotes de 1837-1838. Montréal, Éditions des Dix, 1950.
        433 p. 25cm. Ca. 475 French-Canadians who took part in the
        Canadian Rebellion of 1837-1838 are identified in a biographical
        dictionary beginning on p. 83.

8647   GODBOUT, ARCHANGE
            Nos ancêtres au XVIIe siècle. Dictionnaire généalogique et
        bio-bibliographique des familles canadiennes. Québec [1955?-
        66?] 6 pts. (471 p.) 26cm. Detached from the Rapport de
        l'Archiviste de la province de Québec pour 1953 à 1959/60 and
        the Rapport des Archives du Québec pour 1965. Canadian
        (French) families founded before 1700 with descendents still liv-
        ing; a genealogical and bio-bibliographical dictionary. Covers
        A-Brassard; no more published? Actually a new ed. of the 1st
        vol. of Dictionnaire généalogique des familles canadiennes (by
        Cyprien Tanguay)

8648   GOTTESMAN, ELI, 1932-
            Who's who in Canadian Jewry. Compiled and prepared by
        the Canadian Jewish Literary Foundation for the Jewish Institute
        of Higher Research of the Central Rabbinical Seminary of Cana-
        da. Author and compiler: Eli Gottesman. [Montreal] Jewish
        Institute of Higher Research. Central Rabbinical Seminary of
        Canada, 1965. 525 p. ports. 31cm.

8649   HUGUENIN, ANNE MARIE (GLEASON) 1875-1943.
            Portraits de femmes. [Montréal] La Patrie [1938] 273 p.
        port. Biographical sketches of ca. 200 French-Canadian women
        of accomplishment. Another edition was issued in 1939 (Edition
        scholaire. 188 p.) in which certain biographical notices were
        replaced.

8650   LIVRE D'OR DES CANADIENS. Série nouvelle de portraits et
            de biographies. Montréal, Compagnie de publication Mont
        Royal, 1912-   v. illus., ports. 31cm. Edition for 1915
        called "7. année" (?) The golden book of the French-Canadians;
        with many portraits and biographical sketches.

8651   MORGAN, HENRY JAMES, 1842-1913.
            Types of Canadian women and of women who are or have been
        connected with Canada. Edited by Henry James Morgan. [Vol.
        1] Toronto, W. Briggs, 1903. 382 p. ports. 28cm. Ca. 2000
        women are represented. No more published?

8652   NATIONAL ENCYCLOPEDIA OF CANADIAN BIOGRAPHY.
            Jesse Edgar Middleton [and] W. Scott Downs, directing
        editors. Toronto, Dominion Pub. Co., 1935-37. 2 v. ports.
        28cm. Two editions appeared: 1935 (383 p.); 1937 (336 p.)

8653   THE NEWSPAPER REFERENCE BOOK OF CANADA; embracing
        facts and data regarding Canada and biographical sketches of
        representative Canadian men, for use by newspapers. Toronto,
        Press Pub. Co., 1903. xii, 488 p. 4.º Biographical section:
        p. 81-488.

8654   QUI ÊTES VOUS? Guide du Canada français. Biographies de
        l'élite du Canada français rédigées in collaboration. 1945-
        1946. Montréal, Editions du Canada français, 1945-46. 2 v.
        28cm. No more published? Who's who of important personages
        in French Canada, 1945-1946.

8655   ROY, PIERRE GEORGES, 1870-
        Les officiers d'état-major des gouvernements de Québec,
        Montréal et Trois-Rivières sous le régime français. Lévis
        [Que.] 1919. 270 p. 25cm. Officials of the governments of
        Quebec, Montreal and Three Rivers under the old French re-
        gime (New France).

8656   SHORTT, ADAM, 1859-1931.
        Canada and its provinces; a history of the Canadian people
        and their institutions, by one hundred associates. Adam Shortt,
        Arthur G. Doughty, general editors. [Archives ed.] Toronto,
        Glasgow, Brook and Co. [etc.] 1914-17. 23 v. illus., ports.
        26cm. Vol. 23, the general index volume, includes biographi-
        cal data (in brief form, but of varying length) in its personal
        name index references as well as lists of the Church hierarchy,
        chief justices, etc. accompanied by some biographical data.

8657   STORY, NORAH
        The Oxford companion to Canadian history and literature.
        Toronto, New York, Oxford University Press, 1967. xi, 935 p.
        5 maps. 24cm.

        ---- ----Supplement. General editor: William Toye. Toronto,
        New York, Oxford University Press, 1973. 318 p. 25cm. In-
        cludes many biographical sketches.

8658   SWETTENHAM, JOHN ALEXANDER
        Valient men; Canada's Victoria Cross and George Cross
        winners. Edited by John Swettenham. Toronto, Hakkert, 1973.
        xiii, 234 p. illus., ports. 25cm. (Canadian War Museum.
        Historical publications, 7) 116 Canadian (or associated with
        Canada) heroes from the Crimean War through World War II.
        Arranged chronologically with an alphabetical name index at end.

8659   TASSÉ, JOSEPH, 1848-1895.
        Les Canadiens de l'Ouest. 5. éd. Montréal, Impr. géné-
        rale, 1886. 2 v. illus., 15 ports. 23cm. French-Canadian
        pioneers of the middle and western states of the United States and

western Canada; chronological arrangement of biographies
generally.

8660   VEDETTES; le fait français au Canada. 1952-
            Montréal, Société nouvelle de publicité, 1953-   v.
        24cm. A who's who type biographical dictionary of French Ca-
        nadians (and some French-Americans); emphasis is on intel-
        lectuals and professional people. Issues for 1952, 1958, 1960,
        1962 all that were published?

8661   WOŁODKOWICZ, ANDRZEJ, 1928-
            Polish contributions to arts and sciences in Canada. With
        pref. by Tadeusz Romer. Montreal, 1969. 363 p., xxxii p. of
        illus. 22cm. A biographical dictionary (with several alphabeti-
        cal arrangements).

Local

Alberta

8662   WHO'S WHO IN ALBERTA. Harry Lyone and Douglas Webb,
            editors. Saskatoon, Sask., Western Canada Directories,
        1969. 1 v. Listed in Canadian books in print, 1971.

British Columbia

8663   EDGELOW'S WHO'S WHO IN BRITISH COLUMBIA. 10th-
            ed.; 1969-   Victoria, B. C., G. I. Edgelow.   v.
        24cm. Continues Who's who in British Columbia (v. 1-9, 1931-
        53)

8664   WEBSTER, DAISY DE JONG, 1911-
            Growth of the N. D. P. in B. C., 1900-1970; 81 political
        biographies, by Daisy Webster. [Vancouver? 1970] 103 p.
        103 ports. 21cm. Basically a biographical dictionary of 81
        parliamentarians from British Columbia who were or are memb-
        ers of the New Democratic Party and/or the Cooperative Com-
        monwealth Federation of British Columbia.

8665   WHO'S WHO IN BRITISH COLUMBIA; a biographical directory.
            1971 ed. Saskatoon, Lyone Publications [1971, c1966]
        1 v. (unpaged) illus., ports. 27cm. At head of title: British
        Columbia centennial.

Manitoba

8666   [McRAYE, WALTER] ed.
            Pioneers and prominent people of Manitoba.. Winnipeg, Ca-

nadian Publicity Co., 1925. 353, [13] p. illus. 22cm. A biographical dictionary.

8667   MANITOBA LIBRARY ASSOCIATION.
             Pioneers and early citizens of Manitoba; a dictionary of
        Manitobe biography from the earliest times to 1920. Winnipeg,
        Peguis Publishers [1971] 268 p. map. 24cm.

8668   REPRESENTATIVE MEN OF MANITOBA. History in por-
             traiture. A gallery of men whose energy, ability, enter-
        prise and public spirit have produced the marvelous record of
        the Prairie Province. Winnipeg, Tribune Pub. Co., 1902.
        xxxi p. 151 ports. 24cm. Portraits only. No biographical
        data.

Montreal

8669   ATHERTON, WILLIAM HENRY, 1867-
             Montreal, 1535-1914. Montreal, S. J. Clarke Pub. Co.,
        1914. 3 v. illus., ports. 27cm. Vol. 3 is biographical; prom-
        inent figures in Montreal's history arranged in no particular
        order. Consult index for alphabetical approach.

8670   AUDET, FRANÇOIS JOSEPH, 1867-
             Les députés de Montréal (ville et comtés) 1792-1867; études
        biographiques, anecdotiques et historiques. Montréal, Editions
        des Dix, 1943. 455 p. 25cm. Biographies of 80 Canadian leg-
        islators from Montreal, 1792-1867.

8671   BORTHWICK, JOHN DOUGLAS, 1831 or 2-1912.
             History and biographical gazetteer of Montreal to the year
        1892. Montreal, J. Lovell, 1892. 531 p. illus., ports. 24cm.
        80% of the volume is dedicated to current biography in no parti-
        cular order; index must be consulted for alphabetical approach.

Newfoundland

8672   NEWFOUNDLAND AND LABRADOR WHO'S WHO. Edited by
             James R. Thoms. Centennial ed., 1967/68. St. John's,
        E. C. Boone Advertising [c1968] xxxix, 339 p. illus., ports.
        25cm. First issued in 1961 under title: Newfoundland who's
        who.

Nova Scotia

8673   BLAUVELDT, ROBERT BROOKS, 1894-
             Leaders of Nova Scotia; a "Who's who" of the political, pro-

fessional, commercial and moral leaders of the province. Yarmouth, Loyalist Press, 1936. 82 p. ports. 22cm.

Ontario

8674   THE CANADIAN BIOGRAPHICAL DICTIONARY AND PORTRAIT
        GALLERY OF EMINENT AND SELF-MADE MEN. Ontario
        volume. Toronto [etc.] American Biographical Pub. Co., 1880.
        778 p. illus., ports. 29cm.

8675   CANADIAN BIOGRAPHIES, LIMITED.
        Prominent people of the Province of Ontario. Ottawa [Graphic Publishers] 1925. 273 p. illus., ports. 8.°

8676   MIKA, NICK, 1912-
        Encyclopedia of Ontario [by] Nick and Helma Mika. Belleville, Ont., Mika Pub. Co. [1974-   v. illus. 24cm.
        Vol. 1 (Historic sites of Ontario) contains a large number of
        biographies of Ontarians drawn directly from historical plaques
        at various sites; alphabetical approach thru' index. Vol. 3 will
        be entirely biographical presumably, with the title: People of
        Ontario.

Prairie Provinces

8678   PEEL, BRUCE BRADEN, 1916-
        A bibliography of the Prairie Provinces to 1953, with biographical index. Compiled by Bruce Braden Peel. 2d ed. [Toronto] University of Toronto Press [1973] xxviii, 780 p. 25cm.
        "Author index with biographical notes": p. [627]-776. Includes
        many obscure figures prominent in the cultural and literary life
        of Canada's Prairie Provinces. 1st ed. issued in 1956, with a
        supplement in 1963.

Quebec (City)

8679   ROY, PIERRE GEORGES, 1870-
        Fils de Québec. Lévis, 1933. 4 v. 19cm. Rather detailed biographies of notable persons born in the city of Quebec
        and surrounding area between 1629 and 1843. Index at the end
        of each volume. Arrangement is chronological, by date of birth.

Quebec (Province)

8680   BIOGRAPHIES DU BAS ST.-LAURENT. 2. éd. Rimouski,
        Qué., Editions rimouskoises, 1960. 1 v. (unpaged) ports.
        Biographies of French-Canadians from the Lower Saint Lawrence region. Various fields of endeavor are covered, but few

writers are listed. First ed. (1952) published under title: Biographies de Rimouski.

8681   LE BOTTIN PARLEMENTAIRE DU QUÉBEC. 1. ed. -   ;
        1962-   Montréal, P. E. Parent.   v. illus. ports.
        21cm. annual. Compiler, 1962: P. E. Parent. No more pub-
        lished? The 1962 (1st) edition of this proposed guide to things
        parliamentary in the Province of Quebec (531 p. illus., ports.
        21cm.) contains many portraits and biographical sketches of
        Quebec's legislators, cabinet officers, etc. of the present (as
        well as some retrospective biography) A name index provides
        an alphabetical approach to the persons mentioned.

8682   CANADIAN BIOGRAPHICAL DICTIONARY AND PORTRAIT
            GALLERY OF EMINENT AND SELF-MADE MEN. Quebec
        and the Maritime Provinces volume. Chicago, American Bio-
        graphical Pub. Co., 1881. 759 p. illus., ports. 29cm. In-
        cludes ca. 500 biographical sketches.

8683   MEN OF TODAY IN THE EASTERN TOWNSHIPS. Introductory
            chapters by V. E. Morrill. Biographical section compiled
        by Erastus G. Pierce. [Sherbrooke, Que.] Sherbrooke Record
        Co. [1917] 297 p. illus., ports. 23cm. Biographical sketches
        of persons prominent in the Eastern Townships of the Province
        of Quebec (covering some 15 counties and with an area of some
        9120 square miles extending from Dorchester County in the
        northeast to Missisquoi Co. in the southwest)

8684   ROY, PIERRE GEORGES, 1870-
            La Législature de Québec; galerie des membres du Conseil
        législatif et des députés à l'Assemblée legislative. Lévis, Bul-
        letin des recherches historiques, 1897. 207 p. The Legisla-
        ture of the Province of Quebec ca. 1897; a gallery of the mem-
        bers of the Legislative Council and the deputies at the Legisla-
        tive Assembly.

8685   TURCOTTE, GUSTAVE
            Le Conseil législatif de Québec, 1774-1933. Beauceville,
        l'Eclaireur, 1933. viii, 324 p. 23cm. Bio-bibliographical;
        the Legislative Council of the Province of Quebec's Legislature,
        1774-1933.

8686   VAILLANCOURT, ÉMILE, 1889-
            A partial list of Canadian discoverers, explorers, and
        founders of states and cities of the United States of America
        who proceeded from the Province of Quebec wherein most of
        them were born and others had their home. [Montreal, 1938]
        14 1. 28cm. Cover title. Mimeographed.

8687   WHO'S WHO IN — AU QUÉBEC. v. 1-   ; 1967/68.
       Montreal, Quebec Press Service [c1968] 254 p. 22cm.
       French and English; added t. p. in English (p. 131) Who's who
       in the Province of Quebec.

Saskatchewan

8688   WHO'S WHO IN SASKATCHEWAN. Saskatoon, Western Canada
       Directories.   v. 3d ed., 1970 latest; edited by Harry
       Lyone and Douglas Webb.

CENTRAL AMERICA

8688a GUERRERO CASTILLO, JULIÁN N   1908-
       100 [i. e. Cien] biografías centroamericanas [por] Julián N.
       Guerrero C. [y] Lola Soriano de Guerrero. [Managua, Talleres
       de Litografía y Editorial Artes Gráficas] 1971-   v.
       22cm. 100 Central American biographies; historical person-
       ages. The first volume contains 7 biographies only; the entire
       work is projected for completion in several volumes.

CENTRAL EUROPE

8688b SCHNEIDER, MARIJANA
       Portreti, 1800-1870. Zagreb, Povijesni Muzej Hrvatske,
       1973. 140 p. ports. 22cm. (Provijesni Muzej Hrvatske, Za-
       greb. Katalog Muzejskih zbirki, 9) A catalog of the portraits
       (including reproductions of the portraits with accompanying bio-
       graphical sketches) in the portrait collection of the Historical
       Museum of Croatia. Some 284 portraits are included. Most of
       the figures represented are Central Europeans from prominent
       families (of the Habsburg monarchy, etc.) On pages 15-40 will
       be found a biographical dictionary of the artists responsible for
       the portraits.

CEYLON

See SRI LANKA

CHILE

8688c BIZZARO, SALVATORE
       Historical dictionary of Chile. Metuchen, N. J., Scare-
       crow Press, 1972. 309 p. 22cm. (Latin American historical
       dictionaries, no. 7) Includes biographical entries.

8688d ESPEJO, JUAN LUIS, 1888-
       Nobiliario de la Capitanía General de Chile. [Santiago]
       Editorial Andrés Bello, 1967 [c1966] 946 p. coats of arms.

25cm. The noble families of the Captaincy General of (colonial) Chile; valuable biographical data is given under the families (A-Z). E.g., the 'founder' of the family, his sons and/or daughters, etc. are successively listed and each name is followed by biographical facts whenever available.

8688e   FUENZALIDA, ENRIQUE AMADOR
         Galería contemporánea de hombres notables de Chile (1850-1901) Valparaiso, Impr. del Universo de G. Helfmann, 1901. 356 p. 46 ports. 27cm. "Colaborador: Gustavo Acosta C." Gallery of the notable men of Chile during the years 1850-1901. Intended to be in several volumes, but only the 1st vol. was issued.

8688f   ROJAS, LUIS EMILIO
         Biografía cultural de Chile. Santiago, Chile, Editorial Nascimento, 1974. 278 p. 19cm. Cultural biography of Chile; 104 biographical sketches of Chilean poets, playwrights, essayists, musicians, journalists, historians, educators, literary critics, novelists and short story writers, past and present. Chronological arrangement with an alphabetical index of the biographees.

8688g   VEGA E   , M
         Album de la colonie française au Chili. Cette oeuvre a pour but de faciliter le rapprochement des membres de la colonie; la faire connaître au dedans at au dehors du pays et demontrer par une scrupuleuse statistique le rôle important qu'elle remplit au Chili. Editeur & proprietaire M. Vega E. Santiago de Chile, Impr. et Lithogr. franco-chilienne, 1904. 263, xxix p. illus., ports. 27cm. Contents.--1. ptie. La France au Chili, par Eugene Chouteau.--2. ptie. Profils et biographies (p. 43-204). ... 6. ptie. Guide générale de colonie française. Frenchmen in Chile. Pt. 2 (p. 43-204) yields biographical sketches.

CHINA

Bibliography, Indexes, Portrait Catalogs

8689   CH'EN, T'IEH-FAN
         Sung Yüan Ming Ch'ing ssŭ ch'ao hsüeh an so yin. Taipei, I wen yin shu kuan, 1974. 18, 328, 178, 160 p. 27cm. Index to personal names in the synopsis of Confucian scholars of Sung, Yüan, Ming, Ching dynasties. About 15,000 biographies are indexed with references to the sources consulted. Index of alternative names.

8690   CHU, SHIH-CHIA, 1905-
         Sung Yüan ti fang chih chuan chi so yin. Peking, Chung-hua shu chü, 1963. 182 p. 19cm. An index to several hundred biog-

raphies in more than 30 Chinese gazetteers compiled during the Sung and Yuan dynasties.

8691   CHUANG, TING-I, 1854 or 5-1909.
Liang Han pu lieh chuan jên ming yün pien. Shanghai, Commercial Press, 1935. 1 v. (various pagings) 19cm. An index to the names of persons mentioned in the Ch'ien Han shu and the Hou Han shu (Han Dynasty, 202 B. C. -220 A. D.) but who do not have separate biographies in those works. Alternative names are sometimes given and there is some brief biographical data.

8692   CHUNG YANG T'U SHU KUAN, Taipei.
Chung-kuo chin tai jên wu chuan chi tzŭ liao so yin. Taipei, Chung yang t'u shu kuan, 1973. 2, 14, 430 p. 21cm. Index to periodical articles on 1588 Chinese nationalists in the period 1840 to 1970. Biographees are arranged by family names with author index. Appended with bibliographies of individual and collective biographies.

8693   FANG, CHAO-YING, 1908-   ed.
Tsêng chiao Ch'ing ch'ao chin shi t'i ming pei lu fu yin tê. Peiping, Yen-ching ta hsüeh (Harvard-Yenching Institute) 1941. xxvi, 434 p. 27cm. [Supplement no. 19 of the Harvard-Yenching Institute] A collection of 112 lists of chin-shih, the persons who passed the regular or special civil service examinations held in Peking from 1646 to 1904. Useful for dating the 26,747 chin-shih listed with their native towns. Edited by Fang Chao-ying and Tu Lien-chê. Photocopied in 1966 (Taipei, Ch'eng Wen Pub. Co.)

8694   HU, CHENG-CHIH
Chung-kuo ti hao piao t'i i lan. [Peiping, Index Press, Yenching University] 1939. [vii], 86, 26 p. An index to the personal and other names and the reign titles of 373 Chinese emperors, from Huang-ti to Yüan Shih-k'ai.

8695   KYOTO DAIGAKU. JIMBUN KAGAKU KENKYŪJO.
Rekidai meijin nempu mokuroku. Kyoto, 1951. [6], 163 p. Catalog of 1013 Chinese chronological biographies, beginning with the Duke of Chou and ending with Wen I-to (1899-1946) Also called: Li tai ming jên nien p'u mu lu.

8696   LEI, YEN-SHOU
Ch'ing shih fa k'ao. [n. p., pref. 1924] 2 v. (double leaves) in case. 27cm. Collection of posthumous names of princes and ministers of the Ch'ing Dynasty; ca. 1800 names are listed.

8697   LI, CHOU-WANG, 1669-1730.
Kuo ch'ao li k'o t'i ming pei lu (ch'u-pien) [n. p., pref.

1746] 13 v. Also called: Chin-shih t'i ming pei lu. Compiled by Li Chou-wang and supplemented by Ch'ien Wei-ch'eng and others. List of persons receiving the chin-shih degree, from the Ming Dynasty to the time of publication.

8698 LIU, CH'ANG-HUA, chu jên 1834.
  Li tai t'ung hsing ming lu. [Peiping, Yen-ching ta hsüeh, Yin tê pien tsuan ch'u] 1931. vi, 28 p. 27cm. Lists all important persons with identical names from earliest historical times down to the end of the Ming dynasty. Added t. p.: Index to Li tai t'ung hsing ming lu.

8699 SUNG JEN CHUAN CHI TZǓ LIAO SO YIN. Taipei, Ting wên shu chu [1975-75] 5 v. 22cm. An index to biographical materials of persons prominent during the Sung Dynasty. About 15,000 biographees are included with brief biographical data, dates of birth and death according to the Western calendar. Index of sobriquets. Added title: Index to biographical materials of Sung figures. Edited by Ch'ang Pi-tê.

8700 T'IEN, CHI-TSUNG
  Pa shih chu chung Ming tai chuan chi tsung ho yin tê. [Peiping] Yen-ching ta hsüeh, Yin tê pien tsuan ch'u, 1935. 3 v. in 1. 28cm. (Yen-ching ta hsüeh [Peking] Yin tê pien tsuan ch'u. [Index] 24) A combined index to 89 collections of biographies of persons who lived during the Ming dynasty; approximately 30,000 persons are indexed by the kuei-hsieh system.

8701 TU, LIEN-CHÊ, 1904-
  San shih san chung Ch'ing tai chuan chi tsung ho yin tê. [Peiping] Yen-ching ta hsüeh, 1932. xxi, 392 p. 27cm. (Yen-ching ta hsüeh. Yin tê pien tsuan ch'u. [Index] 9) Added t. p.: Index to thirty-three collections of Ch'ing dynasty biographies. Edited by Fang Chao-ying. Reprinted in 1959.

8702 UMEHARA, KAORU, 1934-
  Ryō Kin Gen-jin denki sakuin. Kyoto, Kyoto Daigaku Jimbunkagaku Kenkyujo, 1972. 13, 219, 103, 24 p. 27cm. Index to biographies of scholars and men of letters of the Liao, Chin, and Yüan dynasties. Alternative names, native places, and relations with other families are given. About 3,200 persons. By Kaoru Umehara and Isuyoshi Koromogawa.

8703 WANG, HUI-TSU, 1731-1807.
  Liao Chin Yüan san shih t'ung hsing ming lu. Taipei, I-wen, 1965. 6 v. (double leaves) 19cm. Also called: San shih t'ung hsing ming lu. Compilation begun by Wang Hui-tsu and completed by his son Wang Chi-p'ei. An index to all biographies in the Liao shih, the Chin shih and the Yüan shih of non-Chinese (Mongols & other tribes & peoples on Chinese soil) whose full names were the same for two or more persons.

8704   WANG, PAO-HSIEN
        Li tai ming jên nien pu tsung mu. [Taichung, Tunghai Uni-
versity Library] 1965. 46, 353 p. 21cm. Index to the chronological biographies of some 1200 famous Chinese arranged in
time sequence from the Duke of Chou to Feng Chien (died 1962).
Gives also alternative names, native place and years of birth
and death.

8705   WANG, TSU-I
        San kuo chih jên ming lu. [Shanghai, Commercial Press]
1957. 265, 18 p. 20cm. Index to 4065 personal names of the
third century in China. Names are arranged by number of
strokes with a four-corner index.

8706   YANG, CHIAO-LO
        Ch'ing jên pieh chi ch'ien chung pei chuan wan yin tê chi pei
chuan chu nien li p'u. [Yangmingshan, Taiwan, Institute for Advanced Chinese Studies] 1965. [4], 3, 410 p. Except for a few
sentences in the preface and the title and publication date, this
Taiwan edition is an exact reproduction of the Peking ed. (Ch'en,
Nai-ch'ien. Ch'ing tai pei chuan wên t'ung chien. Peking,
Chung-hua shu chü, 1959—see Item 546) Index to some 13,000
biographical notes on persons who lived and died during the
Ch'ing dynasty (after 1644).

8707   YEN-CHING TA HSÜEH, Peking.   YIN TÊ PIEN TSUAN CH'U.
        Liao Chin. Yüan chuan chi san shih chung tsung ho yin tê.
[Peking] 1940. xvi, 207 p. 27cm. (Its [Index] 35) Added t. p.:
Combined indices to thrity collections of Liao, Chin and Yüan
biographies.

8708   YEN-CHING TA HSÜEH, Peking.   YIN TÊ PIEN TSUAN CH'U.
        Ssu shi ch'i chung Sung tai chuan chi tsung ho yin tê.
[Peiping] 1939. xxiv, 199 p. 27cm. (Its [Index] 34) Added
t. p.: Combined indices to forty-seven collections of Sung
Dynasty biographies. The biographies of 9204 persons are indexed.

General Works

8709   AJIA KENKYŪJO, TOKYO.
        Chūka Jimmin Kyōwakoku genshoku jimmei jiten. Tokyo,
Ajia Kenkyūjo, 1964. 658 p. 25cm. Biographical dictionary-
directory of current government officials of the People's Republic of China up to Oct. 1963 (8,450 persons). Arranged in
Japanese syllabic order.

8710   ASSOCIATION FOR ASIAN STUDIES. MING BIOGRAPHICAL
        HISTORY PROJECT COMMITTEE.
        Dictionary of Ming biography, 1368-1644 / the Ming Bio-

graphical History Project of the Association for Asian Studies;
L. Carrington Goodrich, editor, Chaoying Fang, associate
editor. New York : Columbia University Press, 1976. 2 v.
(xxi, 1751 p.), [6] leaves of plates : ill., maps ; 27cm. Added
title: Ming tai ming jen chuan. Includes bibliographies and indexes.

8711   BIOGRAPHICAL SKETCHES OF CHINESE COMMUNIST MILI-
        TARY LEADERS. Translated at field level under the auspi-
ces of the Chief of Military History, Dept. of the Army. [n. p.,
197-?] 122 p. Translations of articles published in the periodical Chung kung yen chiu.

8712   CHANG, TING, of Sung Dynasty.
        Ming hsien shih tsu yen hsing lei kao. Shanghai, Shang
wu yin shu kuan, 1935. 24 v. (double leaves) 21cm. Famous
persons up to the Sung Dynasty, arranged by surnames according to the rhymes; sub-arranged in chronological order.

8713   CHANG, TS'AI-T'IEN, 1874-1945.
        Ch'ing lieh ch'ao hou fei chuan kao. Taipei, Wen hai chu
pan she, 1971. 492 p. 19cm. Reprint of 1929 edition. Biographies of the empresses-queens of the Ch'ing Dynasty, 1644-
1912.

8714   CHANG, YÜEH-CH'ING.
        Kuang hsi chao chung lu. Taipei, Hsüeh sheng shu chu,
1972. 2 v. 21cm. Facsimile reprint of 1889 edition. Brief
biographies of Ch'ing officials who died during the Taiping Rebellion, 1850-1864, in Kwangsi Province.

8715   CH'EN, CHI-TS'UNG.
        Chung i chi wên lu. Taipei, Hua wen shu chu [1970?] 2 v.
21cm. Facsimile reprint of 1882 edition. Biographies of slain
('martyred') Chinese of the Ch'ing Dynasty during the Taiping
Rebellion (1850-1864).

8716   CH'EN, TING
        Tung-lin lieh chuan. Taipei, Shang-wu yin shu kuan, 1974.
3 v. 20cm. (Ssu-ku ch'uan shu chen pen 5 chi: 88-90.) Photo-
reprint edition of the Wen Yüan Ko copy. Collection of biographies of about 200 eminent members of the Tung-lin party
during the Ming Dynasty.

8717   CH'EN, T'ING, chin shih 1502.
        T'ang yü chi chuan. Taipei, Hsüeh sheng shu chu, 1969.
471 p. 23cm. Facsimile reprint of 1544 edition. Biographies
of the personalities related to the Kingdom of Nan-t'ang in the
period 936-975 A. D.

8718   CHIA, HU-CH'ENG.
           Chung kuo li tai ti wang pu hsi hui pien. Taipei, Cheng
        chung shu chü, 1966. 4, 5, 357 p. 21cm. Brief biographies
        of 424 Chinese emperors and kings to 1911, with genealogical
        lineage tables. Arranged by date of reigns.

8719   CHINA. HSING CHÊNG YUAN. KUO CHÜN T'UI CH'U I KUAN
        PING FU TAO WEI YUAN HUI.
           Shêng ming ti kuang hui. Taipei [1968?] 2, 12, 894 p.
        ports. 22cm. Biographies of retired generals residing in
        Taiwan.

8720   CHINA (REPUBLIC OF CHINA). KUO FANG PU. SHIH CHÊNG
        CHÜ.
           Kuo chün chung lieh chuan chi. Taipei, 1962-68. 13 v.
        illus. 20cm. Each volume also has distinctive title. Biog-
        raphies of 'martyrs' of the Nationalist (Kuomintang) Armed
        Forces in the struggle with the Chinese Communists.

8721   CHINESE COMMUNIST PARTY CENTRAL COMMITTEE MEM-
           BERS. [n. p.] 1971. 3 l., 94 p. 27cm. (Reference aid)
        "Biographic briefs ... on all full and alternate members of the
        ninth Chinese Communist Party Central Committee elected on
        28 April 1969." In biographical dictionary format.

8722   CHINESE COMMUNIST PARTY PROVINCIAL LEADERS.
           [n. p.] 1971. iv, 130 p. 27cm. (Reference aid) "Biogra-
        phic briefs on all officers of the 29 provincial-level Chinese
        Communist Party committees elected between December 1970
        and August 1971." Provinces arranged alphabetically with bio-
        graphical briefs thereunder; name index at end of volume.

8723   CHINESE COMMUNIST WHO'S WHO. Taipei, Institute of Inter-
           national Relations, 1970-71. 2 v. 27cm. Translation of
        Chung kung jên ming lu.

8724   CHIN-TING SHENG CH'AO HSÜN CHIEH CHU CH'EN LU.
           Compiled by Shu-ho-te and Yu Min-chung. Taipei, Cheng-
        wen ch'u pan she, 1969. 2 v. 20cm. Reprint of 1776 edition.
        Biographies of loyal officials of the Ming Dynasty who sacrificed
        themselves during the troubles of the Chien-wên and late Ming
        periods (ca. 3,600 biographical sketches.

8725   CHUAN CHI CHING HUA. Taipei, Chung wai tu shu ch'u pan
           she, 1972-   v. illus. 22cm. Biographies of
        personalities of modern China. No index. Edited by Niu Hsien-
        ming.

8726 CHŪGOKU JIMMYAKU YŌRAN.
Tokyo, ADI Ajia sogo kaihatsu kenkyujo, 1973. 604 p.
19cm. 1,500 key figures of the People's Republic of China up to
Dec. 1972. Cadets at provincial level are included. Arranged
in Japanese syllabic order.

8727 CHUNG-HUA CHIN TAI MING JÊN CHUAN. Biographies of
prominent Chinese. Prepared under the editorial supervision of A. R. Burt, J. B. Powell and Carl Crow. Shanghai,
Biographical Pub. Co. [1920?] 260 p. ports. 37cm. English
and Chinese. 200 portraits and biographies of prominent Chinese of the late 19th and early 20th century. Alphabetical name
index at end of volume. Reprinted ca. 1970 in an 'Edition de
luxe'?

8728 CHUNG KUNG JÊN MING LU. Taipei, Chung hua min kuo kuo
chi kuan hsi yen chiu so, 1967. 4, 24, 767, 2, 94 p. 27cm.
Biographical record of Communist China; some 2,000 biographies. Issued also in English under title: Chinese Communist
who's who (1970-   ) Edited by Fang Hsüeh-ch'un.

8729 CHUNG-KUO CH'ING NIEN TANG. CHUNG YANG CHIH HSING
WEI YÜAN HUI. HSÜAN CH'UAN TSU.
Chung-kuo ch'ing nien tang hsün kuo ssū nan chi i ku t'ung
chih lüeh chuan. Taipei, Chung-kuo Ch'ing nien tang, 1972.
266 p. 21cm. Biographies of over 100 members of Chung-kuo
Ching nien tang (China Youth Party) who died in the struggle
against the Chinese communists.

8730 CHUNG-KUO JÊN MING TA TZU TIEN. Shang-hai, Shang wu
yin shu kuan, 1938. 1808 p. 23cm. Edited by Fang I.
Cyclopedia of 40,000 (ca.) Chinese biographical names. Supersedes Chung-kuo jên ming ta tz'ŭ tien (Shanghai, 1925, 1933,
etc.?)

8731 CHUNG KUO KUO MIN TANG. CHUNG YANG WEI YÜAN HUI.
Ti hou tang wu kung tso t'ung chih hsün nan shih lüeh hui
pien. [Taipei] 1963. 4, 296 p. illus. 22cm. Brief biographies
of Kuomintang commandos killed in operations on mainland
China after 1949.

8732 CHUNG-KUO KUO MIN TANG. CHUNG YANG WEI YÜAN HUI.
TI 6 TSU.
Kung fei hsin tang ch'üan p'ai. Taipei, 1970. 3 v. 22cm.
Biographical data of Chinese Communist party leaders, govern-
ment officials and military officers, after 1969. Name index by
stroke counts.

8733 CHUNG-KUO KUO MIN TANG. TANG SHIH SHIH LIAO PIEN
TSUAN WEI YÜAN HUI.
Ko ming hsien lieh hsien hsien wei tang hsi shêng fên tou

shih chi. Taipei, 1974-   v. 22cm. Short biographies
of Kuomintang martyrs since the Revolution of 1911. Compiled
by the Historical Archives Commission of the Kuomintang.
Edited by Tu Yüan-tsai.

8734 CHUNG-KUO LI TAI TI HOU HSIANG. Shanghai, Yu-cheng shu
        chü [1927?] 117 ports. 37cm. Added title: Portraits of
emperors and empresses of China. Most of the portraits are
accompanied by guard sheets with descriptive letterpress in
Chinese and English.

8735 CHUNG WAI JÊN MING TZ'U TIEN. Shanghai, Chung hua shu
        chu, 1940. 1300 p. 20cm. Biographical dictionary of Chi-
nese and foreigners (with 5,000 entries for Western names, approximately one-third of the total). Edited by Liu Ping'li.

8736 CHUNG WAI JÊN WU CHUAN CHI. Taipei, Chung wai tu shu
        ch'u pan she, 1971-   v. 19cm. Biographies
of prominent Chinese, mainly of the 20th century. No index.
Edited by Wang Kung-chi.

8737 FEI, SHU
        Lien li chuan. Shanghai, Shang wu yin shu kuan. 1935. 2 v.
(double leaves) 21cm. Biographies of 114 faithful government
officials from the Chou Dynasty to the T'ang Dynasty; arranged
chronologically.

8738 FUJITA, CHIKAMASA.
        Shina mondai jiten. Tokyo, Chuō-koron sha, 1942. 1 v.
(various pagings) 26cm. The biographical section of this dictionary on China has a few hundred names of Chinese active
during the beginning of the Sino-Japanese and World Wars,
especially pro-Japanese puppet government officials.

8739 FUJITA, MASANORI.
        Gendai Chūgoku jimbutsu hyō. Tokyo, Daian, 1969. 3,
226 p. 25cm. Brief biographies of 1,650 Chinese who died
between 1919 and 1967. Indexes in Chinese characters and
in Wade-Giles romanization.

8740 GENDAI CHŪGOKU JIMMEI JITEN. 1958-   Tokyo, Kasumi-
        gaseki Kai [etc.]   v. 22cm. Edited in 1958-1962 by
Kasumigaseki Kai; 1966-   by Kazankai. Issued under the auspices of Gaimushō, Ajiakyoku. 1972 latest edition. Biographical
dictionary of contemporary Chinese & Koreans.

8741 HAN MING CH'EN CHUAN. Taipei, Tai luen kuo feng ch'u pan
        she, 1970. 4 v. (3896 p.) 20cm. State ministers of the

Chinese race in the Ch'ing Dynasty up to the Ch'ien-lung period (1736-1795).

8742   HEMMI, JŪRŌ
        Chūkaminkoku kakumei nijisshunen kinen shi.   [Vol. 1] Keijō, Hemmi Kōenkai Hombu, 1931. 800 p. illus. No more published? A history commemorating 20 years of the Chinese National Revolution. Includes some 300 brief biographies (to p. 356) of prominent Chinese political figures.

8743   HIRAOKA, TAKEO, 1909-
        Redidai meijin nempu. Kyoto, Jimbunkagaku Kenkyūjo, 1951. 163 p. Chronological biographical data for famous men of successive Chinese dynasties; ca. 400 listed on p. 72-105.

8744   HSIANG, CH'ENG
        Hsien tai Hua ch'iao jên wu chih. Taipei, Ta Chung-hua ch'u pan she, 1964-   v. ports. 21cm. Vol. 1 (16, 380 p.) —no more published?) contains 185 biographies of overseas Chinese, still living at the time of the compilation.

8745   HSIANG, TU-SHOU, 1521-1586.
        Chin hsien pei i. Taipei, Shang-wu yin shu kuan, 1972. 2 v. 19cm. Photoreprint edition of the Wen Yuan Ko copy. Biographies of 204 Ming officials from 1368 to early 1500's.

8746   HSÜ, CH'IEN-HSÜEH, 1631-1694.
        Ming shih lieh chuan. Taipei, Hsüeh sheng shu chü, 1970. 10 v. (3 p., 20, 18 l., 4658 p.) 23cm. 'Reprint' of manuscript. Biographies of the Ming Dynasty (1368-1644)—the Hung-wu to the Ch'ung-chen period.

8748   HU, P'U-YÜ.
        Chung-hua li tai ming chiang chuan. Taipei, Sung wu ch'u pan she, 1974. 3 v. 19cm. 200 biographies of famous generals of China from the Chou Dynasty to the Ch'ing (1911), based upon formal histories and arranged chronologically. No index.

8749   HUANG, CHUNG-CHÜN.
        Ch'ou jên chuan ssŭ pien. Shanghai, Shang wu yin shu kuan, 1955. 141 p. 19cm. Supplementing the Ch'ou jên chuan (1-3 pien) with biographies of 275 Chinese, 153 Europeans and 8 wome scientists up to the Ch'ing Dynasty (1644-1911).

8750   HUANG MING MING CH'EN WAN YEN LU. Taipei, Wen Hai ch'u pan she, 1970. 3 v. (1676 p.) 20cm. Facsimile reprint of 1561 edition. Collection of epitaphs of famous officials of the Ming Dynasty from 1368 to 1500. Compiled by Hsü Hung and others.

8751   JAPAN. GAIMUSHŌ. AJIAKYOKU.
        Gendai Chūgoku Chōsen jimmei kan. Tokyo, 1953. 397 p.
Who's who in China and Korea. Some 2,000 Chinese names are
included. Indexed.

8752   K'AI KUO HSIEN CHIN CHUAN. Taipei, Li shih wen hua ch'u
        pan she, 1971. 8, 496 p. illus. 27cm. Revolutionists
active in the formative years of the Republic of China. Compiled by To-nai Hsiang.

8753   KAO, YÜ-T'AI.
        Hsüeh chiao t'ing cheng ch'i lu. Taipei, Taiwan yin hang
Ching chi yen chiu shih, 1970. 2 v. 19cm. (T'ai-wan wen
hsien ts'ung k'an ti 286 chung) Biographies of slain ('martyred')
Chinese of the late Ming Dynasty up to 1664. Arranged in
chronological order.

8754   KASUMIGASEIKAI.
        Gendai Chūgoku jimmei jiten. Tokyo, Konan Shoin, 1957.
718, 73, 129 p. A biographical dictionary of some 7,000 contemporary prominent Chinese in mainland China, Taiwan and
overseas. Indexed.

8755   KENG, TING-HSIANG, 1524-1596.
        Shih fu pao chien. Taipei, Wên hai ch'u pan she, 1970.
4 v. 19cm. Facsimile reprint. Biographies of over 100 Chinese statesmen from ancient times to the Ming Dynasty's end
(1644). Arranged in chronological order with a chronology of
the ministers of the Han, T'ang and Sung Dynasties.

8756   KLEIN, DONALD W
        Biographic dictionary of Chinese communism, 1921-1965 [by]
Donald W. Klein [and] Anne B. Clark. Cambridge, Mass.,
Harvard University Press, 1971. 2 v. maps. 26cm. (Harvard
East Asian series, 57) Contents.--v. 1. Ai Szu-ch'i--Lo I-nung.
--v. 2. Lo Jui-ch'ing--Yun Tai-ying. 433 biographies.

8757   KO MING JÊN WU CHIH. Edited by Huang Chi-lu. Taipei,
        Chung-Kuo kuo min tang, Tang shih shih liao pien tsuan
wei yüan hui, 1969-75. 14 v. 22cm. & index. Biographies of
about 1,500 Kuomintang politicians, military officers and party
members. Name index by stroke count.

8758   KU, SSU-LI, 1669-1722.
        Huang Ming wen hai. [ca. 1700?] 170 vols. Microfilm.
Tokyo, Yushodo, 1962. 24 reels. Collections of biographies
of eminent Chinese during the Ming Dynasty (1368-1644) based
upon anthologies and gravestone inscriptions.

8759   KUO, T'ING-HSÜN
        Pên ch'ao fên shêng jên wu k'ao. Taipei, Cheng wen ch'u
pan she, 1971. 30 v. 21cm. Facsimile reproduction of 1622
edition. Biographies of eminent persons from the beginning of
the Ming Dynasty to the Wan-li period, (1368 - early 17th
century), classified according to native provinces and prefec-
tures. Index of names by stroke count.

8760   LEI, LI, 1505-1581.
        Kuo ch'ao lieh ch'ing chi. Taipei, Cheng Wen ch'u pan
she [1971?] 25 v. 20cm. Reprint of the Ming edition. Includes the biographies of the office-holders in the Grand Secretariat of the Ming Dynasty (period 1368-1592).

8761   LEI, LI, 1505-1581.
        Nei ko hsing shih. Taipei, Hsüeh sheng shu chü, 1970.
4, 562 p. 21cm. (Ming tai shih chi hui k'an, 14) Reprint of
the Ming edition. Biographies of office-holders in the Grand
Secretariat (Nei-ko) of the Ming Dynasty from 1368 to 1521.

8762   LI, CHIH, 1527-1602.
        Hsü ts'ang shu. Peking, Chung-hua shu chu, 1959. 2, 32,
529 p. 21cm. Collection of classified biographies of Ming officials from 1368 to 1560's.

8763   LI, HUAN, 1827-1891.
        Kuo ch'ao ch'i hsien lei cheng ch'u pien. Taipei, Wen-hai
ch'u pan she, 1966. 25 v. 20cm. Reprint of 1884-1890 edition.
Biographies of personalities of the Ch'ing Dynasty to 1850.
Name index.

8764   LI, SHIH-T'AO
        Chung-kuo li tai ming jên nien p'u mu lu. [Shanghai, Com-
mercial Press, 1941] 1 v. (double leaves) in case. 27cm. Lists
chronological biographies of persons living from the Chou period
to the 20th century. 1108 biographies of 964 people are included
and arranged according to the years of birth.

8765   LI, YEN, 1910-
        Tung-lin tang chi k'ao. Peking, Jen min ch'u pan she,
1957. 17, 185 p. 19cm. A collection of biographies of 309
members of Tung-lin shu-yuan, the Tung-lin party during the
Ming Dynasty.

8766   LIU, CHEN.
        Tung kuan Han chi. Taipei, Yi Wen yin shu kuan, 1970.
4 v. (double leaves) 19cm. Collective biography of the later
Han Dynasty (25-220 A. D.); biographies arranged in chronological order.

8767   LIU, PAO.
        Hsien tai Chung-kuo jên wu chih. Shanghai, Po wên shu
tien, 1941. 360 p. 19cm. Over 400 political, military and
other prominent personalities of the Republic of China before
the Second World War.

8768   LIU, TZU-CH'ING.
        Chung-kuo li tai jên wu p'ing chuan. Taipei, Li ming wên
hua shih yeh kung ssu, 1974. 3 v. 22cm. Over 200 biographies of famous Chinese from ancient times to 1912.

8769   P'AN, HSING-HUNG.
        Ma-lai-ya Ch'ao ch'iao t'ung chien. Singapore, Nan tao
chu pan she, 1950. 420 p. illus. 27cm. Over 370 biographies
of Chinese from Ch'ao-chou County, Kwangtung who migrated
to Malaysia. Some portraits.

8770   SHIBATA, MINORU, 1930-
        Gendai Chūgoku jimbutsu hyakusen. Tokyo, Akita Shoten,
1973. 271 p. illus. 19cm. Biographies of 100 leaders of the
People's Republic of China in political, military and diplomatic
fields, with portraits.

8771   SHISŌ UNDŌ KENKYŪJO.
        Chūgoku yōjinroku. Tokyo, Zembosha, 1972. 369 p.
18cm. 500 key figures of the People's Republic of China in
political, military, party and diplomatic circles.

8772   SNOW, HELEN (FOSTER) 1907-
        The Chinese Communists: sketches and autobiographies of
the Old Guard. Book I: Red dust. Book II: Autobiographical profiles and biographical sketches. Introd. to book I by Robert
Carver North. Westport, Conn., Greenwood Pub. Co. [1972]
xxi, 398 p. illus., ports. 24cm. Book I first published in 1952
under title: Red dust. Contains 29 autobiographical sketches and
ca. 117 biographical sketches (the latter in several alphabetical
arrangements).

8773   SUN, CH'ENG-TSE, 1593-1675.
        Yüan ch'ao jen wu lüeh. Taipei, Wen hai ch'u pan she
[1974?] 160 p. 22cm. Reproduced from manuscript copy.
Biographies of famous state ministers of the Yuan Dynasty
(1280-1368).

8774   TSOU, I, fl. 1657.
        Ch'i chen yeh sheng ch'u chi. Peking, Pei-ping ku kung po
wu yuan tu shu kuan, 1936. 4 v. (double leaves) 27cm. Reprint of 1666 edition. Collection of biographies of people prominent during the years 1621 to 1644.

8775   TSUNG, NENG-CHENG
         Sheng kuo tsai fu lu. Taipei, Wen hai chu pan she, ₍1974?₎
237 p. 22cm. 'Reprint' of manuscript copy. Brief biographies
of 222 ministers of the Ming dynasty (1368-1644).

8776   TU, TA-KUEI
         Ming ch'ên pei chuan wan yen chi. Taipei, Wen hai ch'u
pan she, 1969. 3 v. (1644 p.) 20cm. Facsimile reprint of
manuscript. Biographies and epitaphs of statesmen of the Sung
Dynasty (960-1279).

8777   TU, TA-KUEI
         Yüan yen chi shan ts'un fu yin tê. [Peiping] Yen-ching ta
hsüeh, Yin tê pien tsuan ch'u, 1938. 3 v. (double leaves) in
case. 27cm. (Yen-ching te hsüeh. Yin tê pien tsuan ch'u.
[Supplement] 12) Added t. p. : Yüan yen chi abridged. A selection from Tu Ta-kuei's Ming ch'en pei chuan yüan yen chih chi,
which consists of biographies and epitaphs of 221 ministers of
the Sung dynasty. A photocopy of the above work was issued in
1966 by the Ch'eng Wen Publishing Company, Taipei.

8778   UNITED STATES. CONSULATE GENERAL. HONGKONG.
         [Biographical appearance file of Chinese officials, 1951-
1967. Stanford, Calif.] Hoover Institution Microfilms [1971]
87 reels. ports. 16cm. Title on boxes containing reels: Biographic cards. Microfilm copy of an alphabetical card file compiled by the staff of the U. S. Consulate General in Hongkong and
currently held by the Universities Service Centre, Kowloon,
Hongkong. The cards contain biographical data on leaders of
Communist China, prominent persons in Hongkong, foreign diplomatic and business personnel in China and Hongkong as well
as references to newspapers, journals, etc. from which the data
were gathered. The file also includes newspaper clippings.

         ---- ----[Index. Stanford, Calif., Hoover Institution Micro-
films, 1971] 1 v. (unpaged) 28cm.

8779   WANG, PING-HSIEH, 1822-1879.
         Kuo ch'ao ming ch'en yen hsing lu. Taipei, Wen hai ch'u
pan she [1969?] 2 v. 20cm. (Chin tai Chung-kuo shih liao
ıts'ung k'an, 471) Facsimile of 1885 edition. Biographies of 72
famous state ministers of the Ch'ing Dynasty up to the Ch'ien-
lung period (1736-1795).

8780   WHO'S WHO IN CHINA (biographies of Chinese) [Tokyo,
         Ryukei Shosha, 1973-74. 5 v. ports. 25cm. Title also
in Chinese: Chung-kuo jên min lu. Reprint of the 2d-6th editions and supplements of a work published in Shanghai, 1920-
1950 by the China weekly review (earlier: Millard's review)
under title: Who's who in China, containing the pictures and biographies of some of China's political, financial, business and

professional leaders (subtitle varies slightly). See also item
613 in the basic volume of this bibliography.

8781   WHO'S WHO IN THE CHINESE PEOPLE'S POLITICAL CON-
         SULTATIVE CONFERENCE (Chung-kuo jen-min cheng-
         chih hsieh-shang hui-i jen-wu chih) Compiled by Chou-mo pao
         pien wei hui. Washington, Center for Chinese Research Mater-
         ials, Association of Research Libraries, 1970. 2 v. in 1. 28cm.
         Original t. p. reads: Hsin chêng hsieh jên wu chih: v. 2: Chung-
         kuo jên min chêng chih hsieh shang hui i jên wu chih. Chinese
         edition (195- entered under: Chou mo pao, Hongkong in the sup-
         plementary volume (Item 5181) Chinese political figures of the
         Kuomintang and the early years of the Communist regime.

8782   WIEGER, LÉON, 1856-
         China throughout the ages. Translated by Edward Chalmers
         Werner. [Hsien-hsien] Hsien Press, 1928. 508 p. illus. 25cm.
         Translated from the original French edition: La Chine à travers
         les âges, hommes et choses (Sienhsien, 1920) "Biographical
         index" (p. 277-449) is a dictionary of famous Chinese (names
         are romanized, followed by Chinese characters) with quite brief
         biographical data.

8783   YANG, LU-JUNG, fl. 1717.
         Yin wan lu. Taipei, Hsüeh sheng shu chü, 1970. 2, 418 p.
         21cm. (Ming tai shih chi hui k'an, 19) 'Reprint' of a manu-
         script. Biographies of 477 slain ('martyred') Chinese at the
         end of the Ming Dynasty; arranged by death dates.

8784   YU LIEN YEN CHIU SO, KOWLOON.
         Hierarchies of the People's Republic of China, March 1975.
         Kowloon, Union Research Institute, 1975. iii, xi, 262 p. 24cm.
         Includes (on p. 79-260) biographical sketches of over 500 lead-
         ers of the central and local governments of mainland China, the
         Chinese Communist Party, the People's Liberation Army and the
         National People's Congress. In biographical dictionary format.

8785   YÜAN, CHIH, 1502-1547.
         Huang Ming hsien shih. Taipei, Wen hai ch'u pan she, 1970.
         2 v. 19cm. 'Reprint' of a Ming manuscript. Biographies of
         180 prominent persons from the beginning of the Ming Dynasty
         (1368) to the late 16th century.

8786   ZOHO GENDAI CHŪKOGU JITEN. Tokyo, Chūkogu Kenkyūjo,
         1952. 620, 98, 43, 39, 21 p. illus. Supervised by Yoshi-
         tarō Hirano, Wataru Kaji and Tomoyuki Ishihama. An encyclo-
         pedia of contemporary China. On pages 1-98 (2d set) is a who's
         who of modern and contemporary Chinese (arranged by Japanese
         pronunciation).

Local

Honan (Province)

8787   CHU, MU-CHIEH, fl. 1573.
Huang ch'ao chung chou jên wu chih. Taipei, Hsüeh sheng
shu chu, 1970. 2, 490 p. 22cm. Reprint of the 1568 edition.
Over 130 biographies of Chinese of Honan Province from the
early Ming Dynasty up to the Chia-ching period.

Kiangsu (Province)

8788   CHANG, CH'ANG, 1374-1438.
Wu chung jên wu chih. Taipei, Hsüeh sheng shu chu, 1969.
573 p. 21cm. Reprint of the Ming edition. Biographies of personalities of Wu Hsien (Kiangsu Province) from the Chou to the
Ming Dynasty, in 13 categories, sub-arranged in chronological
order.

8789   CHANG, WEI-HSIANG.
Ch'ing tai Pi-ling ming jên hsiao chuan kao. Shanghai,
Ch'ang chou lü Hu t'ung hsiang hui, 1944. 3 v. in 1. 20cm.
Biographies from the Pi-ling district of Kiang-su Province
during the Ch'ing Dynasty.

Shu-Ch'eng

8790   WANG, KUO-FAN.
Shu-ch'êng ch'i chiu lu. [Taipei?] 1963. 150 p. (double
leaves) 25cm. Over 200 biographies of personalities of Shu-
ch'eng County (An-huai Province) since the Han Dynasty. In
chronological order.

COLOMBIA

8791   ARANGO MEJÍA, GABRIEL, 1872-1958.
Genealogías de Antioquia y Caldas. 3. ed. Medellín, Colombia, Editorial Bedout, 1973. 2 v. 24cm. Genealogies of
the departments of Antioquia and Caldas, Colombia. 404 families (with an additional 43 in an appendix to vol. 2) are arranged alphabetically, with a brief biography of the 'founder' of
the Colombian branch of the family.

8792   BARAYA, JOSÉ MARÍA, 1828-1878.
Biografías militares; o, Historia militar del país en medio
siglo. Bogotá, Librería del Ejército, 1962. 542 p. 24cm.
(Ejército de Colombia. Biblioteca del Ejército, v. no. 11) Includes 72 biographies of soldiers prominent in the military history of Colombia.

8793   COBO VELASCO, ALFONSO
                Calendario biográfico y genealógico de Santiago de Cali;
        algunos apuntes relativos a la historia de la ciudad de Santiago
        de Cali, y ligera genealogía de varios de sus hijos y benefac-
        tores, compilados de archivos notariales y parroquiales, de
        libros, revistas y periódicos, 1536-1961. [Cali?] 1962. 223 p.
        illus., ports. 24cm. A biographical, genealogical (and chro-
        nological) calendar of events in the city of Cali, Colombia; ar-
        ranged by month, day and year. Each entry gives brief infor-
        mation on importance of date, and/or biographical data for noted
        Colombians (alphabetical approach thru' index).

8794   CORREA, RAMÓN C
                Diccionario de boyacenses ilustres. Tunja [Colombia] Im-
        prenta Departamental, 1957. 364 p. (Publicaciones de la
        Academia Boyacense de Historia y del Gobierno del Departa-
        mento de Boyacá) Dictionary of illustrious men of the State of
        Boyaca, Colombia. 800 biographies of deceased & living per-
        sonages.

8795   LIBRO AZUL DE COLOMBIA. Blue book of Colombia.
                Bosquejos biográficos de los personajes más eminentes.
        Biographical sketches of the most prominent personages. His-
        toria condensada de la República. Abridged history of the Re-
        public ... [New York, J. J. Little & Ives Co.] 1918. 725 p.
        illus., ports. 32cm. Includes biographical material and spe-
        cial articles on Colombian commerce and economics. The index
        is alphabetical by state. Dedication signed: Jorge Posada Calle-
        jas.

8796   MEJÍA ROBLEDO, ALFONSO, 1897-
                Hombres y empresas de Antioquia. [Medellín, Talleres
        Litográficos de Movifoto, 1971] 573 p. illus., ports. 24cm.
        Men and business enterprises of the Department of Antioquia,
        Colombia. Two biographical dictionaries are included: (1) p.
        29-216--deceased personages; (2) p. 457-573--living personali-
        ties. First published in 1952 (554 p.)

8797   PÁEZ COURVEL, LUIS E
                Precursores, mártires y próceres santandereanos de la
        Independencia colombiana. (In Boletín de historia y antigüeda-
        des; organo de Academia colombiano de Historia, Bogotá. v.
        34, no. 393-395, jul.-sep. 1947. p. [475]-594. 889 persons
        from Santander, Colombia are represented in this biographical
        dictionary of heroes of the Colombian struggle for independence.

8798   PEÑUELA, CAYO LEÓNIDAS, 1864-
                Album de Boyacá. 2. ed. [Tunja, Colombia, Impr. De-
        partmental, 1969-70] 2 v. illus., ports. 24cm. "Homenaje
        de la Comisión Asesora del Gobierno Nacional para la Con-
        memoración de la Campaña Libertadora de 1819." Album of the

Battle of Boyaca (Colombian War of Independence) of 1819. Vol.
2, almost entirely biographical, includes biographical sketches
of participants in the War and the Battle; in places there is a
quasi-alphabetical arrangement of the biographees; the general
index (really a table of contents) at the end of v. 2 gives an over-
all view of the biographees listed.

8799   ROMERO DE NOHRA, FLOR
        Mujeres en Colombia [por] Flor Romero de Nohra [y] Gloria
        Pachón Castro. Bogotá, Editorial Andes, 1961. 287 p. ports.
        28cm. A biographical dictionary of ca. 300 outstanding contem-
        porary Colombian women; photographs accompany most entries.

CONGO (Brazzaville)

8800   THOMPSON, VIRGINIA McLEAN, 1903-
        Historical dictionary of the People's Republic of the Congo
        (Congo-Brazzaville), by Virginia Thompson and Richard Adloff.
        Metuchen, N. J., Scarecrow Press, 1974. viii, 139 p. map.
        23cm. (African historical dictionaries, no. 2) Includes bio-
        graphical entries.

COSTA RICA

8801   FERNÁNDEZ GUARDIA, RICARDO, 1867-
        Diccionario biográfico de Costa Rica. Época del descubri-
        miento y de la conquista. (In Sociedad de Geografía e Historia
        de Costa Rica. Publicación. San José, 1941. no. 1, p. [3]-
        45)

CUBA

8802   BUSTAMANTE, LUIS J
        Enciclopedia popular cubana. La Habana, Cultural, Socie-
        dad Anónima [194-] 3 v. illus., ports. 24cm. Contents.--
        [1] A-Ch. --2. D-M. --3. N-Z. Popular Cuban encyclopedia;
        includes biographical sketches of famous Cubans—dictionary
        format.

8803   DIRECTORY OF PERSONALITIES OF THE CUBAN GOVERN-
        MENT, official organizations, and mass organizations.
        [n. p.] 1971. 994 p. 27cm. (Reference aid) "Brief biographi-
        cal notes on selected personalities are included ... The latest
        date of information is 21 June 1971. " Issued under U. S. Central
        Intelligence Agency auspices (?)

8804   PEZUELA Y LOBO, JACOBO DE LA, 1811-1882.
        Diccionario geográfico, estadístico, histórico de la isla

de Cuba, por Jacobo de la Pezuela. Madrid, Impr. del Estab.
de Mellado, 1863-66. 4 v. 28cm. A geographical, statistical
and historical dictionary of Cuba that includes a substantial
number of biographical entries.

CZECHOSLOVAKIA

(See also SLOVAKIA)

8805   BIOGRAPHISCHES LEXIKON ZUR GESCHICHTE DER BÖH-
           MISCHEN LÄNDER. Hrsg. im Auftrag des Collegium
        Carolinum von Heribert Sturm. München, R. Oldenbourg, 1974-
              v. 25cm. Cover title. Issued in parts. A biographi-
        cal dictionary for the history of Bohemia and its regions, in-
        cluding the 20th century Czechoslovak Republic. Vol. 1, fasc.
        1-3 issued thus far (1976)

8806   BORN, IGNAZ, Edler von, 1742-1791.
              Effigies virorum eruditorum atque artificium Bohemiae et
        Moraviae una cum brevis vitae operumque enarratione. Pragae,
        W. Gerle, 1773-75. 2 v. ports. 4.° Portraits and biographi-
        cal sketches of learned men and artists of Bohemia and Moravia.
        Includes 58 biographies. F. M. Pelzel's Abbildungen böhmi-
        scher und mährischer Gelehrten (q. v.) is a translation of the
        Born's work plus 2 more vols. compiled by Pelzel.

8807   KDO JE KDO V ČESKOSLOVENSKU. Biografie žijících osob
           se stálým bydlištěm v ČSSR. Připr. [kol.] Hl. red.:
        Václav Brož. Red. slov. části: Ol'ga Slušna. 1. vyd. Praha,
        CTK, t. CTK, Brandýs nad Labem, 1969-   v. 24cm.
        Who's who in Czechoslovakia; biographies of persons now living
        in the Czechoslovak Republic.

8808   KUHN, HEINRICH, 1922-
              Biographisches Handbuch der Tschechoslowakei. [Neuaufl.]
        München] R. Lerche, 1969-   v. (loose-leaf) 21cm.
        (Veröffentlichung des Collegium Carolinum) Biographical hand-
        book of present-day leaders of the Czechoslovak Republic. 1st
        ed., issued in 1961 (xiii, 640 p.), was written by H. Kuhn and
        Otto Bloss. Vols. 1-4 complete; v. 5, fasc. 5 issued in 1975.

8809   OTTUV SLOVNÍK NAUČNÝ. Illustrovaná encyklopaedie obec-
           ných vedomosti. V Praze, J. Otto, 1888-1909. 28 v.
        illus., 25-26cm. Vol. 28 is a supplement, A-Z. Issued in
        parts. Otto's encyclopedic dictionary; a general encyclopedia in
        Czech, but extremely valuable for the quite comprehensive list-
        ing of famous figures in Bohemia, medieval and modern (to the
        end of the 19th century). A supplementary set was begun in
        1930 but only 2 vols. were completed as of 1943.

8810   PELZEL, FRANZ MARTIN, 1734-1801.
        Abbildungen böhmischer und mährischer Gelehrten, nebst
kurzen Nachrichten von ihren Leben und Wirken. Praga, J. K.
Hraba, 1773-82. 4 v. ports. 8.º Portraits of Bohemian and
Moravian scholars, with brief notes on their life and works.
The first 2 vols are a translation of Born's Effigies virorum
eruditorum atque artificium Bohemiae et Moraviae (Pragae,
1773-75, 2 v.) q.v. Czerny, R. (Einführung in die tschechoslowakische Bibliographie bis 1918) attributes this work to
Mikulas Adaukt Voigt and F. M. Pelcl (Pelzel).

8811   PERINA, FRANTIŠEK JAROSLAV, 1844-1902.
        Slavín (pantheon) sbírka podobizen, autografů a životopisů
predních mužů československých. Text napsal a uspořadal
František Jar. Peřina. V Praze, F. Bartel [1872] 2 v. in 1.
illus., ports. 23cm. Pantheon of collective biography, portraits and autographs of famous Czechs.

8812   ŠVABINSKÝ, MAX, 1873-1962.
        Svabinského český slavín. Sto portretů M. Švabinského.
Vybral, uspoř. a naps. Ludvík Paleníček. Fot. [portretů]:
František Zahradníček [a kol. 1. vyd. Praha, SPN, 1973.
216, [5] p. ports. 25cm. The Czech 'Pantheon' of Max Sva-
binsky; 100 biographical sketches of famous Czechs past and
present, with portraits.

DAGHESTAN

8813   MAKHACH-KALA. INSTITUT ISTORII PARTII.
        Bortsy za vlast' Sovetov v Dagestane, 1917-1921 gg.; kratkie
biograficheskie spravki. Makhachkala, 1957. 70 p. 17cm.
Brief biographical notices of people in Daghestan who fought for
the establishment of Soviet hegomony in that area during the
years 1917-1921.

DAHOMEY

8814   DECALO, SAMUEL
        Historical dictionary of Dahomey (People's Republic of
Benin) Metuchen, N. J., Scarecrow Press, 1976. xvii, [3],
201 p. maps. 23cm. (African historical dictionaries, no. 7)
Includes biographical entries of persons (native and European)
prominent in the history of Dahomey.

8815   DICTIONNAIRE BIO-BIBLIOGRAPHIQUE DU DAHOMEY.
        [Porto-Novo?] Institut de recherches appliquées du Da-
homey, I. R. A. D., 1969-   v. ports. Bio-bibliographical dictionary of Dahomey.

DENMARK

Bibliography, Indexes, Portrait Catalogs

8816   COPENHAGEN. GARNISONSBIBLIOTEK.
Katalog over det Kongelige Garnisonsbiblioteks officers-
portraetsamling. Udarbejdet paa foranledning af Biblioteket
ved E. Lehmann. Kjøbenhavn, Trykt i Krigsministeriet, 1929.
viii, 172 p. 22cm. Catalog of the collection of Danish Army officers' portraits in the Royal Garrison's Library in Copenhagen.

8817   HOFF, H
Herlufsholm skoles samling af danske portraetter, af H.
Hoff [og P. V. Gøtzsche] Naestved, Ikke i Bogh, 1903-05. 2 v.
(168, 60 p.) A catalog of the Danish portraits in the possession
of Herlufsholm's Grammar School.

8818   HOUMØLLER, SVEN
Biografiske tidsskriftartikler; register til Danske blandende
tidsskrifter (1855-1912) og Dansk tidsskrift-index (1915-49) [Kø-
benhavn] Bibliotekscentralen, 1971. 144, [1] p. 25cm. Index to
biographies (chiefly of Danes) contained in the Danske blandende
tidsskrifter (1855-1912) and the Dansk tidsskrift-index (1915-1949).

8819   LUND, EMIL FERDINAND SVITZER, 1858-   ed.
Danske malede portraeter; en beskrivende katalog. Udg.
under medvirkning af C. Chr. Andersen. København, Gyldendal,
1895-1912. 10 v. plates, ports. 25cm. A descriptive catalog,
with many portraits, of Danish portraiture.

8820   SCHEPELERN, H   D
Portraetsamlingen i Odense adelige Jomfrukloster. Med en
indledning om Klosterets aeldre historie. [København?] Det
Nationalhistoriske museum paa Frederiksborg, 1959. 142 p.
`¹¹us. Catalog of the collection of portraits in Odense's Adelige
Jomfrukloster (home for unmarried ladies of high rank).

8821   WESTERGAARD, PEDER BASSE CHRISTIAN
Danske portraeter i kobberstik, litografi og traesnit; en
beskrivende fortegnelse. København, Haase, 1927-30. 2 v.
(972 & 986 p.) ports. 8.⁰ Issued in 31 fascicles.

---- ----Tillaeg og navnefortegnelse. København, Haase, 1933.
98 p. 8.⁰ Danish engraved portraits on copper, lithographs
and wood; a descriptive catalog.

General Works

8822   BLAEKSPRUTTENS HISTORISKE BLÅ BOG. 168 store og små
danskeres levenedeløb fra Estrup til vor tid. Udg. Gyl-

dendal under medvirken af Blaekspruttens red. Tekst af Knud
Poulsen [et al.] Tegninger af Herluf Jensenius [et al.] København, Gyldendal, 1973. 75 p. illus. 22cm. Blaeksprutten's
(the 'Octopus') historical blue book (or who's who); 168 great
and minor Danish lives from Estrup to the present.

8823   BOECK, HECTOR, 1874-   ed.
        Danmarks haer. Under redaktion of Hector Boeck, S. E.
Johnstad-Møller og C. V. Hjalf. Det biografiske stof under
redaktion af H. Hjorth-Nielsen. København, Selskabet til udgivelse af kulturskrifter, 1934-35. 2 v. illus., ports. 27cm.
Denmark's Army. Includes a biographical section.

8824   DAHL, KAI, 1897-   ed.
        Danmarks flaade. Redigeret af K. Dahl, og for det biogra-
fiske stofs vedkommende af H. Hjorth-Nielsen. København,
Selskabet til udgivelse af kulturskrifter, 1934. 558 p. illus.,
ports. 27cm. Denmark's Navy. Includes biographical sketches.

8825   DANMARKSHISTORIENS BLÅ BOG; 1680 danske maends og kvin-
        ders levnedsløb fra Ansgar til vor tid. Udgivet af Krak
under medvirken af Palle Birkelund [et al.] København, Krak,
1971. 467 p. ports. 24cm. The who's who of Danish history;
1680 Danish men and women from Ansgar to the present. A biographical dictionary (with portraits).

8826   ELBERLING, EMIL, 1835-1927.
        Rigsdagens medlemmer gennem hundrede aar, 1848-1948;
biografier udarb. paa grundlag af materiale indsamlet af
Rigsdagsbibliotekarerne Emil Elberling og Victor Elberling.
København, I kommission hos J. H. Schultz, 1949-50. 3 v.
ports. 27cm. Edited by Victor Elberling (v. 1-2, in collaboration with C. G. Elberling; v. 3 with Magnus Sørensen)

---- ----Rigsdagens medlemmer, 1949-50-1953. Supplement
udg. på foranstaltning af Folketingets praesidium ved Magnus
Sørensen. København, J. H. Schultz, 1958. 31 p. ports. 18cm.
Members of the Danish Parliament, 1848-1953; biographies.

8827   FAEDRENELANDSK NEKROLOG; eller, Efterretninger om de
        ved stilling og virksomhed udmaerkede og ellers bekjendte
afdøde i de sex aar fra 1821-1826. Udg. af etatsraad Frederik
Thaarup. Kjøbenhavn, Forfatteren, 1835-44. x, 520 p. 20cm.
Issued in 8 parts.

---- ----Ny raekke.   hefte. Kjøbenhavn, Forfatteren,
1844-45. 2 pts. 20cm. No more published. A necrology of
notable Danes who died in the years 1821-1845 with remarks on
their offices and activities while alive.

8828   FORLAGET LIBER, Copenhagen.
        De kongelige danske ridderordener og medailler [1964-1968]
        Ordenernes og ordenskapitlets historie ved Albert Fabritius.
        Biografisk redaktion: Forlaget Liber. København, 1970. 591 p.
        illus., ports. 27cm. Continues De kongelige danske ridder-
        ordener og medailler, by Arthur Jensens forlag. Primarily a
        biographical dictionary (in several alphabets) of Danes knighted
        or receiving other honors in the period 1964-1968.

8829   FRIHEDSKAMPENS VETERANER.
        Faldne i Danmarks frihedskamp 1940-45. Udg. af Fri-
        hedskampens veteraner med stotte af Statsministeriet og Fri-
        hedsfondet. Redigeret af Ib Damgaard Petersen i redaktion-
        skomiteen: Sven Seehusen [og] Sven Hoffmann. [København]
        Gyldendal [1970] 461 p. front. 24cm. A biographical dictionary
        of Danish patriots and members of the underground movement
        during World War II who died during that conflict.

8830   GRANDJEAN, LOUIS E   1898-
        Den lille portraetkunst i Danmark siden 1750. [Redaktion:
        Louis E. Grandjean og Albert Fabritius. Medarbejdere: O. H.
        Clementsen et al.] København, Gyldendal, 1949. 221 p. 87 ports.
        (part col.) 22cm. The art of portrait painting in Denmark since
        1750. Includes 87 portraits of famous Danes.

8831   JENSENS (ARTHUR) FORLAG, COPENHAGEN.
        De Kongelige danske ridderordener og medailler. Historisk
        indledning: Louis Bobé. Biografisk redaktion: Arthur Jensens
        forlag. København, 1950-63. 5 v. illus., ports. 27cm. Vols.
        4-5 have imprint: København, Forlaget Liber. Continued by:
        Forlaget Liber, Copenhagen. De kongelige danske ridderordener
        og medailler. Largely a biographical dictionary (in several al-
        phabets) of Danes knighted or receiving other honors in the pe-
        riod 1950-1963.

8832   TÅGHOLT, KNUD
        Hvem var minister. Dansk politik gennem 100 år. [Køben-
        havn] Forlaget Aros [1971] 160 p. illus. 21cm. A handbook of
        Danish politics of the last 100 years which includes a biographical
        dictionary of 230 cabinet officers (p. 33-109).

8833   TOPSOE-JENSEN, THEODOR ANDREAS, 1867-
        Officerer i den dansk-norske søetat 1660-1814 og den danske
        søetat 1814-1932. Oplysninger samlet og udarb. af T. A. Top-
        søe-Jensen og Emil Marquard. København, H. Hagerup, 1935.
        2 v. illus., ports. 26cm. Officers of the Danish-Norwegian
        Navy, 1660-1814, and the Danish Navy, 1814-1932. In alpha-
        betical arrangement.

8834   ZINGLERSEN, BENT
        Københavnske gadenavne og deres historia. København,

Politikens forlag, 1972. 288 p. illus., ports. 18cm. Included
in this dictionary of Copenhagen's streets are brief biographical
(often only identifying) sketches of famous Danes, etc., after whom
many of the streets are named.

DOMINICAN REPUBLIC

8835   FLEURY, VÍCTOR
        Cien dominicanos célebres [por] Víctor Fleury, Gustavo
Ricart [y] Pedro R. Bisono. [1. ed.] Santo Domingo, R. D.,
Publicaciones América [1973] 331 p. 23cm. (Colección "Crisol
dominicano") 100 famous sons of Santo Domingo (Dominican Republic); arranged by activity or profession: educators, scientists, men of letters, statesmen, etc. Lacks an alphabetical approach.

8836   MARTÍNEZ, RUFINO
        Diccionario biográfico-histórico dominicano, 1821-1930.
Santo Domingo, Editora de la Universidad Autónoma de Santo
Domingo, 1971. 541 p. illus. 28cm. (Colección Historia y
sociedad, no. 5) (Publicaciones de la Universidad Autónoma de
Santo Domingo, v. 152) Biographical-historical dictionary of the
Dominican Republic, 1821-1930.

EAST (Far East)

see under ASIA

ECUCADOR

8837   BORK, ALBERT WILLIAM
        Historical dictionary of Ecuador, by Albert William Bork
and Georg Maier. Metuchen, N. J., Scarecrow Press, 1973.
192 p. 23cm. (Latin American historical dictionaries, no. 10)
Includes a large number of biographical sketches.

8838   QUIÉN ES QUIÉN EN QUITO. 1. -   edición; 1966/67-
        [Guayaquil, Artes Gráficas Senefelder]   v. illus., ports.
24cm. Who's who in Quito. Arranged by occupation.

8839   TORO RUIZ, I
        Del pasado ambateño y microbiografías nacionales. [Am-
bato, Ecuador, Impr. Municipal] 1975. 352, [2] p. 18cm.
"Anotaciones al Diccionario biográfico del Ecuador [de Gustavo
Arboleda]": p. 257-352. A history of events in Ambato, Ecuador (city) and national 'microbiographies'; the latter are arranged in biographical dictionary format as annotations to Arboleda's Diccionario biográfico del Ecuador.

EGPYT

(Ancient & Medieval)

8840   HELCK, HANS WOLFGANG
        Lexikon der Ägyptologie. Hrsg. von Wolfgang Helck und
        Eberhard Otto. Wiesbaden, O. Harrassowitz, 1972-
        v. 28cm. Issued in fascicles. Vol. 1 and v. 2, fasc. 1-2
        available as of 1975. Dictionary of Egyptology; includes biogra-
        phies of ancient Egyptians.

8841   AL-KINDĪ, ABŪ 'UMAR MUHAMMAD IBN YŪSUF, 897-961.
        The governors and judges of Egypt; or, Kitāb el 'umarâ' (el
        walâh) wa Kitâb el qudâh of el Kindi, together with an appendix
        derived mostly from Raf' el isr by Ibn Hajar. Edited by Rhuvon
        Guest and printed for the Trustees of the E. J. W. Gibb Memo-
        rial. Leyden, E. J. Brill, 1912. 72, 686, 12 p. 2 fold. maps,
        6 facsims. 25cm. (E. J. W. Gibb Memorial series, v. 19)
        The period covered extends from the conquest of Egypt by the
        Arabs in 641 A. D. down to the author's own day. The supple-
        mentary matter brings it down to 1033. The book of Muslim
        governors and judges in Egypt.

8842   PEREMANS, WILLY, 1907-
        Prosopographia Ptolemaica, par W. Peremans et E. van't
        Dack. Louvanii, Bibliotheca Universitatis, 1950-75. 8 v. 24cm.
        (Studia Hellenistica, 6, 8, 11-13, 17, 20-21) At head of title:
        Universitas Catholica Lovaniensis. Vol. 3-8 by W. Peremans
        [et al.] Vol. 7: Index nominum; v. 8: Addenda et corrigenda
        aux v. 1 & 2. A list (or 'prosopography') of Ptolemaic Egypt
        (332-30 B. C.) containing names of officials, etc. In most cases,
        of course, biographical data is very sparse or almost non-ex-
        istent, but as much data as is available is given so that the work
        has definite biographical value. Alphabetical approach is avail-
        able through the index of names (v. 7).

EUROPE, EASTERN

8843   BIOGRAPHISCHES LEXIKON ZUR GESCHICHTE SÜDOSTEU-
        ROPAS. [Hrsg. von Mathias Bernath und Felix von
        Schoeder] München, R. Oldenbourg, 1972-   v. 25cm.
        (Südosteuropaische Arbeiten, Bd. 75   Biographical diction-
        ary for the history of Southeastern Europe. Issued in fascicles,
        1972-   ; Contents.--Bd. 1. A bis F. 1972.--Bd. 2. G-K. 1976.

8844   FERLUGA, JADRAN
        Glossar zur frühmittelalterlichen Geschichte im östlichen
        Europa. Hrsg. von Jadran Ferluga, Manfred Hellmann [und]
        Herbert Ludat. Redaktion: Dieter Wojtecki [et al.] Wiesbaden,

F. Steiner, 1973-   v. 24cm. Issued in parts. Contents: Ser. A. Lateinische Namen bis 900   v. -- ser. B. Grie-
chische Namen bis 1025. A glossary for the early medieval history of Eastern Europe; this dictionary is largely topographical
in nature, but it does have its uses for identifying and giving
some biographical data for personages of the time. 8 parts issued as of 1976 (ser. A, fasc. 1-6; ser. B, fasc. 1-2)

8845   INTERCONTINENTAL PRESS SERVICE.
        Leading personalities in Eastern Europe; Bulgaria, Czech-
oslovakia, Hungary, Poland, Romania. A desk reference for
editors and journalists. West New York, N. J., 1957. 46 l.
29cm. Includes ca. 180 brief biographies arranged by country
and importance of position.

8846   SEIDMAN, HILLEL
        'Ishim she-hikarti; Demuyot me-'avar karov be-mizrakh
'eyropah, me'et Hillel Seidman. Yerushalayim, Mosad ha-rav
kuk [1970] 12, 508 p. facsims., 31 ports. 22cm. 65 biographies of rabbis from Eastern Europe who lost their lives in the
Nazi Holocaust.

FINLAND

Bibliography, Indexes, Portrait Catalogs

8847   HINTZE, BERTEL, 1901-
        Helsingfors universitets porträttsamling. Beskrivande
förteckning. Helsingfors, 1927. 107 p. The portrait collection
of the University of Helsinki; a catalog.

General Works

8848   BERGHOLM, AXEL
        Keisarillisen Suomen hallitus konseljin ja Senaatin puheen
johtajat, jäsenet ja virkamiehet 1809-1909. Biograafisia tietoja.
Porvoo, W. Söderström, 1912. 440 p. 26cm. The presidents,
the members and the functionaries of the Imperial Council and
Senate of Finland, 1809-1909; biographical data, Register of
functionaries: p. 1-136; biographical section, A-O, p. 139-440.

8849   BOSTRÖM, H   J
        Suomen kaupunkien pormestarit 1800-luvulla. (In Suomen
sukututkimusseura. Vuosikirja. 25cm. v. 6 (1922), p. 1-53;
v. 8 (1924), p. 1-85) Suomen sukututkismusseura. Julkaisuja,
1. Mayors of Finnish cities in the 18th century. Cities in alphabetical order, with mayors listed chronologically thereunder.

8850   ETELÄ-POHJANMAAN MAAKUNTALIITTO.
        Eteläpohjalaisia elämäkertoja. Toimituskunta: Reino Ala-
        Kulju [et al. Vaasa, 1963-65] 2 v. (971 p.) ports. 25cm. A
        biographical dictionary for the province of Etalä-Pohjanmaa
        (better known as Österbotten) Finland.

8851   FINLANDS MINNESVÄRDE MÄN. Samling af lefnadsteckningar.
        Helsingfors, J. C. Frenckell, 1853-55. 2 v. 22cm. Re-
        markable men of Finland; a collection of biographies. Alpha-
        betical table of contents at front of each volume.

8852   GRÅSBECK, ARMAS
             S:t Johannes Logen S:t Augustins matrikel 1762-1808.
        Helsingfors, 1954. 124 p. 26cm. Biographical register of the
        members of the Masonic Lodge of St. Augustine of St. John,
        Helsingfors.

8853   KADETTIKUNTA.
             Kadettikunta, jäsenet 1921-1955. [Mikkeli, 1957] 338 p.
        ports. 25cm. "Varsinaisen toimitustyön on suorittanut ansiok-
        kaasti kapteeni K.-E. Aspara." The Finnish Corps of Cadets,
        1921-1955; a biographical dictionary.

8854   NORDENSTRENG, SIGURD, 1857-1935.
             Borgarståndets medlemmar och sekreterare 1863-1906;
        levnadsteckningar. Helsingfors, Söderström, 1920. 396, v p.
        24cm. (Borgarståndets historia vid Finlands Landtdagar, 1809-
        1906, t. 5) The members and the secretaries of the Commons
        of Finland, 1863-1906; biographies.

8855   PAAVOLAINEN, JAAKKO, ed.
             Karjalainen elämäkerrasto. Porvoo, W. Söderström [1961]
        396 p. illus., ports. 26cm. Biography of Karelia, Finland,
        before that area fell under Russian rule. Chronologically ar-
        ranged; index, p. 391-397.

8856   SUOMEN JÄÄKARIEN ELÄMÄKERRASTO. Porvoo, WSOY,
        1938. xiv, 915 p. illus., ports. 25cm. Biographies of
        Finnish patriot volunteers in the movement for independence
        from Russian rule. Issued by the Ministry of Defence's Bureau
        of Military History (Puolustusministeriön Sotahistoriallinen
        Toimisto).

8857   SUOMEN MATRIKKELI, KUSTANNUSLIIKE.
             Kuka kukin suomalainen; Hämeen lääni, Keski-Suomen
        lääni, Kuopion lääni, Kymen lääni, Lapin lääni, Mikkelin lääni,
        Oulun lääni, Pohjois-Karjalan lääni, Turun ja Porin lääni, Vaasa
        lääni, Uudenmaan lääni. Jyväskylä [1970] 708 p. illus. 30cm.
        A Who's who for the various administrative districts of Finland;
        a biographical dictionary.

8858   SUOMEN MERIKAPTEENIT. Elämäkerrallisia tietoja. Fin-
        lands sjökaptener. Biografiska uppgifter. Helsinki,
        Suomen Laivanpäällystoliitto, 1960. 400 p. illus., ports. 21cm.
        In Finnish or Swedish. Earlier editions issued from 1912 to
        1952. Finnish master mariners—sea captains; biographical
        data.

8859   SUOMEN NAISYHDISTYS.
            Biograafisia tietoja Suomen naisista eri työaloilla. Helsin-
        ki, J. Simeliuksen Perillisten Kirjapaino, 1896. xvi, 198, [2] p.
        19cm. Biographical notices on Finnish women in various pro-
        fessional categories. Index: p. v-xvi.

8860   SUOMEN OMAKOTIASUTUS. Piikkiö, Kirjaseppä [1970-
            v. illus. 26cm. Contents. --1. Hämeen lääni.

        A biographical dictionary of home owners in Finland; each vol-
        ume covers a particular administrative district. Vol. 5 (1972--
        Kymen lääni, Mikkelin lääni) latest one published?

FLANDERS

(See also BELGIUM)

8861   ENCYCLOPEDIE VAN DE VLAAMSE BEWEGING. Redactie:
            Jozef Deleu [et al.] Tielt [Belgium] Lannoo, 1973-75. 2 v.
        illus., ports. 28cm. Encyclopedia of the Flemish movement;
        an alphabetically arranged work that features many biographies
        of leaders in Flemish nationalism, culture, etc. Contents: 1.
        A-L.--2. M-Z.

8862   WINKLER PRINS ENCYCLOPEDIE VAN VLAANDEREN.
            Hoofdredactie: R. F. Lissens [et al. Brussel] Elsevier
        Sequoia [1972-74] 5 v. illus., ports. 27cm. A dictionary-en-
        cyclopedia of Flanders; valuable for the numerous biographical
        sketches of Flemings included in its alphabet.

FRANCE

Bibliography, Indexes, Portrait Catalogs

8863   AUFFRAY, JACQUELINE
            Bibliographie des recueils biographiques de contemporains
        des XIXème et XXème siècles en France. [Paris? 1963] xix,
        152 l. 27cm. Mémoire de fin d'études--Institut national des
        techniques de la documentation, Conservatoire national des
        arts et métiers, Paris. A bibliography of collective biography
        of 19th and 20th century persons of importance in France.

8864   GUIGARD, JOANNIS, 1825-1892.
        Indicateur du Mercure de France, 1672-1789, contenant, par
ordre alphabétique, les noms des personnages sur lesquels on
trouve dans cette collection des notices biographiques et généalogiques, avec renvoi aux années, tomes et pages. Paris, Bache-
lin-Deflorenne, 1869. [6], 142 p. 8.º An index to the Mercure
de France, 1672-1789, containing, in alphabetical arrangement,
names of persons for whom biographical and genealogical notices
are provided (chiefly Frenchmen).

8865   HENNEQUIN, RENÉ
        Avant les photographies. Les portraits au physionotrace
gravés de 1788 à 1830. Catalogue nominatif, biographique et
critique illustré des deux premières séries de ces portraits.
comprenant les 1800 estampes cotées de 1 a R. 27. Troyes,
Impr. J. L. Paton, 1932. 345 p. illus., ports. 25cm. A catalog of French portraits which were engraved from 1788 to 1830.
The subjects of the portraits were prominent figures of the
French Revolution and its aftermath (to 1830), concentrating
especially on Paris.

8866   LE LONG, JACQUES, 1665-1721.
        Bibliothèque historique de la France, contenant le catalogue
des ouvrages, imprimés & manuscrits, qui traitent de l'histoire
de ce royaume, on qui y ont rapport; avec des notes critiques et
historiques. Nouv. éd. rev., corr. & considérablement augm.
par Fevret de Fontette. Paris, Impr. Herissant, 1768-78. 5 v.
40cm. 2d ed. (1st, 1719) Vols. 3-5 issued by Barbeau de la
Bruyère after Fevret de Fontette's death in 1772. Vol. 3 dated
1771, but issued in 1772. A bibliography of the history of France.
Vol. 4, p. 134-285 (2d set) contains an alphabetical listing of
portraits of famous Frenchmen, many of which are located in the
Bibliothèque du Roi and the 'Cabinet de M. Fevret de Fontette'
(and now in the Bibliothèque nationale, Paris?) This listing
yields brief biographical notices.

8867   PARIS. BIBLIOTHÈQUE NATIONAL. DÉPARTEMENT DES
        IMPRIMÉS.
        Catalogue de l'histoire de France. v. 9-10. Paris, Firmin
Didot frères, 1865-70. 2 v. 32cm. In vol. 9, p. 235-794 and
v. 10, p. 1-346 will be found a huge bibliography of individual
French biography.

8868   LES SOURCES DE L'HISTOIRE DE FRANCE DEPUIS LES ORI-
        GINES JUSQU'EN 1815, par A. Molinier [et al.] 3. ptie:
Le XVIIe siècle (1610-1715) par Émile Bourgeois et Louis André.
III: Biographies. Paris, A. Picard, 1923. xii, 372, 10 p. 24cm.
(Manuels de bibliographie historique, 3) Sources for the history
of France. This particular volume (pt. 3, v. 3: Biographies) is
not only a valuable bibliographical guide to collective and individual biography of Frenchmen of the 17th century, but it also contains data for many of the biographers and biographees.

General Works

8869   ACADÉMIE FRANÇAISE, PARIS.
Annuaire de l'Académie française [de l'Institut de France]
Documents et notices sur les membres de l'Académie. Paris,
Firmin-Didot, 1966. 236 p. 21cm. Bio-bibliographical
notices on the members (living) of the French Academy will be
found on p. 43-206.

8870   ANNUAIRE BIOGRAPHIQUE ET DESCRIPTIF DE LA FRANCE
ET DE L'ÉTRANGER. Annuaire des éligibles et des
électeurs. Notices biographiques; descriptions des institutions
politiques et scientifiques; et indications des principaux établissements industriels. Édition de juillet 1843. Paris, A la direction des Archives du 19e siècle, 1843. 3 pts in 1 v. 8.º
No more published? Biographical and descriptive annual for
France and the world, 1st half of the 19th century.

8871   ARCHIVES DE LA LÉGION D'HONNEUR. Paris, Glaesser,
1865. 64 p. 8.º Archives of the Legion of Honor; a biographical dictionary. Was to have been published in 20 fascicles. Only the 1st, Abadie to Bretheau was issued.

8872   L'AUTOGRAPHIE. no. 1-48, 5 déc. 1863-[25 nov.] 1865; 2.
sér., no. 1-52, 2 sept. 1871-24 août 1872. Paris. 3 v.
illus., ports. 30 x 47cm.-36 x 48cm. No. 1-45 semimonthly;
2d series weekly. Title varies: 1863-65: L'Autographe. Prélats,
souverains, hommes d'état ... célébrités, etc. 1871-72,
L'Autographe. Événements de 1870-1871. Edited by H. Villemessant (with G. Bourdin, 1863-65) No more published?
Autographs of famous Frenchmen with numerous portraits.

8873   BEAUVOIR, ROGER DE, 1849-1909.
Nos généraux, 1871-1884. Avec 136 dessins à la plume de
MM. de Haenen et Émile Perboyre. Paris, Berger-Levrault,
1885. viii, 519 p. illus., ports. 23cm. French generals,
1871-1884; portraits and biographical sketches.

8874   BERTRAND, ALPHONSE, 1850-1907.
La Chambre de 1889. Biographies des 576 députés, avec
avertissement et documents divers, la liste des ministères
qui se sont succédé en France depuis 1871, la liste alphabétique
des députés, l'indications de leurs professions etc. Paris, L.
Michaud, 1889. 622 p. 19cm. The French Chamber of Deputies in 1889; biographies of 576 deputies.

8875   BERTRAND, ALPHONSE, 1850-1907.
La Chambre des députés (1898-1902) Biographies des 581
députés, avec avertissement et documents divers, la liste des

ministères qui se sont succédé, la liste alphabétique des députés, etc. Paris, L. H. May, 1899. vi, 593 p. 19cm. The French Chamber of Deputies, 1898-1902; 581 biographical sketches.

8876   BERTRAND, ALPHONSE, 1850-1907.
        Le Sénat de 1894. Biographies des 300 sénateurs, avec avertissement et documents divers, les lois relatives à l'organisation du Sénat et les élections des sénateurs, la liste des ministères qui se sont succédé en France depuis 1871, la liste alphabétique des sénateurs, etc. Paris, Société anonyme de publications périodiques, 1894. xiv, 430 p. 19cm.

        ----Le Sénat de 1897. Supplément à l'ouvrage "Le Sénat du 1894, changements survenus de janvier 1894 à decembre 1897. Paris, Impr. de P. Mouillot, 1898. xvi, 155 p. 15cm.

        ---- ----Le Sénat de 1900. 2. supplément à l'ouvrage; Le Sénat de 1894, changements survenus de décembre 1897 à avril 1900. Paris, Impr. de P. Mouillot, 1900. viii, 167 p. 19cm. The French Senate of 1894; biographies of 300 senators (basic volume).

8877   LE BIOGRAPHE. Publication mensuelle illustrée en photographie, v. 1-11; 1873-88. Bordeaux. 11 v. illus., ports. 8.⁰
        A monthly publication concerned primarily with French biography, heavily illustrated with portraits.

8878   BIOGRAPHIE COMPLÈTE DES REPRÉSENTANTS DU PEUPLE À L'ASSEMBLÉE NATIONALE, avec leurs adresses dans Paris. Paris, A. René, 1848. 1 v. 16.⁰ Preface signed: C.P., H.A., J.B. Complete biography of members of the French National Assembly of 1848, with their Paris addresses.

8879   BIOGRAPHIE COMPLÈTE DES 300 SÉNATEURS, par une député. 2. ed. Paris, Librairie républicaine, 1876. 1 v. 16.⁰ Complete biography of the 300 senators of the French National Assembly of 1876.

8880   BOURDE, PAUL, 1851-1914.
        Les membres de la Commune et du Comité central [par] Paul Delion [pseud.] Paris, A. Lemerre, 1871. xiii, 446 p. 12.⁰ Members of the Paris Commune of 1871 and its Central Committee.

8881   BRUEL, F
        Maréchaux de France; chronologie militaire, 1768-1870. Paris, L. Fournier, 1916. 353 p. illus. (facsims.) 26cm. 85 biographies of marshalls of the French Army from 1768 to 1870; chronologically arranged, with an alphabetical table at end.

8882   BRUHAT, JEAN
        La Commune de 1871. Sous la direction de Jean Bruhat,
Jean Dautry et Émile Tersen. Avec la collaboration de Pierre
Angrand [et al.] 2. éd. revue et complétée. Paris, Éditions
sociales, 1970. 463 p. illus., maps, ports. 29cm. The Paris
Commune of 1871. "Notes biographiques sur les élus, les mili-
tants et les principaux combattants de la Commune" (p. [421]-
446) is a biographical dictionary (154 entries) of principal figures in the Commune.

8883   [CALINAU, L   ] of Metz.
        Dictionnaire des Jacobins vivans, dans lequel on verra les
hauts faits de ces messieurs ... Dédié aux frères et amis, par
Quelqu'un, citoyen français. Hambourg [Impr. de Chartres]
1799. 192 p. front. 17cm. Also attributed to Poulier, aide of
Michel Le Pelletier. Dictionary of living Jacobins of the French
Revolution.

8884   CHARAVAY, JACQUES, d. 1892?
        Les généraux morts pour la patrie, 1792-1871; notices bio-
graphiques, par Jacques Charavay, publiées par son père
[Etienne Charavay] 1. série: 1792-1804. Paris, Siège de la
Société [de l'histoire de la Révolution française, 1893. xx, 120 p.
plates. 25cm. French generals who died in the service of their
country, 1792-1871. The first series only was issued; it contains
77 biographies, in chronological arrangement, for the years
1792-1804, with an alphabetical table at the end for the 2d series,
covering the years 1805-1812, see: Charavay, Noël. Les généraux morts pour la patrie ... 1805-1812.

8885   CHARAVAY, NOËL
        Les généraux morts pour la patrie (armées de terre et de
mer). Notices biographiques. 2. sér. (1805-1812) Paris, N.
Charavay, 1908. vi, 236 p. 24cm. Arranged by date of death;
alphabetical table on p. 211-219. French generals who died in
the service of their country, 1805-1812. For the 1st series, covering the years 1792-1804, see: Charavay, Jacques. Les généraux morts pour la patrie, 1792-1871.

8886   [CHAZET, ANDRÉ RENÉ POLYDORE ALISSAN DE] 1775-1844.
        Le Chambre de mil huit cent vingt; ou, La monarchie sauvée.
Galerie politique des quatre cent vingt-deux députés qui siégent
dans la présente session, par un royaliste. Paris, Ponthieu,
1821. xii, 434 p. The French Chamber of Deputies in 1820; political gallery of the 422 deputies sitting in the present session.

8887   CLERC, A   V
        Nos députés à l'Assemblée nationale, leur biographie et
leurs votes. Documents historiques sur la Législature de 1871-
1872. Paris, A. Le Chevalier, 1872. xxvi, 196 p. 18.º 'Our'
deputies at the National Assembly (France), their biography and
their votes, 1871-1872.

8888   CLÈRE, JULES, 1850-
       Biographie complète des députés, avec toutes les profes-
sions de foi, circulaires électorales, etc. Nouv. éd., augmentée d'un supplément contenant les élections générales du 14
octobre 1877 et les élections complémentaires de 1878 et 1879.
Paris, Garnier frères, 1880. 970 p. 15cm. 1st ed. issued in
1875 under title: Biographie des députés (xv, 848 p. 15cm.)
Complete biography of the deputies (Chambre des députés of the
Assemblée nationale of France) in the latter part of the 1870's.

8889   CLÈRE, JULES, 1850-
       Biographie des députés, avec leurs principaux votes, de-
puis le 8 fevrier 1871 jusqu'au 15 juin 1875. Paris, Garnier
frères, 1875. xv, 848 p. 15cm. Biography of the deputies
(Chamber of Deputies of the French National Assembly) with
their principal votes, after the 8th of February 1871 to June 15,
1875.

8890   CLÈRE, JULES, 1850-
       Biographie complète des sénateurs. Paris [Garnier
frères?] 1876. xiii, 659 p. 15cm. Complete biography of the
senators (Senat of the Assemblee nationale of France) as of
1876.

8891   COLLECTION DE QUATRE-VINGTS PORTRAITS DESTINÉS À
       ORNER LES DEUX ÉDITIONS IN-8° DE L'HISTOIRE DE
FRANCE D'ANQUETIL. Publiées par Janet et Cotelle, libraires.
[Paris, ca. 1819?] 4 p., 80 ports. 18cm. Lettered on cover:
Histoire de France. Gallais. 4. Portraits. In Johns Hopkins
University Library. A collection of 80 portraits of famous
Frenchmen to be used in the two octavo editions of Anquetil's
History of France.

8892   COSTE, JEAN FRANÇOIS, 1741-1819.
       Notices sur les officiers de santé de la Grande Armée,
morts en Allemagne, victimes de leur zèle, depuis le 1. Vende-
miaire an XIV, jusqu'au 1. fevrier 1806. Augsbourg, Roesi,
1806. iv, 61 p. Notes on health officers of Napoleon's Grand
Army who died in Germany, victims of their own zeal, after
Sept. 22, 1805 to Feb. 1, 1806.

8893   COSTON, HENRY
       Dictionnaire de la politique française, publié sous la direc-
tion de Henry Coston. Paris, Publications H. Coston; diffusion:
La Librairie française, 1867-72. 2 v. illus., ports. 25cm. A
dictionary of 20th century French politics; includes numerous
biographical sketches. Each volume is alphabetical in arrangement (each volume goes from A to Z)

8894   DAVONS, A
          Panthéon de la Légion d'honneur, publié par A. Davons avec
          la collaboration de M. Amédée Boudin. Tome 1. Paris, 1864.
          196 p. 8.º No more published. Pantheon of the French Legion
          of Honor; biographical sketches.

8895   DESROCHERS, PIERRE CLAUDE TR
          Biographie des marine français contemporains. Ouvrage
          contenant 800 notices historiques et un précis des évènements
          maritimes contemporains. Paris, Maison, 1837. 128 p. (ca.)
          8.º An incomplete work. Only 1 fascicle was issued. Intended
          to be a biographical dictionary of 800 French naval personages
          of the 18th-early 19th centuries, accompanied by a sketch of
          contemporary naval events.

8896   [DESROCHERS, PIERRE CLAUDE TR]
          Nécrologe de 1832; ou, Notices historiques sur les hommes
          les plus marquants tant en France que dans l'étranger, morts
          pendant l'année 1832. Paris, L'auteur, 1833. vi, iv, 322 p.
          8.º Necrology of 1832, or, Historical notices of the leading
          Frenchmen and foreigners who died during the year.

8897   DICTIONNAIRE DES PERSONNAGES HISTORIQUES FRANÇAIS.
          Paris, Nouvelle histoire de France, 1968, c1962. 142 p.
          illus., ports. 8.º First published in 1962 (Paris, Editions
          Seghers, 381 p. ports. 17cm.) in the series Collection Seghers.
          A biographical dictionary of persons important in French his-
          tory.

8898   DICTIONNAIRE ILLUSTRÉ DES PERSONNAGES HISTORIQUES
          FRANÇAIS. Paris, Seghers, 1962. 384 p. illus., ports.
          19cm. (Collection Seghers, 6) Illustrated dictionary of French
          historical personages.

8899   DORNIC, FRANÇOIS
          La France de la Révolution, 1789/1799. Paris, Denoël,
          1970. 255 p. illus., ports. 23cm. (Histoire de la France)
          France during the Revolution of 1789-1799; includes a dictionary
          (p. [51]-95) which consists largely of biographical sketches of
          persons prominent during the Revolution.

8900   DULEAU, ALPHONSE
          Portraits des membres du Parlement de Paris et des
          maîtres des requêtes vers le milieu du XVIIe siècle, auxquels
          on a joint un armorial et des notes biographiques. Paris, J.-
          B. Dumoulin, 1863. 90 p. illus., ports. 8.º Portraits of
          members of the Parlement of Paris and master-petitioners to-
          wards the middle of the 17th century, accompanied by biographi-
          cal notes.

8901 DUMAY, LÉON
Nos représentants. Portraits-cartes, esquisses biogra-
phiques des députés. Ire [-2e] série. Chalons-sur-Marne, Le
Roy, 1873. 2 v. ports. 12.º "Our representatives"; portraits
and biographical sketches of the deputies of the French National
Assembly of the early 1870's.

8902 FEILLARD,
Livre d'honneur et de gloire; biographie générale des
membres de la Légion d'honneur, par une société de gens de
lettres, publié sous la direction de M. Feillard. 1. livraison.
Paris, Bureaux du Livre d'honneur, 1835. 1 v. 8.º The book
of honor and glory; a general biographical dictionary of the members of the French Legion of Honor (early 19th century) Only
one fascicle was published?

8903 FERET, ÉDOUARD, 1844-
Nos notabilités du XIXe siècle; medaillons bordelais, compositions inédites, planches hors texte d'après les dessins ori-
ginaux à l'encre de Chine de Louis Blayot, avec notices biographiques par Édouard Feret. Bordeaux, Feret et fils, 1896-
1907. 3 v. ports. folio. Notable Frenchmen of the 19th century; folio volumes of portraits, medallions, etc. accompanied
by biographical notices.

8904 FRANCE. PARLEMENT (1946-   ) ASSEMBLÉE NATIONALE.
Notices et portraits. 1- législature; 1946-   Paris,
v. ports. 14cm. annual. Biographical notes and portraits
of members of the French National Assembly (Legislature)

8905 FRANCE. PARLEMENT (1946-   ) SÉNAT. SECRÉTARIAT
GÉNÉRAL DE LA QUESTURE.
Notices et portraits. 1963-   Paris, Impr. nationale.
v. ports. 15cm. Biographical notes and portraits of the
French Senate as constituted beginning with 1963. Intended to be
a continuing publication (but only the 1963 issue was published?)

8906 FROND, VICTOR, 1821-
Panthéon des illustrations françaises au XIXe siècle, comprenant un portrait, une biographie et un autographe de chacun
des hommes les plus marquants dans l'administration, les arts,
l'armée, le barreau, le clergé, l'industrie, les lettres, la
magistrature, la politique, les sciences, etc., etc. Publié sous
la direction de Victor Frond. Paris, A. Pilon (1865-69) 16 v.
illus., ports. 40cm. Comprises portraits, biographical sketches and autographs of Frenchmen prominent in various spheres of
activity in the 19th century; includes an alphabetical name index
at end of vol. 16.

8907   FRONDEVILLE, HENRI DE
        Les présidents du Parlement de Normandie, 1499-1790.
        Recueil généalogique établi sur le base du manuscrit Bigot de la
        Bibliothèque de Rouen. Rouen, A. Lestringant, 1953. 636 p.
        22cm. The presidents of the Parlement of Normandy (Rouen)
        1499-1790; of biographical as well as genealogical import.

8908   GALERIE FRANÇAISE; ou, Potraits des hommes et des
            femmes célèbres qui ont paru en France, gravés en taille-
        douce par les meilleurs artistes, sous la conduite de M.
        Restout. Avec un abrégé de leur vie par une société des gens
        de lettres. Paris, Hérissant, 1771-72. 2 v. and plates (in port-
        folio) Edited by Jean-Baptiste Collet de Messine. The French
        gallery; or, Portraits of famous men and women in France, ac-
        companied by brief remarks on their lives.

8909   GALERIE HISTORIQUE DE LA RÉVOLUTION FRANÇAISE, 1789-
            1793; album de cinquante portraits en pied des personnages
        les plus remarquables de cette grande époque, dessinés et
        gravés par les meilleurs artistes, accompagnés de cinquante
        notices biographiques. Paris, Librairie [1869] [3], 4 p., 50
        ports. 35cm. Historical gallery of the French Revolution, 1789-
        1793; an album of 50 portraits accompanied by 50 brief biographi-
        cal notices.

8910   GALERIE NATIONALE DES NOTABILITÉS CONTEMPO-
            RAINES; annales biographiques ... de la France. Par un
        Société de gens de lettres sous la direction de E. de Saint-Mau-
        rice Cabany. Paris, 1850-51. 3 v. 8.º National gallery of
        contemporary notables of France (mid-19th century)

8911   GEORGES, HENRI
            La nouvelle Chambre, élue les 20 août et 3 septembre 1893.
        581 biographies de députés, par Henri Georges et Jules Guigonet.
        Paris, Fischbacker, 1894. 417 p. 18.º The new Chamber of
        Deputies of the French National Assembly elected 20 August-3
        September 1893; 581 biographical sketches.

8912   HARCOURT, LOUIS, comte d', 1870-
            Connétables et maréchaux de France. [Armoiries en
        couleurs par H. Philippeau] Paris, E. Paul frères, 1912-13.
        2 v. illus., ports. folio. Constables and marshals of France;
        in dictionary format.

8913   HISTOIRE DES GÉNÉRAUX, officiers de tout grade et de tout
            arme, sous-officiers et soldats, qui se sont distingués dans
        les différentes campagnes des armées français. Paris, Lécri-
        vain, 1817. xxii, 225 p. 14cm. Brief history-biography of the
        generals, officers of every rank and branch of the service who
        have distinguished themselves in the various campaigns of the
        French armies.

8914   LES HOMMES D'AUJOURD'HUI; publication illustrée. No. 1-
        468. [1878-98] Paris, Librairie Vanier.   v. col. illus.
        29cm. weekly. Vols. 1-   by Pierre et Paul [pseud.] Félicien
        Champsaur and others. Men of today. Biographical sketches
        and portraits of noteworthy Frenchmen.

8915   HOURIE, PAUL
            Les 557 députés et leurs programmes électoraux, 1881-1885.
        Paris, P. Dupont, 1882. 14, 425 p. 12.º The 557 deputies of
        the French National Assembly of 1881-1885 and their electoral
        programs.

8916   HOZIER, JEAN FRANÇOIS LOUIS D', d. 1793.
            Recueil de tous les membres composant l'ordre royal et
        militaire de Saint-Louis depuis l'année 1693, époque de sa
        fondation. Ouvrage posthume de Jean-François-Louis, comte
        d'Hozier. Paris, J. Smith, 1817-18. 2 v. 8.º No more pub-
        lished. Collection of biographical sketches of all the members
        of the royal and military Order of St. Louis, 1693 to 1817.

8917   HUART, LOUIS, 1813-1865.
            Galerie de la presse, de la littérature et des beaux-arts.
        Directeur des dessins, Charles Philippon. Rédacteur en chef,
        Louis Huart. Paris, Au Bureau de la publication, et chez Au-
        bert, 1839-41. 3 v. ports. 28cm. Biographical-portrait gal-
        lery of the French press, literature and fine arts, early 19th
        century.

8918   IMBERT, JEAN BAPTISTE AUGUSTE, b. 1791.
            Biographie des condamnés pour délits politiques depuis la
        restauration des Bourbons en France jusqu'en 1827. [Par]
        Auguste Imbert et B.-L. Bellet. Bruxelles, A. Imbert, 1827.
        viii, 272 p. 21cm. Biographical dictionary of Frenchmen con-
        victed for political offenses after the restoration of the Bourbons
        (1814) to 1827. The French ed. (Paris, L. Huillier et Pontheiu,
        1828) is incomplete; it covers only A-Louvel.

8919   JEAN, JEAN PIERRE
            Le livre d'or du Souvenir français. Lorraine-Alsace. Lux-
        embourg. Lorraine sarroise. Metz, Impr. des Arts graphiques
        modernes de Jarville-Nancy, 1929. 528 p. plates, ports. 4.º
        Very numerous portraits of French officers and civilians in the
        Franco-Prussian War, 1870-1871, and the first World War (or
        European War) 1914-1918. Some portraits go back to the begin-
        ning of the 19th century.

8920   JOURDAN, LOUIS, 1810-1881.
            Les célébrités du jour, par Louis Jourdan et Taxile Delord.
        1860-61. Paris, Aux Bureaux du journal Le Siècle [1861] 2 v.
        ports. folio. French celebrities of the day (1860-1861) Por-
        traits and biographical sketches.

8921   LABARRE DE RAILLICOURT, DOMINIQUE
        Les généraux des Cent Jours et du Gouvernement Provi-
soire (mars-juillet 1815) Dictionnaire biographique, promotions,
bibliographies et armorial. Préf. de Gaston Saffroy. Paris,
1963. 79 p. illus., 25cm. The generals of the Hundred Days
(1814-1815) and the Provisional Gouvernment of France in March-
July 1815; a bio-bibliographical dictionary.

8922   LACOMBE, L   DE
        Profils parlementaires; biographie complète des députés au
Corps législatif, 1863-1869. Paris, E. Dentu, 1869. 297 p.
23cm. A "2d edition" was issued in the same year under title:
Profils parlementaires: les députés de la France, 1863-1869.
Parliamentary portraits; complete biographical sketches of the
deputies at the French Legislature (Corps législatif) of 1863-1869.

8923   LALANNE, LUDOVIC, 1815-1898.
        Dictionnaire historique de la France, contenant pour l'his-
toire civile, politique et littéraire, la biographie, la chronologie, les assemblées politiques, les parlements, les droits et
usages féodaux, des notices sur les principales familles nobles,
le blason, les institutions et établissements artistiques, littéraires, politiques et scientifiques, la liste des académiciens.
Pour l'histoire militaire, les guerres, les ordres de chevalerie,
les institutions et établissements militaires, etc. Pour l'histoire religieuse, les conciles, les institutions, les usages et les
dignités ecclésiastiques , les ordres monastiques, etc. Pour la
géographie historique, les divisions territoriales et administra-
tives de la Gaule et de la France, etc., etc. 2. ed. Paris,
Hachette, 1877. 2 v. 25cm. Historical dictionary of France;
particularly useful for data on French philosophers, theologians,
religious figures, etc. Reprinted in 1968 (?) by Lenox Hill Pub.
Corp. (Burt Franklin) New York.

8924   LALLIER, JUSTIN H
        Album-contemporain, contenant les biographies sommaires
de trois cents des principaux personnages de notre époque. Portraits photographies par Franck. Paris, 1866. 114 p. mounted
ports. 8.° A volume of mounted portraits with brief biographical notes of 300 of the leading personages of the 19th century (including kings and rulers), chiefly those of French nationality).

8925   LA MADELAINE, STÉPHEN DE, 1801-1868.
        L'Arc de triomphe dédié aux illustrations des armées fran-
çaises, contenant les notices biographiques de tous les guerriers
dont les noms sont inscrits sur le monument de l'Etoile, par Stéphen de La Madelaine [et J. L. Belin] Paris, Chez les editeurs,
1842-47. 2 v. illus., ports. 8.° Bibl. Nat. (Paris) enters this
work under Belin although La Madelaine is first-named author.
The Arch of Triumph in Paris; containing biographical notices of
all the soldiers whose names are inscribed on the monument.

8926   LAMATHIÈRE, THÉOPHILE
        Panthéon de la Légion d'honneur; dictionnaire biographique
des hommes du XIXe siècle. Paris, [1875-1911] 22 v. 28cm.

---- ----Table alphabétique des tomes I-XIV. Washington, 1916.
221 l. 27cm. Typewritten. Only 22 vols. issued? Some bibliographies list 25 vols. Pantheon of the Legion of Honor of France;
a biographical dictionary of men of the 19th century.

8927   [LARDIER, JOSEPH ALEXANDRE] b. 1786.
        Biographie des députés, session de 1828, précédée d'une in-
troduction et d'une notice sur le nouveau ministère. Paris, Chez
les marchands de nouveautés, 1828. xxxv, 428 p. 21cm. Biographical sketches of members of the French Chamber of Deputies in 1828.

8928   LE BIHAN, ALAIN
        Francs-maçons et ateliers parisiens de la Grande loge de
France au XVIIIe siècle (1760-1795) Paris, Bibliothèque nationale,
1973. 509 p. 24cm. (Commission d'histoire économique et so-
ciale de la Révolution française. Mémoires et documents, 28)
The 2d part (p. [227]-388) of this work on French Freemasonary
in the latter part of the 18th century includes 2 biographical dictionaries (1) masters of the Great Masonic Lodge of France (2)
masters of the Paris Lodge (Orient de Paris de la Grande loge
de France).

8929   LEVOT, PROSPER JEAN, 1801-1878.
        Les gloires maritimes de la France. Notices biographiques
sur les plus célèbres marins, découveurs ... par P. Levot et
A. Doneaud. Paris, A. Bertrand, 1866. vi, 559 p. 18.° Biographical notices of the most famous French mariners, explorers, etc.

8930   LIVRE D'OR DE LA SABRETACHE, 1914-1918. Paris, La
        Sabretache, 1923. 2 v. ports. 4.° Portraits of members
of the Sabretache (a French military society) and of their sons
who died in the European War of 1914-1918.

8931   LE LIVRE D'OR DES FEMMES. Cent douze biographies; par
        une société d'hommes de lettres sous la direction d'Edouard
Plouvier. 112 portraits hors texte, dessinés et gravés par Fath
et Dumont. Les dames françaises. Paris, Impr. Jouaust, Librairie internationale, 1870. 330 p. ports. 8.° 112 portraits
and biographical sketches of famous Frenchwomen.

8932   LIVRE D'OR DES MARÉCHAUX DE FRANCE, 1190-1952.
        [Casablanca, Lacour, 1960] 251 p. 183 plates. 31cm.
"Les textes sont de M. Jean Tracou." Edited by G. de Beaure-

gard? Includes portraits and biographical sketches of the great
military leaders of France, 1190-1952.

8933   MASSEY DE TYRONNE, PIERRE FRANÇOIS MARIE, b. 1795.
        Biographie des députés de la Chambre septennale de 1824 à
        1830. Paris, J. G. Dentu, 1826. xvi, viii, 624 p. 22cm. A
        suppressed work in which the printer Dentu collaborated with
        the author. Biography of the septennial French Chamber of
        Deputies, 1824-1830.

8934   MATHIEU-DAIRNVAELL, GEORGES MARIE, b. 1828.
        Biographie satirique de la nouvelle Chambre des députés
        par Satan [pseud.] Paris [1846] 192 p. 32.º Satirical biogra-
        phical sketches of the French Chamber of Deputies for the years
        1846 to 1851.

8935   MATHIEU-DAIRNVAELL, GEORGES MARIE, b. 1828.
        Biographie satirique des députés, suivie de l'indication de
        leurs addresses dans Paris, par Satan [pseud.] Paris, Chez
        l'éditeur, 1847. 175 p. 32.º Another collection of satirical bi-
        ographical sketches of the French deputies (legislators) and
        their Parisian addresses.

8936   MAZAS, ALEXANDRE, 1791-1856.
        Histoire de l'Ordre royal et militaire de Saint-Louis depuis
        son institution en 1693 jusqu'en 1830, par Alex. Mazas. Termi-
        née par Theodore Anne. 2. éd., rev., corr. et considérable-
        ment augm. Paris, Firmin Didot frères, 1860-61. 3 v. 25cm.
        History of the Royal and Military Order of Saint Louis, 1693-
        1830; includes a considerable number of biographical sketches of
        officers of the French Army and Navy of that period.

8937   [MESURÉ, FORTUNÉ]
        Le procuste parlementaire. Portraits satiriques de nos 459
        députés, session de 1845. Par Fortunatus [pseud.] Paris,
        Garnier frères, 1844. 348 p. 16.º Satirical sketches of the
        459 members of the French Chamber of Deputies, session of
        1845.

8938   [MESURÉ, FORTUNÉ]
        Le Rivarol de 1842; dictionnaire satirique des célébrités con-
        temporaines, par Fortunatus [pseud.] Paris, Bureau du Feuille-
        ton mensuel, 1842. 236 p. 19cm. The Rivarol (after Antoine de
        Rivarol's Petit almanach de nos grands hommes pour 1788 in
        which he ridiculed authors of the time) of 1842; satirical diction-
        ary of contemporary celebrities.

8939   MOREAU-NÉLATON, ETIENNE, 1859-
        Les Clouet et leurs émules. Paris, H. Laurens, 1924. 3 v.

ports. 29cm. Jean and François Clouet (16th century) and their rivals; portraits by French portrait painters of the period.

8940 MOREAU-NÉLATON, ETIENNE, 1859-
  Le portrait à la cour des Valois; crayons français du XVIe siècle, conservés au Musée Condé à Chantilly. Introd. par E. Moreau-Nélaton. Paris, Librairie centrale des beaux-arts [190-?] 5 v. plates. folio. Vol. 1: Introduction. The portrait at the Court of Valois; French portrait drawings of the 16th century conserved at the Musée Condé at Chantilly.

8941 NOËL, BERNARD, 1930-
  Dictionnaire de la Commune. Iconographie et légendes de Marie-Jose Villotte. Paris, F. Hazan [1971] 365, [2] p. illus., ports. 24cm. A dictionary of the Paris Commune of 1871 which includes biographical sketches.

8942 ORDRE DE LA LIBÉRATION.
  Mémorial des compagnons de la Libération; compagnons morts entre le a8 juin 1940 et le 8 mai 1945. Paris, Grande Chancellerie de l'Ordre de la Libération, 1961. 582 p. illus. 28cm. Necrology of members of the French liberation movement who died from 18 June 1940 to 8 May 1945.

8943 PAULOUIN, JEAN FRANÇOIS
  La chouannerie du Maine et pays adjacents, 1793, 1799, 1815, 1832, avec la biographie de plus de 120 officiers y compris les généraux d'Andigné, de Frotté, Cadoual, par l'abbé Paulouin. Le Mans, E. Monnoyer, 1875. 3 v. 19cm. The Chouans of the region of Maine and adjoining regions of France and their various revolts against Republican & Napoleonic France; vols. 2-3 comprise a biographical dictionary (with supplement)—ca. 120 biographies in the main dictionary, ca. 180 much briefer sketches in the supplement.

8944 PINARD,
  Chronologie historique-militaire, contenant l'histoire de la création de toutes les charges, dignités et grades militaires supérieurs, de toutes les personnes qui les ont possédés ... des troupes de la maison du roi, et des officiers supérieurs qui y ont servi, de tous les régimens et autres troupes, des colonels qui les ont commandés, les états d'armées par chaque année, les officiers généraux qui y ont été employés depuis la première création des régimens, et les opérations réelles de chaque armée, avec leur véritable époque ... rendues depuis le règne de Louis XIV jusqu'à présent. Paris, C. Hérissart, 1760-78. 8 v. 4.º Contents.--1. Table des rois de France, les secrétaires d'état à la guerre, les sénéchaux, les connétables et les commandans d'armées.--2. Les maréchaux généraux des camps et armées et les maréchaux de France jusqu'à la promotion de 1675.--3. Suite des maréchaux de France, les grands maîtres de l'artillerie, les colonels généraux.--4. Les lieutenants gén-

éraux des armées du roi jusqu'en 1715--5. Suite des lieutenants généraux des armées du roi. --6. Les lieutenants généraux des armées du roi du 25 juillet 1762 et les maréchaux de camp jusqu'en 1715. --7. La suite des maréchaux de camp. --8. Chronologie des brigadiers d'infanterie jusqu'au 24 mars 1772.

----Liste alphabétique des officiers généraux jusqu'en 1762, dont les notices biographiques se trouvent dans la Chronologie-militaire de Pinard, par Léon Lecestre. Paris, A. Picard, 1903. 108 p. 8.º Detached from Bibliographe modern, t. 7, 1903. A chronological account of the military history of France, with numerous biographical notes on French military figures. Lecestre's Alphabetical list of general officers to 1762 gives a relatively quick approach to the biographical data in Pinard's work.

8945   PINASSEAU, JEAN, 1886-1972.
        L'émigration militaire: campagne de 1792. Armée des princes: compagnies de Saintonge, Angoumois et Aunis. Paris, A. et J. Picard, 1971. ix, 95 p. port. 25cm. The French military migration: campaign of 1792. The Army of the Princes. on pages 2-95 is a biographical dictionary of officers of the French Army (emigrés) who remained loyal to the monarchy during the French Revolution.

8946   PINASSEAU, JEAN, 1886-1972.
        L'émigration militaire: campagne de 1792. Armée royale. Paris, A. et J. Picard, 1957-64. 2 v. 26cm. Contents. --1. ptie. Composition. Ordres de bataille. Notices A à C. --2. ptie. Notices D à Z. The French military migration: campaign of 1792. The Royal Army. Chiefly a biographical dictionary of officers of the French Army loyal to the monarchy who became emigrés during the French Revolution.

8947   PINASSEAU, JEAN, 1886-1972.
        L'émigration militaire; emigrés de Saintonge, Angoumois, et Aunis dans le corps de troupe de l'émigration française, 1791-1814. Paris, A. et J. Picard, 1974. 295 p. 24cm. A biographical dictionary of French emigrés from Saintonge, Angoumois and Aunis who served in the emigré (Royalist) Army between 1791 and 1814.

8948   PORTRAITS DES HOMMES ILLUSTRES DES DIX-SEPTIÈME
        ET DIX-HUITIÈME SIÈCLES, dessinés d'après nature, et gravé par Edelink, Lubin, van Schippen, Duflos et Simonneau, avec une notice sur chacun d'eux. Paris, C. Volland, 1805. 2 v. in 1. ports. 42cm. Portraits of famous Frenchmen of the 17th and 18th centuries, with biographical notices accompanying the portraits.

8949   RECUEIL DES HISTORIENS DE LA FRANCE. Publié par l'A-
        cademie des inscriptions et belles-lettres. Obituaires.

Paris, Impr. nationale, 1902-65. 6 v. in 7. 28cm. Each vol.
also has special t. p. Contents. --t. 1. Diocèses de Sens et de
Paris. --t. 2. Diocèses de Chartres. --t. 3. Diocèses d'Orléans,
d'Auxerre et de Nevers. --t. 4. Diocèses de Méaux et de Troyes.
--t. 5. Diocèse de Lyon. --t. 6. Diocèse de Lyon, 2. ptie. Diocèses de Maçon et de Chalon-sur-Saône. A collection of French
obituaries [by diocese] with some identification and biographical
data for a number of the deceased. No more published?

8950 RENÉE, AMÉDÉE, 1808?-1859.
Les princes militaires de la maison de France. Contenant
les états de services et les biographies de près de 300 princes,
l'histoire généalogique et héraldique des diverses branches de
la dynastic capétienne, depuis Robert-le-Fort jusqu'à la Révolution française. Paris, Amyot [1848] viii, 504 p. illus. 4.º
The military princes of the House of France, including biographies of more than 300 princes ... up to the French Revolution.

8951 RIBEYRE, FÉLIX, b. 1831.
Biographie des représentants a l'Assemblée nationale. 2.
éd. Angers, Bureaux de la publication, 1872. 357 p. 18.º
Biographical sketches of the representatives to the French National Assembly ca. 1872.

8952 RIBEYRE, FELIX, b. 1831.
Biographie des sénateurs et des députés. Nouv. éd. contenant la biographie de tous les nouveaux députés élus les 14 et
28 octobre 1877. Angoulême, Au siège de la publication [1878?]
ii, 593 p. 18.º Biographies of the senators and deputies of
the French National Assembly of the late 1870's.

8953 RIBEYRE, FELIX, b. 1831.
La nouvelle Chambre (1889-1893) Biographie des 576
députés. Paris, E. Dentu, 1890. vi, 624 p. 18.º The new
Chamber of Deputies (France) with 576 biographical sketches.

8954 RICHARDSON, HUBERT N   B
A dictionary of Napoleon and his times. Ann Arbor, Mich.,
Gryphon Books, 1971. vi, 489 p. maps, plans. 22cm. Facsimile reprint of the 1921 edition. Yields biographical material
on figures connected with Napoleon and his achievements, some
of them fairly obscure.

8955 RION, ADOLPHE
Biographie nouvelle et complète des pairs de France, comprenant les 76 pairs de la promotion du 5 nov. 1827. Publiée
par A. R. Paris, Marchands du nouveautés, 1828. vi, 279 p.
New and complete biography of the peers of France, comprising
the 76 who were promoted to the peerage on Nov. 5, 1827.

8956   [ROBERT, JEAN BAPTISTE MAGLOIRE] 1766-1820?
Vie politique de tous les députés à la Convention nationale,
pendant et après la Révolution. Ouvrage dans lequel ont trouve
la preuve que dans le procès de Louis XVI la peine de mort avait
été rejetée à une majorité de six voix. Par M. R. Paris, L.
Saint Michel, 1814. xvi, 439 p. 19cm. The political life of all
the deputies at the National Convention during and after the
French Revolution; a biographical dictionary.

8957   SAINT-EDME, EDME THÉODORE BOURG, known as, 1785-1852.
Répertoire général des causes célèbres anciennes et modernes, rédigé par une société d'hommes de lettres, sous la
direction de B. Saint-Edme. Paris, L. Rosier, 1834-35. 13 v.
in 6. 21cm. Vols. 1-4 (1st series, v. 1-4) of this huge collection of French trials comprises a 'biographical dictionary' of
celebrated French criminals, malefactors, etc. in that these
particular volumes of the set are alphabetical (A-Z) in arrangement.

8958   SUSSEL, PHILLIPPE
La France de la bourgeoisie, 1815-1850. Chronologie:
Martine Joly. Dictionnaire: Mme Richard-Arlaud. Filmogra-
phie: Jean-Loup Berger. Paris, Culture, art, loisirs, 1970.
256 p. illus., ports. 24cm. (Histoire de la France) The "Dictionnaire" (p. [179]-233) includes brief biographical sketches of
distinguished Frenchmen of the period, 1815-1850.

8959   TARDIEU, AMBROISE, 1788-1841.
Monument national. Portraits des députés, écrivains et
pairs constitutionnels ... dessinés et gravés par Ambroise
Tardieu. Paris, A. Tardieu, 1820-21. 16 p. 131 plates. 4.º
The national monument. Portraits of French legislators and
writers of the period (early 19th century).

8960   TARDIEU, AMBROISE, 1788-1841.
Portraits des généraux français, faisant suite aux Victoires
et conquêtes des François. [Editées par Charles-Théodore
Beauvais] Paris, C. L. F. Panckoucke, 1818-20. 3 v. ports.
8.º Portraits of the French generals, a volume supplementary
to Victoires et conquêtes des François.

8961   TISSERON, LOUIS
Le Corps législatif de l'Empire français. Documents bio-
graphiques sur tous les Députés. Tome IIIe et dernier de la
collection du Sénat et du Corps législatif. [2. éd. Supplément]
Paris, Dentu, 1864. 380, 8 p. ports. 8.º The Legislative
Corps of the French Empire; biographical documents on all the
Deputies of the Corps (which existed from 1852 to 1870)

8962   TISSERON, LOUIS
          MDCCCLXII [i. e. Mille huit cent soixante-deux] Le Corps
        législatif et le Conseil d'État. Documents historiques sur tous
        les membres de ces deux grands corps de l'Empire français,
        par une société d'hommes des lettres, publiés sous la direction
        de L. Tisseron. Cet ouvrage fait suite à l'Histoire du Sénat.
        Tome Ier [-II] Corps législatif et du Conseil d'État, IIIe [-IVe]
        de la collection des trois grands corps de l'Empire. Paris, Den-
        tu [1862] 2 v. ports. 8.º 1862; the Legislative Corps and
        Council of State of the French Empire. Historical [and biograph-
        ical] documents on all the members.

8963   TISSERON, LOUIS
          MDCCCLX [i. e. Mille huit cent soixante] Le Sénat de
        l'Empire français. Documents historiques sur les membres du
        premier grand corps de l'État. Sous la direction de L. Tisseron.
        Paris, Dentu [1860-61] 2 v. port. 8.º 1860: the Senat of the
        French Empire; historical documents (and biographical data)
        about the members of the first grand Corps of the State.

8964   TODISCO, UMBERTO
          Le personnel de la Cour des comptes (1807-1830) Genève,
        Librairie Droz, 1969. 250 p. 25cm. (Centre de recherches
        d'histoire et de philologie de la IVe Section de l'École pratique
        des hautes études [Paris] 5. Hautes études mediévales et
        modernes, 8) Biographical dictionary (p. [57]-213) of 201 offi-
        cials of the French Accounts or Audit Office for the years 1807-
        1830.

Local

Agenais

8965   ANDRIEU, JULES, 1839-1895.
          Bibliographie générale de l'Agenais et des parties du
        Condomois et du Bazadais incorporées dans le département de
        Lot-et-Garonne, répertoire alphabétique de tous les livres,
        brochures, journaux, etc. ... dus à des auteurs de la région,
        imprimés dans ce pays ou l'Intéressant directement avec dans
        notes littéraires et biographiques. Paris, A. Picard, 1886-91.
        3 v. 24cm. Contents.--t. 1. A-K.--t. 2. L-Z. Supplément.--
        t. 3. Supplément [etc.] A general bibliography of Agenais (a
        former French province) and parts of the Condomois and Baza-
        dais, now incorporated into the department of Lot-et-Garonne;
        includes biographical data.

Ain (Dept.)

8966   DUFÄY, CHARLES JULES, 1808-1887.
          Biographie des personnages notables du département de

l'Ain. Galerie militaire de l'Ain depuis les temps les plus reculés jusqu'à nos jours avec l'indication des hommes de guerre
qui, nés hors du département, s'y sont fait remarquer dans
leurs fonctions ou par leurs écrits. Bourg, L. Grandin, 1874.
511 p. 25cm.

---- ----Supplément. Bourg, F. Martin, 1878. 155 p. 25cm.
Biographical dictionary of notable persons of the Department of
the Ain; military gallery (officers of the French Army)

8967   DUFÄY, CHARLES JULES, 1808-1887.
        Dictionnaire biographique des personnages notables du dé-
partement de l'Ain. Galerie civile (IIe partie), depuis les temps
les plus reculés jusqu'à nos jours ... Bourg-en-Bresse, F.
Martin-Bottier, 1882-84. vi, 524 p. (and supplement) 25cm.
Continuation of his Biographie des personnages notables du département de l'Ain. Biographical dictionary of notable persons
of the Department of the Ain; civilian gallery (that is persons
not in the military branches).

Aisne (Dept.)

8968   DEVISME, JACQUES FRANÇOIS LAURENT
        Manuel historique du département de l'Aisne. Laon, F. Le
Blan-Courtois, 1826. ii, 464 p. 8.º Historical manual of the
Department of the Aisne; with many biographical sketches.

Alpes-Maritimes (Dept.)

8969   ALPES MARITIMES (ET PRINCIPAUTÉ DE MONACO)
        Dictionnaire biographique et ilustré. Paris, E. Flam-
marion, Néauber [189-?] vii, 983 p. illus., ports. 21cm.
(Les Dictionnaires départementaux) Biographical and illustrated dictionary of the department of the Alpes-Maritimes and
the principality of Monaco. The biographical section is on p.
337-929.

Alsace

8970   MEYER, ANTOINE
        Biographies alsaciennes et portraits en photographie, par
Ant. Meyer. Colmar, A. Meyer, 1888-90. 5 v. ports. 8.º
Alsatian biographies and portraits in photographs; 48 in each
volume. Antoine Meyer is the real name of Paul Ristelhuber (?)

8971   STOFFEL, GEORGES, 1819-1880.
        Dictionnaire biographique d'Alsace. Liste préparatoire.

Mulhouse, Impr. de L.-L. Bader, 1869. 111 p. 4.° Biographical dictionary of Alsace; the preparatory list only was
published?

Anjou

8972   LIRON, JEAN, 1665-1749.
        Bibliothèque d'Anjou. Traité historique et critique des au-
teurs de cette province et de leurs ouvrages, avec introd. et
notes par Camille Ballu. Nantes, Société des bibliophiles bretons et de l'histoire de Bretagne, 1897. iii, 100 p. 28cm. A
bio-bibliography of Anjou. Chronological arrangement by date
of death; no index.

Aquitaine

8973   LURBE, GABRIEL DE, d. 1535?
        De illustribus Aquitaniae viris, a Constantino Magno usque
ad nostra tempora, libellus. Burdigaliae, Apud S. Milangium,
1591. 148 p. 8.° Famous Aquitainians, from the time of Con-
stantine the Great up to our day (end of the 16th century).

Aube (Dept.)

8974   SOCARD, ÉMILE, 1818-1889.
        Biographie des personnages de Troyes et du département de
l'Aube. Troyes, L. Lacroix, 1882. 445 p. 21cm. A biographical dictionary for Troyes, France and the Department of Aube.

Auvergne

8975   CHAUMEIL,   abbé
        Biographie des personnes remarquables de la Haute-Au-
vergne, formant la totalité du département du Cantal et du diocèse de Saint-Flour. Précédée d'un essai sur l'histoire religieuse de cette demi-province. Genève, Slatkine Reprints,
1971. 305 p. 22cm. Reprint of the edition of the 1867 (Saint-Flour).
Biographical dictionary of the famous persons of the Auvergne
(Cantal Department & the diocese of Saint-Flour): p. [99]-308.

8976   TARDIEU, AMBROISE, 1840-
        Dictionnaire iconographique de l'ancienne Auvergne. C'est
à-dire liste générale de tous les portraits gravés, lithographiés,
dessinés concernant cette province, y compris les portraits
peints des galeries des châteaux ou familles notables, avec une
suite de personnages vivants dignes de mémoire. Clermont-
Ferrand, Impr. P. Raclot, 1904. vii, 227 p. ports. 31cm.
Iconographic dictionary of old Auvergne. A general list of all

the engraved, lithographed and drawn portraits concerning the province as well as painted portraits from the galleries of the chateaus or of notable families, followed by living people worthy of remembrance.

Aveyron (Dept.)

8977   AFFRE, HENRI, b. 1816.
Biographie aveyronnaise. Rodez, Impr. H. de Broca, 1881. viii, 383 p. 22cm. A biographical dictionary of the Department of Aveyron, France.

Basses-Alpes (Dept.)

8978   BASSES-ALPES. Dictionnaire biographique et historique illus-tré. Paris, E. Flammarion, et Néauber [189-?] vii, 523 p. illus. 20cm. (Les Dictionnaires départementaux) Illustrated biographical and historical dictionary of the department of the Basses-Alpes, France.

Basses-Pyrenees (Dept.)

8979   BASSES-PYRÉNÉES. Dictionnaire biographique et historique illustré. Paris, E. Flammarion, et Néauber [189-?] vii, 523 p. illus. 20cm. (Les Dictionnaires départementaux) Illustrated biographical and historical dictionary of the depart-ment of the Basses-Pyrénées, France.

Bouches-du-Rhone

8980   DICTIONNAIRE, ANNUAIRE ET ALBUM DES BOUCHES-DU-RHÔNE. Paris, E. Flammarion, 1901. 1193 p. illus. 20cm. (Les Dictionnaires départementaux) Dictionary, annual and album of the department of Bouches-du-Rhône. Includes biography.

Brianconnais

8981   ALBERT, ARISTIDE, 1821-
Biographie-bibliographie du Briançonnais. Gap, Impr. Jouglard, 1889-95. 3 v. 22-25cm. Imprint varies: v. [2]: Grenoble, Impr. F. Allier; v. 3: Grenoble, A. Gratier. Biog-raphy-bibliography of the region of Briançonnais, Department of Hautes-Alpes.

Brittany

8982   COUFFON DE KERDELLECH, ALEXANDRE FRANÇOIS
        MARIE, 1814-1893.
            Recherches sur la chevalerie du duché de Bretagne, suivies
        de notices concernant les grands officiers de la couronne de
        France qu'a produits la Bretagne; les grands officiers du duché
        de Bretagne, ainsi qu'un grand nombre de chevaliers bretons.
        Nantes, V. Forest & E. Grimaud, 1877. 2 v. 25cm. Studies
        on the knighthood of the Duchy of Brittany, followed by notices
        of the French Crown's officers in Brittany, Brittany's own of-
        ficials and a large number of Breton knights.

8983   KERVILER, RENÉ POCARD DU COSQUER DE, 1842-1907.
            Cent ans de représentation bretonne: gallerie de tous les
        députés envoyés par la Bretagne aux diverses législatures qui
        se sond succédées depuis 1789 jusqu'à nos jours. Dressée par
        René Kerviler. Paris, Didier [1888]-91. 2 v. in 1. ports.
        22cm. Contents.--1. ser. Les États généraux et l'Assemblée
        constituante (1789-1791).--2. ser. L'Assemblée constituante
        (1791-1792). 100 years of Breton representation: gallery of all
        the deputies sent by Brittany to the various legislative bodies
        after 1789 to the end of the 19th century. However, only these
        2 volumes were published; thus only the representatives to the
        Estates General and the Legislative and Constituent Assemblies
        from 1789 to 1792 are dovered. Each vol. is a biographical dic-
        tionary; v. 1 contains 101 sketches; v. 2, 58.

8984   ROPARTZ, SIGISMOND, 1823-1878.
            Portraits bretons des XVIIe et XVIIIe siècles, d'après des
        documents inédits. Saint-Brieuc, Impr. de S. Prud'homme,
        1857. xiii, 236 p. 12.º Biographical sketches of Bretons
        (Brittany) of the 17th and 18th centuries, based on unpublished
        documents.

Burgundy

8985   MUTEAU, CHARLES FRANÇOIS THÉRÈSE, 1824-1920.
            Galerie bourguignonne, par Ch. Muteau et Joseph Garnier.
        Dijon, J. Picard, 1858-60. 3 v. 15cm. Burgundian gallery; bi-
        ography of men born in Burgundy before 1789 and for the period
        following in the Department of the Côte-d'Or.

Castres

8986   NAYRAL, MAGLOIRE
            Biographie castraise; ou, Tableau historique, analytique et
        critique des personnages qui se sont rendus célèbres à Castres
        ou dans ses environs, par leurs écrits, leurs talens, leurs ex-
        ploits, des fondations utiles, leurs vertus ou leurs crimes,

suivie de chroniques et antiquités castraises. Castres, Impr. de Vidal aîné, 1833-37. 4 v. 20cm. Biographical dictionary of Castres, France and environs (Tarn Department).

Chalons-sur-Marne

8987   LHOTE, AMÉDÉE, 1829-1908.
        Biographie châlonnaise, avec documents inédits et accompagnés de portraits gravés et armoiries. Chalons-sur-Marne, T. Martin, 1870. 378 p. illus., ports. 24cm. Biographical dictionary of Chalons-sur-Marne and the department of the Marne.

Champagne

Bibliography, Indexes, Portrait Catalogs

8988   LIEUTAUD, SOLIMAN, b. 1795.
        Recherches sur les personnages nés en Champagne dont il existe des portraits dessinés, gravés ou lithographiés; liste des portraits ... précédés d'un courte notice biographique. Paris, L'auteur, 1856. iv, 128 p. 8.º Researches on personages born in Champagne for whom there exist portraits, sketches, engraved or lithographed; a list of portraits with brief accompanying biographical sketches.

Charente (Dept.)

8989   LA CHARENTE. Dictionnaire biographique et album. Paris, E. Flammarion, Néauber [189-?] vii, 421 p. illus. 22cm. (Les Dictionnaires départementaux) Biographical dictionary and album of the department of Charente.

Charente-Inferieure (Dept.)

8990   DICTIONNAIRE, ANNUAIRE ET ALBUM DE LA CHARENTE-INFÉRIEURE. Paris, E. Flammarion, 1901. vii, 740 p. illus. 23cm. (Les Dictionnaires départementaux) Dictionary, annual and album of the department of Charente-Inférieure; includes biographies.

8991   FEUILLERET, HENRI, 1817-1879.
        Biographie de la Charente-Inférieure (Aunis & Saintonge) par Henri Feuilleret et L. de Richemond. Niort, L. Clouzot, 1875-77. 2 v. 19cm. Biography of the Department of Charente-Inferieure (especially the old provinces of Aunis and Saintonge)

Chartres

8992   MERLET, LUCIEN VICTOR CLAUDE, 1827-1898.
        Bibliothèque chartraine, antérieure au XIXe siècle. Orlé-
ans, H. Herluison, 1892. 446 p. 24cm. Bio-bibliography of
Chartres before the 19th century. Reprinted in 1971 (Genève,
Slatkine Reprints).

Cher (Dept.)

8993   CHER. Dictionnaire, annuaire et album. Paris, E. Flam-
        marion, 1900. 359 p. illus. 22cm. (Les Dictionnaires
départementaux) Dictionary, yearbook and album of the department of Cher; includes biographies.

Correze (Dept.)

8994   BERGUES LA GARDE, JOSEPH JACQUES MARIE CASIMIR DE
        Dictionnaire historique et biographique des hommes cé-
lèbres et de tous les ilustres de la Corrèze, par De Bergues-
La-Garde. Angers, Impr. de P. Lachèse, Belleuvre et Dol-
beau, 1871. 48 p. 8.º Historical and biographical dictionary
of the famous men and all the illustrious people of the Department of Corrèze.

Cote-d'Or (Dept.)

8995   MICHAUD,   abbé
        Biographie des hommes illustres du département de la
Côte-d'Or. Dijon, Lamarche et Dronelle, 1858. 2 v. 23cm.
Contents.--t. 1. A-Bour.--t. 2. Bour-Desp. No more published? Biographical dictionary of the famous men of the department of Côte-d'Or, France.

Creuse (Dept.)

8997   TARDIEU, AMBROISE, 1840-
        Grand dictionnaire historique, généalogique et biographique
de la Haute-Marche (département de la Creuse). Herment (Puy-
de-Dôme) L'auteur, 1894. iii, 431 p. illus., ports. 8.º
Great historical, genealogical and biographical dictionary of the
region of the Haute-Marche (Department of Creuse)

Dauphine

8998   ALLARD, GUY, 1645-1716.
        Bibliothèque de Dauphiné. Contenant l'histoire des habi-

tants de cette province qui se sont distingués par leur génie,
leur talents & leur connoissances. Nouv. éd., rev. & augm.
Grenoble, V. Giroud, 1680. 340 p. 1st ed. issued in 1680 (II,
224 p. 14cm.) The library of Dauphiné. Contains brief biographical sketches of learned and distinguished natives of the
region.

Deux-Sevres (Dept.)

8999   DEUX-SÈVRES. Dictionnaire biographique et album. Paris,
            E. Flammarion et Néauber [189-?] vii, 547 p. illus. 21cm.
        (Les Dictionnaires départementaux) Biographical dictionary and
        album of the department of Deux-Sèvres.

Franche-Comte

9000   FOURQUET, ÉMILE
            Les hommes célèbres et les personnalités marquantes de
        Franche-Comté du IVe siècle à nos jours. Besançon, Editions
        Séquania, 1929. 589 p. 25cm. A huge number of biographical
        sketches (ca. 1,700) of famous men and outstanding personalities
        of Franche-Comté from the 4th century A. D. to the 'present',
        arranged chronologically by century and within the century. Al-
        phabetical approach through name index at end.

Gard (Dept.)

9001   GARD. Dictionnaire biographique et album. Paris, E. Flam-
            marion, Néauber [189-?] 687 p. illus., 20cm. (Les Dic-
        tionnaires départementaux) Biographical dictionary and album
        of the department of Gard.

Garonne (Dept.)

9002   GARONNE. Dictionnaire biographique et historique illustré.
            Paris, E. Flammarion et Néauber [190-?] 687 p. illus.
        20cm. (Les Dictionnaires départementaux) Illustrated bio-
        graphical and historical dictionary of the department of Garonne.

Gironde (Dept.)

9003   FERET, ÉDOUARD, 1844-
            Statistique générale, topographique, scientifique, admin-
        istrative, industrielle, commerciale, agricole, historique,
        archéologique et biographique du département de la Gironde.
        Bordeaux, Feret et fils, 1874-89. 3 v. illus. 24cm. General
        information about the Department of the Gironde. Only vols.
        1-2 and 3, pt. 1, were published. Vol. 3, pt. 1 is biographi-
        cal.

9004   GUÉRIN, JEAN, 1899-
        Des hommes et des activités autour d'un démi-siècle (1899-
        1957) [par] Jean et Bernard Guérin. Lettre-préf. de François
        Mauriac. [Bordeaux] Éditions B. E. B., 1957. 926 p. 27cm.
        Contents. --1. ptie. Biographies. --2. ptie. Des activités, A-Z
        (p. 705/898) Biographical dictionary for the department of the
        Gironde (1899-1957).

Haute-Saone (Dept.)

9005   SUCHAUX, LOUIS
        Galerie biographique du département de la Haute-Saône.
        Vesoul, Impr. de A. Suchaux, 1864. xxiv, 424 p. 8.º Bio-
        graphical gallery of the Department of Haute-Saône.

Haute Savoie (Dept.)

9006   GRILLET, JEAN LOUIS
        Dictionnaire historique, littéraire et statistique des dé-
        partemens du Mont-Blanc et du Léman, contenant l'histoire
        ancienne et moderne de la Savoie. Chambéry, J.-F. Puthod,
        1807. 3 v. 8.º Historical, literary and statistical dictionary
        of the regions around Mont-Blanc and Léman (Lake Geneva) con-
        taining the ancient and modern history of Savoy (Department of
        Haute-Savoie); includes biographical entries.

9007   HAUTE-SAVOIE. Dictionnaire biographique et historique il-
        lustré. Paris, E. Flammarion et Néauber [190-?] vii,
        583 p. illus. 21cm. (Les Dictionnaires départementaux)
        Illustrated biographical and historical dictionary of the depart-
        ment of Haute-Savoie.

9008   MIQUET, FRANÇOIS
        Répertoire biographique des Savoyards contemporains (1800-
        1898) 1.[-3] sér. Annecy, F. Abry, 1893-98. 3 v. 8.º Re-
        printed from the Revue savoisienne. Biographical collection of
        Savoyards (Department of Haute-Savoie) of the 19th century.

Herault (Dept.)

9009   HÉRAULT. Dictionnaire, annuaire et album. Paris, E. Flam-
        marion et Néauber [190-] 2 v. illus. 21cm. (Les Dic-
        tionnaires départementaux) A biographical and historical dic-
        tionary, yearbook and album of the department of Herault.

Isere (Dept.)

9010   DICTIONNAIRE BIOGRAPHIQUE ET ALBUM DE L'ISÈRE.
        Paris, E. Flammarion et Néauber [190-?] 1093 p. illus.

21cm. (Les Dictionnaires départementaux) Biographical dictionary and album of the department of the Isere.

Landes (Dept.)

9011   CABANNES, GABRIEL
        Galerie des Landais. Mont de Marsan, Chabas, 1930-45.
7 v. ports. 24cm. Gallery of noted persons of the department
of Landes. Contents.--t. 1-2. Les parlementaires, A-W.--t.
3-4. Ceux du passé, A-T.--t. 5. Les contemporains.--t. 6-7.
Suppléments. An extensive collective biography of the department of Landes, France.

Lille

9012   VERLY, HIPPOLYTE, 1838-
        Essai d'une biographie lilloise contemporaine (1800-1869),
augmenté d'un supplément et accompagné de notes historiques
et biographiques. Lille, Leleu, 1869. 250 p. 26cm. Biography of Lille, 1800-1869. Alphabetical table of biographical and
historical notices: p. 243-247.

Limousin

9013   FRAY-FOURNIER, ALFRED
        Catalogue des portraits limousins et marchois reproduits
par la gravure et autres procédés. Limoges, Vve. H. Ducourtieux, 1895. xii, 115 p. 8.º Reprinted from Bulletin de la Société archéologique du Limousin. Catalog of portraits of personages of the old provinces Limousin and La Marche, France,
reproduced by engraving and other processes.

General Works

9014   ARBELLOT, FRANCOIS, 1816-1900.
        Biographie des hommes illustres de l'ancienne province
du Limousin [par] F. Arbellot [et] A. Du Boys. Genève, Slatkine Reprints, 1971. 279 p. 21cm. Reprint of the Limoges edition of 1854. Covers Adam to Frachet only. A biographical
dictionary of Limousin.

Lorraine

Bibliography, Indexes, Portrait Catalogs

9015   LIEUTAUD, SOLIMAN, b. 1795.
        Liste alphabétique de portraits dessinés, gravés et lithographiés de personnages nés en Lorraine, pays Messin et de ceux

appartienment à l'histoire de ces deux provinces. 2. éd. Paris,
L'auteur, 1862. viii, 240 p. 8.º First edition appeared in
1852. Alphabetical list of sketches engraved or lithographed
portraits of persons born in Lorraine or the Messin region, and
of those who belong to the history of these two areas.

9016   LIEUTAUD, SOLIMAN, b. 1795.
        Liste alphabétique des portraits des personnages nés dans
l'ancien duché de Lorraine, celui de Bar et le Verdunois, dont
il existe des dessins, gravures et lithographies. Paris, L'auteur, 1852. iv, 120 p. 8.º Alphabetical list of portraits of
persons born in the ancient duchy of Lorraine and those of Bar
and Verdun; a catalog.

General Works

9017   CHEVRIER, FRANÇOIS ANTOINE, 1721-1762.
        Mémoires pour servir à l'histoire des hommes illustres de
Lorraine. Avec une réfutation de la Bibliothèque lorraine de
Dom Calmet. Bruxelles, 1754. 2 v. 12.º Memoirs serving
to portray the history of the famous men of Lorraine.

9018   MICHEL, LOUIS ANTOINE
        Biographie historique et généalogique des hommes mar-
quans ... de l'ancienne province de Lorraine, formée plus par-
ticulièrement des personnages distingués ... de la Meurthe.
Nancy, 1829. 1 v. 12.º Historical and genealogical biography
of conspicuous personages of Lorraine, more particularly the
region of the Meurthe.

Lyons

Bibliography, Indexes, Portrait Catalogs

9019   AUDIN, MARIUS, 1872-1951.
        Bibliographie iconographiques du Lyonnais. Lyon, A. Rey,
1909-13. 3 v. illus., ports. 24cm. (Bibliothèques de la ville
de Lyon. Collection de travaux de bibliographie) Iconographi-
cal bibliography of Lyons. Vol. 1, pt. 1 contains portraits;
vols. 2-3 contain no portraits or biographical data but only plans
and views. Vol. 2-3 issued in parts.

Maine

9020   BLONDEAU, CLAUDE, d. 1680.
        Les portraits des hommes illustres de la province du Maine.
Le Mans, Impr. de J. Ysambart, 1666. 3 pts in 1 v. ports.
4.º Portraits and biographical sketches of the famous men of
the province of Maine, France.

Marne (Dept.)

9021   MARNE. Dictionnaire biographique et historique illustré.
Paris, E. Flammarion et Néauber [190-?] 2 v. illus.
21cm. (Les Dictionnaires départementaux) Illustrated biographical and historical dictionary of the department of the Marne.

Meuse (Dept.)

9022   LA MEUSE. Dictionnaire, annuaire et album. Paris, H. Jou-
ve, 1895. 1 v. (unpaged) illus. 20cm. (Les Dictionnaires
départementaux) Dictionary, yearbook and album of the department of the Meuse; includes a biography.

Montpellier

9023   LA ROQUE, LOUIS DE, 1830-1903.
Biographie montpelliéraine. Montpellier, Impr. de Hamelin
frères, 1877-93. 3 v. 20cm. Imprint varies: v. 2, Montpellier,
Impr. J. Martel; v. 3, Montpellier, J. Calas. Contents.--[1]
Peintres, sculpteurs et architectes.--[2] Premiers présidents
des cours souveraines (1603-1867).--[3] Les évèques de Mague-
lone et de Montpellier. Biographical sketches of the illustrious
men of Montpellier, France: artists, churchmen (bishops),
presidents of the highest courts.

Morbihan (Dept.)

9024   MORBIHAN. Dictionnaire, annuaire et album. Paris, E.
Flammarion, 1901. vii, 689 p. illus. 20cm. (Les Dictionnaires départementaux) Dictionary, yearbook and album of
the department of Morbihan; includes biographies.

Moselle (Dept.)

9025   PAQUET, RENÉ, 1845-
Dictionnaire biographique de l'ancien département de la
Moselle, contenant toutes les personnes notables de cette région,
avec leurs noms, prénoms et pseudonymes, le lien et la date de
leur naissance, leur famille, leurs débuts, leur profession,
leurs fonctions successives, leurs grades et titres, leurs actes
publics, leurs oeuvres, leurs écrits et les indications bibliographiques qui s'y rapportent, les traits caractéristiques de leur
talent, etc., par Nérée Quépat [pseud.] Paris, A. Picard [etc.]
1887. vi, 620, [3] p. 28cm. Biographical dictionary of the department of the Moselle, France.

Mulhouse

9026   MAY, DENISE RICHTER
          Bio-bibliographie mulhousienne. Mulhouse, Bibliothèque
       municipale de Mulhouse, 1971. xi, 264 p. 30cm. Bio-bibli-
       ography of Mulhouse.

Nancy

9027   DIGOT, PAUL
          Les contemporains de Nancy pour 1883. Nancy, Sidot
       frères, 1882. 55 p. 8.° Biographical sketches of contempo-
       rary figures of Nancy (1883)

Nievre (Dept.)

See Nivernais

Nivernais

9028   NIÈVRE. Dictionnaire, annuaire et album. Paris, E. Flam-
          marion, 1900. vii, 360 p. illus. 21cm. (Les Diction-
       nnaires départementaux) Dictionary, annual and album of the de-
       partment of Nièvre (the old department of Nivernais); includes
       biography.

Nord (Dept.)

9029   NORD. Dictionnaire biographique illustré. 2. éd. Paris, E.
          Flammarion et Néauber [190-?] 3 v. ports. 19cm. (Les
       Dictionnaires départementaux) Illustrated biographical diction-
       ary of the department of Nord.

Normandy

9030   FRÈRE, EDOUARD BENJAMIN, 1797-1874.
          Manuel du bibliographe normand; ou, Dictionnaire historique
       et bibliographique contenant; premièrement: l'indication des
       ouvrages relatifs à la Normandie, depuis l'origine de l'impri-
       merie jusqu'à nos jours; deuxièmement: des notes biographiques,
       critiques et littéraires sur les hommes qui appartiennent à la
       Normandie par leur naissance, leurs actes et leurs écrits;
       troisièmement: des recherches sur l'histoire de l'imprimerie en
       Normandie. Rouen, A. Le Brument, 1857-60. 2 v. 24cm.
       Contents.--t. 1. A-F.--t. 2. G-Z. Contains biographical en-
       tries in its alphabetical arrangement of titles, authors, etc. A
       manual of bio-bibliography of Normandy. Reprinted in 1971 or 2
       by Lenox Hill Pub. Corp., New York.

Oise (Dept.)

9031   OISE. Dictionnaire biographique et historique illustré. Paris,
          E. Flammarion et Néauber [190-?] 787 p. ports. 20cm.
        (Les Dictionnaires départementaux) Illustrated biographical and
        historical dictionary of the department of the Oise.

Orne (Dept.)

9032   ORNE. Dictionnaire biographique et album. Paris, E. Flam-
          marion et Néauber [190-?] 2 v. illus. 20cm. (Les Dic-
        tionnaires départementaux) Contents.--1. A-H.--2. J-Z. Bio-
        graphical dictionary and album of the department of the Orne.

Paris

9033   HURTAUT, PIERRE THOMAS NICOLAS, 1719-1791.
            Dictionnaire historique de la ville de Paris et des ses en-
        virons, dans lequel on trouve la description de tous les monu-
        mens & curiosités; l'établissement des maisons religieuses, des
        communautés d'artistes, d'artisans, &c., &c. ... Paris, Mou-
        tard, 1779. 4 v. fold. maps. 22cm. An historical dictionary
        of Paris and its environs which includes many biographical en-
        tries.

9034   PRONTEAU, JEANNE
            Notes biographiques sur les membres des assemblées mu-
        nicipales parisiennes et des conseils généraux de la Seine de
        1800 à nos jours. [Paris, Impr. municipale, 195- --
            v. 27cm. At head of title: Ville de Paris. Commission des
        travaux historiques. Sous-Commission de recherches d'his-
        toire municipale contemporaine. Contents.--1. ptie. 1800-1971.
        Notices provisoires sur les conseillers municipaux de Paris,
        les conseillers généraux de la Seine, les membres de la Com-
        mission municipale et départementale (1800-1870) et les mem-
        bres de la Commune de 1871. Vol. 1 (only vol. published?) is
        primarily a biographical dictionary of members of various mu-
        nicipal assemblies of Paris and the general councils of Seine
        Dept.

9036   RAUNIÉ, ÉMILE, 1854-1911.
            Épitaphier du vieux Paris: recueil général des inscriptions
        funéraires des églises, couvents, collèges, hospices, cimetiè-
        res et charniers, depuis le moyen âge jusqu'à la fin du XVIIIe
        siècle. Paris, Impr. nationale, 1890-1914. 4 v. illus. 35cm.
        (Histoire générale de Paris; collection de documents) Vol. 4
        revised by Max Prinet. A collection of epitaphs in the churches,
        cemeteries, hospitals, etc. of Paris from the end of the Middle
        Ages to the end of the 18th century. Arrangement is by place
        (A-Z) The epitaphs are successively numbered, 1 to 2053, and
        each vol. has its own alphabetical name index.

Pas-de-Calais (Dept.)

9037   CARDEVACQUE, ADOLPHE DE, 1828-1899.
        Dictionnaire biographique du département du Pas-de-Calais;
ou, Histoire abrégée par ordre alphabétique de la vie publique
et privée d'environ 3,000 personnages nés dans ce départment,
qui se sont faits remarquer par leurs écrits, leurs talents,
leurs vertus ou leurs crimes, avec indication de tous les
ouvrages manuscrits ou imprimés ayant trait à chaque article.
Arras, Sueur-Charrney, 1879. 532 p. 29cm. A biographical
dictionary of ca. 3,000 personages of the Department of Pas-de-
Calais and the old province of Artois.

Perigord

9038   ROUMEJOUX, ANATOLE DE, 1832-1902.
        Bibliographie générale du Périgord [par] Anatole de Roume-
joux, Ph. de Bosredon et Ferd. Villepelet. Périgueux, Im-
primeries de la Dordogne, 1897-1901. 5 v. 24cm. (Publications de la Société historique et archéologique du Périgord) Contents.--1-3. A-Z.--4. Complément. Bio-bibliographies complémentaires.--5. Années 1900 et 1901. Renseignements complémentaires. Bio-bibliographies complémentaires. Bio-bibliographical: Périgord authors and persons from the department of
Dordogne. Based to some extent on De Roumejoux's Essais de
bibliographie périgourdine, 1882.

Poitou

9039   DREUX DU RADIER, JEAN FRANÇOIS, 1714-1780.
        Histoire littéraire du Poitou; précédée d'une introd. et
continuée jusqu'en 1840, par une société d'hommes de lettres.
Niort, Robin, 1842-50. 3 v. 22cm. (Bibliothèque poitevine,
t. 6-8) At head of title: Bibliothèque historique et critique de
Poitou. Contents.--t. 1. Ordre chronologique des évêques de
Poitiers. Ordre chronologique des contes héréditaires de Poi-
tiers. A-D.--t. 2. E-Z. Continuée jusqu'en 1849 par A. de
Lastic-Saint-Jal.--t. 3. Supplément, A-V. Bio-bibliography of
Poitou.

Ponthieu

9040   [DEVÉRITÉ, LOUIS ALEXANDRE] 1743-1818.
        Histoire du comte de Ponthieu, de Montreuil et de la ville
d'Abbéville, sa capitale. Avec la notice de leurs hommes dignes
de mémoire. Londres, J. Nourse, 1765. 2 v. 12.⁰ History of
the comté of Ponthieu, Montreuil and the town of Abbéville,
its capital, with notes on their famous men.

Provence

9041   ACHARD, CLAUDE FRANÇOIS, 1753-1809.
        Dictionnaire de la Provence et du Comté Venaissin.
        Geneve, Slatkine Reprints, 1971. 2 v. 23cm. Reprint of the
        Marseilles, 1787 edition (4 v. "Par une société de gens des
        lettres") A dictionary of biography for Provence and the
        County of Venaissin.

Puy-de-Dome (Dept.)

9042   PUY-DE-DÔME. Dictionnaire, annuaire et album. Paris, E.
        Flammarion, 1900. vii, 414 p. illus. 22cm. (Les Dic-
        tionnaires départementaux) Dictionary, yearbook and album of
        the department of Puy-de-Dôme; includes biographies.

9043   TARDIEU, AMBROISE, 1840-
        Grand dictionnaire biographique des personnages histo-
        riques ou dignes de mémoire nés dans le département du Puy-de-
        Dôme, avec une galerie de 160 portraits, ouvrage faisant suite
        au 'Grand dictionnaire historique du Puy-de-Dôme.' Moulins,
        Impr. de C. Desrosiers, 1878. iv, 116 p. ports. folio. Bio-
        graphical dictionary of historical personages, or memorable
        persons born in the Department of Puy-de-Dôme, with a gallery
        of 160 portraits; accompanying volume to the author's Historical
        dictionary of Puy-de-Dôme.

Reims

9044   DANTON, HENRI
        Biographie rémoise; ou, Histoire des Rémois célèbres,
        depuis les temps les plus reculés jusqu'à nos jours. Reims,
        Brissart-Binet, 1855. ii, 102 p. 8.º Biographical sketches of
        famous citizens of Reims.

Rouergue

9045   BARRAU, HIPPOLYTE DE
        Documents historiques et généalogiques sur les familles et
        les hommes remarquables du Rouergue, dans les temps anciens
        et modernes. Rodez, Impr. de N. Ratery, 1853-60. 4 v. 8.º
        Historical and genealogical documents on the families and note-
        worthy men of the Rouergue (a district and former countship in
        Southern France, now occupied by the department of Aveyron);
        includes numerous and extensive biographical materials.

Saint Malo

9046   MANET, FRANCOIS GILLES PIERRE BARNABÉ, b. 1764?
        Biographie des Malouins célèbres, nés depuis le 15e siècle
        jusqu'à nos jours, précédée d'une notice historique sur la ville

de Saint-Malo, depuis son origine. Saint-Malo, H. Rottier, 1824. viii, 369 p. 8.º Biography of famous citizens of the seaport of Saint Malo (a town of distinctive historical significance) after the 15th century to the early part of the 19th century.

Saone-et-Loire (Dept.)

9047   RAGUT, CAMILLE, b. 1793.
       Statistique de département de Saône et Loire, publiée sous les auspices du Conseil général de ce département et de la Société d'agriculture, sciences et belles-lettres de Maçon, par C. Ragut. Maçon, Impr. de Dejussieu, 1838. 2 v. fold. map (in pocket, v. 1) 31cm. "Biographie" (v. 1, p. 349-406) comprises a biographical dictionary of the Department of Saône-et-Loire, France.

Sarthe

9048   LEGEAY, FORTUNÉ, 1821-
       Nécrologie et bibliographie contemporaine de la Sarthe (1844-1880) La Mans, Leguicheux-Gallienne, 1881. 499 p. 23cm. Necrology, bio-bibliography of Department of the Sarthe, France, from 1844 to 1880.

Savoie (Dept.)

9049   SAVOIE. Dictionnaire biographique et historique illustré.
       Paris, E. Flammarion et Néauber [190-?] vii, 457 p. illus. 21cm. (Les Dictionnaires départementaux) Illustrated biographical and historical dictionary of the department of Savoie.

Seine-Inferieure (Dept.)

9050   SEINE-INFÉRIEURE. Dictionnaire biographique et historique illustré. 2. éd. Paris, E. Flammarion et Néauber [190-?] vii, 1133 p. illus. 20cm. (Les Dictionnaires départementaux) Illustrated biographical and historical dictionary of the department of Seine-Inférieure.

Somme (Dept.)

Bibliography, Indexes, Portrait Catalogs

9051   MACQUERON, HENRI
       Iconographie du département de la Somme; ou, Catalogue des cartes, vues, armoiries, etc., gravés ou lithographiés concernant ce département. Abbeville, Impr. de C. Paillart, 1886. viii, 867 p. 8.º Iconography of the Department

of the Somme; or, Catalog of the maps, views, heraldry, portraits, etc. which relate to this department.

Valenciennes

9052   HÉCART, GABRIEL ANTOINE JOSEPH, 1755-1838.
        Biographie valenciennoise, receuil de notices extraites de
        la "Feuille de Valenciennes" de 1821 à 1826. [Extrait des notes
        biographiques d'Hécart ainé] Valenciennes, Impr. de J.-B.
        Henry, 1826. 112 p. ports. 8.º Biography of personages of the
        City of Valenciennes in Southern France; a collection of notices
        taken from the newspaper 'Feuille de Valenciennes' from 1821 to
        1826.

Vaucluse (Dept.)

9053   VAUCLUSE. Dictionnaire, annuaire et album. Paris, E.
        Flammarion, et Néauber [189-?] vii, 730 p. illus. (Les
        Dictionnaires départementaux) Dictionary, annual and album of
        the department of Vaucluse; biography included.

Vendome

9054   SAINT-VENANT, RAOUL, comte de
        Dictionnaire topographique, historique, biographique,
        généalogique et héraldique du Vendômois et de l'arrondissement
        de Vendôme, par R. de Saint-Venant. Mayenne, J. Floch,
        1969. 4 v. in 2. 25cm. Reprint of the Blois (1912-1917) edi-
        tion. A topographical, historical, biographical, genealogical
        and heraldic dictionary of the Vendome.

Vienne

9055   VIENNE. Dictionnaire biographique et album. Paris, E.
        Flammarion, et Néauber [189-?] vii, 482 p. illus. 20cm.
        (Les Dictionnaires départementaux) Biographical dictionary and
        album of the Department of Vienne.

Yvonne (Dept.)

9056   PIGNARD-PÉGUET, MAURICE
        Histoire de l'Yonne, avec un précis de l'histoire de la
        Troisième République jusqu'au 14 juillet 1912. Histoire des
        communes, guerres, seigneuries, anciens monuments, églises,
        chateaux, archéologie, généalogies, biographies. Paris, Li-
        brairie de l'histoire générale illustrée des départements, 1913.
        xxxiii, 1020 p. map. 27cm. (Histoire générale illustrée des
        départements depuis les temps les plus reculés jusqu'au nos

jours) History of the department of the Yonne. Biographies
(A-Z) are to be found on p. 965-1016.

GALICIA

(Austro-Hungarian Empire)

9057   BADER, GERSHOM, 1868-1953
            Medinah we-bakhameha ... [v. 1; Alef-Camet] New York,
National Booksellers, 1934. 152 p. ports. 24cm. Added t.p.:
Galician Jewish celebrities; an illustrated cyclopedia of noted
Jewish personalities who contributed to Galicia's progress dur-
ing its existence. No more published?

GAMBIA

9058   GAILEY, HARRY
            Historical dictionary of the Gambia. Metuchen, N. J.,
Scarecrow Press, 1975. viii, 172 p. map. 23cm. (African
historical dictionaries, no. 4) Includes biographical entries for
natives and foreigners involved in the historical development of
Gambia.

GEORGIA (Transcaucasia)

9059   BERIDZE, VAKHTANG VUKOLOVICH
            Mastera drevnegruzinskogo iskusstva. Tbilisi, Sabchota
sakartvelo, 1967. 242 p. illus. 22cm. A dictionary of old
Georgian artists. Translated from the Georgian: Dzveli kart-
veli cstatebi (?)

9059a   KARTULI SABCHOTA ENCIKLOPEDIA. Tbilisi, Kartuli Sab-
            chota Enciklopediis Specialuru Samecniero redakcia, 1972-
                  v. illus., ports. 27cm. Contents.--t. 1. A-Atoni.
The Georgian Soviet encyclopedia. The work is presumably to
be complete in 12 vols. Its usefulness is in its large number of
biographical sketches of famous Georgians.

GERMANY

Bibliography, Indexes, Portrait Catalogs

9060   BIELZ, JULIUS
            Porträtkatalog der Siebenburger Sachsen. Hamburg, Ver-
lag Diepenbroick-Grüter und Schulz, 1936. xi, 100 p. ports.
23cm. (Historische Bildkunde, Heft 5) "Erscheint gleich-
zeitig als 1. Heft im 49. Band des Archivs des Vereins für Sieb-

enbürgische Landeskunde in Hermannstadt. " A portrait catalog of Germans in Transylvania.

9061   FRIEDRICHS, ELISABETH
        Lebensbilder-Register. Alphabetisches Verzeichnis der in
den deutschen regionalen Lebensbilder-Sammelbänden behand-
elten Personen. Neustadt/Aisch, Degener, 1971. 177 p. 25cm.
An index to biographical sketches located in various German collective biography volumes. Alphabetical arrangement with
birth/death dates of biographees.

9062   HEITZMANN, JOHANN
        Portraits-Katalog. Verzeichnis aller Portraits welche in
Deutschland bis Ende des Jahres 1857 erschienen und noch vom
Verleger zu beziehen sind. Mit Einschluss einer grossen
Anzahl ausländischer Portraits mit Angabe der Verleger und
Ladenpreise. München, Mey & Widmayer, 1858. iv, 430 p.
23cm. A portrait catalog containing a list of portraits which
have appeared in Germany to the end of the year 1857 and are
still available from their publishers. Also a large number of
foreign portraits which statement of publisher's selling price.

9063   LESSER, FRIEDRICH CHRISTIAN, 1692-1754.
        Besondere Müntzen welche sowohl auf Gelehrte, Gesell-
schaften nemlich Universitäten, Societäten, Seminaria und Gym-
nasia, als auch auf gelehrte Leute, nemlich Theologen, Jure-
Consultos, Medicos und Philosophos, sonderlich auf den theuren
D. Martin Luthern, nach Junckers herausgegebenen güldenen
und silbernen Ehren-Gedächtnisse desselben geprägt worden.
Franckfurt, Leipzig, M. Blochberger, 1739. 830, 128, [40] p.
fold. plates. 18cm. Special coins and medals struck in com-
memoration of schools and societies as well as learned people—
theologians, jurists, physicians, philosophers; a catalog with
reproductions of many of the medals.

9064   MAURER, WILHELM, 1900-
        Namenliste zur deutschen Geschichte des XVI. Jahrhunderts,
als Stichwort-Verzeichnis für die Deutsche Biographie der
Reformationszeit. Leipzig, K. W. Hiersemann, 1941-   v.
24cm. 1st fascicle (A-E) only one published? A check-list of
the persons to be included in a projected work, Deutsche Biographie der Reformationszeit (German biography of the Reformation).

9065   SCHOTTENLOHER, KARL, 1878-1954.
        Bibliographie zur deutschen Geschichte im Zeitalter der
Glaubenspaltung, 1517-1585. Im Auftrag der Kommission zur
Erforschung der Geschichte der Reformation und Gegenreforma-
tion hrsg. Leipzig, K. W. Hiersemann, 1933-66. 7 v. 29cm.
The first volume and part of the 2d volume of this bibliography
of the Reformation and Counter-Reformation in Germany are an

extensive bibliography of individual biographies of persons prominent during the period.

9066 STEINBERG, SIGFRID HENRY, 1899-
Bibliographie zur Geschichte des deutschen Porträts. Hamburg, Von Diepenbroick-Grüter & Schulz, 1934. vii, 166 p. 8.°
(Historische Bildkunde, 1. Heft) Bibliography of the history of the German portrait and portrait painters.

9067 TIEDEMANN, MANFRED VON
Katalog der Leichenpredigtensammlung der Niedersächsischen Staats- und Universitätsbibliothek in Göttingen. Mit einem Vorwort von Wilhelm Wegener. Göttingen, H. Reise, 1954-55. 3 v. 25cm. A catalog of funeral sermons stored in the State and University Library of Lower Saxony in Göttingen. Birth and death dates as well as some identifying data are included for each name listed in the alphabetical catalog.

9068 VERZEICHNIS DER LEICHENPREDIGTEN DER EHEMALIGEN UNIVERSITÄTSBIBLIOTHEK HELMSTEDT. Helmstedt, 1957. 90 leaves, 91-146 p. 29cm. Cover title. At head of title: Landkreis Helmstedt. Ehemalige Universitätsbibliothek. A bibliography of funeral sermons held by the former University Library of Helmstedt, in alphabetical order, with biographical data for the deceased, and thereby a 'biographical dictionary' of distinguished Germans of the past.

9069 WATTENBACH, WILHELM, 1819-1897.
Deutschlands Geschichtsquellen im Mittelalter bis zur Mitte des dreizehnten Jahrhunderts. 6. umgearb. Aufl. Berlin, W. Hertz, 1893-94. 2 v. 23cm. Germany's historical sources in the Middle Ages to the middle of the 13th century; on pages [437]-460 is to be found a very good bibliography of necrologies for this period.

9070 WESTPHAL, MARGARETHE
Die besten deutschen Memoiren. [Lebenserinnerungen und Selbstbiographien aus 7 Jahrhunderten] Univeränderter, berechtigter Nachdruck der 1923 erschienenen Ausg. München-Pullach, Verlag Dokumentation, 1971. 423 p. 19cm. (Kleine Literaturführer, Bd. 5) The best German memoirs. Autobiographies from 7 centuries (14th-20th) A bibliography which includes biographical notes for those who have written autobiographies.

General Works

9071 ALLGEMEINE DEUTSCHE BIOGRAPHIE. Hrsg. durch die Historischen Commission bei der Königlichen Akademie der Wissenschaften. [2., unveränderte Aufl.] Neudruck der 1. Aufl. von 1875-1912. Berlin, Duncker & Humblot, 1967-71. 56 v.

24cm. Biographies of prominent Germans from the earliest
period to the end of the 19th century, edited by R. V. Lilliencron,
assisted until 1897 by F. X. v. Wegele; v. 54 edited by A.
Bettelheim, v. 53 by the Historische Commission. Title of v.
1-8 reads: Allgemeine [etc.] auf Veranlassung und mit Unterstützung Seiner Majestäts des Königs von Bayern Maximilian II.
Hrsg. durch die Historische Commission bei der Königl. Akademie der Wissenschaften. This phrase is printed in roman
capital letters and divided by title vignette coat of arms of Maximilian II. Beginning with v. 27 (1888) each volume has an alphabetical index; the index of v. 27 includes the articles of v. 1-27.
"Generalregister" by Fritz Gerlich: v. 56.

9072   AUBERT, JOACHIM
        Handbuch der Grabstätten berühmter Deutscher, Öster-
reicher und Schweizer. München, Deutscher Kunstverlag,
1973. 201, [18] p. 63 illus. 20cm. Handbook of the burial
places of famous Germans, Austrians and Swiss. Includes
biographical data for the many people included.

9073   BIOGRAPHISCHES LEXIKON ZUR DEUTSCHEN GESCHICHTE.
        Von den Anfängen bis 1917. Hrsg. von Karl Obermann [et
al.] Berlin, Deutschen Verlag der Wissenschaften, 1967. 520 p.
22cm. Biographical dictionary for German history up to 1917.

9074   BIOGRAPHISCHES LEXIKON ZUR DEUTSCHEN GESCHICHTE
        VON DEN ANFÄNGEN BIS 1945. [Herausgeberkollektiv:
Gerhart Hass et al. 2. Druckquote] Berlin, Deutscher Verlag
der Wissenschaften, 1971. 770 p. 25cm. Biographical dictionary for German history from its beginning to 1945. An earlier
edition, under title: Biographisches Lexikon zur deutschen
Geschichte von den Anfängen bis 1917 (q.v.) was issued in 1967.

9075   DIE DEUTSCHE JUGENDBEWEGUNG 1920 BIS 1933; die
        bündische Zeit. Quellenschriften, hrsg. im Auftrage des
Gemeinschaftswerkes Archiv und Dokumentation der Jugendbewegung von Werner Kindt. Mit einem Nachwort von Hans Raupach.
Düsseldorf, E. Diederichs, 1974. 1840 p. 24cm. (Dokumentation der Jugendbewegung, 3) The German youth movement from
1920 to 1933. "Kurzbiographien" (p. 1753-1807) comprise
a biographical dictionary of leaders in the youth movement (over
200 biographical sketches).

9076   DEUTSCHE MÄNNER. 200 Bildnisse und Lebensbeschreibung-
        en. Mit einer Einführung von Wilhelm Schüssler. Berlin,
E. Steiniger, 1938. 424 p. ports. 25cm. Text and full-page
portraits on opposite pages. 200 portraits and brief lives of
famous Germans.

9077   EISGRUBER, HEINZ, 1894-
        Völkische und deutschnationale Führer. 100 Heldenbilder.

Leipzig. E. Oldenbourg, 1925. 68 p. German leaders of the first quarter of the 20th century; 100 biographical sketches.

9078   FASTENRATH, JOHANNES, 1839-1908.
La Walhalla y las glorias de Alemania. [Noticia de todos los personajes que alcanzaron honrosa celebridad e fama, asé en la guerra como en la política; asé en las ciencias como en las artes y en las letras, por] Juan Fastenrath. Prólogo de M. R. Blanco-Belmonte. Madrid, Estab. Tip. Sucesores de Rivadeney-ra, 1910. 6 v. fronts. 19cm. The Valhalla and the glories of Germany; notes on all the personages who attained celebrity and fame in war and politics, the sciences, arts and letters. First issued in 5 v. in 1873-1879?

9079   GALLERIE DER ZEITGENOSSEN. Neue Folge, oder Die natur-getreuen Bildnisse der Männer des deutschen Volks und der benachbarten freien Nationen ... Lief. 1-55. Hildburghausen [etc.] 1848-53. 55 fascicules. 110 ports. 4.º 2 portraits and biographical sketches in each fascicle. 'Gallery of contempo-raries' (mid-19th century) 'True to life' portraits and biographi-cal sketches (2 to a fascicle; 110 in all) of prominent Germans as well as figures from neighboring nations.

9080   GENEALOGISCHES TASCHENBÜCHER DER ADELIGEN
HÄUSER. 1.-19. Jahrg., 1870-1894. Brunn. 19 v. illus. 12-14cm. Title varies: 1870-81, Genealogisches Taschenbuch der Ritter- und Adelsgeschlechter. Publication suspended from 1871 to 1876 inclusive. A genealogical yearbook for the noble houses of Germany; entry is by family, with biographical-genea-logical sketches of family members thereunder.

9081   GERMANY. REICHSTAG.
Amtliches Reichstags-Handbuch. 1890/92-1912. Hrsg. von Reichstags-Bureau. Berlin, Trowitzsch.   v. ports., plans. 17cm. On cover: Reichstags Handbuch. Amtliche Ausg. Began with Legislative period 8, 1890/92 and continued until the end of the 13th Legislative period in 1912; began again as Reichstags-Handbuch, Election period 1, 1920 (q. v.) Extensive biographi-cal sections were included in this official handbook of the Ger-man Parliament (Reichstag). E. g., 1890/1895 vol., p. [135]-279, is a biographical dictionary of members of the Reichstag for that period as are p. 173-356 for the 1903-1908 volume.

9082   GERMANY. REICHSTAG.
Der Deutsche Reichstag. [1933]-   [1]-   Wahlperiode nach dem 30. Januar 1933-   Berlin.   v. illus., ports. 19-21cm. Vols. for 1933-   have title: Reichstags-Handbuch. VIII.-IX. Wahlperiode. Ceased ca. 1939? Continues Reichstags-Handbuch, I.1VII. Wahlperiode (q. v.) The German Reichstag ('Parliament') 1933-   ; includes portraits and biographical sketches of the members of the Reichstag.

9083   GERMANY. REICHSTAG.
        Reichstags-Handbuch. I.-VII Wahlperiode; 1920-1932. Ber-
lin, Reichsdruckerei, 1920-33. 6 v. illus., ports. 19cm. Preceded by its Amtliches Reichstags-Handbuch (q. v.), continued
by its Der Deutsche Reichstag (q. v.). Some supplements were
also published. The German Reichstag ('Parliament') 1920-1932;
includes portraits and biographical sketches of members of the
body for those years.

9084   GLENZDORF, JOHANN CASPAR
        Henker, Schinder und arme Sünder [von] Johann Glenzdorf
[und] Fritz Treichel. Bad Münster am Deister, W. Rost, 1970.
2 v. ports. 22cm. "Hangmen (executioners), punishers and
poor sinners"; the major portion of this work consists of a biographical-genealogical dictionary of German executioners and
men who served as the instruments of punishment of criminals
sentenced by the courts.

9085   HAMBURGER, ERNST, 1890-
        Juden im öffentlichen Leben Deutschlands. Regierungsmit-
glieder, Beamte und Parlamentarier in der monarchischen Zeit,
1848-1918. Tübingen, J. C. B. Mohr (P. Siebeck) 1968. xxii,
595 p. 24cm. Jews in the public life of Germany; members of
the government, officials and parliamentarians during the monarchy, 1848-1918. Biographical data is merged into the text, but
is quite extensive; use the index for alphabetical approach.

9086   HOHLFELD, JOHANNES, 1888-
        Zwanzig Jahre deutsches Ringen; vom Weltkrieg über Ver-
sailles zur nationalen Erneuerung, von Johann von Reichenbrand
[pseud.] Berlin, P. Franke [1934] 398 p. illus., ports. 26cm.
"Drittes Buch: Kriegslexikon" (p. 257-398) includes many brief
biographies of Germans and world figures instrumental in the
development of German history from the early years of the 20th
century up to and including the early years of the Nazi period.

9087   JANTZEN, HINRICH
        Namen und Werke; Biographien und Beiträge zur Soziologie
der Jugendbewegung. [1. Aufl.] Frankfurt am Main, Dipa-Ver-
lag [1972-   v. illus., ports. 23cm. (Quellen und Beiträge zur Geschichte der Jugendbewegung, Bd. 12
"Names and works"; biographies and contributions towards the
sociology of the youth movement. A bio-bibliographical dictionary of leaders in the 20th century German youth movement (vol.
1, A-Z, contains 61 biographies; v. 2, A-Z, 51 biographies): v.
3 (1975), Alverdes to Zacharias, 46 biographies.

9088   KAZNELSON, SIEGMUND
        Juden im deutschen Kulturbereich; ein Sammelwerk. Mit
einem Geleitwort von Richard Willstätter. 2., stark erweiterte
Ausg. Berlin, Jüdischer Verlag [1959] xx, 1060 p. 25cm.

Jews in German cultural life. Biographical sketches arranged
by subject: Theater, Films, Philology, etc., with a name index
at the end of the volume.

9089   KLEIN, ANTON, EDLER VON, 1748-1810.
        Leben und Bildnisse grosser Deutschen, von verschiedenen
Verfassern und Künstlern. 2. Ausg. Mannheim, 1803-05. 5 v.
ports. folio. 1st ed. issued in 1785-180-? A one-volume extract
from the above work was issued in French in 1806 under title:
Galerie historique des illustres Germains depuis Arminius
jusqu'à nos jours (Paris, A.-A. Renouard) The lives and like-
nesses of great Germans, by various authors and artists.

9090   KLINKICHT, MOR
        300 berühmte Deutsche. Bildnisse in Holzschnitten von
M. Klinkicht. Lebensbeschreibungen von Karl Siebert. Stuttgart, S. Greiner, & Pfeiffer, 1912. 622 p. ports. 8.º 300
famous Germans; portraits and biographical sketches.

9091   KRAUSHAAR, LUISE
        Deutsche Widerstandskämpfer 1933-1945. Biographien und
Briefe. Berlin, Dietz Verlag, 1970. 2 v. facsims., ports.
24cm. Contents.--Bd. 1. A-M.--Bd. 2. N-Z. Ergänzungen
A-Z. "Diese Biographien wurde geschrieben von Luise Kraushaar unter Mitarbeit von Hans Dress [et al.] Herausgeber: Institut für Marxismus-Leninismus beim Zentralkomitee der SED."
Biographical dictionary, in part, of the Anti-Nazi Resistance.

9092   KUNOWSKI, JOHANNES VON
        Deutsches Soldatentum; 100 Lebensbilder grosser deutscher
Soldaten. Berlin, Verlag für Volkstum, Wehr und Wirtschaft
[1940] 223 p. illus. 31cm. German military figures; 100 lives
of famous German soldiers.

9093   LEFRANK, M
        Die Zeitgenossen Friedrichs des Grossen; Ehre und Grosse
des preussischen Staats. Biographien sämmtlicher auf dem
Denkmal Friedrichs des Grossen zu Berlin dargestellten und
namentlich aufgeführten Helden, Staatsmänner, Gelehrten und
Künstler. Berlin, Sacco, 1853. xvi, 944 p. 8.º The contemporaries of Frederick the Great. With biographies of all those
whose names are inscribed on the monument to Frederick in Berlin: heroes, statesmen, scholars and artists.

9094   RÖSSLER, HELLMUTH, 1910-1968.
        Biographisches Wörterbuch zur deutschen Geschichte. Be-
gründet von Hellmuth Rössler und Günther Franz. 2., völlig
neubearb. und stark erw. Aufl. bearb. von Karl Bosl,
Günther Franz, Hanns Hubert Hofmann. München, Francke Verlag [1973-75] Biographical dictionary of German history; first
edition, issued in 1952, was by Rössler and Franz with the col-

laboration of Willy Hoppe. Contents. --1. Bd. A-H. --2. Bd. I-
R. --3. Bd. S-Z. Register.

9096   SIEBS, BENNO EIDE, 1891-
         Lebensbilder von der Elb- und Wesermündung. Ein Quer-
         schmitt durch acht Jahrhunderte. Hrsg. vom Heimatbund der
         Männer vom Morgenstern, Bremerhaven. Bremerhaven, Nord-
         westdeutscher Verlag, 1966. 116 p. 24cm. 8 centuries of bi-
         ography of persons who lived near the mouth of the Elbe and
         Weser Rivers. Arranged by date of birth; list of personal names:
         p. 111-114.

9097   SNYDER, LOUIS LEO, 1907-
         Encyclopedia of the Third Reich. New York, McGraw-Hill
         [1976] [22], 410 p. illus., ports. 25cm. Includes entries "for
         every person of importance in the history of the Third Reich
         [Nazi Germany]. "

9098   WEBERSTADT, HANS, 1875-
         Gedenkhalle für die Gefallenen des Dritten Reiches. Unter
         Mitarbeit der Gauleitungen der NSDAP und Angehörige der
         Gefallenen ... [Von] Hans Weberstadt und Kurt Langner. Mit
         zahlreichen Bildern und Dokumenten aus dem Kampf der Beweg-
         ung. 2. Aufl. München, Zentralverlag der NSDAP, F. Eher
         Nachf, 1936. 240 p. illus., ports. 25cm. A memorial to
         the fallen heroes of the Third Reich. Biographical sketches of
         members of the Nazi Party (before 1936).

GERMANY, EAST

(German Democratic Republic)

9099   BUCH, GÜNTHER
         Namen und Daten; Biographien wichtiger Personen der DDR.
         Bearb. von Günther Buch. Berlin, J. H. W. Dietz, 1973. xv,
         332 p. 22cm. Names and dates; biographies of important per-
         sons in the German Democratic Republic. A biographical dic-
         tionary.

9100   OSTDEUTSCHE GEDENKTAGE. 1968-   [Bonn, Bund der
         Vertriebenen]   v. ports. 19cm. annual. A yearbook
         of biography for contemporary East Germany and Germans in
         Eastern Europe issued by the Association of Refugees in West
         Germany.

GERMANY, WEST

(German Federal Republic)

9101   GERMANY (FEDERAL REPUBLIC, 1949-   ) BUNDES-
        MINISTERIUM DER VERTEIDIGUNG.
            Handbuch der Bundeswehr. [Stand: 10. August 1972. Bonn]
        Bundesministerium der Verteidigung, Informations- und Presse-
        stab [1972] 1 v. (unpaged) ports. 20cm. Handbook of the West
        German Armed Forces; includes biographical notes on leading
        figures in the Armed Forces.

9102   GERMANY (FEDERAL REPUBLIC, 1949-   ) PRESSE UND
        INFORMATIONSAMT.
            The German Federal Republic. [Bonn?] Published on be-
        half of the Press- and Information Office of the Federal Govern-
        ment [1970?] 93 p. ports. 21cm. Portraits and biographical
        sketches (54 in all) of the German Federal Republic's ministers,
        parliamentary state secretaries and permanent state secretaries
        as of 22nd October 1969.

9103   GOYKE, ERNST
            Die 100 [i. e. Hundert] von Bonn: 1972-1976. Bergisch-Glad-
        bach, Lübbe, 1973. 303 p. 100 ports. 23cm. 100 key political
        figures (statesman, etc.) of the West German Government,
        1972-1976.

9104   KENKELS, WALTER
            Bonner Köpfe. [7. Aufl.] Düsseldorf, Econ Verlag [1970]
        379 p. 23cm. First-4th ed. has title: 99 Bonner Köpfe, and
        5th-6th ed. has title: 111 Bonner Köpfe. Prominent political
        figures in the Federal Republic of Germany.

9104a   SAUR, KARL OTTO
            Who's who in German politics; a biographical guide to 4,500
        politicians in the Federal Republic of Germany. New York, R.
        R. Bowker, 1971. x, 342 p. 22cm. In German; preface also
        in English. Issued also under title: Who's who in der Politik
        (München, Verlag Dokumentation, 1971)

Local

Baden

9105   RAPP, ALFRED, 1880-
            Die Badischen Landtagsabgeordneten 1905/1929. Mit Bibli-
        ographie und Statistiken zur Geschichte des badischen Landtags.
        Hrsg. vom Badischen Landtag. Karlsruhe, Badenia, 1929. 109 p.
        8.⁰ Members of the Legislative Assembly of Baden, 1905 to
        1929.

Bavaria

9106   BAYERN'S HELDEN- UND EHRENBUCH. Dekorirte und
        Belobte der nach Frankreich ausmarschirten bayerischen
        Armee; ein Gedenkbuch des deutsch-französischen Krieges 1870-
        1871. Nach Mitteilungen der verschiedenen Heeresabtheilungen.
        München, Huber, 1872-73. 280 p. No more published? A me-
        morial book for Bavaria's decorated soldiers in the Franco-
        Prussian War of 1870-1871.

Berlin

9107   [KNÜPPELN, JULIUS FRIEDRICH] 1757-1840.
        Busten Berlinscher Gelehrten und Künstler mit Devisen.
        Leipziger Ostermesse [Stendal, Franzen] 1787. xiv, 396 p.
        17cm. Written in collaboration with C. C. Nencke and C. L.
        Paalzow. Sketches of German artists and scholars in Berlin,
        with mottos.

9108   KULLINICK, HEINZ
        Berliner und Wahlberliner; Personen und Persönlichkeiten
        in Berlin von 1640-1914. Berlin, A. W. Hayn's Erben, 1961.
        268 p. 20cm. Persons and personalities in Berlin from 1640 to
        1914. Arranged alphabetically for each of the 10 last reigning
        sovereigns from Frederick William, the Great Elector to Wil-
        liam II; rather brief biographical facts.

Bremen

9109   BREMISCHE BIOGRAPHIE, 1912-1962. Hrsg. von der His-
        torischen Gesellschaft zu Bremen und dem Staatsarchiv
        Bremen. In Verbindung mit Fritz Peters and Karl H. Schwebel
        bearb. von Wilhelm Lührs. Bremen, H. M. Hauschild, 1969.
        xv, 573 p. 26cm. A biographical dictionary of prominent per-
        sons of Bremen, Germany, covering the years 1912 to 1962.

Cologne

9110   IN KÖLN VERLIEBT, UM KÖLN VERDIENT; biographisch-bi-
        bliographisches Lexikon des Heimatvereins Alt-Köln.
        [Köln, Heimatverein Alt-Köln, 1973] 271, [32] p. 20cm. (Bei-
        träge zur kölnischen Geschichte, Sprache und Eigenart, Bd. 54)
        Title on Spine: Alt-Köln-Lexikon. A bio-bibliographical diction-
        ary of Cologne, past and present; entries are very sparse, giv-
        ing only basic biographical data.

Franconia

9111   CHROUST, ANTON, 1864-1945, ed.
        Lebensläufe aus Franken. Erlangen, Palm & Enke, 1919-

60. 6 v. 26cm. (Veröffentlichungen der Gesellschaft für Fränkische Geschichte, 7. Reihe) Includes a substantial number of biographies of people prominent in Franconia's civilization and history (e.g., vol. 5 contains 51 biographies) Each vol. alphabetical, A-Z.

Heidelberg

9112 NEUMÜLLERS-KLAUSER, RENATE
Die Inschriften der Stadt und des Landkreises Heidelberg. Stuttgart, A. Druckenmüller, 1970. xxii, 413 p. illus. 28cm. (Die Deutschen Inschriften, Bd. 12. Heidelberger Reihe, Bd. 4) Included among the 621 inscriptions from the churches, etc. of the City of Heidelberg and environs are epitaphs which yield biographical data. An alphabetical approach to the above data is afforded by the "Orts- und Personennamen" [index] on p. 387-398.

Konigsberg

Bibliography, Indexes, Portrait Catalogs

9113 TIESLER, KURT
Verzeichnis von Lebensläufen vorwiegend des Handwerker- und Kaufmannstandes aus der Zeit von 1579-1729, entnommen den in der Stadtbibliothek Königsberg i Pr. befindlichen 507 handschriftlichen Leichenpredigten. Leipzig, Zentralstelle für Deutsche Personen- und Familiengeschichte, 1927. xii, 128 p. 25cm. (Mitteilungen der Zentralstelle für Deutsche Personen- und Familiengeschichte ... 34. Heft) A list of lives, especially of artisans and merchants, 1579-1724, taken from 507 manuscript funeral sermons in the Municipal Library of Königsberg; with brief biographical notes.

General Works

9114 WEISFERT, JULIUS NICOLAUS.
Biographisch-litterarisches Lexikon für die Haupt- und Residenzstadt Königsberg und Ostpreussen. Hildesheim, New York, G. Olms, 1975. 259 p. 19cm. Reprint of the 1897 ed. (Königsberg, G. Schadlofsky). a 2d ed. of the original work (259, v p.) was issued in 1898 (Königsberg, Bon)? A biobibliographical-literary dictionary of Königsberg (now Kaliningrad, Russia) and East Prussia.

Mainz

9115 ARENS, FRITZ VIKTOR, 1912-
Die Inschriften der Stadt Mainz von frühchristlicher Zeit bis 1650. Stuttgart, A. Druckenmüller, 1958. 743 p. illus.

29cm. (Die Deutschen Inschriften. 2. Bd.; Heidelberger Reihe, 2. Bd.) Issued in 10 fascicles, 1951-58. Among the 1603 inscriptions in this volume gathered from the Cathedral at Mainz and other churches and buildings of the city (from ca. 1000 to 1650) are a huge number of epitaphs which in themselves provide biographical data; when the epitaphs are in Latin, German translations are given. An alphabetical approach to the personal names is given on pages 719-727. Bibliographical references to other sources of information about individuals are often given.

Munich

9116   HUFNAGEL, MAXIMILIAN JOSEPH, 1919-
Berühmte Tote im Südlichen Friedhof zu München. 500 Zeugen des Münchner kulturellen, geistigen und politischen Lebens im 19. Jahrhundert. München, Manz Verlag [1969] 312 p. plan (in pocket) 20cm. Famous deceased persons interred in the South Cemetery in Munich. Non-alphabetically arranged, but with an index. 500 witnesses of Munich's cultural, intellectual and political life in the 19th century.

9117   KLOOS, RUDOLF, 1926-
Die Inschriften der Stadt und des Landkreises München. Stuttgart, A. Druckenmüller, 1958. xxvi, 370 p. illus. 28cm. (Die Deutschen Inschriften, 5. Bd. Münchener Reihe, 1. Bd.) 667 inscriptions and epitaphs from churches and buildings of the City of Munich (ca. 1200 to ca. 1650). German translation of Latin epitaphs for numerous individuals are given, yielding in some cases fairly substantial biographical data; occasionally biographical facts are elaborated on by the compiler. Alphabetical approach to personal names is given by "Orts- und Personennamen" (p. 525-558)—a 'phonetical alphabet' index. Sources for further data are often listed.

Nassau (Duchy)

9118   BONNET, RUDOLF, 1889-
Männer aus und in Nassau nebst einigen Frauen; ein Quellenweiser. Frankfurt am Main, 1940-   v. 25cm. (Nassovica; Bausteine zur nassauischen Familien- und Ortsgeschichte, Bd. 6, 14
Each vol. (two published as of 1969) forms a biographical dictionary of prominent persons in the Duchy of Nassau; most of the entries are quite brief, but contain references to sources for more biographical detail.

Nuremberg

9119   ZAHN, PETER
Die Inschriften der Friedhöfe St. Johannis, St. Rochus und Wöhrd zu Nürnberg. Gesammelt und bearb. von Peter Zahn.

München, A. Druckenmüller, 1972. xxiii, 441 p. illus. 28cm.
(Die Deutschen Inschriften, Bd. 13. Münchener Reihe, Bd. 3)
Gravestone inscriptions from 3 burial grounds in the city of
Nuremberg. The compiler gives other biographical data and
references when available. Alphabetical approach thru' "Orts-
und Personennamen" (p. 377-427)

Osnabruck

9120   STUVE, JOHANN EBERHARD
        Beschreibung und Geschichte des Hochstifts und Fürstent-
hums Osnabrück, mit einigen Urkunden. Osnabrück, In der
Schmidtschen Buchhandlung, 1789. [6[, 480, lxv p. 17cm.
Description and history of the diocese and principality of Osnabrück. Biographical notices are to be found on p. 148-480, arranged by date of entry into function.

Prussia

9121   KROLLMANN, CHRISTIAN ANTON CHRISTOPH, 1866-1944.
        Altpreussische Biographie. Hrsg. im Auftrage der His-
torischen Kommission für Ost- und Westpreussische Landes-
forschung. Königsberg, Gräfe und Unzer, 1936-67. 2 v. 26cm.
A biographical dictionary of deceased Prussians. Vol. 2 has
imprint: Marburg: N. G. Elwert. Contents.--Bd. 1. Abegg-
Malten.--Bd. 2. Maltig-Z. Another earlier ed. appeared in
1941 in 3 vols.

9122   MILITÄRISCHES PANTHEON; oder, Biographisches Lexikon
        aller preussischen Helden. Berlin, 1790-99. 4 v. 8.°
The military pantheon; or, Biographical dictionary of Prussian
heroes.

9123   OSTPREUSSISCHE KÖPFE. Königsberg, Königsberger
        Allgemeine Zeitung und Verlagsdruckerei, 1928. 270 p.
ports. 20cm. "Vorwort" signed: Ulrich Baltzer. Portraits
and biographical notes on famous East Prussians. Arranged by
date of birth; use contents note for approach to individuals
sketched.

9124   PRIESDORFF, KURT VON
        Soldatisches Führertum. Hamburg, Hanseatische Verlags-
Anstalt, 1936-42. 10 v. ports. 4.° Portraits and biographies
of generals of the armies of Brandenburg-Prussia and Germany;
an extensive collection. Accompanied by an alphabetical list to
vols. 1-5.

Rhine Valley

9125   AUGEL, JOHANNES
        Italienische Einwanderung und Wirtschaftstätigkeit in
        rheinischen Städten des 17. und 18. Jahrhunderts. Bonn, L.
        Röhrscheid, 1971. 482 p. 23cm. (Rheinisches Archiv, 78)
        Originally presented as the author's thesis, Bonn. Italian im-
        migration and economic activity in the Rhine Valley of Ger-
        many in the 17th and 18th centuries. "Anhang 1: Namenver-
        zeichnis" (p. 310-451) an alphabetical name-listing, gives
        dates and some brief biographical data for many of the entries.

9126   NEKROLOGE AUS DEM RHEINISCH-WESTFÄLISCHEN INDUS-
            TRIEGEBIET. Essen, Essener Verlagsanstalt, 1940-55.
        2 v. ports. 22-24cm. (Schriften der Volks- und Betriebs-
        wirtschaftlichen Vereinigung im Rheinisch-Westfälischen In-
        dustriegebiet, n. F., Heft 4, 16) Contents.--Bd. 1. 1937 &
        1938. Bearb. von Walter Bacmeister.--Bd. 2. 1939-51. Bearb.
        von Fritz Pudor (Düsseldorf, A. Bagel) Necrologies from the in-
        dustrial region of the Rhine Valley and Westphalia. Alphabeti-
        cally arranged within each year. Vol. 2 has title: Lebensbilder
        aus dem rheinisch-westfälischen Industriegebiet.

Saar Valley

9127   RAUMER, KURT VON, 1900-
        Saarpfälzische Lebensbilder. Hrsg. im Auftrag der Pfäl-
        zischen Gesellschaft zur Förderung der Wissenschaften von Kurt
        von Raumer und Kurt Baumann. Bd. 1: 990-1901. Kaiser-
        slautern, Verlag der Pfälzischen Gesellschaft zur Förderung
        der Wissenschaften, 1938. v, 245 p. 23cm. Arranged by date
        of birth. No more published? Lives of famous personages of
        the Saar Valley-Palatinate.

9128   SAARLAND. LANDTAG.
        Handbuch. [Neuauflage. Saarbrücken] 1971-   1 v.
        (loose-leaf) ports. 19cm. Handbook for the Legislature of the
        Saarland. "Teil H" (p. 431-484) comprises a biographical dic-
        tionary of representatives to the Landtag and ministers of the
        government of the Saarland (53 in all)

Saxony

9129   VOLGER, BRUNO, 1875-   ed.
        Sachsens Gelehrte, Künstler und Schriftsteller im Wort und
        Bild. [Leipzig?] 1907-08. 2 v. ports. A biographical diction-
        ary, with many portraits, of Saxony's famous scholars, artists
        and authors. This work is listed in Kosch's Deutsches Litera-
        tur-Lexikon (2d ed., v. 4, under Volger) but is not mentioned in

the standard trade bibliographies. The Deutsches Museum,
Munich, owns a copy.

Schleswig-Holstein

9130   SCHLESWIG (CITY) SCHLESWIG-HOLSTEINISCHES LANDES-
        MUSEUM.
        Schleswig-holsteinische Porträts. Neuerwerbungen für die
        Porträtsammlung des Schleswig-Holsteinischen Landesmuseums
        seit 1964. Ausstellung, 31. 1.-7.3. 1971. [Katalog: Paul Zu-
        bek] Schleswig [1971] 53 p. illus., ports. 21cm. Some 60
        portraits (with biographical data) of persons prominent in the
        history and culture of Schleswig-Holstein, as well as a number
        of unknown individuals.

9131   SCHLESWIG-HOLSTEINISCHES BIOGRAPHISCHES LEXIKON.
        Hrsg. im Auftrage der Gesellschaft für Schleswig-Holstein-
        ische Geschichte von Olaf Klose. Neumünster, K. Wachholtz,
        1970-   v. ports. 24cm. Biographical dictionary of
        Schleswig-Holstein. 3 vols. have appeared thus far (1970-74)
        Each vol. is a biographical dictionary, A-Z.

Westphalia

9132   WEGMANN, DIETRICH
        Die leitenden staatlichen Verwaltungsbeamten der Provinz
        Westfalen, 1815-1918. Münster in Westf., Aschendorff, 1969.
        xv, 352 p. 24cm. (Geschichtliche Arbeiten zur westfälischen
        Landesforschung. Wirtschafts- und sozialgeschichtliche Gruppe,
        Bd. 1) (Veröffentlichungen der Historischen Kommission West-
        falens, 22a) Leading government officials in the Province of
        Westphalia from 1815 to 1918; a biographical dictionary of 252
        administrative officials is to be found on pages 239-351.

9133   WESTFÄLISCHE LEBENSBILDER. Im Auftrage der Historischen
        Kommission des Provinzialinstituts für Westfälische Landes-
        und Volkskunde. Münster, Aschendorffsche Verlagsbuchhand-
        lung, 1930-70. 10 v. illus. 23cm. Lives of famous West-
        phalians. Vols. 1-5 contain ca. 20-25 biographies each; v. 6-
        10, ca. 10 biographies to a volume. 10 vols. issued up to 1970.

Wurttemberg

9134   BERNHARDT, WALTER
        Die Zentralbehörden des Herzogtums Württemberg und ihre
        Beamten 1520-1629. Stuttgart, W. Kohlhammer, 1972. 2 v.
        (xxxii, 1070 p.) 23cm. (Veröffentlichungen der Kommission
        für Geschichtliche Landeskunde in Baden-Württemberg. Reihe
        B: Forschungen, Bd. 70-71) An enlargement of the author's

thesis, Tübingen, 1970. Government officials of the Duchy of Württemberg, 1520-1629; a major portion of the work is a biographical dictionary.

Wuppertal

9135   STRUTZ, EDMUND
        Die Ahnentafeln der Elberfelder Bürgermeister und Stadt-
richter von 1708-1808. 2. Aufl. Neustadt an der Aisch, Verlag
Degener, Inhaber Gerhard Gessner, 1963. 231 p. ports., fold.
table (in pocket) 25cm. (Bergische Forschungen, Bd. 3) Genealogy of the mayors and city magistrates of Elberfeld (now part
of the city of Wuppertal) 1708-1808; contains portraits and biographical material on 83 officials. Chronological arrangement
(by date of entry into office).

GHANA

9136   THE DIPLOMATIC PRESS GHANA TRADE DIRECTORY. 1st-
            1959-   London, Diplomatic Press and Pub. Co.
    v. illus., ports. 23-29cm. Title varies slightly. Cover
title: 1959, Directory of Ghana--1960-61/62, Directory of the
Republic of Ghana.--1964, Trade directory of the Republic of
Ghana.--1967-   Ghana trade directory. The issues for 1960
and 1961-62 include biographical sections of a who's who type,
with ca. 200 biographies in each, i.e. biographical sketches of
persons who were prominent in Ghana at the time the directory
was issued.

9137   GHANA WHO'S WHO. Accra, Bartels Publications (Ghana)
        Ltd.   v. illus. 25cm. Annual. Began 1972/73?

GREAT BRITAIN

Bibliography, Indexes, Portrait Catalogs

9138   BATTS, JOHN STUART
        British manuscript diaries of the nineteenth century; an
annotated listing. Totowa, N. J., Rowman and Littlefield, 1976.
xi, 345 p. 23cm. Supplements William Matthews British di-
aries; an annotated bibliography, 1442-1942. Includes brief
identifying data for autobiographees.

9139   [EVANS, EDWARD]
        Catalogue ... London, E. Evans, 1836-53. 2 v. 22cm.
Vol. 2 has imprint: London, A. E. Evans. Contents.—v. 1.
Catalogue of a collection of engraved portraits ... comprising
nearly twenty thousand portraits of persons connected with the

history and literature of this country ... with an enumeration of
the circumstances connecting the most eminent persons with the
various counties of Great Britain, preferably of the clergy ...
Alphabetically arranged ... --v. 2. Catalogue of engraved portraits, comprising thirty thousand portraits of persons connected
with the history and literature of Great Britain, the British colonies and the United States of America, accompanied by concise
biographical notices. A sales catalog of nearly 20,000 prints.
The biographical notices are very brief.

9140   HAMILTON, EDWARD, 1824-1899.
        The engraved works of Sir Jushua Reynolds; a catalogue
raisonné of the engravings made after his paintings from 1755-
1822, with descriptions of the states of each plate, biographical
sketches of the persons represented, a list of pictures which
have been engraved, names of the possessors, and other particulars. New, enl. ed. with addition of plates and an index.
Amsterdam, G. W. Hissink [1973] vi, 200 p. illus. 23cm.
[Scripta artis monographia, 15) Reprint of the London, 1884 ed.,
published under title: A catalogue raisonné of the engraved works
of Sir Joshua Reynolds. The biographical notes (covering ca.
400 persons) are arranged in 2 alphabets: pt. 1, Male portraits &
pt. 2, Female portraits--and serve as a type of biographical dictionary of prominent British of the 18th century.

9141   HEPWORTH, PHILIP
        Select biographical sources: the Library Association manu-
scripts survey. London, Library Association, 1971. 154 p.
illus. 30cm. (Library Association research publications, 5)
"Entries represent material relating to 3,135 persons (chiefly
British, some Americans, etc.) in 231 repositories; a finding
list of manuscripts containing information of a biographical nature."

9142   LONDON. NATIONAL PORTRAIT GALLERY.
        Concise catalogue, 1856-1969; edited and arranged by Mau-
reen Hill. London, National Portrait Gallery, 1970. v, 346 p.
21cm. An index to the collection of British portraits in the Gallery; includes sitters' birth/death dates and phrases descriptive
of occupation, etc.

9143   REEL, JEROME V
        Index to biographies of Englishmen, 1000-1485, found in
dissertations and theses [by] Jerome V. Reel, Jr. Westport,
Conn., Greenwood Press [1975] xiii, 689 p. 25cm. An index
to biographical data about "obscure persons" in British history;
sheriffs, gentry, members of episcopal households, etc. found
in theses accepted in Great Britain, Canada and the United
States between 1930 and 1970.

General Works

9144   BAILEY, CONRAD
        Harrap's guide to famous London graves. With a foreword
        by John Betjeman. Photos. by Philip Sayer. London, Harrap,
        1975. 157 p. illus. 20cm. Includes biographical data about
        various famous Britons buried in London.

9145   CAMBRIDGE. UNIVERSITY. KING'S COLLEGE.
        A register of admission to King's College, Cambridge,
        1945-1970. Compiled with short biographical notes by R. H.
        Bulmer and L. P. Wilkinson for the King's College Association.
        London, King's College Association, 1973. vi, 387 p. 23cm.
        Contains 3,381 brief biographical sketches; arrangement is al-
        phabetical under year of entry into the College. Alphabetical
        name index at end of volume.

9146   CAMBRIDGE. UNIVERSITY. PETERHOUSE.
        Admissions to Peterhouse in the University of Cambridge,
        January 1931-December 1950; a register consisting of abstracts
        from the College Historical registers, supplemented by informa-
        tion from other sources, compiled by the late Evelyn Ansell.
        With a pref. by Sir Herbert Butterfield. Cambridge, Peter-
        house, 1971. xxxixm, 292 p. 27cm. Biographical sketches ar-
        ranged by year; alphabetical approach through index.

9147   CAPP, B   S
        The Fifth Monarchy men; a study in seventeenth-century
        English Millenarianism. London, Faber and Faber, 1972.
        315 p. 22cm. "Biographical appendix" (p. 239-270) is a biogra-
        phical dictionary of English millenialists (many of them quite
        obscure) from the Reformation to the 1680's.

9148   THE COMPACT EDITION OF THE DICTIONARY OF NATIONAL
        BIOGRAPHY. Complete text reproduced micrographically.
        London, Oxford University Press, 1975. 2 v. (3149 p.) 31cm.
        "Includes the complete and unaltered text of the 22 volumes of
        the main D. N. B. and of the six volumes which make up the
        twentieth-century D. N. B." In slip case.

9149   DASENT, ARTHUR IRWIN, 1859-1939.
        The speakers of the House of Commons from the earliest
        times to the present day ... With notes on the illus. by John
        Lane & a portrait of every speaker where one is known to exist.
        London, New York, J. Lane, 1911. xl, 455 p. illus., ports.
        22cm. "Catalogue of speakers, from the earliest times to the
        present day, with the places they sat for, the dates of their ap-
        pointment to and close of office, etc.": p. [341]-415. Contains
        ca. 90 portraits of speakers, clerks, etc. of the House of Com-
        mons. Biographical material is scattered thru' text and must
        be approached thru' index.

9150   THE DIPLOMATIC SERVICE LIST. 1966-   London, H. M.
        Stationery Off.   v. 22cm.   annual.   Supersedes in part
        the Foreign Office list and the Commonwealth Relations Office
        yearbook. Issued by the Diplomatic Service Administration Of-
        fice of Great Britain. Includes biographical sketches of mem-
        bers of the British diplomatic and consular service; e.g., in the
        1973 edition—"Biographical list": p. 155-472.

9151   DODWELL, EDWARD, 1767-1832.
        Alphabetical list of the Honourable East India Company's
        ... civil servants ... London, Longman, Orme, Brown, 1839.
        3 v.   Contents. --[1] Bengal, from the year 1780 to the year 1838.
        --[2] Bombay, from the year 1798, to the year 1839.   Distin-
        guishing, with dates, the several high and important offices
        held by them during their official career; also the dates of their
        retirement, resignation, or death, to which is attached a list of
        the Governors of Bombay from the year 1773, to the year 1839.
        --[3] Madras, 1780 to 1839.

9152   EMDEN, ALFRED BROTHERSTON, 1888-
        A biographical register of the University of Oxford, A. D.
        1501 to 1540. Oxford, Clarendon Press, 1974. xxiv, 742 p.
        24cm.

9153   ETON COLLEGE.
        The Eton College register; alphabetically arranged and
        edited with biographical notes. Eton, Spottiswoode, Ballantyne,
        1921-43. 3 v. 24cm. Contents. —[1] 1441-1698, by Sir W.
        Sterry. --[2] 1698-1752, by R. A. Austen-Leigh. --[3] 1753-1790,
        by R. A. Austen-Leigh.

9154   [FINDEN, WILLIAM, 1787-1852.
        Portraits of the female aristocracy of the court of Queen
        Victoria. London, J. Hogarth, 1849. 2 v. ports. 36cm. Each
        portrait accompanied by a biographical notics.

9155   FRY, PETER GEORGE ROBIN SOMERSET, 1931-1973.
        They made history: great men and women from Britain's
        past [by] Plantagenet Somerset Fry [pseud.] Colour illus.
        by Michael Whittlesea [and others] London, New York, Hamlyn,
        1970. 237 p. col. illus., col. ports. 29cm. Profiles of 270
        British men and women whose significant contributions to their
        country were also important to the general welfare and advance-
        ment of mankind.

9156   THE GALLERY OF ONE HUNDRED FAMOUS PORTRAITS OF
        GREAT MEN AND WOMEN. First [-fourth] series. Lon-
        don, Museum Galleries, 1923-29. 4 portfolios of col. portraits.
        60cm. Each portrait accompanied by leaf of descriptive letter-
        press. British portraits.

9157   GUIDE TO THE HOUSE OF COMMONS. 1970-   London,
          Times Newspapers, ltd.   v. ports. 26cm. At head of
          title, 1970-   : The Times. Supersedes: The Times, London.
          House of Commons, with full results of the polling, biographies
          of members and unsuccessful candidates ... (q. v., main vol.,
          1967).

9157a   HUGGETT, FRANK EDWARD
          A dictionary of British history, 1815-1973. Oxford [Eng.]
          Blackwell, 1974. x, 297 p. 24cm. "This dictionary gives a
          comprehensive coverage to the main personalities, the events
          and the trends in the different fields of British history during
          the last 150 years."--Book jacket.

9158   [KIMBER, EDWARD] 1719-1769.
          The new peerage; or, Ancient and present state of the no-
          bility of England, Scotland and Ireland. Containing a genealogi-
          cal account of all the peers, together with their paternal coats
          of arms. To which is added, the extinct peerage, comprehend-
          ing an authentic account of all the peers who have ever existed
          from the earliest times. 2d ed. London, W. Owen, 1778. 3 v.
          coats of arms. 19cm. A revised ed. of the author's The peer-
          age of England (1766), The peerage of Scotland (1767) and The
          peerage of Ireland (1768)

9159   KINNEY, ARTHUR F   1933-
          Titled Elizabethans; a directory of Elizabethan state and
          church officers and knights, with peers of England, Scotland,
          and Ireland, 1558-1603. [Hamden, Conn.] Archon Books, 1973.
          ix, 89 p. port. 23cm. The primary value of this work lies in
          its "British peers during Elizabeth's reign" (p. 25-63) an al-
          phabetical listing, by title, which does include brief biographical
          notes for many of the peers and indicates which titles lapsed.

9160   KNAPP, ANDREW
          The new Newgate calendar; being interesting memoirs of
          notorious characters, who have been convicted of outrages on the
          laws of England, during the eighteenth century, brought down to
          the present time. Chronologically arranged ... With occas-
          ional essays on crimes and punishments, original anecdotes and
          observations on particular cases; the speeches, confessions,
          and last exclamations of sufferers, to which is added a correct
          account of the various modes of punishment of criminals in dif-
          ferent parts of the world. By Andrew Knapp and William Bald-
          win. London, J. Robins [1826?] 6 v. illus., ports. 22cm.
          Subtitle varies slightly. Biographies of numerous criminals of
          the 17th and to the early 19th centuries in Great Britain. Each
          volume (with possible exception of v. 1) is separately indexed;
          the indexes must be used for an alphabetical approach to the bi-
          ographies. See also note under: Wilkinson, G. T. The Newgate
          calendar improved.

9161   LIVES OF THE STUART AGE, 1603-1714. Compiled by
              Laurence Urdang Associates. Editor, Edwin Riddell;
        managing editor, Patrick Hanks. Lonson : Osprey Pub. Ltd.,
        1976. xi, 500 p. ports. 24cm. First published vol. in a
        series of period-by-period dictionaries of English biography;
        322 major personalities are presented.

9162   LLOYD, DAVID, 1635-1692.
              State-worthies; or, The statesmen and favourites of Eng-
        land ... 2d ed. London, Printed by T. Milbourn for S. Speed,
        1670. 1051, [4] p. 17cm. First ed. published in 1665 with title:
        The statesmen and favourites of England since the Reformation.
        Contains well over a 100 biographies arranged by reign: Henry
        VIII through Charles I.

9163   LONDON. NATIONAL PORTRAIT GALLERY.
              Early Victorian portraits [by] Richard Ormond. London,
        H. M. Stationery Off., 1973. 2 v. ports. 29cm. Contents. --
        v. 1. Text. --v. 2. Plates. The text volume includes brief bio-
        graphical data for the over 500 portrait sitters active in Great
        Britain between the years 1830-1860. The 2d volume contains
        the portraits catalogued in detail in the text volume.

9164   LUMMIS, WILLIAM MURRELL.
              Honour the Light Brigade : a record of the services of offi-
        cers, non-commissioned officers and men of the five Light Cav-
        alry Regiments, which made up the Light Brigade at Balaclava
        on October 25th 1854 and saw service in the Crimea from Septem-
        ber 1854 to the end of the war, by William Murrell Lummis ; edi-
        ted, arranged and additional material supplied by Kenneth G.
        Wynn. London, J. B. Hayward, 1973. 320 p., [16] p. of plates.
        illus., ports. 26cm. Includes biographical data for British sol-
        diers of the Light Cavalry Regiments in the Crimean War from
        1854 to 1856.

9165   MANWARING, GEORGE ERNEST, 1882-
              A bibliography of British naval history; a biographical and
        historical guide to printed and manuscript sources. London, G.
        Routledge, 1930. xxii, 163 p. 24cm. A guide to naval material
        (essays) in books, in periodicals and magazines, in transactions
        of learned societies, in manuscripts in various archives, and in
        publications of the Navy Records Society. Not a guide to individ-
        ual books. Includes brief biographical data for British naval fig-
        ures. Contents. --pt. 1. Authors. --pt. 2. Subjects.

9166   THE MAYORS OF ENGLAND AND WALES; with portraits of
              mayors and mayoresses, 1902. Coronation year, King Ed-
        ward VII. Brighton, W. T. Pike [1902] 632 p. ports. 22cm.
        Edited by F. A. Barnes (?)

9167   MILLAR, OLIVER, 1923-
         The later Georgian pictures in the collection of Her Majesty
the Queen. [London] Phaidon Press [1969] 2 v. illus., ports.
31cm. Contents. —[1] Text. --[2] Plates. Yields biographical
data and portraits for sitters (chiefly British) and biographical
facts for the portrait-painters. There is an index of portraits,
subjects (sitters), etc. at the end of vol. 1.

9168   PINE, LESLIE GILBERT
         The new extinct peerage, 1884-1971. Containing extinct,
abeyant, dormant & suspended peerages with genealogies and
arms. Baltimore, Genealogical Pub. Co. , 1973. xxv, 313 p.
illus. 25cm. Includes substantial biographical material for last
surviving members of British peerages which have recently be-
come extinct. Forms a continuation of J. B. Burke's A genealogical history of the dormant, abeyant, forfeited, and extinct
peerages of the British Empire (new ed. , 1883).

9169   POTTED BIOGRAPHIES; a dictionary of anti-national biography.
         4th ed. London, Boswell Print. & Pub. Co. [foreword
1930] 127, 10 p. 22cm. A biographical dictionary of British
socialists, 'anti-establishment' figures, etc. of the period (1st
third of the 20th century).

9170   ROTH, ANDREW
         The business background of M. P. s. 1972 ed. by Andrew
Roth and Janice Kerbey. London, Parliamentary Profile Services, 1972. [4], xii, 494 p. facsims., port. 23cm. (Parliamentary profiles) First published in 1957 under title: The business background of members of Parliament. In biographical dictionary format; contains interesting biographical data for members of the present House of Commons, but not birth dates or
education.

9171   [RYALL, HENRY THOMAS] 1811-1867.
         Portraits of eminent conservatives and statesmen, with
genealogical and historical memoirs. 1st[-2d] series. London,
G. Virtue [1836-46?] 2 v. 72 ports. 36 x 26cm. British
statesmen of the 19th century, with 72 portraits.

9172   SEDGWICK, ROMNEY, 1894-
         The House of Commons, 1715-1754; the history of Parlia-
ment. New York, Published for the History of Parliament Trust
by Oxford University Press, 1970. 2 v. illus. 25cm. At head
of title: The history of Parliament. "Members, A-D" (v. 1, p.
405-630) and "Members, E-Y" (all of vol. 2) is a biographical
dictionary.

9173   TAYLOR, WILLIAM COOKE, 1800-1849.
         The National portrait gallery of illustrations and eminent

personages, chiefly of the nineteenth century, with memoirs by
W. C. Taylor. London [1846-48] 4 v. illus., ports. 4.º
British portraits.

9175   THOMPSON, GODFREY
        London's statues. [London] J. M. Dent [1971] 126 p.
        illus. 13 x 19cm. Description of 95 statues in London erected
        in honor of famous men and women (chiefly British) accompanied
        by biographical sketches.

9176   WILKINSON, GEORGE THEODORE
        The Newgate calendar improved; being interesting memoirs
        of notorious characters who have been convicted of offences
        against the laws of England, during the seventeenth century; and
        continued to the present time, chronologically arranged ... Lon-
        don, Printed for T. Kelly [ca. 1821-24?] 6 v. illus., ports.
        22cm. The first three volumes especially include numerous bi-
        ographies of British criminals of the 17th to the early 19th cen-
        turies. Each volume is separately indexed; the indexes must be
        used for an alphabetical approach to the biographies. The first
        3 volumes contain many of the same biographies (in the same
        words) as Knapp and Baldwin's The new Newgate calendar (q. v.).

9178   Y. M. C. A. WHO'S WHO AND ANNUAL. London, Shaw Pub.
        Co., 1934. 128 p. 8.º The Young Men's Christian As-
        sociation in Great Britain; officials, etc. No more published?

Local

Bedfordshire

Bibliography, Indexes, Portrait Catalogs

9179   CONISBEE, LEWIS RALPH
        A Bedfordshire bibliography, with some comments and bio-
        graphical notes [by] L. R. Conisbee. [Luton?] Bedfordshire
        Historical Record Society, 1962. 333 p. 35cm.

        ---- ----1967 supplement. [Luton?] Bedfordshire Historical
        Record Society, 1967. 85 p. 24cm. "Biography" (main work,
        p. 219-314 & supplement, p. 67-80) lists collective and individ-
        ual biographies. Under the individual biographical references
        are often given brief biographical data for the individuals listed.

Berkshire

9180   GRANT, JOHN, historian
        Berkshire and Oxfordshire: historical, biographical and
        pictorial. London, London & Provincial Pub. Co., 1912. 1 v.
        (unpaged) illus., ports.

Buckinghamshire

9181   GRANT, JOHN, historian
          Buckinghamshire: a short history, with genealogies and current biographies. Published only for subscribers. London, London & Provincial Pub. Co., 1911. 2 v. illus., ports. Cover title: Buckinghamshire and some neighbouring records, historical, biographical and pictorial.

Devon

9182   GASKELL, ERNEST
          Devonshire leaders: social and political. London, Queenhithe Print. and Pub. Co. [1907] 1 v. (unpaged) ports. 28cm.

East Anglia

9183   SMITH-DAMPIER, JOHN LUCIUS
          East Anglian worthies. Oxford, B. Blackwell, 1949. xiv, 210 p. 23cm. Two hundred biographical sketches of persons of varying importance in the history of East Anglia (Norfolk and Suffolk); each sketch occupies a single page.

Essex

9184   ADDISON, WILLIAM, 1905-
          Essex worthies; a biographical companion to the county. London, Phillimore, 1973. [7], 212 p., [5] p. of plates. ports. 23cm. A biographical dictionary.

9185   GASKELL, WILLIAM
          Essex leaders (social and political, by William Gaskell and C. A. M. Press) London, Queenhithe Print. & Pub. Co. [19--?] 1 v. (unpaged) ports. 28cm.

9186   THE LIVES OF EMINENT & REMARKABLE CHARACTERS,
          born or long resident in the counties of Essex, Suffolk, & Norfolk. Embellished with 68 portraits. London, Printed for Longman, Hurst, Rees, Orme, and Brown [etc.] 1820. [140] p. 68 ports.

Guernsey

9187   WHO'S WHO IN GUERNSEY. 1937-   Jersey, 1938-
          v. No more published?

Herefordshire

9188   HEREFORDSHIRE PORTRAITS (past and present) illustrated by
            reproductions from photographs of Herefordshire men or
        men connected with Herefordshire. Hereford, Jakeman and Car-
        ver, 1908. 1 v. ports. 32cm.

Ipswich

9189   WHO'S WHO IN IPSWICH. London, Pullman Press [1960]
            89 p. 22cm. (Pullman biographical series)

Jersey

9190   WHO'S WHO IN JERSEY. 1937-   Jersey, 1938-
            v. No more published?

Lancashire

9191   GASKELL, ERNEST
            Lancashire leaders: social and political. London, Queen-
        hithe Print. and Pub. Co. [190-?] 1 v. (unpaged) ports. 28cm.
        Privately printed.

Liverpool

9192   "IN MEMORIAM;" or, Funeral records of Liverpool celebrities.
            Containing many interesting reminiscences of local men ...
        Liverpool, A. Bowker, 1876. 13 1., 272 p. 22cm.

London

9193   LEADING MEN OF LONDON: a collection of biographical ske-
            tches. London, British Biographical Co., 1895. xii, 444 p.
        port. 32cm. Contemporary biography; outstanding Londoners at
        the end of the 19th century.

Norfolk

Bibliography, Indexes, Portrait Catalogs

9194   RYE, WALTER, 1843-1929.
            A short list of works relating to the biographies of Norfolk
        men and women ... preserved in the Free Library, at Norwich.
        Norwich [Eng.] 1908. 34 p. 8.º

General Works

9195   GASKELL, ERNEST
       Norfolk leaders, social and political. London, Queenhithe
Print. and Pub. Co. [190-?] 1 v. (unpaged) ports. 28cm.
"Published solely for private circulation."

Northamptonshire

9196   GASKELL, ERNEST
       Northamptonshire leaders, social and political. London,
Queenhithe Print. and Pub. Co. [190-?] 1 v. (unpaged) ports.
28cm. "Published solely for private circulation."

9197   WHO'S WHO IN NORTHAMPTON. London, Pullman Press
       [1961] 85 p. 22cm. (Pullman biographical series)

Norwich

9198   COZENS-HARDY, BASIL
       The mayors of Norwich, 1403-1835; being biographical
notes on the mayors of the old corporation, by Basil Cozens-
Hardy and Ernest A. Kent. Norwich [Eng.] Jarrold, 1938.
188 p. ports. 26cm.

9199   WHO'S WHO IN NORWICH. London, Pullman Press [1961]
       105 p. 22cm. (Pullman biographical series)

Nottingham

9200   MELLORS, ROBERT, 1835-
       Men of Nottingham and Nottinghamshire. [Being biographi-
cal notes of five hundred men and women who were born, or
worked, or abode, or died in the County or City of Nottingham,
and who, in some way, were distinguished for usefulness to
others] Wakefield, Eng.] Republished by S. R. Publishers,
1969. viii, 368 p. 20cm. [County history reprints] First published in 1924 by J. & H. Bell, printers, Nottingham.

Reading

9201   WHO'S WHO IN READING. London, Pullman Press [1960]
       74 p. 22cm. (Pullman biographical series) Biographi-
cal dictionary of the City of Reading, England.

Somerset

9202   HUMPHREYS, ARTHUR LEE, 1865-1946.
        The Somerset roll; an experimental list of worthies, un-
        worthies and villains born in the county. Compiled by A. L.
        Humphreys. London, Strangeways, 1897. 124 p. 27cm.

Warwickshire

9203   GASKELL, WILLIAM
        Warwickshire leaders: social and political, by William
        Gaskell and George Pickwood. London, E. R. Alexander [1906]
        1 v. (unpaged) ports. 28cm.

Wiltshire

9204   JACKSON, JOHN EDWARD, 1805-1891
        A list of Wiltshire shefiffs. Devizes [Eng.] Printed by H.
        Bull, 1856. 47 p. 4.° Biographical data for sheriffs of the
        English county of Wiltshire.

Worcestershire

9205   GASKELL, ERNEST
        Worcestershire leaders: social and political. London,
        Queenhithe Print. and Pub. Co. [1920] 1 v. (unpaged) ports.
        28cm. "Published solely for private circulation. "

GREECE, ANCIENT

9206   BAUMEISTER, AUGUST, 1830-1922.
        Denkmäler des klassischen Altertums zur Erläuterung des
        Lebens der Griechen und Römer in Religion, Kunst und Sitte.
        Lexikalisch bearb. von B. Arnold [et al.] und dem Herausgeber
        A. Baumeister. München, R. Oldenbourg, 1885-88. 3 v. illus.
        27cm. A dictionary of classical antiquities with biographical
        sketches of Greek and Roman historical figures.

9207   DAVIES, J   K
        Athenian propertied families, 600-300 B. C. Oxford,
        Clarendon Press, 1971. xxi, 653 p. 24cm. "A selective bio-
        graphical dictionary" comprises the main portion of this work.
        "Rich families are entered under the name of their most promi-
        nent member (with extensive cross-referencing, and each entry
        sets out the available evidence for dates of births, marriages,
        and deaths, and for the changing extent and nature of family
        property and public disbursements. "--Book jacket.

9208   EFFIGIES VIRORUM AC FOEMINARUM ILLUSTRIUM, quibus
        in Graecis aut Latinis monumentis aliqua ... pars datur ...
        ex antiquis marmoribus ... numismatibus, gemmisque expres-
        sae ... A collection of 300 plates, first published with the The-
        saurus of J. Gronovius, now re-published by P. van der Aa.
        Lugduni Batavorum, P. van der Aa [1724?] 3 l., 311 plates.
        folio. First published in the 16th century? Portraits of famous
        men and women of the Classical (Greek & Roman) world.

9209   RADICE, BETTY
        Who's who in the ancient world; a handbook to the survivors
        of the Greek and Roman classics. Selected with an introd. by
        Betty Radice. Rev. [ed. Harmondsworth, Middlesex, Eng.,
        Baltimore] Penguin Books [1973] 336, [32] p. illus. 20cm.
        (Penguin reference books, R55) A dictionary of Greek and Ro-
        man personalities and of mythological characters. First edition
        →New York, Stein and Day, 1971, had collation: xlvi, 225 p.
        illus. 27cm.

9210   WOLOCH, MICHAEL
        Roman citizenship and the Athenian elite, A. D. 96-161.
        Two prosopographical catalogues. Amsterdam, Hakkert, 1973.
        xviii, 315 p. 23cm. The 1st prosopographical and alphabetical
        catalog includes biographical data for all Athenians with Roman
        citizenship, 96-161 A. D. The 2d: a selective group of Athenian
        holders of Roman and Athenian magistracies and priesthoods in
        the same period.

GREECE, MODERN

9211   CHIOTĒS, PANAGIOTES, 1814-1896.
        Historika apomnēmoneumata 'Eptanesou 'upo P. Hiotou
        Tomos 6os (seiras) Periechōn tēn ethikēn katastasin apo
        Benetokratias mechri tōn 'emeron 'emon. En Zakunthoi, Tupo-
        grafeion 'o Foskolos, 1887. 468 p. 23cm. Historical memoirs
        of the Ionian Islands. Famous men of the Islands, A-I (p. 285-
        453) Biographies for letters K-Z were issued in the periodical
        "Ai Mousai."

9212   GOUDAS, ANASTASIOS N   1816-1882.
        Vioi paralleloi tōn epi tēs anagennēseos tēs Hellados
        diaprepsantōn andrōn. 'Athenai, Týpois Ch. N. Philadelphéōs,
        1870-76 [v. 1, 1872. Athenai, Phototypiche anatyposis B. N.
        Grēgoriádēs, 1971] 8 v. ports. 22cm. A collective biographi-
        cal work on modern Greece with ca. 100 lives (usually accom-
        panied by portraits).

9213   MAZARAKĒS, ANTHIMOS
        Biografiai tōn endoxon andron tēs nēsou Kefallenias. En
        Benetia, Ek tēs Ellenikes Tupografias tou Foinikos, 1843. [15],
        672 p. 21cm. Biographies of illustrious men of the Island of

Cephalonia. Arranged by type of activity: scholars, politicians
and soldiers.

9214   THŌMOPOULOS, SŌZ
        Korinthiako biografiko leksiko. Athenai, Tupois "Nik.
        Izitze, " 1969-   v. 24cm. Biographical dictionary
        of Corinth, Greece. Vol. 1 (54 p. —A-O).

9215   TSITSELĒS, ELIAS A
        Symbolai eis tēn istorian kai laograffan tēs nēsou Kefal-
        lenias. Tomos A. En Athenais, Tupois Paraskeua Leone, 1904.
        xx, 940 p. 24cm. Contributions to the history and folklore of
        the Island of Cephalonia. Part 1 (p. 1-842) includes biographies
        and the history of families.

9216   ZOES, LEŌNIDAS CH
        Lexikon istorikon kai laografikon Zakunthou. Tomos A :
        Istorikon-biografikon. Athenai, Ek tou Ethnikou Tupografeiou,
        1963. 709, [5], i' p. 25cm. Historical and folkloric dictionary
        of the Island of Zante. Vol. A: Historical-biographical. A 2d
        ed., complete and posthumous.

9217   ZOLOTAS, GEORGIOS I
        Istorike topografia kai genealogia. Suntahtheisa epimeleia
        tēs thugatros autou Aimilias K. Sarrou kai ekdotheisa tej
        frontidi F. P. Argente, L. M. Kalbokorese, D. P. Petrokok-
        kinou kai tej horegiaj filopatridon kai filomouson Hion en te
        Aggliaj kai allahou. Athenai, Tupois P. D. Sakellariou, 1921-
        28. 3 v. in 4. 24cm. History of the Island of Chios, with his-
        torical topography and genealogy. Includes biographical notices
        under the names of the families. British Museum gives title
        as: Istoria tēs Chios ... Suntahtheisa epimeleia tēs Thugatros
        aytoy.

GUATEMALA

9218   MOORE, RICHARD E   1932-
        Historical dictionary of Guatemala. Rev. ed. Metuchen,
        N. J., Scarecrow Press, 1973. 285 p. 23cm. (Latin Ameri-
        can historical dictionaries, no. 1) Includes many biographical
        sketches of Guatemalans important in the development of the
        country. First edition (187 p.) issued in 1967.

HUNGARY

9219   BUDAPEST LEXIKON. Szerkesztő bizottság: Bernat György,
        Berza László, főszerkesztő [et al.] 1335 p. illus., ports.
        25cm. Dictionary of Budapest; includes biographies of persons
        prominent in the history and culture of the city.

9220   FEKETE, MÁRTON
            Prominent Hungarians: home and abroad. London, Fehér
        Hollo Press, 1973. 480 p. 22cm. A biographical dictionary of
        contemporary Hungarians in Hungary and those in foreign coun-
        tries.

9221   KI KICSODA?   Életrajzi lexikon magyar és külföldi személyisé-
            gekröl, kortársainkról. [Szerk.: Fonó Györgyné] 2. átdolg.
        bőv. kiad. [Budapest] Kossuth Könyvkiadó, 1972. 611 p. 25cm.
        A who's who. Biography of Hungarian contemporaries; includes
        some world coverage. 1st ed. appeared in 1969.

9222   PAYER, HUGÓ
            Bibliotheca Carpatica. A Magyarországi Kárpátegylet
        megbizásából összeálliótotta Payer Hugó.   Igló, Schmidt J.,
        1880. 378 p. 23cm. A bio-bibliographical handbook on the
        lives & works of persons prominent in the cultural life of the
        Carpathian regions of Hungary in the latter part of the 19th cen-
        tury (now in Slovakia, Russia & Romania).

9223   RADISICS, ELEMÉR, 1884-
            Hungary; pictorial records of a thousand years. Budapest
        [Athenaeum] 1944. xv, 190 p. illus., ports. 27cm. French
        translation has title: La Hongrie millénaire. Includes ca. 120
        portraits of and paintings by Hungarian artists accompanied by
        biographical notes. Alphabetical approach available thru' index
        at end.

9224   REICH, IGNAZ
            Beth-El. Ehrentempel verdienter ungarischer Israeliten.
        2. verb. Aufl. Pest, Druck von A. Buczansky [1868?] 3 v.
        ports. 24cm. British Museum gives collation: 2 pts in 1 v.
        (573 p.) Temple of honor of meritorious Hungarian Jews. Ar-
        ranged more or less chronologically (18th & 19th centuries) Con-
        tents (alphabetical) at end of first two volumes. Contents (non-
        alphabetical) at beginning of vol. 3.

9225   [SZILÁGYI, SÁNDOR] 1827-1899.
            A Magyar forradalom férfiai 1848/9 bol. 2. átdolgozott
        kiadás. Pest, G. Heckenast, 1850. vi, 345 p. 22cm. Men of
        the Hungarian Revolution, 1848-1849. A series of biographical
        sketches arranged by profession; no index.

INDIA

General Works

9226   ABD AL-RAZZĀQ SAMSĀM AL-DAULAH SHĀH-NAVĀZ KHAN.
            The Maathir-ul-umara; being biographies of the Muhamma-

dan and Hindu officers of the Timurid sovereigns of India from
1500 to about 1780 A. D. 2d ed. Translated by H. Beveridge.
Rev., annotated and completed by Baini Prashad. Calcutta,
Baptist Mission Press, 1911-52. 2 v.   (Bibliotheca
Indica, no. 202) Also issued in earlier editions by the Asi-
atic Society (1888-96 and 1911 [v. 1 only?] under title: The
Massir al-umara or Maasiru-1-umarā.

9227   'ABDU LHA'Ī IBN FAKHRUDDĪN AL-HASANĪ, 1869-1923.
            Nuzhat al-khawātir ... Hyderabad, India. Osmania Ori-
        ental Publications Bureau, 1930-70. 8 v. in 5. 26cm.
        (Dāiratu'l-Ma'ārif-il-Osmania publications. New series, 10)
        Vols. 5-8 have added t. p.: Nuzhatu'l-khwātir, biographies of
        eminent Indians, by 'Abdu-1-Hayy b. Fākhru'd-Din al-Hasani
        (varies slightly) Biographies of eminent persons of India: schol-
        ars, political figures, writers, etc. of the Islamic faith.

9228   BHĀRATOKOSHA. Calcutta, Bangiya Sahitya Parishad,
            1964-   v. illus. 26cm. An encyclopedia of India,
        especially Bengal, with biographies of eminent deceased Indians
        and Bengalis. To be in 5 vols. (3 vols. issued as of 1967). In
        Bengali. Edited by Sushil Kumar De.

9229   BRITISH PEOPLE BOOK COMPANY.
            The Indian Empire Royal Book. Edited and compiled by
        Charles Feilden. [London, 1912?] 310 p. illus., ports. 32cm.
        Contains brief biographies and portraits of many of the native
        rulers of India. Includes advertising matter.

9230   CHITRAV, SIDDHESHVARSHASTRI VISHNU, 1894-
        _ Bhāratavarshīya arvācīna caritrakośa. Poona, Bhāratavar-
        sīya Caritrakośa Maṇḍala, 1946. 12, 600 p. 26cm. In Marathi.
        A dictionary of Indian biography (from 1818 to 1945).

9231   CHITRAV, SIDDHESHVARSHASTRI VISHNU, 1894-
        _ Bhāratavarshīya prācīna caritrakośa. Poona, Bhāratavar-
        shīya Caritrakośa Maṇḍal, 1964. 12, 1204 p. facsim. 25cm.
        In Hindi. A dictionary of ancient Indian biography (literary
        especially) translated from Marathi. Goes up to Chandragupta
        Maurya. The original Marathi work bore the title: Bhāratavar-
        shīya-madhyayugina-charitra-kosha. A multi-vulome edition
        was begun in 1968 (?)

9232   CURRENT AFFAIRS; India, Pakistan and the world, a year book
            and book of general knowledge. 1949-1963. Calcutta, A.
        Mukherji. 15 v. maps. 18cm. annual. Includes a section de-
        voted to a Who's who in India (as well as Pakistan in the earlier
        volumes) and Indian obituaries.

9233   DIRECTORY OF KEY PERSONNEL IN PUBLIC ENTERPRISES
        & 'WHO IS WHO' IN PUBLIC SECTOR. New Delhi, Standing
        Conference of Public Enterprises, 1975. viii, 283, B1-B52, A1-
        A52, 20 p. ports. 24cm. "Who is who in public sector" (p. B1-
        B52) comprises a biographical dictionary, with portraits, of
        leading figures in business enterprises of the Government of
        India.

9234   FAMOUS INDIA; nation's who's who. Ravi Bhushan, compiling
        editor. Delhi, Famous India Publications [pref. 1975]
        [40], 384 p. 22cm. Circa 1300 living Indians are presented;
        not in alphabetical arrangement, but there is an alphabetical
        name index at the front of the volume.

9235   GODBOLE, R   B
        Bharatvarshiya prachin aitihasik kosh. Poona, Chitrasala
        Press, 1928. 448 p. 2d ed.; 1st ed. issued in 1876. A diction-
        ary of ancient India. Includes biography. In Marathi.

9236   INDIA. INTELLIGENCE BUREAU.
        Politico-criminal who's who. Compiled in the Office of the
        Director, Criminal Intelligence. [n. p.]; Simla, G. M. Press,
        1914. 212 p. At head of title: Secret. Available in microfilm
        (made by the India Office Library) at the Center for Research
        Libraries, Chicago. A who's who of political agitators against
        British rule in India, compiled ca. the outbreak of the First
        World War.

9237   INDIA (REPUBLIC). MINISTRY OF INFORMATION AND BROAD-
        CASTING.
        Bhārata ke gaurava. Delhi, Publications Division, 1965-
        v. ports. 21cm. In Hindi. Biographies of celebrities of
        India. Five volumes published thus far, with ca. 20-25 biogra-
        phies per vol.

9238   INDIA (REPUBLIC). PARLIAMENT.
        Who's who. 1950. Delhi, Manager of Publications. 139 p.
        17cm. Superseded in 1952 by: India (Republic) Parliament.
        House of the People. Who's who and India (Republic) Parlia-
        ment. Council of States. Who's who. No more published?

9239   INDIA (REPUBLIC). PARLIAMENT. COUNCIL OF STATES.
        Who's who. 1952-   New Delhi, Rajya Sabha Secretariat.
        v. ports. 17cm. Supersedes in part: India (Republic) Par-
        liament. Who's who. Vols. for   issued by the Council
        under a variant name: Rajya Sabha.

9240   INDIA AT A GLANCE; twenty years of freedom, 1947-1967.
        Editor: Sudershan K. Savara. Editorial advisor: Attar

Singh. [New Delhi, Commercial Publications Bureau, 1967]
[336] p. col. map, ports. 26cm. Includes a who's who in India.

9241   THE INDIAN BIOGRAPHICAL DICTIONARY, 1915. Madras,
        Pillar [1916] 472 p. 8.° Circa 2,000 Europeans and Indians
        living at the time of the dictionary's compilation. Intended to be
        an annual, but this volume only was published. Edited by Con-
        jeevaram Hayavadana Rao.

9242   INDIAN WHO'S WHO, 1935. Bombay, 1935. xxxvi, 600 p. 8.°
        1,200 biographies of men and women of Indian or British
        descent. Edited by Warman (Vāmana) P. Kabadi.

9243   JEHANGIR, SORABJI, 1857-1916.
        Representative men of India; a collection of memoirs, with
        portraits of Indian princes, nobles, statesmen, philanthropists,
        officials, and eminent citizens. With an introd. by Sir George
        C. M. Birdwood. 2d ed. Bombay, Education Society's Press
        [1891] xvi, 172 p. ports. 38cm.

9244   KOTHARI, HEMRAJ, 1933-
        Who's who in India. Edited by H. Kothari. 1st ed. Cal-
        cutta, Kothari Publications, 1973. vii, 464 p. (p. 425-448 ad-
        vertisements) 23cm.

9245   KULKARNI, VASANT SITARAM, 1920-
        India's Parliament, 1971: who's who of Indian M. P.'s; en-
        cyclopaedia of India's Parliament, 1971. Editors: Vasant S.
        Kulkarni, Sunita Kulkarni [and] Prakash Kokil. [1st ed.] Poona,
        Law Book House [1971] 432, 93 p. illus. 19cm.

9246   KUNJUKRISHNAN, PALLIPATTU, 1905-
        Mahaccarita samgrahasāgaram. The great historical Indi-
        ans; a biographical dictionary. Alleppey, E. K. Raghu Rama
        Chandran, 1965-   v. 22cm. In Malayalam. Vols. 1-9
        published (to 1966). To be in 12 vols.

9247   KURIAN, GEORGE THOMAS.
        Historical and cultural dictionary of India. Metuchen, N. J.,
        Scarecrow Press, 1976. xxii, 306 p. map. 23cm. (Historical
        & cultural dictionaries of Asia, no. 8) There are over 2,000
        entries in the dictionary; something less than a quarter of them
        are biographical.

9248   MAKERS OF MODERN INDIA. [Text and sketches by A. K.
        Gupta, Z. A. Nizami, N. N. Nagaraj] 2d rev. ed. New
        Delhi, Indian Council of Historical Research; distributors: Thom-

son Press (India); Delhi, Publication Division, 1974, c1973. xiv,
125 p. [14] leaves of plates. 21 x 28cm. Contains ca. 170 brief
biographical sketches and many portraits of India's leaders in
its struggle for independence (19th-20th centuries). Topical arrangement: e. g., The pioneers, The moderates, The extremists,
Thinkers and philosophers, etc., etc.

9249   RAMA RAO, T   V
        India at a glance (a comprehensive reference book on India)
by G. D. Binani, managing editor and T. V. Rama Rao, editor.
Compiled by Binani Printers ltd. [Calcutta] Orient Longmans
[1953] 1896 p. illus., ports. 28cm. Includes biographical
sections, e. g.: House of the People (Lok Sabha) who is who,
biographical sketches of ministers of the various states, a general Who is who (in India).

9250   RĀMĀRĀVU, PADĀLA, 1924-
        Bhārata svātantrya sāyudha samara caritra. Rajahmundry,
Andhrasri Publications, 1966-67. 3 v. in 2. 19cm. Brief biographies of those who lost their lives in India's independence
movements. In Telugu. Contents.--1. 1757.--2. 1857.--3.
1947.

9251   REFERENCE GUIDE OF INDIA (Who's who) incorporating Men
        of library science in India (III), Men of science & technology
in India (III), Men of education in India (III). v. 1-   1973-
New Delhi, Premier Publishers (India)   v. ports. 24cm.
annual/irregular. A who's who type of publication for contemporary educators, etc. in India. Vol. 1-   edited by Raj J.
Khosla.

9252   SEN, SIBA PADA, 1915-
        Dictionary of national biography. Edited by S. P. Sen, di-
rector, Institute of Historical Studies. Calcutta, Institute of
Historical Studies, 1972-74. 4 v. 25cm. A dictionary of biography for India, covering the period 1800-1947; includes biographies of ca. 1400 persons. Modeled after the British Dictionary
of national biography. Contents.--v. 1. A-D.--v. 2. E-L.--v.
3. M-R.--v. 4. S-Z.

9253   SHĀHID HUSAINI
        Amar jivan. Hyderabad, Anjumane-Taraqui-e-Urdu;
Andhra Pradesh, 1964-67. 2 v. in 1. ports. 19cm. Vol. 2 by
Mir Hasan. Biographical sketches of prominent Indians, chiefly
politicians, of the 19th & 20th centuries. In Urdu.

9254   SHARMA, JAGDISH SARAN, 1924-
        Encyclopaedia of India's struggle for freedom. Foreword
by Shriman Narayan. [1st ed.] New Delhi, S. Chand [1971]
xii, 258 p. 24cm. (National bibliography, no. 8) Alphabeti-

cally arranged; includes biographical sketches of many persons
prominent in India's independence movement.

9255   SHARMA, JAGDISH SARAN, 1924-
        The national biographical dictionary of India [by] Jagdish
Saran Sharma. [1st ed.] New Delhi, Sterling Publishers [1972]
302 p. 22cm. Ca. 1500 entries, covering a period of about
5,000 years.

9256   UPADHYAYA, J   M   1900-
        Gandhiji's early contemporaries and companions. [1st ed.]
Ahmedabad, Navajivan Pub. House [1971] vii, 54 p. [49] p. of
ports. 17 x 25cm. Portraits and biographical sketches of 48
early Indic associates of Mohandas K. Gandhi.

9257   WHO'S WHO (IN INDIA) New Delhi, Guide Publications, 1967.
        viii, 182 p. ports. 22cm. Issued irregularly.

Local

Andhra Pradesh

9258   ANDHRA PRADESH ALMANAC. 1967-   Madras, Educa-
        tional Products of India.   v. 19cm. annual. 1967 vol.
(only one issued?) edited by B. Subbarayan. Includes a Who's
who ("Current biography") of eminent people of Andhra Pradesh.

9259   ĀNDHRADĒŚA CARITRA, BHŪGŌLA SARVASVAMU.
        Hyderbad, Andhra Rachaita Sangamu, 1969-   v.
25cm. In Telugu. Added t.p.: Encyclopaedia of the history
and geography of Andhra. Vol. 1 contains names of persons
and places.

Bombay (Province)

9260   HOUSTON, JOHN, ed.
        Representative men of the Bombay Presidency; a collection
of biographical sketches, with portraits, of the princes, chiefs,
philanthropists, and other leading residents of the Presidency.
Philadelphia, Historical Pub. Co. [1897] 1 v. illus., ports. 8.º

Delhi

9261   WHO'S WHO OF DELHI FREEDOM FIGHTERS. Editor: Prabha
        Chopra. Advisory committee chairman: Mir Mushtaq
Ahmad. Members: C. Krishna Nair [and others] Delhi, Gazet-
teer Unit, Delhi Administration, 1974-   v. 21cm.
Vol. 1 contains ca. 3,500 very brief biographical sketches of

patriots (natives of Delhi) who participated in India's fight for
freedom in the 20th century.

Gujarat

9262   MAJITHIA, SUDARSHAN, 1932-
        The Gujarat directory, including who's who. Chief editor
        & compiler: Sudarshan Majithia. [1st ed.] Bhavnagar, Gujarat
        Pub. House [1973] 472 p. 25cm. "Who's who" (p. [441]-472)
        contains 118 biographical sketches; not in alphabetical order, but
        a preliminary listing gives alphabetical approach.

Haryana

9263   HARYANA DIRECTORY AND WHO'S WHO, 1967/68-
        Ambala, Indian Book Agency.   v. maps, port. 22cm.

Hyderabad (State)

9264   OUR LEGISLATORS; who's who in the Hyderabad Legislative
        Assembly, and Hyderabad representatives in the Parlia-
        ment. [Rev. and enl. ed.] Hyderabad, Issued by the Dept. of
        Information and Public Relations [1953] 66 p. illus. 22cm.
        Cover title: Our legislators: MCS, MPS, MLAS.

Jammu and Kashmir

9265   J & K YEARBOOK & WHO'S WHO. 1970-   Jammu, Ranbir
        Publications.   v. illus., ports. 25cm. Editor-in-chief:
        1970-   Mulk Raj Saraf. Includes a who's who (with portraits)
        for Jammu and Kashmir.

Kerala (State)

9266   KERALA, INDIA (STATE). LEGISLATIVE ASSEMBLY.
        Who's who. 1968-   Trivandrum, Public Relations
        Dept.   v. ports. 18cm.

9267   PAVANAN, 1926-
        Paricayam. [Quilon, Jana Yugom Books, 1968] 359 p.
        19cm. Brief biographies of Kerala's politicians. In Malayalam.

Madras (Presidency)

9268   JUSTICE PARTY GOLDEN JUBILEE SOUVENIR, 1968. [Ma-
        dras, Copies available with K. Paramasivam, secretary,

Justice Party, 1968?] lxv, 404 p. , [182] p. of ports. (part col.)
26cm. Advertising matter included in paging. In English or
Tamil. This souvenir publication of the Justice Party of Madras
Presidency, India, includes (among other portraits) some 213
portraits of leading men of the Party as well as officials of the
Presidency (past and present)

Midnapore (District)

9269   MAITY, SACHINDRA KUMAR
        Freedom movement in Midnapore. Calcutta, Firma K. L.
Mukhopadhyay, 1975-   v. 22cm. "Biography of free-
dom-fighters and social reformers" (v. 1, chapter 3, p. [79]-
162) is a biographical dictionary of the Midnapore District of India (20th century and contemporary).

Mysore

9270   MYSORE. LEGISLATIVE COUNCIL.
        Who's who. [ca. 1968?-   Bangalore, Printed by the
Director of Print. and Publications at the Govt. Press.   v.
ports. 22cm.

9271   MYSORE. LEGISLATURE. LEGISLATIVE ASSEMBLY.
        Who's who. [ca. 1968?-   Bangalore, Printed by
the Director of Print. , Stationery and Publications at the Govt.
Press.   v. ports. 22cm.

9272   WHO'S WHO IN KARNATAKA. 1972-   Mysore, Pravin
        Prakashan.   v. illus. 19cm. annual. Continues
Who's who in Mysore.

9273   WHO'S WHO IN MYSORE. 1971-   Mysore, Pravin
        Prakashan.   v. ports. 22cm. annual. Superseded
by Who's who in Karnataka, 1972-

Punjab

9274   BAJWA, FAUJA SINGH
        Eminent freedom fighters of Punjab [by] Fauja Singh. 1st
ser. Patiala, Punjabi University, Dept. of Punjab Historical
Studies, 1972. xvi, 246 p. ports. 22cm. Life sketches, in
brief, of 92 freedom fighters in pre-1947 Punjab; a biographical dictionary.

9275   PUNJAB, INDIA (STATE). LEGISLATURE. LEGISLATIVE
        COUNCIL.
            Who's who. Chandigarh.   v. ports. 19cm. Began
        1966?   Over 1,000 biographical sketches.

9276   PUNJABI UNIVERSITY. DEPT. OF HISTORY AND PUNJAB
        HISTORICAL STUDIES.
            Who's who: Punjab freedom fighters. Chief editor: Fauja
        Singh: editors: C. L. Datta [and others] Patiala, Dept. of Pun-
        jab Historical Studies, Punjabi University [1972-   v.
        26cm. To be complete in 2 v. Entries, by 'forename,' are very
        brief; includes just about every Punjabi who fought for India's
        freedom from the British Raj.

9277   SINGH, GURMUKH, 1899-
            Wihawin sadi de shahid. New Delhi, Vidya Prakashan
        Bhawan, 1968. 350 p. 111 life sketches of distinguished Pun-
        jabis. In Punjabi.

Tamil Nadu

9278   TAMIL NADU. LEGISLATURE. LEGISLATIVE ASSEMBLY.
            Tamilnātu Cattap Pēravai "yar-evar". Tamil Legislative
        Assembly: Who's who. 1971-   Madras, Tamil Nadu Legis-
        lative Assembly Dept.   v. ports. 23cm. In English and
        Tamil. Supersedes Madras (State). Legislature. Legislative
        Assembly. Who's who.

9279   TAMIL NADU. LEGISLATURE. LEGISLATIVE COUNCIL.
            Who is who. Madras.   v. illus. 19cm. 1970/71 edi-
        tion has 75 p.

9280   WHO'S WHO OF FREEDOM FIGHTERS, [TAMIL NADU].
            [Madras, Stree Seva Mandir Press, 1973] 3 v. 26cm.
        Vols. 2-3 have imprint: Printed by the Director of Stationery
        and Print., Madras, on behalf of the Govt. of Tamil Nadu. Pre-
        pared by the State Govt. of Tamil Nadu on the initiative of the
        Central Govt., in connection with the silver jubilee of Indian in-
        dependence, 1972. Arranged alphabetically under each district
        of the State. Citizens of Tamil Nadu (active in the 20th century)
        who contributed to India's struggle for independence from the
        British Raj.

INDOCHINA

9281   SOUVERAINS ET NOTABILITÉS D'INDOCHINE; notices par ordre
            alphabétique. Hanoi, Editions du Gouvernement général de
        l'Indochine, IDEO, 1943. xix, 108 p. ports. Native rulers and
        notables of Vietnam; a biographical dictionary(Duong-Sam-An

to M. Pann-Yung) preceded by 8 biographical sketches of the
ruling family (Bao-Dai, etc.) Available on microfilm at Cornell
University Libraries.

INDONESIA

9282   BIOGRAFI PAHLAWAN NASIONAL. Para penjusun: Mardanas
[et al.] Djakarta, Lembaga Sedjarah dan Antropologi, 1972.
2 v. 32cm. (Seri pahlawan nasional) Biography of Indonesia's
national heroes.

9283   INDONESIA. LEMBAGA PEMILIHAN UMUM.
Riwayat hidup anggota-anggota Majelis Permusyawaratan
Rakyat hasil pemilihan umum 1971. [Jakarta, 1973?; (kata
pengantar 1972)] 1277 p. illus., ports. 22cm. Biographical
sketches, accompanied by portraits, of 920 members of Indonesian People's Consultative Assembly.

9284   INDONESIA. PUSAT SEDJARAH ABRI.
Siapa-apa (who's who) pedjabat teras HANKAM/ABRI.
Edisi 3. [Djakarta] 1971. 299 l. 33cm. Cover title. "Pener-
bitan sementara." At head of title: Departemen Pertahanan-
Keamanan. A who's who of the officials of the Indonesian Gov-
ernment's Department of Defense and Security and the Armed
Forces.

9285   KLOOT, M   A   VAN RHEDE VAN DER
De Gouverneurs-Generaal en Commissarissen-Generaal van
Nederlandsch-Indië 1610-1888. Historisch-genealogisch beschreven door M. A. van Rhede van der Kloot. Met wapen-afbeel-
dingen door M. J. Lion. Uitg. met ondersteuning van het Min-
isterie van Koloniën. 's-Gravenhage, W. P. van Stockum, 1891.
xi, 335 p. plates. 28cm. The Governors-General and Commis-
sioners-General of the Dutch East Indies, 1610-1888. Arranged
by date of entry into office. Index of names mentioned (p. 345-
351) Ca. 75 biographical sketches.

9286   LANGEN, KAREL FREDERIK HENDRIK VAN, 1848-1915.
Beknopt alfabetisch informatieboekje betreffende Groot
Atjehsche personen en aangelegenheden. Kota Radja, 1897.
200 p. illus. 13cm. A biographical and historical dictionary
for Atjeh (or Aceh) Indonesia.

9287   ROEDER, O   G
Who's who in Indonesia; biographies of prominent Indonesian personalities in all fields. Compiled by O. G. Roeder.
[1st ed.] Djakarta, Gunung Agung, 1971. xxxii, 544 p. ports.
22cm.

9288   SURYADINATA, LEO
        Prominent Indonesian Chinese in the twentieth century; a
        preliminary survey. [Athens, Ohio University Center for Inter-
        national Studies, Southeast Asia Program, 1972] xi p., 62 l.
        28cm. (Papers in international studies. Southeast Asia series,
        no. 23) Primarily a biographical dictionary.

IRAN

9289   JUSTI, FERDINAND, 1837-1907.
        Iranisches Namenbuch. [Reprografischer Nachdruck der
        Ausgabe Marburg 1895] Hildesheim, G. Olms, 1963. xxvi,
        526 p. 25cm. A dictionary of Persian proper names which
        yields identifying data for many prominent personages in Per-
        sian history and culture as well as references to where fuller
        biographical data may be found (e. g., sources listed in "Ab-
        kürzungen" at front of vol.).

General Works

9290   IRAN WHO'S WHO. 1972-   1st-   ed. [Tehran?] Echo
        of Iran.   v. 21cm.

9291   WILBER, DONALD NEWTON
        Four hundred forty-six kings of Iran. Shiraz [Pahlavi Uni-
        versity, 1972] 189 p. illus. 25cm. At head of title: Publica-
        tions of Pahlavi University for the celebration of 2500 years of
        Kingship in Iran.

IRAQ

9292   AL-ĀLŪSĪ, 'ALĪ 'ALĀ' AL-DĪN, 1861-1922.
        al-Durr al-muntathir fī rijal al-qarn al-thānī 'ashar wa-al-
        thālith 'ashar. Bāgdād, Dar al-Ghumhūriyya Wazārat at-Taqafa
        wa-al-Isrād, 1387 [1967] 260, 6 p. facsims. 24cm. Muslim
        personalities of Iraq in the 12th-13th to the 18th-19th centuries.
        Non-alphabetical arrangement, with index of names cited in the
        work (p. 213-225)

IRELAND

9293   DE BURGH, U   H   HUSSEY
        The landowners of Ireland; an alphabetical list of owners of
        estates of 500 acres or £500 valuation and upwards, in Ireland,
        with the acreage and valuation in each county. And also contain-
        ing a brief notice of the education and official appointments of
        each person, to which are added his town and country addresses,
        and clubs. Dublin, Hodges, Foster and Figgis, 1878. xxviii,
        486 p. 23cm.

9294   FITZGERALD, THOMAS W   H   1848-
        Ireland and her people; a library of Irish biography together
        with a popular history of ancient and modern Erin to which is
        added an appendix of copious notes and useful tables supplement-
        ed with a dictionary of proper names in Irish mythology, geog-
        raphy, genealogy, etc. ... Embracing a period of forty centu-
        ries of legend, tradition and history ... Chicago, Fitzgerald
        Book Co., 1909-11. 5 v. ports. 25cm. Vols. 1-3: Biography.
        Alphabetical index at the end of the first 3 volumes.

9295   WHO'S WHO, WHAT'S WHAT AND WHERE IN IRELAND.
        [Compiled by Zircon Publishing] in association with the
        Irish Times. [1st ed.] London, Geoffrey Chapman Publishers,
        1973. 735 p. illus. 24cm. Issued also in the U. S. by Macmil-
        lan Library Services, Riverside, N. J. (640 p.) Includes over
        3,500 entries for leading contemporary Irish personalities in all
        fields of endeavor. "Who's who in the Republic of Ireland": p.
        13-362. "Who's who in Northern Ireland": p. 539-630.

ISLAMIC COUNTRIES

9296   AL-'AYDARUS, 'ABD AL-QĀDIR IBN SHAYKH, 1570-1627.
        Tarīkh al-mūr al-sāfir 'an akhbār al-qarn al-'āshir.
        Bagdad, al-Maktaba al-'Arabiyya, 1335 [1934] 508 p. facsim.
        25cm. A first volume only was published? Events of the 10th
        century A. D. in Southern Arabia particularly. Includes biog-
        raphies of Arab scholars, judges, etc. arranged by death-dates.
        Table to the biographies on p. 481-508. Edited by Muhammad
        Rāshid al-Saffār.

9297   AL-BŪRĪNĪ, HASAN IBN MUHAMMAD, 1556-1615.
        Tarajim al-a'yān min abnā' al-zamān. Damashq [Damas-
        cus] Matbū'at al-Majma' al-'Ilmī al-'Arabi bi Dimashq, 1959-
                v. 24cm. Edited by Salah al-Dīn al-Munajjid. Cele-
        brated men of the epoch; biographies of famous Muslims of the
        16th-17th centuries A. D.

9298   CAETANI, LEONE, principe di Teano, 1869-1935.
        Onomasticon Arabicum; ossia, Repertorio alfabetico dei
        nomi di persona e di luogo contenuti nelle principali opere
        storiche, biografiche e geografiche, stampate e manoscritte,
        relative all'Islam, compilato per cura di Leone Caetani e Giu-
        seppe Gabrieli. Roma, Casa editrice italiana, 1915. 2 v.
        34cm. This alphabetical list of names of persons prominent in
        Islamic civilization includes Persian, Mongolian, Hindustani and
        Turkish names as well as Arabic. Only 2 vols. were published? ;
        v. 2 ends with: 'Abdallah ibn Ziyād ibn Abi Sufyan. Biographical
        data is available for a substantial number of the entries.

9299   AL-DHAHABĪ, MUHAMMAD IBN AHMAD, 1274-1348.
        Kitāb tadhkirat al-huffāz. Hyderabad, Osmania Oriental

Publications Bureau, 1955-58. 4 v. 25cm. Moslem traditionalists; arranged by 'generation'; table of biographies at head
of vols. 1, 2 & 4.

9300   AL-DHAHABĪ, MUHAMMAD IBN AHMAD, 1274-1348.
        Siyar al'lam al-nubala'. al-Qāhira, Institut des manu-
scrits arabes [1956? -57] 2 v. facsims. 25cm. (Dhakhā'ir
al-Arab, 19) Biographical dictionary of famous Muslims from
the origins of Islam to the 8th century after the Hegira. Arranged by 'generations' with entries chiefly by forenames and
an index of biographies, etc., in each volume.

9301   AL-DHAHABĪ, MUHAMMAD IBN AHMAD, 1274-1348.
        Tārikh al-Islām wa tabaqāt al-mashāhir wa-l-a'lām.
al-Qāhira, Maktabat al-Qudsi, 1947-48. 5 v. 24cm. History
of Islam and the 'Generations' of its famous men. A chronology
with biographical entries chronologically arranged.

9302   AL-FĀSĪ, TAQĪ AL-DĪN MUHAMMAD IBN AHMAD, 1373-1429.
        Tarikh 'ulamā' Baghdād ... Baghdād, Matba 'at al-Ahāli,
1357 [1938] 286 p. 26cm. Cover title: Muntakhab al-Mukhtar,
choix historiques des ulemas de Baghdad, par Abi-l-Ma'āli
Muhammad ibn Rafi'. 201 biographies of men of Baghdad arranged alphabetically, drawn from al-Sallāmī's al-Mukhtār al-
mudhayyal, which was composed as a supplement to Ibn al-
Najjar's supplement (dhayl) to a work by al-Khatib al-Baghdad.
Edited by 'Abbas al-Azzawi.

9303   IBN AL-ABBĀR, MUHAMMAD IBN 'ABD ALLĀH, 1199-1260.
        al-Mu'jam fī ashāb al-Qādi al-Imām Abi 'Ali al-Sadafi.
al-Qāhirah, Dār al-Kātib al-Arabi, 1967. 15, 336 p. 25cm.
Biographical sketches of colleagues and students of Husayn ibn
Muhammad ibn Sukkarah al-Sadafi (d. 1220), Muslim scholar
who lived in Spain.

9304   IBN AL-ABBĀR, MUHAMMAD IBN 'ABD ALLĀH, 1199-1260.
        At-Takmila li Kitāb as-Sila. [al-Qāhirah] 'Izzat al-Attar al-
Husayni: Maktabat al-Hāngī, 1375 [1955-56] 2 v. 24cm. Complement of the book "Lien"; biographies of famous men (Muslims)
of Andalusia). Alphabetical by forename.

9305   IBN AL-ATHĪR, 'IZZ AL-DĪN, 1160-1233.
        Usd al-jaba fi ma'rifat as-sahāba. [Cairo] 1868-71. 5 v.
Biographical dictionary of the companions of Muhammad, the
Prophet.

9306   IBN AL-JAZARĪ, MUHAMMAD IBN MUHAMMAD, 1350-1429.
        Kitāb ghāyat al-nihāyah fi tabaqāt al-qurrā'. [Cairo]
Matba'at as-Sa'āda [1933-35] 2 v. 26cm. (Biblioteca Islami-

ca, 8) Added t. p. : Das biographische Lexikon der Koranlehrer.
Edited by Gotthelf Bergsträsser and Otto Pretzl. Biographical
dictionary of scholars of the Koran.

9307   IBN AL-QĀDĪ, AHMAD IBN MUHAMMAD, 1552 or 3-1616.
        Durrat al-hijal, répertoire biographique d'Ahmad ibn al-
Quadi. Texte arabe, publié par la première fois, avec une introd. et trois index par I. S. Allouche. Rabat, F. Moncho,
1934-36. 2 v. (iv, 618 p.) 26cm. (Collection de textes arabes
publiée par l'Institut des hautes études marocaines, v. 4-5) Biography of celebrated Muslim personages: traditionists, jurists,
scholars, saints, poets, men of the Maghreb and Andalusians.

9308   IBN AL-ZUBAYR, ABŪ JA'FAR AHMAD IBN IBRĀHĪM, 1229 or
        30-1308.
        al-Qism al-akhir min kitāb Silat al-silah ... [Rabat, 1937]
12, 285 p. 25cm. Cover title: Silat as-sila [par] Ibn al-Zubair.
Edited by E. Levi-Provençal. Biographies of Muslims in Andalusia in the 13th century (7th century after the Hegira).

9309   IBN 'ASKAR, 'ABD AL-RAHMĀN IBN MUHAMMAD, 1246-1332.
        La "Daouhat an-Nâchir, " sur les vertus éminentes des
chaikhs du Maghrib au dixième siècle. Traduction de A. Graulle.
Paris, E. Leroux, 1913. 342 p. plate. 8.º (Archives marocaines, v. 19) Biographical sketches of ca. 150 Sheikhs of the
Maghreb to the 10th century after the Hegira: Muslim scholars,
men of letters, saints, theologians, etc.

9310   IBN KHALLIKĀN, 1211-1282.
        Wafayāt al-a'lyān wa-anbā' abnā' al-zamān. Edited by Ihsān
'Abbās. Beirut, Dār Sādr [1968? -72?] 8 v. illus. 25cm. Vol.
5 has added t. p. : Wafayat el-a'yān (Biographies of illustrious
men) [by] Ibn Khallikān; v. 8 has subtitle: al-fahāris al-amāh,
i'dād Wadād al-Qadhī [and] 'Iz-al-Din Ahmad Mūsa, under the
supervision of Ihsān 'Abbās. Biographical dictionary of Islamic
personalities of the Middle Ages; see also English translation.

9311   IBN SA'ĪD, 'ALĪ IBN MŪSÁ AL-MAGHRIBĪ, 13th cent.
        al-Mughrib fi hulā al-Maghrib 'Kitāb washy al-turus fi hulā
jazirat al-Andalus. al-Qāhirah, Dar al-Ma'ārif, 1953-55. 2 v.
25cm. 'The extraordinary among the ornaments of the Maghreb. '
Chiefly biographies of Arabs in Spain and North Africa: sovereigns, statesmen, judges, etc.

9312   'INĀN, MUHAMMAD 'ABD ALLĀH, 1896-
        Tarājim Islamiyah sharqiyah wa-al-Andalusiyah. al-
Qāhirah, Dār al-Ma'ārif, 1366 [1947] 271 p. illus. 25cm.
Moslem biographies (kings, rulers, etc.): Eastern and Andalu-
sian (and Maghrebian). Chronologically arranged, with an index
of names.

9313   ISLÂM ANSIKLOPEDISI. Islâm âlemi coğrafya, etnoğrafya ve
            biyografya lûgati. Beynelmilel Akademiler Birliğinin
        yardımı ve tanımmis müstersriklerin istiraki ile nesredenler:
        M. Th. Houtsma [et al.] Istanbul, Maarif Matbassı, 1940-
            v. illus., ports. 27cm. Issued in parts: v. 1, pt. 7-
        have title: Islam ansiklopedisi. Islam âlemi tarih, coğrafya,
        etnoğrafya ve biyografya lûgati. Turkish edition (with some ex-
        pansion?) of the Encyclopaedia of Islam (q. v.) Goes up to
        Mescid (v. 8, pt. 1, 1957) only?

9314   ISLÂM-TÜRK ANSIKLOPEDISI MECMUASI.   cild 1-   (no. 1-
            64); [29   Ekim [1940 or 1]-   [Istanbul]   v.
        ports., facsims. 29cm. irregular. Title varies: no. 1-8,
        Islâm-Türk muhitülmaarif necmuasi; no. 9-44, Islam-Türk
        ansiklopedisi muhitülmaarif; no. 45-50, Islam-Turk muhitülmaa-
        rifi. Editor: 1941-   E. Edib. A periodical publication de-
        voted to Muslim and Turkish biography. Ceased with no. 64 (?)

9315   'IYĀD IBN MŪSĀ, 1083-1149.
            Tarājim Aghlabīyah. Tunis, al-Jāmia'tut Tūnīsya, 1968.
        568, 62 p. 25cm. Added t. p.: Biographies aghlabides; ex-
        traites des Madārik du Cadi 'Iyād. Complete work known under
        title: Tartīb al-madārik wa-taqrīb al-masālik. Introductory
        matter in Arabic and French. Edited by Muhammad al-Talibi.
        Biographies of 173 followers/disciples of the Maliki school of
        Islamic traditionalism and legalism.

9316   JAMIL AHMAD, KHWAJA
            Hundred great Muslims [by] Jamil Ahmad. [1st ed.] La-
        hore, Ferozsons [1971] ii, 716 p. 23cm. Great figures in Is-
        lamic civilization through the centuries: religious leaders, phi-
        losophers, scientists, statesmen, etc. —the Near East and India
        especially.

9317   AL-JUNDĪ, ANWAR
            Tarājim al-a'lam al-mu'āsirīn fe al-'alām al-Islami.
        [al-Qāhira] Maktabat al-Anglū al-Misriyya, 1970-   v.
        24cm. Biographical dictionary of contemporary (20th century)
        figures in the Muslim world; entry by forename.

9318   KAHHĀLAH, 'UMAR RIDĀ
            A'lām an-nisā' fī ālamay al-'Arab wa al-Islām. Dimāshq
        (Damascus) al-Matba'ahal-Hashimiyyah, 1958-59. 5 v. 25cm.
        Famous women in the Arabic-Muslim world. A 2d edition (1st,
        1940, 3 v.) Entries primarily by forename, some by 'kunyah. '

9319   AL-KATTĀNĪ, 'ABD AL-HAYY IBN 'ABD AL-KABĪR
            Kitāb Fihris al-fahāris ... Fās, 1346-47 [1927-28] 2 v.
        28cm. Dictionary of dictionaries, of lists and of collections of

traditions; dictionary of biographies of Muslim traditionists and
their collections, from the middle of the 9th to the middle of the
14th century A. H. (15th-20th century A. D.) Arranged alphabetically by forename, 'surname,' kunyah, misbah, etc.

9320   AL-KUTUBĪ, MUHAMMAD IBN SHĀKIR, d. 1363.
        Fawāt al-wafayāt. al-Qāhirah, Maktabat an-Nahdah al-
Misriyyah, 1951. 2 v. 25cm. Edited by Muhammad Muhyi al-
Dīn 'Abd al-Hamid. Supplement to Ibn Khallikān's Kitāb wafayāt
al-'ayan, necrology of Muslim notables and chronicle of contemporaries (13th-14th centuries A. D.) Entries by forename;
a biographical dictionary.

9321   LEXIKON DER ISLAMISCHEN WELT. [Hrsg. von] Klaus
        Kreiser, Werner Diem, Hans Georg Majer. Stuttgart,
Kohlhammer, 1974. 3 v. illus. 19cm. (Urban-Taschenbücher,
Reihe 80) Dictionary of the Islamic countries' civilization and
history; with biographical sketches.

9322   MAŁY SŁOWNIK KULTURY ŚWIATA ARABSKIEGO. [Autorzy
        haseł: Józef Bielawski et al. Wyd. 1.] Warszawa, Wiedza
Powszechna, 1971. 596 p. illus. 21cm. A dictionary of Arab
civilization and antiquities which includes biographical sketches.

9323   MANSOOR, MENAHEM
        Political and diplomatic history of the Arab world, 1900-
1967; a biographical dictionary. [Washington] Microcard Editions Books, 1974. xvi, 144 p. 29cm. The term 'biographical
dictionary' must be carefully considered; actually "the purpose
of this biographical dictionary is to describe briefly the political
and diplomatic role of all persons who are mentioned either in the
seven volumes of The political and diplomatic history of the Arab
world published in 1971 or in The political and diplomatic documents of the Arab world: 1900-1967, shortly to be published.
The aim here is not to provide complete biographical data ...
but to provide basic information on the office and function of
those personalities in a given year."

9324   MAZAS, ALEXANDRE, 1791-1856.
        Les hommes illustres de l'Orient rangés par ordre chrono-
logique depuis l'établissement de l'islamisme jusqu'à Mahomet
II, le conquérant de Constantinople. Paris, J. Lecoffre, 1847.
2 v. 8.° Famous men of the Islamic Empire and the Muslim
East arranged in chronological order from the founding of Islam
to Mahomet II, conqueror of Constantinople.

9325   AL-MUHIBBĪ, MUHAMMAD AMĪN IBN FADL ALLĀH, 1651-
        1699.
        Khulāsat al-athar. Beirut, Dār Şādir [1969?] 4 v. 26cm.
(Rawā'i' al-turāth al-'Arabi) Photo-offset reproduction of the

Cairo ed. of 1868. Biographical dictionary of famous personalities in Islamic countries, 1590-1690.

9326   NĀJĪ, MU'ALLIM
        Asāmi. [Constantinople, 1890] 452 p. 12.° An alphabeti-
        cally arranged account of 700 famous Moslems. In Turkish.

9327   AL-NAWAWĪ, 1233-1277.
        The biographical dictionary of illustrious men, chiefly at
        the beginning of Islamism. Now first edited, from the collation
        of two MSS. at Göttingen and Leiden, by Ferdinand Wüstenfeld.
        Göttingen, Printed for the London Society for the Publication of
        Oriental Texts, and sold by Dieterich, 1842-47. 878 p. 25cm.
        The manuscript contains a second part which was never publish-
        ed. Cf. Bankipore. Orient Pub. Lib. Arabic MSS., v. 12, p.
        4, no. 648. Biographical dictionary of men prominent in the
        Islamic Empire of the Middle Ages.

9328   AL-SAFADI, KHALĪL IBN AYBAK, 1297 (ca.)-1363.
        Nakt al-himyān fi nukat al-'umyān. al-Qāhirah, al-Matr-
        ba'ahal - Ghammāliyyah, 1911. 320, 16 p. 25cm. Curiosities
        concerning the blind; a biographical dictionary of the famous
        sightless men of the Islamic East. Entries by forename.

9329   SHAHĀBĪ, INTIZĀMULLĀH
        Khavātin-i Islām. Karachi, Madina Pub. Co., [1965]
        304 p. 22cm. In Urdu. Imprint date from jacket. Biographies
        of 152 famous Muslim women.

9330   AL-SHA'RĀNĪ, 'ABD AL-WAHHĀB IBN AHMAD, 1493 (ca.)-
        1565 or 6.
        al-Tabaqāt al-kubrā: "Lawāqih al-anwār fi tabaqāt al-akhyār."
        al-Qāhirah, Maktabat wa Matba'at Muhammad 'Ali Subayh [1954?]
        2 v. in 1. 28cm. Biographies of the Moslem saints and mys-
        tiques.

9331   AL-SHA'RĀNĪ, 'ABD AL-WAHHĀB IBN AHMAD, 1493 (ca.)-
        1565 or 6.
        Vite e detti di santi musulmani. A cura di Virginia Vacca.
        Torino, Unione tipografico-editrice torinese, 1968. 413 p.
        plates. 23cm. (Classici delle religioni. Sezione 3. La re-
        ligione islamica [6]) Classici U. T. E. T. Abridged transla-
        tion of Lawāqih al-anwār fi tabaqāt al-akhyār, better known un-
        der title: al-Tabaqāt al-kubrā. The lives and deeds of the Mos-
        lem saints.

9332   AL-SHAWKĀNĪ, MUHAMMAD IBN 'ALĪ, 1759-1839.
        Al-Badr al-tāli' bi mahāsin man ba'd al-qarn as-sābi'. al-
        Qāhirah, Ma'ruf 'Abd Allāh Bāsandūh, 1348 [1929-30] 2 v. 25cm.

Muslim biography; men who flourished after the 7th century A. H. Arranged alphabetically by forename.

9333   ZAYDAN, JIRJI, 1861-1914.
        Tarajim mashahir al-sharq fi al-qarn at-tasi' 'ashar. [al-Qahira] Matba'at al-Hilal, 1910-11. 2 v. in 1. 24cm. 2d edition; 1st ed. issued in 1902-03. Biographies of famous men of the East (Near East) in the 19th century. Vol. 1: khedives of Egypt, kings & princes, military leaders, administrators and political figures. Vol. 2, protagonists of the Muslim cultural renaissance, writers, journalists, litterateurs, poets. Chronologically arranged within each category; entries under forenames & index to biographies at end of volume.

9334   AL-ZIRIKLI, KHAYR AL-DIN, 1893-
        al-A'lam ... al-Qahirah, 1954-59. 10 v. facsims., ports. 25cm. Names; biographical dictionary of the most famous men and women: Arabs, Arab philologists & Orientalists. Alphabetical by forename.

ISRAEL

9335   FAERBER, MEIR, 1908-
        Die Israel führen. Tel Aviv, Olamenu, 1971. 213 p. ports. 24cm. A biographical dictionary of 72 leaders in contemporary Israeli political life.

9336   NIZKOR; sefer zikaron le-talmidim, 'ovedim umorim ba-Universitah ha-'Ivrit bi-Yerushalayim she-nafelu be-milhemet sheshet ha-yamin uvisheloh ha-shanim 'iyar tav shin kaf zayin—ciyar tav shin lamed. [Ri'aynu, liktu ve-khatevu Avraham Benmelekh, Shelomoh Laufer u-Shelomoh Rozner. Ba-' arikhat Yehudah Ha'ezrahi] Yotse' la-'or 'al-yede ha-mahlakah le-hasbarah ve-yahase tsibur shel ha-Universitah ha-'Ivrit, ve-Histadrut ha-studentim shel ha-Universitah ha-'Ivrit. Yerushalayim, 730 [1970] 338 p. ports. 24cm. Biographies of 80 students, staff members and teachers of the Hebrew University killed in action during the Six-Day Israel-Arab War of 1967 or its aftermath. Alphabetical approach thru' index on p. 337-338.

ITALY

Bibliography, Indexes, Portrait Catalogs

9337   GHENO, ANTONIO
        Contributo alla bibliografia genealogica italiana. Bologna, Forni, 1971. 297 p. 24cm. Reprint of the 1924 Rome edition. Not only a bibliography of Italian families; it also includes bibliography of many individuals who belonged to the various families listed.

General Works

9338   AICHELBURG, ERRADO DI
Medaglie d'oro. Bergamo, Societa anonimà A. Savoldi,
1927. 2 v. illus., ports. 24cm. Contents. --t. 1. Lombardia,
3 Venezie, Liguria-Emilia. --t. 2. Toscano e Lazio, Umbria-
Marche, Abruzzi, Campania-Basilicata-Puglia. Calabria-
Sicilia-Sardegna. Italians decorated with the gold medal for
valor in the Wars of 1848-1849, 1859, 1860-1861 and 1870 & the
African and Chinese campaigns. Notices arranged by region;
alphabetical name index by region at front of each volume.
Numerous portraits are included.

9339   ARGEGNI, CORRADO
Condottieri, capitani, tribuni. Milano, E. B. B. I., Istituto
editoriale italiano B. C. Tosi, 1936-37. 3 v. illus., ports.
28cm. (Enciclopedia biografica e bibliografica 'Italiana, ' ser.
19) A biographical dictionary of military leaders in Italy.

9340   AYALA, MARIANO D', 1808-1877.
Vite degli italiani benemeriti della libertà e della patria.
Firenze, Col tipi di M. Cellini, 1868-83. 2 v. 25cm. Contents. --[1] Morti combattendo. --[2] Uccisi dal carnefice. Vol.
2 has imprint: Torino, Fratelli Bocca. A dictionary of Italian
military biography; Italians who fought and died for their country's freedom, especially during the Risorgimento.

9341   CAIVANO-SCHIPANI, FELICE
Dizionario biografico de' soci dell' Accademia pittagorica.
2. ed. interamente riveduta, ampliata e divisa in I e II serie.
Napoli, R. Rinaldi e G. Sellito, 1884. 199 p. 27cm. Biogra-
phical dictionary of associates of the Pythagorean Academy in
Naples.

9342   CAPUTO, VINCENZO
Figure del Risorgimento (1820-1870); biografie. Milano,
Gastaldi, 1960. 247 p. 20cm. (Collana Cultura) A biographical dictionary of leading figures in the Italian Risorgimento
(1820-1870)

9343   I DEPUTATI E SENATORI DEL PRIMO-SESTO PARLAMENTO
REPUBBLICANO. Roma, La Navicella, 1949-72. 6 v.
ports. 17-19cm. Biographical dictionaries of the deputies and
senators of the 1st-6th Italian Parliament (1948-1972—)

9344   DIZIONARIO GEOGRAFICO, STORICO, BIOGRAFICO ITALIANO.
Firenze, Poligrafia italiana, 1848. 2 v. 8.° A dictionary
of Italian geography, history and biography.

9345   DIZIONARIO STORICO POLITICO ITALIANO. Diretto da Er-
        nesto Sestan. Firenze, Sansoni, 1971. 1458 p. 23cm. A
        dictionary of Italian political history, much of it biographical.

9346   DORIA, GINO, 1888-
            La strade di Napoli. Saggio di toponomastica storica. 2.
        ed. riveduta e accresciuta. Milano, R. Ricciardi, 1971. 506 p.
        plates. 23cm. The streets of Naples; a dictionary which in-
        cludes biographical data for persons after whom streets are
        named (often entered under their forenames, i. e. the streets'
        names) Surname approach available through the "Indice ono-
        mastico. " The persons listed are chiefly prominent Italian his-
        torical and cultural figures.

9347   ERCOLE, FRANCESCO, 1884-
            Il Risorgimento italiano. Milano, E. B. B. I., Istituto
        editoriale italiano B. C. Tosi, 1939-42. 4 v. illus., ports.
        28cm. (Enciclopedia biografica e bibliografica 'Italiana,' ser.
        42) Contents.--v. 1. I martiri.--v. 2-4. Gli uomini politici. A
        biographical dictionary of leading figures in the Italian Risorgi-
        mento (19th century)

9348   FABRONI, ANGELO, 1732-1803.
            Vitae Italorum doctrina excellentium qui saeculis XVII. et
        XVIII. floruerunt. Pisis, Excudebat C. Genesius, 1778-1805.
        20 v. 21cm. Imprint varies. Vol. 19-20 published after the
        death of the author by D. Pacchi. A collection; contains 154
        lives of famous Italians who flourished in the 17th-18th centuries.

9349   GAZZINO, GIUSEPPE
            Indice cronologico e bibliografico d'illustri italiani dal
        secolo XI al XIX. Come appendice alla Storia della poesia in
        Italia del professore B. Cereseto. Milano, G. Silvestri, 1857.
        146 p. 16.º Chronological and bibliographical index of famous
        Italians of the 11th to the 19th century; a biographical dictionary
        actually.

9350   GRUPPO MEDAGLIE D'ORO AL VALOR MILITARE D'ITALIA.
            Le medaglie d'oro al valor militare. Roma, Tip. regionale,
        1965. 2 v. 21cm. The Gold Medal of Military Valor, Italy,
        and its recipients. Contents.--t. 1. Bandiere (1929-1954) ...
        Individuali (1925-1941).--t. 2. Individuali (1942-1959). Arranged
        by the date of nomination of the recipients.

9351   MALATESTA, ALBERTO, 1879-
            Ministri, deputati, senatori dal 1848 al 1922. Milano
        E. B. B. I., Istituto editoriale italiano B. C. Tosi [1940-41]
        3 v. illus., ports. 28cm. (Enciclopedia biografica e biblio-
        grafica 'Italiana,' ser. 43) A biographical dictionary of Italian
        statesmen (cabinet ministers, Parliamentary deputies and sena-
        tors) from 1848 to 1922.

9352   MANNO, ANTONIO, barone, 1834-1918.
L'opera cinquantenaria della R. Deputazione di storia patria
di Torino; notizie di fatto storiche, biografiche e bibliografiche
sulla R. Deputazione e sui deputati nel primo mezzo secolo dalla
fondazione. Torino, Fratelli Bocca, 1884. xvii, 524 p. 27cm.
(Biblioteca storica italiana, pubblicata per cura della R. Deputazione di storia patria, 1) Pt. 2 of the volume contains biographies of associates of the Deputazione and bio-bibliographies of
the "deputati," the historians and authors who contributed to the
gathering and exposition of material concerning the history of the
Province of Turin.

9353   1,508 [i. e. MILLE CINQUECENTO OTTO] DEPUTATI AL
PARLAMENTO PER LA XXIII LEGISLATURA; biografie e
ritratti ... Milano, Fratelli Treves, 1910. 512 p. 485 ports.
13cm. 1,508 deputies to the Italian Parliament for the 23d Legislative session; biographies and 485 portraits.

9354   1,535 [i. e. MILLE CINQUECENTO TRENTACINQUE] DEPUTATI
AL PARLAMENTO PER LA XXVI LEGISLATURA; biografie
e ritratti. Milano, Treves, 1922. 555 p. 521 ports. 14cm.
1,535 biographical sketches and 521 portraits of deputies to the
Italian Parliament for the 26th legislative session.

9355   1,535 [i. e. MILLE CINQUECENTO TRENTACINQUE] DEPU-
TATI AL PARLAMENTO PER LA XXVII LEGISLATURA ...
Biografie e ritratti ... Milano, Fratelli Treves, 1924. 547 p.
515 ports. 14cm. 1,535 biographical sketches and 515 portraits
of deputies to the Italian Parliament for the 27th legislative session.

9356   MONGRUEL, L   P
Dictionnaire militaire, topographique, géographique, stra-
tégique, historique et biographique de la guerre d'indépendance
en Italie ... 1. ed. Paris, Éditeur du Dictionnaire de la guerre
[1859] 180 p. 16.º Military, topographical, geographical,
strategic, historical and biographical dictionary of the War of
Independence in Italy (ca. 1849-1859) The biographies include
native Italians as well as other Europeans involved in Italian affairs of the period.

9357   MUZZI, SALVATORE, 1808-1884.
Vite d'Italiani illustri da Pitagora a Vittorio Emmanuele II.
3. ed., con aggiunte. Bologna, N. Zanichelli, 1880. 1016 p.
19cm. Circa 300 chronologically arranged lives of famous Italians from Pythagoras (sic) to Victor Emmanuel II. 3d ed.,
with additions. Alphabetical name index at end.

9358   THE NEW CENTURY ITALIAN RENAISSANCE ENCYCLOPEDIA.
Edited by Catherine B. Avery. Editorial consultants: Mar-

vin B. Becker [and] Ludovico Borgo. New York, Appleton-Century-Crofts [1972] xiii, 978 p. illus. 26cm. In large part a biographical dictionary of Italy during the Renaissance.

9359   ORESTANO, FRANCESCO, 1873-
        Eroine, ispiratrici e donne di eccezione. A cura di Francesco Orestano. Milano, E. B. B. I., Istituto editoriale italiano B. C. Tosi [1940] 399 p. illus., ports. 28cm. (Enciclopedia biografica e bibliografica 'Italiana, ' ser. 7) A biographical dictionary of women in Italy; heroines, exceptional women who have inspired their country.

9360   PANTEON DEI MARTIRI DELLA LIBERTÀ ITALIANA, compilato da vari letterati, pubblicata per cura di una società di emigrati italiani. Torino, Fontana, 1861. Pantheon of martyrs of Italian liberty in the Risorgimento for the years 1750-1860.

9361   SARTI, TELESFORO
        Il Parlamento italiano nel cinquantenario dello statuto; profili e cenni biografici. Roma, Tip. Agostiniana, 1898. 592 p. 16.º The Italian Parliament in the fiftieth anniversary of the Constitution; biographical profiles.

9362   SARTI, TELESFORO
        Il Parlamento subalpino e nazionale. Profili e cenni biografici di tutti i deputati e senatori eletti e creati dal 1848 al 1890 (legislature XVI), con appendice contenente i profili e cenni biografici dei deputati e senatori eletti e creati durante le legislature XVII, XVIII e XIX. Terni, Tip. dell'Industria, 1890. 977 p. 8.º Profiles and biographical sketches of all the deputies and senators, elected and appointed, from 1848 to 1890; the Italian National and "Subalpine" (Northern Italy) Parliament.

9363   STOPITI, GIACOMO
        Galleria biografica d'Italia. Roma, Stab. tip. Italiano, 1877-80. 101 pts. ports. folio. Biographical gallery of famous Italians.

9364   TOMASINI, JACOPO FILIPPO, 1597-1654.
        Elogia virorum literis & sapientia illustrium ad viuum expressis imaginibus exornata. Patavii, Typ. S. Sardi, 1644. 411 p. ports. 21cm. 73 biographies, most accompanied by portraits, of Italian scholars and authors. Index of names (alphabetical by forenames) at end.

9365   VALORI, ALDO, 1882-
        Condottieri e generali del Seicento. Milano, E. B. B. I., Istituto editoriale italiano B. C. Tosi [194-] xx, 464 p. illus.,

ports. 28cm. (Enciclopedia biografica e bibliografica 'Italiana,' ser. 20) A biographical dictionary of captains (military leaders) and generals in the 17th century in Italy.

9366   VANNUCCI, ATTO, 1810-1883.
        I martiri della libertà italiana dal 1794 al 1848. Memorie. 7. ed. Milano, L. Bortolotti, 1887. 3 v. 19cm. Not a dictionary, but a running biographical account of martyrs to Italian freedom from 1794 to 1848; contains an 'alphabetical index of martyrs' that leads one to biographical data in the main text.

9367   VITE E RITRATTI DI ILLUSTRI ITALIANI. Padova, Tip. Bettoni, 1812-20. 2 v. ports. 34cm. Vol. 2 has imprint: Milano, Tip. Bettoni. Contents. --1. Agnesi-Doria. --2. Filangieri-Vespucci. A biographical dictionary (with portraits) of 60 of the most famous Italians of all periods.

Local

Bergamo

9368   CALVI, DONATO
        Campidoglio de guerrieri ed altri illustri personaggi di Bergamo. Milano, F. Vigone, 1668. 374 p. 19cm. Biographical data for military leaders and other famous personages of Bergamo.

Bologna

9369   GUIDICINI, GIUSEPPE DI GIOVANNI BATTISTA, 1763-1867.
        I riformatori dello stato di libertà della città di Bologna dal 1394 al 1797. Opera di Giuseppe di Gio. Battista Guidicini, pubblicata dal figlio Ferdinando. Bologna, Regia tip., 1876. 3 v. 28cm. Political reformers and men of affairs in the city of Bologna, 1394 to 1797. Many biographical sketches, approached alphabetically through an index of family names which gives references to individuals in the various families (but not the forenames of these individuals).

Calabria

9370   GRISOLIA, LUIGI
        Cizionario dei calabresi nel mondo. Repertorio biografico. 1. ed. Roma, Edisud, 1965. 15, 209 p. 21cm. (Collana biografica moderna, 1) Dictionary of famous Calabrians.

Cremona

9371   LANCETTI, VINCENZO, 1767?-1851.
        Biografia cremonese; ossia, Dizionario storico delle fa-

miglie e persone ... memorabili e chiare spettanti alla città di
Cremona dai tempi più remoti fino all'età nostra. Milano, 1819-
22. 3 v. 4.º Fasc. 1 only of vol. 3 published? Biography of
Cremona.

Ferrara

9372   UGHI, LUIGI
        Dizionario storico degli uomini illustri ferraresi. Bologna,
        Forni, 1969. 231, 232 p. 22cm. Facsimile of the 1804 (Fer-
        rara) ed. Historical dictionary of the famous men of Ferrara.

Genoa

9373   CAPPELLINI, ANTONIO
        Dizionario biografico di Genovesi illustri e notabili,
        cronologia dei governi di Genova ed indice alfabetico-analitico.
        Bologna, Forni editore, 1969. 171 p. 22cm. Reprint of the
        Genoa edition of 1932. Biographical dictionary of famous peo-
        ple of Genoa.

Liguria

9374   ENCICLOPEDIA DEI LIGURI ILLUSTRI. Genova, Realizza-
            zioni grafiche Artigiana, 1970-   v. illus.
        24cm. (Collana La Randa) Editors: Vito Elio Petrucci and
        Cesare Viazzi. An encyclopedia of biography of famous
        Ligurians (Region of Liguria, Italy).

Lodi

9375   MOLOSSI, GIAMBATTISTA
        Memorie d'alcuni uomini illustri della città di Lodi. Bo-
        logna, Forni, 1969. 2 v. illus., ports. 24cm. Reproduction
        of the Lodi 1776 ed. Memories (biographical data) and portraits
        of ca. 90 famous men of the City of Lodi. Arrangement is
        chronological, from medieval times to the middle of the 18th
        century.

Lombardy (Kingdom)

9376   JARNUT, JÖRG
        Prosopographische und sozialgeschichtliche Studien zum
        Langobardenreich in Italien (568-774) Bonn, L. Röhrscheid,
        1972. 427 p. 23cm. (Bonner historische Forschungen, Bd. 38)
        This work is primarily a register of known persons in the Lom-
        bard Kingdom, 568-774, but on pages [336]-398 will be found bio-
        graphical notes on higher officials of the Kingdom; the notes are
        in 3 alphabets (A-Z) and comprise a total of 213 brief sketches.

Lucania

9377   PEDIO, TOMMASO, 1917-
            Dizionario dei patrioti lucani. Artefici e oppositori (1700-
        1870) Trani, Vecchi, 1969-   v. 25cm. At head of
        title: Società di storia patria per la Puglia. Contents.--v. 1.
        A-C.--v. 2. D-I (1972)
        Biographical dictionary of Lucania (patriots and leaders in the
        Italy of 1700 to 1870 and the Risorgimento)

Lucca

9378   SFORZA, GIOVANNI, conte, 1846-1922.
            Ricordi e biografie lucchesi. Lucca, Tip. editrice Baroni,
        1916 [i.e. 1918] xlviii, 839 p. 25cm. Biographical sketches
        of Luccans: p. 525-796, preceded by Sforza's memoirs.

Manuta

9379   VOLTA, LEOPOLDO CAMMILLO, 1751-1825.
            Biografia dei Mantovani illustri nelle scienze, lettere ed
        arti. Corretta e riordinata da A. Mainardi (?) Mantova, 1845-
        46. 64 p. 4.º Biography of Mantuans famous for their labors
        in the sciences and letters; no more published?

Martina Franca

9380   MARINO, ANGELO   •
            Repertorio bio-bibliografico degli scrittori, artisti e sci-
        enziati martinesi. Martina Franca, 1970. 101 p. 24cm. (Col-
        lana di studi martinesi, 1) A bio-bibliographical dictionary of
        the writers, artists and scientists of the city of Martina Franca,
        Italy.

Mirandola

9381   CERETTI, FELICE
            Biografie mirandolesi. Mirandola, Tip. di Grilli Candido,
        1901-05. 4 v. 25cm. [Memorie storiche della città e dell-antico
        ducato della Mirandola, v. 13-16] Biographical dictionary for
        the city and former dukedom of Mirandola.

Modena

9382   BARBIERI, ALBERTO
            Modenesi da ricordare. Modena, Società tip. editrice
        modenese, 1966-69. 3 v. plates. 31cm. Biographical sketches
        of famous citizens of Modena. Vol. 1: Musicians, architects,
        sculptors, painters; v. 2: Scientists; v. 3: Churchmen. Ar-
        ranged chronologically by category; contains index of persons.

Piedmont

9383   PAROLETTI, MODESTO, 1765-1834.
Vita e ritratti di sessanta Piemontesi illustri. Torino, F.
Festa, 1824. 1 v. (unpaged) 60 ports. folio. Lives and por-
traits of 60 famous persons of Italian Piedmont.

Pisa

9384   FABRONI, ANGELO, 1732-1803.
Memorie storiche de più uomini illustri pisani. Pisa,
1790-92. 4 v. 4.° Historical memorials of the most famous
men of Pisa.

Pistoia

9385   CAPPONI, VITTORIO
Biografia pistoiese; o, Notizie della vita e delle opere dei
pistoiesi illustri nelle scienze, nelle lettere, nelle arti, per
azioni virtuose, per la santità della vita ec., dai tempi più
antichi fino a' nostri giorni. Pistoia, Tipografia Rossetti, 1878.
x, 471 p. 25cm. A bio-bibliographical dictionary of notable citizens of the City of and region around Pistoia. Reprinted in 1972
(Bologna, Forni).

Sannio

9386   ZAZO, ALFREDO
Dizionario bio-bibliografico del Sannio. Napoli, F. Fioren-
tino, 1973. 7, 397 p. illus., ports. 24cm. Bio-bibliographical dictionary of the Sannio, a region in South-Central Italy.

Sardinia

9387   MARTINI, PIETRO, 1800-1866.
Biografia sarda. Bologna, Forni editore, 1971. 3 v. 21cm.
(Italica gens, n. 26) Reproduction of the Cagliari ed. of 1837-38.
A biographical dictionary of Sardinia.

Sicily

9388   AURIA, VINCENZO, 1625-1710.
Historia cronologica delli signori vicere di Sicilia dal
tempo che mancò la personale assistanza de' Serenissimi Rè di
quella, cioè dall'anno 1409, sino al 1697, presente ... Palermo,
Per P. Coppola, 1697. [18], 316 p. 30cm. Biographies of 73
viceroys of Sicily, 1409 to 1697, arranged in chronological order; chronological index to the biographies at front of volume.

Trapani

9389   FERRO, GIUSEPPE M   DI
        Biografia degli uomini illustri trapanesi dall'epoca norman-
na sino al corrente secolo. Trapani, Presso Mannone e Solina,
1830-50. 4 v. in 2. Biography of the famous men of Trapani.

Umbria

9390   FABRETTI, ARIODANTE, 1816-1894.
        Biografie de capitani venturieri dell'Umbria, scritte ad
illustrate con documenti. Montepulciano, A. Fumi, 1842. 4 v.
in 2. ports. 19cm.

        ———— ————Note e documenti che servono ad illustrare le Biogra-
fie ... Montepulciano, A. Fumi, 1842. 631 p. 19cm. Biographies of military leaders of Umbria.

Urbino (Duchy)

9391   [GROSSI, CARLO] 1787-1855.
        Degli uomini illustri di Urbino comentario ... Urbino, V.
Guerrini, 1819. [16], 287, [6] p. 25cm. On p. [6] (3d set):
Pubblicato il di XXIII, Marzo MDCCCXX. Well over 200 biographical sketches of famous men of the Duchy of Urbino; alphabetical approach thru' index.

Venetia

9392   [BRUNATI, GIUSEPPE]
        Dizionarietto degli uomini illustri della Riviera di Salò,
considerata qual era sotto la Rep. Veneta cioè formata dalle sei
quadre o distretti antichi di Gargnano, Maderno, Salò, Mon-
tagna, Valtenese, e Campagna. Milano, 1837. 177 p. Little
dictionary of the famous men of a region around Salo, Italy,
which included six districts: Gargnano, etc., formerly in the
Venetian Republic.

Vercelli

9393   DIONISOTTI, CARLO, 1824?-1899.
        Notizie biografiche dei Vercellesi illustri. Biella, Amosso,
1862. 292 p. 23cm. Biographical notices of famous persons
from Vercelli.

JAMAICA

9394   ROBERTSON, GLORY
        Members of the Assembly of Jamaica from the general elec-

tion of 1830 to the final session, January 1866. Kingston [Institute of Jamaica, West India Reference Library] 1965. 59 p. 28cm. Memeographed.

9395   WRIGHT, PHILIP
         Monumental inscriptions of Jamaica. London, Society of Genealogists, 1966. x, 361 p. 21cm. Persons who lived and died in Jamaica, 1655-188-. Some of the inscriptions yield brief descriptions of the activities of the named, although most give only birth and/or death dates. Arrangement is by parish, with a comprehensive name index at end.

JAPAN

Bibliography, Indexes, Portrait Catalogs

9396   HOSEI DAIGAKU, TOKYO. BUNGAKUBU. SHIGAKU KENKYU-SHITSU.
         Nihon jimbutsu bunken mokuroku. Tokyo, Heibonsha, 1974. 4, 1199 p. 27cm. Bibliography of Japanese biographical literature from 1868 to 1966. Arranged by biographies in Japanese syllabic order.

9397   KOKURITSU KOKKAI TOSHOKAN, Tokyo. SANKO SHOSHIBU.
         Jimbutsu bunken sakuin. Horitsu seiji hen. Tokyo, Kokuritsu Kokkai Toshokan, 1972. 397 p. 27cm. A bibliography of Japanese biographical literature on 1,870 Japanese and 380 non-Japanese in politics, government, law-making and legal thought; army generals are included. Collective biographies are also listed.

General Works

9398   AOMORI-KEN JIMMEI DAIJITEN. Aomori, Tōō Nippō Sha, 1969. 899 p. 27cm. Numerous biographies of noted people in the Prefecture of Aomori.

9399   BAN, KŌKEI, 1733-1806.
         Kinsei kijin den. Zoku kinsei kijin den Katen Mikuma. Tokyo Heibonsha, 1972. 9, 512 p. illus. 18cm. Short biographies of Japanese eccentrics of the Edo period (1603-1868).

9400   DAI NIHON JIMMEI JITEN (Shimban) Tōkyō, Dōjinsha Shoten, 1927. 3 v. 27cm. Biographical dictionary of Japan. New edition.

9401   DAI NIHON JIMMEI JITEN (Teisei zōho) Tōkyō, Keizai Zasshi Sha, 1903. 2244, 8 p. 27cm. Biographical dictionary of

Japan. Augmented and corrected edition. First edition issued in 1885.

9402   HAGA, YAICHI, 1867-1927.
Nihon jimmei jiten. Kyoto, Shibungaku, 1972. 95, 83, 13, 1174 p. 19cm. Reprint of 1914 edition. Includes persons not listed in Dai Nihon jimmei jisho, pseudonyms, aliases and nicknames. Listing by personal names in Japanese syllabic order. Stroke indexes of personal names and syllabic index of surnames.

9403   HIOKI, SHOICHI, 1904-
Nihon rekishi jimmei jiten. Tokyo, Meicho Kankokai, 1973. 2, 4, 40, 991 p. 22cm. Reprint of 1938 edition. Includes ca. 5,000 Japanese personalities from ancient times to 1938. In Japanese syllabic order.

9404   INAMURA, TETSUGEN, 1928-
Taishō kakochō. Tokyo, Tokyo Bijutsu, 1973. 1 v. (various pagings) 22cm. By Tetsugen Inamura, Makoto Maruyama & Hiroshi Imon. A who was who of Japanese of Taisho era (1912-1926). Name index.

9405   ISHIDA, SEITARŌ, 1874-1945.
Ōsaka jimbutsushi. Zoku Ōsaka jimbutsushi. Kyoto, Rinsen Shoten, 1974. 2 v. 23cm. Reprint of 1927 edition (published by Ishida Bunko, Osaka). Dictionary of over 1200 persons born or active in Osaka and environs who contributed to the cultural heritage of the region. Indexed.

9406   KIKUCHI, AKISHIRŌ, 1884-
Hoten nijūnenshi. [Mukden] Fengtien, Hōten Nijunenshi Kankōkai, 1926. 770, 124, 172 p. illus. By Akishirō Kikuchi and Ichiro Nakajima. A history of 20 years of the City of Mukden. The last 172 pages contain a who's who of the local Japanese leadership.

9407   KOKUSHO KANKOKAI.
Keizu sōran. Tokyo, Meisaku Kankokai, 1964. 2 v. 22cm. Photocopy of 1915 edition. Contains more than 150 important genealogies-biographies of Japanese nobles, with titles, birth and death dates and achievements of each individual listed.

9408   KUZUU, YOSHIHISA, 1874-
Tōa senkaku shishi kiden. [Tokyo?] Kokuryūkai, 1935-36. 3 v. illus. 23cm. Memoirs of pioneer East Asian patriots, by the Amur [River or 'Black Dragon'] Society. Includes biographies of ca. 1,000 persons active in Japanese expansion into Korea, Manchuria and China.

9409   MORI, SENZŌ, 1895-
        Taishō jimbutsu itsuwa jiten. Tokyo, Tokyodo, 1966.
        438 p. 19cm. A dictionary of anecdotes about persons who
        were active in the Taisho period (1912-1926).

9410   ŌUE, SHIRŌ, 1896-
        Meiji kakocho. Tokyo, Tokyo Bijutsu, 1971. 6, 167,
        1264 p. 22cm. A who was who of Japanese of the Meiji era
        (1868-1912). Name index.

9411   SAKAMOTO, TAKEO.
        Kugyō jiten. Tokyo, Kokusho Kankokai, 1974. 107, 183,
        97 p. illus. 22cm. Gives the lineage, rank, achievements
        and death year of about 2,000 court nobles and some high rank
        officials from Heian Period up to 1868, in Japan.

9412   SHIZUOKA, JAPAN (PREFECTURE)
        Shizuoka-ken jimbutsu shi. Kyoto, Rinsen Shoten, 1974.
        536, 37, 21 p. 22cm. Reprint of the 1924 ed. Biographies
        of personalities of Shizuoka Prefecture. With name index and
        chronological table.

9413   TAI-SHI KŌRŌSHA DENKI HENSANKAI.
        Tai-Shi kaikoroku. [Tokyo?] 1936. 2 v.

        ---- ----Zoku Tai-Shi kaikoroku. Tokyo, Dai Nippon Kyōka
        Tosho, 1941-42. 2 v. A record looking back on China, by the
        Japanese Commission for the Compilation of Biographical
        Memoirs of Those Who Rendered Service in China. Vol. 2
        yields biographies of some 830 Japanese (deceased) active in
        regard to China since 1868; v. 2 of the supplement (Zoku) gives
        214 more biographies.

9414   TAJIRI, TASUKU, 1863-1929.
        Zōi shoken den. Tokyo, 1975. 2 v. 20cm. Reprint of
        1927 edition, with additions. Brief biographies of 2,372 Japa-
        nese awarded noble rank, etc. posthumously from the Meiji
        period to 1944. Arranged in Japanese syllabic order.

9415   TAKAYANAGI, MITSUTOSHI, 1892-1969.
        Sengoku jimmei jiten. Tokyo, Yoshikawa Kobunkan, 1973.
        325 p. 20cm. By Mitsutoshi Takayanagi & Toshikazu Matsudai-
        ra. A biographical dictionary of Japanese in the Sengoku period
        (1482-1558)

9416   TAKEUCHI, RIZŌ, 1907-   ed.
        Nihon kodai jimmei jiten. Tokyo, Yoshikawa Kobunkan,
        1965-73. 6 v. A biographical dictionary of early Japanese
        up to 781 A. D., based upon given historical sources. Arranged
        in Japanese syllabic order.

9417   TANI, SHIN'ICHI, 1905-
Shôzô senshû. Tokyo, Yoshikawa Kôbunkan, 1962. 335 p.
ports. 19 x 22cm. Includes representations, either in painting
or sculpture, of 160 persons significant in Japan's history, and
notes on the sitters and the portraits.

9418   TEIKOKU JIMMEI JITEN. Tōkyō, Tōkyō Tosho Shuppan, 1899.
    1784, 120 p. 23cm. Biographical dictionary of the Japanese
Empire.

JEWS

General Works

(For Jews in specific countries or areas,

see under the country or area)

9419   'ANSHE HA-'ALIYAH HA-SHENIYAH; pirke zikhronot. 'Arkhu
    Ya'akov Sharet ve-Nahman Tamir. Tel-Avic, ha-Merkaz
le-tarbut vele-hinukh, 1970-   v. 25cm. 144 biographies
of men from the second wave of immigration (Second 'Aliyah)
to Israel (Palestine) 1904-1914. Short accounts of their lives
in their country of origin and in Palestine after immigration.
Vol. 1 contains 55 biographies; v. 2 has 89. There is a table
of names at the beginning of each vol.

9420   BADER, GERSHOM, 1868-1953.
    The Jewish spiritual heroes; the lives and works of the
rabbinical teachers from the beginning of the "Great Syna-
gogue" to the final completion of the Talmud. Seven centuries
of Jewish thought. New York, Pardee Pub. House, 1940. 3 v.
24cm. English translation by Solomon Katz. Contents. --1.
The creators of 'Mishna'. --2. The 'Amoraim' of Palestine and
the Jerusalem Talmud. --3. The 'Amoraim' of Babylon and
the Babylonian Talmud.

9421   BREZA, EUGEN, Graf von
    Gallerie der ausgezeichneten Israeliten aller Jahrhunderte,
ihre Portraits und Biographien. Hrsg. von Eugen Grafen Breza.
Redigirt von Richard Otto Spazier. Stuttgart, Fr. Brodhag'sche
Buchhandlung, 1834-38. 5 pts. in 1 v. plate, ports. 28cm. A
gallery of outstanding Jews of all centuries, their portraits and
biographies.

9422   COMAY, JOAN
    Who's who in Jewish history after the period of the Old
Testament. [1st American ed.] New York, D. McKay Co.,
1974. 448 p. illus., ports. 26cm. Over 1,000 biographies
are included.

9423   ELAM, YIGAL, 1936-
        Elef Yehudim ba-'et ha-hadashah; leksikon. Tel-Aviv,
        Zemora, Beitan, Modan, 1974. 367 p. 24cm. On verso of
        half title page: Thousand Jews in modern times. A biographi-
        cal dictionary.

9424   ENCICLOPEDIA JUDAICA CASTELLANA; el pueblo judio en el
        pasado y el presente: su historia, su religión, sus costum-
        bres, su literatura, su arte, sus hombres, su situación en el
        mundo. Obra realizada con la cooperación de centenares de
        colaboradores. Director: Eduardo Weinfeld. Gerente: Isaac
        Babani. México, Editorial Enciclopedia Judaica Castellana,
        1948-51. 10 v. illus., ports. 28cm. An encyclopedia of Jewish
        history and culture published in Spain; includes biography.

9425   ENCYCLOPAEDIA JUDAICA. Jerusalem, Encyclopaedia
        Judaica; [New York] Macmillan, 1972. 16 v. illus., ports.
        32cm. Cecil Roth, editor-in-chief. In English. Includes nu-
        merous biographies of Jews prominent in world history and
        civilization.

9426   ENCYCLOPEDIA OF ZIONISM AND ISRAEL. Edited by Raphael
        Patai. New York, Herzl Press, 1971. 2 v. (xxiii, 1292 p.)
        illus., ports. 29cm. Includes many biographical entries for
        leaders in the Zionist movement and in the creation of the State
        of Israel.

9427   EVERYMAN'S JUDAICA; an encyclopedic dictionary. Edited by
        Geoffrey Wigoder. Jerusalem, Keter Pub. House, 1975.
        xi, 673 p. illus., ports. 29cm. Includes many quite brief bio-
        graphical sketches of distinguished Jews past and present. A-
        merican ed. (New York, L. Amiel, 1974) issued under title:
        Encyclopedic dictionary of Judaica.

9428   EVREISKAIA ENTSIKLOPEDIIA; svod znanii o evreistvie i ego
        kul'turie v proshlom i nastoiashchem. S.-Petersburg, Izd.
        Ob-va dlia nauch. evreiskikh izd. i Izd-va Brokgauz-Efron
        [1906-   The Hague, Mouton, 1969-   v. illus.,
        ports. 26cm. (Slavistic printings and reprintings, 193) En-
        cyclopedia of the Jewish people (in Russian) that includes a
        large number of biographies of famous Jews.

9429   ISAACSON, BEN
        The popular Jewish encyclopedia, by Rabbi Ben Isaacson
        [and] Deborah Wigoder. Jerusalem, Massada Press [1973] 336 p.
        illus. 27cm. Includes biographical notes on famous Jews living
        and dead. American ed. issued in the same year by Prentice-
        Hall under title: The international Jewish encyclopedia.

9430   JÜDISCHER PLUTARCH; oder, Biographisches Lexicon der
        markantesten Männer und Frauen jüdischer Abkunft. Hrsg.
        von Franz Gräffer und Simon Deutsch. Nachdruck der Ausg.
        Wien 1848 [-1849?] Hildesheim, New York, Olms, 1975. 2 v. in
        1. illus., ports. 15cm. Reprint of the Vienna ed. published by
        U. Klopf and A. Eurich in 2 volumes (1848-1849?) The Jewish
        Plutarch; a biographical dictionary of noted persons of Jewish
        ancestry with especial concentration on the Austrian Empire.

9431   KRESSEL, GETZEL, 1911-
        Ishim u-sefarim. Ramat-gan, Masada [1971] 178 p. 19cm.
        (Leksikon le-toda'ah yehudit) A bio-bibliographical dictionary of
        famous Jews of the last 250 years (deceased) who have contri-
        buted significantly to Jewish civilization and to Palestinian and
        Israeli society in the fields of the arts, religion and the social
        and political science, etc.

9432   LEXIKON DES JUDENTUMS. Chefredakteur: John F. Oppen-
        heimer. Mitherausgeber: Emanuel Bin Gorion, E. G.
        Lowenthal [und] Hanns G. Reissner. [2. Aufl. Gütersloh]
        Bertelsmann Lexikon-Verlag [1971] 960 columns. illus., ports.
        25cm. A dictionary of the Jews, with many biographical en-
        tries. First edition issued in 1967.

9433   MORAIS, HENRY SAMUEL, 1860-
        Eminent Israelites of the nineteenth century; a series of bio-
        graphical sketches. Philadelphia, E. Stern, 1880. 371 p. 21cm.
        100 famous Jews. Arranged alphabetically.

9434   THE NEW STANDARD JEWISH ENCYCLOPEDIA. Cecil Roth
        and Geoffrey Wigoder, editors-in-chief. [4th] new rev. ed.
        Garden City, N. Y., Doubleday, 1970. 2028 columns. illus.,
        ports. 28cm. Includes many biographies of outstanding Jewish
        personalities, past and present. Also published in Jerusalem
        in the same year (Massada Pub. Co.) Prior to 1970 published
        under title: The standard Jewish encyclopedia.

9435   SEMIGOTHAISCHES GENEALOGISCHES TASCHENBUCH.
        1.-3. Jahrg.; 1912-14. München [etc.] Kyffhäuser.   v.
        geneal. tables. 15cm. Title varies: 1912-13, Weimarer his-
        torisch-genealoges Taschenbuch des gesamten Adels jehudäi-
        schen Ursprunges. No more published? A genealogical hand-
        book of prominent Jewish families (some of noble lineage) in
        Germany especially; the work has an anti-Semitic aura, but
        might be of some use in gathering biographical data.

9436   WALDEN, AARON, b. ca. 1835.
        Shem ha-gedolim he-hadash ... [Jerusalem, 1964/65] 2 v.
        in 1. 24cm. Photo-offset ed. of Warsaw, 1879/80 ed. Contin-
        uation of Azulai's Shem ha-gedolin ha-shalem. Edited by J. A.
        L. Walden. Bio-bibliography of Jews and Hebrew writers.

9437   WOMEN'S INTERNATIONAL ZIONIST ORGANIZATION. DEPT.
        OF ORGANISATION AND EDUCATION.
            Who's who in Wizo, 1966-1970. Tel-Avic [1970] v, 156 l.
        27cm.

        ---- ----Supplement, 1972. Tel-Aviv [1972] 20 l. 27cm. Not
        in alphabetical arrangement. Seems to be arranged, first of all,
        by office held and then, secondly, by country (of origin?).

KAZAKHSTAN

9438   GEROI SOTSIALISTICHESKOGO TRUDA--KAZAKHSTANTSY.
            [Redaktsionnaia kollegiia: Beisembaev, A. B. ... Dzhanga-
        lin, M. O. (otvet. redaktor) i dr.] Alma-Ata, Izd-vo "Kazakh-
        stan," 1969-70. 4 v. ports. 21cm. A huge collection of bio-
        graphical sketches of Heroes of Socialist Labor in Kazakhstan;
        ca. 1200 biographies. Each volume has its own table of con-
        tents, with names listed alphabetically by district.

9439   QAZAQ SOVET ENTSIKLOPEDIIASY. Bas redaktor M. K. Ka-
            rataev. Almaty, Qazaq sovet entsiklopediiasynyn bas
        redaktsiiasy, 1972-   v. illus., ports. 27cm. On
        page facing t. p.: Qazaq SSR ghylym akademiiasy. The Kazakh
        Soviet encyclopedia; a general encyclopedia useful for its many
        biographical entries for notable personages in Kazakhstan's civi-
        lization and history. Contents.--1. A-Aiapov.

KOREA

9440   SOHN, POW-KEY
            Biographical tables of the Koryo period. Berkeley, East
        Asia Studies, Institute of International Studies, University of
        California, 1958. v, 179 p. 28cm. The tables, alphabetical
        in arrangement, yield names, other names used, descent, sons,
        highest offices held and biographical sources for officials, etc.
        of the Koryo period of Korean history, 918-1392 A. D.

General Works

9441   HAN'GUK INMYONG TAESAJON. Seoul, Sin'gu Munhwasa
            [1967] 72, vii, 1390 p. illus., ports. 26cm. The 'Great'
        Korean biographical dictionary. Edited by Yi Hui-sung. With
        some 10,000 biographies. No living persons are included.

9442   HAN'GUK UI IN'GANSANG. Seoul, Sin'gu Munhwasa, 1965.
            6 v. illus., ports. 19cm. A selective biographical dic-
        tionary of some 200 persons who were important in Korean civi-
        lization and history.

9443   KOREA (GOVERNMENT-GENERAL OF CHOSEN, 1910-1945).
        CHŪSUIN.
        Chosen jimmei jisho. Kyoto, Rinsen Shoten, 1972. 2 v.
        21cm. Reprint of 1938 edition. A biographical dictionary, in
        Japanese, of about 13,000 Koreans from ancient times to about
        1930, arranged by Chinese stroke counts, with index in Japa-
        nese.

9444   KOREAN ANNUAL. 1970 (7th ed.) Seoul, Hapdong News
            Agency, 1970. 1 v. illus. Has an extensive Who's who
        section.

9445   TAEBAEKKWA SAJŌN. Korean encyclopedia.   Seoul,
            Hakwŏnsa [1958]165. 8 v. illus. 27cm. In Korean.

        ---- ----[Index] Seoul, 1965. 534 p. 27cm. Useful for the
        large amount of Korean biography included.

9446   YI, HONG-JIK, 1909-
            Kuksa taesajŏn. Seoul, Chimungak, 1962-63. 2 v. (2085 p.)
        illus. 27cm. Historical dictionary of Korea with many bio-
        graphical entries; a one-volume edition was prepared in 1968.

9447   YI, KA-WŎN, 1917-
            Yijo myŏngin yŏichŏn. Seoul, Uryu Munhwasa, 1965.
        42, 932, 16 p. 21cm. The Korean Yi dynasty biographical dic-
        tionary; 1,670 persons who lived in the 14th century to the end
        of the dynasty in 1910. Arranged by date of birth.

LATIN AMERICA

9448   COVARRUBIAS, RICARDO
            Las calles de Monterrey. Monterrey, México, Tip. Garza
        y Jiménez, 1947-   v. illus. 24cm. A dictionary
        which gives portraits & biographical sketches of individuals for
        whom most of the streets are named. For example, vol. 3 (A-
        Z) has ca. 45 biographies of world figures, although most of the
        persons are Latin American. 3 vols. issued as of 1970.

9449   DICTIONARY OF LATIN AMERICAN AND CARIBBEAN BIOG-
            RAPHY. Hon. general editor: Ernest Kay. 2d ed. Lon-
        don, Melrose Press, 1971. 458 p. 26cm. First ed. published
        in 1970 under title: Dictionary of Caribbean biography. Con-
        temporary Latin Americans and persons living in the Caribbean
        area.

9450   ENCYCLOPEDIA OF LATIN AMERICA. Edited by Helen Del-
            par. New York, McGraw-Hill, 1974. ix, 651 p. illus.

29cm. This dictionary-encyclopedia is strong in the extent and completeness of its biographical coverage of political and historical persons.

9451   GARCÍA BRUGOS, MANUEL
Héroes, apóstoles y gigantes españoles en el Nuevo Mundo; los pueblos hispanoamericanos no son latinos. Buenos Aires, Editorial Plus Ultra [1970] 151 p. illus. 24cm. Spaniards in colonial Latin America; pt. 2 (p. 67-151) is a biographical dictionary of explorers, conquistadors, churchmen, etc.

9452   INTERNATIONALE PROMINENZ. International prominence.
Importantes personalidades del mundo. Ausg. Lateinamerika. [Herausgeber: Rolf K. W. Schellhorn] Köln, Deutscher Wirtschaftsdienst [1966-   2 v. ports. 23cm. Kept up to date by loose-leaf supplements. Biographical sketches of prominent contemporary Latin Americans.

9453   LATIN AMERICAN GOVERNMENT LEADERS. 2d ed. Edited by David William Foster. Tempe, Center for Latin American Studies, Arizona State University, 1975. viii, 135 p. 23cm. First edition, issued in 1970, edited by L. A. Tambs and others. Biographical sketches arranged alphabetically under country: Argentina to Venezuela.

9454   QUIÉN ES QUIÉN EN HISPANOAMÉRICA. (In Anuario hispanoamericano. Madrid, Ediciones Mundus. t. 1., 1953/54, p. [659]-975; t. 2 [1954/55] p. [503]-647) Who's who in Spanish America; v. 1 contains 6,000 brief biographies. Vol. 2 is a revised but abridged version of v. 1.

9455   WHO'S WHO IN LATIN AMERICA; a biographical dictionary of notable living men and women of Latin America. Edited by Ronald Hilton. 3d ed. Stanford, Calif., Stanford University Press. Detroit, B. Ethridge, 1971 [c1945] 2 v. 24cm. Contents.--1. Mexico, Central America, and Panama. Cuba, Dominican Republic and Haiti, Colombia, Ecuador and Venezuela.--2. Brazil, Bolivia, Chile, and Peru. Argentina, Paraguay, and Uruguay.

LATVIA

9456   ALBUM LETTONORUM, 1870-1882-1930. Riga, 1930.
xxi, 168 p. plates, ports. folio. Plates printed on both sides. Preface signed: Lettonias konvents, Lettonias fil. pal. biedr. valde. An album of portraits and biographical notes on noteworthy Latvians from 1870 to 1930.

9457   LATVIJAS PSR MAZĀ ENCIKLOPĒDIJA. [Galvenais redaktors
        V. Samsons] Rīgā, Zinātne, 1967-70. 3 v. illus., ports.
        27cm. Contents. --1. Abava-Juveris. --2. Kabile-Pianino. --
        3. Piebalga-Zivigule.

        ---- ----Personu un priekšmetu alfabētiskais rādītājs. Rīgā,
        Zinātne, 1972. 306 p. 27cm. A Latvian encyclopedia with
        many biographical entries for famous Latvians.

9458   RIGASCHE BIOGRAPHIEEN; nebst einigen Familien-Nach-
             richten, Jubiläums-Feiern, etc.; aus den Rigaschen Stadt-
        Blättern vom Jahre 1810-1879 incl., mit Ergänzungen und
        Zusätzen, zum Theil aus dem seit den Jahren 1858 in Riga
        erscheinenden Rigaschen Almanach bis 1880 incl. [par] J. G. F.
        Nachdruck der Ausg. Riga, Schnakenburg, 1881-1884. Han-
        nover-Döhren, Von Hirschheydt, 1973. 3 v. in 1. 19cm. Con-
        tents. --1. Bd. 1810-1829. --2. Bd. 1830-1855. --3. Bd. 1856-
        1879 incl. Biographies of noteworthy 19th century citizens of
        Riga as well as an almanac of events in the City.

LIBERIA

9459   DIRECTORY WITH WHO'S WHO IN LIBERIA. 1970/71-
             Monrovia, A. & A. Enterprises Incorporated.   v.
        illus. 24cm. Cover title, 1970/71-   : A & A directory
        and who's who.

LITHUANIA

9460   ENCYCLOPEDIA LITUANICA. Edited by Simas Sužiedelis.
             Boston, J. Kapocius, 1970-   v. illus., ports. 25cm.
        Contents. --v. 1. A-C. --v. 2. D-J. --v. 3. K-M. --v. 4. N-R.
        1975.
        Valuable for its many biographies of Lithuanian personalities
        and persons of surrounding countries involved in Lithuanian
        history and culture.

9461   LIETUVOS ALBUMAS. [Berlin, O. Elsner, 19--] 435 p. illus.,
             ports. 21 x 23cm. An album of early 20th century Lithuan-
        ians; pages 5-285 contain portraits, with captions in Lithuanian
        and English; pages 291-435 comprise a biographical dictionary.

9461a   MAGGID, HILLEL NOAH, 1829-1903.
             'Ir Wilna ... [Vilna, 1900] xiv, 304 p. 23cm. In Yiddish.
        Vol. 1 only was published. Materials for the history of the Jew-
        ish community in Vilna in biographical sketches with bibliogra-
        phical notices.

9462   MAŽOJI LIETUVIŠKOJI TARBINĖ ENCIKLOPEDIJA. J. Matu-
         lis, vyriausiasis redaktorius. [Vilnius, Mintis, 1966-70
         3 v. illus., ports. 27cm. At head of title: Lietuvos TSR Mokslų
         Akademija. Contents. --1. A-J. --2. K-P. --3. Pie-Z. An en-
         cyclopedia of Lithuanian history that includes many biographical
         sketches.

LIVONIA

9463   KRUSENSTJERN, GEORG VON
         Die Landmarschälle und Landräte der livländischen und der
         öselschen Ritterschaft in Bildnissen. Gesammelt, Zusammen-
         gestellt und mit historischem Text versehen. Hrsg. von der
         Livländischen Ritterschaft und von der Öselschen Ritterschaft.
         Hamburg, Verlag Harry von Hoffmann, 1963. 243 p. ports.
         24cm. Marshalls and councillors of Livonia and Osel Island in
         portraits and biographical sketches.

LUSATIA

9464   SERBSKI BIOGRAFSKI SLOWNIK. Budyšin, Domowina [1970]
         301 p. ports. 19cm. By A. Brankačk and others. A bio-
         graphical dictionary of Lusatia.

MALAWI

9465   MALAWI. DEPT. OF INFORMATION.
         Biographies of his Excellency the Life President Dr. H.
         Kamuzu Banda, cabinet ministers, regional ministers, parlia-
         mentary secretary and members of Parliament of the Republic
         of Malawi. [Blantyre, 1971] 47 p. ports. 28cm. Cover title.

MALAYSIA

9466   WHO'S WHO IN MALAYSIA AND GUIDE TO SINGAPORE.
         1971/72-   Kuala Lumpur, J. V. Morais.   v.
         illus. 28cm. Biennial. Continues The Who's who in Malaysia
         and [The] Who's who [in] Malaysia and Singapore. Latest vol.,
         1975-1976.

MALTA

9467   BONNICI, ROBERT MIFSUD
         Dizzunarju bijo-bibljografiku nazzjonali. Valletta, Dept. of
         Information, 1960-68. v, 459 p. In Maltese. Bio-bibliogra-
         phical dictionary of Malta.

MANCHURIA

9468   GIBERT, LUCIEN
        Dictionnaire historique et géographique de la Mandchourie.
        Hongkong, Impr. de la Société des missions-étrangères, 1934.
        xx, 1040 p. illus., ports. 23cm. Arranged alphabetically by
        French transcription followed by Chinese characters. An his-
        torical and geographical dictionary of Manchuria, with a sub-
        stantial number of biographical entries.

MEXICO

Bibliography, Indexes, Portrait Catalogs

9469   IGUÍNIZ, JUAN BAUTISTA, 1881-
        Bibliografía biográfica mexicana. México, Universidad
        Nacional Autónoma de México, Instituto de Investigaciones His-
        tóricas, 1969. 431 p. 24cm. (Instituto de Investigaciones His-
        tóricas. Serie bibliográfica, 5) A bibliography of Mexican bio-
        graphical literature. An enlargement of the 1930 ed., which in-
        cluded only vol. 1: Repertorio bibliográfico.

General Works

9470   DICCIONARIO BIOGRÁFICO DE MÉXICO. 1. ed. Monterey,
        Editorial Revesa, 1968-70. 2 v. 24cm. Biographical
        dictionary of Mexico. The 1st volume covers colonial and early
        independent Mexico (A-Z); vol. 2 (A-Z) covers present-day
        Mexico.

9471   DICCIONARIO PORRUA DE HISTORIA, BIOGRAFÍA Y GEOG-
        RAFÍA DE MÉXICO. 3. ed. corr. y aumentada. México,
        Editorial Porrua, 1971, c1970. 2 v. (xxxi, 2465 p., p. 2455-
        2465 advertisements) fold. col. maps. 26cm. A dictionary of
        Mexican history, biography and geography. 1st ed., 1964; 2d,
        1965.

9472   ENCICLOPEDIA REGIONAL ILUSTRADA COAHUILA. Dic-
        cionario castellano. México, Fernández, 1966. 95, 217 p.
        illus., ports. 17cm. The first 95 pages (also entitled: Dic-
        cionario enciclopédico regional del Estado de Coahuila) are a
        dictionary of the State of Coahuila and include 153 biographical
        entries.

9473   ICAZA, FRANCISCO A   DE, 1863-1925.
        Conquistadores y pobladores de Nueva España; diccionario
        autobiográfico sacado de los textos originales. Madrid, 1923.
        2 v. 26cm. The conquistadors and settlers of New Spain (1,385

notices); a dictionary of autobiography drawn from the original
texts. Not in alphabetical arrangement; index of names (v. 1,
p. lix-xci) gives alphabetical approach.

9474   MÁRQUEZ MONTIEL, JOAQUÍN, 1895-
         Hombres célebres de Chihuahua. México, Editorial Jus,
1953. 304 p. illus., ports. 18cm. Famous men of the State of
Chihuahua, Mexico.

9475   MÁRQUEZ MONTIEL, JOAQUÍN, 1895-
         Hombres célebres de Puebla. México, Editorial Jus,
1952-   v. illus., ports. 18cm. Contents.--t. 1. Por
nacimiento.
Famous men of the State of Puebla, Mexico.

9476   MORALES DÍAZ, CARLOS
         Quién es quién en la nomenclatura de la ciudad de México
(apuntes biográficos de las personas cuyos nombres aparecen en
dicha nomenclatura) 2. ed., aumentata. México, B. Costa-
Amic, 1971. 650 p. illus. 24cm. Who's who in the nomenclature of the City of Mexico. A biographical dictionary of persons
whose names have been used for the names of the streets of the
city (universal, in scope, but with chief emphasis, of course, on
famous Mexicans)

9477   PASQUEL, LEONARDO
         La generación liberal veracruzana. [México] Editorial Cit-
laltepetl, 1972. viii, 366 p., ports. 18cm. (Colección Suma
veracruzana. Serie Biografía) A biographical dictionary of 80
notable Vera Cruzans (a state of Mexico) of the 19th and early
20th centuries.

9478   PASQUEL, LEONARDO
         Xalapeños distinguidos. México, Editorial Citlaltepetl,
1975. xix, 692 p. ports. 19cm. (Colección Suma veracruzana.
Serie Biografía) A biographical dictionary of distinguished natives of the City of Jalapa, Mexico. Includes portraits for 78 of
the biographies.

9479   PEÑALOSA, JOAQUÍN ANTONIO
         Cien mexicanos y Dios. 1. ed. México, JUS, 1975. 275 p.
19cm. 100 living Mexicans give their views on God and religion;
each statement is preceded by a biographical sketch. Arrangement is alphabetical by surnames.

9480   PERAL, MIGUEL ANGEL, 1900-
         Diccionario histórico, biográfico, geográfico e industrial
de la República. México, Editorial Pac, 1960-   v.
illus., ports. 23cm. An historical, biographical, geographi-

cal and industrial dictionary of Mexico. Vol. 1, fasc. 1-2, covering Aatzin Ahatl to Ancona Albertos, only ones issued?

9481 SIERRA, CARLOS J   1933-
Historia de la administración hacendaria en México, 1821-1970 [por] Carlos J. Sierra. [México, Secretaría de Hacienda y Crédito Público, Dirección General de Publicaciones, 1970] 93 p. ports. 33cm. Contains biographical sketches of the 100 secretaries of public finance in Mexico, 1821-1911.

9482 UROZ, ANTONIO, 1894-
Hombres y mujeres de México. [1. ed.] México, Editorial Lic. A. Uroz, 1972. 318 p. illus., ports. 24cm. Men and women in the history of Mexico; over 100 biographical sketches are included in this chronologically arranged work, which, unfortunately, has no alphabetical index.

9483 WHO'S NOTABLE IN MEXICO. v. 1-   1972-
Mexico, Who's Who in Mexico.   v. 24cm. Lucien F. Lajoie, editor; Jack D. Myer, assistant editor; Francisco Castillo Najera, special consultant.

MOLDAVIA

9484 ENCHIKLOPEDIIĂ SOVETIKĖ MOLDOVENIĂSKE. Redaktor-shef IĂ. Grosul. Kishinèu, Red. Principalė a Enchiklopedieĭ Sovetichė Moldovenesht, 1970-   v. illus., ports. 27cm. Issued by the Akademiiă de Shtlintse a RSSM. An encyclopedia of Soviet Moldavia, of great value for its many biographical entries for leading figures in Moldavia's past and present civilization. Vol. 4 (1974)--L to Nianiùl--latest published.

MOROCCO

9485 IBN AL-QĀDĪ, AHMAD IBN MUHAMMAD, 1552 or 3-1616.
Hādhihi Jadhwat al-iqtibās fī-man halla min al-a'lam madīnat Fās. [Fez, 1891-92] 355, 3-5 p. 23cm. Biographies of personages of medieval Fez (or Fes or Fas), Morocco.

MOZAMBIQUE

9486 PINTO, FREDERICO DA SILVA
Roteiro historico-biografico da cidade de Lourenço Marques. [Lourenço Marques, Moçambique Editora] 1965. 206 p. 19cm. (Colectanea biografica) A biographical survey of important men in the history of Lourenço Marques, Mozambique.

NEAR EAST

9487   HERAVI, MEHDI
            Concise encyclopedia of the Middle East. Mehdi Heravi,
        editor. Washington, Public Affairs Press [1973] 336 p. 24cm.
        Includes many biographical entries for important figures in the
        recent and contemporary political history of the area.

9488   SHIMONI, YAACOV, 1915-
            Political dictionary of the Middle East in the 20th century.
        Edited by Yaacov Shimoni and Evyatar Levine. Supplement
        edited by Itamar Rabinovich and Haim Shaked. [Rev. and up-
        dated paperback ed. New York] Quadrangle/New York Times
        Book Co. [1974] 510 p. illus., ports. 24cm. Includes articles
        on leading personalities, Arab, Israeli, etc. in the Middle East
        and northern Africa. First ed. published in 1972; London
        (Weidenfeld and Nicolson) ed. of 1974 had collation: 434 p. illus.,
        ports. 25cm.

NEPAL

9489   HEDRICK, BASIL CALVIN, 1932-
            Historical and cultural dictionary of Nepal, by Basil C.
        Hedrick and Anne K. Hedrick. Metuchen, N. J., Scarecrow
        Press, 1972. vii, 198 p. 22cm. (Historical and cultural dic-
        tionaries of Asia series, no. 2) Includes biographical entries.

9490   WHO IS WHO—NEPAL, 1972-74 : [a biographical dictionary of
            the distinguished Nepali personalities] / Editors, Aryal,
        Deepak Kumar ... [et al.]. --1st ed.--Kathmandu : Kathmandu
        School of Journalism, 1974. xxxiv, 392 p., [1] leaf of plates :
        ill., maps (1 on lining paper) ; 25cm. Advertising matter in-
        cluded in paging. Includes index. Rs100.00 "About 400 person-
        alities who have earned their name or fame in social, political,
        economic, administrative, scientific and other important fields."

NETHERLANDS

9491   ETTE, A   J   H   VAN
            Onze ministers sinds 1798. Samengesteld door A. J. H.
        van Ette. Alphen aan den Rijn, N. Samson, 1948. [4], 125 p.
        21cm. Dutch cabinet-officers since 1798. Chronologically ar-
        ranged by ministerial department & then an alphabetical listing
        of names (p. 61-125) Biographical information very brief.

9492   JONGE, JOHANNES CORNELIS DE, 1793-1853.
            L'Union de Bruxelles, année 1577, selon l'original publié
        par J. C. de Jonge, avec les additions et corrections que cet au-

teur y a faites: traduite par Laurent Deleville-Baussart. Rotterdam, Chez la veuve Allart, 1829. 288 p. 22cm. Originally published in Dutch under title: De Unie van Brussel des jaars 1577. The major portion of this work consists of brief biographical sketches of the signers of the Union of Brussels (a pact made between patriots of the northern and southern halves of the Low Countries against the Spanish, 1577). An alphabetical approach to the over 200 biographical sketches is available through the "Table" at the end.

9493   MOLHUYSEN, PHILIP CHRISTIAAN, 1870-1944.
        Holandeses no Brasil; verbetes do Novo dicionário holandês de biografias. Traduzidos por Francisco José Moonen. Com uma introd. por José Antonio Gonsalves de Melo. Recife, Universidade Federal de Pernambuco [Instituto de Ciencias do Homen, Divisão de História] 1968. 170 p. 21cm. (Coleção Textos traduzidos, 1) The Dutch in Brazil; a biographical dictionary which consists of translations of selected biographies from Molhuysen's Nieuw Nederlandsch biografisch woordenboek (Leyden, 1911-37)

9494   NAGTGLAS, FREDERIK, 1821-
        Levensberichten van Zeeuwen. Zijnde een vervolg op P. de la Rue, Geletterd, staatkundig en heldhaftig Zeeland. Voor het Zeeuwsch Genootschap der Wetenschappen uitg. door F. Nagtglas. Middelburg, J. C. & W. Altorffer, 1890-93. 2 v. 23cm. Issued in 4 parts, 1888-1893. A bio-bibliographical dictionary of Zealand, Netherlands.

9495   REINSMA, R
        Van Goor's woordenboek der Vaderlandse geschiedenis. Den Haag, Van Goor [1973] 464 p. 19cm. A dictionary of Dutch history which includes a huge number of biographical sketches.

NETHERLANDS ANTILLES

9496   ENCYCLOPEDIE VAN DE NEDERLANDSE ANTILLEN.
        Hoofdredacteur: H. Hoetink. Amsterdam, Elsevier, 1969. 708 p. illus., ports. 26cm. An encyclopedia-dictionary of the Netherlands Antilles with biographies of persons involved in the islands' history & culture scattered through the text.

NEW ZEALAND

9497   CHAMBERLAIN, WALTER MAX
        Victoria Cross winners of New Zealand. 2d ed. Ormond East, Victoria, Military History Society of Australia, 1968. ii, 45 p. illus. Brief biographical sketches of heroic New Zealanders.

9498   GUDGEON, THOMAS WAYTH, d. 1890.
        The Defenders of New Zealand; being a short biography of
colonists who distinguished themselves in upholding Her Majes-
ty's supremacy in these islands. Auckland, H. Brett, 1887.
620, xxxvi p. illus., ports. 26cm. Biographical sketches of
many New Zealand colonists, especially those who fought in the
Maori Wars, 1843-1870.

NICARAGUA

9499   MEYER, HARVEY KESSLER, 1914-
        Historical dictionary of Nicaragua. Metuchen, N. J.,
Scarecrow Press, 1972. xiii, 503 p. illus. 22cm. (Latin A-
merican historical dictionaries, no. 6) Includes biographical
entries.

NIGERIA

Bibliography, Indexes, Portrait Catalogs

9500   NATIONAL LIBRARY OF NIGERIA.
        A bibliography of biographies and memoirs on Nigeria. La-
gos, 1968. 11 p. 22 x 9cm. (National Library publications, 9)

General Works

9501   AYENI, PETER M
        Who's who in Midwestern Nigeria Legislature. Compiled
by Peter M. Ayeni. 1st ed. Benin City, 1964. 81 p. ports.

9502   EASTERN NIGERIA. MINISTRY OF INFORMATION.
        Know your legislators: biographical notes, 1963. Enugu,
Govt. Printer, 1963. 118 p. ports. 25cm. Latest or only vol.
published?   Portraits and biographies of the governor, premier,
ministers, provincial commissioners, parliamentary secretaries, and members of the House of Assembly and the House of
Chiefs of Eastern Nigeria in 1963.

9503   WHO'S WHO IN NIGERIA; a biographical dictionary. [2d ed.
        Apapa, Nigeria, Printed by Times Press, 1971] 232 p.
illus. 21cm. "A Daily times' Magazine Division publication."

9504   WHO'S WHO, NORTHERN REGION OF NIGERIA LEGISLATURE.
        Kaduna, 1961. 107 p. ports.

9505   WHO'S WHO OF THE FEDERAL HOUSE OF REPRESENTA-
        TIVES. Lagos, 1958. 124 p. illus., ports. Nigerian
        House of Representatives; a who's who.

NORWAY

Bibliography, Indexes, Portrait Catalogs

9506   ANKER, CARL JOHAN, 1835-1903.
        Katalog over malede portraeter i Norge, hvorom anmel-
        delse er indkommen til C. J. Anker og H. J. Huitfeldt-Kass.
        Christiania, Dybwad, 1886. 164 p. Catalog of portrait paint-
        ings in Norway.

General Works

9507   AAGAARD, ADOLF
        De vernepligtige sjøofficerer og marinen. Utarb. i
        anledning av foreningens 25 aars. jubilaeum 23/2 1920.
        Kristiania, 1919. 176 p. Norwegian naval and maritime offi-
        cers, early 20th century.

9508   BARTH, BJARNE KEYSER, 1892
        Norges militaere embedsmenn 1929. Oslo, A. M. Hanche,
        1930. 656 p. ports. 25cm. Biographical sketches of Nor-
        wegian military officers (Army & Navy) active in 1929.

9509   EGGE, NILS MARTINSEN, 1880-
        Biografialbum 1764-1930. Underofficerer og underofficer-
        sutdannede m. fl. ved Feltartilleriregiment nr. 2 og tidligere
        avdelinger av artilleriet i Oslo og omegn. Oslo, Merkantile
        boktr., 1937. 543 p. illus. Album of biography (1764-1930) of
        non-commissioned officers serving with the 2nd Field Artillery
        Regiment (Norwegian Army) or with former sections of the ar-
        tillery in Oslo and environs.

9510   NORGES VERNEPLIKTIGE SJØOFFICERER [1879-1934] Utg.
        av Vernepliktige sjøofficerers forening. Oslo, Merkantile
        boktr., 1938. 200 p. illus. Norwegian naval officers, 1879-
        1934.

9511   OFFICERSKULLET 1919. Biografiske medelelser samlet i
        anledning af 10-årsjubileet. Tr. som ms. Oslo, J. Chr.
        Gundersen, bok- og notetr., 1929. 95 p. Biographical infor-
        mation on the Army Officers' School in Oslo in 1919.

9512   PETERSEN, ALF
        Den norske haers vernepliktige officerer, 1864-1933. Utg.

ved Vernepliktige officerers forenings 40-års jubileum 1936.
Oslo, 1936. 632 p. illus., ports. 8.° Brief biographical
sketches of Norwegian Army officers, 1864-1933.

PAKISTAN

9513   BIOGRAPHICAL SKETCHES OF GOVERNMENT OF WEST
            PAKISTAN OFFICERS. [n. p., 1960?] 1 v. (unpaged)
        27cm.

9514   PAKISTAN.
            History of services of officers holding gazetted appoint-
        ments in the Government of Pakistan ... Karachi, Manager of
        Publications, 196--   v. 24cm. A series of volumes,
        in 4 sections, which gives pertinent biographical information for
        living Pakistani officials & civil service officers: e.g., date of
        birth (when known), service history, domicile, religion, etc.
        The 4 sections: 1. Ministry of Law & Parliamentary Affairs,
        National Assembly & Cabinet Secretariat. 2. Ministries of
        Home & Kashmir Affairs & Defence. 3. Ministries of Agricul-
        ture & Works Communications and Education and Scientific Re-
        search. 4. Ministries of Health, Labour and Family Planning,
        Industries and Natural Resources, and Information & National
        Affairs.

PANAMA

9515   HEDRICK, BASIL CALVIN, 1932-
            Historical dictionary of Panama, by Basil C. and Anne K.
        Hedrick. Metuchen, N. J., Scarecrow Press, 1970. 105 p.
        22cm. (Latin American historical dictionaries, no. 2) Includes
        biographies.

PAPUA — NEW GUINEA

(Territory)

9516   ENCYCLOPAEDIA OF PAPUA AND NEW GUINEA. Edited by
            Peter Ryan. Melbourne, Melbourne University Press in
        association with the University of Papua and New Guinea, 1972.
        3 v. illus. 27cm. Contents.--v. 1. A-K.--v. 2. L-Z.--v. 3.
        Index. Includes biographies of persons influential in the areas'
        modern development.

PARAGUAY

9517   FRANCO PREDA, ARTEMIO
            El Guairá y su aporte a la cultura paraguaya; historia cul-
        tural del Guairá. Prólogo del Dr. Hermógenes Rojas Silva.

[Asunción? 1972] 460 p. 20cm. A cultural history of the Province of Guaira, Paraguay, with ca. 85 biographies (chronologically arranged).

9518   KOLINSKI, CHARLES J
        Historical dictionary of Paraguay. Metuchen, N. J.,
        Scarecrow Press, 1973. vi, 282 p. 22cm. (Latin American
        historical dictionaries, no. 8) Biographical sketches are in-
        cluded.

PERU

Bibliography, Indexes, Portrait Catalogs

9519   OJEDA, OLIVIA
        Iniciación de una bibliografía biográfica del Perú. (In
        Fénix, revista de la Biblioteca Nacional, Perú. Lima. No. 2,
        1. sem., 1945. p. [297]-311) The beginnings of a biographical
        bibliography of Peru; 108 works listed, with annotations.

General Works

9520   BARRETO VILLAVISENCIO, CARLOS A   1892-
        Diccionario biográfico de figuras contemporáneas, por C.
        A. Barreto V. y G. de la Fuente Chávez. Lima, Lit. Tip. T.
        Scheuch, 1926-28. 2 v. ports. 24cm. Vol. 2 has imprint:
        Lima, Tall. Gráf. de la Penitencaria. A biographical diction-
        ary of contemporary figures in Peru.

9521   BARRIOS, D   WALTER
        Diccionario histórico geográfico de Tacna [por] D. Walter
        Barrios [y] José Antezana. 1. ed. popular. Tacna [Peru] J. H.
        Girón Flores, 1974. 170 p. 22cm. Historical and geographi-
        cal dictionary of Tacna, Peru. Includes biographical entries for
        the city & province of Tacna.

9522   BUSTO DUTHURBURU, JOSÉ ANTONIO DEL
        Diccionario histórico biográfico de los conquistadores del
        Perú. Lima, Editorial Arica, 1973-   v. 21cm. (Co-
        lección Perú historia. Serie anaranjada: La Conquista, 1
        A biographical dictionary of the Spanish conquistadors in Peru
        in the 16th century. Contents.--t. 1. Abadia-Azpeitia.

9523   LOCKHART, JAMES MARVIN
        The men of Cajamarca; a social and biographical study of
        the first conquerors of Peru, by James Lockhart. Austin, Pub-
        lished for the Institute of Latin American Studies by the Univer-
        sity of Texas Press [1972] xvi, 496 p. map. 23cm. (Latin A-

merican monographs, no. 27) "Part II: The men" (p. [119]-455)
includes 168 biographies, of varying lengths, of Spaniards prominent in the Peruvian conquest (1522-1548) Arrangement is alphabetical under such categories as: Leaders, Hidalgos, Clerks,
Artisans, etc.

9524   LOHMANN VILLENA, GUILLERMO
        Los ministros de la Audiencia de Lima en el reinado de los
Borbones (1700-1821); esquema de un estudio sobre un núcleo
dirigente. Sevilla, Escuela de Estudios Hispano-Americanos de
Sevilla, 1974. cxxiv, 200 p. plates (2 fold.) 25cm. (Publicaciones de la Escuela de Estudios Hispano-Americanos de Sevilla, 222) The ministers of the Royal Audiencia of Lima during
the reign of the Spanish Bourbons, 1700-1821. "Cédulas per-
sonales de los ministros de la Audiencia de Lima (1700-1821)"
(p. [1]-145) is a biographical dictionary ("identification papers")
of the 158 ministers; the appendix (p. [149]-195) yields 51 more
brief biographies (in biographical dictionary arrangement) of
native Peruvian officials of the 16th-17th centuries who were
sons of various Spanish dignitaries.

9525   ROMERO, EMILLIA
        Apuntes para una cronología peruana; relación de fechas de
nacimiento y muerte de algunos peruanos que se han distinguido
en el campo de sus respectivas actividades y de algunos extranjeros cuya obra en algún punto se relaciona con el Perú. (In
Fénix; revista de la Biblioteca Nacional, Peru. Lima. No. 3,
2. semestre, 1945. p. [554]-600). This work on the historical
chronology of Peru includes brief biographical data for many
Peruvians and foreigners who had some connection with Peru;
as well as references under the biographies to periodical articles, etc. where more information may be found about them.

PHILIPPINE ISLANDS

9525a   MANILA. NATIONAL LIBRARY. BIBLIOGRAPHY DIVISION.
        Constitutional Convention 1970 campaign materials; a re-
search guide. [Rev. and enl. ed.] Manila, 1972. iv, 225 1.
33cm. (TNL research guide series, no. 4) "National Library
Heritage Project." Includes a comprehensive index to biographical data of 1,580 candidates from 66 electoral provinces for
the 1970 Philippine Constitutional Convention. This biographical
material is stored in the National Library along with posters,
leaflets, etc., all pertaining to the 1970 election.

General Works

9526   GALANG, ZOILO M   ed.
        Encyclopedia of the Philippines. [3d ed.] Manila, E.
Floro [1950-58] 20 v. illus., ports. 24cm. Partial contents.
--v. 3-4. Biography.--v. 17-18. Builders. The 4 volumes noted

above contain numerous biographies of Filipino leaders of the
present and figures (Filipino and foreign) of the past connected
in various ways with Philippine history.

9527   MARING, ESTER G
        Historical and cultural dictionary of the Philippines, by
        Ester G. Maring and Joel M. Maring. Metuchen, N. J., Scare-
        crow Press, 1973. vii, 240 p. 22cm. (Historical and cultural
        dictionaries of Asia, no. 3) Includes biographical sketches of
        outstanding figures in Philippine history and civilization.

9528   PERALTA, LAVERNE Y   1948-
        Who is who: Philippine guerrilla movement, 1942-1945.
        [Manila? 1972] xii, 458 p. illus., ports. 23cm. Philippine
        guerrilla fighters against the Japanese during the Second World
        War; in majority of the cases dates of birth and/or death are not
        given.

POLAND

9529   CIOŁEK, GERARD
        Materiały do słownika twórców ogrodów polskich. Wyd. 1.
        Warszawa, Państwowe Wydawn. Naukowe, [Oddz. w Łodzi]
        1968. 136 p. 24cm. (Instytut Podstawowych Problemów Plan-
        owania Przestrzennego Politechniki Warszawskiej. Materiały i
        studia) At head of title: Gerard Ciołek i Witold Plapis. A dic-
        tionary of city planners in Poland.

9530   ENCYKLOPEDIA WARSZAWY. Wyd. 1. Warszawa, Państwowe
        Wydawn. Naukowe, 1975. 815 p. illus., ports. 25cm.
        Encyclopedia of Warsaw; a dictionary that includes a huge num-
        ber of biographical sketches of Poles who were intimately con-
        nected with the history and culture of the city.

9531   ENCYKLOPEDYJA POWSZECHNA. Warszawa, 1859-68. 28 v.
        8.° A general encyclopedia in Polish, included because of
        its many biographies of famous Poles from Poland's beginnings
        to the middle of the 19th cent. A new edition under the title
        Encyklopedja powszechna Ultima Thule was begun in 1930. Of
        this new edition only 9 vols. were completed (v. 9, R-Spa) be-
        cause of the interruption caused by the outbreak of World War II.
        A good reason for listing this item is that the Polski słownik
        biograficzny (the Dictionary of Polish biography) is still in
        progress.

9533   NISSENBAUM, SALMON BARUCH, 1866-1926.
        Sefer le-korot ha-Yehudim be-Lubin; ziyunim le-nefashot
        shel ge'one gedole u-farnase 'irenu u-kezat mi-toldot hayehem,
        gam me'at mi-korot 'adatenu bi-zmanim 'avaru. 'asafti ve-
        likatti 'ani mi-sefarim u-mikhtavim 'atikim Shlomo Baruch Nis-

senbaum. 'im he'arot u-milu'im m'et David Koyfman, A. A.
Harekhavi ve- SH. Baber. Lublin, bi-defus shel A. Pheder u-B.
Zetser, 660 [1899 Mahadura 2. 'im nosafim u-milu'im besof ha-
sefer be-shem "Rehovot 'ir" ve-'Hutsot Kiryah" ... Yerushalayim?] 728 [1967 or 8] 175, iv, 11 p. 25cm. Includes biographical sketches of more than 200 Jews and rabbis of Lublin, Poland. With an alphabetical index of names.

9534   OD AGRYKOLI DO ZYWNEGO; mały słownik patronow ulic
        warszawskich. Red. Grażyna Kieniewiczowa, Alina Soko-
łowska. Wyd. 1. Warszawa, Ludowa Społdzielnia Wydawnicza,
1968. 202 p. ports. 21cm. Issued by the Museum Historyczne,
Warsaw. From Agricola to Zywn; dictionary of the 'patrons' of
Warsaw's streets.

9535   OSTROWSKA, RÓŻA
        Bedeker kaszubski. Róża Ostrowska, Izabella Trojanowska.
Wyd. 2., poszerzone i uzup. Gdańsk, Wydawn. Morskie, 1974.
493 p. illus., ports. 20cm. A dictionary of persons, places,
etc. of the Kaszuby region of Poland.

9536   PERLICK, ALFONS, 1895-
        Beuthener Biographien. Lebensbilder verdienstvoller Per-
sönlichkeiten aus dem Beuthener Stadt- und Landraume. (In
Beuthener Geschichts- und Museumsverein. Mitteillungen.
Dortmund, 1954/55. 24cm. Heft 15/16, p. 45-97. ports.)
Biographical sketches (ca. 200) of personalities from the city
and district of Beuthen, Silesia (now Bytom, Poland) arranged
by activity. No index.

9537   SŁOWNIK HISTORII POLSKI. [Red. nacz. Tadeusz Łepkowski]
        Wyd. 5. Warszawa, Wiedza Powszechna, 1969. xv, 815 p.
maps. 20cm. (Wydawnictwa popularno-encyklopedyczne) First-
4th editions published under title: Mały słownik historii Polski.
A dictionary of Polish history which includes numerous biographical entries.

9538   SZYMANOWSKI, WOJCIECH
        300 portretów zasłuzionych w narodzie Polaków i Polek z
dodaniem krótkich wspomnienich żywotów, zebranych i napisa-
nych W. S. Warszawa, W. Drukarnie Jana Psurskiego, 1860.
vii, 339, lx p. illus., 19cm. 300 biographies and portraits of
eminent Poles. The portraits are from wood-engravings by
Władysław Bakalowicz & Kazimierz Górnicki.

9539   ZAKRZEWSKI, ZBIGNIEW
        Nazwy osobowe i historyczne ulic Posnania. [Wyd. 1:
Poznań] Wydawn. Poznańskie, 1971. 107 p. 20cm. Personal
and historical names of the streets of Posen (Poznań) Biographical data is included for those famous persons (majority

are polish) after whom streets are named (Alphabetical arrangement by surname chiefly but sometimes by forename: p.
9-94)

POLYNESIA

9540   O'REILLY, PATRICK
        Tahitiens; répertoire biographique de la Polynésie Fran-
çaise [par] Patrick O'Reilly & Raoul Teissier. 2. éd. revue,
corrigée et augmentée. Illus. et portraits de J. Boullaire [et
al.] Paris, Musée de l'Homme, 1975. 670 p. illus., ports.
27cm. (Publications de la Société des Océanistes, no. 36)
Tahitians; a biographical dictionary of French Polynesia; includes 1, 875 entries. 1st ed. issued in 1962 with a supplement
in 1965.

PORTUGAL

9541   ENCICLOPEDIA HISTÓRICA DE PORTUGAL. Direcção de
        Duarte de Almeida. Lisboa, J. Romano Torres, 1938.
12 v. illus., ports. 19cm. An historical encyclopedia or Portugal with numerous biographical sketches.

9542   ESTEVES PEREIRA, JOÃO MANUEL
        Portugal; diccionario historico, chorographico, heraldico,
biographico, bibliographico, numismatico e artistico ... per
Esteves Pereira e Guilherme Rodrigues. Lisboa, J. Romano
Torres, 1904-15. 7 v. illus., ports. 28cm. An historical,
biographical [etc.] dictionary of Portugal.

9543   FERREIRA MARTINS, JOSÉ FREDERICO, 1874-
        Os vice-reis da India, 1505-1917. Obra ilustrada com 118
fotogravuras e 106 'fac'similes' de assinaturas. [Lisboa] Imprensa Nacional de Lisboa, 1935. viii, 326 p. illus., ports.
25cm. The viceroys of Portuguese possessions on the Indian
subcontinent, 1505-1917.

9544   FONSECA, MARTINHO AUGUSTO FERREIRA DA, 1869-1934.
        Aditamentos ao Dicionário bibliográfico português de
Inocencio Francisco da Silva. Coimbra, Imprensa da Universidade, 1927. 377 p. 23cm. Part of the material was published
in the Boletim da Sociedade de'Bibliophilos Barbosa Machado,
v. 3-4, 1915-1917, and also as a separate. Additions to the Portuguese bio-bibliographical dictionary of I. F. da Silva (q. v.)

9545   GALLIS, JOAQUIM ALFREDO, 1859-1910.
        Synopse dos homens celebres de Portugal desde a fundação
da monarchia. Lisboa, Typ. de J. C. d'Ascensão Almeida, 1883.
149 p. ports. 17cm. Biographical synopses of the famous men
of Portugal from its origin to the foundation of the monarchy.

9546   LAFUENTE FERRARI, ENRIQUE
        Iconografía lusitana. Retratos grabados de personajes
portugueses. Madrid, Juanta de Iconografía Nacional, 1941.
169 p. plates, ports. 26cm. Portuguese iconography; engraved
portraits of Portuguese personages.

9547   LAGOA, JOÃO ANTONIO DE MASCARENHAS JUDICE,
           visconde de, 1898-1957.
        Grandes e humildes na epopeia portuguesa do Oriente (sécu-
los XV, XVI e XVII) Lisboa [Gráfica Lisbonense] 1942-
v. illus., ports. 26cm. Biographical dictionary of the
Portuguese in India and the East, 15-17th centurie. Contents.
--v. 1. Abarca, Bartolomeu-Acosta, Baltasar. --v. 2. Adamo,
João Mateus-Albuquerque, Afonso de (1943) Two volumes (or
two fascicles) only have ever been published? Presumably
enough material was collected for a work of some 22 vols.
(50,000 items).

9548   NOBREZA DE PORTUGAL; bibliografia, biografia, cronologia,
           filatelia, genealogia, heráldica, historia, nobiliarquia,
numismática. [Direcção, coordenação e compilação de Afonso
Eduardo Martins Zuquete, com a colaboração de Acácio Casimiro, et al.] Lisboa, Editorial Enciclopédia, 1960-61. 3 v. illus., ports. 26cm. Issued in 36 parts. The nobility of Portugal; bibliography, biography, etc. Vols. 2-3, in biographical
dictionary arrangement, include biographical sketches of the
first holders of the patent of nobility.

9549   RETRATOS E ELOGIOS DOS VARÕES E DONAS, que illustra-
           ram a nação portugueza em virtudes, letras, armas, e
artes, assim nacionaes, como estranhos, tanto antigos, como
modernos. Lisboa, Officina de S. T. Ferreira, 1817-[22] 2 v.
in 1. ports. 21cm. Consists of 79 biographical sketches of
famous Portuguese men and women (with portraits) written chiefly by P. J. de Figueiredo and published in 19 nos.

9550   SERRÃO, JOEL
        Dicionario de história de Portugal. Lisboa, Iniciativas
Editoriais, 1963-71. 4 v. ports. 25cm. Contents. --1. A-D.
--2. E-Ma. --3. Me-Sin. --4. Sis-Zurara e adenda. Dictionary
of Portuguese history; with many biographical entries.

9551   ZÚQUETE, AFONSO EDUARDO MARTINS, 1907-
        Tratado de todos os vice-reis e governadores da India.
Lisboa [Editorial Enciclopédia] 1962. 317 p. illus., ports.
26cm. "Serie cronologica e biográfica dos vice-reis e governadores da India" p. [59]-266. Biographies and portraits of all
the viceroys and governors of Portuguese India.

PUERTO RICO

9552   FARR, KENNETH R
          Historical dictionary of Puerto Rico and the U. S. Virgin
          Islands. Metuchen, N. J., Scarecrow Press, 1973. vii, 148 p.
          22cm. (Latin American historical dictionaries, no. 9) Includes
          biographical sketches.

9553   MELÓN DE DÍAZ, ESTHER M   1933-
          Puerto Rico: figuras del presente y del pasado y apuntes
          históricos. Rio Piedras, Editorial Edil, 1972. 225 p. ports.
          23cm. Puerto Rico: figures of the present and the past; a bio-
          graphical dictionary (410 sketches), p. 9-200.

9554   PUERTO RICO. OFFICE OF THE HISTORICAL INDEX.
          Tesauro de datos históricos; índice compendioso de la litera-
          tura histórica de Puerto Rico, incluyendo algunos datos inéditos,
          periodísticos y cartográficos. San Juan, Impr. del Gobierno de
          Puerto Rico, 1948-49. 2 v. 25cm. At head of title: Gobierno
          de Puerto Rico. Oficina del Historiador Oficial. Treasury of
          historical data; a dictionary of and index to the history of Puerto
          Rico. Includes biographical entries; biographical information is
          brief, with references to sources for further material on indi-
          viduals. Only 2 vols. (covering Abacoa to Cuyón) were issued?
          Geoghegan, A. B. Obras de referencia de América Latina (Bue-
          nos Aires, 1965) seems to indicate the issuing of 3 vols. (v. 3,
          1951)

9555   RIBES TOVAR, FEDERICO
          100 [i. e. Cien] biografías de puertorriqueños ilustres.
          [New York] Plus Ultra Educational Publishers [c1973] 304 p.
          ports. 18cm. (Plus Ultra books, 9) 100 biographies of famous
          deceased Puerto Ricans; arranged chronologically from Aguey-
          bana I (d. 1510). No alphabetical index of names.

9556   ROSA-NIEVES, CESÁREO, 1901-
          Biografías puertorriqueñas: perfil histórico de un pueblo,
          por Cesáreo Rosa-Nieves y Esther M. Melon. Sharon,
          Conn., Troutman Press [1970 or 71] 487 p. 27cm. (Puerto
          Rico: realidad y anhelo, no. 12) Puerto Rican biographies; his-
          torical profile of a people. Contains more than 300 biographical
          sketches of notable men and women past and present in biogra-
          phical dictionary arrangement.

RHODESIA

9557   ENCYCLOPAEDIA RHODESIA. Contributing editors: Peter
          Bridger [and others] Salisbury, Rhodesia, College Press,
          1973. 448 p. illus. 25cm. Includes biographical entries.

9558   FEDERATED RHODESIA NYASALAND. Salisbury [The Rho-
            desian graphic] 1954. 100 p. ports. Edited by S. H. Veats.
            Includes biographical notes with portraits of members of the
            Federal Assembly.

9559   TABLER, EDWARD C
            Pioneers of Rhodesia. Cape Town, C. Struik, 1966. viii,
            185 p. illus., port. 25cm. A biographical dictionary of "adult
            male foreigners (including Griquas and other Coloureds and a few
            Africans) who arrived in the defined area [present-day Southern
            Rhodesia, the Caprivi Strip, Barotse Valley, Victoria Falls
            Region, the Tati Concession and part of Bechuanaland Protec-
            torate]... 1836, till 1880. "

ROMAN EMPIRE

9560   ALFÖLDY, GEZA
            Fasti Hispanienses; senatorische Reichsbeamte und Offi-
            ziere in den spanischen Provinzen des Romanischen Reiches von
            Augustus bis Diokletian. Wiesbaden, F. Steiner, 1969. xv,
            335 p. facsims. 25cm. Included in the "Prosopographische
            Listen" (p. [3]-190) are many biographical sketches of Roman
            Imperial officials in Rome's Spanish provinces, arranged
            chronologically under office held.

9561   BROUGHTON, THOMAS ROBERT SHANNON, 1900-
            The magistrates of the Roman Republic, by T. Robert S.
            Broughton with the collaboration of Marcia L. Patterson.
            Cleveland, Ohio, Published for the American Philological As-
            sociation by the Press of Case Western Reserve University,
            1968. 2 v. 25cm. (Philological monographs, no. 15) "Orig-
            inally published by the Association in 1951. Reprinted 1968. "
            Contents. --v. 1.509-100 B.C. --v. 2. 99-31 B.C. In chrono-
            logical arrangement, the work gives details of the careers of
            consuls, censors, praetors, etc., of the Roman Republic. The
            2d vol. includes an alphabetical listing of the names from the
            chronological sections.

9562   CALZA, RAISSA
            Iconografia romana imperiale. Da Carausio a Giuliano
            (287-363 d. C.) A cura de Raissa Calza. Roma, L'Erma di
            Bretschneider, 1972. 434 p. illus., ports. 26cm. (Quaderni
            e guide di archeologia, 3) Imperial Roman iconography; in-
            cludes biographical sketches and portraits of 48 Roman emper-
            ors and empresses from 287-363 A. D.

9563   CEBEILLAC, MIREILLE
            Les "Quaestores principis et candidati" aux Ier et IIeme
            siecles de l'Empire. Milano, Cisalpino-Goliardica, 1972.
            287 p. 24cm. (Biblioteca storica universitaria. Monografie a
            supplemento degli Atti, 4) Roman officials (quaestors) of the

1st and 2d centuries of the Roman Empire (40 B. C. -161 A. D.)
In the main text biographical data for 72 quaestors are given
(chronologically arranged). In the appendices data for some 20
candidates for the office of quaestor (from the reign of Augustus
to Marcus Aurelius) are given.

9564   DE VIRIS ILLUSTRIBUS URBIS ROMAE. English and Latin.
        Deeds of famous men (De viris illustribus) A bi-lingual
edition, translated and edited by Walter K. Sher-
win, Jr. 1st ed. Norman, University of Oklahoma Press, 1972,
c1973. xvi, 206 p. 19cm. A series of 77 anonymous biographical sketches of men significant in Roman history from Proca to
Pompey. The work is contained in Sexti Aurelii Victoris Liber
de Caesaribus, published in 1911, corrected by R. Gruendel, and
reprinted in 1961.

9565   ECK, WERNER
        Senatoren von Vespasian bis Hadrian. Prospographische
Untersuchungen mit Einschluss des Jahres und Provinzialfasten
der Statthalter. München, Beck, 1970. viii, 284 p. 24cm.
(Vestigia, Bd. 13) Revision of the author's thesis, Universität
Erlangen-Nürnberg, Erlangen. Roman senators from Vespasian
to Hadrian. A prosopography; actually a listing with biographical data more or less confined to footnotes under the lists;
chronological arrangement.

9566   JONES, ARNOLD HUGH MARTIN, 1904-
        The prosopography of the Later Roman Empire, by A. H. M.
Jones, J. R. Martindale and J. Morris. Cambridge [Eng.] University Press, 1971-   v. geneal. tables. 24cm. Contents. --v. 1. A-D. 260-395.
Biographical data for the governing classes of the Later Roman
Empire taken from inscriptions, papyri, Patristic and hagiogra-
phical literature, literary and historical texts, etc. Each vol. is
in alphabetical arrangement, A-Z (to be in 3 vols.) Continuation
of the Prosographia Imperii Romani. Vol. 1 only available as of
1976.

9567   VOLLENWEIDER, MARIE LOUISE
        Die Porträtgemmen der romanischen Republic. Mainz, P.
von Zabern [1974] 2 v. plates, ports. 30cm. Contents. --[1]
Text. --[2] Katalog und Tafeln. In addition to portraits of vari-
our persons prominent in the Roman Republic found on the plates
of vol. 2 of this work, the 1st vol. (text) contains a biographical
index of the historical persons, medallists, artists, authors,
poets, gods and mythological figures mentioned in the work (v.
1, p. 264-302)

9568   WISEMAN, TIMOTHY PETER
        New men in the Roman Senate, 139 B. C. -A. D. 14. Lon-
don, Oxford University Press, 1971. xi, 325 p. 23cm. (Ox-

ford classical and philosophical monographs) The "prosopography" (p. [205]-283) lists the senators in alphabetical order and
contains some biographical data as well as references to sources
for biographical facts about the senators.

ROMANIA

9569   CAMARIANO-CIORAN, ARIADNA
        Les académies princières; de Bucarest et de Jassy et
leurs professeurs. Thessaloniki, Institute for Balkan Studies,
1974. 730 p. illus. 25cm. (Hetaireia Makedonikōn Spoudōn.
Hidryma Meletōn. Chersonēsou tou Haimou. Ekdoseis, 142)
The learned institutions of Bucharest and Jassy, Romania and
their professors; pages 363-662 are devoted to biographies
(chronologically arranged) of over 90 professors.

9570   MAFTEI, IONEL
        Personalități ale stiintei, culturii, si artei românesti. Iasi,
Comitetul de Cultură si Arta al Jud. Tasi, 1968-   v.
21cm. Contents.--pt. 1. Prezentări bibliografice. Personalities of Rumanian science, culture and art. Part 1 (319 p.): bibliographical presentation. Ca. 200 notices. No further vols. issued? Searched Romanian bibliographies thru' 1974.

9571   MICUL DICTIONAR ENCICLOPEDIC. Bucuresti, Editura
        Enciclopedică română, 1971. 1800 p. 17 x 24cm. A one-
volume Romanian encyclopedia with ca. 3000 biographies, em-
phasizing Romanians.

9572   PERSONALITIES OF THE ROMANIAN SCIENCE AND CULTURE.
        Bucharest, Romanian Institute for Cultural Relations with
Foreign Countries, 1973. 63 p. illus., ports. 30cm.

9573   ROSETTI, DIMITRIE
        Dictionarul contimporanilor din România, 1800-1898.
Bucuresti, 1898. 207 p. Dictionary of 'contemporaries' (i. e.
personages of the 19th century) in Romania.

9574   STOICESCU, NICOLAE
        Dictionar al marilor dregatori din Tara Românesca si
Moldova. Sec. SIV-XVII. Bucuresti, Editura enciclopedica
româna, 1971. 456 p. 21cm. A biographical-genealogical dictionary of Romanian and Moldavian nobility, 14th-18th centuries.
In 2 parts: (1) Romania (2) Moldavia, with alphabetical arrangement under each century.

RUSSIA

Bibliography, Indexes, Portrait Catalogs

9575   GEROI VELIKOĬ OTECHESTVENNOĬ VOĬNY; rekomendatel'nyĭ
            ukazatel' literatury. [Sostavitel'-redaktor: N. A. Shokina.
        Sostaviteli: N. I. Beketova, i dr.] Moskva, Izd-vo "Kniga,"
        1970. 128 p. (Stranitsy biografii) At head of title: Gosudarstven-
        naia publichnaia istoricheskaia biblioteka RSFSR. Soviet Heroes
        of the Great Patriotic War (World War II); a recommended list
        of collective biographies, autobiography, individual biography.

General Works

9576   BEREZHNOĬ, ALEKSANDR FEODOSEEVICH
            Boĭtsy revoliutsii. Sotrudniki bol'shevistskoĭ pechati.
        Biobibliogr. spravochnik. Leningrad, Lenizdat, 1969. 275 p.
        17cm. At head of title: A. F. Berezhnoĭ, S. V. Smirnov.
        Bio-bibliography of Russian journalists active in the Russian
        Revolution.

9577   CONTEMPORARY BIOGRAPHIES FROM THE LARGE SOVIET
            ENCYCLOPEDIA YEARBOOK FOR 1971. Arlington, Va.,
        Joint Publications Research Service; may be ordered from Na-
        tional Technical Information Service, Springfield, Va., 1972.
        a, 493 p. 28cm. (JPRS-56377) Cover title. A biographical
        dictionary of prominent living Russians.

9578   DEĬATELI SOĬUZA SOVETSKIKH SOTSIALISTICHESKIKH
            RESPUBLIK I OKTIABR'SKOI REVOLIUTSII; avtobiografii
        i biografii. Prilozhenie k tsiklu "Soiuz Sovetskikh Sotsialistiche-
        skikh Respublik." [Moskva, 1926?] 350, 233, 304 columns (on
        double leaves) 22cm. A Xerox copy (Ann Arbor, Mich., Uni-
        versity Microfilms, 1963) of the original work. A biographical
        dictionary of persons active in the Russian Revolution of October,
        1917 and in the early years of the Soviet Republic (to ca. 1925).

9579   EKZEMPLIARSKIĬ, ALEKSANDR VASIL'EVICH, 1846-1900.
            Velikie i udiel'nye kniaz'ia sievernoi Rusi v tatarskii
        period, s 1238 po 1505 g. Biograficheskie ocherki po pervois-
        tochnikam i glavnieishim posobiiam A. V. Ekzempliarskago.
        Sanktpeterburg, Tip. I. Akademii nauk, 1889-91. 2 v. fold.
        geneal. tables. 29cm. "Izdanie grafa I. I. Tolstago." Con-
        tents.--t. 1. Velikie kniaz'ia vladimirskie i vladimiro-moskov-
        skie.--t. 2. Vladietel'nye kniaz'ia vladimirskikh i moskovskikh
        udielov i velikie i udiel'nye vladietel'nye kniaz'ia suzdal'sko-
        nizhego-rodskie, tverskie i riazanskie. A rather extensive col-
        lection (vol. 2 especially; v. 1 has 20 biographies only) of bio-
        graphical sketches of early Russian princes and rulers in nor-
        thern Russia during the Tatar period (1238-1505).

9580   FITZPATRICK, SHEILA
        The Commissariat of Enlightenment: Soviet organization of
        education and the arts under Lunacharsky, October 1917-1921.
        New York, Cambridge University Press, 1970. xxii, 380 p.
        ports. 23cm. (Soviet and East European studies) The appen-
        dix contains well over 100 brief biographies of people involved in
        the affairs of Narkompros (Commissariat of Public Enlighten-
        ment--Narodnyĭ komissariat po prosveshcheniiŭ).

9581   GALERIE DES PORTRAITS GRAVÉS DES GÉNÉRAUX, officiers,
           etc., qui, par leur valeur, leurs talens militaires et leur
        patriotisme, ont contribué aux succès des armes russes, pend-
        ant la guerre commencés en 1812. St.-Petersbourg, Impr. de
        Pluchart, 1813. 1 v. (unpaged) ports. Text in French; t. p. and
        captions in Russian and French. Portraits of Russian Army of-
        ficers who performed heroically during the Napoleonic invasion
        of Russia.

9582   GEROĬAM RODINY—SLAVA. [Podgotovleno N. A. Grininym,
           I. M. Mullo i E. D. Rybakom. Izd. 2., ispr. i dop.
        Petrozavodsk, Izd-vo "Kareliiȃ," 1970] 334 p. ports. 22cm.
        A biographical dictionary (with portraits) in 2 alphabets, of 162
        Heroes of the Soviet Union (World War II, 1939-1945) The first
        section (alphabetical) features those who fought on the Karelian
        front; the 2d, on the general Russian front.

9583   IMENA MOSKOVSKIKH ULĬTS. Pod obshcheĭ red. A. M. Pe-
           gova; avtorskiĭ kollektiv S. V. Evgenov [et al.] Izd. 2.,
        perer. i dop. Moskva, Moskovskiĭ rabochiĭ, 1975. 535 p.
        illus. 21cm. A dictionary of Moscow's streetnames which in-
        cludes biographical sketches of the famous persons (primarily
        Russians) after whom many of the streets are named.

9584   INSTITUT ZUR ERFORSCHUNG DER UdSSR.
           Who was who in the USSR; a biographic directory containing
        5,015 biographies of prominent Soviet historical personalities.
        Compiled by the Institute for the Study of the USSR, Munich,
        Germany. Edited by Heinrich E. Schulz, Paul K. Urban [and]
        Andrew I. Lebed. Metuchen, N. J., Scarecrow Press, 1972.
        677 p. 28cm.

9585   KALININ, VENIAMIN VASIL'EVICH
           Geroi podvigov na Khar'kovshchine. Khar'kov, "Prapor,"
        1970. 463 p. maps, ports. 21cm. At head of title: V. V.
        Kalinin, L. G. Makarenko. Heroes of the Soviet Union at the
        Battle of Kharkov, 1943. Includes ca. 200 portraits and brief
        biographical sketches of Russian soldiers; with an alphabetical
        index at end of vol.

9586   KLEVENSKIĬ, MITROFAN MIKHAĬLOVICH, 1877-
           Gertsen-izdatel' i ego sotrudniki. (In: Literaturnoe nasled-
        stvo, t. 41-42. A. I. Gertsen, kn. 2, p. 581-620. ports. Mos-

kva, 1941) A biographical dictionary of collaborators with Alexander Hertzen in his various publishing ventures.

9587   LEWYTZKYJ, BORYS, comp.
        The Stalinist terror in the Thirties; documentation from the
Soviet press. Compiled with pref. and introd. by Borys Levyt-
sky. Stanford, Calif., Hoover Institution Press [1974] xxvii,
521 p. ports. 24cm. (Hoover Institution publications, 126) Included are 234 biographical sketches, arranged alphabetically
by categories: e. g., military figures, Communist Party leaders, statesmen, industrialists, Chekhists. These people disap-
peared in the Stalinist purge of the 1930's.

9588   LIUDI BESSMERTNOGO PODVIGA. Ocherki o dvazhdy,
        trizhdy i chetyrezhdy Geroiakh Sovetskogo Soiuza. Izd. 3.,
ispr. i dop. Moskva, Politizdat, 1973. 2 v. illus., ports.
20cm. 123 Heroes of the Soviet Union ('people of immortal exploits') in World War II (1939-1945) In biographical dictionary-
type arrangement. Portraits and biographical sketches are followed by detailed accounts of particular exploits. 2d ed. (1965)
included 111 biographies. Edited by A. Sinitsyn; biographical
sketches by A. Sinitsyn and V. Evstigneev.

9589   LOBANOV, DMITRII IVANOVICH
        Russkie sovremennye dieiateli; sbornik portretov zamiecha-
tel'nikh lits nastoiashchago vremeni s biograficheskimi ocher-
kami. S.-Peterburg, Izd. A. O. Baumana, 1876-78. 3 v. in 2.
ports. 24cm. Portraits of Russians prominent in the latter
half of the 19th century accompanied by biographical sketches.

9590   THE MODERN ENCYCLOPEDIA OF RUSSIAN AND SOVIET
        HISTORY. Edited by Joseph L. Wieczynski. Gulf Breeze,
Fla., Academic International Press, 1976-   v.
25cm. Contents: v. 1. Aachen-Anichkov.

        A dictionary of Russian history; biographical entries are numer-
ous. However, "personalities from the Russian past whose sole
importance is limited to the areas of literary work, the hard
sciences and other realms not of direct concern to students of
history will not be cited in this collection. "

9591   MODZALEVSKII, LEV BORISOVICH, 1902-
        Materialy dlia biografii I. L. Lobachevskogo. Moskva,
1948. 828 p. illus., ports. 27cm. (Akademiia nauk SSSR.
Trudy Komissii po istorii Akademii nauk SSSR) Material for the
biography of L. B. Lobachevskii: includes ca. 800 notices of
personages from Kazan, end of the 19th century to the beginning
of the 20th.

9592   NAVECHNO V STROIU. [Sbornik ocherkov o Geroiakh Velikoi
        Otechestvennoi voiny. Sostavitel' I. Roschin] Moskva,

Voen. izd-vo, 1957-66. 5 v. ports. 21cm. Contains circa 100 biographies of substantial length of Heroes of the Great Patriotic War (1939-1945)

9593   ORLOVSKÝ, DEZIDER
       Album, významnych výročí a osobností ZSSR v roku 1973. Úvod Anna Sakáčová. Martin, Matica slovenská, t. Tlač. SNP, 1973. 419, [2] p. illus., ports. 13 x 18cm. A biographical dictionary of famous Russians (in Czech) issued on the occasion of the 50th anniversary of the USSR.

9594   SEMEVSKIĬ, MIKHAIL IVANOVICH, 1837-1892.
       Znakomye. Al'bom M. I. Semevskogo, izdateliā-redaktora istoricheskogo zhurnala "Russkaiā starina." Kniga avtobiograficheskikh sobstvennoruchnykh zametok 850 lits. Vospominaniiā, stikhotvoreniiā, epigrammy, shutki, podpisi, 1867-1888. Sankt-Peterburg [Tip. V. S. Balasheva] 1888. xxxi, 415 p. 26cm. "Acquaintances." An album containing autobiographical pieces from 850 persons in Russia of the latter half of the 19th century (1867-1888)—memoirs, poetry, epigrams, jests, autographs, etc.

9595   SERISEV, INOCENTO
       Album of great outstanding and eminent personalities of Russia: with short biographies. [Sydney, W. C. Penfold] 1945-53. 3 v. ports. 29cm. No more published?

9596   SOVETSKAIĀ VOENNAIĀ ĖNTSIKLOPEDIIĀ. Moskva, Voennoe izd-vo, 1976- v. illus., ports. 27cm. On leaf preceding t. p.: Ministerstvo oborony SSSR. Institut voennoi istorii. Contents: 1. A-Biŭro.

Soviet military encyclopedia (alphabetical arrangement); includes biographies of Soviet military figures.

9597   VENKOV, BORIS STEPANOVICH
       Geroi Karpat. Uzhgorod, Izd-vo "Karpati," 1972. 206 p. ports. 21cm. Heroes of the Soviet Union in World War II from the Carpathian Mountain region and Bukovina; experiences of 75 soldiers and guerrillas preceded by portraits and biographical sketches. At end is an alphabetical list of names with date and place of exploit, but no page references to the more extensive description in the text.

Local

(For constituent republics of the U.S.S.R.,

see e.g.: Kazakhstan, Ukraine, etc.)

Adygeyskaia Avtomnaya Oblast

9598   ZOLOTYE SVEZDY ADYGEI. Maikop, Adygeĭskoe otd-nie
        Krasnodarskogo knizhnogo izd-va, 1972. 207 p. ports.
        20cm. 91 biographies and portraits of Heroes of the Soviet
        Union in World War II and Heroes of Socialist Labor from
        Adygeyskaiã avtonomnaya oblast'. By N. G. Aparin and others.

Bukhara (Province)

9600   TAGGER, NISSIM
        Toldot Yehude Bukhara be-Bukhara uvi-Ysra'el [mi-shenat
        600 'ad 1970 me'et] Nisim Tagger. Tel-Aviv, 731 [1970] 128,
        154 p. illus., ports. 25cm. Short biographies (with many por-
        traits) of Jews in Bukhara (now a province or "oblast" of Russia)
        Alphabetical approach thru' index, p. 149-153.

Caucasus

9601   TUMANOV, G   M
        Slovar' kavkazskikh deiãtelei. Tiflis, Tip. M. Vartaniãntsa,
        1890. 85 p. 21cm. "Prilozheniiã k spravochnoi knige staro-
        zhila 'Kavkaz,' No. 1." Dictionary of famous persons of the
        Caucasus.

Don Valley

9602   OTVAZHNYE SYNY DONA; ocherki o Geroiãkh Sovetskogo
        Soiuza. [Sostavitel' i avtor spravochnogo materiala N. I.
        Sychkov. Rostov na/Donu] Rostovskoe knozhnoe izd-vo, 1963.
        289 p. ports. 23cm. 'Courageous sons of the Don'; Heroes of
        the Soviet Union (ca. 150) in World War II from the Don Valley.

9603   OTVAZHNYE SYNY DONA. Ocherki o Geroiãkh Sovetskogo
        Soiuza. [Vstupit, stat'iã Marshala Sovetskogo Soiuza trizdhy
        Geroiã Sovetskogo Soiuza S. Budennogo. Rostov n/D., Kn. izd-
        vo, 1970] 503 p. illus., ports. 22cm. Compiled by I. A.
        Kalinin, S. D. Kravchenko and S. D. Shvetsov. 'Courageous
        sons of the Don'; Heroes of the Soviet Union in World War II
        from the Don Valley. An enlargement or new edition of the work
        of the same title issued in 1963 (q. v.)?

Gorki

9604   GEROI SOVETSKOGO SOIUZA—GOR'KOVCHANE. Avtory
        teksta L. K. Tiul'nikov, IA. I. Basovich. Gor'kii, Volgo-
        Viãtskoe knizhnoe izd-vo, 1972. 349 p. ports. 18cm. Heroes
        of the Soviet Union in World War II from the Province of Gorki,
        Russia; a biographical dictionary.

Kalinin (Province)

9605   DOLGOV, IVAN ALEKSEEVICH
        Zolotye zvezdy kalinintsev. Lit. obrabotka N. Mazurina.
        Izd. 2., dop. Moskva, Moskovskii rabochii, 1969. 566 p.
        ports. 20cm. 279 'Gold stars' from the Province of Kalinin,
        Heroes of the Soviet Union in World War II (1939-1945)

9606   GEROI TRUDA—KALININTSY. [Sostavitel' knigi N. Arapova.
        Moskva] Moskovskii rabochii, 1970. 378 p. illus., ports.
        22cm. 54 sketches with biographical data on 'Heroes of Social-
        ist Labor' (Geroi Sotsialisticheskogo Truda) of the Province of
        Kalinin.

Kirov (Province)

9607   KIROVCHANE—GEROI SOVETSKOGO SOIUZA; [sbornik. 2.,
        dop. i perer. izd. Avtorskii kollektiv: M. A. Ardashev i
        dr. Sostaviteli I. I. Monoszon i N. G. Komarov. Kirov] Kirov-
        skoe knizhnoe izd-vo, 1962. 446 p. ports. 21cm. 100 persons
        from the Province of Kirov, Heroes of the Soviet Union in the 2d
        World War (1939-1945)

9608   VYDAIUSHCHIESIA UROZHENTSY I DEIATELI KIROVSKOI
        OBLASTI. Rekomendatel'nyi ukazatel' literatury. Kirov,
        Kirovskoe knizhnoe izd., 1955-62. 5 v. 21cm. Contents. --t. 1.
        Izobretateli i tekhniki. --t. 2. Uchenie. --t. 3. Deiateli iskus-
        stva. --t. 4. Obshchestvenno-politicheskie i voennye deiateli. --
        t. 5. Literatory. Famous natives of the region of Kirov; in-
        cludes 105 biographies indeterminately arranged, with no index.

Kuban (Province)

9609   KUBANI SLAVNYE SYNY; ocherki o Geroiakh Sovetskogo Soiuza,
        kubantsakh, sovershivshikh podvigi v gody Velikoi Otechest-
        vennoi Voiny. [Sost. V. Ivanenko, A. Kostenkov, K. Obishchi-
        kov. Krasnodar] Krasnodarskoe kn izd-vo, 1963. 414 p. illus.,
        ports. 21cm. More than 300 Heroes of the Soviet Union in World
        War II from the Province of Kuban ('Kuban's glorious sons').

Kuybyshevskaya Oblast'

9610   PODVIG VO IMIA RODINY. [Redkollegiia: S. S. Barsukov i dr.
        Kuibyshev] Kuibyshevskoe knizhnoe izd-vo, 1965-68. 2 v.
        ports. 21cm. More than 150 biographical sketches of Heroes of
        the Soviet Union from Kuybyshevskaya oblast' in World War II
        (1939-1945) are included in this volume.

Leningrad

9611   BUROV, ABRAM VENIAMINOVICH
        Tvoi geroi, Leningrad. Izd. 2., dop. Leningrad, Leniz-
        dat, 1970. 637 p. illus. 23cm. At head of title: A. V. Burov.
        Includes portraits and sketches of the lives & activities of a
        large number of Soviet war heroes during the siege of Leningrad,
        1941-1944. With alphabetical list of names and page references
        at end.

Moscow

9612   GEROI GRAZHDANSKOĬ VOĬNY; kniga o moskvichakh, uchast-
            nikakh Grazhdanskoĭ voĭny [Avtory: A. S. Abramov, et al.
        Nauch. red N. I. Rodionova] Moskva, Moskovskiĭ rabochiĭ,
        1974. 415 p. illus., ports. 22cm. On leaf preceding t. p.:
        Institut istorii partii MGK i MK KPSS, filial Instituta marksizma-
        leninizma pri TSK KPSS. Heroes of the Russian Civil War, 1917-
        1921; sons and daughters of Moscow who participated heroically
        in the Revolution in Moscow.

Odessa

9613   ALEKSEEV, MIKHAIL PAVLOVICH, 1896-
        Materialy dlia biograficheskogo slovaria odesskikh
        znakomykh Pushkina. Sost. kruzhkom odesskikh pushkinistov.
        Odessa, 1927. 98 p. 25cm. Materials for a biographical dic-
        tionary of the friends of Pushkin in Odessa.

Omsk, Siberia

9614   SHLEVKO, GALINA MIKHAĬLOVNA
        Radi zhizni na zemle. Èto kniga o Geroiakh Sovetskogo
        Soiuza, tekh, kto rodilsia, zhil i zhivet v g. Omske i Omskoĭ
        oblasti. Omsk, Zapadno-Sibirskoe knizhnoe izd-vo, Omskoe
        otd-nie, 1972. 462 p. illus., ports. 21cm. Heroes of the
        Soviet Union in World War II from the City and Province of Omsk;
        a biographical dictionary (with portraits) of 123 soldiers and re-
        sistance fighters.

Perm' (Province)

9615   ALIKHINA, NADEZHDA ALEKSEEVNA
        Revoliutsionery Prikam'ia. [150 biografii deiatelei revo-
        liutsionnogo dvizheniia, rabotavshik v Prikam'e] Sostaviteli:
        N. A. Alikina, I. G. Gorovaia. Redaktsionnaia kollegiia: N.
        A. Alikina, B. N. Nazarovskiĭ, V. F. Popov. Perm', Perm-
        skoe knizhnoe, 1966. 823 p. ports. 23cm. At head of title:
        TSentral'nyi arkhiv Permskogo obkoma KPSS. Gosudarstven-

nyĭ archiv Permskiĭ oblasti. Permskiĭ gosudarstvennyĭ universitet ... Permskii oblastnoĭ kraevedcheskiĭ muzei. The Province of Perm in the Russian Revolution of 1917-1921; 150 biographies of activists.

9616   OTCHIZNY VERNYE SYNY. Permiaki--Geroi Sovetskogo
        Soiuza. Perm', Perm'skoe knizhnoe izd-vo, 1964. 472 p.
ports. 'Loyal sons of the Fatherland.' 140 Heroes of the Soviet Union (World War II, 1939-1945) from the Province of Perm'.

9617   ZOLOTYE ZVEZDY PRIKAM'IA; [sbornik. 2. dop. i pererabot.
        izd.] Perm', Kn. izd-vo, 1969. 500, [6] p. illus., ports.
21cm. Compiled by I. Kondaurov and S. Mokrousov. 1st ed. published in 1964 under title: Otchizny vernye syny. 190 bioraphies (with portraits) of 190 Heroes of the Soviet Union from the Province of Perm.

Saratov

9618   KHOVANSKIĬ, NIKOLAĬ FEDOROVICH
        Ocherki po istorii goroda Saratova i Saratovskoĭ gubernii,
s biografiiami. Saratov, Tip. Ishchenko, 1884. 238 p. 19cm. The history of Saratov City and Saratov Government, with biographical sketches of writers, scholars, military men and government officials on pages 37-184.

Stavropol'

9619   IKH IMENA NIKOGDA NE ZABUDUTSIA. Stavropol'tsy: Geroi
        Sovetskogo Soiuza, 1941-1945 g. Stavropol', Knizhnoe
izdanie, 1968-69. 2 v. illus., ports. Heroes of the Soviet Union, World War II, from Stavropol and environs; 180 biographical sketches.

Tula

9620   TULIAKI—Geroi Sovetskogo Soiuza. Tula, Priokskoe knizhnoe
        izd-vo, 1967. 445 p. illus., ports. 27cm. 200 people
from Tula, Russia, Heroes of the Soviet Union in World War II (1939-1945)

Volgograd (Province)

9621   GEROI—VOLGOGRADTSY. [Sbornik podgotovlen A. M.
        Borodinym i dr.] Volgograd, Nizhne-Volzhskoe Kn. izd-vo,
1967. 470 p. ports. 21cm. 156 Heroes of the Soviet Union in the World War (1939-1945) from the Province of Volgograd.

Volgda (Government)

9622   VESELOVSKIĬ, ALEKSANDR
        Vologzhane-kraevedy; istochniki slovaria. Vologda, Gos.
        izd-vo Vologod. otd-nie, 1923. xvi, 166 p. ports. 21cm. At
        head of title: Aleksandr i Alekseĭ Veselovskiĭ. Well-known peo-
        ple of the Vologda region; materials for a dictionary (77 notices).

Yaroslavl' (Province)

9623   GOLOVSHCHIKOV, KONSTANTIN DMITRIEVICH, 1835-1900.
        Deiateli IAroslavskago kraia. Sostavil K. D. Golovshchikov.
        Izdanie IAroslavskoĭ Uchenoĭ arkhivnoĭ kommissii. IAroslavl',
        Tipo-lit. E. G. Fal'k, 1898-99. 2 v. 25cm. Contents.--1.
        Aaron-Andrei.--2. Andrei-Bashmakovy. No more published?
        A biographical dictionary of the famous people of Yaroslavl'
        Province.

SAINT HELENA

9624   CHAPLIN, ARNOLD, 1864-
        A St. Helena who's who; or, A directory of the island during
        the captivity of Napoleon. 2d ed., rev. and enl. New York, E.
        P. Dutton, 1919. xi, 257 p. ports. 25cm. A biographical dic-
        tionary on p. 48-141 consists primarily of English Army and
        Navy personnel and the French attendants of Napoleon.

SALVADOR

9625   FLEMION, PHILIP F
        Historical dictionary of El Salvador. Metuchen, N. J.,
        Scarecrow Press, 1972. 157 p. 22cm. (Latin American histori-
        cal dictionaries, no. 5) Includes biographical sketches of noted
        personalities in Salvadorian civilization and history.

9626   MOLINA Y MORALES, ROBERTO
        Guión histórico del poder legislativo de El Salvador; con-
        stituyentes-legislaturas, síntesis biográficas de sus presidentes.
        San Salvador, Asamblea Legislativa [1966-   v. ports.
        25cm. Contents.--pt. 1. 1822-1870.--pt. 2. 1870-1900. Histori-
        cal guide to the national legislature in Salvador. Biographical
        sketches of presiding officers of the National Assembly (Asam-
        blea Nacional). In chronological arrangement. Part 2 issued in
        1969.

9627   SAN SALVADOR Y SUS HOMBRES. [2. ed.] San Salvador,
        Ministerio de Educacion, Direccion General de Publica-
        ciones [1967] 424 p. fold. map, ports. 25cm. (Coleccion
        Historia, v. 10) "Preparado ... por la Academia Salvadorena

de la Historia. " History and biography of San Salvador. "Bocetos biográficos" (p. 311-337) is a biographical dictionary with
sketches of some of the most prominent figures in San Salvador's
history. In the main text, however, there are a substantial
number of longer biographical sketches of San Salvadorians other than those listed in the "Bocetos biográficos. " The work as
a whole is, unfortunately, not indexed.

SAN MARINO

9628   MONTALBO, LUIGI DE, conte, 1848-
         Dizionario bibliografico iconografico della reppublica di
San Marino, contenente le indicazioni delle opere pubblicate in
varie lingue, con note illustrative, biografiche, rettificative,
preceduto da un blasonario e da una carta topografica, per il
barone Luigi de Montalbo, il duca Amedeo Astraudo ed il conte
Amedeo Galati di Riella ... Parigi, Protat frères, 1898. xxv,
321 p. illus., ports. 30cm. A bibliographical-iconographical-
genealogical dictionary of the Republic of San Marino; includes
biographical data.

SAUDI ARABIA

9629   RILEY, CARROLL L
         Historical and cultural dictionary of Saudi Arabia. Metu-
chen, N. J., Scarecrow Press, 1972. vi, 133 p. 22cm. Historical and cultural dictionaries of Asia, no. 1) Includes biographical sketches of persons (native and foreign) who played a
part in the history and cultural life of Saudi Arabia.

SCANDINAVIA

Bibliography, Indexes, Portrait Catalogs

9630   OLSO. NORSKE NOBELINSTITUTT. BIBLIOTEKET.
         Biografier i Nobelinstituttets bibliotek; en bibliografi: nor-
diske personer. [Utarb. av Berit Wille] Oslo, 1964. 14 1.
28cm. Cover title. A bibliography of Scandinavian (and Finnish)
biographies held by the Library of the Nobel Institute in Oslo.

General Works

9631   DICTIONARY OF SCANDINAVIAN BIOGRAPHY. Hon. general
         editor: Ernest Kay. With a memoir on the work of the
Nordic Council by G. F. D. Dawson, and with the full text of
the treaty of cooperation between Denmark, Finland, Iceland,
Norway and Sweden. London, Melrose Press, 1972. xxxv, 467 p.
25cm. Some 3,600 biographical sketches of contemporary men
and women; a who's who.

SCOTLAND

9632   ABERDEEN. UNIVERSITY.
        Roll of service in the Great War, 1914-1919. Edited by
        Mabel Desborough Allardyce. Aberdeen, Aberdeen University
        Press, 192]. ix, 441 p. ports. 26cm. (Aberdeen University
        studies, no. 84) Includes portraits and some biographical data
        for many of the former students, etc. mentioned.

9633   ANDERSON, WILLIAM PITCAIRN
        Silences that speak. Records of Edinburgh's ancient
        churches and burial grounds, with biographical sketches of the
        notables who rest there. Edinburgh, A. Brunton, 1931. 748 p.
        23cm.

9634   DISTINGUISHED MEN OF THE COUNTY; or, Biographical
        annals of Kinross-shire. Kinross, Scot., Kinross-shire
        advertiser, 1932. vii, 114 p. 8.°

9635   DONALDSON, GORDON, 1913-
        Who's who in Scottish history, by Gordon Donaldson and
        Robert S. Morpeth. Oxford, B. Blackwell, 1973. xx, 254 p.
        illus., ports. 22cm.

9636   GEDDES, JOHN, 1910-
        Great Scots; a condensed biographical dictionary of 1450
        notable Scots. Ilfracombe, Scot., Stockwell, 1974. 139 p.
        22cm.

9637   HOWIE, JOHN, 1735-1793.
        The Scots worthies; their lives and testimonies, with an
        historical introd. and appendix. Also a supplement containing
        memoirs and historical sketches of Ladies of the Covenant [by
        James Anderson] London, Blackie, 1876. xii, lxxii, 748, xvi,
        236 p. illus., ports. 26cm. Many earlier, less comprehensive
        editions issued under title: Biographia Scotiana (1775, etc.) In
        the main text are 72 biographies of noteworthy figures in Scottish
        church history (especially the Church of Scotland) Additional bi-
        ographies are found in Anderson's Ladies of the Covenant.

9638   IN MEMORIAM; an obituary of Aberdeen and vicinity, for the
        year 1890 [and 1891] with biographical notes of prominent
        citizens. Aberdeen, 1891. 2 v. 8.° No more published?

9639   JERVISE, ANDREW, 1820-1878.
        Epitaphs & inscriptions from burial grounds & old buildings
        in the north-east of Scotland, with historical, biographical, gen-
        ealogical and antiquarian notes, also an appendix of illustrative

papers. Edinburgh, Edmonston and Douglas, 1875-79. 2 v.
illus. 21cm. Vol. 2 has imprint: Edinburgh, D. Douglas.

9640   KIMBER, EDWARD, 1719-1769.
The peerage of Scotland; a genealogical and historical account of all the peers of that ancient kingdom. Together with a
like account of all the attainted peers; and a list of those nobles
whose titles are extinct. London, Printed for J. Almon, etc.,
1767. [4], 337 p. 96 coats-of-arms.

9641   KNIGHT, WILLIAM ANGUS, 1836-1916.
Some nineteenth century Scotsmen; being personal recollec-
tions. Edinburgh, Oliphant, Anderson & Ferrier, 1903. 456 p.
ports. 24cm. 62 biographies. Non-alphabetical; contents, p.
11-14.

9642   MACFARLANE, MARGARET E
The Scottish radicals tried and transported to Australia for
treason in 1820, by Margaret and Alistair Macfarlane. Sydney,
Wentworth Books, 1975. 75 p. illus., ports. 26cm. (Studies
in Australian and Pacific history, no. 5) A biographical dictionary of 19 Scotchmen convicted of treason for their part in the up-
rising of 1820 in Scotland against depressive economic conditions
in Great Britain generally.

9643   MacINNES, JOHN
The brave sons of Skye; containing the military records
[from authentic sources] of the leading officers, non-commis-
sioned officers, and private soldiers, whom Eilean a Cheo has
produced. London, 1899. xxiv, 230 p. ports. 8.⁰ Portraits
and military records and other biographical data of military persons from the island of Skye, Inner Hebrides, Scotland.

9644   MEMOIRS AND PORTRAITS OF ONE HUNDRED GLASGOW MEN
WHO HAVE DIED DURING THE LAST THIRTY YEARS, and
in their lives did much to make the city what it now is. Glasgow,
J. Maclehose, 1886. 2 v. ports. 34cm. Brief biographies contributed by 54 authors.

9645   PINKERTON, JOHN, 1758-1826.
Iconographia Scotica; or, Portraits of illustrious persons
of Scotland, engraved from the most authentic paintings, etc.,
with short biographical notices. London, J. Herbert, 1794-97.
2 v. 8.⁰ Issued in parts, at first monthly. A different work
from his The Scotish gallery (which contained 50 portraits and
biographies).

9646   ROSS, JOHN DAWSON, 1853-1939.
Who's who in Burns. Stirling [Scot.] E. Mackay, 1927.

[New York, AMS Press, 1973] 335 p. map. 19cm. In large
part biographical sketches of friends and associates of the poet,
Robert Burns, although fictional characters in Burns' works are
included.

9647   SCOTT, Sir JOHN, Lord SCOTSTARVET, 1585-1670.
        The staggering state of the Scots statesmen, for one hundred
        years, viz. from 1550 to 1650. By Sir John Scot of Scotstarvet.
        Now first published from an original manuscript. Edinburgh,
        Printed by W. Ruddiman, Jun., 1754. xxxiv, 190 p. 18cm. 87
        brief biographies of Scotch statesmen from 1550 to 1650, classi-
        fied under headings: chancellors, secretaries, admirals, etc.

9648   STARK, JOHN, of Edinburgh.
        Biographica Scotica; or, Scotish biographical dictionary;
        containing a short account of the lives and writings of the most
        eminent persons and remarkable characters, natives of Scotland,
        from the earliest ages to the present time. By J. Stark. Edin-
        burgh, A. Constable, 1805. [428] p. 5 ports. 15cm.

9649   TAYLER, ALISTAIR NORWICH, 1870-
        Morayshire M. P. s since the Act of Union, by Alister
        and Henrietta Taylor. [Elgin, Scot.] J. A. Yeadon, 1930. 59 p.
        port. 19cm.

SERBIA

(See also Yugoslavia)

9650   STOJANOVIČ-VOKS, VOJA
        Zaslužni sinovi. Biografija zaslužnih ljudi za teritorija
        Istočne Srbije i Pemoravlja. Knj. 1. Beograd, Stamparija
        Minerva, 1940. 192 p. 21cm. Worthy sons; biographies of
        people of merit from eastern Serbia and the region of the Mora-
        va River. Alphabetically arranged, with entries by forename.

SLOVAKIA

9651   FLORIAN, THEO H
        Oravci v slovenskej kulture. Dolný Kubín, Okres Dom
        osvety, 1961. 144 p. Leading figures of Slovakian culture; a
        dictionary.

9652   JABLONICKÝ, JOZEF
        Slovník Slovenského národného povstania. Autori: J[ozef]
        Jablonický, M[iroslav] Kropilák. 2. upr. a dopl. vyd. Bratisla-
        va, Epocha, t. Pravda Zilina, 1970. 337, [2] p. 17cm. A dic-
        tionary of the history of the Slovakian Uprising of 1944 (World

War II) which includes numerous biographical sketches. 1st ed.
(1964) issued under title: Malý slovník slovenského národného
povstania.

9653   REPREZENTAČNY LEXIKON SLOVENSKA A PODKARPATSKEJ
        RUSI. Spracoval redakčny výbor Reprezentačného lexikona.
        V. Bratislave, Academia, 1936. 375 p. 24cm. Representative
        (biographical) dictionary of Slovakia and Sub-Carpathian Russia
        (Ruthenia); includes biographical sketches of many personalities
        prominent before 1918.

SLOVENIA

9654   SEZNAM IMEN ZA SLOVENSKI BIOGRAFSKI LEKSIKON.
        Ljubljana, Zadružna gosp. banka, 1922. 117 p.   A listing
        or catalog of names for a Slovenian biographical dictionary.

SOMALIA

9655   CASTAGNO, MARGARET, 1922-
        Historical dictionary of Somalia. Metuchen, N. J., Scare-
        crow Press, 1975. xxviii, 213 p. map. 23cm. (African his-
        torical dictionaries, no. 6) Includes some biographical data
        about natives as well as foreigners who participated in the his-
        torical development of Somalia.

SOUTH AFRICA

9656   THE AFRICAN YEARLY REGISTER. 1922-
        Johannesburg.   v. 1931 ed., edited by Mweli T. D.
        Skota, the last issue of this particular periodical that appeared
        (?) although see M. T. D. Skota's The African who's who
        (196-) which carries the running title: The African yearly regi-
        ster. A biographical compilation of Africans in the Republic
        of South Africa (with some emphasis on the Transvaal).

9657   AFRIKAANSE KINDERENSIKLOPEDIE. [2.] hersiene uitg.
        Redakteur: E. F. Albertyn. Met medewerking van voor-
        aanstaande wetenskapelikes en opvoedkundiges. Kaapstad,
        Nasionale Boekhandel, 1963-64. 10 v. illus. A major South
        African encyclopedia in the Afrikaans language. Intended
        chiefly for juveniles it is still invaluable for the history,
        biography, etc. of South Africa.

9658   BOYENS, A   J   H
        Album van Suid-Afrikaanse volksfigure en prominente per-
        sone [1956-1958] A. J. H. Boyens en Adam Johannes Boyens,
        samenstellers. 2. uitg. Brakpan, Historiese Uitgewers, 1958.

472 p. ports. 25cm. 1st ed. issued in 1956 (396 p.) Album of
national figures and prominent persons in the Republic of South
Africa, 1956-1958.

9659   THE NATAL WHO'S WHO; an illustrated biographical sketch
        book of Natalians. Durban, Natal Who's Who Pub. Co.,
        1906. 223 p. ports. 25cm.

9660   SKOTA, MWELI T. D.
        The African who's who; an illustrated classified register
        and national biographical dictionary of the Africans in the Trans-
        vaal. Contributions by leading Africans. Edited and compiled
        by T. D. Mweli Skota. [Johannesburg] Distributed by Central
        News Agency [196-] 373 p. ports. 23cm. Running title: The
        African yearly register. "3rd edition, revised and enlarged [of
        the Transvaal section of the African register]. "

9661   VILLIERS, CHRISTOFFEL COETZEE DE, 1850-1887.
        Genealogies of old South African families. Completely rev.
        ed., augmented and rewritten by C. Pama. Cape Town, Bal-
        kema, 1966. 3 v. An important source for retrospective bi-
        ography and genealogy. 1st ed., issued in 1893-94 in Afrikaans
        (Geslacht-register der oude Kaapsche familien. 3 v.) was sup-
        plemented by J. Hoge's Byrdraes tot die genealogie van ou
        Afrikaanse families (1958—224 p.)

SOUTH AMERICA

9662   DICCIONARIO BIOGRÁFICO CONTEMPORÁNEO SUD-AMERI-
        CANO QUE CONTIENE LOS DATOS BIOGRÁFICOS MÁS
        COMPLETOS SOBRE LA VIDA Y LAS OBRAS DE LOS HOMBRES
        DE ESTADO, de ciencias, literatos, artistas, militares, in-
        dustriales, etc., etc., que han figurado o figuran en el conti-
        nente desde el principio de este siglo hasta nuestros días ...
        tomo I. Buenos Aires, H. Lacquaniti, 1898. 96, 70, 95, 10 p.
        ports. 33cm. Edited by Rafael Barreda. No more published.
        A biographical dictionary of South America; contemporary fig-
        ures flourishing in the latter part of the 19th century.

9663   LACQUANITI, HECTOR
        Diccionario biografico de contemporáneos sudamericanos.
        Buenos Aires, 1898. Suárez, 1930. 2 v. Biographical diction-
        ary of contemporary South Americans (living in 1898) A-E only.
        No more published.

SPAIN

9664   ANUARIO DE LA ARISTOCRACIA Y ALTA SOCIEDAD.
        Edición hispano-argentina. 1971-72--   Madrid.
        v. 21cm. "(Quién es quién)." Continues Anuario de la
        aristocracia y alta sociedad española. Editor:

J. R. de Lahoz y Sánchez de Valero. A periodical (annual)
devoted to the aristocracy and social elite of Spain and Argentina which takes the guise of a biographical dictionary.

9665   ANUARIO DE LA ARISTOCRACIA Y ALTA SOCIEDAD ES-
          PAÑOLA. Madrid.   v. 21cm. Superseded by Anuario
        de la aristocracia y alta sociedad. Edición hispano-argentina.
        Began in 1959? Ceased ca. 1970? A periodical (annual) de-
        voted to the aristocracy and high society of Spain with biogra-
        phical sketches a large part of its content. Superseded by
        Anuario de la aristocracia y alta sociedad (q. v.).

9666   BRAVO MORATA, FEDERICO
          Los nombres de las calles de Barcelona. Madrid, Fenicia,
        1971. 5 v. 18cm. (Colección de bolsillo) Cover title: Historia
        de los nombres de las calles de Barcelona. A history of street-
        names of Barcelona. A dictionary which has utility as a bio-
        graphical dictionary also, since a majority of the streets are
        named after famous persons the world over, but especially for
        persons of Spanish nationality. Entries are by order of street
        name, so that many personal names begin with forename.

9667   BRAVO MORATA, FEDERICO
          Los nombres de las calles de Madrid. Madrid, Fenicia,
        1970. 2 v. plates. 20cm. (Colección de bolsillo Fenicia, v.
        5-6) A dictionary of the street names of Madrid, with biogra-
        phical data for those individuals (chiefly Spanish) after whom
        streets are named.

9668   [CARRETERO, JOSÉ MARÍA] 1888-
          Galería; más de cien vidas extraordinarias contadas por
        sus protagonistas y comentadas por el Caballero audaz [pseud.]
        Madrid, Ediciones Caballero Audaz, 1943-46. 3 v. 22cm.
        A Spanish 'gallery'; more than 100 extraordinary Spanish lives
        as told by their protagonists and commented upon by Carretero.

9669   DÍAZ, NICOMEDES PASTOR, 1811-1863.
          Galería de españoles célebres contemporáneos; o, Biogra-
        fías y retratos de todos los personages distinguidos de nuestros
        días en la ciencia, en la política, en las armas, en las letras y
        en las artas, publicadas por Nicomedes Pastor Díaz y Francisco
        de Cárdenas. Madrid, Impr. de Sánchez, 1841-46. 9 v. ports.
        18cm. Imprint varies: v. 1, fasc. 1, Madrid, Impr. de Sánchez;
        v. 1, fasc. 2-4 and v. 2, Madrid, Impr. de V. de Lalama; v. 8-9,
        Madrid, Boix. 150 biographies of famous Spaniards of 1st half
        of the 19th century.

9670   DICCIONARIO BIOGRÁFICO ESPAÑOL CONTEMPORÁNEO.
          Madrid, Círculo de Amigos de la Historia, 1970. 3 v.
        ports. 21cm. Contents.--v. 1. A-D.--v. 2. E-M.--v. 3. N-Z.
        A biographical dictionary of contemporary Spaniards.

9671   EQUIPO MUNDO.
        Los 90 [i. e. Noventa] ministros de France. Prólogo de
        Emilio Romero. 18 entrevistas de Manuel del Arco. Epílogo de
        Amando de Miguel. Barcelona, Dopesa, 1970. 527 p. illus.,
        ports. 21cm. (Testimonio de actualidad, 2) Biographies and
        portraits of the 90 ministers in the various governments of Fran-
        cisco Franco, 1938-1970. Equipo Mundo is the pseudonym of
        Eduardo Alvarez Puga, José Carlos Clemente and José Manuel
        Girones.

9672   LOS ESPAÑOLES. Madrid, Publicaciones Controladas.
                        no. illus. 29cm. weekly. Began ca. 1972 or 3? The
        Spanish; a periodical devoted to biography.

9673   FERNÁNDEZ DE LOS RÍOS, ANGEL, 1821-1880.
                Biografías de todos los representantes de la Nación. Redac-
        tadas por Manuel Prieto y Prieto y otros distinguidos escritores.
        Madrid, Rey, 1869. 515 p. illus. 31cm. At head of title: La
        Asamblea Constituyente de 1869. Biographies of all the repre-
        sentatives of the Spanish Nation (the Constituent Assembly of
        1869 in Spain).

9674   GIRONELLA, JOSE MARÍA
                100 [i. e. Cien] españoles y Dios. [Barcelona] Ediciones
        Nauta [1969] 687 p. ports. 24cm. (Serie Documentos, 1 (Nau-
        ta)) An alphabetically arranged work, with many portraits, of
        100 well-known contemporary Spaniards who express their views
        on God and religion. Valuable especially for its portraits (sev-
        eral for each individual).

9675   KAYSERLING, MEYER, 1829-1905.
                Biblioteca española-portugueza-judaica and other studies in
        Ibero-Jewish bibliography by the author and by J. S. da Silva
        Rosa; with a bibliography of Kayserling's publications by M.
        Weisz. Selected with a prolegomenon by Yosef Hayim Yerushal-
        mi. [Augm. ed.] New York, Ktav Pub. House, 1971. xxxii,
        272 p. 24cm. (Studia Sephardica) Includes a bio-bibliographi-
        cal dictionary of Spanish-Portuguese Jews on p. 23-140.

9676   LONGHURST, JOHN EDWARD, 1918-
                Luther's ghost in Spain (1517-1546) [by] John E. Longhurst.
        [Lawrence, Kan.] Coronado Press, 1969. 393 p. 22cm. "Di-
        rectory of Spanish 'Lutherans'": p. [295]-363 (biographical
        notes on Spanish Protestants persecuted by the Inquisition—bio-
        graphical dictionary format).

9677   MARCO, CONCHA DE, 1916-
                La mujer española del Romanticismo. León, Editorial Eve-
        rest [1969] 2 v. (351 p.) illus., ports. 20cm. (Club Everest,
        3-4) Spanish women of the Romantic period; ca. 111 biographies

of varying lengths. There is no strict alphabetical approach.
Contents note at end of vol. 2 must be searched. Arrangement
by subject; e. g., Infantas, aristocracy, wives of public men,
writers, etc.

9678   PORCEL, BALTASAR, 1937-
            Los encuentros. 1.-2. serie. [Barcelona] Ediciones
        Destino [1969-71] 2 v. ports. 22cm. (Ser o no ser; biografías)
        "Encounters" or interviews, with 100 contemporary Spanish
        writers, artists, etc., which contain reminiscences, views, etc.
        of those with whom the author talked.

9679   QUIÉN ES QUIÉN EN LAS CORTES ESPAÑOLAS; una informa-
            ción general sobre los grupos constitutivos de las Cortes y
        de sus comisiones, con la relación nominal de sus miembros.
        Una documentación biográfica exclusiva de todos los procuradores
        en Cortes pertenecientes a la IX Legislatura (1967-71), en fecha
        31 de diciembre de 1970 ... 1. ed. Madrid, Documentación Es-
        pañola Contemporánea, 1971. 901 p. illus., ports. 22cm.
        Who's who in the Spanish Cortes as of December 1970; biogra-
        phies and portraits.

9680   SEGOVIA, ANGEL MARÍA
            Figuras y figurones. Biografías de los hombres que más
        figuran actualmente así en la política como en las armas,
        ciencias, artes, magistratura, alta banca ... 2. ed. corregida
        y aumentada. Madrid, Jaramillo, 1881-86. 43 v. ports. 16.º
        'Figures and pretentious characters.' Biographies of men who
        have played prominent political, military [etc.] roles in the
        world.

9681   SPAIN. SERVICIO HISTÓRICO MILITAR.
            Medalla militar, 1939-1969. Madrid, 1970-   v.
        illus., ports. 28cm. (Galería militar contemporánea, v. 2

        Contents. --1. pt. Generales y coroneles.

        Biographical sketches and portraits of winners of Spain's mili-
        tary Medal of Honor, 1939-1969.

Local

Alicante

9682   MILEGO É INGLADA, JOSÉ MARÍA, 1859-
            Alicantinos ilustres. Apuntes biográficos, por José M.
        Milego y Antonio Galdó López. Alicante, Impr. de El Graduador,
        1905. xv, 446 p. 21cm. 54 biographical sketches of famous
        people of Alicante, Spain.

Aragon

9683   BIOGRAFÍAS ARAGONESAS. Zaragoza, Institución 'Fernando
        el Católico', 1967-   v. 26cm. (Anejo de Zaragoza,
        7) Institución 'Fernando el Católico. ' Publicación no. 429.
        Biographies of famous persons of Aragon. Arranged in chrono-
        logical order.

Asturias

9684   GRAN ENCICLOPEDIA ASTURIANA. [Gijón, Gran Enciclo-
        pedia Asturiana, 1970-   v. illus. (part col.)
        30cm. An encyclopedia for the Province of Asturias, Spain,
        which includes many biographical entries. 12 vols., covering A
        to Salme, were issued as of ca. 1974 or 5.

Basque Provinces

9685   ENCICLOPEDIA GENERAL ILUSTRADO DEL PAÍS VASCO.
        San Sebastián, Editorial Auñamendi [196-   v.
        ports. 28cm. A general illustrated encyclopedia of the Basque
        Provinces of Spain which includes portraits and biographical ma-
        terial for prominent figures in Basque civilization. 4 vols.
        (v. 4: Balzola-Bi) issued up to 1973.

Cantabria

9686   PEREDA DE LA REGUERA, MANUEL
        Indianos de Cantabria. Prólogo del Excmo. Sr. D. Pedro de
        Escalante y Huidobro. Santander, Publicaciones de la Excma.
        Diputación Provincial, 1968. 144 p. illus., ports. 24cm. Na-
        tives of Cantabria, Spain who migrated to the New World (Spanish
        colonies of America and the newly independent Latin American
        states) some of whom returned to Spain. Pages 75-144 comprise
        a biographical dictionary of these persons.

Cartagena

9687   VICENT Y PORTILLO, GREGORIO
        Biblioteca histórica de Cartagena; colección de obras,
        memorias, discursos, folletos, manuscritos, bibliografía y
        biografía de sus hijos más ilustres ... t. 1. Madrid, 1889.
        xvi, 760 p. plates. 8.º Historical library of Cartagena,
        Spain; a collection of works, memoirs ... bibliography and bi-
        ography of the most famous sons of this city. Vol. 1 only was
        published.

Galicia

9688   POLO, CARLOS
            Galicia, en sus hombres de hoy. [Madrid, Gráf. Virgen
        de Loreto, 1971-   v. 24cm. Galicia in its men
        of today; interviews by the author with contemporary Galicians,
        wherein the interviewees reveal biographical information about
        themselves; the first volume contains 50 interviews. Arranged
        in no particular order.

Malaga (Province)

9689   DÍAZ DE ESCOVAR, NARCISO, 1860-1935.
            Galería literaria malagueña; apuntes para un índice biográ-
        fico bibliográfico, relativos a escritores hijos de esta provincia,
        residentes en ella o que han escrito respecto a la misma. Mala-
        ga, Poch y Creixell, 1898. 648 p. 17cm. Brief notes (unfortu-
        nately, with numerous errors) on many Arab and Christian writ-
        ers native to or residing in the province of Malaga, Spain.
        Notes for a bio-bibliographical index.

Valencia

9690   101 [i. e. CIENTO UN] HIJOS ILUSTRES DEL REINO VALEN-
            CIANO. Vicente Añón Marco, dirección y realización;
        notas biográficas Rafael Gayano Abad, Juan Soriano Esteve;
        illustraciones, Fernando Cabedo Torrents. Valencia, V. Añón,
        1973. 6, 101 leaves. illus. 24cm. Cover title. 101 famous
        men prominent in the history of the old Kingdom of Valencia.

9691   GRAN ENCICLOPEDIA DE LA REGIÓN VALENCIANA. [Direc-
            ción y producción: Manuel Mas. Valencia, Gran Enciclo-
        pedia de la Región Valenciana, 1973-   v. illus., ports.
        30cm. An encyclopedia for the Valencia region of Spain (includ-
        ing the provinces of Valencia, Alicante and Castellón) Included
        is a large number of biographical sketches of natives of those
        provinces. Seven volumes, covering A to Nob, were issued as
        of ca. 1976.

Vizcaya

9692   DELMAS, JUAN EUSTAQUIO, 1820-1892.
            Diccionario biográfico de claros varones de Vizcaya. In-
        trod. por Juan Ramón de Urquijo y Olano. Prólogo, notas e
        índices por Angel Rodríguez Herrero. Bilbao [Editorial La Gran
        Enciclopedia Vasca] 1970. xvi, [9]-293 p. illus., ports. 24cm.
        (Colección Separatas de La Gran enciclopedia vasca, 3) Text is
        that of the previously unpublished manuscript written in 1892 and
        entitled: Biografía universal de claros varones de Vizcaya. Bio-
        graphical dictionary of famous men of Vizcaya (Basques, etc. of

a province in northern Spain off the Bay of Biscay) **Also publish-**
ed in La Gran enciclopedia vasca, Bilboa, 1970 (v. **4, p. [5]-**
200).

SRI LANKA

9693   ABEYESOORIYA, SAMSON
Who's who of Ceylon. 3d ed. Colombo, The author, 1928.
xxvi, 234, xxviii p. 95 illus.(ports.) The illustrations are
portraits of "Ceylon's dead" with laudatory notices or some
other biographical data appended. The chief alphabetical section contains 5 or 6-line biographies. First ed. covers 1916-
1917; 2d, 1918-1920.

9694   CEYLON. JĀTIKA RĀJYA SABHĀVA. PUSHTAKĀLAYA.
Members of the legislatures of Ceylon, 1931-1972. [Colom-
bo] Library, National State Assembly, 1972. ii, 235 p. 25cm.
Cover title. An alphabetical listing with birth and/or death
dates, political affiliation, data concerning service in the Parliament (House of Representatives or State Council) etc.

9695   THE CEYLON DAILY NEWS.
Ceylon State Council, 1931. With full results of the polling,
biographies and photographs of the members and a complete
analysis and statistical tables. Colombo, Associated Newspapers of Ceylon, 1931. 56 p. ports.

9696   THE CEYLON DAILY NEWS.
Parliament of Ceylon; with full results of the polling, biographies and photographs of winning candidates, and a complete
analysis ... of the general election. Colombo, 1947-   v.
ports. 20cm. Vols. for 1947, 1952, 1956, 1960 and 1965 (and beyond?) have been issued.

9697   THE CEYLON DAILY NEWS.
The State Council of Ceylon, 1936. Colombo, 1936. [4],
93 p. ports. Includes portraits and biographical sketches of
members of the State Council in 1936.

9698   CEYLON NATIONAL CONGRESS.
The handbook of the Ceylon National Congress, 1919-1928.
Edited by S. W. R. D. Bandaranaike. Colombo, H. W. Cave,
1928. xiv, 912, 165 p. ports. 8.° Appendices A-H (165 p.)
at end. Includes portraits and biographical sketches of leaders
of the National Congress.

9699   KANDYAN ANNUAL AND DIRECTORY.   Kandy [Ceylon] [1947]
1 v. Biographical directory of prominent figures of the
City of Kandy, Ceylon: p. 59-76.

9700   LEWIS, JOHN PENRY, 1854-1923.
        List of inscriptions on tombstones and monuments in Ceylon,
        of historical or local interest, with an obituary of persons un-
        commemorated. Colombo, Printed by H. C. Cottle, 1913. x,
        462 p. front. 33cm. Contains biographical data, in addition to
        inscriptions for those commemorated, for over 2,000 Europeans
        who lived or traveled in Ceylon.

9701   LIYANAGE, GUNADASA, 1930-
        Kavda mē? [Colombo, 1968-   v. ports. 19cm.
        Biographical sketches of politicians, artists and scholars of
        Ceylon. In Sinhalese. Vol. 1 only published?

9702   MARTYN, JOHN H
        Notes on Jaffna: chronological, historical, biographical,
        etc. With an appendix. Tellippalai, American Ceylon Mission
        Press, 1923. [8], 363, lxvi, xx p. 8.° Jaffna, Ceylon, is a
        city of ca. 70,000 inhabitants.

9703   RAJA SINGAM, S   DURAI
        A hundred years of Ceylonese in Malaysia and Singapore
        (1867-1967) [by] S. Durai Raja Singam. Kuala Lumpur [1967 or
        8] xxviii, 532, xxx-xlix p. illus., ports. 32cm. Valuable for
        its many hundreds of portraits (which are indexed on p. xlvi-
        xlix); also includes biographical sketches scattered through the
        general text.

9704   SENANAYAKE, C   D   P
        The encyclopaedia of Ceylon's prominent personalities.
        2d ed. Panadura, City Press, printers, 1952. 60 p.

9705   WIJEYESINGHE, H   R   H
        Biographies of Ceylon residents. (In Ceylon in corporation
        year. Compiled and edited by H. R. H. Wijeyesinghe. Colom-
        bo, 1937. p. 25-108; 208-243. illus. (ports))

9706   WRIGHT, ARNOLD, ed.
        Twentieth century impressions of Ceylon; its history, peo-
        ple, commerce, industries and resources. London, Durban
        [etc.] 1907. 916 p. illus., ports. 32cm. "A special note
        should be made of the biographical element in the book. The
        list of subjects embraces practically every personage of im-
        portance in the island, and as the most scrupulous care has been
        taken to compile the notices, it may be claimed for the feature
        that it will be of enduring value."--Editor's preface. Biogra-
        phies are scattered thru' pages 425-862 (along with company
        histories) Index at end yields biographical approach.

SWAZILAND

9707   GROTPETER, JOHN J
        Historical dictionary of Swaziland. Metuchen, N. J.,
        Scarecrow Press, 1975. xiv, 251 p. map. 23cm. (African
        historical dictionaries, no. 3) Persons, places, organizations
        and events of significance in the history of Swaziland; however,
        birth and death dates are not given for individuals.

SWEDEN

Bibliography, Indexes, Portrait Catalogs

9708   BJÖRKBOM, CARL, 1898-
        Svensk porträttlitteratur; bibliografisk förteckning av Carl
        Björkbom och Boo von Malmborg. [Gävle, 1941] 171 p. 24cm.
        [Svenska porträttarkivets publikationer, 3) Swedish portrait
        literature; a bibliography.

9709   STOCKHOLM. NATIONALMUSEUM. SVENSKA PORTRÄTT-
        ARKIVET.
        Index över svenska porträtt, 1500-1850, i Svenska porträtt-
        arkivets samlingar ... på uppdrag av stiftelsens arbetsutskott
        och Nationalmusei chef utgiven av Sixten Strömbom. Medar-
        betare: Evald E:son Uggla och Carl Johan Lamm. Redaktions-
        sekreterare: Lennart Sandberg. [Stockholm] Nordisk roto-
        gravyr [1935-43] 3 v. ports. 24cm. Index of Swedish portraits
        (1500-1850) in the collections of the Swedish Portrait Archives
        of the National Museum. Vol. 3 has title: Svenska kungliga por-
        trätt i Svenska porträttarkivets samlingar (i.e. Swedish royal
        portraits in the collections of the Swedish Portrait Archives).

General Works

9710   COLLIN, JOHAN GABRIEL, 1794-1879.
        Lefnadsteckningar öfver de utmärktare personerna under
        kriget emot Ryssland åren 1808 och 1809. Stockholm, J. L.
        Brudin, 1861-62. 2 v. 21cm. Contents.--t. 1. A-K.--t. 2.
        L-O. Biographical sketches of the most remarkable Swedish fig-
        ures in Sweden's war against Russia, 1808-1809; a biographical
        dictionary.

9711   FRYXELL, ANDERS, 1795-1881.
        Berättelser ur svenska historien. XLIII: Adolf Frederik och
        Lovisa Ulrika, deras samtida statsmän, krigare, ambetsmän
        och prester. Stockholm, 1875. 278 p. 8.° The 43d volume of
        Fryxell's 45-vol. narratives of Swedish history is devoted to
        biographical sketches of statesmen, soldiers, public officials
        and clergymen of the reign of Adolphus Frederick and Louisa
        Ulrica (1751-1771)

9712   HIRN, HANS, 1896-
        Från Lantingshausen till Jägerhorn; ett värvat regemente i
        Finland, 1751-1808. Helsingfors, Svenska litteratursällskapet i
        Finland [1970] 285 p. illus., ports. 25cm. (Skrifter utg. av
        Svenska litteratursällskapet i Finland, nr. 441) History of a
        Swedish regiment in Finland for the years 1751 to 1808; includes
        a biographical appendix (p. 228-273) in the form of a dictionary
        (3 alphabets) for officers, non-commissioned officers and civil-
        ians attached to the military.

9713   ISER, CARL, 1785-1809.
        Genealogiske och biografiske anteckningar hörande till Nor-
        rköpings stads historia. Första delen, utg. 1806. Stockholm,
        Bokförlaget Rediviva, 1969. 88, xx p. 20cm. (Suecica redi-
        viva, 3) No more published. Facsimile reprint. Genealogical
        and biographical notes for the history of Norrköping. Ca. 90 bi-
        ographies, chronologically arranged, are included.

9714   KLINGSPOR, CARL ARVID, 1829-1903.
        Sveriges adel under 1600-1700 talen. Samtids minnesteck-
        ningar jemte anmärkningar. Utgifna af C. A. Klingspor. Up-
        sala, W. Schultz, 1876-77. 2 v. 23cm. Issued in 8 parts.
        Swedish nobility, 1600-1700. Contemporary biographies with
        notes.

9715   MELLIN, GUSTAF HENRIK, 1803-1876.
        Sveriges store män, snillen, statsmän, hjeltar och foster-
        landsvänner samt märkvärdigaste fruntimmer framställda i
        tvåhundrafyrtio bilder jemte lefnadsteckningar. Redaktör: G. H.
        Mellin. Tecknare: A. C. Wetterling och O. Wallgren m. fl.
        Stockholm [1840]-49. [9], 240 p. 240 ports. 4.° Sweden's
        great men: geniuses, statesmen, heroes and patriots as well
        as its most remarkable women in 240 portraits together with
        outlines of their lives.

9716   SJÖBERG, NILS
        Svenska porträtt i öffentliga samlingar. Utgifna under med-
        verkan af Personhistoriska samfundet. Stockholm, H. W. Tull-
        berg [1905-07] 2 v. 100 ports. 33cm. With a French summary.
        Contents. --1. Drottningholm. --2. Gripsholm. Vasatiden.
        Swedish portraits in public collections.

9717   SUEVIA-TÜBINGEN, 1831-1931. Bd. 3: Lebensbilder. Tübin-
        gen, Selbstverlag des Corps Suevia, 1931. xxi, 549 p. 4.°
        Swedish students at the University of Tübingen. Vol. 3: Bio-
        graphical sketches.

9718   SVENSKAR I UTLANDET: biografisk uppslagsbok. Utg. av
        Utlandssvenskarnas förening och Riksföreningen for svensk-
        hetens bevarande i utlandet. Stockholm, P. Norstedt, 1969.

267, [3] p. 20cm. Swedes in foreign countries; a biographical
reference work arranged alphabetically-geographically. Index of
persons: p. 251-264. First edition issued in 1929; 2d ed., 1959.

SWITZERLAND

9719   ANNUAIRE SUISSE DU MONDE ET DES AFFAIRES. Wer ist
              wer in der Schweiz? (Jahrbuch führender schweizerischer
         Persönlichkeiten). Swiss biographical index of prominent per-
         sons. Annuaire svizzero del mondo e degli affari. 1972/73-
              Lausanne, Editions Léman.   v. 25cm. A biographical
         dictionary of "the most important living Swiss personalities as
         well as those of well known foreigners who either reside in
         Switzerland or who visit the country regularly. Also included
         are the biographies of prominent Swiss persons who reside a-
         broad. " In French, German or English, depending on the na-
         tive tongue of the biographee.

9720   BERTSCHY, ANTON, 1929-
              237 [i. e. Zweihundert siebenunddreissig] Biografien zum
         kulturellen Leben Deutschfreiburgs 1800-1970. Geleitwort von
         Gonzague de Reynold. Freiburg im Üchtland, Deutschfrei-
         burgische Arbeitsgemeinschaft; gedruckt in der Paulusdruck-
         erei, 1970. xi, 286 p. 21cm. (Schriftenreihe der Deutsch-
         freiburgische Arbetisgemeinschaft, Bd. 5) 237 biographies of
         contributors to the German cultural life of Fribourg Canton,
         Switzerland; a biographical dictionary.

9721   EGLI, JEAN, 1828-1870.
              Der ausgestorbene Adel von Stadt und Landschaft Zürich.
         Zürich, Farbendruck von Egli-Schätti, Buchdruck von Gebr.
         Gull, 1865. 224 p. 41 col. plates. 28cm. The deceased no-
         bility of the City and Canton of Zürich; biographical and heral-
         dic.

9722   ESCHER, KONRAD, 1882-
              Zürcher Porträts aller Jahrhunderten. Hrsg. von Conrad
         Escher unter Mitwirkung von A. Corrodi-Sulzer. Basel, Fro-
         benius, 1920. 2 v. ports. (part col.) 33cm. Portraits of
         famous persons of the City and Canton of Zürich from all the
         centuries. Each portrait is accompanied by a brief biographical
         note.

9723   GILIBERT, FRANÇOISE.
              Biographies neuchâteloises: bibliographie analytique de re-
         cueils de biographies. Neuchâtel, Bibliothèque de la Ville, 1971.
         ii, vi, 82 p. 30cm. A bibliography of collective biographies (or
         works where biographical data may be found) for the Canton of
         Neuchâtel, Switzerland. Includes a personal name index with
         references to the collective biographical works in which data a-
         bout the individuals listed may be found.

9724   HÜRLIMANN, MARTIN, 1897-
        Grosse Schweizer. 110 Bildnisse zur eidgenössische
        Geschichte und Kultur. Unter Mitarbeit von Gerold Ermatinger
        und Ernst Winkler hrsg. von Martin Hürlimann. Zürich, At-
        lantis-Verlag [1938] 768 p. illus. 4.º Famous Swiss; 100 bi-
        ographies.

9725   MEYER, CONRAD, d. 1689.
        Portraets der Zürcher Bürgermeister von 1336. [Zürich?]
        1734. 60 mounted ports. folio. Title from cover. Many of the
        portraits are signed by Johann Meyer. This work is in the Har-
        vard College Library. Portraits of the mayors of Zürich from
        1336 to 1734.

SYRIA

9726   AL-SAFADI, KHALĪL IBN AYBAK, 1297 (ca.)-1363.
        Umarā' Dimashq fi al-Islām. Dimashq, al-Maghma' al-
        'Ilmī al-'Arabi, 1374 [1955] [15, 5], 221 p. facsims. 24cm.
        The emirs of Damascus in Islam. Alphabetical by forename.

9727   AL-SHATTĪ, MUHAMMAD JAMĪL, 1882-
        Rawd al-bashar fi a'yān Dimashq fi al-qarn al-thālith 'a-
        shar. Dimashq, Dār al-Yaqzah al-Arabbiyah li at-Ta'līf wa at-
        Tarjama wa an-Nashr, 1365 [1946] 7, 270 p. 22cm. 'The
        garden of men'; about the notables of Damascus in the 13th cen-
        tury A. H. (1786-1883) Alphabetical arrangement (by forename).

9728   AL-SHATTĪ, MUHAMMAD JAMĪL, 1882-
        Tarājim a'yān Dimashq fi al-qarn ar-rābi' 'ashar. Dimashq,
        Dār al-Yaqzah al-'Arabbiyah li at-Ta'lif wa at-Tarjama wa an-
        Nashr, 1365 [1948] 123 p. 22cm. Biographies of notables of
        Damascus in the first half of the 14th century A. H. (1883-1932)
        Chronologically arranged by date of death, with an index of
        names (by forenames)

TAIWAN

(Including REPUBLIC OF CHINA)

9729   PU, YU-FU.
        T'ai-wan feng yün jen wu. Hong Kong, Hsin wen t'ien ti
        she, 1962. 3, 2, 226 p. ports. 26cm. Biographies of 66
        famous persons in Taiwan in the 1960's. No index.

9730   WU, HSIANG-HSIANG, 1913-
        Min ko pai jên chuan. Taipei, Chuan chi wen hsüeh she,
        1971. 4 v. illus. 22cm. 100 famous persons of the Republic
        of China.

9731   YING, WEI-CH'IH
        I wên jên wu. Taipei, K'ung chung tsa chih she, 1972.
        8, 240 p. 19cm. Short biographies of 120 personalities of the
        Republic of China (Taiwan).

THAILAND

9732   THAILAND. SAṬHĀBAN BANDIT PHATTHANA BỌRIHĀN SĀT.
        SAMNAK WIČHAI.
        Ratthasaphā Thai, Ph. S. 2513; chī waprawat samāchik ...
        The National Assembly of Thailand, 1970; biographies of mem-
        bers. Compiled and edited by A. Clarke Hagensick (and others,
        ... Bangkok, 1970] 185, 125 p. 27cm. In Thai and English.
        383 extremely brief biographical sketches, giving only basic in-
        formation.

9733   WHO'S WHO IN THAILAND. May 1973-
        [Bangkok, International Pub. and Marketing Co.]   v.
        illus. 27cm. monthly.

TIBET

9734   KHETSUN SANGPO, 1921-
        Biographical dictionary of Tibet and Tibetan Buddhism.
        Dharamsala, H. P., Library of Tibetan Works and Archives,
        Headquarters of H. H. the Dalai Lama, 1973-   v.
        illus. 22cm. In Tibetan; foreword in English. Contents.--v. 1.
        The arhats, siddhas, and panditas of India.

TOGO

9735   DECALO, SAMUEL
        Historical dictionary of Togo. Metuchen, N. J., Scarecrow
        Press, 1976. xviii, 243 p. maps. 23cm. (African historical
        dictionaries, 9) Includes biographical sketches.

TRANSYLVANIA

9736   ERDÉLYI LEXIKON. Szerk.: Osvát Kálmán. Oradea-Nagy-
        varád, Szabadsatjo Könyv- es Lapkiadó Rt., 1928. 318 p.
        illus., ports. 18cm. Transylvanian [biographical] encyclo-
        pedia.

TRINIDAD AND TOBAGO

9737   WHO'S WHO IN TRINIDAD AND TOBAGO. 2d ed., 1972-1973.
        Compiled and edited by Carlton N. Comma. [Port of Spain,
        Published biennially by Carlton Comma, 1973] 470 p. port.
        22cm. Advertising matter interspersed.

TURKEY

9738   ATALAY, BESIM, 1882-
        Türk büyürkleri veya türk adlari. 2. basim. Istanbul,
        Deblet besimevi, 1935. 177 p. 24cm. Turkish personal names,
        with brief biographical sketches of their bearers.

9739   ATĀYĪ, ATĀULLAH NEV'IZADE, 1583-1634.
        Hadā'iq ul-haqā'iq fī takmilat ash-Shaq'iq [Constanti-
        nople, 1852?] 387-771 p. 4.° Lives of the learned and holy
        men of Turkey. A continuation, up to 1634, of Tashkupri Za-
        dah's al-Shakā'ih al-nu'māniyyah.

9740   GÖVSA, IBRAHIM ALAETTIN, 1889-1949.
        Meshur adamlar, hayathlari, esslerı, yazan Ibrahim
        Alâettin, hazırııyan ve qikaran Sedat Simavī. Istanbul, 1933-36.
        4 v. (1064 p.) A Turkish dictionary of famous personalities in
        world history and civilization.

9741   MEHMED SUREYYA, BEY, 1845-1909.
        Osmanli devletinde kim kimdi? Sicill-i Osmanī; yahud,
        Tezkire-i Misahir-i Osmaniyye-min düzeltilip genisletilmis
        edimsel yeni basımı. Ankara, Küğ Yayını, 1969-   v.
        geneal. tables. 24cm. [Küğ yayini, 11-
        Parts of this work appeared in 1969-70; nothing further issued
        as of 1975? Contents: 1. cild. Osmanoğullari. The Ottoman
        Empire's national biography; a dictionary of rulers, etc. An
        earlier edition [1890-98] was issued in Constantinople (Istanbul)
        --4 vols. (in 2).

9742   RESIMLI TÜRK VE DÜNYA MESHURLARE ANSIKLOPEDISI.
        [Istanbul] Altın Kitaplar Yayinevi [1958] 390 p. illus. 29cm.
        (Altın Kitaplar aylık ansiklopedisi, 1-[6]) "Kemal Zülfü Tameri
        baskanlığında bir heyet tarafından hazırlanmıstır." Cover title:
        Türk ve dünya meshurları ansiklopedisi. Illustrated encyclo-
        pedia of Turkish and world biography.

UKRAINE

9743   BOEVYE ZVEZDY KIEVLIAN; ocherki o Geroiakh Sovetskogo
        Soiuza. Kiev, Politzdat Ukrainy, 1968. 499 p. ports.
        21cm. Compiled by A. P. Mushta, M. D. Maksimtsov and K.
        I. Klepsik. 197 biographical sketches of Heroes of the Soviet
        Union in World War II (1939-1945) from the Province of Kiev.

9744   ENTSYKLOPEDIIA UKRAINOZNAVSTVA, v dvokh tomakh.
        Pid golovniu red. Volodymyra Kubiiovycha i Zenona Kuzeli.
        Miunkhen, Naukove tovarystvo im. Shevchenka, 1949-   v.

illus., ports. 26cm. A general Ukrainian encyclopedia extremely useful because 50% of it is devoted to biography with
emphasis on native Ukrainians as well as non-Ukrainians who
were involved in some way with Ukrainian civilization and history. From the latest information (as given by Dr. Kubiľovych)
the encyclopedia is now being published in France & will even-
tually contain 8 or 9 volumes plus a supplement and an index.
The first volume may have been reprinted (in revised format?)
in 1955 to accompany the set issuing from France [Sarcelles,
Naukove t-vo Shevchenka-Société scientifique Ševčenko) Vol.
7 (1975) is the latest volume to appear; v. 8 is in preparation.

9745   RADIĂNS'KA ENTSYKLOPEDIĬA ISTORII UKRAINY. Red. kol.
        A. D. Skaba [ta inshi] Kyiv, Gol. red. Ukr. Rad. entsyk-
        lopediĭ, 1969-72. 4 v. illus., ports. 25cm. An encyclopedic
        dictionary of Ukrainian history which includes biographies and
        portraits of noted Ukrainians.

9746   UKRAIN'SKA RADIĂNS'KA ENTSYKLOPEDIĬA. Golovna red.
        kolegiĭa: M. P. Bazhan [ta in.] Kyiv, Akademii nauk URSR,
        1959-65. 17 v. illus., ports. 27cm.

        ---- ----Alfavitnyĭ predmetno-imennyĭ pokazhchyk. Kyiv [1968]
        579 p. 27cm. Ukrainian Soviet encyclopedia; useful for the
        large number of biographical sketches of native Ukrainians.

UNITED STATES

Bibliography, Indexes, Portrait Catalogs

9747   THE AMERICAN GENEALOGICAL-BIOGRAPHICAL INDEX
        to American genealogical, biographical and local history
        materials. Middletown, Conn., Published under the auspices
        of an advisory committee representing the cooperating sub-
        scribing libraries by Godfrey Memorial Library, 1952-
             v. 26cm. Editors, 1952-   Fremont Rider
        Indexes published genealogies, the genealogical columns of the
        old Boston Transcript, etc. Vol. 91 (latest as of 1975): Jacobs,
        Daniel--Jennings, Willard.

9748   BELL, BARBARA L
             Black biographical sources; an annotated bibliography, by
        Barbara L. Bell, New Haven, Yale University Library, 1970.
        20 p. (Yale University Library. Bibliography series, 1) Most
        of the titles listed are located in libraries at Yale University;
        some are in the Schomburg Collection, New York Public Library.

9749   BRIGNANO, RUSSELL CARL
             Black Americans in autobiography: an annotated bibliogra-
        phy of autobiographies and autobiographical books written since

the Civil War. Durham, N. C., Duke University Press, 1974.
ix, 118 p. 25cm. Includes descriptions of 291 post-bellum autobiographies plus 126 autobiographical books.

9750   DAVIS, LENWOOD G
        The Black woman in American society; a selective annotated
        bibliography. Boston, Mass., G. K. Hall, 1975. xi, 159 p.
        25cm. Items 1-350 of the bibliography are collective and indi-
        vidual biographies and autobiographies of Black women in A-
        merica.

9751   DORNBUSCH, CHARLES EMIL, 1907-
        Military bibliography of the Civil War. New York, New
        York Public Library, 1961-72. 3 v. 26cm. Vol. 1 has title:
        Regimental publications and personal narratives of the Civil
        War; a checklist. Contents.--v. 1. Northern States.--v. 2.
        Southern, Border, and Western States and Territories. Feder-
        al troops. Union and Confederate biographies.--v. 3. General
        references; Armed Forces; and campaigns and battles. Bibli-
        ographies of individual biographies and autobiographies of the
        American Civil War follow the regimental histories, etc. which
        are listed state by state. Each volume has an index of personal
        names (with birth and/or death dates when known included in the
        index to vol. 1). Especially see v. 2 (p. 165-248) for "Union [and
        Confederate] biographical and personal narratives; [a bibliog-
        raphy]"

9752   FILBY, P   WILLIAM, 1911-
        American & British genealogy & heraldry; a selected list
        of books. 2d ed. Chicago, American Library Association,
        1975. xxi, 467 p. 25cm. Includes a number of biographical
        dictionaries and a few "mug" books (i.e. portrait and biographi-
        cal history books)

9753   HOTCHKISS, JEANETTE
        American historical fiction and biography for children and
        young people. Metuchen, N. J., Scarecrow Press, 1973. 318 p.
        22cm. Covers North and South America, with emphasis on the
        United States.

9754   JOHNSON, ROBERT OWEN
        An index to profiles in The New Yorker. Metuchen, N. J.,
        Scarecrow Press, 1972. vi, 190 p. 22cm. Indexes biographical
        sketches of contemporaries in vols. 1-46 (Feb. 21, 1925 thru' Feb.
        13, 1971) of The New Yorker.

9755   LIFSCHUTZ, E
        Bibliografye fun amerikaner un kanader yidishe zikhroynes
        un 'oitabeyagrafyes 'oyf yidish, hebreysh un 'english, tsuzamen-
        geshtelt fun Y. Lifschutz. Nyu-Yark, Yidisher Visnshaftlekher
        'Institut-Yivo, 1970. 74, 2, 75-[76] p. 28cm. Added t. p.:

Bibliography of American and Canadian Jewish memoirs and autobiographies in Yiddish, Hebrew and English.

9756   NATIONAL PORTRAIT GALLERY, Washington, D. C.
        Checklist of the permanent collection, National Portrait
Gallery, Smithsonian Institution. Washington, Smithsonian Institution Press, 1975. 72 p. 26cm. (Smithsonian Institution
Press publication no. 6109. A catalog of portraits of "men and
women who have made significant contributions to the history,
development, and culture of the people of the United States and
[an index] of the artists who created such portraits. " Birth and
death dates are given. Replaces 1973 edition (54 p.) which included all portraits acquired by the Gallery thru' 30 June 1972.

9757   NEVINS, ALLAN, 1890-1971.
        Civil War books; a critical bibliography. Edited by Allan
Nevins, James I. Robertson, Jr. [and] Bell I. Wiley. Baton
Rouge, Published for the U. S. Civil War Centennial Commis-
sion by Louisiana State University Press [1967-69] 2 v. 29cm.
"Biographies, memoirs and collected works [by] Robert W. Jo-
hannsen": vol. 2, p. 35-103.

9758   NEW YORK HISTORICAL SOCIETY.
        Catalogue of American portraits in the New-York Historical
Society. New Haven, Published for the New-York Historical Society by Yale University Press, 1974. 2 v. (ix, 964 p.) ports.
29cm. Description of 2,420 paintings, drawings, sketches and
busts accompanied by biographical material for the sitters. In
the form of a biographical dictionary, alphabetical by subjects
of the portraits.

9759   NEW YORK HISTORICAL SOCIETY.
        Catalogue of American portraits in the New-York Historical
Society: oil portraits, miniatures, sculptures. New York City,
1941. vii, 374 p. 879 ports. 24cm. Compiled by A. J. Wall.

9760   NEW YORK HISTORICAL SOCIETY.
        List of 500 portraits of men, made in New York City, 1900-
1942, by Pirie MacDonald, photographer of men, in the collections of the New-York Historical Society. New York City, 1943.
23 p. port. 20cm. Most of the portraits listed in the catalog
are of prominent Americans of the period 1900-1942; the re-
mainder are primarily British.

9761   NOTABLE NAMES IN AMERICAN HISTORY; a tabulated regis-
        ter. 3d ed. of White's Conspectus of American biography.
[Clifton, N. J.] J. T. White, 1973. 725 p. 29cm.

9762   PENNSYLVANIA. UNIVERSITY.
        Portraits in the University of Pennsylvania. Edited by Ag-
        nes Addison. Philadelphia, University of Pennsylvania Press,
        1940. 67 p. ports. 29cm.

9763   PENNSYLVANIA ACADEMY OF THE FINE ARTS, PHILA-
           DELPHIA.
        Loan exhibition of historical portraits, Dec. 1, 1887-Jan.
        15, 1888. Catalogue. 2d ed. Philadelphia, 1887. 148 p. 18cm.
        Biographical notes are provided for individuals who sat for por-
        traits (chiefly Americans, some Europeans). Alphabetical ar-
        rangement. Also includes: "Alphabetical list of artists ... with
        biographical notes" (p. 115-148).

9764   SHAW, THOMAS SHULER, 1906.
        Index to profile sketches in New Yorker magazine, 1925-
        1970. 2d rev. ed. Westwood, Mass., F. W. Faxon, 1972.
        x, 206 p. 23cm. (Useful reference series, no. 98) "Revision
        of Index to profile sketches in New Yorker magazine [Boston,
        1946] ... which covered those appearing in volume 1, number
        1, February 21, 1925 to volume 16, no. 1, February 17,
        1940, bringing it up to date to volume 46, number 1, February
        21, 1970."

9765   SMITH COLLEGE.
        Picture catalog of the Sophia Smith collection. Northamp-
        ton, Mass. [c1972] 128 p. (chiefly illus., ports.] 23cm. Under
        such headings as: Arts-Humanities, Biography, Social Reform,
        Women's Rights [etc.] can be found many portrait-prints (with
        identifying captions) of notable American women (and a few
        British) as well as prominent men of American history (19th
        century). Index at end yields an alphabetical approach.

General Works

9766   ACTON, JAY
        Mug shots; who's who in the New Earth, by Jay Acton,
        Alan Le Mond [and] Parker Hodges. Photos. by Raeanne Ru-
        benstein. New York, World Pub. Co., 1972. 244 p. illus.
        29cm. "A Meridian book." "A compendium of short biogra-
        phies of more than 200 [American] cartoonists, activists, edu-
        cators, rebels, musicians, writers, et al. who have made a
        name for themselves in the counter-culture" ... from Abolafia
        (Louis) to Zinn.

9767   ANDREWS, RALPH WARREN, 1897-
        Indian leaders who helped shape America. 1st ed. Seattle,
        Superior Pub. Co., 1971. 184 p. illus., ports. 28cm. This
        volume's value resides in its many portraits of American Indian
        chiefs, etc. Alphabetical approach to portraits and biographi-
        cal data thru' general index.

9768   BAKELESS, JOHN EDWIN, 1894-
           Signers of the Declaration [of Independence, by] John and
Katherine Bakeless. Boston, Houghton Mifflin, 1969. xiv,
300 p. 22cm. Biographies of the 56 signers, arranged by
state, Massachusetts thru' Georgia.

9769   BARONE, MICHAEL
           The almanac of American politics; the Senators, Repre-
sentatives; their records, States and districts, by Michael
Barone, Grant Ujifusa and Douglas Matthews. 2d ed. Boston,
Gambit, 1974, c1973. xxiii, 1240 p. illus., ports. 22cm.
1st ed. (xxv, 1030 p.) issued in 1972. Includes a brief biography,
with portrait, of each of the Senators and Representatives of
the U. S. Congress (ca. 535) as of 1974.

9770   BARONE, MICHAEL
           The almanac of American politics, 1976; the Senators, the
Representatives, the governors--their records, States, and
districts, by Michael Barone, Grant Ujifusa and Douglas Matthews. New York, Dutton, c1975. xviii, 1054 p. illus., ports.
21cm. (A Sunrise book) Like the earlier editions (especially
the "2d," 1974 ed., q. v.) the work includes a brief biography,
with portrait, of each of the Senators and Representatives of
the U. S. Congress as of 1975.

9771   BIOGRAPHICAL DIRECTORY OF AMERICANS AND CANADIANS
           OF CROATIAN DESCENT. 1973-   Calgary, Alta.,
Research Centre for Canadian Ethnic Studies.   v. 28cm.
(Research Centre for Canadian Ethnic Studies. Occasional
monograph, no. 1   Continues Biographical directory of
scholars, artists, and professionals of Croatian descent in the
United States and Canada (3 v., 1963-1970). Edited by Vladimir
Markotic.

9772   BIOGRAPHICAL DIRECTORY OF THE UNITED STATES EXEC-
           UTIVE BRANCH, 1774-1971. Robert Sobel, editor-in-chief.
Westport, Conn., Greenwood Pub. Co., 1971. x, 491 p. 24cm.
500 detailed biographies of executive officers of the Federal
Government serving from the Continental Congress to the Nixon
administration.

9773   BOATNER, MARK MAYO, 1921-
           Encyclopedia of the American Revolution, by Mark Mayo
Boatner III. Bicentennial ed. New York, D. McKay Co., 1974.
xviii, 1290 p. 22cm. A dictionary with ca. 2,000 entries; approximately a third of the entries are biographical (Continental
Army and Navy officers, statesmen (American and British),
Loyalists, British, French and German officers, physicians,
jurists, and clergymen) Revision of the 1st (1966) ed.

9774   BOYCE, RICHARD FYFE
        American Foreign Service authors; a bibliography, by
        Richard Fyfe Boyce and Katherine Randall Boyce. Metuchen,
        N. J. , Scarecrow Press, 1973. x, 321 p. 22cm. Brief bio-
        graphical notes are included for each author.

9775   BROWN, EVERIT
        A dictionary of American politics: comprising accounts of
        political parties, measures and men, and explanations of the
        Constitution, divisions and practical workings of the govern-
        ment, together with political phrases, familiar names of per-
        sons and places, noteworthy sayings, party platforms, etc. ,
        etc. By Everit Brown and Albert Strauss. New York, A. L.
        Burt, 1908, c1907. iv, 620 p. ports. 20cm. Includes brief
        biographical sketches of the more important American political
        figures of the 18th and 19th centuries. First published in 1888.

9776   CHASE, JOSEPH CUMMINGS, 1878-1965.
        Speaking of heroes; portraits of men of the A. E. F.
        from generals to privates in both world wars and Korea. The
        collection in the Smithsonian Institution painted by Joseph Cum-
        mings Chase, official portrait painter with the A. E. F. [Mil-
        waukee? c1972] 173 p. illus. , ports. 24cm. Includes 192 por-
        traits of American soldiers with some biographical data espe-
        cially of war experiences. Congressional Medal of Honor win-
        ners, etc. Copyrighted by Rudolph Binzel and Marion Lemonds.

9777   CLEPPER, HENRY EDWARD, 1901-   comp.
        Leaders of American conservation. Edited by Henry Clep-
        per. New York, Ronald Press Co. , 1971. vii, 353 p. 24cm.
        363 short biographies (period from 1900 to 1960) are included.

9778   COMMUNITY LEADERS AND NOTEWORTHY AMERICANS.
        Raleigh, N. C. , American Biographical Institute.   v.
        25cm. annual. Continues Community leaders of America. Be-
        gan with 1973/74 issue. A biographical dictionary of contempo-
        rary noteworthy Americans.

9779   DAVIS, ROBERT RALPH
        Lexicon of Afro-American history, by Robert R. Davis, Jr.
        New York, Simon and Schuster, 1975. 175 p. 24cm. The dic-
        tionary includes biographies of outstanding Afro-Americans past
        and present.

9780   DENNIS, HENRY C
        The American Indian, 1492-1970; a chronology & fact book.
        Compiled and edited by Henry C. Dennis. Foreword by Robert
        L. Bennett. Dobbs Ferry, N. Y. , Oceana Publications, 1971.
        xv, 137 p. 23cm. (Ethnic chronology series) "Indians of the
        past" (p. 81-94) contains 30 biographical sketches (alphabetically

arranged); "Contemporary Indians" (p. 91-109) is a biographical
dictionary of 50 prominent Indians of the 20th century (most are
still living).

9781   DIAMONSTEIN, BARBARALEE
        Open secrets; ninety-four women in touch with our time.
        New York, Viking Press, 1972. xxxvi, 474 p. ports. 25cm.
        A "biographical dictionary" (with portraits) of 94 living Ameri-
        can women of achievement who comment on social, political,
        etc. questions of the day, offering in the process autobiographi-
        cal data.

9782   DICTIONARY OF AMERICAN BIOGRAPHY. Under the auspices
        of the American Council of Learned Societies. New York,
        C. Scribner, 1928-   v. 26cm. "No living persons ...
        have biographies in the Dictionary." Edited by Allen Johnson,
        Dumas Malone and others. Contents.--v. 1-20. A-Z.--v. 21.
        Supplement one (To Dec. 31, 1935).--v. 22. Supplement two (To
        Dec. 31, 1940).--[v. 23] Supplement three (1941-1945)--[v. 24]
        Supplement four (1946-1950) with an index guide to [all] the sup-
        plements. 24 vols. issued as of 1974.

9783   DOUTH, GEORGE
        Leaders in profile: the United States Senate. 1972-
        New York, Speer & Douth, inc.   v. ports. 18cm. annual.
        Biographical profiles, with portraits, of present members of
        the U. S. Senate.

9784   DEPUY, TREVOR NEVITT, 1916-
        People & events of the American Revolution. Edited by
        Trevor N. Dupuy and Gay M. Gammerman. New York, Bowker,
        1974. xi, 473 p. maps (on lining papers) 24cm. Second part
        of the volume is a biographical dictionary: "People of the Amer-
        ican Revolution" (Loyalists, patriots, Indian leaders, people
        known locally at the time, etc.) with brief biographical data (ca.
        1,400), p. 279-432.

9785   THE EBONY SUCCESS LIBRARY, by the editors of Ebony.
        Chicago, Johnson Pub. Co., 1973. 3 v. illus., ports.
        29cm. Contents.--v. 1. 1,000 successful Blacks.--v. 2. Fa-
        mous Blacks give secrets of success.--v. 3. Career guide.
        Vol. 1 is in biographical dictionary arrangement; articles aver-
        age 1/3 of a page. Portrait accompanies each biography.

9786   EDMONDS, HELEN G
        Black faces in high places; Negroes in government. New
        York, Harcourt Brace Jovanovich, 1971. vi, 277 p. illus.,
        ports. 22cm. Not a biographical dictionary but a good source
        for brief biographical notes on several hundred Negroes in Fed-
        eral, State and municipal government in the United States.

These notes are under topics (government departments, activities, etc.) with an alphabetical approach through the "Index of officeholders (page numbers in italic type refer to pictures [portraits])": p. 271-277.

9787   ENCYCLOPEDIA OF AMERICAN HISTORY. [Editor: Ernest
         Kohlmetz] Guilford, Conn., Dushkin Pub. Group, 1973.
         405 p. illus. 24cm. Includes biographies, especially of more
         recent figures (e. g. , Betty Friedan).

9788   ENGELBARTS, RUDOLF
         Women in the United States Congress, 1917-1972; their ac-
         complishments, with bibliographies. Littleton, Colo. , Librar-
         ies Unlimited, 1974. 184 p. 24cm. A bio-bibliographical list-
         ing in chronological arrangement (with alphabetical lists toward
         end) of the 81 women who have served in the U. S. Congress,
         1917-1972.

9789   THE EVENING STAR, Washington, D. C.
         The New Frontiersmen; profiles of the men around Kennedy.
         With a foreword by I. William Hill and an introd. by M. B.
         Schnapper. Washington, Public Affairs Press, 1961. 254 p.
         24cm. Biographical sketches (chiefly of the who's who type, ar-
         ranged by executive branch: Dept. of State, Commerce Dept. ,
         etc.)

9790   FAILOR, KENNETH M
         Medals of the United States Mint, by Kenneth M. Failor and
         Eleanora Hayden. Rev. [Washington] Dept. of the Treasury;
         [for sale by the Supt. of Docs. , U. S. Govt. Print. Off.] 1972.
         v, 312 p. illus. , ports. 28cm. Includes ca. 160 medallions
         with portraits of famous Americans, with biographical sketches
         thereof. 1st ed. issued in 1969.

9791   FAMILY ENCYCLOPEDIA OF AMERICAN HISTORY. Pleasant-
         ville, N. Y. , Reader's Digest Association [1975] 1370 p.
         maps. 27cm. At head of title: The Reader's digest. Biography
         is a major part of the dictionary, with entries for explorers,
         Indians, government leaders, etc.

9792   FAMOUS LIVING AMERICANS. Los Angeles, C. Webb, 1915-
         [41] 2 v. ports. 25cm. Contents. --[1] Famous living A-
         mericans; edited by Mary Griffin Webb and Edna Lenore Webb. --
         [2] Famous Americans, 2d series; edited by Warren Huff and
         Edna Lenore Webb Huff. Biographies (e. g. , 2d series contains
         50) of prominent Americans who flourished from 1915 through
         the first 2 administrations of Franklin D. Roosevelt.

9793   FEDERAL WRITERS' PROJECT.
        The American slave; a composite autiobiography. George
        P. Rawick, general editor. Westport, Conn., Greenwood Pub.
        Co. [1972] 19 v. 23cm. (Contributions in Afro-American and
        African studies, no. 11) Vols. 1-17 reprinted from typewritten
        records prepared in 1941 under title: Slave narratives, and with
        sponsorship of the Library of Congress; v. 18-19 were first is-
        sued by Fisk University as its Social science source documents,
        no. 1-2. A huge collection of autobiographies and narratives
        from former slaves (in vols. 2-17) Each of these volumes is de-
        voted to a Southern state or states, with an alphabetical list of
        narrators at the front of each volume.

9794   FOREMOST WOMEN IN COMMUNICATIONS; a biographical
        reference work on accomplished women in broadcasting,
        publishing, advertising, public relations, and allied professions.
        [New York] Foremost Americans Pub. Corp. in association with
        R. R. Bowker Co. [1970] xvii, 788 p. ports. 25cm. Ameri-
        can women, leaders in communications; biographical sketches of
        more than 7,000 individuals.

9795   FRANK, BENIS M
        Marine Corps oral history collection catalog. Compiled by
        Benis M. Frank. Rev. Washington, History and Museums Di-
        vision, Headquarters, U. S. Marine Corps, 1975. xi, 42 p.
        26cm. (Marine Corps historical reference pamphlet) Primarily
        a biographical dictionary of officers and some non-commissioned
        officers of the 20th century U. S. Marine Corps. The brief bio-
        graphical sketches are the result of interviews conducted by oral
        history researchers.

9796   GARRATY, JOHN ARTHUR, 1920-
        Encyclopedia of American biography. John A. Garraty,
        editor. Jerome L. Sternstein, associate editor. [1st ed.]
        New York, Harper & Row [1974] xiv, 1241 p. 25cm. Includes
        ca. 1,000 biographies of historical and living personnages.

9797   GATELY, JAMES J
        A register of the governors of the states of the United States
        of America, 1776-1974. [Collingswood, N. J.] Gateford Publica-
        tions, 1974. ii, 123 p. 28cm. A listing that includes birthplace,
        dates of birth and death (if deceased), political affiliation, dates
        of administration.

9798   GELLÉRT, IMRE
        Amerikai Magyar karrierek albuma. Cleveland [1923] 1 v.
        (unpaged) illus., ports. An album of successful Hungarians in
        America; contemporary portraits (1920's) and guide.

9799   GREENE, ROBERT EWELL, 1931-
         Black defenders of America, 1775-1973; [a reference and
         pictorial history] Chicago, Johnson Pub. Co., 1974. 416 p.
         illus. 28cm. Includes brief biographies and photographs of
         several hundred American Blacks who served in the Armed
         Forces. Name index serves as an alphabetical approach to the
         biographies.

9800   HORAN, JAMES DAVID, 1914-
         The McKenney-Hall portrait gallery of American Indians.
         New York, Crown Publishers, 1972. 373 p. illus., ports. (part
         col.) 31cm. Includes 128 portraits in full color of American
         Indians reproduced from the works of American artists more
         than 150 years ago (1st published in 1836 in 3 portfolios) Biogra-
         phical sketches accompany the portraits when such information
         is available.

9801   JACKSON, MARGARET (YOUNG) 1918-
         An investigation of biographies and autobiographies of A-
         merican slaves published between 1840 and 1860, based upon the
         Cornell Special Slavery Collection. [Ithaca, N. Y.] 1954. vi,
         393 l. 28cm. Thesis--Cornell University. The appendices in-
         clude "Biographical sketches of [161] slaves" (l. [342]-356) with
         references to sources giving greater detail, and an extensive
         bibliography of slave narratives, biographies and autobiographies.

9802   JUDSON, LEVI CARROLL
         The sages and heroes of the American Revolution. Including
         the signers of the Declaration of Independence. Two hundred and
         forty three of the sages and heroes are presented in due form and
         many others are named incidentally. Port Washington, N. Y.,
         Kennikat Press, 1970. 480 p. 24cm. (Kennikat American bicen-
         tennial series) Biographical dictionary (in 2 alphabets); pt. 1: 75
         fairly lengthy biographies--pt. 2: 165 shorter biographies. Re-
         print of the 1851 ed.

9803   KERRIGAN, EVANS E
         The Medal of Honor in Vietnam. Noroton Heights, Conn.,
         Medallic Pub. Co. [1971-   v. ports. 23cm. Vol. 1 con-
         tains over 100 portraits, birth dates (or birth/death dates) and
         description of exploits of recipients of the Medal.

9804   LEONARD, EUGENIE (ANDRUSS) 1888-
         The American woman in Colonial and Revolutionary times,
         1565-1800; a syllabus with bibliography [by] Eugenie Andruss
         Leonard, Sophie Hutchinson Drinker [and] Miriam Young Holden.
         Philadelphia, University of Pennsylvania Press [1962] 169 p.
         24cm. "104 outstanding Colonial women" (p. 111-125) gives name
         of colony in which the individual was born, her significant con-
         tribution, dates of birth and death (when known), names of her
         husband or husbands, and specific page references to numbered

items in the bibliography which follows. "Bibliography" (p. 126-169) includes 1082 items.

9805   LÉVESQUE, LÉO ALBERT, 1900-
        Silhouettes franco-americaines [par] Rosaire Dion-Lévesque [pseud.] Manchester, N. H., Association canado-américaine, 1957. 933, 6 p. 23cm. Includes biographical sketches of A-merican public men of French ancestry (New England especial-ly).

9806   LITHUANIAN ALLIANCE IN AMERICA.
        Susivientijimo lietuvių Amerikoje auksinio jubiliejaus al-bumas. Isleidimu rūpinosi SLA Jubiliejaus komisija. Redagavo ir tekstus parašė S. E. Vitaitis. Vinietes nupiešė ir medžiaga surinko A. B. Strimaitis. New York, Išleido Susivienijimas Lietuvių Amerikoje, 1936. 303 p. illus., ports. 24 x 31cm. Most of this volume consists of group and individual portraits of Lithuanians in the United States. Many of the individual portraits have captions of some biographical interest. There is an index to the portraits at the end of the volume.

9807   LO, SAMUEL E
        Asian who? in America. Compiled and edited by Samuel E. Lo. [Roseland, N. J.] East-West Who? [1971] 329 p. 23cm. Biographical dictionary of distinguished persons of Asian birth or ancestry now resident in the United States.

9808   MAGYAR-AMERIKA ÍRÁSBAN ÉS KÉPBEN. Amerikai Magyar úttörők es vezető férfiak arcképes életrajza. Magyar egy-házak, egyletek, közin tézmények története és müködése. Szerk.: Káldor Kálmán. [St. Louis, Hungarian Pub. Co., 1937-39. 2 v. illus., ports. 31cm. Hungarian-America in words and pictures; photographs and biographies of American-Hungari-an pioneers and civic leaders. Arranged by regions and locali-ties.

9809   MAJORS, MONROE ALPHUS, 1864-
        Noted Negro women, their triumphs and activities. [Free-port, N. Y., Books for Libraries Press, 1971] 364 p. ports. 23cm. (The Black heritage library collection) Reprint of the 1893 ed. (Chicago, Donohue & Henneberry). Includes within its pages biographical sketches of ca. 300 Black women prominent in American life from the late 18th to the late 19th century. Al-phabetical approach via Contents (p. 11-16).

9810   MORRIS, DAN
        Who was who in American politics; a biographical dictionary of over 4,000 men and women who contributed to the United States political scene from colonial days up to and including the immediate past, by Dan and Inez Morris. New York, Hawthorne Books [c1974] 637 p. 25cm.

9811   MORRIS, RICHARD BRANDON, 1904-   ed.
        Encyclopedia of American history; edited by Richard B.
        Morris. Associate editor: Jeffrey B. Morris. Bicentennial
        [5th] ed. New York, Harper & Row [1976] xiv, 1245 p. maps.
        24cm. 1st ed., 1953; 2d, 1961; 3d, 1965; 4th, 1970. "Five hun-
        dred notable Americans" [past and present; a biographical dic-
        tionary]: p. [961]-1191.

9812   MYERS, ROBERT MANSON, 1921-
        The children of pride; a true story of Georgia and the Civil
        War. Edited by Robert Manson Myers. New Haven, Yale Uni-
        versity Press, 1972. xxv, 1845 p. maps (on lining papers)
        26cm. "[Selected] from the voluminous family papers of the
        Rev. Dr. Charles Colcock Jones (1804-1863) of Liberty County,
        Georgia." "Who's who" (p. [1449]-1738) presents a biographical
        sketch of every individual mentioned in the text, chiefly Ameri-
        cans and Southerners of the period, but also world figures of the
        time, etc.

9813   NASH, JAY ROBERT
        Bloodletters and badmen; a narrative encyclopedia of A-
        merican criminals from the Pilgrims to the present. New York;
        M. Evans; distributed in association with J. B. Lippincott,
        Philadelphia [1973] 640 p. illus., ports. 29cm. A biographi-
        cal dictionary.

9814   NATIONAL PORTRAIT GALLERY, Washington, D. C. HIS-
            TORIAN'S OFFICE.
        "The dye is now caste"; the road to American independence,
        1774-1776. Text by Lillian B. Miller, historian, National Por-
        trait Gallery, and the staff of the Historian's Office. Russell
        Bourne, editor. Washington, Published for the National Por-
        trait Gallery by the Smithsonian Institution Press, 1975. xvi,
        328 p. illus. 28cm. Includes ca. 110 portraits and biographies
        of figures (American, British, French, etc.) who played promi-
        nent roles in the American Revolutionary War; there is a name
        index at the end of the volume.

9815   NOTABLE AMERICAN WOMEN, 1607-1950; a biographical dic-
            tionary. Edward T. James, editor. Janet Wilson James,
        associate editor. Paul S. Boyer, assistant editor. Cambridge,
        Mass., Belknap Press of Harvard University Press, 1971. 3 v.
        26cm. "Prepared under the auspices of Radcliffe College."
        1,359 biographies of American women who died no later than the
        end of 1950. Contents.--v. 1. A-F.--v. 2. G-O.--v. 3. P-Z.

9816   100 GREATEST AMERICAN WOMEN [by] Roseann C. Hirsch,
            editorial director; Susan Gilman, associate editor. New
        York, Lexington Library, 1976-   v. illus. 28cm.

9817   1,000 SUCCESSFUL BLACKS, by the editors of Ebony. Nash-
           ville, Tenn., Southwestern Co. by arrangement with John-
    son Pub. Co., 1973. 341 p. ports. 29cm. (The Ebony suc-
    cess library, v. 1) A biographical dictionary of 1,000 distin-
    guished living Black Americans.

9818   OUTSTANDING AMERICAN HIGH SCHOOL STUDENTS; a bio-
           graphical compilation of the most outstanding high school
    seniors in America. [Birmingham, Ala.] Outstanding American
    High School Students [1969] 306 p. 24cm.

9819   PANORAMA; a historical review of Czechs and Slovaks in the
           United States of America. Cicero, Ill., Czechoslovak Na-
    tional Council of America [1970] 328 p. illus. 27cm. A bio-
    graphical dictionary of prominent living and deceased Czechs and
    Slovaks in the United States will be found on p. 187-313.

9820   PENNSYLVANIA. HISTORICAL SOCIETY.
           Paintings and miniatures at the Historical Society of Pennsyl-
    vania. Rev. ed. compiled by Nicholas B. Wainwright. Phila-
    delphia, 1974. xx, 334 p. illus. (part col.), ports. 29cm.
    Published in 1872 under title: Catalogue of the paintings and other
    objects of interest belonging to the Historical Society of Pennsyl-
    vania; and in 1942 under title: Catalogue, descriptive and criti-
    cal, of the paintings and miniatures in the Historical Society of
    Pennsylvania. The main portion of the text is a biographical dic-
    tionary of the subjects of the portraits painted by chiefly Ameri-
    can artists of the 18th-20th centuries. Most of the biographies
    are, of course, of Americans too.

9821   PENNSYLVANIA ACADEMY OF THE FINE ARTS, PHILA-
           DELPHIA.
           Catalogue of an exhibition of portraits by Charles Sillson
    Peale and James Peale and Rembrandt Peale. Final ed. Phila-
    delphia, 1923. 239 p. illus. 26cm. With biographical sketches
    of over 250 sitters for the Peales.

9822   PLOSKI, HARRY A
           Afro USA; a reference work on the Black experience, com-
    piled and edited by Harry A. Ploski and Ernest Kaiser. [New
    York] Bellwether Pub. Co.; distributed by Afro-American Press
    [1971] 1110 p. illus. 29cm. "An expanded and enlarged ver-
    sion of the ... Negro almanac, first published in 1967 and now
    completely revised and updated for the 1970's." Includes a sec-
    tion on famous Negro personalities.

9823   RALPH NADER CONGRESS PROJECT.
           Citizens look at Congress. [Washington, Grossman Pub-
    lishers, 1972-74. 9 v. 30cm. Individual profiles, biographical

and political data on 484 Congressmen (92d Congress, 1971-72)
Alphabetical arrangement by states. Project director: Robert
C. Fellmeth; profile directors: Joan Claybrook and Dale Pullen;
editor: Deanna Nash. On spine: Congress Project, 92d Congress.

9824   REFERENCE ENCYCLOPEDIA OF THE AMERICAN INDIAN.
          Bernard Klein and Daniel Icolari, editors. With an introd.
          by Robert L. Bennett. 2d ed. Rye, N. Y., Todd Publications
          [1973-74] 2 v. 26cm. Vol. 2, edited by D. Icolari, has sub-
          title: Who's who, and is a biographical dictionary of prominent
          contemporary Indians as well as non-Indians active in Indian af-
          fairs.

9825   RIPPEY, JOSEPH
          Historical biography of the United States, classified. Con-
          taining all the historical, noted events, and interesting incidents
          connected with the settlement of the United States since its first
          discovery, up to the present time. Baltimore, J. Rippey & Co.
          [1885] 401 p. 24cm. Advertisements on business houses inter-
          spersed throughout the text.

9826   RUTGERS UNIVERSITY, NEW BRUNSWICK, N. J. CENTER
          FOR THE AMERICAN WOMAN AND POLITICS.
          Women in public office; a biographical directory and statis-
          tical analysis. Compiled by Center for the American Woman and
          Politics, Eagleton Institute of Politics, Rutgers ... Project
          staff: Sara B. Chrisman [and others] New York, Bowker, 1976.
          iii, 455 p. 29cm. 13,000 profiles of the nation's most political-
          ly powerful and influential women in a state-by-state listing. In-
          cludes date and place of birth, political affiliation, education,
          organization, memberships, previous political positions, occu-
          pation, etc.

9827   SMITH, HELEN AINSLIE
          One hundred famous Americans. Rev. to date with article
          on "Hall of Fame" by H. M. MacCracken. New York, G. Rout-
          ledge [1902] viii, 574 p. illus., ports. 23cm. The 100 de-
          ceased Americans whose achievements were recognized by the
          Hall of Fame at New York University (as of 1902). Since that
          time additional persons of achievement in science, literature,
          art, government, theology, etc. have been elected.

9828   SOEDINENNYE SHTATY AMERIKI; slovar'-spravochnik. [Pod
          obshchei red. A. A. Arzumaniana, N. V. Mostovets, M. A.
          Kharlamova. Moskva, Gos. izd-vo polit. lit-ry, 1960] 611 p.
          illus., ports. 23cm. An encyclopedic Russian work on the
          United States. On pages [541]-598 is a biographical dictionary
          of figures important in the political and cultural life of the U.S.

9829   SONS OF THE REVOLUTION. PENNSYLVANIA SOCIETY.
        Decennial register of the Pennsylvania Society of Sons of
        the Revolution, 1888-1898. Philadelphia, Printed by F. B. Lip-
        pincott, 1898. 457 p. illus., ports. 26cm. The "Roll of an-
        cestors, 1775-1783" (p. [237]-448) is a 'biographical dictionary'
        of soldiers of all ranks in the American Revolution, ca. 1100
        names in all, from whom members of the Society claimed de-
        scent. Birth and death dates, and some details of military and
        civilian careers are given.

9830   TOPPIN, EDGAR ALLAN, 1928-
        A biographical history of Blacks in America since 1528, by
        Edgar A. Toppin. New York, D. McKay Co. [1971] x, 499 p.
        25cm. "Based on a series of articles that appeared weekly in
        the Christian science monitor, March 6 to June 12, 1969. "
        "Biographies of notable Americans" (p. 241-483) is a biographi-
        cal dictionary, with 145 biographies of contemporary men &
        women.

9831   UKRAINIANS IN NORTH AMERICA; a biographical directory of
        noteworthy men and women of Ukrainian origin in the United
        States and Canada. Editor: Dmytro M. Shtohryn. Editorial
        board: Jurij Fedynskyj [and others] 1st ed. Champaign, Ill.,
        Association for the Advancement of Ukrainian Studies, 1975.
        xxiv, 424 p. 25cm. Covers the United States and Canada. In-
        cludes obituaries of 35 biographees who died during the course
        of publication (p. 387-398).

9832   UNION SAINT-JEAN-BAPTISTE D'AMÉRIQUE.
        Le Bureau général de l'Union Saint-Jean-Baptiste d'Amé-
        rique (de mars 1900 à septembre 1937); notes historiques [et]
        biographies des officiers, et directeurs généraux des membres
        du Bureau médical [par Élie Vezina] Woonsocket, R. I. 1937.
        213 p. illus. ports. 23cm. History of a French-American,
        French-Canadian society and biographies of ca. 120 of its of-
        ficers, living and deceased.

9833   UNITED STATES. ARCHITECT OF THE CAPITOL.
        Art in the United States Capitol. Prepared by the Architect
        of the Capitol under the direction of the Joint Committee on the
        Library. Washington, U. S. Govt. Print. Off., 1976. xi, 453 p.
        illus., ports. (part col.) 27cm. Pages [1]-127 contain colored
        portraits of presidents of the U. S., vice-presidents, senators,
        speakers of the House, chairmen of the House Committee on Ap-
        propriation, architects of the Capitol, and other prominent in-
        dividuals. Additional portraits (busts, statues, etc.) are scat-
        tered thru' the volume. Index leads one to the various individual
        portraits.

9834   UNITED STATES. CIVIL SERVICE COMMISSION. LIBRARY.
        Fifty United States Civil Service Commissioners; biographi-

cal sketch, biographical sources, writings. Washington, 1971,
275 p. 27cm. Cover title. In chronological arrangement; alphabetical name index at end of volume.

9835   UNITED STATES. CONGRESS.
            Biographical directory of the American Congress, 1774-1971,
        the Continental Congress, September 5, 1774, to October 21,
        1778, and the Congress of the United States, from the First
        through the Ninety-first Congress, March 4, 1789 to January 3,
        1971, inclusive. [Washington] U. S. Govt. Print. Off., 1971.
        1972 p. 30cm. (92d Congress, 1st session. Senate document,
        no. 92-8) Rev. ed. (1961) covered 1774-1961. Compiled by
        Lawrence F. Kennedy.

9836   UNITED STATES. CONGRESS. SENATE. COMMITTEE ON
            VETERANS' AFFAIRS.
            Vietnam era Medal of Honor recipients, 1964-1972. Wash-
        ington, U. S. Govt. Print. Off., 1973. xix, 236 p. illus.
        24cm. At head of title: 93d Cong., 1st sess. Committee Print
        no. 8. Biographical dictionary of over 100 Medal of Honor re-
        cipients during the Vietnamese Conflect, 1964-1972 (p. 18-157).

9837   UNITED STATES. NAVY. ATLANTIC FLEET. SUBMARINE
            FORCE.
            United States ship Thresher. In memoriam April 10, 1963.
        [Compiled by the staff, Deputy commander, Submarine Force,
        U. S. Atlantic Fleet. New York, 1964] xiv, 146 p. illus.,
        ports. 27cm. Biographical dictionary (2 parts: (1) officers
        (2) ship's crew) of the 129 men who went down with the nuclear-
        powered attack submarine U. S. S. Thresher in April 10, 1963.

9838   UNITED STATES. SOCIAL SECURITY ADMINISTRATION.
            America's centenarians: reports of interviews with social
        security beneficiaries who have lived to 100. [Washington]
        1963-   v. ports. 27cm. 13 volumes published as
        of 1972. Vol. 11 has title: America's centenarians; reports of
        interviews with social security beneficiaries who reached 100
        from January 1969 through December 1969. Biographical
        sketches and portraits.

9839   VAN DOREN, CHARLES LINCOLN, 1926-
            Webster's American biographies, Charles Van Doren, editor.
        Robert McHenry, associate editor. Springfield, Mass., G. &
        C. Merriam Co. [1974] xii, 1233 p. 26cm. A biographical dic-
        tionary with ca. 3,000 entries.

9840   VEXLER, ROBERT I
            The vice-presidents and cabinet members; biographies ar-
        ranged chronologically by administration. Dobbs Ferry, N. Y.,
        Oceana Publications, 1975. 2 v. (xix, 887 p.) 26cm. Vice-

presidents and cabinet members of the United States Government from its beginnings to the present (1975).

9841   WANDYCZ, DAMIAN S
       Register of Polish American scholars, scientists, writers & artists. Edited by Damian S. Wandycz. New York, Polish Institute of Arts and Sciences in America, 1969. 80 p. 23cm. Living scholars, etc.: includes birth dates and brief occupational data.

9842   WEBSTER'S GUIDE TO AMERICAN HISTORY: a chronological, geographical, and biographical survey and compendium. [Editors: Charles Van Doren and Robert McHenry] Springfield, Mass., G. & C. Merriam Co. [1971] 1428 p. illus., maps. 24cm. Includes a biographical dictionary with 1,035 half-column biographical sketches (p. [793]-1349).

9843   WESLEYAN UNIVERSITY, MIDDLETOWN, CONN.
       Alumni record of Wesleyan University, Middletown, Conn. Centennial (sixth) ed., 1931. Edited by Frank W. Nicolson. Middletown, Pelton & King, printers [1931] xxxvi, 1245 p. 24cm. Biographical sketches for alumni (1831-1931) arranged alphabetically under class.

9844   WHO WAS WHO IN AMERICAN HISTORY, ARTS AND LETTERS.
       Chicago, Marquis Who's Who, 1975. xiii, 604 p. 27cm. Entries are taken from the first six Who was who in America volumes; American artists of the past.

9845   WHO'S WHO AMONG AMERICAN HIGH SCHOOL STUDENTS.
       6th-   1971/72-   Northfield, Ill., Educational Communications, inc.   v. 28cm. annual. Continues Merit's who's who among American high school students.

9846   WHO'S WHO AMONG BLACK AMERICANS. 1st-   ed.; 1975-1975--   Northbrook, Ill., Who's Who among Black Americans. inc. Pub. Co., 1976-   v. 29cm. 1st-   ed.: Edited by William C. Matney. Vol. for 1975-1976 contains biographies of 10,000 contemporary Black Americans at all levels of endeavor.

9847   WHO'S WHO AMONG STUDENTS IN AMERICAN VOCATIONAL AND TECHNICAL SCHOOLS. 1974/75-
       Tuscaloosa, Ala., Randall Pub. Co.   v. 24cm. annual.

9848   WHO'S WHO IN GOVERNMENT. 1st ed. -   1972/72-
       Chicago, Marquis Who's Who.   v. 31cm. Contemporary American statesmen, officials, etc. Supersedes the

publication with the same title issued by the Biographical Research Bureau. The 2d ed. (1975) expands the 1st (1972) by
some 25 percent.

9849   WHO'S WHO OF AMERICAN WOMEN. 6th-   ed.:
              1970/71-   Chicago, Marquis Who's Who.   v.
        31cm. biennial. Continues Who's who of American men and
        women of Canada. Title varies slightly.

9850   WILLIAMS COLLEGE.
              Williams College in the World War. [Williamstown, Mass.]
        President and Trustees of Williams College, 1926. 500 p.
        illus., ports. 27cm. Primarily a roster of service records of
        alumni, faculty, etc. of Williams College in the World War of
        1914-1918: its value lies in the many hundreds of photographs
        of the persons listed.

Local

Alabama

9851   DU BOSE, JOEL CAMPBELL, 1855-   ed.
              Notable men of Alabama, personal and genealogical, with
        portraits. Atlanta, Ga., Southern Historical Association, 1904.
        2 v. ports.

9852   NORTHERN ALABAMA, historical and biographical. Birming-
              ham, Smith & DeLand, 1888. 776 p. ports. 27cm. In-
        cludes many biographical sketches of persons prominent in
        Northern Alabama in the 2d half of the 19th century.

9853   STEWART, JOHN CRAIG
              The governors of Alabama. Gretna [La.] Pelican Pub.
        Co., 1975. viii, 232 p. ports. 23cm. Brief biographies of
        the 75 individuals who (from the French, British and Spanish
        colonial regimes to George Corley Wallace) have served as gov-
        ernors in the 270 years of Alabama's existence. Arranged
        chronologically.

Arizona

9854   ARIZONA, THE GRAND CANYON STATE; a history of Arizona.
              [Compiled by Florence Wachholtz] Westminster, Colo.,
        Western States Historical Publishers, 1975. 2 v. (vii, 956 p.)
        illus., ports. 29cm. Pages 161-476 and 639-949 are exclu-
        sively devoted to biographical sketches of 895 20th century per-
        sonalities of Arizona (some deceased, most living). Alphabeti-
        cal approach thru' 'Biographical' [index] on p. 952-956.

Birmingham, Ala.

9855   DU BOSE, JOHN WITHERSPOON, 1836-1918, ed.
Jefferson County and Birmingham, Alabama: historical and
biographical. Birmingham, Teeple & Smith, 1887. 595 p.
ports. 4.º Biographies comprise a substantial part of the
volume.

Buffalo

9856   BUFFALO EVENING NEWS.
A history of the City of Buffalo: its men and institutions;
biographical sketches of leading citizens. Buffalo, 1908. 252 p.
illus., ports. 31cm.

9857   [DEVOY, JOHN] 1842-1928.
A history of the City of Buffalo and Niagara Falls, including
a concise account of the aboriginal inhabitants of the region; the
first white explorers and missionaries; the pioneers and their
successors ... Biographical sketches ... Buffalo, The Times,
1896. 304, 62 p. illus., ports. 32cm. "Compiled for the Buffalo times by John Devoy"--Verso of t. p. 146 biographies and
portraits of prominent citizens of Buffalo and Niagara Falls
(U. S.) at the end of the 19th century scattered thru' the text,
with a biographical index and index of portraits.

9858   SMITH, HENRY PERRY, 1839-1925.
History of the City of Buffalo and Erie County, with illustrations and biographical sketches of some of its prominent men and
pioneers. Syracuse, D. Mason, 1884. 2 v. illus., ports. 26cm.
Contents. --1. History of Erie County [with 52 portraits, 50 biographical sketches, and "Brief personals" (p. [709]-769) alphabetical under towns]--2. History of Buffalo [with 88 portraits,
and 91 biographical sketches]

California

9859   DAVIS, ELLIS ARTHUR
Davis' commercial encyclopedia of the Pacific Southwest:
California, Nevada, Utah, Arizona. Edited and published by
Ellis A. Davis. Berkeley, Calif. [1918?] 840 p. illus., ports.
38cm. "Men of California": p. 372-840. First published in
1910?

9860   RHOADES, ELIZABETH R
Foreigners in Southern California during the Mexican period. [San Francisco, R and E Research Associates, 1971]
170 p. 29cm. Originally presented as the author's thesis, University of California, 1924. The "Appendix" (p. 49-[153]) consists of 4 "biographical dictionaries"--1. Pioneers by sea. 2.

Hide and tallow merchants. 3. Overland trappers: New Mexico
traders. 4. Ranchers and agriculturists. —for a total of 72 biographies.

Colorado

9861   HISTORY OF CLEAR CREEK AND BOULDER VALLEYS,
            COLORADO. Containing a brief history of the State of
        Colorado ... and biographical sketches. Chicago, O. L. Baskin,
        1880. 713 p. illus., ports. 26cm. Includes portraits and bio-
        graphical sketches of prominent people in 4 counties in Colorado.

9862   HISTORY OF THE ARKANSAS VALLEY, COLORADO. Chicago,
            O. L. Baskin, 1881. 889 p. illus., ports. 26cm. Includes
        many biographical sketches of prominent citizens and early set-
        tlers of the Valley which covers the following counties: Lake, El
        Paso, Fremont, Custer, Pueblo and Bent and the Ten Mile re-
        gion.

Connecticut

9863   ENCYCLOPAEDIA OF BIOGRAPHY OF CONNECTICUT.
            Chicago, Century Pub. and Engraving Co., 1892. 211 p.
        ports. 30cm.

Florida

9864   BLACKMAN, LUCY (WORTHINGTON)
            The women of Florida. Jacksonville, Southern Historical
        Pub. Associates, 1940. 2 v. illus., ports. 28cm. Contents. --
        v. 1. The narrative. --v. 2. The biographies.

9865   MAKERS OF AMERICA, an historical and biographical work by
            an able corps of writers. Jacksonville, Fla., Published
        under the patronage of the Florida Historical Society [by] A. B.
        Caldwell, Atlanta, 1909. 2 v. illus., ports. 25cm. At head of
        title: Florida edition. These 2 vols. are devoted to Florida bi-
        ography and economic history.

9866   MARKS, HENRY S
            Who was who in Florida. Written and compiled by Henry S.
        Marks. Huntsville, Ala., Strode Publishers [1973] 276 p.
        front. 27cm.

9867   WHO'S WHO IN FLORIDA. 1st-   ed.; 1973/74-
            Lexington, Ky., Names of Distinction, inc.   v. 28cm.

Galveston, Tex.

9868   HAYES, CHARLES W   d. 1905.
          Galveston; history of the island and the city. Austin, Tex.,
          Jenkins Garrett Press; distributed by the Jenkins Pub. Co.,
          1974. 2 v. (xiii, 1044 p.) plate. 24cm. Printed from the
          original page proofs of the 1879 ed. (unpublished) with title: His-
          tory of the island and the city of Galveston, from the discovery
          of the island in 1526, from the founding of the city in 1837, down
          to the year 1870. A biography section at the end of vol. 2 (p.
          [811]-983) includes ca. 100 biographies (some quite extensive) of
          founders and movers of Galveston. The biographies are arrang-
          ed in no discernible order and index must be used to get at them
          alphabetically.

Georgia

9869   CHANDLER, ALLEN DANIEL, 1834-1910.
          Georgia; comprising sketches of counties, towns, events,
          institutions, and persons, arranged in cyclopedic form. Edited
          by Allen D. Chandler and Clement A. Evans. Atlanta, State
          Historical Association, 1906. Spartanburg, S. C., Reprint Co.,
          1972. 4 v. ports. 23cm. Cover title of 1972 reprint ed.: Cy-
          clopedia of Georgia. Vol. 4: Supplemental vol. The first 3
          vols. are in dictionary arrangement and include biographies.
          Vol. 4 consists entirely of "personal sketches of representative
          Georgians for whom special portraits have been executed on
          steel."

9870   NATIONAL SOCIETY OF THE COLONIAL DAMES OF AMERICA.
          GEORGIA. HISTORICAL ACTIVITIES COMMITTEE.
          Early Georgia portraits, 1715-1870. Compiled by the His-
          torical Activities Committee, Marion Converse Bright, state
          chairman, for the National Society of the Colonial Dames of A-
          merica in the State of Georgia. Athens, University of Georgia
          Press, c1975. xiii, 338 p. ports. 29cm. Includes over 600
          individual portraits accompanied by biographical sketches in bio-
          graphical dictionary arrangement. Prominent members of Geor-
          gia society dominate the earlier portraits; the later ones feature
          people from all ranks: doctors, farmers, lawyers, bankers,
          artisans, soldiers, their ladies and their progeny.

9871   WHO'S WHO IN GEORGIA. 1st-   ed.; 1973-
          Atlanta, United States Public Relations Service.   v.
          24cm.

Hartford, Con.

9872   SILVERMAN, MORRIS, 1894-
          Hartford Jews, 1659-1970. Hartford, Connecticut Histori-
          cal Society [1970] xii, 448 p. illus., ports. 29cm. "Who was

who" (p. [117]-314) is a biographical dictionary, with many portraits, of prominent Hartford Jews of the past.

Houston, Tex.

9873 HOUSTON PRESS CLUB.
Men of affairs of Houston and environs. Houston, Tex.,
1913. 192 p.

Illinois

9874 CLAYTON, JOHN, 1892-
The Illinois fact book and historical almanac, 1673-1968.
Carbondale, Southern Illinois University Press, 1970. vii, 568 p.
maps. 21cm. Includes 2 biographical sections: (1) "State officers"--p. 96-158, a chronologically arranged (by administration) series of biographical sketches of officials of the State and
(2) "Famous Illinoisans" p. 490-511 (a brief biographical dictionary).

9875 ILLINOIS BIOGRAPHICAL ASSOCIATION.
Illinois and its builders. A work for newspaper and library
reference. Compiled under the direction of the James O. Jones
Company. [Chicago] 1925. 358 p. illus., ports. 30cm.

Indiana

9876 BIOGRAPHICAL AND GENEALOGICAL HISTORY OF CASS,
MIAMI, HOWARD AND TIPTON COUNTIES, INDIANA.
Chicago, Lewis Pub. Co., 1898. [Evansville, Ind., Unigraphic, 1974] 2 v. illus., ports. 26cm.

9877 HISTORY OF NORTHEAST INDIANA: La Grange, Steuben,
Noble and De Kalb Counties. Under the editorial supervision of Ira Ford [and others] Chicago, Lewis Pub. Co., 1920.
2 v. illus., ports. Includes biographical sections.

9878 [HOUGH, C   C   ]
Biographical sketches of members of the Indiana State
Government, State and judicial officials, and members of the
54th Legislative Assembly, 1885. [Indianapolis] Indianapolis
Sentinel Co. [1885?] 215 p. Preface signed: C. C. Hough.

9879 HUBBARD, FRANK McKINNEY, 1868-1930, ed.
A book of Indiana; the story of what has been described as
the most typically American state in the American democracy
told in terms of biography. Kin Hubbard, editor-in-chief. Associate editors: L. G. Ellingham [and others] Published by the
Indiana Biographical Association. [n. p.] Compiled under the
direction of the James O. Jones Co., 1929. 694 p. illus., ports.

Iowa

9880   BRIGHAM, JOHNSON, 1846-1936.
Iowa: its history and its foremost citizens. Cleveland, S.
Clark Pub. Co., 1915. 3 v. illus., ports. 32cm. Vols. 2-3
contain biographical sketches.

9881   THE IOWA PRESS ASSOCIATION'S WHO'S WHO IN IOWA; a
biographical record of Iowa's leaders in business, professional and public life. Des Moines, Iowa Press Association
[1940-   v. 28cm. Only one volume of this publication
(1940) was issued (?)

9882   LAKE, FRANK C
Who's who in Iowa, by Frank C. Lake and Lloyd N. Prince.
Sioux City, Lake and Prince, 1920. 1 v. Listed in: Petersen,
William J. Iowa history reference guide (Iowa City, State His-
torical Society of Iowa, 1952)

9883   A MEMORIAL AND BIOGRAPHICAL RECORD OF IOWA.
Chicago, Lewis Pub. Co., 1896. 1187 p. ports. 29cm.
In double columns.

Kansas City, Mo.

9884   KANSAS CITY, MISSOURI: pictorial and biographical. Chicago,
S. J. Clarke Pub. Co., 1908. 327 p. illus., ports. 32cm.

9885   KANSAS CITY PRESS CLUB, KANSAS CITY, MO.
Men of affairs in greater Kansas City, 1912; a newspaper
reference work. Kansas City, Mo. [1912] 273 p. illus., ports.
31cm.

Kentucky

9886   WHO'S WHO IN KENTUCKY: a compilation of biographical
information on outstanding citizens of the State of Kentucky.
1st ed. Atlanta, United States Public Relations Service [1974]
xiv, 526 p. ports. 24cm.

Louisiana

9887   BRUNS, THOMAS NELSON CARTER, Mrs.
Louisiana portraits, compiled by Mrs. Thomas Carter Bruns
for the Historical Activities Committee, the National Society of
the Colonial Dames of America in the State of Louisiana. Bicentennial ed. New Orleans, National Society of the Colonial Dames

of America in the State of Louisiana, 1975. 317 p. ports. 29cm.
In addition to the many portraits accompanied by biographical
data for the individuals portrayed the volume includes an "Index
of illustrated artists" which contains short biographical notes.

9888   DAVIS, ELLIS ARTHUR
        The historical encyclopedia of Louisiana. [n. p.] Louisiana
        Historical Bureau [194-] 2 v. illus., ports. 29cm. Paged con-
        tinuously. "Biographies of representative citizens": p. 211-1438.

9889   LOUISIANA HISTORICAL AND BIOGRAPHICAL ASSOCIATION.
        Louisianians and their state; a historical and biographical
        text book of Louisiana, its notable men and leading institutions.
        D. D. Moore, editor. [New Orleans? 1919] 144 l. ports. 29cm.

9890   REEVES, MIRIAM G
        The Governors of Louisiana. [3d ed.] Gretna, La. , Peli-
        can Pub. Co. , 1972. 128 p. ports. 23cm. Chronologically
        arranged biographies of ca. 75 Governors or acting Governors
        of Louisiana from the Spanish and French periods to the present;
        included are 63 portraits.

9891   WHO'S WHO IN LOUISIANA. 1st-   ed. ; 1974-
        Atlanta, Ga. , United States Public Relations Service.   v.
        24cm.

9892   WHO'S WHO IN LOUISIANA AND MISSISSIPPI; biographical
        sketches of prominent men and women of Louisiana and
        Mississippi. [New Orleans] Times-Picayune, 1918. 286 p.
        20cm.

Maine

9893   MAINE GENEALOGIST AND BIOGRAPHER; a quarterly journal,
        published under the direction of the Maine Genealogical and
        Biographical Society. Wm. Berry Lapham, editor. v. 1-3; Sept.
        1875-June 1878. Augusta, The Society [1875-78] 3 v. ports.
        24cm. No more published.

Maryland

9894   CORDELL, EUGENE FAUNTLEROY, 1843-1913.
        University of Maryland, 1807-1907; its history, influence,
        equipment and characteristics, with biographical sketches and
        portraits of its founders, benefactors, regents, faculty and
        alumni, by Eugene Fauntleroy Cordell. Associate editors: Wil-
        liam Calvin Chesnut [and others] New York, Lewis Pub. Co. ,
        1907. 2 v. illus., ports. 28cm.

9895   WHITE, FRANK P
        The governors of Maryland, 1777-1970, by Frank F. White,
        Jr. Annapolis, Hall of Records Commission, State of Maryland,
        1970. xxv, 351 p. illus., ports. 26cm. (Maryland. Hall of
        Records Commission. Publication no. 15) Portraits and biog-
        raphies of the 56 governors of Maryland.

Massachusetts

Bibliography, Indexes, Portrait Catalogs

9896   MASSACHUSETTS HISTORICAL SOCIETY, BOSTON.
        Portraits of women, 1700-1825. Boston, 1954. unpaged.
        illus. 20cm. (A Massachusetts Historical Society picture book)
        Portraits of American women (chiefly from Massachusetts) in
        the collections of the Massachusetts Historical Society; catalog of
        an exhibition, with accompanying portraits.

General Works

9897   HISTORY OF THE CONNECTICUT VALLEY IN MASSACHU-
        SETTS, with illustrations and biographical sketches of some
        of its prominent men and pioneers. Philadelphia, L. H. Everts,
        1879. 2 v. illus., ports. 32cm.

Michigan

9898   ALBUM OF THE MICHIGAN STATE OFFICERS AND LEGIS-
        LATURE, 1877-8. C. H. Mead, photographer. [n. p.,
        1878?] 157 photos in 1 v. In the Burton Historical Collection
        of the Detroit Public Library.

9899   HISTORY OF THE LAKE HURON SHORE. With illus. and bio-
        graphical sketches of some of its prominent men and pio-
        neers. Chicago, H. R. Page, 1883. 280 p. illus., ports.
        35cm. Includes Bay, Tosco, Alpena and Alcona Counties in
        Michigan.

9900   HISTORY OF THE UPPER PENINSULA OF MICHIGAN, contain-
        ing a full account of its early settlement, its growth, devel-
        opment and resources, an extended description of its iron and
        copper mines. Also accurate sketches of its counties, cities,
        towns and villages, biographical sketches, portraits of promi-
        nent men and early settlers. Chicago, Western Historical Co.,
        1883. 549 p. illus., ports. 32cm.

9901   WHO'S WHO IN MICHIGAN; a compilation of biographical infor-
        mation on outstanding citizens of the State of Michigan.

Atlanta, Ga. , United States Public Relations Service [1974]
xxvi, 556 p. 24cm.

Missouri

9902   HISTORY OF COLE, MONITEAU, MORGAN, BENTON, MILLER,
           MARIES AND OSAGE COUNTIES, MISSOURI ... Chicago,
Goodspeed Pub. Co. , 1889. 1172 p. illus. , ports. 26cm. Includes a substantial number of biographies and portraits of
prominent figures in Missouri life of the time.

9903   HISTORY OF SOUTHWEST MISSOURI. Embracing an historical
           account of the counties of Ste. Genevieve, St. Francois
Perry, Cape Girardeau, Bollinger, Madison, New Madrid,
Pemiscot, Lunklin, Scott, Mississippi, Stoddard, Butler,
Wayne and Iron. Chicago, Goodspeed Pub. Co. , 1888. 1215 p.
plates. ports. 26cm. Includes numerous biographical sketches.

Nevada

9904   NEVADA, THE SILVER STATE. Carson City, Western States
           Historical Publishers, 1970 [c1969] 2 v. (1088 p.) illus. ,
ports. 28cm. "Silver State biographical sketches": v. 1, p.
179-654; v. 2, p. 803-1051. With an index to the biographies at
the end of v. 2.

New Hampshire

9905   BROWN, LEONARD BOARDMAN, 1844-1914.
        Biographical sketches of the governor, councilors and
members of the Senate and House of Representatives of the
N[ew] H[ampshire] Legislature for 1883-4. Compiled by L. B.
Brown. Concord, N. H. , 1883. 48 p. 24cm. "Vol. II. " The
Governor, 5 councillors, 24 senators and 312 representatives
comprise the biographical sketches.

9906   FOSS, GERALD D   1910-
        Three centuries of Freemasonry in New Hampshire, by
Gerald D. Foss. Edited by Enzo Serafini. With biographical
dictionary compiled by Gerald D. Foss [and] Woodbury S. Adams.
[Concord, N. H. , Available from Grand Lodge of New Hampshire, 1972] xxiv, 546 p. illus. , ports. 24cm. "Biographical
dictionary": p. 379-518.

9907   METCALF, HENRY HARRISON, 1841-
        One thousand New Hampshire notables; brief biographical
sketches of New Hampshire men and women, native or resident,
prominent in public, professional, business, educational, fra-
ternal or benevolent work. Edited and compiled by Henry Har-

rison Metcalf, assisted by Frances M. Abbott. Concord, N. H.,
Rumford Print. Co., 1919. viii, 558 p. ports. 20cm.

New Mexico

9908   CHAVEZ, ANGELICO, 1910-
          Origins of New Mexico families in the Spanish colonial pe-
riod: in two parts, the seventeenth (1598-1693) and the eighteenth
(1693-1821) centuries. With four illus. by José Cisneros. Santa
Fe, N. M., W. Gannon, 1975. xvii, 339 p. illus. 28cm. On
spine: New Mexico families. Reprint of the ed. published by the
Historical Society of New Mexico, Santa Fe, in 1954. Families
are listed alphabetically within the century. Although primarily
a volume of genealogy, much biographical data for individuals
within the various old Spanish-Mexican families is available.

9909   THE HISTORICAL ENCYCLOPEDIA OF NEW MEXICO. Ellis
          Arthur Davis, editor. Albuquerque, New Mexico Historical
Association, 1945. 2 v. illus., ports. 29cm. Includes an extensive biographical section.

New York (State)

9910   EMPIRE STATE NOTABLES, 1914. New York, Hartwell Staf-
          ford, Publisher, 1914. 701 p. (chiefly ports.) 23cm. A
volume of some 2,680 portraits of notable New York Staters of
the early 20th century: index to portraits at front of volume.

9911   ENCYCLOPAEDIA OF CONTEMPORARY BIOGRAPHY OF NEW
          YORK. 2d ed. New York, Atlantic Pub. and Engraving Co.,
1878-85 [c1887] 4 v. ports. 30cm. Cover title: Contemporary
biography of New York.

9912   MOORE, WALTER BURRITT
          The public service of the State of New York during the year
1883. Historical, descriptive, biographical. Illustrated with
views and portraits. Walter Burritt Moore, editor. Boston, J.
R. Osgood, 1883. xiii, 315 p. illus., ports. 36cm. At head of
title: State of New York. Biographical for the most part, with
biographies of persons active in the Executive, Legislative and
Judicial branches of the State Government in 1883.

North Carolina

Bibliography, Indexes, Portrait Catalogs

9913   NORTH CAROLINA. STATE LIBRARY, RALEIGH.
          Marriages and death notices in Raleigh register [and] North
Carolina State gazette, Daily sentinel, Raleigh observer, and

News and observer. 1799-1825--   [Raleigh]   v.
23cm. Vols. for 1826-45--   issued as the Library's
Bulletin. Title varies: 1799-1825--1856/57, Marriage and death
notices in Raleigh register and North Carolina State gazette (varies slightly) Vol. for 1799-1825 is a reprint from the Library's
Report 1942-44, and published in Baltimore by Genealogical Pub.
Co. Compiler: 1799-1825--   C. L. Broughton. Indexes
obituaries and marriage notices in various North Carolina newspapers from 1799.

General Works

9914   MANARIN, LOUIS H
        North Carolina troops, 1861-1865; a roster. Compiled by
Louis H. Manarin. Raleigh, N. C., State Dept. of Archives
and History, 1966-   v. 27cm. Contents. v. 1. Artillery.
--v. 2. Cavalry.--v. 3-5. Infantry. Not only a roster, but also
yields some biographical data beyond military careers; each vol.
has an alphabetical name index. Five vols. issued as of 1975.
Vols. 4-5 are compiled by W. T. Jordan; unit histories for those
vols. by L. H. Manarin.

9915   SPEIDEL, FREDERICK G
        North Carolina Masons in the American Revolution. [Ox-
ford, N. C.] Press of Oxford Orphanage, 1975. 77 p. illus.
22cm. "Biographical sketches ... "(p. 49-75) contains 99
brief biographies (alphabetical in arrangement) of Masons who
adhered to the American cause.

9916   WHO'S WHO IN NORTH CAROLINA. 1st-   ed.; 1973-
        Lexington, Ky., Names of Distinction, inc.   v. 28cm.

9917   WHO'S WHO IN NORTH CAROLINA. 1st-   ed.; 1973-
        Atlanta, Ga., United States Public Relations Service.   v.
24cm.

Northwest, Pacific

Bibliography, Indexes, Portrait Catalogs

9918   APPLETON, MARION BRYMNER
        Index of Pacific Northwest portraits. Edited by Marion B.
Appleton. Seattle, Published for Pacific Northwest Library
Association, Reference Division, by the University of Washington Press, 1972. x, 210 p. 29cm. Indexes portraits of over
12,000 men and women identified with the history of the Pacific
Northwest: Alaska, British Columbia, Idaho, Montana, Oregon,
and Washington, found in some 324 books.

Ohio

9919   DUFF, WILLIAM ALEXANDER, 1872-
        History of north central Ohio, embracing Richland, Ashland,
Wayne, Medina, Lorain, Huron and Knox Counties. Topeka,
Indianapolis, Historical Pub. Co., 1931. 3 v. illus. ports.
28cm. Includes large biographical sections.

9920   FESS, SIMEON DAVIDSON, 1861-1936, ed.
        Ohio; a four-volume reference library on the history of a
great State. Under the editorial direction of Simeon D. Fess.
Chicago, Lewis Pub. Co., 1937. 4 v. illus., ports. 27cm.
Vol. 4 has special title: Ohio's three hundred [biographies]

---- ----Supplemental biographical volume. Chicago, New
York, Lewis Pub. Co., 1937. 629 p. ports. 27cm.

9921   GALBREATH, CHARLES BURLEIGH, 1858-1934.
        History of Ohio. Chicago, American Historical Society,
1925. 5 v. illus., ports. 28cm. Vols. 3-5 contain numerous
biographies of distinguished Ohioans; index to the set is in vol.
1.

9922   HISTORY OF LOWER SCIOTO VALLEY, OHIO, together with
        sketches of its cities, villages and townships, educational,
religious, civil, military, and political history, portraits of
prominent persons, and biographies of representative citizens.
Chicago, Inter-State Pub. Co., 1884. 875 p. illus., ports.
26cm.

9923   HOLLINGSWORTH, Mrs. EMMA J
        Capitol guide catalog of the paintings and portraits of the
governors of Ohio in the Ohio State Capitol. Columbus, F. J.
Heer Print. Co., 1910. 105 p. plates, ports. 23cm. Contains
also portraits and sketches of other prominent men of Ohio.

9924   LEWIS, THOMAS WILLIAM, 1851-
        History of southeastern Ohio and the Muskingum Valley,
1788-1929, covering Athens, Belmont, Coshocton, Guernsey,
Locking, Meigs, Monroe, Morgan, Muskingum, Noble, Perry
and Washington Counties. Chicago, S. J. Clarke Pub. Co.,
1928. 3 v. illus., ports. 27cm. Vol. 3: biographical.

9925   MEN OF OHIO. [Cleveland] Cleveland news [and] Cleveland
        leader [191-] 193 p. illus., ports. 27cm. Portraits and
biographical sketches of leaders in Ohio life at the turn of the
20th century.

9626   MERCER, JAMES KAZERTA, 1850-
        Representative men of Ohio, 1896-97, by James K. Mercer
        and C. N. Vallandigham. Columbus, Mercer & Vallandigham,
        1896. 175 p. ports. 24cm.

9927   MERCER, JAMES KAZERTA, 1850-
        Representative men of Ohio, 1900-1903, by James K. Mer-
        cer and Edward K. Rife. Columbus, J. K. Mercer, 1903. viii,
        222 p. ports. 24cm.

9928   MERCER, JAMES KAZERTA, 1850-
        Representative men of Ohio, 1904-1908: administration of
        Myron T. Herrick, Governor of Ohio, 1904-5. Columbus, Press
        of F. J. Heer [1908] viii, 315 p. ports. 24cm. Ca. 127 bio-
        graphical sketches; alphabetical approach thru' index at front of
        volume.

9929   OHIO. GENERAL ASSEMBLY.
        Biographical notices of the members of the fifty-fifth Gener-
        al Assembly of the State of Ohio. Columbus, J. Wallace, 1862.
        132 p. 8.°

9930   THE OHIO BLUE BOOK; or, Who's who in the Buckeye State.
        A cyclopedia of biography of men and women of Ohio, com-
        piled under the direction of C. S. Van Tassel. Norwalk, Ohio,
        American Publishers' Co., 1917. 479 p. 24cm.

9931   OHIO'S PROGRESSIVE SONS; a history of the State. Sketches
        of those who have helped to build up the Commonwealth.
        Cincinnati, Queen City Pub. Co., 1905. 843 p. illus. 32cm.

9932   TAYLOR, WILLIAM ALEXANDER, 1837-1912.
        Ohio in Congress from 1803 to 1901, with notes and sketches
        of senators and representatives, and other historical data and
        incidents. Columbus, XX. Century Pub. Co., 1900. 318 p.
        ports. 21cm.

9933   VAN TASSEL, CHARLES SUMNER, 1858-
        Familiar faces of Ohio; a souvenir collection of portraits
        and sketches of well-known men of the Buckeye State. Bowling
        Green, C. S. Van Tassel [1891] 183, [89] p. illus. ports.
        31cm. On cover: Men of Wood County and familiar faces of
        Ohio. "Men of Wood County and other familiar faces" : p. [99]-
        183.

9934   VAN TASSEL, CHARLES SUMNER, 1858-
        Men of northwestern Ohio; a collection of portraits and bi-

ographies of well known men in this section of the professional,
business and commercial world. Centennial ed. Bowling Green
& Toledo, Van Tassel, 1898. 373, 192 p.

9935   VAN TASSEL, CHARLES SUMNER, 1858-
            Story of the Maumee Valley, Toledo, and the Sandusky re-
        gion. Also special articles by able writers, and individual his-
        tories of northwestern Ohio counties by well known authorities.
        Chicago, S. J. Clarke Pub. Co., 1929. 4 v. illus., ports.
        28cm. Vols. 3-4 contain biographies.

9936   WHO IS WHO IN AND FROM OHIO; a history of the development
            of the State, sketches of those who have helped build up the
        Commonwealth. The book of Ohio ... Cincinnati, Queen City
        Pub. Co., 1910-12. 2 v. illus., ports. 41cm.

9937   WHO IS WHO IN OHIO. 1961-   Los Angeles, Moore's
        Who Is Who Publications.   v. 24cm.

9938   WHO'S WHO IN OHIO. 1st-   ed.; 1974-   Atlanta,
        Ga., United States Public Relations Service.   v. 24cm.

9939   WINTER, NEVIN OTTO, 1869-
            A history of northwest Ohio; a narrative account of its his-
        torical progress and development from the first European explo-
        ration of the Maumee and Sandusky Valleys and the adjacent
        shores of Lake Erie, down to the present time, by Nevin O.
        Winter assisted by a board of advisory and contributing editors.
        Chicago, Lewis Pub. Co., 1917. 3 v. illus., ports. 28cm.
        Vols. 2-3 contain biographies.

9940   WOMEN OF OHIO; a record of their achievements in the history
            of the State. Ruth Neely, editor in chief. Sponsored by the
        Ohio Newspaper Women's Association. [Cincinnati] S. J. Clarke
        Pub. Co. [1939]-   v. illus., ports. 27cm. A
        least 4 vols. have been published.

9941   WRIGHT, GEORGE FREDERICK, 1838-1921.
            Representative citizens of Ohio. Memorial, genealogical.
        Cleveland, Memorial Pub. Co., 1913. 660 p. illus., ports.
        folio.

Ohio Valley

9942   HISTORY OF THE OHIO FALLS CITIES AND THEIR COUNTIES,
            with illustrations and bibliographical [i. e. biographical]
        sketches. Cleveland, L. A. Williams, 1882. 2 v. illus. ports.

28cm. Includes Jefferson County and Louisville, Kentucky and
Clark and Floyd Counties, Indiana. 40 biographies and portraits
in vol. 1, 85 in vol. 2, scattered through the volumes. At front
of each vol. is an alphabetical index to the biographies in the
volume.

Oregon

9943   HISTORY OF OREGON. Deluxe supplement. Chicago, Pioneer
Historical Pub. Co., 1922. 367 p. ports. 32cm. Possibly
a supplement to C. H. Carey's History of Oregon. Chiefly biographical in content.

Pennsylvania

9944   EGLE, WILLIAM HENRY, 1830-1901.
Pennsylvania women in the American Revolution. Cotton-
port, La., Polyanthos, 1972. 208 p. 23cm. Reprint of the 1898
ed. published under title: Some Pennsylvania women during the
War of the Revolution. A biographical dictionary (69 biographies).

9945   ENCYCLOPAEDIA OF CONTEMPORARY BIOGRAPHY OF
PENNSYLVANIA. New York, Atlantic Pub. & Engraving
Co., 1889-93. 3 v. ports. 30cm.

9946   ENCYCLOPAEDIA OF GENEALOGY AND BIOGRAPHY OF THE
STATE OF PENNSYLVANIA, with a compendium of history.
New York, Lewis Pub. Co., 1904. 2 v. ports.

Philadelphia

9947   COLLINS, HERMAN LEROY, 1865-1940.
Philadelphia, a story of progress, by Herman LeRoy Collins ("Girard") and Wilfred Jordan. New York, Lewis Historical Pub. Co., c1941. 4 v. illus., ports. 28cm. Vol. 4, containing biographies, was written by the staff of the Lewis Historical Publishing Company.

9948   DISTINGUISHED MEN OF PHILADELPHIA AND OF PENNSYL-
VANIA. Philadelphia, Press Co., 1913. 102 p. ports. 4.º
Reproduction in half-tones of photographs of men prominent in
the commercial, professional, official, political and social activity of Philadelphia and Pennsylvania. Biographically the work
contains salient facts furnished by the subjects themselves.

9949   WHO'S WHO IN GREATER PHILADELPHIA IN THE NEGRO
COMMUNITY. Philadelphia, Urban Market Developers,
inc. [1968-   v. 1968-   ed. edited by Napoleon
M. Vaughn.

Pittsburgh

9950   FLEMING, GEORGE THORNTON, 1855-1928.
        History of Pittsburgh and environs, from prehistoric days
to the beginning of the American Revolution. New York, American Historical Society, 1922. 5 v. illus., ports. 28cm. Vols.
2-[5] by special contributors and members of the editorial staff.
Vols. 3-[5] contain biographical data.

Rochester, N.Y.

9951   DEVOY, JOHN, 1842-1928.
        Rochester and the Post express; a history of the City of
Rochester from the earliest times; the pioneers and their pre-
decessors--frontier life in the Genessee country--biographical
sketches, with a record of the Post express. Rochester, N. Y.,
Post Express Print. Co., 1895. 286 p. illus., ports. 32cm.
Includes biographies and portraits of prominent citizens of Rochester, New York (in the late 19th century), with a biographical
index and index of portraits.

St. Louis (and Environs)

9952   DEVOY, JOHN, 1842-1928.
        A history of the City of St. Louis and vicinity, from the
earliest times to the present. The pioneers and their successors, biographical sketches. St. Louis, 1898. 415 p. illus.,
ports. 32cm. Includes biographies and portraits of prominent
citizens of St. Louis (late 19th century) scattered thru' the text,
with a biographical index and an index of portraits.

9953   WHO'S WHO IN NORTH ST. LOUIS. St. Louis, Mo. [Printed
        by A. S. Werremeyer] 1925. 356, [1] p. illus., ports.
31cm. Edited by the North St. Louis Business Men's Association.

San Francisco

9954   BLOCK, EUGENE B
        The immortal San Franciscans for whom the streets were
named. San Francisco, Chronicle Books, 1971. xii, 244 p.
illus., ports. 24cm. 60 biographies and over 100 names listed
in the appendix (with some biographical data) Alphabetical approach through index.

9955   STARR, LANDO
        Blue book of San Franciscans in public life. Compiled and
edited by Lando Starr. San Francisco, McLaughlin Pub. Co.
[1941] xxiv, 308 p. ports. 20cm. A biographical dictionary of

San Franciscans active in the public life of the city, State of California and the nation to 1940, during the first half of the 20th century.

South Carolina

9956   BIOGRAPHICAL DIRECTORY OF THE SOUTH CAROLINA
HOUSE OF REPRESENTATIVES. Walter B. Edgar, editor.
Inez Watson, research consultant. 1st ed. Columbia, University of South Carolina Press, 1974-   v. maps. 26cm.
"Compiled under the direction of the House Research Committee." Contents. --Sessions lists, 1692-1973, by J. S. R. Faunt
and R. E. Rector, with D. K. Bowden.

9957   GARLINGTON, J   C
Men of the time; sketches of living notables. A biographical
encyclopedia of contemporaneous South Carolina leaders. Spartanburg, S. C., Garlington Pub. Co., 1902. [Spartanburg, Reprint Co., 1972] iii, 467 p. ports. 23cm. Prominent South
Carolinians of the 19th & early 20th century.

9958   WHO'S WHO IN SOUTH CAROLINA. 1st-   ed.; 1974-
Atlanta, United States Public Relations Service.   v.
23cm.

Southern States

9959   MEN OF THE SOUTH; a work for the newspaper reference
library. Editors: D. D. Moore [and others] Compiled under
the direction of the James O. Jones Company. New Orleans,
Southern Biographical Association, 1922. 792 p. ports. 32cm.
Prominent Southerners active in the first 2 decades of the 20th
century.

9960   WARNER, EZRA J
Biographical register of the Confederate Congress, by Ezra
J. Warner & W. Buck Yearns. Baton Rouge, Louisiana State
University Press, 1975. xxii, 319 p. illus. 25cm. Five hundred-word sketches of the 267 members of the Congress are the
major part of this volume.

Syracuse, N.Y.

9961   SYRACUSE AND ONONDAGA COUNTY, NEW YORK; pictorial
and biographical. [New York, etc.] S. J. Clarke Pub. Co.,
1908. 200 p. ports. 32cm. 62 biographies with full-page
portraits of prominent citizens of Syracuse and Onondaga County
at the turn of the 20th century; in biographical dictionary arrangement.

Tennessee

9962   DYER, GUSTAVUS WALKER
        Library of American lives. Tennessee edition; a source
        edition recording the contemporary history of the nation through
        the medium of the life history of it's [sic] most constructive
        contributors. Chronicling the genealogical and memorial rec-
        ords of its prominent families and personages. Nashville, His-
        torical Record Association, 1949. 2 v. (1117 p.) illus. 27cm.
        Biographical sketches of leading Tennesseans living in the 1940's
        are in substantial number.

9963   HISTORY OF TENNESSEE FROM THE EARLIEST TIMES TO
            THE PRESENT ... Nashville, Goodspeed Pub. Co., 1886-
        87. 15 v. illus., ports. 26cm. Each vol. in this set includes
        historical and biographical data for anywhere from one to thirty-
        one counties (74 in all)

9964   MEN OF TENNESSEE. Chattanooga, 1930. 180 p. Biographical
        sketches of Tennesseans still active in the 1930's.

9965   TENNESSEE LIVES: the Volunteer State historical record.
            Written and prepared under the supervision of William T.
        Alderson assisted by an editorial advisory board composed of
        eminent Tennesseans. Hopkinsville, Ky., Historical Record
        Association, 1971. 448 p. ports. 27cm.

Texas

9966   DAVIS, ELLIS ARTHUR
            The historical encyclopedia of Texas. Ellis Arthur Davis,
        editor. Rev. ed. [n. p.] Texas Historical Society [1948?] 2 v.
        illus., ports. 29cm. "Men of Texas": v. 1, p. 203-546; v. 2.
        Some issues of this work (first issued ca. 1920? with title: The
        encyclopedia of Texas) have cover title and t. p.: The new ency-
        clopedia of Texas.

9967   HISTORY OF TEXAS, together with a biographical history ...
            Chicago, Lewis Pub. Co., 1893-95. 2 v. illus., ports.
        28cm. Contents. --[1] Milan, Williamson, Bastrop, Travis, Lee
        and Burleson Counties. --[2] Tarrant and Parker Counties.
        "With portraits and biographies of prominent citizens of the above
        named counties and personal histories of many of the early set-
        tlers and leading families. "

9968   HISTORY OF TEXAS, together with a biographical history of
            the cities of Houston and Galveston; containing a concise
        history of the State, with portraits and biographies of prominent

citizens of the above named cities, and personal histories of
many of the early settlers and leading families. Chicago, Lewis
Pub. Co., 1895. 730 p. plates, ports. 18cm.

9969   JOHNSON, FRANCIS WHITE, 1799-1884.
        A history of Texas and Texans, by Frank W. Johnson. Ed-
ited and brought to date by Eugene C. Barker with the assistance
of Ernest William Winkler. To which are added historical, statistical and descriptive matter pertaining to the important local
divisions of the state, and biographical accounts of the leaders
and representative men of the state. Chicago, American Historical Society, 1914. 5 v. illus., ports. 28cm. Vols. 3-5 contain
biographies.

9970   WHO'S WHO IN TEXAS. 1st-   ed.; 1973/74-
        Atlanta, Ga., United States Public Relations Service.   v.
24cm.

9971   WOMEN IN EARLY TEXAS. Edited by Evelyn M. Carrington;
        sponsored by American Association of University Women,
Austin Branch. Austin, Tex., Jenkins Pub. Co., 1975. 308 p.
ports. 23cm. Biographies of 50 pioneer women in Texas (covering the years ca. 1820-1955); in biographical dictionary arrangement, A-Z.

Vermont

9972   GILMAN, MARCUS DAVIS, 1820-1889.
        The bibliography of Vermont; or, A list of books and pamph-
lets relating in any way to the State. With biographical and other
notes. Prepared by M. D. Gilman, with additions by other hands.
Burlington, Vt., Printed by the Free Press Association, 1897.
vii, 349 p. 27cm. Over 7,000 titles (including 3,452 Vermont
imprints) arranged alphabetically by authors, with some form
and subject headings. Appeared first in the Montpelier Argus
and patriot, 1879-1880. Edited from the corrected proof-slips
in the possession of the Vermont State Library, by George Grenville Benedict, who added 563 titles and 73 biographical sketches,
also incorporating material furnished by Thos. L. Wood.

Virginia

Bibliography, Indexes, Portrait Catalogs

9973   VIRGINIA. STATE LIBRARY, RICHMOND.
        Index to obituary notices in the Richmond enquirer from
May 9, 1804 through 1828, and the Richmond Whig, from
January, 1824 through 1838. [Originally prepared by several
members of the apprentice class of the Virginia State Library,
1904, under the direction of John P. Kennedy, librarian]; edited
by H. R. McIlwaine. [Rev.] Baltimore, Genealogical Pub. Co.,

1974. 87 p. 21cm. "Originally published as Bulletin of the
Virginia State Library, vol. XIV, no. 4, October, 1921. Richmond, 1923. " On spine: Obituary notices, Richmond enquirer
and Richmond Whig.

General Works

9974   BARRINGER, PAUL BRANDON, 1858-1939, ed.
        University of Virginia; its history, influence, equipment
and characteristics, with biographical sketches and portraits
of founders, benefactors, officers and alumni. Editorial staff:
Historical, Paul Brandon Barringer, James Mercer Garnett.
Biographical, Rosewell Page. New York, Lewis Pub. Co.,
1904. 2 v. illus. , ports. 28cm. Caption title: A history of
the University of Virginia ... "Founders, visitors and benefactors": v. 1, p. 313-530; "Officers and alumni": v. 2 in its
entirety.

9975   NORFLEET, FILLMORE
        Saint-Mémin in Virginia: portraits and biographies. Illus-
trated with reproductions of fifty-six crayon portraits and one
hundred and forty-two engravings by Saint-Mémin. Richmond,
Dietz Press, 1942. xix, 235 p. illus. , ports. 28cm. The
value of this volume rests in its portraits and biographical
sketches ("Biographical notes on Virginians whose portraits were
drawn by Fevret de Saint-Mémin": p. [137]-226), the latter in
biographical dictionary format.

9976   NORRIS, J   E
        History of the Lower Shenandoah Valley: counties of Fred-
erick, Berkeley, Jefferson and Clarke; their early settlement
and progress to the present time ... portraits of some of the
prominent men, and biographies of many of the representative
citizens. Edited by J. E. Norris. Chicago, A. Warner, 1890.
Berryville, Virginia Book Co. [1972?] viii, 925 p. illus. 26cm.
Includes a new index. "Genealogy and biography": p. 557-804.
The biographical data is not in any formal order; the two indexes
give the only alphabetical approach to the many biographical
sketches. Frederick and Clarke County are in Virginia; Jefferson and Berkeley in West Virginia.

9977   WHO'S WHO IN VIRGINIA, 1974/75; a composite of biographical
        sketches of outstanding men and women of the State of Vir-
ginia. 1st ed. Acworth, Ga. , Names of Distinction, inc.
[1975] 320 p. ports. 28cm.

The West

9978   HAFEN, LE ROY REUBEN, 1893-
        The mountain men and the fur trade of the Far West; biogra-
phical sketches of the participants by scholars of the subject and
introductions by the editor. Under the editorial supervision of

LeRoy R. Hafen. Glendale, Calif., A. H. Clark Co., 1965-72.
10 v. illus., ports. 25cm. Vol. 10 has title: Analytical index to
the series with an extensive bibliography, series contents and
contributing personnel and a statistical review of the mountain
men. Contains 292 biographies, alphabetically indexed in v. 10.

9979   McLOUGHLIN, DENIS
        Wild and woolly; an encyclopedia of the Old West. 1st ed.
Garden City, N. Y., Doubleday, 1975. 570 p. illus. 24cm.
2,500 entries; covers famous and infamous persons, pioneer
towns, events, etc. in the old American West.

West Virginia

9980   ATKINSON, GEORGE WESLEY, 1845-1925.
        Prominent men of West Virginia. Biographical sketches
of representative men in every honorable vocation, including
politics, the law, theology, medicine, education, finance, jour-
nalism, trade, commerce and agriculture. The growth and advancement of the State as shown in the history of her distinguished representatives. A succinct but comprehensive statement of the advantages, resources and development of the State.
A compendium of returns of every election, national, State and
Congressional. A record of every State officer, executive, legislative and judicial. By Geo. W. Atkinson and Alvaro F. Gibbens. Wheeling, W. Va., W. L. Callin, 1890 [c1884] xiv,
1022 p. illus., ports. 24cm.

Western Reserve

9981   HISTORY OF THE GREAT KANAWHA VALLEY, with family
        history and biographical sketches. A statement of its nat-
ural resources, industrial growth and commercial advantages.
Madison, Wis., Brant, Fuller, 1891. 2 v. ports. 27cm. "Biographical sketches" in vol. 2. Some chapters signed: John P.
Hale [and others]

9982   UPTON, Mrs. HARRIET (TAYLOR)
         History of the Western Reserve, by Harriet Taylor Upton;
H. G. Cutler and a staff of leading citizens collaborated on the
counties and biographies. Chicago, Lewis Pub. Co. [1910] 3 v.
illus., ports. 27cm. Vols. 2-3 are primarily biographical; index to the set is found in vol. 1.

Wichita, Kan.

9983   WHO'S WHO IN GREATER WICHITA, 1963. Biographical
        sketches of men and women of achievement listed alpha-
betically. [Wichita, Kan.] Wichita Historical Museum Association [1964] 1 v. illus. 31cm.

Wyoming

9984   THE HISTORICAL ENCYCLOPEDIA OF WYOMING. Cheyenne,
Wyoming Historical Institute [c1970] 2 v. (1669 p.) illus.,
ports. 28cm. "Representative citizens of Wyoming [past and
present]": p. 245-[1661] Alphabetical approach to these many biographies through index at end of vol. 2.

URUGUAY

9985   MONTEVIDEO. BIBLIOTECA DEL PODER LEGISLATIVO.
SECCIÓN IDENTIFICACIÓN DE AUTORES.
Uruguayos contemporáneos; noticias biográficas. Montevi-
deo, 1965. 4 v. 25cm. Contents. --1. A-Ch. --2. D-K. --3.
L-Q. --4. R-Z. Contemporary Uruguayans; a biographical dic-
tionary.

9986   MONTEVIDEO. INTENDENCIA MUNICIPAL.
Gobernantes municipales de Montevideo; datos biográficos-
fotografías. Montevideo, Intendencia Municipal de Montevideo,
Dirección de Publicaciones y Prensa, 1972. 72 p. illus., ports.
24cm. 30 portraits with facing biographical sketches of municipal supervisors and presidents of the departmental council of
Montevideo.

9987   WILLIS, JEAN L
Historical dictionary of Uruguay. Metuchen, N. J., Scarecrow Press, 1974. vii, 275 p. 22cm. (Latin American historical dictionaries, no. 11) Includes biographical sketches of
persons prominent in Uruguayan history and civilization.

UZBEKISTAN

9988   UZBEK SOVET ÉNTSIKLOPEDIĪASI. Toshkent, Uzbek sovet
entsiklopediiāsi bosh redaktsiiāsi, 1971-   v.
illus., ports. 27cm. On page facing t. p.: Uzbekiston SSR fanlar akademiiāsi. The Uzbek Soviet encyclopedia; a general encyclopedia useful for its many biographical entries for notable
personages in Uzbekistan's civilization and history. Contents. --
1. A-Akhkar. --2. B-Bakf. --3. Bakfnoma-Dekhli. --4. Dekhnav-
Industriiā. --5. Industriiālash-Konkurentsiiā. 1974. --6. Kon-
kurs-Marmar. 1975.

VENEZUELA

9989   AMEZAGA ARESTI, VICENTE DE, 1901-
El elemento vasco en el siglo XVIII venezolano. Caracas,
Comisión Nacional del Cuatricentenario de la Fundación de

Caracas, Comité de Obras Culturales, 1966. 372 p. 23cm.
(Ediciones del cuartricentenario de Caracas) Alphabetically arranged list of Basques who resided in 18th century Venezuela
with brief biographical and genealogical data.

9990   DÁVILA, VICENTE, 1874-
            Próceres trujillanos; obra dedicada a la antigua Provincia
        trujillana. Caracas, Impr. Bolivar, 1972. Caracas, Oficina
        Central de Información, Dirección de Publicaciones, 1971. viii,
        368 p. illus., ports. 24cm. (Biblioteca de autores y temas
        tachirenses, 55) "Reedición. " "Arbol de los Briceños": p.
        [301]-365. Ca. 73 biographies of leading figures in the history
        of the State of Trujillo, Venezuela.

9991   M. S. DE VENEZUELA, la biografía del mérito y el trabajo.
            1. ed. Caracas, Edit. Cediaz, 1972. 946 p. 23cm. Bio-
        graphical dictionary of noteworthy Venezuelans.

9992   PERSONAJES ILUSTRES DE VENEZUELA; hombres heroicos,
            apasionados que han forjadò nuestra historia. [Caracas]
        Ediciones Edime [1967 or 8-   v. illus., col.
        ports. 31cm. Cover title. Vol. 2-   also paged separately.
        Issued in parts. Persons famous in Venezuelan history and cul-
        ture.

9993   RUDOLPH, DONNA KEYSE, 1934-
            Historical dictionary of Venezuela, by Donna Keyse Ru-
        dolph and G. A. Rudolph. Metuchen, N. J., Scarecrow Press,
        1971. 142 p. 23cm. (Latin American historical dictionaries,
        no. 3) Includes many brief biographical entries.

9994   SANTIAGO, PEDRO A   DE, 1889-
            Biografías trujillanas; homenaje a Trujillo en el cuarto cen-
        tenario de su fundación, 1557-1957. Caracas, Ediciones Edime
        [1956] 357 p. illus. 22cm. A collection (in alphabetical ar-
        rangement) of 74 biographies of famous individuals with histori-
        cal significance for the State of Trujillo, Venezuela.

9995   VANNINI DE GERULEWICZ, MARISA
            Italia y los italianos en la historia y en la cultura de Vene-
        zuela. Caracas [Oficina Central de Información] 1966. 629 p.
        24cm. Italians in Venezuela; includes ca. 100 biographical
        sketches with a helpful table of contents but no index, so there
        is no alphabetical approach.

9996   VARGAS, FRANCISCO ALEJANDRO, 1908-
            Nuestros próceres navales. Caracas, 1964. 722 p. ports.
        23cm. Biographies and biographical sketches of 113 naval he-
        roes of Venezuela instrumental in the Wars of Independence from
        Spain.

9997 VENEZUELA. ARCHIVO GENERAL DE LA NACIÓN.
Hojas militares. Caracas, Tip. Americana, 1930-
v. 24cm. At head of title, v. 1: Vicente Dávila; v. 2-
Archivo General de la Nación. Vol. 2- has imprint: Caracas,
Impr. Nacional. "Contiene las hojas de servicio de las antiguas provincias, que constiuyeron en 1777 la Capitanía General
de Venezuela, desde 1768, año en que se estableció en Caracas
el primer regimiento español, hasta 1810 en que se inició la independencia nacional. " Only 3 vols. were published? Includes
biographical data for Venezuelan military personalities from
1768 to 1810.

VIETNAM

9998 BIOGRAPHIE DES MEMBRES DU GOUVERNEMENT RÉVOLU-
TIONNAIRE PROVISOIRE DE LA RÉPUBLIQUE DU SUD
VIETNAM ET DE SON CONSEIL DES SAGES. [n. p., Editions
Giai Phong, 1969] 54 p. ports. 24cm. Biographies (with portraits) of 38 members of the Provisional Revolutionary Government of the Republic of South Vietnam and its Advisory Council.

9999 HỒ ĐẮC HÀM
Việt-Nam nhân-vật-chỉ vùng biên. Hồ Đắc Hàm và Thái Văn
Kiểm biên soan. [Saigon] Bộ Quốc-Gia Giáo-Dục, 1962. 2 v. in
1 (285 p.) 24cm. (Văn-hóa tùng-thư, tập so 13-14) A dictionary
of Vietnamese biography.

10000 WHITFIELD, DANNY J
Historical and cultural dictionary of Vietnam. Metuchen,
N. J., Scarecrow Press, 1976. viii, 369 p. maps. 23cm.
(Historical and cultural dictionaries of Asia, no. 7) Includes a
substantial number of biographical sketches of famous Vietnamese past and present.

10001 WHO'S WHO IN NORTH VIETNAM. [Washington] 1972. xxiv,
342 l. ports. 28cm. "Prepared in the U. S. Government
from Central Intelligence Agency files and released by the Office of External Research, U. S. Department of State. " Chiefly
political and military leaders.

10002 WHO'S WHO OF THE REPUBLIC OF SOUTH VIET NAM.
[n. p.] Giai Phong Editions [1969] 54 p. ports. 26cm.
Biographies and portraits of 38 members of the Provisional
Revolutionary Government of the Republic of South Viet Nam and
of the Advisory Council (Viet Cong).

WALES

10003 GRANT, JOHN, historian
Flintshire; a short history with genealogies and current biographies. London, London & Provincial Pub. Co. [191-?]
224 p. illus., ports.

WEST INDIES

10004 JONES, ANTHONY MARK
    Caribbean men. [Port of Spain? Trinidad, W. I.] A. M.
Jones [197-] 73 p. map, ports. 27 x 15cm. (Educo series, no.
2. Political history) In its brief compass this pamphlet contains biographical sketches of 54 prominent historical figures,
past and present, of the West Indies. Arranged by Island--from
Cuba to Trinidad & Tobago. Written for young people.

WHITE RUSSIA

10005 BELARUSKAIĀ SAVETSKAIĀ ENTSYKLAPEDYIĀ. Red.
    kalegiiā: P. U. Broŭka (galoŭny red.) [i inshyiā] Minsk,
1969-75. 12 v. illus., ports. 25cm. At head of title: Akademiiā navuk BSSR. Galoŭnaiā redaktsyiā Belaruskai savetskai
entsyklapedyi. White Russian Soviet encyclopedia: valuable for
its many biographies of distinguished White Russians of the past
and present.

YAKUTIA

10006 KALENDAR' ZNAMENATEL'NYKH I PAMIĀTNYKH DAT
    IAKUTSKOĬ ASSR. 1963-   IĀkutsk, IĀkutskoe knizhnoe
izd-vo. v. illus. 20cm. Issued by IĀkutskaiā respubli-
kanskaiā biblioteka im. A. S. Pushkina. A calendar of famous
prople and memorable events in Yakutia. Periodically issued
in numbers that generally contain one or more brief biographies
and a chronology of happenings.

10007 ZA VLAST' SOVETOV V IĀKUTII; biograficheskiĭ sbornik o
    borfsakh pogibshikh v 1918-1925 godakh. Izd. 2., perer. i
dopelnennoe pod red. P. U. Petrova. IĀkutsk, IĀkutskoe
Gosudarstvennoe izd-vo, 1958. 260 p. 21cm. For Soviet
power (the Revolution) in Yakutia; biographical collection of
those who died in combat between 1918 and 1925.

YEMEN

10008 ZABĀRAH, MUHAMMAD IBN MUHAMMAD
    Nayl al-watar min tarajim rijal al-Yaman fi al-qarn at-tā-
lit 'ashar, min hijrat sayyid al-bashar. al-Qāhirah, al-Matba'a
as-Salafiyyah, 1929-32. 2 v. 24-26cm. Biographical dictionary (by forename) of Yemen in the 13th century A. H.

YUGOSLAVIA (See also Serbia)

10009 BIOGRAFSKI LEKSIKON: Narodno pretstavništvo. Senat,
    Narodna skupština. Beograd, Sedma sila, 1939. 366 p.

ports. 21cm. Added title pages: (1) Lexique biographique: Assemblée nationale. Sénat, Chambre des députés. (2) Biographisches Lexikon: Volksvertretung. Senat, Abgeordnetenhaus. Biographical dictionary of the pre-World War II (1939) Senate and Chamber of Deputies of Yugoslavia; in two alphabets. Biographies in Serbian, French and German (abbreviated versions in the latter two languages). Few copies in existence.

10010   DRUSTVENO-POLITIČKE ZAJEDNICE. Priredio za stampu: Dragoljub Đurovic. Urednik: Nine Opačić. Tekstove napisali: Svetozar Vukmanović Tempo [i dr.] Beograd, "Medunarodna stampa-Interpress," 1968-   v. illus., ports. 28cm. At head of title: Jubilarno izdanje. Contents.--t. 1. Federacija. --t. 2. Socijalisticke republike: autonomne pokra jine. The social-political community of Yugoslavia. In part a register of Yugoslav Government officials and employees with some biographical data therefor.

10011   JUGOSLOVENSKI SAVREMENICI. Ko je ko u Jugoslaviji. [Redakcioni odbor: Milan Joksimović [i dr.] Glavni redaktor i "Reč urednika" napisao Radošin Rajović. Milan Bartoš, predgovor] Beograd, Hronometar, 1970. [16], 1208, [66] p. 24cm. (Biblioteka Leksikon) Contemporary Yugoslavs. Who's who in Yugoslavia; a biographical dictionary.

10012   LIKOVI REVOLUCIJE. [Redakcioni odbor: Mirko Milojković [i dr.] Beograd, Prosveta, 1962-66. 3 v. 21cm. Ca. 40 biographies (A-Z) in each volume. Revolutionary figures in Yugoslav history.

10013   PRVO JUGOSLOVENSKO NARODNO PRETSTAVNISTVO IZABRANO 8 NOVEMBRA 1931 GODINE. [Uredio i izdao C. Mitrinović] Beograd, 1931. 181 p. ports. 26cm. Contains ca. 200 biographies and portraits of Yugoslav legislators and statesmen living in 1931.

BIOGRAPHY BY VOCATION

BIOGRAPHY BY VOCATION

THE ARTS

Fine Arts

Bibliography, Indexes, Artists' Marks

10014   HAVLICE, PATRICIA PATE
Index to artistic biography. Metuchen, N. J., Scarecrow
Press, 1973. 2 v. (viii, 1362 p.) 22cm. Guide to biographical
information on 70,000 artists in 64 reference works published
between 1902 and 1970.

General Works

10015   AN ANNUAL OF NEW ART AND ARTISTS, 1973/74-
New York, H. N. Abrams.   v. illus. 30cm. The
first issue is an anthology of the works of 53 contemporary artists from 18 countries. Editors: 1973-74--   Willem
Sanberg.

10016   BIHALJI-MERIN, OTO, 1904-
Masters of naive art: a history and worldwide survey.
Translated by Russell M. Stockman. New York, McGraw-Hill,
1971. 304 p. illus. 33cm. Includes 207 brief biographies of
primitive artists, 111 of which are not in Anatole Jakovsky's
Peintres naifs (q. v.). Translated from the author's unpublished
manuscript.

10017   [BONI, FILIPPO DE] 1816-1870.
Biografia degli artisti; ovvero, Dizionario della vite e delle
opere dei pittori, degli scultori, degli intagliatori, dei tipogra-
fi e dei musici di ogni nazione che fiorirono da' tempi più remoti sino a' nostri giorni. 2. ed. Venezia, Presso A. Santini,
1852. viii, 1109 p. 30cm. Biographies of artists; or, Dictionary of the lives and works of the painters, sculptors, engravers,
printers and musicians of all nations and times.

10018   CODEX MAGLIABECCHI, XVIII, 17.
         Il Codice magliabecchiano. Hrsg. von Carl Frey, Berlin,
1892. Farnborough, Hants., Eng., Gregg International Publishers, 1969. xvix, 404 p. facsims. 21cm. Includes biographical
sketches of artists of antiquity and more especially of Floren-
tine artists from Cimabue to Michelangelo. This anonymous
manuscript is in the Biblioteca nazionale, Florence. Alphabetical approach to the artists thru' the modern index.

10019   COYSH, ARTHUR WILFRED
         The antique buyer's dictionary of names, by A. W. Coysh.
New York, Praeger, 1970. 278 p. illus. 23cm. Arranged alphabetically by topics--Book illustrations to Silver --with biographical dictionary arrangement under each topic. A dictionary of
artists and craftsmen.

10020   DIZIONARIETTO DEI PIÙ CELEBRI PITTORI, SCULTORI,
         ARCHITETTI. Milano, Casa editoriale Sonzogno [1933]
64 p. 16.º Little dictionary of the most celebrated painters,
sculptors and architects.

10021   ÉBER, LÁSZLÓ, 1871-1935, ed.
         Művészeti lexikon: épitészet, szobrászat, festészet,
iparművészet. Társszerkestő Gombosi György. 2., lényegesen
megbőv. és átdolg. kiad. Budapest, Győző A., 1935. 2 v.
illus. 21cm. A dictionary of universal art and artists: sculpture, painting, industrial arts. 1st ed. issued in 1926.

10022   ENCICLOPEDIA GARZANTI DELL'ARTE. Milano, Redazione
         Garzanti, 1973. 863 p. illus. 18cm. On cover: Enciclo-
pedia dell'arte Garzanti. An Italian encyclopedia of art, with
biographies of artists included in its alphabetical arrangement.

10023   ENCICLOPEDIA UNIVERSALE SEDA DELL'ARTE MODERNA
         ... Milano, IDAF [1971?] 8 v. (2985 p.) illus. 30cm.
"Direzione generale Vero Pizzigoni, coordinatore Mino Mazzo-
leni, direzione redazionale Lisetta Belotti." An encyclopedia of
modern art with many biographical entries.

10024   GALERIE CONTEMPORAINE, LITTÉRAIRE, ARTISTIQUE.
         1.- année; 1876-   v. illus. ports. 36cm. 1.
année, 1. semestre, 1876; 2. semestre, 1878; 2. année, 1877;
3. année, 1. semestre, 1880; 2. semestre, 1878; 4. année, 1879.
The 2d part of '5. année' has title: Galerie contemporaine,
artistique ... Nouvelle série. An art periodical especially useful for its portraits of artists, musicians and authors of the day
(latter half of the 19th century).

10025   GALERIE DES ARTISTES; ou, Portraits des hommes célèbres
        dans la peinture, la sculpture, la gravure et la musique,
        pendant les trois siècles de la Renaissance. Cinquante-deux
        gravures par différents maîtres ... avec de courtes notices.
        Paris, Société des amis des arts, 1836. 110 p. 52 plates. 27cm.
        Portraits of artists of the Renaissance--52 painters, sculptors,
        engravers and musicians; with biographical notices.

10026   GALERIE SECHSUNDSECHZIG HOFHEIM.
        Miniaturen '70 [i. e. Siebzig] International. [Hofheim am
        Taunus, 1970] 1 v. (chiefly illus.; part col.) 19cm. Catalog
        of an art exhibition held in 1970 at the Galerie 66 in Hofheim;
        included are portraits and brief biographical notes on the 214
        artists (all of them born in the 20th century and now living) who
        exhibited their works.

10027   GUILMARD, DÉSIRÉ, b. 1810.
        Les maîtres ornemanistes, dessinateurs, peintres, archi-
        tectes, sculpteurs et graveurs, écoles françaises, italiennes,
        allemandes et des Pays-Bas (flamande et hollandaise) Ouvrage
        renfermant le répertoire général des maîtres ornemanistes avec
        l'indication précise d'ornement qui se trouvent dans les cabinets
        publics et particuliers de France, de Belgique, etc. ... Précédée
        d'une introd. par le baron Duvillier. Paris, E. Plon, 1880-81.
        xvi, 560 p. and atlas of 180 plates. illus. 30cm. Notices
        grouped by schools (division by centuries) and chronologically
        arranged; alphabetical index, p. 545-558. French, German,
        Italian, Flemish and Dutch artists.

10028   HARMON FOUNDATION, INC.
        Negro artists; an illustrated review of their achievements,
        including exhibition of paintings by the late Malvin Gray Johnson
        and sculptures by Richmond Barthé and Sargent Johnson. Pre-
        sented by the Harmon Foundation in cooperation with the Delphic
        Studios, April 22-May 4, 1935, inclusive. Freeport, N. Y.,
        Books for Libraries Press, 1971. 59 p. illus., ports. 23cm.
        (The Black heritage library collection) Reprint of the 1935 ed.
        "Directory of Negro artists" (p. 41-59) is a biographical diction-
        ary of over 100 artists active in the first third of the 20th cen-
        tury.

10029   HÉBERT,
        Dictionnaire pittoresque et historique. Genève, Minkoff
        Reprint, 1972. 2 v. in 1 (216 p.) 31cm. Reprint of the Paris 1756
        edition. An art dictionary; the 1st part is devoted to buildings,
        their architecture, the paintings and sculpture in them, etc.
        On pages 154-216 (in double columns) will be found alphabetical
        lists of architects, painters, sculptors, engravers, numismatists,
        and gold and silversmiths, with biographical notes for many of
        them, although quite often death dates or dates when the artist
        flourished only are given.

10030   INTERNATIONAL WHO'S WHO IN ART AND ANTIQUES. Hon.
         general editor: Ernest Kay. Cambridge [Eng.] Melrose
         Press [1972] viii, 679 p. illus. 25cm. More than 4,000 de-
         tailed biographies of living painters, sculptors, engravers, art
         and antique collectors, dealers and restorers, art educators,
         gallery and museum directors, specialist publishers and book-
         sellers, etc. from 58 countries. American edition published in
         1973 by Rowman & Littlefied.

10031   JACOBS, JAY
         The color encyclopedia of world art. New York, Crown
         Publishers [1975] 324 p. illus. (part col.) 29cm. Contains
         primarily 2,400 brief entries for artists and works of art plus
         numerous large color reproductions.

10032   JALARD, MICHEL-CLAUDE
         Post-Impressionism. [Translated from the French by Anne
         J. Cope] London, Heron Books, 1968. 208 p. illus., ports.
         28cm. (History of art, history of painting, v. 18) "Dictionary"
         (p. [145]-[203]) contains some terms but consists chiefly of bio-
         graphical sketches of ca. 86 artists, writers, etc. (French pri-
         marily, but also other nationals) who related to Post-Impres-
         sionism. Translation of Post-impressionisme.

10033   LUGT, FRITS, 1884-
         Les marques de collections de dessins & d'estampes;
         marques estampillées et écrites de collections particulières et
         publiques. Marques de marchands, de monteurs et d'imprimeurs.
         Cachets de vents d'artistes décédés. Marques de graveurs ap-
         posées après le tirage des planches. Timbres d'édition, etc.
         Avec des notices historiques sur les collectionneurs, les col-
         lections, les ventes, les marchands et éditeurs, etc. Amster-
         dam, Vereenigde Drukkerijen, 1921. xi, 598 p. illus. 30cm.

         ---- ----Supplément. Le Haye, M. Nijhoff, 1956. xi, 463 p.
         illus. 30cm. A catalog of art collector' marks, but also in-
         cludes, in a 'semi-alphabetical' arrangement, biographical no-
         tices of collectors, art dealers, etc. Comprehensive index at
         end of each volume.

10034   MARSY, FRANCOIS MARIE DE, 1714-1763.
         Dictionnaire abrégé de peinture et d'architecture. Genève,
         Minkoff Reprints, 1972. 2 v. in 1 (214 p.) 31cm. "Réimpres-
         sion des éditions de Paris, 1746." "Abbreviated" dictionary of
         painting and architecture. While largely a dictionary of termi-
         nology there is a substantial number of biographical sketches
         included.

10035   MŰVÉSZETI LEXIKON. Főszerkesztők: Zádor Anna és Genthon
         István. [Szerkesztők: Balogh Jolán, et al.] Budapest,
         Akadémiai Kiadó, 1965-   v. illus. ports. 25cm. A
         dictionary of art and artists; in Hungarian.

10036   NEW INTERNATIONAL ILLUSTRATED ENCYCLOPEDIA OF
             ART. New York, London, Greystone Press, 1967-72. 24 v.
         illus. 27cm. Includes many biographies.

10037   THE OXFORD COMPANION TO ART. Edited by Harold Osborne.
             Oxford, Clarendon Press, 1970. xii, 1277 p. illus. 25cm.
         Includes many biographical listings.

10038   PHAIDON DICTIONARY OF TWENTIETH CENTURY ART.
             London, New York, Phaidon [Press, 1973] 420 p. illus.
         26cm. Over 1,600 artists are included in this dictionary.

10039   PIERRE, JOSE, 1927-
             A dictionary of surrealism. Translated by W.-J. Strachan.
         [London] Eyre Methuen [1974] 168 p. illus. (part col.) 19cm.
         Much of the dictionary is devoted to artists prominent in the
         surrealist movement.

10040   PRAEGER ENCYCLOPEDIA OF ART. New York, Praeger,
             1971. 5 v. (2139 p.) illus (part col.) 29cm. The English-
         language ed. is an updated translation, with additional new ma-
         terial, of Dictionnaire universel de l'arte et des artistes. In-
         cludes ca. 3,000 biographical articles.

10041   REISER, WALTER
             Begegnung; Maler und Bildhauer der Gegenwart. Encoun-
         ters; contemporary artists and sculptors. Einführung von Die-
         trich Mahlow. [Stuttgart] Belser Verlag [c1970] 1 v. (unpaged)
         illus. (part col.), ports. 23cm. Portraits, biographical
         sketches and examples of the work of 135 contemporary artists.

10042   SCHENCK, AXEL
             Künsterlexikon; Biographien der Grossen Maler, Bildhauer
         und Baumeister. Reinbek (bei Hamburg), Rowohlt, 1973. 2 v.
         illus. 19cm. (Rokoko-Handbuch) Contents: Bd. 1. Hans von
         Aachen-Filippino Lippi. --Bd. 2. Fra Filippo Lippi-Francisco de
         Zurbaran. A dictionary of artists; biographies of the great
         painters, sculptors and architects.

10043   SERIE DEGLI UOMINI I PIÙ ILLUSTRI NELLA PITTURA,
             SCULTURA E ARCHITETTURA, con i loro elogi, e ritratti
         incisi in rame, cominciando dalla sua prima restauratione fino
         ai tempi presenti ... Firenze, 1769-75. 12 v. in 6. ports.
         29cm. Imprint varies. The portraits are from drawings by
         Ignazio Hugford, most of them engraved by G. B. Cecchi. The
         accompanying biographical notes of painters, sculptors and ar-
         chitects, written by Hugford's friends, are chiefly summaries
         from Vasari, Malvasia, and others.

---- ----Supplemento; o sia, Abecedario pittorico dall'origine delle belle arti a tutto l'anno MDCCLXXV ... Firenze, Nella Stamperia Allegrini, Pisoni, 1776. 1 v. in 2. 3 plates, port. 28cm.

10044   SHOREWOOD PUBLISHERS, inc., New York.
        The Shorewood art reference guide. Written by Matila Simon. Prepared under the direction of the editors of Shorewood Publishers, inc. Rev. and enl. 3d ed. New York, Shorewood Reproductions [1970] xviii, 600 p. illus. 24cm. In large part can be used as a 'biographical dictionary' with the aid of the index of artists at the end of the volume. Actually the artists are arranged in alphabetical order under each of the several countries or geographical areas which are the basis of chapter headings.

10045   A VISUAL DICTIONARY OF ART. [General editor: Ann Hill]
        Greenwich, Conn., New York Graphic Society [1974] 640 p. illus. (part col.) 27cm. In part also a biographical dictionary of artists.

Painting And Engraving

General Works

10046   BASAN, PIERRE FRANÇOIS, 1723-1797.
        Dictionnaire des graveurs anciens et modernes depuis l'origine de la gravure. 2. éd., mise par ordre alphabétique, considérablement augmentée et ornée de cinquante estampes par différens artistes célèbres, ou sans aucune, au gré de l'amateur. Paris, L'auteur, et Cuchet, 1789. 2 v. illus., ports. 22cm. 1st ed. issued in Paris in 1767. Contents.--t. 1. A-L.-- t. 2. M-Z. A dictionary of engravers, ancient and modern.

10047   BLANC, CHARLES, 1813-1882.
        Histoire des peintres de toutes les écoles. Paris, Loones, Renouard successeur, 1865-84 [v. 1, 1883] 17 v. in 12. illus., ports. 35cm. Imprint varies. First published 1849-76 (issued in 631 parts). A huge collection; several hundred biographies and critical assessments of painters of all schools. Alphabetical approach through listings of artists at end of each volume. Some of the volumes were written in collaboration with other critics: P. Mantz, etc.

10048   BREMEN, KUNSTHALLE
        Katalog der Gemälde des 19. und 20. Jahrhunderts in der Kunsthalle Bremen. Bearb. von Gerhard Gerkens und Ursula Heiderich. Bremen, Kunstverein Bremen, 1973. 2 v. 679 illus. 22cm. Vol. 1 (Text) of this catalog of 19th and 29th cen-

tury paintings in Bremen's Kunsthalle is in dictionary format
and contains biographical data about the artists followed by ex-
planations of their paintings.

10049   BRUNSWICK (CITY). HERZOG ANTON-ULRICH-MUSEUM.
         Verzeichnis der Gemälde. Braunschweig, Klinkhardt &
         Biermann, 1969. 156 p. 123 plates (part col.) 21cm. A cata-
         log of the paintings held by the Museum; on pages 25-152 is a
         bio('bibliographical') dictionary of the painters represented in
         the collection.

10050   COLOGNE. WALLRAF-RICHARTZ-MUSEUM.
         Katalog der Gemälde des 20. [i.e. zwanzigsten] Jahr-
         hunderts; die alteren Generationen bis 1915 im Wallraf-Richartz-
         Museum, mit Teilen der Sammlung Ludwig, und im Kunst-
         gewerbermuseum. Von Evelyn Weiss mit Vorarbeiten von Oth-
         mar Metzger und Ingrid Jenderko. Köln, 1974. 207 p., [143]
         leaves of plates. illus. 24cm. (Kataloge des Wallraf-Richartz-
         Museums, 7) A catalog of paintings of the 20th century in the
         Wallraf-Richartz-Museum and the Kunstgewerbemuseum in
         Cologne; pages 15-188 comprise a 'bio-bibliographical' diction-
         ary of painters of the earlier part of the 20th century--i.e., a
         brief biographical sketch of each painter is followed by descrip-
         tions of his paintings held by the museums.

10051   ENCYCLOPEDIA OF PAINTING; painters and painting of the
         world from prehistoric times to the present day. Bernard
         S. Myers, editor. Shirley D. Myers, assistant editor. Contri-
         buting associates: Milton W. Brown [and others] 3d rev. ed.
         New York, Crown Publishers, 1970. 511 p. illus. (part col.)
         29cm.

10052   ESSEN, MUSEUM FOLKWANG.
         Katalog der Gemälde des 19. Jahrhunderts. Bearb. von
         Jutta Held. Essen, 1971. 105 p. illus., 78 plates (part col.)
         24cm. An exhibition catalog of paintings of the 19th century;
         serves also as a biographical dictionary: 100 nineteenth century
         European painters are briefly sketched in words.

10053   ESSEN. MUSEUM FOLKWANG.
         Katalog der Gemälde des 20. Jahrhunderts. Bearb. von
         Uta Laxner-Gerlach. Essen, 1971. 144 p. illus., 77 plates
         (part col.) 24cm. An exhibition catalog of paintings of the 20th
         century; serves also as a biographical dictionary: 107 20th cen-
         tury painters are briefly sketched in words.

10054   FÉLIBIEN, ANDRÉ, sieur des Avaux et de Javercy,
         1619-1695.
         Noms des peintres les plus célèbres et les plus connus
         anciens et modernes. Genève, Minkoff Reprint, 1972. 81,

[31] p. 22cm. Reprint of the Paris edition of 1679. A chronologically arranged listing of painters from ancient times to the
end of the 17th century. Biographical data is available (in quite
brief form) for a substantial number of the names and an alphabetical approach is available through the 31-page index of names
at the end of the volume.

10055 FRANKFURT AM MAIN. STÄDELSCHES KUNSTINSTITUT.
        Die Gemälde des 19. Jahrhunderts. Hrsg. von Ernst
Holzinger. Bearb. von Hans-Joachim Ziemke. Frankfurt am
Main, G. Schulte-Bulmke, 1972. 2 v. illus. 25cm. (Its Kataloge der Gemälde, 1) Painting in the 19th century; vol. 1, the
"Textband," is a dictionary of painters of the 19th century with
biographical notes and descriptions of their works as listed in
the Institute's catalog.

10056 LE BLANC, CHARLES, 1817-1865.
        Manuel de l'amateur d'estampes, contenant le dictionnaire
des graveurs de toutes les nations dans lequel sont décrites les
estampes rares, précieuses et intéressantes, avec l'indication
de leurs différents états et des prix auxquels ces estampes ont
été portées dans les ventes publiques, en France et à l'étranger,
depuis un siècle ... Ouvrage destiné à faire suite au Manuel du
libraire et de l'amateur de livres par J.-Ch. Brunet. Paris, E.
Bouillon, 1854/58-90. 4 v. 25cm. Originally issued in 17 parts.
Imprint varies. Manual for lovers and collectors of engravings
which contains a dictionary of engravers; a supplement to J. C.
Brunet's Manuel du libraire et de l'amateur de livres. Reprinted
in 1970 by G. W. Hissink, Amsterdam (4 v. in 2).

10057 LEXIKON MODERNÉHO MALIARSTVA. Red. B. Grečnerová.
        Vyd. 1. Bratislava, Tatram, 1968. 412 p. 21cm. A dic-
tionary of modern painting and painters.

10058 MITCHELL, PETER
        Great flower painters; four centuries of floral art. Wood-
stock, N. Y., Overlook Press [1973] 272 p. illus. (part col.)
29cm. Biographical dictionary of the world's flower painters:
p. 33-262.

10059 NOUVEAU DICTIONNAIRE DE LA PEINTURE MODERNE.
        [3. ed.] Paris, F. Hazan, 1963. 416 p. illus. First is-
sued in 1960 under title: Dictionnaire de la peinture moderne.
New dictionary of modern painting; with many biographical entries.

10060 NUREMBERG. KUNSTHALLE.
        Graphik der Welt; internationale Druckgraphik der letzten
25 Jahre. Ausstellung der Kunsthalle Nürnberg vom 28. August
bis 28. November 1971 im Künstlerhaus am Königstor. St. Gal-

len, Erker-Verlag [1971] 227 p. illus. (part col.) 25cm. An
exhibition catalog of prints of the last 25 years sponsored by
Nuremberg's Kunsthalle. Includes a biographical dictionary of
75 modern painters-lithographers (p. [13]-31)

10061 PAPILLON DE LA FERTÉ, DENIS PIERRE JEAN, 1727-1794.
Extrait des différents ouvrages publiés sur la vie des
peintres. Genève, Minkoff Reprint, 1972. 2 v. illus. 22cm.
Reprint of the 1776 ed. (Paris, Ruault) Lives of painters from
ancient times to the ca. the mid-18th century, as digested by the
author from various works. Each volume has its own alphabetical name index. The work is arranged by painting schools.

10063 THE PORTRAITS OF THE MOST EMINENT PAINTERS, and
other famous artists, that have flourished in Europe. Cu-
riously engraved on above one hundred copper plates. by F.
Boultats [and others] From original paintings by Sir Anthony
Van Dyck ... and other celebrated masters. With an account of
their lives, characters, and most considerable works. To
which is now added, An historical and chronological series of
all the most eminent painters for near five hundred years.
Chiefly collected from a manuscript of the late Father Resta.
London, J. Duke, 1739. 63, 18 p. ports. 27cm. "An historical and chronological series of the most eminent painters" has
special t. p. and separate paging.

10064 PREMIO INTERNAZIONALE BIELLA PER L'INCISIONE 1971.
Aprile-maggio 1971. Circolo degli artisti, Museo civico,
Biella. Biella, Tip. lib. Unione biellese, 1971. xxv, 116 p.
illus. 21 x 21cm. A catalog of an exhibition (International
Biella Prize for Engraving, 1971) held in the Civic Museum and
at the Artists' Circle (Circolo degli artisti) Biella, Italy. The
main body of the volume yields biographical notes on ca. 230 engravers of the present day, arranged alphabetically under country. Complete alphabetical approach given by index at end.

10065 SANTINI, PIER CARLO
Modern landscape painting. [Translated by P. S. Falla
[London] Phaidon [1972 350 p. illus. 29cm. "Biographies [of
modern landscape painters] ... compiled by Franca Geri and
translated by Barbara Thompson": p. 291-338--a biographical
dictionary (133 painters) Translation of Il paesaggio nella pittura contemporanea.

10066 VALSECCHI, MARCO
Landscape painting of the 19th century. [Translated from
the Italian by Arthur A. Coppotelli] Greenwich, Conn., New
York Graphic Society [1971, c1969] 387 p. illus. (part col.)
29cm. "Biographies" (p. 325-376) is a biographical dictionary
of some 150 landscape painters.

10067   VICTORIA AND ALBERT MUSEUM, SOUTH KENSINGTON.
         Catalogue of foreign paintings. [Compiled by] C. M. Kauf-
         fmann. London, 1973. 2 v. illus. 25cm. Contents: 1. Before
         1800.--2. 1800-1900. Includes biographical and other data a-
         bout the painters represented; arrangement is alphabetical un-
         der the various schools (e. g. , Dutch, Flemish, French, Ger-
         man and Austrian, Italian, Spanish). Each volume has a "List
         of artists by schools" at end which gives a quick overview of the
         artists included.

10068   WALLACE COLLECTION, LONDON.
         Wallace Collection catalogues; pictures and drawings, with
         historical notes, short lives of the painters, and 380 illus. By
         authority. [14th ed.] London, H. M. Stationery Off. , 1920.
         xxxii, 408 p. illus. , ports. 25cm. Does service as a bio-
         graphical dictionary of painters, although the biographical notes
         are quite brief. Preface signed: D. S. M. (i. e. D. S. MacColl).

10069   WARD, MARTHA EADS
         Illustrators of books for young people, by Martha E. Ward
         and Dorothy A. Marquardt. 2d ed. Metuchen, N. J. , Scare-
         crow Press, 1975. 223 p. 22cm. A biographical dictionary.
         First edition issued in 1970 (with 370 biographies). This edi-
         tion includes 750 biographical sketches.

10070   WORCESTER ART MUSEUM.
         European paintings in the collection of the Worcester Art
         Museum. [Worcester, Mass.] Published by the Worcester Art
         Museum in cooperation with the University of Massachusetts
         Press, 1974. 2 v. illus. 25cm. Contents. --[1] Text. --[2]
         Plates. The text volume includes biographical notes on painters
         of the various schools: British, Dutch, Flemish, French, Ger-
         man, Italian, Spanish, Austrian, Belgian, Greek, Hungarian,
         Icelandic, Russian, Swedish & Turkish. The biographical
         sketches are listed alphabetically under the particular school.
         Total alphabetical approach thru' index at end of vol. 2.

Local

Australia

10071   BENKO, NANCY
         Art and artists of South Australia. Adelaide, Published
         under the patronage of the Lidums family, 1969. 163 p. illus.
         (part col.) ports. 28cm. A biographical dictionary.

10072   GLEESON, JAMES
         Masterpieces of Australian painting. [Melbourne] Lands-
         downe [1969] 222 p. 21 illus. , 96 plates. 32cm. (Australian
         art library) The reproductions of the paintings are accompanied

by biographical sketches of the 76 Australian artists represented:
arrangement is chronological.

10073   HORTON, MERVYN
         Present day art in Australia. Edited by Mervyn Horton.
Introd. by Daniel Thomas. Sydney, Ure Smith [1969] 244 p.
illus. (part col.) ports. 25cm. A biographical dictionary of
living Australian artists with portraits and reproductions of
their works.

Austria

10074   GRIMSCHITZ, BRUNO, 1892-1964.
         The Old Vienna school of painting. Wien, Kunstverlag
Woldrum [1961] 38 p.   124 mounted plates [part col.] 31cm.
Opposite each mounted plate is a brief biography of the artist
(124 in all) Translation of Die Altwiener Maler (Wien, 1961)
Continued by the author's Austrian painting from Biedermeier
to modern times.

10075   LIST, RUDOLF, 1901-
         Kunst und Künstler in der Steiermark. Ein Nachschlage-
werk. Ried im Innkreis, Oberösterreichischer Landesverlag,
1967-   pts. illus. 25cm. Contents.--Fasc. 1-3. A-
Ferrabosco (p. 1-120)
Art and artists in Styria.

10076   SCHMIDT, RUDOLF, 1894-
         Österreichisches Künstlerlexikon von den Anfängen bis zur
Gegenwart. Verfasst von Rudolf Schmidt. [Wien] Edition Tusch
[1974-   v. 24cm. Dictionary of Austrian artists from
the beginnings to the present. Vol. 1, pt. 1 only (covering A-
Bacher, R.) has been issued as of 1976.

Belgium

(See also Flanders)

10077   DELEPIERRE, JOSEPH OCTAVE, 1802-1879.
         Galerie d'artistes brugeois; ou, Biographie concise des
peintres, sculpteurs et graveurs célèbres de Bruges. Ornée de
portraits par P. de Vlamynck. Bruges, Impr. de Vandeca-
steele-Werbrouck, 1840. 163 p. ports. 24cm. Gallery of the
artists of Bruges, Belgium. A concise biographical collection
of the famous painters, sculptors and engravers of Bruges.

10078   DESMAZIÈRES, ÉMILE, 1825-1896.
         Bibliographie tournaisienne; recherches sur la vie et les
travaux des imprimeurs et des libraires de Tournai. Tournai,

Casterman, 1882. 768 p. plates. 26cm. 80 copies only printed? A bibliography of Tournai that includes extensive notes on
the lives and works of the printers and booksellers of that Belgian city.

10079   EEMANS, MARC
            L'art vivant en Belgique. [Bruxelles] Meddens [1972] 208 p.
         illus. (part col.) 29cm. Twentieth century art in Belgium, with
         a who's who on pages 169-200 ("Qui est qui? ").

Brazil

10080   CAVALCANTI, CARLOS, 1909-
            Dicionário brasileiro de artistas plásticos. Brasilia, In-
         stituto Nacional do Livro, 1973-   v. illus., ports.
         28cm. (Coleção Dicionários especializados, 5
         A biographical dictionary of the Brazilian fine arts. Contents:
         1. A-C.

10081   PONTUAL, ROBERTO, 1939-
            Arte Brasil/hoje: 50 anos depois. [São Paulo, Collectio
         Artes, 1973] 401 p. illus., ports. 21 x 23cm. A biographi-
         cal dictionary of contemporary Brazilian artists (175 in all);
         entry by forename[s] with surname index at front of volume.

10082   PONTUAL, ROBERTO, 1939-
            Dicionário das artes plásticas no Brasil. Introd. histórico-
         crítica de Mario Barata [et al. Rio de Janeiro] Civilização Bra-
         sileira [1969] 559 p. illus. 29cm. Dictionary of art and artists
         in Brazil.

Burma

10083   HLA MAUNG, G
            Kaba pāngyi thi-Bama pāngyi thi: Myamma pāngyi saya myā
         hnin pāngyi pyinya abidan. A dictionary of art and artists (Bur-
         ma) Rangoon, Shwei Hla Myaing Sapei, 1968. 348 p. illus.,
         ports. 19cm. In Burmese. Covers modern Burmese artists
         from ca. 1869 to 1968.

Canada

10084   CANADIAN BIOGRAPHIES; artists, authors and musicians.
            Ser. 1-   Ottawa, Canadian Library Association, 1948-
               v. 28cm. Reproduced from typewritten copy. Ser. 1
         has title: Canadian biographies: artists and authors.

10085   CREATIVE CANADA; a biographical dictionary of twentieth-
            century creative and performing artists. Compiled by

Reference Division, McPherson Library, University of Victoria.
Toronto, Published in association with McPherson Library, University of Victoria by University of Toronto Press, 1971-
v. 26cm. Each vol. covers A-Z. Two vols. (v. 1-2, complete?) issued as of 1973.

10086   HARPER, JOHN RUSSELL
Early painters and engravers in Canada. [Toronto] University of Toronto Press [c1970] xv, 376 p. 26cm. A biographical
dictionary of Canadian artists born before 1867; includes also
foreign artists who resided in Canada.

10087   HUBBARD, ROBERT HAMILTON, 1916-
Peintres du Québec: Collection Maurice et Andrée Corbeil.
Painters of Quebec: Maurice and Andrée Corbeil Collection. Ot-
tawa, Galerie nationale du Canada, 1973. 212 p. illus. 26cm.
In French and English. 37 French-Canadian painters; biogra-
phies in chronological order. Alphabetical name index at end.

10088   HUBBARD, ROBERT HAMILTON, 1916-
Three hundred years of Canadian art. Trois cents ans
d'art canadien. An exhibition arranged in celebration of the cen-
tenary of Confederation. Catalogue by R. H. Hubbard and J. R.
Ostiguy. Ottawa, National Gallery of Canada, 1967. v, 254 p.
illus. 25cm. Text in English and French. "Biographies of
artists" (p. 222-254) comprises a biographical dictionary containing ca. 187 brief biographies.

10089   NORMAN MACKENZIE ART GALLERY.
Saskatchewan: art and artists. [Regina, 1971] 106 p.
illus. (part col.) 22 x 26cm. Catalogue of an exhibition, April
2-July 31, 1971, at the Norman MacKenzie Art Gallery and
Regina Public Library Art Gallery. Includes a 'biographical'
dictionary (98 names)

10090   ONTARIO. ART GALLERY.
Art Gallery of Ontario; the Canadian collection. Toronto,
New York, McGraw-Hill Co. of Canada [1970] xvi, 603 p. illus.
(part col.) 26cm. A catalog that also serves as a biographical
dictionary of Canadian artists, past and present (biographical
data is brief, concise).

10091   WHO'S WHO IN ONTARIO ART. Nov. 1947-51. Toronto
[Ontario library review] 16 pts. in 1 v. (Canadian National Library copy) 26cm. In part, consists of reprints from the
Ontario library review. Contains ca. 175 biographies of artists
active in Ontario in the mid-20th century. Pt. 16 is an alphabetical index to the preceding 15 parts.

China

Bibliography, Indexes, Portrait Catalogs

10092   FU, PAO-SHIH, 1905-1965.
      Chung-Kuo mei shu nien piao. Hongkong, T'ai p'ing shu
chü, 1963. [12], 148 p. 18cm. First published in 1937 or 8
(Shanghai, Commercial Press); reprinted (photocopied) in 1968
(Taipei, Wu chou ch'u pan she) A table summarizing facts about
Chinese art; includes biographical information about famous
artists. Covers the period from 2697 B. C. to 1911 A. D. A
useful checklist for those interested in Chinese art.

10093   HUNG, WILLIAM, 1893-
      Ch'ing hua chuan chi-i san chung, fu yin tê. Peiping, Yen-
ching ta hsüeh (Harvard-Yenching Institute) 1941. 42, 18 p. 27cm.
(Harvard-Yenching Institute. Supplement no. 8) "Reproduces
three rare collections containing 373 short biographies of Ch'ing
painters. Their names and alternative names are indexed."--
Teng & Biggerstaff. ... Chinese reference works (3d ed., 1971)
Reproduced in 1966 by photocopy (Taipei, Ch'eng Wen Pub. Co.)
First published in 1934 (1 v. of double leaves in case) with added
t. p.: Biographies of Ch'ing dynasty painters in three collections.

10094   SHANG, CH'ÊNG-TSU, 1902-
      Chung-kuo li tai shu hua chuan ko chia tzŭ hao so yin.
[Peking] Jên min mei shu ch'u pan shê, 1960. 2 v. 21cm.
Compiled by Shang Ch'êng-tsu and Huang Hua. Index to the alternative names of some 16,000 calligraphers, painters, seal
artists and engravers from the Ch'in dynasty to the Republican
period.

10095   TS'AI, CHIN-CHUNG
      Ch'ing tai shu hua chia tzu hao yin tê. [Peiping] Yen-ching
ta hsüeh, 1934. xxxii, 179 p. 27cm. (Yen-ching ta hsüeh.
Yin tê pien tsuan ch'u. [Index] 21) Added t. p.: Index to the
fancy names of the calligraphers and painters of the Ch'ing
dynasty. The names of 5787 painters and calligraphers are indexed.

General Works

10096   LIN, CHIEN-T'UNG, 1911-
      Tang tai Chung-kuo hua jên ming lu. Hong Kong, Mei hua
shu wu, 1971. 6, 7, 274 p. illus. 22cm. A biographical dictionary of contemporary Chinese painters, mainly from South
China and Hong Kong. Names by stroke counts. By Lin Chien-
t'ung and Lin Chi-k'ai.

10097   ŌNISHI, RINGORŌ
        Shina shoga jimmei jisho. Tokyo, Daiichi Shobo, 1975.
        75, 549 p. 22cm. Reprint of 1919 edition. 10,000 Chinese
        calligraphers and painters listed by the order of names.

10098   YAMAMOTO, TEIJIRŌ, 1870-1937.
        Sō Gen Min Shin shoga meiken shoden. Kyoto, Shibungaku,
        1973. 4 v. illus. 22cm. Reprint of 1926 edition. Biographies
        of 558 Chinese painters and calligraphers, in chronological or-
        der. Name index. By Teijirō Yamamoto and Toraichi Kisei.

Colombia

10099   PINILLA AGUILAR, JOSÉ I
        Antología artística colombiana; ciento ocho biografías y cien
        reseñas de artistas colombianos. Bogotá, Ediciones Escorial
        R. Usme F., 1973. 272 p. ports. 23cm. Cover title. A bio-
        graphical dictionary of 108 contemporary Colombian performing
        artists with an additional 'dictionary' of lesser sketches of 100
        additional artists.

Croatia

10100   PEIĆ, MATKO
        Hrvatski umjetnici. Zagreb, Znanje, 1968. 408 p. illus.
        17cm. (Biblioteka Gledišta) Croatian artists; arranged under
        periods.

Czechoslovakia

10101   STERNBERG-MANDERSCHEID, FRANZ JOSEPH, Graf von,
        1763-1830.
        Beiträge und Berichtigungen zu Dlabacž Lexikon böhmischer
        Künstler. Hrsg. und durch Anmerkungen ergänzt von Paul Berg-
        ner. Prag, André, 1913. 64 p. 26cm. Additions and correc-
        tions to Dlabac's Dictionary of Bohemian artists.

10102   ZOLAROVÁ, IRENA,
        Artistický slovnik. Praha, Div. úst., 1964. 110 p. A
        dictionary of Czech/Bohemian artists.

Eskimo

10103   GRAY, PHILIP HOWARD, 1926-
        A directory of Eskimo artists in sculpture and prints.
        Bozeman, Mont., Gray [1974] iv, 264 p. 14 x 24cm. A direc-
        tory with brief biographical information for over 500 Eskimo
        artists; alphabetical arrangement.

Finland

10104   PAISCHEFF, ALEKSANDER
        Suomen kuvaamataiteilijat. Julkaisija: Suomen Taiteili-
jaseura. [Helsinki] Kustannusosakeyhtiö Kirjamies [1943]
192 p. ports. 26cm. A dictionary of Finnish artists.

10105   TIRRANEN, HERTTA
        Suomen taiteilijoita; elämäkertoja Porvoo,
Helsinki, Soderstrom, 1955. 2 v. illus., ports. 25cm.
Contents. --[1] Juho Rissasesta Jussi Mäntyseen. --[2] Alvar
Cawénista Waino Aaltoseen. Finnish artists; chronologically
arranged with index of names at end of each volume.

Flanders

(See also Belgium)

10106   BALKEMA, C   H
        Biographie des peintres flamands et hollandais qui ont exi-
sté depuis Jean et Hubert van Eyck jusqu'à nos jours, pour
servir de guide aux peintres et aux amateurs de tableaux. Gand,
H. Hoste, 1844. vii, 366 p. front. 26cm. A biographical
dictionary of Flemish and Dutch painters who flourished after
Jan and Hubert van Eyck to the 1840's.

10107   INSTITUT NÉERLANDAIS, Paris.
        Vlaamse tekeningen uit de zeventiende eeuw; Verzameling
Frits Lugt, Institut Néerlandais, Paris. Tentoonstellingen:
Londen, Victoria and Albert Museum [etc.]... 1972. [Ledeberg/
Gent, Drukkerij Erasmus, 1972] li, 205 p. illus., 128 plates.
26cm. Flemish drawings from the 17th century; an exhibition
catalog, but also serves as a biographical dictionary of 51
Flemish painters of the period.

France

Bibliography, Indexes, Portrait Catalogs

10108   JOUIN, HENRI AUGUSTE, 1841-1913.
        Musée de portraits d'artistes: peintres, sculpteurs, archi-
tectes, graveurs, musiciens, artistes dramatiques, amateurs,
etc., nés en France ou y ayant vécu, état de 3,000 portraits,
peints, dessinés ou sculptés, avec l'indication des collections
publiques ou privées qui les renferment, par Henry Jouin.
Paris, H. Laurens, 1888. xx, 241 p. port. 26cm. A catalog
of 3,000 portraits of French artists: painters, sculptors, architects, engravers, musicians, theatrical performers, etc.

General Works

10109   ANNUAIRE BIOGRAPHIQUE DES ARTISTES FRANÇAIS, pein-
        tres, sculpteurs, architectes, graveurs, musiciens,
        contenant: 1. des notices sur les principaux artistes ... avec
        des portraits ou des planches d'après leurs ouvrages. 2. une
        liste générale alphabétique de tous les artistes vivants ...
        Publié par Guyot de Fère et B. de Boissy. Paris, Bureau du
        Journal des beaux-arts, 1841-42. 2 v. 8.º Continuation of
        Annuaire des artistes français and Annuaire statistique des
        artistes français, 1836. Biographical annual of contemporary
        French artists, painters, sculptors, architects, engravers,
        musicians.

10110   L'ART ET LA VIE EN FRANCE À LA BELLE ÉPOQUE.
        Bendor, septembre-octobre 1971. [n. p., Impr. spéciale
        Paul Ricard, 1971?] 1 v. (unpaged) illus. 27cm. Cover title.
        On spine: Fondation Paul Ricard. A catalog of French art of
        the 'Belle Époque' (late 19th and early 20th century) and Art
        nouveau, compiled by Jean Pierre Camard and Lynne Thornton.
        The catalog includes biographical notes (in 3 'biographical dic-
        tionaries') for most of the over 170 artists represented. There
        is an alphabetical index to all artists represented.

10111   BELLIER DE LA CHAVIGNERIE, ÉMILE, 1821-1871.
        Les artistes français du XVIIIe siècle oubliés ou dédaignés.
        Genève, Minkoff Reprints, 1973. 180 p. 23cm. "Réimpression
        de l'édition de Paris, 1865." The forgotten or disdained French
        artists of the 18th century. A biographical dictionary with 225
        entries.

10112   BRUNE, PAUL, 1862-1920.
        Dictionnaire des artistes et ouvriers d'art de la Franche-
        Comté. Paris, Bibliothèque d'art et d'archéologie, 1912.
        xxviii, 337 p. 27cm. (Dictionnaire des artistes et ouvriers
        d'art de la France par provinces) (Publications pour faciliter
        les études d'art en France) Cover title: Dictionnaire des
        artistes et ouvriers d'art de la France. Franche-Comté. Dic-
        tionary of artists and artisans in the historical region of the
        Franche-Comté.

10113   COGNIAT, RAYMOND, 1896-
        A dictionary of impressionism. With an introd. by Jean
        Selz; biographies by Raymond Cogniat, Frank Elgar and Jean
        Selz. London, Eyre Methuen, 1973. 168 p. illus. (part col.)
        19cm. Translation of L'Impressionisme. Primarily a biogra-
        phical dictionary of French impressionism (flourishing 1874-1886)

10114   FONVIEILLE, RENÉ, 1913-
        La vieux Grenoble, ses artistes, ses trésors d'art. Gre-
        noble, Roissard, 1970. 325 p. illus. 30cm. Old Grenoble.

France, its artists and art treasures. On pages 11-136 are biographical sketches (in several alphabets, arranged by subject,
e. g., sculptors, gold and silversmiths, etc.) of Grenoble's
artists.

10115   FRANCE. ARCHIVES NATIONALES.
         Documents du Minutier central concernant les peintres, les
sculpteurs et les graveurs au XVIIe siècle (1600-1650) [par]
Marie-Antoinette Fleury. Paris, S. E. V. P. E. N., 1969-
         v. illus. 23cm. At head of title: Ministère des affaires
culturelles. Direction des archives de France. Archives nationales. Summaries of materials in documents (housed in the
French National Archives) concerning French painters, sculptors
and engravers of the 17th century. Arrangement is alphabetical
under name of the artist. Vol. 1 only available as of 1976.

10116   FRENCH SYMBOLIST PAINTERS: Moreau, Puvis de Chavannes,
         Redon and their followers; [catalogue of an exhibition held
at the] Hayward Gallery, London, 7 June-23 July 1972 [and at the]
Walker Art Gallery, Liverpool, 9 August-17 September 1972; [or-
ganized by the Association française d'action artistique in association with the Arts Council of Great Britain] London, Arts
Council, 1972. 170, 7 p. illus. (part col.) 30cm. In the form
of a dictionary lists French symbolist painters with brief lives
and description of their works (ca. 54 artists)

10117   GRANDMAISON, CHARLES L   DE, 1824-1903.
         Documents inédits pour servir à l'histoire des arts en
Touraine. Tours, Guilland-Verger, 1870. xxiv, 368 p. 25cm.
(Mémoires de la Société archéologique, t. 20) Quotations, extracts, etc. from source material for the biography of medieval
and early modern French painters of Touraine. Topical arrangement with alphabetical approach thru' the comprehensive
index at the end.

10118   GRANGES DE SURGÈRES, ANATOLE, marquis de, 1850-1902.
         Les artistes nantois, architectes, armuriers, brodeurs,
fondeurs, graveurs, luthiers, maitres d'oeuvre, peintres,
potiers d'étain, sculpteurs, tapissiers, gentilshommes verriers
... du moyen âge à la Révolution. Notes et documents inédits.
Paris, Charavay, 1898. xii, 456 p. 22cm. A dictionary of
French artists of Nantes.

10119   [HERLUISON, HENRI] 1835-1905.
         Artistes orleanais, peintres, graveurs, sculpteurs, archi-
tectes. Liste sous forme alphabétique des personnages nés pour
la plupart dans la province de l'Orleanais suivie de documents inédits. Par H. H. *** Orléans, H. Herluison, 1863. 129 p.
20cm. Artists from the former province of Orléanais; an alphabetical listing with brief biographical notes.

10120   HORSIN-DÉON, LÉON
         Essai sur les portraitlistes français de la Renaissance,
contenant un inventaire raisonné de tous les portraits du XVIe
siècles des musées de Versailles et du Louvre. Paris, Impr.
Ve. P. Larousse, 1888. 212 p. 22cm. A treatise on the French
portrait painters of the Renaissance, with an inventory of all
the portraits of the 16th century in the museums of Versailles and
the Louvre.

10121   JACQUOT, ALBERT, 1853-
         Essai de répertoire des artistes lorrains. Paris, J.
Rouan [etc.] 1900-13. 11 pts. illus., ports. 24cm. Artists of
Lorraine. Contents.--fasc. 1. Peintres, peintres verriers,
faienciers, émailleurs.--fasc. 2. Sculpteurs.--fasc. 3. Architectes, ingénieurs, maîtres d'ouvrés, maitres maçons.--fasc.
4. Luthiers.--fasc. 5. Les musiciens, chanteurs, compositeurs, etc.--fasc. 6. Les comédiens, les auteurs dramatiques,
les poètes et les littérateurs lorrains.--fasc. 7. Les orfèvres,
les joailliers, les argentiers, les potiers d'étain lorrains.--
fasc. 8. Les graveurs.--fasc. 9. Les facteurs d'orgue et de
clavecins lorrains.--fasc. 10. Imprimeurs, relieurs.--fasc.
11. Dessinateurs et directeurs de jardins.

10122   LAVIGNE, HUBERT, 1818-1881, comp.
         Etat civil d'artistes françaises; billets d'enterrement ou de
décès depuis 1823 jusqu'à nos jours. Paris, J. Baur, 1881. vi,
216 p. 22cm. At head of title: Société de l'histoire de l'art française. Notes on the burial or death or French artists from 1823
to 1881.

10123   MAIGNIEN, EDMOND AUGUSTE, 1847-1915.
         Les artistes grenoblois: architectes, armuriers, brodeurs,
graveurs, musiciens, orfèvres, peintres, sculpteurs, tapissiers,
tourneurs, etc. Notes et documents inédits. Grenoble, X. Dre-
vet, 1887. 384 p. 24cm. The artists of Grenoble, France,
with notices and documents.

10124   MARTIN, JULES, 1860-
         Nos peintres et sculpteurs, graveurs, dessinateurs, por-
traits et biographies, suivis d'une notice sur les salons français depuis 1673, les sociétés de beaux-arts, la propriété artistique, etc. Paris, E. Flammarion, 1897-98. 2 v. in 1. ports.
14cm. French painters, sculptors, engravers, designers; portraits and biographies.

10125   ROBERT-DUMESNIL, A   P   F   1778-1864.
         Le peintre-graveur français; ou, Catalogue raisonné des
estampes gravées par les peintres et les dessinateurs de l'école
français. Ouvrage faisant suite au Peintre-graveur de M.
Bartsch. Paris, G. Warée, 1835-71. 11 v. in 6. illus. 21cm.
Vols. 9-10, "publié d'après les désirs de l'auteur, par M.

Georges Duplessis. " Vol. 11: Supplément aux dix volumes du Peintre-graveur français, par Georges Duplessis. French painters-engravers; a catalog that includes short biographies of the artists represented. A continuation of Adam von Bartsch's Le peintre graveur.

10126   SÉRULLAZ, MAURICE
Encyclopédie de l'impressionisme [par] Maurice Sérullaz avec la collaboration de Georges Pillement, Bertrand Maret [et] François Duret-Robert. Paris, Somogy, 1974. 286 p. illus. (some col.) 24cm. An encyclopedia of French impressionism and impressionist painters.

10127   WILDENSTEIN, DANIEL, 1917-
Documents inédits sur les artistes français du XVIIIe siècle, conservés au Minutier central des notaires de la Seine, aux Archives nationales et publiés avec le concours de la Fondation Wildenstein de New York. Paris, Les Beaux arts, 1966. 174 p. 27cm. Unpublished documents on French artists of the 18th century; in dictionary arrangement, thus the volume serves in part as a 'biographical dictionary'.

Germany

10128   DIENST, ROLF GUNTER
Deutsche Kunst, eine neue Generation. Köln, M. DuMont Schaubert, 1970. 1 v. (unpaged) illus., ports. 31cm. (DuMont aktuell) Art from the Federal Republic of Germany; includes a biographical dictionary of 61 pages (with portraits of the artists) at the end of the volume.

10129   DRESDEN. KUPFERSTICHKABINETT.
Graphik in der DDR. Ausstellung zum zwanzigsten Jahrestag der Deutschen Demokratischen Republik, Kupferstich-Kabinett der Staatlichen Kunstsammlungen Dresden. Dresden, Staatliche Kunstsammlungen, 1969. 108 p. illus. 26cm. Text by Wolfgang Winter. An exhibition of engravings by artists in the Democratic Republic of Germany. Pages 75-95 contain a biographical dictionary of the 86 engravers represented.

10130   HARVARD UNIVERSITY. BUSCH-REISINGER MUSEUM OF GERMANIC CULTURE.
German master drawings of the nineteenth century. [Cambridge, Mass., 1972] 1 v. (unpaged) 93 illus. 24cm. Catalog of an exhibition held at the Busch-Reisinger Museum, Harvard University, Cambridge, Oct. 5-Nov. 18, 1972, and other museums. Serves also as a biographical dictionary of 52 master drawers of the nineteenth century.

10131   HEYDORN, VOLKER DETLEF
         Maler in Hamburg. [Herausgeber: Berufsverband Bildender
Künstler, Hamburg] Hamburg, Christians [1974] 3 v. illus.
24cm. Contents: 1. 1886-1945.--2. 1945-1966.--3. 1966-1974.
"Biographische Übersicht Hamburger Maler und Graphiker"
(v. 3, p. 116-147) is a biographical dictionary of Hamburg's
painters and graphic artists, 1866-1974. The notices are very
brief, 1 to 15 lines.

10132   ROH, JULIANE
         Deutsche Kunst der 60er Jahre; Malerei, Collage, Op-Art,
Graphik. München, Bruckmann [1971-   v. illus.
(part col.) 25cm. "Kurzbiographien der Künstler": v. 1, p.
273-284—a biographical dictionary of 110 modern German artists of the Federal Republic, treated at greater length in the
main text.

10133   SCHMIED, WIELAND, 1929-
         Malerei nach 1945 in Deutschland, Österreich und der
Schweiz. Mit Beiträgen von Peter F. Althaus, Eberhard Roters
und Anneliese Schröder. [Frankfurt am Main, Berlin, Wien]
Propyläen [Verlag, 1974] 336 p. illus., ports. 30cm. Painting in Germany, Austria and Switzerland after 1945. "Bio-Bibliographie" (p. [81]-311) comprises a "bio-bibliographical" dictionary of the painters represented.

Great Britain

10134   ARTS COUNCIL OF GREAT BRITAIN.
         British painting '74; [exhibition] 26 September-17 November
1974. London, 1974. ca. 203 p. illus. 25cm. An exhibition
catalogue which is arranged alphabetically by artist and includes
bio-bibliographical notes for each painter; 122 artists are included.

10135   CANADA. PUBLIC ARCHIVES.
         Image of Canada. Documentary watercolours and drawings
from the permanent collection of the Public Archives of Canada.
Visage du Canada. Aquarelles et dessins historiques tirés de
la collection permanente des Archives publiques du Canada. Ottawa, Information Canada, 1972. 1 v. (unpaged) illus. 21cm.
Includes a biographical dictionary arrangement of the some 42
painters (chiefly British and Canadian) whose works dealt primarily with the Canadian scene of 1750-1850.

10136   EDE, HAROLD STANLEY, 1895-
         A chart of British artists, 1560-1860. With short lives of
the principal artists. London, Faber & Faber, 1934. table 44
x 55cm. fold. to 15 x 23cm. Cover title. Biographical sketches
on verso of the chart.

10137   FISHER, STANLEY W
             A dictionary of watercolour painters, 1750-1900. London,
         New York, W. Foulsham [1972] 245, [16] p. illus. 26cm.
         British watercolour painters.

10138   FOSKETT, DAPHNE
             A dictionary of British miniature painters. New York,
         Praeger, 1972. 2 v. illus. 29cm. "Vol. 1 is the dictionary
         itself, listing nearly 4500 miniaturists who were born or worked
         in Great Britain and Ireland from 1520 to 1910."--Library journal,
         June 15, 1972.

10139   HALL, MARSHALL
             The artists of Northumbria: a dictionary of Northumber-
         land and Durham painters, draughtsmen and engravers, born
         1647-1900. Newcastle-upon-Tyne, Marshall Hall Associates,
         1973. 72, 32 p. illus., ports (on lining papers) 29cm. (Art-
         ists of the regions series [1])

10140   HAMMELMANN, HANNS
             Book illustrators in eighteenth-century England [by] Hanns
         Hammelmann. Edited and compiled by T. S. R. Boase. New
         Haven, Published for the Paul Mellon Centre for Studies in Brit-
         ish Art by Yale University Press, 1975. xiv, 120 p. illus. 26cm.
         A biographical dictionary of 263 artists involved in book illustra-
         tion in 18th-century England (1700-1800)

10141   HARDIE, MARTIN, 1875-1952.
             Water-colour painting in Britain. Edited by Dudley Snel-
         grove with Jonathan Mayne and Basil Taylor. London, Bats-
         ford [1967-68] 3 v. plates (part col.) 31cm. Contents. --1.
         The eighteenth century. 2d ed. --2. The Romantic period. --3.
         The Victorian period. Basically a sizeable collection of bio-
         graphical sketches of British water-color painters. Indexes at
         the end of each volume yield an alphabetical approach to the bi-
         ographies (via dark-print page references).

10142   MORRIS, SIDNEY
             A catalogue of Birmingham & West Midlands painters of
         the nineteenth century. Compiled by Sidney Morris and Kathleen
         Morris. Stratford-upon-Avon [Eng.] S. Morris, 1974. [87] p.
         illus., plates. 29cm.

10143   REDGRAVE, SAMUEL, 1802-1876.
             A dictionary of artists of the English school from the Middle
         Ages to the nineteenth century; painters, sculptors, architects,
         engravers and ornamentists, with notices of their lives and work.
         New and rev. ed. Amsterdam, G. W. Hissink, 1970. xiv,
         497 p. port. 24cm. Reprint of the London, 1878 ed. First
         published in 1874.

10144   WATERS, GRANT M
         Dictionary of British artists, working 1900-1950. East-
bourne [Eng.] Eastbourne Fine Art, c1975. [2], 368 p. 26cm.

10145   WOOD, CHRISTOPHER
         Dictionary of Victorian painters; with guide to auction
prices ... an index to artists' monograms. [Woodbridge, Eng.]
Antique Collectors' Club [1971] xvi, 435 p. illus. 28cm.

10146   WOOD, JOHN CLAIRMONT
         A dictionary of British animal painters [by] J. C. Wood.
Leigh-on-Sea, F. Lewis, 1973. 75 p., [40] l. illus. 30cm.

10147   WOODHOUSE, CHARLES PLATTEN
         The Victoriana collector's handbook. New York, St. Mar-
tin's Press [1972, c1970] xiv, 238 p. illus. 26cm. "Artists,
craftsmen, designers & firms" (p. 3-50) yields brief biographical data in its alphabetical listing.

Greece, Ancient

10148   THE NEW CENTURY HANDBOOK OF GREEK ART AND ARCHI-
         TECTURE. Edited by Catherine B. Avery. New York, Ap-
pleton-Century-Crofts [1972] ix, 213 p. illus. 21cm. "Selected from The New Century classical handbook, edited by Catherine B. Avery ... 1962." Includes entries for Greek artists and
architects.

Hungary

10149   STETTNER, BELA
         Ungarische Grafik. Magyar grafika. Grafique hongroise.
Dürer emlékezetére születésének 500 évfordulóján. [Gyula,
1971] 1 v. (unpaged) illus. 23cm. In Hungarian and German.
Catalog of an exhibition of Hungarian prints held in Magyar Nemzeti Galéria, Budapest and in Ferenc Erkel Múzeum, Gyula. A
major part of the volume is a bio-bibliographical dictionary of
66 Hungarian engravers of the present day.

10150   SZANA, TAMÁS, 1844-1908.
         Magyar müvészek. Mütörténelmi vázlatok képekkel. Uj
sorozat. Budapest, Hornyánszky V., 1889. 251 p. illus.,
ports. 31cm. Hungarian artists; sketches of the history of art—
new series.

10151   SZENDREI, JÁNOS, 1857-
         Magyar képzőmüvészek lexikona; magyar és magyarországi
vonatkozású müvészek életrajzai a XII. századtól napjainkig.

313

Irták: Szendrei János és Szentiványi Gyula. 1. kot. Abadi-Gunther. Budapest, Endrényi, 1915. 616 p. illus. 27cm. No more published. Encyclopaedia of Hungarian artists & artisans; 2953 biographies are included in this only volume published.

Israel

(See also Jews)

10152   TALPHIR, GABRIEL, 1899-
Me'ah omanim be-Yisrael she-halkhu le-'olamam ba-shanim tav resh samekh het-tav shin lamed (1908-1970) Tel-Aviv, 731 [1971] 100 p., 108 p. of plates (part col.), 16 p. illus. 28cm. In Hebrew; introd. also in English. Added t. p.: 100 artists in Israel who passed away in the years 1908-1970.

Italy

10153   ANDREINI, IVO
La pittura italiana del 1970 [i. e. millenovecentosettanta] A cura del pittore Ivo Andreini. Milano, Industrie grafiche L. Rosio, 1971. 428, vii p. illus. 30cm. Italian painting of the 20th century; with bio-bibliographical sketches; in part a biographical dictionary of ca. eight hundred 20th century Italian painters.

10154   ARCO, CARLO D', conte, 1799-1872.
Delli arti e degli artefici di Mantova; notizie raccolte ed illustrate con disegni e con documenti. Mantova, G. Agazzi, 1857. 2 v. 59 plates (part fold.) 34cm. The artists and the artisans of Mantua.

10155   BALDINUCCI, FILIPPO
Notizie dei professori del disegno da Cimabue in qua per le quali si dimostra come, e per chi le belle arti di pittura, scultura e architettura, lasciata la rozzezza delle maniere greca e gotica, si siano in questi secoli ridotte all'antica loro perfezione. Firenze, Per V. Batelli, 1846-47. 5 v. illus. 23cm. Italian masters of artistic design from the time of Cimabue, 1570-1670. Arranged by years when artist flourished; chronological index at end of each volume with alphabetical index to all volumes at end of vol. 5 (p. 709-720) First ed., Florence, 1681-1728 (6 v.); 2d, Florence, 1767-74 (22 v. in 10); 3d, Turin, 1768-1817 (5 v.)

10156   BARUFFALDI, GIROLAMO, 1740-1817.
Vite de' pittori e scultori ferraresi, con annotazioni. Ferrara D. Taddei, 1844-46. 2 v. ports. 24cm. Lives of the painters & sculptors of Ferrara. Principally in chronological arrangement; general index, by surname, at end of v. 2 (p. 597-604)

10157   BERENSON, BERNARD, 1865-1959.
          Italian painters of the Renaissance: a list of the principal
          artists and their works, with an index of places. Central Ital-
          ian and North Italian schools. By Bernard Berenson. London,
          Phaidon Press, 1968. 3 v. illus. 27cm. Distributed in the
          U. S. by Praeger. Contents. --v. 1. Text. --v. 2-3. Plates.
          The first volume contains a list of artists and the location of
          their works; the 'list' is bio-bibliographical in format, although
          the biographical data are quite brief.

10158   BIENNALE NAZIONALE D'ARTE CITTÀ DI MILANO, 27th,
             Milan, 1971-72.
          XXVII [i.e. Ventisettesima] Biennale nazionale d'arte Città
          di Milano. Situazione dell'uomo, contraddizioni a confronto.
          Dicembre 1971-gennaio 1972. Palazzo della Permanente, Milano.
          Milano, Società per la belle arti ed Esposizione permanente,
          1971. xv, 288 p. illus. 24cm. Catalog edited by M. De Mi-
          cheli. Catalog of the Biennial Exhibition of Italian Art (the 27th)
          held in Milan, 1971-1972. Serves also as a biographical diction-
          ary of modern Italian artists, Valerio Adami to Giuseppe Zigaina
          (some 93 artists in all)

10159   BINDI, VINCENZO, 1853-
          Artisti abruzzesi; pittori, scultori, architetti, maestri di
          musica, fonditori, cesellatori, figuli dagli antichi a' moderni.
          Notizie e documenti. Napoli, G. de Angelia, 1883. 302 p.
          24cm. Artists from Abruzzi; painters, sculptors, architects,
          musicians, etc. Biographical notes and documents. Index of
          artists by surname: p. 293-300.

10160   BRENZONI, RAFFAELLO
          Dizionario di artisti veneti; pittori, scultori, architetti,
          etc. dal XII al XVIII secolo. Firenze, L. S. Olschki, 1972.
          304 p. illus. 27cm. Dictionary of Venetian artists; painters,
          sculptors, architects, etc. from the 12th to the 18th century.

10161   CALVI, GIROLAMO LUIGI, 1791-1872.
          Notizie sulla vita e sulle opere dei principali architetti,
          scultori, e pittori che fiorirono in Milano durante il governo dei
          Visconti e degli Sforza. Milano, Tip. Ronchetti, 1859-69. 3 v.
          Imprint varies. Bio-biographical notices of the principal archi-
          tects, sculptors and painters who flourished in Milan during
          the reign of the Viscontis and the Sforzas.

10162   CATALOGO BOLAFFI DELLA PITTURA ITALIANA DELL'800
          (Ottocento). [Direttore: Enrico Piceni] Torino,
          G. Bolaffi, c1974. viii, 473 p. illus., ports. 29cm. (I Cata-
          loghi Bolaffi d'arte) This catalog of Italian painting of the 19th
          century is arranged alphabetically under painter and with its
          'biobibliographical' notes does service as a 'biographical dic-
          tionary.'

10163   COMANDUCCI, AGOSTINO MARIO, 1891-1940.
          Dizionario illustrato dei pittori, disegnatori e incisori
          italiani moderni e contemporanei. 4. ed., completamente
          rifatta e ampliata a cura di una redazione diretta da Luigi Ser-
          volini. Milano, L. Patuzzi, 1970-   v. 30cm. Con-
          tents. --t. 1. A-Cau. 1st ed., 1935 (under title: I pittori italiani
          dell'Ottocento); 2d, 1945 (under title: Dizionario illustratato dei
          pittori e incisori italiani moderni, 1800-1900); 3d, 1962 (in 4 v.)
          Illustrated dictionary of modern and contemporary Italian paint-
          ers, drawers and engravers (1800 on).

10164   [CRESPI, LUIGI] d. 1779.
          Felsina pittrice; vite de' pittori bolognesi tomo terzo ...
          Roma, Nella Stamperia de di M. Pagliarini, 1769. xx, 344 p.
          ports. 25cm. Binder's title: Felsina pittrice t. III. Issued al-
          so under title: Vite de' pittori bolognesi non descritte nella Fel-
          sina pittrice. Includes a great many lives of Bolognese painters
          not included in Malvasia's Felsina pittrice and issued as supple-
          mentary to that work. Alphabetical index to painters portrayed
          at end of volume.

10165   DEBIAGGI, CASIMIRO
          Dizionario degli artisti valsesiani dal secolo XIV al XX.
          Varallo, Società conservazione opere arte monumenti Valsesia,
          1968. v, 216 p. 25cm. Dictionary of Italian artists of the Sesia
          Valley from the 14th to the 20th century.

10166   DIZIONARIO ENCICLOPEDICO BOLAFFI DEI PITTORI E
          DEGLI INCISORI ITALIANI. Dall' XI al XX secolo ...
          Torino, G. Bolaffi, 1972-   v. illus. 28cm. (I Di-
          zionari Bolaffi) A dictionary of Italian painters and engravers
          from the 11th to the 20th century. 11 vols., covering A-Zuppelli
          published as of 1976.

10167   DONINI, MAURO
          Firmamento artistico. Autori italiani. Bologna, Tipogra-
          fia moderna, 1970. 79 p. illus. 25cm. A dictionary of mod-
          ern Italian artists and authors (and especially those who
          are involved in both writing and painting, sculpture, etc.)

10168   FREMANTLE, RICHARD
          Florentine Gothic painters from Giotto to Masaccio; a guide
          to painting in and near Florence. With 1335 illustrations and 13
          pages of maps. London, M. Secker and Warburg [1975] xxv,
          665 p. illus. 32cm. Provides biographical data for 108 Floren-
          tine painters in chronological arrangement, and full bibliographi-
          cal references for further information about the artists. The bio-
          graphical data is in the form of quotations from various authori-
          ties on the specific artists. Many of the 'biographies' are about
          pseudonymous artists (e.g., Master of Santa Cecilia, Pseudo
          Ambrogio di Baldese, etc.).

10169   GUALDO, GIROLAMO, 1599-1656.
        1650 [i. e. Mille seicento cinquanta] Giardino di Cha
Gualdo. A cura di Lionello Puppi. Firenze, L. S. Olschki
[1972] lxiv, 135 p. illus. 25cm. (Civiltà veneziana. Fonti e
testi, 11. Serie 1.: Fonti e documenti per la storia dell'arte
veneta, 8) On page preceding t. p.: Fondazione Giorgio Cini.
Centro di cultura e civiltà. Scuola di San Giorgio per lo studio
della civiltà veneziana. Istituto di storia dell'arte. Ca. 130
sketches of Italian artisans and artists whose works were represented in the collections of the Gualdo family. In chronological
arrangement.

10170   LONDON. NATIONAL GALLERY.
        The seventeenth and eighteenth century Italian schools, by
Michael Levey. London, National Gallery, 1971. 274 p. 25cm.
(Its Catalogues) A catalog of Italian paintings in the National
Gallery; it also serves as a biographical dictionary of Italian
painters of the 17th-18th centuries.

10171   LUCIANI, LIDIA
        Dizionario dei pittori italiani dell'800 [di] Lidia e Franco
Luciani. Firenze, Vallecchi, 1974. xxxviii, 428 p. 56 plates.
24cm. Dictionary of Italian painters of the 19th century.

10172   MALVASIA, CARLO CESARE, conte, 1616-1693.
        Felsina pittrice. Vite de' pittori bolognesi. Con aggiunte,
correzioni e note inedite dell'autore, di Giampietro Zanotti e di
altri scrittori. Bologna, Forni, 1967. 2 v. 24cm. Reproduction of the 1841 Bologna ed. This work was first issued in 1678
and has been reprinted many times (the latest is a 1971 ed. by
ALFA, Bologna) This 1967 ed. contains biographical sketches of
ca. 120 Bolognese painters. A third volume of the work was issued by Luigi Crespi (Rome, 1769) with title: Felsina pittrice;
vite de' pittori bolognesi tomo terzo; and Vite de' pittori bolognesi non descritte nella Felsina pittrice.

10173   MICHELI, MARIO DE
        I naifs italiani. Pref. di Cesare Zavattini. Note critiche
di Nevio Iori. Progetto grafico di Franco Benedetti e Mauro
Buzzi. Parma, Passera & Agosta Tota, 1972. 391 p. illus.
34cm. At head of title: Mario De Micheli, Renzo Margonari.
Reproductions of the painting of 93 contemporary Italian primitive artists, accompanied by portraits of the artists and brief
biographical data. Alphabetical arrangement, A-V.

10174   PASCOLI, LIONE, 1674-1744.
        Vite de' pittori, scultori, ed architetti perugini. Roma, A.
de Rossi, 1732. 259 p. 24cm. Painters, sculptors and architects of Perugia. In the main chronologically arranged, with an
index to surnames.

10175   PIETRUCCI, NAPOLEONE
        Biografia degli artisti padovani. Bologna, Forni, 1970.
        295 p. 25cm. (Italica gens, n. 9) A biographical dictionary
        of the artists of Padua. A reprint of the Bologna edition of 1858.

10176   ROLI, RENATO
        I disegni italiani del Seicento. Scuole emiliana, toscana,
        romana, marchigiana e umbra. [Treviso] Libreria editrice
        Canova, 1969. lxxx, 167 p. 90 plates. 27cm. (Il Disegno
        italiano) Italian drawings of the 16th century. "Biografie e
        catalogo" (p. 167 p. at end) includes biographical sketches (in
        chronological arrangement) of 111 Italian masters of drawing
        and engraving.

10177   SAGGIO DI UN DIZIONARIO BIOGRAFICO DI ARTISTI VICENTINI.
        Vicenza, Rumor, 1885-86. 2 fasc. 8.º An essay at a
        biographical dictionary of the artists of Vicenza. Only 2 fasci-
        cles were published?

10178   TASSI, FRANCESCO MARIA, 1716-1782.
        Vite de' pittori, scultori e architetti bergamaschi ... A
        cura di Franco Mazzini. [Ristampa anastatica] Milano, Edi-
        zioni Labor [1969-70] 2 v. port. 24cm. (Gli Storici della
        letteratura artistica italiana, 31-32) Facsimile of the 1793 edi-
        tion. Contents.--[1] Facsimile. 2 v. in 1.--[2] Saggio bio-
        bibliografico. Appendici. Indice analitico generale. Lives of
        painters, sculptors and architects of Bergamo, city and province.
        The index at the end of the 2d (facsimile) volume yields an alpha-
        betical approach to the many biographical sketches in the main
        text. But there is also a biographical dictionary (in part) com-
        piled by the editor of the reprint edition, Franco Mazzini, on
        pages 219-420 of the 'third' (i.e. 2d physical) volume.

10179   ZANNANDREIS, DIEGO, 1768-1836.
        Le vite dei pittore, scultori e architetti veronesi. Pubbli-
        cate e corredate di pref. e di due indici da Giuseppe Biadego.
        Bologna, Forni [1971] xxv, 559 p. 21cm. (Italica gens, n. 23)
        Reprint of the Verona, 1891 ed. Lives of the painters, sculp-
        tors and architects of Verona; ca. 260 biographies; in non-al-
        phabetical arrangement. Alphabetical approach through index of
        the lives at the end of the volume.

10180   ZERI, FREDERICO
        Italian paintings in the Walters Art Gallery. With condition
        notes by Elisabeth C. G. Packard. Edited by Ursula E. Mc-
        Cracken. Baltimore, Published by the Trustees [of the Walters
        Art Gallery] 1976. 2 v. (xx, 647 p. , 299 plates) 28cm. The
        catalog is arranged chronologically and includes biographical
        notes for the over 200 Italian painters represented. Alphabeti-
        cal approach to these biographical notes thru' index at end of
        vol. 2 (heavy print indicates page where biography and critical
        apparatus are located).

Japan

10181   ARALO, TADASJO
        Dai Nihon shoga meika taikan. Tokyo, Dai'ichi Shobo,
        1975. 4 v. 22cm. Reprint of 1934 edition. 20,000 biographies
        of Japanese artists, painters, calligraphers, seals, signatures,
        of artists, genealogies of different schools of art are given.
        Name indexes in Japanese syllables and stroke counts of Chinese
        characters.

10182   ASAOKA, OKISADA, 1800-1856.
        Koga bikō. Kyoto, Shimonkaku, 45 [1970] 4 v. illus.
        23cm. Facsimile edition, with revisions by Ōta Kin. A dic-
        tionary of Japanese and Korean painters, artists' marks and
        Japanese seals (numismatics).

10183   BARBOUTAU, PIERRE
        Biographies des artistes japonais dont les oeuvres figurent
        dans la collection Pierre Barboutau. Amsterdam. R. W. P.
        de Vries, 1904. 2 v. plates. 36 x 28cm. Preface signed:
        Arsène Alexandre. First published in 1904 (Paris, S. Bing).
        Contents. --t. 1. Peintures. --t. 2. Estampes et objets d'art. Bi-
        ographies of the Japanese artists represented in the collection
        of Pierre Barboutau.

10184   BLAKEMORE, FRANCES
        Who's who in modern Japanese prints. New York, Weather-
        hill, 1975. 263 p. illus. 22cm. A biographical dictionary of
        20th century Japanese printmakers.

10185   HORI, NAONORI, 1806-1880.
        Fusō meiga den. Tokyo, Tetsugaku Shoin, 1899. 2 v.
        23cm. Biography of approximately 1,900 Japanese painters and
        art-lovers, classified according to their social standings into 14
        groups. Written by Naonori Hori and Harumura Kurokawa. Re-
        vised by Mamichi Kurokawa.

10186   MITCHELL, C   H
        The illustrated books of the Nanga, Maruyama, Shijo and
        other related schools of Japan; a biobibliography by C. H. M
        Mitchell, with the assistance of Osamu Ueda. Los Angeles,
        Dawson's Book Shop, 1972. 623 p. 27cm. Part I was published
        in 1968 under the title Guide to the illustrated books of the Nanga,
        Maruyama and Shijo school of Japan. "Alphabetical listing of
        artists": p. [9]-204. Biographical information is fairly substan-
        tial for the better known artists, but very brief for little known
        ones.

10187   MORRISON, ARTHUR, 1863-1945.
        The painters of Japan. New York, F. A. Stokes [1911] 2 v.
        122 plates (part col.) 39cm. The work is divided into large

sections which deal with particular schools of painting. These
sections are almost entirely devoted to biographies of Japanese
painters (in chronological order) The comprehensive name-
subject index at the end of vol. 2 yields an alphabetical approach
to the many biographies.

10188   SAWADA, AKIRA, 1876-1934.
         Nihon gaka jiten. Kyoto, Daigakudo Shoten, 1970. 2 v.
         illus. 22cm. Reprint of 1927 edition. A biographical diction-
         ary of Japanese artists who died before 1927, with references.
         Vol. 1: painters; v. 2, artists' marks. Includes an index of
         names other than real names.

10189   YOSHIA, TERUJI, 1901-1972.
         Ukiyoe jiten. Tokyo, 1965-71. 3 v. illus. 27cm. A
         dictionary of the Ukiyoe school of Japanese painting, including
         biographies of painters.

Jews

(See also Israel)

10190   KLINGER, RUTH, 1906-
         ha-Omanut veha-omanim be-Eerets-Yisrael. [Tel-Aviv]
         1946. 104, 144 p. (p. [121]-144 advertisements) 18cm. Added
         t. p.: Art and artists in Palestine; comprises theatre, music,
         dance, painting and sculptural art. Planned by Maxim Sakas-
         hansky.

Korea

10191   KIM, YŎNG-YUN
         Hanguk sŏhwa inmyŏng sasŏ. Biographical dictionary of
         Korean artists and calligraphers, by Young-Yun Kim. Seoul,
         Hanyang Munhwasa, 1959. 43, 566 p. 26 plates. 22cm.

Netherlands

10192   BODART, DIDIER
         Les peintres des Pays-Bays méridionaux et de la principau-
         té de Liège à Rome au XVIIème siècle. Bruxelles, Institut his-
         torique belge de Rome, 1970. 2 v. illus. 27cm. (Études d'his-
         toire de l'art, t. 2) Vol. 2, p. [5]-70 contains a list, with some
         biographical data (and in dictionary format) of Dutch and Flemish
         painters and engravers and artists of Liège who sojourned in
         Rome in the 17th century.

10193   DUTUIT, EUGENE, 1807-1886.
         Manuel de l'amateur d'estampes; introduction générale
         contenant un essai sur les plus anciens gravures et les estampes
         en manière criblée, sur les livres xylographiques et les livres,
         à figures du XVe siècle. Accompagnée d'un catalogue raisonné
         des nielles ou gravures d'orfèvre. Continué par Auguste Dutuit
         et Gustave Pawlowski. Suivi du dictionnaire biographique des
         graveurs des Écoles flamande et hollandaise, avec descriptions
         raisonnées de leur oeuvre. Amsterdam, G. W. Hissink, 1970-
                         v. illus. 23cm. Reprint of Paris edition of 1881-88.
         The work was originally intended to be published in 8 v. and an
         atlas, but vols. 2, 3, 7 & 8 never appeared. Cf. Lorenz, Cata-
         logue générale de la librairie française, and Vicaire, Manuel de
         l'amateur des livres du XIXe siècle. Contents. --t. 1. Intro-
         duction générale. --t. 2. Dictionnaire. A manual of engraving
         and engravings. The reprint edition contains a vol. 2 (and be-
         yond?) which includes the dictionary (biographical) of the Flem-
         ish and Dutch schools of engravers. The so-called biographies
         are, in most cases, extremely brief. 5 vols. issued as of 1972.

10194   KELLEN, JOHAN PHILIP VAN DER, 1831-1906.
         Le peintre-graveur hollandais et flamand; ou, Catalogue
         raisonné des estampes gravées par les peintres de l'école hol-
         landaise et flamande. Ouvrage faisant suite au Peintre-graveur
         de Bartsch. Par J. Philip van der Kellen ... avec des facsim-
         ilé, gravés à l'eau-forte par J. A. Boland. Utrecht, Kemink et
         fils [1867-73] vii, 242 (i.e. 246), [2] p. 36 mounted plates
         (incl. ports.) 41 x 31cm. Dutch and Flemish painters-engrav-
         ers; a supplement to Adam von Bartsch's Le peintre graveur.

10195   LEWIS, FRANK
         A dictionary of Dutch & Flemish flower, fruit, and still life
         painters, 15th to 19th century. Leigh-on-Sea [Eng.] F. Lewis,
         1973. 83 p., 48 leaves. illus. (part col.) 30cm. Cover title:
         A dictionary of Dutch & Flemish flower & still life painters, 16th-
         19th centuries.

10196   PARIS. PALAIS DES BEAUX-ARTS.
         Le siècle de Rembrandt; tableaux hollandais des collec-
         tions publiques françaises, Musée du Petit palais, 17 novembre
         1970-15 fevrier 1971. [Paris] Réunion des musées nationaux
         [1970] xxxi, 278 p. 24cm. "Catalogue rédigé par Arnauld
         Bréjon de Lavergnée [et al.] Exhibition catalog of Dutch paint-
         ings of the age of Rembrandt in French public collections. The
         catalog also serves as a biographical dictionary of the painters,
         since it is alphabetically arranged by name of painter and in-
         cludes biographical notes on each.

10197   PRESTON, RUPERT
         The seventeenth century marine painters of the Netherlands.
         Leigh-on-Sea, F. Lewis, 1974. viii, 103 p. illus., 47 leaves
         of plates. 30cm.

10198   WILLIGEN, ADRIAAN VAN DER, 1810-1876.
         Les artistes de Harlem; notices historiques avec un précis
sur la gilde de St. Luc. Ed. rev. et augm. Nieuwkoop, B. de
Graaf, 1970. xiv, 366 p. facsims., geneal. tables. 23cm.
"Reprint of the edition Harlem-La Haye, 1870. " Translation of
Geschiedkundige aanteekeningen over Haarlemsche schilders.
The artists of Haarlem, the Netherlands; historical notices with
an essay on the Gild of Saint Luke. Pages [66]-351 contain a
biographical dictionary.

Peru

10199   UGARTE ELSPURU, JUAN MANUEL, 1911-
         Pintura y escultura en el Perú contemporáneo. Lima,
Ediciones de Difusión del Arte Peruano, 1970. 248 p. illus.
23cm. (PeruArte) Painting and sculpture in contemporary
Peru; the "Indice onomástico" (p. [213]-238) is a biographical
dictionary (brief data).

Poland

10200   GROŃSKA, MARIA
         Nowoczesny drzeworyt polski (do 1945 roku) Wrocław,
Zakład Narodowy im. Ossolińskich, 1971. 510 p. illus. (part
co.) 26cm. Polish wood-engraving of the 20th century (up to
1945) Includes a dictionary of wood-engravers (Słownik artystow)
on p. 391-[464]. With a summary of the text in English.

10201   RASTAWIECKI, EDWARD, baron, 1805-1874.
         Słownik rytowników polskich tudziez obcych w Polsce osiad-
łych lub czasowo w niej pracupacych. Wydany Staraniem To-
warzystwa Przyjacioł Nauk Poznańskiego z Funduszów Sp. Nor-
berta Bredkrajcza. Poznan, Z drukarni J. I. Krasjewskiego
(Dr. W. Lebiński) 1886. viii, 316 p. front. 24cm. Dictionary
of Polish engravers and foreign engravers living in Poland or
working there temporarily.

10202   SŁOWNIK ARTYSTÓW POLSKICH I OBCYCH W POLSCE
         DZIAŁAJACYCH; malarze, rzeźbiarze, graficy. Zespół
redakcyjny: Jolanta Maurin-Białostocka [et al.] Konsultant
naukowy: Andrzez Ryskiewicz. Wrocław, Zakład Narodowy im.
Ossolińskich, 1971-   v. 26cm. At head of title: v.
1-   Instytut Sztuki Polskiej Akademii Nauk. Dictionary of
Polish artists and foreigners active in Poland: painters, sculptors, engravers. Contents.--t. 1. A-G.

10203   ZWIAZEK POLSKICH ARTYSTÓW PLASTYKÓW. OKREG
         WARSZAWSKI.
         Słownik artystów plastyków. Artyści plastycy Okregu
Warszawskiego ZPAP 1945-1970. Słownik biograficzny. Red.

M. Serafińska. Wyd. 1. Warszawa, Okreg. Warszawski ZPAP,
1972. 714 p. illus. 33 x 18cm. A biographical dictionary of
ca. 2600 artists connected with Warsaw and the surrounding area
from 1945 to 1970 and members of the Warsaw District (Section)
of the Society of Polish Artists.

Portugal

10204   GUIA DE PORTUGAL ARTÍSTICO. v. 1-8. Lisboa [M. Costa
Ramalho, 1933-41?] 8 v. illus. Guide to art and artists in
Portugal, 1933-1941. Vol. 5 is especially biographical. No
more published?

Russia

10205   IVENSKIĬ, SEMEN GEORGIEVICH
Mastera russkogo ėkslibrisa. [Leningrad, "Khudozhnik
RSFSR," 1973] 333 p. illus. 21cm. Masters of the Russian ex
libris; pages [73]-302 include, in alphabetical arrangement, biographical sketches of 83 Russian designers of book-plates.

10206   KHUDOZHNIKI NARODOV SSSR; biobibliograficheskiĭ slovar'.
Moskva, Iskusstvo, 1970-   v. 27cm. On leaf preceding t. p.: Akamediiā khudozhestv SSSR. Nauchno-issledovatel'skiĭ institut teorii i istorii izobrazitel'nykh iskusstv. To be
in 6 vols. Vol. 1-   compiled by O. E. Vol'tsenburg. Edited by
T. N. Gorina. Contents.--t. 1. Aavik-Boĭko.--t. 2. Boĭchenko-
Geondzhian (1972) Artists of the USSR; a bio-bibliographical dictionary.

10207   KONEČNÁ, GALINA
Maƚy slovnĭk sovětských maliřů. Praha, Vyd. Svaz čs.-
sovět pratelství, 1956. 63 p. 8.° Little dictionary of Soviet
Russia's artists-painters.

10208   KORNILOV, PETR EVGEN'EVICH, 1896-
Slovar' khudozhnikov Arzamasskoi shkoly zhivopisi (1797-
1862) (In his Arzamasskaiā shkola zhivopisi pervoĭ poloviny XIX
veka. Moskva, Iskusstvo, 1947. 22cm. p. 191-197) 118 very
brief notices of painters of the Arzamas School of Painting, Arzamas, Russia in biographical dictionary format.

10209   LEONOV, ALEKSEĬ IVANOVICH, 1898-
Russkoe iskusstvo; ocherki o zhizni i tvorchestve khudozhnikov. Moskva, Iskusstvo, 1962-   v. illus., ports.
27cm. Edited by A. I. Leonov. An extensive collection of biographies of Russian painters, with about 40 to 50 lives in each
volume. The first 5 volumes (1962-1971) cover the 18th and 19th
centuries.

10210   USPENSKIĬ, ALEKSANDR IVANOVICH, 1873-
         TSarskie ikonopistsy i zhivopistsy XVIII v. Moskva, 1910-
         16. 4 v. illus. 35cm. Vol. 1: Slovar' tsarskikh ikonopistsev
         i zhivopistsev XVIII v. Russian Imperial icon and portrait
         painters of the 18th century; vol. 1 is a dictionary of these paint-
         ers.

Scandinavia

10211   RABEN & SJÖGRENS LEXIKON ÖVER MODERN SKANDINA-
         VISK KONST. [Huvudredaktör: Jesper Engelstoft] Stock-
         holm, Raben & Sjögren [1958] 239 p. illus. 22cm. In Danish,
         Norwegian or Swedish. Danish ed. has title: Gyldenals leksi-
         kon over moderne nordisk kunst. A dictionary of modern
         Scandinavian art; with biographical entries.

Silesia, Upper

10212   IWANEK, WITOLD
         Słownik artystów na Slasku Cieszyńskim. [Wyd. 1. Bytom]
         1967. 175 p. 24cm. (Rocznik Muzeum Gornoslaskiego w By-
         tomiu. Sztuka, zesz. 2) Dictionary of artists of Upper Silesia.

10213   KRAUSE, WALTER
         Grundriss eines Lexikons bildender Künstler und Kunsthand-
         werker in Oberschlesien von den Anfängen bis zur Mitte der
         neunzehnten Jahrhundert. Oppeln, Verlag "Der Oberschlesier",
         1933-35. 2 v. 8.° (Schriftenreihe der Vereinigung für Ober-
         schlesische Heimatkunde, 8-9) A basic dictionary of artists and
         artisans in Upper Silesia from the earliest times to the middle
         of the 19th century.

Slovakia

10214   SLOVNÍK SÚČASNÉHO SLOVENSKÉHO UMENIA. Dictionnaire
         de l'art contemporain slovaque. [Hlavný redaktor Marian
         Váross. 1. vyd. Bratislava] Vyd-vo Slovenského fondu výt-
         varných umeni [1967] 1 v. (unpaged) illus. (part col.) 17cm.
         Preface and legends also in French. Dictionary of contemporary
         Slovak art; Slovak artists of the 20th century.

South Africa

10215   BERMAN, ESMÉ
         Art and artists of South Africa; an illustrated biographical
         dictionary and historical survey of painters and graphic artists
         since 1875. Cape Town, A. A. Balkema, 1970. xvi, 368 p.
         illus., ports. 28cm. Includes more than 300 biographies of
         painters and graphic artists.

10216   MIRVISH, DOREEN BELLE
        South African artists, 1900-1958; a bibliography. [Cape
Town] University of Cape Town Libraries, 1970. vi, 40 p. 23cm.
(University of Cape Town, School of Librarianship. Bibliogra-
phical series) Pages 9-37 contain the bibliography of works a-
bout 20th century individual South African painters and sculptors.
First published in 1959 and reprinted in 1970.

                              Spain

10217   ALDANA FERNÁNDEZ, SALVADOR
        Guía abreviada de artistas valencianos. Valencia, Ayun-
tamiento de Valencia, 1970. 382 p. 25cm. (Publicaciones del
Archivo Municipal de Valencia. Ser. 1.: Catálogos, guías y
repertorios, 3) A biographical dictionary (brief sketches) of
Valencian artists.

10218   CAMPOY, ANTONIO MANUEL
        Diccionario crítico del arte español contemporaneo. Ma-
drid, Ibérico Europea de Ediciones, 1973. 490 p. illus. (part
col.) 31cm. (Colección Arte contemporáneo español, 5) A biographical dictionary of contemporary Spanish artists (most living, a few deceased)

10219   MADARIAGA, LUIS
        Pintores vascos. San Sebastián, Editorial Auñamendi [1971]
2 v. plates. 19cm. (Colección Auñamendi, 81-82) A biographical dictionary of painters from the Basque Provinces of Spain.

10220   MORENO GALVÁN, JOSÉ MARÍA
        The latest avant-garde. Text by José María Moreno Galván.
Translation by Neville Hinton. [n. p.] Magius [Art Publications;
published in the U. S. by New York Graphic Society, Greenwich,
Conn., 1972?] 273 p. illus. (part col.) 33cm. On half-title
page: Spanish painting; collection. Translation of La última van-
guardia. Spanish avant-garde painting of the 20th century; includes a biographical dictionary: "Biographical appendix" (p.
251-267)

10221   ORELLANA, MARCOS ANTONIO DE
        Biografía pictórica valentina; o, Vida de los pintores, ar-
quitectos, escultores y grabadores valencianos. Obra filoló-
gica. 2. ed., preparada por Xavier de Salas. Valencia, Ayun-
tamiento de Valencia, 1967. xlvii, 654 p. 24cm. 1st issued
in Valencia in 1950. Artists of Valencia, Spain; a chronological
listing.

10222   PINTORES ESPAÑOLES CONTEMPORÁNEOS: desde 1881,
        nacimiento de Picasso. Diccionario. Bajo la dirección de

J. I. de Blas. Madrid, Estiarte [1972] 250 p. illus. (part
col.) 29cm. A dictionary of contemporary Spanish painters
from 1881, the date of birth of Picasso. Biographical details
are quite brief, often only an identifying phrase, and are primarily critical.

Sweden

10223   BJURSTRÖM, PER, comp.
          90 [i.e. Nittio] grafiker. Grafik i svart och vitt. Utg.:
Nationalmuseum och Föreningen för grafisk konst. Stockholm,
1974. [189] p. illus. 20cm. Pref. in English and Swedish.
Biographical sketches of 90 Swedish printmakers with examples
of their work.

10224   BJURSTRÖM, PER
          Svenska illustratörer. Red.: Per Bjurström. Utg.: Na-
tionalmuseum och Föreningen Svenska tecknare. Stockholm,
Utgivaren: Solna, Seelig, 1972. 95, [1] p. illus. 20cm. A
dictionary of Swedish book illustrators of the 20th century.

10225   SVENSKA KONSTNÄRER; biografisk handbok. [Ny suppl.]
          Stockholm, Eden bokförlag [1969] 535 p. 21cm. 3d ed.,
1947; 5th ed., 1955. Swedish artists; a biographical handbook.

10226   WRETHOLM, EUGEN, 1911-
          Moderna svenska konstnärer från 1940-, 50- och 60-talen.
Stockholm, Bokförlaget Forum, 1969. 164 p. ports. 17cm.
A dictionary of modern Swedish artists of the 1940's, 1950's
and 1960's.

Switzerland

10227   BIRKNER, OTHMAR
          Der Weg ins 20. Jahrhundert. [Aus der Entwicklungs-
geschichte der modernen Raumgestaltung in der Schweiz, 1870-
1918. Ausstellung] Gewerbemuseum Winterthur, 15. June-10.
August 1969. Katalog. Von Othmar Birkner und Robert Steiner.
Winterthur, 1969. 128 p. illus. 22cm. 'Biographie" (p. 49-
79) yields 130 biographical sketches of Swiss artists (largely
followers of the Art nouveau movement) who flourished in the
years 1870-1918. In biographical dictionary format. The compiler (Birkner) states that his list is a 'modest' supplement to
the Schweizerisches Künstlerlexikon and the Künstlerlexikon
der Schweiz, XX. Jahrhundert.

Ukraine

10228   SLOVNYK KHUDOZHNYKIV UKRAINY. Vidp. redaktor M. P.
          Bazhan. Kyiv, Hol. red. Ukrains'skoi Radians'koi Entsik-

lopedii, 1973. 267 p. illus. (part col.), ports. 27cm. At head
of title: Akademiia nauk Ukrains'koi Radians'koi Sotsialistychnoi
Respubliky. A dictionary of Ukrainian artists (painters, etc.)

United States

Bibliography, Indexes, Portrait Catalogs

10229   ST. LOUIS. PUBLIC LIBRARY.
             An index to Black American artists. [St. Louis, 1972?]
         50 p. 28cm. Cover title: Black American artists index.

General Works

10230   AFRO-AMERICAN ARTISTS: New York and Boston; [exhibition]
             The Museum of the National Center of Afro-American
         Artists, the Museum of Fine Arts [and] the School of the Mu-
         seum of Fine Arts, Boston, 19 May-23 June 1970. [Boston?
         1970] 1 v. (unpaged) illus. 26cm. A 'biographical dictionary'
         at the back of the volume lists 70 artists.

10231   AMERICAN EXPRESS CO.
             Art '65: Lesser known and unknown painters. Young Amer-
         ican sculpture, East to West. New York, Printed by Star Press,
         1965. 131 p. illus. 20cm. An exhibition catalog of young
         American painters and sculptors which includes two 'biogra-
         phical dictionaries': one for 35 painters and the 2d for 24
         sculptors. The exhibit was held in the American Express Pa-
         vilion at the New York World's Fair, 1965.

10232   BELKNAP, HENRY WYCKOFF, 1860-
             Artists and craftsmen of Essex County, Massachusetts.
         Salem, Essex Institute, 1927. viii, 127 p. illus., ports. 25cm.
         A biographical dictionary, i.e., alphabetical arrangement of
         biographies under various topics, e.g., architects, engravers,
         photographers, etc.

10233   BOLTON, THEODORE, 1889-
             Early American portrait draughtsmen in crayons. New
         York, Kennedy Graphics, 1970 [c1923] xii, 111 p. ports. 24cm.
         (Library of American art) Reprint of the 1923 edition. A bio-
         graphical dictionary of early American portrait-painters, with
         lists of portraits drawn by them.

10234   THE BRITANNICA ENCYCLOPEDIA OF AMERICAN ART.
             Chicago, Encyclopaedia Britannica Educational Corp.;
         world book trade distribution by Simon and Schuster, New York,
         1973. 699 p. illus. (part col.) 29cm. "A Chanticleer Press

edition. " An alphabetically arranged encyclopedia of American
art and artists; 1100 entries.

10235   BROOKLYN INSTITUTE OF ARTS AND SCIENCES. MUSEUM.
        A century of American illustration. Exhibition, the Brook-
lyn Museum, March 22-May 14, 1972. Brooklyn, 1972. 155 p.
illus. (part col.) 23cm. On pages 141-153 is a biographical
dictionary of American illustrators (114 in all)

10236   CEDERHOLM, THERESA DICKASON
        Afro-American artists: a bio-bibliographical directory.
Boston, Trustees of the Boston Public Library, 1973. 348 p.
24cm. Some 2,000 Afro-American artists from the slave
craftsmen of the 18th century to the present are represented.

10237   COLLINS, JIMMIE LEE, 1934-
        Women artists in America: eighteenth century to the pres-
ent. Chattanooga, Dept. of Art, University of Tennessee, 1973.
1 v. (unpaged: ca. 430 p.) illus. 24cm. More than 4,000 very
brief sketches of women artists of the United States from the
1700's to the present.

10238   CONTEMPORARY ART SOCIETY, INDIANAPOLIS.
        Painting & sculpture today. Indianapolis, 1970. v, 120 p.
illus. 26cm. Catalog of the 1970 annual exhibition presented at
the Indianapolis Museum of Art; includes very brief biographical
data and lists of exhibitions for 149 contemporary American
painters and sculptors, with alphabetical index.

10239   CONTEMPORARY SOUTHERN PLAINS INDIAN PAINTING.
        With an essay by Rosemary Ellison. Edited by Myles Lib-
hart. Anadarko, Oklahoma Indian Arts and Crafts Cooperative,
1972. 80 p. col. illus., ports. 24cm. "An exhibition organized by the Indian Arts and Crafts Board of the U. S. Department of the Interior. " "Biographical directory of the artists,
compiled by Rosemary Ellison": p. 65-79. 42 biographies with
portraits for most of the artists.

10240   CUMMINGS, PAUL
        A dictionary of contemporary American artists. 2d ed.
New York, St. Martin's Press, 1971. xv, 368 p. illus. 24cm.
787 American artists. First edition issued in 1966.

10241   DAWDY, DORIS OSTRANDER
        Artists of the American West; a biographical dictionary.
1st ed. Chicago, Sage Books, 1974. viii, 275 p. 24cm. Lists
more than 1300 artists and illustrators born before 1900, but
provides biographical sketches (100 to 150 words in length) for
ca. 300 of them.

10242   EBERT, JOHN
        American folk painters, by John & Katherine Ebert. New
York, Scribner, 1975. viii, 225 p. illus. 27cm. A history of
folk painting in America, with an appendix: Selected list of A-
merican folk painters (p. 205-214) which gives brief biographical notes (in alphabetical arrangement on 91 painters.

10243   FIELDING, MANTLE, 1865-1941.
        Dictionary of American painters, sculptors and engravers,
by Mantle Fielding. Enl. ed., with over 2,500 new listings of
seventeenth, eighteenth and nineteenth century American artists.
Edited by Genevieve C. Doran. Greens Farms, Coon., Modern
Books and Crafts [c1974] vi, 455 p. 24cm. Supersedes the 1st
ed. of 1945 and the 1965 ed. enlarged by James F. Carr.

10244   GERDTS, WILLIAM H
        Revealed masters; 19th century American art. [Catalogue
of] an exhibition organized by American Federation of Arts, New
York. New York, American Federation of Arts [1974] 152 p.
illus. (part col.) 28cm. "AFA exhibition number 74-1; circu-
lated September 1974-September 1975." "Illustrations, biographies and checklist" (p. [43]-[129]) includes a biographical dictionary of 43 artists.

10245   GIBSON, ARTHUR HOPKIN
        Artists of early Michigan; a biographical dictionary of
artists native to or active in Michigan, 1701-1900. Compiled by
Arthur Hopkin Gibson. Research assistants: Beverly Bassett
and Jean Spang. Detroit, Wayne State University Press, 1975.
249 p. illus. 24cm.

10246   GOSHEN COLLEGE, GOSHEN, IND. ART GALLERY.
        Mennonite artists contemporary, 1975: [exhibition] Goshen
College Art Gallery, Goshen, Indiana, February 2-March 16.
Compiled and edited by Abner Hershberger. Goshen, The College, 1975. [112] p. illus. 18cm. A dictionary arrangement; 54
artists listed with accompanying biographical notes and reproductions of art work.

10247   HEMPHILL, HERBERT W
        Twentieth-century American folk art and artists, by Herbert
W. Hemphill, Jr. [and] Julia Weissman. New York, E. P. Dutton, 1974. 237 p. illus. (part col.) 29cm. "An essential feature ... is the biographical material provided wherever possible" (Book jacket) 145 artists are included; alphabetical approach via "Index to artists" (p. 234-235).

10248   LEWIS, SAMELLA S
        Black artists on art [edited by] Samella S. Lewis and Ruth
G. Waddy. [Los Angeles, Contemporary Crafts Publishers,

1969-   v. illus., ports. 27cm. Includes portraits of Black American artists as well as a biographical dictionary at the end of each volume. 2 vols. issued as of 1971.

10249   MOURE, NANCY DUSTIN WALL
       Dictionary of art and artists in Southern California before 1930, by Nancy Dustin Wall Moure with research assistance by Lyn Wall Smith. Introd. by Carl Shaefer Dentzel. Glendale, Calif., Dustin Publications, 1975. xxvi, 306 p. illus. 28cm. (Publications in Southern California art; no. 3)

10250   NORDNESS, LEE, ed.
       Art: USA: now. Text by Allan S. Weller. New York, Viking Press [1963] 2 v. (475 p.) illus., ports. 25cm. (A Studio book) Includes biographical sketches of 102 contemporary American painters.

10251   O'SULLIVAN, JUDITH
       The art of the comic strip. With an introductory note by Don Denny. [College Park] University of Maryland Dept. of Art [1971] 95 p. illus. 22 x 27cm. Exhibition held at University of Maryland Art Gallery, Apr. 1-May 9, 1971. "Biographies" (p. 60-87) is a biographical dictionary of 114 American comic strip creators.

10252   SHERIDAN, MARTIN, 1914-
       Comics and their creators: life stories of American cartoonists. [Rev. ed., 1944] New York, Luna Press [Reprinted 1971] 304 p. illus. 23cm. Includes biographical facts for some 88 American cartoonists, creators of the best known comic strips of the 1930s and 40s; index must be used for alphabetical approach.

10253   SHERMAN, FREDERIC FAIRCHILD, 1874-1940.
       Early American painting. New York, Century Co. [1932] xxi, 289 p. illus., ports. 21cm. [Century library of American antiques] Chiefly a biographical collection containing ca. 140 American painters' lives. Arranged chronologically and/or by painting types—genre, portrait, landscape, etc. Alphabetical approach to the artists through the index.

10254   UNITED STATES. INDIAN ARTS AND CRAFTS BOARD.
       Contemporary Indian artists, Montana, Wyoming, Idaho; an exhibition organized by the Indian Arts and Crafts Board of the U. S. Dept. of the Interior. Selected by Myles Libhart and Ramon Gonyea. With an essay by Ramon Gonyea. Edited by Dorothy Jean Ray. [Rapid City, S. D., Tipi Shop, 1972] 80 p. illus., ports. 25cm. A circulating exhibition released through the Museum of the Plains Indian, Browning, Mont. Included are biographical sketches and portraits of some 47 Indian artists (in no particular arrangement and unfortunately no index of names).

10255   VAN DEVANTER, ANN C
        American self-portraits, 1670-1973. Introd. and [exhibi-
tion] catalogue by Ann C. Van Devanter and Alfred V. Frankenstein with the assistance of Shirley S. Simpson. [Washington]
International Exhibitions Foundation, 1974. 247 p. illus.,
ports. 28cm. Exhibition held at the National Portrait Gallery
and the Indianapolis Museum of Art. Includes portraits and biographical notes on American artists or artists in America (ca.
107) in chronological arrangement with an alphabetical index of
artists at the end of the volume.

10256   WEHLE, HARRY BRANDEIS, 1887-
        American miniatures, 1730-1850; one hundred and seventy-
three portraits, selected with a descriptive account by Harry B.
Wehle ... & a biographical dictionary of the artists by Theodore
Bolton. Garden City, N. Y., Garden City Pub. Co. [1937] xxv,
127 p. ports. 29cm. For an alphabetical approach to the portraits themselves use the index.

10257   WIESENDANGER, MARTIN
        19th century Louisiana painters and paintings from the col-
lection of W. E. Groves [by] Martin and Margaret Wiesendanger, curators of the collection. Gretna [La.] Pelican Pub.
Co., 1971. 118 p. illus. 25cm. A "biographical dictionary"
of 64 painters active in Louisiana in the 19th century, American, French, etc. Biographical notes are brief since a large
part of the work is devoted to reproductions of paintings.

Venezuela

10258   DICCIONARIO BIOGRÁFICO DE LAS ARTES PLÁSTICAS EN
        VENEZUELA, SIGLOS XIX Y XX. Caracas, Instituto Na-
cional de Cultura y Bellas Artes, 1973. 300 p. illus. (part
col.) 27cm. Cover title: Diccionario de las artes plásticas en
Venezuela. Biographical dictionary of the plastic arts in Venezuela in the 19th and 20th centuries.

10259   DUARTE, CARLOS F
        Materiales para la historia de las artes decorativas en
Venezuela. Caracas, 1971. 230 p. plates. 23cm. (Biblioteca
de la Academia Nacional de la Historia, 104) (Fuentes para la
historia colonial de Venezuela) Materials for the history of the
decorative arts in Venezuela. Pages 61-208 contain a biographical dictionary of joiners, cabinetmakers, woodcarvers and
sculptors.

Yugoslavia

10260   KUKULJEVIĆ-SAKCINSKI, IVAN, 1816-1889.
        Slovnik umjetnikah jugoslavenskih. U Zagrebu, Tiskom
Narode Tiskarne Ljudevita Gaja, 1850-60. 5 v. in 1. ports.
Dictionary of artists in Yugoslavia.

10261   MAZALIC, ĐOKA
         Leksikon umjetnika slikara, vajara, graditelja, zlatara,
kaligrafa i drugih koji su radili u Bosni i Hercegovini. Sarajevo,
Veselin Masleša, 1967. 153 p. 28cm. (Biblioteka Kulturno
nasljede) Dictionary of artists of Bosnia and Herzegovina.

Architecture

10262   BRIGGS, MARTIN SHAW, 1882-
         Everyman's concise encyclopaedia of architecture, by Mar-
tin S. Briggs. London, J. M. Dent; New York, Dutton, 1969,
c1959. xi, 372 p. illus. 20cm. (Everyman's reference library) Includes biographical sketches of famous architects.

10263   DAVID DE PENANRUN, LOUIS THÉRÈSE
         Les architectes, élèves de l'École des beaux-arts. Par
David de Penanrun, Roux et Delaire. 2. éd. par E. Delaire.
Préf. de J. L. Pascal. Paris, Librairie de la construction
moderne, 1907. xii, 484 p. illus., ports. 24cm. At head of
title: 1793-1807. French architects, students of the School of
Fine Arts, Paris, in the years 1793-1807. Very brief biographical notices may be found on pages 157-431.

10264   DÉZALLIER D'ARGENVILLE, ANTOINE NICOLAS, d. 1794.
         Vies des fameux architectes depuis la Renaissance des
arts. Genève, Minkoff Reprint, 1972. 2 v. 22cm. Reprint of
the 1787 Paris edition. On spine: Vies des fameux architectes
et sculpteurs. Vol. 2 has title: Vies des fameux sculpteurs depuis la Renaissance des arts. Lives of famous architects and
sculptors after the Renaissance of the arts. Vol. 1 contains 42
biographies of architects (Italian, English, German, French);
v. 2, 62 sculptors (44 at length, 18 mentioned briefly within the
biographies of their masters).

10265   FLEMING, JOHN, 1919-
         The Penguin dictionary of architecture [by] John Fleming,
Hugh Honour [and] Nikolaus Pevsner. Drawings by David Ether-
ton. 2d ed. [Harmondsworth, Eng.] Penguin Books) 1972.
315 p. illus. 20cm. (Penguin reference books) Includes brief
biographies of architects. 1st ed. issued in 1966 (248 p.)

10266   HATJE, GERD
         Encyclopedia of modern architecture. New York, H. N.
Abrams, 1964. 336 p. illus., ports. 22cm. "Originally published as Knaurs Lexikon der modernen Architektur." Includes
biographies of architects.

10267   HATJE, GERD
         Lexikon der modernen Architektur. Hrsg. von Gerd Hatje.
[Redaktion: Wolfgang Pehnt. Mitarbeiter: Kyösti Alander et al.

Vollständige Taschenbuchausg. München] Droemer/Knaur
[1966] 349 p. 18cm. (Knaur-[Taschenbücher] 119) First ed.
published in 1963 under title: Knaur's Lexikon der modernen
Architektur. French ed. (Paris, F. Hazan) has title: Dictionnaire de l'architecture moderne. Italian ed.: Enciclopedia
dell'architettura moderna (Milano, Garzanti, 1967) Issued in
English with title: Encyclopaedia of modern architecture (New
York, H. N. Abrams, 1964) A dictionary of modern architecture
that includes biographies of architects.

10268   MILIZIA, FRANCESCO, 1725-1798.
         The lives of celebrated architects, ancient and modern:
with historical and critical observations on their works, and on
the principles of the art. Translated from the Italian by Mrs.
Edward Cresy. With notes and additional lives. London, J.
Taylor, 1826. 2 v. 22cm. Translation of Memorie degli architetti antichi e moderni. A collective biographical volume with
many brief lives in chronological arrangement.

10269   OUDIN, BERNARD
         Dictionnaire des architectes. [Paris] Seghers [1970] 478 p.
illus. 24cm. A dictionary of architects of all times and countries.

10270   PEVSNER, NIKOLAUS, Sir, 1902-
         A dictionary of architecture [by] Nikolaus Pevsner, John
Fleming and Hugh Honour. Rev. and enl. Woodstock, N. Y.,
Overlook Press, 1976. 554 p. illus. 24cm. Includes biographies of architects. 1st ed. issued in 1966 under author and
title: Fleming, John, 1919-   The Penguin dictionary of
architecture (248 p.)

10271   RAVENEL, BEATRICE ST. JULIEN.
         Architects of Charleston. Introd. by William Watts Ball.
Photographs by Carl Julien. Charleston, Carolina Art Association [1945] xvi, 329 p. illus. 26cm. Includes in a chronological arrangement biographical sketches of varying length of ca.
72 Charleston, South Carolina architects.

10272   ROLAND LE VIRLOYS, CHARLES FRANÇOIS, 1716-1772.
         Dictionnaire d'architecture, civile, militaire et navale,
antique, ancienne et moderne, et de tous les arts et métiers
qui en dépendent; dont tous les termes sont exprimés, en français, latin, italien, espagnol, anglois et allemand; enrichi de
cent une planches de figures en taille-douce ... auquel on a
joint une notice des architectes, ingénieurs, peintres, sculpteurs, graveurs, & autres artistes les plus célèbres, dont on
rapporte les principaux ouvrages. Paris, Libraires associés,
1770. 3 v. and atlas of plates. 28cm. A dictionary of architecture that includes numerous biographical entries for architects, engineers and artists of all countries and periods (to the
mid-18th century).

10273   SIR BANISTER FLETCHER LIBRARY.
        Catalogue of the drawings collection of the Royal Institute of
British Architects. [London] [Farnborough, Eng.] Gregg International Publishers [1968-   v. plates. 34cm. At
head of title: Royal Institute of British Architects. Running title:
RIBA drawings collection. This catalog of architectural drawings is generally in alphabetical arrangement by architect-draw-
er and includes biographical sketches. However some volumes
of the set are devoted entirely to one or two architects. Contents. --[1] A. --[2] B. --[3] C-F. --[4] Inigo Jones & John Webb.
[etc.] Vols. 1-10, 13-14, 16, & 18 (1972) available as of 1976.

Sculpture

10274   DIZIONARIO BOLAFFI DEGLI SCULTORI ITALIANI MODERNI.
        Torino, G. Bolaffi, 1972. xci, 415 p. illus., ports. 28cm.
(I Dizionari Bolaffi) A biographical dictionary of 20th century
Italian sculptors.

10275   ESCULTURA ITALIANA CONTEMPORÁNEA : bronces; [catá-
        logo] Exposición organizada por la Quadriennale nazionale
d'arte di Roma y el Museo Nacional de Bellas Artes de Buenos
Aires. Buenos Aires, Museo Nacional de Bellas Artes, junio-
julio 1971. Buenos Aires, Asociación Amigos del Museo Nacional de Bellas Artes de Buenos Aires, 1971. 1 v. (unpaged)
illus. 24cm. Contemporary Italian sculpture in bronze; catalog
of an exhibition in Buenos Aires, 1971. The main body of the
catalog consists of biographical and critical notes and lists of
works of 83 sculptors, arranged alphabetically.

10276   KEYSER, EUGÉNIE DE
        Le sculpture contemporaine en Belgique. Bruxelles, La-
conti [1972] 250 p. illus. 24cm. (Belgique, art du temps)
Contemporary sculpture in Belgium. "Notices biographiques"
(p. 216-251) is a biographical dictionary of ca. 150 Belgian
sculptors.

10277   NEW DICTIONARY OF MODERN SCULPTURE. General editor:
        Robert Maillard. [Translated from the French by Bettina
Wadia] New York, Tudor Pub. Co. [1971] 328 p. illus. 24cm.
A new edition of Dictionary of modern sculpture (1962) with 200
additional sculptors' biographies (but others have been deleted,
so that this edition covers only 56 more artists than the first).
Translation of Nouveau dictionnaire de la sculpture moderne,
first published in 1960 under title: Dictionnaire de la sculpture
moderne.

10278   PANORAMA DE LA SCULPTURE AU QUÉBEC, 1945-1970.
        Paris [Presses artistiques, 1970?] 1 v. (unpaged) illus.
22cm. Catalog of an exhibition organized by the Quebec Dept. of
Cultural Affairs and the French Ministère d'État chargé des

affaires culturelles and held at the Musée Rodin. In part a biographical dictionary (66 biographies) of 20th century Canadian
and French-Canadian sculptors from Quebec.

10279   PYKE, E   J
        A biographical dictionary of wax modellers. Oxford,
Clarendon Press, 1973. lxvi, 216 p. illus. 24cm. Covers
the Renaissance to the present. Includes artists who used wax
in preparation for their finished works of art as well as professional wax modellers.

10280   SCULTORI ITALIANI CONTEMPORANEI. Mostra graziosa-
        / mente prestata dalla Quadriennale d'arte di Roma come
contributo all'attività dell'Università internazionale dell'arte.
Firenze, La Gradiva, 1970. 215 p. illus. 25cm. At head of
title: Università internazionale dell'arte di Firenze e Venezia.
In part a biographical dictionary (by J. Recupero) of some 65
contemporary Italian sculptors.

Decorative And Applied Arts

10281   BÖSKEN, SIGRID
        Die Mainzer Goldschmiedezunft; ihre Meister und deren
Werke vom Ende des 15. bis zum ausgehenden 18. Jahrhundert.
Mainz, Stadtbibliothek, 1971. 140 p. illus. 29cm. (Beiträge
zur Geschichte der Stadt Mainz, Bd. 21) A history of the gold
and silversmiths' guilds in Mainz. "Verzeichnis der Gold- und
Silberschmiede" (p. 35-65) is a biographical dictionary of
Mainz's gold and silversmiths.

10282   BOGER, LOUISE ADE
        The dictionary of world pottery and porcelain. New York,
Scribner, 1971. 533 p. illus. (part col.) 28cm. The entries
cover factories, companies and individual potters, modellers,
painters and engravers, etc.

10283   BORG, TYRA
        Guld- och silversmeder; Finland; deras stämplar och ar-
beten, 1373-1873. Helsingfors, Ab. F. Tilgmann, 1935. 528 p.
illus. 29cm. Gold and silversmiths of Finland: their marks
and their works. Biographical notices grouped by cities and
towns and arranged chronologically. Index of the notices: p.
516-525.

10284   BULGARI, COSTANTINO G
        Argentieri, gemmari e orafi d'Italia. Notizie storiche e
raccolta dei loro contrassegni con la reproduzione grafica dei
punzoni individuali e dei punzoni di Stato. Roma, L. del Turco,

1958-   2 v. illus. 30cm. Contents.--pt. 1. Roma. 2 v.
In part a dictionary of Italian silversmiths, gem-workers and
goldsmiths with their marks and reproductions of their tools
and dies.

10285   BURTON, E   MILBY
          South Carolina silversmiths, 1690-1860. Rutland, Vt., C.
Tuttle Co., 1968. xvii, 311 p. illus., ports. 24cm. (Contributions from the Charleston Museum, 10) Reprint of the 1942
ed. Includes 320 biographical entries of varying length; the
biographies are arranged alphabetically under 21 geographical
areas.

10286   CALASIBETTA, CHARLOTTE MANKEY
          Fairchild's dictionary of fashion. Edited by Ermina Stim-
son Goble [and] Lorraine Davis. New York, Fairchild Publications, 1975. xiv, 693 p. illus. 25cm. Includes biographies of
250 fashion designers, 50 of them Americans.

10287   CHAMPEAUX, ALFRED DE, 1833-1903.
          Dictionnaire des fondeurs, ciseleurs, modeleurs en bronze
et doreurs, depuis le moyen-âge jusqu'à l'époque actuelle.
Paris, J. Rouan, 1886. 357 p. 16cm. Dictionary of French
smelters, carvers, modellers in bronze and gilders from the
end of the Middle Ages to the end of the 19th century. An incom-
plete work; covers letters A-C only.

10288   CITROEN, KAREL   A
          Amsterdamse zilversmeden en hun merken. Amsterdam,
Noord-Hollandsche Uitgeversmij., 1975. xxiv, 254 p. illus.
25cm. Amsterdam's silversmiths and their marks; includes
biographical data. Arrangement is 'alphabetical' by mark (when
letters are involved in the mark). Name index at end of volume
gives an alphabetical approach to the silversmiths.

10289   CURRIER, ERNEST M   1867-1936.
          Marks of early American silversmiths, with notes on silver,
spoon types & list of New York City silversmiths, 1815-1841 ...
Edited with introductory note by Kathryn C. Buhler. Watkins
Glen, N. Y., American Life Foundation; distributed by Century
House, 1970. 171, [5] p. illus. 24cm. Reprint of the 1938 ed.
published by the Southworth-Anthoensen Press, Portland, Me.,
with most of the preliminary matter omitted and a new bibliography added. Includes brief biographical data for many of the
alphabetically-listed silversmiths.

10290   ERIKSEN, SVEND
          Early neo-classicism in France; the creation of the Louis
Seize style in architectural decoration, furniture and ormolu,
gold and silver, and Sèvres porcelain in the mid-eighteenth

century. Translated from the Danish and edited by Peter Thornton. London, Faber and Faber, 1974. 432 p. plates. 28cm. "Select biographies"(p. [145]-225) is a biographical dictionary of ca. 125 artisans, arbiters of taste for the period, etc.

10291   FALLON, JOHN P
         Marks of London goldsmiths and silversmiths: Georgian period (c. 1697-1837) Newton Abbot [Eng.] David & Charles [1972] 420 p. 15cm. An alphabetical listing (by owner of mark) accompanied by genealogical and biographical notices.

10292   FRIED, FREDERICK
         Artists in wood; American carvers of cigar-store Indians, show figures, and circus wagons. New York, C. N. Potter [1970] xiv, 297 p. illus., ports. 31cm. On pages 115-247 are given biographies of 37 carvers (only 2 of which appear in the Dictionary of American painters, sculptors and engravers); on p. 263-269 are listed 53 show-figure carvers with dates of birth and death (when known) and working addresses. Most of the latter also appear in the general biographical section.

10293   LES GRAVEURS D'ACIER ET LA MÉDAILLE DE L'ANTIQUITÉ À NOS JOURS. [Avant-propos par Pierre Dehaye] Paris, Musée de la monnaie, 1971. xxiv, 731 p. illus. 24cm. Catalog of an exhibition held at the Musée de la monnaie, June-October 1971. Engravers in metal and medals and numismatics from antiquity to the present. "Les graveurs en médaille d'aujourd'-hui" (Medal engravers of today)--p. [485]-627—is a biographical dictionary (with portraits) of ca. 60 engravers.

10294   GRIMWADE, ARTHUR
         London goldsmiths, 1697-1837; their marks and their lives, from the original registers at Goldsmith's Hall and other sources, by Arthur G. Grimwade. London, Faber, 1976. ix, 728 p. illus. 26cm. The biographical section has entries of varying lengths and acts as an index to the nearly 4,000 marks taken from the Goldsmith's Hall registers.

10295   HERITAGE FOUNDATION.
         The Heritage Foundation collection of silver; with biographical sketches of New England silversmiths, 1625-1825. [By] Henry N. Flynt and Martha Gandy Fales. Old Deerfield, Mass., 1968. xiv, 391 p. illus., ports. 27cm. "Biographies and touch-marks" (p. [139]-364) is a biographical dictionary (with marks, when available).

10296   HONEY, WILLIAM BOWYER, 1889-
         European ceramic art, from the end of the Middle Ages to about 1815. London, Faber & Faber [1952-63] 2 v. plates. 29cm. Vol. 1: 2d ed., 1963; v. 2: 1st ed., 1952, has sub-title:

A dictionary of factories, <u>artists</u>, technical terms, etc. It includes a large number of brief biographies of potters and artists; some of the personal name entries are only 2 or 3 lines in length.

10297   HOUSE & GARDEN DICTIONARY OF DESIGN & DECORATION.
        Editor: Robert Harling. Art editor: Alex Kroll. Editorial
associates: Ann Barr [and others] Rev. and enl. ed. London,
Collins in association with Conde Nast Publications, c1973. 538p.
illus., ports. 30cm. Includes biographical entries for designers
and architects, living and deceased. American ed. (New York,
Viking Press) issued under title: Studio dictionary of design &
decoration.

10298   JANNEAU, GUILLAUME, 1887-
        Les ateliers parisiens d'ébenistes et de menuisiers aux
XVIIe et XVIIIe siècles. Publication dirigée par J. Fréal. [n.
p.] Editions S. E. R. G. [1975] 273 p. illus. 24cm. The history of the furniture industry and trade in Paris in the 17th-18th
centuries has distinctive biographical value and interest, because, although not a 'biographical dictionary', prominent names
are given in the left margin throughout the volume and biographical data is found opposite these names. A comprehensive index
of names leads one to all furniture and cabinet-makers for whom
biographical data is available with the most prominent names
starred or otherwise marked.

10299   JEDDING, HERMANN
        Europäisches Porzellan. München, Keysersche Verlagsbuchhandlung [1971-   v. illus. 23cm. Contents.--Bd. 1.
Von den Anfängen bis 1800. Each vol. is in dictionary format
(with a pictorial supplement at end) and includes numerous biographical sketches of Europeans (manufacturers, artists, etc.)
involved in the making of porcelain ware and art objects. Vol. 1
only available as of 1976.

10300   MACKAY, DONALD CAMERON
        Silversmiths and related craftsmen of the Atlantic provinces.
Halifax, Petheric Press, 1973. vi, 133 p., [27] leaves of plates.
illus. 27cm. Silversmiths, etc. of eastern Canada.

10301   MASON, ANITA
        An illustrated dictionary of jewellery. Illustrated by Diane
Packer. New York, Harper and Row, 1974. 389 p. illus. 24cm.
Includes biographies of notable jewellers of the past.

10302   MAYER, LEO ARY, 1895-1959.
        Islamic woodcarvers and their works. Geneva, A. Kundig,
1958. 99, [6] p. illus. 26cm. A biographical dictionary (roll
of woodcarvers): p. [21]-68.

10303   NEUMANN, WILHELM, 1849-
        Verzeichnis baltischer Goldschmiede, ihrer Merkzeichen
und Werke. Riga, Druck von W. F. Häcker, 1905. 75 p. 22cm.
Biographical listing of Baltic goldsmiths, their marks & works.
In geographical arrangement; no index.

10304   NORDNESS, LEE
        Objects: USA. New York, Viking Press [1970] 360 p. il-
lus. (part col.), ports. 25cm. (A Studio book) With the use of
the index at the end of the vol. this work can be used as a "biographical dictionary" of 20th century Americans in the art industries and trades, since the illustrative matter is accompanied by biographical sketches of and photographs of the artists.

10305   NORRIS, ANDREA S
        Medals and plaquettes from the Molinari Collection at
Bowdoin College, by Andrea S. Norris & Ingrid Weber. With
an introd. to the medals catalogue by Graham Pollard. Brunswick, Me., President and Trustees of Bowdoin College, 1976.
xi, 292 p. illus., ports. 29cm. Includes biographical notes
for medallists and makers of plaquettes (in chronological arrangement) and reproductions of medals and plaquettes, a
large number of which are portraits of Renaissance and early
modern (thru' the 18th century) European personages.

10306   THE OXFORD COMPANION TO THE DECORATIVE ARTS.
        Edited by Harold Osborne. Oxford, Clarendon Press, 1975.
xiv, 865 p. illus. 24cm. A dictionary that includes numerous
biographies of craftsmen outstanding in the decorative arts and
design.

10307   PLEASANTS, JACOB HALL, 1873-1957.
        Maryland silversmiths, 1715-1830, with illustrations of
their silver and their marks and with a facsimile of the design
book of William Faris, by J. Hall Pleasants and Howard Sill.
And including a publisher's foreword by Robert Alan Green.
Harrison, N. Y., R. A. Green, 1972. xiv, 324 p. illus. 29cm.
Reprint of the 1930 Baltimore edition. Includes biographical
sketches in several alphabets (e. g., chapter headings: Annapo-
lis silversmiths, Baltimore silversmiths, Eastern Shore silversmiths, etc.).

10308   ROHDE, ALFRED, 1892-
        Goldschmiedekunst in Königsberg. Bearb. von Ulla Stöver.
Stuttgart, W. Kohlhammer, 1959. 160 p. illus. 26cm. (Bau-
und Kunstdenkmäler des deutschen Ostens, Reihe B, Bd. 2)
Goldsmithing in Königsberg. List of masters mentioned (a biographical dictionary of ca. 60 goldsmiths): p. 43-70.

10309   SCHOEFFLER, O   E   1899-
        Esquire's encyclopedia of 20th century men's fashions, by
        O. E. Schoeffler and William Gale. New York, McGraw-Hill,
        1973. x, 700 p. illus., ports. 28cm. Includes a section con-
        taining a biographical dictionary of 80 outstanding designers.

10310   STUDIO DICTIONARY OF DESIGN & DECORATION. [Editor:
        Robert Harling. Art editor: Alex Kroll. American research
        and contributions: Julius Trousdale Sadler, Jr., Edith Gaines
        and the staff of Studio Books. Editorial associates: Ann Barr and
        others. Rev. and enl. ed.] New York, Viking Press [1973]
        538 p. illus., ports. 30cm. Includes portraits and biographical
        sketches of architects, furniture designers, decorators, etc.
        London ed. (Collins) issued under title: House & garden diction-
        ary of design & decoration.

10311   THUILE, JEAN
        Histoire de l'orfèvrerie du Languedoc; généralités de Mont-
        pellier et de Toulouse. Répertoire des orfèvres depuis le moyen-
        âge jusqu'au début du XIXe siècle. Paris, T. & F. Schmied,
        1964-69. 3 v. illus. 28cm. Contents.--[1] A à C.--[2] D à L.
        --[3] M à Z. History of goldsmithing and silversmithing in
        Languedoc. These 3 vols. comprise a biographical dictionary
        of gold and silversmiths.

10312   WOLFBAUER, GEORG
        Meisterverzeichnis der steirischen Goldschmiede. Graz,
        1935. 98 p. Taken from the Zeitschrift des Historischen
        Vereins für Steiermark, Schriftenreihe des Kunstgewerbemu-
        seums, 2. Master list of Styrian goldsmiths; actually a bio-
        graphical dictionary.

Performing Arts

(See Also Music)

Bibliography, Indexes, Portrait Catalogs

10313   SCHUSTER, MEL
        Motion picture directors; a bibliography of magazine and
        periodical articles, 1900-1972. Metuchen, N. J., Scarecrow
        Press, 1973. 418 p. 22cm. An index to biographical and ca-
        reer-oriented information on some 2,300 directors, filmmak-
        ers and animators found in 340 magazines.

10314   SCHUSTER, MEL
        Motion picture performers; a bibliography of magazine and
        periodical articles, 1900-1969. Metuchen, N. J., Scarecrow
        Press, 1971. 702 p. 22cm. Indexes periodical articles about

movie actors.

---- ----Supplement no. 1: 1970-1974. Metuchen, N. J.,
Scarecrow Press, 1976. 793 p. 22cm.

General Works

10315   BALCAR, ALEXANDER J
         Knaurs Ballett Lexikon. Vorwort von Pavel Ludikar.
München, Droemersche Verlagsanstalt, Th. Knaur Nachf.,
1958. 379 p. illus., ports. 22cm. Knaurs ballet dictionary;
includes biographies of dancers.

10316   BARIL, JACQUES
         Dictionnaire de danse. Paris, Éditions du Seuil, 1964.
273, [15] p. illus. ports. 18cm. (Collection Microcosme.
Dictionnaires, 2) A dictionary of dance. Dancers (A-Z): p.
50-205.

10317   BARSACQ, LÉON, 1906-1969.
         Le décor de film. Préf. de René Clair. Paris, Seghers,
1970. 375 p. plates. 21cm. (Cinéma club) A handbook of film
design which includes a biographical dictionary of 100 noted film
designers (p. 238-260).

10318   BEVENEY'S WHO'S WHO IN FILMDOM. 1947-   London,
         Beveney Pub. Co.   v. 8.º Edited by June Steyning.
Nos. 1-2 (1947-48) only ones issued? Chiefly motion picture
actors and actresses (British especially).

10319   BLECH, RICHARD
         Malá encyklopédia filmu; zahraničná tvorba. 1. vyd. Bra-
tislava. Obzor, 1974. 802 p. illus. 25cm. Encyclopedia of
motion pictures: foreign (non-Czech) film activities. Includes
biographical data.

10320   THE BLUE BOOK OF THE SCREEN. Ruth Wing, editor. Hol-
         lywood, Calif., Blue Book of the Screen, inc., c1923. 415 p.
illus., ports. 28cm. Actors and actresses of the silent screen.

10321   BROŽ, JAROSLAV
         555 [i. e. Pět set pades'at pět] profilů zahraničních rezisé-
rů. Autoři: Jaroslav Brož, Myrtil Frída. Praha, Čes. filmový ustav, rozmn. Služby města Ostravy, Ostrava, 1971. 2 v.
21cm. 555 profiles of foreign (non-Czech) film directors. An
expansion of Broz's Profily zahraničních rezisérů.

10322   BROŽ, JAROSLAV
         Profily zahraničních režisérů; 400 filmografii. V Praze,
Filmový ústav, 1967. 331 p. 20cm. At head of title: Jaroslav
Brož, Myrtil Frída. Profiles of foreign film directors; 400
filmographies.

10323   BRUSENDORFF, OVE
         Filmen, dens navne og historie. Copenhagen, Universal-
forlaget, 1939. 3 v. illus., ports. 24cm. The film, its
celebrities and history (to 1940). Vol. 2 is a dictionary listing
the world's moving-picture actors and actresses (silent and
talking films) with filmographies, dates, identifying statements
and many portraits.

10324   CAMPBELL, OSCAR JAMES, 1879-   ed.
         The reader's encyclopedia of Shakespeare. Edited by Os-
car James Campbell. Associate editor: Edward G. Quinn. New
York, T. Y. Croweell, 1966. xv, 1014 p. illus., ports. 26cm.
Included are biographical sketches of Shakespearean scholars,
critics, actors, directors of Shakespeare's dramas, etc. and
contemporaries of Shakespeare.

10325   CAWKWELL, TIM
         The world encyclopedia of film. Associate editors: Tim
Cawkwell and John M. Smith. London, Studio Vista, 1972. xi,
444 p. illus., ports. 28cm. American ed. (New York, World
Publishing) has J. M. Smith as first named editor on t. p.
Paper back ed. (A & W Visual Library, New York) issued in
1974. A dictionary of people involved in the production of moving pictures.

10326   DANCE WORLD. v. 1-2. 1966-1967. New York, Crown Pub-
         lishers. 2 v. illus., ports. 24cm. annual. Editor: 1966-
1967, J. Willis. Includes many photographs of dancers in America as well as biographies of choreographers and featured dancers (dictionary at end of each volume) No more published?

10327   DICTIONNAIRE DU CINÉMA, suivi d'un répertoire des princi-
         paux films. 2. éd. Paris, Seghers, 1965, c1962. 414 p.
ports. 17cm. A dictionary of the cinema, followed by a list of
outstanding films. Supersedes Dictionnaire du cinéma (Paris,
Seghers, 1962—388 p. ports. 17cm.) Includes biography.

10328   ENCICLOPEDIA ILUSTRADA DEL CINE. Barcelona, Editorial
         Labor, 1970-72. 3 v. illus., ports. 28cm. Contents.--
t. 1. A-F.--t. 2. G-O.--t. 3. P-Z. Vocabulario técnico. An
illustrated dictionary of the moving-pictures; includes biographical entries.

10329   FILM KISLEXIKON. Szerk: Ábel Péter. Fömunkatársak:
         Nemeskürthy István és Pozsonyi Gábor. Budapest, A-
         kadémiai Kiadó [1964] 981 p. illus., ports. 25cm. Biographi-
         cal dictionary of motion picture actors, directors, etc.

10330   FILM-KURIER, BERLIN.
         Das grosse Bilderbuch des Films. Berlin [1925] 400 p.
         illus., ports. 30cm. Picture-book of silent films; contains a
         section on directors and actors, with portraits. Edited by Hu-
         bert Miketta. Other editions appeared in 1922, 1928.

10331   FILM STAR PARADE; a glittering galaxy of your screen favor-
         ites, emphasis on glamour. [London, W. H. Allen, 1944]
         60 ports. 22 x 19cm. Cover title. Descriptive text on verso of
         each portrait.

10332   FILM STARS OF THE WORLD. [London, Amalgamated Press,
         193-] 160 ports. 23cm. Cover title. Each portrait ac-
         companied by short biography.

10333   FOX, CHARLES DONALD
         Who's who on the screen. Edited by Charles Donald Fox and
         Milton L. Silver. New York, Ross Pub. Co. [c1920] 415 p.
         illus., ports. 22cm. Actors and actresses of the silent screen.

10334   GRAHAM, FRANKLIN
         Histrionic Montreal; annals of the Montreal stage, with
         biographical and critical notices of the plays and players of a
         century. 2d ed. New York, B. Blom [1969] 303, iv p. illus.,
         ports. 24cm. This 2d ed. first published in 1902. A major
         part of the volume consists of biographical notices of actors and
         actresses of the English and world theater who appeared on the
         Montreal stage in the 19th century.

10335   THE INTERNATIONAL ENCYCLOPEDIA OF FILM. General
         editor: Roger Manvell. American advisory editor: Lewis
         Jacobs ... New York, Crown Publishers [1972] 574 p. illus.
         29cm. Includes biographical data: actors, directors, etc.

10336   INTERNATIONALER TONFILM-ALMANACH (ITA) 1929/30-
         1935/36. Berlin, H. Wendt. 6 v. ports. 23cm. Ceased
         publication with 6th ed., 1935/36? 1935/36 ed. has title: Erster
         internationaler Tonfilm-Almanach (ITA) An international motion
         picture almanach with substantial biographical sections.

10337   JEANNE, RENÉ, 1887-
         Dictionnaire du cinéma universel [par] René Jeanne et

Charles Ford. Paris, R. Laffont [1970] 711 p. ports. 24cm.
Dictionary of world cinema; a biographical dictionary of moving-
picture actors, directors, etc.

10338   MCDONAGH, DON
          The complete guide to modern dance. 1st ed.
          Garden City, N. Y., Doubleday, 1976. x, 534 p. illus. 24cm.
          Individual artists are presented thru' brief biographies & de-
          scriptions of their outstanding works.

10339   MAGYAR SZÍNMŰVÉSZETI LEXIKON; a magyar színjátszás és
             drámairodalom enciklopediája. Budapest, Országos Színés-
          zegyesület és Nyugdíjintézete, 1929-31. 4 v. Edited by Aladár
          Schöpflin. Hungarian dictionary of theatrical arts with theatrical
          biography.

10340   MARTIN, MICHAEL RHETA, 1917-
             The concise encyclopedic guide to Shakespeare, by Michael
          Rheta Martin and Richard C. Harrier. New York, Horizon
          Press [1971] 450 p. illus. 27cm. "Critics and scholars of
          Shakespeare" [a biographical dictionary]: p. 369-384. "People
          of the theater" [actors, actresses, directors and producers of
          Shakespeare's plays]: p. 385-408. "A selected list of composers
          of music based on the works of Shakespeare": p. 416-426.

10341   MITRY, JEAN
             Dictionnaire du cinéma. Paris, Larousse [1964, c1963]
          327 p. illus. 18cm. (Dictionnaire de l'homme du XXe siècle.
          A dictionary of movie terms. etc. that includes brief descrip-
          tions of persons in the cinema; emphasis on French personali-
          ties.

10342   THE NEW YORK TIMES DIRECTORY OF THE FILM. New
             York, Arno Press [and] Random House, 1971. 1243 p.
          ports. 32cm. Includes a portrait gallery containing 2,000 por-
          traits of movie actors and actresses (primarily American and
          British).

10343   OTTŮV DIVADELNÍ SLOVNÍK. [Za součinnosti Karla Engel-
             müllera redig. Karel Kamínek. Praha, J. Otto, 1914-18]
          944 p. illus. 25cm. A Czech encyclopedia of the theatre which
          includes biographies of individual theatrical figures of the past;
          covers A-G only. No more published; issued in parts.

10344   THE OXFORD COMPANION TO FILM. Edited by Liz-Anne
             Bawden. New York, London, Oxford University Press,
          1976. ix, 742 p. illus. 24cm. Includes biographies of actors,
          directors, writers, composers, producers of motion pictures
          (worldwide). 1974 is cut-off date.

10345   ÖZÖN, NIJAT
         Ansiklopedik sinema sözlüğö. Istanbul, Tan Matbaasi,
         1958. vii, 464 p. illus. 8.° A dictionary-encyclopedia of mo-
         tion pictures; in Turkish; biographies are included.

10346   PASINETTI, FRANCESCO
         Filmlexikon. Piccola enciclopedia cinemotografica redatta
         sulla base del Kleines Filmlexikon di Charles Reinert. [Milano]
         Filmeuropa, 1948. 715 p. illus. 21cm. The 2d part of this
         3 part film dictionary (based on Reinert's Kleines Filmlexikon)
         contains brief biographies of persons involved in the movies (p.
         [669]-708).

10347   PICTURE SHOW ANNUAL.
         Who's who on the screen. London, Amalgamated Press,
         1956] 160 p. ports. British and American film actors and
         actresses chiefly.

10348   PIES, EIKE
         Prinzipale: zur Genealogie des deutschsprachigen Berufs-
         theaters vom 17. bis 19. Jahrhundert. Ratingen, A. Henn
         [1973] 398 p. illus., ports. 25cm. A biographical-genealogi-
         cal dictionary of the German-speaking theater of Europe from the
         17th to the 19th century.

10349   RASMUSSEN, BJØRN
         Filmens hvem-hvad-hvor. [Ny. udg.] København, Politiken,
         1968-70. 5 v. illus. 18cm. Contents: bind 1. Danske titler og
         biografier. Udarb. af B. Rasmussen og L. Roos.--bind 2-3.
         Udenlandske film 1950-1967. Udarb. af B. Rasmussen.--bind
         4. Udenlandske biografier. Udarb. af B. Rasmussen.--bind 5.
         Verdens beste film. Beskrevet og vurderet af B. Rasmussen.
         In part a biographical dictionary of Danish and foreign moving-
         picture luminaries, past and present (talking pictures primar-
         ily).

10350   REICHOW, JOACHIM
         Filmkünstler A-Z. Leipzig, Bibliographisches Institut,
         1967. 334 p. 20cm. (Meyers Taschenlexikon) A biographical
         dictionary (international) of motion picture artists (actors, di-
         rectors, etc.)

10351   REYNA, FERDINAND
         Concise encyclopedia of ballet. Translated [from the
         French] by Andre Gateau. London, Collins, 1974. [3], 250 p.
         illus., ports. 23cm. Includes many biographical sketches of
         dancers, choreographers, etc. A translation, with revisions,
         of Dictionnaire des ballets.

10352   SADOUL, GEORGES, 1904-1967.
             Dictionary of film makers. Translated, edited and updated
         by Peter Morris. Berkeley, University of California Press
         [1972] viii, 288 p. 24cm. 1,000 entries: directors, script-
         writers, cinematographers, art directors, composers and pro-
         ducers only. Translation of Dictionnaire des cinéastes.

10353   SCREEN WORLD. 1949-   New York.   v. illus., ports.
             22cm. annual. Edited by Daniel Blum (1949-1966): John
         Willis (1967-   At the end of each volume very brief biogra-
         phical data for film stars (chiefly American and British) are
         given, but most useful are the many portraits in the volumes and
         the longer biographical sketches under the obituary notices of
         the year section. Some early issues also known by title: Daniel
         Blum's screen world.

10354   SZINHÁZI KISLEXIKON. Főszerkesztő Hont Ferenc. Szer-
             keszette Staud Géza. Budapest, Gondolat, 1969. 535 p.
         illus., plates, ports. 25cm. A dictionary of the theater that in-
         cludes numerous biographical entries; in Hungarian.

10355   TEICHMAN, JOSEF, 1896-1958.
             Divadelni slovník. Činohra. Praha, Orbis, 1949. 343 p.
         Dictionary of the theater: drama. Includes bio-bibliographies.

10356   THOMSON, DAVID, 1941-
             A biographical dictionary of film. New York, Morrow,
         1976. ix, 629 p. 24cm. British ed. published in 1975 under
         title: A biographical dictionary of the cinema (London, Secker
         & Warburg).

10357   TRUITT, EVELYN MACK, 1931-
             Who was who on screen. New York, R. R. Bowker, 1974.
         vii, 363 p. 29cm. 6,000 screen personalities covered, pri-
         marily American, English and French, who died between the
         years 1920 and 1971. The biographical facts are, however,
         very brief in most cases.

10358   TURCONI, DAVIDE, 1911-
             Le vite e i film; biografie e autobiografie della gente del
         cinema. A cura di Davide Turconi e Camillo Bassotto. Introd.
         di Luigi Chiarini. Venezia, Edizioni Mostra Cinema, 1966.
         315 p. illus., ports. A bio-bibliography of moving-pictures;
         actors, directors, etc.

10359   WALDEKRANZ, RUNE
             Filmen växer upp. Stockholm, Geber, 1941. 411 p. illus.,
         ports. 8.º This work on motion pictures includes a section
         called "Filmgalleri" (p. 301-392) which contains biographical

sketches of persons involved in the movie scene, especially ca.
1940.

10360   WILSON, GEORGE BUCKLER LAIRD
        A dictionary of ballet. 3d ed. New York, Theatre Arts
Books, 1974. xi, 539 p. 21cm. 1st ed., 1957; 2d (completely
rev. ed.) 1961. Includes definitions of terms and titles of bal-
lets but is largely a biographical dictionary of dancers, composers, teachers, etc.

10361   YOUNG, WILLIAM C   1928-
        Famous actors and actresses on the American stage. New
York, R. R. Bowker Co., 1975. 2 v. (xxi, 1298 p.) illus.,
ports. 26cm. (Documents of American theatre history) Re-
veals the personal & professional lives of 225 stage immortals
(American, British, etc.) thru' reviews, articles & interviews
of theater writers and critics.

Local

Argentine Republic

10362   FOPPA, TITO LIVIO, 1884-1960.
        Diccionario teatral del Río de la Plata. Buenos Aires,
Argentores, 1961. 1046 p. 25cm. Theatrical dictionary of the
Río de la Plata region (Argentine Republic and Uruguay) Part
1 (p. [43]-764) is a biographical dictionary of Argentine and
Uruguayan theatrical personages.

Armenia

10363   PĒSHIKT'ASHLIAN, NSHAN, 1898.
        T'aterakan dēmk'er. [Antilias, 1969] 1140 p. illus.,
ports. 25cm. (Gēorg Melitinets'i Grakan Mrts'anak. Hrata-
rakowt'iwn, t'iw 4) Personalities of the Armenian theater: in
chronological order.

Asia

10364   ASIAN FILM DIRECTORY AND WHO'S WHO. 1952-
        New Delhi.   v. illus. 26cm. The who's who section
focuses largely on Indian film luminaries.

Australia

10365   PORTER, HAL
        Stars of Australian stage and screen. Adelaide, Rigby Ltd.
[1965] 304 p. illus., ports. 23cm. Not a biographical diction-

ary nor a reasonable facsimile thereof, but a chronologically arranged series of biographical sketches, several to a chapter,
with a total of ca. 100 lives, some fairly lengthy. A name index
affords an alphabetical approach. Unfortunately it lists every
name in the text, biography or no, and one had best look for the
number and successive length of page references to determine
whether the person has received a biographical sketch.

Austria

10366   50 [i.e. FÜNFZIG] JAHRE HOFTHEATER. Geschichte der
         beiden Wiener Hoftheater unter der Regierungszeit des
Kaisers Franz Joseph I, von Rudolph Lothar und Julius Stern
unter Mitwirkung von Hermann Bahr [et al.] Neue verm. Aufl.
Wien, Schallehn & Wollbrück, 1900. 2 v. illus., ports. folio.
Illustrated by Alexander Duschnitz. 50 years of the Hoftheater
(now Burgtheater) of Vienna, at one time split into 2 theaters (1)
the Hofburgtheater (2) the Hof-Operntheater. Included in the
text are ca. 100 biographies of actors, directors, etc. and hun-
dreds of portraits.

10367   GESEK, LUDWIG
         Kleines Lexikon des österreichischen Films. [Wien] Öster-
reichischer Bundesverlag in Kommission [1959] 71 p. illus. 8.º
(Filmkunst, 1959, Nr. 22/30) Little dictionary of the Austrian
cinema; includes biographical data.

10368   HAFENRICHTER, WILHELM
         77 [i.e. Siebenundsiebzig] Portratskizzen der Mitglieder
des Burgtheaters. Wien, 1935. 1 v. (chiefly ports.) 77 portraits of persons involved with the activities of Vienna's Burgtheater.

10369   LOTHAR, RUDOLPH, 1865-
         Das Wiener Burgtheater. Leipzig, E. A. Seemann, 1899.
212 p. illus., ports. 26cm. (Dichter und Darsteller, 2) A
history of Vienna's Burgtheater, valuable because of its over
200 portraits of actors, directors, etc. who worked at the theater. There is biographical material in the text, the index includes personal dates and heavy printed page numbers indicating
location of the various portraits.

Brazil

10370   COSTA, MARCELO FARIAS, 1948-
         História do teatro cearense. Fortaleza, Imprensa Univer-
sitaria da Universidade Federal do Ceará, 1972. 286 p. illus.
22cm. History of the theater in the State of Ceará, Brazil.
"Quem é quem no teatro cearense" (Who's who in the theater of
Ceará): p. 229-284—155 biographical sketches of actors, directors, etc. in several alphabets.

10371   GONÇALVES, AUGUSTO DE FREITAS LOPES, 1896-1968.
         Dicionário histórico e literário do teatro do Brasil. Rio
         de Janeiro, Livraria Editora Cátedra, 1975-   v. port.
         23cm. Contents: v. 1. Letra A.
         Historical and literary dictionary of theater in Brazil; biographi-
         cal entries are included, although the data under personal names
         is often very minimal.

Canada

10372   BEATTIE, ELEANOR GALE, 1937-
         A handbook of Canadian film. Toronto, P. Martin Asso-
         ciates, 1973. vii, 280 p. illus. 20cm. (Take one film book
         series, 2) "Filmmakers" (p. 20-167) is an alphabetical listing
         containing short biographies, filmographies and bibliographies.
         The book contains other short biographies of persons active in
         Canadian filmmaking, but in no particular order other than a
         topical one.

10373   LE DICTIONNAIRE DE NOS VEDETTES DE T.V., RADIO,
             THÉÂTRE, CABARET, MUSIC-HALL ET CINÉMA.
         1958-59—1960-61. Montréal, Janin Productions, 1958-59.
         2 v. No more published? A dictionary of French-Canadian stars
         of TV, radio, theater, the night club scene, music-halls and
         movies.

10374   PONTAUT, ALAIN, 1925-
         Dictionnaire critique du théâtre québécois. [Montréal]
         Leméac [1972] 161 p. 21cm. (Collection Documents) Bio-
         bibliographical dictionary of the principal dramatists of the
         Quebec theater.

Czechoslovakia

10375   DEWEY, LANGDON
         Outline of Czechoslovakian cinema. London, Informatics,
         1971. 122 p. illus., ports. 14 x 22cm. (Informatics' original
         paperbacks on the cinema) This work is in large part 'bio-bib-
         liographical,' i.e. it contains many sketches of the careers and
         work of Czech motion picture figures. Chronologically arranged,
         the biographies are best approached thru' index (page numbers
         in heavy type indicate biographical or background notes on per-
         sons).

Europe, Eastern

10376   HIBBIN, NINA
         Eastern Europe; an illustrated guide. London, A. Zwemmer;
         New York, A. S. Barnes [c1969] 239 p. illus., ports. 21cm.
         (Screen series) 404 post-World War II personalities of East
         European moving-pictures.

France

10377   ANNUAIRE DU SPECTACLE: théâtre, cinéma, musique, radio,
          télévision. 1.- année; 1942/43-   v. illus., ports.
         22-25cm. A directory of the French entertainment business;
         about one-third of each volume contains photographs of chiefly
         French film, theatrical, television and variety performers.
         Title varies: 1942/43-1944, Annuaire général du spectacle in
         France.--1945-   Annuaire du théâtre, musique, radio,
         télévision (varies slightly)

10378   CAMPARDON, ÉMILE, 1837-1915.
             Les Comédiens du roi de la troupe française pendant les
         deux derniers siècles; documents inédits recueillis aux Archives
         nationales. Paris, H. Champion, 1879. xvi, 336 p. 24cm.
         (Société de l'histoire de Paris [et de l'Ile de France] Documents,
         2 [i.e. 4]) The 'Actors of the king': the French theatrical troupe
         during the last two centuries. In part a "biographical diction-
         ary" with brief biographical sketches of French & Italian actors
         followed by documents.

10379   CAMPARDON, ÉMILE, 1837-1915.
             Les Comédiens du roi de la troupe italienne pendant les
         deux derniers siècles; documents inédits recueillis aux ar-
         chives nationales. Paris, Berger-Levrault, 1880. 2 v. 25cm.
         The 'Actors of the King': the Italian theatrical troups during the
         last two centuries; in part a 'biographical dictionary' of Italian
         and French actors in France—brief biographical sketches fol-
         lowed by documents concerning the various individual actors.

10380   CAMPARDON, ÉMILE, 1837-1915.
             Les spectacles de la foire. Théâtres, acteurs, sauteurs,
         et danseurs de corde, monstres, géants ... des foires Saint-
         Germain et Saint-Laurent, des boulevards et du Palais-Royal
         depuis 1595 jusqu'à 1791. Documents inédits recueillis aux Ar-
         chives nationales. [Réimpression de l'édition de Paris, 1877]
         Genève, Slatkine Reprints, 1970. 2 v. in 1. 23cm. Almost en-
         tirely a 'biographical dictionary' of entertainers at carnivals
         and fairs of France from 1595 to 1771.

10381   GALERIE DRAMATIQUE; ou, Acteurs et actrices célèbres qui
             se sont illustrés sur les trois grands théâtres de Paris.
         Ornée de soixante portraits. Paris, Mme. Veuve Hocquart,
         1809. 2 v. col. ports. 14cm. Actors and actresses of the
         Parisian theater at the turn of the 19th century; with 60 colored
         portraits.

10382   GALERIE THÉÂTRALE; collection de 144 portraits en pied des
             principaux acteurs et actrices qui ont illustré la scène
         française depuis 1552 jusqu'à nos jours. Paris [1872]-73. 2 v.

144 ports. folio. Theatrical gallery; a collection of 144 full-length portraits of the principal actors and actresses of the French theater after 1552 to the last quarter of the 19th century.

10383   LE FLÂNEUR, GUILLAUME, pseud.
Petite biographie dramatique, silhouette des acteurs, actrices, chanteurs ... Paris, Lemonnier, 1821. viii, [5]-229 p. 18cm. Attributed by Quérard (Les supercheries littéraires) to A. Vilain de Saint-Hilaire and in La France littéraire to E. Marc de Saint-Hilaire. Biographical sketches of the actors and actresses, singers, etc. of the French stage in the early part of the 19th century.

10384   LÉRIS, ANTOINE DE, 1723-1795.
Dictionnaire portatif historique et littéraire des théâtres, contenant l'origine des différens théâtres de Paris; le nom de toutes les pièces qui y ont été représentées depuis leurs établissement, & celui des pièces jouées en province, ou qui ont simplement paru par la voie de l'impression depuis plus de trois siècles; avec des anecdotes & des remarques sur la plupart: le nom, & les particularités intéressantes de la vie des auteurs, musiciens & acteurs; avec le catalogue de leurs ouvrages, & l'exposé de leurs talens: une chronologie des auteurs, & des musiciens; avec une chronologie de tous les opéra, & des pièces qui ont paru depuis trente-trois ans. Par M. de Léris. 2. éd. rev., corr. & considérablement augm. Paris, C. A. Jombert, 1763. xxxiv, 730 p. 18cm. A dictionary of the theater in France. "Seconde partie, contenant le nom des auteurs, musiciens & acteurs" (p. 495-701) is a biographical dictionary of French dramatists, librettists, musicians and actors of the period. 1st ed. (1754) issued under title: Dictionnaire portatif des théâtres ...

10385   LYONNET, HENRY, 1853-1933.
Dictionnaire des comédiens français (ceux d'hier) Biographie, bibliographie, iconographie. Genève, Slatkine Reprints, 1969. 2 v. illus., ports. 23cm. Reprint of the edition of 1902-08 [or 12?] (Paris, Librairie de l'art du théâtre—issued in 85 parts) Contents.--v. 1. A à D.--v. 2. E à Z. Dictionary of French actors of the late 19th and early 20th century; biography, bibliography, iconography.

10386   MAHALIN, PAUL, 1838-1899.
Les jolies actrices de Paris. Série [1]-5. Paris, Pache & Deffaux [etc.] 1868-89. 5 v. illus., ports. 18cm. Actresses on the Parisian stage in the latter part of the 19th century; biographies and portraits.

10387   MARTIN, JULES, 1860-
Nos artistes; annuaire des théâtres et concerts, 1901-1902. Portraits et biographies, suivis d'une notice sur les droits d'au-

teur, la censure, les associations artistiques, les principaux
théâtres, etc. Préf. par Alfred Capus. Paris, P. Ollendorff,
1901. 410 p. ports. 16cm. French actors, actresses, & musicians flourishing in 1901-1902; a biographical dictionary.

10389   MARTIN, JULES, 1860-
   Nos artistes; portraits et biographies, suivis d'une notice
sur les droits d'auteurs, l'Opéra, la Comédie-Française, les
associations artistiques, etc. Préf. par Aurélien Scholl. Photo-
gravure de H. Reymond. Paris, Librairie de l'Annuaire universel, 1895. 448 p. ports. 13cm. Half-title: Nos artistes des
théâtres & concerts. Advertising matter interspersed. French
actors and actresses of the 19th century; includes portraits and a
biographical dictionary.

10390   MARTIN, MARCEL
   France; [an illustrated guide to 400 key figures in the French
cinema] London, Zwemmer; New York, A. S. Barnes, 1971.
191 p. illus., ports. 21cm. (Screen series) Performers and
directors, past & present.

10391   SIMON, ALFRED
   Dictionnaire du théâtre français contemporain. Paris, Larousse [1970] 255 p. illus. 18cm. (Les Dictionnaires de
l'homme du XXe siècle, D39) A dictionary of the contemporary
French theater, with biographical entries for actors, dramatists, directors, etc.

Germany

10392   DEUTSCHES BÜHNEN-JAHRBUCH; theatergeschichtliches
   Jahr- und Adressenbuch. 1.-   Jahrg.; 1890-   Berlin,
F. A. Günther [etc.]   v. illus., ports. 21-23cm. Title
varies: 1890-1914, Neuer Theater-Almanach. Edited successively by the Genossenschaft Deutscher Bühnen-Angehöriger
(and the Deutscher Bühnen-Verein) and the Fachschaft Bühne in
der Reichstheaterkammer. German theater yearbook; contains
numerous portraits of German theatrical personalities with bio-
bibliographical notices in various listings, some of them arranged in alphabetical order.

10393   FUCHS, GOETZ JOACHIM
   Die Künstler der Deutschen Oper am Rhein; 109 Biographien
(und zwei Nachträge) hrsg. von Goetz-Joachim Fuchs in Zusammenarbeit mit der Generalintendanz der Deutschen Oper am
Rhein. Düsseldorf, Goetz-Joachim Fuchs-Verlag, 1966. 157 p.
ports. 22cm. The artists of the Deutsche Oper am Rhein,
Düsseldorf/Duisburg. 109 biographies. Notices alphabetically
arranged under 8 groupings, representing various aspects of
theatrical activity: directors, scene designers, dancers, singers, etc.

10394   KÜNSTLER ALMANACH; das Handbuch für Bühne, Konzert,
            Film und Funk. 1932. Berlin, Theater und Film Verlags-
        Gesellschaft, 1932. 424 p. ports. 23cm. Edited by Wilhelm
        Ritter. The artists' almanac; handbook for stage, concert,
        film and radio. Includes a dictionary of musicians (German) and
        many portraits.

10395   VIRCHOW, MARTIN
            Die 100 [i. e. Hundert] von Fernsehen; von Peter Alexander
        bis Eduard Zimmermann. Ein Buch z. Nachschlagen. Bergisch
        Gladbach, Lübbe, 1973. 185 p. 100 ports. 23cm. 100 key
        figures in television broadcasting in West Germany; a biographi-
        cal dictionary.

10396   WEINSCHENK, HARRY ERWIN
            Wir von Bühne und Film. Hrsg. von Harry E. Weinschenk.
        [Frankfurt a. M.] Limpert [1941] 383 p. illus. 8.° We of the
        stage and motion pictures; German actors and actresses.

Great Britain

Bibliography, Indexes, Portrait Catalogs

10397   ARNOTT, JAMES FULLARTON
            English theatrical literature, 1559-1900; a bibliography,
        incorporating Robert W. Lowe's A bibliographical account of
        English theatrical literature, published in 1888, by James Ful-
        larton Arnott and John William Robinson. London, Society for
        Theatre Research, 1970. xxii, 486 p. 26cm. "Biography"
        (p. 212-354) is not only a bibliography of English theatrical per-
        sonages, but also, in the section on 'individuals,' serves to
        some extent as a bio-bibliographical dictionary.

General Works

10398   [CROSBY, BENJAMIN]
            Crosby's pocket companion to the playhouses. Being the
        lives of all the principal London performers. To be re-printed
        at the commencement of each winter, with the addition of those
        new performers ... London, Printed for B. Crosby, 1796.
        xi, 105 p. illus. 16cm.

10399   CUMBERLAND'S THEATRICAL ILLUSTRATIONS: consisting of
            portraits of celebrated performers, engraved from original
        drawings by Thomas Wageman; and interesting scenes from the
        most popular acting plays, engraved by G. W. Bonner, from
        drawings taken in the theatre by Robert Cruikshank. London,
        J. Cumberland [1831?] 1 v. (unpaged) illus., ports. 14cm.

Illustrations of Cumberland's British and minor theatre in one volume, published by subscription.

10400   HIGHFILL, PHILIP H
       A biographical dictionary of actors, actresses, musicians, dancers, managers & other stage personnel in London, 1660-1800, by Philip H. Highfill, Jr., Kalman A. Burnim and Edward A. Langhans. Carbondale, Southern Illinois University Press, [1973-   v. illus., ports. 26cm. Contents.--v. 1. Abaco to Belfille.--v. 2. Belfort to Byzand. To be completed in 12 vols.; will include information on more than 8,500 persons who contributed their talents to London theaters, pleasure gardens, opera houses, etc.

10401   REID, ERSKINE
       The dramatic peerage, 1891-[1892] Personal notes and professional sketches of the actors and actresses of the London stage. Compiled by Erskine Reid and Herbert Compton. London, General Pub. Co. [1891-92] 2 v. 17cm. (The "Peerage" series) A biographical dictionary. Vol. 2 (1892) revised and corrected by the profession.

10402   STARS OF THE SCREEN. 1931-1934. London, H. Joseph.
       4 v. ports. 8.⁰ British and American moving-picture actors and actresses in the 1930's. Ceased publication with the 4th vol. (1934) Vols. for 1931 thru' 1933 edited by C. O. Birmingham; 1934 vol. edited by J. S. Ross.

10403   WHO'S WHO IN DANCING, 1932. London, Dancing Times, 1932. 143 p. 8.⁰ No more published? British ballroom dancers, instructors, etc.

10404   WHO'S WHO ON THE SCREEN. London, Amalgamated Press, 1931. 74 p. 8.⁰ No more published in this edition, but see the same title entered under Picture show annual in 1956 (no. 10347). British and American screen personalities of the early talkies.

10405   WHO'S WHO ON THE WIRELESS. 1934-   London, Amalgamated Press [1933-   v. 8.⁰ British radio personalities of the early 1930's. 1934 volume only one published?

Hungary

10406   VOGL, FERENC
       Theater in Ungarn, 1945 bis 1965. Unter Mitarbeit von Peter Brochow. Köln, Verlag Wissenschaft und Politik [1966] 198 p. 22cm. Biographical dictionary of Hungarian actors and authors active 1945 to 1965: p. 169-189 (ca. 96 notices).

India

10407   PARICAYAM; Keralettile ralakaranmarude lagujivacaritra
         kuruppu. Trichur, Kerala Sangeetha Nataka Akademy
         [1967] 209 p. ports. 22cm. In Malayalam. Who's who of mu-
         sical and theatrical performers of Kerala, India.

10408   SHYAMLAL
         Kalākāra sangama. Mathura, Hindi Seva Sadan, 1968.
         194 p. 19cm. Biographical sketches of India's film artists
         and articles on the film industry in India. In Hindi.

Israel

10409   IGUD HA-OMANIM.
         Omane bamah be-Yisrael. [Tel-Aviv] 1970. vi, 326, vi p.
         ports. 28cm. Added t. p.: Israel actors' guide [by] the Actors'
         Union. In Hebrew and English. A directory of Israeli actors;
         no birth dates or educational information, but a portrait of each
         actor is included as well as some career information.

Italy

10410   LEONELLI, NARDO
         Attori tragici, attori comici. Con pref. di Renato Simoni.
         Milano, E. B. B. I., Istituto editoriale italiano B. C. Tosi
         [1940-44] 2 v. illus., ports. 28cm. (Enciclopedia biografica
         e bibliografica 'Italiana,' ser. 9) A biographical dictionary of
         Italian tragic and comic actors.

10411   RONDOLINO, GIANNI
         Dizionario del cinema italiano 1945-1969. Torino, G.
         Einaudi, 1969. 417 p. 18cm. (Piccola biblioteca Einaudi, 128)
         A biographical dictionary of the Italian cinema, 1945-1969.

Japan

10412   SVENSSON, ARNE
         Japan. London, A. Zwemmer; New York, A. S. Barnes
         [1971] 189 p. illus., ports. 21cm. (Screen series) "Main
         entries" (p. 9-118) is a dictionary that includes entries for
         major films, directors, actors, etc. of the Japanese motion
         picture industry.

Mexico

10413   ENCICLOPEDIA CINEMATOGRÁFICA MEXICANA, 1897-1955.
         [Editores: Ricardo Rangel y Rafael E. Portas] México,
         Publicaciones Cinematográficas, 1957. 1322 p. ports. 22cm.

An encyclopedia of Mexican motion picture activities including
biographies of actors, etc.

Peru

10414   MONCLOA Y COVARRUBIAS, MANUEL
Diccionario teatral del Perú. Indice de artistas nacionales
y extranjero, autores y sus obras, escenógrafos, empresarios,
tecnicismo, fraseologia, teatros del Perú, apuntes históricos,
anecdotas, etc., etc. Lima, Badiola y Berrio, 1905. 198 p.
plates, ports. 22cm. At head of title: Manuel Moncloa y Covarrubias (Cloamón) Dictionary of the Peruvian theater; an index
of Peruvian and alien theatrical figures, dramatists, empresarios, phraseology, etc.

Philippine Islands

10415   SALUMBIDES, VICENTE
Motion pictures in the Philippines. [Manila?] 1952. 3 pts.
in 1 v. illus., ports. 24cm. Included in this volume are over
120 portraits and biographical sketches of Filipino motion picture actors, actresses, directors, exhibitors, etc. However,
the work lacks an index, so approach must be made thru' topical
chapters: "Acting and the stars" (for actors), etc.

Poland

10416   JANICKI, STANISŁAW, writer on moving-picture industry.
Film polski od A do Z. Słowniczek biofilmograficzny,
realizatorzy i aktorzy, oprac. Irena Nowak-Zaorska. Bibliografia oprac.: Elzibieta Moszoro, Alicja Debowska, Ilona
Szuster. [Wyd. 2., propawione i uzup.] Warszawa, Wydawnictwa Artystyczne i Filmowe, 1973. 299 p. illus., ports.
22cm. The Polish film from A to Z. The biographical dictionary is on pages 181-[264] and includes actors, directors, etc.

10417   SŁOWNIK BIOGRAFICZNY TEATRU POLSKIEGO, 1765-1965.
[Na podstawie materiałow Stanisława Dabrowskiego opracowała redakcja w składzie: Zbigniew Raszewski (redaktor
naczelny) [et al.] Warszawa, Państwowe Wydawn. Naukowe,
1973. xvi, 905 p. illus., ports. 25cm. At head of title: Polska Akademia Nauk. Instytut Sztuki. Biographical dictionary of
the Polish theater, 1765-1965. Contains 6,298 biographies of
actors, dancers, singers, stage directors, dramatists, etc.

Roman Empire

10418   GARTON, CHARLES
Personal aspects of the Roman theatre. Toronto, Hakkert,
1972. xv, 338 p. illus. 23cm. "A register of Republican

actors": p. [231]-265. "A register of Augustan actors": p.
[267]-283. The two registers contain 204 entries (in alphabetical arrangement) and yield biographical data, whenever available; included are a number of entries labeled "anonymous."

Russia

10419   AKTERY SOVETSKOGO KINO. 1-   Moskva, Iskusstvo,
         1964-   v. illus., ports. 22cm. Actors and ac-
         tresses of the Soviet cinema. Each vol. contains 19 to 23 biog-
         raphies and critical assessments. Eight vols. were issued as
         of 1972.

10420   DEGEN, ARSEN BORISOVICH
         Mastera tantsa. Materialy k istorii leningradskogo baleta,
         1917-1973. [Slovar'-spravochnik. Leningrad] "Muzyka," Len-
         ingradskoe otd-nie, 1974. 248 p. illus. 17cm. At head of
         title: A. B. Degen, I. V. Stupnikov. Masters of the dance; ma-
         terial for the history of ballet in Leningrad, 1917-1973; a diction-
         ary-handbook of dancers, choreographers, ballet-masters, etc.

Slovenia

10421   SLOVENSKI GLEDALIŠKI LEKSIKON. Uredil [in] "Uvodna
         beseda" [napisal] Smiljan Samec. Ljubljana, Mestno
         gledališče, 1972. 3 v. (866 p.) 16cm. (Knjižnica Mestnega
         gledališča ljubljanskega, 56-58) A dictionary of the Slovenian
         theater and its prominent figures.

10422   SMOLEJ, VIKTOR
         Slovenski dramski leksikon. Ljubljana, 1961-62. 2 v.
         ports. 17cm. (Knjižnica Mestnega gledališča, zv. 16, 20)
         "Dodatek k I. zv.": v. 2, p. 223-234. Contents: 1. A-L.--2.
         M-Z. A dictionary of the Slovenian theater; biography of theat-
         rical personalities and dramatists.

Sweden

10423   WINQUIST, SVEN G   1924-
         Svenskt filmskådespelarlexikon. 5000 svenska skådespelare
         i svenska och utländska filmer. 500 utländska skådespelare i
         svenska filmer. [Av] Sven G. Winquist [och] Torsten Jungstedt.
         Stockholm, Forum, 1973. 946 p. illus. 21 x 22cm. (Svenska
         filminstitute. Skrifter från dokumentationsavdelningen, nr. 15)
         A dictionary of Swedish film actors and actresses; 5,000 Swedish
         actors in Swedish and foreign films and 500 foreign actors in
         Swedish films. More of a filmography than a biographical dic-
         tionary, but most useful for the many portraits included.

United States

10424   BILLINGS, PAT
        Hollywood today, by Pat Billings and Allen Eyles. London,
Zwemmer; New York, A. S. Barnes, 1971. 192 p. ports. 16cm.
(The International film guide series) A biographical dictionary
of the active film colony of Hollywood (372 biographies).

10425   CAMERON, IAN ALEXANDER, 1937-
        Dames, by Ian & Elisabeth Cameron. New York, Praeger,
1969. 144 p. illus., ports. 18cm. London ed. (Studio Vista)
has title: Broads. Portraits and biographical sketches of 72
Hollywood actresses of the last 25 years who specialized in
'heavy' roles: gangsters' molls, 'tarts,' etc.: biographical dictionary format.

10425a   CAMERON, IAN ALEXANDER, 1937-
        The heavies [by] Ian & Elisabeth Cameron. [New York]
Praeger [1969, c1967] 143 p. illus., ports. 17cm. (Praeger
film library) Books that matter. A biographical dictionary of
84 motion picture actors (chiefly American) who specialize in
the portrayal of villians.

10426   CLAPP, JOHN BOUVÉ
        Players of the present, by John Bouvé Clapp and Edwin
Francis Edgett. New York, Dunlap Society, 1899-1901. 3 v. in
1 (405 p.) ports. 24cm. (Dunlap Society. Publications, new
ser., no. 9, 11, 13) Biographical dictionary of American actors
and actresses (19th century).

10427   CORNEAU, ERNEST N
        The Hall of Fame of western movie stars. North Quincy,
Mass., Christopher Pub. House [1969] 307 p. illus. 27cm.
Nearly 150 American actors and actresses who were featured in
western films.

10428   GALLERY OF PLAYS AND PLAYERS FROM THE ILLUSTRA-
        TED AMERICAN. no. 1-10; 1894-95. New York. 10 nos.
illus., ports. 32cm. The first 10 numbers contain portraits
and biographies of 220 actors and actresses (chiefly American)
active during the last decade of the 19th century. Title varies:
nos. 1-9, Gallery of players.

10429   HOLLYWOOD GLAMOR PORTRAITS; 145 portraits of stars,
        1926-1949. Edited by John Kobal. New York, Dover Pub-
lications, 1976. xiv, 144 p. ports. 29cm.

10430   LAHUE, KALTON C
Gentlemen to the rescue; the heroes of the silent screen.
South Brunswick, N. J., A. S. Barnes [1972] 244 p. illus.,
ports. 26cm. A biographical dictionary of 30 motion picture
actors who starred in American silent films.

10431   HOLLYWOOD ALBUM; the wonderful city and its famous inhabitants. 1st-   London, S. Low, Marston, 1941-
v. illus., ports. 28cm. Editor: 1st-   Ivy Crane Wilson.
Includes many portraits and biographical sketches of Hollywood
stars of the early 1940's. 1947 vol. last one published?

10432   McCLURE, ARTHUR F
Heroes, heavies and sagebrush; a pictorial history of the
"B" western players, by Arthur F. McClure and Ken D. Jones.
South Brunswick, N. J., A. S. Barnes, 1972. 350 p. illus.,
ports. 29cm. With numerous portraits and biographical data
for actors in Hollywood "B" western films.

10433   PARISH, JAMES ROBERT
Hollywood players: the Forties, by James Robert Parish
and Lennard DeCarl, with William T. Leonard and Gregory W.
Mank. Introd. by Jack Ano. Editor, T. Allan Taylor. Research associates, John Robert Cocchi and Florence Solomon.
New Rochelle, N. Y., Arlington House Publishers, 1976. 544 p.
illus., ports. 29cm. 85 Hollywood actors and actresses of the
1940's; arranged in biographical dictionary format.

10435   SPRINGER, JOHN SHIPMAN, 1916-
They had faces then; [Annabella to Zorina] Superstars,
stars and starlets of the 1930's, by John Springer and Jack
Hamilton. 1st ed. Secaucus, N. J., Citadel Press, 1974.
342 p. illus., ports. 32cm. 900 photographs of movie actresses from the Hollywood of the Thirties accompany this biographical dictionary.

10436   TAYLOR, JOHN RUSSELL
The Hollywood musical [by] John Russell Taylor [and] Arthur Jackson. New York, McGraw-Hill Book Co. [1971] 278 p.
illus., ports. 25cm. Includes a biographical [dictionary] "index of names" [of actors, directors, etc. of musicals]: p. 157-
234.

10437   WHO'S WHO IN THE FILM WORLD. Edited and compiled by
Fred C. Justice and Tom R. Smith. Los Angeles, Film
World Pub. Co., 1914. 230 p. ports. Actors, directors, etc.
of the American silent screen.

Yugoslavia

10437a NARODNO POZORIŠTE SARAJEVO.
Narodno pozorište Sarajevo 1921-1971. Glavni red urednik:
Lěsić Josip. [Saradnici: Besarović Risto [i dr. Vlajko Ubavič:
Uvod] Urednik fotografije: Gaković Mirjana. Sarajevo, Narodno
pozorište [1972] xi, 599 p. illus., ports. 25cm. A dictionary
of performances, performers, etc. (Yugoslav & foreign) at the
National Theater in Sarajevo. The biographical sketches are a
large proportion of the volume.

Music

Bibliography, Indexes, Portrait Catalogs

10438 BULL, STORM
Index to biographies of contemporary composers. New
York, Metuchen, N. J., Scarecrow Press, 1964-74. 2 v. 22cm.
Vol. 1: 5,800 composers listed & more than 60 books indexed.
Vol. 2: 8,000 composers listed (4,000 of them were in v. 1) and
more than 100 works are indexed.

10439 DRUGULIN, W., LEIPZIG.
Verzeichniss von Portraits zur Geschichte des Theaters
und der Musik, welche zu den beigesetzten Preisen von dem
Leipziger Kunst-Comptoir (W. Drugulin) zu beziehen sind.
Walluf bei Wiesbaden, M. Sändig, 1973. 210 p. 21cm. Reprint
of the 1864 ed. published by Kunst-Comptoir, Leipzig. A sales
catalog of portraits of musicians and actors; useful as a bibliography of portraits.

10440 HIXON, DONALD L
Women in music; a biobibliography, by Don L. Hixon and
Don Hennessee. Metuchen, N. J., Scarecrow Press, 1975.
xiii, 358 p. 23cm. An index to biographies of women musicians
in 45 music dictionaries and encyclopedias. Classical music
only is cited; each entry gives name, birth and death places and
dates, very brief identification, and a list of sources containing
biographical data. Includes musicians, choreographers, dancers,
singers and instrumentalists.

10441 SCHAAL, RICHARD
Musiker-Monogramme; ein Verzeichnis. Mit einem Quel-
len-Anhang, Kataloge und Literatur. Wilhelmshaven, Heinrichshofen's Verlag [1976] 122 p. 18cm. (Taschenbücher zur
Musikwissenschaft, 27) Identifies monograms used by musicians
from the 15th to the middle of the 19th century. The major part
of the book consists of two lists: (1) the monograms with user in
opposite column, (2) the musicians, with their birth-death dates,
and monograms they used in opposite column.

10442   SCHAAL RICHARD
         Die Tonkünstler-Porträts der Wiener Musiksammlung von
Aloys Fuchs. Unter Benutzung der Originalkataloge bearb. von
Richard Schaal. Mit einem Anhang von 178 Abbildungen. Wilhelmshaven, Heinrichshofen's Verlag [1970] 126 p. (p. 65-126
ports.) 30cm. (Quellen-Kataloge zur Musikgeschichte, 3) A
catalog (with birth/death dates & descriptive ephthets) of portraits of musicians in the collection of Aloys Fuchs (1799-1853);
also included are 178 portraits from the collection (p. 65-126).

General Works

10443   ALBUM [of photographs of musicians, chiefly women. n. p.,
         1867?] 1 v. (unpaged) 89 ports. 24 x 16cm. 89 portraits
of 19th century performing musicians, chiefly women—singers,
etc. The album is in the Boston Public Library.

10444   ALTMANN, WILHELM, 1862-1951.
         Kurzgefasstes Tonkünstler-Lexikon für Musiker und
Freunde der Musik, begründet von Paul Frank, neu bearb. und
erg. von Wilhelm Altmann, mit einem Vorwort von Helmut
Roesner. 15. Aufl. Wilhelmshaven. Heinrichshofen's Verlag,
c1971-   v. 26cm. First-11th ed. entered under: Merseburger, Carl Wilhelm, 1816-1885. Kleines Tonkünstlerlexikon,
enthaltend kurze Biographien der Tonkünstler früherer und
neuerer Zeit. Part 1 is a reprint of the 14th ed. published in
Ratisbon by G. Bosse, 1936. Pt. 2 (1974): Ergänzungen und
Erweiterungen seit 1937. Bd. 1: A-K. A dictionary of musicians.

10445   AMMER, CHRISTINE
         Harper's dictionary of music. Drawings by Carmela M.
Ciampa & Kenneth L. Donlon. New York, Harper, 1972.
414 p. illus. 24cm. Includes biographical entries for major
musical figures; seems designed primarily for young people.

10446   AUERBACH, ERICH
         An eye for music. Introd. by Lord Goodman. London, R.
Hart-Davis, 1971. 248 p. (chiefly illus., ports.) 31cm. Contains ca. 200 portraits (photographs) of contemporary musicians and a few other celebrities. Alphabetical index at front
of volume.

10447   BERGL, M
         ABC skladatelů, textařů, interpretů, publicistů. Praha,
Státní hud. vydav., 1962. 38 p. Supplement to the collection:
Taneční hudba a jazz, 1962. An ABC (dictionary) of modern
composers, musical interpreters, publicists and librettists.

10448   BETTOLI, PARMENIO, 1835-1907.
         I nostri fasti musicali: dizionario biografico. Parma, Tip.

Gazzetta di Parma, 1875. 228 p. 16.⁰ Our musical records; a biographical dictionary of famous musicians.

10449   BLOM, ERIC, 1888-1959.
         Everyman's dictionary of music. 5th ed., rev. by Sir Jack Westrup, with the collaboration of [others] London, Dent, 1971. xiii, 793 p. music. 20cm. (Everyman's reference library) Includes biographical sketches, especially of many composers of secondary interest. First issued in 1946 (?)

10450   BOHLÄNDER, CARLO, 1919-
         Reclams Jazzführer. Von Carlo Bohländer und Karl Heinz Holler. Stuttgart, Reclam, 1970. 991 p. illus. 16cm. (Universal-Bibliothek, Nr. 10185-10186) Primarily a bio-bibliographical dictionary of jazz musicians.

10451   ČERNY, ARNOŠT J,
         Kapesní hudební slovník. 2 vyd. Třebíč, J. Lorenz, 1914. 201, xxi p. A pocket music dictionary; includes brief biographical entries. In Czech.

10452   COOPER, MARTIN, 1910-
         The concise encyclopedia of music and musicians. Edited by Martin Cooper. 2d ed., rev. London, Hutchinson, 1972. xix, 481 p. illus. 23cm. First edition appeared in 1958.

10453   DAVALILLO, MARÍA
         Músicos célebres; 99 biografías cortas [por] M. Davalillo. Dibujos de J. Vinyals y E. C. Ricart. 8. ed. Barcelona, Editorial Juventud, 1973. 240 p. illus., ports. 22cm. (Colección Grandes biografías) On spine: 99 [i.e. Noventa y nueve] biografías de músicos célebres. Brief biographies of 99 famous musicians (composers). In biographical dictionary arrangement.

10454   DICTIONARY OF CONTEMPORARY MUSIC. John Vinton,
         editor. New York, E. P. Dutton, 1974. xiv, 834 p. 25cm. Includes over a thousand articles on countries, composers and technical and interdisciplinary subjects.

10455   DICTIONNAIRE DE LA MUSIQUE. Publié sous la direction de
         Marc Honneger. Paris, Bordas, 1970-   v. illus., ports. 25cm. Contents.--1-2. Les hommes et leurs oeuvres. A dictionary of music. Vols. 1-2 are a biographical dictionary of musicians.

10456   ENCICLOPEDIA DE LA MÚSICA POP, 1900-1973. Dirigida
         por José María Iñigo & Jesús Torbado. Madrid, Akal,

c1973. 1 v. (unpaged) illus. 27cm. Cover title: Gran enciclopedia de la música pop, 1900-1973. Encyclopedia of pop music,
1900-1973; a bio-bibliography.

10457   ENCICLOPEDIA GARZANTI DELLA MUSICA. 1. ed. Milano,
            Redazioni Garzanti, 1974. 808 p. illus., ports. 18cm.
        Cover title: Enciclopedia della musica Garzanti. A dictionary
        of music and musical bio-bibliography.

10458   EWEN, DAVID, 1907-
            Composers since 1900; a biographical and critical guide.
        New York, H. W. Wilson Co., 1969. 639 p. ports. 27cm.
        This volume replaces: Composers of today, American compos-
        ers today, and European composers today, originally published
        in 1934, 1949, and 1954, respectively. A biographical dictionary
        of 20th century composers.

10459   EWEN, DAVID, 1907-
            The new encyclopedia of the opera. New York, Hill and
        Wang, 1971. viii, 759 p. 24cm. Previous editions have title:
        Encyclopedia of the opera. Includes biographies of composers,
        librettists, singers, conductors, impresarios, state directors,
        critics, teachers and musicologists in its alphabetical arrange-
        ment.

10460   FISHER, RENEE B
            Musical prodigies; masters at an early age. New York,
        Association Press [1973] 240 p. illus., ports. 23cm. A series
        of biographical sketches within such chapter headings as: The
        prodigy composers, The violin prodigies, The piano prodigies,
        etc. "Supplement: Other musical prodigies" (p. 195-231) lists
        and sometimes gives biographical data, beyond dates, for those
        not expanded upon in the main text. Although not a biographical
        dictionary, the work is useful to anyone who might be interested
        in what or who consitutes a musical 'prodigy.' The "Index of
        names" (p. [237]-240) lists over 400 persons mentioned in main
        text and supplement.

10461   FITZPATRICK, HORACE
            The horn and horn-playing and the Austro-Bohemian tradi-
        tion from 1680 to 1830. London, New York, Oxford University
        Press, 1970. xiii, 256 p. illus. 26cm. Includes two biogra-
        phical sections: Register of players, pt. 1: First and second
        generations, 1680-1760 (p. [90]-124) and pt. 2: Third and fourth
        generations, 1750-1830 (p. [195]-216) The biographical sketches
        are, for the most part, quite brief, and in chronological ar-
        rangement within each part.

10462   GATHY, AUGUST, 1800-1858.
            Musikalisches Conversations-Lexikon; Encyklopädie der

gesamten Musik-Wissenschaft für Künstler, Kunstfreunde und
Gebildete. Redigirt von A. Gathy unter Mitwirkung von J.
Schmidt [et al.] 2. verm. und verb. Aufl. Hamburg, G. W.
Niemeyer, 1840. 528, xii p. , 24 p. of music. 22cm. A dic-
tionary of music: terms and biographical sketches.

10463   GEALY, FRED D
          Companion to the Hymnal; a handbook to the 1964 Methodist
        Hymnal. Texts: Fred D. Gealy. Tunes: Austin C. Lovelace.
        Biographies: Carlton R. Young. General editor: Emory Stevens
        Bucke. Nashville, Abingdon Press [1970] 766 p. 22cm. "Part
        III: Biographies" (p. [467]-720) includes brief biographies of
        composers, arrangers, authors and translators of hymns includ-
        ed in the Methodist Hymnal.

10464   GOODENOUGH, CAROLINE LOUISA (LEONARD) 1856-
          High lights on hymnists and their hymns. New York, AMS
        Press [1974] 505 p. 22cm. Reprint of the 1931 ed. (Rochester,
        Mass.) A repository of biographical material about several
        hundred hymn-writers, with emphasis on British and Americans.
        Semi-chronological arrangement with an alphabetical name index.

10465   GRISCHOW, JOHANN HEINRICH, 1685-1754.
          Kurzgefasste Nachricht von ältern und neuern Liederver-
        fassern. Anfangs von Johann Heinrich Grischow im Druck
        ertheilet, nunmehro aber verb. und vermehrter hrsg. von Jo-
        hann Georg Kirchner. Halle, Im Verlag des Waisenhauses,
        1771. [10] l., 56, [50] p. 19cm. First ed., "Verzeichniss der
        bekannt gewordenen Verfasser derer Lieder, so in den beyden
        Theilen des Freilinghausischen Gesangbuchs in länglich 12mo
        befindlich," printed in 1753 for private circulation only, without
        t. p. or preface. Brief notices on 279 hymn-writers.

10466   HATFIELD, EDWIN FRANCIS, 1807-1883.
          The poets of the church; a series of biographical sketches of
        hymn-writers, with notes on their hymns. Boston, Milford
        House [1972] vii, 719 p. 22cm. Reprint of the 1884 ed. A bio-
        bibliographical dictionary of hymn writers of all periods (but
        chiefly British Protestants).

10467   HEMEL, VICTOR VAN
          De viool, geschiedenis, bouw, vervaardigers, componisten,
        virtuozen, methodes e. a. 2. bijewerkte druk. Antwerpen,
        Cupido [1955] 96 p. illus. 21cm. The violin, its history, con-
        struction, makers, composers, virtuosos, methods, etc. In-
        cludes ca. 190 brief biographical sketches (chronologically ar-
        ranged under country of origin, lists, etc., with an alphabetical
        name index at end).

10468   HEMMING, ROY
          Discovering music; where to start on records and tapes,

the great composers and their works, today's major recording artists. New York, Four Winds Press, 1974. xiii, 379 p. ports. 25cm. "Part three: Major music-makers on discs and tapes" (p. [271]-355) is a bio-bibliographical dictionary (with recommended recordings) of major recording artists of the 20th century (most of them living).

10469 HERIOT, ANGUS, 1927-
        The castrati in opera. New York, Da Capo Press, 1974. 243 p. ports. 23cm. (Da Capo music reprint series) Reprint of the 1956 ed. (London, Secker & Warburg). "Careers of some well-known castrati" (p. [84]-199) comprises a biographical dictionary of 32 castrati (Annibali to Velluti).

10470 HUNGÁRIA ZENEI LEXIKON. Szer.: Lányi Viktor. Budapest, Hungária, 1945. 911 p. Hungarian musical encyclopedia; with biographies of European and Hungarian musicians. Appendix: 1. Európa zeneje.--2. A magyar zene.

10471 JACOBS, ARTHUR
        A new dictionary of music. 3d ed. [Harmondsworth, Eng.] Penguin Books [1973] 425 p. music. 18cm. (A Penguin reference book) With many bio-bibliographical entries for musicians. 2d ed. issued in 1962.

10472 EIN JAHRTAUSEND LATEINISCHER HYMNENDICHTUNG.
        Eine Blutenlese aus den Analecta hymnica mit literar-historischen Erläuterungen von Guido Maria Dreves. Nach des Verfassers Ableben revidiert von Clemens Blume. Bologna, Forni, 1969. 2 v. 21cm. (Bibliotheca musica Bononiensis. Sezione 6, n. 10) Reproduction of the 1909 (Leipzig) edition. A millenium of Latin hymnology; a collection of Latin hymns (without music) with analyses and, in vol. 1, a chronologically arranged listing of hymn writers from Ambrose, Bp. of Milan (d. 397) to Johannes Mauburnus, Abbot of Livry (d. 1503) with examples of their hymns and biographical and bibliographical sketches (109 hymn writers in all).

10473 KARP, THEODORE
        Dictionary of music. [New York, Dell Pub. Co., 1973] 448 p. music. 18cm. Includes biographies of composers.

10474 KINSKY, GEORGE, 1882-1951.
        Album musical. Publié par George Kinsky avec la collaboration de Robert Haas, Hans Schnoor, Henry Prunières et de plusieurs musicologues français et étrangers. Iconographie contenant 1560 reproductions de portraits, autographes, instruments. scènes, exemples musicaux, ets., se rapportant aux grands musiciens et à la musique de tous le temps et tous les pays. Paris, Librairie Delagrave, 1930. vii, 364 p. illus.,

ports. 32cm. A musical iconography useful for its many portraits of musicians, which include legends giving dates and
some biographical data. The index to names of persons yields
an alphabetical approach. Translated into English under title:
A history of music in pictures (q. v.).

10475   KUTSCH, K   J
        Unvergängliche Stimmen; Sängerlexikon [von] K. J. Kutsch
        [und] Leo Riemens. Bern, München, Francke Verlag, 1975.
        731 p. 22cm. A biographical dictionary of singers, past and
        present.

10476   LONGSTREET, STEPHEN, 1907-
        Knaurs Jazzlexikon [von] Stephen Longstreet [und] Alfons M.
        Dauer. Zeichmungen von Stephen Longstreet. München, Droe-
        mersche Verlagsanstalt [1957] 324 p. illus., ports. 22cm. A
        major part of this dictionary of jazz is devoted to jazz musi-
        cians.

10477   LUEKEN, WILHELM
        Lebensbilder der Liederdichter und Melodien. Unter Benut-
        zung eines Manuskriptes von Otto Michaelis bearb. von Wilhelm
        Lueken. Göttingen, Vandenhoeck & Ruprecht, 1957. 300 p.
        24cm. (Handbuch zum Evangelischen Kirchengesangbuch, Bd. 2,
        1. T.) Biographical sketches of 236 writers and composers of
        German and Latin hymns, in chronological arrangement, with an
        alphabetical name-index at the end of the volume.

10478   MANÉN, JUAN, 1883-1971.
        Diccionario de celebridades musicales. Barcelona, R.
        Sopena [1973] 699 p. illus., ports. 22cm. (Biblioteca Hispa-
        nia) A dictionary of famous musicians; contains 323 biographies.

10479   MOSAIK JAZZLEXIKON. [Hrsg. von] John Jörgensen [und]
        Erik Wiedemann. [Ins Deutsche übertragen und bearb. von
        Hans-Georg Ehmke]   Hamburg, Mosaik Verlag [1966] 399 p.
        22cm. Translation of Jazzens hvem, hvad, hvor—who's who
        in the world of jazz.

10480   LA MUSICA. Sotto la direzione di Guido M. Gatti. A cura di
        Alberto Basso. [Torino] Unione tipografico-editrice tori-
        nese [1966-71] 6 v. illus. 27cm. Contents.--pt. 1. Enciclo-
        pedia storica. 4 v.--pt. 2. Dizionario. 2 v. An encyclopedia
        of music; pt. 2 (in 2 vols.) is a biographical dictionary of the
        world's musicians.

10481   PICKA, FRANTIŠEK, 1873-1918.
        Operní skladatelé a jejich díla. Praha, F. A. Urbánek
        [1910] 32 p. 8.º [Knihovna Smetany, čís. 9) Opera composers
        and their works; brief bio-bibliographical dictionary.

10482   POBLETE VARAS, CARLOS
         Diccionario de la música. Valparaiso, Ediciones Universi-
tarias de Valparaiso, Universidad Católica del Valparaiso, 1972.
376 p. illus. 19cm. A dictionary of musical terminology and
biography.

10483   PÖSSIGER, GUNTER
         Die grossen Sänger und Dirigenten; Kurzbiographien der
bedeutendsten Sänger und der führenden Dirigenten unserer
Zeit mit den wichtigsten persönlichen Daten, Angaben über Aus-
bildung und künstlerische Entwicklung, über Stimmlage, Glanz-
parteien, Opernhäuser und internationale Erfolge. Umfang-
reiche Schallplattenhinweise auf lieferbare historische und moderne Aufnahmen. Originalausgabe. München, W. Heyne, 1968.
220 p. illus., ports. 18cm. (Das Heyne Sachbuch, Nr. 95)
Contents. --Sänger, A-Z (p. 13-146). Dirigenten, A-Z (p. 147-
218) The great singers and conductors of the 20th century; short
biographies.

10484   PORTRAITS OF GREAT COMPOSERS, with biographical
         sketches. Chicago, Hall & McCreary Co. [1936-
v. ports. 24cm. Vol. 2 (in portfolio) by Ned Hadley, with
biographical sketches by W. B. Lindsay.

10485   REIMANN, HUGO, 1849-1919.
         Reimanns Musik Lexikon. Personenteil. 12. völlig neu-
bearb. Aufl. Hrsg. von Willibald Gurlitt. Mainz, B. Schott's
Söhne; New York, Schott Music Corp., 1959-61. 3 v. 27cm.

         ---- ----Ergänzungsband. Personenteil. Hrsg. von Carl Dahl-
haus. Mainz, B. Schott's Söhne; New York, Schott Music Corp.,
1972-75. 2 v. 27cm. Contents. --[1] A-K. --[2] L-Z. A dictionary of musicians.

10486   RORORO MUSIKHANDBUCH. Hrsg. und bearb. von Heinrich
         Lindlar in Zusammenarbeit mit der Fachredaktion Musik
des Bibliographischen Instituts. [Hamburg] Rowohlt [1973, c1971]
c1971] 2 v. (759 p.) illus. 19cm. (Rororo Handbuch 6167-
6168) Originally issued under title: Meyers Handbuch über die
Musik (4. verb. Aufl.) q. v. A dictionary of music. Vol. 2 is
a dictionary of composers and performing musicians (the latter
primarily a listing).

10487   ROSTAND, CLAUDE
         Dictionnaire de la musique contemporaine. Paris, La-
rousse, 1970. 250 p. illus. 18cm. (Les Dictionnaires de
l'homme du XXe siècle, 40) A dictionary of 20th century music
that includes bio-bibliographical entries.

10488   SASKA, ROBERT
         Operní skladetelé. Život a dílo. Brno, O. Pazdírek, 1920.
         80 p. 8.º "Otisk ze "Zpěvoherního repertoiru. "" Opera
         composers; lives and works.

10489   SCHLEMAN, HILTON R
         Rhythm on record; a complete survey and register of all the
         principal recorded dance music from 1906 to 1936, and a who's
         who of the artists concerned in the making. London, Melody
         Maker, 1936. 333 p. , 48 plates. illus.

10490 . SCHOLES, PERCY ALFRED, 1877-1958.
         The concise Oxford dictionary of music. 2d ed. [reprinted
         with corrections] Edited by John Owen Ward. London, New
         York, Oxford University Press, 1973. xxx, 636 p. illus. 20cm.
         Condensation of Scholes' Oxford companion to music, with new-
         ly added biographical entries.

10491   SEEGER, HORST, 1926-
         Kleines Musik Lexikon. [2. Aufl.] Berlin, Henschelverlag
         [1959] 192 p. illus. 21cm. Little music dictionary; bio-bib-
         liographical also.

10492   SIEGMEISTER, ELIE, 1909-
         The new music lover's handbook. Edited by Elie Sieg-
         meister. Irvington-on-Hudson, N. Y. , Harvey House [1973]
         620 p. illus. 29cm. Includes biographical articles on compos-
         ers who flourished from the 17th century to the present day.
         "1st ed. " issued in 1943 under title: The music lover's handbook
         (New York, W. Morrow).

10493   SLAGMOLEN, GERRIT, 1914-1971.
         Muzieklexicon. 3. herz. druk. Utrecht, Bruna [1974]
         2 v. 18cm. (Zwarte beertjes, 1367-1368) A dictionary of music
         and musicians.

10494   SUPPAN, WOLFGANG, 1933-
         Lexikon des Blasmusikwesens. Im Auftrage des Bundes
         Deutscher Blasmusikverbände hrsg. im Zusammenarbeit mit
         Fritz Thelen und Weiteren Fachkollegen von Wolfgang Suppan.
         Freiburg im Breisgau, Blasmusikverlag Fritz Schulz, 1973.
         306 p. illus., ports. 23cm. A dictionary of the wind instru-
         ments. The biographical section of the work (p. [107]-306) lists
         players, composers, etc. of wind instruments.

10495   THOMPSON, KENNETH
         A dictionary of twentieth-century composers (1911-1971)
         London, Faber and Faber [1973] 666 p. 25cm. A bio-biblio-
         graphical dictionary of "thirty-two of the most influential com-
         posers of the century excluding those still living. " From Bartok
         to Webern.

10496   THOMPSON, OSCAR, 1887-1945.
          The international cyclopedia of music and musicians. Edi-
tor in chief: Oscar Thompson. Editor, 5th-8th editions: Nicholas Slonimsky. Editor, 9th ed.: Robert Sabin. Editor, 10th
ed.: Bruce Bohle. New York, Dodd, Mead, 1975. 2511 p.
29cm. 1st ed. issued in 1939; new ed., rev. and enl., 1943;
3d, 1944; 4th, 1946; 5th, 1949; 6th, 1952; 7th, 1956; 8th, 1958.

10497   VAĬNKOP, ĬULĬAN ĬAKOVLEVICH
          Kratkiĭ biograficheskiĭ slovar' kompozitorov; klassiki
russkoĭ i zarubezhnoĭ muzyki, sovetskie i sovremennye zaru-
bezhnye kompozitory. Izd. 2., dop. Leningrad, "Muzyka"
[Leningradskoe otd-nie] 1971. 207 p. 20cm. Biographical dictionary of composers: classical Russian and foreign, Soviet and
contemporary_foreign composers. 1st ed. issued in 1967. At
head of title: ĬU. Vaĭnkop, I. Gusin.

10498   WASSERBERGER, IGOR
          Jazzový slovník. [1. vyd.] Bratislava, Štátne hudobné
vydavatel'stvo, 1966. 350 p. illus., ports. and phonodisc (2 s.
7 in. 45 rpm.) 20cm. (Edície hudobnej literatúry) At head of
title: Igor Wasserberger a kolektív. A dictionary of jazz music
and musicians.

10499   WEISSENBÄCK, ANDREAS, 1880-
          Sacra musica; Lexikon der katholischen Kirchenmusik.
Klosterneuburg bei Wien. Verlag der Augustinus-Druckerei,
1937. viii, 419 p. music. 23cm. A dictionary of Catholic
sacred music, with biographies and technical terms included in
one alphabet.

10500   WILLEMZE, THEO, 1931-
          Spectrum   muzieklexicon. Utrecht, Het Spectrum, 1975.
4 v. (1953 p.) illus. 18cm. A dictionary of music, much of
it biobibliographical.

Musical Instruments Makers

10501   BALZ, HANS MARTIN
          Orgeln und Orgelbauer im Gebiet der ehemaligen hessischen
Provinz Starkenburg; ein Beitrag zur Geschichte des Orgel-
baues. Marburg, 1969. 604 p. 20 plates, fold. map. 21cm.
(Studien zur hessischen Musikgeschichte, Bd. 3) Organs and
organ-builders in the region of the former Hessian province of
Starkenburg. Ca. 110 biographical sketches are included.

10502   BOALCH, DONALD HOWARD
          Makers of the harpsichord and clavichord, 1440-1840. 2d
ed. Oxford, Clarendon Press, 1974. xxi, 225 p. illus. 28cm.

First ed. issued in 1956. This 2d ed. records over 1,200 makers of early keyboard instruments, half as many again as the 1st ed. A biographical dictionary.

10503   BURGEMEISTER, LUDWIG, 1863-1932.
Der Orgelbau in Schlesien. 2., erw. Aufl. bearb. von Hermann J. Busch, Dieter Grossman und Rudolf Walter; mit einem Beitrag über den Orgelbau zwischen den beiden Weltkriegen von Rudolf Walter. Frankfurt a. M., W. Weidlich, 1973. 376 p. illus. 27cm. (Bau- und Kunstdenkmäler des deutschen Ostens. Reihe C: Schlesien, Bd. 5) Organ construction in Silesia. "Verzeichnis der Orgelbauer" (List of organbuilders), p. 122-332, is in alphabetical dictionary format and includes both personal names and firms. Biographical information is generally brief: two to twenty lines.

10504   DOLGE, ALFRED, 1848-
Pianos and their makers: a comprehensive history of the development of the piano from the monochord to the concert grand player piano. New York, Dover Publications, 1972. 478 p. illus., ports. 22cm. (Dover books on music) Reprint of the 1911 ed. (Covina, Calif.) "Part three--Men who have made piano history" (p. [211]-382) includes biographical data for over 150 piano manufacturers (individuals & firms) in narrative form, but an alphabetical approach is available through the "Index of names" at the end of the volume.

10505   FAIRFIELD, JOHN HOUGHTON, 1899-
Known violin makers. [New York, Designed & produced by the Bradford Press, 1942] xiv, 192 p. 24cm. A biographical dictionary in two alphabets: (1) European makers, (2) American makers.

10506   GOŁOS, JERZY
Zarys historii budowy organów w Polsce. Bydgoszcz, 1966. 249 p. 11 plates. 21cm. (Z dziejów muzyki polskiej, 12) At head of title: Bygodskie Towarzystwo Naukowe. Filharmonia Pomorska im. Paderewskiego. With a summary in English. Historical sketch of organ construction in Poland. "Słownik organmistrzów działających w dawnej Polsce" (p. 99-131) is a dictionary of the activity of master organ builders in former times. Not much biographical data is given, but included are references to books and periodicals where more information about these craftsmen is given.

10507   GRÉGOIR, EDOUARD GEORGES JACQUES, 1822-1890.
Historique de la facture et des facteurs d'orgue avec la bibliographie musicale. Avec une introd. et une nomenclature par G. Potvlieghe. Amsterdam, F. Knuf, 1972. [13], 304, 16, [62] p. port. 23cm. (Biblioteca organologica, v. 25) Facsimile of the Anvers, 1865 ed. History of organ manufacture and

organ-makers. Largely a biographical dictionary in several alphabets, e. g.: "Les facteurs d'orgues néerlandais et belges"
(p. [72]-214): "Notices sur les organistes belges et néerlandais"
(p. [215]-254); etc.

10508   GRILLET, LAURENT, 1851-1901.
         Les ancêtres du violon et du violoncelle; les luthiers et les
fabricants d'archets, précédées d'une préf. par Théodore Du-
bois. Paris, C. Schmid, 1901. 2 v. 27cm. Contents. --t. 1.
Histoire des instruments du musique. --t. 2. Histoire ... Suite.
Les luthiers (p. 167-392) L'archet (et les fabricants d'archets):
p. 393-409. Ancestors of the violin & violoncello; v. 2 (in part)
contains biographical sketches of makers of stringed instruments (grouped by nationality & alphabetical thereunder) and
bow-makers. Notices often very, very brief.

10509   HAMMA, FRIDOLIN
         Meister deutscher Geigenbaukunst. 2. erweiterte Aufl.
Stuttgart, Schuler Verlagsgesellschaft, 1961. 71 p. illus.
29cm. 1st ed. issued in 1948. Includes a biographical dictionary of German master violin-makers.

10510   HAMMA, WALTER
         Meister italienischer Geigenbaukunst. [Neue Ausg.] Stutt-
gart, Schuler Verlagsgesellschaft, 1965. 728 p. illus. 28cm.
1st ed. by Fridolin Hamma, issued in 1931. American ed. (New
York, Bärenreiter) issued in 1964 (i.e. 1965). Masters of the
Italian violin-making art.

10511   JACQUOT, ALBERT, 1853-
         La lutherie lorraine et française depuis ses origines jusqu'à
nos jours d'après les archives locales. Préf. de M. J. Mas-
senet. Paris, Fischbacher, 1912. xxix, 357 p. illus., ports.
28cm. Biographical dictionary (in 2 parts) of French stringed-
instrument and bow-makers largely from Lorraine.

10512   JALOVEC, KAREL
         The violin makers of Bohemia, including craftsmen of Mo-
ravia and Slovakia. London, Anglo-Italian Publication ltd.
[1959] 128 p. plates. 31cm. A German version was issued under title: Böhmische Geigenbauer. Biographical dictionary on
p. 25-101.

10513   LANGWILL, LYNDESAY GRAHAM, 1897-
         An index of wind-instrument makers. 4th ed. , rev. & enl.
Edinburg [The author, 1974] xv, 272 p. illus. 26cm. Many of
the entries have biographical data appended. 1st ed.: 1960; 2d
ed.: 1962; 3d ed.: 1972.

10514   VIDAL, ANTOINE, 1820-1891.
        La lutherie et les luthiers. New York, Broude Bros. [1969]
        ii, 347 p. illus. 27cm. Reprint of the Paris 1889 ed. At vari-
        ous points in this history of the violin and its makers there are
        sections which are 'biographical dictionaries' (although many of
        the 'biographies' are only a line or two in length) for particular
        countries, especially Italy, Germany, Great Britain and France.

Local

Africa

10515   HUSKISSON, YVONNE
        The Bantu composers of Southern Africa. Die Bantoe-
        komponiste van Suider-Afrika. [1st ed. Johannesburg, South
        African Broadcasting Corp., 1969] 335 p. illus., ports. 25cm.
        In English and Afrikaans. A bio-bibliographical dictionary.

Armenia

10516   AT'AYAN RHOBERT A
        Armiănskie kompozitory. Erevan, Armiănskoe gosudar-
        stvennoe izd-vo, 1956. 182 p. ports. 20cm. At head of title:
        R. A. Ataĭan, M. O. Muradiăn, A. G. Tatevosiăn. 47 Armen-
        ian composers; in chronological arrangement.

10517   BROWTYAN, TS'ITS'ILIA
        Sp'yowrhk'i hay erazhistnerĕ. Erivan, "Hayastan," 1968.
        623 p. ports. 21cm. Summaries in English and Russian. Mu-
        sicians of the Armenian 'diaspora.''

Australia

10518   GLENNON, JAMES
        Australian music & musicians. [Adelaide] Rigby [1968]
        291 p. ports. 22cm. Includes 115 biographical sketches and '40
        "profiles" of contributors to Australian musical life: singers;
        pianists, organists, instrumentalists, conductors, conserva-
        torium directors, teachers. The sketches are not in alphabeti-
        cal arrangement; the profiles are.

10159   McCREDIE, ANDREW D
        Catalogue of 46 Australian composers and selected works
        [by] Andrew D. McCredie. Canberra, Advisory Board, Com-
        monwealth Assistance to Australian Composers, 1969. 20 p.
        21 x 30cm. [Music by Australian composers, survey no. 1] A
        biographical dictionary, in part, of 20th century (chiefly) Aus-
        tralian composers.

10520   MURDOCH, JAMES
         Australia's contemporary composers. [Melbourne] Mac-
         millan [1972] xiii, 223 p. ports. 25cm. A biographical dic-
         tionary, with portraits, bibliography and discography of 33
         composers.

Austria

10521   HAFENRICHTER, WILHELM
         Die Träger des Wiener Liedes; 45 Porträtskizzen Wiener
         Komponisten, Schriftsteller und Sänger. Mit einem Vorwort von
         Ernest Decsey. [Wien, Druck der Waldheim-Eberle, 1933. [4]p.,
         45 ports. on 44 l. 38cm. Issued in portfolio. Sponsored by the
         Gesellschaft zur Hebung und Förderung der Wiener Volkskunst.
         Index includes data from autobiographical and other sources. A
         volume consisting almost entirely of 45 portraits of Viennese
         composers, authors and singers.

10522   MUSIKBUCH AUS ÖSTERREICH; ein Jahrbuch der Musikpflege
         in Österreich und den bedeutendsten Musikstädten des Aus-
         landes. 1.-10. Jahrg.; 1904-1013. Wien und Leipzig, C. Fromme.
         10 v. 18 x 14cm. Edited by Richard Heuberger and Josef Reit-
         ter. Continuation of Kalender für die musikalische Welt. The
         music book of Austria; a yearbook of musical activity in Austria
         and the most important musical centers of the world. Each vol-
         ume contains a comprehensive list of contemporaries with
         birth and/or death dates and characterising phrases. Each vol-
         ume also contains a necrology of the world's musicians.

Azerbaijan

10523   KHALILOV, R
         Kompozitory Azerbaĭdzhana. Baku, Azerneshr, 1959. 131 p.
         ports. 20cm. 45 composers of Azerbaijan.

Belgium

10524   HEMEL, VICTOR VAN
         Voorname Belgische toonkunstenaars uit de 18de, 19de en
         20ste eeuw. Beknopt overzicht van hun leven en oeuvre. 3.
         bijgewerkte druk. Antwerpen, Cupido-Uitgave [1958] 84 p.
         21cm. A biographical dictionary of 101 Belgian musicians of the
         18th, 19th and 20th centuries. Supersedes his Voorname Bel-
         gische toonkunstenaars uit de XVIIIe, XIXe en XXe eeuw.
         (Antwerp, 1933—59 p. ports. 21cm.)

Canada

Bibliography, Indexes, Portrait Catalogs

10526   CANADIAN MUSIC CENTRE, TORONTO.
Catalogue of chamber music available on loan from the Library of the Canadian Music Centre. Catalogue de musique de chambre diponible à la musicothèque du Centre musical canadien. Toronto, 1967. 288 p. 25cm. "Detailed index, alphabetically by composers" (p. 47-267) is actually a bio-bibliographical compilation (with data in English and French) of Canadian composers of chamber music.

10527   NAPIER, RONALD
A guide to Canada's composers. Willowdale, Ont., Avondale Press [1973] 50 p. 24cm. An alphabetical list of Canadian composers, living and dead, which includes dates of birth or birth-death, place of birth, type of compositions issuing from the composer and publisher of the composer's works.

General Works

10528   CONTEMPORARY CANADIAN COMPOSERS. Edited by Keith MacMillan and John Beckwith. Toronto, New York, Oxford University Press, 1975. xxiv, 248 p. 25cm. Produced under the sponsorship of the Canadian Music Centre. A bio-bibliographical dictionary of 144 composers who have produced most of their works since 1920.

10529   MAHON, A   WYLIE
Canadian hymns and hymn writers. [St. John, N. B., "Glove," 1908] 56 p. mounted plates & ports. 17cm.

Colombia

10530   ZAPATA CUÉNCAR, HERIBERTO
Compositores antioqueños. [n. p., Editorial Granamérica, 1973] 130 p. ports. 24cm. A biographical dictionary of 158 Colombian composers past and present, specifically those from the Department of Antioquia.

10531   ZAPATA CUÉNCAR, HERIBERTO
Compositores nariñenses. [Medellín, Impreso en Editorial Granamérica, 1973] 41 p. ports. 24cm. A biographical dictionary of 37 composers of music from the Dept. of Nariño, Colombia.

Czechoslovakia

10532   KOZÁK, JAN, doctor of music.
Československi koncertni umělçi a komorni soubory; sbornik.
Praha, Statni hudebni vydavatelstvi, 1964. 482 p. illus., ports.
22cm. Czech concert artists and chamber music groups. Includes bibliographies and discographies.

Denmark

10533   LYNGE, GERHARDT
Danske komponister i det 20. aarhundredes begyndelse,
med portraeter og faksimilenodetryk efter komponisternes manu-
skripter. 2. omarbejdede og noget forkortede udg. Aarhus, E.
H. Jung, 1917. 279 p. illus., ports. 28cm. A bio-bibliographical dictionary of Danish composers at the beginning of the
20th century; portraits are included. 44 composers.

Finland

10534   GRANHOLM, ÅKE
Finnish jazz; history, musicians, discography. [Helsinki]
Foundation for the Promotion of Finnish Music, Finnish Music
Information Centre, 1974. 39 p. illus., ports. 21cm. Pri-
marily a biographical dictionary of 25 Finnish jazz musicians or
groups.

France

10535   BRUNSCHWIG, CHANTAL
100 [i. e. Cent] ans de chanson française; par Chantal
Brunschwig, Louis-Jean Calvet [et] Jean-Claude Klein. Paris,
Éditions du Seuil, 1972. 384 p. illus., ports. 22cm. 100
years of French song; a dictionary which includes biographical
sketches (often accompanied by portraits) of French singers
(popular music, folk-songs, etc.), song composers, librett-
tists, etc.

Georgia (Transcaucasia)

10536   TORADZE, GULBAT GRIGOR'EVICH
Kompozitory Gruzii. Tbilisi, Merani, 1968. 132 p. ports.
21cm. The composers of Georgia (Transcaucasia).

Germany

10537   DEUTSCHLANDS, ÖSTERREICH-UNGARNS UND DER
SCHWEIZ MUSIKER IN WORT UND BILD. Eine illus-

trierte Biographie der gesamten alldeutschen Musikwelt. Hrsg.
und bearb. von Ernst Mann [et al.] Leipzig-Gohlis, B. Volger,
1909. vi, 525 p. ports. Musicians of Germany, Austria-
Hungary and Switzerland at the turn of the 20th century in text
and portraits; an illustrated biography of the world of German
music.

10538   FISCHER, ALBERT FRIEDRICH WILHELM, 1829-1896.
         Kirchenlieder-Lexikon; hymnologisch-literarische Nach-
weisungen über ca. 4500 der wichtigsten und verbreitesten
Kirchenlieder aller Zeiten in alphabetischer Folge, nebst einer
Übersicht der Liederdichter. Hildesheim, G. Olms, 1967. 2 v.
in 1. 25cm. Reprint of the Gotha edition of 1878. A dictionary
of hymns. "Alphabetisches Verzeichniss der Dichter und ihre
Lieder": v. 2, p. [425]-486—a bio-bibliography in dictionary
format (biographical notices are very brief, often just place and
dates of birth and death) of German hymn-writers.

10539   MUSIK UND MUSIKER AM MITTELRHEIN; ein biographisches,
         orts- und landesgeschichtliches Nachschlagewerk, in Ver-
bindung mit der Musikwissenschaftlichen Institut der Universität
Frankfurt am Main ... [et al.] under Mitarbeit zahlreichen Mu-
sik- und Lokalgeschichtsforscher und mit Unterstützung durch
Franz Bösken hrsg. von Hubert Unverricht. Mainz, Schott,
1974-   v. illus. 21cm. (Beiträge zur mittelrheini-
schen Musikgeschichte, Nr. 20) Music and musician on the
Middle Rhine; a biographical dictionary; (e. g., v. 1, A-Z, 41
biographies)

Great Britain

10540   DUFFIELD, SAMUEL WILLOUGHBY, 1843-1887.
         English hymns, their authors and history. New York, Funk
& Wagnalls, 1886. vii, 675 p. 23cm. An alphabetical listing by
titles of hymns, with biographical notices of the hymn-writers
thereunder, so that the index of authors (p. [641]-648) must be
used to gain access to these notices.

10541   FOSTER, MYLES BIRKET, 1851-1922.
         Anthems and anthem composers; an essay upon the develop-
ment of the anthem from the time of the Reformation to the end
of the nineteenth century. New York, Da Capo Press, 1970.
225 p. ports. 24cm. (Da Capo Press music reprint series)
Reprint of the 1901 ed. Includes bio-bibliographical lists of English anthem composers (alphabetical by century)

10542   GRAY, ANDY
         Great pop stars. London, New York, Hamlyn [1973] 160 p.
of ports. (some col.) 31cm. Text covers "the most successful
recording artists and their records ... from 1955 to the present
day." Useful for its portraits of pop singers (singles and groups,
British and American).

Hungary

10543   CONTEMPORARY HUNGARIAN COMPOSERS. Responsible
editor: Gyula Czigány. Budapest, Editio Musica, 1970.
156 p. ports. 24cm. A bio-bibliographical dictionary of 73
composers, with portraits.

India

10544   GARGA, LAKSHMĪNĀRĀYANA.
Hamāre sangīta ratna. 2d ed. Hathras, U. P., Sangīta
Karyālaya, 1969-   v. ports. 22cm. In Hindi. Vol.
1 contains biographies of 337 ancient and modern Indian musicians, instrumentalists, and dancers.

10545   WHO'S WHO OF INDIAN MUSICIANS. New Delhi, Sangeet Natak
Akademi [1968] 100 p. 23cm.

Italy

10546   BEDESCHI, D
Prontuario biografico dei più illustri musicisti italiani e
stranieri. Florenzuola d'Arda, Pennaroli, 1897. 31 p. 16.º
Biographical reference booklet for the most famous Italian and
foreign musicians.

10547   GASPARI, GAETANO, 1807-1881.
De' musicisti bolognesi al XVI e XVII secolo e delle loro
opere a stampa; ragguagli biografici e bibliografici. Modena,
G. T. Vicenti, 1877. 85 p. 25cm. Caption title: Continuazione
delle Memorie biografiche e bibliografiche sui musicisti bolognesi del secolo XVI. Detached from Atti e memorie delle Depu-
tazioni di storia patria dell' Emilia, nuova ser., v. 1, 1877.
Biobibliography of musicians of Bologna in the 16th and 17th centuries.

Jews

10548   FRIEDMANN, ARON, 1855-   ed.
Lebensbilder berühmter Kantoren. Berlin, C. Boas Nachf.,
1918-27. 3 v. illus., ports. 23cm. Vol. 3 has imprint: Berlin, Im Selbstverlag der Hilfskasse. Lives of famous Jewish
cantors. Arranged by date of death in each vol. Contents note
at front of each vol. lists cantors.

10549   NULMAN, MACY
Concise encyclopedia of Jewish music. New York, McGraw-
Hill [1975] xii, 276 p. illus., ports. 24cm. Contains 500 en-

tries, a large number of which are bio-bibliographical. Concerns terminology of and contributors to the musical heritage of Judaism and the distinctively Jewish musical idiom.

Korea

10550   YI, WŎN-GI, ed.
         Kugak yesul inmyŏnggam. Seoul, Kugak Kyesa, 4292
         [1961] 235 p. illus., ports. 22cm. A manual of Korean musicians.

Latin America

10551   GIORDANO, ALBERTO
         Cien músicos de América. Buenos Aires, Ediciones Morán
         [1946] 347 p. 24cm. 100 musicians of North and South America.

10552   SLONIMSKY, NICOLAS, 1894-
         Music of Latin America. New York, T. Y. Crowell [1945]
         vi, 374 p. illus., ports. 24cm. "Dictionary of Latin American
         musicians, songs and dances, and musical instruments": p. 295-
         325. At the end of each of the 20 chapters in part II (Music of
         the twenty republics) is a biographical dictionary of musicians,
         each of which is treated also (much more briefly) in the 'Dictionary' (p. 295-325).

Latvia

10553   PADOMJU LATVIJAS MŪZIKAS DARBNIEKI. [Autoru kolektīvs:
         Rita Afanasjeva et al. Sastādijis: O. Grāvitis] Riga,
         Izdevnieciba "Liesma," 1965. 663 p. ports. 18cm. Musicians of Soviet Latvia.

10554   VITOLIŅŠ, JĒKABS
         Latvju skaņu mākslinieku portrejas. Sastadijis Jēkabas Vitoliņš un Roberts Koders. Jekaba Poruka ievads. Riga, J. Ozolins, 1930. 172 p. ports. 20cm. Portraits (biographical notices) of Lettish (Latvian) musicians; arranged by type of musical activity.

Moravia

10555   ELVERT, CHRISTIAN, Ritter d', 1803-1896.
         Geschichte der Musik in Mähren und Oesterr. —Schlesien
         mit Rücksicht auf die allgemeine, böhmische und österreichische Musik-Geschichte. Brünn, In Commission der Buchhandlung von C. Winiker, 1873. vi, 258, 252 p. 25cm. "Bildet

auch den 5. Band meiner Beiträge zur Culturgeschichte Mährens und Oesterr. Schlesiens und den 21. Band der Schriften der Histor. Sektion [der K. K. Mährisch-Schlesischen Gesellschaft zur Beförderung des Ackerbaues, der Natur- und Landeskunde in Brünn]" A history of music in Moravia and Austrian Silesia that includes a biographical dictionary of musicians on p. 65-205 (2d set).

Norway

10556 OVAMME, BÖRRE, 1911-
Norwegian music and composers. London, Bond Pub. Co. [1949] 64 p. ports., music. 20cm. Not a biographical dictionary, but the work consists almost entirely of biographical sketches to which a name index gives an alphabetical approach.

Peru

10557 BARBACCI, RODOLFO
Apuntes para un diccionario biográfico musical peruano. (In Fénix. Lima. 25cm. v. 6 (1949) p. [414]-510) A biographical dictionary of Peruvian musicians (A-Z)

10558 RAYGADA, CARLOS
Guía musical del Perú. (In Fénix. Lima. 25cm. 1956-57. v. 12 (1956-57) p. [3]-77; v. 13 (1963) p. [1]-82; v. 14 (1964) p. 3-95) A dictionary (A-V) of musical life in Peru, with many biographies included.

10559 SAS ORCHASSAL, ANDRÉS
La música en la Catedral de Lima durante el Virreinato. Lima, Universidad Nacional Mayor de San Marcos, 1971-72. 3 v. 22cm. (Colección de documentos para la historia de la música en el Perú) Contents. --1. pt. Historia general. --2. pt. Diccionario biográfico. 2 v. Music in the Cathedral of Lima during the Spanish colonial period; part 2 in 2 vols. is a biographical dictionary of musicians.

Poland

10560 BŁASZCZYK, LEON TADEUSZ
Dyrygenci polscy i obcy w Polsce, działajacy w XIX i XX wieku. [Wyd. 1. Kraków] Polskie Wydawn. Muzyczne [1964] 358 p. ports. 25cm. Polish and foreign orchestral conductors in Poland, active in the 19th & 20th centuries. Ca. 1,000 names included.

Portugal

10561   SOUSA VITERBO, FRANCISCO MARQUES DE, 1845-1910.
Subsídios para a historia da música em Portugal. Coimbra,
Imprensa da Universidade, 1932. 603 p. 25cm. A biographical
dictionary of Portuguese musicians.

Romania

10562   COSMA, VIOREL
Muzicieni romãni. Compozitori și muzicologi. Lexicon.
Bucuresti, Editura muzicală, 1970. 475 p. 21cm. First ed.
published in 1965 under title: Compositori și muzicologi romãni.
Preface in English, French, German, Spanish, Italian, Romanian, and Russian. A dictionary of Romanian composers and
musicologists.

Russia

10563   BAJER, JIŘÍ
Maly slovník sovětských hudebníků. Praha, Ustř. výbor
Svazu československ. přátelstvi, 1956. 67 p. Little dictionary of
Soviet musicians.

10564   BERNANDT, GRIGORIĬ BORISOVICH
Kto pisal o muzyke; bio-bibliograficheskii slovar' muzykal'-
nykh kritikov i lits, pisavshikh o muzyke v dorevoliutsionnoĭ
Rossii i SSSR. Moskva, Vsesoiûznoe izd-vo 'Sovetskii kom-
positor,' 1971-   v. 22cm. Contents.--t. 1. A-I. At
head of title: G. G. Bernandt, M. M. IAmpol'skii. Those who
write about music; a bio-bibliographical dictionary of Russian
music critics in pre-revolutionary and in in Soviet Russia.

10565   BOLOTIN, SERGEĬ VASIL'EVICH
Biograficheskii slovar' muzykantov-ispolnitelei na dukhov-
nykh instrumentakh. Leningrad, Muzyka, 1969. 200 p. ports.
21cm. Biographical dictionary of Russian musical performers
on wind instruments.

Scandinavia

10566   YOELL, JOHN H
The Nordic sound; explorations into the music of Denmark,
Norway, Sweden. Foreword by Antal Dorati. Boston, Crescen-
do Pub. Co. [1974] viii, 264 p. illus. 24cm. "Composers
gallery" (p. 59-229) comprises a biographical dictionary of 43
Scandinavian composers past and present.

Scotland

10567   BAPTIE, DAVID, 1822-1906.
Musical Scotland, past and present. Being a dictionary of
Scottish musicians from about 1400 till the present time. To

which is added a bibliography of musical publications connected
with Scotland from 1611. Compiled and edited by David Baptie.
Hildesheim, New York, G. Olms, 1972. iv, 253 p. 22cm. Reprint of the 1894 edition (Paisley, Scot., J. and R. Parlane)

Serbia

10568 PERIČIĆ, VLASTIMIR
        Muzički stvaraoci u Srbiji. [Napisao] Vlastimir Peričić uz
saradnju Dušana Kostića i Dušana Skovrana. [Prevod rezimea
na engelski: Caslav Stojanović] Beograd, Prosveta [1969] 663 p.
music, ports. 23cm. Summaries in English. Composers of
music in Serbia; a biographical dictionary (75 Yugoslav musicians)

Sweden

10569 ENGLUND, BJÖRN
        Svenska violinister på skiva (1907-1955) [av] Björn Englund
och Tage Ringheim. Stockholm, Kungliga biblioteket, 1973. 42
leaves. 31cm. (Nationalfonotekets diskografier, 504) A discography of 50 20th-century Swedish (or naturalized Swedes)
violinists, alphabetically arranged by surname of violinist,
which includes brief biographical notes.

Tajikistan

10570 KOMPOZITORY TADZHIKISTANA; [kratkiĭ biograficheskiĭ
        spravochnik] Dushambe, Irfon, 1966. 82 p. ports. 14cm.
Composers of Tajikistan; a brief biographical reference work.

Turkey

10571 ÖZTUNA, T   YILMAZ
        Turk musikisi ansiklopedisi [yazan] Yilmaz Öztuna. [Is-
tanbul] M. E. B. Devlet Kitaplari, 1969-   v. illus.,
ports. 29cm. Based on the author's Türk musikisi lugati. A
dictionary of Turkish music, with bio-bibliographical entries
included. Vol. 2 (Mabeyn-Öztoprak) 1974, latest one issued.

10572 RONA, MUSTAFA
        20. [i.e. Yirminci] yüzyıl Türk musikisi; bestekârları ve
bestleri güftelerile. [İlâveli 3. baskı. Istanbul] Türkiye
Yayınevi [1970] 828 p. ports. 25cm. First two editions published under title: 50 yıllık Türk musikisi. 20th century Turkish
music; 258 Turkish composers and lyricists and their compositions. Chronological arrangement; alphabetical name index at
end.

United States

Bibliography, Indexes, Portrait Catalogs

10573   BARNES, EDWIN NINYON CHALONER, 1877-
         American women in creative music; tuning in on American
music. Washington, Music Education Publications, 1936. 44 p.
21cm. Cover title. Useful primarily as a source of names for
further research, with the biographical sketches in no logical
arrangement.

10574   JACKSON, RICHARD, 1936-
         United States music; sources of bibliography and collective
biography. [Brooklyn] Institute for Studies in American Music,
Dept. of Music, Brooklyn College of the City University of New
York [c1973] vii, 80 p. 22cm. (I. S. A. M. monographs, no. 1)

General Works

10575   BAXTER, CLARICE (HOWARD)
         Gospel song writers biography, compiled by Mrs. J. R.
(Ma) Baxter and Videt Polk. Dallas, Tex., Stamps-Baxter
Music & Print. Co., 1971. 306 p. ports. 21cm. Biographical
sketches of ca. 109 American gospel song writers, primarily of
the 20th century.

10576   BROWN, LEN
         The encyclopedia of country and western music, by Len
Brown and Gary Friedrich. New York, Tower Publications,
1971. 191 p. ports. 18cm. (A Tower book) Bio-bibliographical dictionary of individuals and groups of prominent in American
country and western music (most of them living, a few deceased).

10577   BROWN, LEN
         Encyclopedia of rock & roll, by Len Brown and Gary Fried-
rich. [New York, Tower Publications, 1970] 217 p. ports.
18cm. (A Tower book) A bio-bibliographical dictionary of A-
merican singers and singing groups, rock and roll music, 1954-
1963.

10578   CHILTON, JOHN, 1931 or 2-
         Who's who of jazz: Storyville to Swing Street. London,
Bloomsbury Book Shop, 1970. [8], 447 p. ports. 22cm. A-
merican jazz musicians; American ed. (Philadelphia, Chilton
Book Co., 1972) has foreword by Johnny Simmen and collation:
419 p.

10579   CLAGHORN, CHARLES EUGENE
            Biographical dictionary of American music. West Nyack,
         N. Y., Parker Pub. Co., 1974. 491 p. 24cm. Entries are
         brief but numerous; includes many names and groups from the
         world of popular music that are not found easily elsewhere.

10580   ELLINWOOD, LEONARD WEBSTER, 1905-
            The history of American church music. New York, More-
         house-Gorham, 1935. xiv, 274 p. music, ports. 24cm. A
         biographical dictionary in the appendix (p. 201-242) gives sketch-
         es (or references to main text) of 98 church music composers,
         tune book compilers, etc.

10581   EWEN, DAVID, 1907-
            New complete book of the American musical theater. New
         York, Holt, Rinehart and Winston, 1970. xxv, 800 p. illus.
         24cm. Revised edition of the Complete book of the American
         musical theater (1958] "Librettists, lyricists and composers"
         (p. [607]-734) is a bio-bibliographical dictionary of some 160
         musicians and writers.

10582   EWEN, DAVID, 1907-
            Popular American composers from Revolutionary times to
         the present; a biographical and critical guide. New York, H.W.
         Wilson, 1962. 217 p. ports. 26cm.

            ---- ----First supplement. New York, H. W. Wilson, 1972.
         121 p. ports. 26cm. The supplement includes composers in the
         fields of rock, country and western music.

10583   KINKLE, ROGER D   1916-
            The complete encyclopedia of popular music and jazz, 1900-
         1950. New Rochelle, N. Y., Arlington House [1974] 4 v. illus.,
         ports. 24cm. Includes 2,105 biographical sketches of singers,
         composers, bandleaders, actors, musicians, impresariors,
         arrangers--the American musical scene for the 1st half of the
         20th century. Contents.--v. 1. Music year by year, 1900-1950.
         --v. 2-3. Biographies, A-Z.--v. 4. Indexes & appendices.

10584   KROHN, ERNST CHRISTOPHER, 1888-
            Missouri music, by Ernest C. Krohn. New York, Da Capo
         Press, 1971. xl, 380 p. 24cm. (Da Capo Press music reprint
         series) "An unabridged republication of Ernst C. Krohn's A
         century of Missouri music ... 1924 [with] a new introduction, a
         supplementary list of Missouri composers, musicians and musi-
         cologists, and a bibliography of the writings and compositions of
         Ernst C. Krohn, all specially prepared for this edition by the au-
         thor." The "Index" and "Supplementary list" (p. [101]-161) in-
         cludes brief biographical sketches.

10585   SIMON, GEORGE THOMAS
         The big bands [by] George T. Simon. With a foreword by
         Frank Sinatra. [Rev. enl. ed.] New York, Macmillan [1971]
         xvi, 584 p. ports. 25cm. "Biographies" of over 400 dance
         bands in the United States. Includes portraits and sketches of
         the band leaders. First ed. issued in 1967 (xvi, 537 p.)

10586   STAMBLER, IRWIN
         Encyclopedia of pop, rock and soul. New York, St. Martin's
         Press [1974] 609 p. ports. 24cm. In 500 entries traces the
         careers of individual and group performers from the Allman
         Brothers to Paul Zappa (pop, rock and soul singers on the Amer-
         ican scene—chiefly American, some British).

10587   THOMSON, VIRGIL, 1896-
         American music since 1910. With an introd. by Nicolas
         Nabokov. [1st ed.] New York, Holt, Rinehart and Winston
         [1971] xvi, 204 p. illus., ports. 23cm. (Twentieth century
         composers, v. 1) "106 American composers": p. 118-185—a
         biographical dictionary of past and present composers.

10588   WHO'S WHO AMONG MUSIC STUDENTS IN AMERICAN HIGH
         SCHOOLS. 1st-   ed.; 1974/75-   Tuscaloosa,
         Ala., Randall Pub. Co.   v. 24cm. " A biographical dic-
         tionary of outstanding music students in American high schools."

10589   WOOD, GRAHAM.
         An A-Z of rock and roll. London, Studio Vista, 1971.
         128 p. illus., ports. 21cm. A biographical dictionary of rock
         singers and rock groups (American and British)

Yugoslavia

(See under Serbia)

ATHLETICS AND GAMES

General Works

10590   ANDHRA PRADESH KREEDA DARSHINI. 1963/64-
         Hyderabad, Kreeda Publications, 1965-   v. In Telugu.
         Edited by Eka Venkata Subbarao. Includes brief sketches of
         sportsmen in Andhra Pradesh.

10591   BOROWIK, HANS, 1887-
         Olympiakämpfer 1940; 1000 Kurzbiographien von Sportlern
         aller Länder. Hrsg. von Hans Borowik. Berlin, W. Limpert,
         1939. 224 p. 15cm. 1,000 Olympic Games' athletes, 1940.

10592   BRITISH ATHLETES, 1951. Foreword by the Rt. Hon. the Lord
         Burghley. Action photos. of more than 200 famous British
         athletes with biographies by N. D. McWhirter; Walkers, by F. W.
         Blackmore. Rochester, Eng., Athletic and Sporting Publica-
         tions [1951?] 1 v. (unpaged) illus. 27cm.

10593   ENCICLOPEDIA DELLO SPORT. [Direttore responsabile:
         Giordano Goggioli] Roma, Edizioni sportive italiane, 1969-
         70 [c1964] 4 v. illus., ports. 31cm.

         ----Statistiche. Roma, Edizioni sportive italiane, 1969 [c1964]
         3 v. illus., ports. 31cm.

         ----Monografie. Roma, Edizioni sportive italiane [196 , c1964-
                    v. illus. 31cm. Includes portraits and biographi-
         cal sketches of leading figures in world sports.

10594   GŁUSZEK, ZYGMUNT
             Polscy Olimpijczycy. Warszawa, Wydawn. "Sport i
         Turystyka, " 1971. 352 p. illus., ports. 17cm. The Polish
         Olympiads; dictionary of Polish participants in the Olympic
         Games (p. 123-349).

10595   HICKOK, RALPH
             Who was who in American sports. New York, Hawthorne
         Books, 1971. xlii, 338 p. illus., ports. 24cm.

10596   MEZŐ, FERENC, 1885-
             Golden book of Hungarian Olympic champions. Livre d'or
         des champions olympiques hongrois. Budapest, Sport Lap- es
         Könyvkiadó, 1955. 131 p. ports. 25cm. (Hungarian Olympic
         library, 1) Biographies and portraits of Hungarian Olympic
         champions arranged chronologically by order of the Games
         (1896-1952).

10597   OUTSTANDING COLLEGE ATHLETES OF AMERICA.
             1969-   [Chicago, Outstanding Americans Foundation]
         v. 26cm. annual.

10598   SCHELENZ, KARL
             Deutschlands Olympiakämpfer 1928 in Wort und Bild. 300
         Biographien deutscher Olympiakandidaten, von Karl Schelenz
         und Karl Scharping. Dresden, W. Limpert, 1928. 175 p. illus.,
         ports. 8.⁰ Germany's Olympic Games competitors for 1928
         in words and pictures; 300 biographies of German Olympic can-
         didates.

10599   SLOVENSKA ATLETIKA, 1945-1970. Uredil uredniški odbor:
         Marko Račic [in dr.] Fotografije: Svetozar Busić [in dr.]

Ljubljana, Atletska zveza Slovenije, 1970. 183, 40 p. illus., ports. 20cm. Slovenian athletics, 1945-1970; includes biographical sketches and portraits of athletes.

10600   WHO'S WHO IN SPORTS IN MALAYSIA AND SINGAPORE.
Editor-in-chief: Thomas R. P. Dawson. Petaling Jaya, Malaysia, Who's Who in Sports, 1975. xvi, 724 p. illus. 27cm. "Bio-data" (p. 417-505) comprises the biographical dictionary section of the volume.

10601   WHO'S WHO IN THE SPORTING WORLD: Witwatersrand and
Pretoria. Johannesburg [1933-   v. 4.°
Sports figures of the early 1930's from the Witwatersrand and Pretoria, South Africa.

Auto Racing

10602   CUTTER, BOB, 1930-
The encyclopedia of auto racing greats, by Robert Cutter and Bob Fendell. Englewood Cliffs, N. J., Prentice-Hall, 1973. viii, 675 p. illus. 29cm. Includes about 550 biographies, some illustrated with black and white photos, of men and women connected with motor racing.

10603   THE ENCYCLOPEDIA OF MOTOR SPORT. Edited by G. N.
Georgano. Advisory editor: Albert R. Bochroch. Foreword by Stirling Moss. New York, Viking Press, 1971. 656 p. illus. 29cm. (A Studio book) Auto racing. Over 300 biographies are included. Issued also in London (Studio Books) as the Encyclopaedia of motor sport.

Baseball

10604   DAVIS, MAC, 1905-
100 greatest baseball heroes. New York, Grosset & Dunlap, 1974. 151 p. illus. 29cm. (Illustrated true books) Biographical sketches of such stars as Babe Ruth, Pete Gray, Connie Mack, Jackie Robinson, Warren Spahn and 95 others.

10605   KARST, GENE, 1906-
Who's who in professional baseball [by] Gene Karst [and] Martin J. Jones, Jr. New Rochelle, N. Y., Arlington House, 1973. 919 p. 24cm. 1,500 biographies of players, coaches, managers, umpires and executives from baseball's beginnings to the present.

Basketball

10606   CASTRILLO DE CABO, EUSEBIO
         272 [i.e. Dosciento setenta y dos] encuentros, 1923-1973:
         125 jugadores, 50 aniversario del baloncesto español [by] Euse-
         bio Castrillo de Cabo con la colaboración de la Asociación
         Española de Baloncestistas Internacional. Madrid, 1973. 215 p.
         illus. 21cm. 50 years of basketball in Spain, 1923-1973, with
         biographical data and records of 125 players.

10607   HOLLANDER, ZANDER
         The modern encyclopedia of basketball. Edited by Zander
         Hollander. New York, Four Winds Press (1969) xxi, 468 p.
         illus., ports. 27cm. "An Associated Features book." Includes
         portraits, records, etc. of American basketball players.

10608   MENDELL, RONALD L   1943-
         Who's who in basketball. New Rochelle, N. Y., Arlington
         House [1973] 248 p. 25cm. Facts and figures for over 900
         American college and professional players, coaches and offi-
         cials, 1891 to the present.

10609   STAINBACK, BERRY
         Basketball stars. New York, Pyramid Books.   v. illus.,
         ports. 18cm. annual. Vols. for 19   -65 by B. Gottehrer; 1966
         by Stainback and S. Gelman. American basketball players; por-
         traits and biographies.

Boxing

10610   BURRILL, BOB
         Who's who in boxing. New Rochelle, N. Y., Arlington
         House, 1974. 208 p. 24cm. Some 400 boxers (chiefly Ameri-
         can) are listed in alphabetical order, with biographical data
         averaging one quarter to half a page.

10611   McCALLUM, JOHN DENNIS, 1924-
         The encyclopedia of world boxing champions since 1882. 1st
         ed. Radnor, Pa., Chilton Book Co., 1975. xix, 337 p. illus.
         29cm. Biographical sketches range from several pages for the
         more famous heavyweights to a few lines for the lesser known
         in the lighter weight classes.

Bull-Fighting

100612   BAGÜES, VENTURA, 1880-
         Historia de los matadores de toros, por Don Ventura
         [pseud.] Barcelona, De Gasso Hnos., 1970. 476 p. col. ports.

23cm. (Enciclopedias De Gasso. Extra) History of matadors.
870 biographies of Spanish and Latin American bullfighters
chronologically arranged, with an alphabetical index.

10613   MULAS PÉREZ, I
Diccionario taurino. [Barcelona, J. Marí Torres, 1970]
510 p. illus. 24cm. A dictionary of bullfighting, chiefly terminology, but does include a bio-bibliographical dictionary of writers on bullfighting ("Escritores taurinos": p. 137-146) and a list
of matadors ("Matadores de toros ... ": p. 442-479) which includes pseudonyms used, place and date of birth, place and date
of "alternativa" ceremonies, names of bulls fought & their breed-
ing, and patron.

Contract Bridge

10614   AMERICAN CONTRACT BRIDGE LEAGUE.
The official encyclopedia of bridge. Authorized by the
American Contract Bridge League and prepared by its editorial
staff. Richard L. Frey, editor-in-chief. Alan F. Truscott,
executive editor. Thomas M. Smith, managing editor. New,
rev. and expanded ed. New York, Crown Publishers, 1971.
793 p. 25cm. Includes biographies of all leading players
(more than 600 new biographies added in this edition).

Cricket

10615   INDIAN CRICKET-FIELD ANNUAL. [19--] Bombay, D. B.
Taraporevala.   v. illus. 19cm. Who's who of Indian
cricket at end of volume.

Football

10616   BORSTEIN, LARRY
Football stars. New York, Pyramid Books.   v. illus.,
ports. 18cm. annual. Began with vol. for 1969. Supersedes a
publication of the same title by B. Stainback (q. v.). Not to be
confused with Football stars (Dell Pub. Co., New York, 1952-
), q. v. American football players; portraits and biographical data.

10617   COHANE, TIM
Great college football coaches of the Twenties and Thirties.
New Rochelle, N. Y., Arlington House, 1973. xv, 329 p. illus.,
ports. 26cm. Arranged alphabetically; biographical sketches,
portraits, etc. of 42 American football coaches of the 1920's and
1930's.

10618   MENDELL, RONALD L   1943-
Who's who in football [by] Ronald L. Mendell [and] Timothy

B. Phares. New Rochelle, N. Y., Arlington House [1974] 395 p.
24cm. A biographical dictionary of American football with over
1,400 names; collegiate and professional players, coaches and
officials.

10619   PREP ALL-AMERICA FOOTBALL YEARBOOK. [Montgomery,
        Ala., Coach and athlete]   v. illus., ports. 27cm. A
biographical dictionary of high school & preparatory school football players and coaches.

10620   STAINBACK, BERRY
        Football stars. New York, Pyramid Books [etc.]   v.
illus., ports. 18cm. annual. Each vol. carries also in the
title the year of issue, i.e. Football stars of 1967 [etc.] Began
with vol. for 1965? American football players; biographies and
portraits.

10621   SULLIVAN, GEORGE, 1927-
        Pro football A to Z; a fully illustrated guide to America's
favorite sport. New York, Winchester Press, 1975. 341 p.
illus. 24cm. A dictionary of teams, players, coaches, rules
and terminology of American and Canadian football.

10622   WHO'S WHO IN NATIONAL ATHLETICS HIGH SCHOOL FOOT-
        BALL. 1973/74-   [Denver, Colo., Josep Com-
munications, inc.]   v. ill. 28cm. annual. Continues
Who's who in national high school football.

10623   WHO'S WHO IN NATIONAL HIGH SCHOOL FOOTBALL.
        Pueblo, Colo., National Josep Pub. Co.   v. illus.
28cm. annual. Began ca. 1970(?) Continued by Who's who in
national athletics high school football (1973/74-   )

Golf

10624   EVANS, WEBSTER
        Encyclopedia of golf. Rev. ed. New York, St. Martin's
Press, 1974. 320 p. illus. 24cm. Includes brief biographical
sketches of professional golfers. First ed. issued in 1972.

10625   GOLF MAGAZINE'S ENCYCLOPEDIA OF GOLF. Edited by
        Robert Scharff and the editors of Golf magazine, assisted by
Peter D. Eaton. [1st ed.] New York, Harper & Row [1970]
vi, 424 p. illus., ports. 27cm. Includes a section: Golfdom's
who's who.

Hockey

10626   FISCHLER, STAN
         Fischlers' hockey encyclopedia [by] Stan & Shirley Fischler.
         New York, Crowell [1975] 628 p. ports. 24cm. Primarily a
         biographical dictionary of 1,000 past and present professional
         hockey players and other hockey personalities.

10627   HOLLANDER, ZANDER
         The complete encyclopedia of ice hockey; the heroes, teams,
         great moments, and records of the National Hockey League.
         Edited by Zander Hollander and Hal Bock. Englewood Cliffs, N.
         J., Prentice-Hall [1970] xi, 623 p. illus., ports. 25cm. "An
         Associated Features book."

10628   KARIHER, HARRY C   1932-
         Who's who in hockey. New Rochelle, N. Y., Arlington
         House [1973] 189 p. 24cm. Brief profiles of ca. 600 hockey
         players, coaches, owners, officials and general managers, 1870
         to 1973 (National Hockey League primarily).

10629   NATIONAL HOCKEY LEAGUE.
         NHL action players, 74/75; [the official 96 page word and
         picture album of NHL players and teams] [Montreal?] NHL,
         c1974. 96 p. col. illus. 28cm.

10630   THE POCKET HOCKEY ENCYCLOPEDIA; a complete and
             illustrated handbook on hockey: records, rules, statistics
         and results. New York, Scribner [c1972] 254 p. illus. In-
         cludes biographies.

10631   PRO AND SENIOR HOCKEY GUIDE. Herb Elk, editor. 1970-71
             ed. St. Louis, Sporting news [1970?] 575 p. illus. Most
         of the book consists of biographical and career information on
         each player.

Horsemanship

10632   [ETREILLIS,   baron de] b. ca. 1822.
         Dictionnaire du sport français. Courses, chevaux, entraine-
         ment, langue du turf, célébrités du turf, Paris et parieurs,
         reglements, hippodromes, par Ned Pearson [pseud.] Paris,
         C. O. Lorenz, 1872. 676 p. 19cm. Dictionary of French horse-
         racing, including biographical sketches of celebrities of the
         turf.

10633   STRATTON, CHARLES
         The international horseman's dictionary. London, New

York, Hamlyn, 1975. 256 p. illus., ports. 31cm. Includes
biographies in its 2,500 entries.

Martial Arts

10634   20th CENTURY WARRIORS; prominent men in the Oriental
fighting arts, from the pages of Black belt magazine and
Karate illustrated. Illus. by Geraldine Simon. Los Angeles,
Ohara Publications [1971] 254 p. illus. 24cm. 36 biographies
(with portraits) of masters of judo, karate, and aikido.

10635   WALL, BOB, 1939-
Who's who in the martial arts and directory of black belts.
Beverly Hills, Calif., R. A. Wall Investments, inc., 1975.
xix, 254 p. illus. 22cm. "The main section of the volume of-
fers photographs and one-page biographies of [131] well-known
martial artists" [chiefly Americans or living in the U. S. A.]--
Library Journal, Feb. 1, 1976.

Mountaineering

10636   UNSWORTH, WALTER
Encyclopedia of mountaineering. Compiled by Walt Unsworth. London, Robert Hale; New York, St. Martin's Press,
1975. 272 p. illus. 25cm. (Sports encyclopaedias) In large
part a biographical dictionary for some 400 mountain climbers,
with emphasis on British and European mountaineers.

Physical Education

10637   ENCYKLOPAEDISCHES HANDBUCH DES GESAMTEN TURN-
WESENS UND DER VERWANDTEN GEBIETEN. In Verbindung mit zahlreichen Fachgenossen hrsg. von Carl Euler.
Wien, Pichler, 1894-96. 3 v. illus., ports. 23cm. Encyclopedic handbook of gymnastics and related activities; includes
portraits and biographies of famous gymnasts (mostly from
German-speaking countries).

Soccer

10638   THE CLIPPER ANNUAL OF WHO'S WHO IN FOOTBALL.
London, Clipper Press. v. The 1970 ed. (issued in
1969) had collation: 127 p. illus., ports. 28cm. It was edited
by Brian Wright. Who's who in British soccer (association
football).

10639   DASS, SITA RANJAN
Bharatiya football. Calcutta, Gyanatirtha, 1967. 103 p.
In Bengali. Life sketches of present-day football (soccer) play-
ers in India.

10640   FAMOUS FOOTBALLERS AND ATHLETES.   1-14; 1895-1896.
         London, Hudson & Kearns [etc.] 14 pts. illus. folio.
         Edited by C. W. Alcock and R. Hill. British soccer players at
         the end of the 19th century; a periodical that lasted for 14 issues
         only.

10641   FOOTBALL MANIA: who's who in soccer. London, Century 21
         House, 1969. 125 p. (chiefly illus., ports.) 27cm. Cover
         title. British soccer (association football) players (chiefly il-
         lustrations and portraits).

10642   FUMYK, ANDRE
         Futbol y sus reyes. Madrid, Editorial Rollán, 1969. 451 p.
         illus. 23cm. Football (i.e. soccer) and its stars. Alphabeti-
         cal index at end.

10643   STARS OF SOCCER. 1952-   Windsor, Eng.   v.
         ports. 8.⁰ English soccer stars. Edited by Cedric Day.

10644   WHO'S WHO IN FOOTBALL. Hertford, Eng., Barnes, New-
         berry & Co.   v. illus. 27cm. Biographical dictionary
         of British soccer players. Began ca. 1970?

Swimming

10645   BESFORD, PAT
         Encyclopaedia of swimming. Compiled by Pat Besford.
         New York, St. Martin's Press, 1971. 235 p. illus. 23cm.
         A dictionary that includes a substantial amount of biography
         of swimming champions, chiefly those of the present.

Tennis

10646   UNITED STATES LAWN TENNIS ASSOCIATION.
         Official encyclopedia of Tennis. Edited by the staff of the
         U. S. L. T. A. [1st ed.] New York, Harper & Row [1972]
         viii, 472 p. illus., ports. 27cm. "Lawn tennis greats" (p.
         [367]-455) includes biographical sketches under such headings
         as: National Lawn Tennis Hall of Fame [American players], The
         Samuel Hardy Award [an American prize], World tennis roll of
         honor [alphabetically arranged]

Track

10647   HANLEY, REID M   1945-
         Who's who in track and field. New Rochelle, N. Y., Arling-
         ton House [1973] 160 p. 25cm. Biographical sketches and

statistics for over 400 runners, hurdlers, shot-putters, jumpers, etc. from the 1870's to 1973.

EDUCATION AND SCHOLARSHIP

General Works

10648   ANDRÉ, VALÈRE, 1588-1655.
Imagines doctorum virorum e variis gentibvs, elogijs breuibus illustratae. Valerivs Andreas desse; ius Brabantus publicabat. Antverpiae, Apud D. Martinium, anno 1611. [108] p. ports. 13cm. 78 portraits with brief biographical notes of learned men in Europe, 12 of them physicians.

10649   ASSOCIATION FOR ASIAN STUDIES.
Membership directory (and manpower survey) Ann Arbor, Mich., 1973. 333 p. 28cm. A directory of scholars in the field (chiefly American and Canadian) in the format of and with the content of a bio-bibliographical dictionary.

10650   BILDNISSE DER BERÜHMTESTEN UND VERDIENST-
VOLLSTEN PÄDAGOGEN UND SCHULMÄNNER ÄLTERER UND NEUERER ZEIT. Quedlinburg, G. Basse, 1833-41.   pt. in   facsims., ports. Paged continuously; exact collation unknown. Each part except the first has title: Bildnisse und Lebensbeschreibungen der berühmtesten und verdienstvollsten Pädagogen und Schulmänner. Includes biographies. Portraits (with biographical notes) of the most famous and meritorious teachers and schoolmen of the older and modern times (early 19th century).

10651   DIMBERG, RONALD
A Ming directory---1968: scholars, Taiwan publications. Compiled by Ronald Dimberg, Edward L. Farmer and Robert L. Irick. Taipei, Chinese Materials and Research Aids Service Center, 1968. 39 p. 22cm. A directory of Ming scholars the world over, but with some biographical data (date of birth, position, field of specialization, current projects).

10652   EAST INDIES INSTITUTE OF AMERICA, NEW YORK.
A list of lecturers on Southeast Asia (Burma, Siam, French Indo-China, Malay Peninsula, Malay Archipelago, Philippines) and adjacent areas. New York, 1945. 75 p. 23cm. A bio-bibliographical dictionary of 92 American scholars, etc. who specialized in Southeast Asian civilization, etc.

10653   EMINENT ORIENTALISTS: Indian, European, American.
1st ed. Madras, G. A. Natesan, 1922. viii, 378 (i.e. 406) p. 17cm.

10654 ENCYCLOPAEDIA BRITANNICA
        A book of portraits; containing photographs of 564 of the
        1500 contributors to the Encyclopaedia Britannica. New York,
        Cambridge University Press [1910?] 1 v. (unpaged) 564 ports.
        29cm. Cover title.

10655 GALLE, PHILIPPE, 1537-1612.
        Imagines L doctorum virorum qui bene de studiis literarum
        servere; cum singulorum elogiis nunc primum editae et seri in-
        cisae opera Philippi Gallaei. Antverpiae, [Raphelengius] 1587.
        2 p. l., 50 ports. 25cm. Reprinted in 1606 ([4]) p. 50 ports.
        31cm.) Intended as a supplement to Galle's earlier Virorum
        doctorum ... effigies (see below)

        ---- ----Virorum doctorum de disciplinis benemerentium effi-
        gies XLIIII. [Cum singulorum elogiis opera Benedicti Ariae
        Montani] Antwerpiae [Apud Raphelengium] 1572. 49 plates. 4.º
        Together these 2 volumes offer 93 portraits of learned men in
        Europe (men of letters, humanists, etc.) of the early modern
        period.

10656 HENNICKE, KARL AUGUST
        Beiträge zur Ergänzung und Berichtigung des Jöcher'schen
        Allgemeinen Gelehrten-Lexikon's und des Meusel'schen Lexikon's
        der von 1750 bis 1800 verstorbenen teutschen Schriftsteller.
        [Reprografischer Nachdruck der Ausg. Leipzig, Vogel, 1811-
        1812] Hildesheim, G. Olms, 1969. 3 v. in 1. 23cm. Cover
        title: Ergänzungen zu Jöcher und Meusel. Additions and correc-
        tions to Jöcher's dictionary of scholars and Meusel's dictionary
        of German authors, 1750 to 1800.

10657 THE INTERNATIONAL SCHOLARS DIRECTORY. John Warwick
        Montgomery, general editor. Strasbourg, France [Deer-
        field, Ill.] International Scholarly Publishers, 1973. xix, 288 p.
        28cm. Includes bio-bibliographical data on scholars, scientists
        and researchers in all fields throughout the 'free world.' Keyed
        to other biographical reference sources.

10658 INTERNATIONAL WHO'S WHO IN ASIAN STUDIES. 1975-76--
        Hong Kong, Asian Research Service, c1975-
        v. ports. 27cm. A "worldwide directory ... an annual
        publication designed to provide concise biographical information
        on scholars and specialists in Asian studies." 1st vol. (1975-
        1976) has 201 p.

10659 LEXIKON DER PÄDAGOGIK. [Hrsg. vom Deutschen Institut
        für Wissenschaftliche Pädagogik, Münster, und dem Insti-
        tut für Vergleichende Erziehungswissenschaft, Salzburg. Verant
        wortlich für die Schriftleitung: Heinrich Rombach. Freiburg
        [i. B.] Herder, 1952-55. 4 v. 25cm. A dictionary of education,
        including biographies of famous educators.

10660   OSS, ADRIAAN VAN
        Latinoamericanistas en Europa; un registro de datos bio-
bibliográficos sobre 443 especialistas activos en los estudios
Latinoamericanos en Europa, resultados de una encuesta reali-
zada en el otoño de 1973. Compilado por Adriaan van Oss.
Amsterdam, Centro de Estudios y Documentación Latinoamericanos [1974?] 84 p. 25cm. Biobibliographical dictionary of
443 European Latin Americanists.

10661   ROCKEFELLER FOUNDATION.
        Directory of fellowships and scholarships, 1917-1970. [New
York, 1972] xvii, 412 p. 26cm. Very brief 'biographies' of ca.
9,500 individuals around the world who received fellowships or
scholarships (or both) from the Foundation.

10662   SÁNCHEZ SARTO, LUIS
        Diccionario de pedagogía. Publicado bajo la dirección de
Luis Sánchez Sarto con la colaboración de eminentes especialis
tas españoles y extranjeros. Barcelona, Editorial Labor, 1936.
2 v. illus., ports. 27cm. In double columns. A dictionary of
education that includes biographies of famous educators.

10663   SCHWARTZ, HERMANN
        Pädagogisches Lexikon. In Verbindung mit der Gesellschaft
für Evangelische Pädagogik und unter Mitwirkung zahlreicher
Fachmänner hrsg. von Hermann Schwartz. Bielefeld, Leipzig,
Velhagen & Klasing, 1928-31. 4 v. 27cm. A dictionary of education which includes biographical sketches of educators (featur-
ing those of the Germanic countries).

10664   YUNESUKO HIGASHI AJIA BUNKA KENKYU SENTA, TOKYO.
        Research institutes and researchers of Asian studies in:
Cambodia, Laos, Malaysia, Singapore and the Republic of Vietnam. [Tokyo] Centre for East Asian Cultural Studies, 1970.
vii, 183 p. 21cm. (Centre for East Asian Cultural Studies.
Directories no. 8) Includes bio-bibliographical sketches of the
researchers.

Local

Austria

10665   [DOLENZ, KARL]
        Scriptores antiquissimae, ac celeberrimae Universitatis
Viennensis ordine chronologico propositi. Viennae Austriae,
Kaliwoda, 1740-42. 3 v. (with a total of 422 p.) Writers connected with the University of Vienna from its foundation (1365)
to 1665; in chronological arrangement. Ca. 120 bio-bibliographies.

10666   HÖLBING, FRANZ, 1932-
         300 [i. e. Dreihundert] Jahre Universitas Oenipontana. Die
         Leopold-Franzens-Universität zu Innsbruck und ihre Studenten.
         Zur 300-Jahr-Feier hrsg. von der Österreichischen Hochschuler-
         schaft an der Universität Innsbruck. Franz Hölbing: Text. Wulf
         Stratowa: Bildteil, Biographien. 158 Bilder davon 41 in Farben.
         Innsbruck, Verlag der Tiroler Nachrichten, " 1970. 280 p. il-
         lus., ports. 27cm. 300 years of the University of Innsbruck.
         Interspersed throughout the text on special plates are biographi-
         cal sketches of 92 distinguished faculty and scholars (with por-
         traits for most) associated with the University from 1689 to the
         present.

10667   MAYRÖCKER, FRANZ
         Von den Stillen im Lande. Pflichtschullehrer als Dichter,
         Schriftsteller und Komponisten. Wien, 1938. 137 p. Bio-biblio-
         graphical dictionary of Austrian teachers (contemporary) as po-
         ets, authors and composers.

Belgium

10668   LE ROY, ALPHONSE, 1822-1896.
         Liber memorialis: l'Université de Liége depuis sa fonda-
         tion ... Liége, H. Vaillant-Carman, 1869. 80, lxxix p. 1180
         columns, clxvi p. 25cm. Includes biographical notices of mem-
         bers of the faculty, etc. of the University of Liége arranged al-
         phabetically in five categories: administrators, deceased profes-
         sors & professors emeriti, those who were at the University but
         left, non-teaching associates, and teaching faculty to 1867. Par-
         tial contents. --2. -3. ptie. La famille universitaire. I. Les
         professeurs et leur auxiliaire. II. Les élèves.

Bulgaria

10669   BŬLGARSKA AKADEMIIA NA NAUKITE, SOFIA. BIBLIOTEKA.
         100 [i. e. Sto] godini Bŭlgarska akademiia na naukite, 1869-
         1969. Pol red. P. Zarev (otgovoren redaktor) [i dr.] Sofiia,
         Izd-vo na Bŭlgarskata akademiia na naukite, 1969-72. 3 v.
         ports. 25cm. A hundred years of the Bulgarian Academy of Sci-
         ences, 1869-1969. The 1st volume is devoted entirely to bio-bib-
         liographical information about academicians and corresponding
         members of the Academy since its founding to the present; the
         2d, social scientists; the 3d volume yields bio-bibliographical
         data for professors and contributors to the older sciences and
         the natural, mathematical and applied sciences.

10670   SOFIA. UNIVERSITET.
         Almanakh na Sofiiskiia universitet Sv. Kliment Okhridski;
         zhivotopisni i knigopisni svedeniia za prepodavatelite. 2. izd.
         Za petdesetgodishninata na universiteta, 1888-1939. Sofiia,
         Pridvorna pechatnitsa, 1940. 726 p. 24cm. (Universitetska

biblioteka, No. 207) First edition published in 1929 under title:
Almanakh na Sofiĭskiĭa universitet, 1888-1929. Almanac of
Sofia University which includes a large bio-bibliographical sec-
tion for members of the faculty, 1888-1939.

China

10671   CHUNG-KUO CHIN TAI HSÜEH JÊN HSIANG CHUAN. Taipei,
         Ta lu tsa chih she, 1971-   v. 22cm. Vol. 1
contains 160 short biographies of scholars in modern China,
with portraits. No index.

10672   HUA, CHU, of Ch'ing Dynasty.
         I min chuan. Taipei, Kuang-wen shu chü, 1974. 461 p.
22cm. Photocopy of manuscript. Biographies of 262 Chinese
scholar-hermits up to the end of the Ch'ing Dynasty, (1911).

10673   SHÊN, CHIA, chin shih 1688.
         Ming ju yen hsing lu. Taipai, Shang wu yin shu kuan, 1972.
4 v. 19cm. Facsimile reprint. Biographies of 208 Confucian
scholars of the Ming Dynasty in chronological order. No index.

10674   SUN, YÜ-HANG.
         Chin ssŭ pai nien lai An-hui hsüeh jên lu. Taipei, 1965.
80, 18 p. 19cm. Biographies of 337 scholars from An-hui
Province for the last 400 years (since the late Ming period).
Chronological order. No index. Also known under title: Ch'ing
tai Huan chiang kuan hsüan lu.

10675   TUNG, CH'I-SHENG.
         Hsüeh hsiao jên wu chih. Taipei, Kuang wen shu chu, 1975.
2 v. 22cm. Reprint of 1718 edition. Biographies of Confucian
scholars who are officially worshipped in Confucian temples.

Czechoslavakia

10676   KUDĚLKA, MILAN
         Československé práce o jazyce, dějinách a kultuře slovan-
ských narodů od r. 1760; biograficko-bibliografický slovnik.
[Vyd. 1. V Praze] Státni pedagogické nakl, [1972] 560 p. 25cm.
[Edice Slovanské knihovny) By Milan Kudělka and Zdeněk Šimeček. A bio-bibliographical dictionary of scholars in the field of
Slavic studies in Bohemia and the Czechoslovak Republic from
the year 1760 to the present.

10677   LEBENS- U. ARBEITSBILDER SUDETENDEUTSCHER LEHRER.
         Pohrlitz, Lehrerverein, 1932-33. 2 v. illus., ports. 8.°
Biographical sketches and portraits of teachers of German extraction in the Sudetenland.

10678   PRAŽÁK, FRANTIŠEK
        Spisovatelé učitelé. Praha, Nákl. České grafické unie
        [1946] 202 p. ports. 22cm. Author-teachers in Czechoslo-
        vakia; a dictionary.

Denmark

10679   MAGISTER-STATEN. [6. udg.] 1967. Under red. af Hans Hald
        Jensen og Tage Kaarsted. København, Magisterforbundet,
        1968. 690 p. 26cm. First ed. published in 1907 under title: Fi-
        lolog- og magister-stat; 2d-3d ed. under title: Magister-stat.

        ---- ----Tillaeg IV, under redaktion af Hans Held Jensen. Kø-
        benhavn, Magisterforbundet, 1970. 59 p. 25cm. "Tillaeg I og
        II er optaget i Magister-staten 1967, s. 664-682 [i.e. 690]" A
        biographical dictionary of prominent living Danes, especially
        those who graduated from the University of Copenhagen and have
        some interest in or are active in education.

Finland

Bibliography, Indexes, Portrait Catalogs

10680   DAHLSTRÖM, LOTTEN
        Porträtt från den forna Åbo akademi. Åbo, Åbo akademi,
        1940. 13 p. 24cm. (Acta Academiae Aboensis. Humaniora,
        XIII, 5). A catalog of portraits of professors, etc. of the Acad-
        emy at Åbo, 17th-19th centuries. The alphabetical listing in-
        cludes birth-death dates, and some identifying data.

General Works

10681   CARPELAN, TOR HARALD, 1867-
        Helsingin Yliopisto opettajat ja virkamiehet vuodesta 1828.
        Helsingissä, Söderström, 1925-26. 2 v. (viii, 1128 p.) ports.
        26cm. At head of title: Tor Carpelan ja L. O. Th. Tudeer.
        Issued in 7 parts, 1921-1926.

        ---- ----Täydennys vuoden 1938 loppuun, toimittaneet Solmu
        Sola ja L. O. Th. Tudeer. Helsinki, Söderström, 1940. 2 v.
        (948 p) ports. 26cm. Biographical dictionary of professors
        and members of the administration in the University of Helsinki
        (Helsingfors, 1828-1938) Issued also in Swedish under title:
        Helsingfors universitet, lärare och tjänstemän ...

10682   SUNDMAN, CARL ERIC, 1912-
        Åbo akademis lärare och tjänsteman 1918-1968 [av] C. -E.
        Sundman. [Åbo, 1968] vii, 277 p. illus., ports. 25cm. A
        biographical dictionary of the faculty of Åbo Academy (Turku,
        Finland) for the years 1918-1968, with a further listing of teach-

ing assistants, office personnel, technicians, etc. (p. 259-[278]
that includes birth and/or death dates.

France

10683   BERTHE, LÉON NOËL
        Dictionnaire des correspondants de l'Académie d'Arras au
temps de Robespierre. Arras, L'auteur, 1969. 224 p. illus.
24cm. A biographical dictionary of 1,103 correspondents of the
Academy of Sciences, Letters and the Arts of Arras at the time
of Robespierre.

10684   FIERVILLE, CHARLES, 1833-
        Archives des lycées. Proviseurs et censeurs, ler mai
1802-ler juillet 1893. Documents administratifs recueillis et
classés pour la première fois. Paris, Firmin-Didot, 1894.
lxxxv, 526 p. 8.° The 4th part is a biographical dictionary of
French educators, vice-principals and headmasters of lycées.

10685   GOUJET, CLAUDE PIERRE, 1697-1767.
        Mémoire historique et littéraire sur le Collège royal de
France. Genève, Slatkine Reprints, 1971. 3 v. in 1 (441 p.)
31cm. Each volume contains major biographical sections, giving
notices of professors, etc. of the Royal College of France. Reprint of the Paris edition of 1758 (3 v. 17cm.)

Germany

10686   BARDONG, OTTO
        Die Breslauer an der Universität Frankfurt (Oder); ein
Beitrag zur schlesischen Bildungsgeschichte 1648-1811. Würz-
burg, Holzner-Verlag [1970] xxxii, 368 p. 24cm. (Quellen und
Darstellungen zur schlesischen Geschichte, hrsg. von der
Historischen Kommission für Schlesien, Bd. 14) Students from
Breslau at the University of Frankfurt an der Oder, 1648-1811.
"Lebensläufe" (p. 191-348) is a biographical dictionary of the
more prominent students.

10687   BECMANN, JOHANN CHRISTOPH, 1641-1717.
        Notitia Universitatis Francofurtanae una cum iconibus per-
sonarum aliquot illustrium aliorumque virorum, qui eam pre-
sentia sua ac meritis illustrarunt, professorum denique ordi-
nariorum qui anno seculari Universitatis secundo vixerunt.
Francofurti ad Viadrum, 1707. 2 v. ports. folio. Notices and
portraits of the faculty at the University of Frankfurt on the
Oder.

10688   BONNER GELEHRTE. Beiträge zur Geschichte der Wissen-
        schaften in Bonn. Bonn, Bouvier, 1968-70. 7 v. illus.,

ports. 25cm. (150 Jahre Rheinische Friedrich-Wilhelms-Universität zu Bonn, 1818-1968) Contents. --[1] Evangelische Theologie. --[2] Katholische Theologie. --[3] Staatswissenschaften. --[4] Mathematik und Naturwissenschaften. --[5] Philosophie und Altertumswissenschaften. --[6] Geschichtswissenschaften. --[7] Sprachwissenschaften. Biographical sketches of scholars at the University of Bonn, 1818-1968.

10689   CELLIUS, ERHARD, 1546-1606.
Imagines professorum Tubingensium Senatorii praecipue ordinis, qui, hoc altero Academiae seculo, anno 1577, inchoato, in ea & hodie anno [1596] vivunt ac florent ... & interea mortui sunt. Tubingae, Typis auctoris, 1596. [135] p. 73 p. 20cm. A part 2 (sig. A-F^4) has special t. p.: Sequuntur imagines professorum ... mortuorum. Includes 73 portraits with biographical notes of professors at the University of Tübingen in the latter part of the 16th century.

10690   HÄNSEL, WILLY
Catalogus professorum Rinteliensium; die Professoren der Universität Rinteln und des Akademischen Gymnasiums zu Stadthagen 1610-1810. Bearb. von Willy Hänsel. Rinteln, C. Bösendahl, 1971. xiii, 94, [8] p. illus. 24cm. (Schaumburger Studien, Heft 31) A catalog (actually biographical sketches) of professors at the University of Rinteln, Germany, 1610-1810, and the adjunct Academic Gymnasium in Stadthagen. Arranged by faculty, with an alphabetical index at end.

10691   HAID, JOHANN JACOB, 1704-1767.
Neue Sammlung von Bildnissen Gelehrter um die Kirche, um das gemeine Wesen und um die Wissenschaften verdienter noch lebender Männer nach Original-Malereien mit Fleiss entworfen und mit historischen Nachrichten von ihrem Leben, Schriften und Verdiensten begleitet. Erstes Fünfzig, Augusburg, 1757. 22 p. ports. 42cm. No more published? Intended as a supplement to J. J. Brucker's Ehren-Tempel der deutschen Gelehrsamkeit (?) A new collection of portraits of living learned men in the Church, in everyday life and in the sciences, accompanied by historical facts concerning their lives, works and meritorious achievements. Concerned primarily with German scholars.

10692   HELMSTEDT, GER. UNIVERSITÄT.
Album Academiae Helmstadiensis. Bearb. von Paul Zimmermann. Hannover, Selbstverlag der Historischen Kommission; Kommissionsverlag für Deutschland: A. Lax, Hildesheim, 1926-   v. 30cm. (Veröffentlichungen der Historischen Kommission für Hannover, Oldenburg, Braunschweig, Schaumburg-Lippe und Bremen, 9
Contents. --Bd. 1. Album Academiae Juliae. Abt. 1: Studenten, Professoren, etc. der Universität Helmstedt von 1574-1636. Voran geht ein Verzeichnis der Schüler und Lehrer des Pädagogium Illustre in Gandersheim 1572-74.

10693   KUHN, WERNER, 1943-
         Die Studenten der Universität Tübingen zwischen 1477 und
         1534; ihr Studium und ihre spätere Lebensstellung. Göppingen,
         A. Kümmerle, 1971. 2 v. (xv, 579 p.) 21cm. (Göppinger aka-
         demische Beiträge, Nr. 37/38) Students at the University of
         Tübingen between 1477 and 1534; their studies and their later po-
         sition in life. Whenever the information is available, the author
         gives brief biographical data; in many cases, because of such
         lack, only a line or two is given under the entry. Arrangement
         is semi-alphabetical; i. e., the author uses the format followed
         in: Die Matrikeln der Universität Tübingen 1477-1600, as well as
         a 'phonetic' alphabet arrangement (A, B. & P, C & K, D & T,
         etc.)

10694   SAUPE, EMIL, 1872-
         Deutsche Pädagogen der Neuzeit; ein Beitrag zur Geschichte
         der Erziehungswissenschaft zu Beginn des 20. Jahrhunderts.
         Osterwieck, A. W. Zickfeldt, 1929. viii, 412 p. 35 plates.
         First issued in 1924 (226 p.)? German educators at the begin-
         ning of the 20th century; a biographical reference work.

10695   VOIT, MAX
         Bildnisse Göttinger Professoren aus zwei Jahrhunderten.
         Festgabe des Universitätbundes zum Jubiläum der Georgia Au-
         gusta. Göttingen, Vandenhoeck & Ruprecht, 1937. 24 p. 113
         plates. 20 x 30cm. Portraits of professors at the University of
         Göttingen, 19th & 20th centuries.

10696   WENZ, RICHARD
         Dichter im deutschen Schulhaus. Betrachtungen ihres
         Schaffens und Proben aus ihren Werken. Leipzig, F. Moeser
         Nachfolger, 1915. 397 p. 8.º Bio-bibliographical dictionary
         of German and Austrian teachers who also are writers, with
         samples of their work.

10697   WIDMANN, HORST, 1927-
         Exil und Bildungshilfe; die deutschsprachige akademische
         Emigration in die Türkei nach 1933. Mit einer Bio-Bibliogra-
         phie der emigrierten Hochschullehrer im Anhang. Bern, H.
         Lang [1973] 308 p. 21cm. German-speaking academicians
         (primarily Germans and Austrians) who migrated to Turkey aft-
         er 1933. The bio-bibliography (p. 252-293) includes 75 names
         in the main alphabet along with brief sketches of other academi-
         cians associated with the chief biographees.

Great Britain

10698   THE ACADEMIC WHO'S WHO; university teachers in the
         British Isles in the arts, education and social sciences.
         1st-   ed.; 1973-74 —   London, A. & C. Black,
         1974-   v. 26cm. biennial. 1973/74 ed. (xxvii,

521 p.); 1975/76 ed. (784 p.) issued in the U. S. by Gale Research Company, Detroit. The 2d (1975/76) ed. contains ca. 7,000 biographical sketches.

10699   WHO'S WHO IN EDUCATION. Editor: Robert Bradfield. Research: Margaret Connolly. London, Mercury House Reference Books, 1974. xxiii, 926 p. 26cm. British educators of today.

Greece, Medieval and Modern

10700   ARABANTINOS, PANAGIŌTĒS, 1809-1870.
Biographikē syllogē logion tēs Tourkokratias. Eisagōgē-epimeleiai K. Th. Dēmara. Iōannina, Ekd. Hetaireias Epeirō-tikōn Meletōn, 1960. 249, [7] p. port. 25cm. Biographies of Greek scholars who flourished during the Turkish domination of Greece in the early 19th century, with an alphabetical index (names of persons): p. 225-249. A posthumous work.

10701   KURIAKIDĒS, TH   EPAMEINONDAS
Biografiai tōn ek Trapezountos kai tēs peri auten chopas apo tēs 'alōseōs mechris 'emon akmasantōn logiōn meta shediasuratos 'istorikou peri tou 'ellēnikou frontistēriou tōn Trapezountiōn. En Athēnais, Ek tou Tupografeiou Paraskena Leonē, 1897. 276 p. 22cm. 139 numbered notices of learned men (chiefly Greeks) of Trebizond and the surrounding area from the fall of Constantinople to 1897.

Hungary

10702   MAGYAR TANÍTÓK LEXIKONA. Budapest, 1939. vii, 456 p. Edited by Lajos Bene. Encyclopedia of Hungarian teachers.

India

10703   BISWAS, ARABINDA, 1925-
Encyclopaedic dictionary and directory of education; with special reference to India [by] A. Biswas & J. C. Aggarwal. New Delhi, Academic Publishers, 1971-   v. 26cm. Vol. 1 includes 3 brief biographical dictionaries: (1) World educators and educationists. (2) Great teachers of ancient India. (3) Who's who in Indian education.

10704   EMINENT EDUCATIONISTS OF INDIA. 1969-   New Delhi, National Book Organisation.   v. ports. 25cm. A bio-bibliographical dictionary; 1969 vol. contains sketches of ca. 1700 contemporary Indian educators.

Islamic Countries

10705   AL-QIFTĪ, 'ALĪ IBN YŪSUF, 1172 or 3-1248.
Tarīh al-hukamā. Auf Grund der Vorarbeiten Aug. Müller's

hrsg. von Julius Lippert. Leipzig, Dietrich'sche Verlagsbuch-
handlung (T. Weicher) 1903. 22, 496 p. 25cm. Biographical
dictionary of Islam's learned men (philosophers and scientists)
Abridged by Muhammad ibn 'Ali al-Khatibi al-Zauzani.

10706   AL-TAMĪMĪ, ABŪ AL-'ARAB MUHAMMAD IBN AHMAD
         Classes des savants de l'Ifriqiya, par Abu l'Arab Moham-
med ben Ahmad ben Tamim et Mohammed ben al-Harit ben
Asad al-Hosani.   Text arabe publié avec une traduction fran-
çaise et des notes par Mohammed ben Cheneb. t. 1. Paris,
Leroux, 1915. [4], 300, [2] p. (Publications de la Faculté des
lettres d'Alger. Bulletin de correspondance africaine, t. 51)
Vol._1 only published?   The texts of the Kitāb Tabaqāt 'ulamā
Ifriqīyah and the Kitāb Tabaqāt 'ulamā Tūnis of Abū l-'Arab
al-Tamīmī and the Kitāb tabaqāt 'ulamā Ifriqīyah of al-Khushani.
Muslim men of learning of North Africa.

10707   WÜSTENFELD, HEINRICH FERDINAND, 1808-1899.
         Die Academien der Araber und ihre Lehrer. Nach Aus-
zügen aus Ibn Schohba's Klassen der Schafeiten bearb. von
Ferdinand Wüstenfeld ... Göttingen, Vandenhoeck und Ruprecht,
1837. viii, 136, 22 p. 21cm. Extracts in Arabic from Ibn
Shuhbah's Tabakāt al-shāfi 'iyat (22 p. at end).   254 biographical
notices of Arabic educators and authors divided by academies
in Arabia & Cairo (which are named after their founders).

Italy

10708   CODIGNOLA, ERNESTO, 1885-
         Pedagogisti ed educatori. A cura di Ernesto Codignola.
Milano, E. B. B. I., Istituto editoriale italiano B. C. Tosi,
1939. 451 p. illus., ports. 28cm. (Enciclopedia biografica e
bibliografica 'Italiana,' ser. 38) A biographical dictionary of
Italian educators.

10709   MEMORIE E DOCUMENTI PER LA STORIA DELL'UNIVERSITÀ
         DI PAVIA E DEGLI UOMINI PIÙ ILLUSTRI CHE V'INSEG-
NARONO. Bologna, Forni, 1970. 3 v. 32cm. (Athenaeum, 12)
Reproduction of the Pavia 1877-78 ed. This history of the University of Pavia includes in vol. 1 (with title: Serie dei rettori e
professori con annotazioni) lists of the rectors and professors
of the various faculties; some biographical data is included in
the lists, but more extensive biographies are given in sections
following the lists. There are indexes of names by faculty at the
end of the volume.

10710   ROME (CITY) PONTIFICIO ATENEO ANTONIANO.
         Pontificium Athenaeum Antonianum, ab origine ad praesens.
Roma, Ed. Antonianum [1970] 797 p. illus. 25cm. Pref. in
English, French, German, Italian, Latin, and Spanish; text in
English, German, Italian, Latin or Spanish. "Bio-bibliographia
professorum" (p. 267-392) is a bio-bibliographical dictionary of
the professors (58) at the Pontificio Ateneo antoniano in Rome.

Latvia

10711   BIRKERTS, PĒTERIS, 1881-
           1905 [i. e. Tükstotis devini simti piektāj] g. revolucijā
cientusie Latvijas skolotāji. Riga, 1927. _ 222 p. illus., ports.
24cm. (Latvijas vēstures pētisanas biedribas raksti, no. 2)
Latvian teachers in the Revolution of 1905.

Netherlands

10712   ONZE HOOGLEERAREN; portretten en biografieën. Rotterdam,
           Nijgh & Van Ditmar [1898] 363 p. ports. 13cm. Our pro-
fessors; portraits and biographical notes (361 in all) on distinguished Dutch scholars.

10713   REGTEREN ALTENA, JOHAN QUIRLJN VAN, 1899-
           De portret-galerij van de Universiteit van Amsterdam en
haar stichter Gerard van Papenbroeck, 1673-1743. In opdracht
van de Historische Commissie der Universiteit beschreven door
I. [sic] Q. van Regteren Altena en P. J. J. van Thiel. Met een
voorwoord van H. Engel. Amsterdam, Swets en Zeitlinger,
1964. xii, 387 p. illus., ports. 30cm. Summary in English.
The portrait gallery of the University of Amsterdam and the collector Gerard van Papenbroeck. This catalog (which contains
many portraits) refers chiefly to Dutch professors but also includes poets and other persons (primarily of Dutch nationality)
involved in intellectual pursuits.

Philippine Islands

10714   DOWN MEMORY'S LANE (biographical sketches; memoirs or
           profiles of members of the BORTEMA. Board of editors:
Geronimo Mejia, editor-in-chief [and others] Tagbilaran City,
Philippines, Bohol Retired Teachers-Employees Mutual Association, 1972. 155, [16] p. ports. 23cm. Contains some 400
biographical sketches of members of the Bohol Retired Teachers-
Employees Mutual Association, Bohol Island, Philippines. A ˇ-
rangement is alphabetical under city of town of the island.

10715   QUEZON, PHILIPPINES. UNIVERSITY OF THE PHILIPPINES.
           LIBRARY.
           U. P. biographical directory. Quezon City, 1964. ix,
190 p. 26cm. Biographical dictionary of faculty and professional staff members of the University of the Philippines.

           ---- ----Supplement 1-   Quezon City, 1970-   v.
28cm.

Poland

10716   JANOWSKI, LUDWIK
        Słownik bio-bibliograficzny dawnego Uniwersytetu Wileń-
skiego wydany pod kierunkien Ryszarda Mienickiego przy spółud-
ziaŁe Marty Burbianki i BogumiŁa Zwolskiego. Wilno, Towarzystwo PrzyjacioŁ Nauk w Wilnie, 1939. 528 p. 25cm. (ZrodŁa
i materjaly historyczne. Wydawnictwa wydziaŁu III. Towar-
zystwa PrzyjacioŁ Naul w Wilnie, t. 5) A bio-bibliographical
dictionary of the faculty of the University of Vilna.

10717   NIECIOWA, ELŻBIETA HELENA
        CzŁonkowie Akademii Umiejetności, oraz Polskiej Akademii
Umiejetności, 1872-1952. OpracowaŁa Elżbieta Helena Nieciowa. Kraków, ZakŁad Narodowy im. Ossolińskich [Oddz. w
Krakowie] 1973. 169 p. ports. 20cm. At head of title: Polska
Akademia Nauk. OddziaŁ w Krakowie. Primarily a biographical dictionary of the members of the Polish Academy of Sciences
at Krakow. The biographical sketches are very brief.

Romania

10718   CÂNDEA, SANDA
        Bibliografia lucrarilor stiintifice ale cadrelor didactice.
Universitatea Bucuresti. Seria istorie. Bucuresti, 1970. 2 v.
(xxix, 663 p.) 20cm. At head of title: Biblioteca Centrală
Universitară. Sectorul de Documentae Universitara. A bio-
bibliographical dictionary of the faculty of the University of
Bucharest (19th-20th centuries) Contents. --v. 1. A-L. --v. 2.
M-Z.

Russia

10719   BIOGRAPHIC REPORT: USSR Institute of the United States of
        America and Canada. [Washington] Central Intelligence
Agency, 1976. ix, 144 p. ports., fold. chart. 27cm. "Biographic sketches on 71 Soviet personalities who are professional
staff members of the Institute of the USA and Canada and/or
members of the editorial board on the Institute's journal, USA:
economics, politics, ideology." Biographical dictionary format.

10720   LVOV. UNIVERSYTET. NAUKOVA BIBLIOTEKA.
        Drukovani pratsi professoriv, vykladachiv i spivrobitnykiv
L'vivs'kogo Universytetu za 1944-1960 roky. Bibliografichnyi
pokazhchyk. L'viv, Vid-vo L'vivs'kogo Universytetu, 1962.
768 p. 21cm. Actually a bio-bibliographical guide to the professors and instructors of the University of Lvov, 1944-1960.
Notices arranged alphabetically under faculties.

Spain

10721   ESPERABÉ ARTEAGA, ENRIQUE, 1868-
Historia pragmática e interna de la Universidad de Salamanca. Salamanca, F. Nuñez Izquierdo, 1914-17. 2 v. 26cm.
Contents. --t. 1. La Universidad de Salamanca y los reyes. --
t. 2. La Universidad de Salamanca: Maestros y alumnos más
distinguidos. A history of the University of Salamanca, Spain:
vol. 2 is devoted primarily to numerous biographical sketches
of the faculty and distinguished alumni of the University. Unfortunately the biographical sketches are not in alphabetical arrangement and no name index is provided.

Sweden

10722   MOLIN, GÖSTA GIDEON
Smolandi Upsalienses; Smålandsstudenter i Uppsala på 1500-
och 1600-talen: biografier med genealogiska notiser. Lund, C.
Bloms boktr.; [Smålands nation, Uppsala] 1955-
25cm. Vol. 2, by G. G. Molin and P. Wilstadius, and v. 3
have imprint: Karlskrona, A. Abrahamsons boktryckeri. Students from Småland, Sweden at the University of Uppsala in the
16th and 17th centuries; biographical notices, etc.

Switzerland

10723   ADUMBRATIO ERUDITORUM BASILIENSIUM MERITIS APUD
EXTEROS OLIM HODIEQUE CELEBRIUM. Apendicis
loco Athenis Rauricis addita. Basiliae, Sumtibus C. A. Serini,
1780. 180 p. 20cm. A bio-bibliographical dictionary of 54
scholars in Basel in the 18th century.

Ukraine

10724   ISTORIIA AKADEMII NAUK UKRAINS'KOĬ RSR. Paton, B. E.,
gol. redaktor. [Kyiv, Gol. red. rad. entsiklopedii AN URSR,
1967] 2 v. illus., ports. 25cm. At head of title: Akademiia
nauk Ukrains'koĭ RSR. A history of the Academy of Sciences of
the Ukrainian Soviet Republic. In vol. 2, p. 175-673, is to be
found a biographical dictionary of academicians and correspondents past and present of the Academy ("Korotki narysy pro zhytti
zhyttia i naukovu diial'nist' akademikiv ta chleniv-korespondentiv
Akademii nauk Ukrains'koĭ RSR")--in 2 alphabets, A-IA.

10725   POPOV, V   M
Ucheni vuziv Ukrains'koĭ RSR. [Avtors'kii kolektyv: V. M.
Popov (keerivnyk) V. I. Polurez, IU. P. Diachenko. Kyiv] Vyd-
vo Kyivs'kogo universytetu, 1968. 515 p. ports. 23cm. A biographical dictionary, with some portraits, of contemporary
scholars in the universities of the Ukrainian Soviet Socialist Republic.

United States

10726   CORNELL UNIVERSITY. SOUTHEAST ASIA PROGRAM.
          Alumni directory. Ithaca, N. Y., Southeast Asia Program,
          Dept. of Asian Studies, Cornell University, 1970. 119 p. 25cm.
          A bio-bibliographical dictionary (in part) of specialists in South-
          east Asian studies.

10727   DIRECTORY OF AMERICAN SCHOLARS. Edited by Jaques Cat-
          tell Press. 6th ed. New York, R. R. Bowker, 1974. 4 v.
          29cm. Includes ca. 38,000 brief biographies of American and
          Canadian scholars. First published as a single volume work in
          1942, 1951 (2d ed.), 1957 (3d ed.); 4th ed. (1963-64) in 2 volumes;
          5th ed. (1969) in 4 vols. Contents. --v. 1. History. --v. 2. Eng-
          lish, speech, and drama. --v. 3. Foreign languages, linguistics,
          and philology. --v. 4. Philosophy, religion, and law.

10728   ILIOPOULOS, NICHOLAS D
          Who's who of Greek origin in institutions of higher learning
          in United States and Canada. New York, Greek Orthodox Arch-
          diocese of North and South America, Office of Education, 1974.
          xiv, 186 p. 22cm. Cover title: Who's who; who is who of Greek
          origin in institutions of higher learning in the United States &
          Canada. 1, 173 educators of Greek origin.

10729   JOINT COMMITTEE ON THE FOREIGN AREA FELLOWSHIP
          PROGRAM.
          Directory: Foreign area fellows, 1952-1972, of the Joint Com-
          mittee on the Foreign Area Fellowship Program of the American
          Council of Learned Societies and the Social Science Research
          Council, 1962-1972, formerly administered by the Ford Founda-
          tion, 1951-1962. Compiled and edited by Dorothy Soderlund. As-
          sistant editor: Leslie Wendell. [3d ed. New York, Social Science
          Research Council, Foreign Area Program, c1973] [23], 397 p.
          28cm. Biographical sketches, in alphabetical who's who format,
          of 2,050 American scholars who have had fellowships under
          a foreign area study program inaugurated by the Ford Foundation
          and later administered by the above named organizations.

10730   LEADERS OF AMERICAN ELEMENTARY & SECONDARY EDU-
          CATION. [Chicago]   v. ports. 26cm. (Outstanding
          Americans biographical compilation series) Began in 1972 (?)

10731   LEADERS OF AMERICAN SECONDARY EDUCATION, including
          outstanding elementary teachers. [Washington]   v.
          26cm. annual. (Outstanding Americans biographical series)
          Began ca. 1973?

10732   OUTSTANDING EDUCATORS OF AMERICA. 1970-
         [Chicago]   v. 26cm. annual. Contemporary American
         educators; a biographical dictionary.

10733   OUTSTANDING SECONDARY EDUCATORS OF AMERICA.
         [Washington]   v. illus. 26cm. Began ca. 1973 or 4?
         High school teachers of the United States; living persons.

10734   RECHCIGL, EVA EDWARDS, 1932-
         Biographical directory of the members of the Czechoslovak
         Society of Arts and Sciences in America, inc. Compiled and
         edited by Eva Rechcigl and Miloslav Rechcigl, Jr. [New ed.]
         New York, Czechoslovak Society of Arts and Sciences in A-
         merica, 1972. viii, 134 p. 25cm. Gives the following infor-
         mation: name, occupational title (including professional affil-
         iation or discipline, where indicated), institutional address,
         residence, date and place of birth, degrees received (field,
         institution and year), major field of competence.

10735   WHO'S WHO AMONG ELEMENTARY SCHOOL PRINCIPALS.
         [Arlington, Va.] National Association of Elementary School
         Principals.   v. illus. 28cm. annual. Vols. for
         include the Association's Membership directory and annual re-
         port. Began ca. 1971 or 1972?

10736   WHO'S WHO IN INDUSTRIAL ARTS TEACHER EDUCATION.
         John M. Pollock, editor [and] Charles A. Bunten, editor.
         [2d ed. Oxford, Ohio] American Council on Industrial Arts
         Teacher Education [1969] 352 p. Published as a supplement to
         the American Council on Industrial Arts Teacher Education's
         Yearbook series.

LANGUAGE AND LITERATURE

Bibliography, Indexes, Portrait Catalogs

10737   COMBS, RICHARD E
         Authors: critical and biographical references; a guide to
         4,700 critical and biographical passages in books, by Richard
         E. Combs. Metuchen, N. J., Scarecrow Press, 1971. ix,
         221 p. 22cm.

10738   HAVLICE, PATRICIA PATE
         Index to literary biography. Metuchen, N. J., Scarecrow
         Press, 1975. 2 v. (viii, 1300 p.) 22cm. Guide to biographical
         information for over 68,000 authors world-wide, from ancient
         times to the present; indexes 50 standard literary reference
         works. Minimum entries include the author's name, pseudo-
         nyms (if any), birth and death dates, nationality, and form of
         writing typically known for.

Anonyms and Pseudonyms

10739   BAUER, ANDREW
        The Hawthorn dictionary of pseudonyms, compiled by An-
drew Bauer. New York, Hawthorn Books, 1971. vi, 312 p.
24cm. Nearly 10,000 cross-referenced entries; real names &
pen-names, pseudonyms, cognomens, abbreviations, Latiniza-
tions, etc. of writers, poets, philosophers & politicians from
ancient times to the present.

10740   CHRISTENSEN, FOLMER
        Literaturleksikon. 2000 definitioner af litteraere begreber
og bogfaglige udtryk samt 500 forfatterpseudonymer. Under
medvirken af Lotte Eskelund. København, Gjellerup, 1969.
300 p. 21cm. A dictionary of literature, chiefly of terms, but
also includes a section of 500 authors' pseudonyms (p. 261-300)
and real names.

10741   GEISSLER, FRIEDRICH, 1636-1679.
        De nominum mutatione et anonymis scriptoribus ... ex-
hibuit Fridr. Geisler ... Lipsiae, J. E. Hahn, 1679. [72] p.
19cm. At head of title: ... Dissertatio ductu L. un C. de
mutat. nomin. First published as dissertation (Leipzig, 1669--
[60] p.) with Daniel Schrock as joint author. Concerned with
authors who have changed their names and with anonymous-
pseudonymous authors.

10742   McGHAN, BARRY
        Science fiction and fantasy pseudonyms. [With 1973 supple-
ment] Compiled by Barry McGhan. [n. p.] Misfit Press, 1973.
iv, 34, iii, 21 p. 27cm.

10743   SHARP, HAROLD S
        Handbook of pseudonyms and personal nicknames. Com-
piled by Harold S. Sharp. Metuchen, N. J., Scarecrow Press,
1972. 2 v. (xi, 1104 p.) 23cm. With some 15,000 real-name
entries and 25,000 nicknames & pseudonyms.

        ---- ----1st-   supplement. Metuchen, N. J., Scarecrow
Press, 1975-   2 v. 23cm. The 2 vols. of the 1st supplement
add another 18,000 real-name entries plus 30,000 nicknames
and/or pseudonyms.

10744   TAYLOR, ARCHER, 1890-
        The bibliographical history of anonyms and pseudonyms, by
Archer Taylor and Frederic J. Mosher. Chicago, Published
for the Newberry Library by the University of Chicago Press,
1951. ix, 288 p. front. 24cm. "Bibliography of anonyma and
pseudonyma": p. 207-279.

General Works

10745   ANGELIEVA, FANI
       Bio-bibliografiia na prepodavatelite ot Fakulteta po zapadni
filologii. Sofiia, SU Kliment Okhridski, 1973. 522 p. 20cm.
At head of title: Sofiiski universitet "Kliment Okhridski." Uni-
versitetska biblioteka. By F. Angelieva, A. Paunova and V.
Khrusanova. Ttile also in English: Bio-bibliography of the Philological Faculty members. Bio-bibliography of ca. 136 members, past & present, of the Faculty of Philology of Sophia University in Bulgaria. Chronologically arranged but with an alphabetical listing by surname at end of vol.

10746   ASH, BRIAN
       Who's who in science fiction. New York, Taplinger Pub.
Co., 1976. 219, [1] p. 23cm. More than 400 of the world's
leading writers, editors, artists, etc. past & present.

10747   AUTHORS IN THE NEWS; a compilation of news stories and fea-
       ture articles from American newspapers and magazines
covering writers and other members of the communications
media. By the staff of Biography news. Barbara Nykoruk,
editor. Detroit, Gale Research Co., 1976-   v.
illus., ports. 29cm. Provides illustrated biographical articles
on novelists, nonfiction writers, playwrights, etc. Each volume reproduces ca. 350 new stories and feature articles selected from over 90 American newspapers and magazines.

10748   BERNARDES BRANCO, MANOEL, 1832-1900.
       Portugal e os estrangeiros. Lisboa, Imprensa Nacional,
1893-95. 3 v. 25cm. A new, enlarged edition of the work
first issued in 1879 in 2 vols. Half title: Diccionario dos
escriptores estrangeiros que escreveram ácerca de assumptos
portuguezes. A dictionary of foreign authors who have written
about Portugal; arranged alphabetically by authors. Many bio-
bibliographical notes and copious extracts from the works described.

10749   BOISSARD, JEAN JACQUES, 1528-1602.
       Bibliotheca chalcographica, hoc est virtute et eruditione
clarorum virorum imagines, collectore Iano-Iacobo Boissardo.
Vesunt, sculptore Theodoro de Bry, Leod., primum editae, et
ab ipsorum obitu hactenus continuatae. Heidelbergae, Impensis
Clementis Ammoni, 1669. 5 v. in 1. 446 ports. 21cm. The
first volume contains the plates of the author's Icones virorum
illustrium (5th ed.) The 2d to 5th vols (each with special t. p.)
are designated as "pars VI-IX of the Bibliotheca, and "Contin-
uatio I-[IV]" of the Icones. Imprints vary. With portraits (446
in all) of the famous writers and scholars of the Middle Ages
and the Reformation.

10750   BRUNET, GUSTAVE, 1807-1896.
         Les fous littéraires. Essai bibliographique sur la littéra-
ture excentrique, les illuminés, visionnaires, etc. Genève,
Slatkine Reprints, 1970. xii, 229 p. 22cm. A bio-bibliographical dictionary of eccentrics, Illuminati, visionaries, etc.
in world literature (emphasis on French literature). A reprint
of the Brussels, 1880 ed.

10751   CASSELL'S ENCYCLOPEDIA OF WORLD LITERATURE. Ed-
         ited by S. H. Steinberg in two volumes. Rev. and enlarged
in three volumes. General editor: J. Buchanan-Brown. New
York, W. Morrow, 1973. 3 v. 24cm. "First published in two
volumes in 1953 as Cassell's encyclopedia of literature." Vols.
2-3: Biographies, A-Z.

10752   CATHOLIC AUTHORS IN MODERN LITERATURE, 1880-1930.
         Loretto, Pa., St. Francis College, 1930. 230 p. 27cm.
(Mariale, v. 6 (1930)) Actually the half-title of the 1930 (v. 6)
ed. of Mariale. Short biographical sketches of 200 authors are
included.

10753   CHERPAKOV, AVGUST IVANOVICH
         Les fous littéraires; rectifications et additions à l'Essai
bibliographique sur la littérature excentrique, les illuminés,
visionnaires, etc. de Philomneste junior. Par Av. Iv. Tcherpakoff. Moscou, 1883. 89 p. 19cm. Corrections and additions
to Brunet's bio-bibliographical dictionary of eccentrics (Les
fous littéraires, q. v.)

10754   THE CONCISE ENCYCLOPEDIA OF MODERN WORLD LITERA-
         TURE. Edited by Geoffrey Grigson. 2d ed. New York,
Hawthorn Books, 1971 [c1963] 430 p. 26cm. Writers of the
20th century; a bio-bibliographical work which concentrates on
the longer and better known authors and bypasses many of the
most recent claimants to fame. The first edition was issued in
1963 (512 p.)

10755   CONSTANT, ALPHONSE LOUIS, 1810-1875.
         Dictionnaire de littérature chrétienne ... Paris, J. P.
Migne, 1861. 1250 columns. 29cm. (Nouvelle Encyclopédie
théologique, ou deuxième série de dictionnaire sur toutes les
parties de la science religieuse ... t. 7) A dictionary of Christian literature that includes biographical-critical sketches of
Christian authors from the earliest history of the church to the
mid-nineteenth century.

10756   CONTEMPORARY AUTHORS; a bio-bibliographical guide to
         current authors and their works. James M. Ethridge [and]
Barbara Kopala, editors. 1st revision. Detroit, Gale Research
Company, 1967-   v. 26cm. Contents.--[1] v. 1-4 (1962-
63).--[2] v. 5-8 (1963).--[3] v. 9-12 (1974).--[4] v. 13-16 (1975).
--[5] v. 17-20 (1976).

10757   CONTEMPORARY AUTHORS. Permanent series; [a bio-biblio-
          graphical guide to current authors and their works] v. 1-
          Detroit, Gale Research Co., 1975-   v. 29cm. Con-
          tains listings that will not require revision in the future: de-
          ceased authors, older authors past retirement age who report
          no works in progress or who have no works in print. Sketches
          have been revised from the basic set of Contemporary authors.

10758   CROWELL'S HANDBOOK OF CONTEMPORARY DRAMA, by
          Michael Anderson ... and others. New York, Crowell,
          1971. vi, 505 p. 24cm. (A Crowell reference book)

10759   ČUBELIĆ, TVRTKO
          Književni leksikon. Osnovni teorijsko-književni pojmovi i
          bio-bibliografske bilješke o piscima. 3., nadop. i proš. izd.
          Zagreb, 1972. lvi, 558 p. 21cm. First-2d editions published
          under title: Književnost. A dictionary of world literature; in-
          cludes bio-bibliography and definitions of terms.

10760   DANSKE SPROG- OG LITTERATURSELSKAB, COPENHAGEN.
          Det Danske sprog- og litteraturselskab, 1911-1961. Medlem-
          mer og medarbejdere. København, 1961. xii, 109 p. ports.
          23cm. Contains numerous portraits and some biographical data
          for members and collaborators of the Danish Philological Soci-
          ety. Edited by Albert Fabritius.

10761   DE MONTREVILLE, DORIS
          Third book of junior authors. Edited by Doris de Montre-
          ville and Donna Hill. New York, H. W. Wilson Co., 1972.
          320 p. ports. 27cm. (The Authors series) "Continues the
          work of Stanley J. Kunitz and Howard Haycraft in The junior
          book of authors, 1963." Includes a cumulative index to the 3
          works (p. 314-320) A biographical dictionary, chiefly of Amer-
          ican authors of books for children; many of the sketches are au-
          tobiographical.

10762   DÉZSI, LAJOS, 1868-   ed.
          Világirodalmi lexikon (külfoldi irodalom) Budapest,
          "Studium" [1931?-34?] 3 v. illus., ports. 25cm. An encyclo-
          pedia of world literature; foreign (non-Hungarian) literature,
          with entries and portraits for major literary figures.

10763   DICTIONNAIRE DES LITTÉRATURES ÉTRANGÈRES CONTEM-
          PORAINES. Paris, Editions universitaires, 1974. vii,
          817 p. 24cm. "Comment lire" (p. v-vii) signed: Dominique
          Roux. Dictionary of foreign contemporary literature; a bio-
          bibliographical work arranged alphabetically by language group
          and alphabetically by author thereunder. Ca. 360 authors are
          included.

10764   DICTIONNAIRE LITTÉRAIRE: extrait des meilleurs auteurs
         anciens et modernes. Avec la permission des supérieurs.
Liége, Libraires associés, 1768.   v. 22 x 28cm. Reproduced from a copy of the 1768 ed. Printed in double columns on
one side of leaf only. Contents. --v. 1. A-K. --v. 2. L-Q. --v. 3.
R-V. A dictionary of literature based on material from the better ancient and modern authors; with biographical data.

10765   DĬUGMEDZHIEVA, PETĬA TRIFONOVA
         Chuzhdestranni pisateli na bŭlgarski ezik. 1945-1970. Bio-
bibliografski ukazatel. Sustav. P. Dĭugmedzhieva i St. Ivanov.
Red. (s predg.) Benko Khristov. Sofiĭa, Narodna biblioteka
Kiril i Metodii, 1973. 812 p. 24cm. A bio-bibliographical
compilation covering foreign authors of the modern period (chiefly 19th-20th centuries) who have been translated into Bulgarian.
Arrangement is alphabetical under country, with a name index at
end.

10766   DIZIONARIO BIOGRAFICO DEGLI AUTORI DI TUTTI I TEMPI.
         Letterati, filosofi, scienziati, musicisti, storici, politici.
Milano, Fabbri, Bompiani [1970] 4 v. illus. 26cm. "Nuova
edizione ... aggiornata." Originally published under title:
Dizionario letterario Bompiani degli autori di tutti i tempi e di
tutte la letterature. A biographical dictionary of all times and
literatures, including men of letters, philosophers, scientists,
musicians, historians and political scientists/statesmen.

10767   DIZIONARIO DI BELLE LETTERE. Ed. 2. Venezia, 1816. 3 v.
         in 1. An early 19th century dictionary of literature, in Ital-
ian, with biographical entries.

10768   DUPIN, LOUIS ELLIES, 1657-1719.
         Bibliothèque des auteurs separez de la communion de l'Eg-
lise romaine du XVIème et XVIIème siècle. Paris, A. Pralard,
1718-19. 2 v. in 4. 20cm. Bio-bibliography of authors separa-
ted from the Catholic Church, 16th-17th centuries. Arranged by
church & chronologically thereunder; alphabetical table of authors at end of vols. 1, pt. 2 & 2, pt. 2. Reprinted in 1969/70 by
Gregg Publishers, Farnborough, Eng.

10769   ENCICLOPEDIA DE LA LITERATURA. Recopilado bajo la
         dirección de Benjamín Jarnés. México, Editora Central
[1946?] 6 v. 25cm. Encyclopedia of literature and the world's
famous authors.

10770   ENCICLOPEDIA GARZANTI DELLA LETTERATURA. Milano,
         Garzanti, 1972. 963 p. illus. 18cm. Cover title: Enciclo-
pedia della letteratura Garzanti. An encyclopedia of world
literature; with biographical sketches.

10771   ENCYCLOPEDIA OF WORLD LITERATURE IN THE 20th
         CENTURY. General editor: Wolfgang Bernard Fleisch-
         mann. New York, F. Ungar Pub. Co., 1967-75. 4 v. ports.
         29cm. Translation and expansion of Lexikon der Weltliteratur
         im 20. Jahrhundert; bio-bibliographical. Vol. 4; Supplement
         and index, edited by F. Ungar and Lina Mainiero.

10772   ENZIKLOPEDIAH LE-SIFRUTH YISRAELITH U-KELALITH.
         Tel-Aviv, Mizpah Pub. Co., 1942-47. 4 v. ports. 23cm.
         Added t. p.: Hebrew encyclopedia of Hebrew and foreign litera-
         ture. Edited by Baruch Krupnik with the assistance of promi-
         nent writers and scholars. Includes entries for many authors,
         foreign and Jewish.

10773   ENZYKLOPÄDIE DES MÄRCHENS; Handwörterbuch zur his-
         torischen und vergleichenden Erzählforschung. Hrsg. von
         Kurt Ranke zusammen mit Hermann Bausinger [et al.] Redak-
         tion: Lotte Baumann [et al.]   v. 25cm. Issued in fascicles.
         An encyclopedia (dictionary) of the tale (folktales, fairy tales,
         mythology, etc.) which includes biographies of classical, medi-
         eval and modern writers (that is, tellers and collectors of tales
         primarily).

10774   FINOTTI, JOSEPH MARIA, d. 1879.
         Bibliographia Catholica Americana; a list of works written
         by Catholic authors and published in the United States. Pt. I:
         from 1784 to 1820 inclusive. New York, Catholic Publication
         House, 1872. 318 p. 25cm. No more published. Both authors
         and title of works in one alphabet. Biographical information
         is given under many of the authors (not all of them).

10775   HARTE, BARBARA, comp.
         200 contemporary authors; bio-bibliographies of selected
         leading writers of today with critical and personal sidelights.
         Barbara Harte, Carolyn Riley, editors. Detroit, Mich., Gale
         Research Co. [1969] 306 p. 26cm. "All of the sketches ...
         are revisions of listings currently included in the ... semi-
         annual series Contemporary authors."

10776   HENNEQUIN, PIERRE, b. 1772.
         Cours de littérature ancienne et moderne, contenant un
         traité complet de poétique, extrait des meilleurs critiques et
         commentateurs; enrichi de 700 notices sur les poètes les plus
         célèbres de tous les temps et de toutes les nations ... Moscou,
         Impr. d'A. Semen, 1821-22. 4 v. 25cm. A 'course' in ancient
         and modern literature with a treatise on poetics, supplemented
         with biographical notes on famous poets; the 700 biographical
         notices originally projected were extended to 950 by the addition
         of the fourth volume.

10777   HETTLER, AUGUST, 1860-
        Philologenlexikon. Lebensnachrichten und Schriftenver-
        zeichnisse. 1. Lfg. Halle, 1916. 16 p. 8.º No more published?
        Dictionary of philologists; a bio-bibliographical work.

10778   THE INTERNATIONAL AUTHORS AND WRITERS WHO'S WHO.
        Edited by Ernest Kay. Totowa, N. J., Rowman and Little-
        field, 1976. 676 p. 26cm. English ed. issued by the Melrose
        Press, Cambridge, Eng. Incorporates The Authors and writers
        who's who (published in 6 editions since 1934) and includes
        10,000 biographical entries, a list of pseudonyms of included
        authors and a list of literary agents. Future editions are con-
        templated.

10779   INTERNATIONAL WHO'S WHO IN POETRY. 2d ed. 1970-1971.
        Edited by Ernest Kay. With an appreciation of the late John
        Masefield by G. Wilson Knight. London, International Who's
        Who in Poetry [c1970] [24], 519 p. port. 25cm. More than
        3,000 living poets.

10780   JÜNGER, HARRI
        Literaturen der Völker der Sowjetunion. Hrsg. von Harri
        Jünger. [2., durchgesehene Aufl.] Leipzig, VEB Biblio-
        graphisches Institut [1968] 439 p. 20cm. (Meyers Taschen-
        lexikon) Literature of the peoples of the Soviet Union. Pages
        [120]-433 comprise a bio-bibliographical dictionary of 19th-20th
        century writers of those literatures (Russian, Armenian, Esto-
        nian, Uzbek, Moldavian, Ukrainian, etc.).

10781   JÜNGER, HARRI
        The literatures of the Soviet peoples; a historical and bio-
        graphical survey. Edited by Harri Jünger. [Translated from
        the German] New York, F. Ungar Pub. Co. [1971, c1970] xii,
        482 p. ports. 22cm. Translation of Literaturen der Völker
        der Sowjetunion. Pages 99-482 comprise a bio-bibliographical
        dictionary of 19th-20th century writers of those literatures (Rus-
        sian, Armenian, Estonian, Uzbek, Moldavian, Ukrainian, etc.).

10782   KAISER, FRANCES E
        Translators and translations: services and sources in sci-
        ence and technology. Frances E. Kaiser, editor. 2d ed. [New
        York] Special Libraries Association, 1965. x, 214 p. 28cm.
        Project jointly sponsored by the Special Libraries Association's
        Translations Activities Committee and its Georgia Chapter.
        "Free lance translators" (p. 1-53) comprises a 'biographical dic-
        tionary' of a sort (standardized information, but with no birth
        dates).

10783   LEXIKON DER KINDER- UND JUGENDLITERATUR; Personen-,
        Länder-und Sachartikel zu Geschichte und Gegenwart der

Kinder- und Jugendliteratur. Hrsg. von Klaus Doderer. Wein-
heim, Basel, Beltz; Pullach (bei München), Verlag Dokumentation, 1975-   v. illus. 25cm. To be in 3 vols. Dictionary of the literature of children and young people; includes
entries for persons, countries and subjects.

10784   LEXIKON DER WELTLITERATUR IM 20. JAHRHUNDERT.
         Freiburg i. B., Herder [1960-61] 2 v. ports. 27cm.
"Gestaltet vom Forschungsinstitut für Europäische Gegenwartskunde, Wien, und vom Lexikographischen Institut des Verlags
Herder." Contents.--1. Bd. A-J. [2. Aufl.]--2. Bd. K-Z. 1.
und 2. Aufl. Mit ... Personenregister. Dictionary of world
literature in the 20th century; chiefly a bio-bibliographical dictionary.

10785   McGRAW-HILL ENCYCLOPEDIA OF WORLD DRAMA; an inter-
         national reference work. New York, McGraw-Hill [1972]
4 v. (2150 p.) illus. 29cm. A biographical dictionary of 910
dramatists.

10786   MAGILL, FRANK NORTHERN, 1907-
         Cyclopedia of world authors. Rev. ed. Edited by Frank N.
Magill. Associate editors: Dayton Kohler, Tench Francis Tilgh-
man. Englewood Cliffs, N. J., Salem Press [c1974] 3 v. (vii,
1973, xi p.) 24cm. First ed. under this title issued in 1958.
"An earlier edition of this work appears under the title of: Mas-
terplots cyclopedia of world authors." Contents.--v. 1. A-Gab.
--v. 2. Gal-Oco.--v. 3. Ode-Z. Index. "Considers the lives
and works of about one thousand ... creative individuals, writers." Covers all periods although "almost half of the authors
included for the first time [since earlier edition] are contemporary writers whose major works have been written since 1950."

10787   MAŁY SŁOWNIK LITERATURY DLIA DZIECI I MŁODZIEZY.
         Pod red. Krystyny Kuliczkowskiej i Ireny Słonskiej. [Wyd.
1.] Warsawa, Wiedza Powszechna, 1964. 436 p. 20cm.
(Wydawnictwa popularno-encyklopedyczne) Dictionary of authors
of children's literature.

10788   MAŁY SŁOWNIK PISARZY ŚWIATA. [Redaktorzy: Kazimierz
         Hanulak, Henryk Olszewski] Wyd. 2., popr. i rozsz. War-
szawa, Wiedza Powszechna, 1972. 544 p. ports. 21cm. 1st ed.
published in 1968 under the editorship of Leon Bielas. A dictionary of the world's writers (some 2,000 entries).

10789   MARCHMONT, FREDERICK
         A concise handbook of ancient and modern literature, issued
either anonymously, under pseudonyms, or initials. London,
The author, 1896. 164 p. port. 19cm. "Offered for use as a
supplementary volume to Lownde's Bibliographer's manuel."

10790   MATLAW, MYRON, 1924-
            Modern world drama; an encyclopedia. New York, Dutton,
         1972. xxi, 960 p. illus., ports. 25cm. A dictionary that in-
         cludes bio-bibliographical entries for 688 playwrights of the 19th
         and 20th centuries.

10791   MEYER-BROCKMANN, HENRY, 1912-
            Brockmanns gesammelte Siebenundvierziger. 100 Karika-
         turen literarischer Zeitgenossen. [Texte von Henri M.-Brock-
         mann und Jürgen von Hollander. München] Deutscher Taschen-
         buch Verlag [1967] 115 p. ports. 18cm. (Dtv [-Taschenbücher]
         447) 100 caricatures of contemporary literary figures.

10792   MEYERS HANDBUCH ÜBER DIE LITERATUR. Ein Lexikon der
            Dichter und Schriftsteller aller Literaturen. Hrsg. von der
         Lexikonredaktion des Bibliographischen Instituts. Redaktionelle
         Leitung: Ingrid Adam und Gisela Preuss. 2., neu bearb. Aufl.
         Mannheim, Bibliographisches Institut [1970] 987 p. illus.,
         ports. 23cm. (Meyers Handbücher der grossen Wissenschafts-
         gebiete) A bio-bibliographical dictionary of world literature.

10793   OLLES, HELMUT, 1929-
            Literaturlexikon 20. [i.e. zwanzigstes] Jahrhundert. Hrsg.
         von Helmut Olles. [Reinbek bei Hamburg] Rowohlt [1971] 850 p.
         24cm. Dictionary of literature of the 20th century; a bio-biblio-
         graphical dictionary of world literature. Issued also as a paper-
         back in 3 volumes.

10794   PALLAS, GUSTAV, 1882-
            Slovníček literární. Praha, J. Otto, 1923. 366 p. 8.º
         (Ottovy malé slovníky) A dictionary of world literature; bio-
         bibliographical in large part.

10795   THE PENGUIN COMPANION TO EUROPEAN LITERATURE.
            Edited by Anthony Thorlby. New York, McGraw-Hill [1971,
         c1969] 907 p. 24cm. (The Penguin companion to world litera-
         ture) Largely a bio-bibliographical dictionary for European
         literature of all periods.

10796   THE PENGUIN COMPANION TO LITERATURE. [Harmonds-
            worth, Middlesex, Eng.] Penguin Books [1969-71] 4 v.
         20cm. (Penguin reference books, R35) Contents.--1. Britain
         and the Commonwealth.--2. Europe, edited by A. Thorlby.--3.
         U. S. A. and Latin American, edited by Eric Mottram, Malcolm
         Bradbury and Jean Franco.--4. Classical and Byzantine, edited
         by D. R. Dudley. Oriental and African, edited by D. M. Lang.
         Largely a set of bio-bibliographical dictionaries.

10797   THE READER'S COMPANION TO WORLD LITERATURE.
             [Contributed materials by] Sterling A. Brown [and others]
         Editor: Lillian Herlands Hornstein. Co-editor: G. D. Percy.
         2d ed. , rev. and updated by Lillian Herlands Hornstein, Leon
         Edel and Horst Franz. New York, New American Library [1973]
         977 p. 18cm. (A Mentor book) A dictionary of literature which
         includes biographies of the major figures in world literature.

10798   RECLAMS HÖRSPIELFÜHRER. Hrsg. von Heinz Schwitzke
             unter Mitarbeit von Franz Hiesel, Werner Klippert [und]
         Jürgen Tomm. Stuttgart, P. Reclam Jun. [1969] 670 p. 16cm.
         (Universal-Bibliothek Nr. 10161-68) A bio-bibliographical dic-
         tionary of world authors for the medium of television.

10799   SHIPLEY, JOSEPH TWADELL, 1893-
             Encyclopedia of literature. Edited by Joseph T. Shipley.
         New York, Philosophical Library [1946] 2 v. 25cm. "Biogra-
         phical notices" (v. 2, p. 1055-1188)—a biographical dictionary
         of famous authors in world literature.

10800   SINHA, SHRI MURARI, 1915-
             Nobel laureates of literature, 1901-1973 (with a note on the
         laureates of 1974). New Delhi, S. Chand, 1975. xlviii, 397 p.
         port. 23cm. Biographies of the 71 winners of the Nobel prize
         in literature from 1901 to 1974. Chronological arrangement.

10801   SOMETHING ABOUT THE AUTHOR: facts and pictures about
             contemporary authors and illustrators of books for young
         people. v. 1-   Detroit, Gale Research Co. , 1971-   v.
         illus., ports. 29cm. Each volume covers ca. 200 authors and
         illustrators of juvenilia. Nine volumes issued as of 1976.

10802   STEINER, GERHARD, 1905-
             Fremdsprachige Schriftsteller. Hrsg. von Gerhard Steiner.
         Wissenschaftliche Redaktion: Herbert Greiner-Mai. Leipzig,
         Bibliographisches Institut, 1971. 712 p. 20cm. (Meyers Tasche-
         nlexikon) Bio-bibliography of world literature (excluding German
         authors). See also the author's Lexikon der Weltliteratur: fremd-
         sprachige Schriftsteller ...

10803   STEINER, GERHARD, 1905-   ed.
             Lexikon der Weltliteratur. Fremdsprachige Schriftsteller
         und anonyme Werke von den Anfängen bis zur Gegenwart. Hrsg.
         von Gerhard Steiner unter Mitarbeit zahlreicher Fachwissen-
         schaftler. 2. Aufl. Leipzig, VEB Bibliographisches Institut,
         1965. 903 p. ports. 20cm. 1st ed. (1963) issued by Volks-
         verlag, Weimar (xvi, 812 p.) Dictionary of world literature;
         foreign (non-German) authors and anonymous works from the be-
         ginnings of literature to the present.

10804   SZYMUSIAK, JAN MARIA
         Słownik wczesnochrześcijańskiego piśmiennictwa. Jan Ma-
ria Szymusiak, Marek Starowieyski. Wyd. 1. Poznań, Ksie-
garnia Sw. Wojciecha, 1971. 659 p. 25cm. (Starożytna mysl
chrześcijańska, t. 2) Illustrative matter in pocket. A dictionary
of early Christian literature (350 entries) with bio-bibliographical entries.

10805   VERSINS, PIERRE, 1923-
         Encyclopédie de l'utopie, des voyages extraordinaires et de
la science fiction. [Lausanne, Switzerland] L'Age d'homme
[1972] 997 p. illus. 28cm. Encyclopedia of utopias, fantastic
voyages and travels and science fiction; included in this dictionary are biographies of many writers of these genres as well as
other people who have a connection with the themes of the encyclopedia.

10806   VINSON, JAMES, 1921-
         Contemporary dramatists. With a pref. by Ruby Cohn.
Editor: James Vinson. London, St. James Press; New York,
St. Martin's Press [1973] xv, 926 p. 25cm. (Contemporary
writers of the English language) A bio-bibliographical dictionary, with critical comments, of some 300 living playwrights
using the English language.

10807   VINSON, JAMES, 1921-
         Contemporary novelists. With a pref. by Walter Allen.
Editor: James Vinson. Associate editor: D. L. Kirkpatrick.
[2d ed.] London, St. James Press; New York, St. Martin's
Press [1976] xvii, 1636 p. 25cm. (Contemporary writers of
the English language, v. 2) Over 600 novelists (American, English, Commonwealth of Nations primarily) are included in this
bio-bibliography. 1st ed. appeared in 1972 (xvii, 1422 p.).

10808   WAKEMAN, JOHN
         World authors, 1950-1970; a companion volume to Twen-
tieth century authors. Edited by John Wakeman. Editorial consultant: Stanley J. Kunitz. New York, H. W. Wilson Co., 1975.
1594 p. ports. 26cm. (The Authors series) A biographical
dictionary with entries for 959 authors most of whom came into
prominence between 1950 and 1970.

10809   WALSH, THOMAS, 1875-1928, comp.
         The Catholic anthology; the world's great Catholic poetry.
Rev. ed. New York, Macmillan, 1943. xii, 584 p. 21cm.
Revised ed. first issued in 1932. Includes a brief biographical
dictionary (p. 515-564) of Catholic poets.

10810   WARD, ALFRED CHARLES, 1891-
         Longman companion to twentieth century literature. 2d ed.

London, Longman, 1975. 597 p. 23cm. 20th century literature; a dictionary with biographical sketches. First English edition issued in 1970.

10811   WEBSTER GROVES, MO. GALLERY OF LIVING CATHOLIC
        AUTHORS.
        The Gallery of Living Catholic Authors in the Catholic
literary center of the world ... By Sister Mary Joseph. Webster Groves [1945] 97 p. 21cm. Brief bio-bibliographical data
is given for over 400 names.

African

10812   HERDECK, DONALD E   1924-
        African authors; a companion to Black African writing, by
Donald E. Herdeck. Contributors: Abiola Irele, Lilyan Keste-
loot, Gideon Mangoaela. Rockville, Md., Black Orpheus Press.
1973-   v. illus., ports. 24cm. [Dimensions of the
Black intellectual experience] Contents.--v. 1. 1300-1973. "Bio-
bibliographical entries, A-Z"; v. 1, p. [15]-471. "[The first]
volume represents the first of a series of biennial reference
companions to Black African writing. Future volumes will up-
date and perfect the entries of previous years, add more authors ... "

10813   JAHN, JANHEINZ
        Who's who in African literature; biographies, works, com-
mentaries [by] Janheinz Jahn, Ulla Schild [and] Almut Nordmann. Tübingen, Published for the German Africa Society [by]
H. Erdmann, 1972. 406, [3] p. ports. 21cm. A bio-bibliographical dictionary of more than 400 Sub-Saharan African writers.

10814   ZELL, HANS M
        A reader's guide to African literature. Compiled and edited
by Hans M. Zell and Helene Silver. With contributions by Barbara Abrash and Gideon-Cyrus M. Mutiso. New York, Africana
Pub. Corp. [1971] xxi, 218 p. ports. 23cm. "Biographies"
(p. 114-199) is a biographical dictionary (with a number of portraits) of 51 of the most prominent African writers (writing in
English or French).

American

Anonyms and Pseudonyms

10815   GAINES, PIERCE WELCH
        Political works of concealed authorship relating to the Unit-
ed States, 1789-1810, with attributions. 3d ed. rev. and enl.
Hamden, Conn., Shoe String Press, 1972. xx, 226 p. 22cm.
First published in 1959 under title: Political works of concealed

authorship during the administrations of Washington, Adams, and Jefferson, 1789-1809. Rev. and enl. ed. (1965) issued under title: Political works of concealed authorship in the United States, 1789-1810, with attributions. Includes a list of pseudonyms, with real name immediately following and reference to literary work in the bibliographical main text.

General Works

10816   ADOFF, ARNOLD, comp.
The poetry of Black America; anthology of the 20th century. Edited by Arnold Adoff. Introd. by Gwendolyn Brooks. New York, Harper & Row, 1973. xxi, 552 p. 24cm. "Biographical notes" (p. [517]-538) is a bio-bibliographical dictionary.

10817   AMERICAN WRITERS; a collection of literary biographies.
Leonard Unger, editor in chief. New York, Scribner, 1974. 4 v. 29cm. The biographies were originally published as the University of Minnesota pamphlets on American writers. 97 bio-bibliographies, alphabetically arranged. Contents. --v. 1. Henry Adams to T. S. Eliot. --v. 2. Ralph Waldo Emerson to Carson McCullers. --v. 3. Archibald MacLeish to George Santayana. --v. 4. Isaac Bashevis Singer to Richard Wright.

10818   BAILEY, LEAONEAD PACK
Broadside authors and artists; an illustrated biographical dictionary. Compiled and edited by Leaonead Pack Bailey. 1st ed. Detroit, Mich., Broadside Press, 1974. 125 p. ports. 22cm. 192 chiefly Black authors and artists (183 are Americans, 184 are authors) who wrote or write (or illustrate) for the Broadside Press.

10819   BARKSDALE, RICHARD, comp.
Black writers of America; a comprehensive anthology by Richard Barksdale and Keneth Kimmamon. New York, Macmillan, 1972. xxiii, 917 p. 26cm. Included are bio-bibliographical sketches of 84 authors (in chronological arrangement).

10820   BARNS, FLORENCE ELBERTA
Texas writers of today. Foreword by Robert Adger Law. Ann Arbor, Mich., Gryphon Books, 1971. 513, [1] p. 22cm. Reprint of the 1935 ed. A bio-bibliographical dictionary of 1,180 Texas authors plus representative selections from their writings.

10821   BRAWLEY, BENJAMIN GRIFFITH, 1882-1939.
The Negro genius; a new appraisal of the achievement of the American Negro in literature and the fine arts. New York, Biblo and Tannen, 1966 [c1937] xiii, 366 p. illus., ports. 21cm. Collective biography arranged under such chapter head-

ings as : Poetry and the arts, Literature, Drama and stage, etc. Contains ca. 80 fairly full bio-bibliographies with brief notes on other Negro artists. Alphabetical approach through the index.

10822 BRÜNING, EBERHARD
       Amerikanische Literatur. Mit einem Anhang: Die englische Sprache in den Vereinigten Staaten, von Albrecht Neubert. [3. neubearb. und erw. Aufl.] Leipzig, Bibliographisches Institut, 1967. 230 p. illus. 20cm. (Meyers Taschenlexikon) A dictionary of American literature; includes bio-bibliographies.

10823 BURKE, WILLIAM JEREMIAH, 1902-
       American authors and books. 1640 to the present day [by] W. J. Burke and Will D. Howe. Rev. by Irving Weiss and Anne Weiss. 3d rev. ed. New York, Crown Publishers [c1972] 719 p. 25cm. Ca. 17,000 entries, mostly bio-bibliographical.

10824 CHESTER, LAURA, comp.
       Rising tides; 20th century American women poets. Edited by Laura Chester and Sharon Barba. New York, Washington Square Press, Pocket Books, 1973. xxxi, 410 p. ports. 18cm. An anthology of poetry with a short biography and a portrait accompanying the work of each of the 70 poets represented. Chronologically arranged, from Gertrude Stein to Laura Chester. Alphabetical approach through names in heavy print in index.

10825 ELLMANN, RICHARD, 1918-   comp.
       The Norton anthology of modern poetry. Edited by Richard Ellmann and Robert O'Clair. 1st ed. New York, Norton, 1973. xlvi, 1456 p. 24cm. Included because of its 155 biographical and critical sketches of American and British poets of the first half of the 20th century and the last decades of the 19th century. Arrangement is chronological by date of poet's birth.

10826 FLAGG, MILDRED (BUCHANAN) 1886-
       Profiles of New York authors. New York, Carlton Press [1972] 182 p. 21cm. (A Hearthstone book) Over a hundred biographical sketches of "major writers who were either born in the Empire State or lived the major portion of their professional life there, or whose literary careers are inseparable from that great state's history." In alphabetical arrangement.

10827 FOX, HUGH, 1932-   comp.
       The living underground; an anthology of contemporary American poetry. Edited by Hugh Fox. Troy, N. Y., Whitston Pub. Co., 1973. xi, 479 p. 24cm. "Biographical notes" (p. 447-479) comprises a biographical dictionary (without birth dates) of 20th century (living) American underground poets.

10828   HOPKINS, LEE BENNETT
         More books by more people; interviews with sixty-five au-
thors of books for children. New York, Citation Press, 1974.
xx, 410 p. ports. 20cm. Continues his earlier Books are by
people (1969); like the latter it is a 'bio-bibliographical dictionary,' in part (chiefly American authors and illustrators).

10829   MALKOFF, KARL
         Crowell's handbook of contemporary American poetry. New
York, Crowell [1973] ix, 338 p. 24cm. In large part a bio-bibliographical dictionary of American poets flourishing since 1940.

10830   THE PENGUIN COMPANION TO AMERICAN LITERATURE.
         Edited by Malcolm Bradbury, Eric Mottram and Jean Fran-
co. New York, McGraw-Hill [1971] 384 p. 24cm. (The Penguin companion to world literature) English edition (Harmonds-
worth, Penguin Books) has title: The Penguin companion to literature: U. S. A. ... Latin America. With biographical sketches
of notable writers.

10831   RUSH, THERESSA GUNNELS, 1945-
         Black American writers past and present; a biographical
and bibliographical dictionary, by Theressa Gunnels Rush,
Carol Fairbanks Myers and Esther Spring Arata. Metuchen, N.
J., Scarecrow Press, 1975. 2 v. (865 p.) ports. 22cm. Contents: v. 1. A-I.--v. 2. J-Z. Detailed information (it is a bio-
bibliographical dictionary) on more than 2,000 Black American
authors.

10832   SHOCKLEY, ANN ALLEN
         Living Black American authors; a biographical directory
[by] Ann Allen Shockley and Sue P. Chandler. New York, R. R.
Bowker, 1973. xv, 220 p. 24cm. A bio-bibliographical dictionary.

10833   TAYLOR, WELFORD DUNAWAY
         Virginia authors, past and present. Welford Dunaway Tay-
lor, general editor, with Maurice Duke, bibliographical editor
[and others. Richmond] Virginia Association of Teachers of
English, 1972. xiv, 125 p. map (on lining papers) 23cm. A
bio-bibliographical dictionary.

10834   THOMPSON, DONALD EUGENE, 1913-
         Indiana authors and their books, 1917-1966; a continuation of
Indiana authors and their books, 1816-1916, and containing additional names from the earlier period. Compiled by Donald E.
Thompson. Crawfordsville, Ind., Wabash College, 1974. xvi,
688 p. 29cm. A bio-biobibliographical dictionary.

10835   WHO'S WHO AMONG PACIFIC NORTHWEST AUTHORS. 2d ed.
         Edited with a pref. by Frances Valentine Wright. [Mis-
         soula? Mont.] Pacific Northwest Library Association, Reference
         Division, 1969. 105 p. 29cm. (Libri montani)

10836   WHO'S WHO ON THE WORLD. [New York, The World, 1922]
              35 p. illus., ports. 26cm. Cover title. "Biographical
         sketches [of newspapermen on The World, a newspaper in New
         York City, that existed from 1860 to 1931] ... reproduced from
         ... Who's who in America. "

10837   WILLIAMS, MILLER, comp.
              Contemporary poetry in America. [1st ed.] New York,
         Random House [1973] xxviii, 189 p. ports. 28cm. An anthol-
         ogy which also includes biographical sketches and portraits of
         96 living American poets. "Index of poets" (p. 189) yields al-
         phabetical approach to the works and biographies.

Arabic

10838   IBN AL-KHATĪB, d. 1374.
              Al-Katībah al-kāminah ... [Beirut, Lebanon] Dār at-Taqafa
         [1963] 320 p. 24cm. Biographies of Andalusian (Moslem) poets
         of the 8th century A. H. /14th century A. D.

10839   IBN AL-NADĪM, MUHAMMAD IBN ISHĀQ, fl. 987.
              The Fihrist of al-Nadīm; a tenth-century survey of Muslim
         culture. Bayard Dodge, editor and translator. New York, Co-
         lumbia University Press, 1970. 2 v. (xxxiv, 1149 p.) facsims.,
         geneal. table. 24cm. (Records of civilization: sources and
         studies, no. 83) An encyclopedic bio-bibliography of early Mus-
         lim scholars, writers, etc. The "Biographical index" (p. [931]-
         1135 at the end of vol. 2) gives a 'who's who' type of approach to
         persons listed in the main text.

10840   ISMAIL, pasa, 1839-1920.
              Hadiyyat al-'arifin ... [Istanbul] Matba'at al-Ma'arif [1951-
         55] 2 v. 34cm. Added t. p.: Hadiyyat al-'arifin, asma' al-
         mu'allifin va asr al-musannifin ... A bio-bibliographical diction-
         ary of Arabic authors.

10841   KAHHĀLAH, 'UMAR RIDA
              Mu'jam al-mu'allifin tarajim musannifi al-kutub al-Arabiy-
         yah. Dimashq [Damascus] al-Maktabah al-Arabiyyah bi Dimashq
         [1957-61] 15 v. 25cm. A dictionary of authors of Arabic litera-
         ture; bio-bibliographical.

10842   AL-KHAFĀJĪ, AHMAD IBN MUHAMMAD, d. 1659.
              Hādhā kitāb rayhānat al-alibbā ... Bulaq, 1273 A. H.

[1856/57] 8,439 p. An anthology of Arabic poetry of the 11th
century A. H. (ca. 1590-1650) accompanied by biographical notices and anecdotes about the poets.

10843   AL-MARZUBĀNĪ, MUHAMMAD IBN 'IMRĀN, 909?-994?
        Die Gelehrtenbiographien des Abū 'Ubaidallāh al-Marzu-
bānī, in der Rezension des Hāfiz al-Yagmūrī. Hrsg. von Rudolf
Selheim. Wiesbaden, In Kommission bei F. Steiner, 1964-
        v. facsims. 26cm. (Bibliotheca Islamica, Bd. 23
Added t. p.: Nūr al-gabas al-mukhtasar min al-Muqtabas ...
Muslim grammarians, men of letters, poets and scholars. Vol.
1 (Arabic text) only one available as of 1976?

10844   AL-MARZUBĀNĪ, MUHAMMAD IBN 'IMRĀN, 909?-994?
        Mu'jam al-shu'arā'. al-Qāhirah [Cairo] Dār Ihya' al-
Kutub al-Arabiyyah, 1379 A. H. [1960] 13,590 p. 25cm. A dictionary of Arabic poets.

10845   AL-QIFTĪ, 'ALĪ IBN YŪSUF, 1172 or 3-1248.
        Inbāh al-ruwāt 'alā anbāh al-nuhāt. al-Qāhirah [Cairo]
1950-73. 4 v. 28cm. A biographical dictionary of Arab grammarians. Edited by Muhammad Abū al-Fadl Ibrāhim. Vol. 4
published by Dār al-Kutub wa-al-Wathā'iq al-Qawmīyah.

10846   AL-SUYŪTĪ, 1445-1505.
        Bughyat al-wu'ah fi tabaqat al-lugawiyyim wa an-nuha. al-
Qāhira, Matba'at 'Isa al-Babī al-Halabī, 1964-65. 2 v. 25cm.
A biographical dictionary of Arabic linguists and philologists.

10847   YĀQŪT IBN 'ABD ALLĀH AL HAMAWĪ, 1179?-1229.
        The Irshād al-arib ilā ma'rifat al-adib; or, Dictionary of
learned men of Yāqút. Edited by D. S. Margoliouth, and printed
for the trustees of the E. J. W. Gibb Memorial. Leyden, E. J.
Brill, 1907-27. 7 v. 25cm. (E. J. W. Gibb memorial series,
v. 6) Vol. 4 dated 1927.

Argentine

10848   FIDALGO, ANDRÉS
        Panorama de la literatura jujeña. Buenos Aires, Ediciones
La Rosa Blindada [1975] 191 p. illus. 21cm. (Colección de
ens[a]yos Los tiempos nuevos) A bio-bibliography of ca. 100
Argentine authors from (or originally from) the Province of
Jujuy.

10849   ORGAMBIDE, PEDRO G
        Enciclopedia de la literatura argentina. Dirigida por
Pedro Orgambide y Roberto Yahni. Buenos Aires, Editorial

Sudamericana [1970] 639 p. 20cm. An encyclopedia-dictionary of Argentine literature consisting chiefly of bio-bibliographical entries.

Armenian

10850   CH'RAK'IAN, K'EROVBĒ, 1877-1970.
Hay matenagirner tasninnerord darow. Venetik, Surp Ghazar, 1904. 192 p. illus., ports. 18cm. Cover title. Bio-bibliography of Armenian authors of the 19th century. Non-alphabetical arrangement; without contents note or index.

10851   GASPARYAN, GASPAR KARAPETI
Hay barharangrowt 'yan patmowt'yown. Erivan [Institute of Linguistics H. Acharian] 1968. 564 p. facsims., ports. 23cm. Bio-bibliographical history of Armenian dictionaries, i. e. Armenian lexicographers and their work. Chronological in arrangement.

10852   HAY NOR GRAKANOWT'YAN PATMOWT'YOWN. Erivan, Haykakan SSR GA Hradkts., 1962-   v. illus., ports. 27cm. Added t. p.: Istoriia novoi armianskoi literatury. Edited by A. A. Asatryan and issued by the Institute of Literature (Grakanowt'yan Institowt) A history of modern Armenian literature from 1772, but with entire sections devoted to biographical-critical sketches of Armenian authors: e. g., v. 1, p. 151-194, 197-236, 273-528; v. 2, p. 67-493. Contents. --1. 1772-1850. --2. 1851-1870. --3. 1871-1890. --v. 1891-early 20th century. 4 vols issued as of 1972.

10853   MELIK, ROUBEN, comp.
La poésie arménienne; anthologie des origines à nos jours. Réalisée sous la direction de Rouben Melik. Paris, Editeurs français réunis [1973] 563 p. illus. 20cm. An anthology of Armenian poetry from its origins to the present; in chronological arrangement, the anthology also includes brief biographical sketches of 88 poets.

10854   POGHARIAN, NORAYR
Hay groghner, E-zhi dar. Erowsaghēm, Tparan Srbots' Hakobeants', 1971. 16, 616 p. 19cm. In Armenian. Biographical sketches of 153 Armenian authors; arranged chronologically, from ca. 355 to 1700.

10855   SOVETAHAY GRAKANOWT'YAN PATMORT'YOWN. Erivan, Haykakan SSR GA Hradkts., 1961-65. 2 v. 23cm. Edited by Sowren Aghababyan, Ed. T'op'ch'yan and Lewon Hakhverdyan and issued by the Soviet Literature Section of the Literature Institute (Sovetskan Grakanowt'yan Sektor, Grakanowt'yan Institowt). Contents. --1. 1917-1941. --2. 1941-1964. A history of

Armenian literature under Soviet rule. Extensive biographical-critical sections will be found in v. 1, p. 220-449, 626-798 and v. 2, p. 64-331, 589-772.

10856   T'EOLEOLIAN, MINAS
         Dar me grakanowt'iwn, 1850-1950. Gahire [Yolsaber] 1955-56. 2 v. illus., ports. 25cm. A century of Armenian literature, 1850-1950. Contains a substantial number of sections devoted to bio-bibliography (v. 1, p. 97-312, 341-473, 509-723; v. 2, p. 55-287, 421-501)

Assamese

10857   SHASTRI, P   N   1923-
         The Writers Workshop handbook of Assamese literature [by] P. N. Shastri & P. Lal. Calcutta, Writers Workshop, c1972-   v. 23cm. Title on spine: Assamese literature. Running title: The WW handbook of Assamese literature. A dictionary of Assamese literature which consists for the major part of bio-bibliographical entries, but also includes titles of literary works, journals, etc. Vol. 1 only (A-D) available as of 1976.

Australian

Anonyms and Pseudonyms

10858   NESBITT, BRUCE
         Australian literary pseudonyms; an index, with selected New Zealand references, compiled by Bruce Nesbitt and Susan Hadfield. Adelaide, Libraries Board of South Australia, 1972. viii, 134 p. 23cm.

General Works

10859   ANDERSON, HUGH, 1927-
         The singing roads: a guide to Australian children's authors and illustrators. Arr. and edited by Hugh Anderson. 2d ed. [Sydney]. Wentworth Press, 1966. xiv, 117 p. 26cm. First ed. published in 1965. A bio-bibliographical dictionary of Australian children's authors and illustrators.

Austrian

Bibliography, Indexes, Portrait Catalogs

10860   STOCK, KARL FRANZ
         Personalbibliographien österreichischer Dichter und Schriftsteller von den Anfängen bis zur Gegenwart. Mit Auswahl einschlägiger Bibliographien, Nachschlagewerke, Sammel-

biographien, Literaturgeschichten und Anthologien. [Von] Karl
F. Stock, Rudolf Heilinger [und] Marylene Stock. Pullach bei
München, Verlag Dokumentation, 1972. xxiii, 703 p. 22cm. A
bibliography of biographies and bio-bibliographies of Austrian
authors, collective and individual. Includes also anthologies
that contain biographical data about the authors represented.

General Works

10861   BINDER, LUCIA
        Lexikon der Jugendschriftsteller in deutscher Sprache.
Hrsg. von Lucia Binder. Wien, Leimüller, 1968. 219 p.
21cm. (Schriften zur Jugendlektüre, Bd. 6) "Sonderdruck aus
Die Barke, 1968." A dictionary of Austrian writers of children's literature.

10862   FRANZOS, KARL EMIL, 1848-1904, comp.
        Deutsches Dichterbuch aus Oesterreich. Hrsg. von Karl
Emil Franzos. Leipzig, Breitkopf und Härtel; Stuttgart, A.
Bonz, 1883. xl, 338 p. 24cm. An anthology of German poetry
from Austria, with bio-bibliographical sketches of the 99 poets
represented.

10863   GALL, FRANZ
        Universitas poetarum. (In Österreichische Hochschulkunde;
Festgabe zur Sechshundertjahrfeier der Alma Mater Rudolphina.
Wien, 1965. 126 p. illus. 8.º p. 25-57) On pages 29-57 is a
biographical dictionary of 167 Austrian poets and authors.

10864   GASSER, VINZENZ
        Erstes biographisch-literarisches Schriftstellerlexikon von
Tirol; oder, Kurze Lebensbeschreibung der Schriftsteller,
welche geborene Tiroler waren oder sich längere Zeit in Tirol
aufgehalten haben, mit Angabe ihrer Werke. Senale-Innsbruck,
1896. 4 v. The first biographical-literary author dictionary of
the Tyrol; or, Brief biographies of authors who were born in the
Tyrol or have lived there a long time. A manuscript set of volumes in the Bibliothek des Museums Ferdinandeum, Innsbruck.

10865   HANDBOOK OF AUSTRIAN LITERATURE. Introduced and edited
        by Frederick Ungar. New York, F. Ungar Pub. Co., 1973.
xvi, 322 p. 25cm. Primarily articles from Hermann Kunisch's
Handbuch der deutschen Gegenwartsliteratur, in English translation. Bio-bibliographical dictionary of 79 authors born in the
territory of the Austro-Hungarian monarchy who wrote or write
in German.

10866   HASSENBERGER, EDUARD
        Österreichisches Kaiser-Jubiläums-Dichterbuch (50 Jahre
österreichischer Literatur) Huldigungsgabe zur 50. Jahres-

wende der Thronbesteigerung Sr. Maj. des Kaisers Franz
Joseph I. Hrsg. von Eduard Hassenberger. Redigiert von Hans
Maria Truxa. Mit 96 Porträts und Original–Beiträgen in hoch-
deutscher Sprache und in allen deutsch-österreichischen Mund-
arten. Wien, E. Hassenberger, 1899. viii, 325 p. ports. 4.º
An Austrian literary jubilee book celebrating the 50th year of
Emperor Franz Joseph's reign; it includes 234 "biograms" of
contemporary writers and poets living in Austria and writing in
German.

10867 HAUER, JOHANNES, comp.
       Am Quell der Muttersprache; österreichische Mundart-
dichtung der Gegenwart. [Graz] Staisny Verlag [1955] 555 p.
illus. 21cm. Writers of German literature (poetry) in Austrian
dialects; an anthology. Pages [493]-549 contain a biographical
dictionary (in several alphabets--by region: Styria, Burgenland,
etc.) of ca. 178 authors.

10868 LANGER, NORBERT
       Dichter aus Österreich. Wien, Österreichischer Bundesver-
lag [1956-67] 5 v. illus., ports. 20cm. German-writing authors
(20th century, living and deceased) from Austria; the five volumes (no more published?) contain 103 bio-bibliographical essays.
Each volume is arranged alphabetically.

10869 LEBENDIGE STADT. 1-10; 1954-1963. Wien, Hrsg. von Amt
       für Kultur, Volksbildung und Schulverwaltung der Stadt Wien.
10 v. Vol. 10, 1963 (263 p.) is a bio-bibliographical dictionary
of ca. 450 living poets, writers, artists and scholars of Austria,
all of whom were contributors to the first nine volumes of the almanac.

10870 LUCA, IGNAZ DE, d. 1799.
       Wiens gegenwärtiger. Zustand unter Josephs Regierung.
Wien, 1787. 323 p. (ca.) 8.º Contemporary Vienna (1787) under the Emperor Joseph. A work in the form of a dictionary;
pages 295-323 contain a biographical dictionary with 225 brief
sketches of Viennese authors of the 18th century.

10871 MAYR, AMBROS, comp.
       Tiroler Dichterbuch. Hrsg. im Auftrage des Vereins zur
Errichtung eines Denkmals Walthers von der Vogelweide in
Bozen. Innsbruck, Wagner, 1888. xii, 311 p. illus. 34cm.
Book of Tyrolean poetry; selections from the works of 123 Austrian poets from the Tyrol and 12 "friends" (non-Tyroleans). Selections are preceded by brief biographical sketches of the poets
represented. Chronologically arranged, from the Middle Ages
to the latter part of the 19th century.

10872 MOSENTHAL, SALOMON HERMANN, Ritter von, 1821-1877.
       Museum aus den deutschen Dichtungen österreichischer
Lyriker und Epiker der frühesten bis zur neuesten Zeit, aus-

gewählt und in neuhochdeutscher Sprache zusammengestellt.
Wien, Gerold, 1854. xvi, 515 p. An anthology of 130 Austrian
poets of all periods with accompanying biographical sketches.

10873 NAGL, JOHANN WILLIBALD, 1856-
        Deutsch-österreichische Literaturgeschichte; ein Handbuch
zur Geschichte der deutschen Dichtung in Österreich-Ungarn.
Unter Mitwirkung hervorragender Fachgenossen hrsg. von J. W.
Nagl und Jakob Zeidler. Wien, C. Fromme, 1899-[1937] 4 v.
illus., ports. 24cm. Vols. 2-4 edited and continued by Eduard
Castle. A comprehensive history of Austrian literature; included
here because of the great number of portraits of writers contained in vols. 2-4.

10874 NIGG, MARIANNE
        Biographien der österreichischen Dichterinnen und Schrift-
stellerinnen; ein Beitrag zur deutschen Literatur in Österreich.
Kornauburg, J. Kühkopf, 1893. 64 p. A biographical dictionary
of Austrian women as authors; German literature in Austria.

10875 DER ÖSTERREICHISCHE PARNASS VERSPOTTET IN WORT
        UND BILD. Hrsg. von Richard Maria Werner. Wien, 1912.
vi, 52 p. ports. 1st ed., Vienna, 1841, issued under title:
Oesterreichischer Parnass, bestiegen von einem herunter-
gekommenen Antiquar [Uffo Horn?] The Austrian Parnassus
mocked in word and picture; ca. 100 Austrian authors treated in
light-hearted fashion.

10876 P. E. N. CLUB. AUSTRIA.
        Österreichischer P. E. N. Club. Austrian P. E. N. Club.
P. E. N. Club autrichien. Bibliographie seiner Mitglieder.
Bibliography of its members ... Bearb. von Johann Gunert. 2.
verb. und erw. Aufl. Wien, 1959. 263 p. 8.º The Austrian
P. E. N. Club, with bio-bibliographical notices of its members.
1st ed., 1955.

10877 SCHEYRER, LUDWIG, 1811-1874.
        Die Schriftsteller Oesterreichs in Reim und Prosa auf dem
Gebiete der schönen Literatur; aus der ältesten bis auf die neu-
este Zeit. Mit biografischen Angaben und Proben aus ihren
Werken. Wien, Typographisch-Literarisch-Artistische Lehranstalt, 1858. iv, 595 p. The writers of Austria in verse and
prose; an anthology in chronological arrangement with biographical notes for the 230 authors represented. Includes an alphabetical index.

10878 SCHLOSSAR, ANTON, 1849-
        Steiermark im deutschen Liede. Eine poetische Anthologie.
Zwei Theile mit biographisch-literarhistorischem Anhang. Graz,
1880. 2 v. Styria in German poetry; an anthology. On pages

309-353 of vol. 2 are biographical sketches of 83 poets, chiefly
natives of Styria, but also including poets of other countries who
have written about Styria.ᵀ

10879   STERN, JULIUS, 1858-1912.
Journalisten- und Schriftsteller-Verein "Concordia" 1859-
1909. Eine Festschrift. I. Werden und Walten der "Concordia,"
von Julius Stern. II. Die soziale Arbeit der "Concordia," von
Sigmund Ehrlich. Wien, 1909. 262 p. ports. The Journalists'
and Writers' Association "Concordia," a Viennese group. The
volume contains many brief biographies and portraits of Austrian
journalists and authors as well as a necrology.

10880   STIMMEN DER GEGENWART. 1951-1956. Wien, 1951-56.
5 v. illus. 21cm. "Herausgegeben im Auftrag der Gesellschaft für Freiheit der Kultur." Volume for 1955 never published. Ceased publication. Austrian German literature of the
20th century; an anthology. At the end of each volume is a bio-
bibliographical dictionary of the authors included in the particular volume.

10881   STRATOWA, WULF, comp.
Österreichische Lyrik aus neun Jahrhunderten. Wien, P.
Neff, 1948. 407 p. 8.° An anthology of Austrian lyrics from
9 centuries; on pages 355-408 will be found a bio-bibliographical
dictionary of the 180 poets represented.

10882   STRELKA, JOSEPH, 1927-
Das zeitlose Wort; eine Anthologie österreichischer Lyrik
von Peter Altenberg bis zur Gegenwart. Eingeleitet und ausgewählt von Joseph Strelka, mit einem Nachwort von Ernst Schön-
weise. Graz, Stiasny Verlag, 1964. 256 p. 19cm. (Stiasny-
Bücherei, Bd. 125) An anthology of Austrian lyrics from Peter
Altenberg to the present, with a brief bio-bibliographical dictionary at the end of the volume covering 96 poets.

10883   SZYSZKOWITZ, GERALD
Dramatiker in der Steiermark. Redaktion: Gerald Szyszkowitz und Regine Friedrich. Graz, 1969. 32 p. ports. (Ve-
reinigte Bühnen Graz. Sonderheft) 120 dramatists in Styria
(natives or residents); with biographical notices.

Bashkir

10884   GAĬNULLIN, MIDKHAT FAZLYEVICH
Pisateli Sovetskoĭ Bashkirii. Biobibliograficheskiĭ spravochnik. Ufa, Bashkirskoe knizhnoe izd-vo, 1969. 403, [5] p.
ports. 21cm. At head of title: M. Gaĭnullin, G. Khusaĭnov. A
bio-bibliographical dictionary of contemporary Bashkirian authors.

Belgian

10885   ANDRÉ, VALÈRE, 1588-1655.
Bibliotheca Belgica. [De Belgis vita scriptisq. claris]
Facsimile of the Edition Louvain, 1643. Nieuwkoop, B. de
Graff, 1973. 900 p. illus. 23cm. (Monumenta humanistica
Belgica, v. 5) At head of title: Valerius Andreas. Bio-bibliography of Belgian authors, primarily active in the 16th-17th
centuries, and most often writing in Latin. Entry is by forename with a list of all the writers by surnames at front of
volume.

10886   LE MIRE, AUBERT, 1573-1640.
Illustrium Galliae Belgicae scriptorum icones et elogia.
Ex museio Auberti Muraei. Antverpiae, Apud T. Gallaeum,
1608. 58 ports., coat of arms. 23cm. Portraits and biographical sketches of 58 famous Belgian authors of the early modern
period who wrote in Latin. Succeeded by Le Mire's Elogia
Belgica (q. v.).

Bengali

10887   MITRA, SHIVRATAN, 1872-
Bangiya sahitya sevak. Calcutta, 1906. 1 v. Biographical
dictionary of Bengali authors. In Bengali.

10888   MUKHOPADHYAY, HARIMOHAN
Bangabhasar lekhak. Calcutta, Natabehari Rai, 1904.
1008 p. Biographical account of noted Bengali litterateurs. In
Bengali.

10889   SĀHITYA-SĀDHAKA-CARITAMĀLA.
[1943-no. 1, 1957] Calcutta.   nos. in   v. ports.
19cm. Edited by Brajendra Nath Banerjee and others. In Bengali. Includes biographical data for many Bengali authors with
annotated bibliographies for each.

Bohemian

See Czech

Bolivian

10890   COSSÍO SALINAS, HÉCTOR, comp.
La poesia en Cochabamba; selección, prólogo y notas de
Héctor Cossío Salinas. Cochabamba, Editorial Los Amigos del
Libro, 1972. 333 p. illus. 21cm. (Biblioteca IV [i.e. Cuarto]
centenario, 11) An anthology of Bolivian poetry by 74 authors

native to or related in some way with the City of Cochabamba.
Includes brief bio-bibliographical sketches of the poets (with an
alphabetical index to the poets at end of volume).

10891 GUZMÁN, AUGUSTO
        Poetas y escritores de Bolivia. La Paz, Editorial Los
Amigos del Libro, 1975. 293 p. ports. 20cm. 71 poets and
writers of Bolivia from the colonial period to the present; in
chronological arrangement.

10892 QUIRÓS, JUAN, comp.
        Las cien mejores poesías bolivianas. [Selección de] Juan
Quiros. [1. ed.] La Paz, Editorial y Librería Difusion, 1968.
239 p. 22cm. The 100 major Bolivian poets; an anthology that
includes bio-bibliographical sketches of the poets.

Brazilian

10893 FERNANDES, APARÍCIO, comp.
        Trovadores do Brasil. Rio de Janeiro, Editora Minerva
[1966]-70. 3 v. 27cm. Includes biographical notes on 1100
modern Brazilian poets and balladeers as well as selections
from their work.

10894 FERNANDES, NABOR, comp.
        Antologia de poetas valencianos (o que nos conta o passado
e o que se vê no presente). Rio de Janeiro, Editora Pongetti,
1974. 322 p. 19cm. An anthology of Brazilian poetry by writers from the city of Valenca (or Marques de Valenca), State of
Rio de Janeiro. Selections are preceded by biographical sketches (79 in all) of the poets (contemporary and dead). No alphabetical approach; arrangement is somewhat chronological.

10895 SOUSA, JOSÉ GALANTE DE, 1913-
        O teatro no Brasil. Rio de Janeiro, Ministério da Educação
e Cultura, Instituto Nacional do Livro, 1960. 2 v. illus., ports.
24cm. Vol. 2: Subsidios para uma biobibliografia do teatro no
Brasil. The theater in Brazil; v. 2 is entirely devoted to bio-
bibliographies of Brazilian dramatists, chiefly, and is in the format of a biographical dictionary.

Bulgarian

10896 BULGARSKI PISATELI-69; iûbileino izdanie. [Redaktor Grigor
        Grigorov. Sŭstaviteli Todor IÂnchev, Ivan Sarandev] So-
fiîa, Do "Bŭlgarska kniga, 1969. 178 p. illus., ports. 21cm.
A critical-bibliographical work with some biographical data and
portraits for Bulgarian writers (primarily living authors). Arranged in 3 sections with authors in alphabetical order in each
section.

10897   KONSTANTINOV, GEORGI
      Bŭlgarski pisateli. Biografiia. Bibliografiia. Sofiia,
Bŭlgarskii pisatel', 1961. 787 p. 21cm. At head of title: G.
Konstantinov, TSv. Minkov, St. Velikov. Bio-bibliography of
Bulgarian authors. Arranged by date of birth; index of biogra-
phical notices and names cited at end of each volume. First is-
sued in 1947 (viii, 454 p.).

10898   KONSTANTINOV, GEORGI
      Bulgarski pisateli; tvortsy na literatura za detsa i iunoshi;
bio-bibliografski ocherki. Sofiia, Narodna mladek, 1958. 471p.
illus. 21cm. Bulgarian authors; a bio-bibliography for children
and youth.

10899   NICOLOFF, ASSEN
      Bulgarian folklore and fine literature translated into Eng-
lish, French and German; a selected bio-bibliography. Cleveland, 1971. 79 p. 28cm. 40 Bulgarian authors are represented;
the bibliographies under the biographical sketches of the authors
are titles of translated works only.

10900   SOFIA. NARODNA BIBLIOTEKA.
      Bŭlgarska bŭzrozhdenska knizhinna; analitichen repertoar
na bŭlgarskite knigi i periodichni izdaniia 1806-1878. Sustavil
Man'o Stoianov. Pod red. na Aleksandur K. Burmov. Sofiia,
Nauka i izkustvo, 1957-   v. illus. 31cm. At head
of title, v. 1: Dŭrzhavna biblioteka "Vasil Kolarov." Otdel
"Rukopisi i staropechatni knigi"; v. 2: Narodna biblioteka. In
its main (alphabetical) listing, vol. 1 (p. [1]-382) contains a
large number of bio-bibliographical sketches of Bulgarian authors.

Canadian

(See also French-Canadian)

Anonyms and Pseudonyms

10901   AMTMANN, BERNARD
      Contributions to a dictionary of Canadian pseudonyms and
anonymous works relating to Canada. Contributions à un dictionnaire des pseudonymes canadiens et des ouvrages anonymes
relatifs au Canada. Montreal, B. Amtmann, 1973. 144 p. 2
facsims. 23cm. On spine: Pseudonymes canadiens/Canadian
pseudonyms. Text in English or French. Attempts to identify
pseudonyms, initialisms, etc. of Canadian (English) and French-
Canadian authors.

General Works

10902 CASWELL, EDWARD SAMUEL, 1861-
Canadian singers and their songs; a collection of portraits,
autograph poems and brief biographies. 3d ed. Toronto,
McClelland & Stewart, c1925. 268 p. ports. 22cm. Canadian
poets and writers of ballads and songs; an anthology with biographical notes on p. 225-269.

10903 DAVEY, FRANKLAND WILMOT, 1940-
From here to there; a guide to English-Canadian literature
since 1960, by Frank Davey. Erin, Ont., Press Porcepic, 1974.
288 p. illus. 21cm. (Our nature, our voices, 2) A bio-bibliographical dictionary of 60 living Canadian writers in English.

10904 MacMURCHY, ARCHIBALD, 1832-1912.
Handbook of Canadian literature (English) Toronto. W.
Briggs, 1906. v, 236 p. 20cm. Actually a bio-bibliography of
Canadian writers (in English) chronologically arranged from 1770
to ca. 1906. "Index to authors" at end of vol. gives an alpha-
betical approach.

10905 RHODENIZER, VERNON BLAIR, 1886-
Canadian literature in English. [Montreal, Printed by
Quality Press, c1965] 1055 p. 24cm.

---- ----Index. Compiled by Lois Mary Thierman. Edmonton,
Printed by La Survivance Print. [1968] ix, 469 p. 24cm. Bio-
bibliography of Canadian authors writing in English.

Chilean

10906 FIGUEROA, PEDRO PABLO, 1857-1909.
Galería de escritores chilenos. Santiago de Chile, Impr.
Ahumada 37 E., 1885. 272 p. 12.º A gallery of Chilean au-
thors.

10907 MEDINA, JOSÉ TORIBIO, 1852-1930.
Biblioteca hispano-chilena (1523-1817) Santiago de Chile,
Impreso y grabado en casa del autor, 1897-99. 3 v. illus. 23cm.
A bio-bibliography of early Chilean literature from its beginnings
to 1817; fairly extensive biographical data follow many of the individual bibliographical citations; each vol. has a personal name
index to authors, biographees, etc.

10908 MENGOD, VICENTE
Historia de la literatura chilena. [Santiago de Chile] Zig-
Zag [1967] 253 p. 21cm. (Colección Textos de estudio) This
history of Chilean literature actually takes a bio-bibliographical

form; that is, it consists chiefly of biographical-critical-biblio-
graphical sketches of many Chilean authors in chronological arrangement.

10909   POETAS CHILENOS DEL SIGLO XX. Carlos René Corres
         [editor] 1. ed. Santiago de Chile, Zig-Zag, 1972. 2 v.
         (621 p.) 19cm. (Libros de bolsillo Zig-Zag, 8) A chronologi-
         cally arranged anthology of Chilean poetry of the 20th century;
         biographical-critical notes are given for the 212 poets repre-
         sented. Alphabetical approach to the authors is available through
         an index at the end of vol. 2.

10910   SANTIAGO DE CHILE. BIBLIOTECA NACIONAL.
         Bibliografía general de Chile. Por Emilio Vaisse, jefe de
         sección en la Biblioteca Nacional de Chile. 1. parte: Diccion-
         ario de autores y obra (biobibliografía y bibliografía) ... Abalos-
         Barros, Araba. Santiago de Chile, Impr. Universitaria, 1915.
         lxix, 331, x p. 24cm. No more published. General bibliogra-
         phy of Chile; the first part: Dictionary of authors and their work
         (covering Abalos to Barros, Araba only)

Chinese

Bibliography, Indexes, Portrait Catalogs

10911   HUNG, WILLIAM, 1893-
         Ch'üan shang ku san tai Ch'in Han San-kuo Liu ch'ao wên
         tso che yin tê. Peiping, Yen-ching ta hsüeh (Harvard-Yenching
         Institute) 1932. iv, 2, 40 p. 27cm. Photocopies and republish-
         ed in 1966 (by Ch'eng Wen Pub. Co., Taipei) Edited by William
         Hung and others. A kuei-hsieh index to brief biographical notes
         about 1497 pre-T'ang authors whose writings are collected in the
         Ch'üan shang-ku san tai Ch'in Han San-kuo Liu ch'ao wen, a 746-
         chüan anthology of pre-T'ang prose collected by Yen K'o chün
         (1762-1834).

10912   LIN, SSŬ-TÊ
         Ch'üan T'ang shih wen tso chia yin te ho pien. [Tsingtao,
         Library of the National Tsingtao University] 1932. 215 p. A
         combined number-of-strokes index to the names of writers of
         the poems collected in the Ch'üan T'ang shih (900 chüan) and of
         the essays collected in the Ch'üan T'ang wen (1000 chüan)

10913   RACHEWILTZ, IGOR DE
         Index to biographical material in Chin and Yüan literary
         works [by] Igor de Rachewiltz and Miyoko Nakano. Canberra,
         Centre of Oriental Studies in association with Australian Nation-
         al University Press, 1970-   v. 25cm. (Australian
         National University, Canberra. Centre of Oriental Studies.
         Oriental monograph series, no. 6

In English and Chinese. "To be used in conjunction with, and
as a supplement to, the Combined indices to thirty collections
of Liao, Chin and Yüan biographies." Vol. 2 (2d ser.) by Rachewiltz and May Wang.

10914   YEN-CHING TA HSÜEH, PEKING. YIN TÊ PIEN TSUANG
          CH'U.
               Ch'üan Han San-kuo Chin Nan-pei ch'ao shih tso che yin tê.
          [Peiping] Yen-ching ta hsüeh, Yin tê pien tsuan ch'u, 1941.
          x, 14 p. 27cm. (Its [Index] 39) Added t. p.: Index to the authors
          in Chu'an Han San-kuo Chin Nan-pei ch'ao shih. A kuei-hsieh
          index to brief biographical notes for ca. 3497 pre-T'ang authors
          in the work collected by Yen K'e-chün. Compiled by Ts'ai Chin-
          chung, William Hung and others.

10916   YEN-CHING TA HSÜEH, PEKING. YIN TÊ PIEN TSUANG CH'U.
               Sung shih chi shih chu che yin tê. [Peiping] Yen-ching ta
          hsüeh, Yin tê pien tsuan ch'u, 1934. xviii, 127 p. 27cm. (Its
          [Index] 19) Added t. p.: Index to the authors in the Sung shih
          chi shi. Edited by William Hung and others. A kuei-hsieh in-
          dex to the names of more than 6800 writers whose best poems
          are collected in the Sung shih chi shih and in the Sung shih chi
          shih pui.

10917   YEN-CHING TA HSÜEH, PEKING. YIN TÊ PIEN TSUAN CH'U.
               T'ang shih chi shih chu chê yin tê. [Peiping] Yen-ching ta
          hsüeh, 1934. xii, 15 p. 27cm. (Yen-ching ta hsüeh. [Index]
          18) Added t. p.: Index to authors in T'ang shih chi shih. In-
          dexes 1150 writers whose best poems are collected in the T'ang
          shih chi shih. Edited by William Hung and others.

10918   YEN-CHING TA HSÜEH, PEKING. YIN TÊ PIEN TSUAN CH'U.
               Yüan shih chi shih chu chê yin tê. [Peking] 1934. xii, 16 p.
          27cm. (Its [Index] 20) Added t. p.: Index to the authors in Yüan
          shih chi shih. A kuei-hsieh index to the names of 1000 writers
          whose poems are collected in an anthology of Yüan dynasty poet-
          ry, compiled by Ch'ien Ta-hsin. Edited by William Hung and
          others.

Anonyms and Pseudonyms

10919   CHANG, T'AI-KU
               Pi ming yin tê. Tai-pei, Wen-ha ch'u pan shê, 60 [1971]
          89, 174 p. 21cm. Chinese pseudonyms and personal names; a
          compilation.

10920   CH'EN, TÊ-YÜN, d. 1947, ed.
               Ku chin jên wu pieh ming so yin. Taipei, I wen yin shu kuan,
          1965. 630 p. 27cm. (Ling nan ta hsüeh [Canton] T'u shu kuan.
          Ling nan ta hsüeh t'u shu kuan ts'ung shu) Added t. p.: A synon-

ymy of names of distinguished Chinese, ancient and modern.
First published in Canton in 1937. Anonyms and pseudonyms;
characters are classified under thirteen outstanding strokes,
with a number-of-strokes index at the end of the volume. Under
each alternative name the person's ordinary name and the dynasty under which he lived are given.

10921   MA, YUNG-I.
        Shih pin lu. [Shanghai] Shang wu yin shu kuan, 1935. 6 v.
(double leaves) in case. 21cm. Chinese anonyms and pseudonyms, including biographical sketches, to ca. 1300 A. D.

10922   SHU, AUSTIN C   W
        Modern Chinese authors: a list of pseudonyms. Compiled
by Austin C. W. Shu. 2d rev. ed.   [Taipei] Chinese Materials
and Research Aids Service Center, 1971. 84 p. 27cm. (Chinese Materials and Research Aids Service Center. Occasional
series, no. 9) First ed. (1969) was issued by the Asian Studies
Center, Michigan State University and had collation: xi, 108 p.
28cm.

10923   YÜAN, YUNG-CHIN
        Hsien tai chung-kuo tso chia pi ming lu. A list of pseudo-
nyms of modern Chinese authors, compiled by Yuan Yeong-jinn.
[Peiping] Library Association of China, 1936. 144 p. 19cm.
(Publications of the Library Association of China, no. 11) Names
and pseudonyms of ca. 550 modern Chinese authors. Reissued
in 1968 by Daian Bookstore, Tokyo. In Chinese.

General Works

10924   CH'EN, CH'ÊNG-CHIH
        Chung-kuo chu tso chia tz'u tien. A biographical & biblio-
graphical dictionary of Chinese authors. Compiled by Charles
K. H. Chen. Hanover, N. H., Oriental Society, 1971-76. 3 v.
21 cm. Vols. [2-3]: Supplement, pt. 1: A-K; pt. 2, L-Y. Text
in Chinese, with names of biographees also listed in romanized
form.

10925   CHUNG-HUA MIN KUO TANG TAI WÊN I TSO CHIA MING LU.
        Taipei, National Central Library, 59 [1970] 318 p. 21cm.
Added t. p.: Directory of contempor[ar]y authors of the Republic
of China. Chinese and English. Primarily a directory, but
does give date and place of birth and sometimes a few other
facts, as well as a list of the author's works.

10926   HUANG, CHÜN-TUNG, 1934-
        Hsien tai Chung-kuo tso chia chien ying. Hong Kong, Yu
lien ch'u pan she, 1972. 1, 7, 314 p. illus. 16cm. Profiles
70 modern and contemporary Chinese writers.

10927 KONDŌ, HARUO, 1914-
        Gendai Chūgoku no sakka to sakuhin. [Tokyo?] Shinsen
Shōbo, 1949. 374, 6 p. Contemporary Chinese writers and
writings; brief biographies are to be found on 115 pages of the
work.

10928 OGAWA, TAMAKI, 1910-
        Tōdai no shijin -- so no denki. Tokyo, Taishukan Shoten,
1975. 6, 714, 16 p. 22cm. Biographies of 62 poets of T'ang
Dynasty of China. Translated in Japanese. Includes a chronology of important events and the poets.

10929 SCHWARZ, ERNST, fl. 1967-   comp.
        Chrysanthemen im Spiegel; klassische chinesische Dicht-
ungen. Hrsg. aus dem Chinesischen, übertragen und nach-
gedichtet von Ernst Schwarz. [1. Aufl.] Berlin, Rütten &
Loening [1969] 473 p. illus. 28cm. "Über die Dichter" (p.
409-452) gives biographical data for 102 classical Chinese poets
in dictionary format.

10930 SHIH, TUAN-CHIAO, 1603-1674.
        T'ang shih yün hui p'u. Taipei, Kuang wen shu chu, 1973.
402 p. 22cm. Photocopy. Biographies of poets of the Tang
Dynasty, arranged by period. No index.

10931 TSÊNG, CHI-HUNG.
        Wu ch'ao Hsiang shih chia shih yung. Taipei, 1974.
273, 25 p. illus. 21cm. Biographies of 118 poets from Hunan
Province (Tang Dynasty to 1911).

Chuvashian

10932 IUR'EV, MIKHAIL IVANOVICH
        Chăvash pisatelēsem. Bio-bibliografi spravochnike.
Shupashkar, Chăvash ASSR kĕneke izd-vi, 1968. 370 p. ports.
21cm. In Chuvash. An edition in Russian (Chuvashkie pisateli)
appeared in 1964 (325 p.) See also a 1975 Russian ed. in this
volume. Chuvashian authors; a bio-bibliography.

10933 IU'REV, MIKHAIL IVANOVICH
        Pisateli Sovetskoĭ Chuvashii. Cheboksary, Chuvashskoe
knizhnoe izd-vo, 1975. 455, [1] p. ports. 21cm. A bio-bibliographical dictionary of authors in Soviet Chuvashia who write
in Russian and/or Chuvashian.

Circassian

10934 PISATELI KARACHAEVO-CHERKESSII. [Sost. V. Turov]
        Cherkessk, Stavropol'skoe knizhnoe izd., 1966. 45 p.

ports. 20c. . The writers of the Karachayeva-Cherkesskaya
region (Circassian, etc. authors)

Classical

10935   FEDER, LILLIAN
        Crowell's handbook of classical literature. New York,
Crowell [1964] viii, 448 p. maps. 23cm. (A Crowell reference
book) Includes biographical data for Greek and Latin authors.

10936   KROH, PAUL, 1925-
        Lexikon der antiken Autoren. Stuttgart, A. Kröner [1972]
xvi, 675 p. 18cm. (Kröners Taschenausgabe, Bd. 366) Dictionary of ancient (classical) authors.

10937   THE PENGUIN COMPANION TO CLASSICAL, ORIENTAL &
        AFRICAN LITERATURE. Edited by D. M. Lang and D. R.
Dudley. New York, McGraw-Hill [1971, c1969] 359 p. 24cm.
(The Penguin companion to world literature) Includes biographi-
cal entries.

Colombian

Anonyms and Pseudonyms

10938   OTERO MUÑOZ, GUSTAVO, 1894-
        Seudónimos de escritores colombianos. (In Thesaurus;
boletín del Instituto Caro y Cuervo, Bogotá, Colombia, t. 13,
1958, p. 112-131) Pseudonyms of Colombian writers.

General Works

10939   ANTOLOGÍA CRÍTICA DE LA POESÍA COLOMBIANA, 1874-
        1974. [por] Andrés Holguin. 1. ed. Bogotá, Banco de
Colombia [1974?] 2 v. illus., ports. 21cm. (Biblioteca del
centenario del Banco de Colombia) A critical anthology of Colombian poetry, 1874-1974; each chapter is devoted to a particular poet and biographical data is given at the beginning of each
chapter; 72 poets are represented; arrangement is chronological.

10940   PACHECO QUINTERO, JORGE, comp.
        Antología de la poesía en Colombia. Bogotá, Instituto Caro
y Cuervo, 1970-73. 2 v. 21cm. (Publicaciones del Instituto
Caro y Cuervo. Series minor, 14-15) Contents: t. 1. Época colonial.   Períodos renacentista y barroco.--t. 2. El neoclas-
icismo. Los romances tradicionales. An anthology of Colombian poetry from the colonial period (beginning with the 16th cen-

tury) to the 19th century. Biobibliographical data are given for the 109 known poets represented; arrangement is chronological.

10941 VILLA LÓPEZ, FRANCISCO
Poemas de Antioquia; Antioquia y sus poetas. Medellín, 1962. 417 p. An anthology of 77 poets of Antioquia with biographical sketches for each entry. Useful for obscure writers of the 20th century.

Costa Rican

10942 DUVERRÁN, CARLOS RAFAEL, 1935-   comp.
Poesía contemporánea de Costa Rica; antología. Selección y prólogo: Carlos Rafael Duverrán. Colaboradores: Laureano Alban, Carlos Luis Altamirano, Arturo Montero Vega. 1. ed. San José, Editorial Costa Rica, 1973. 443 p. 19cm. An anthology of contemporary Costa Rican poetry; selections are preceded by bio-bibliographies of the 53 poets represented in the collection; in chronological arrangement.

Croatian

10943 MIHALIĆ, SLAVKO, 1928-   comp.
La poésie croate des origines à nos jours [par] Slavko Mihalić et Ivan Kusan. Préf. de Slavko Mihalić. [Paris] Seghers [1972] 307 p. 18cm. (Anthologie "Autour du monde") An anthology of Croatian poetry (translated into French) from its origins to the present; included are bio-bibliographical sketches of 67 poets.

Czech

Anonyms and Pseudonyms

10944 PROCHÁZKOVÁ, MARIE
Autorské šifry v českých časopisech, 1959-1964. Zprac. Marie Procházková. V Praze, Státní knihovna ČSSR, 1965. 758 p. 21cm. (Bibliografický katalog ČSSR. České knihy, 1965. Zvláštní seš. 7, říjen 1965) Anonyms and pseudonyms in Czech writings for the years 1959-1964.

10945 TAUŠ, KAREL
Slovník cizích slov, zkratek, novinářských šifer, pseudonymů a časopisů pro čtenáře novin. 2., opr. a dopl. vyd. Blansko, K. Jelínek, 1947. 830 p. 1st ed. published in 1946 (724 p.) Dictionary of foreign words, abbreviations, journalistic usage, Czech pseudonyms and periodicals for new readers.

General Works

10946 ČESKOSLOVENSKÁ AKADEMIE VĚD. ÚSTAV PRO ČESKOU
LITERATURU.
Dějiny české literatury. Hlavní redaktor: Jan Mukařovský.
Praha, Československá akademie věd, 1959-   v. 25cm.
A history of Czech literature. "Soupis spisovatelů s údaji
životopisnými a bibliografickými" (v. 3, p. [547]-611) com-
prises a list of Czech authors with biographical and bibliogra-
phical data. Vols. 1-3 (1959-1961) only vols issued thus far?

10947 ČEŠTÍ SPISOVATELÉ Z PŘELOMU 19. A 20. STOLETÍ.
Napsal autorský kolektiv za redakce Zdeňka Pešata. Vyd.
1. Praha, Československý spisovatel, 1972. 187 p. 21cm. 48
deceased Czech authors who wrote at the end of the 19th and into
the 20th century: a bio-bibliographical work in alphabetical arrangement.

10948 CZECHOSLOVAK REPUBLIC. KOMISE PRO KNIHOPISNÝ
SOUPIS ČESKÝCH A SLOVENSKÝCH TISKŮ AŽ DO KONCE
XVIII. STOLETÍ.
Knihopis československých tisků od doby nejstarší až do
konce XVIII. století. V Praze, V komisi knihkupectvi F.
Topiče, 1925-   v. in   facsims. 31-46cm. Issued in
parts; v. 1 (pt. 1-2), v. 2 (pt. 1-9) issued to 1967. Vols. 1-2,
pt. 1-4 edited by Zdeněk Tobolka; v. 2, pt. 5- edited by
František Horák. Vol. 2, pts. 1- , have title: Knihopis českých
a slovenských tisku od doby nejstarší až do konce XVIII. století.
Vol. 2 of this bibliography of Czech and Slovak imprints, covering the years 1501 to 1800, is actually bio-bibliographical in
scope; authors and anonymous and pseudonymous works are alphabetically interfiled; under personal authors there is often to
be found biographical data of varying length.

10949 FRABŠA, FRANTIŠEK S., 1887-
Ceski spisovatelé dnešní doby. Praha, Lidová tribuna,
1923. 159 p. ports. 23cm. Czech authors of today (1920's).

10950 JIREČEK, JOSEF, 1825-1888.
Rukovět k dejinám literatury české do konce XVIII. věku.
Ve způsobě slovníku životopisného a knihoslovného. V Praze,
Nakl. B. Tempského, 1875-76. 2 v. 22cm. Contents.--t. 1.
A-L.--t. 2. M-Z. A manual of Czech literature to the end of
the 18th century, arranged like a bio-bibliographical dictionary.
Includes variants of names and pseudonyms.

10951 JUNGMANN, JOSEF JAKUB, 1773-1847.
Josefa Jungmanna Historie literatury české. Aneb: Sa-
ustawný prehled spisů českých s krátkau historii národu, os-
wiceni a jazyka. 2. wydání. (Nákladem Českého museum číslo
XXXII.) W Praze, W kommissí Kněhkupectwi F. Řiwnáče, 1849.

vi, 771 p. port. 26cm. Edited with memoir of the author by
V. V. Tomek. First edition issued in 1825. "Popis spisowatelů
českých": p. [529]-659. A history of Czech (Bohemian) literature with bio-bibliographical notes (in dictionary arrangement)
as indicated in the preceding note, p. [529]-659.

10952   KRYŠPÍN, VOJTĚCH, 1844-
        Obraz činnosti literární učitelstva ceskoslovenského za
posledních 100 let. Od r. 1780 do r. 1882. S doplňkem za léta
1883 a 1884. Přispěvek k historii české literatury a českeho
skolstvi. V Praze, M. Knapp, 1885. viii, 422 p. 11 ports.
21cm. Scholars (teachers) of a century (1780-1884); a bio-bibliography of Czech literature and scholarship.

10953   KUNC, JAROSLAV
        Česká literární bibliografie, 1945-1963; soupis článku, statí
a kritik z knižních publikaci a periodického tisku let 1945-1963 o
dilech soudobých českých spisovatelů. V Praze, Státní knihovna
ČSSR, 1963-   v. ports. 21cm. (Bibliografický katalog
ČSSR. Česke knihy, 1963-   Zvláštni seš. 6, 5, prosinec
1963-
A bibliography of historical and critical works on 20th century
(1945-1963) Czech literature useful for its many portraits of authors. The authors' birth dates and birth/death dates are given,
but no other biographical data. Vol. 1-2 only available as of
1976?

10954   KUNC, JAROSLAV
        Kdy zemřeli ... ? Přehled českých spisovatelů a publicistů
zemřelých 1967-1970, 1935-1936 a dodatek do "Kdy zemřeli 1937-
1966." Zprac. Jaroslav Kunc. V Praze, Státní knihoyna ČSR,
1970. 247 p. 21cm. (Bibliografický katalog ČSSR. České knihy
1970. Zvláštni seš. 3, 1970) When did he die? Czech authors
and publicists who died in the years 1937-1970. A bio-bibliographical dictionary; continues work with the same title by Kunc issued in 1962 (q. v.) which covered the years 1937-1962.

10955   VAVROUŠEK, BOHUMIL, 1875-
        Literární atlas ceskoslovensky. Sebral a sest. Bohumil
Vavroušek a literárním přispenim Arna Nováka. V Praze, J.
Otto, 1932-38. 2 v. (chiefly illus., ports.) 44cm. Vol. 2
published by Prometheus, Prague. An invaluable Czech-Slovak
literary atlas that contains a huge number of portraits and iconography of authors as well as bio-bibliographical sketches.
Chronological and alphabetical name indexes are at the end of
vol. 2.

Danish

10956   BØRNENES HVEM SKREV HVAD. [Dansk og udenlandske bør-
        nebøger efter 1900. Hovedred.: Gudrun Paaske. 2. udg.

København, Politiken, 1974. 448 p. illus. 18cm. (Politikens litteraturhandbøger) Bio-bibliographical dictionary of Danish and foreign children's literature after 1900.

10957 DANSK CENTRALBIBLIOTEK FOR SYDSLESVIG.
Dansk skønlitteratur i 60'erne og på taersklen til 70'erne. Flensborg, Udg. af Dansk centralbibliotek, 1971. 71 p. illus., ports. 23 x 11cm. "Udgivet ... i anledning af udstillingen 28. oktober til 20. november 1971." Danish literature in the 1960's and forward to the 70's; a bibliography, with portraits of 150 authors (novelists and poets) including birth dates.

Dominican

Anonyms and Pseudonyms

10958 FLORÉN LOZANO, LUIS
Algunos seudónimos dominicanos; aportación a un diccionario de seudónimos de escritores nacionales [por] Luis Florén. (In Anales de la Universidad de Santo Domingo, Santo Domingo, República Dominicana. v. 14, no. 49-52, enero-dic. 1949, p. 95-122; v. 15, no. 53-56, enero-dic. 1950, p. 125-131) Contains 276 pseudonyms with lists of true names (writers of the Dominican Republic).

Dutch

10959 AA, ABRAHAM JACOB VAN DER, 1792-1857.
Niew biografiesch, anthologiesch en kritiesch woordenboek van Nederlandsche dichters, onder medewerking van J. T. Bodel Nyenhuis, I. Da Costa, H. O. Feith en anderen, bij-een-gebracht door A. J. van der Aa. Uitmakende tevens een vervolg op Witsen Geysbeeks Woordenboek der Nederlandsche dichters. Nieuwe uitg., met ... eene voorreden van J. A. Alberdingk Thijm. Amsterdam, C. L. van Langenhuysen, 1864. 3 v. port. 22 cm. 1st edition issued in 1844-46. A new, biographical, 'anthological' and critical dictionary of Dutch poets; continues Geysbeeks' Biographisch, anthologisch en critisch woordenboek der Nederduitsche dichters.

Ecuadorian

Anonyms and Pseudonyms

10960 ROLANDO, CARLOS A   1881-
Pseudónimos de escritores nacionales y extranjeros en la prensa nacional. (In his Cronología del periodismo ecuatoriano. Guayaquil, Impr. Monteverde & Velarde, 1920. p. [87]-161) Pseudonyms of national and foreign writers in the Ecuadorian press.

10961 ROLANDO, CARLOS A   1881-
       Pseudónimos en la prensa del Ecuador. (In his Cronología
del periodismo ecuatoriano. Guayaquil, Tip. y Lit. de la Sociedad Filantrópica del Guayas, 1934. p. 43-87) Continuation
and amplification of the preceding work on pseudonyms in Ecuador's press.

General Works

10962 BARRIGA LÓPEZ, FRANKLIN
       Diccionario de la literatura ecuatoriana [por] Franklin
Barriga López [y] Leonardo Barriga López. Quito, Editorial
Casa de la Cultura Ecuatoriana, 1973. 590 p. 22cm. A dictionary of Ecuadorian literature which is entirely bio-bibliographical in format.

10963 GALLO ALMEIDA, LUIS
       Literatos ecuatorianos. 3. ed. Quito, Tall. Gráf. del
Colegio Militar, 1938. 338 p. ports. 20cm. A bio-bibliography of Ecuadorian writers (literary figures, historians, journalists & political orators) with selections from the works of the
more important authors; arranged by genre and periods.

10964 JARAMILLO, MIGUEL ANGEL, 1874-1953.
       Indice bibliográfico de la Biblioteca "Jaramillo" de escri-
tores nacionales. Tomo 1. Cuenca, Ecuador, Impr. de la Universidad, 1932. ii, 356 p. 24cm. No more published. An annotated bibliography of ca, 1,800 Ecuadorian publications in alphabetical order by author; biographical data accompany each
author entry.

English

Anonyms and Pseudonyms

10965 ATKINSON, FRANK, 1922-
       Dictionary of pseudonyms and pen-names; a selection of
popular modern writers in English. London, C. Bingley; Hamden, Conn., Linnet Books of the Shoe String Press, 1975. 166 p.
23cm. In 2 parts: (1) some 2,500 writers active since 1900,
along with pseudonyms and pen-names they have used; (2) arrangement by pseudonym, with real name for each.

General Works

10966 BROOK, DONALD
       Writers' gallery; biographical sketches of Britain's greatest
writers, and their views on reconstruction. London, Rockliff

Pub. Corp., 1944. 168 p. ports. 22cm. A biographical dictionary of 25 writers.

10967   THE CONCISE OXFORD DICTIONARY OF ENGLISH LITERA-
            TURE. 2d ed., rev. by Dorothy Eagle. Oxford, Clarendon
        Press, 1970. [10], 628 p. 21cm. An abridgment based on the
        4th ed. of Sir Paul Harvey's Oxford companion to English litera-
        ture. Includes biographical sketches of British and American
        authors.

10968   CONTEMPORARY POETS. Editor: James Vinson. Associate
            editor: D. L. Kirkpatrick. 2d ed. With a pref. by C. Day
        Lewis. London, St. James Press; New York, St. Martin's
        Press, 1975. xv, 1849 p. 24cm. Bio-bibliography of ca. 800
        living poets of the English language; with an appendix of 200
        more poets recently deceased. First ed. issued in 1971 under
        title: Contemporary poets of the English language (Rosalie Mur-
        phy, editor) had ca. 1,000 poets listed in the text.

10969   ENCYCLOPEDIA OF MYSTERY AND DETECTION. Chris
            Steinbrunner and Otto Penzler, editors-in-chief. Marvin
        Lachman and Charles Shibuk, senior editors. New York,
        McGraw-Hill [1976] 436 p. illus., ports. 24cm. Primarily a
        bio-bibliographical dictionary of more than 500 authors of mys-
        tery and detective literature (almost exclusively British and
        American).

10970   FLEAY, FREDERICK GARD, 1831-1909.
            A biographical chronicle of the English drama, 1559-1642.
        London, Reeves and Turner, 1891. 2 v. 24cm. A bio-bibliog-
        raphy of English dramatists of the period. The authors are ar-
        ranged alphabetically, with only such biographical particulars
        as bear upon the history of the drama. Reprinted (1972 or 3?)
        by Lenox Hill Pub. Corp., New York (?).

10971   GILLIE, CHRISTOPHER
            Longman companion to English literature. [London] Long-
        man, 1972. xiv, 881 p. illus., ports. 24cm. "The reference
        section" (p. [373]-880) is a dictionary of English literature which
        includes bio-bibliographical entries (English authors) and brief
        biographies of some famous historical world figures.

10972   HANDLEY-TAYLOR, GEOFFREY, 1920-
            Authors of Wales today: being a checklist of authors born in
        Wales, together with brief particulars of authors born elsewhere
        who are currently working or residing in Wales--an assemblage
        of more than 600 authors together with addresses and (where ap-
        plicable) their pseudonyms. General editor: Geoffrey Handley-
        Taylor. London, Eddison Press, 1972. xiii, 76 p. 22cm.
        (County authors today series)

10973   HANDLEY-TAYLOR, GEOFFREY, 1920-
        Berkshire, Hampshire and Wiltshire authors today, being a
checklist of authors born in these counties together with brief
particulars of authors born elsewhere who are currently working
or residing in these counties; an assemblage of more than 650
authors together with their addresses, and (where applicable)
their pseudonyms. General editor: Geoffrey Handley-Taylor.
London, Eddison Press, 1973. xiv, 111 p. 22cm. (County authors today series)

10974   HANDLEY-TAYLOR, GEOFFREY
        Cheshire, Derbyshire and Staffordshire authors today: being
a checklist of authors born in these counties, together with brief
particulars of authors born elsewhere who are currently working
or residing in these counties--an assemblage of more than 460
authors, together with their addresses and (where applicable)
their pseudonyms. General editor: Geoffrey Handley-Taylor.
London, Eddison Press, 1972. xiv, 70 p. 22cm. (County authors today series)

 10975 HANDLEY-TAYLOR, GEOFFREY, 1920-
        Devon, Dorset and Somerset authors today; being a check-
list of authors born in these counties together with brief particulars of authors born elsewhere who are currently working or residing in these counties. An assemblage of more than 400 authors together with their addresses and (where applicable) their
pseudonyms. Hon. general editor: Geoffrey Handley-Taylor.
London, Eddison Press, 1973. xii, 84 p. 22cm. (County authors today series)

10976   HANDLEY-TAYLOR, GEOFFREY
        Kent authors today; being a checklist of authors born in Kent
together with brief particulars of authors born elsewhere who are
currently working or residing in Kent--an assemblage of more
than 530 authors together with their addresses and (where applicable) their pseudonyms. London, Eddison Press, 1973. xiv,
96 p. 22cm. (County authors today series).

10977   HANDLEY-TAYLOR, GEOFFREY
        Lancashire authors today; being a checklist of authors born
in Lancashire together with brief particulars of authors born
elsewhere who are currently working or residing in the County
Palatine. London [County Authors Today Series] 1971. vii, 68 p.
illus. 22cm. (County authors today series) Biographical data
is quite scant; largely bibliographical. Includes pseudonyms
where applicable.

10978   HANDLEY-TAYLOR, GEOFFREY
        Scottish authors today; being a checklist of authors born in
Scotland together with brief particulars of authors born elsewhere who are currently working or residing in Scotland--an

assemblage of more than 700 authors together with their addresses and (where applicable) their pseudonyms. General editor:
Geoffrey Handley-Taylor. London, Eddison Press, 1972. xii,
82 p. 22cm. (County authors today series)

10979 HANDLEY-TAYLOR, GEOFFREY
          Sussex authors today; being a checklist of authors born in
       Sussex together with brief particulars of authors born elsewhere
       who are currently working or residing in Sussex--an assemblage
       of more than 620 authors together with their addresses and (where
       applicable) their pseudonyms. London, Eddison Press, 1973.
       xiv, 113 p. 22cm. (County authors today series)

10980 HANDLEY-TAYLOR, GEOFFREY
          Yorkshire authors today: being a checklist of authors born
       in Yorkshire, together with brief particulars of authors born
       elsewhere who are currently working or residing in the county,
       an assemblage of more than 700 authors together with their ad-
       dresses and (where applicable) their pseudonyms. General ed-
       itor: Geoffrey Handley-Taylor. London, Eddison Press, 1972.
       xiv, 77 p. 22cm. (County authors today series) Biographical
       data scant; largely bibliographical.

10981 HARDWICK, JOHN MICHAEL DRINKROW, 1924-
          A literary atlas & gazetteer of the British Isles [by]
       Michael Hardwick. Cartography by Alan G. Hodgkiss. Newton
       Abbot [Eng.] David & Charles [1973] 216 p. col. maps. 25cm.
       Biographical sketches of authors connected in some way with
       particular places are arranged in semi-alphabetical order under
       particular place names. "Index I: of people, in alphabetical
       order" (p. [189]-202)

10982 HERMAN, LINDA
          Corpus delicti of mystery fiction; a guide to the body of the
       case, by Linda Herman and Beth Stiel. Metuchen, N. J., Scare-
       crow Press, 1974. viii, 180 p. 23cm. A bio-bibliographical
       dictionary of mystery story writers--"Fifty representative au-
       thors and their works" (p. 30-128)--chiefly of British or Ameri-
       can origin.

10983 JACOB, GILES, 1686-1744.
          An historical account of the lives and writings of our most
       considerable English poets. New York, Garland Pub. Co., 1970.
       xxvi, 328 p. ports. 22cm. Originally issued as a continuation
       of the Poetical register; or, The lives and characters of the Eng-
       lish dramatic poets, first published in 1719. Original imprint
       reads: London, Printed for E. Curll, 1720.

10984 JACOB, GILES, 1686-1744.
          The poetical register; or, The lives and characters of the

English dramatic poets. New York, Garland Pub., 1970. vii, 433 p. (i. e. 334 p.) ports. 22cm. Facsim. of the Yale University Library copy with imprint: London, Printed for E. Curli, in Fleetstreet, 1719. Originally continued by An historical account of the lives and writings of our most considerable English poets ... first published in 1720.

10985   KENNEDY, X. J., comp.
         Messages; a thematic anthology of poetry. Edited by X. J. Kennedy. Boston, Little, Brown [1973] xix, 386 p. illus. 22cm. On pages [335]-367 of this anthology of English and American poetry is a bio-bibliographical dictionary with facts for ca. 170 of the poets represented in the collection.

10986   MAŁY SŁOWNIK PISARZY ANGIELSKICH I AMERYKAŃSKICH.
         [Redaktor: Elżbieta Piotrowska. Wyd. 1.] Warszawa, Wiedza Powszecha, 1971. 545 p. ports. 21cm. Little dictionary of English and American authors (ca. 800).

10987   MYERS, ROBIN, fl. 1967-
         A dictionary of literature in the English language, from Chaucer to 1940. Compiled and edited by Robin Myers for the National Book League. [1st ed.] Oxford, New York, Pergamon Press [1970] 2 v. (xvii, 1497 p.) illus. 26cm. Biographical (brief) and bibliographical details on writers in English throughout the world. Vol. 2: Title-author index.

10988   THE PENGUIN COMPANION TO ENGLISH LITERATURE.
         Edited by David Daiches. New York, McGraw-Hill [1971] 575 p. 24cm. (The Penguin companion to world literature) Contains many entries for Commonwealth of Nations authors of the past and present whose written language was/is English (or chiefly English).

10989   QUENNELL, PETER, 1905-
         A history of English literature. Springfield, Mass., G. & C. Merriam Co. [1973] 512 p. illus. 25cm. Actually a reference work of the dictionary type, with many biographical entries.

10990   RUOFF, JAMES E
         Crowell's handbook of Elizabethan Stuart literature. New York, T. Y. Crowell [1975] x, 468 p. 24cm. An alphabetical guide with biographical entries for writers from about the time of Sir Thomas More to that of John Milton.

10991   SIMMS, RUPERT, 1853-
         Bibliotheca Staffordiensis; or, A bibliographical account of books and other printed matter relating to--printed or published in--or written by a native, resident, or person deriving a title

from--any portion of the County of Stafford: giving a full collation and biographical notices of authors and printers. Together
with as full a list as possible of prints, engravings, etchings,
&c., of any part thereof; and portraits of persons so connected.
Lichfield, Printed for the complier by A. C. Lomax, 1894.
xxv, 546 p. 29cm.

10992 SPENDER, STEPHEN, 1909-   ed.
    The concise encyclopedia of English and American poets and
poetry. Edited by Stephen Spender and Donald Hall. [2d ed.
(rev. in new format) London, Hutchinson [1970] [11], 388 p.
23cm.

10993 STANFORD, ANN, comp.
    The women poets in English; an anthology. Edited, with an
introd. by Ann Stanford. New York, McGraw-Hill [1972] xlix,
374 p. 24cm. On pages 335-363 of this anthology are bio-bibliographical notes on some 135 women poets from the United States
and the British Commonwealth and Ireland. The notes are arranged chronologically—from the Anglo-Saxon period in England
to the present.

10994 WEBSTER'S NEW WORLD COMPANION TO ENGLISH AND
    AMERICAN LITERATURE. Edited by Arthur Pollard. As-
sociate editor for American literature; Ralph Willett. New
York, World Pub. [1973] 850 p. 24cm. Includes brief descriptions of over 1,000 authors and brief articles on literary genres.

Estonian

10995 MÄGI, ARVO
    Eesti kirjandus paguluses, 1944-1972 [kirj.] Arvo Mägi,
Karl Ristikivi [jac] Bernard Kangro. [Lund, Sweden] Eesti
Kirjanike Kooperatiiv [1973] 180 p. illus., ports. 23cm. With
a summary in English. A history of Estonian literature in exile,
1944-1972. "Bio- ja bibliograafilised markmed" (p. 133-166) is
a bio-bibliographical dictionary of 93 Estonian authors of the
20th century.

10996 MAUER, MARE
    Estonskaia literatura; rekomendatelnyi ukazatel' literatury.
Moskva, "Kniga," 1975. 223 p. ports. 20cm. At head of title:
Gosudarstvennaia biblioteka SSSR imeni V. I. Lenina. Gosudarstvennaia biblioteka Estonskoi SSR imeni Fr. R. Kreitsval'da.
Bio-bibliographies and portraits of 58 Estonian authors (from
the late 18th century to the present) Arranged chronologically,
with an alphabetical name index.

10997 NIRK, ENDEL, 1925-
    Estonian literature; historical survey with bio-bibliographi-

cal appendix. [Translated from the Estonian by V. Hain, A. R. Hone and O. Mutt. Tallinn, Eesti Raamat, 1970] 414 p. illus., ports. 21cm. On page facing t. p.: Institute of Languages and Literature, Academy of Sciences of the Estonian S. S. R. "Biographical notes concerning the principal authors" (p. 380-[405]) is a bio-bibliographical dictionary for 63 writers who are treated at greater length in the main text. There are also bio-bibliographical sketches of other authors in the main text who may be located alphabetically via a name index.

10998   ORAS, ANTS, 1900-
         Estonian literature in exile; an essay, by Ants Oras, with a bio-bibliographical appendix by Bernard Kangro. Lund, Eesti Kirjanika Kooperativ, 1967. 88 p. 23cm. "Biographical notes" (p. 71-88): a bio-bibliographical dictionary (38 authors)

French

10999   ANNUAIRE BIO-BIBLIOGRAPHIQUE DES JEUNES ÉCRIVAINS
         DE FRANCE ET DES COLONIES. Publié sous la direction technique de Marcel Conrath. Toulouse, "Les Pyrénées littéraires [1927?] 104 p. ports. 22cm. No more published? The bio-bibliographical annual of the young writers of France and its colonies.

11000   [BOSSANGE, HECTOR] 1795-1884.
         Ma bibliothèque française. Paris, H. Bossange et fils, 1855. vii, 480 p. 18cm. Half title: Catalogue de la bibliothèque française. A selection of over 1100 standard French works (7000 vols.) with bio-bibliographical notes (arranged in the form of a bio-bibliographical dictionary) A companion volume to Henry Stevens' My English library, 1853.

11001   BOURIN, ANDRÉ, 1918-
         Dictionnaire de la littérature française contemporaine [par] André Bourin [et] Jean Rousselot. Paris, Larousse, 1966. 256 p. illus. 17cm. (Les Dictionnaires de l'homme du XXe siècle) Dictionary of 20th century French literature and authors.

11001a   CARRIAT, AMÉDÉE
         Dictionnaire bio-bibliographique des auteurs du pays creusois et des écrits le concernant des origines à nos jours. Guéret, Impr. Leconte et les Presses du Massif Central, 1965-
              p. 25cm. A bio-bibliographical dictionary of the authors of the department of Creuse, France. Issued in fascicles (560 p. issued as of 1971)

11002   CARTERET, LÉOPOLD
         Le trésor du bibliophile romantique et moderne, 1801-1875. Édition revue, corrigée et augmentée. Éditions originales.

[Gargenville (or Paris?)] Éditions du Vexin français et
Laurent Carteret, 1976. 4 v. 25cm. Reprint of the Paris edition of 1924-1928. The 1st two volumes are alphabetically arranged by author; brief biographical notes are given for many of
the lesser known French authors of the 19th century, 1801-1875
(Romantic & 'modern' period).

11003   CIORANESCU, ALEXANDRE
           Bibliographie de la littérature française du dix-huitième
siècle. Paris, Éditions du Centre national de la recherche
scientifique, 1969. 3 v. 28cm. A bibliography of French literature of the 18th century which often provides a line or several
of biographical information about lesser-known authors.

11004   CLÉMENT-SIMON, GUSTAVE, 1833-1909.
           Curiosités de la bibliographie limousine. Genève, Slat-
kine Reprints, 1972. 226 p. 23cm. Reprint of the Limoges
edition of 1905. Curiosities of the bibliography of Limousin,
France. Actually a bio-bibliographical dictionary of 50 authors
native to Limousin.

11005   DAIRE, LOUIS FRANÇOIS, 1713-1792.
           Histoire littéraire de la ville d'Amiens. Genève, Slatkine
Reprints, 1970. ii, viii, 669 p. 23cm. Literary history of the
city of Amiens. The work is in large part a bio-bibliography of
French literature by persons associated with the city. The arrangement is generally chronological; alphabetical approach
through "Table des noms et des matières" at end. Reprint of
the Paris edition of 1782.

11006   DENIS, AUGUSTE, 1827-
           Recherches bibliographiques en forme de dictionnaire sur
les auteurs morts et vivants qui ont écrit sur l'ancienne province de Champagne; ou, essai d'un manuel du bibliophile
Champenois. Chalons-sur-Marne, Impr. de T. Martin, 1870.
vi, 190 columns. 25cm. H. Stein (Manuel de bibliographie générale) has a low opinion of this work. Biographical and descriptive notes. Two other parts were projected, but were never
published. (Bio)-bibliographical researches (in the form of a
dictionary) on authors living and dead who have written about
Champagne.

11007   DESEILLE, ERNEST, 1835-
           Galerie des écrivains boulonnais. 1. ptie.: Les contempo-
rains. Boulogne-sur-Mer, Battut, 1863. 52 p. 12.° A gallery
of the writers of Boulougne-sur-Mer; pt. 1: Contemporaries.
No more published.

11008   DICTIONAR AL LITERATURII FRANCEZE. Autori: Alexandru
           Dimitriu-Pausesti [et al.] Bucuresti, Editura Stintifica,

1972. 535 p. 20cm. A dictionary of French literature from
Romania; includes bio-bibliographical entries.

11009   GALERIE DES PORTRAITS; recueil des notices publiées de 1928
        à 1972 sur les membres de l'Académie. Bruxelles, Palais
        des Académies, 1972. 4 v. ports. 18cm. Gallery of portraits;
        a collection of notices (with portraits) of members (deceased)
        of the Academy, published from 1928 to 1972. In dictionary ar-
        rangement (A-Z). Represented are 74 distinguished writers and
        scholars in the field of French language and literature from
        Europe and America.

11010   GAUTIER, TOUSSAINT FRANÇOIS ANGE
        Bibliothèque générale des écrivains bretons. 2. ptie,
        contenant la biographie des auteurs bretons qui ont vécu ou sont
        morts depuis 1789 jusqu'à nos jours (1850) Brest, Impr. de J.
        -B. Lefournier aîné, 1850. 47 p. 8.º No more published?
        Bio-bibliography of Breton authors; the 2d part, containing those
        who resided in Brittany or died after 1789 to 1850.

11011   GUYOT DE FÈRE, FRANÇOIS FORTUNE, 1792-1866.
        Statistique des gens de lettres et des savants existant en
        France, contenant la liste de leurs productions et de leurs tra-
        vaux ... des notices sur tous les établissemens littéraires et
        scientifiques des départemens, des tables systématiques de tous
        des savans et littérateurs classés suivant l'ordre des connais-
        sances humaines. 2. éd. corr. et considérablement augm.
        Paris, Au Bureau de la statistique, 1837-40. 2 v. 22cm. This
        'statistical' work on French letters and scholarship of the early
        19th century is also bio-bibliographical in nature.

11012   HAURÉAU, BARTHÉLEMY, 1812-1896.
        Histoire littéraire du Maine. Nouv. éd. Paris, Dumoulin,
        1870-77. 10 v. 19cm. Literary history of Maine, France; a bio-
        bibliographical dictionary. 1st ed. issued in 4 v. (Paris, J.
        Lanier, 1843-52)

11013   LABLÉE, JACQUES, 1751-1841.
        Tableau de nos poètes vivants, par ordre alphabétique.
        Année 1789-1790. À Londres, Chez l'auteur, 1789-[90?] 2 v.
        20cm. Vol. 2 has imprint: Paris, Desenne. France's living
        poets (latter part of the 18th century, arranged alphabetically--
        years 1789-1790.

11014   LA BOURALIÈRE, AUGUSTE DE, 1838-1907.
        Bibliographie poitevine; ou, Dictionnaire des auteurs poite-
        vins et des ouvrages publiés sur le Poitou, jusqu'à la fin du 18e
        siècle. Genève, Slatkine Reprints, 1972. x, 581 p. 23cm. Re-
        print of the Poitiers edition of 1907. A bibliography (in alpha-
        betical arrangement--author and title entries) of Poitou, but, as

the alternative title suggests, the work also contains brief biographical notes under author entries (writers from Poitou).

11015 LACHÈVRE, FRÉDÉRIC, 1855-
       Bibliographie des recueils collectifs de poésies publiés de
1597 à 1700. Paris, H. Leclerc, 1901-05. 4 v. 28cm. Contents. --1. 1597-1635. --2. 1636-1661. --3. 1662-1700. --4. Supplément. Additions. Corrections. Tables générales. A bibliography of collections of French poetry, individual and collective,
from 1597 to 1700 with bio-bibliographies (in alphabetical arrangement) of the poets whose works have been collected and
published.

11016 LACHÈVRE, FRÉDÉRIC, 1855-
       Les recueils collectifs de poésies libres et satiriques pub-
liés depuis 1600 jusqu'à la mort de Théophile (1626) Bibliographie de ces recueils et bio-bibliographie des auteurs qui y fig-
urent ... Paris, Champion, 1914. xiv, 597 p. 29cm. (His La
libertinage au XVIIe siècle, 4)

---- ----Supplément; additions et corrections, Paris, Champion,
1922. 95 p. 29cm. A bibliography of collections of French poetry from 1600 to 1626 (largely erotic and satirical) with bio-bibliographies (alphabetical in arrangement) of the poets whose
works have been collected & published.

11017 [LA PORTE, JOSEPH DE] 1713-1779.
       Dictionnaire dramatique, contenant l'histoire des théâtres,
les règles du genre dramatique, les observations des maitres
les plus célèbres. Paris, Lacombe, 1776. 3 v. 20cm. By J.
de La Porte and Sébastien R. N. Chamfort. Primarily a dictionary of plays performed in the French theater, but in vol. 3, p.
[501]-615, one finds "Notices des poètes et musiciens qui on tra-
vaillé pour le théâtre, avec la liste de leurs ouvrages," a dictionary of dramatists, musicians, etc. active in the French theater.

11018 LAUGIER, ADOLPHE
       Galerie biographique des artistes dramatiques des théâtres
royaux. Paris, Ponthieu, 1826-27. fasc. 1-3. 8.º No more
published. Contents. --1. Académie royale de musique. --2.
Théâtre royal italien. --3. Théâtre-français. A biographical
gallery of dramatists of the royal theaters of France, 18th-19th
centuries.

11019 LIRON, JEAN, 1665-1749.
       Bibliothèque chartraine. Genève, Slatkine Reprints, 1971.
xii, xxxvi, 370 p. 23cm. Reprint of the Paris edition of 1719.
Bio-bibliography of Chartres, France. Index of authors and
famous men at end of volume.

11020   LIRON, JEAN, 1665-1749.
Bibliothèque générale des auteurs de France. Livre premier, contenant la Bibliothèque chartraine; ou, Le traité des auteurs et des hommes illustres de l'ancien diocèse de Chartres:
qui ont laissé quelques monumens a la posterite, ou qui ont ex-
celle dans les beaux arts. Avec le catalogue de leurs ouvrages;
le denombrement des differentes editions qui en ont ete faites &
un jugement sur plusieurs des memes ouvrages. Paris, J. M.
Garnier, 1719. xxxvi, 364, [4] p. 26cm. No more published.
Reissued under title: Bibliothèque chartraine. General library
of the authors of France: the 1st volume, containing a bio-bibliography of authors and famous men of the diocese of Chartres.

11021   LONGEON, CLAUDE, 1941-
Les écrivains foréziens du XVIe siècle, repertoire bio-
bibliographique. [Saint-Etienne] Centre d'études foréziennes,
1970. 456 p. map. 24cm. [Collection Thèses et mémoires
publiée par le Centre d'études foréziennes, 1] 61 authors from
Forez of the 16th century; a bio-bibliographical work. Alphabetical approach through name index at end, with names of authors for whom bio-bibliographical sketches are given (as well
as page references) in dark letters and numerals.

11022   MALIGNON, JEAN, 1906-
Dictionnaire des écrivains français. [Paris] Editions du
Seuil [1971] 552 p. illus., ports. 22cm. A bio-bibliographical
dictionary of French writers.

11023   MAŁY SŁOWNIK PISARZY FRANCUSKICH, BELGIJSKICH I
PROWANSALSKICH. Warszawa, Wiedza Powszechna, 1966.
259 p. ports. 21cm. Dictionary of French, Belgian and Provençal writers (ca. 400 entries).

11024   MANDET, FRANCISQUE, b. 1811.
Histoire poétique et littéraire de l'ancien Velay. Paris,
Rozier, 1842. lii, 448 p. 27cm. Poetical history and literary
history of the old region of Velay; a bio-bibliography. Chronological arrangement; index of biographical notices at end.

11025   MARTIN, JULES, 1860-
Nos auteurs et compositeurs dramatiques; portraits et biographies, suivis d'une notice sur les sociétés d'auteurs, droits,
règlements, statistique, et sur les transformations de l'affiche
théâtrale, reproductions, d'affliches des XVIIe, XVIIIe et XIX
siècles. Préf. par Maurice Donnay. Paris, E. Flammarion,
1897. 623 p. illus., ports. 15cm. Bio-bibliography of French
dramatists and composers; portraits and a biographical dictionary.

11026   MERLET, LUCIEN VICTOR CLAUDE, 1827-1898.
        Poètes beaucerons antérieurs au XIXe siècle. Notices.
Chartres, Impr. Durand, 1894. 2 v. 21cm. (Bibliothèque chartraine) A bio-bibliography of the poets of Beauce before the 19th
century. Table of contents (listing biographical notices) at end
of each volume.

11027   MONSELET, CHARLES, 1825-1888.
        Le lorgnette littéraire. Augmenté du complément Diction-
naire des grands et des petits auteurs de mon temps. Geneve,
Slatkine Reprints, 1971. xviii, 240 p. 29cm. Reprint of the
Paris editions of 1857 and 1870. A dictionary of French authors
of the 19th century. Generally lacks dates of authors' activities;
primarily critical. A '2d edition' was issued in 1859.

11028   NICOLAS, MICHEL, 1810-1886.
        Histoire littéraire de Nimes et des localités voisines qui
forment actuellement le département du Gard. Nimes, Ballivet
et Fabre, 1854. 3 v. 19cm. Literary history of Nimes and
neighboring localities forming the Department of the Gard; bio-
bibliographical in nature. Chronologically arranged with table
of contents at end of each vol.; no general index.

11029   OLIVIER, PAUL, 1871-   comp.
        Cent poètes; lyriques précieux ou burlesques du 17e siècle
[par] Paul Olivier. Avec en guise de préf. un poème de Jean
Richepin. Genève, Slatkine Reprints, 1971. xx, 581 p. 22cm.
Reprint of the Paris edition of 1898. An anthology of 100 [i. e.
103] French poets of the 17th century, with bio-bibliographical
data for each poet. In chronological arrangement.

11030   PALISSOT DE MONTENOY, CHARLES, 1730-1814.
        Mémoires pour servir à l'histoire de notre littérature, de-
puis François 1er jusqu'à nos jours. Par M. Palissot. Paris,
Gérard, an XI, 1803. 2 v. 20cm. A biographical dictionary of
French authors from the reign of Francis I to the latter part of
the 18th century.

11031   PICOT, EMILE, 1844-1918.
        Les Francais italianisants au XVIe siècle. Paris, H.
Champion, 1906-07. 2 v. 23cm. 61 biographies of practitioners of Italian literature in France; i. e. Frenchmen who wrote
in Italian.

11032   LA POÉSIE CONTEMPORAINE DE LANGUE FRANÇAISE
        DEPUIS 1945; études critiques, par Serge Brindeau [et al.
Paris] Editions Saint-Germain-des-Prés [1973] 927 p. illus.,
ports. 22cm. Contemporary French poetry after 1945; critical
studies. The usefulness of the volume lies in its many portraits

of poets writing in French (France, Belgium, former French colonies in Africa and Asia, etc.) The critical notes are foot-noted with date and place of birth of the poet, and bibliography of the poet's works. Alphabetical approach through dark page print in name index.

11033   QUIRIELLE, ROGER DE, b. 1848.
         Bio-bibliographie des écrivains anciens du Bourbonnais. [Chatillon-sur-Seine ?] La Roue à livres, 1974. xiv, 240 p. illus., ports. 23cm. A bio-bibliographical dictionary of the older authors of Bourbonnais, France. Reprint of the 1899 edition (Moulins, H. Durond)

11034   SLOVNÍK SPISOVATELŮ. Francie, Švýcarsko, Belgie, Lucem-
         bursko. [Zprac. kolektiv autorů za vedení O. Nováka. Praha, Odeon, 1966. 699 p. 20cm. A dictionary of French, Swiss, Belgian and Luxemburg authors.

11035   VIER, JACQUES, comp.
         La poésie bretonne d'expression française; anthologie XVe-XXe siècle. [Saint-Brieuc] Presses universitaires de Bretagne [c1971-   v. 17cm. (Les Classiques bretons, 3-4
         Contents. --t. 1. XVe-XVIIIe siecle.

An anthology of French poetry by authors from Brittany, 15th-20th century. Includes bio-bibliographical notes; there are 63 poets in vol. 1. Vol. 1 only available as of 1976.

French Canadian

Anonyms and Pseudonyms

11036   VINET, BERNARD, 1924-
         Pseudonymes québécois. Édition basée sur l'oeuvre de Audet et Malchelosse intitulée Pseudonymes canadiens. Qué-bec, Editions Garneau, [1974] xiv, 361 p. 20cm. Quebec pseudonyms; based on Pseudonymes canadiens, by F. J. Audet and G. Malchelosse.

General Works

11037   BARBEAU, VICTOR, 1896-
         Dictionnaire bibliographique du Canada français, par Victor Barbeau et Andre Fortier. Montréal, Académie canadienne française, 1974. 246 p. 32cm. A bio-bibliographical dictionary of French-Canadian authors from the beginning of French litera-ture in Canada to the present. The biographical data is brief but informative.

11038   BIOGRAPHIES ET PORTRAITS D'ÉCRIVAINS CANADIENS.
1. sér. Montréal, Beauchemin, 1913. 140 p. illus., ports.
20cm. (Bibliothèque canadienne. Collection Montcalm) No
more published. Biographies and portraits of French-Canadian
authors. 1st series only was issued.

11039   LE RÉPERTOIRE NATIONAL; ou, Recueil de littérature canadienne. Compilé et publié par J. Husten. 2. éd.,
précédée d'une introd. par M. le juge Routhier. Montréal, J.
M. Valois, 1893. 4 v. 21cm. This anthology of literary texts
of French Canada, 1734 to 1848, includes interesting biographical notices of the authors of the texts.

Frisian

11040   SUFFRIDUS, PETRUS, 1527-1597.
De scriptoribus Frisiae, decades XVI et semis: in quibus
non modo peculiares Frisiae, sed et totius Germaniae communes
antiquitates plurimae indicantur, et veterum historicorum ac
geographorum loci, hactenus non intellecti, explicantur. Caus-
aeque redduntur dilucidae, cur veteres Germani praeter meritum
ruditatis et imperitiae a quibusdem in literaria arguantur.
Franequerae, J. Horreus, 1699. lxxxviii, 498 p. 14cm. The
writers of Friesland (Frisian authors) through 16 and a half decades (15th-16th centuries). Arranged by years when writers
flourished; alphabetical listing, p. lxxi-lxxxviii. 1st ed. published in Coloniae Agrippinae (Cologne) by H. Falkenburgh in
1593.

Georgian

Anonyms and Pseudonyms

11041   MIKADZE, GIVI
Slovar' psevdonimov; nerasshifrovannye psevdonimy 'Gru-
zinskoĭ knigi." Izd. 1. Tibilisi, Metŝniereba, 1969. 64 p. A
dictionary of about 400 pseudonyms of Georgian (Caucasia) authors.

German

Bibliography, Indexes, Portrait Catalogs

11042   FRIEDRICHS, ELISABETH
Literarische Lokalgrössen, 1700-1900. Verzeichnis der in
regionalen Lexika und Sammelwerken aufgeführten Schriftsteller.
[Stuttgart] Metzler [1967] x, 439 p. 24cm. (Repertorien zur
deutschen Literaturgeschichte, Bd. 3) An alphabetically ar-

ranged listing of German local writers, 1700-1900, with birth/
death dates, pseudonyms (if any) and references to dictionaries
and other works which contain bio-bibliographical data about
them.

Anonyms and Pseudonyms

11043   PATAKY, SOPHIE, 1860-
         Verzeichnis der Pseudonyme, welche von deutschen Frauen
der Feder seit etwa 200 Jahren gebraucht worden sind. Berlin,
Schuster & Loeffler, 1898. 72 p. List of pseudonyms used by
German women authors in the last 200 years. 3,500 entries.
Taken from the author's Lexikon deutscher Frauen der Feder
(q. v.).

General Works

11044   DENINA, CARLO, 1731-1813.
         La Prusse littéraire sous Frédéric II; ou, Histoire abrégé
de la plupart des auteurs, des académiciens et des artistes qui
sont nés ou qui ont vécu dans les Etats prussiens depuis 1740
jusqu'à 1786. Par ordre alphabétique. Précédé d'une introd.,
ou, D'un tableau général des progrès qu'ont faits les arts et les
sciences dans les pays qui constituèrent la Monarchie prussiene.
Berlin, H. A. Rottmann, 1790-91. 3 v. 21cm. Writers (German and French primarily) native to or residing in Prussia
during the reign of Frederick II (1740-1786). A biographical dictionary.

11045   DURZAK, MANFRED
         Die deutsche Exilliteratur 1933-1945. Hrsg. von Manfred
Durzak. Stuttgart, P. Reclam jun., 1973. 624 p. 21cm. German literature in exile, 1933-1945. Bio-bibliographical dictionary of writers in exile: p. [521]-592 (in double columns)

11046   FORMANN, WILHELM
         Sudetendeutsche Dichtung heute. München, Aufstieg-Ver-
lag [1961] 160, [1] p. ports. 19cm. Sudeten German literature
today; "Kurzbiographien von A bis Z" (p. 113-160) is a bio-bibliographical dictionary of contemporary writers in German in
Bohemia (Sudetenland area).

11047   FRANKE, KONRAD, 1938-
         Die Literatur der Deutschen Demokratischen Republik.
Neubearb. Ausg. mit 3 einführenden Essays von Heinrich Vormweg. München, Kindler, 1974. 678 p. illus., ports. 25cm.
(Kindlers Literaturgeschichte der Gegenwart) The literature of
the German Democratic Republic. In large part a bio-bibliographical work with entensive essays on prominent East German
writers in the main text (alphabetical approach through the in-

dex) and a section of short biographies ("Kurzbiographien") on
pages [633]-660 (ca. 190 sketches) and numerous portraits.

11048   FRANKFURT AM MAIN. DEUTSCHE BIBLIOTHEK.
        Exil-Literatur, 1933-1945. Ausstellung, Mai bis August
1965. [Ausstellung und Katalog: Werner Berthold; Mitarbeiterin:
Christa Wilhelmi. Frankfurt am Main, 1966] 324, 40 p. illus.,
ports. 21cm. (Its Sonderveröffentlichungen, Nr. 1) "Zweite
Auflage 1966. 1st ed. published in 1965. "Ergänzungen und
Berichtigungen (Beilage zur 2. Aufl. 1966)": 7 p. inserted at
end. An exhibition of German literature in exile during the Nazi
regime. Bio-bibliographical; authors arranged under field of
endeavor or activity, i. e., Social Democrats, Communists, political writers, scientists, etc. Alphabetical approach thru' index at end (dark-printed numbers indicate biographical sketches).

11049   GARLAND, HENRY BURNAND
        The Oxford companion to German literature, by Henry and
Mary Garland. Oxford, Clarendon Press, 1976. vii, 977 p.
24cm. Includes biographies of writers.

11050   GROSS, HEINRICH, b. 1849.
        Deutsche Dichterinen und Schriftstellerinen in Wort und
Bild. Berlin, F. Thiel, 1885. 3 v. ports. 25cm. Anthology
with bio-bibliographical sketches of over 240 German women as
authors, with 113 portraits. 1st appeared in the Jahresbericht
über das K. K. Gymnasium in Triest, 30 (1880) and 31 (1881) A
"2d ed." was issued in Berlin in 1882 (iv, 290 p.)

11051   JÄGER, CAJETAN
        Literarisches Freiburg im Breisgau; oder, Verzeichnis der
gegenwärtig zu Freiburg im Breisgau lebenden Schriftsteller
mit Angabe der Hauptzüge ihrer Laufbahn und der von ihnen im
Drucke erschienenen Schriften. Freiburg, Druck und Verlag von
F. X. Wangler, 1839. xii, 214 p. 18cm. (Gelehrtes Baden;
oder, Verzeichnis des im Grossherzogthum Baden lebenden
Schriftsteller mit Angabe der Hauptzüge ihrer Laufbahn und der
von ihnen im Drucke erschienenen Schriften, Heft 1) Literary
Freiburg im Breisgau; or, A list of the authors now living in
that city, with data on their careers and writings.

11052   KAPP, ERNST
        Hundert Lebensbilder deutscher Dichter, mit Proben aus
ihren Werken. Für Schule und Haus bearb. Hrsg. vom Würt-
tembergischen Evangelischen Lehrer-Unterstützungsverein. 3.
und 4. Aufl. Stuttgart, A. Bonz, 1925. 266 p. 8.° Biographies
of 100 German authors, with examples from their work.

11053   KESTEN, HERMANN, 1900-
        Deutsche Literatur im Exil. Briefe europäischer Autoren

1933-1949. Wien, K. Desch [1964] 380 p. 21cm. Correspond-
ence to and from Kesten with German authors (and a few British
and American) living abroad during the Nazi era and shortly
thereafter; each letter is accompanied by short bio-bibliographical notices about the persons named. Name index on p. 373-379.

11054   KNOBLOCH, ERHARD JOSEPH, 1923-
Kleines Handlexikon. Deutsche Literatur in Böhmen, Mäh-
ren, Schlesien von den Anfängen bis heute. München, Europa-
Buchhandlung, 1968. 91 p. 19cm. A handbook-dictionary of
German literature in Bohemia, Moravia and Silesia from its be-
ginnings to the present.

11055   KÖNNECKE, GUSTAV, 1845-1920.
Bilderatlas zur Geschichte der deutschen Nationalliteratur;
eine Ergänzung zu jeder deutschen Litteraturgeschichte. Nach
den Quellen bearb. 2. verb. und verm. Aufl. Marburg, N. G.
Elwert [1895] xxvi, 423 p. illus., ports. 42cm. A pictorial
history of German national literature. A great number of portraits and biographical sketches of leading figures in German
literature are included. Alphabetical approach thru' name index
at end of volume. First ed. issued in 1887 (xxxvi, 316 p.)

11055a   KÖNNECKE, GUSTAV, 1845-1920.
Deutscher Literaturatlas. Mit einer Einführung von Christian Muff. Marburg, N. G. Elwert; New York, G. E. Stechert,
1909. xii, 156 p. illus., ports. 35cm. An abbreviated, cheap-
er edition of the author's Bilderatlas zur Geschichte der deutsch-
en Nationallitteratur. A pictorial history of German national
literature. A large number of portraits and biographical sketches of German writers are included. Alphabetical approach thru'
name index at end of volume.

11056   KOSEL, HERMANN CLEMENS, 1867-   comp.
Der Lehrer als Dichter. Gesammelte Dichtungen aus der
Lehrerwelt Deutsch-Oesterreichs, von Hermann Clemens Kosel
und Emil Hofmann. Mit einem Geleitsbriefe von Peter Rosegger.
Wien, Sallmayer'sche Buchhandlung, 1901. iv, 197 p. ports.
8.º The teacher as author; an anthology with 132 brief biogra-
phies of writers from the profession of teaching in Germany and
Austria.

11057   KÜHN, HUGO JOHANN WILHELM
Lehrer als Schriftsteller; Handbuch der schriftstellernden
Lehrer, mit Biographien und Angabe ihrer litterarische Erzeug-
nisse. Leipzig, Siegismund & Volkening, 1888. 192 p. 12.º
Teachers as authors; a bio-bibliographical dictionary of German
and Austrian (primarily) writer-teachers.

11058   KÜRSCHNERS DEUTSCHER LITERATUR-KALENDER. Nekro-
           log 1936-1970. Hrsg. von Werner Schuder. Berlin, New
           York, W. de Gruyter, 1973. xiv, 871 p. 21cm. The 1901-1935
           Nekrolog is entered under Kürschners Deutscher Literatur-Kal-
           ender with title: Nekrolog zu Kürschners Literatur Kalender.
           Kürschner's German literary calendar; necrology of German au-
           thors for the years 1936-1970.

11059   KUNISCH, HERMANN, 1901-
           Handbuch der deutschen Gegenwartsliteratur. 2., verb. und
           erw. Aufl. Redaktion Herbert Wiesner in Zusammenarbeit mit
           Helge Kähler, Christoph Stoll und Irena Zivsa. München,
           Nymphenburger Verlagshandlung [1968-70. 3 v. 26cm. Con-
           tents.--Bd. 1. A-K.--Bd. 2. L-Z.--Bd. 3. Bibliographie der
           Personalbibliographien. Handbook of contemporary (20th cen-
           tury) German literature; a bio-bibliographical dictionary.

11060   LEIMBACH, KARL LUDWIG
           Die deutschen Dichter der Neuzeit und Gegenwart. Biogra-
           phien, Charakteristiken und Auswahl ihrer Dichtungen. Kassel,
           T. Kay, 1884-[1909] 10 v. 21cm. (His Ausgewählte deutsche
           Dichtungen für Lehrer und Freunde der Litteratur, 5.-1 Bd.)
           Imprint varies: v. 5-10 (2. Lfg.), Leipzig, Kesselringsche Hof-
           buchhandlung (E. v. Mayer) German poets of the modern era and
           the present (end of the 19th century). An anthology arranged al-
           phabetically (vols. 1-9: Alexander, Graf von Württemberg-Scher-
           er, Georg). Selections are preceded by quite substantial bio-
           bibliographical outlines of the authors. No more published after
           the 2d fascicle of vol. 10?

11061   LEXIKON SOZIALISTISCHER DEUTSCHER LITERATUR, von
           den Anfängen bis 1945. Monographisch-biographische
           Darstellungen. [Verfasser der Artikel, Wilfried Adling, et al.;
           der literaturgeschichtliche Überblick wurde von Silvia Schlen-
           staedt verfasst]. 's-Gravenhage, Van Eversdijck; Giessen,
           Prolit-Buchvertrieb [in Kommission] 1973. 592 p. 21cm.
           (Rotdruck, 20) Dictionary of German socialist (communist) lit-
           erature from its beginnings to 1945, with monographic-biogra-
           phical entries.

11062   MINCKWITZ, JOHANNES
           Der neuhochdeutsche Parnass, 1740-1860. Eine Grundlage
           zum besseren Verständnisse unserer Literaturgeschichte in
           Biographien, Charakteristiken und Beispielen unserer vorzüg-
           lichsten Dichter. 2. Aufl. Leipzig, Arnold, 1864. xvi, 895 p.
           illus. 1st ed. issued in 1861. An anthology of German poetry,
           1740-1860, arranged alphabetically by author, with brief bio-
           graphical sketches of the authors (includes many Austrians).

11063   OEHLKE, WALDEMAR, 1879-
           Deutsche Literatur der Gegenwart. Berlin, Deutsche Bibli-

othek Verlagsgesellschaft [1942] 479 p. 20cm. A bio-bibliography of German literature (including Austria) of the 1st half of
the 20th century.

11064   SCHERER, GEORG, 1828-1909.
          Deutscher Dichterwald. Lyrische Anthologie. Mit 152
Medaillon-Porträten und 32 Vollbildern von Arnold Böcklin,
Franz von Defregger [et al.] 18. Aufl. Jubiläums-Ausg. Stuttgart, Deutsche Verlags-Anstalt, 1902. viii, 568 p. illus.,
ports. An anthology of German lyric poetry, with 152 medallion-
portraits and 32 full-page plates. Pages 537-562 contain an al-
phabetically-arranged list of the poets represented, with biographical data.

11065   SCHLÖSSER, MANFRED, comp.
          An den Wind geschrieben; Lyrik der Freiheit, 1933-1945.
[Gesammelt, ausgewählt und eingeleitet von Manfred Schlösser
unter Mitarbeit von Hans-Rolf Ropertz. 2., verb. Aufl.] Darmstadt, Agora [1961, c1960] 372 p. 22cm. (Agora; eine human-
istische Schriftenreihe, Bd. 13/14) An anthology of German
poetry ("lyrics of freedom") which appeared during the years of
the Nazi regime, 1939-1945, and written primarily by exiles
from Germany for those years. "Biographien-Bibliographien"
(p. 323-372) is a bio-bibliographical dictionary of the 175 poets
represented.

11066   SCHRIFTSTELLER DER DDR [von] Günter Albrecht [et al.]
          [Leitung des Autorenkollektivs und Gesamtredaktion: Kurt
Böttcher in Zusammenarbeit mit Herbert Greiner-Mai] Leipzig,
Bibliographisches Institut, 1974. 656 p. 20cm. (Meyers
Taschenlexikon) Treats over 700 writers of the German Demo-
cratic Republic (deceased and living).

11067   SOERGEL, ALBERT, 1880-
          Dichtung und Dichter der Zeit; vom Naturalismus bis zur
Gegenwart [von] Albert Soergel [und] Curt Hohoff. [Neubear-
beitung] Düsseldorf, A. Bagel [1961-63] 2 v. illus., ports.
25cm. German literature from naturalism to the present; late
19th and 20th century German literature in bio-bibliographical
essays. Valuable too for its many portraits of writers, autographs, etc. Each topic (chapter) starts out with a critical-his-
torical description and then is followed by the bio-bibliographies.
The work was first issued in a single volume in 1911 (by Soergel
alone) followed by a "Neue Folge" (new series) in 1925 and a
"Dritte Folge" (3d series) in 1934.

11068   STERNFELD, WILHELM, 1888-
          Deutsche Exil-Literatur 1933-1945; eine Bio-Bibliographie
[von] Wilhelm Sternfeld [und] Eva Tiedemann. 2., verb. und
stark erw. Aufl. Mit einem Vorwort von Hanns W. Eppelsheimer.
Heidelberg, L. Schneider, 1970. 606 p. 24cm. (Veröffent-

lichung der Deutschen Akademie für Sprache und Dichtung, Darmstadt [29a]) A bio-bibliographical dictionary of German writers who left Germany during the Nazi regime, 1933-1945.

11069   WEISS, KARL, 1846-
Deutsche Dichterinnen und Schriftstellerinnen in Böhmen, Mähren und Schlesien. Ein Beitrag zur Geschichte der deutschen Dichtung in Österreich-Ungarn, von Karl Schrattenthal [pseud.] Brünn, 1885.   89 p. 8.° Bio-bibliography of women writing in German in Bohemia, Moravia and Silesia.

11070   WILPERT, GERO VON
Deutsche Literatur in Bildern. 2. erw. Aufl. Mit 970 Abbildungen. Stuttgart, Kröner [1965] viii, 352 p. of illus. (with text) 26cm. German literature in pictures; an iconography with many of the illustrations consisting of portraits of literary figures. Alphabetical approach through text and portrait index at end.

Greek, Ancient

11071   HEINOLD, ANT
Kurze Biographien alter bekannten griechischen und lateinischen Schriftsteller vom Anfang der Wissenschaften bis ins 5. Jahrhundert. In alphabetischer Ordnung zusammengetragen. Wien, F. Haas, 1807. 292 p. Brief biographies of the Greek and Latin authors from the earliest times to the 5th century A. D.; a biographical dictionary.

11072   MANTINBAND, JAMES H
Concise dictionary of Greek literature. New York, Greenwood Press, 1969 [c1962] 409 p. 23cm. Includes biographies (for the most part very brief) of classical Greek authors.

Greek, Modern

Anonyms and Pseudonyms

11073   NTELOPOULOS, KYRIAKOS
Neoellēnika philologika pseudonyma. 1. ekd. Athēnai [Athens] Kollegion Athenōn, 1969. 143 p. 21cm. (Bibliothēkē Kollegion Athenōn. Encheiridia bibliothēkonomias, 3) Modern Greek pseudonyms.

General Works

11074   DĒMĒTRAKOPOU LOS, ANDRONIKOS K ̦   d. 1872.
Epanorthōseiș sfalmátōn paratērēthéntōn en tēj Neoellenikēj
filologiaj toū K. Sátha, metà kai tinōn prosthēkōn. Tergéstēj,
Túpois toū Austriakoū Loüd, 1872._ 53 p. 2lcm. Corrections
and additions to Sathas' Neoellēnikē filologia (q. v.) which contains bio-bibliographical material on modern Greek literature.

11075   DĒMĒTRAKOPOU LOS, ANDRONIKOS K   d. 1872.   ̦
Prosthēkai kai diorthōseiș eis tēn Neoellēnikēn filologian
Kōnstantinou Sátha. En Leipsia, Túpois Métzger kai Bittig,
1871. 119 p. 2lcm. Supplement and corrections for K. N.
Sathas' Neollēnike filologia (q. v.) which contains bio-bibliogra-
phical material on modern Greek literature.

11076   KASDAGLĒS, EMMANOUĒL CH
Autographa Hellēnōn syngropheōn. [Athens] Hetaireia
Spoudōn, Scholē Mōraitē, 1974. 159 p. ports. 34cm. A volume of autographs (accompanied by biographical facts) of modern Greek writers.

11077   LEGRAND, ÉMILE LOUIS JEAN, 1841-1903.   ̦
Bibliographie hellénique; ou, Description raisonnée des
ouvrages publiés par des Grecs au dix-septième siècle. Bruxelles, Culture & civilisation, 1963. 5 v. illus. 25cm. Reprint
of the Paris (Picard) edition of 1894-1903. A bibliography of
Greek literature of the 17th century; includes biographical notices
(v. 3, p. 92-477--88 notices; v. 4, p. 1-521--7; v. 5, p. 173-498
--98) with alphabetical index of the biographical notices at front
of vols. 3 & 5.

11078   VRETOS, ANDREAS PAPADOPOU LOS, 1800? -1876.
Neoellēnike filologia; ētoi, Katalogos tōn apo ptōseōs tēs
Byzantinēs autokratorias mechri egkathidryseōs tēs en Elladi
Basileias typōthenton Bibliōn par Ellēnon eis tēn omiloumenēn,
ē eis archaian ellēnikēn glossan. En Athenais, L. D. Bilaras
kai B. P. Lioumēs, 1854-57. 2 v. 2lcm. Neohellenic philology; a bibliography of modern Greek philology with biographical sketches of authors in vol. 1 (p. 171-251)--A-O) and v. 2
(p. 239-351--A-O)

11079   ZABIRAS, GEŌRGIOS IŌANNOU, 1744-1804.
Néa 'Ellàs e 'Ellēnikon theatron ekdothen. 'Athenesi,
Tupois 'Efemeridos tōn Suzētēseōn, 1872. 561 p. 23cm. At
head of title: ... Anekdota suggrammata. Modern Greece; or,
The Greek theater. Bio-bibliography of modern Greek litera-
ture. Edited by G. P. Kremos. Reprinted in 1972.

Gujarati

11080   DESAI, RAMNIK SRIPATRAY, ed.
Prachin kavio ane temni kritio. Baroda, Luhana Mitra
Print. Press, 1949. 369 p. In Gujarat. Bio-bibliographical
sketches of Gujarati authors.

11081   GUJARAT VERNACULAR SOCIETY.
Granth ane granthakar. Ahmedabad, 1930-52. 10 v. In
Gujarati. Bio-bibliography of Gujarati authors.

Hebrew

See under Jewish

Hindi

11082   TANDON, PREM NARAYAN, 1915-   ed.
Hindī-sevī-samsara. Lucknow, Hindi Sevi Samsara Karya-
lay, 1963-65. 2 v. port. 22cm. In Hindi. Vol. 1 has added
title: Hindī sahityakāra kośa. Vol. 1 includes biographies of
some 2749 living Hindi writers. Supplementary biographies are
also in appendices I to IV. Vol. 2 is a directory of institutions
and libraries connected with Hindi research study.

Hungarian

11083   BENEDEK, MARCELL, 1885-   ed.
Magyar irodalmi lexikon. Főszerkesztő Benedek Marcell.
Budapest, Akademiai Kiado, 1963-65. 3 v. 24cm. A diction-
ary of Hungarian literature, in large part bio-bibliographical.

11084   HÖHL, MARTHA
Ungarische Literatur des 20. Jahrhunderts; ein Auswahlver-
zeichnis. Mit einem Beitrag von Miklós Beládi. Dortmund,
Stadtbücherei, 1971. xv, 62 p. 21cm. (Völker im Spiegel der
Literatur, Folge 14) Hungarian literature of the 20th century; a
bio-bibliography of 93 authors in chronological order with an alphabetical index at end.

11085   LATOGATÓBAN; kortárs magyar írók vallomásai; új gyujte-
mény. [Szerk.: Lengyel Péter. A bibliográfiát összeál-
litotta: X Zalán Vince] Budapest, Gondolat Kiadó, 1971. 475 p.
ports. 21cm. Visitations with and statements by 59 contemporary Hungarian writers; a bio-bibliographical work, with portraits of the authors.

11086 MOENICH, KÁROLY
Magyar írók névtára. Életrajzi és könyvészeti adatok
gyüjteménye. Különféle kutfőkből szerkesztették Moenich
Károly es Vutkovich Sándor. Pozsony, Nirschy Ferenc Köny-
vnyomdája, 1876. xiv, 577, xxix p. 23cm. List of Hungarian
authors, a bio-bibliographical collection of data from various
sources, arranged according to day of birth (Jan. 1-Dec. 31)

11087 PÁL, OTTÓ
Írók és olvasók; író-olvasó találkozók rendezésenek
módszertana. Budapest, A Tudományos Ismeretterjesztő Tarsulat Könyvkiadója, 1964. 102 p. 19cm. "A methodology of
the arrangement of meetings between writers and readers"--a
literal translation of the title. Actually the chief section of the
work is the "Életrajzi jegyzetek" (Biographical notes), p. 33-
102, which contains brief bio-bibliographical data on many 20th
century Hungarian authors not listed in the standard sources.

11088 S KÉT SZÓ KÖZÖTT A HALLGATÁS; magyar mártir írók anto-
lógiája. [Válogatta és szerk. Keresztury Desző és Sik
Casba] Budapest, Magvető Kiadó, 1970. 2 v. 19cm.
"And two words amid the silence"; anthology of Hungarian 'mar-
tyr' authors with bio-bibliographical notices. 50 authors who
died during World War II and selections from their works in vol.
1 (e. g.)

11089 SLOVNÍK SPISOVATELŮ. Maďarsko. Za ved. Petra Rákose
zprac. [kol.] Úv. studii naps., chronologický přehl. sest.
P. Rákos. 1. vyd. Praha, Odeon, 1971. 386, [22] p. 20cm.
Dictionary of Hungarian authors.

11090 SLOVNÍK SVĚTOVÝCH DRAMATIKU. Maďarsti autoři. Red.
Ludmila Kopáčová. a kol. 1. vyd. Praha, Svoboda, 1973.
357 p. 21cm. Dictionary of the world's dramatists; Hungarian
authors.

11091 TOLDY, FERENCZ, 1805-1875.
A magyar költeszet kézikönyve, a Mohácsi vésztöl a jelen-
korig, vagyis az utóbbi negyedfél század kithünőbb költői életra-
jzokban és jellemző mutatványokban; feltüntetve Toldy Ferenc
által. Második, átdolgozott, kiadás ... Budapest, Franklin-
tarsulat, 1876 [i. e. 1875] 5 v. port. 19cm. 2d rev. ed. of A
magyar nyelv és irodalom kézikönyve (Pest, 1855-57. 2 v.) An
even earlier edition in German (Handbuch der ung[a]rischen
Poesie) was issued in 1828. Manual of Hungarian language and
literature after the disaster of Mohacs to the middle of the 19th
century. An anthology with bio-bibliographical notices, in
chronological arrangement.

Icelandic

11092   JÓNSSON, JÓN, Borgfirðingur, 1826-1912.
        Stutt rithöfundatal á Íslandi 1400-1882. Reykjavík, Prent-
smiðju Ísafoldar, 1884. [6], iv, 141, [5] p. Icelandic writers
from 1400 to 1882; arranged by century and by specialty. Alphabetical index with entries by forename, p. 131-141.

Indic

(See also Bengali, Hindi, etc.)

Anonyms and Pseudonyms

11093   VIRENDRA KUMAR, 1933-
        Dictionary of pseudonmys [sic] in Indian literature. Edited
by N. K. Goil. [Delhi] Delhi Library Association, 1973. x,
163 p. 25cm. (Delhi Library Association. English series, no.
7) Running title: Pseudonyms in Indian literature. Chiefly 20th
century pseudonyms with some from 18th-19th centuries.

General Works

11094   GARCIN DE TASSY, JOSEPH HÉLIODORE SAGESSE VERTU,
        1794-1878.
        Histoire de la littérature hindouie et hindoustanie; [biogra-
phie, bibliographie, et extraits] 2. éd. rev., corr., et considérablement augm. New York, Burt Franklin [1968] 3 v.
23cm. (Oriental Translation Fund. [Publications]) (Essays in
literature and criticism, 23) (Burt Franklin research & source
works series, 326) "Originally published ... 1870." History of
Hindu and Hindustani literature; actually a bio-bibliographical
dictionary.

11095   PARDESI, RAM GOPAL, 1937-
        Bhāratīya lekhaka kośa. [1. ed. Agra, Sāntvanā Prakashan;
distributors: Pragati Prakashan, 1970-   v. illus.
23cm. In Hindi. Who's who of living Indic writers. Arrangement is by forenames. To be complete in 3 vols.

Iraqui

11096   'AWWĀD, KŪRKĪS
        Mu'jam al-mu'allifīn al-'Irāqīyīn. [Baghdad, al-Irshad
Press, 1969. 3 v. 26cm. Added t. p.: A dictionary of Iraqi
authors during the ninetieth [sic] and twentieth centuries, 1800-
1969 A. D., by Gurguis Awwad. Vol. 3: Supplementary.

Irish

11097   CLEEVE, BRIAN TALBOT, 1921-
         Dictionary of Irish writers. Cork, Ire., Mercier Press,
         1967-71. 3 v. 18cm. (A Mercier paper-back) Contents. --v. l.
         Fiction, novelists, playwrights, poets, short story writers in
         English. --v. 2. Non-fiction. --v. 3. Writers in the Irish lan-
         guage.

11098   O'REILLY, EDWARD, d. 1829.
         A chronological account of nearly four hundred Irish writ-
         ers, with a descriptive catalogue of their works. Introd. by
         Gearoid S. MacEoin. New York, Barnes & Noble [1971]
         ccxxxvii p. 26cm. On spine: 400 Irish writers. Reprint of the
         1820 ed. Includes an index which gives an alphabetical approach
         to the writers.

Italian

Anonyms and Pseudonyms

11099   EDMAR.
         Pseudonimi di giuliani friulani e dalnati. Scrittori, gior-
         nalisti, artisti, musicisti. Trieste, Libreria internazionale
         Italo Svevo, 1972. 60 p. 10cm. [Collezione Millerighe, 7]
         Pseudonyms of artists and writers from Friuli-Venezia Giulia,
         Italy and Dalmatia.

11100   FRATTAROLO, RENZO
         Dizionario degli scrittori italiani contemporanei pseudonimi
         (1900-1975); con un repertorio delle bibliografie nazionali di
         opere anonime e pseudonime. Ravenna, Longo, 1975. 325 p.
         25cm. (Bibliografia e storia della critica, 1) A dictionary of
         pseudonymous Italian writers of the 20th century (1900-1975);
         biographical and bibliographical.

11101   GIULIARI, GIOVANNI BATTISTA CARLO, conte, 1810-1892.
         Gli anonimi veronesi. Verona, H. F. Münster, (G. Gold-
         schagg success.) 1895. 192 p. 8.º The anonyms of authors
         from the City of Verona.

General Works

11102   ANGELIS, LUIGI DE
         Biografia degli scrittori sanesi. Siena, Rossi, 1824-27.
         2 v. plate. 4.º Vol. 1 and v. 2, fasc. 1 only ones published;
         ceased with the letter L. A biographical dictionary of authors
         from Siena.

11103   BANDINI BUTI, MARIA (FERRARI) 1896-
        Poetesse e scrittrici. A cura di Maria Bandini Buti.
        Roma, E. B. B. I., Istituto editoriale italiano B. C. Tosi,
        1941-42. 2 v. illus., ports. 28cm. (Enciclopedia biografica
        e bibliografica 'Italiana, ' ser. 6) A biographical dictionary of
        women poets and authors of Italy.

11104   BONU, RAIMONDO
        Scrittori sardi nati nel secolo XVIII. Con notizie stori-
        che e letterarie dell'epoca. 2. ed. ampliata. Cagliari, Editi-
        rice sarda Fossataro, 1972-   v. plates. 24cm. Sar-
        dinian authors born in the 18th century; on pages 179-344 of vol.
        1 are bio-bibliographical studies of 55 writers (arranged by date
        of birth). Despite the above title, presumably a second vol.
        will be published that will contain authors born in the 19th cen-
        tury (4 of the authors mentioned in vol. 1 are in a supplement
        entitled: "Supplemento I al vol. II: Scrittori sardi (1' '800). "
        An earlier edition (Oristano, 1952-   ) covered Sardinian au-
        thors from 1746 to 1950.

11105   CAGNACCI, FR
        Scritti, scrittori e uomini celebri della provincia di Gros-
        setto. Grossetto, Baralli, 1874. 68 p. 8.⁰ Writings, writers
        and famous men of the Province of Grossetto; bio-bibliographi-
        cal.

11106   CALVI, DONATO
        Scena letteraria degli scrittori bergamaschi, aperta alla
        curiosità dei suoi concittadini. Bergamo, Marc' Antonio
        Roffi, 1664. 2 v. illus., ports. 22cm. A bio-bibliography of
        writers from Bergamo, Italy.

11107   CANTALAMESSA-CARBONI, GIACINTO, 1789-1858.
        Memoria intorno i letterati e gli artisti della città di As-
        coli nel Piceno. Ascoli, Tip. di L. Cardi, 1830. viii, 304 p.
        27cm. Bio-bibliography of authors and artists from the city of
        Ascoli Piceno.

11108   CATANZARO, CARLO
        La donna italiana nelle scienze, nelle lettere, nelle arti;
        dizionario biografico delle scrittrici e delle artiste viventi. Con
        pref. di Giovanni Manzi. Firenze, Biblioteca editrice della Ri-
        vista italiana [1892] 285 p. ports. 8.⁰ Italian women in the
        sciences, literature and arts; a biographical dictionary of living
        writers and artists (late 19th century).

11109   [CERRI, LEOPOLDO]
        Memorie per la storia letteraria di Piacenza, in continua-
        zione al Poggiali. Piacenza, Stamperia F. Solari, di G. Tononi,
        1895-97. 2 pts. in 1 v. (v, 215, 43, [4] p.) 28cm. Bio-bibliog-

raphy of the city of Piacenza, especially men of letters. A continuation of C. Poggiali's work of the same title (q. v.)

11110   CHI SCRIVE; repertorio bio-bibliografico e per specializzazioni
         degli scrittori italiani. 2. ed. Milano, IGAP, 1966. 699 p.
         25cm. (Collana Personalità, 2) 1st ed. (Milano, Istituto Librario editoriale. 1235 p.) was issued in 1962. A bio-bibliography of contemporary Italian authors.

11111   COLOMO, GAVINO, comp.
         Poeti, scrittori ed artisti degli anni '70. Antologia a cura
         di Gavino Colomo. Firenze, BIE, 1970. 523 p. illus. 22cm.
         Italian poets, writers and artists of the 1970's (51 painters, 91
         authors); an anthology, with rather extensive bio-bibliographical notes.

11112   COLOMO, GAVINO
         Poeti, scrittori ed artisti degli anni '70. Dizionario bio-
         bibliografico, a cura di Gavino Colomo. Firenze, BIE, 1970.
         253 p. plates. 22cm. Italian poets, writers and artists of the
         1970's; a bio-bibliographical dictionary.

11113   DE LEO, ERNESTO, 1899-   comp.
         Antologia dei poeti, narratori, scrittori d'Italia al 1971.
         Genova, Ass. ital. poeti-narratori e scrittori, 1972. 102 p.
         ports. 24cm. Anthology of works by 89 lesser-known contemporary Italian authors, accompanied by portraits and biographical sketches for 44 of them; alphabetical name index at
         end.

11114   DIZIONARIO BIO-BIBLIOGRAFICO DEGLI SCRITTORI ITALIANI.
         Ser. 1, fasc. 1. Bergamo, Istituto d'arti grafiche, 1898.
         64 p. 16.º No more published? Bio-bibliographical dictionary
         of Italian writers.

11115   DIZIONARIO CRITICO DELLA LETTERATURA ITALIANA.
         Diretto da Vittore Branca. Redattori,Armando Balduino,
         Manlio Pastore Stocchi, Marco Pecoraro. Torino, Unione
         tipografico editrice torinese [1974?] 3 v. plates. 26cm. Critical dictionary of Italian literature; bio-bibliographical.

11116   DIZIONARIO DELLA LETTERATURA ITALIANA CONTEMPO-
         RANEA. Firenze, Vallecchi, 1973. 2 v. 18cm. (Tascabili
         Vallecchi, 34-35) Edited by E. Ronconi. Contents.--1. Movimenti letterari, scrittori.--2. Repertorio. A dictionary of contemporary Italian literature; included in vol. 1 is a biographical
         dictionary of writers.

11117   DIZIONARIO GENERALE DEGLI AUTORI ITALIANI CONTEM-
        PORANEI. Firenze, Vallecchi, 1974. 2 v. (xliv,1551 p.)
        illus. 23cm. "Coordinamento Enzo Ronconi." Contents.--1.
        Movimenti letterari, Abba-Luzzatto Fegiz.--Maccari-Zumbini,
        Influenze e corrispondenze. Dictionary of contemporary Italian
        authors.

11118   FOSCARINI, AMILCARE
        Saggio di un catalogo bibliografico degli scrittori Salentini,
        le cui opere sono state messe a stampa. Lecce, Lazzaretti,
        1894. xvi, 310 p. 8.º Attempt at a (bio)-bibliographical catalog
        of writers from the Peninsula of Salentina whose works are in
        print.

11119   GAMBA, BARTOLOMMEO, 1776-1841.
        De' Bassanesi illustri, con un catalogo degli scrittori di
        Bassano del secolo XVIII. Bassano, Dalla Remondiniana, 1807.
        108 p. 24cm. Authors of the 18th century from Bassano, Italy.
        Narrative (with notices arranged chronologically), p. 7-66; al-
        phabetical catalog of writers of the 18th century, p. 67-104.

11120   GINANNI, PIETRO PAOLO, 1698-1744.
        Memorie storico-critiche degli scrittori ravennati. Faenza,
        G. A. Archi, 1769. 2 v. 25cm. Bio-bibliography of writers
        from Ravenna.

11121   GUSSAGO, GERMANO JACOPO
        Biblioteca Clarense; ovvero, Notizie istorico-critiche in-
        torno agli scrittori e letterati di Chiari. Chiari, 1820. 3 v.
        8.º Includes bio-bibliographical material on the writers and
        literati of Chiari.

11122   [MAFFEI, FRANCESCO SCIPIONE, marchese] 1675-1755.
        Verona illustrata. Verona, J. Vallarsi e P. Berno, 1731-32
        [v. 1, 1732] 4 v. illus., maps. 40cm. Text in double columns.
        Vol. 2 ('parte seconda') is devoted to a large number of brief bi-
        ographical notices of authors connected with Verona, from Ro-
        man times to the author's time. Alphabetical approach thru'
        name index at end of the volume.

11123   MANZANO, FRANCESCO DI
        Cenni biografici dei letterati ed artisti friulani dal secolo
        IV al XIX. Udine, Tip. G. B. Doretti, 1884. 227 p. 24cm. A
        biographical dictionary of literati and artists of Friuli.

11124   MAŁY SŁOWNIK PISARZY WŁOSKICH. Red. J. Gałuszka.
        Warszawa, Wiedza Powszechna, 1969. 213 p. 20cm. A
        dictionary of ca. 250 Italian authors.

11125   PASSANO, GIOVANNI BATTISTA
         I novellieri italiani in prosa, indicati e descritti da Giam-
battista Passano. 2. ed. migliorata e notevolmente accresciuta.
Torino, G. B. Paravia, 1878. 2 v. 24cm. A bio-bibliography
of Italian writers of fiction, a companion volume to the author's
I novellieri italiani in verso (Bologna, 1868).

11126   PASSANO, GIOVANNI BATTISTA
         I novellieri italiani in verso, indicati e descritti da Giam-
battista Passano. Bologna, G. Romagnoli, 1868. viii, 306 p.
28cm. A bio-bibliography of Italian poets, a companion volume
to the author's I novellieri italiani in prosa (Torino, 1878).

11127   ROLANDIS, GIUSEPPE MARIA DE
         Notizie sugli scrittori Astigiani. Asti, Della Tip. di A.
Garbiglea, 1839. 158, [2] p. 24cm. Bio-bibliographical notes
on the writers of Asti.

11128   RUSSO, LUIGI, 1892-1961.
         I narratori (1850-1950) Nuova ed. integrata e ampliata.
Milano, G. Principato [1951] 406 p. 22cm. Bio-bibliography
of Italian writers of fiction, 1850-1950.

11129   SPIRITI, SALVADORE, marchese di Casabona, 1712-1776.
         Memorie degli scrittori Cosentini. Napoli, Stamperia de'
Muzj, 1750. 190, [17] p. 24cm. Arranged chronologically,
with author and subject indexes; the writers of Cosenza--a bio-
bibliography.

11130   TREVISANI, CARLO
         La vita e le opere dei 360 più noti scrittori d'Italia. Roma,
Verdesi, 1886. 268 p. 16.º The life and works of the 360
most noted Italian authors.

11131   TROISI, LUIGI
         Il Novecento; aspetti letterari. Roma, O. Barjes [1970]
378 p. 22cm. Bio-bibliography of Italian literature in the 20th
century. Topical arrangement. The index of names yields an
alphabetical approach although the index of critical notes (non-
alphabetical; follows page order) is the only specific listing of
those writers for whom the work contains bio-bibliographical
data.

11132   VECCHIETTI, FILIPPO
         Biblioteca Picena; o sia, Notizie istoriche delle opere e
degli scrittori piceni. Osimo, D. A. Quercetti, 1790-96. 5 v.
27cm. Ceased publication at the letter L. In collaboration
with Tommaso Moro. Bio-bibliography of the authors of Piceno,
Italy.

Jagataic

11133   HOFMAN, H   F
         Turkish literature; a biobibliographical survey. Section III:
         Moslim Central Asian Turkish literature being in the main a list
         of Chaghatayan authors and works in Chaghatay as registered in
         Professor M. F. Köprülü's article: Çagatay edebiyati, IA. vol.
         I II (270-) (with some additions, Navā'iāna, however excepted)
         By H. F. Hofman. [Utrecht, Published by the University of
         Utrecht under the auspices of the Royal Asiatic Society of Great
         Britain and Ireland, 1969-   v. in   24cm. Contents.
         --pt. 1. Authors.   v.

Japanese

Anonyms and Pseudonyms

11134   WAKIMIZU, KEN'YA.
         Senken meika betsugō beshō jiten. Tokyo, 35 [1960] 278p.
         illus. 19cm. A dictionary of pseudonyms and real names of
         Japanese calligraphers, artists, tea masters, writers, etc.

General Works

11135   GENDAI SAKKA JITEN. Tokyo, Tokyodo, 1973. 417 p. 19cm.
         A dictionary of biographies of modern Japanese writers,
         with emphasis on post-1945 authors. In Japanese syllabic order.

11136   HISAMATSU, SEN'ICHI, 1894-1976.
         Biographical dictionary of Japanese literature. 1st ed.
         [Tokyo] Kodansha International in collaboration with the Interna-
         tional Society for Educational Information [1976] 437 p. 22cm.
         320 writers are represented. Arrangement is alphabetical with-
         in periods of the development of Japanese literature: e. g.,
         Archaic period, Early period, Middle period, Early modern
         period, Modern period.

11137   SENGO SAKKA NO RIREKI. Tokyo, Shibundo, 1973. 346 p.
         23cm. Biography of post-war (1945-   ) Japanese writ-
         ers, with portraits.

11138   TAKAGI, SOGO
         Haikai jimmei jiten. Tokyo, Gannando, 1970. 17, 660 p.
         19cm. Reprint of 1960 edition. Brief biographies and evalua-
         tions of Japanese poets specializing in haiku from Sōkan to 1959.
         Arranged by periods and schools, with an index of pen names.

Jewish

Anonyms and Pseudonyms

11139   CHAJES, SAUL, 1884-
Thesaurus pseudonymorum quae in litteratura Hebraica et
Judaeo-Germanica inveniuntur. Pseudonymen-Lexikon der
hebräischen und jiddischen Literatur. Wien, Bamberger &
Wahrman, 1933. xiv, 335, [10], 66 p. 25cm. (Veröffentlich-
ungen der Oberrabiner Dr. H. P. Chajes-Preisstiftung an der
Israelitisch-Theologischen Lehranstalt in Wien) Added t.p.:
Ozer beduye ha-shem ... Text in Hebrew or Yiddish. A thesau-
rus of Hebrew and Yiddish anonyms and pseudonyms.

General Works

11140   CAZES, DAVID
Notes bibliographiques sur la littérature juive-tunisienne.
Tunis, Impr. internationale, 1893. 370 p. 17 x 26cm. [Bio]-
bibliographical notes on the literature of Jews in Tunisia.

11141   GALLERY OF HEBREW POETS. [5485-5663, 1725-1903] London, Greenberg [190-] 94 l. ports. 26cm. Text in Hebrew and English.

11142   HAZAN, SOLOMON, d. 1856.
Sefer ha-ma'aloth li-Shelomoh ... [Alexandria, Egypt,
1894] 116 l. 22cm. Bio-bibliography of modern Jewish authors
of the East. Bio-bibliographical appendix of Alexandrian rabbis:
l. 113-116.

11143   ZOHN, HARRY
Österreichische Juden in der Literatur; ein bio-biblio-
graphisches Lexikon. Tel-Aviv, Olamenu, 1969. 61 p. ports.
24cm. (Schriftenreihe des Zwi Perez Chajes Instituts, 1)
Austrian Jews in the world of literature; a bio-bibliographical
dictionary of ca. 270 authors with portraits and bibliographies.

Kannada

11144   HEGADE, N   K   1933-
Uttara Kannada jilheya granthakāraru. Kasaragodu,
Sahitya Sangha Janata Vidyalay, 1969. xxiv, 502, xxvi (i. e.
xxiv) p. In Kannada. Biographical sketches of Kannada writers
of North Kanara district, by N. K. Hegade and I. S. Bhatta.

11145   SANGALI, VENKATESA
Srigannada granthakartara charitrakosa. Mysore, Usha

Sahityamale, 1960-   v. In Kannada. Biographies
of Kannada authors. Vol. 1 covers the years 1882-1920. Published in collaboration with Sahitya Akademi, New Delhi and
Karnatak University, Dharwar.

Karelian

11146   SOĨUZ PISATELEĨ KAREL'SKOI ASSR.
         Pisateli Karelii. Spravochnik. [Izd. 2., ispr. i dop.]
Petrozavodsk, "Kareliiă," 1971. 159 p. ports. 17cm. "Avtor-
sostavitel' A. A. Ivanov.   First ed. published in 1959 under
title: Pisateli Sovetskoi Karelii. The writers of Karelia.

Kazakh

11147   ĚL'KONINA, FAINA IOSIFOVNA
         Kazakhskaiă literatura; rekomendatel'nyĭ ukazatel'. Mos-
kva, "Kniga," 1973. 177 p. ports. 20cm. At head of title:
Gosudarstvennaiă biblioteka SSSR im. V. I. Lenina. Gosudarstvennaiă biblioteka Kazakhskoi SSR im. A. S. Pushkina. A recommended reading list of Kazakh literature which includes bio-
bibliographical sketches and portraits of 50 Kazakh authors, all
but two of whom flourished under the Soviet regime. Alphabetical listing of authors and their works at end of volume.

Kirghiz

11148   SAMAGANOV, DZHENBAĬ, 1915-
         Pisateli Sovetskogo Kirgizstana. [Biobibliogr. spravochnik]
Frunze, "Kyrgyzstan," 1969. 643 p. ports. 21cm. Writers
of Soviet Kirghizstan. A bio-bibliography of 145 Kirghiz authors
of the 20th century.

Korean

11149   THE HAKWŎNSA DICTIONARY OF LITERATURE. Munye tae
         sajŏn. Seoul, Hakwŏnsa, 1962. viii, 1255 p. ports. 21cm.
Korean literature; a dictionary of authors (in Korean) with various indexes (including one in the Latin alphabet).

Latin, Ancient

11150   MANTINBAND, JAMES H
         Dictionary of Latin literature. New York, Philosophical
Library [1956] vi, 303 p. 22cm. (Midcentury reference library) Includes biographies (for the most part very brief) of classical Latin authors.

Latin, Medieval and Modern

11151   LECOUVET, FERDINAND, 1828-1864.
Hannonia poetica; ou, Les poètes latins du Hainaut. Genève,
Slatkine Reprints, 1971. xii, 226 p. 22cm. Reprint of the Tournai edition of 1859. Latin poets of Hainaut, Belgium; a biographical dictionary (38 poets)

11152   PEERLKAMP, PETRUS HOFMAN, 1786-1865.
Liber de vita, doctrina et facultate Nederlandorum qui car-
mina Latina composuerunt. Editio 2. emendata et aucta. Lug-
duni Batavorum, H. W. Hazenberg, 1843. xii, 575 p. 22cm.
Edition of 1838 with new title page? Running title: De poetis
Latinis Nederlandiarum. Bio-bibliography of Dutch authors who
wrote in Latin.

11153   RUKOVĚT' HUMANISTICKÉHO BÁSNICTVÍ ČECHÁCH A NA
MORAVĚ. Založili Antonín Truhlář a Karel Hrdina. Pokra-
čovali Josef Hejnic a Jan Martínek. [1. vyd.] Praha, Academia,
1966-   v. facsims., ports. 25cm. Added title
pages, v. 1-   :Enchiridion renatae poesis Latinae in Bohemia
et Moravia cultae. Latin or Czech. "První svazek Rukověti ob-
sahuje druhé, podstatně přepracované vydání hesel A-Collinus a
první vydání hesel Colonius-Czyrtner. Hesla A-Caucalius vydal
r. 1908 A. Truhlář, hesla Cautius-Collinus r. 1918 z Truh-
lářovy pozůstalosti K. Hrdina." Contents.--t. 1. A-C.--t. 2.
C-J.--t. 3. K-M.--t. 4. N-R (1973).
Humanists of Bohemia and Moravia, especially poets of those
regions who wrote in Latin; a bio-bibliographical dictionary.

Latin American

Anonyms and Pseudonyms--Bibliography

11154   MOORE, ERNEST RICHARD
Anónimos y seudónimos hispanoamericanos. (In Revista
iberoamericana, organo del Instituto Internacional de Literatura
Iberoamericana, México, v. 5, no. 9, mayo 1942, p. 179-197)
Analyzes 40 collections of Spanish-American anonyms and
pseudonyms.

General Works

11155   AMICO, ALICIA D'
Retratos y autoretratos: escritores de América Latina
Fotografías: Alicia d'Amico, Sara Facio. Textos: Miguel Angel Asturias [et al.] Buenos Aires, Ediciones Crisis, 1973.
192 p. (chiefly ports.) 28cm. Portraits and self-portraits;

writers of Latin America. A volume of portraits of Latin A-
merican authors of the present day with some accompanying
biographical-autobiographical data.

11156   BACIU, STEFAN, comp.
             Antología de la poesía latinoamericana, 1950-1970. Albany,
State University of New York Press, 1974. 2 v. (lviii, 1244 p.)
24cm. This anthology of Latin American poetry for the years
1950-1970 includes biobibliographical sketches of the 125 poets
represented in the collection. Arrangement is by country (alphabetically: Argentina to Venezuela).

11157   COLL, EDNA, 1906-
             Indice informativo de la novela hispanoamericana. 1. ed.
[Río Piedras]: Editorial Universitaria, Universidad de Puerto
Rico, 1974-   v. 25cm. Contents: t.1. Las Antillas.
A bio-bibliography of Spanish American fiction. Biographical
dictionary arrangement, e.g., vol. 1, covering the Antilles, has
3 alphabets: (1) Puerto Rican authors; (2) authors of the Dominican Republic; (3) Cuban authors.

11158   FOSTER, DAVID WILLIAM
             A dictionary of contemporary Latin American authors.
Tempe, Center for Latin American Studies, Arizona State University, 1975. vi, 110 p. 27cm. A bio-bibliographical dictionary of living Spanish American authors.

11159   REICHARDT, DIETER
             Lateinamerikanische Autoren; Literaturlexikon und Bibli-
ographie der deutschen Übersetzungen. [Hrsg. vom Institut für
Iberoamerika-Kunde, Hamburg] Tübingen, H. Erdmann [1972]
718 p. 21cm. Latin American authors; a literary dictionary
and a bibliography of German translations of Latin American literature.

Latvian

11160   ANERAUDS, JĀNIS
             Fifty encounters; short information about fifty Latvian So-
viet men of letters. Translated from the Latvian by J. Cērps.
Riga, Liesma Pub. House, 1973. 159 p. ports. 17cm. Translation of Piecdesmit tikšanās. Portraits and biographical
sketches.

11161   BĒRSONS, ILGONIS
             Latviesu padomju rakstnieki. Rigā, Latvijas Valsts
Izdevnieciba, 1963. 529 p. ports. 18cm. The writers of Soviet Latvia; a bio-bibliography.

11162   LATVIJAS PADOMJU SOCIALISTISKĀS REPUBLIKAS ZINĀTNU
         AKADĒMIJA. VALODAS UN LITERATŪRAS INSTITŪTS.
         Valodas un literatūras darbinieki; biogrāfiska vārdnīca.
         [Autoru kolektīvs: B. Gudrike, et al. Atbildīgais redaktors J.
         Kalniņs] Riga, Zinātne, 1965. 375 p. 22cm. A bio-bibliogra-
         phical dictionary of Latvian literature.

Lithuanian

11163   VAIČIULAITIS, ANTANAS
         Outline history of Lithuanian literature. With a foreword
         by Alfred Senn. Chicago, 1942. 54 p. ports. 23cm. (Publi-
         cations of the Lithuanian Cultural Institute. Section I: Lithuanian
         language and literature, no. 1) A lot in a small compass; in-
         cludes bio-bibliographical sketches of over 75 writers, with
         some portraits. Arrangement is strictly topical and chronologi-
         cal. There is no alphabetical index, but the table of contents of-
         fers some guidance.

Macedonian

11164   JOVANOVSKI, METO, 1928-
         Mal literaturen leksikon. Skopje, "Prosvetno delo, " 1971.
         184 p. 20cm. A dictionary of modern Macedonian literature that
         includes bio-bibliographical entries. An earlier edition was pub-
         lished in 1963 under title: Koj e koj i sto i sto.

Malayalam

11165   SREEDHARAN, C   P   1931-
         Innatte sāhityakarānmār. [Kottayam, Sahityavedi Publica-
         tions, 1969] x, 1088 p. 22cm. In Malayalam. Who's who of
         contemporary Malayalam writers.

Marathi

11166   KHANOLKAR, G   D
         Arvācina Marāthī vāṅmayasevaka. Bombay, Swastic Pub.
         House, 1930-62. 5 v. 19cm. In Marathi. A biographical dic-
         tionary of modern Marathi authors. A 2d ed. was begun in 1966,
         with vol. 1, pt. 1 issued.

Mexican

Anonyms and Pseudonyms

11167   CASTILLO, IGNACIO B   DEL
         Catálogo de seudónimos, anagramas, iniciales, etc., de
         escritores mexicanos y de extranjeros incorporados a las letras

mexicanas. (In Boletín de la Biblioteca Nacional, México. 2.
epoca, t. 4, no. 4, oct. -dic. 1953, p. 31-48) A catalog of pseudonyms, anagrams, initials, etc. of Mexican writers and of alien writers who had a relationship with Mexican literature. A
list alphabetical by pseudonym, etc., with true name in opposite
column. Continues the catalogs of Iguíniz and Juana Manrique
de Lara and Guadalupe Monroy (q. v.)

11168   STOWELL, ERNEST E
             More Mexican writers and pseudonyms. (In Hispanic re-
         view. [Philadelphia] 1943. v. 11, p. 164-174) In large part
         Stowell's lists supplement R. L. Grismer's Reference index to
         twelve thousand Spanish American authors.

11169   SUÁREZ, VICTOR M
             Iniciación para un catálogo de seudónimos, anagramas e
         iniciales de autores yucatecos. (In Revista de estudios yuca-
         tecos. México. No. 1, feb. 1949, p. 33-50) Beginnings of a
         catalog of the pseudonyms, anagrams and initials of the authors
         of Yucatan.

11170   VALLES, ROBERTO
             Indice de anónimos de la Bibliografia mexicana del siglo
         XVIII del Dr. don Nicolás León. México, Vargas Rea, 1946.
         43 p. 31cm. (Biblioteca Aportación histórica) Index to the
         anonyms in the Bibliografia mexicana del siglo XVIII (Mexican
         bibliography of the 18th century) of Nicolás León.

General Works

11171   ANDRADE, CAYETANO, 1890-
             Antología de escritores Nicolaitas (IV centenario del
         Colegio Primitivo y Nacional de San Nicolás de Hidalgo) 1540-
         1940. Obra conmemorativa. México, Editorial Vanguardia
         Nicolaita, 1940. 800 p. plates, ports. 23cm. An anthology
         of writers from the City of Morelia, Mexico, more especially
         those connected with the Colegio Primitivo y Nacional de San
         Nicolás de Hidalgo, Morelia. Includes bio-bibliographical ma-
         terial about the authors.

11172   CORDERO Y TORRES, ENRIQUE, 1904-
             Poetas y escritores poblanos (por origen o adopción) 1900-
         1943. Puebla, "Nieto" [1943] 562 (i. e. 542) p. ports. 21cm.
         Poets and writers (by origin or by adoption) of the State of
         Puebla, 1900-1943.

11173   ILLESCAS, FRANCISCO R   ed.
             .Escritores veracruzanos; reseña biográfico-antológica
         [por] Francisco Illescas y Juan Bartolo Hernández. Veracruz

[Impr. Veracruzana] 1945. xv, 796 p. ports. 24cm. Writers native to or involved with the State of Vera Cruz, Mexico. An anthology with bio-bibliographies of contributing authors.

11174   SANTAMARÍA, FRANCISCO JAVIER, 1889-
Semblanzas tabasqueñas. [Méjico] Gobierno Constitucional de Tabasco, 1946. 159 p. 20cm. (Contribución de Tabasco a la cultura nacional, 9) Collective biography (brief sketches) of famous sons of the State of Tabasco, Mexico, especially its writers.

11175   SOCIEDAD DE AMIGOS DEL LIBRO MEXICANO.
Directorio de escritores mexicanos. México, 1956. 347 p. ports. 30cm. At head of title: SALM. A directory (with bio-bibliographical data) of Mexican authors of the day.

Moldavian

11176   KISHINEV, BESSARABIA. GOSUDARSTVENNAĬA RESPUBLI-KANSKAIA BIBLIOTEKA MSSR.
Skriitorii sovetski' moldoven'; indiche biobibliografik. [Alketuitor: I. Shpak] Kishineu, Kartía moldoveniaske, 1965. 257 p. ports. 21cm. At head of title: Ministerul kulturii AL RSS Moldovenesht.' Biblioteka republikane de stat "N. K. Krupskaĭa." Bio-bibliographical indices of authors in Soviet Moldavia. A 2d ed. (265 p. 20cm.) was issued in 1969 (?)

11177   MADAN, IVAN KONSTANTINOVICH
Moldavskaĭa literatura. Rekomendatel'nyĭ ukazatel'. Moskva, "Kniga," 1972. 208 p. ports. 20cm. At head of title: Gosudarstvennaĭa biblioteka SSSR im. V. I. Lenina. Gosudarstvennaĭa respublikanskaĭa biblioteka MSSR im. N. K. Krupskoĭ. I. K. Madan, I. I. Shpak. Bio-bibliography and portraits of 51 Moldavian authors, 19th century to the present.

Mordvinian

11178   KUZNETSOVA, A   G
Pisateli sovetskoi G Mordovii. Biobibliograf. spravochnik. [Vstupit. stat'ia V. Gorbunova i B. Kiriushkina] Izd. 2., ispr. i dop. Saransk, Mordovskoe kn. izd-vo, 1970. 207 p. ports. 17cm. At head of title: Ministerstvo kul'tury Mordovskoi ASSR. Respublikanskaĭa biblioteka A. S. Pushkina. A bio-bibliography of Soviet Mordovia; authors of Mordvinian literature.

Norwegian

11179   DAHL, WILLY
Nytt norsk forfatterleksikon. Oslo, Gyldendal Norsk forlag, 1971. 267 p. 22cm. A dictionary of Norwegian authors.

Oriental

11180   DICTIONARY OF ORIENTAL LITERATURES. General editor:
Jaroslav Průšek. New York, Basic Books, 1974. 3 v.
24cm. Contents.--v. 1. East Asia. Volume editor: Zbigniew
Słupski.--v. 2. South and Southeast Asia. Volume editor: Dušan Zbavitel.--v. 3. West Asia and North Africa. Volume editor: Jiří Bečka. In large part bio-bibliographical.

11181   A GUIDE TO EASTERN LITERATURES. Edited by David M.
Lang. New York, Praeger [1971] x, 500 p. 24cm. Divided into chapters, each of which discusses a particular literature, e. g., Arabic, Jewish, Persian, Turkish, Armenian and
Georgian, Ethiopic, Indian, Chinese, Burmese, etc., etc. At
the end of each chapter is a bio-bibliography (alphabetically arranged) of the leading writers of that literature.

Panamanian

11182   SAZ SÁNCHEZ, AGUSTÍN DEL, comp.
Antología general de la poesía panameña, siglos XIX-XX.
Estudio prelim., bibliografía y selección de Agustín del Saz.
[1. ed.] Barcelona, Editorial Bruguera [1974] 604 p. 18cm.
(Libro clásico, 122) This general anthology of Panamanian
poetry of the 19th-20th centuries includes bio-bibliographical
data for 55 poets.

Persian

11183   'AWFI, MUHAMMAD, fl. 1228.
The Lubābu 'l-albāb of Muhammad 'Awfi. Edited in the
original Persian with pref., indices and variants by Edward G.
Browne. London, Luzac, 1903-1906. 2 v. facsims. 24cm.
(Persian historical texts, v. 2, 4) Vol. 2 edited by E. G.
Browne and Mizá Muhammad ibn 'Abdu'l 1-Waháb-i-Qazwīnī.
An anthology of Persian poetry with bio-bibliographical sketches.

11184   HĀSHIMĪ SANDĪLAVĪ, AHMAD 'ALĪ KHĀN, 1749-1809?
Tazkirah-'i makhzan al-ghara'ib. [Lahore, Pakistan,
Panjab University Oriental Publications Fund, 1968-   v.
26cm. (Panjab University Oriental publication, no. 40, 41
Added t. p.: Tazkerah-ye makhzan-al-gharaib; an unpublished
biographical work on Persian poets of Shaikh Ahmad 'Alī
Hāshimī of Sandilah, compiled in A. H. 1218 (A. D. 1803), and
now reproduced from the oldest manuscript dated A. H. 1219 (A.
D. 1804), with an introd. and notes by Mohammad Baqir. Biographical anthology of Persian poets, alphabetically arranged by
pseudonyms, 874-1802 A. D. Vol. 1-2 only issued as of 1970?

Peruvian

Anonyms and Pseudonyms

11185   ANGELES CABALLERO, CÉSAR AUGUSTO
         Diccionario de seudónimos peruanos [y primera adición]
(In Boletín bibliográfico de la Universidad Nacional Mayor de
San Marcos, Biblioteca Central, Lima. v. 32, no. 1-2, jun.
1962, p. [37]-90 & v. 33, no. 3-4, dec. 1962, p. [162]-215)
Dictionary of Peruvian pseudonyms; 1,472 pseudonyms; in dou-
ble columns, 1st, pseudonyms, 2d, true names.

11186   TAURO, ALBERTO
         Contribución al catálogo de seudónimos peruanos. (In Bole-
tín de la Biblioteca Nacional, Lima. año 15, no. 23, 3. trimes-
tre, 1962. p. [1]-15) Contribution to the catalog of Peruvian
pseudonyms; 219 pseudonyms, with an index of true names.

Philippine

11187   MOJARES, RESIL B
         Cebuano literature; a survey and bio-bibliography with
finding list. Cebu City, Philippines, University of San Carlos,
1975. vii, 194 p. 24cm. (San Carlos publications. Ser. A:
Humanities, no. 10) "Cebuano writers: a biographic index"
(p. [134]-161) comprises a biographical dictionary of 116 writers of Cebú literature living and deceased.

Polish

11188   BARTELSKI, LESŁAW M
         Polscy pisarze współcześni; informator 1944-1970. Wyd.
nowe, poszerzone. Warszawa, Agencja Autorska, 1972. 367,
[1] p. 21cm. 1st ed. (covering the years 1944-1968) issued in
1970. Bio-bibliographical dictionary of 20th century Polish literature.

11189   HERTZ, PAWEŁ, comp.
         Zbiór poetów polskich XIX w. [Warszawa] Państwowy In-
stytut Wydawniczy [1959-75] 7 v. 18cm. (Biblioteka poezji i
prozy) This comprehensive collection of 19th century (1795-1918)
Polish poetry includes bio-bibliographical data for many poets in
the main text (vols. 1-5) as well as further bio-bibliographical
data in v. 6 in the form of emendations and supplements to that
found in the first 5 vols. Vol. 6 in fact has two sections arranged
alphabetically by authors: the first, the aforementioned emendations and supplements (p. 23-[325]) and the 2d (p. 329-[1073]) a
bio-bibliographical dictionary for poets, versifiers and translators of foreign poetry not found in the main volumes. Vol. 7
consists largely of an index to the poets, poems, etc.

11190   KRZYŻANOWSKI, JULIAN, 1892-
        Neoramantyzm polski, 1890-1918. Bibliografie opracowały
Teresa Brzozowska i Maria Bokszczanin. Wrocław, Zakład
Narodowy im. Ossolińskich, 1971. 475 p. ports. 24cm. Polish Neoramanticism, 1890-1918. The bibliography of pages 352-
459 is actually a bio-bibliography (with emphasis, however, on
bibliography) in dictionary arrangement of Polish writers of the
period.

11191   LITERATURA POZYTYWIZMU I MŁODEJ POLSKI. Opracowal
        zespół pod kierownictwem Zygmunta Szweykowskiego i
Jarosława Maciejewskiego. [Zespoł autorski: Wiesława Al-
brecht et al. Warszawie] Państwowy Instytut Wydawniczy, 1970-
                v. 25cm. (Bibliografia literatury polskiej "Nowy
Korbut," 13
At head of title: v. 1-   : Instytut Badań Literackich Polskiej
Akademii Nauk. Contents. --[1] Hasła ogólne. Hasła osobowe:
A-F. --2. G-Ł. 1973.
In part a bio-bibliographical dictionary of Polish authors (posi-
tivists and adherents of the 'Young Poland' movement (ca. 1865-
1920).

11192   MAŁY SŁOWNIK PISARZY POLSKICH. [Autory haseł: Maria
        Grabowska et al. Redaktor: Maria Goszczyńska] Wyd. 3.
Warszawa, Wiedza Powszechna, 1972-   v. ports. 20cm.
Vol. 1, A-Z. A bio-bibliographical dictionary of Polish authors.
1st ed. issued in 1966 (208 p.)

11193   MILSKA, ANNA
        Pisarze Polscy; wybór sylwetek 1543-1890. Warszawa,
Instytut Wydawniczy CRZZ, 1974. 287 p. illus., ports. 21cm.
'Silhouettes' of Polish writers, 1543-1890. 100 biographical
sketches arranged chronologically.

11194   OŚWIECENIE; hasła ogólne, rzeczowe i osobowe. Opracowała
        Elżbieta Aleksandrowska z zespołem. Redaktor tomy do v.
1958 Tadeusz Mikulski. [W Warszawie] Państwowy Instytut
Wydawniczy, 1966-72. 3 v. in 4. 25cm. (Bibliografia literatury polskiej "Nowy Korbut," 4-6) At head of title: Instytut Badań
Literackich Polskiej Akademii Nauk. Contents. --[1] A-H. --[2]
I-O. --3. P-Z. Addenda A-O. --[4] Uzupełnienia. Indeksy. A
bio-bibliographical dictionary of Polish literature of the En-
lightenment (18th century and first half of the 19th).

11195   ROMANTYZM. Opracował zespół pod kierownichtwem Irminy
        Sliwińskiej i Stanisława Stupkiewicza. [W Warszawie]
Państwowy Instytut Wydawniczy, 1968-72. 3 v. 25cm. (Bibliografia literatury polskiej. Nowy Korbut, 7-9) At head of title:
Instytut Badań Literackich Polskiej Akademii Nauk. Contents.
--[1] Hasła ogolne i rzeczowe. Hasła osobowe: A-J. --[2] Hasła

osobowe: K-O. --[3] Hasła osobowe: P-Z. Uzupełnienia. A
bio-bibliographical dictionary of Polish literature in the 19th
century (Romantic period)

11196   SLOVNÍK SPISOVATELŮ: Polsko. [Zprac. kol. za ved. Otakara
         Bartoše; úv. studie naps. O. Bartoš] 1. vyd. Praha,
         Odeon, 1974. 468, [50] p. 20cm. Bio-bibliographical diction-
         ary of Polish authors.

11197   STAROWOLSKI, SZYMON, 1588-1656.
         Setnik pisarzów polskich albo pochwały i żywoty stu najzna-
         komitszych pisarzów polskich. Przeł. i komentarzen opatrzył
         Jerzy Starnawski. Wstep napisali: Franciszek Bielak i Jerzy
         Starnawski. [Wyd. 1. Kraków] Nakładem Wydawn. Literackiego,
         1970. 364 p. facsims., ports. 22cm. Translation of Centum
         illustrium Poloniae scriptorum elogia et vitae (1627) Bio-bibli-
         ography of 100 famous writers of Poland to the mid-17th century.

11198   STAROWOLSKI, SZYMON, 1588-1656.
         Simonis Starovolsci Scriptorum Polonicorum hechatontas;
         seu, Centum illustrium Poloniae scriptorum elogia et vitae.
         Frncoforti [sic] Sumptibus Iacobi de Zetter, 1625. 132 p. 19cm.
         Bio-bibliography of 100 famous writers of Poland to the mid-17th
         century.

Portuguese

11199   ANUÁRIO ARTÍSTICO E LITERÁRIO DE PORTUGAL. 1. -
         ano; 1948-   Lisboa, União Portuguesa de Imprensa.
         v. 20cm. An annual of the arts and literature for Portugal
         with emphasis on biography.

11200   ANUÁRIO DOS ESCRITORES. 1. -2. ano; 1941-1942. Pôrto,
         Portucale.   v. 20cm. An annual containing bio-biblio-
         graphical data for living Portuguese authors. No more pub-
         lished?

11201   MOISÉS, MASSAUD
         Literatura portuguesa moderna; guia biográfico, crítico e
         bibliográfico. Direção e organização: Moisés Massaud. [Co-
         laboradores: Alvaro Cardoso Gomes et al.] São Paulo, Editora
         Cultrix [1973] 202 p. 20cm. A bio-bibliographical dictionary
         of 20th century Portuguese literature.

Provencal

Bibliography, Indexes, Portrait Catalogs

11202   CHABANEAU, CAMILLE, 1831-1908.
         Liste alphabétique de tous les poètes ou auteurs provençaux

dont les noms ont été conservés jusqu'à la fin du XVe siècle.
(In Vic, Claude de et Vaissète, J.   Histoire du Languedoc.
Nouv. éd.   Paris, 1872-92. 28cm.   t. 10 (1885), p. 324-409)
An alphabetical list, with some sketchy biographical data, of
Provençal poets or authors to the end of the 15th century; gives
references to sources for biographical facts about the authors
listed.

11203   CHAMBERS, FRANK M
Proper names in the lyrics of the troubadours. Chapel
Hill, University of North Carolina Press, 1971. 269 p. 24cm.
(Studies in the Romance languages and literatures, no. 113)
Useful, although this work is primarily an index of personal and
geographical names found in the troubadour's' poems. Some
biographical material is occasionally given for historical and
literary personal names as well as references to biographical
material for the troubadours listed.

General Works

11204   BAYLE, LOUIS
Histoire abrégée de la littérature provencale moderne.
Toulon, L'Astrado, 1971. 136 p. 21cm. (Bibliothèque d'histoire littéraire et de critique) An abbreviated history of modern
Provencal literature; but actually the work is almost entirely
bio-bibliographical with sketches of 151 authors, 68 at some
length, 83 very briefly. Generally arranged chronologically
there is an alphabetical approach through an index of names cited at the end of the volume.

11205   NOSTREDAME, JEAN DE, fl. ca. 1507-1577.
Les vies des plus célèbres et anciens poètes provencaux.
Nouv. éd. accompagnée d'extraits d'oeuvres inédites du même
auteur préparée par Camille Chabaneau et publiée avec introd.
et commentaire par Joseph Anglade. Paris, H. Champion,
1913. [176], 406 p. 21cm. Arranged by years when biographees flourished, with an index of names cited (references in
parentheses are those poets from whom biographical data are
given). Contains the lives of 76 Old Provencal poets.

Puerto Rican

11206   HILL, MARNESBA D
Puerto Rican authors: a biobibliographic handbook, by
Marnesba D. Hill and Harold B. Schleifer. With an introd. by
Maria Teresa Babin. Translations of entries into Spanish by
Daniel   Maratos.   Metuchen, N. J., Scarecrow Press, 1974.
x, 267 p. 22cm. English and Spanish. Added title: Autores
puertorriqueños; una guía biobibliográfica. Each entry contains
basic biographic information and short descriptive evaluations
of the author's works.

11207   LÓPEZ DE VEGA, MAXIMILIANO, comp.
         Las cien mejores poesías de Puerto Rico (joyas poéticas del
         arte boricua). [1. ed.] Río Piedras, Editorial Edil, 1970. xv,
         309 p. 19cm. (Colección Poética Edil) The 100 major poems &
         poets of Puerto Rico; an anthology with biographical sketches of
         the poets preceding their works. Chronologically arranged.

Romanian

11208   PIRU, AL
         Panorama deceniului literar românesc, 1940-1950.
         [Bucuresti] Editura Pentru Literatura, 1968. vi, 535 p. 20cm.
         Panorama of a decade of Rumanian literature, 1940-1950. Ca.
         160 biographical sketches are included.

11209   POPA, MARIAN
         Dictionarul de literatura româna contemporana. [Bucuresti]
         "Albatros," 1971. 672 p. 17cm. A dictionary of contemporary
         (20th century) Romanian literature; bio-bibliographical.

Russian

Anonyms and Pseudonyms

11210   PETRIAEV, EVGENII DMITRIEVICH
         Psevdonimy literatorov-sibiriakov; materialy k "Istorii rus-
         skoi literatury Sibiri." Novosibirsk, "Nauka," Sibirskoe otd-
         nie, 1973. 74 p. 22cm. At head of title: Akademiia nauk SSSR.
         Sibirskoe otdelenie. Institut istorii, filologii i filosofii. Pseu-
         donyms of litterateurs of Siberia; materials to accompany the
         "History of Siberian Russian literature."

General Works

11211   ANASHKINA, V   T   comp.
         Pisateli Srednego Urala; bio-bibliograficheskii spravoch-
         nik. Sostavitel' V. T. Anashkina. Sverdlovsk, Sredne-Ural'-
         skoe knizhnoe izd-vo, 1965. 201 p. ports. 21cm. Bio-bibli-
         ography of Russian writers of the Ural Mountain region.

11212   ARMIANSKIE SOVETSKIE PISATELI; spravochnik. [Redaktor:
         A. Salakhian] Erevan, Armianskoe Gosudarstvennoe izd-
         vo, 1956. 196 p. 16cm. Authors of Russian literature in So-
         viet Armenia.

11213   BUDOVNITS, ISAAK URIELEVICH
         Slovar' russkoi, ukrainskoi, belorusskoi pis' mennosti i

literatury do XVIII veka. Moskva, Izd-vo Akademii naul SSSR,
1962. 397 p. 27cm. At head of title: Akademiia nauk SSSR.
Sovetskii komitet slavistov. Bio-bibliographical dictionary of
Russian, Ukrainian and White Russian writers, Slavicists, collectors of manuscripts, etc. to the 18th century. Biographical
data is very limited in most cases, altho' references to sources
for augmented information are often given. The alphabetical
list includes authors and titles of anonymous works.

11214 IGNATOV, IL'IA NIKOLAEVICH, 1858-1921.
         Entsiklopediia russkikh pisatelei. Tekst I. Ignatova. Steit
       Kaledzh, Pa., 1972. 420 p. illus., ports. 25cm. Added t. p.:
       The encyclopedia of Russian writers. Arranged quasi-chrono-
       logically with an alphabetical name index at end of volume.

11215 KRASNOIARSKIE PISATELI. Rekomendatel'nyi ukazatel'
         literatury. Krasnoiarsk, Tip. Sibir', 1969. 64 p. ports.
       18cm. Authors from Krasnoyarsk.

11216 LASHMANOV, M   I   1912-
         Kuibyshevskie pisateli; bio-bibliograficheskii ukazatel'.
       [Sostaviteli M. I. Lashmanov, E. I. Lebedeva. Kuibyshev]
       Kuibyshevskoe knizhnoe izd-vo, 1967. 125 p. illus., ports.
       14cm. At head of title: Kuibyshevskaia oblastnaia biblioteka.
       Kuibyshevskoe otdelenie Soiuz pisatelei. Kuybyshev's writers;
       a bio-bibliography of Russian authors native to or living in
       Kuybyshevskaya oblast'.

11217 LENINGRAD. UNIVERSITET. KAFEDRA RUSSKOGO IAZYKA.
         Russkoe iazykoznanie v Peterburgskom-Leningradskom uni-
       versitete. Pod red. N. A. Meshcherskogo. Leningrad, Izd-vo
       Leningr. un-ta, 1971. 168 p. 22cm. At head of title: Lenin-
       gradskii ordena Lenina i ordena Trudovogo Krasnogo Znameni
       gosudarstvennyi universitet imeni A. A. Zhdanova. Filologi-
       cheskii fakul'tet. Kafedra russkogo iazyka. 104 Russian philolo-
       gists at St. Petersburg (and later Leningrad) University.

11218 MAL'SAGOV. A   U
         Pisateli Sovetskoi Checheno-Ingushetii. [Biobibliogr. spra-
       vochnik] Groznyi, Checheno-Ingush Knizhnoe izd-vo, 1969.
       148 p. 20cm. Compiled by A. U. Mal'sagov and N. V. Turkaev.
       Writers of Russian literature in Chechen-Ingush A. S. S. R.

11219 MALÝ SLOVNÍK SOVĚTSKÝCH SPISOVATELŮ. Praha, Svaz
         čes.-sovět. přatelstvi, 1959. 120, 88, 110 p. Contents.--
       čast 1. Rusti spisovatelé.--čast 2. Ukrajinšti a bělorusti spi-
       sovatelé.--čast 3. Neslovanšti spisovatelé. Dictionary of Sovi-
       et authors: Russian, Ukrainian, White Russian and non-Slavic
       writers.

11220   MAŁY SŁOWNIK PISARZY NARODÓW EUROPEJSKICH ZSSR.
         [Komitet redakcyjny: Mieczysław Brahmer, et al. Wyd. 1.]
         Warszawa, Wiedza Powszechna, 1966. 327 p. ports. 20cm.
         (Wydawnictwa popularno-encyklopedyczne) Little dictionary (bio-
         bibliographical) of the writers of European Russia.

11221   NOVOSIBIRSK. OBLASTNAĬA BIBLIOTEKA.
         Pisateli Sibiri; kratkii bibliograficheskiĭ ukazatel'. [Sos-
         tavlen: T. A. Vorob'evoi i dr. Novosibirsk] Novosibirskoe
         knizhnoe izd-vo, 1956. 74 p. 20cm. At head of title: K. so-
         veshchaniiu sibirskikh pisatelei. A bio-bibliographical list of
         Russian authors from Siberia.

11222   PETRIĀEV, EVGENIĬ DMITRIEVICH
         Kraevedy i literatury Zabaĭkal'iā. Materialy dliā biobibliogr.
         slovar'. [Irkutsk-Chita] Vostochnoe –Sibirskoe knizhnoe izd-vo,
         1965.-   v. Contents.--ch. 1. Dorevoliūtsionnyĭ period.
         (No more published?) Students of local lore and the literature of
         the Lake Baikal region; materials for a bio-bibliographical dic-
         tionary.

11223   PISATELI KABARDINO-BALKARII; [biobibliograf. ukazatel'
         Sost. A. G. Sozaeva, T. B. Nagoeva] Redaktor: A. S.
         Shumakhova. Nal'chik, Kabard.-Balkar. knizhnoe izd-vo, 1965.
         135 p. 20cm. Authors of Soviet literature of Kabardia and Bal-
         karia; a bio-bibliography.

11224   PISATELI VORONEZHA; biobibliograficheskiĭ ukazatel'. [Sost.
         N. Ishutinova] Pod obshchei red. N. T. Strel'nikovoĭ.
         Voronezh, TSentr. Chernozem. knizhnoe izd-vo, 1969. 169 p.
         17cm. Russian authors of Voronezh; a bio-bibliographical list.

11225   PISATELI VOSTOCHNOĬ SIBIRI; biobibliograficheskii ukazatel'.
         Irkutsk, Vostochno-sibirskoe knizhnoe izd-vo, 1973. 330 p.
         27cm. At head of title: Zonal'noe ob'edinenie bibliotek Vostoch-
         noi Sibiri. Irkutskaiā oblastnaiā biblioteka im. I. I. Molchanova-
         Sibirskogo. Writers of eastern Siberia, living and deceased; a
         bio-bibliographical listing, alphabetical under chronological per-
         iods.

11226   RUSSKIE PISATELI; biobibliograficheskiĭ slovar'. [Spravochnik
         dliā uchiteliā. Red. kollegii: D. S. Likhachev i dr.] Mos-
         kva, Prosveshchenie, 1971. 728 p. ports. 27cm. Has ca.
         300 bio-bibliographies of Russian writers from the Middle Ages
         to the early 20th century. Compiled by A. P. Spasibenko and N.
         M. Gaidenkov.

11227   SLOVNÍK RUSKÝCH SPISOVATELŮ OD POČATKŮ RUSKÉ
         LITERATURY DO ROKU 1917. Zprac. kol., odb. red. Eva

Hermanová. 1. vyd. Praha, Lid. nakl., t. Tisk 1, Brno, 1972.
316, [2] p. 21cm. Dictionary of Russian writers from the beginnings of Russian literature to the year 1917.

11228   SOKOLOV, SEMION DMITRIEVICH
         Saratovtsy pisateli i uchenye. Materialy dlia bio-biblio-
grafícheskogo slovaria. (In: Saratovskaia uchenaia arkhivnaia
komissiia. Trudy. Saratov, 1913-16. 22cm. t. 30, p. 257-
366 (A-Kazem-bek); t. 32, p. 221-284 (Kamenskii-Lopukhin);
t. 33, p. 135-196 (Lonin-Pavel)) No more published. The
writers and learned men of Saratov; materials for a bio-bibliographical dictionary.

11229   STSENARISTY SOVETSKOGO KHUDOZHESTVENNOGO KINO,
         1917-1967. Spravochnik. Moskva, "Iskusstvo," 1972.
439 p. 21cm. At head of title: Gosfil'mofond SSSR. By V. N.
Antropov and others. A bio-bibliographical dictionary of Soviet
screen writers, 1917-1967.

11230   TROFIMOV, IVAN TROFIMOVICH
         Pisateli Smolenshchiny. [Biobibliograficheskii spravochnik]
Moskva, Moskovskii rabochii, 1973. 359 p. ports. 20cm. A
bio-bibliography of Russian writers (19th-20th centuries) from
the province of Smolensk. The main body of the text contains
76 major bio-bibliographies (with portraits) while at the end of
the volume are 41 bio-bibliographies of lesser-known authors.

11230a   VOKHRYSHEVA, M   G   comp.
         Pisateli Altaia; biobibliograficheskii spravochnik. [Sost.
M. G. Vokhrysheva i L. S. Pankratova] Barnaul, Altaiskoe
knizhnoe izd-vo, 1967. 150 p. ports. 21cm. At head of title:
Altaiskaia kraevaia biblioteka. Spravochno-bibliograficheskii
otdel. Bio-bibliography of writers using the Russian language
who are native to or reside in Altayskiy, Kray.

11231   ZDOBNOV, NIKOLAĬ VASIL'EVICH, 1888-1942.
         Materialy dlia sibirskogo slovaria pisatelei. Material for
a dictionary of Siberian writers. Letchworth [Eng.[Prideaux
Press, 1972. [2], 62 p. 25cm. (Russian titles for the special-
ist, no. 40) Reprint of the 1922 Moscow ed. This work is itself
a biographical dictionary (very brief entries, in most cases, of
Russian authors in Siberia).

11232   ZERNOV, NICOLAS
         Russkie pisateli emigratsii: biograficheskie syedeniia i
bibliografiiakh ikh knig po bogosloviiu, religioznoi filosofii,
tserkovnoi istorii i pravoslavnoi kul'ture, 1921-1972. Sostavitel'
Nikolai Zernov. Boston, G. K. Hall, 1973. xl, 182 p. 27cm.
Added t. p.: Russian emigré authors: a biographical index and
bibliography of their works on theology, religious philosophy,

church history and Orthodox culture, 1921-1972. Text in Russian; prefatory matter also in English. A bio-bibliographical dictionary of more than 200 Russian emigré writers on religious themes.

Sanskrit

11233   BANERJI, SURES CHANDRA, 1917-
A companion to Sanskrit literature; spanning a period of over three thousand years, containing brief accounts of authors, works, characters, technical terms, geographical names, myths, legends, and twelve appendices. 1st ed. Delhi, Motilal Banarsidass, 1971. xvi, 729 p. 23cm. "Part I: Authors': p. [9]-117; a bio-bibliographical dictionary.

11234   EASWARAN NAMPOOTHIRY, E   1930-
Sanskrit literature of Kerala; an index of authors with their works. Trivandrum; distribution: College Book House, 1972. xii, 162 p. 22cm. A bio-bibliographical dictionary (with minimum biographical data) of writers in Sanskrit (from the 9th century to the present) whose sphere of activity was more or less confined to the present-day State of Kerala.

Scandinavian

11235   RUNNQUIST, ÅKE
Moderna nordiska författare; en översikt över nordisk litteratur under fyra årtionden. Danmark, Färöarna, Finland, Island, Norge. Stockholm, Forum, 1966. 224 p. ports. 17cm. (När—var—hur--serien) Bio-bibliography (with portraits) of 127 20th century Danish, Finnish, Icelandic, Faroese and Norwegian authors (alphabetically arranged by country).

Serbian

(See also Yugoslav)

11236   KALIĆ, MITA
Srpski književnici. Novi Sad, Nakladom Srp. Knižare i Stamparije sprače M. Popopica, 1890-95. 4 v. 19cm. Serbian authors from 1726 to 1848; arranged in somewhat chronological order.

11237   NOVINARI. Izbor i predgovor ("Zapisi o srpskim novinarima") Siniša Paunović. Novi Sad, Matica srpska, 1967. 484 p. 20cm. (Biblioteka Srpska književnost u sto knjiga, knj. 88) Includes at the end of the volume biographical sketches of 63 Serbian journalists.

Slavic

11238   KURZ, JOSEF
       Slovanská filologie na Universitě Karlově. Josef Kurz,
Felix Vodička, Zdeňka Havránková. Uvod: Bohuslav Havránek.
1. vyd. Praha [Universita Karlova] 1963. 371 p. plates. 22cm.
Text partly in Russian. A history of the study of Slavic philology
in the Charles University of Prague. On pages [313]-357 there
is a biographical dictionary of 20th century professors and teachers of Slavic studies at that University (ca. 90 biographies).

11239   MAŁY SŁOWNIK PISARZY ZACHODNIOSŁOWIAŃSKICH I
       POŁUDNIOWOSŁOWIAŃSKICH. [Redaktor: Bożena Chiciń-
ska. Wyd. 1.] Warszawa, Wiedza Powszechna, 1973. 505 p.
ports. 20cm. "Pocket" dictionary of writers of Western and
Southern Slavdom.

11240   SLOVNÍK ČESKÝCH A SLOVENSKÝCH SLAVISTOV. Ukážky
       hesiel. Materiál pre diskusiu na 5. mezinár. sjazde slavis-
tov v Sofii. Pripr. K. Habovstiaková. Red. M. Kudělka.
Brno, Slovan ust. Československ akademie věd, 1963. 102 p.
Dictionary of Czech and Slovak Slavists. Material for discussion
at the 5th International Congress of Slavists in Sofia.

11241   SOFIA. UNIVERSITET. FAKULTET PO SLAVIANSKOĬ
       FILOLOGII.
       Biografsko-bibliografski sbornik; izdalen po sluchaĭ Mezh-
dunaroden slavistichen kongres v Prage, 1968. [Red. kolegiiã
G. Veselinov, K. Kuev i St. Stoiãnov] Sofiiã, Nauka i izkustvo,
1968. 214 p. 21cm. At head of title: Sofiiski universitet "Kliment Okhridski." Fakultet po slaviãnski filologii. Bio-bibliography of 103 Slavic philologists (of Bulgarian nationality, chiefly)
present at the 6th International Congress of Slavists, Prague,
1968.

Slovak

11242   BRTÁŇ, RUDO
       Slovenski novinári a publicisti (1700-1850) Bratislava,
Obzor, 1971. 185 p. illus., ports. 21cm. (Edicia Ne) A biographical dictionary of 47 Slovak journalists and publicists
(1700-1850)

11243   KUDĚLKA, VIKTOR
       Slovník slovinských spisovatelů s nástinem hlavních vývo-
jových etap slovinské literatury. 1. vyd. Praha, SPN, 1967.
84 p. 8.° Dictionary of Slovak writers.

11244   RIZNER, L'UDOVÍT VLADIMIR, 1849-1913.
       Bibliografia písomníctva slovenského na spôsob slovníka od
najstarších čias do konca r. 1900. S pripojenou bibliografiou

archeologickou, historickou, miestopisnou a prírodovedeckou.
Sostavil L'udovít V. Rizner. Vydáva Matična správa ... V
Turcianskom Sv. Martine, Nákladom Matice slovenskej, 1929-
34. 6 v. 24cm. Edited by Jaroslav Vlček, and after his death
in 1930 by Ján V. Ormis. A bibliography of Slovak literature
that has some bio-bibliographical features, since it does yield
variants of names and pseudonyms in addition to very brief
biographical data.

11245   SLOVNÍK SLOVENSKÝCH SPISOVATEL'OV PRE DETI A
        MLÁDEŽ. Zost. Ondrej Sliacky. 1. vyd. Bratislava,
Mladé letá, 1970. 428 p. 21cm. (Otázky detskej literatúry)
Dictionary of Slovak authors writing for children.

Slovenian

11246   KOTNIK, STANKO
        Pisatelji in njihova dela ter osnove besedne umetnosti.
Ljubljana, Državna založba Slovenije, 1971. 40 p. ports. 20cm.
Cover title. At head of title: Kotnik-Mihelič. Bio-bibliography
of 42 Slovenian writers, from the 16th century to the present;
chronological arrangement, in part.

11247   PAVLETIĆ, VLATKO, comp.
        100 [i. e. Sto] djela književnosti jugoslavenskih naroda.
Sastavio [i Predgovor napisao] Vlatko Pavletić. Izbor iz make-
donske književnosti: Petar Kepeski. Izbor iz slovenskie književnosti: Jože Pogačnik. 4., dop. izd. Zagreb, "Stvarnost," 1970.
xi, 584 p. 16 ports. 23cm. 100 years of the literature of the
Yugoslav peoples. Works of Slovenian and Macedonian authors
in Serbo-Croatian translation. Includes biographical-critical notices of 88 authors. Arrangement is chronological, from the
late 15th century to the middle of the 20th. Alphabetical name
index at end.

Soyot

11248   SOBOLEVA, L   M
        Pisateli Tuvy. [Biobibliogr. spravochnik] Kyzyl, Tuv-
knigoizdat, 1970. 115 p. ports. 17cm. At head of title:
Tuvinskaia respublikanskaia biblioteka im. A. S. Pushkina.
Tuvinskii nauchno-issledovatel'skii institut iazyka, literatury i
istorii. By L. M. Soboleva and A. V. Stepanova. Writers from
the Tannu-Tuva Republic of the Soviet Union utilizing the Soyot
and/or the Russian language.

Spanish

11249   ALLISON, ANTONY FRANCIS.
        English translations from the Spanish and Portuguese to
the year 1700; an annotated catalogue of the extant printed ver-

sions, excluding dramatic versions. London, Dawson of Pall
Mall, 1974. 224 p. 23cm. An alphabetically arranged (by
original author) catalog, with brief bio-bibliographical notes
for Spanish and Portuguese authors who flourished before 1700,
and thus a bio-bibliographical dictionary for those authors.
Includes also a "biographical index of translators" (p. 194-215).

11250   CASTRO, JOSÉ RAMÓN
         Autores e impresos tudelanos, siglos XV-XX. Pamplona,
Patronato José María Quadrado, Institución "Príncipe de Viana,"
1963. 489 p. illus., ports. 26cm. (Bibliografías locales, no.
1) "Apuntes biográficos" (p. [321]-454): a bio-bibliographical
dictionary of authors and imprints associated with Tudela,
Spain.

11251   COLMENARES, DIEGO DE, 1585-1651.
         Historia de la insigne ciudad de Segovia y compendio de las
historias de Castilla. Ilustrada con notas ... Segovia, Baeza,
1846-47. 4 v. illus. Vol. 4 has subtitle: Vidas y escritos de
escritores segovianos y cronologia de los obispos ... añadida
con algunas biografias ... First published in 1637; 2d ed., 1640.
A later edition than the above was issued in 1921 (Segovia, Impr.
de "La Terra de Segovia." 3 v. in 1. ports. 20cm.) Vol. 4
of this history of the City of Segovia comprises a bio-bibliography of Segovia's writers and a chronology of the diocese's bishops.

11252   CONDE ABELLÁN, CARMEN, comp.
         Antología de poesía amorosa contemporánea. Recopilación
de Carmen Conde. 1. ed. Barcelona, Editorial Bruguera, 1969.
783 p. 18cm. (Libro amigo) An anthology of contemporary
Spanish love poetry that includes bio-bibliographical notices of
the 108 authors represented: the collection is arranged alphabetically by author, so that the work serves as a bio-bibliographical dictionary.

11253   DICCIONARIO DE LITERATURA ESPAÑOLA. Dirigido por
         Germán Bleiberg [y] Julián Marías. 4. ed. corregida y
aumentada. Madrid, Ediciones de la Revista de Occidente,
1972. 1191 p. maps, plates. 23cm. Dictionary of Spanish literature; a major portion of the work is allotted to bio-bibliographies of Spanish writers.

11254   FUENTE, JOSÉ JULIO DE LA
         Memoria acerca del estado del Instituto Vizcaíno que, en
el acto solemne de la apertura del curso académico de 1871 a
1872 ... Bilbao, Impr. de Juan E. Delmas, 1867-72. 7 nos.
20cm. "Apéndice I: Catálogo bio-bibliográfico de 150 escritores,
por orden alfabético de nombres" (p. 46-96), i. e. Bio-bibliographical catalog of 150 writers of the province of Vizcaya,
Spain (alphabetical arrangement).

11255   GALLEGO MORELL, ANTONIO, 1923-
         Sesenta escritores granadinos, con sus partidas de bautis-
mo. [Granada] Caja General de Ahorros de Granada, 1970. 121p.
25cm. A bio-bibliographical dictionary of 70 Spanish authors of
the City of Granada.

11256   INSTITUTO NACIONAL DEL LIBRO ESPAÑOL.
         Quién es quién en las letras españolas. 2. ed. Madrid
[1973] 546 p. 24cm. Who's who in Spanish letters; bio-bibliography of living Spanish authors.

11257   IRIBARREN, MANUEL
         Escritores navarros de ayer y de hoy. Pamplona, Editorial
Gómez [1970] 223 p. 21cm. (Colección IPAR, 35) A bio-bibliographical dictionary of Spanish writers of Navarre, yesterday
and today.

11258   RÍOS RUIZ, MANUEL, 1934-
         Diccionario de escritores gaditanos. [Cadiz, Instituto de
Estudios Gaditanos, Diputación Provincial, 1973] 217 p. port.
25cm. Bio-bibliographical dictionary of the writers of the Spanish province of Cadiz.

11259   SÁNCHEZ PORTERO, ANTONIO, 1934-
         Noticia y antología de poetas bilbilitanos. Selección y notas
de Antonio Sánchez Portero. Calatayud, 1969. 420, [2] p. ports.
25cm. Biographical notices and an anthology of ca. 80 Spanish
poets from the City of Calatayud (old Roman name: Bilbilis); alphabetical approach thru' index on p. [421-422] Includes portraits
for a number of the poets.

Swedish

Anonyms and Pseudonyms

11260   BYGDÉN, ANDERS LEONARD, 1844-1929.
         Svenskt anonym- och pseudonymlexikon; bibliografisk för-
teckning öfver uppdagade anonymer och pseudonymer i den
svenska litteraturen, af Leonard Bygdén. [Utg. av Sune Lund-
qvist] Stockholm, Rediviva; Nordiska bokhandeln (distr.), 1974.
ix p., 942, 1052 columns, 127 p. 23cm. (Suecica rediviva, 40)
Added t. p.: A dictionary of anonymous and pseudonymous
Swedish literature. Facsimile reprint of the original ed. of
1898-1915 (2 v.) with corrections and supplement together with
index of real names and pseudonyms. Preface also in English.

General Works

11261   RUNNQUIST, ÅKE
         Moderna svenska författare. En samlad översikt över

svensk litteratur under fyra ärtionden. 2. omarb., utökade
uppl. Stockholm, Forum, 1967. 256 p. illus., ports. 17cm.
Modern Swedish authors. Illustrated with 183 photographs.
First ed. issued in 1959 (176 p.)

11262   STIERNMAN, ANDERS ANTON VON, 1695-1765.
        Aboa literata, continens omnes fere scriptores qui aliquid
ab Academiae ejusdem incunabulis a. C. 1640 in lucem publicam
edidisse pro tempore deprehenduntur; cum praecipuorum potio-
rumque vivorum vitis, brevi subjuncta Academiae historia ...
Holmiae, Typis J. L. Horrn, 1719. 172 p. 4.º Biographical
sketches of almost all the authors of the Academy at Åbo (or
Turku) Finland, from the year 1640.

11263   SVENSKT LITTERATURLEXIKON. 2. utvidgade uppl. Lund,
        C. W. K. Gleerup, 1970. xi, 643 p. 23cm. Dictionary of
Swedish literature; includes bio-bibliographies. 1st ed. issued
in 1964.

Swiss

11264   BERNER SCHRIFTSTELLER-VEREIN
        Berner Schrifttum der Gegenwart, 1925-1950. Bern, A.
Francke, 1949. 189 p. ports. 21cm. Bio-bibliography of
writers who use German from Bern, Switzerland, 1925-1950.

11265   BERNER SCHRIFTSTELLER-VEREIN
        Dichter und Schriftsteller der Heimat, Autoren des Berner
Schriftsteller-Vereins und ihre Werke. Bern, Buchverlag
Verbandsdruckerei, 1943. 164 p. ports. 21cm. Native poets
and writers; Swiss (German) authors belonging to the Writers'
Club of Bern and their works.

11266   BERNER SCHRIFTSTELLER-VEREIN
        Lexikon des Berner Schriftstellervereins, 1961. Bern, P.
Haupt, 1962. 70 p. ports. 21cm. A dictionary of Swiss writ-
ers in German of the Writers' Club of Bern; the material in the
dictionary is taken from two earlier publications of the Club:
Dichter und Schriftsteller der Heimat and Berner Schrifttum der
Gegenwart (q. v.)

11267   SENEBIER, JEAN, 1742-1809.
        Histoire littéraire de Genève. Genève, Barde, Manget,
1786. 3 v. 20cm. A bio-bibliography of the writers of Geneva,
Switzerland. Chronologically arranged.

11268   DIE ZEITGENÖSSISCHEN LITERATUREN DER SCHWEIZ.
        Hrsg. von Manfred Gsteiger. Zürich und München, Kindler

Verlag [1974] 752 p. illus., ports. 25cm. (Kindlers Literaturgeschichte der Gegenwart, [Bd. 4]) Contemporary literature
of Switzerland (German, French, Italian, Raeto-Romance). Although primarily an historico-critical compilation, it has particular bio-bibliographical usefulness because of its "bio-bibliographical overview" (p. 681-724) which contains short sketches
about the authors mentioned more fully in the main text and their
work. Use of index in conjunction with the "overview" will direct
user to those fuller assessments.

Syryenian

11269 PISATELI KOMI ASSR. Sostavitel'
         G. I. Torlopov. Syktyvkar, Komi knizhnoe izd-vo, 1970.
264 p. ports. 17cm. Authors of Komi ASSR, Russia, who
write in the Syryenian language. First edition issued in 1961
(150 p.).

Tajik

11270 PISATELI TADZHIKISTANA; [kratkie biograficheskie spravki]
         Dushambe, Irfon, 1966. 291 p. ports. 17cm. The writers
of Tajikistan; a brief biographical dictionary of Tajik authors.

11271 ZAND, MIKHAIL ISAAKOVICH
         Pisateli Tadzhikistana. Stalinabad, Tadzhikgosizdat, 1957.
84 p. ports. 22cm. At head of title: Soiuz pisatelei Tadzhikistana. A bio-bibliographical dictionary, with portraits of
Tajik authors (45 in all).

Tamil

11272 KANAPATIPPILLAI, TENPULOLIYUR M
         Ilanattin Tamilc cutarmanikal. Madras, Paari Nilayam,
1967. 242 p. In Tamil. Who was who of 19th century Tamil
writers.

11273 KANDAYYA PILLAI, N   C
         Tamizp pulavar akarati. [Madras, Teachers Pub. House,
1952] 442 p. In Tamil. Dictionary of Tamil poets.

11274 MUDALIYAR, M   BALASUBRAHMANYA
         Canka nurpulavarkal peyar akarati. Madras, Saivasiddhan-
ta, 1934. 53 p. In Tamil. A dictionary of the Sangam poets.

11275 RAMASWAMY PULAVAR, SUBRAMANIA ARITTIRU, 1907-
         Tamilppulavar akaravaricai ... Madras, Saivasiddhanta,

1962. 3 v. (7, 995, 2 p.) 19cm. Includes bio-bibliographies
of Tamil authors and poets. In Tamil. The 2d series of a set,
the 3d vol. of which comprises a list of works by the poets listed
in the 3 vols. of the 1st series, the first 2 vols. of the 2d series,
and the 25 vols. of a set published earlier under the title: Ta-
milppulavar varicai.

11276   SINGERVEL MUDALIAR, A
        Apitan Chintamani. Madurai, Tamil Sangham, 1910. 1640 p.
In Tamil. An encyclopaedia of Tamil literature; includes biographical sketches.

Tatar

11277   GINIIATULLINA, ASIIA KASHAFUTDINOVNA
        Pisateli Sovetskogo Tartarstana. Biobibliograficheskii
spravochnik. Kazan', Tatar kn. izd-vo, 1970. 511 p. ports.
21cm. Writers of Soviet Tartaria; a bio-bibliographical dictionary. An earlier edition appeared in 1957 (485 p.).

Telugu

Anonyms and Pseudonyms

11278   RAJU, ADDEPALLI APPALA NARASIMHA, 1940-
        Handbook of pseudonymous authors in Telugu. Hyderabad
[India] Distributors: Booklinks Corp., 1974. xiv, 64 p. 22cm.

General Works

11279   RAMALAKSHMI, K   1930-
        Andhra racayitrula samācāra sūcika. Hyderbad, Andhra
Pradesh Sahitya Akademi, 1968. 1 v. (unpaged) ports. 18cm.
In Telugu. A Who's who of modern Telugu women authors (66
in all).

Turkish

(See also Jagataic, Turko-Tataric)

11280   MUHAMMAD TĀHIR IBN RIF'AT (BRUSALI)
        'Osmānli mu'allifleri. [Istanbul, 1914-28] 3 v. The lives
and works of Turkish writers. With an index entitled: Miftāh
al-Kutub wa asāmi mu'allifin fihrisi, compiled by Ahmad Ramzi.

11281   ŠABANOVIĆ, HAZIM
        Književnost Muslimana BiH na orijentalnim jezicima. Bio-

bibliografija. Redigovao, za štampu pripremio [i "Napomena redaktora" napisao] Ahmed S. Aličić. Nacrt za korice: Dragan Dimitrijević. Sarajevo, "Svjetlost," 1973. 726 p. 19cm. (Biblioteka Kulturno nasljeđe) A bio-bibliography of 239 authors resident in Bosnia and Herzegovina who wrote in Turkish or Arabic.

11282   SALĪM, EFENDI
        Tezkiri Salim. [Istanbul] Ikdam Matbaas, 1900] 727, [6] p. (Kitaphana-i Ikdam. Adet, 10) Biographical notices of Turkish writers, with selections from their works.

Turkoman

11283   SEIDOV, ASHIR
        Biobibliograficheskiĭ spravochnik dorevoliutsionnykh turkmenskikh poetov. Ashkabad, "Turkmenistan," 1965. 150 p. 20cm. Biobibliography of pre-revolutionary Turkoman poets.

Turko-Tataric

11284   KONONOV, ANDREĬ NIKOLAEVICH, 1906-
        Biobibliograficheskiĭ slovar' otechestvennykh tiurkologov : dooktiabr'skiĭ period. Pod red. i s vvedeniem A. N. Kononova. Moskva, Glavnaia redaktsiia vostochnoi lit-ry, 1974. 340 p. 22cm. On leaf preceding t. p.: Akademiia nauk SSSR. Institut vostokovedeniia. Pages 95-[297] comprise a bio-bibliographical dictionary of philologists whose chief interest was Turko-Tataric philology and who flourished before the Russian Revolutionary period (19th century primarily).

Ukrainian

11285   ROMANENCHUK, BOHDAN
        Azbukovnyk; entsyklopediia ukrainsk'koi literatury. Kyiv, Filiadelfiia, 1969 [i. e. 1966?]-   v. ports. 24cm. Added t. p.: Alphabetarion: a concise encyclopedia of Ukrainian literature and literary terms. Contents.--t. 1. A-B.--t. 2. V-G.
        Includes biographies and portraits of writers.

Urdu

11286   ABU AL-KASIM MIR KUDRAT ALLAH KASIM
        Majmu'a-i-naghz; or, Biographical notices of Urdu poets, by Hakim Abu'l Qasim Mir Quadratullah Qasim. Edited by Hafiz Mahmud Shairani. Lahore, University of the Punjab,

1933. 46, 400, 456 p. 25cm. (Punjab University, Lahore.
Oriental publications, no. 19) Text in Hindustani.

11287   BALOCH, NABI BAKHSH
          Sindh men Urdū shā'irī. 1st ed. Hyderabad, Pakistan,
          Mehran Arts Council, 1970. 7, 284 p. 22cm. In Urdu. In-
          cludes bibliographical references. 66 Urdu poets from the
          Sindh.

11288   NIZAMI BADAUNI, pseud.
          Qamus-al-mashahir. Badaun, Nizami Press, 1924. 2 v.
          A biographical dictionary of Urdu authors.

Venezuelan

Anonyms and Pseudonyms

11289   MACHADO, JOSE E
          Escarceos bibliográficos; lista de seudónimos y anónimos
          en la literatura y en la política venezolana. (In Boletín de la
          Biblioteca Nacional, Caracas, Venezuela. v. 1, no. 5, oct.
          1924, p. 131-134; v. 2, no. 6, enero 1925, p. 163-167; v. 2, no.
          7, abr. 1925, p. [193]-196; v. 2, no. 9, oct. 1925, p. 262-266;
          v. 2, no. 10, enero 1926, p. 299-303; v. 3, no. 11, abr. 1926,
          p. 333-336; v. 3, no. 12, jul. 1926, p. 264-366; v. 5, no. 19,
          abr. 1928, p. 587-591) A list of the pseudonyms and anonyms in
          Venezuelan literature and politics.

General Works

11290   DICCIONARIO GENERAL DE LA LITERATURA VENEZOLANA.
          Mérida, Centro de Investigaciones Literarias, Universidad
          de los Andes, 1974-   v. 24cm. A dictionary of Venez-
          uelan literature; bio-bibliographical entries included.

11291   MANCERA GALLETTI, ANGEL
          Quienes narran y cuentan en Venezuela; fichero bibliográ-
          fico para una historia de la novela y del cuento venezolano. [1.
          ed.] Caracas, Ediciones Caribe, 1958. xv, 654 p. 24cm. Ca.
          142 Colombian writers in all fields (contemporary, 20th century)
          are represented in this bio-bibliographical work; arranged in no
          particular order, by chapters headings: e. g. Women as au-
          thors, etc.

11292   TEJERA, FELIPE
          Perfiles venezolanos. Prólogo de Pedro Díaz Seijas.
          Caracas, Presidencia de la República, 1973. 445 p. 22cm.
          (Fuentes para la historia de la literatura venezolana, no. 5) Bio-
          bibliographical profiles of 94 Venezuelan authors, arranged
          chronologically, from Andrés Bello (born 1781) to Santiago Gon-
          zález Guinán (born 1854?).

Vietnamese

11293   TRÂN-VĂN-GIÁP, 1902-
        Luoc truyên các tác giả Viêt Nam. In lân thú 2, có sửa
chữa, bô sung. Hà-nòi, Khoa Hoc Xã Hôi, 1971-   v.
19cm. Contents. --tâp 1. Tác giả các sach Han,· Nôm tù thê ky
XI đên đâu thê ky XX.

        Biographical sketches of Vietnamese authors (2d ed.). The ar-
rangement is chronological within each volume. Vol. 1: Authors
of books in Chinese from the 11th to the 20th century (735 authors).

Wendic

11294   ŽUR, HUBERT
        Komuž muza pjero wodži. Budyšin, Domowina; [wudal
Lektorat za powšitkownu literaturu] 1963. 242 p. ports. 20cm.
What person is hidden under the pen(name)? A bio-bibliography
of Wendic literature.

White Russian

11295   PIS'MENNIKI SAVETSKAĬ BELARUSI; karotki biiàgrafichny
        davednik. [Sklali: IA. Kazeka, R. Niàkhai, A. Esakou]
Minsk, Dziàrzh. vyd-va BSSR, 1959. 499 p. ports. 18cm.
The writers of Soviet White Russia; a brief biographical diction-
ary.

11296   PIS'MENNIKI SAVETSKAĬ BELARUSI. Karotki biiàbibliiagr.
        davednik. Minsk, "Belarus," 1970. 439 p. ports. 17cm.
By A. Hardzitski, IA. Kazeka, and others. Bio-bibliography of
White Russian authors. A later edition of a work with the same
title issued in 1959 (q. v.)

11297   VYTOKI PESNI; aŭtabiiahrafii belaruskikh pis'mennikaŭ.
        [Skladanie i padrykhtoŭka tekstaŭ IA. Kazeki. Minsk,
Mastatskaià lit-ra, 1973. 335 p. ports. 21cm. Cover title:
Aŭtabiiahrafii belaruskikh pis'mennikaŭ. Autobiographies of
55 White Russian authors (living) accompanied by portraits. In
alphabetical arrangement.

Yakut

11298   PROTOD'IAKONOV, VASILIĬ ANDREEVICH, 1912-
        Pisateli IAkutii. Kratkii biobibliograficheskii spravochnik.
Otv. redaktor: G. G. Okorokov. 2. dop. izd. IAkutsk, IAkut-
skoe knizhnoe izd-vo, 1972. 398 p. ports. 17cm. At head of
title: Soiuz pisatelei IAkutii. Respublikanskii literaturnyi muzei

im. P. A. Oiunskogo. IÁkutskaiâ respublikanskaiâ biblioteka
im. A. S. Pushkina. V. Protod'iàkonov, N. Alekseev. A bio-
bibliographical dictionary of contemporary Yakut literature and
Russian literature by authors of Yakut origin. 1st ed. (168 p.)
issued in 1963.

Yugoslav

(See also Croatian, Macedonian, Serbian)

11299   DRENOVAC, NIKOLA
         Pisci govore. Bibliografija i literature: Zivorad P. Jovano-
vić. Beograd, Grafos, 1964. 525 p. ports. 21cm. "The authors speak"; a bio-bibliography of Yugoslav literature.

11300   JUGOSLOVENSKI KNJIŽEVNI LEKSIKON. Redakcija: Zivojin
         Boškov [et al.] Urednik: Živan Milisavac. [Novi Sad]
Matica Srpska, 1971. 598 p. illus., ports. 24cm. Yugoslav
literary dictionary; bio-bibliographical.

11301   LEKSIKON PISACA JUGOSLAVIJE. [Glavni urednik Živojin
         Boškov. Korice: Ivan Boldižar. Novi Sad] Matica srpska,
1972-   v. illus., ports. 29cm. A bio-bibliographical
dictionary of Yugoslav authors.

11302   LUKIĆ, SVETA
         Contemporary Yugoslav literature; a sociopolitical approach.
Edited by Gertrude Joch Robinson. Translated by Pola Triandis.
Urbana, University of Illinois Press [1972] xvi, 280 p. map.
24cm. Translation of Savremena jugoslovenska literatura. "Biographical notes on contemporary Yugoslav writers": p. 185-207.

LAW

Local

Canada

11303   ROY, PIERRE GEORGES, 1870-
         Les avocats de la région de Québec. Lévis, 1936. 487 p.
Short biographies of lawyers of the judicial districts of Quebec,
Beauce, Chicoutimi, Montmagny, Arthabaska, Gaspé, Rimouski, Kamouraska, Saguenay, Roberval & Abitibi from origins
to 1936.

11304   ROY, PIERRE GEORGES, 1870-
         Les juges de la province de Québec. Québec, Service des

archives du Gouvernement de la province de Québec, 1933.
xxvii, 588 p. ports. 27cm. Brief biographies of the judges of
the Province of Quebec up to 1933.

11305   WILKIE, GEORGE, 1867-
            The bench and bar of Ontario. Editors: George Wilkie,
        John A. Cooper [and] C. W. Benedict. Toronto, Brown-Searle
        Print. Co., 1905. 445 p. of ports. 24cm. A huge collection
        of portraits of the judges and lawyers of Ontario.

Courland

11306   RÄDER, WILHELM
            Die Juristen Kurlands im 17. Jahrhundert. Marburg/Lahn
        [Johann Gottfried Herder-Institut] 1957. viii, 104 p. 20cm.
        (Wissenschaftliche Beiträge zur Geschichte und Landeskunde
        Ost-Mitteleuropas, Nr. 28) A biographical dictionary with 193
        brief sketches of lawyers in Courland in the 17th century.

Czechoslovakia

11307   NAVRÁTIL, MICHAL
            Almanach československých právniku. Životopisný slovnik
        čs. pravniků kteři působili v uméni, védé, krasném pisemnict-
        vi a politice od Karla IV. až na naše doby. V Praze, Nákl.
        vl., 1930. 559 p. 4.⁰ Almanac of Czech lawyers and jurists
        from the beginnings to 1930; a biographical dictionary.

Denmark

11308   HJORTH-NIELSEN, HENNING, 1878-
            Danske prokuratorer med kongelig bevilling 1660-1869; samt
        et tillaeg indeholdende oplysninger om en del prokuratorer uden
        kongelig bevilling. Udg. med støtte af Det Danske sagførersam-
        fund. København, I kommission hos Levin & Munksgaard, 1935.
        446 p. 27cm. Danish lawyers licensed by the Crown, 1660-1869.

11309   JURIDISK OG STATSVIDENSKABELIG STAT. København [etc.]
            V. Richter [etc.]   v. 23-26cm. Title varies: some
        issues, Juridisk stat. 23d ed. dated 1965. Issued by Jurist-
        forbundet in some years. Danish lawyers, political scientists
        and economists, especially graduates of Copenhagen University.

Finland

11310   HONKA, OLAVI, 1894-
            Prokuraattori. Oikeuskansleri, 1809-1959. Juhlajulkaisu.

Helsinki [Valtioneuvoston Kirjapaino] 1959. 330 p. illus., ports.
25cm. The chancellor of justice in Finland, 1809-1959. Biographical notices on pages 237-320 (by K. K. Vuorisalo)

11311   LAGUS, WILHELM GABRIEL, 1786-1859.
         Biographiska anteckningar om Åbo Hofrätts presidenter och
ledamöter; jemte forteckning öfver secretare och advokatfis-
caler derstädes intill den 12 nov. 1823, da Hofrätten firade Sin
andra Secularfest. Helsingfors, J. C. Frenckell, 1836. xxxiii,
596 p. 22cm. Biographical notes concerning the presidents and
members of the Court of Appeals of Åbo, together with lists of
the secretaries & lawyers in the service of this court (to Nov.
12, 1823). Added t. p.: Åbo Hofrätts historia ...

11312   MALI, MATTI, ed.
         Korkein Øikeus, 1809-1959. Tietoja hallituskonseljin ja
senaatin oikeusosaston sekä korkeimman oikeuden historiasta,
toiminnasta ja virkakunnasta. Helsinki, Valtioneuvoston Kir-
japaino, 1959. 503 p. illus., ports. 25cm. The Supreme Court
of Finland, 1809-1959. Information on the Council of State and
the juridical section of the Senate, and history of the Supreme
Court, its activities and its personnel. Index of persons, p.
473-503.

11313   SUOMEN LAKIMIEHET. FINLANDS JURISTER. [Vammala,
         etc.]   v. ports. 22-26cm. Vols. for 1949-   issued
as Suomen Lakimiesliiton kirjasarja, no. 3, 11
Began publication with 1879 issue. Title varies:
Finlands jurister.--1939, Lakimiesmatrikkeli, elämäkerrallisia
tietoja Suomen lakimiehistä. Juristmatrikel, biografiska uppgifter om Finlands jurister. Compilers: A. W. Westerlund.--   J. E. Wilskman.--1949, E. I. Lammin-Koskinen.--1958-   E. Schrey. Finlands jurists; a biographical
directory-compilation.

11314   WESTERLUND, ADOLF WILHELM, 1852-
         Åbo hovrätts presidenter, ledamöter och tjänstemän 1623-
1923. Biografiska och genealogiska anteckningar. Åbo, Åbo
tryckeri och tidnings AB, 1923. 2 v. (xiv, 812, 15, vii, 48 p.)
ports. 25cm. Presidents, members & officials of the Court of
Appeals of Åbo (now Turku) 1623-1923; biographical & genealogical notes.

France

11315   BLUCHE, FRANCOIS
         L'origine des magistrats du Parlement de Paris au XVIIIe
siècle (1715-1771); dictionnaire généalogique. Paris, Fédération
des sociétés historiques et archéologiques de Paris et de l'Ile-
de-France, 1956. 412 p. 23cm. (Paris et Ile-de-France.
Mémoires, t. 5-6, 1953-54) A genealogical-biographical dictionary of the magistrates of the Parlement in Paris, 1715-1771.

11316   STRAYER, JOSEPH REESE, 1904-
         Les gens de justice du Languedoc sous Philippe le Bel.
Toulouse, Association Marc Bloch, 1970. 211 p. 24cm. (Association Marc Bloch de Toulouse. Cahiers. Etudes d'histoire
méridionale, 5) The appendix of 150 p. comprises short biographical notes on some 420 royal seneschals, judges, lawyers
(avocats) and procureurs who held office in the 5 seneschalships
of the Midi of France between 1280 and 1320.

Islamic Countries

11317   FLÜGEL, GUSTAV LEBERECHT, 1802-1870.
         Die Classen der hanefitischen Rechtsgelehrten. (In Sächs-
ische Gesellschaft der Wissenschaften. Philologisch-Historische
Classe. Abhandlungen. Leipzig, 1861. 28cm. 3. Bd., p.
[267]-358) Biographical notes on Hanafis (experts in Islamic
law) divided into 24 classes with a comprehensive name list (index) of the jurists mentioned.

11318   IBN ABĪ AL-WAFĀ' AL-QURASHĪ, 'ABD AL QADIR IBN MU-
         HAMMAD, 1297-1373.
         al-Jawāhir al-mudiyah. [Hyderabad] Silsalat Matbu'at da-
irat al-Ma'arif al-'Utmāniyya [1914] 2 v. 26cm. Biographical
dictionary of Hanafis, followers of a Muslim school of religious
law.

11319   IBN HAJAR AL-'ASQALĀNĪ, AHMAD IBN 'ALĪ, 1372-1449.
         Raf' al-isr 'an qudāt misr. al-Qahirah [Cairo] 1957-
         v. 24cm. Biographies of Egyptian judges. A biographical
dictionary; two volumes issued as of 1961.

11320   IBN QUTLŪBŪGHA, AL-QĀSIM IBN 'ABD ALLAH, 1399 or 1400-
         1474 or 5.
         Die Krone der Lebensbeschreibungen enthaltend die Classen
der Hanefiten, von Zein-ad-din Kasim ibn Kutlûbuga. Zum
ersten Mal hrsg. und mit Anmerkungen und einem Index begleitet
von Gustav Flügel. Leipzig, In Commission bei F. A. Brock-
haus, 1852. xvi, 192 p. 23cm. [Abhandlungen der Deutschen
Morgenländischen Gesellschaft, 2. Bd., No. 3] Arabic title at
head of t. p.; text in Arabic. Biographical dictionary of Hanafis.
Another edition (in Arabic: Tāj at-tarajim fi tabaqāt al-Hunafi-
yah) appeared in Baghdad in 1962.

11321   IBRĀHĪM IBN 'ALĪ, called IBN FARHŪN.
         Kitāb al-dībāj al-mudhab fī ma'rifat a'yān 'ulamā' al-madhab.
[Fez, 1892] 304 p. 8.° A collection of biographies of prominent Malikite jurists, Muslim lawyers who put into practice the
teachings of Malik ibn Anas.

11322   AL-SAKHĀWĪ, MUHAMMAD IBN 'ABD AL-RAHMĀN, 1427 or 8-
        1497.
            al-Dhayl 'alā Raf' al-isr. al-Qāhirah [Cairo, 1966] 40,
        588 p. 27cm. Composed as a supplement to Raf' al-isr 'an
        qudāt Misr by Ibn Hajar al-'Asqalānī. Cover title: az-Zaylu ála
        Rafá el-isr; or, Bughyatul ulamaa' warruwah, by al-Imam Abdul
        Ruhmān al-Sakhāwi. Biographical dictionary of judges, schol-
        ars of Islamic law. Edited by Hilāl Jūdah and Muhammad Ma-
        hmūd Subh.

11323   WAKĪ', MUHAMMAD IBN KHALAF, d. 918.
            Akhbàr al-qudah. al-Qāhirah 1947-50. 3 v. 24cm. Bi-
        ographies of Moslem judges and traditionists during the first
        three centuries after the Hegira. Edited by 'Abd al-'Aziz
        Mustafá al-Marāghi.

Philippine Islands

11324   LEON-PARAS, CORAZON DE
            The justices of the Supreme Court of the Philippines (a bio-
        graphical directory) Compiled and edited by Corazon de Leon-
        Paras and Ma. Corona Salcedo-Romero. Manila, Rex Book
        Store [1971] vi, 180 p. ports. 23cm. A biographical diction-
        ary (in part) of 62 justices.

Russia

11325   KHARKOV. UNIVERSITET.
            IŪridicheskii fakul'tet Khar'kovskogo universiteta za pervye
        sto let ego sushchestvovaniiā (1805-1905) I. Istoriiā fakul'teta.
        II. Biograficheskii slovar' professorov i prepodavatelei, pod
        red. M. P. Chubinskogo i D. I. Bagaleiā. Khar'kov, Izd. Uni-
        versiteta, 1908. viii, 310, iv p. 25cm. Pt. 3 is a biographical
        dictionary of the professors and teachers on the Faculty of Law
        of Kharkov University, 1805-1905.

Scotland

11326   GRANT, SIR FRANCIS JAMES, 1863-
            The Faculty of Advocates in Scotland, 1532-1943, with gene-
        alogical notes. Edinburgh, Scottish Record Society, 1944. iv,
        228 p. 8.° (Scottish Record Society. [Publications] v. 70)
        A 'biographical dictionary' of Scottish lawyers, although biogra-
        phical data are confined to just a few lines for each individual.

Sweden

11327   BOSTRÖM, H   J
            Wasa Hofrätts presidenter, ledamöter och tjänstemän samt

hofrätten underlydande lagniän och häradohöfdingar 1766-1914.
Helsingförs, Lilius och Hertzberg, 1915. 354 p. ports. 25cm.
Presidents, members and officials of the Court of Appeals of
Wasa, and the judges of second instance and presidents of tri-
bunals of first instance dependent on the Court of Appeals, 1766-
1914.

United States

11328   BERRYMAN, JOHN R., 1849-1914, ed.
         History of the bench and bar of Wisconsin. Prepared under
direction of John R. Berryman. Chicago, H. C. Cooper, Jr.,
1898. 2 v. ports. 28cm. Includes a large proportion of biographical sketches.

11329   BIOGRAPHICAL DICTIONARY OF THE FEDERAL JUDICIARY.
         Compiled by Harold Chase [and others] Detroit, Gale
Research Co., 1976. 381 p. 1,600 biographical sketches of
American Federal judges from 1789 to the present.

11330   FRIEDMAN, LEON, comp.
         The justices of the United States Supreme Court, 1789-1969,
their lives and major opinions. Leon Friedman & Fred L. Israel,
editors. With an introd. by Louis H. Pollak. New York, Chel-
sea House in association with Bowker, 1969. 4 v. (xxiv, 3373 p.)
25cm. Includes biographies of 97 justices (to Chief Justice Warren Burger)

11331   HISTORY OF THE BENCH AND BAR OF OREGON. Portland,
         Historical Pub. Co., 1910. 286 p. ports. 27cm. His-
torical, p. [7]-77; biographical, p. [79]-286. Compiled chiefly
by Montagu Colmer.

11332   MARSHALL, CARRINGTON TANNER, 1869-   ed.
         A history of the courts and lawyers of Ohio. New York,
American Historical Society, 1934. 4 v. illus., ports. 28cm.
Includes many biographical sketches of lawyers and judges in
Ohio's past up to the 1930's.

LIBRARY SCIENCE AND BOOK ARTS

11333   BONNET, RUDOLF, 1889-
         Männer der Kurzschrift; 572 Lebensabrisse von Vorkämp-
fern und Führern der Kurzschriftbewegung. Darmstadt, Winkler, 1935. 228 p. 22cm. Men who pioneered in shorthand;
572 biographical sketches of people involved in the shorthand
movement.

11334   BRIELS, J G C A
          Zuidnederlandse boekdrukkers en boekverkopers in de Re-
publiek der Verenigde Nederlanden omstreeks 1570-1630: een
bijdrage tot de kennis van de geschiedenis van het boek. Met in
bijlage bio- en bibliografische aantekeningen betr. Zuid- en
Noordnederlandse boekdrukkers, uitgevers, boekverkopers,
lettergieters etc., en andere documenten. Met een voorrede
van H. de la Fontaine Verwey. Nieuwkoop, B. de Graaf, 1974.
xvi, 649 p. illus. 25cm. (Bibliotheca bibliographica Neerlandica, v. 7) Printers and booksellers in the Republic of the
United Netherlands (southern part), 1570-1630. Pages 163-554
comprise a bio-bibliographical dictionary of printers, publishers, booksellers, typographers, etc.

11335   CHYBA, KARLE
          Slovník knihtiskařů y Československu od nejstarsich dob do
roku 1860. Praha, Památnik Narodniho pisemnictvi, 1966/68-
                    v. 22cm. Dictionary of printers in Czechoslo-
vakia from the origins of printing to 1860.

11336   CORRARD DE BREBAN,   b. 1792.
          Recherches sur l'établissement et l'exercice de l'imprim-
erie à Troyes [contentant la nomenclature des imprimeurs de
cette ville depuis la fin du XVe siècle jusqu'à 1789 et des notices
sur leurs productions les plus remarquables ... 3. éd. revue
et considérablement augmentée d'après les notes manuscrites
de l'auteur par Olgar Thierry-Poux. Chatillon-sur-Seine?] La
Roue à livres, 1973. 200 p. illus. 22cm. "Notice alphabétique des imprimeurs troyens de 1483 à 1789": p. [45]-177. Reprint of the 1873 (Paris, A. Chossonnery) ed. Chiefly a dictionary of printers in Troyes, with brief biographical notes and a
listing of the printers' works.

11337   FLETCHER, WILLIAM YOUNGER, 1830-1913.
          English book collectors. Edited by Alfred Pollard. New
York, B. Franklin [1969] xviii, 448 p. illus., ports. 22cm.
(Burt Franklin bibliography and reference series, 209) Reprint of the 1902 ed. "Alphabetical list of collectors'''' p. [xiii]-
xvi. 100 biographies are included.

11338   GYLLENBERG, GIDEON
          Finlands bokhandlare. En samling biografiska data över
Finlands forna och nutida förlags- och sortimentsbokhandlare
samt librister. Borga, Den Finska bokhandels centralorganisa-
tion och W. Soderström, 1923. 172 p. ports. 25cm. Finland's
booksellers, a collection of biographical facts. Added t. p.:
Suomen kirjakauppaiaita.

11339   HANDBUCH ÖSTERREICHISCHER BIBLIOTHEKEN. II. Statis-
          tik und Personalverzeichnis. Stand 1960, 1966, 1971
Hersg. von der Vereinigung Österreichischer Bibliothekare.

Wien, Österreichische Nationalbibliothek, 1961-   v. 21cm.
(Biblos-Schriften, Bd. 31, 47, 71
A handbook of Austrian libraries: section II: Statistics and list
of personnel. The work is in large part a biographical dictionary
of Austrian librarians, issued every 5 or 6 years.

11340   HAZLITT, WILLIAM CAREW, 1834-1913.
         A roll of honour. A calendar of the names of over 17,000
men and women who throughout the British Isles and in our early
colonies have collected mss. and printed books from the XIVth
to the XIXth century, with topographical and personal notices
and anecdotes of many of them and their libraries, and introductory remarks. To which are added indexes of localities, and
of ranks and occupations. London, B. Quaritch, 1908. viii,
273, 276-279 numb. l., xi p. illus. 22cm. Reprinted 1972 or 3
by Lenox Hill Pub. Corp. (B. Franklin) New York.

11341   HUMPHRIES, CHARLES
         Music publishing in the British Isles, from the beginning
until the middle of the nineteenth century; a dictionary of engravers, printers, publishers, and music sellers, with a historical
introd., by Charles Humphries and William C. Smith. 2d ed.,
with suppl. New York, Barnes & Noble, 1970. vii, 392 p.
facsims. 26cm. 1st ed. (London, Cassell) issued in 1954.

11342   HUNT, CHRISTOPHER JOHN
         The book trade in Northumberland and Durham to 1860; a
biographical dictionary of printers, engravers, lithographers,
booksellers, stationers, publishers, mapsellers, printsellers,
musicsellers, bookbinders, newsagents and owners of circulat-
ing libraries. Newcastle upon Tyne, Thorne's Students' Book-
shop for the History of the Book Trade in the North, 1975. xviii,
116 p. illus. 25cm.

11343   LANG, HELMUT W
         Die Buchdrucker des 15. bis 17. Jahrhunderts in Österreich.
Mit einer Bibliographie zur Geschichte des österreichischen
Buchdrucks bis 1700. [1. Aufl.] Baden-Baden, V. Koerner,
1972. 103 p. 24cm. (Bibliotheca bibliographica Aureliana, 42)
Printers in Austria from the 15th to the 17th century. Brief biographies of ca. 150 printers; arrangement is under city (Bregenz
to Wimpassa/Leitha) where printing activities were carried on.

11344   MAIGNIEN, EDMOND AUGUSTE, 1847-1915.
         L'imprimerie les imprimeurs et les libraires à Grenoble du
XVème au XVIIIeme siècle. Grenoble, Impr. G. Dupont, 1884.
cxiv p. 21cm. (Bulletin de l'Académie Delphinale, 3. sér., t.
18, 1883) Printing, printers and booksellers at Grenoble, 15th-
18th centuries. Biographies of printers (p. xxi-lxix); biographies of booksellers, p. lxx-cxiv. Chronological arrangement;
no index.

11345   MARIACHER, BRUNO, 1922-
Who's who in publishing. A biographical dictionary containing 241 biographies of publishers attending the 13th Congress of
the International Publisher's Association at Zürich from June
21st-25th, 1954. [Bern-Bümpliz, Benteli, 1954] 63 p. 8.° In
English, French and German.

11346   MEN OF LIBRARY SCIENCE AND LIBRARIES IN INDIA.
1967-   New Delhi, Premier.   v. 1967-   vols.
edited by R. K. Khosla. The 1967 vol. is in 3 parts: pt. 1 includes a who's who section with brief sketches of distinguished
librarians and teachers of library science.

11347   MOES, ERNST WILHELM, 1864-1912.
De Amsterdamsche boekdrukkers en uitgevers in de zestiende
eeuw. Amsterdam, C. L. van Langenhuysen, 1900-15. 4 v.
illus. 22cm. Vol. 2 by Moes and C. P. Burger, Jr.; v. 3-4 by
C. P. Burger, Jr. Vol. 4 has imprint: 's Gravenhage, M. Ni-
jhoff. Amsterdam's printers and booksellers in the 16th century;
includes printers' marks.

11348   NIKOLAEV, VALERIĬ ALEKSEEVICH
Bibliografy Sibriri i Dal'nego Vostoka. Biobibliograficheskiĭ
slovar'. Otv. redaktor H. N. IAnovskiĭ. Novosibirsk, "Nauka, "
Sibirskoe otd-nie, 1973. 174 p. 22cm. At head of title: Akade-
miiã nauk SSSR. Sibirskoe otd-nie. Gos. publichnaiã nauchno-
tekhnicheskaiã biblioteka. A bio-bibliographical dictionary of
some 95 Russian bibliographers interested in Siberian and Central Asian studies.

11349   PACHNICKE, GERHARD
Gothaer Bibliothekare; dreissig Kurzbiographien in chrono-
logischer Folge. [Gotha] Landesbibliothek Gotha, 1958. 32 p.
ports. 21cm. (Veröffentlichungen der Landesbibliothek Gotha,
Heft 5) Librarians of Gotha, Germany; 30 biographies (with portraits) arranged chronologically.

11349a   PORTA, FREDERICO
Diccionario de artes gráficas. Porto Alegre, Editôra
Globo [1958] vi, 424 p. illus., ports. 24cm. (Enciclopédias
e dicionários Globo) A dictionary of the printing arts; included
are biographies and portraits of printers, engravers, etc.

11350   ROUZET, ANNE
Dictionnaire des imprimeurs, libraires et éditeurs des XVe
et XVIe siècles dans les limites géographiques de la Belgique
actuelle, par Anne Rouzet avec la collaboration de Micheline
Coline-Boon [et al.] Nieuwkoop, B. de Graaf, 1975. 287 p.
29cm. (Collection du Centre national de l'archéologie et de l'histoire du livre, Bruxelles. Publications, 3) A biographical dic-

tionary of printers, booksellers and publishers in Belgium in the 15th and 16th centuries.

11351   SABZWARI, GHANIUL AKRAM
        Who's who in librarianship in Pakistan. Compiled by Gha-niul Akram Sabzwari and M. Wasil Usmani. 1st ed. Karachi, Library Promotion Bureau, 1969. xxiii, 273 p. ports. 25cm.

11352   SŁOWNIK PRACOWNIKÓW KSIĄŻKI POLSKIEJ. [Pod red.
        Ireny Treichel. Wyd. 1.] Warszawa, Państwowe Wydawn. Naukowe, 1972. xviii, 1042 p. 25cm. A biographical diction-ary of ca. 3,000 deceased Polish librarians, bibliographers, bibliophiles, book illustrators, copyists, printers, publishers, etc.

11353   VARELA VELÁSQUEZ, MARGARITA
        Quién es quién en la bibliotecología colombiana. Medellín, Escuela Interamericana de Bibliotecología, 1960. vii, 266 l. A biographical dictionary of 334 Colombian librarians or people who work in libraries in Colombia.

11354   VERNAZZA, GIUSEPPE, barone di Freney, 1745-1822.
        Dizionario dei tipografi e dei principali correttori ed in-tagliatori che operarono negli stati sardi di terraferma e più specialmente in Piemonte sino all'anno 1821. Opera e stampa che rimasta imperfetta per la morte dell'autore barone Ver-nazza di Freney, viene in luce per cura d'una società anonima. Torino, Stamperia reale, 1859. 328 p. 27cm. Dictionary of the printers, editors and engravers who were active in the Sardinian states and especially the Piedmont up to the year 1821.

11355   WAKEMAN, GEOFFREY
        A guide to nineteenth century colour printers [by] Geoffrey Wakeman & Gavin D. R. Bridson. [Loughborough, Eng.] Plough Press [1975] xii, 127 p. illus. 22cm. An alphabetically ar-ranged listing of printing firms in Great Britain that specialized in color printing. The firm names are generally those of the founders and biographical data for these printers are given under the entries for the firm.

11356   WHO'S WHO IN BOOK MANUFACTURING; a compilation of the
        men and machinery in book printing, typesetting, edition binding, and complete book manufacturing, for the book publish-ing industry in the United States. Philadelphia, North American Pub. Co., 1972. 188 p. illus., ports. 29cm.

11357   WHO'S WHO IN LIBRARIANSHIP AND INFORMATION SCIENCE.
        Edited by T. Landau. 2d ed. London, New York, Abelard-

Schuman [1972] v, 311 p. 25cm. 1st ed. issued in 1954.
British librarians.

11358   WHO'S WHO IN NEW ZEALAND LIBRARIES. 1954/55-
        Wellington, New Zealand Library Association, 1955-
        v.

MEDICINE

Bibliography, Indexes, Portrait Catalogs

11359   BALL, ROBERT
        Katalog der vom verstorbenen Numismatiker Herrn Robert
        Ball in Berlin ... hinterlassenen Sammlung von Münzen und
        Medaillen auf Aerzte, Medizin, Naturforscher, Kongresse und
        verwandte Gebiete mit beigefügten Nettopreisen. Berlin, 1905.
        72 p. A catalog of coins and medallions featuring portraits of
        doctors and scientists, owned by Robert Ball but put forward
        for sale by the Robert Ball firm (dealers in numismatics) after
        his death.

11360   GARRISON, FIELDING HUDSON, 1870-1935.
        Available sources and future prospects of medical biography.
        (In Bulletin of the New York Academy of Medicine, ser. 2, v. 4:
        p. 586-607. New York, 1928) Reprinted in the author's Contri-
        butions to the history of medicine, New York, Hafner, 1966 (p.
        697-718) A bibliography of collective biographies, autobiogra-
        phies, and dictionaries of anonymous and pseudonymous works.

11361   HOLZMAIR, EDUARD
        Katalog der Sammlung Dr. Josef Brettauer, Medicina in
        nummis. Hrsg. vom Kuratorium der Dr. Josef Brettauer-
        Stiftung. Wien, Im Selbstverlag, 1937. xvi, 384 p. illus.
        29cm. A catalog of the medical medallions, etc. of the Dr.
        Josef Brettauer-Stiftung at the University of Vienna. "Per-
        sonen" (p. 1-99) includes short identifying biographical data and
        description of the medallions.

11362   KAATHOVEN, CORNELIUS WILLEM HENDRIK VAN
        Catalogue de la collection très-importante de portraits de
        médecins, naturalistes et mathématiciens et de gravures illus-
        trant l'histoire de la médecine. Amsterdam & Leide, F. Mul-
        ler, 1879-80. 2 v. (iv, 88, 140 p.) 8.º Catalog of the very im-
        portant collection of C. W. H. Kaathoven containing portraits of
        physicians, naturalists and mathematicians and engravings il-
        lustrating the history of medicine.

11363   KISCH, BRUNO, 1890-
        Iconographies of medical portraits. (In Journal of the his-
        tory of medicine and allied sciences. New York, 1957. v. 12,
        p. 366-387, 524) The bibliography (p. 376-387), arranged

chronologically, includes over 160 items from 1570 to 1957, works
that contain a substantial number of portraits of the physicians.

11364   LEVINSON, ABRAHAM, 1888-1955.
          Medical medallions. [Baltimore] c1943. [3]-34 p. illus.
24cm. "Reprinted from the Bulletin of the Medical Library Association, vol. 31, no. 1, January, 1943." 74 medical medallions in the author's collection of which 67 are portrait medallions of 67 physicians. Many of the medallions are reproduced
as portraits. Brief biographical notes are included.

11365   PAULY, ALPHONSE, 1830-
          Bibliographie des sciences médicales ... London, D. Ver-
schoyale, 1954. xix p., 1758 columns, [72] p. 24cm. (Derek
Verschoyle Academic and Bibliographical Publications, ltd.,
London. 1st ser., no. 3) Reprint of the Paris, Tross, 1874 ed.
A bibliography of the medical sciences; columns 47-87 contain
bibliography of general biographical collections of physicians,
etc. Columns 87-442: bibliography of individual physicians, etc.

11366   RUDOLPHI, KARL ASMUND, 1771-1832.
          Recentioris aevi numismata virorum de rebus medicis et
physicis meritorum memoriam servantia collegit et recensuit.
Denno edidit, emendavit et auxit Carol. Ludov. de Duisburg.
Cum supplemento. Dantisci, T. Bertling, 1862-63. xiii, 257,
14 p. 8.°

          ---- ----Supplementum II. Gedani, Sumtibus Auctoris, 1868.
32 p. 8.° Numismatic representations of physicians and men
of medicine of the recent period; a catalog.

11367   STORER, HORATIO ROBINSON, 1830-1922.
          Medicina in nummis; a descriptive list of the coins, medals,
jetons relating to medicine, surgery, and the allied sciences.
Edited by Malcom Storer. [Boston, Wright & Potter Print. Co.,
1931] 1146 p. plates, port. 25cm. "Personal medals": p. 43-
520. "Addenda [to] Personal medals": p. 1079-1106.

11368   THORNTON, JOHN LEONARD
          A select bibliography of medical biography. With an intro-
ductory essay on medical biography. 2d ed. London, Library
Association, 1970. 170 p. illus., ports. 22cm. (Library Association. Bibliographies, no. 3) Restricted to books in English published since 1900. Over 1,000 collective and individual
biographies are listed.

General Works

11369   BAAS, JOHANN HERMANN, 1838-1909.
          Outlines of the history of medicine and the medical profes-

sion. Translated in conjunction with the author and rev. and
enl. by H. E. Handerson. New York, J. H. Vail, 1889. 117 p.
24cm. Translation of Grundriss der Geschichte der Medizin
und des heilenden Standes (Stuttgart, 1876). Includes biobibliographical notices of important physicians of each period and
specialty, arranged by nationality, at the end of each historical
'essay.' These extensive biographical sections are comprehen-
sively indexed at the end of the volume.

11370   BARRAUD AND JERRARD, PHOTOGRAPHERS, LONDON.
         The medical profession in all countries, containing photo-
graphic portraits from life. London, Churchill, 1873-75. 2 v.
ports. 8.°

11372   BISHOP, WILLIAM JOHN
         Medicine and science in postage stamps, by W. J. Bishop
and N. M. Matheson. London, Harvey & Blythe, 1948. 82 p.
illus., ports. 19cm. A treatise with some portraits on stamps
followed by a dictionary of famous physicians and scientists
who have been honored by the issuance of postage-stamps bearing their portraits, etc. (p. 60-82).

11373   BRADFORD, THOMAS LINDSLEY, 1847-1918.
         The pioneers of homoeopathy. Philadelphia, Boericke &
Tafel, 1897. xii, 677 p. 24cm. Includes biographical data for
ca. 500 physicians the world over who practiced homeopathy
before 1835.

11374   CHOULANT, JOHANN LUDWIG, 1791-1861.
         History and bibliography of anatomic illustration in its re-
lation to anatomic science and the graphic arts, by Ludwig
Choulant. Translated and edited with notes and a biography by
Mortimer Frank. With a biographical sketch of the translator
and two additional sections by Fielding H. Garrison and Edward
C. Streeter. Chicago, University of Chicago Press, 1920.
xxvii, 435 p. illus. 26cm. Translation of Geschichte und
Bibliographie der anatomischen Abbildung (Leipzig, Weigel,
1852) Pages 88-350 yield brief biographical data, arranged
chronologically, about some 84 anatomic illustrators from Mon-
dino de' Luzzi (early 14th cent.) to Julien Fau (middle of the
19th cent.).

11375   ENCICLOPEDIA SALVAT DE CIENCIAS MÉDICAS. Dirigida
         por J. Valero-Ribas. Barcelona, Salvat Editores, 1955-57.
5 v. illus., ports. 28cm.

---- ----Apéndice. Barcelona, Salvat, 1963. 518 p. 28cm.
An encyclopedia of medicine that includes biographies of doctors
(universal in scope).

11376   FERNER, HELMUT RICHARD, 1912-
         Anatomia in nummis [von] Helmut Ferner. [München]
Urban & Schwarzenberg [1972] 159 p. illus., ports. 26cm. 89
anatomists; biographical sketches and reproductions of their
portraits on commemorative medals, etc. Alphabetical name
index on p. 7.

11377   FREUND, HUGO, ed.
         Geschichte der Mikroskopie: Leben und Werk grosser
Forscher. Hrsg. von Hugo Freund und Alexander Berg unter
Mitarbeit namhafter Autoren. Frankfurt a. M., Umschau Verlag, 1963-   v. illus. 24cm. Each vol. includes biographies by various authors, arranged alphabetically (v. 1 contains 30 biographies; v. 2: 46 and v. 3: 58) A history of microscopy which is actually the lives and work of famous medical
researchers and pioneers of microscopy. Vol. 3 (latest?) issued
in 1966.

11378   GALERIE HERVORRAGENDER ÄRZTE UND NATURFORSCHER.
         Beilage zur Münchener medizinischen Wochenschrift.
Munich, J. F. Lehmann [1890-1914] 342 ports. (and index) 8.⁰
A collection of portraits, with index, of outstanding physicians
and scientists (mostly German) The British Museum & the John
Crerar Library, Chicago, have a copy of this work which was is-
sued in sheets over a period of 25 years.

11379   GERONTOLOGICAL SOCIETY.
         International directory of gerontology. Bethesda, Md., U.
S. Dept. of Health, Education and Welfare, National Institute of
Child Health and Human Development [1969] xiv, 339 p. 27cm.
Includes biographical sketches of persons who do research on
aging. Part 1: Biographies, United States; part 2: Biographies,
foreign.

11380   GOTFREDSEN, EDVARD, 1899-1963.
         Medicinens historie. 2. udg. Kjøbenhavn, Nyt nordisk
forlag, A. Busck, 1950. 697 p. illus. 25 cm. The history of
medicine; not a dictionary but largely a biographical compilation.
The comprehensive name index at the end of the volume leads
the reader to the many biographical sketches in the text.

11381   GOULIN, JEAN, 1728-1799.
         Mémoires littéraires, critiques, philologiques, biogra-
phiques et bibliographiques, pour servir à l'histoire ancienne &
moderne de la médecine ... Paris, Jean-François Bastien,
1777. 2 v. in 1. 26cm. Vol. [1] was first published serially in
52 parts in 1775; v. [2] was first published in 36 parts in 1776.
Literary, critical, philological, biographical and bibliographical
memoirs of the ancient and modern history of medicine; chiefly
medical bio-bibliography.

11382   GURLT, ERNST JULIUS, 1825-1899.
        Geschichte der Chirurgie und ihrer Ausübung. Volks-
chirurgie, Altertum, Mittelalter, Renaissance. Hildesheim, G.
Olms, 1964. 3 v. illus. 25cm. "Reprographischer Nachdruck
der Ausgabe Berlin 1898." A history of surgery and its practice.
The work is also, in large part, a comprehensive work of collective biography, containing over 500 lives of surgeons from
antiquity to the Renaissance. Alphabetical approach is thru' the
"Namen-Register" (p. [818]-823, v. 3).

11383   HANIN, L. (or J. L.)
        Vocabulaire médical; ou, Recueil et définition de tous les
termes employés en médecine par les auteurs anciens et modernes; suivi d'un dictionnaire biographique des médecins
célèbres de tous les temps, avec l'indication des meilleurs
ouvrages qu'ils ont publiés, et d'un tableau des signes chimiques.
Paris, Caille & Ravier, 1811. viii, 455 p. plate. 8.º A dictionary of medical terminology followed by a bio-bibliographical
dictionary of famous physicians.

11384   HERRLINGER, ROBERT, 1914-1968.
        Die Nobelpreisträger der Medizin; ein Kapitel aus der
Geschichte der Medizin. 2., erg. Aufl. [Durchgesehen und erg.
von Jorg-Dieter Herrlinger] München, H. Moos [c1971] 91 p.
ports. 25cm. Nobel Prize winners in medicine (physicians,
physiologists), 1901-1970; 106 portraits with very brief biographical data.

11385   INTERNATIONAL MEDICAL CONGRESS, 14th, MADRID, 1903.
        Recuerdo del 14. Congreso Internacional de Medicina, Ma-
drid, abril, 1903. [Leipzig, 1903] 40 groups of ports. mounted
on 40 l. 30 x 42cm. Includes 187 photographs of prominent physicians at the Congress.

11386   JOHNS HOPKINS UNIVERSITY. JOHN WORK GARRETT
        LIBRARY.
        Medals relating to medicine and allied sciences in the nu-
mismatic collection of the Johns Hopkins University. A catalogue
by Sarah Elizabeth Freeman. Baltimore, Evergreen House Foundation, 1964. xx, 430 p. 32 plates. 30cm. (Evergreen House
Foundation. Publication no. 2) 922 items described. First section, "Medals of individuals" (p. 3-274), contains an alphabetical
list (with biographical notes) of physicians and scients for whom
medals were struck.

11387   JUSTUS, WOLFGANG, 1521-1573.
        Chronologia, sive Temporum supputatio, omnium illustrium
medicorum tam veterum quam recentiorum ... a primis artis
medicae inventoribus et scriptoribus, usque ad nostram aetatem
... Francophorti ad Viadrum, J. Eichhorn, 1556. x, 174 p. 8.º
Chronology of famous men of medicine of past and present who
contributed to the art through their writings and inventiveness.

11388   KAGAN, SOLOMON ROBERT, 1881-
         The modern medical world. Portraits and biographical
sketches of distinguished men in medicine. Boston, Medico-
Historical Press, 1945. 223 p. ports. 24cm.

11389   KESTNER, CHRISTIAN WILHELM, 1694-1747.
         Medicinisches Gelehrten-Lexicon. Nebst einer Vorrede von
Gottlieb Stolle. Hildesheim, New York, G. Olms, 1971. 940 p.
22cm. Reprint of the edition published in Jena in 1740. A bio-
bibliographical dictionary of famous physicians.

11390   KILLIAN, HANS, 1892-
         Meister der Chirurgie und die Chirurgenschulen im deutsch-
en Raum: Deutschland, Österreich, deutsche Schweiz, von H.
Killian und G. Krämer. Stuttgart, G. Thieme, 1951. vii, 231 p.
25cm. Masters of surgery and schools of surgery in German-
speaking countries; includes sections on biographies of professors of medicine (surgery), chiefly 19th-20th centuries; alphabetical approach thru' index.

11391   KOLLE, KURT, 1898-   ed.
         Grosse Nervenärzte; Lebensbilder. In Gemeinschaft mit
H. J. de Barahona [et al.] hrsg. von Kurt Kolle. Stuttgart, G.
Thieme, 1956 [i. e. 1955]-63. 3 v. illus. 25cm. 66 biogra-
phies of famous neurologists-psychiatrists.

11392   LEAKE, CHAUNCEY DEPEW, 1896-
         Some founders of physiology; contributors to the growth of
functional biology. Washington, 1956. x, 122 p. illus., ports.
A souvenir publication for the 200th International Physiological
Congress, Brussels, 1956. Contains portraits and biographical
notes on over 300 deceased physiologists or contributors to the
science. Chronological arrangement, with alphabetical approach
thru' the index.

11393   LINDEN, JOHANNES ANTONIDES VAN DER, 1609-1664.
         Lindenius renovatus; sive, Johannis Antonidae van der
Linden De scriptis medicis libri duo, quorum prior, omnium,
tam veterum, quam recentiorum, Latino idiomate, typis unquam
expressorum scriptorum medicorum, consummatissimum cata-
logum continet ... posterior vero cynosuram medicam, sive,
rerum & materiarum indicem, omnium titulorum vel thematum
medicorum potiorum loca communia alphabetico ... ordine ...
exhibet ... Noviter praeter haec addita plurimorum authorum
... vitae curriculorum succincta descriptione ... Continuati,
dimidio pene amplificati, per plurimum interpolati, & ab extan-
tioribus mendis purgati a Georgio Abrahamo Mercklino. Norim-
bergae, Impensis Johannis Georgii Endteri, 1686. 1097, 160 p.
21cm. Book 2 has also separate t. p.: Cynosura medica; sive,
De scriptis medicis liber II. First published in 1662 under title:
De scriptis medicis. Concerning medical writings. Linden re-

vised; primarily bibliographical in nature, but there is biographical data for a number of the entries (ancient to early modern medicine), none for many (probably the data was not available to Linden). Arrangement is alphabetical by forename of the various writers on medicine, with an index by surname at the end of the volume.

11394   MAJOR, RALPH HERMON, 1884-
        A history of medicine. Springfield, Ill., C. C. Thomas, 1954. 2 v. (1155 p.) illus. 22cm. Includes major biographical sketches in the main text as well as "biographical addenda' at end of each section.

11395   MANSCH, ANTON
        Medical world gallery of contemporaries in the field of medical science. Berlin [19--] 1 v. 101 portraits. folio. The 101 portraits are accompanied by brief identifying sketches.

11396   LES MÉDECINS CÉLÈBRES. [Genève[Mazenod [1947] 371 p. ports. (part. col.) 30cm. (La Galerie des hommes celebres, 3) Edited by René Dumensil and Flavien Bonnet-Roy. 82 biographies and portraits of famous physicians of the world.

11397   MEDICINSKA ENCIKLOPEDIJA. [Glavni redaktor Ante Šercer] Zagreb, Izdanje i nakl. Leksikografskog zavoda FNRJ, 1957-65. 10 v. illus., ports. 30cm. A medical dictionary-encyclopedia in Serbo-Croatian which includes biographical sketches of distinguished physicians in world medical history.

11398   MOURE, JEAN GABRIEL ÉMILE, 1855-
        Galerie internationale des oto-rhino-laryngologistes. Bordeaux, G. Gounovilhou, 1908. 3 p. 188 ports. 8.° 188 portraits with short biographies. At head of title: Revue hebdomadaire de laryngologie, d'otologie et de rhinologie. International gallery (188 portraits with brief accompanying biographical sketches) of otorhinolaryngologists (late 19th, early 20th century), specialists in diseases of the nose & larynx.

11399   NEWERLA, GERHARD J   1906-
        Medical history in philately and numismatics, by Gerhard J. Newerla. [2d ed. Waltham, Mass., 1971] v, 473 p. 22cm. "Physicians on stamps: Biographies" (p. 17-170) is a biographical dictionary. "Paramedical persons of interest: Biographies" (p. 171-214) is another biographical dictionary. Farther on there are other groups of biographical sketches (e. g., Charity seals of medical interest: Biographies). There is no name index to the work as a whole, however.

11400   PAZZINI, ADALBERTO
        Bio-bibliografia di storia della chirurgia. Roma, Edizioni
Cosmopolita, 1948. 524 p. illus., ports. 21cm. Part 1, p.
21-333 contains bio-bibliographical notices of 475 surgeons from
Hippocrates to Harvey Cushing, arranged by periods and nationalities.

11401   RIEGER, HEINRICH
        Professoren der Chirurgie unserer Zeit an den Univer-
sitäten von Oesterreich-Ungarn, Deutschland, Schweiz, Belgien, Holland, Dänemark. Für das 25jährige Professoren-
Jubiläum Theodor Bilroth's gesammelt und hrsg. von Heinrich
Rieger. Nach den Original-Photographien in Lichtdruck ausge-
führt. Wien, M. Jaffé, 1893. 88 ports. on 8 plates. 4.° Professors of surgery of our time (last decade of the 19th century)
at the universities of Austria-Hungary, Germany, Switzerland,
Belgium, Holland & Denmark; a collection of 88 portraits with
signatures of the surgeons.

11402   RIVERAIN, JEAN, 1907-
        Dictionnaire des médecins célèbres. Paris, Larousse,
1969. 144 p. illus., ports. 23cm. A biographical dictionary
of famous physicians from ancient times to modern. Profusely
illustrated and accompanied by portraits.

11403   SAMBUCUS, JOHANNES, 1531-1584.
        Icones veterum aliqvot, ac recentivm medicorvm, philo-
sophorvmqve elogiolis svis editae, opera I. Sambvci. Nagedrukt
in fac-simile volgens de uitgave van Plantin van 1574, met eene
inleiding door Max Rooses. Antwerpen, Nederlandsche Boek-
handel [etc.] 1901. vii p., facsim.: 69 l. incl. plates, ports.
39cm. (Maatschappij der Antwerpsche Bibliophilen. Uitgave nr.
21) Pref. in Dutch and French. "La manière des gravures in-
dique à toute évidence que Pierre van der Borcht les exécuta à
l'eau-forte ... Tout permet d'affirmer que van der Borcht ne
grava pas seulement, mals dessina également les planches."--
Pref. Iconography (chiefly portraits, 64 in all) of some old and
recent (to the middle of the 16th century) physicians and philosophers accompanied by some words ('eulogies') about them.

11404   SCHIFFMANN, GENEVIEVE
        Medical research institutions named after medical men.
Compiled by Genevieve Schiffmann and Jaroslav Nemec. Bethes-
da, Md. [U. S. National Institutes of Health, 1969?] 79 p. 26cm.
At head of title: National Library of Medicine. Reference Services Division. Includes 311 quite brief biographical sketches of
physicians, medical researchers, etc. after whom medical lab-
oratories, research facilities, etc. are named.

11405   STILL, Sir GEORGE FREDERIC, 1868-1941.
        The history of paediatrics; the progress of the study of the

diseases of children up to the end of the XVIIIth century. London, Oxford University Press, 1931. xviii, 526 p. illus. 23cm. A general survey presented chiefly in biobibliographical format (ca. 110 biographies); alphabetical approach thru' "Index of names." Reprinted in 1965 by Dawsons of London.

11406   STIRLING, WILLIAM, 1851-1932.
Some apostles of physiology, being an account of their lives and labours. Labours that have contributed to the advancement of the healing art as well as to the prevention of disease. London, Prov. printed by Waterlow, 1902. iv, 129 p. illus., ports. 33cm. Includes 74 portraits with short biographies of ca. 90 physiologists from Vesalius to the end of the 19th century.

11407   SZÉKELY-KOVÁCS, OLGA, illus.
Caricatures of 88 pioneers in psychoanalysis, drawn from life at the eighth International Psychoanalytic Congress [by] Olga Székely-Kovács and Robert Berény. New York, Basic Books [1954] [96] p. (chiefly illus.) 23cm.

11408   TALBOTT, JOHN HAROLD, 1902-
A biographical history of medicine: excerpts and essays on the men and their work [by] John H. Talbott. New York, Grune & Stratton [1970] 1211 p. illus., ports. 27cm. Lives and portraits of several hundred physicians of the past arranged chronologically from Hammurabi and his laws concerning the practice of medicine (2250 B. C.) to F. G. Banting (1891-1941).

11409   VIERORDT, HERMANN, 1853-
Medizin-geschichtliches Hilfsbuch, mit besonderer Berücksichtigung der Entdeckungsgeschichte und der Biographie. Tübingen, H. Laupp'sche Buchhandlung, 1916. vii, 469 p. 23cm. A handbook for the history of medicine with a good deal of emphasis on bio-biographical data.

11410   ZAPRIANOV, N
Meditsinski biografichen spravochnik. [1. izd.] Plovdiv, Khristo G. Danov, 1972. 347 p. ports. 21cm. At head of title: N. Zaprianov, Gr. Naidenov. Added t. p.: Medical biographical reference book. A dictionary of medical biography.

Local

Arab

11411   AHMAD 'ISĀ.
Mu'jam al-attibā'. al-Qahirah, Matba'at Fath-Allāh al-Yās, 1942 (1361 A. H.) 527 p. 24cm. (Jāmi-ah Fu'ād al-Awwal. Kulliyāt al-Tibb, 18) A biographical dictionary of physicians

(chiefly Arab) from 650 A. H. to the early 20th century. A
supplement to the 'Uyūn al-anbā' of Ibn Abī- Usaibi'ah.

11411a IBN ABĪ USAYBI'AH, AHMAD IBN AL-QĀSIM, d. 1269 or 70.
'Uyūn al-anbā' fī tabaqāt al-atibbā'. Bayrut, Dar Maktabat
al-Hayāh, 1965. 792 p. 29cm. Sources of information on Arab
physicians; entry by forename or by best-known surname. Table of biographees at front of each volume.

Argentine Republic

11412   DICCIONARIO MÉDICO ARGENTINO. 1932-   Buenos Aires.
v. illus., ports. Editor: 1932-   E. Gajardo Cru-
gat. Argentine medical dictionary; that is, a biographical directory, with portraits, of Argentine physicians.

Austria

11413   FOSSEL, VIKTOR, 1846-1913.
Geschichte der Medizinischen Fakultät in Graz von 1863 bis
1913. Festschrift zum Feier des 50jährigen Bestandes. Im
Auftrage der Professorenkollegiums verfasst von Viktor Fossel.
Graz, Verlag der Medizinischen Fakultät; in Kommission von
Leuschner & Lubensky, 1913. 71 p. illus. 32cm. History of
the Medical Faculty of the University of Graz, 1863-1913; contains brief biographies of the most important members of the
teaching faculty and a list of professors.

Belgium

11414   FAIDHERBE, ALEXANDRE JOSEPH, 1867-
Les médecins et les chirurgiens de Flandre avant 1789.
Lille, Danel, 1892. 347 p. illus. 4.° Issued also as thesis,
Lille. Includes biographical sketches and biobibliography (the
latter on p. 296-336) of physicians of Flanders prior to 1789.

Brazil

11415   GIFFONI, O   CARNEIRO, 1912-
Dicionario bio-bibliografico brasileiro de escritores médi-
cos (1500-1899) [por] O. Carneiro Giffoni. São Paulo, Livraria
Nobel, 1972. 298 p. 24cm. A bio-bibliographical dictionary of
Brazilian medical writers, 1500-1899.

Bulgaria

11416   VISSH MEDITŜINSKI INSTITUT "I. P. PAVLOV."
         Bio-bibliografski ukazatel na nauchnite trudove na sŭtrud-
nitŝite ot instituta, 1945-1970. Sŭstaviteli: Khristina Lazarova
[i] Liŭba Dimitrova-Bozhkova. Otg. redaktor: Todor Tashev.
Bibliogr. konsultant: B. Boshinova-Troiânova. Plovdiv, Danov,
1971. 634 p. Added t. p.: Biobibliographical index of the scientific publications of the Institute members, 1945-1970, Higher
Medical Institute "I. P. Pavlov." Bulgarian physicians.

Canada

11417   AHERN, MICHAEL JOSEPH, 1844-1914.
         Notes pour servir à l'histoire de la médecine dans le Bas-
Canada depuis la fondation de Québec jusqu'au commencement
du XIXe siècle, par M.-J. & Geo. Ahern. Québec, Impr.
Laflamme, 1923. 563 p. 27cm. Notes illustrating the history
of medicine in Lower Canada after the founding of Quebec to
the beginning of the 19th century; chiefly biographical notes,
arranged alphabetically.

11418   CANNIFF, WILLIAM, 1830-1910.
         The medical profession in Upper Canada, 1783-1850: an his-
torical narrative, with original documents relating to the profession, including some brief biographies. Toronto, W. Briggs,
1894. 688 p. illus., 19 ports. 23cm. Biographical sketches:
p. 217-677.

Chile

11419   LAVAL MANRÍQUEZ, ENRIQUE
         Noticias sobre los médicos en Chile en los siglos XVI,
XVII, y XVIII. Santiago, Universidad de Chile, Centro de In-
vestigación de Historia de la Medicina, 1958. 137 p. (Biblioteca de historia de la medicina en Chile, 3) Biographical notices
of physicians in Chile in the 16th, 17th & 18th centuries.

China

11420   HUARD, PIERRE ALPHONSE, 1901-
         Bio-bibliographie de la médecine chinoise [par] Pierre Huard
et Wong. [Saigon, 1956] [181]-246 p. Reprinted from Bulletin
de la Société des études indochinoises, nouv. ser., t. 31, no.3.
A bio-bibliography of Chinese medicine; 247 names are listed,
some with several lines of biographical data, many with only a
line or two.

11421   UNITED STATES. LIBRARY OF CONGRESS.
         Chinese personalities in biomedicine; a publication of [the]

Geographic Health Studies [Project] by the John E. Fogarty International Center for Advanced Study in the Health Sciences, prepared under an interagency agreement with the Library of Congress. [Bethesda? Md.] U. S. Dept. of Health, Education and Welfare, Public Health Service, National Institutes of Health, 1975. v, 87 p. 27cm. (DHEW publication no. (NIH) 75-783) A bio-bibliographical dictionary (biographical data is primarily confined to educational and professional data, birth dates are not given) of biomedical specialists in the People's Republic of China.

Croatia

11422   BAZALA, VLADIMIR, 1901-
           Poviestni razvoj medicine u hrvatskim zemljama. Zagreb, Hrvatski izdavački bibliografski zavod, 1943. 285 p. 19cm. (Znanstvena knjižnica, 2) The historical development of medicine in Croatia; biographical dictionary (" Biografski leksikon"): p. 229-273.

Czechoslovakia

11423   MATOUŠEK, MILOSLAV, 1900-
           Malý biografický slovník československých lékařů. [Vyd. 1.] Praha, Státni pedagogické naklad, 1964. 198 p. 20cm. (Učebni texty vysokých škol) At head of title: Palackého universita v Olomouci. Fakulta lékařská. 'Little' biographical dictionary of Czech physicians.

Denmark

11424   DANSK FARMACEUTISK STAT. Odense, Dansk farmaceutforening. v. illus. 23cm. Began publication in 1898 under title: Fortegnelse over farmaceuter og apotekere i Denmark. 6th (latest?) ed., 1964, published in 1965 and edited by S. A. Simonsen. A directory, with biographical data, of Danish pharmacists.

Finland

11425   GRATSCHOFF, LOUIS, 1863-
           Finlands läkarekår jämte Finlands tandläkare; biografiska anteckningar. Mariehamn, Lundström, 1900. 236 p. 8.°
Finlands physicians and dentists; biographical notes.

11426   JOHNSON, GUNNAR, 1904-
           Suomen piirilääkarit 1749-1927. Helsinki, Suomen Sukututkimusseura, 1928. 188 p. 24cm. (Eripainos Suomen Sukututkimusseuran vuosikirjasta, 11) Finnish physicians in Finland's various departments (districts).

France

11427   ACADÉMIE NATIONALE DE MÉDECINE, PARIS.
Index biographique des membres, des associés et des
correspondants de l'Académie de médecine de 1820 a 1970,
par Maurice Genty, bibliothécaire. 2. ed. revue et complétée
par Geneviève Nicole-Genty et Monique Chapuis. Paris, Doin,
1972. xvi, 261 p. 25cm. A directory of members, associates
and correspondents of the National Academy of Medicine in
Paris from 1820 to 1970. Biographical dictionary format; very
brief biographical notations. 1st ed. was issued in 1939 and
covered the years 1820 to 1939.

11428   BALLAND, JOSEPH ANTOINE FÉLIX, 1845-
Notices biographiques sur les anciens pharmaciens in-
specteurs de l'Armée. Paris, H. Charles-Lavauzelle, 1892.
40 p. 24cm.
            and
His Travaux scientifiques des pharmaciens militaires
français. Paris, Asselin, 1882 (xxiv, 125 p. 25cm) Both of
these works were predecessors of his Les pharmaciens militaires français and contain, like it, bio-bibliographical sketches
of French military pharmacists.

11429   BEDEL, CHARLES
Figures pharmaceutiques français. Notes historiques et
portraits, 1803-1953. Paris, Masson, 1953. 275 p. ports.
29cm. Figures in French pharmacy; historical notes and portraits.

11430   BERGER, CHARLES VICTOR
Répertoire bibliographique des travaux des médicins et des
pharmaciens de la Marine française, 1698-1873, suivi d'une table méthodique des matières, par Charles Berger [et] Henri
Rey. Paris, J.-B. Baillière, 1874. iv, 282 p. 22cm. (Archives de médicine navale, t. 21. Appendice) A bibliography of
the medical & pharmaceutical works of French naval personnel.
Does include very brief biographical notes.

11431   CHEREAU, ACHILLE, 1817-1885.
Le parnasse médical francaise; ou, Dictionnaire des méde-
cins-poètes de la France, anciens ou modernes, morts ou vivants. Amsterdam, B. R. Grüner, 1972. xxiv, 552 p. 24cm.
Reprint of the Paris (A. Delahaye) 1874 edition. The French
medical Parnassus; or, Dictionary of physician-poets of France.

11432   DULIEU, LOUIS
La chirurgie à Montpellier de ses origines au début du
XIXe siècle. [Avignon?] Presses universelles [1975] 345 p.
illus. 24cm. "Biographie des chirurgiens et des chirurgiens

barbiers ayant exercé à Montpellier depuis le XIIe siècle
jusqu'à la Révolution": p. [229]-315. Surgery at Montpellier,
France from its origins to the beginning of the 19th century.
Pages [229]-315 contain a biographical dictionary of surgeons
and barber-surgeons who practiced in Montpellier from the
13th century to the French Revolution.

11433   DULIEU, LOUIS
         La pharmacie à Montpellier de ses origines à nos jours.
[Avignon? France] Presses universelles, 1973. 343 p. illus.,
ports. 24cm. Pharmacy in Montpellier, France from its origins to the present day. "Biographie des apothicaires de
Montpellier depuis le haut moyen âge jusqu'au XIXe siècle" (p.
[227]-290); "Biographie succincte des maîtres ayant enseigné
à l'École et à la Faculté de pharmacie de Montpellier" (p. [291]-
302); and "Biographie ... XIXe et au XXe siècle" (p. [303]-314)
are three biographical dictionaries of pharmacists of the City of
Montpellier in various time periods and at the School and Faculty of Pharmacy of the University of Montpellier.

11434   FLORANGE, CHARLES
         Les jetons des doyens de l'ancienne Faculté de médecine de
Paris, 1636-1793. Paris, Jules Florange, 1933. x, 54 p. illus.
26cm. Medals portraying the senior members and deans of the
old Faculty of Medicine of the University of Paris, 1636-1793.

11435   FOURNIÉ, H
         Les jetons des doyens de l'ancienne Faculté de médecine de
Paris. Chalon-sur-Saone, E. Bertrand, 1907. iii, 180+ p.
plates, ports. 8.º Reprinted from Gazette numismatique.
Brussels, 1906, t. 12, p. 225-383; 1907, t. 13, p. 1-27. Medals
portraying the members of the old Faculty of Medicine of the
University of Paris.

11436   LACHAISE, CLAUDE, b. 1797.
         Les médecins de Paris jugés par leurs oeuvres; ou, Stati-
stique scientifique et morale des médecins de Paris. Contenant,
par ordre alphabétique, indépendamment de tout ce qu'on trouve
dans les annuaires, l'exposé exact et l'appréciation impartiale
des travaux et des opinions de tous les professeurs de l'école,
de tous les membres de l'Académie ou médecins des hôpitaux,
de tous les spécialistes ou praticiens connus, voire même des
charlatans, par C. Sachaile [pseud.] Paris, Chez l'auteur, 1845.
634 p. 23cm. The physicians of Paris judged by their works.
In alphabetical arrangement the work contains numerous facts of
biographical significance.

11437   ROGER, JULES, 1839-
         Les médecins bretons du XVIe au XXe siècle; biographie
et bibliographie. Paris, J.-B. Baillière, 1900. xiii, 198 p.
ports. 25cm. Bio-bibliographical sketches of 51 physicians in
Brittany, 14th to the 20th century.

11438   ROGER, JULES, 1839-
Les médecins normands du XIIe au XIXe siècle. Biographie
et bibliographie. Paris, G. Steinheil, 1890-95. 2 v. ports.
25cm. Bio-bibliography of French physicians from Normandy,
12th to the 19th century. Vol. 1, e. g., includes 121 bio-bibliographical sketches of physicians in the department of Seine-Inférieure. Contents. --[t. 1] Seine-Inférieure. --t. 2. Calvados,
Manche, Orne, et Eure.

Germany

11439   DEUTSCHE APOTHEKER-BIOGRAPHIE.   Hrsg. von Wolf-
gang-Hagen Hein und Holm-Dietmar Schwarz. Stuttgart,
Wissenschaftliche Verlagsgesellschaft, 1975-   v.
21cm. (Veröffentlichungen der Internationalen Gesellschaft für
Geschichte der Pharmazie, neue Folge, Bd. 43
A biographical dictionary (to be in 2 vols.) of German pharmacists from the Middle Ages to 1950; a contemplated supplementary volume will cover pharmacists who died between 1950 and
1970. Contents. --Bd. 1. A-L.

11440   DEUTSCHER CHIRURGEN-KALENDER. Verzeichnis der
deutschen Chirurgen und Orthopäden mit Biographien und
bibliographischen Skizzen. Hrsg. von A. Borchard und W. v.
Brunn. Leipzig, J. A. Barth, 1920. iv, 277 p. 19cm. A calendar of German surgeons; a list of German surgeons and or-
thopedists with biographies and bibliographical sketches.

11441   FREY, RUDOLF, 1917-
Verzeichnis der Fachärzte fur Anaesthesiologie in Deutschland, Österreich und in der Schweiz. In Einvernehmen mit der
Deutschen Gesellschaft für Anaesthesie und Wiederbelebung [et
al.] hrsg. von R. Frey und H. Kronschwitz. Berlin, Springer,
1966. xii, 229 p. ports. 24cm. List of anaesthesiologists in
Germany, Austria and Switzerland (with brief biographical information and publications).

11442   GAUSS, CARL J
Die deutschen Geburtshelferschulen; Bausteine zur
Geschichte der Geburtshilfe[von]C. J. Gauss und B. Wilde.
München, Banaschewski, 1956. 333 p. ports. German schools
of obstetrics. Brief biographies on p. 90-326.

11443   GOTTLIEB, BERNWARD JOSEF
Das Antlitz des germanischen Aerztes in vier Jahrhunderten, von Bernward J. Gottlieb und Alexander Berg. Berlin,
Rembrandt-Verlag [1942] 212 p. 200 ports. 27cm. The face
of the German physician in 4 centuries; 200 portraits included.

11444   KIRCHHOFF, THEODOR, 1853-1922.
        Deutsche Irrenärzte: Einzelbilder ihres Lebens und Wirkens.
        Hrsg. mit Unterstützung der Deutschen Forschungsanstalt für
        Psychiatrie in München, sowie zahlreicher Mitarbeiter. Ber-
        lin, J. Springer, 1921-24. 2 v. ports. 25cm. Contains biogra-
        phical studies of 118 German psychiatrists, primarily of the 18th
        through the early 20th century.

11445   MEDICINISCHES DEUTSCHLAND; Gallerie von Zeitgenossen
        auf dem Gebiete der medicinischen Wissenschaften. Ber-
        lin, A. Eckstein, 1902. 1 v. (unpaged) ports. folio. Medicine
        in Germany; a gallery of contemporaries in the field of the medi-
        cal sciences.

11446   SCHOLZ, HARRY, 1879-1969.
        Ärzte in Ost- und Westpreussen; Leben und Leistung seit
        dem 18. Jahrhundert. Zusammengestellt und hrsg. von Harry
        Scholz und Paul Schroeder. Würzburg, Holzner, 1970. x, 330 p.
        illus., ports. 22cm. (Ostdeutsche Beiträge aus dem Göttinger
        Arbeitskreis, Bd. 48) Physicians in East and West Prussia since
        the 18th century. Includes ca. 75 biographical sketches as well
        as many even briefer ones buried in the text, but reclaimable
        through the index. Useful too for its fairly numerous portraits.

11447   WHO'S WHO IN MEDICINE. Edition Germany. Ottobrunn [bei
        Munich] Who's Who-Book and Pub. GmbH, 1973. xi, 509 p.
        This 'Edition 1' is a biographical dictionary containing some
        4700 biographies of prominent people in the sector of medicine,
        within Germany and 246 organizations.

Great Britain

Bibliography, Indexes, Portrait Catalogs

11448   ROYAL COLLEGE OF PHYSICIANS OF LONDON.
        Catalogue of engraved portraits in the Royal College of Phy-
        sicials, by A. H. Driver. London, 1952 [i. e. 1953] 219 p. 8.°
        A list of 4500 prints of physicians & scientists (largely British)
        with alphabetical arrangement by person. Identifies and gives
        dates for subjects of the portraits, painter and engraver.

11449   ROYAL COLLEGE OF PHYSICIANS OF LONDON.
        A descriptive catalogue of the portraits, busts, silver and
        other objects of interest in the Royal College of Physicians of
        London. [By Arnold Chaplin] London, 1926. 70 p.

11450   ROYAL COLLEGE OF PHYSICIANS OF LONDON.
        Index of portraits in books; physicians, surgeons, and oth-

ers, maintained in the Library of the Royal College of Physicians. London, Royal College of Physicians and Micro Methods,
ltd., 1964. microfilm (2 reels, 35mm.) Copy of a card file;
portraits in serials or in individual biographies not indexed.

General Works

11451   MONRO, THOMAS KIRKPATRICK, 1805-
        The physician as a man of letters, science, and action. 2d
ed. Edinburgh, E. & S. Livingstone, 1951. 259 p. 23cm. Short
biographical sketches of ca. 550 physicians, primarily British,
who gained fame in fields other than medicine. Arranged under
subjects, e. g., drama, saints, soldiers, crime, etc. First
edition issued in 1933.

11452   ROBINSON, RONALD HENRY OTTYWELL BETHAM
        Lives of the fellows of the Royal College of Surgeons of
England, 1952-1964, by R. H. O. B. Robinson and W. R. Le
Fanu. With a foreword by Sir Cecil Wakeley. Edinburgh, E.
& S. Livingstone, 1970. 470 p. 25cm. 3 earlier volumes
covering the years 1843-1951 were compiled by Victor G. Plarr
& Sir D'Arcy Power. A biographical dictionary; ca. 800 entries.

11453   SMITH, ROBERT WILLIAM INNES
        English speaking students of medicine at the University of
Leyden. With a foreword by John D. Comrie. Edinburgh,
Oliver & Boyd, 1932. xxiii, 258 p. port. 24cm. A 'biographical dictionary'; biographical notes are often extremely brief,
reflecting the scarcity of biographical data available.

Hungary

11454   WESZPRÉMI, ISTVÁN, 1723-1799.
        Magyarország és Erdély orvosainak rövid életrajza. Suc-
cincta medicorum Hungariae et Transylvaniae biographia.
Budapest, Medicina Könyvkiadó, 1960-70. 4 v. illus. 19cm.
(Ovostörténeti könyvek) First published in Vienna (J. O. Trat-
tner) 1774-1787. Brief biographies of the earliest Hungarian
and Transylvanian physicians. Each volume (covering a century) is alphabetical in arrangement (A-Z).

India

11455   DIRECTORY & WHO'S WHO OF HOMOEOPATHIC PRACTI-
        TIONERS. 1970-71--   New Delhi, M/S. B. Jain.
        v. ports. 25cm. irregular. Included are two sections:
(1) Leading foreign homoeopathic practitioners--primarily a
listing, with some portraits and biographical sketches, and (2)
Leading Indian homoeopathic practitioners--a biographical dictionary, with portraits, of India's leaders in the field.

11456   GIRINDRANATH MUKHOPADHYAYA.
        History of Indian medicine, containing notices, biographical
and bibliographical, of the ayurvedic physicians and their works
on medicine, from the earliest ages to the present time. 2d ed.
New Delhi, Oriental Books Reprint Corp. ; distributed by Mun-
shiram Manoharlal Publishers, 1974. 3 v. 23cm. Includes
passages in Sanskrit. Reprint of the 1923-29 ed. (University of
Calcutta). Vols. 2-3 are biographical; they contain over 100 bio-
bibliographical notices of ancient Indic physicians skilled in
herbal medicine, materia medica, etc. (some of the entries are
of mythological personages).

11457   SRIKANTA MURTHY, K   R   1929-
        Luminaries of Indian medicine, from the earliest times to
the present day. Foreword by P. M. Mehta. [1st ed. Mysore]
1968. xii, 152 p. 22cm. Published serially in the National
medical journal, Mysore. Includes quotations in Sanskrit. In
3 sections: (1) Mythological personages: 16 names. (2) Semi-
historical personages: 27. (3) Historical personages: 130. Alphabetical approach thru' the index at end.

Italy

11458   BRAMBILLA, GIAN ALESSANDRO, 1750-1800.
        Storia delle scoperte fisico-medico-anatomiche-chirur-
giche fatte dagli nomini illustri italiani. [Milano, A. Maggiore,
1780-82] 2 v. in 3. illus. 30cm. A history of medical discoveries made by Italian physicians, physiologists and anatomists
which is actually an extensive collection of biographical sketches
arranged chronologically in v. 1 and geographically in v. 2.
Each part of v. 2 (which is in 2 parts) contains an alphabetical
index to the biographies.

11459   MITARITONNA, ONOFRIO
        Notizie, poco conosciute, di vita quotidiana riguardanti medi-
ci, alcuni noti altri meno noti, dal secolo X al secolo XIX. Roma, Arti grafiche E. Cossidente, 1968. 209 p. 24cm. At head
of title: Istituto di storia della medicina dell'Università di Roma.
Little-known notices on the daily life of Italian physicians, 10th
to the 19th century. Gives references to sources of the notices
as well as biographical data for some of the physicians. Broken
down by century; alphabetical listing within each century.

Jews

Bibliography, Indexes, Portrait Catalogs

11460   KOREN, NATHAN
        Jewish physicians; a biographical index. Jerusalem, Is-
rael Universities Press, 1973. 275 p. 28cm. Physicians who

lived and worked from the 1st century B. C. E. to the present;
indexes 152 collective biographical volumes and histories of
medicine.

11461   STEINSCHNEIDER, MORITZ, 1816-1907.
        Jüdische Aerzte. (In Zeitschrift für hebräische Bibliog-
        raphie. Berlin, S. Calvary; Frankfurt a. M., M. J. Kauff-
        mann. Jahrg. 17 (1914) p. 63-96, 121-167; Jahrg. 18 (1915),
        p. 25-57; Jahrg. 19 (1916), p. 22-36; Jahrg. 20 (1917), p. 44-
        48, 69-71; Jahrg. 22 (1919), p. 76-89; Jahrg. 23 (1920), p. 40-
        62; Jahrg. 24 (1921), p. 1-21)   A list of 3,014 Jewish physi-
        cians throughout history, with biographical references, complet-
        ed by A. Freimann and L. Lewin. The periodical in which this
        work was found was reprinted in 1973 by G. Olms, Hildesheim
        and New York.

General Works

11462   FRIEDENWALD, HARRY, 1864-1950.
        Jewish luminaries in medical history, and a Catalogue of
        works bearing on the subject of Jews and medicine from the pri-
        vate library of Harry Friedenwald. Baltimore, Johns Hopkins
        Press, 1946. viii, 199 p. plates. 24cm. Part 1 of the Catalogue
        is a 'bio-bibliographical' (but chiefly bibliographical) dictionary;
        it "lists the writings of individual physicians and publications
        concerning them" as well as a line or several lines about their
        lives and achievements.

Netherlands

11463   BANGA, JELLE
        Geschiedenis van de geneeskunde en van hare beoefenaaren
        in Nederland, vóór en na de stichting der Hoogeschool te Leiden
        tot aan den dood van Boerhaave; uit de bronnen toegelicht.
        Leeuwarden, Eckhoff, 1868. 2 v. (viii, 903 p.) 8.⁰   History of
        medicine and its practitioners in the Netherlands. Documented
        biographies of Dutch physicians to the time of Boerhaave. In
        chronological arrangement.

11464   KRUL, R
        Haagsche doctoren, chirurgen en apothekers in den ouden
        tijd. Archief-studien. 's-Gravenhage, W. P. van Stockum,
        1891. 220 p. 8.⁰   Physicians, surgeons and pharmacists in
        The Hague of former times.

Norway

11465   KOBRO, ISAK, 1867-
        Norges laeger, 1909-1925. Oslo, H. Aschehoug, 1927.

434 p. ports. 25cm. Continues his Norges laeger, 1800-1908.
A biographical dictionary of Norway's physicians, 1909-1925.
Kobro also issued a less comprehensive edition for the years
1909-1915 (Kristiana, A. Cammermeyer, 1916—114 p.)

11466   NORGES LEGER. 1967. Red. Bernhard Getz. [Utg. av Den
         Norske laegeforening] Oslo, Centraltrykkeriet, 1968.
         567 p. ports. 25cm. Earlier editions are entered under:
         Kobro, Isak, 1867-1953. Norges laeger. Norway's physicians
         as of 1967.

11467   NORSKE MILITAERLAEGER, 1882-1932. Biografier og bil-
            leder. Oslo, Grøndahl, 1932. 203 p. ports. Norwegian
         military and naval doctors.

Peru

11468   VALDIZÁN, HERMILIO, 1885-1929.
            Diccionario de medicina peruana. A-C. Lima [i. e.
         Magdalena del Mar] Hosp. Victor Larco Herrera, 1923-38.
         3 pts. in 2 v. A dictionary of Peruvian medicine which includes
         historical, topical, and biographical entries. No more publish-
         ed?

Poland

11469   ALBUM ZASŁUŻONYCH LEKARZY POLSKICH.
            Warszawa, Redakcja Albumu Zasłużonych Lekarzy Polskich,
         1925. 136 p. 19 x 38cm. Album of eminent Polish physicians.

11470   GASIOROWSKI, LUDWIK, 1807-1863.
            Zbiór wiadomości do historyi sztuki lekarskiéj w Polsce od
         czasów najdawniejszych, aż do najnowszych. W Poznaniu, 1839-
         55. 4 v. 8.º Collected material for a history of medicine in
         Poland from the most ancient to the most recent period; mainly
         devoted to bio-bibliographic material on Polish physicians or
         alien physicians active in Poland. Groupings are by medical
         specialties.

11471   GIEDROYĆ, FRANCISZEK, 1860-
            Zródła biograficzno-bibliograficzne do dziejów medycyny w
         dawnej Polsce. Warszawa, Druk K. Kowalewskiego, 1911. 942,
         xxiv p. 22cm. Bio-bibliographical sources for the history of
         medicine in old Poland.

11472   HERMAN, EUFEMIUSZ J
            Neurolodzy polscy. [Wyd. 1.] Warszawa, Państwowy
         Zakład Wydawnictw Lekarskich, 1958. 462 p. ports. 20cm.
         Polish neurologists. Includes a large number of portraits.

Portugal

11473   FONSECA BENAVIDES, IGNACIO ANTONIO DA, 1788-1857.
Bibliographia medica portuguesa. [Lisboa] Jornal da Sociedade de [i. e. das] Sciencias Medicas de Lisboa, 1840-4) 1 v.
(various pagings) Taken from the Jornal of the Sociedade for
1840-42. Bio-bibliography of Portuguese medicine.

Russia

11474   KHARKOV. UNIVERSITET.
Meditsinskiĭ fakul'tet Khar'kovskogo universiteta za pervye
sto let ego sushchestvovaniiā (1805-1905) I. Istoriiā fakul'teta.
II. Istoricheskie ocherki kafedr. III. Biograficheskiĭ slovar'
professorov i prepodavateleĭ. Pod red. I. Skvortsova i D. I.
Bagaleiā. Khar'kov, Izd. Universiteta Khar'kova, 1905-06.
vi, 472, 374, xvi p. 25cm. Pt. 3 is a biographical dictionary
of the professors and teachers on the Faculty of Medicine of
Kharkov University, 1805-1905.

11475   RICHTER, WILHELM MICHAEL VON, 1767-1822.
Geschichte der Medicin in Russland. [Unveränderter
Nachdruck der Originalausgabe 1813-1817] Moskwa, Gedruckt
bei N. S. Wsewolojsky, 1813-[17. Leipzig, Zental-Antiquariat
der Deutschen Demokratischen Republik, 1965] 3 v. port.
21cm. This history of medicine in Russia is largely a series of
biographical sketches of physicians who served at the courts of
or during the reigns of the various Russian sovereigns; arrangement of the biographies is, in fact, chronological by reign. The
index at the end of vol. 3 affords an alphabetical approach to the
many biographies.

11476   SOVIET PERSONALITIES IN BIOMEDICINE. [Washington]
U. S. Dept. of Health, Education and Welfare, Public Health
Service, National Institutes of Health, 1974. xx, 968 p. 27cᵐ.
"A publication of the Geographic Health Studies Program of th.
John E. Fogarty International Center for Advanced Study in the
Health Sciences. Prepared under an interagency agreement with
the Library of Congress."

Savoy

11477   MALACARNE, VINCENZO, 1744-1816.
Delle opere de' medici, e de' cerusici che nacquero o
fiorirono prima del secolo XVI negli Stati della real casa di
Savoja monumenti. [Torino] Stamperia reale, 1786-89. 2 v.
4.° Physicians and surgeons who were born or flourished in
the lands of the House of Savoy prior to the 16th century.

Slovakia

11478   RIPPA, B   K ,
        K histórii mediciny na Slovensku. Bratislava, Vyd-vo Slo-
        venskej akadémie vied, 1956. 200 p. illus., ports. The 2d
        part of this history of medicine in Slovakia contains a bio-bibli-
        ographical overview of physicians, chiefly Slovakians.

South Africa

11479   BURROWS, EDMUND H
        A history of medicine in South Africa up to the end of the
        nineteenth century. Cape Town, Published under the auspices
        of the Medical Association of South Africa by A. A. Balkema,
        1958. 389 p. illus. 25cm. A major portion of the volume con-
        sists of biographical sketches; alphabetical approach thru' index.

Spain

11480   GRANJEL, LUIS S
        Indice de médicos españoles, por Luis Sánchez Granjel y
        Ma. T. Santander Rodríguez. Salamanca [Universidad de Sala-
        manca] 1962. 111 p. 25cm. (Acta Salmanticensia. Medicina,
        t. 7, no. 1) Index to biographies of Spanish physicians; analyzes
        66 collective biographical works.

General Works

11481   AGULLÓ Y COBO, MERCEDES
        Documentos sobre médicos españoles de los siglos XVI al
        XVII. Salamanca, Universidad de Salamanca, Ediciones del
        Seminario de Historia de la Medicina Española, 1969. 111 p.
        25cm. (Cuadernos de historia de la medicina española. Mono-
        grafías, 12) In biographical dictionary format; contains short
        biographical notes on Spanish physicians of the 16th-17th centu-
        ries, with excerpts from manuscripts that further document
        biographical data.

11482   ÁLVAREZ-SIERRA, JOSÉ
        Diccionario de autoridades médicas. Madrid, Editora ,
        Nacional, 1963. xii, 593 p. 24cm. (Colección Mundo cientí-
        fico. Série médical) Dictionary of Spanish medical experts.

11483   ARCHIVOS MÉDICO-BIOGRÁFICOS; doctorado médico. Bar-
        celona [195-?]   no. illus., ports. Medical-biographi-
        cal archives of Spain; a periodical.

11484   CHINCHILLA, ANASTASIO, 1801-1865.
        Anales históricos de la medicina en general y biográfico-
bibliográficos de la española en particular. With a new introd.
by Francisco Guerra, and Indices de las obras de Hernández
Morejón y Chinchilla, by Rafael Sancho de San Román. New
York, Johnson Reprint Corp., 1967. 4 v. facsims., ports.
24cm. (The Sources of science, no. 8) Facsim. of the Valencia 1841-46 ed. Historical annals of medicine in general and bio-
bibliography of Spanish medicine in particular. Contains a huge
amount of biographical material; the alphabetical approach to
this material must be made through the index preceding the text
of vol. 1.

11485   DICCIONARIO BIOGRÁFICO MÉDICO MUNDIAL. 1-   ed.;
        1958-   Barcelona.   v. illus., ports. Editor: 1958-
        G. Monge Muley. Directory and biographical dictionary of
contemporary medical men in Spain and Spanish-speaking Countries.

11486   GARCÍA DEL REAL, EDUARDO, 1870-
        Historia de la medicina en España. Madrid, Editorial
Reus, 1921. 1148 p. 23cm. (Biblioteca médica de autores
españoles y extranjeros, v. 23) A comprehensive biographical
survey of Spanish medicine up to & through the 19th century.

11487   PLATA Y MARCOS, MIGUEL DE LA, 1837-1885.
        Colección bio-bibliográfica de escritores médicos españoles.
(In Gaceta de sanidad militar. Madrid, 1880. t. 6) A bio-bibliographical collection of Spanish medical authors.

Sweden

11488   SJÖBERG, NILS
        Porträtt af svenska läkare och apotekare, beskrifna af N.
Sjöberg. Utg. af Svenska läkaresällskapet. Stockholm, Nordisk
bokhandel, 1911. viii, 128 p. 209 ports., 6 plates. Issued in
3 fascicles. Portraits of 209 Swedish physicians and pharmacists.

11489   SVERIGES LÄKAREHISTORIA IFRÅN KONUNG GUSTAF DEN
        I:s TILL NÄVARANDE TID. 1.-   följden. Stockholm,
Norstedt [etc.] 1822-   v. Editors: [1. foljden] and
suppl., Joh. Fredr. Sacklen.--[1. följden] nytt suppl., A.
Hilarion Wistrand.--[2. följden, A. Hilarion Wistrand [et al.]--
3. följden, A. J. Bruzelius.--4. följden, A. Widstrand.
3. följden has added title: Svensk läkare-matrikel. 3. följden,
4. delen includes Förteckning öfver svenska läkare intill år 1901,
tillika utgörande register till Sveriges läkarehistoria ... 1., 2.,
3. foljden. Last volume appeared in 1935? (V-Ö, jämte supplement; utg. på uppdrag av Svenska läkaresällskapet). History of
Swedish physicians from the reign of King Gustav I (1523-1560)
to ----; actually a biographical dictionary.

Switzerland

11490   BUESS, HEINRICH, 1911-
         Schweizer Aerzte als Forscher, Entdecker und Erfinder.
         Basel, Ciba A. G., 1946. 137 p. 60 ports. Swiss physicians
         as researchers, discoverers and inventors; 60 portraits and
         biographies. On cover: Ausstellung von Büchern und hand-
         schriftlichen Dokumenten veranstaltet mit Unterstützung der
         Ciba Aktiengesellschaft, Basel, von der Zentralbibliothek,
         Zürich.

United States

Bibliography, Indexes, Portrait Catalogs

11491   HUME, EDGAR ERSKINE, 1889-
         The medals of the United States Army Medical Department
         and medals honoring Army medical officers. New York, Ameri-
         can Numismatic Society, 1942. 146 p. 23 plates on 12 l., port.
         (Numismatic notes and monographs, no. 98)

General Works

11492   AMERICAN GYNECOLOGICAL SOCIETY.
         Album of the fellows of the American Gynecological Society,
         1876-1930. Floyd Elwood Keene, editor. Philadelphia, W. J.
         Dornan, 1930. 640 p. ports. 23cm. Brief biographies, with
         portraits. An earlier edition covering the years 1876-1917 was
         issued in 1918.

11493   BLANTON, WYNDHAM BOLLING, 1890-1960.
         Medicine in Virginia in the seventeenth century. New York,
         Arno Press, 1972 [c1930] 337 p. illus. 23cm. (Medicine &
         society in America) "A brief biographical dictionary of 17th
         century Virginia physicians": p. 260-297. Information is often
         identifying data only.

11494   BRADFORD, THOMAS LINDSLEY, 1847-1918.
         Biographical index of the graduates of the Homoeopathic
         Medical College of Pennsylvania and the Hahnemann Medical
         College and Hospital of Philadelphia, including a history of the
         College and Hospital. A list of all the graduates arranged by
         years of graduation. Also a list of the graduates who are now
         in the medical military service of the United States. Philadel-
         phia, Published by subscription, 1918. xix, 436 p. 24cm.

11495   CORDELL, EUGENE FAUNTLEROY, 1843-1913.
         The medical annals of Maryland, 1799-1899. Prepared for

the centennial of the Medical and Chirurgical Faculty. Baltimore, Press of Williams & Wilkins Co., 1903. 889 p. illus., ports. 25cm. In part a revision of Quinan's Medical annals ot Baltimore from 1608 to 1880 (q.v.). Includes ca. 2400 biographical sketches and detailed memoirs of 12 founders and leaders in medicine in Maryland and the University of Maryland.

11496   COWEN, DAVID LAURENCE
          The New Jersey Pharmaceutical Association, 1870-1970; containing a history of the Association, historical vignettes of New Jersey pharmacy, a biographical register of the members of the Association [by] David L. Cowen. Trenton, New Jersey Pharmaceutical Association, 1970. xii, 239 p. illus., ports. 26cm. "The biographical register": p. 138-228; a biographical dictionary of New Jersey pharmacists.

11497   DIRECTORY OF OSTEOPATHIC SPECIALISTS. 1st ed. Chicago, Published for the American Osteopathic Association by Marquis Who's Who, 1974. xvi, 247 p. 24cm. A biographical directory of osteopaths in the United States.

11498   FISHBEIN, MORRIS, 1889-
          A history of the American Medical Association, 1847 to 1947, by Morris Fishbein; with the biographies of the presidents of the Association, by Walter L. Bierring; and with histories of the publications, councils, bureaus and other official bodies [by various authors] Philadelphia, Saunders [1947] xvi, 1226 p. illus., ports. 26cm. Biographies and portraits of the 101 presidents of the Association: p. [567]-830.

11499   FRANK, LOUIS FREDERICK, 1857-1941.
          The medical history of Milwaukee, 1834-1914. Milwaukee, Germania Pub. Co., 1915. xvi, 272 p. illus., 27cm. "Contents: Biographies of deceased physicians, 1834-1914" leads the user, via an alphabetical listing, to 184 biographical sketches (often accompanied by portraits).

11500   GOLDSTEIN, MAX AARON, 1870-
          One hundred years of medicine and surgery in Missouri; historical and biographical reviews of the careers of the physicians and surgeons of the State of Missouri, and sketches of some of its notable medical institutions. 364 p. illus., ports. 25cm. Biographies on p. 208-360.

11501   HERRINGSHAW, THOMAS WILLIAM, 1858-
          The American physician and surgeon blue book. A distinct cyclopedia of 1919. Five thousand medical biographies. Chicago, American blue book publishers, 1919. 478 p.

11502   JACKSON, RUSSELL LEIGH
        The physicians of Essex County. (In Essex Institute, Salem,
    Mass. Historical Collections. v. 83 (1947) p. 162-177, 249-272,
    377-392; v. 84 (1948) p. 75-90, 169-192, 277-292, 331-348.
    ports.) A biographical dictionary of medical doctors of Essex
    County, Massachusetts.

11503   JOHNSON AND JOHNSON, INC. ETHICON SUTURE DIVISION.
        Portraits of great American surgeons by famous American
    artists. [New Brunswick, N. J., 1944-   v. col. ports.
    30 x 26cm. Short biography of subject and of artist on versos
    facing each portrait. Contents. --1st ser. From the collection of
    the School of Medicine, University of Pennsylvania. Introd. by
    William Pepper III. No more published?

11504   KAGAN, SOLOMON ROBERT, 1881-
        American Jewish physicians of note; biographical sketches.
    Illustrated with 129 ports. Boston, Boston Medical Pub. Co.,
    1942. 304 p. 129 ports. 24cm. A supplement to the author's
    Jewish contributions to medicine in America.

11505   KEMPER, GENERAL WILLIAM HARRISON, 1839-
        A medical history of the State of Indiana. Chicago, Ameri-
    can Medical Association Press, 1911. xxv, 393 p. illus., ports.
    21cm. Includes biographical data in its historical sketches of
    counties and cities, and a list of deceased physicians (with bio-
    graphical data and publications) on p. 231-371: "Alphabetical list
    of deceased physicians").

11506   LARSELL, OLOF, 1886-1964.
        The doctor in Oregon; a medical history. Portland, Bin-
    fords & Mort for the Oregon Historical Society, 1947. x, 671 p.
    illus., ports. 25cm. Physicians to 1900 (biographies, by coun-
    ty): p. 161-342. Women physicians to 1900: p. 414-419.

11507   MEDICAL SOCIETY OF THE DISTRICT OF COLUMBIA.
        History of the Medical Society of the District of Columbia.
    Washington, 1909-47. 2 v. ports. 24cm. Contents. --[pt. 1]
    1817-1909. --pt. 2. 1833-1944. Includes biographies and lists of
    members. Compiled by committees under the chairmanship of
    Daniel S. Lamb and John B. Nichols.

11508   MEDICAL WORLD; biographical sketches of notable physicians
        and surgeons of the present. New York, Berlin Pub. Co.
    [1910?] [142] p. ports. 40cm. 109 portraits and brief biogra-
    phies; chiefly American physicians.

11509   NEW YORK ACADEMY OF MEDICINE.
         Collection of portraits of fellows. New York [1896?] 1 v.
(168 plates (ports.)) American physicians of the 19th century;
portraits.

11510   OHIO. STATE UNIVERSITY, COLUMBUS. COLLEGE OF
         MEDICINE.
         The Ohio State University College of Medicine. Blanchester,
Ohio, Brown Pub. Co., 1934-61. 2 v. illus., ports. 24cm.
Vol. 2 has imprint: Columbus, Ohio State University. Vol. 1
edited by Harlow Lindley; v. 2 by N. Paul Hudson. Contents.--
v. 1. A collection of source materials covering a century of
medical progress, 1834-1934.--v. 2. 1934-1958. Vol. 1 includes extensive medical biographical sketches.

11512   PHILLIPS, PAUL CHRISLER, 1883-1956.
         Medicine in the making of Montana. Written by Paul C.
Phillips from his own researches and the pioneer manuscripts
of Llewellyn L. Callaway. Additional researches and notes by
contributors. Missoula, Published by Montana State University
Press [for] the Montana Medical Association, 1962. 564 p.
illus. 24cm. In large part a biographical compilation, with
many biographical sketches in the main text and supplementary
biographical notes arranged by county.

11513   QUEBBEMAN, FRANCES E
         Medicine in Territorial Arizona. Phoenix, Arizona Histori-
cal Foundation, 1966. xxi, 424 p. illus., ports. 24cm. Includes biographical notes (p. 325-381) in the form of a biographical dictionary.

11514   RED, MRS. GEORGE PLUNKETT
         The medicine man in Texas, by George Plunkett Red (Mrs.
S. C. Red) [Houston, Standard Print & Lithographing Co.
1930] 344 p. illus., ports. 20cm. Collected biographies of
Texas physicians: p. 111-340.

11515   STRIKER, CECIL, 1897-
         Medical portraits. Edited by Cecil Striker. Cincinnati,
Academy of Medicine of Cincinnati, 1963. 279 p. ports. 22cm.
Biographical sketches of 79 Ohio physicians reprinted from the
Cincinnati journal of medicine.

11516   TYLER, ALBERT FRANKLIN, 1881-1944.
         History of medicine in Nebraska. Albert F. Tyler, editor.
Ella F. Auerbach, compiler. Omaha, Magic City Print. Co.,
1928. 662 p. illus., ports. A 'biographic history,' with a
directory of living physicians (p. 549-662)

11517   UNDERWOOD, FELIX JOEL, 1882-
         Public health and medical licensure in the State of Missis-
sippi, [by] Felix J. Underwood and R. N. Whitfield. Jackson
[Tucker Print. House] 1938-[51] 2 v. illus., ports. 24cm.
Contents. --v. 1. 1798-1937.--v. 2. 1938-1947. Includes biographies of physicians and lists of officials.

11518   WALSH, JAMES JOSEPH, 1865-1942.
         History of medicine in New York; three centuries of medi-
cal progress. New York, National Americana Society, 1919.
5 v. illus., ports. 24cm. Vols. 4-5 are devoted to bio-bibliographies of New York State physicians.

11519   WARING, JOSEPH IOOR, 1897-
         A history of medicine in South Carolina, 1670-1825. With
a foreword by Richard H. Shryock. Charleston, South Carolina
Medical Association, 1964. xviii, 407 p. illus., ports. 24cm.
Biographical section (South Carolina physicians): p. 173-330, in
dictionary arrangement.

11520   WICKES, STEPHEN, 1813-1889.
         History of medicine in New Jersey, and of its medical men,
from the settlement of the province to A. D. 1800. Newark, N.
J., Dennis, 1879. 449 p. 24cm. A comprehensive biographical dictionary of New Jersey physicians is included on p. 123-
438.

Venezuela

11521   ARCHILA, RICARDO, 1909-
         Diccionario biográfico de médicos venezolanos: ensayo:
letro A. Caracas, Tip. Vargas, 1974. 105 p. 23cm. An at-
tempt at a dictionary of Venezuelan physicians, covering the
letter A.

11522   ARCHILA, RICARDO, 1909-
         La literatura venezolana y su historia; presencia de médi-
cos. Caracar [i.e. Caracas] 1971. xv, 421 p. ports. 23cm.
A bio-bibliographical dictionary of Venezuelan physicians, psychiatrists, pharmacists and other persons in the medical sciences who were also writers.

11523   CARRILLO, PEDRO EMILIO
         Médicos trujillanos. Valera, 1974. 269 p. illus., ports.
21cm. Short biographies of 76 deceased physicians from the
State of Trujillo, Venezuela. Non-alphabetical arrangement,
but with alphabetically arranged name index at end.

DENTISTRY

11524   DANSKE TANDLAEGER. 3. udg. Udg. af Dansk tandlaege-
forenings hovedbestyrelse. Redigeret af F. Orth og Kai
Storm. København, Dansk videnskabs forlag, 1953. 684 p.
ports. Danish dentists of the present.

11525   INTERNATIONAL ASSOCIATION FOR DENTAL RESEARCH.
Journal of dental research: its fifty years history; and, International Association for Dental Research: Biographical directory of members. History written and directory compiled
under the direction of Frank J. Orland. Chicago, 1969. 29, xxi,
209 p. illus., ports. 24cm. (Journal of dental research, v. 48:
Special commemorative supplement)

---- ----Addendum to the Biographical directory of members.
Worcester, Mass., 1971. 48 p. 24cm. (Journal of dental research, v. 50: Supplement)

11526   KOCH, CHARLES RUDOLPH EDWARD, ed.
History of dental surgery; contributions by various authors;
edited by Charles R. E. Koch. Chicago, National Art Pub. Co.,
1909. 2 v. illus., ports. 28cm. Vol. 3: Biographies of pioneer American dentists and their successors, by B. L. Thorpe.

11527   ROMEICK, DIETRICH, 1914-
Die Erfurter Zahnärzte von 1587 bis 1967   Erfurt, Freier
Deutscher Gewerkschaftsbund, 1968.   271 p. illus., ports.
22cm. Dentists in Erfurt from 1587 to 1967. Scattered thru'
the text are successively numbered (chronological arrangement)
biographical sketches of 295 dentists ("Die Auistellung der Erfurter Zahnärtzte ... "). Alphabetical approach thru' index at
end.

11528   SVENSKA TANDLÄKARE I ORD OCH BILD; porträttgalleri med
biografiska uppgifter över alla nu levande svenska legiti-
merade tandläkare. Stockholm, Biografisk galleri, 1939. 584 p.
Swedish dentists in word and picture; a portrait gallery with biographical particulars for Swedish dentists living in 1939.

PHILOSOPHY, PSYCHOLOGY, OCCULTISM

11529   ASAHI JĀNARU.
Nihon no shisoka. Tokyo, Asahi Shimbunsha, 1962-63.
3 v. 19cm. Biographies of 67 modern Japanese thinkers and
authors who have flourished since the Meiji era.

11530   BLANC, ÉLIE, 1846-1927.
Dictionnaire de philosophie ancienne, moderne et contemporaine, contenant environ 4,000 articles disposés par ordre

alphabétique dans le cours de l'ouvrage, complété par deux
tables méthodiques. Paris, P. Lethielleux, 1909. xvi p., 1248
numb. columns, vi p., 154 numb. columns. 24cm. "Edition
1909, avec supplément allant de janvier 1906 à decembre 1908. "
A dictionary of philosophy which includes articles on individual
philosophers. Reprinted in 1972 by Burt Franklin, New York.

11531   CHRZANOWSKI, IGNACY, 1866-1940.
         Wiek XIX. Sto lat myśli polskiej. Życiorysy, streszcze-
nia, wyjatki. Pod red. Ignacego Chrzanowskiego, Henryka
Gallego, Stanisława Krzemińskiego. Warszawa, Nakład Ge-
bethnera i Wolffa, 1906-24. 9 v. 24cm. The 19th century; 100
years of Polish thought: biographies, resumés, extracts from
works. Table of contents in each volume is the best approach
to the biographies.

11532   DALMOR, E   R
         Quién fue y quién es en ocultismo. Diccionario biográfico
de ocultistas, registro de entidades y publicaciones y compendio
de materias afines. Buenos Aires, Editorial Kier, 1970. 602 p.
23cm. (Colección Horus) Who was who and who is who in oc-
cultism. Biographical dictionary of occultists, etc.

11533   DAY, HARVEY
         Occult illustrated dictionary. London, Kaye & Ward; New
York, Oxford University Press, 1975. iv, 156 p. illus., ports.
21cm. Includes biographies of people involved in the occult sciences (both founders of movements and researchers).

11534   ESZTÉTIKAI KISLEXIKON. 2., átdog., bóv. kiad. [Főszer-
         kesztő: S. Nyiro József. Szerkesztő: Szerdahelyi István és
Zoltai Dénes. A kislexikon szerzói: Aradi Nóra et al. Buda-
pest] Kossuth Könyvkiadó, 1972. 718 p. 25cm. A dictionary of
aesthetics (especially Communist aesthetics) which includes biographies of famous philosophers of aesthetics. 1st ed. was issued in 1969 (400 p.)

11535   FILOZOFIA W POLSCE; słownik pisarzy. [Komitet redakcyjny:
         Bronisław Baczko et al. Opracowanie bibliograficzne:
Andrzej Przymusiała] Wrocław, Zakład Narodowy im.
Ossolińskich, 1971. 461 p. ports. 26cm. At head of title:
Instytut Filozofii i Socjologii Polskiej Akademii Nauk. A dic-
tionary of ca. 600 Polish philosophers.

11536   GELDSETZER, LUTZ
         Philosophengalerie. 1. Bildnisse und Bibliographien von
Philosophen aus dem 11. bis 17. Jahrhundert. [Düsseldorf]
Philosophia Verlag [1967]   240 p. ports. 21cm. Portraits
and bio-bibliographical sketches of the Western world's great

philosophers from the 11th to the 17th century. Vol. 1 contains
material on 114 philosophers. No more published?

11537   GRLIĆ, DANDO
        Leksikon filozofa. [Opremio Zoltan Gabor] Zagreb,
        "Naprijed, " 1968. 574, [2] p. ports. 20cm. A dictionary of
        philosophers (in Serbo-Croatian)

11538   GROOTEN, JOHAN, d. 1957.
        New encyclopedia of philosophy [by] J. Grooten & G. Jo
        Steenbergen. With the cooperation of K. L. Bellon [and others]
        Translated from the Dutch, edited & rev. by Edmond van den
        Bossche. New York, Philosophical Library [1972] 468 p. 24cm.
        Translation of Filosofisch lexicon. A combination of dictionary
        of terms, biographical dictionary & encyclopedia.

11539   HVEM TAENKTE HVAD. Filosofens hvem-hvad-hvor. [Af
        Henrik Thomsen. Billedredaktion: Poul Henning Traustedt. 3.
        [staerkt udvid.] udg. København, Politiken, 1967. 416 p. illus.
        18cm. Who though what? A dictionary of philosophers. 1st ed.
        issued in 1961 (390 p.)

11540   JAKATDAR, SHRIKRISHNA ANANT, 1919-
        Jyotirvaibhava, direktari. Poona, Phal-Jyotish Abhyas
        Mandal [1967] 1 v. (various pagings) illus., ports. 26cm. In
        Marathi. Biographical directory of astrologers, chiefly Maha-
        rashtrian, and a collection of articles on astrological topics.

11541   JÉHAN, LOUIS FRANÇOIS, b. 1803.
        Dictionnaire de philosophie catholique. Paris, J. -P.
        Migne, 1860-64. 3 v. 28cm. (Troisième et dernière encyclo-
        pédie théologique, t. 48-50. Encyclopédie théologique, t. 150-
        152) A dictionary of Catholic philosophy; includes biographical
        sketches of philosophers (Catholic especially)

11542   KRUG, WILHELM TRAUGOTT, 1770-1842.
        Allgemeines Handwörterbuch der philosophischen Wissen-
        schaften nebst ihrer Literatur und Geschichte. Faksimile-
        Neudruck der 2., verb. und verm. Aufl., Leipzig [Brockhaus]
        1832-1838. Stuttgart-Bad Canstatt, Frommann (Holzboog) [1969]
        4 v. 21cm. A 19th century dictionary of philosophy that includes
        biographies of philosophers.

11543   MARIEL, PIERRE
        Dictionnaire des sociétés secrètes en Occident. [Paris,
        Culture, art, loisirs, 1971] 478 p. illus., ports. 21cm. (His-
        toire des personnages mystérieux et des sociétés secrètes) A
        dictionary of secret societies in the Western civilization; includes

biographies and some portraits of founders of the societies and
occult movements.

11544   MAI, CHUNG-KUEI.
Sung Yüan li hsüeh chia chu shu sheng tsu nien piao. Hong
Kong, Hsin ya shu yüan Chung wen yen chiu so, 1968. 4, 443,
20 p. 21cm. Chronological table of bio-bibliographical data on
neo-Confucian philosophers from 960 to 1367. Name index.

11545   MASSACHUSETTS BOARD OF CERTIFICATION IN PSYCHOL-
OGY.
Biographical directory of certified psychologists in Massa-
chusetts. [Boston] 1964. [56] p. 22cm.

11546   MENCHACA, JOSE A
Diccionario bio-bibliografico de filosofos [por] Jose A.
Menchaca. Bilbao, El Mensajero del Corazon de Jesus, 1965
[i. e. 1966-   v. 25cm. (Publicaciones de la Universidad de Deusto. Seccion de Filosofia) A bio-bibliographical
dictionary of philosophers. 2 vols. available thus far (as of
1975) ?

11547   MIERS, HORST E
Lexikon des Geheimwesens. Das umfassende Nachschlag-
werk zur Deutung, Erklärung und Erläuterung der Begriffe,
Ausdrücke, Symbole und Namen aus allen Gebieten der Geheim-
lehren und Grenzwissenschaften nebst Darstellungen der Geschichte, Zielsetzungen und Tendenzen der einschlägigen Verein-
igungen und den Lebensdaten der mit ihnen verbundenen Persönlichkeiten. Mit 2790 Stichwörtern, 223 Abbildungen [und] 3960
Literaturhinweisen. Freiburg i. Br., Verlag H. Bauer [1970]
xiii, 453 p. illus., ports. 25cm. A dictionary of the occult
sciences which includes biographical data for persons prominent
in occult movements.

11548   NAUMAN, ST. ELMO
Dictionary of American philosophy, by St. Elmo Nauman,
Jr. Totowa, N. J., Littlefield,Adams, 1974 [c1973] viii, 273 p.
21cm. (A Littlefield, Adams quality paperback, no. 275) "147
significant contributors to the development of American thought."
Useful for sketches of obscure 18th & 19th century thinkers; not
very useful for recent philosophers.

11549   PHILOSTRATUS, FLAVIUS.
Vitae sophistarum. Textum recensuit, epitomam Romanam
et Parisinam ineditas adiecit commentarium et indices concin-
navit Carolus Ludovicus Kayser. Hildesheim, New York, G.
Olms, 1971. xiii, 416 p. 20cm. Reprint of the 1838 ed. (Heidelberg, J. C. B. Mohr) Text in Greek. Recounts, in two
books, the lives of 59 Sophist philosophers; written in the 3d
century A. D.

11550   ROZENTAL', MARK MOISEEVICH
A dictionary of philosophy. Edited by M. Rosenthal and P.
Yudin. [Translated from the Russian. Edited by Richard R.
Dixon and Murad Saifulin] Moscow, Progress Publishers, 1967.
494 p. 22cm. Translation of Filosofskii slovar'. Does not in-
clude portraits of philosophers, as does the Russian ed. (q. v.).
Includes biographical data for philosophers.

11551   ROZENTAL' MARK MOISEEVICH
Kratkii filosofskii slovar'. Pod red. M. Rozental' i P.
IUdina. Izd. 4, dop. i ispr. Moskva, Gos. izd-vo polit. lit-
ry, 1955. 567 p. ports. 23cm. A brief biographical dictionary. Includes biographical data and portraits for philosophers.

11552   SŁOWNIK FILOSOFÓW. Warszawa, Państwowe Wydawn.
Naukowe, 1966-   v. 31cm. Vol. 1 (vi, 500 p.)
by Kazimierz Ajdukiewicz and Irena Krońska. A dictionary of the
world's philosophers.

11553   THE STEINERBOOKS DICTIONARY OF THE PSYCHIC, MYSTIC
OCCULT. Blauvelt, N. Y., Rudolf Steiner Publications,
1973. 235 p. illus. 18cm. (Steinerbooks, 1767) Provides
brief information about concepts, personalities, and terms.

11554   VOELKEL, TITUS, 1849-
Einführung in der Geschichte des freien Gedankens in
hundert Lebensabrissen seiner Vorkämpfer, von S. E. Verus
[pseud.] Frankfurt a. M., Neuer Frankfurter Verlag, 1914.
xvi, 224 p. 24cm. Introduction to the history of free thought
in a hundred life sketches of its champions.

11555   WHO'S WHO IN THE PSYCHIC WORLD. 1971-
Phoenix, Ariz.   v. illus. 21cm. Vols. for
include the "Annual directory of the psychic register international."

11556   ZUSNE, LEONARD, 1924-
Names in the history of psychology: a biographical source-
book. Washington, Hemisphere Pub. Corp.; distributed by
Wiley [1975] xvii, 489 p. ports. 25cm. Arranged chronologically, by birth dates, the work lists 526 psychologists and their
place and date of birth, highest degree, major positions held, a
narrative of life, and a selective group of sources of biographical data. An alphabetical list of names is placed at the front of
the volume.

RELIGION

General Works

11557   LECANU, AUGUSTE FRANÇOIS, 1803-
        Dictionnaire des prophéties et des miracles ... précédé
d'une introduction sur les véritables prophéties et les vrais miracles ... et suivi du tableau général des prophéties bibliques et
d'un table analytique. Paris, J.-P. Migne, 1852. 2 v. 27cm.
(Nouvelle encyclopédie théologique, par l'abbé Migne, t. 24-25)
A dictionary of prophets (Christian, Moslem, secular) and miracles. Contents.--1. Abd-El-Melech-Krudener.--2. Labarum-
Zorobabel.

11558   PARRINDER, EDWARD GEOFFREY
        A dictionary of non-Christian religions, by Geoffrey Par-
rinder. Philadelphia, Westminster Press [1973? c1971] 320 p.
illus. 24cm. Includes biographical sketches of notable religious figures, philosophers, etc. in Judaism, Hinduism, Buddhism and other non-Christian religions.

11559   SCHLOSSER, KATESA
        Propheten in Afrika. Braunschweig, A. Limbach, 1949.
426 p. map. 21cm. (Kulturgeschichtliche Forschungen, Bd. 3)
Prophets in Africa; 69 biographies, arranged by country or area,
of native Africans who led various religious movements (Islam,
native religions, etc.)from ca. 700 A. D. to the near mid-20th
century.

By Faith

Buddhism

Bibliography, Indexes, Portrait Catalogs

11560   HACKMANN, HEINRICH FRIEDRICH, 1864-1935.
        Alphabetisches Verzeichnis zum Kao sêng ch'uan. Leiden,
E. J. Brill, 1923. [81]-112 p. 24cm. "Sonderabzug aus den
Acta Orientalia, vol. II." Alphabetical index to the Kao sêng
chuan, a collection of material on Chinese Buddhism and Buddhists.

General Works

11561   CHOU, YUNG-NIEN, 1582-1647.
        Wu tu fa ch'eng. [n. p.] 1936.   14 v. (double leaves) in
2 cases. 27cm. Biographies of Buddhists in Wu-chiang County,
Chiang-su. No index.

11562   HUI-HUNG, 1071-1128.
             Ch'an lin seng pao chuan. Taipei, Hsin wên feng ch'u pan
         she, 1973. 1 v. (various pagings) 20cm. Reprint ed. Biog-
         raphies of 81 Buddhist priests of the Zen school in the period
         1056-1111. No index.

11563   MIKKYŌ JITEN HENSANKAI MIKKYŌ DAIJITEN. Kyoto,
             Hozōkan, 49 [1974] 6 v. illus. 27cm. Reprint of the
         1933 ed. (issued by Mikkyō Gakkai?) A dictionary of Tantric
         Buddhism with biographical entries.

11564   MING-FU.
             Chung-kuo Fo hsüeh jên ming tz'ǔ tien. Taipei, Fang chou
         ch'u pan she, 1974. 16, 95, 670, 190 p. 22cm. A biographical
         dictionary of 5,326 Chinese Buddhists; arranged by radicals and
         stroke counts.

11565   PEIRIS, WILLIAM
             The Western contribution to Buddhism. With a foreword by
         H. Saddhatissa Maha Thera. [1st ed.] Delhi, Motilal Banarsi-
         dass [1973] xxviii, 278 p. 48 ports. 23cm. Chiefly biographi-
         cal sketches of 87 Western scholars of Buddhism, arranged by
         country; alphabetical approach through Index.

11566   SHÊN SÊNG CHUAN. Taipei, I-wen yin shu kuan [1967]
             4 v. (double leaves) 19cm. Includes biographies of 208
         Buddhist priests who performed miracles during the Han to the
         Sung Dynasties; arranged in chronological order.

11567   TAO-HSÜAN, 596-667.
             Hsü Kao sêng chuan. [Shanghai] Yin song ban zang jing hui
         yinching, 1935. 4 v. 15cm. Continuation of Hui-chao's Kao
         sêng chuan (Biographies of Chinese Buddhist priests). An ear-
         lier edition was published in 1890 in 10 v. (on double leaves) in
         block print.

11568   WASHIO, JUNKEI, 1868-1941.
             Nihon bukke jimmei jisho. Tokyo, Tokyo Bijutsu, 1973.
         364, 1319, 181 p. geneal. tables, ports. 22cm. A biographi-
         cal dictionary of Buddhists in Japan up to Meiji era. Genealo-
         gical tables and portraits are included. Index by Japanese
         syllabic order.

11569   YÜ, CH'IEN
             Hsin hsü Kao sêng chuan. Taipei, Liu li ching fang 1967.
         4 v. (1884 p.) 19cm. New supplement to Hui-chao's Kao sêng
         chuan (biographies of Chinese Buddhist priests).

Christianity

General Works

11570   AKADEMIĬA NAUK SSSR. INSTITUT FILOSOFII.
Kratkii nauchno-ateisticheskii slovar'. Izd. 2., peresm.
i dop. [Redakts. kollegiĩa: I. P. TSameriãn (glavn. redaktor)
i dr.] Moskva, Nauka, 1969. 798 p. 21cm. 1st ed. (641 p.)
issued in 1964. A dictionary of atheism that includes biographies of religious leaders as well as prominent agnostics and
atheists.

11571   ALTANER, BERTHOLD, 1885-
Patrology. Translated by Hilda C. Graef. New York,
Herder and Herder, 1960. xxiv, 659 p. 23cm. Bio-bibliography of the Fathers of the Church; for alphabetical approach index
must be used. "Based on the fifth German edition of Patrologie
[1958]"

11572   AURENHAMMER, HANS
Lexikon der christlichen Ikonographie. Wien, Brüder
Hollinek, 1959-   v. 22cm. Issued in fascicles, 1959-
67--   Contents. --Bd. 1. A-Chr. Saints, Biblical characters, concepts and objects are covered in one alphabet in
this dictionary of Christian iconography.

11573   BARKER, WILLIAM PIERSON
Who's who in church history, by William P. Barker. Old
Tappan, N. J., F. H. Revell, 1969. 319 p. 24cm.

11574   BARR, GEORGE, 1916-
Who's who in the Bible. Middle Village, N. Y., Jonathan
David Publishers, 1975. 177 p. 22cm.

11575   BAUTZ, FRIEDRICH WILHELM
Biographisch-bibliographisches Kirchenlexikon. Bearb.
und hrsg. von Friedrich Wilhelm Bautz. Hamm (Westf.), T.
Bautz, 1970-   v. 27cm. Issued in fascicles. Biographi-
cal-bibliographical dictionary of the Christian Church.

11576   BIOGRAFÍA ECLESIÁSTICA COMPLETA. Vidas de los personajes del Antiguo y Nuevo Testamento; de todos los santos que venera la Iglesia, papas y eclesiásticos célebres por
sus virtudes y talentos, en órden alfabético. Redactada por
una reunión de eclesiásticos y literatos. Revisada por una
comisión nombrada por la autoridad superior eclesiástica.
T. 1-[14] Barcelona, J. M. Grau, 1848-56; Madrid, Librería
de Olamendi, 1857-63. 14 v. 93 ports. 4.º No more pub-

lished; goes from Aaron to O'Gavan. 'Complete' ecclesiastical
biography. Extensive lives of Bible characters, Popes, saints,
etc. in dictionary arrangement. Chief editor: Basilio Sebastián
Castellanos.

11577   BROWNRIGG, RONALD
Who's who in the New Testament. New York, Holt, Rinehart & Winston, 1972. 448 p. illus. 26cm. Published in England in 1971 (London, Weidenfeld and Nicolson).

11578   CATHOLIC BIBLICAL ENCYCLOPEDIA: Old and New Testaments, by John E. Steinmueller and Kathryn Sullivan. Introd. by Athanasius Miller. New York, J. F. Wagner, 1956.
2 v. in 1. illus. 26cm. Covers biography of Biblical characters etc.; two separate dictionaries, one for the Old, one for
the New Testament.

11579   THE CATHOLIC ENCYCLOPEDIA; a general work of reference
for art, biography, education, history, law, literature,
philosophy, the sciences, religion, and the Church. Rev. and
enl. ed. Editors: Edward A. Pace [and others] New York,
Gilmary Society, 1936. 1 v. illus. 26cm. No more published.

11580   THE CATHOLIC ENCYCLOPEDIA FOR SCHOOL AND HOME.
New York, McGraw-Hill, 1965. 12 v. illus., ports.
25cm. A popular work for general readers and use in school.
"It augments general encyclopedias in its biographies of religious figures" (Booklist and SBB, LXIII, July 1967, p. 1113)

11581   COMAY, JOAN
Who's who in the Old Testament together with the Apocry-
pha. Advisory editors for this volume: Michael Graetz and
Leonard Cowie. New York, Holt, Rinehart & Winston, 1971.
448 p. illus. 26cm.

11582   CORPUS DICTIONARY OF WESTERN CHURCHES. Edited by T.
C. O'Brien. Washington, Corpus Publications, 1970. xviii,
820 p. 25cm. A dictionary of the theology of Western Christianity; includes biographical articles.

11583   DÖRING, HEINRICH, 1789-1862.
Die deutschen Kanzelredner des achtzehnten und neunzehn-
ten Jahrhundert, nach ihrem Leben und Wirken dargestellt.
Neustatt a. d. Orla, J. K. G. Wagner, 1830. viii, 590 p. 21cm.
The German preachers of the 18th & 19th centuries; indexed in
vol. 4 of the author's Die gelehrten Theologen Deutschlands (?)

11584   DOLLAR, GEORGE W
         A history of fundamentalism in America. Greenville, S. C.,
Bob Jones University Press, 1973. xiii, 415 p. 23cm. "Biographical index" (p. [299]-375) provides not only references to
the text but also brief biographical data for many fundamentalist
preachers as well as leading figures in American church history
in the 19th and 20th centuries.

11585   DUPIN, LOUIS ELLIES, 1657-1719.
         Nouvelle bibliothèque des auteurs ecclésiastiques contenant
l'histoire de leur vie, le catalogue, la critique, et la chronologie de leurs ouvrages; le sommaire de ce qu'ils contiennent:
un jugement sur leur style, et sur leur doctrine, et le dénom-
brement des différentes éditions de leurs oeuvres. Paris, A.
Pralard, 1693-1715. 19 v. 25cm. A bio-bibliography of Christian authors from the origins of the Church through the 17th
century. Reprinted in 1970 by Gregg Publishers, Farnborough,
Eng.

11586   DUPIN, LOUIS ELLIES, 1657-1719.
         Table universelle des auteurs ecclésiastiques, disposez par
ordre chronologique et de leurs ouvrages véritables ou supposez.
Paris, A. Pralard, 1704. 4 v. 19cm. Contents. --1. Auteurs
des 16 premiers siècles (disposés par ordre chronologique).--2.
Auteurs du XVIIe siècle. --3. Table alphabétique des auteurs
contenus dans les 2 tomes précedens... --4. Table universelle
des auteurs héretiques du XVIe et du XVIIe siècle. Universal
table of religious authors and their works, arranged in chronological order.

11587   EERDMAN'S HANDBOOK TO THE BIBLE. Edited by David
         Alexander [and] Pat Alexander. Consulting editors: David
Field [and others. 1st ed.] Grand Rapids, Mich., Eerdmans
Pub. Co., 1973. 680 p. illus. 23cm. Included in Pt. 4 of the
work is a Who's who in the Bible.

11588   ENCICLOPEDIA DE LA BIBLIA. Barcelona, Ediciones Garriga,
         1963. 6 v. Encyclopedia of the Bible; with rather long
signed articles, including proper names (biographical data).

11589   ENCICLOPEDIA DEL CRISTIANISMO. Diretta da Silvio Romani.
         Segretario di redazione: Rodolfo Sommaruga. Roma, Casa
editrice Taraffi, 1947. lxiii, 1356 p. 22cm. A dictionary of
Christianity, covering Church doctrines, biography and terms.

11590   THE ENCYCLOPAEDIA OF MISSIONS. Descriptive, historical,
         biographical, statistical. 2d ed. Edited under the aus-
pices of the Bureau of Missions by Henry Otis Dwight, H. Allen
Tupper and Edwin Munsell Bliss. Detroit, Gale Research Co.,

1975. xii, 851 p. 23cm. First edition (1891) edited by E. M.
Bliss. Includes biographical sketches of famous missionaries
and converts. Reprint of the 1904 ed. (New York, Funk & Wagnalls).

11591 ENCYCLOPEDIC DICTIONARY OF THE BIBLE. A translation
and adaptation of A. van den Born's Bijbels woordenboek.
2d rev. ed., 1954-57, by Louis F. Hartman. New York,
McGraw-Hill, 1963. xv p., 2634 columns. illus. 25cm. Includes biographies of Biblical personages.

11592 ENCYCLOPÉDIE DES SCIENCES RELIGIEUSES. Publiée sous
la direction de F. Lichtenberger. Paris, Sandoz et Fischbacher, 1877-82. 13 v. 25cm. Encyclopedia of the religious
sciences; vol. 13 (p. 1-233) includes a biographical dictionary of
theologians, etc. ("Dictionnaire des contemporains") of the
19th century.

11593 FISCHLIN, LUDWIG MELCHIOR, 1672-1729.
Memoria theologorum Wirtembergensium ressuscitata, h. e.
Biographia praecipuorum virorum qui a tempore Reformationis
usque ad hanc nostram aetatem partim in Ducatu Wirtenbergico
Verbum Domini docuerunt, partim extra suam hanc patriam
vocati Ecclesiae Christi aliis in terris inservierunt ... Ulmae,
Sumptibus G. W. Kühnen, 1709. 2 v. 8.º

---- ----Supplementa. Ulmae, Sumptibus G. W. Kühnen, 1710.
403 p. 8.º Memorials of Württemberg's theologians from the
Reformation to the beginning of the 18th century.

11594 FRANCK, KASPAR, 1543-1584.
Catalogus haereticorum. Das ist: Warhafftige Erzelung der
namhafften Irrthumb und Ketzer welche von Anfang der Welt biss
auff unsere Zeit entstanden ... Ingolstat, D. Schneider, 1576.
[8] l., 529, [97] p. 17cm. A dictionary of heresies and heretics,
with biographical sketches comprising a large part of the volume.

11595 FULLER, THOMAS, 1608-1661.
Abel redevivus; or, The dead yet speaking. The lives and
deaths of the modern divines. A new ed., with notes by William
Nichols. London, W. Tegg, 1867. 2 v. illus. 20cm. "A
large proportion of these lives are translations, in an abridged
form, from Melchior Adam's Vitae Germanorum Theologorum."
Brief lives of theologians of the Protestant Reformation (e. g.,
v. 1 contains 50 biographies.

11596 GAINET, JEAN CLAUDE, 1805-1890.
Dictionnaire d'ascétisme, comprenant: 1º Un discours pré-
liminaire résumant l'histoire générale de l'ascétisme ... 2º

L'exposé et la solution de toutes les questions ... de la théologie mystique; 3º Les notices biographiques et bibliographiques
des principaux auteurs ascétiques... 4º L'histoire sommaire
des faux mystiques et de leurs erreurs; 5º Le catalogue général,
par ordre chronologique, des principaux auteurs et ouvrages
mystiques; 6º Une table méthodique des matières propre à fa-
ciliter l'étude raisonnée de la théologie mystique. Par les abbés
J.-C. G. et J.-C. P. Paris, J.-P. Migne, 1865. 2 v. 28cm.
(Nouvelle encyclopédie théologique, t. 45-46. Encyclopédie
théologique, t. 95-96) A dictionary of asceticism which includes
bio-bibliographies of the chief ascetic authors.

11597   GOUJET, CLAUDE PIERRE, 1697-1767.
         Bibliothèque des auteurs ecclésiastiques du XVIIIe siècle,
pour servir de continuation à celle de M. Du Pin. Paris,
Pralard & Quillau, 1736. 3 v. 20cm. A bio-bibliography of
Christian authors of the 18th century; a supplement to L. E.
Dupin's Nouvelle bibliothèque des auteurs ecclésiastiques (q. v.).

11598   HAAG, HERBERT, 1915-
         Bibel-Lexikon. Hrsg. von Herbert Haag in Verbindung mit
A. van den Born und zahlreichen Fachgelehrten. Einsiedeln,
Benziger [1956] xiii p., 1784 columns. illus. 26cm. A dictionary of the Bible that includes biographical sketches of persons
mentioned in the Bible. Translated into Spanish under title: Diccionario de la Biblia (Barcelona, 1963) with some adaptations.

11599   THE INTERNATIONAL STANDARD BIBLE ENCYCLOPEDIA.
         James Orr, general editor. John L. Nuelson, Edgar Y.
Mullins, assistant editors. Morris O. Evans, managing editor.
Chicago, Howard-Severance Co., 1915. 5 v. illus., ports.
28cm. A Bible dictionary with entries for Biblical personages
and contemporaries.

11600   JAENCKE, JOHANN DAVID, 1702-1752.
         Gelehrtes Pommer-Land, worin die Historie, sowohl aller
in Pommern gebohrnen, als auch anderer in Pommern gestand-
enen oder verstorbenen Gelehrten, die sich durch Schrifften
bekandt gemacht haben, zum gemeinen Nutzen und Vergnügen
mitgetheilet wird. Der erste Tomus, von denen gelehrten The-
ologis. Das erste Stück. Alten-Stettin, H. G. Essenbahrten,
1734. 16, 192 p. 19cm. No more published. Learned Pomerania; presumably the work was to cover biographical data for
scholars and authors native to Pomerania, living and deceased,
but only vol. 1, theologians, was issued.

11601   JÉHAN, LOUIS FRANÇOIS, b. 1803.
         Dictionnaire des origines du Christianisme; ou, Histoire des
trois premiers siècles de l'Église chrétienne. Etablissement du
christianisme en Orient et en Occident. Paris, J.-P. Migne,
1856. 1260 columns. 28cm. (Troisième et dernière encyclo-

pédie théologique, t. 15. Encyclopédie théologique, t. 117) Dictionary of Christianity's origins; the early Christian church and
some of its leading figures.

11602   JONES, JOHN ANDREWS, 1779-1868, ed.
          Bunhill memorials. Sacred reminiscences of three hundred
ministers and other persons of note, who are buried in Bunhill
Fields, of every denomination. With the inscriptions on their
tombs & gravestones and other historical information respecting
them, from authentic sources. Edited by J. A. Jones. London,
J. Paul, 1849. vi, 384, [4] p. 20cm. Clergy of a section of the
City of London.

11603   KEMPNER, BENEDICTA MARIA
          Priester vor Hitlers Tribunalen. München, Rütten &
Loening [1966] 496 p. ports. 21cm. Priests before Hitler's
tribunals; a biographical dictionary of German clergymen who
resisted the Nazis.

11604   KÜNSTLE, KARL, 1859-
          Ikonographie der christlichen Kunst. Freiburg i. B., Herd-
er, 1926-28. 2 v. illus. 27cm. Vol. 2 is a dictionary of the
iconography of saints that includes biographical data.

11605   LECONTE, JACQUES ROBERT
          Aumôniers militaires belges de la guerre 1914-1918 [par]
J.-R. Leconte. [Bruxelles, Musée royal de l'Armée et d'histoire militaire, 1969] 395 p. illus., ports. 24cm. (Centre
d'histoire militare. Travaux, 5) Pages 92-335 contain a biographical dictionary of 572 Belgian military chaplains of the first
World War (or European War) of 1914-1918.

11606   McCLINTOCK, JOHN, 1814-1870.
          Cyclopaedia of Biblical, theological, and ecclesiastical lite-
rature, by John M'Clintock and James Strong. New York, Arno
Press [1969] 10 v. in 5. illus. 32cm. Title on spine: Cyclo-
paedia of Biblical literature. Reprint of 1867-81 ed. Includes
biographical sketches of some minor figures which may not be
found elsewhere.

11607   MEHLIG, JOHANN MICHAEL, 1716-1777.
          Historisches Kirchen- und Ketzer-Lexicon, aus den besten
Schriftstellern zusammen getragen. Chemnitz, Stössel, 1758.
2 v. 18cm. A dictionary of church history and heretical movements; includes biographical entries.

11608   MILLER, MADELEINE (SWEENY) 1890-
          Harper's Bible dictionary, by Madeleine Miller and J. Lane
Miller. Rev. by eminent authorities. [8th ed.] New York,

Harper & Row, 1973. ix, 853 p. illus. 25cm. Includes biographical entries for historical Biblical personalities.

11609   NEILL, STEPHEN CHARLES, Bp.
             Concise dictionary of the Christian world mission. Edited
         by Stephen Neill, Gerald H. Anderson [and] John Goodwin.
         Nashville, Abingdon Press [1971] xxi, 682 p. 23cm. (World
         Christian books) Includes biographies of many missionaries.

11610   O'LEARY, DE LACY EVANS, 1872-
             The saints of Egypt: an alphabetical compendium of martyrs,
         patriarchs and sainted ascetes in the Coptic calendar, com-
         memorated in the Jacobite synaxarium with bio-bibliographical
         annotations and preceded by a general introduction on the Church
         of Alexandria, on Egyptian monasticism, and on the Coptic lan-
         guage and calendar. Amsterdam, Philo Press, 1974. vii, 290 p.
         23cm. Reprint of the 1937 ed. published by the Society for Pro-
         moting Christian knowledge, London, and Macmillan Co., New
         York. The 'alphabetical catalogue', the chief part of the book,
         is a biographical dictionary.

11611   ORTIZ DE URBINA, IGNACIO
             Patrologia Syriaca. Romae, Pont. Institutum Orientalium
         Studiorum, 1965. 268 p. 23cm. 1st issued in 1958 (250 p.)
         Covers Syriac Fathers of the Church, heretical, Orthodox,
         anonymous and some post-Patristic writers with extensive bio-
         bibliographies for each.

11612   THE OXFORD DICTIONARY OF THE CHRISTIAN CHURCH.
             Edited by F. L. Cross. 2d ed. edited by F. L. Cross and
         E. A. Livingstone. London, New York, Oxford University
         Press, 1974. xxi, 1518 p. 25cm. Includes many biographical
         sketches of theologians, clergy, etc. prominent in Christian-
         ity's history and thought. First ed. was issued in 1957.

11613   RÉAU, LOUIS, 1881-
             Iconographie de l'art chretien. Paris, Presses universi-
         taires de France, 1955-59. 3 v. in 6. plates. 24cm. Vol. 3,
         pts. 1-3 (in 3 v.) comprise a dictionary of the saints.

11614   ROTBERG, ROBERT I
             Christian missionaries and the creation of Northern Rho-
         desia, 1880-1924. Princeton, N. J., Princeton University
         Press, 1965. xi, 240 p. illus. 21cm. Missionary biographi-
         cal sketches in the appendices (p. 163-195)--a biographical dic-
         tionary (with ca. 200 names) with sketches varying from 2 to
         27 lines.

11615   SAXON, KURT
        The instant who's who in the Bible. [Eureka, Calif.: Atlan
Formularies, 1974] 302 p. 28cm. Cover title.

11616   SEVESTRE, A   abbe
        Dictionnaire de patrologie; ou, Répertoire des saints pères,
des docteurs et de tous les autres écrivains des douze premiers
siècles de l'Église, contenant ... avec la biographie des auteurs,
l'analyze raisonné de leurs oeuvres ... Petit-Montrouge, J. P.
Migne, 1851-59. 5 v. 4.º Contents.--1. A-C.--2. D-G.--3.
H-M.--4. N-Z.--5. [Supplementary volume going up to part of
the 13th century] A dictionary of early Church history containing data on the Church Fathers, theologians and other writers
of the first 12 centuries of the Church.

11617   SIANDA, GIOVANNI
        Lexicon polemicum in quo potiorum haereticorum vita
perstringitur, omnes contra fidem errores colliguntur, inserta
conciliabulorum omnium schismatum et controversiarum quae
ad ecclesiasticam historiam pertinent notitia; addita demum
bibliotheca polemicum. Editio ab auctore recognita et adaucta.
Augustae Vindelicorum, Sumptibus M. Rieger, 1761. 3 v. 8.º
Another ed. issued in 1760 (Editio 2.: Romae). Contents.--1.
A-F.--2. G-Q.--3. Q-Z. A dictionary of heresies and heretics.

11618   SPOL, EUGÈNE
        Dictionnaire de la Bible; ou, Explication de tous les noms
propres historiques et géographiques de l'Ancien et du Nouveau
Testament. Paris, Gaume, 1876. 228 p. 18.º Dictionary of
the Bible; or, Explanation of all the proper historical and geographical names in the Old and New Testaments.

11619   UHSE, ERDMANN
        Curieuses Lexicon derer Geistlich-Gelehrten oder berühm-
testen Kirchen-Lehrer und Scribenten welche im XVI. und XVII.
Jahr-Hundert nach Christi Geburth gelebet. Leipzig, 1714. 1 v.
8.º An 'odd' item, presumably a dictionary of theologians and
religious leaders of the 16th-17th centuries. 1st issued in 1710
under title: Leben der berühmtesten Kirchen-Lehrer und Scribenten des XVI. und XVII. Jahr-Hunderts nach Christi Geburth.

11620   VIGOUROUX, FULCRAN GRÉGOIRE, 1837-1915.
        Dictionnaire de la Bible, contenant tous les noms de per-
sonnes, de lieux, de plantes, d'animaux mentionnés dans les
Saintes Ecritures, les questions théologiques, archéologiques
... [etc.] publié par F. Vigouroux avec le concours d'un grand
nombre de collaborateurs ... Paris, Letouzey et Ané [1907]-12.
5 v. illus. 28cm. Issued in 39 parts.

        ---- ----Supplément, publié sous la direction de Louis Pirot
avec le concours de nombreux collaborateurs ... Paris, Le-

touzey et Ané, 1928-   v. 29cm. Issued in fascicles;
of the supplement 8 vols. & 2 fascicles of v. 9 had been issued
up to 1976. A dictionary of the Bible; not only does it contain
biographical material on Biblical personages, but also included
are a large number of biographical, critical sketches of Biblical
scholars, theologians, etc.

11621   WATERS, CLARA ERSKINE CLEMENT, 1834-1916.
        A handbook of Christian symbols and stories of the saints
as illustrated in art. Edited by Katherine E. Conway. Boston,
Ticknor, 1886. Detroit, Gale Research Co., 1971. xiv, 349 p.
illus., ports. 22cm. Pages [37]-323 constitute a biographical
dictionary of the saints of the Church.

11622   THE WESTMINSTER DICTIONARY OF CHURCH HISTORY.
        Editor: Jerald C. Brauer. Associate editors: Brian Gerrish
[and others] Philadelphia, Westminster Press [1971] xii, 887 p.
25cm. Includes biography.

11623   WILLIAMS, ETHEL L
        Biographical directory of Negro ministers, by Ethel L.
Williams. 3d ed. Boston, G. K. Hall, 1975. 578 p. 22cm.
First ed. (1965) and 2d ed. (1970) issued by Scarecrow Press
(New York & Metuchen, N. J.)

Christianity-By Demonination

Anglican Communion

11624   CASSAN, STEPHEN HYDE
        Lives and memoirs of the bishops of Sherborne and Salis-
bury from the year 705-1824. Salisbury [Eng.] Printed and
sold by Brodie and Dowding, 1824. 3 pts. in 1 v. illus. 22cm.
100 lives, chronologically arranged, with an alphabetical index
of names at the front of the 1st part of the volume.

11625   CHURCH OF ENGLAND. NATIONAL ASSEMBLY.
        The official year-book of the National Assembly of the
Church of England. 1st-   1882-   London, Society for Pro-
moting Christian Knowledge.   v. illus. Title varies: 1882,
The year book of the Church; 1883-1921, The official year book
of the Church of England; 1922-   Official year-book of the National Assembly of the Church of England. Includes a Who's who
in the Church's Assembly and some of its boards, councils, etc.

11626 FELLOWES, EDMUND HORACE, 1870-
        The vicars or minor canons of His Majesty's Free Chapel
of St. George in Windsor Castle, by Edmund H. Fellowes.

Windsor. Published for the dean and canons of St. George's
Chapel in Windsor Castle by Oxley [1945] 118 p. 22cm. [His-
torical monographs relating to St. George's Chapel, Windsor
Castle] The list of clergy (for the years 1352-1944) on p. 55-113
yields some biographical data. The arrangement is chronological (with alphabetical approach available via index). For names
of clergymen after 1600 the biographical matter is lengthier.

11627   LAWLOR, HUGH JACKSON, 1860-1938.
        The fasti of St. Patrick's, Dublin. With an appendix on the
French congregation in the Lady Chapel of St. Patrick's Cathedral, 1666-1816, by Thomas Philip Le Fanu. Dundalk [Ire.] Published by W. Tempest for the Standing Committee of the General
Synod of the Church of Ireland, 1930. 336 p. 23cm. Includes
many biographical notes on clergy of the Church of Ireland.

Baptists

11628   CATHCART, WILLIAM, 1826-1908.
        The Baptist encyclopaedia. A dictionary of the doctrines,
ordinances, usages, confessions of faith, sufferings, labors and
successes, and of the general history of the Baptist denomination in all lands. With numerous biographical sketches of distinguished American and foreign Baptists, and a supplement.
Rev. ed. Philadelphia, L. H. Everts, 1883. 2 v. 1366 p. illus.
28cm. First ed. issued in 1881 (1328 p. 28cm.)

        ---- ----Index to names in the Baptist encyclopaedia, compiled
by Elizabeth Hayward. Chester, Pa., American Baptist Historical Society, 1951. 58 p. 28cm.

11629   ENCYCLOPEDIA OF SOUTHERN BAPTISTS. Nashville,
        Broadman Press, 1958-71. 3 v. (xxviii, 2064 p.) ports.
27cm. Includes biographies of many leading Southern Baptists,
past and present. On spine of vol. 3: Supplement, A-Z.

11630   PAXTON, WILLIAM EDWARD, 1825-1883.
        A history of the Baptists of Louisiana, from the earliest
times to the present. With a biographical introduction by F.
Courtney. St. Louis, C. R. Barns Pub. Co., 1888. 622 p.
port. 20cm. "Part II. Biographical sketches" (p. [491]-617)
contains ca. 110 brief biographies of ministers, elders and other
leaders of the Baptist Church in Louisiana.

Catholic Church

Bibliography, Indexes, Portrait Catalogs

11631   MAULVAULT, ACHILLE
        Répertoire alphabétique des personnes et des choses de

Port-Royal. Paris, H. Champion, 1902. 280 p. 23cm. Alphabetical list of persons and events concerned with Port Royal and Jansenism; a bibliography which has its uses as a bibliography of biography.

11632   TAURISANO, INNOCENZO M., 1877-1960.
         Catalogus hagiographicus Ordinis Praedicatorum. Editio altera. Roma, 1918. 78 p. 8.º Very useful for identifying manuscript sources, bibliography, etc. concerning Dominican saints.

11633   TRUDEAU, PAUL ALBERT
         Index alphabétique des biographies des profès et des novices décédés, 1831-1970. [2. éd. corr. et augm.] Joliette, 1970. 118 p. Clerics of Saint Viator (Viatorians) of all the provinces of the community; an alphabetical index giving dates of birth and death. The Viatorians (a teaching order primarily) in Canada are centered in Joliette and Montreal.

General Works

11634   ACTA SANCTORUM ORDINIS S. BENEDICTI DOMINI
         JOANNIS MABILLON nunc tandem tertio post Parisinam Venetianamque editionem Solesmensium monachorum curis impressa nec non variis documentis ac notis ornata ... Matiscone, Fratres Protat Typographi Matisconenses, 1935-
         v. 41 cm. At head of title: Armarium Solesmense. Vol. 2- issued in parts. With reproductions of title pages of original ed. (Paris, 1668-   ) The original ed. (6 v. in 9) went up to the year 1100. Contents. --1. Ab anno D ad annum DC. --2. Ab anno DC ad annum DCC. --3. pars 1. Ab anno DCC ad annum DCCLIII. Extensive collective biography of the saints of the Benedictine Order; a work in the tradition of the Bollandists' Acta sanctorum. 3 vols. issued up to 1939.

11635   ALVAREZ, PAULINO
         Santos, bienaventurados, venerables de la Orden de Predicadores. Vergara, Tip. del Santísimo Sacramento, 1920-23. 4 v. illus. 25cm. The saints, the Blessed and the Venerable of the Dominican Order. Vol. 3 is especially biographical.

11636   AMBROGIO A S. TERESA, 1886-
         Bio-bibliographia missionaria ordinis Carmelitarum Discalceatorum. [Extracta ex Analectis Ord. Carm. Disc. 14-16] Romae, Apud Curiam Generalitam, 1941. 495 p. 24cm. Bio-bibliography of Discalced Carmelite missionaries.

11637   AMBROGIO A S. TERESA, 1886-
         Hierarchia Carmelitana; seu, Series illustrium praesulum

ecclesiasticorum ex ordine Carmelitarum discalceatorum.
Romae, Apud Curiam Generalitam, 1933-[39?] 384 p. 25cm.
Hierarchy of the Carmelite Order; that is, brief biographical
data of missionaries in Asia, etc. Issued in 5 fascicles. Extracted from Analecta Carmelitarum Discalceatorum, v. 6-14.

11638 BATTEREL, LOUIS, 1679 or 80-1752.
Mémoires domestiques pour servir à l'histoire de l'Oratoire; les pères de l'Oratoire recommandables par la piété ou
par les lettres. Publié par A.-M.-P. Ingold. Genève, Slatkine
Reprints, 1971. 5 v. in 4. 23cm. Vols. 2-4: Publiés par
A.-M.-P. Ingold et E. Bonnardet. Reprint of the Paris edition
of 1902-1911. 233 biographies of members of the Oratory of Jesus Christ and of Mary the Immaculate (Oratoire de Jésus-
Christ et de Marie Immaculée). Table of names at end of each
volume, with index to the whole at the end of vol. 4.

11639 BENEDICTINES.
SS. patriarchae Benedictae familiae confoederatae ...
Sublaci, Typis Proto-Coenobii [etc.] 1869-   v. illus.,
ports. 19-25 cm. Title varies: 1869, Album Benedictinum;
seu, Catalogus exhibens seriem sacrorum antistitutum ac
monachorum ... 1880, Album Benedictinum, nomina exhibens
monachorum ... Imprint varies. A directory of the Benedictine Order that includes bio-bibliographical sections.

11640 BERNAD, MARCEL, 1860-
Bibliographie des Missionaires oblats de Marie Immaculée.
Liège, H. Dessain, 1922-   v. 24cm. [Bio-]bibliography
(alphabetical by author) of the Oblates of Mary Immaculate.
Vol. 1: Ecrits des Missionaires oblats, 1816-1915 (147 p.). Un-
able to locate further volumes.

11641 BLÉMUR, MARIE JACQUELINE BOUETTE DE, 1618-1696.
L'année bénédictine; ou, Les vies des saints de l'ordre de
Saint-Benoît pour tous les jours de l'année. Paris, L. Billaine,
1667-73. 12 v. in 6. 4.º The Benedictine year; or, The lives
of the saints of the Benedictine order for every day of the year.

11642 BRUSHER, JOSEPH STANISLAUS, 1906-
Popes through the ages; photos. Collected and edited by
Emanuel Borden. Princeton, N. J., Van Nostrand, 1959. xiii,
530 p. illus., ports. 29cm. A pictorial history with one-page
biographies (in chronological arrangement) of the Popes and 259
portraits.

11643 CATALOGO ALFABETICO DI TUTTI I PADRI DEL CONCILIO
I. ECUMENICO VATICANO. Roma, Tipi dell' Osservatore
romano, 1870. 72 p. Biographical dictionary-catalog of all the
participants in the 1st Vatican Council of 1869-1870.

11644   CATHOLIC ALMANAC. [First]-   year of publication;
        1904-   Paterson, N.J., St. Anthony's Guild, 1903-
        v. illus., ports. 20-27cm. 1931-33 issued as no. 1, v.11-13
        of the Franciscan. No volumes issued for the years, 1930, 1934-
        35. Title varies: 1904-1910, St. Antony's almanac; 1911, Fran-
        ciscan almanac; 1912-1926, St. Antony's almanac; 1927-1929, St.
        Anthony's almanac; 1931-1933, The Franciscan ... almanac edi-
        tion; 1936-1939, the ... Franciscan almanac; 1940-1968, The Na-
        tional Catholic almanac. Editors: 1904-1929, Published by the
        Franciscan Fathers of the Province of the Most Holy Name; 1940-
                compiled by the Franciscan Clerics of Holy Name College,
        Washington, D.C. Imprint varies. Still being published; 1975
        ed. latest? Contains several biographical dictionary sections;
        e.g., in the 1971 ed.: "Biographies of Catholics" (p. 371-390);
        Missionaries to the Americas" (p. 477-498); "American bishops
        of the past" (p. 499-511).

11645   THE CATHOLIC ENCYCLOPEDIA AND ITS MAKERS. New
                York, Ency[c]lopedia Press, 1917. vii, 192, 6 p. ports.
        26cm. Brief biographies and portraits of the 1,452 contributors
        to the Catholic encyclopedia.

11646   CATHOLICISME, hier, aujourd'hui demain. Encyclopédie,
                dirigée par G. Jacquemet. Paris, Letouzey et Ané, 1947-
                v. 28cm. Issued in parts. Six vols. and fasc. 28-
        31 issued as of 1976. An encyclopedia of the Catholic Church
        which includes many biographical sketches of persons promi-
        nent in church history and Catholicism.

11647   CECCARONI, AGOSTINO, 1867-
                Piccola enciclopedia ecclesiastica: agiografia, biografie,
        missione cattoliche, ordini religiosi, liturgia, inni sacri ...
        aneddoti. Appendice aggiornata a tutto il 1952 dal don Angelo
        Ciceri. Milano, A. Vallardi, 1953. 1294, 301 p. illus. 20cm.
        First published in 1898 as: Dizionario ecclesiastico illustrato.
        An encyclopedia of the Church with the lives of saints, biography,
        Catholic missions, etc.

11648   CEILLIER, REMI, 1688-1761.
                Histoire générale des auteurs sacrées et ecclésiastiques,
        qui contient leur vie, le catalogue, la critique, le jugement, la
        chronologie, la l'analyse et le dénombrement des différentes
        éditions de leurs ouvrages; ce qu'ils renferment de plus in-
        teressant sur le dogme, sur la morale et sur la discipline de
        l'église; l'histoire des conciles ... et les actes choisis des
        martyrs, par Remy Ceillier. Nouv. éd. soigneusement rev.,
        cor., complétée et terminée par une table générale des
        matières, par un directeur de Grand séminaire. Paris, L.
        Vivès, 1853-63. 14 v. in 15. 18cm. Vols. 11-14, Nouv. éd.,
        "par l'abbé Bauzon."

        ---- ----Table générale des matières ... rédigée par Laur.-
        Et. Rondet ... [et] revue, corrigée et augm. par l'abbé Bauzon.

Paris, L. Vivès, 1868-69. 2 v. 28cm. Lives and commen-
taries on the works of religious writers (Fathers of the Church,
etc.) from the Old Testament to the end of the 13th century.
Chronological arrangement but with indexes in each volume, as
well as the 2-vol. general index.

11649 CHAUGY, FRANÇOISE MADELEINE DE, 1611-1680.
L'année sainte des religieuses de la Visitation. Annecy,
1686. 3 v. 4.º For each day of the year the life of a Catholic
religious personage is recounted.

11650 CHÈVE, CHARLES FRANÇOIS, 1813-1875.
Dictionnaire des conversions; ou, Essai d'encyclopédie
historique des conversions au catholicisme depuis dix-huit
siècles et principalement depuis le protestantisme; Paris, J. -
P. Migne, 1852. 1672 columns. 28cm. (Nouvelle encyclopédie
théologique, t. 33) (Encyclopédie théologique, t. 83) A dictionary of converts to Catholicism (chiefly after the advent of Protestantism).

11651 DACIO, JUAN
Diccionario de los papas. Pref. de Vintila Horia. [1. ed.]
Barcelona, Ediciones Destino, 1963. 267 p. illus., ports.
25cm. A dictionary of the Popes, with portraits.

11652 DICCIONARIO DE SANTOS. Presentación de Florentino Pérez.
Madrid, Circulo de Amigos de la Historia, 1969. 188 p.
19cm. Dictionary of the saints of the Church.

11653 DICCIONARIO DEL HOGAR CATÓLICO. Barcelona, Editorial
Juventud, 1962. 1179 p. 22cm. A dictionary of Catholicism
which includes biographical data. Translation and revision of
the French Dictionnaire du foyer catholique (Paris, 1956)

11654 DICTIONNAIRE DES AUTEURS CISTERCIENS. Sous la direction de Emile Brouette, Anselme Dimier et Eugène Manning. Rochefort [France] Abbaye Notre-Dame de St. -Rémy,
1975-   v. 26cm. (La Documentation cistercienne, v.
16, t. 1   Issued in parts.
A biographical dictionary of authors, past and present, members of the Cistercian Order.

11655 DICTIONNAIRE DU FOYER CATHOLIQUE. Apporte, sous le
classement alphabétique, les responses à toutes les questions que peut se poser un catholique de XXe siècle. Paris,
Librairie des Champs-Élysées, 1956. xv, 892 p. 23cm. A
popular Catholic dictionary covering terms, concepts, biography, etc. Spanish edition has title: Diccionario del hogar catò-

lico (Barcelona, Editorial Juventud, 1962), a revision of the
French work.

11656   DICTIONNAIRE HISTORIQUE DES SAINTS PERSONNAGES, où
        l'on peut prendre une notion exacte & suffisante de la vie &
des actions mémorables des héros du christianisme: de apôtres,
des pontifes, des patriarches ... de tout ceux enfin dont les
églises grecque & latin ont conservés les noms dans leurs
fastes, ou consacré la mémoire par un culte public. Paris,
Vincent, 1772. 2 v. An historical dictionary of the saints of the
Church: the Apostles, popes, patriarchs, etc. of the Greek and
Latin Churches, but largely devoted to the Roman Catholic
Church.

11657   DIZIONARIO DELLE RELIQUIE E DEI SANTI DELLA CHIESA
        DI ROMA. 1. ed. italiana. 2. ed. Firenze, Tip. Claudi-
ana, 1888. 179 p. 16.º 1st ed. issued in 1871 (238 p. 17cm.)
Dictionary of reliquaries and saints of the Catholic Church.

11658   DIZIONARIO ECCLESIASTICO. Sotto la direzione dei rev.mi
        mons. Angelo Mercati [e] mons. Augusto Pelzer, con la
collaborazione di numerosi e noti specialisti. Redattore capo
Antonio M. Bozzone. Torino, Unione tipografico-editrice, 1953-
58. 3 v. illus., ports. 31cm. An ecclesiastical dictionary,
with many biographies, especially of minor Italian functionaries
in the Catholic Church.

11659   DOLS, JEAN MICHEL ÉMILE, 1905-
        Bibliographie der Moderne Devotie. Nijmegen, Centrale
Drukkerij, 1936-41. 2 v. 22cm. Includes bio-bibliography of
authors of works on the Devotio Moderna movement (the Brethren of the Common Life were one of its principal exponents).

11660   DOYÉ, FRANZ VON SALES, 1860-
        Heilige und Selige der römisch-katholischen Kirche, deren
Erkennungszeichen, Patronate und lebensgeschichtliche Bemer-
kungen. Leipzig, Vier Quellen-Verlag, 1930. 2 v. illus.
24cm. A biographical dictionary of the saints and the pious of
the Roman Catholic Church.

11661   ENCICLOPEDIA DE LA RELIGIÓN CATHÓLICA. Barcelona,
        Dalmau y Jover, 1950-56. 7 v. illus. 30cm. A poorly
conceived encyclopedia of Catholicism; what value it has re-
sides in its Spanish viewpoint and the large number of biographical articles it contains.

11662   ENCICLOPEDIA DEL CATTOLICO. [Milano] A. Mondadori,
        1953. 3 v. illus., ports. 23cm. Edited by Giustino Boson.
Encyclopedia of Catholicism. Vol. 1 is a series of popular es-

says. Vols. 2-3 are an encyclopedia of short articles (with biographies)

11663   ENGLEBERT, OMER, 1893-
           The lives of the saints. Translated by Christopher and
Anne Fremantle. New York, D. McKay Co., 1951. xi, 522 p.
23cm. Short articles on major saints in the calendar arrangement. Minor saints are listed with dates and places of birth
and death. Translation of Les saints. Index of names included.

11664   ESCOLAPIOS INSIGNES POR SU PIEDAD RELIGIOSA DESDE
           EL ORIGEN DE LAS ESCUELAS PÍAS HASTA NUESTROS
DÍAS. Madrid, Impr. de San Francisco de Sales, 1899-1900.
4 v. 26cm. Preface signed: E. Llanas del Rosario. Based on
Jericó de la Concepcion's Varones insignes en santidad de vida
del Instituto y religión de clérigos pobres de la Madre de Dios
de las Escuelas Pías, 1751, and continued to 1900. Members of
the Piarist Order from its origins to 1900.

11665   FERNÁNDEZ ESPINOSA, LUIS MARÍA
           Año seráfico; o sea, Santoral de la primera Orden Franciscana. Barcelona, J. Vilamala, 1932. 2 v. front. 15cm.
(Biblioteca franciscana) Brief biographies of the saints and
blessed of the Franciscan Order and a calendar of said saints
and blessed.

11666   [FORESTIER, PIERRE] 1654-1723.
           Les vies des saints, patrons, martirs et évêques d'Autun.
Dijon, C. Robustel, 1713. 2 pts. in 1 v. 12.° Lives of the
saints, patrons and bishops of the diocese of Autun.

11667   GARGIULO, BONAVENTURA
           Il paradiso serafica; ossia, Il martirologio francescano,
coi santi, beati e venerabili di tutto l'ordine dei Minori. Napoli,
Festa, 1898. xii, 171 p. 8.° A Franciscan martyrology as well
as a biographical synopsis of the saints, blessed and venerable
of the order.

11668   GIORDANI, IGINO, 1894-
           I grandi convertiti. [Roma] Apollon [1945] vi, 326 p. 23cm.
(Collezione Fari) Biographical data for more than 200 converts
to the Catholic faith.

11669   I GRANDI DEL CATTOLICESIMO; enciclopedia biografica. A
           cura di P. Gini, G. Roschini e A. Santelli con la collaborazione di oltre 130 insigni studiosi diretta da C. Carbone. Roma,
Ente Libraio italiano, 1955-58. 2 v. illus. A biographical encyclopedia of Catholicism with major emphasis on Italian Catholics.

11670   GUARNACCI, MARIO
            Vitae, et res gestae Pontificum Romanorum et S. R. E.
Cardinalium a Clemente X usque ad Clementem III ... quibus
perducitur ad nostra haec tempora historia eorumdem ab
Alphonso Ciacconio, Ord. Praed. aliisque descripta a S. Petro
ad X Clementem IX. Romae, Sumptibus Venantii Monaldini, 1751.
2 v. illus., ports. 42cm. The lives and deeds of the 8 Popes
from Clement X to Clement XII, and of 244 cardinals who served
the Church during these Popes' reign. In chronological arrangement, with indexes at front of vol. 1. Valuable too for the portraits that accompany each biography.

11671   GUÉRIN, LOUIS FRANÇOIS, 1814-1872.
            Dictionnaire de l'histoire universelle d l'Église, embrassant
... par ordre alphabétique, l'histoire des idées, des faits, des
actes, des personnages, etc., qui appartiennent aux annales de
l'Église catholique, depuis la naissance de Notre-Seigneur
jusqu'au temps présent ... Paris, J.-P. Migne, 1854-73. 6 v.
27cm. (Encyclopédie théologique, 3. sér., t. 51-56) A dictionary of the history of the Catholic Church, including entries for
outstanding personages of the Church.

11672   HAIDACHER, ANTON
            Geschichte der Päpste in Bildern. Mit einem geschichtlich-
en Überblick von Josef Wodka. Eine Dokumentation zur Papst-
geschichte von Ludwig Freiherr von Pastor. Heidelberg, F. H.
Kerle [1965] 780 p. illus., ports. 27cm. Iconography and portraits of 62 Popes--from Bonifacius VIII (1294-1303) to Pius VI
(1775-1799) but of more use and value are the iconography and
portraits of cardinals, members of the Popes' families, papal officials etc. Consult the index for alphabetical approach (dark-
printed page numbers).

11673   HOLY GHOST FATHERS.
            Nécrologe de la Congrégation du Saint-Esprit et du Saint-
Coeur de Marie, 1709-1965. [Paris] Maison-Mère, 1966. 410 p.
Necrology of the Congregation of the Holy Ghost and of the Sac-
red Heart of Mary (the Holy Ghost Fathers) 1709-1965.

11674   IBERTIS, ENRICO, 1891-
            Figure domenicane; o, Piccola enciclopedia domenicana.
Torino, San Domenico, 1970. 340 p. 19cm. A biographical dictionary of the Dominican Order.

11675   DE KATHOLIEKE ENCYCLOPAEDIE. 2. druk, onder redactie
            van P. van der Meer, F. Baur [en] L. Engelbregt. Amster-
dam, Uitg. Mij. Joost van den Vondel, 1949-55. 25 v. illus.,
ports. 26cm. An encyclopedia-dictionary of the Catholic Church,
with many biographical entries for Church and world figures.

11676   KRUG, VIKTOR
         Unsere Namenspatrone; über 1300 Heilige und Selige nach
Name, Leben und Verehrung. Bamberg, St. Otto-Verlag, 1929.
702 p. col. plates. 8.º In alphabetical arrangement this work
portrays over 1300 saints and other religious figures.

11677   LACROIX,   official at the Ministry of Finance.
         Dictionnaire des missions catholiques, contenant 1º une
notice biographique sur les saints ou pieux personnages auxquels .
... l'Église doit la propagation de la foi, par M. Lacroix ... 2º
une introduction ... 3º une énumération des missions protes-
tantes ... 4º une description de l'état religieux des contrées ou
le catholicisme n'est pas encore dominant; 5º une histoire a-
brégés de tous les ordres ... 6º un appendice ... par Etienne
Djunkovskoy. Petit-Montrouge, J.-P. Migne, 1863-64. 2 v.
8.º (Troisième et dernière encyclopédie théologique, t. 59-60)
Dictionary of Catholic missions, containing biographical notices
of the saints or pious persons who were instrumental in the propagation of the faith, etc., etc.

11678   LEAL, JUAN
         Año cristiano. 2. ed. Madrid, Escelicer, 1961. 867 p.
22cm. "The Christian year. " A calendar of the saints with biographical data. Follows the calendar of the Roman missal. Includes useful indexes for names of saints, categories of saints,
etc.

11679   LECHNER, PETRUS, 1805-1874.
         A Benedictine martyrology, being a revision of Peter Lech-
ner's Ausführliches Martyrologium des Benedictiner-Ordens und
seiner Verzweigungen, by Alexius Hoffmann. Collegeville, Minn.,
St. John's Abbey, 1922. 341 p. 27cm.

11680   LE VASSEUR, LÉON
         Ephemerides Ordinis Cartusiensis. Monstrolii [i. e.
Montreuil-sur-Mer, Chartreuse de Notre-Dame des Prés]
1890-93. 5 v. 4.º Includes 1,620 biographies of members of
the Carthusian Order.

11681   LIBER PONTIFICALIS.
         The book of the popes. Liber Pontificalis. Translated with
an introd. by Louis Ropes Loomis. New York, Octagon Books,
1965-   v. 24cm. (Records of civilization: sources and
studies, no. 3
Contents. --[1] To the pontificate of Gregory I.

A chronologically arranged source for the lives of the Popes,
originally written in Latin. Reprint of the 1916 ed. by the Columbia University Press of which vol. 1 only was published.

11682   LIBER PONTIFICALIS.
         Le Liber Pontificalis. Texte, introd. et commentaire par
         l'abbé Duchesne. Paris, E. Thorin, 1886-92. 2 v. illus.
         32cm. (Bibliothèque des Ecoles françaises d'Athènes et de
         Rome, 2. sér., [3]) The Book of the popes; chronologically ar-
         ranged brief lives. This is the best of the many editions of the
         original Latin text.

11683   LIPPOMANO, LUIGI, Bp., 1500-1559.
         De vitis sanctorum, ab Aloysio Lipomano ... olim con-
         scriptis. Nunc primum a F. Laurentio Surio emendatis &
         auctis ... Venetiis, 1581. 6 v. 31cm. Earlier editions appear-
         ed under various titles: 1551-60, Sanctorum priscorum patrum
         (8 v.); 1564-68, Historiae Aloysii Lipomani ... De vitis sanc-
         torum; etc. A quite extensive collection of biographies of the
         saints of the Church, the predecessor of Laurentius Surius'
         Historiae; seu, Vitae sanctorum and the Bollandists' Acta sanc-
         torum.

11684   MARCELLINO DA CIVEZZA, d. 1906.
         Saggio di bibliografia, geografica storica, etnografica,
         sanfrancescana. Prato, R. Guasti, 1879. xiv, 698 p. 26cm.
         A bio-bibliography of 819 Franciscan writers many of whose
         works deal with Spanish American colonial history; arranged al-
         phabetically by authors.

11685   MARTÈNE, EDMOND, 1654-1739.
         La vie des Justes. Ligugé, Abbaye Saint Martin; Paris, A.
         Picard, 1924-26. 3 v. 25cm. (Archives de la France monas-
         tique, v. 27-28, 30). 232 biographical notices of 'righteous men'
         (Catholic religious figures). Edited by Benjamin Heurtebize.

11686   MELCHERS, ERNA, ed.
         Das Jahr der Heiligen: Geschichte und Legende. Unter
         Mitarbeit von Hans Melchers. München, Südwest Verlag [1965]
         840 p. illus. 24cm. A calendar of the saints, with alphabeti-
         cal approach thru' index.

11687   METODIO DA NEMBRO, Father
         Quattrocento scrittori spirituali. Milano, Centro studi
         Cappuccini lombardi, 1972. xvi, 465 p. 24cm. (Centro studi
         Cappuccini lombardi. Pubblicazioni, 18) At head of title: Me-
         todio da Nembro (Carobbio Mario) 400 writers of the Capuchin
         Order in Europe from the 16th to the 20th century; a bio-bibli-
         ography, arranged by nationality and century. Alphabetical in-
         dex of authors at end of volume.

11688   MINOCCHERI, LUIGI ·
         Catalogo di nomi di santi e beati, compilato per ordine alfa-
         betico. Roma, Filiziani, 1898. 112 p. 16.° A [biographical]

catalog of the names of the saints and the blessed, arranged in
alphabetical order.

11689   PECORINI, CARLO
        Florilegio di paradiso; o, Raccolta di circa 300 vite di
santi. Genova, Tip. della Gioventu, 1868. 2 v. 8.º A collection of circa 300 lives of saints of the Church.

11690   PETREJUS, THEODORUS, 1567-1640.
        Bibliotheca Cartvsiana; siue, Illustrivm sacri Cartvsiensis
Ordinis scriptorvm catalogvs. Accesservnt origines omniu per
Orbem Cartvsiarvm, quas eruendo publicauit Reuer. D. Al-
bertvs Miraevs. Coloniae, Apud Antonium Hieratum, 1609.
[Farnborough, Hants., Eng., Gregg International Publishers,
1968] 310, 73 p. port. 18cm. A bio-bibliographical dictionary-catalog of writers of the Carthusian Order.

11691   PONSONAILHE, CHARLES, 1860- ̬
        Les saints, par les grands maîtres; hagiographie et icono-
graphie du saint de chaque jour. Tours, A. Mame, 1897.
viii, 415 p. illus. 8.º Reissued in 1902 (399 p.) The saints,
by the great masters; hagiography and iconography of the saints
day-by-day.

11692   POPP, GEORG, ed.
        Die Grossen der Kirche; Männer und Frauen der Kirche,
die jeder kennen sollte. [3. Aufl.] Würzburg, Arena-Verlag
[1957] 476 p. illus. 24cm. The famous of the Church; men and
women of the [Catholic] Church "whom everyone should know.'
Brief biographical sketches arranged by vocation and including
saints of the Church.

11693   PRADIER,   abbé
        La vie des saints pour tous les jours de l'année. Lille,
Impr. de Desclée, de Brouwer, 1889. 535 p. illus. 8.º Lives
of the saints for all the days of the year.

11694   PROVOST, JOSEPH
        Fleurs des petits Bollandistes; vie des saints pour tous les
jours de l'année. Paris, Bloud et Barral, 1889. 2 v. 8.º
Contains lives of the saints day-by-day through the year.

11695   RACCOLTA TASCABILE DI VITE DI SANTI PER CIASCUN
        GIORNO DELL'ANNO. Nuova ed. Modena, Tip. dell'Im-
maculata Concezione, 1894. 452 p. 24.º A pocketbook collection of the lives of the saints for each day of the year.

11696   ROHRBACHER, FRANÇOIS RENÉ, 1789-1856.
         Vies des saints pour tous les jours de l'année, à l'usage du
clergé et du peuple fidèle. Paris, Garnier frères, 1853-54.
6 v. 8.° Lives of the saints for each day of the year.

11697   ROSCHINI, GABRIELE MARIA
         Dizionario di mariologia. Roma, Editrice Studium, 1961.
xii, 517 p. 22cm. A dictionary of Mariology which includes biographies of scholars in the field of studies of the Virgin Mary.

11698   ROUILLARD, PHILIPPE
         Dictionnaire des saints de tous les jours, établi et présenté
par Philippe Rouillard, suivi d'une étude sur les miracles par
Pierre Teilhard de Chardin. [Paris] R. Morel [c1963] 415 p.
14cm. Another ed. was issued in the same year by R. Morel
(361 p. ports.) A dictionary of the saints for each day of the
year.

11699   SAGGI, LUDOVICO, comp.
         Santi del Carmelo. Biografie da vari dizionari a cura e con
introd. di Ludovico Saggi. Pref. di Valentino Macca. Roma,
Institutum Carmelitanum, 1972. 403 p. 24cm. Carmelite
saints. Lives taken from various dictionaries; pages [154]-380
comprise a biographical dictionary of 72 saints.

11700   SCHWAB, GREGOR
         Kurze Lebensgeschichten heiliger und verdienstvoller
Männer aus dem Hospital-Orden des heiligen Johannes von Gott.
Hrsg. von Gregor Schwab. Altötting, Gebr. Geiselberger,
1927. 3 v. 8.° Brief biographical sketches of members of
the Hospitaller Order of St. John of God.

11701   SMITH, EDWARD FRANCIS, 1891-
         Baptismal and confirmation names containing in alphabetical
order the names of saints with Latin and modern language equiv-
alents, nicknames, brief biography, representation in art and
pronunciation, with a daily calendar of feasts and lists of patron
saints. New York, Benziger Bros., 1935. viii, 280 p. 19cm.
Includes cross references to other forms of names.

11702   STABELL, THEODOR
         Lebensbilder der Heiligen. In der Ordnung des bürger-
lichen Kalenders kritisch-historisch dargestellt. Biographical
sketches of the Saints of the Church arranged by the regular calendar.

11703   STORNI, GIOCONDO
         Le vite dei santi per tutti i giorno dell'anno. Einsiedeln,

Benziger, 1896.   810 p.   16.º   The lives of the saints for each day of the year.

11704   SURIUS, LAURENTIUS, 1522-1578.
Historiae; seu, Vitae sanctorum juxta optimam Colonien-sem editionem, nunc vero ex recentioribus et probatissimis monumentis numero auctae, mendis expurgatae et notis exornatae, quibus accedit Romanum martyrologium breviter illustratum, Taurinensi presbytero e Congreg. Clerr. Regg. S. Paulli curante. Augustae Taurinorum, Ex Typ. Petri Marietti, 1875-80.   13 v. 23cm.   Lives of the saints of the Church based on "Sanctorum priscorum patrum vitae," by Aloysius (Luigi) Lippomano.   Pref. signed: Camillus Aloisius Bracco.   First issued in 1618 in 12 vols. (?)

11705   VALENTINI, EUGENIO
Dizionario biografico dei salesiani.   Redazione: Eugenio Valentini, Amedeo Rodinò.   Revisione: Guido Borra.   Segre-tario redazionale: Giovanni Magdic.   Arichivio fotografico: Lu-igi Dotta.   Torino, A cura dell'Ufficio stampa salesiano [1973?] 302, [114] p.   illus., ports.   28cm.   A biographical dictionary of the Salesian order.

11706   VEZZOSI, ANTONIO FRANCESCO
I scrittori de' cherici regolari detti teatini d'Antonio Fran-cesco Vezzosi della loro congregazione.   [Farnborough, Eng., Gregg Press, 1966 (i. e. 1967)]   2 v.   24cm.   Facsimile of 1st ed., Rome, Sacra Congregazione di Propaganda Fide, 1780.   A bio-bibliographical dictionary of the Theatines (a congregation of regular clerics established in 1524 to check Lutheranism).

11707   WADDING, LUKE, 1588-1657.
Scriptores Ordinis Minorum quibus accessit syllabus illorum qui ex eodem ordine pro fide Christi fortiter occubuerunt.   Priores atramento, posteriores sanguine Christianam, religionem as-seruerunt.   Recensuit Lucas Waddingus.   Editio novissima. Romae, A. Nardecchia, 1906.   243 p.   39cm.   (Bibliotheca his-torico-bibliographica, 1)

---- ----Supplementum et castigatio ad scriptores trium Ordi-num S. Francisci a Waddingo, aliisve descriptos.   Cum adnota-tionibus ad syllabum martyrum eorundem Ordinum.   Opus post-umum Jo: Hyacinthi Ebaraleae.   Editio nova variis additamentis et indice scriptorum chronologico locupletata.   Romae, A. Nar-decchia, 1908-   The main work was first published in Rome in 1650.   The supplement first appeared in 1806, together with the 1806 edition of Wadding's work.   This famous bibliogra-phy of Franciscans does contain some biographical data for the authors listed.   No birth or death dates are given, however, and the biographical facts are of varying length and usefulness.

11708   ZIMMERMANN, ALFONS M
        Kalendarium Benedictinum. Die Heiligen und Seligen des
Benediktinerordens und seiner Zweige. Im Auftrage der Bayeri-
schen Benediktinerkongregation verfasst von Alfons M. Zimmermann. Metten, Druck und Verlag der Abtei, 1933-37. 4 v.
23cm. Calendar of notable Benedictine (saints, etc.).

Catholic Church-Local

Africa

11709   DELLAGIACOMA, VITTORINO
        An African martyrology. Verona, Italy, Nigrizia Print.
Press, 1965. 243 p. Extracted from the 4th ed. of The book of
saints, compiled by the Benedictine monks of St. Augustine's
Abbey, Ramsgate, Eng. Saints of the Church martyred for their
faith in Africa while serving as missionaries, etc.

Argentine Republic

11710   FURLONG CARDIFF, GUILLERMO, 1889-
        Diócesis y obispos de la iglesia argentina, 1570-1942. Bue-
nos Aires, 1942. 58 p. ports., map. 20cm. The dioceses and
bishops of the Catholic Church in the Argentine Republic; includes
biographical data on 131 bishops. Detached from the Anuario
católico argentino, 1942.

11711   GALERÍA BIOGRÁFICA; obispos y arzobispos de Buenos Aires
        (1622-1897) Buenos Aires, J. A. Berra, 1897. 126 p. ports.
Biographies and portraits of the bishops and archbishops of the
Archdiocese of Buenos Aires, 1622 to 1897.

Austria

11712   ERDINGER, ANTON
        Bibliographie des Clerus der Diocese St. Polten von der
Gründung derselben bis auf die Gegenwart (1785-1889) 2. Aufl.
St. Pölten, B. Trauner, 1889. 305 p. A bio-bibliography of the
clergy of the Diocese of St. Polten, Lower Austria, from its
founding to the 'present' (near the end of the 19th century) Ca.
440 brief biographies alphabetically arranged, are included.

11713   GUPPENBERGER, LAMBERT, b. 1839.
        Bibliographie des Clerus der Diöcese Linz von deren
Gründung bis zur Gegenwart, 1785-1893. Linz, F. I. Ebenhöch,
1893. ix, 270 p. A bio-bibliographical dictionary of the Catholic clergy of the Diocese of Linz, Austria, 1785-1893.

11714   LEARDI, PETER
Reihe aller bisherigen Erzbischöfe zu Salzburg, wie auch
der Bischöfe zu Gurk, Seckau, Lavant und Leoben, sammt einer
kurzen Geschichte dieser Bisthümer vom Jahre 582 bis 1817.
Gratz, 1818. 144 p. plates. Ca. 200 brief biographies of Austria's archbishops at Salzburg as well as bishops at Gurk, Seckau, Lavant und Leoben (and Styria) from earliest times to the
present (1817).

11715   NEUNER, KASSIAN
Literarische Tätigkeit in der Nordtiroler Kapuzinerprovinz.
Bio-bibliographische Notizen. [Neudruck] Innsbruck, 1929.
160 p. Literary activity in Capuchin Province of the North Tyrol; bio-bibliographical dictionary of 220 authors. First printing, 1927.

11716   OBERSTEINER, JAKOB
Die Bischöfe von Gurk, 1072-1822. Klagenfurt, Verlag des
Geschichtsvereins für Kärnten, 1969. 544 p. illus., ports.
24cm. (Aus Forschung und Kunst, Bd. 5) Biographies (in
chronological order) of the 54 bishops of the diocese of Gurk,
Austria, for the years 1072-1822.

Belgium

11717   BOGAERTS, AMBROSIUS M   1908-
Dominikanen in Belgïe, 1835-1958. Door A. M. Bogaerts.
Brussel, Uitg. "Dominikaans Archief," 1969. x, 530 p. maps.
27cm. (Bouwstoffen voor de geschiedenis der Dominikanen in
de Nederlanden, [A]) Dominicans in Belgium, 1835-1958. Includes on pages 219-405 over a thousand brief sketches (birth
date, family, date of entry into the order, activities, death
date, if any) arranged by date of entry into the Dominican order.
On p. 407-484 are 276 biographical sketches of Dominicans in
the Congo.

Bohemia

See under Czechoslavakia

Brazil

11718   NÓBREGA, APOLONIO CARNEIRO DA CUNHA
Dioceses e bispos do Brasil. (In Revista do Instituto Histórico e Geographico Brasileiro, Rio de Janeiro. v. 222, jan.-
mar. 1954, p. [3]-328). On p. [78]-320 are biographies of 345
bishops and 5 cardinals of Brazil.

Canada

11719   BERGERON. ARTHUR, 1898-
         Le clergé du diocèse de Nicolet, 1885-1958. Wickham,
Qué., 1958. xxxii, 335 p. illus. 24cm. The clergy of the
Catholic diocese of Nicolet, province of Quebec, 1885-1958; 475
biographical notices.

11720   FRENETTE, FRANÇOIS XAVIER EUGÈNE, 1867-
         Notices biographiques et notes historiques sur le diocèse de
Chicoutimi. Chicoutimi, 1945. 243 p. ports. 23cm.

         ---- ----Supplément. Liste des prêtres seculiers et reguliers
et des frères et religieuses des différentes communautés du
Canada originaires du diocèse de Chicoutimi. Chicoutimi, 1947.
415 p. ports. 23cm. Secular and regular clergy of the Diocese
of Chicoutimi, Province of Quebec.

11721   GAUTHIER, HENRI, 1864-
         Sulpitiana. Montréal, Bureau des oeuvres paroissiales de
St. -Jacques, 1926. 276 p. 24cm. The 2d part of this work contains a "Dictionnaire sulpicien" (p. 163-276), a biographical dictionary which includes sketches of Canadian Sulpicians from the
origins of the order in Canada to 1926.

11722   GRAVEL, ALBERT, 1894-
         Obituaire du clergé séculier de l'archidiocèse de Sher-
brooke, de 1874 à 1968. Sherbrooke, 1969. 24, 71, 17, 2 l.
map, ports. 29cm. Obituary of the secular clergy of the Archdiocese of Sherbrooke, Province of Quebec.

11723   PANNETON, GEORGES
         Le diocèse de Trois-Rivières, 1962 [par] Georges Panneton
[et] Antonio Magnon. [Trois-Rivières, Qué.] Editions du Bien
public [1962] 513, [5] p. illus., ports. 23cm. "Biographies
sacerdotales": p. [13]-217. The diocese of Trois-Rivières,
Quebec, 1852 to 1962; with biographical sketches of clergy of the
diocese. Supersedes an earlier volume which covered the years
1852-1952.

11724   PLOURDE, ANTONIN MARIE
         Qui sont-ils et d'ou viennent-ils? Nécrologe dominicain,
1882-1964. Préf. par Thomas-M. Rondeau. Montréal, Editions du Lévrier [1965] 411 p. illus. 22cm. Who are they and
from whence to they come? Dominican necrology, 1882-1964.
Dominicans of the Canadian Province; brief biographies, with
dates of birth and death. Arranged in order of date of death.

11725   SAINTE-MARIE-DE-PONTMAIN, Sister
         Bio-bibliographie analytique des imprimés des Soeurs de la

Congrégation de Notre-Dame de Montréal. Lettre-préf. de
soeur Sainte-Marie-Madeleine-du-Sacré-Coeur. Québec, 1952.
xiv, 175 p. Bio-bibliography of the imprints of the Sisters of
Notre-Dame, Montreal province.

11726   SIMARD, ANDRÉ, 1922-
     Les évèques et les prêtres séculiers au diocèse de Chicou-
timi (1878-1968); notices biographiques. Chicoutimi, Chancellerie de l'évêche, 1969. 812 p. coats of arms, ports. 25cm.
The bishops and the clergy of the diocese of Chicoutimi, Quebec,
Canada.

11727   TANGUAY, CYPRIEN, 1819-1902.
     Répertoire général du clergé canadien par ordre chronolo-
gique, depuis la fondation de la colonie jusqu'à nos jours. [2.
éd.] Montréal, E. Senécal, 1893. xiv, 526, xlvi p. 23cm.
A list of all clergy who have served the Catholic Church in Canada, with very brief biographical notes. Arranged chronologically with an alphabetical name index at end. First ed. (Québec, C. Darveau, 1868) has collation: 321, xxix p. 23cm.

Chile

11728   CATÁLOGO BIOGRÁFICO ECLESIÁSTICO CHILENO. Santiago
     de Chile, Proveedora del Culto.   v. 19cm. The Catho-
lic Church in Chile; a biographical catalog and directory of its
clergy. Began in 1963?

11729   HANISCH ESPÍNDOLA, WALTER
     Itinerario y pensamiento de los jesuitas expulsos de Chile,
1767-1815 [por] Walter Hanisch. Santiago de Chile, Editorial
Andrés Bello, c1972. 332 p. 24cm. History and thought of
Jesuits expelled from Chile in the years 1767 to 1815. "Catálogo
alfabético de biografías (p. 257-329) comprises a biographical
dictionary with brief sketches.

11730   MUÑOZ OLAVE, REINALDO
     Rasgos biográficos de eclesiásticos de Concepción 1552-
1818. Santiago de Chile, Impr. "San José," 1916. 548 p. 20cm.
Biographical features of the clergy of the Archdiocese of Concepción, Chile.

China

11731   HSÜ-CHIA-HUI TS'ANG SHU LOU, SHANGHAI.
     Clergé chinois au Kiang-nan sous les Ta-tsing en excluant
les jésuites et les élèves du séminaire de Nan-king. Bureau
sinologique de Zi-ka-wei. Shanghai, Impr. de T'ou-sè-wè près
Zi-ka-wei, 1933. 67 p. 25cm. A biographical dictionary (ca.

77 names) of native Catholic clergy in China (exclusive of Jesuits and students of the Seminary of Nanking).

11732   MOIDREY, JOSEPH TARIF DE, 1858-
La hiérarchie catholique en Chine, en Corée et au Japon (1307-1914); essai. Zi-ka-wei près Chang-hai, Impr. de l'Orphelinat de T'ou-sè-wè, 1914. ii, 301 p. maps. 25cm. (Variétés sinologiques, no 38) The Catholic hierarchy in China, Korea and Japan, 1307-1914; includes numerous biographical sketches arranged under place; the biographies can be located alphabetically through the name index at end of volume.

11733   WANG, GIUSEPPE
Martirologio della Chiesa Cattolica in Cina. Città del Vaticano, Edizione Alma Mater [1967] 178 p. 21cm. Martyrology of the Catholic Church in China; includes biographical sketches of ca. 90 Chinese Catholic martyrs beatified by the Church from 1900 to 1955. Chronological arrangement.

Colombia

11734   BOTERO RESTREPO, JUAN
El clero sonsonés. [2. ed. Medellín, Editorial Granamérica, 1972 or 1973] 273 p. 24cm. (Ediciones Centro de Historia de Sonsón) Biographical sketches (some very brief, some fairly extensive) of 154 Catholic clergy in Sonson, Colombia. Chronological arrangement; no index. 1st ed. had title: Sonsoneses ilustres.

11735   BUITRAGO TRUJILLO, RUBÉN, 1921-
Memorias biográficas de la Provincia de Nuestra Señora de la Candelaria de la Orden de Recoletos de San Agustín. Años 1663-1963. Bogotá, Editorial Pax, 1965, 844 p. 24cm. Biographical memoirs of the Augustinians in Colombia, 1663-1963.

11736   RESTREPO POSADA, JOSÉ
Arquidiócesis de Bogotá; datos biográficos de sus prelados. Bogotá, Editorial Lumen Christi, 1961-   v. illus., ports. 25cm. (Biblioteca de historia eclesiásticos "Fernández Caycedo y Florez," v. 2-3, 5-6 Biographical data on the Archdiocese of Bogotá and its bishops and clergy. Vol. 4 (Cabildo eclesiástico) issued in 1971, includes 198 biographical notices.

11737   URIBE VILLEGAS, GONZALO
Los arzobispos y obispos colombianos desde el tiempo de la colonia hasta nuestros días. Bogotá, Impr. de "La Sociedad," 1918. 792 p. 24cm. The 89 archbishops and bishops of Colombia from the time of the colony to 1918; in alphabetical arrangement.

Crotia

11738   TUMPIC, MIHAEL
Pavlini varaždinci. Rim, Institut crkvenih studija, 1966.
4, 31 p. 24cm. (Archivum Ordinis Sancti Pauli Primi Eremitae
Dissertationes, 3) (Studia ecclesiastica, 2) (Historica, 4)
Pages [7]-25 comprise a biographical dictionary of 56 Hermits
of St. Paul active in Varaždin, Croatia in the 17th-18th centuries.

Czechoslavakia

11739   SCHALLER, JAROSLAUS
Kurze Lebensbeschreibung jener verstorbenen gelehrten
Männer aus dem Orden der Frommen Schulen, die sich durch
ihr Talent und besondere Verdienste um die Literatur und Wissenschaften ... vorzüglich ausgezeichnet haben. Prag, Fr.
Jeřábek, 1799. viii, 170 p. 8.º   Bio-bibliography of deceased
learned men of the Piarists (Clerks Regular of the Pious Schools)
in Bohemia.

11740   VONDRUSKA, ISIDOR
Životspisy svatých v pořadi dějin cirkenvích. Praha, Kun-
cíř, 1930-31. 5 v. illus. 8.º   The lives of saints in the course
of church history; emphasizes Bohemian saints.

France

11741   ALBERT, ANTOINE, 1717-1804.
Dictionnaire portatif des prédicateurs français, dont les
sermons, homélies, panégyriques, et oraisons funèbres sont
imprimés. Avec de courts analyses de tous les traites de
l'éloquence de la chaire ont paru en françois. Lyon, P. Bruy-
set-Ponthus, 1757. xx, 488 p. 8.º   By A. Albert and Jean
Francois de La Cour.   A dictionary of French Catholic clergy
noted for their preaching.

11742   ARRAS, FRANCE. SAINT-VAAST (ABBEY)
Nécrologe de l'Abbaye de St. Vaast d'Arras. Publié van
E. van Drival. Arras, 1878. xxiii, 501 p. 8.º   Published by
the Société royale pour l'encouragement des sciences, des lettres et des arts, afterwards Académie d'Arras. A necrology
of the Benedictine abbey of Saint-Vaast in Arras.

11743   BARTHÉLEMY, CHARLES, 1825-1888, ed.
Annales hagiologiques de la France. Les vies de tous les
saints de France, depuis le premier siècle du christianisme
jusqu'à nos jours. Tr. des actes les plus anciens et des auteurs contemporaines sous la direction de Ch. Barthélemy.
Versailles (Seine-et-Oise) Bureau des Annales hagiologiques de

France, 1860-70. 10 v. 8.º Annals of the saints of France.
The lives of all the French saints from the origins to the mid-
19th century. Collective biography on a comprehensive scale.

11744   BENEDICTINES. CONGREGATION DE FRANCE (SOLESMES)
Bibliographie des Bénédictines de la Congrégation de
France, par des pères de la même Congrégation. Nouv. éd.
entièrement refondue, accompagnée des portraits en héliogra-
vure de dom Guéranger et dom Pitra. Paris, H. Champion,
1906. xxviii, xi, 179 p. front., ports. 26cm. Bio-bibliography and portraits of Benedictines of the Congregation of France.

11745   BENEDICTINES. PARIS.
Vies des saints et des bienheureux selon l'ordre du calendrier, avec l'histoire des fêtes, par les Bénédictins de
Paris. Paris, Letouzey et Ané, 1935-59. 13 v. 24cm. A
calendar of the lives of the saints and the blessed of the Church,
arranged by month (one month per volume; v. 13, index) Edited by J. L. Baudot and Léon Chaussin.

11746   BILDLICHE DARSTELLUNGEN DER HEILIGEN DES EHEMALI-
GEN ELSASSES, begreifend die Bisthümer Strassburg und
Basel, nach historischen Skizzen und Urquellen, mit Beachtung
der Trachten ihres Zeitalters. Strassburg [1820?] 16 p. 59
plates. 8.º Issued also in French under title: Galerie des
saints de la ci-devant Alsace, comprenant les évêches de
Strasbourg et de Bâle (Strasbourg, Lith. de M.-F. Boehm,
1841) Portraits of the saints of former Alsace, encompassing
the dioceses of Strasbourg and Basel.

11747   BOUSQUET, JEAN LOUIS ETIENNE, abbé
Tableau chronologique et biographique des cardinaux,
archévêques et évêques originaires de l'ancienne province du
Rouergue. Rodez, Impr. de N. Ratery, 1850. 120 p. 8.º Extracted from the Mémoires de la Société des lettres, sciences
et arts de l'Aveyron. A chronological and biographical tableau
of the cardinals, archbishops and bishops of the former province of Rouergue.

11748   CHAMARD, FRANÇOIS, 1828-1908.
Les vies des saints personnages de l'Anjou. Paris, J.
Lecoffre, 1863. 3 v. 18cm. Lives of the saintly persons of
Anjou.

11749   COLLÈGE DE SAINT-FRANÇOIS-XAVIER, BESANÇON,
FRANCE.
Vie des saints de Franche-Comté, par les professeurs du
college Saint-Francois-Xavier de Besançon. Besançon, Tur-
bergue, 1854-56. 4 v. 8.º Lives of the saints (men of the
church and pious figures) of Franche-Comté.

11750   COLLIN, JEAN, abbé
Histoire sacrée de la vie des saints principaux et autres
personnes plus vertueuses qui ont pris naissance, qui ont vecu,
ou qui sont en vénération particulière en divers lieux du diocèse
de Limoges. Limoges, M. Barbou, 1672. 708 p. 12.° Lives
of the chief saints and other persons of virtue who were born or
resided in the diocese of Limoges or were held in special vener-
ation in the diocese.

11751   COSTE, HILARION DE, 1595-1661.
Histoire catholique où sont décrites les vies, faits, et
actions heróiques et signalées des hommes et dames illustres,
qui, par leur piété ou sainteté de vie, se sont rendus recommandables dans les XVIe et XVIIe siècles. Paris, Chez p. Chevalier, 1625. [30], 804 p. illus. 35cm. Includes the lives of
114 Catholic Frenchmen and Frenchwomen of the 16th (especially) and the 17th centuries who distinguished themselves by their
saintly Christian lives.

11752   CROSNIER, AUGUSTIN, 1804-1880.
Hagiologie nivernaise; ou, Vie des saints et autres pieux
personnages qui ont édifié le diocèse de Nevers par leurs vertus.
Nevers, Impr. de I.-M.Fay, 1858. xxx, 593 p. 28cm. At
head of title: Publication de la Société nivernaise. Hagiography
of the diocese of Nevers; or, lives of saints and other pious persons of the diocese.

11753   GALLIA CHRISTIANA IN PROVINCIAS ECCLESIASTICAS DIS-
TRIBUTA QUA SERIES & HISTORIA ARCHIEPISCOPORUM,
episcoporum & abbatum Franciae vicinarumque ditionum ab
origine ecclesiarum ad nostra tempora deducitur et probatur ex
authenticis instrumentis ad calcem positis. Parisiis, V. Palme,
1856-99 [v. 1, 1870] 16 v. maps. 41cm. Variously edited by D.
de Saint-Marthe, P. L. Piolin and B. Hauréau. Vols. 6-10, 12
are a facsimile ed. of the 1739 ed. Original t. p. reads: Opera
et studio Monachorum Congregationis S. Mauri Ordinis S. Benedicti. Vols. 14-16 have imprint: Paris, Firmin-Didot frères.
This reprinted compendium of French Catholic Church history
contains a huge mass of biography of ecclesiastical figures. The
work is arranged by ecclesiastical province, diocese, etc., with
biographical sketches of clergy, officials, etc. thereunder.
Each vol. has its own general index.

11754   GARABY, MALO JOSEPH DE
Vies des bienheureux et des saints de Bretagne pour tous
les jours de l'année. Saint-Brieuc, L. Prud'homme, 1859.
544 p. 12.° Lives of the blessed and saintly persons of Brittany
for each day of the year.

11755   GLORIEUX, PALÉMON, 1892-
Répertoire de maîtres en théologie de Paris au XIIIe siècle.

Paris, Librairie philosophique J. Vrin, 1933-34. 2 v. fold.
tables. 26cm. (Études de philosophie mediévale, 17-18) Bio-
bibliographies of 425 theologians at the University of Paris in
the 13th century; arranged by religious orders.

11756   GODEFROY, JEAN ERNEST, 1886-
      Bibliothèque des Bénédictins de la Congrégation de Saint-
Vanne et Saint-Hydulphe. Paris, A. Picard, 1925. xxiii, 239 p.
ports. 25cm. (Archives de la France monastique, v. 29) Bio-
bibliography of the Benedictines of the Congregation of Saint-
Vanne et Saint-Hydulphe.

11757   HAMY, ALFRED, 1838-
      Province de Lyon, 1582-1762. Noms, prénoms, lieu d'ori-
gine, dates de naissance, d'entreé, de degré, lieu et date de
mort de tous les Jesuites demeurés fidèles à leurs voeux jusqu'à la fin. Paris, H. Champion, 1900. 197 p. 29cm. Chronologie biographique de la Compagnie de Jésus, l. sér.) Consists of a list of the Jesuits of the Province of Lyon, France
from 1582 to 1762, with place & date of birth, death and entry into the Order, degree attained and place of death.

11758   JARNOUX, ALPHONSE
      La Loire leur servit de linceul; les prêtres victimes de la
première noyade, 16 novembre 1793 [par] A. Jarnoux. [Quimper,
Impr. cornouaillaise, 1972] 413 p. plates. 24cm. "Les con-
fesseurs de la foi" (p. 64-336) contains biographies of 83 clergymen (in part alphabetically arranged) of the Catholic Diocese
of Nantes who were persecuted and lost their lives during the
French Revolution in Nantes.

11759   LAMA, CARL VON, 1841-1920.
      Bibliothèque des écrivains de la Congrégation de Saint-Maur,
ordre de Saint-Benoît en France. Ouvrage publié avec le concours d'un Bénédictin de la Congrégation de France de l'abbaye
de Solesmes. 2. éd. Munich, C. de Lama; Paris, V. Palme,
1882. 261 p. 29cm. A bio-bibliography of the Benedictines of
the Congregation of St. Maur, 1620 to 1830. Authors arranged
chronologically: Bénard, d. 1620 to Bévy, d. 1830. "Abrégé de
l'ouvrage du Dom Tussin": Jahresb. d. Geschichtswiss. 1882.
Reprinted in 1971 (Geneve, Slatkine Reprints)

11760   PEQUEGNOT, F   E
      Legendaire d'Autun; ou, Vies des saints et autres pieux
personnages des diocèses d'Autun, Châlon et Maçon, disposées
selon l'orde du calendrier. Lyon, Girard et Guyet [1846] 2 v.
illus. 12.⁰ Legendary of Autun, giving the lives of the saints
and other pious persons of the dioceses of Autun, Chalon and
Maçon arranged by calendar sequence.

11761   PORT-ROYAL DES CHAMPS (ABBY OF CISTERCIAN NUNS)
        Nécrologe de l'abbaye de Notre-Dame de Port-Royal des
        Champs, Ordre de Citeaux, Institut du Saint-Sacrement; qui
        contient les éloges historiques avec les épitaphs des fondateurs
        & bienfaiteurs de ce monastere, & des autres personnes de dis-
        tinction, qui l'ont oblige par leurs services, honoré d'une af-
        fection particuliere, illustré par la profession monastique,
        édifie par leur penitence & leur pieté, sanctifié par leur mort,
        ou par leur sepulture. Amsterdam, Chez N. Potgieter, 1723.
        lxxii, 498, [11] p. 25cm. Edited by Antoine Rivet.

        ----Supplément ... première partie contenant, outre de nou-
        veaux éloges, des corrections & des additions a la plupart des
        articles des six premiers mois du Nécrologe, avec un receuil
        des pièces intéressantes. [n. p.] 1735. 690 p. 26cm. No more
        published. Attributed to C. H. Lefebvre de Saint-Marc and C. P.
        Goujet as joint editors, also to each separately. Necrology,
        epitaphs, etc. of the nuns of the Abbey of Notre-Dame de Port-
        Royal des champs, Cistercian Order, and of other persons of
        distinction connected in some way with the Abbey.

11762   ROY, JEAN, 1744-1805.
        Nouvelle histoire des cardinaux francais. Ornée de leurs
        portraits. Paris, Chez l'auteur, 1785-88. 10 v. ports. 8.º
        New history of the French cardinals of the Church; with their
        portraits. Collective biography of large scope.

11763   SABATIER, AGATHON
        Vies des saints du diocèse de Beauvais. Beauvais, V. Pi-
        neau, 1866. 541 p. 12.º Lives of the saints of the Diocese of
        Beauvais.

11764   THUILIER, RENÉ, d. 1714.
        Diarium patrum, fratrum et sororum ordinis Minimorum
        Provinciae Franciae sive Parisiensis qui religiose obierunt ab
        anno 1506 ad annum 1700. Parisiis, Apud P. Giffart, 1709.
        2 v. 4.º Divided by months and days, with biographical data
        for many Minim Friars (founded by St. Francis of Paola) of the
        French Province, especially Paris.

Germany

11765   EBELING, FRIEDRICH WILHELM, 1822-1893.
        Die deutschen Bischöfe bis zum Ende des 16. Jahrhunderts.
        Biographisch, literarisch, historisch und kirchenstatistisch
        dargestellt. Leipzig, O. Wigand, 1857-59. 2 v. 23cm. The
        German bishops to the end of the 16th century (with biographical
        sketches).

11766   GESTERKAMP, DESIDERIUS, 1913-1971.
        Liber mortuorum; die Verstorbenen der rheinisch-schwä-

bischen Augustinerproving und der neuen deutschen Ordensprov-
ing 1650-1950. Würzburg, Augustinus-Verlag, 1972. 788 p.
23cm. (Cassiciacum, Bd. 25) Obituaries of Augustinians in
the Rhine-Swabian province from 1650 to 1950. The alphabetical
listing yields birth/death dates (with place of birth/death) and
pertinent facts about careers--the work has a columnar format.

11767   SCHWAIGER, GEORG
          Bavaria sancta. Zeugen christliches Glaubens in Bayern.
          Hrsg. von Georg Schwaiger. Regensburg, Pustet [1970-
            v. illus. 23cm. 'Holy Bavaria'; witnesses of the Christian
          faith in Bavaria. Comprehensive biography of Catholic saints
          and prominent churchmen in Bavaria's past. Vol. 3 (1973)
          latest issued as of 1976.

Great Britain

11768   SNOW, TERENCE BENEDICT, 1838-1907.
          Obit book of the English Benedictines, 1600-1912. With a
          new introd. by Maurus Lunn. [Farnborough? Eng.] Gregg. In-
          ternational Publishers, 1970. xli, 414 p. 21cm. At head of
          title: Henry Norbert Birt. Reprint of the Edinburgh ed. of 1913.
          Original t. p. reads: Obit book of the English Benedictines from
          1600 to 1912; being the necrology of the English Congregation of
          the Order of St. Benedict from 1600 to 1883, compiled by Abbot
          Snow. Rev., enl. and continued by Henry Norbert Birt. Edin-
          burgh, Privately printed by J. C. Thomson at the Mercat Press,
          1913. Pages [1]-242 contain biographical sketches, chronologi-
          cally arranged (by death of biographee) of deceased monks and
          nuns.

11769   WARK, K   R
          Elizabethan recusancy in Cheshire. Manchester [Man-
          chester University Press] for the Chetham Society, 1971. viii,
          200 p. map. 22cm. (Remains historical and literary connected
          with the Palatine Counties of Lancaster and Chester, 3d series,
          v. 19) Includes a list of Cheshire recusants (Catholics) with bio-
          graphical notes on pages 138-173.

Italy

11770   CAPASSO, GAETANO
          Cultura e religiosità ad Aversa nei secoli XVIII-XIX-XX.
          [Contributo bio-bibliografico alla storia ecclesiastica meridion-
          ale] Napoli, Athena mediterranea, 1968. 501 p. illus. 21cm.
          Includes much biographical material on the clergy of Aversa,
          Italy, 18th-20th centuries. There is no alphabetical name guide
          to the many figures portrayed briefly, but there is a fairly com-
          prehensive "Indice-guida" (actually a table of contents).

11771   CIPRIANO DA SERRACAPRIOLA, O. F. M. Cap.
Necrologia dei Frati minori cappuccini della provincia
religiosa di Foggia (1530-1968) Foggia, Curia provinciale dei
Cappuccini, 1969. 782, lxxxiii p. 24cm. Necrology of Capuchins of the Province of Sant'Angelo, 1530-1968. A day-by-day
listing, with some biographical material for more prominent
figures. Alphabetical name indexes at end: one·list for surnames and one for names in religion.

11772   D'ANDREA, GIOACCHINO
Repertorio bibliografico dei frati minori napoletani. Napoli, Edizioni Dehoniane, 1974. 369 p. plates. 24cm. (Documenti, studi e sussidi, n. 1) Actually a bio-bibliographical dictionary (alphabetical by name in religion) of Franciscans in the
province of Naples.

11773   FEDELE, BENEDETTO
Missionari francescani; sintesi storica bio-bibliografica,
con sommario geografico-cronologico. 2. ed. rifusa e ampliata.
L'Aquila, A cura della Procura delle missioni francescane,
1966. 384 p. illus., ports. 22cm. (Cattedra Bernardiniana,
L'Aquila. [Pubblicazioni] n. 5) Italian Franciscan missionaries;
an historical, bio-bibliographical synthesis. The 'Geographical-
chronological summary' (p. 265-341) lists missionaries in order
of date of death and yields some biographical data. In the historical text itself bio-bibliographical facts are given, with the
alphabetical name index as the means of locating particular individuals.

11774   FERRARIUS, PHILIPPUS, d. 1626.
Catalogvs sanctorvm Italiae in menses duodecim distributus;
in qvo vitae illorvm ex particvlarivm ecclesiarum monumentis
compendio describuntur, adiectis vbique scholijs, notisq ...
Mediolani [Milan] 1613. 822 p. Catalog of the Italian saints
distributed through the 12 months of the year, giving brief lives
compiled from the records of particular churches.

11775   KAMP, NORBERT
Kirche und Monarchie im staufischen Königreich Sizilien.
München, W. Fink, 1973-   v. 28cm. (Münstersche
Mittelalter-Schriften, Bd. 10-
Contents. --I. Prosopographische Grundlegung; Bistümer und
Bischöfe des Königreichs 1194-1266. 1. Abruzzen und Kam-
panien. 2. Apulien und Kalabrien. The first section of this
study of Church and State in medieval Sicily and Southern Italy
is a prosopography of bishops of the various dioceses. Biographical data is concerned primarily with activities of the bishops
during their terms in office. Vol. 1, pts. 1-2 issued as of 1975.

11776   MELLONI, GIOVAMBATTISTA, 1713-1781.
Atti o memorie degli uomini illustri in santità nati o morti

in Bologna ... Volume postumo a cura di A. Benati e M. Fanti.
Roma, Multigrafica editrice, 1971. lvii, 548 p. 26cm. (Monumenta Italiae ecclesiastica. Hagiographica, 1) A volume supplementary to Melloni's 6-vol. work of the same title (Bologna,
1773-1818) This vol. contains ca. 90 biographies of prominent
figures of the Catholic Church in Bologna as well as table of
contents for the earlier 6 vols.

11777   ZAVERIO, FRANCESCO (de S. Lorenzo della Costa)
         I cappuccini genovesi. Note biografiche. t. 1. Genova,
Tip. della Gioventu, 1912. vii, 530 p. illus., ports. 25cm.
No more published? A biographical dictionary (in several al-
phabets) of Capuchins in Genoa.

Japan

11778   CATALOGO E BREVI MEMORIE DEI DUECENTO E CINQUE
         BEATI MARTIRI NEL GIAPPONE. Roma, Coi tipi della
Civiltà Cattolica, 1867. 124 p. 15cm. Catalog and brief mem-
o. ⁓ ꝛf the 205 blessed Catholic martyrs in Japan.

Mexico

11779   ANDRADE, VICENTE DE PAULA, 1844-1915.
         Datos biográficos de los señores capitulares de la Santa
Iglesia Catedral de México. México, 1908. 279 p. 17cm.
Biographical facts concerning the capitulars (members of the
ecclesiastical chapter) of the Cathedral of Mexico City.

11780   GUTIÉRREZ CASILLAS, JOSÉ
         Jesuitas en México durante el siglo XIX. Con 220 retratos.
[1. ed.] México, Editorial Porrua, 1972. 542 p. illus., ports.
24cm. (Biblioteca Porrua, 52) On pages [275]-409 of this monograph on the Jesuits in Mexico during the 19th century is a biographical dictionary of said Jesuits (facts are given in a columnar chronological arrangement) followed by 220 portraits of near
contemporary Mexican Jesuits.

11781   VALLE, RAFAEL HELIODORO, 1891-
         Jesuitas de Tepozotlán. Bogotá, Instituto Caro y Cuervo,
1955. 109 p. 25cm. "De Thesaurus, boletín del Instituto Caro
y Cuervo, tomo IX, números 1, 2 y 3, 1953." Jesuits of the
Colegio of Tepotzotlán, Mexico; a bio-bibliographical work.

Moluccas

11782   WESSELS, CORNELIUS
         Catalogus patrum et fratrum e Societate Iesu qui in missione
Moluccana ab A. 1546 ad A. 1677 adlaboraverunt. [n. p., 1932]

[237]-253 p. 25cm. Cover title. Reprinted from Archivum historicum Societatis Iesu, I, 1932. A collection of 81 brief biographies of Jesuit missionaries who served in the Moluccas from 1546 to 1677; in chronological arrangement.

Netherlands

11783   AXTERS, STEPHANUS GÉRARD, 1901-
   Bibliotheca Dominicans Neerlandica manuscripta, 1224-1500, door Stephanus G. Axters. Louvain, Bureaux de la R. H. E., Bibliothèque de l'Université, 1970. 381 p. 25cm. (Bibliothèque de la Revue d'histoire ecclésiastique, fasc. 49) In two main parts; bio-bibliographical listing of Dutch Dominicans, their manuscripts and very brief notes on their lives, 1224-1500, and a similar listing for Dominicans outside of the Netherlands. The arrangement in each part is alphabetical by forename.

11784   TROEYER, BENJAMIN DE, 1913-
   Bio-bibliographia franciscana neerlandica saeculi XVI. Nieukoop, B. De Graaf, 1969-74. 3 v. illus., facsims. 25cm. Contents. --1. Pars biographica. De auteurs van de uitgegeven werken. --2. Pars bibliographica. De edities. --3. Pars bibliographica (Illustrationes incunabulorum). Bio-bibliography of 74 Dutch Franciscans of the 16th century (10 of them anonymous).

Palestine

11785   GOLUBOVICH, GIROLAMO, 1865-1941.
   Serie cronologica dei reverendissimi superiori di Terra Sancta; ossia, dei provinciali custodi e presidenti della medesima, già commissari apostolici dell'Oriente e sino al 1847 in officio di gran maestri del S. Militare Ordine dal SS. Sepolcro, attuali prelati mitrati, provinciali e custodi di T. S., guardiani del S. Monte Sion e del SS. Sepolcro di N. S. G. C. ecc. Nuova serie, con due appendici di documenti e firmani arabi inediti, e d'un sunto storico de' conventi, santuari ed istituti di beneficenza dipendenti da Terra Santa. Gerusalemme, Tip. del Convento di S. Salvatore, 1898. xxxii, 272 p. 31cm. Biographical data (in chronological arrangement) on Franciscan superiors and other officials of that order in the Holy Land.

Poland

11786   HAGIOGRAFIA POLSKA; słownik bio-bibliograficzny. Dzieło zbiorowe pod red. Romualda Gustawa. [Wyd. 1] Poznań, Ksieg. św. Wojciecha [1971] 2 v. 25cm. A bio-bibliographical dictionary of 100 Polish saints and prominent figures in Polish church history.

Portugal

11787   CARDOSO, JORGE, 1606-1669
Agiologio lvsitano dos sanctos, e varoens illvstres em
virtvde do reino de Portvgal, e svas conqvistas. Lisboa, Officina Craesbeekiana, 1652-1744. 4 v. 29cm. Vol. 4 written by
Antonio Caetano de Sousa. No more published. Imprint varies.
Portuguese saints and famous Portuguese, arranged by the
months of the calendar. Goes up through the month of August
only.

11788   CASTRO, JOSÉ DE, 1886-
O cardial nacional. Lisboa, Divisão de Publicações e
Biblioteca, Agência Geral das Colonias, 1943. 456 p. facsims.
23cm. At head of title: República Portuguesa. Ministério das
Colonias. Bishops and cardinals of Lisbon.

Scotland

11789   WATT, DONALD ELMSLIE ROBERTSON
Fasti Ecclesiae Scoticanae Medii Aevi ad annum 1638.
Second draft, by D. E. R. Watt. Edinburgh, Printed for the
Society by Smith and Ritchie, 1969. xxi, 411 p. 22cm. (Scottish Record Society. [Publications] new ser., 1) In large part
a listing and register of medieval Scottish clergy arranged under
diocese; however some biographical material is provided for
major figures, as well as references to sources for these figures. Detailed name index at end of volume.

Spain

11790   COLLELL COSTA, ALBERTO
Escritores dominicos del principado de Cataluña. Barcelona, Casa Provincial de Caridad, Impr. Escuela, 1965. 304 p.
facsims. 24cm. Writers of the Dominican Order in the 'principality' of Catalonia.

11791   DICCIONARIO DE HISTORIA ECLESIÁSTICA DE ESPANA.
Dirigido por Quintín Aldea Vaquero, Tomás Marín Marti-
nez, José Vives Gatell. Madrid, Instituto Enrique Florez,
Consejo Superior de Investigaciones Cientificas, 1972-75. 4 v.
illus. 28cm. Contents. --1. A-C. --2. Ch-Man. --3. Man-Ru. --
4. S-Z. A dictionary of Spanish church history; biographies of
Spanish churchmen constitute a large part of the dictionary.

11792   ESCRITORES CARTUJANOS ESPAÑOLES, por un cartujo de
Aula Dei e Ildefonso M. Gómez. Abadia de Montserrat,
1970. 228 p. 25cm. (Scripta et documenta, 19) "Este volumen

constituye una separata de Studia monastica, IX (1967)-XI (1969),
con algunas correcciones de detalle, un nuevo prólogo del P.
General de la Cartuja y cinco índices." Spanish Carthusian
authors; a bio-biographical dictionary of 224 writers, chiefly
from the 14th to the 18th centuries.

11793   NIETO, A
         Adiciones a los Escritores franciscanos de la Provincia de
Cartagena. (In Archivo ibero-americano. Madrid, 1933-35.
XXXVI, p. 94-144; XXXVIII, p. 76-102) Additions to the work of
Antonio Martín: Apuntes bio-bibliográficos sobre los religiosos
escritores hijos de la provincia seráfica de Cartagena ... (q. v.
--item 8046, 1st supplement)

11794   ROBLES, LAUREANO
         Escritores dominicos de la Corona de Aragón (siglos XIII-
XV). Salamanca [Imp. Calatrava] 1972. 304 p. 24cm. In
Latin or Spanish. Dominican writers of the Kingdom of Aragon
in the 13th-15th centuries; a bio-bibliography.

11795   SALAMANCA. PONTIFICIA UNIVERSIDAD ECLESIÁSTICA.
         INSTITUTO DE HISTORIA DE LA TEOLOGÍA.
         Repertorio de historia de las ciencias eclesiásticas en
España. Salamanca, 1967-   v. 25cm. (Corpus
scriptorum sacrorum Hispaniae. Estudios, v. 1-
Principally a bio-bibliography of Spanish Church figures, including members of various monastic orders, from the Church's
origins. Entries are under names in religion or surnames.
The arrangement is, in general, chronological and/or under religious order. There is an alphabetical name index at the end of
each vol. Entries vary in length from little or nothing, insofar
as biographical data is concerned, to a page. 4 vols, covering
the 13th to the 16th centuries, were issued up to 1972.

11796   SOLLANA, EMILIO MARÍA DE
         Escritores capuchinos de Alicante y su provincia. Alicante,
Comisión Provincial de Monumentos Históricos y Artísticos,
1958. 65 p. 22cm. (Bibliografía Alicantino, 24. Concurso
bibliográfico, 4) Capuchin writers of Alicante, Spain and its
province.

11797   VARONES INSIGNES DE LA CONGREGACIÓN DE VALLADOLID,
         según un manuscrito del siglo XVIII. Prologado y com-
pletado por Justo Pérez de Urbel. [Pontevedra, España] Museo
Provincial de Pontevedra [1967] 370 p. 25cm. Published from
the manuscript conserved in the Museo Provincial de Pontevedra
with title: Varones memorables de la Congregación de San Beni-
to de España llamada de Valladolid. Possibly the work of Ramón
Alvarez, monk and later abbot of the Monastery of San Pedro de
Cardeña in the 18th century. A bio-bibliographical dictionary of
Benedictines, Congregation of Valladolid, Spain, to the 18th cen-

tury; the work has several alphabetical arrangements: pt. 1, writers; pt. 2, translators; pt. 3, bishops and famous authors; pt. 4, authors of unpublished works; a 5th part with no particular designation.

Switzerland

11798   HELVETIA SACRA. Begründet von Rudolf Henggeler. Hrsg. von Albert Bruckner. Bern, Francke [1972-   v. in maps. 24cm. Contents: Abt. 1, Bd. 1. Schweizerische Kardinäle. Das apostolische Gesandtschaftswesen in der Schweiz. Erzbistümer und Bistümer I, A-Ch.

Abt. 5. Der Franziskusorden.   v. --Abt. 6. Die Karmeliter in der Schweiz. --Abt. 7. Die Somasker in der Schweiz.   The Catholic Church in Switzerland. Each volume contains extensive biographical sections on bishops and other church officials, clergy, monks, etc. Alphabetical approach available only thru' indexes at end of each vol. Sect. 1, v.1 ; sect. 5, v.2; and sect. 6-7 available as of 1976. Supersedes a work of the same title authored by R. Henggeler (Zug, Switzerland, 1961: 288 p. 25cm.)

United States

11799   BRASSARD, GERARD
        Biographical and heraldic dictionary of the Catholic bishops in America. Worcester, Mass., Stobbs Press, 1960-   v. illus., ports. 29cm. Contents. --
v.2. The South Atlantic States. --v. 3. The New England States. Also issued within his Armorial of the American hierarchy; the Roman Catholic Church in the United States of America (?)

11800   CLARKE, RICHARD HENRY, 1827-1911.
        Lives of the deceased bishops of the Catholic Church in the United States, with an appendix and an analytical index. Author's rev., enl. and corrected ed. New York, R. H. Clarke, 1888. 3 v. 25cm. In chronological arrangement; over 100 bishops' lives are treated.

11801   REUSS, FRANCIS XAVIER
        Biographical cyclopedia of the Catholic hierarchy of the United States, 1784-1898. Milwaukee, Diederich-Schaefer Co., 1898. 129 p.

11802   THE ZACATECAN MISSIONARIES IN TEXAS, 1716-1834; excerpts from the Libros de los decretos of the Missionary College of Zacatecas, 1707-1828. Translated by Fr. Benedict Leutenegger. And A biographical dictionary, by Fr. Marion A. Habig. Austin, Tex., 1973. [12], 181 p. illus. 28cm. (Texas

Historical Survey Committee. Office of the State Archeologist reports, no. 23) The biographical dictionary (p. [105]-156) contains 119 biographies of the Zacatecan (Franciscan) missionaries in Texas (18th-early 19th centuries).

Friends, Society of

11803   A COLLECTION OF MEMORIALS CONCERNING DIVERS DE-
            CEASED MINISTERS AND OTHERS OF THE PEOPLE
         CALLED QUAKERS, in Pennsylvania, New-Jersey, and parts
         adjacent, from nearly the first settlement thereof to the year
         1787. With some of the last expressions and exhortations of
         many of them. Philadelphia, Printed by Crukshank, 1787. viii,
         439 p. 20cm.

Lutheran Church

11804   BÄTZING, GERHARD
            Pfarrergeschichte des Kirchenkreises Wolfhagen von An-
         fängen bis 1968. Bearb. von Gerhard Bätzing. Marburg, N.
         G. Elwert (Kommissionsverlag), 1975. xxiii, 314 p. 2 geneal.
         tables (in pocket) 25cm. (Kurhessisch-Waldeckisches Pfarrer-
         buch, 1. Bd.) (Veröffentlichungen der Historischen Kommission
         für Hessen, 33) Biographical-genealogical data for clergy of
         Wolfhagen, Hesse, from the 12th century to 1968. Majority of
         the clergy covered are Lutheran.

11805   A BIOGRAPHICAL DIRECTORY OF CLERGYMEN OF THE
            AMERICAN LUTHERAN CHURCH. Arnold R. Mickelson,
         editor. Robert C. Wiederaenders, associate editor. Minne-
         apolis, Augsburg Pub. House, 1972. ix, 1054 p. ports. 24cm.
         Published in 1962 under title: A biographical directory of pas-
         tors of the American Lutheran Church, compiled by J. M. Jen-
         sen, C. E. Linder and G. Giving.

11806   DEN DANSKE PRAESTEFORENING.
            Teologisk stat. [Ny udg.] 1965-66. Udg. af Dan Danske
         praesteforening i samarbejde med Kirkeministeriet. Hillerød,
         R. Pallesens bogtr., 1965-67. 2 v. 25cm. Contents.--bd. 1.
         Dansk kirkeret, af August Roesen. 2. udg.--bd. 2. Danske
         teologer og praester. Med en oversigt over Danmarks prae-
         steembeder. Redigeret af Sven Houmøller. A directory-biog-
         raphy of the Danish clergy (Danske folkekirke) and theologians
         of today.

11807   JENSEN, JOHN MARTIN, 1893-
            A biographical directory of pastors of the American Luther-
         an Church. Compiled by John M. Jensen, Carl E. Linder [and]
         Gerald Giving. Minneapolis, Augsburg Pub. House [1962] 857 p.
         ports. 24cm.

11808   KIRKELIG HAANDBOG. Udg. paa foranledning af den Danske
            praesteforening. København, Gyldendal.   v.
            25cm. Handbook for the Danish folkekirke which includes bio-
            graphical sketches of the Danish clergy, especially graduates of
            Copenhagen University. 1972 and 1975 editions are the latest
            issues published.

11809   LUTHERAN CHURCH IN AMERICA. SOUTH CAROLINA SYNOD.
            HISTORY OF THE SYNOD COMMITTEE.
            A history of the Lutheran Church in South Carolina. [Co-
            lumbia, S. C.] South Carolina Synod of the Lutheran Church in
            America, 1971. xiii, 966 p. illus., ports. 24cm. "Biographi-
            cal sketches of pastors" (a biographical dictionary): p. 831-915.

11810   LUTHERAN CYCLOPEDIA. Erwin L. Lueker, editor. Rev.
            ed. St. Louis, Concordia Pub. House [1975] xiv, 845 p.
            27cm. Includes many biographical sketches of historical church
            personages with emphasis on Lutherans and special emphasis on
            American Lutherans. 1st ed. was issued in 1954 (xii, 1160 p.
            24cm.)

11811   NORSK MISJONSLEKSIKON. Utg. med tilslutning fra Norsk
            misjonsrad og de misjoner dette representerer. Redaksjon:
            Fridtjov Birkeli [m. fl.] Stavanger, Nomi, 1965-67. 3 v. illus.,
            ports. 28cm. A biographical dictionary of Norwegian mission-
            aries.

11812   WHITE UNTO HARVEST: a survey of Lutheran United Mission,
            the China mission of the Norwegian Lutheran Church of
            Ameriea. Written by missionaries in the field. Editorial Com-
            mittee: T. Ekeland, Albert Anderson, Olive T. Christensen.
            Minneapolis, Board of Foreign Missions, 1919. 253, [3] p.
            illus., ports. 23cm. "Biographies of the missionaries ... "
            (p. [221]-245) forms a biographical dictionary (with portraits)
            of 92 missionaries of the Norwegian Lutheran Church of Ameri-
            ca in China.

Mennonites

11813   KAUFMAN, EDMUND GEORGE
            General Conference Mennonite pioneers. North Newton,
            Kan., Bethel College, 1973. xii, 438 p. illus., ports. 24cm.
            Biographies of 58 American members of the General Conference
            Mennonite Church (19th-20th centuries)

Methodists

11814   THE ENCYCLOPEDIA OF WORLD METHODISM. Sponsored by
            the World Methodist Council and the Commission on Ar-
            chives and History of the United Methodist Church. Nolan B.

Harmon, general editor. Albea Godbold [and] Louise L. Queen,
assistants to the general editor. Nashville, Tenn., United
Methodist Pub. House, 1974. 2 v. (2814 p.) illus., ports.
29cm. A large proportion of the work is devoted to biographies
of prominent Methodists throughout the world, past and present.

11815   A HISTORY OF THE METHODIST CHURCH IN CEYLON, 1814-
         1964. Colombo, Wesley Press [1971] 666 p. 22cm. "A
         biographical list of Methodist ministers in Ceylon, 1814-1964":
         p. [607]-647. British and native clergymen.

11816   THE METHODIST LOCAL PREACHERS' WHO'S WHO.
             1934-   A complete record of the lives and careers of
         Methodist local preachers. With an introd. by John Scott Lidgett.
         [London] Published by Shaw Pub. Co. with the co-operation of
         the Methodist Church Connexional Local Preachers' Committee
         and the Methodist Local Preachers' Mutual Aid Association,
         1934-   v. ports. 23cm. 1934 vol. (631 p.) was the only
         one ever issued? English Methodist ministers living in 1934.

11817   WALLS, WILLIAM JACOB, Bp., 1885-
             The African Methodist Episcopal Zion Church; reality of
         the Black church. Charlotte, N. C., A. M. E. Zion Pub. House
         [1974] 669 p. illus., ports. 24cm. "Part VII: Paramount
         functionalities; the bishops" (p. 565-619) gives biographical
         sketches of the 75 bishops of the Church (accompanied mostly by
         portraits) in chronological arrangement.

Mormons

Bibliography, Indexes, Portrait Catalogs

11818   MERRILL LIBRARY. SPECIAL COLLECTIONS DEPT.
             Name index to the Library of Congress collection of Mormon
         diaries. Logan, Utah State University Press, 1971. 391 p. 28cm.
         (Western Text Society series, v. 1, no. 2)

General Works

11819   FLAKE, LAWRENCE R
             Mighty men of Zion: General Authorities of the last dispen-
         sation. Salt Lake City, K. D. Butler, 1974. xx, 536 p. ports.
         24cm. Includes ca. 190 biographies of prominent figures in the
         Church of Jesus Christ of Latter-Day Saints (Mormons). Not in
         alphabetical arrangement, but there is an alphabetical index at
         the end.

Orthodox Eastern Church

11820   DEMETRAKOPOULOS, ANDRONIKOS K   d. 1872.
        Orthodoxos Hellas; etoi Peri ton Hellenon ton grapsanton
kata Latinon kai peri ton syngrammaton auton. En Leipsia,
Typois Metzger kai Wittig, 1872. Athenai, Bibliopoleion N.
Karabia, 1968. 12, 204 p. 22cm. (Bibliotheke historikon mele-
ton, 26) Bio-bibliography of Orthodox Eastern Church writers
who opposed the positions of the Roman Catholic Church; in
chronological arrangement; over 200 authors are considered.

Orthodox Eastern Church, Russian

11821   SLOVAR' ISTORICHESKII O SVIATYKH, proslavlennykh v
        rossiiskoi tserkvi, i o niekotorykh podvizhnikakh blago-
chestiia, miestno chtimykh. Izd. 2. (ispr. i dop.) S.-Peter-
burg, V. Tip. II Otd-iia Sobstvennoi E. I. V. Kantseliarii, 1862.
xii, 260, 14 p. 28cm. Historical dictionary of the Saints of the
Russian Orthodox Church. 1st ed. issued in 1835 or 6 (collation: viii, 303 p. 28cm.).

Presbyterians

11822   BURY CLASSIS (PRESBYTERIAN)
        Minutes of the Bury Presbyterian Classis, 1647-1657. Ed-
ited by William A. Shaw. Manchester, Eng., Chetham Society,
1896-98. 2 v. 23cm. (Remains, historical and literary, connected with the Palatine counties of Lancaster and Chester, new
ser., v. 36, 41) Paged continuously. "An account of the ministers mentioned in the Bury minutes": p. 205-265--a biographical dictionary of English Presbyterian clergymen of the 17th century.

11823   DEDHAM CLASSIS (PRESBYTERIAN)
        The Presbyterian movement in the reign of Queen Elizabeth
as illustrated by the Minute book of the Dedham Classis, 1582-
1589. Edited for the Royal Historical Society, from the MS. in
the possession of J. F. Gurney ... by Roland G. Usher. London, Royal Historical Society, 1905. li, 105 p. 22cm. (Royal
Historical Society. Publications. Camden series, 3d ser., v. 8)
"A list of Puritan ministers concerned in the classical movement": p. xxxv-li--a biographical dictionary of English Presbyterian clergymen of the latter part of the 16th century (chiefly
from the County of Essex) with references to biographical
sources.

11824   A HISTORY OF THE WESTMINISTER ASSEMBLY OF DIVINES.
        Embracing an account of its principal transactions, and
biographical sketches of its most conspicuous members. Com-

piled for the Board of Publication from the best authorities.
Philadelphia, Presbyterian Board of Publication, 1841. 430 p.
20cm. "Part II: Biographical sketches of the Westminister divines" (p. [183]-430) is a biographical dictionary to p. 420—105
clergymen attending the Assembly of British Presbyterians in
1643-1646.

11825   MANCHESTER CLASSIS (PRESBYTERIAN)
         Minutes of the Manchester Presbyterian Classis [1646-1660]
Edited by William A. Shaw. [Manchester, Eng.] Chetham Society, 1890-91. 3 v. 23cm. (Remains, historical and literary,
connected with the Palatine counties of Lancaster and Chester,
new ser., v. 20, 22, 24) Paged continuously. "An account of
the ministers mentioned in these minutes": v. 3, p. 402-451--a
biographical dictionary of English Presbyterian clergymen (County of Lancashire) in the 17th century.

11826   NEVIN, ALFRED, 1816-1890, ed.
         The encyclopaedia of the Presbyterian Church in the United
States of America: including the Northern and Southern Assemblies. Alfred Nevin, editor, assisted by B. M. Smith, W. E.
Schenck and other eminent ministers of the church. D. R. B.
Nevin, managing editor. Philadelphia, Presbyterian Encyclopaedia Pub. Co., 1884. 1248 p. illus., ports. 29cm. Largely
devoted to biographical sketches of American Presbyterian
clergy.

11827   REFORMED PRESBYTERIAN CHURCH OF IRELAND.
         Fasti of the Reformed Presbyterian Church of Ireland.
Compiled and edited by Adam Loughridge. [Belfast, Published
jointly by the Committee on Church History of the Reformed
Presbyterian Synod of Ireland and the Presbyterian Historical
Society, 1970-   v. 22cm. A biographical dictionary; pt. 1: Aiken, Samuel to Young, Robert. Vol. 1 only available as of 1976?

11828   WILSON, JOHN, Clerk to the Synod of Perth and Stirling.
         The Presbytery of Perth; or, Memoirs of the members,
ministers of the several parishes within the bounds, from the
Reformation to the present time, compiled from the records of
the Presbytery and other sources. Perth, Mrs. C. Paton,
1860. xiii, 292 p. 8.° Ministers of the Church of Scotland in
the Presbytery of Perth.

Protestant Churches

General Works

11829   CUMMINGS, PRESTON, 1800-1875.
         A dictionary of Congregational usages and principles accord-

ing to ancient and modern authors: to which are added brief notices of some of the principal writers, assemblies and treatises
referred to in the compilation. Stereotype ed., rev., collated
and enl. Boston, S. K. Whipple, 1853. 432 p. 20cm. "Notices" (p. [391]-432] comprise a biographical dictionary of various
figures in English and American church history, especially New
England & Massachusetts ministers of the 17th-19th centuries.

11830   PUAUX, FRANÇOIS, 1806-1895.
         Galerie des personnages célèbres qui ont figuré dans l'his-
toire du protestantisme français, par F. Puaux. Strasbourg,
Impr. de Vve. Berger-Levrault, 1862-64. 3 v. ports. 8.°
Gallery of famous persons who have been prominent in the history of French Protestantism; biographies with portraits.

11831   VALLÉE, LOUIS
         Dictionnaire du protestantisme; ou, Histoire de l'établis-
sement de la Réforme depuis son origine jusqu'à nos jours.
Petit-Montrouge, J.-P. Migne, 1858. 1384 columns. illus.
8.° (Troisième et dernière Encyclopédie théologique, t. 36)
Dictionary of Protestantism from the Reformation to 1858; includes biographical entries.

11832   [WYLIE, ALEXANDER] 1815-1887.
         Memorials of Protestant missionaries to the Chinese: giving
a list of their publications, and obituary notices of the deceased.
Shanghai, American Presbyterian Mission Press, 1867. vi,
331 p. 24cm. Bio-bibliographical sketches of 338 English and
American missionaries to China (chiefly 19th century).

St. Thomas Christians

11833   THE ST. THOMAS CHRISTIAN ENCYCLOPAEDIA OF INDIA.
         Edited by George Menachery. Board of editorial consult-
ants: E. R. Hambye [and others] Trichur, St. Thomas Christian Encyclopaedia of India, 1973-   v. -illus. 29cm.
Vol. 2 (and presumably vol. 1 and succeeding volumes) has a
section: "Minor articles," which is a dictionary of persons,
place names, etc. connected with the St. Thomas Christians.
As of 1976 only v. 2 (1973) has been issued.

Unitarians

11834   CARTER, GEORGE
         Unitarian biographical dictionary; being short notices of the
lives of noteworthy Unitarians, and kindred thinkers, brought
down to the year 1900. London, Unitarian Christian Pub. Office, 1902. vi, 144 p. 19cm.

United Brethren In Christ

11835   KOONTZ, PAUL RODES, 1890-
The bishops, Church of the United Brethren in Christ,
from the organization in 1800 to the merger with the Evangelical
Church in 1946, thereby forming the Evangelical United Brethren
Church. By Paul Rodes Koontz and Walter Edwin Roush. Day-
ton, Ohio, Otterbein Press, 1950. 2 v. illus., ports. 21cm.

Hinduism

11836   BHATTACĀRYA, PRAMATHANĀTHA
Bharatera sādhaka. Calcutta, Prachi Publications, 1961-
v. illus., ports. 23cm. Biographies of holy men of
India. In Bengali. 11 vols. published as of 1968, with from 5
to 12 biographies in each.

11837   SHAMA RAO, TALLAK SUBBANNA, 1906-
Sivasarana kathāratnakośa. Mysore, Tulukinavenkaneya
Smarat Granthmala, 1967. xx, 647 p. illus. 25cm. In Kan-
nada. Encyclopedia of Lingayat saints.

11838   VIDYALANKAR, SASHI BHUSHAN
Jeevanikosha; short biographical sketches of personalities
mentioned in Vedas, Upanishads, Ramayana, Mahabharata,
Puranas, Tantras, etc. Calcutta, 1932. 5 v. In Bengali.
Biographical dictionary of important personalities mentioned in
Hindu scriptures and classics.

Islam

11839   AHMAD IBN 'ALI, AL-NAJASHI
Kitab al-rijāl. [Bombay, 1899] 340 p. Bio-bibliographical dictionary of narrators of Islamic tradition and of Shiites.

11840   AL-AZDI (ABD AL-GHANĪ IBN SA'ID IBN 'ALI IBN SA'ĪD)
Kitāb al-Mu'talif wa'l-muhtalif fī asmā' naqalat al-Hadīt
wa-Kitāb Mushtabih al-nisbah. [Allahabad, 1909] 136, 80, 4,
12, 4 p. 4.º A dictionary, arranged alphabetically, of the
names of traditionalists which can easily be confounded; to
which is attached the author's Mushtabih al-nisbah, a similar
dictionary dealing with gentilic names. Edited by Muhammad
Muhyī al-Dīn al'Ja'fazi al-Zainabī.

11841   AL DULĀBĪ, MUHAMMAD IBN AHMAD
Kitāb al-Kunā wa 'l-asmā. Haidarabad, 1904-05. 2 pts. in
1 v. 13". A dictionary-index of surnames of traditionists, con-

taining a number of traditions in the isnāds (chain of tɪ ɪdition-
ists) of which these surnames occur. Indexed and partly edited
by Muhammad Sharīf al-Dīn al-Fālamī.

11842   IBN AL-MURTADĀ AHMAD IBN YAHYA, 1363-1437.
         Kitāb tabaqāt al-mu'tazilah. [Beirut, Deutsche Morgen-
ländische Gesellschaft] 1961. xviii, 189, xx p. 25cm. (Bibliotheca Islamica, Bd. 21) The book of the 'lasses' of Mutazilites;
arranged by 'generation' Added t. p.: Die Klassen der Mu'-
taziliten. Edited by Suzanne Diwald-Wilzer.

11843   IBN AL-QAYSARĀNĪ, MUHAMMAD IBN ṬĀHIR, 1056-1113.
         Hādhā kitāb al-Jam' bayna kitābay Abi Nasr al-Kalābādhī
wa-Abī Bakr al-Isbahāni. [Hyderabad, 1905] 2 v. in 1 (638, 70 p.)
25cm. Biographies of the Muslim traditionists (ahl al-Hadith)
based on material from the works of al-Kalābādhī and al-Isbahānī.

11844   IBN HAJAR AL-'ASQALĀNĪ, AHMAD IBN 'ALĪ, 1372-1449.
         Kitāb lisān al-mizān. [Hyderabad, 1911-13] 6 v. in 3.
25cm. Biographies of the Muslim traditionists; authorities on
the Hadith, the narratives or traditions that relate the sayings
or actions of Mohammed & his companions.

11845   IBN HAJAR AL-'ASQALĀNĪ, AHMAD IBN 'ALĪ, 1372-1449.
         Tahdhib al-Tahdhib. Beirut, Dar Sadr,
[1968] 12 v. 25cm. Added title page: Tahdib at-Tahdib [by] Ibn
Hagar al-'Asqalāni. Reprint of the ed. published in Hyderabad,
1325-37 A. H. Based on al-Mizzi's Tahdhib al-Kamāl, itself a
revision of al-Jammā'ili's al-Kamāl fi ma'rifat asmā' al-rijāl.
Biographical dictionary of Muslim traditionists.

11846   IBN RAJAB, 'ABD AL-RAHMĀN IBN AHMAD, d. 1393.
         Kitāb al-dhayl 'alā Tabaqāt al-Hanābilah. [Damascus]
[1951-   v. facsims. 25cm. On cover: Histoire des
hanbalites, par Ibn Rağab al-Bāgdadi. History and biography of
the Hanbalites, followers of the Muslim school of theology, law,
& morality based on the teachings of Ahmad ibn Hanbal; supplement to Ibn Abi Ya'la's work: Tabaqat al-Hanabilah.

11847   KHAZRAJĪ, AHMAD IBN ABD ALLĀH
         Khulasat tadhib al-kamāl fi asmā' al-rijal. [Cairo, 1905]
431 p. 4.° A dictionary of the names of traditionists, with short
notes as to date, credibility and other matters, being an abridge-
ment of al-Dhahabi's Tadhib al-tahdib.

11848   MUHAMMAD BĀQĪR IBN ZAIN AL-'ABIDĪN, AL-MŪSAWĪ AL-
         KHWĀNSARI
         Ahsan al-wadi'ah ... [Baghdad, 1348 A. H., 1929] 2 v.

Biographies of famous Shiites; being a continuation of the author's Raudāt al-jannat.

11849   MUHAMMAD BĀQIR IBN ZAIN AL-'ĀBIDĪN, AL-MŪSAWĪ AL-
        KHWANSĀRĪ
            Raudāt al-jannāt fī akhwal al-'ulamā' wa's-sādāt. [Tehe-
        ran, 1888] 4 v. in 1. Biographical dictionary of learned men
        (scholars and writers) chiefly Shittes.

11850   MU'IN AL-DIN JUNAID AL-SHIRĀZĪ
            Shadd al-izār fī hatt al-awzār 'an zuwwār al-mazār. [Te-
        heran] 1910-11. vi, 631 p. 24cm. Pilgrimage to the holy places
        of Shiraz, Iran; 315 biographical sketches of the saints and mys-
        tics of Shiraz.

11851   MUSTAFĀ IBN AL-HUSAIN AL-HUSAINI AL-TAFRISHĪ, 17th
        cent.
            Naqd ar-rijāl. [Teheran, 1900/01] 427 p. 4.º Biographi-
        cal dictionary of Shiite traditionists.

11852   AL-SADR, HASAN IBN HĀDĪ, 1856-1935.
            Ta'sis al-Shi'ah li-'ulūm al-Islām. al-Kazimiyyah [Iraq,
        1951] 445 p. 24cm. Chiefly bio-bibliography of the Shiites.

11853   AL-SULAMĪ, MUHAMMAD IBN AL-HUSAYN, d. 1021.
            Kitab tabaqāt al-Sūfiyya. Texte arabe, avec une introd. et
        un index par Johannes Pedersen. Leiden, E. J. Brill, 1960.
        97, 590 p. 25cm. Added t. p. in Arabic. The book of the 'gen-
        erations' of Sufi mystics; 105 biographical notices.

11854   AL-SUYŪTĪ, 1445-1505.
            Specimen a litteris orientalibus, exhibens Sojutii librum De
        interpretibus Korani, ex MS. codice Bibliothecae Leidensis
        editum et annotatione illustratum, quod ad publicam disceptation-
        em proponit Albertus Meursinge. Lugduni Batavorum, Apud S.
        & J. Luchtmans, 1839. [Teheran, M. H. Asadi, 1960] [2] p.,
        facsim.: 188, [4], 43 p. 29cm. (Arabic and Persian texts se-
        ries, 1) Added t. p.: Tabaqat al-mufassirin, by Jalalu'ddin as-
        Suyuti, edited by A. Meursinge. Photographically reproduced
        from the Leyden edition. Biographical sketches of critics and
        commentators on the Koran.

11855   AL-TĀDILĪ, ABŪ YA'QŪB YŪSUF IBN YAHYĀ, d. 1929 or 30.
            al-Tashawwuf ilā rijāl al-tasawwuf. Ar-Ribāt (Rabat) In-
        stitut des hautes études marocaines, 1377 [1958] 10,551 p.
        26cm. Cover title: at-Tašawwuf ilä rijāl at-tasawwuf. Vies
        des saints du sud marocain. Texte arabe établi et publié par A.
        Faure. Biographies of Sufi saints of South Morocco, 5th-7th
        century after the Hegira. Indeterminate arrangement (entries

by kunya) with an alphabetical name index to the biographies on
p. 483-498.

11856   AL-TAHRĀNĪ, AGHĀ BUZURK
          Tabakat (or Tabaqāt) a'lam al'shi'at. Nejet (Iraq), al-
        Matba'at al-'ilmiyat, 1954-56. 2 v. 25cm. Biographical dic-
        tionary of Shiites.

Jainism

11857   HASTIMALLA, fl. 1290.
          Pattāvalī parabandha sangraha. Jaipur, Jain Itihas Nirman
        Samity, 1968. 39, 872 p. 22cm. (Jaina Itihāsa Nirmāna
        Samiti prakāśana, 1) Edited by Narendra Bhanawat. Biographi-
        cal data for Jain gurus of the Lanka and Sthanakavasi lineages of
        the Swetambara School. In Marathi.

Judaism

11858   JERUSHALMI, JOSEPH
          'Ishim u-sefarim ba-Mikra. Haifa, La student, 1970. v,
        125 p. 24cm. On verso of t. p.: Bibliography of persons and
        books in the Bible; articles from Hebrew periodicals and col-
        lections.

General Works

11859   BUBER, SALOMON, 1827-1906.
          Anshe shem ... Cracow, 1895. xxviii, 249 p. 24cm.
        Added t. p.: Anshe shem. Biographien und Leichensteinin-
        schriften von Rabbinen, Lehrhausvorstehern, Religionsweisern,
        Rabbinatsassessoren und Gemeindevorstehern, die während
        eines Zeitraumes von vierhundert Jahren (1500-1890) in Lemberg
        lehrten und wirkten ... Krakau, 1895. Biographies and epi-
        taphs of rabbis, teachers, etc. in Lemberg, Poland, 1500-1890.
        Reprinted in 1967 or 8 in Jerusalem (?)

11860   KAMELHAR, JEKUTHIEL ARYEH, 1869 or 70-1937.
          Sefer Dor de'ah, Peri 'eto shel Jekuthiel Aryeh Kamelhar.
        [Yerushalayim? 1969 or 70] 3 v. ports. 23cm. Reprint of
        Bilgoraj, 1932 or 3-1934 or 5 edition. Vol. 3 originally publish-
        ed in Piotrków. General survey of methods and actions of the
        standard-bearers of Hasidism. Vol. 1 contains 16 biographies
        of major figures. Vols. 2-3 each contain ca. 200 biographical
        sketches.

11861   KOHN, DAVID, 1838-1915.
          Toldot ha-mekubalim, ha-Shabeta'im veha-Hasidim. 'Al-

pi mekor כt yeshanim va-hadashim ('im toledot ha-mehaber u-
temunato) be-'arba'ah sefarim. Mahadurah 2. be-hosafot ve-
tikunim rabim 'im 'eser temunot 'atikot shel r'ashe ba'ale ha-
me'ora'ot haba'im ba-sefarim ha-hem. 'Odisah, Moriyah, 673-
74 [1913-14] Yerushalayim, Makor, 730 [1969 or 70] 2 v. ports.
25cm. Biographies of ca. 85 Cabalists, Sabbatians and Hasadists
(16th-18th century). Indexes of proper names at end of vol. 2.

11862   NAFTAL, ABRAHAM MOSES.
        ha-Talmud ve-yotsrav; sifrut ha-Talmud behithavutah, ha-
reka' ha-ruhani, ha-hevrati vehamedini, ba-'arets uva-tefutsot,
yeshivot Bavel ve-'erets Yisrael ... me'atsve ruah ha-doroth,
toldotam, 'ishiyutam u-fo'olam [me'et] Avraham Mosheh Naftal.
Tel-Aviv, Yavneh [1969-70] 2 v. maps. 25cm. Vol. 1: A substantial number of biographies of commentators on the Mishnah
(Tana'im) and initiators of its compilation (from 70 to 200 A. D.)
Vol. 2: Intellectual biographies of Talmudic scholars ('Amora'im)
and their contributions to the Babylonian and Jerusalem Talmud
(from 200 to 500 A. D. '.

11863   RAPHAEL, ITZHAK, 1914-   ed.
        Sefer ha-hasidut. Tel-Aviv, 'Avraham Ziyoni, 1955. 19,
564 p. illus., ports. 25cm. Includes short biographies and
selections from the works of 100 Hasidim, members of a Jewish
religious sect.

11864   RESEARCH INSTITUTE OF RELIGIOUS JEWRY, NEW YORK.
        Eleh ezkerah ... New York, 1956-65. 6 v. ports. 26cm.
Added t. p.: These will I remember; biographies of leaders of
religious Jewry in Europe who perished during the years 1939-
1945.

11865   ROSMARIN, AARON, 1896-
        Arn Rozmarin's Tanakh entsiklopedye. Perzenlikhten,
proges un entfers loit Talmud, Midrash, Zoar, Rishonim un
Aharonim. [New York] Um Pab, 724-   [1964-   v.
27cm. Added t. p.: Aaron Rosmarin's Bible encyclopedia. Primarily a dictionary (in Yiddish) of Biblical (Old Testament--
Talmud, Midrash, etc.) biography.

Roman Empire

11866   SZEMLER, G   J
        The priests of the Roman Republic; a study of interactions
between priesthoods and magistracies. Brussels, Latomus,
1972. 224 p. illus. 25cm. (Collection Latomus, v. 127) A
prosopographical study of all known priests from ca. 300 B. C.
to the death of Julius Caesar; includes, in chronological arrangement, all the available data concerning ca.226 priests. Alphabetical approach through the general index.

Shinto

11867   ANZU, MOTOHIKO, 1912-
        Shintō jiten. Tokyo, Hori Shoten, 1974. 666, 60 p. 23cm.
        Contains short biographies of several hundred Shintoists, with
        portraits. By Motohiko Anzu & Yoshihiko Umeda.

11868   SHINTO DAIJITEN. Tokyo, Heibonsha, 1937-40. 3 v. (1474 p.)
        illus. 27cm. A dictionary of Shinto; includes biographies
        of prominent Shinto priests and scholars. Reprinted in 1974(?)

SCIENCE

Bibliography, Indexes, Portrait Catalogs

11869   BARR, E   SCOTT
        An index to biographical fragments in unspecialized sci-
        entific journals. University, Ala., University of Alabama
        Press, 1973. vii, 294 p. 25cm. Covers about 7,700 individ-
        uals, providing about 15,000 citations and about 1,500 portrait
        locations which are found in: American journal of science, 1819-
        1920; Proceedings of the Edinburgh Royal Society, 1832-1920;
        Proceedings of the Royal Society of London, 1800-1933, Nature,
        1869-1918; Popular science monthly, 1872-1915; Philosophical
        magazine, 1798-1902; Science, 1883-1894; and Science, new se-
        ries, 1895-1919.

11870   ISIS CUMULATIVE BIBLIOGRAPHY. Edited by Magda Whitrow.
        Chairman of Editorial Committee: I. Bernard Cohen. [Lon-
        don] Mansell in conjunction with the History of Science Society,
        1971-   v. 29cm. Vols. 1-2 have subtitle: A bibliography
        of the history of science formed from Isis critical bibliographies
        1-90, 1913-65. Contents.--v. 1. Personalities, A-J.--v. 2, pt.
        1. Personalities, K-Z. pt. 2. Institutions, A-Z. Vol. 1-2, pt.
        1 comprise a bibliography of the biography of scientists and schol-
        ars.

General Works

11871   ASIMOV, ISAAC, 1920-
        Asimov's biographical encyclopedia of science and tech-
        nology; the lives and achievements of 1195 great scientists from
        ancient times to the present, chronologically arranged. New
        rev. ed. Garden City, N. Y., Doubleday, 1972. xxviii, 805 p.
        ports. 24cm. First edition appeared in 1964.

11872   BOBER, JURAJ
         Malá encyklopédia bádatel'ov a vynálezcov. Zostavil a
spracoval Juraj Bober. 1. vyd. Bratislava, Obzor, 1973.
742 p. illus., ports. 21cm. A biographical dictionary of scientists and inventors. In Czech.

11873   BOGGI, FRANCESCO
         Album di 57 ritratti di scienziati intervenuti al primo Con-
gresso in Pisa nell'ottobre 1839. Lucca, 1840. 1 v. (57 ports.)
57 lithographed portraits of scientists at the 1st International
Science Congress in Pisa, October, 1839.

11874   JEHAN, LOUIS FRANÇOIS, b. 1803.
         Dictionnaire historique des sciences physiques et naturelles
depuis l'antiquité la plus reculée jusqu'à nos jours. Paris, J.
-P. Migne, 1857. 1108 columns. 28cm. (Troisième et dernière
encyclopédie théologique, t. 30. Encyclopédie théologique, t.
132) Historical dictionary of the physical and natural sciences
from ancient to modern times; with biographical entries.

11875   JOŚĪ, PRALHĀDA NARAHARA, 1924-
         Śāstrajñañcā caritrakośa. Poona, Anand Karyalay Praka-
shan, 1969. 12, [4], 493 p. ports. 23cm. Biographical dictionary (in Marathi) of scientists and inventors. Includes an English
index.

11876   ORDEN POUR LE MERITÉ FÜR WISSENSCHAFTEN UND
         KÜNSTE.
              Die Mitglieder des Ordens. Berlin, Gebr. Mann, 1975-
                   v. ports. 24cm. Contents: Bd. 1. 1842-1881.

         Members of the Prussian Order of Merit for the Sciences and
Arts (founded by King Friedrich Wilhelm IV); distinguished
Europeans (and several Americans) with emphasis on German-
speaking countries. Vol. 1 contains ca. 190 portraits and biographical sketches.

11877   WHO'S WHO IN SCIENCE IN EUROPE; a reference guide to
              European scientists. 2d ed. Guernsey (Channel Islands)
F. Hodgson, 1972. 4 v. 29cm. Nearly 40,000 entries, including scientists from Eastern Europe. The 1st ed. (3 v.
1967) was issued under title: Who's who in science in Europe;
a new reference guide to West European scientists.

11878   WILLIAMS, TREVOR ILLTYD
         A biographical dictionary of scientists. Edited by Trevor
I. Williams. Assistant editor: Sonia Withers. 2d ed. New
York, Wiley [1975] xv, 641 p. 25cm. "A Halsted Press book."
1st ed. issued in 1969. Well over 1,000 biographies of eminent scientists & technologists, past and present.

Local

Colombia

11879 FONDO COLOMBIANO DE INVESTIGACIONES CIENTÍFICAS Y
       PROYECTOS ESPECIALES FRANCISCO JOSÉ DE CALDAS.
       UNIDAD DE RECURSOS HUMANOS.
           Directorio de científicos y profesionales en Colombia; "quién
       es quién en ciencia y tecnología en Colombia." Ed. prelim.
       Bogotá, Colciencias, 1971. 435 p. 27cm. (Serie Directorios y
       repertorios. Colciencias, no. 1) Cover title: Quién es quién en
       ciencia y tecnología en Colombia; directorio profesional. Di-
       rectory of scientists, engineers and social scientists in Colom-
       bia; a who's who type of publication with basic biographical infor-
       mation.

Czechoslovakia

11880 ČLENOVÉ ČESKOSLOVENSKÉ AKADEMIE VĚD A ČLENOVÉ
       ČESKÝCH VĚDECKÝCH INSTITUCÍ NA NĚŽ ČSAV
       NAVAZUJE VE SVÉ ČINNOSTI. [1. vyd.] Praha, ČSAV, 1968.
       178 p. 24cm. Biographical register of scientists attached to
       the Czech Academy of Sciences; Czech and Slovak scientists of
       today.

France

11881 JEANDET, ABEL
           Recherches bio-bibliographiques pour servir à l'histoire des
       sciences naturelles en Bourgogne et particulièrement dans le
       département de Saone-et-Loire, depuis le XVIe siecle jusqu'a
       nos jours. Macon, Impr. de Protat frères, 1892. 133 p. plate.
       22cm. Bio-bibliographical researches to assist in the history of
       the natural sciences in Burgundy, and, in part, the department
       of Saone-et-Loire.

11882 MAINDRON, ERNEST, 1838-1908.
           L'ancienne Académie des sciences. Les académiciens,
       1666-1793. Paris, B. Tignol, 1895. ii, 90 p. 25cm. The old
       Academy of Sciences, Paris, and its academicians, 1666-1793.
       "Liste des membres ... ": p. [7]-90 (a 'biographical dictionary,'
       although data is quite limited.

Great Britain

11883 ARCHIVES OF BRITISH MEN OF SCIENCE. London, Mansell
           Information Pub. Co., 1972. 59 microfiches. "Each mi-
       crofiche has biographical data on 60 people, A-Z by name. The
       complete work is indexed in an accompanying booklet."
       --Walford, A. J. Guide to reference material. 3d ed.

11884   ROYAL SOCIETY OF LONDON.
Obituaries of deceased fellows, chiefly for the period 1898-
1904. (In Its Proceedings, v. 75, London, 1905) Quite extensive biographies of 76 fellows, arranged by date of birth; alphabetical name index at end of volume.

India

11885   INDIAN NATIONAL SCIENCE ACADEMY.
Biographical memoirs of fellows. v. 3-   1973-
[New Delhi]   v. ports. 26cm. Continues Biographical
memoirs of fellows of the National Institute of Sciences of India.
Each vol. contains 12 to 17 biographies.

11886   WHO IS WHO. Hyderabad, India, Andhra Pradesh Akademi of
Sciences [1975] 59 p. illus. 29cm. Cover title. "World
Telugu Conference publications." A biographical dictionary of
contemporary Indian scientists from Andhra Pradesh.

Russia

11887   KORNEEV, STEPAN GAVRILOVICH
Sovetskye uchenye—pochetnye chleny inostrannykh nauch-
nykh uchrezhdenii. Moskva, "Nauka," 1973. 295 p. 20cm.
Soviet scientists and their honorary memberships in foreign
scientific societies, institutions, etc. Part 1 (p. 7-119) lists in
alphabetical order the scientists, gives birth or birth-death dates,
brief identifying statement and then honorary memberships.

Sweden

Bibliography, Indexes, Portrait Catalogs

11888   SVENSKA VETENSKAPSAKADEMIEN, STOCKHOLM.
Vetenskapsakademiens konstsamlingar. Förteckning över
porträtt, medaljer och överiga konstföremål. Upprättad av
Brita Stina Nordin-Pettersson. Stockholm, Almqvist & Wiksell,
1971. 119 p. illus., ports. 22cm. (Its Bidrag till Kungl.
Svenska vetenskapsakademiens historia, 10) A catalog of portraits, portrait medallions, etc. in the Swedish Academy of
Science. Included are biographical notes for many Swedish
scientists. Index of names at end of volume yields an alphabetical approach.

Switzerland

11889   HÖHN, WALTER, naturalist.
Schweizerische und ausländische Naturwissenschaftler im

Bild. 63 Porträtskizzen gezeichnet von Walter Höhn in den Jahren 1908-1963. Mit Lebensabrissen versehen von C. H. Eugster, E. Müller [und] E. A. Thomas. Auf Anregung der Naturforschenden Gesellschaft in Zürich hrsg. von der Stiftung von Schnyder v. Wartensee. Zürich, Kommissionsverlag H. Rohr, 1971. 127 p. illus., ports. 21cm. 63 portraits and biographical sketches of Swiss and foreign scientists. For alphabetical approach to the volume the list on p. 7 must be used.

United States

11890   AMERICAN MEN AND WOMEN OF SCIENCE.
Formerly American men of science, a biographical directory founded in 1906. Edited by the Jaques Cattell Press. 12th ed. New York, Jaques Cattell Press/R. R. Bowker, 1971-73. 9 v. 29cm. Contents: [pt. 1] The physical and biological sciences. (A-Z). 6 v. --[pt. 2] The social and behavioral sciences (A-Z) 2 v. --[pt. 3] Discipline index: the physical and biological sciences.

11891   INSTITUTE OF ECOLOGY.
Directory of environmental life scientists. Prepared by the Institute of Ecology (TIE) for the U. S. Army Corps of Engineers. Washington, 1974-   v. 27cm. Contents.--

v. 3. Missouri River region.
v. 5. North central region
v. 7. North Atlantic region.
American ecologists; yields birth date, address, fields of competence, work experience, research activities, etc.

11892   NATIONAL ACADEMY OF SCIENCES, WASHINGTON, D. C.
Biographical memoirs. v. 1-   Washington, 1877-19
v. ports. 22cm. Each volume contains from ca. 12 to ca. 15 biographies of leading American scientists. 47 vols. issued thru' 1975.

Biology and Geology

Bibliography, Indexes, Portrait Catalogs

11893   FRUTON, JOSEPH STEWART, 1912-
Selected bibliography of biographical data for the history of biochemistry since 1800. Philadelphia, American Philosophical Society Library, 1974. viii, 140 p. 28cm. (American Philosophical Society Library. Library publication no. 6)

General Works

11894   AMERICAN MALACOLOGISTS; a national register of professional and amateur malacologists and private shell col-

lectors and biographies of early American mollusk workers
born between 1618 and 1900. [R. Tucker Abbott, editor-in-
chief] 1st ed., 1973-1974. Falls Church, Va., American Malacologists, 1973. iv, 494 p. illus. 21cm. Ca. 1,000 biographical sketches are recorded.

11895   BACKER, CORNELIS ANDRIES, 1874-
         Verklarend woordenboek der wetenschappelijke namen van
de in Nederland en Nederlandsch-Indie in het wild groeiende
en in tuinen en parken gekweekte varens en Hoogere planten.
Groningen, P. Noordhoff [etc.] 1936. xii, 664 p. 28cm.
Gives scientific names of plants growing in the Netherlands and
the Dutch East Indies (Indonesia) with biographical information
about the persons for whom they are named (p. [644]-664--in
double columns)

11896   BAROT, ALEXANDRE
         Dictionnaire biographique international des naturalistes.
Ouvrage rédigé par un comité de naturalistes sous la direction
de Alexandre Barot. Paris, Impr. de l'Amorial français, 1895.
49 p. ports. At head of title: Société des grands dictionnaires
biographiques. International biographical dictionary of naturalists. Reissued in 1903 with Carnoy's Dictionnaire biographique international des médecins et chirurgiens, and Dictionnaire biographique international des physiciens et chimistes
under the collective title: Dictionnaire biographique international
des médecins, chirurgiens, physiciens, chimistes et naturalistes.

11897   BIOLOGEN-KALENDER. 1. -   Jahrg.; 1914-   Leipzig, B.
         G. Teubner.   v. illus. 19cm. Vol. for 1914 edited by
B. Schmid and C. Thesing. 1914 vol. only one published? The
"Adressenverzeichnis" (v. 1, p. [157]-357) is actually a bio-
bibliographical dictionary of biologists (largely of German or
Central European nationality)

11897a   BRIQUET, JOHN ISAAC, 1870-1931.
         Biographies des botanistes à Genève de 1500 à 1931, par
John Briquet. Redaction: Fr. Cavillier. Genève, Impr. A.
Kundig, 1940. ix, 494 p. port. 22cm. (Berichte der Schweizerischen Botanischen Gesellschaft, 50a) Biographies of botanists
is Geneva from 1500 to 1931; list of authors (by date of birth): p.
491-494

11898   DICTIONNAIRE DES SCIENCES NATURELLES, dans lequel on
         traité méthodiquement des différens êtres de la nature,
considérés soit en eux-mêmes, d'après l'état actuel de nos connoissances, soit rélativement a l'utilité qu'en peuvent retirer la
médecine, l'agriculture, le commerce et les arts. Suivi d'une
biographie des plus célèbres naturalistes. Par plusieurs professeurs du Jardin du roi, et des principales écoles de Paris.
Strasbourg, F. G. Levrault [etc.] 1816-1845. 61 v. and atlas of

plates (12 v.) 22cm. "M. F. Cuvier est chargé de la direction
générale de l'ouvrage. " Vol. 61 contains the biographical sketches that accompany this dictionary of natural history.

11899   FEDOROWICZ, ZYGMUNT
         Dzieje zoologii na Uniwersytecie Jagiellónskim w latach
1780-1960. Kraków, Nakładen Uniwersytetu Jagiellońskiego,
1965. 143 p. 22cm. History of zoology at Jagiellon University
in Cracow; includes biographical sketches of zoologists grouped
by specialty and then chronologically. Alphabetical index of
names: p. 137-141.

11900   GRIGOR'EV, SERGEĬ VLADIMIROVICH
         Biograficheskiĭ slovar'; estestvoznanie i tekhnika v Karelii.
Petrozavodsk, "Kareliiâ, " 1973. 291 p. port. 27cm. At head
of title: Gosudarstvennaiâ publichnaiâ biblioteka KASSR. Karel'-
skiĭ filial Akademii nauk SSSR. A biographical dictionary of naturalists in Karelia.

11901   HUNT INSTITUTE FOR BOTANICAL DOCUMENTATION.
         Biographical dictionary of botanists represented in the Hunt
Institute portrait collection--Rachel McMasters Miller Hunt Bo-
tannical Library. Boston, G. K. Hall, 1972. viii, 451 p. 29cm.
Identifies over 11, 000 botanists and horticulturists and plantsmen
whose portraits are included in the collection; brief biographical
data is also provided. Based on the collections of the Hunt Institute for Botanical Documentation, which was the Hunt Botanical
Library prior to 1971.

11902   INTERNATIONAL MINERALOGICAL ASSOCIATION.
         World directory of mineralogists. Compiled by M. Font-
Altaba and Marjorie Hooker with the help of the representatives
of the national mineralogical societies. Barcelona, Published
for the I. M. A. by Editorial Jover, 1970. xi, 170 p. 22cm. Includes quite brief biographical data. A new edition of a work the
first edition of which was published in 1962.

11903   KÖPPEN, FEDOR PETROVICH, 1833-1908.
         Biographieen solcher Schriftsteller (Naturforscher, Geo-
graphen, Statistiker, Reisender, Aerzte, etc.) welche über die
Thierwelt, Jagd und Fischfang Russlands, bis zum Schlusse von
1885, gehandelt haben, und überhaupt solcher Autoren, deren
Schriften im vorliegenden Werke verzeichnet sind. (In Köppen's
Bibliotheca zoologica Rossica. S. -Peterburg, 1907. Bd. 2, 1.
Hälfte. p. 43-239) 1098 names. Biographical notes on naturalists, geographers, statisticians, travelers, physicians, etc.
who have written about Russia's natural history (to 1885).

11904   MAFFEI, EUGENIO
         Apuntes para una biblioteca española de libros, folletos y

articulos, impresos y manuscritos, relativos al conocimiento y
explotación de las riquezas minerales y a las ciencias auxiliares.
... Acompañados de reseñas biográficas y de un ligero resúmen
de la mayor parte de las obras que se citan, por Eugenio Maffei
y Ramon Rua Figueroa. Madrid, J. M. Lapuente, 1871-[72] 2 v.
25cm. A bibliography of Spanish books and articles on the geol-
ogy, mineralogy and mineral resources of Spain and Latin A-
merica accompanied by biographical sketches of many of the authors.

11905   TARDIEU, AMBROISE, 1788-1841.
        Iconographie universelle ancienne et moderne; ou, Collec-
        tion complète et du même format des portraits de tous les per-
        sonnages célèbres, français et étrangers, dessinés et gravés
        par Ambroise Tardieu. Série des naturalistes. Paris, A. Tar-
        dieu, 1823-24. 6 fasc. ports. 8.°-4.°   Universal iconography,
        ancient and modern; or, Collection of portraits of famous per-
        sonages, French and alien--naturalists.

11906   UNITED NATIONS EDUCATIONAL, SCIENTIFIC AND CULTUR-
        AL ORGANIZATION. REGIONAL CENTER FOR THE AD-
        VANCEMENT OF SCIENCE IN LATIN AMERICA.
        Directorio latinoamericano de ciencias geológicas. Monte-
        video, Centro Regional de la Unesco para el Fomento de la
        Ciencia en América Latina, 1968. 661, lix p. 22cm. This di-
        rectory of the geological sciences in Latin America, arranged by
        country, includes a biographical section under each country,
        wherein dates of birth, academic career, present activities and
        special research interests are given.

Chemistry

11907   AMERICAN CHEMISTS AND CHEMICAL ENGINEERS.
        Wyndham D. Miles, editor. Washington, American Chemi-
        cal Society, 1976. x, 544 p. 25cm. A biographical dictionary
        of 517 deceased men and women who have contributed signifi-
        cantly to the development and progress of chemistry and chemi-
        cal engineering over the past 300 years in the United States.

11908   BUGGE, GÜNTHER, 1885-
        Das Buch der grossen Chemiker. Unter Mitwirkung nam-
        hafter Gelehrter hrsg. von Günther Bugge. Unveränderter
        Nachdruck. Weinheim, Verlag Chemie, 1955. 2 v. illus.,
        ports. 24cm. First issued in 1929. The book of great chem-
        ists. Vol. 1: Zosimos to Schönbein (4th-19th centuries--38 biog-
        raphies); v. 2: Liebig to Arrhenius (19th-20th centuries--30 bi-
        ographies).

11909   CAMPBELL, WILLIAM ALEC
        Contemporary British chemists, by W. A. Campbell and
        N. N. Greenwood. London, Taylor & Francis, 1971. 286 p.

ports. 27cm. A biographical dictionary of ca. 140 outstanding living British chemists.

11910   FARBER, EDUARD, 1892-
Nobel Prize winners in chemistry, 1901-1961. Rev. ed. London, New York, Abelard-Schuman, 1963. 341 p. ports. 23cm. (The Life of science library, no. 41) Includes 65 biographical sketches arranged by date of award.

Mathematics

Bibliography, Indexes, Portrait Catalogs

11911   MAY, KENNETH OWNSWORTH, 1915-
Bibliography and research manual on the history of mathematics. [Toronto] University of Toronto Press [1973] 818 p. 26cm. "Biography" (p. [41]-391) contains a bibliography of biographical collections, portrait volumes, biographical reference sources, and biographical sources for individual mathematicians (A-Z, p. 47-391)

General Works

11912   ANDONIE, GEORGE ST
Istoria matematicii in România. Bucuresti, Editura Stiintifică, 1965-67. 2 v. illus., ports. The history of mathematics in Romania, with biographical notices grouped within the various chapters by specialty and date of birth. Many portraits are included.

11913   ANDONIE, GEORGE ST
Istoria matematicilor aplicate clasice din România. Mecanică si astronomie. Bucuresti, Editura Academiei Republicii Socialiste România, 1971. 640 p. illus., ports. 24cm. History of mathematics in Romania, especially as applied to mechanics and astronomy; a major portion of the work is devoted to bio-bibliography of 87 Romanian mathematicians and scientists.

11914   BIOGRAPHIC INFORMATION ON SOVIET SCIENTISTS IN THE FIELD OF MATHEMATICS. New York, U.S. Joint Publications Research Service, 1961. 208 p. (JPRS: 6802) "Translation of selected biographic entries on Soviet scientists in the field of mathematics from the Russian-language book Matematika v SSSR za sorok let 1917-1957 (Forty years of mathematics in the USSR, 1917-1957), Moscow, vol. 2, 1959, p. 27-816. "

11916   FANG, JOONG
Mathematicians from antiquity to today [by] J. Fang, in col-

laboration with U. Dudley. A prelim. ed. [Hauppauge, N. Y.]
Paideia [Press, c1972-   v. 24cm. (Paideia; studies
in the nature of modern mathematics, 12
Contents. --v. 1. Introduction. [Biographies] A-D.

11917   MATEMATIKA V SSSR, 1958-1967. Pod red. Pravleniiā Mos-
         kovskogo matematicheskogo ob-va. Otv. redaktory: S. V.
         Fomin i G. E. Shilov. Moska, Nauka, 1970-   v. 26cm.
         Mathematics in the Soviet Union from 1958 to 1967. Vol. 2 (in 2
         parts, the only vol. published thus far) is bio-bibliographical,
         A-IA; however, biographical data, when available (some authors
         are merely listed by name) are generally rather sparse.

11918   MATEMATIKA V SSSR ZA SOROK LET 1917-1957. Pod red. A.
         G. Kurosha [i dr.] Moskva, Gos. izd-vo fiziko-mate-
         maticheskoi lit-ry, 1959. 2 v. illus. 27cm. Mathematics in
         the Soviet Union, 1917-1957. Vol. 2 is biobibliographical, A-IA;
         however, biographical data, when available (some authors are
         merely listed by name) are generally rather sparse.

11919   MESCHKOWSKI, HERBERT
         Mathematiker-Lexikon. 2., erw. Aufl. Mannheim, Biblio-
         graphisches Institut, 1973. 328 p. illus. 21cm. A dictionary
         of mathematicians (2d, enlarged edition).

11920   SMITH, DAVID EUGENE, 1869-1944.
         Rara arithmetica; a catalogue of the arithmetics written be-
         fore the year MDCI, with a description of those in the library
         of George Arthur Plimpton of New York. [4th ed., including A.
         De Morgan's Arithmetical books, published at London in 1847]
         New York, Chelsea Pub. Co., 1970. xviii, 725 p. illus. 21cm.
         Includes the author's "Addenda to Rara arithmetica which de-
         scribed in 1908 such European arithmetics printed before 1601 as
         were then in the library of the late George Arthur Plimpton" (p.
         [490]-548) first published in 1939. First edition appeared in 2
         vols. in 1908. Chiefly bibliographical, but does include a lim-
         ited amount of biographical data (1-8 lines generally) Arranged
         chronologically (by date of publication of the various arithmetics)
         with alphabetical approach to authors through an index.

11921   SUTER, HEINRICH, 1848-1922.
         Die Mathematiker und Astronomen der Araber und ihre
         Werke. Leipzig, B. G. Teubner, 1900. ix, 277 p. 24cm.
         (Abhandlungen zur Geschichte der Mathematischen Wissen-
         schaften mit Einschluss ihrer Anwendungen, 10. Heft) The
         Arabian mathematicians and astronomers and their work; a bio-
         bibliography.

11922   WHO'S WHO IN COMPUTER EDUCATION AND RESEARCH.
         Edited by T. C. Hsiao. 1st ed. Washington, Science and

Technology Press, 1975. xi, 312 p. 29cm. Issued as v. 3, Faculty and research staff, of the Directory of computer education and research. Presents biographical sketches of some 2,000 educators and researchers in computer sciences in institutions in the United States.

11923   WHO'S WHO IN COMPUTERS AND DATA PROCESSING, 1971: a biographical dictionary of leading computer professionals. 5th ed. New York, The New York times, Book and Educational Division; Newtonville, Mass., Computers and Automation, Berkeley Enterprises, inc., of New York [and] Quadrangle Books [1971] 3 v. 29cm. Previous editions issued under title: Who's who in the computer field. Contents. --v. 1. Systems analysts and programmers. --v. 2. Data processing managers and directors. --v. 3. Other computer professionals.

Physics and Astronomy

11924   BILDNISSE ZEITGENÖSSISCHER PHYSIKER Herrn Viktor von Lang zu seinem 70. Geburtstag (2. März 1908) gewidmet. [Wien? 1908] 341 ports. on 44 l. 17 x 25cm. Cover title. Portraits of contemporary physicists (late 19th, early 20th century)

11925   EHRENBUCH DER RÖNTGENOLOGEN UND RADIOLOGEN ALLER NATIONEN. Hrsg. von Hermann Holthusen, Hans Meyer und Werner Molineus. 2. erg. und wesentlich erw. Aufl. München, Urban & Schwarzenberg, 1959. xi, 268 p. mounted illus. 25cm. (Sonderbände zur Strahlentherapie, Bd. 42) A work honoring Röntgenologists and radiologists of all countries; contains ca. 350 brief biographies of those who died while experimenting with radium and X-rays. 1st ed. issued in 1937.

11926   HERMANN, ARMIN, 1933- Lexikon Geschichte der Physik A-Z; Biographien, Sachwörter, Originalschriften und Sekundärliteratur. Köln, Aulis Verlag, 1972. 423 p. illus. 25cm. A dictionary of the history of physics with the emphasis on biography and terms. Although most major figures in the history of physics are mentioned, there are surprising gaps; e. g., Oppenheimer, Urey, Goddard, et al. are not included.

11927   JÜAN, YÜAN, 1794-1849. Ch'ou jên chuan. Shanghai, Shang wu yin shu kuan, 1955. 4 v. Includes Ch'ou jên chuan, ch'u pien, hsu pien, san pien and Ch'ou jên chu shu chi by Hua, Shih-fang. 400 Chinese astronomers and mathematicians from ancient period to the Ch'ing Dynasty with biographical data for 52 European scientists and works by some scientists of the Ch'ing Dynasty. Arranged chronologically; no index.

11928   KHARKOV. UNIVERSITET.
Fiziko-matematicheskiĭ fakul'tet Khar'kovskogo universiteta
za pervye sto let sushchestvovaniia (1805-1905) I. Istoriia fakul'teta. II. Ocherk otdel'nykh kafedr. III. Biograficheskiĭ slovar' professorov i prepodavateleĭ pod red. I. P. Osipova i D. I.
Bagaleia. Khar'kov, Izd. Universiteta, 1908. vi, 358, 248,
xvi p. 25cm. Pt. 3 is a biographical dictionary of the professors and teachers on the Faculty of Physical Sciences and Mathematics of Kharkov University, 1805-1905.

11929   MATEU SANCHO, PEDRO
Diccionario de astronomía y astronáutica. Barcelona, Ediciones Destino [1962] 345 p. illus., ports. A dictionary of
astronomy and astronautics; with portraits and biographical
sketches of astronomers.

11930   MAYER, LEO ARY, 1895-1959.
Islamic astrolabists and their works. Geneva, A. Kundig,
1956. 128 p. 26 plates. 27cm. "Roll of astrolabists" (p. [23]-
87) is a biographical dictionary.

11931   SATTERTHWAITE, GILBERT ELLIOTT
Encyclopedia of astronomy. New York, St. Martin's Press,
1971. ix, 537 p. illus. 24cm. Includes biographies of astronomers.

11932   SOURCES FOR HISTORY OF QUANTUM PHYSICS.
Sources for history of quantum physics; an inventory and
report [by] Thomas S. Kuhn [and others] Philadelphia, American Philosophical Society, 1967. ix, 176 p. 28cm. (Memoirs
of the American Philosophical Society, v. 68) "Author catalog
of principal sources"(p. 12-99) serves as a bio-bibliographical
dictionary of quantum physicists.

11933   WHO'S WHO IN ATOMS; an international reference book.
[1st]-   ed.; 1959-   London, Vallancey Press,
etc.   v. 26cm. The 5th ed. (London, Harrap), 1969, was
issued in 2 volumes and contained more than 22,000 entries on
nuclear scientists and engineers in 78 countries.

11934   WHO'S WHO IN INDIAN RADIOLOGY. Poona, Organising Committee, 23rd Indian Congress of Radiology, 1970. 187 p.
Gives brief biographical data and photographs for 300 specialists with a listing of 400 more.

SOCIAL AND HISTORICAL SCIENCES, ETC.

General Works

11935   DICIONÁRIO DE SOCIOLOGIA. Rio de Janeiro, Editora
        Globo, 1961. 377 p. 22cm. (Enciclopedias e dicionários
        Globo) A dictionary of sociology; includes biographies of soci-
        ologists, philosophers, etc.

11936   ECHÁNOVE TRUJILLO, CARLOS A   1907-
        Diccionario de sociología. 2. ed. rev. y aum. México,
        J. M. Cajica, 1957. 316 p. illus. .   (Biblioteca Cajica de
        derecho, economía, sociología y política) A dictionary of soci-
        ology; includes bio-bibliographical articles.

11937   HARRISON, BRIAN HOWARD
        Dictionary of British temperance biography [by] Brian Har-
        rison. Sheffield, Society for the Study of Labour History, 1973.
        xviii, 139 p. 24cm. (Society for the Study of Labour History
        bulletin. Supplement, no. 1)

11938   INTERNATIONAL WHO'S WHO IN COMMUNITY SERVICE.
        1973/74-   ed. London, Eddison Press.
        v. 26cm. "Incorporating Directory of public affairs, Ré-
        pertoire d'affaires publiques, Who's who in public affairs, Dic-
        tionnaire biographique de service public, and Who's who in Sus-
        sex." Biographical dictionary of contemporary social service
        workers, public administrators, and educators. 1973/74 volume
        contains 6,400 names.

11939   POPULÁRNÍ POLITICKÝ SLOVNÍK. Ekonomie, filosofie,
        mezinárodní vztahy. Politika vnitřní a zahraniční. Kdo je
        kdo. [Zprac. za red. Václava Kocourica tito autoři: Oldřich
        Babický et al. 2. vyd.] Praha, Mladá fronta, 1964. 548 p.
        17cm. (Svazácká knihovna, sv. 13) 1st ed. issued in 1962
        (464, 2 p.) A dictionary of political and social science. In-
        cludes a "who's who" section.

11940   UNITED STATES. LIBRARY OF CONGRESS. HISPANIC
        FOUNDATION.
        National directory of Latin Americanists; biographies of
        2,695 specialists in the social sciences & humanities. Compiled
        by the Hispanic Foundation, Reference Dept., Washington, Li-
        brary of Congress, 1971 [i. e. 1972] 684 p. 24cm. (Hispanic
        Foundation bibliographical series, no. 12) First edition, issued
        in 1966, covered 1,884 specialists.

Economics, Commerce, Labor

General Works

11941   BERKA. HANS
Lebensmittelarbeiter als berühmte Zeitgenossen; hundert
Lebensbilder mit 91 Porträtzeichnungen. Wien, Verlag des Österreichischen Gewerkschaftsbundes, 1959. 263 p. ports.
21cm. Workers in the food industry and trade as famous contemporaries; 100 lives, with 91 portraits.

11942   DICTIONNAIRE DU MOUVEMENT OUVRIER, par Gérard Adam
[et al.] sous la direction de André Nataf. Paris, Editions
universitaires, 1970. 541 p. illus., ports. 22 x 11 cm. (Dictionnaires de culture) A dictionary of the labor movement in
Europe that includes biographies of labor leaders, socialists,
economic theorists, etc.

11943   EKONOMICHESKAĬA ĖNTSIKLOPEDIĬA. Politicheskaia ekono-
miiă. Glavnyĭ redaktor A. M. Rumiàntsev. Moskva,
"Sovetskaia entsiklopediiă, 1972-   v. illus. 27cm.
(Entsiklopedii, slovari, spravochniki) At head of title: v. 1-
Nauchno-redaktsionnyĭ sovet Izdatel'stva "Sovetskaia entsiklopediiă. " Otdelenie ekonomiki Akademii nauk SSSR. A dictionary of economics (Marxian economics especially) which includes many biographical entries for economists.

11944   IKONOMICHESKA ENTSIKLOPEDIĬA. Otg. red. Ivan Stefanov.
Obshcha red. Emiliiă Ivanova. Sofiiă, Nauka i izkustvo,
1971-   v. illus. 23cm. A Bulgarian dictionary of economics that includes biographical sketches of famous economists;
to be in 2 volumes when completed.

11945   KOCH, PETER, 1935-
Pioniere des Versicherungsgedankens; 300 Jahre Versicher-
ungsgeschichte in Lebensbildern 1550-1850. Wiesbaden, Be-
triebswirtschaftlicher Verlag [1968] 336 p. illus., ports.
20cm. 57 biographies of pioneers of the concepts of social insurance from 1550 to 1850 in chronological arrangement. Alphabetical index to persons mentioned at end of volume.

11946   LEADERS IN DEVELOPMENT. 1968-   Atlanta, Conway
Research.   v. ports. 23cm. "The international guide
to professional development executives [in the United States]"

11947   MAI, LUDWIG H
Men and ideas in economics; a dictionary of world economists, past and present. Totowa, N. J., Littlefield, Adams,

1975. xii, 270 p. 22cm. (A Littlefield, Adams quality paperback, no. 284)

11948   MAITRON, JEAN
Dictionnaire biographique du movement ouvrier international. Publié sous la direction de Jean Maitron et Georges Haupt.
Paris, Editions ouvrières [1971-   v. illus. 25cm. Biographical dictionary of the international labor movement, with
concentration particularly on socialists. 4 vols. issued as of
1975 (A-Mar).

11949   MUNKÁSMOZGALOMTÖRTÉNETI LEXIKON. [Szerkesztők:
Vass Henrik et al. Budapest] Kossuth Könyvkiadó, 1972.
637, [1] p. 25cm. On page facing t. p.: Magyar Szocialista
Munkáspárt. Központi Bizottságának Párttörténeti Intézete. A
dictionary of the history of the world's labor movement; biographical sketches comprise a major part of the dictionary which
focuses primarily on socialism and communism.

11950   STATISTICA (BOLOGNA)
Bibliografie con brevi cenni biografici. [Bologna] Cappelli
[1959] 550 p. 25cm. (Biblioteca di "Statistica," 2) Bio-bibliography of 129 statisticians-economists of the 20th century (biographical data is quite brief, appearing at the head of the list of
the individual's writings)

11951   WHO'S WHO IN RAILROADING AND RAIL TRANSIT. [1st]-
ed.; 1885-   New York, Simmons-Boardman Pub.
Corp.   v. 23cm. First published in 1885-1913 under title:
Biographical directory of the railroad officials of North America;
1930, Who's who in railroading, United States, Canada, Mexico,
Cuba; 19   Who's who in railroading in North America; 1971
(17th ed.) Who's who in railroading and rail transit. Imprint
varies.

Africa

11952   THE ADVERTISING & PRESS ANNUAL OF AFRICA.
1949/50(?)-   Capetown.   v. illus. 25cm.
Title varies: 1949/50(?)-55: The African press & advertising
annual; 1967-   : Advertising & press annual of all Africa;
the blue book of advertising in Africa (Johannesburg, National
Pub. Co. , 1968) Includes a "Who's who in advertising &
publishing" (e.g., 1967 ed. , p. 377-406 -- in triple columns);
emphasizes South Africans of British and Afrikaans extraction.

11953   PRÉSIDENTS ADMINISTRATEURS ET DIRECTEURS GÉNÉRAUX
DES SOCIÉTÉS PUBLIQUES ET PRIVÉES D'AFRIQUE
NOIRE. PDG-AFRIQUE 1969. Paris, EDIAFRIC, La Documen-
tation africaine [1969?] 471 p. 27cm. "Numéro spécial du

Bulletin de l'Afrique noire." Covers former French Africa and France, arranged by country. Includes brief biographies (alphabetical) of key officials concerned with a country's economy (largely business executives, directors of corporations, etc.)-- 1,500 individuals in all.

Austria

11954   GRANICHSTAEDTEN-CZERVA, RUDOLF VON, 1885-
Altösterreichische Unternehmer; 110 Lebensbilder
[von] R. Granichstaedten-C[z]erva, J. Mentschl [und] G. Otruba.
[Wien, Bergland Verlag [1969] 153 p. 19cm. (Österreich-Reihe,
Bd. 365/367) Entrepreneurs of "old" (chiefly 18th-19th, early
20th century) Austria; 110 biographical sketches.

Canada

11955   WHO'S WHO IN CANADIAN PLACEMENT. [Toronto] University
Career Planning Association. 1966-   v. ports.
23cm. Spiral binding. Vols. for 1966, (1967-68? 1968-69?)
1969-70, 1970-71.

China

11956   HSU, WAN-CH'ENG.
Shang-hai pai yeh jen ts'ai hsiao shih. Shanghai, Lung wen
shu tien, 1945. 483 p. ports. 18cm. Directory with portraits
of industrialists and businessmen in Shanghai in 1945.

Colombia

11957   OTERO MUÑOZ, GUSTAVO, 1894-
El Banco de la República, 1923-1948 ... [Bogotá] Tall.
Gráf. e Impr. del Banco de la República [1948] 330 p. col.
ports. 28cm. Includes 90 biographies of members of the Board
of Directors of the Colombian Bank of the Republic from 1923 to
1948 (p. [267]-308).

Denmark

11958   DANSK FORSIKRINGS-STAT. København, O. Rechendorff.
v. 19cm. biennial. 25th ed. covers the years 1966-67.
Directory, with biographical data, of leading Danish insurance
men.

11959   DANSK ØKONOMSTAT 1966. Under redaktion af Erik Hjelmar.
København, Danske økonomers forening, 1967. 192 p.
26cm. Danish economists of the present.

11960   DANSKE STATSAUTORISEREDE REVISORER. 5. udg. Udg. af
         Foreningen af statsautoriserede revisorer. København,
         1968. 296 p. illus. 25cm. "Tillaeg 1969": 19 p. in pocket.
         Biographical dictionary of auditors in Denmark.

France

11961   DICTIONNAIRE DES DYNASTIES BOURGEOISES ET DU MONDE
         DES AFFAIRES. Publié sous la direction de Henry Coston.
         Paris, Editions A. Moreau, c1975. 599 p. illus. 25cm. Bio-
         graphical dictionary of persons prominent in French commercial
         and business affairs.

11962   FRANCE. CONSEIL ÉCONOMIQUE ET SOCIAL.
            Notices et portraits. Paris.   v. ports. 15cm. Began
         ca. 1954? Vols. for 1954-   issued by the Council under its
         earlier name: Conseil économique. Notices and portraits of
         French economists.

11963   SZRAMKIEWICZ, ROMUALD
            Les régents et censeurs de la Banque de France nommés
         sous le Consulat et l'Empire. Genève, Droz, 1974. lxiii, 422 p.
         25cm. (Hautes études médiévales et modernes, 22) At head of
         title: Centre de recherches d'histoire et de philologie de la IVe
         section de l'École pratique des hautes études V. Primarily a bi-
         ographical dictionary of 43 of the chief officials of the Bank of
         France under the consulate (of Napoleon) and the Empire.

Germany

11964   PUDOR, FRITZ
            Lebensbilder aus dem rheinisch-westfälischen Industriege-
         biet ... Düsseldorf, A. Bagel, 1957-66. 4 v. ports. 22cm.
         (Schriften der Volks- und Betriebswirtschaftlichen Vereinigung
         im Rheinisch-Westfälischen Industriegebiet, n. F., Hauptreihe,
         Heft 21-24) Vol. 4 has imprint: Köln, Westdeutscher Verlag.
         Contents. --[1] Jahrg. 1952-1954. --[2] Jahrg. 1955-1957. --[3]
         Jahrg. 1958-1959. --[4] Jahrg. 1960-1961. Neue Folge der
         Nekrologe aus dem Rheinisch-Westfalischen Industriegebiet.
         Biographies of businessmen in the Ruhr Valley. Successor to
         the author's Nekrologe aus dem rheinisch-westfälischen Indus-
         triegebiet.

Great Britain

11966   BELLAMY, JOYCE M
            Dictionary of labour biography [by] Joyce M. Bellamy and
         John Saville. Clifton, N. J., A. M. Kelley; [London] Macmil-
         lan, 1972-   v. 25cm. British labor biography from

1790 to the present (but living persons are excluded) Expected
to be complete in 15 or 20 volumes. Each volume complete in
itself (A-Z) Vol. 1 issued in 1972; v. 2, 1974.

11967   CAVERLEY, ROBERT BOODEY, 1806-1887.
         Leading insurance men of the British Empire [by] R. B.
Caverly and R. B. Bankes. London, Index Pub. Co., 1892.
xii, 585 p. illus., ports. 25cm. Arranged by position, e.g.:
main headquarters officials, fire loss assessors, etc. Alphabetical index on p. v-xii.

11968   FOX, W   E
         Who's who in Bristol? London, Labour Research Dept.,
1935. 27 p. 17cm. A who's who of businessmen of Bristol,
England.

11969   WHO'S WHO IN FINANCE. 1972-   [Epping, Eng.] Gower
         Press,   v. 24cm. Information about the personal
and professional lives of over 3,000 men and women in British
finance. Issued in the U. S. (New York, R. R. Bowker Co.)
under title: Who's who in British finance.

11970   WHO'S WHO IN THE MOTOR AND COMMERCIAL VEHICLE
         INDUSTRIES: an annual directory of the British motor and
commercial vehicle industries, and of the professional, commercial and sporting organizations associated with the British
automotive world. 1964-   London, Temple Press (later
issued by Kelly's Directories, Kingston)   v. 23cm. annual.
Previous issues published under title: Who's who in the motor
industry. Biographies (including obituaries) are included in the
4th section of the work (e. g., 1970/71 ed.: p. 361-468, with ca.
800 entries).

India

11971   COMMERCE YEAR BOOK OF PUBLIC SECTOR. 1970-
         Bombay, Commerce (1935) Limited.   v. 29cm. annual.
Includes a who's who of India's commerce.

11972   GUPTA, BADLU RAM, 1920-
         The Aggarwals; a socio-economic study. New Delhi, S.
Chand, 1975. viii, 146 p. ports. 22cm. "Eminent Aggarwals"
(p. [47]-146) contains 120 biographical sketches of members
(chiefly businessmen) of that prominent community of India.

11973   INSTITUTE OF SCIENCES AND INDUSTRIAL PUBLICATIONS.
         Directory and who is who of Ghaziabad industries. Editor
in chief: B. M. Soni. Ghaziabad [1974] 1 v. (various pagings)

illus. 25cm. Title on spine: Directory: Ghaziabad industries. Survey conducted by the Institute of Sciences and Industrial Publications in collaboration with the All India Manufacturers' Organization, U. P. State Board, Ghaziabad. Section 4 (Bio-data of entrepreneurs) contains biographical sketches of 173 businessmen (with portraits for many) prominent in an industrial suburb of Delhi.

11974   SUNEJA'S BANKING YEAR BOOK AND WHO'S WHO.
        [1st-   ed.]: 1969-   New Delhi, Suneja Publishers.   v. 23cm. annual. Banks and banking in India; Who's who section at the end of each annual volume (e. g., 1973 (4th ed.) has biographical sketches on pages 453-499—in double columns).

Italy

11975   CREATORI DI LAVORO. 3. ed. Roma, A cura della Confederazione generale dell'industria italiana, 1968. 587 p. illus. 24cm. Edited by Rino Carassiti. 2d ed. published in 1954 by Gazzetta per i lavoratori. Businessmen of Italy.

11976   IL DIZIONARIO INDUSTRIALE ITALIANO. 2. ed., con una minuta descrizione di 10,000 enti industriali ... Roma, V. Giacchetti, 1927. iv, 600 p. illus. 4.º The dictionary of Italian industry; with a biographical section for leaders of Italian commerce and industry.

11977   IL MOVIMENTO OPERAIO ITALIANO: dizionario biografico, 1853-1943. [A cura di] Franco Andreucci, Tommaso Detti. 1. ed. Roma, Editori riuniti, 1975-   v. illus., ports. 24cm. Contents: v. 1. A-Cec.

        A biographical dictionary of the Italian labor movement and Italian socialism, 1853-1943.

11978   WHO'S WHO IN ITALIAN ECONOMIC LIFE, 1964. Under the sponsorship of the Italian Foreign Trade Ministry. Milano, Casa editrice Nuova Mercurio, 1964. 573 p. illus., ports. 18cm. 1959 edition issued under title: Who's who in the Italian economic life.

11979   WHO'S WHO IN THE ITALIAN ECONOMIC LIFE (Who's who in the Italian section of the I. C. C.) Servizio informazioni estero, sotto il patrocinio della Sezione italiana della Camera di commercio internazionale. Milano, Nuova Mercurio, 1959. 343 p. illus., ports. 18cm. A later edition was issued in 1964 under title: Who's who in Italian economic life, 1964.

Pakistan

11980   PAKISTAN INSURANCE SURVEY & WHO'S WHO. 1975-
                    v. ports. 29cm. Advertising matter interspersed.
         The 1975 edition, e. g., includes a "Who's who in Pakistan in-
         surance" with 92 biographies in alphabetical (by surname) order.

Poland

11981   SŁOWNIK BIOGRAFICZNY DZIAŁACZY POLSKIEGO RUCHU
         ROBOTNICZEGO. Red. Feliks Tych. Wyd. 1. Warszawa,
         Muzeum Historii Polskiego Ruchu Rewolucyjnego, Zakład His-
         torii Partii przy KC PZPR, 1967-.   v. 21cm. Dic-
         tionary of biography of leaders in the Polish labor movement.
         Vol. 1 contains ca. 130 biographies on 138 pages.

Taiwan
(Republic of China)

11982   TAIWAN WEN HUA FU WU SHE, TAIPEI.
                    Chung hua min kuo ming jèn chuan chih 4. Taipei, Taiwan
         wen hue fu wu she, 1957. 255 p. ports. 26cm. Over 100 bi-
         ographies of persons in commercial and industrial circles in
         Taiwan in the post-1945 period.

11983   TUI T'AI-WAN CHING CHI CHIEN SHÊ TSUI YU KUNG HSIEN
         TI KUNG SHANG JÊN MING LU. Taiwan business who's
         who, 500. [Taipei] China Credit Information Service [1973]
         575 p. ports. 28cm. Cover title. Portraits and biographical
         sketches of 500 prominent businessmen of Taiwan (Formosa).

United States

11984   BEACH, MOSES YALE, 1800-1868.
                    The wealthy citizens of New York. New York, Arno Press,
         1973. 32, 83 p. 23cm. (Big business: economic power in a
         free society) Reprint of the 1845 ed. (New York, Sun Office)
         which was issued under title: Wealth and biography of the wealthy
         citizens of New York City, comprising an alphabetical arrange-
         ment of persons estimated to be worth $100,000 and upwards ...;
         and of the 1855 ed. (New York, Sun Office) with title: The wealth
         and biography of the wealthy citizens of the City of New York.
         Birth and death dates are not given, but biographical data of an
         informal sort is available for many of those listed.

11985   BUSINESS PEOPLE IN THE NEWS; a compilation of news stories
         and feature articles from American newspapers and maga-

zines covering people in industry, finance, and labor. v. 1-
Edited by Barbara Nykoruk. Detroit, Gale Research Co., 1976-
            v. illus., ports. Each vol. contains ca. 200
current illustrated articles and interviews. Personality profiles on corporation presidents, union leaders, financiers, etc.

11986 FINK, GARY M
            Biographical directory of American labor leaders. Editor-
        in-chief: Gary M. Fink. Advisory editor: Milton Cantor. Con-
        tributing editors: John Hevener [and others] Westport, Conn.,
        Greenwood Press [1974] xiv, 559 p. 24cm. Provides sketches
        of over 500 men and women influential in the American labor
        movement, past & present.

11987 WHO'S WHO AMONG INNKEEPERS; a biographical reference
            work about hotel, motel, and resort managers and owners
        in America. 1st ed., 1974-1975. [New York, Rating Publica-
        tions, 1974] 210 p. 23cm. American hotel, motel, and resort
        managers; 800 biographical sketches selected from over 100,000
        candidates.

11988 WHO'S WHO IN CONSULTING; a reference guide to professional
            personnel engaged in consultation for business, industry
        and government. Paul Wasserman, managing editor. Janice
        McLean, associate editor. 2d ed. Detroit, Gale Research Co.,
        1973 [c1974] xvii, 1011 p. 29cm. "Serves as a companion to
        Consultants and consulting organization, 2d edition." A bio-
        graphical dictionary of American business and government con-
        sultants. 1st ed. issued in 1968 (Ithaca, N. Y., Graduate
        School of Business and Public Administration, Cornell Univer-
        sity—ix, 395 p. 29cm.)

11989 WHO'S WHO IN FINANCE AND INDUSTRY. 17th-   ed.;
            1972/73-   Chicago, Marquis Who's who.   v.
        24-31cm. Continues World who's who in finance and industry.
        Title varies: 1936-59, Who's who in commerce and industry;
        1961-67, World who's who in commerce and industry; 1970/71,
        World who's who in finance and industry. Issued 1936-38 by the
        Institute for Research in Biography, inc., New York; 1940-
        by Marquis Who's who. "An extension of Who's who in America
        and a component volume of the Marquis biographical library."
        Primarily American (and Canadian) businessmen.

11990 WHO'S WHO IN LABOR. 1st ed. New York, Arno Press,
            1976. xxi, 807 p. 25cm. Labor union officials and leaders
        in the United States.

Yugoslavia

11991 ZADRUŽNI LEKSIKON FNRJ. The Yugoslav co-operative en-
            cyclopedia. [Red.: Vučković Mihajlo et al. Zagreb,

Zadružna stampa, 1956-57] 2 v. illus., ports. 25cm. Preface also in English; summary in English. Contents. --knjiga 1. A-Lj. --knjiga 2. M-Z. Includes biographies and portraits of leaders in the Yugoslav co-operative movement.

Geography and Travel

Bibliography, Indexes, Portrait Catalogs

11992   MOROZOVA, M   N
        Fizicheskaiä geografiiä; annotirovannyĭ perechen' otechest-
vennykh bibliografii, izdannykh v 1810-1966 gg. [Sostaviteli: M.
N. Morozova i E. A. Stepanova] Moskva, Kniga, 1968. 308 p.
22cm. At head of title: Gosudarstvennaia ordena Lenina biblioteka SSSR im. B. I. Lenina. Institut geografii Akademii nauk
SSSR. Sektor seti spetsial'nykh bibliotek Akademii nauk SSSR.
Pages 43-86 (entries 136-339) contain data leading to 207 published biographies and lists of publications of Russian geographers and travelers in Russia.

General Works

11993   ADELUNG, FRIEDRICH VON, 1768-1843.
        Kritisch-literarische Übersicht der Reisenden in Russland
bis 1700, deren Berichte bekannt sind. St. Petersburg, Eggers,
1846. 2 v. illus. 26cm. Edited by N. F. Adelung. Critical-
literary overview of foreign travellers in Russia in 1700 who
have written reports. In some measure bio-bibliographical,
although the biographical data is relatively scanty, bearing primarily on activity in Russia and reasons for being there.

11994   BAGROW, LEO, 1881-1957.
        A. Ortelii Catalogus cartographorum. Bearb. von Leo
Bagrow. Gotha, J. Perthes, 1928-30. 2 v. facsim., maps.
28cm. (Ergänzungsheft Nr. 109, 210 zu Petermanns Mitteilung-
en) Extended bio-bibliographical notices (87) of the cartographers in the Catalogus cartographorum from the Theatrum
orbis of Ortelius. In dictionary arrangement (v.1, A-L; v.2,
M-Z)

11995   DICTIONARY OF LAND SURVEYORS AND LOCAL CARTOG-
        RAPHERS OF GREAT BRITAIN AND IRELAND, 1550-1850.
Compiled from a variety of sources by Francis Steer [and others]
and edited by Peter Eden. Folkestone, Eng., Dawson, 1975-76.
3 v. (377 p.) 23cm. Actually more of a directory than a biographical dictionary, but the work does contain some useful data
for the more prominent names represented.

11996   ENCICLOPEDIA GENERAL DEL MAR. Bajo la dirección de
        José Ma. Martínez-Hidalgo y Terán. Madrid, Ediciones

Garriga, 1957-58. 6 v. illus., ports. 26cm. Encyclopedia of
the sea and of naval art and science. Includes many biographical sketches and portraits of persons prominent in naval affairs,
exploration of the ocean, etc.

11997   ENCYCLOPAEDIA OF SHIPS AND SHIPPING. Edited by Her-
             bert B. Mason. London, Shipping Encyclopaedia, 1908.
         707 p. plates (part col.) 28cm. Includes biographies of sail-
         ors, navigators, etc., with emphasis on British personalities.

11998   GUTHORN, PETER J
             British maps of the American Revolution. Monmouth Beach,
         N. J., Philip Freneau Press, 1972. 79 p. illus., maps. 32cm.
         The first section of this work (Manuscript and printed maps, p.
         9-48) lists over 150 British and Loyalist cartographers and their
         works and includes biographical data for all those for which bio-
         graphical material has been found. Format is that of a bio-bib-
         liographical dictionary.

11999   HENNEQUIN, JOSEPH FRANÇOIS GABRIEL, 1775-1842.
             Biographie maritime; ou, Notices historiques sur la vie et
         les campagnes des marins célèbres français et étrangers.
         Paris, Regnault, 1835-37. 3 v. ports. 24cm. Maritime biog-
         raphy; or, Historical notes on the lives and campaigns of famous
         French and foreign seamen.

12000   HENZE, DIETMAR
             Enzyklopädie der Entdecker und Erforscher der Erde.
         Graz, Akademische Druck- u. Verlagsanstalt, 1975-   v.
         28cm. Issued in fascicles. Contents.--1. Lfg. A.--2. Lfg.
         Bab-Bock.
         Encyclopedia of discoverers and explorers of the earth; a bio-
         graphical dictionary.

12001   KRATKAIÀ GEOGRAFICHESKAIÀ ENTSIKLOPEDIIÀ. [Glav.
             redaktor A. A. Grigor'ev] Moskva, Izd-vo Sovetskaià ent-
         siklopediià," 1960-66. 5 v. illus. 27cm. (Entsiklopedii,
         slovari, spravochniki) Vol. 5, p. 410-544 of The Short geo-
         graphical encyclopedia contain about 3,000 names of geographers,
         explorers and workers in related disciplines from all periods
         and countries (but emphasizing Russians); biographical sketches
         are included along with bibliographies and references to pages
         in the encyclopedia where the names are mentioned.

12002   MATVEEVA, T   P
             Russkie geografy i puteshestvenniki. Fondy Arkhiva Geogr.
         obshchestva. [Spravochnik] Sost. T. P. Matveeva, T. S. Fi-
         lonovich, L. I. IArukova. Leningrad, "Nauka," Leningradskoe
         otd-nie, 1971. 175 p. illus. 22cm. At head of title: Akademiià

nauk SSSR. Geograficheskoe obshchestvo SSSR. A bio-bibliographical dictionary of 64 Russian geographers and travelers.

12003   NEWBY, ERIC
          World atlas of exploration. Introd. by Sir Vivian Fuchs.
          South Melbourne, Victoria, Macmillan; London, Mitchell Beaz-
          ley, 1976. 288 p. illus. 30cm. Includes capsule biographies
          of 600 explorers. American ed. has title: The Rand McNally
          world atlas of exploration.

12004   OLSZEWICZ, BOLESŁAW, 1893-
          Wykaz polskich pracownikow na polu kartografii. (In Studia
          i materiały z dziejow nauki polskiej. Seria C: Historia nauk
          matematycznych, fizykochemicznych i geologiczno-geograficz-
          nych. Warsaw, Pánstwowe Wydawn. Naukowe. zesz. 4 (1961),
          p. [35]-59; zesz. 13 (1968), p. 57-61) A list of Polish cartog-
          raphers; the biographical notes are brief for the most part. The
          list is in two alphabets, A-Z.

12005   OXFORD COMPANION TO SHIPS AND THE SEA. Edited by
          Peter Kemp. London, New York, Oxford University Press,
          1976. vii, 971 p. illus. 24cm. Includes biographies of men
          of the sea (navigators, pirates, explorers, etc.).

12006   POLIEVKTOV, MIKHAIL ALEKSANDROVICH
          Europeiskie puteshestvenniki ... Tbilisi, Akademiia nauk
          SSSR, Nauchno-issledovatel'skii institut kavkazovedeniia, 1935-
          46. 2 v. 21cm. Vol. 2 published by: Arkhivnoe upravlenie
          MVD Gruzinskoĭ SSR, and reprinted in part from the journal
          Istoricheskii vestnik (t. 1) Contents. --[1] XIII-XVIII. vv. po
          Kavkazu. [Russian travellers, B-IA. Non-Russian, A-Z]--
          [2] Po Kavkazu, 1800-1830 gg. [Russian travellers, A-IA. Non-
          Russians, A-Z]. European travellers in the Caucasus, 13th
          century to 1830.

12007   TOOLEY, RONALD VERE, 1898-
          Some portraits of geographers and other persons associated
          with maps. With notes, by R. V. Tooley. London, Map Col-
          lector's Circle, 1975. 2 v. ([66]) p. chiefly illus., ports.
          25cm. (Map Collector's series, v. 11, no. 104-105) Portraits
          of 59 geographers and cartographers from ancient to early mod-
          ern times (accompanied by some biographical data).

12008   ZIELIŃSKI, STANISŁAW, bibliographer.
          Mały słownik pionerów polskich kolonjalnych i morskich;
          podróznicy, odkrywcy, zdobywcy, badacze, eksploratorzy,
          emigranci-pamietnikarze, dzialacze i pisarze migracyjni.
          Warszawa, 1932 [cover 1933] 680 p. 17cm. "Niniejszy 'Mały
          słownik' jist rozszerzonym 'Słownikiem biograficznym,' pub-
          likowanym w 'Morzu' [1931-1933]." Dictionary of Polish ex-
          plorers and mariners.

History, Archaeology, Anthropology, Etc.

12009   ÅSTRÖM, PAUL
        Who's who in Cypriote archaeology. Biographical and
        bibliographical notes. Göteborg, P. Aströms forlag, 1971.
        88 p. ports. 31cm. (Studies in Mediterranean archaeology,
        v. 23)

12010   ALISHAN, GHEWOND, 1820-1901, comp.
        Hayapatown ... Venedig, Impr. S. Ghazarow, 1901 [i. e.
        1902] 142, 649 p. illus., ports. 34cm. Armenian history
        [and Armenian chroniclers] Biographical section (p. 69-349)
        chronologically arranged; alphabetical index (by forenames) to
        the chroniclers, p. 353-357.

12011   ARKAEOLOGISK ABC. Handbog i dansk forhistorie. Red. :
        Mogens Rud. København, Politikens forlag, 1972. 351 p.
        illus., ports. 18cm. A dictionary of Danish archaeology: pre-
        historic man in Denmark (and Europe). Includes portraits and
        biographical sketches of leading Danish archaeologists of the
        past and present.

12012   FIFTH INTERNATIONAL DIRECTORY OF ANTHROPOLOGISTS.
        Pref. by Sol Tax. Chicago, University of Chicago Press,
        1975. x, 496 p. 29cm. In double columns. Actually a bio-
        graphical dictionary-directory of living anthropologists. 3d ed.
        appeared in 1950.

12013   HAMBURG. UNIVERSITÄT. COLLEGIUM POLITICUM.
        Geschichtswissenschaftler in Mitteldeutschland. Hrsg. vom
        Collegium Politicum an der Universität Hamburg, Arbeitsgruppe
        Historiographie. Bonn, F. Dümmlers [1965] 100 p. 21cm. His-
        torians in Middle Germany; a bio-bibliographical dictionary of
        present-day German historians.

12013a HISTORISCHE KOMMISSION WESTFALENS.
        Die Mitglieder der Historischen Kommission Westfalens.
        Zusammengestellt von Wilhelm Kohl. Münster in Westfalen,
        Aschendorff, 1972. 62 p. 22cm. (Schriften der Historischen
        Kommission Westfalens, 8) At head of title: 75 Jahre Histor-
        ische Kommission Westfalens. 226 German historians, ar-
        chivists, etc. who were members of the Historical Commission
        of Westphalia, 1896-1971; biographical data is sparse, but refer-
        ences to biographies are given under each member.

12014   HURZHII, IVAN OLEKSANDROVYCH
        Vydatni radians'ki istoryky. [Narysy napysaly i pidgotuvaly
        po druku ... I. O. Hurzhii i V. S. Petrenko. Redaktor: Z. O.
        IErmakova] Kyiv, Vyd-vo Rad. shkola, 1969. 244 p. ports.

23cm. (Biblioteka vchytelia istorii) Portraits and biographies of 96 contemporary Soviet Russian historians, living and deceased.

12015   LUNIYA, BHANWARLAL NATHURAM, 1917-
Some historians of medieval India [by] B. N. Luniya. Agra, Lakshmi Narain Agarwal [1969] vii, 200 p. 23cm. Bio-bibliographical sketches of ca. 50 historials who lived and wrote in India during that country's medieval period.

12016   MÜLINEN, EGBERT FRIEDRICH VON, Graf
Podromus einer schweizerischen Historiographie in alphabetischer Reihenfolge die Historiker aller Cantone und aller Jahrhunderts umfassend. Bern, Hubert, 1874. x, 240 p. 24cm. Very brief biographical notices of Swiss historians.

12017   PRĀCYAVIDYĀ-TARANGINĪ; golden jubilee volume of the Department of Ancient Indian History and Culture. Edited by D. C. Sircar. [Calcutta] University of Calcutta, 1969. xix, 540 p. illus., ports. 23cm. Pages 327-483 contain autobiographical-biographical sketches of 66 teachers, students, etc. connected with the Dept. of Ancient Indian History and Culture of the University of Calcutta.

12018   ROY, SACHIN, 1920-
Anthropologists in India; short-biography, bibliography, and current projects. Compiled and edited by Sachin Roy. New Delhi, Indian Anthropological Association, 1970. xx, 218 p. 25cm. "Chapter I: Biography" (p. [1]-63) is a biographical dictionary of 20th century Indic anthropologists.

12019   SHVEDOVA, OL'GA IVANOVNA, 1900-
Istoriki SSSR; ukazatel' pechatnykh spiskov ikh trudov. Pod red. I. N. Koblentsa. Moskva [Vsesoiuznaia knizhnaia palata] 1941. 152 p. 18cm. (Nauchno-issledovatel'skii kabinet bib-liograficheskogo istochnikovedeniia i istorii bibliografii. [Trudy] No. 1) The historians of Russia; intent of the work is primarily bibliographical, but it does contain brief biographical data (dates, professional activities, etc.) of Russian historians of the 18th-20th centuries.

12020   WILGUS, ALVA CURTIS, 1897-
The historiography of Latin America; a guide to historical writing, 1500 to 1800. Metuchen, N. J., Scarecrow Press, 1975. xv, 333 p. 22cm. 227 bio-bibliographical sketches of historians of various nationalities who wrote about Latin America. Arranged by century in which the authors flourished and thereunder by country, etc. Alphabetical approach thru' the General index of names.

Political Science

12021   CANKAYA, ALI, 1920-
Yeni Mülkiye târihi ve Mülkiyeliler (Mülkiye seref kitabi)
Ankara, Mars Matbaasi, 1968-71. 8 v. facsims., ports. 24cm.
At head of title: "Son asir Türk tarihinin önemli olaylari ile
birlikde." A history of the Faculty of Political Sciences (and
Public Administration) at the University of Ankara, Turkey
(v. 1-2); v. 3-7 contain biographies (and, in many cases, portraits) of 5,993 graduates (from 1860 to 1967), 103 teachers, 10
directors and 5 deans. The last volume (8) includes an index
which yields an alphabetical approach to the biographies in v.
3-7, which have a chronological arrangement.

TECHNOLOGY AND APPLIED SCIENCE

Bibliography, Indexes, Portrait Catalogs

12022   BELL, S   PETER
A biographical index of British engineers in the 19th century. New York, Garland Pub., 1975. x, 246 p. 22cm. (Garland reference library of social science, v. 5) An index of o-
bituaries of some 3500 British engineers which appeared in
British engineering journals before 1901.

12023   HIGGINS, THOMAS JAMES
A biographical bibliography of electrical engineers and
electrophysicists. (In Technology and culture. Chicago. 24cm.
v. 2 (1961) p. 28-32, 146-165) In 2 parts: 1. Books. 2. Periodical items.

General Works

12024   AKADEMIA NAUK TECHNICZNYCH, WARSAW.
Akademia Nauk Technicznych, 1933-1937. Warszawa,
1937. 169, [3] p. 22cm. Includes biographical notices of
members of the Academy of Technology in Warsaw (1933-1937)
grouped by discipline and alphabetical thereunder.

12025   ALBUM ACADEMICUM DES POLYTECHNIKUMS ZU RIGA,
1862-1912. Riga, Jonck & Poliewsky, 1912. 826 p. illus.,
ports. Academic album of the Polytechnicum (later the Poly-
technical Institute) in Riga for the years 1862-1912. Many photographs and biographical notes are given for students and faculty.

12026   CARTER, ERNEST FRANK, 1899-
Dictionary of inventions and discoveries. 2d rev. ed.
London, F. Muller [1974] 208 p. 23cm. 1st ed., 1966; rev.

ed., 1969. Includes brief biographical sketches of noted inventors and research scientists. Surnames in biographical entries are in capital letters.

12027   CENTRE DE CRÉATION INDUSTRIELLE. Design française.
Paris, 1971. 246 p. illus. 14 x 21cm. Cover title. Catalog of an exhibition organized by the Center and held at the Union centrale des arts décoratifs, Oct. 22-Dec. 21, 1971. "Le catalogue établi par le CCI a été rédigé grâce au concours de Danielle Ceria [et al.]" Scattered through the catalog are many biographical sketches of industrial designers active in France. There is an "Index biographique" to these sketches at the front of the volume.

12028   DIZIONARIO DELLE ORIGINI, invenzioni e scoperte nelle arti, nelle scienze, nella geografia, nel commercio, nell' agricoltura ecc. , ecc. Opera compilata da una società di letterati italiani. Milano, A. Bonfanti, 1828-31. 4 v. Dictionary of inventions and discoveries in the arts, sciences, geography, commerce, agriculture, etc. With biographical data.

12029   HEPPNER, ERNST
Juden als Erfinder und Entdecker. Berlin-Wilmersdorf, Welt-Verlag, 1913. 126 p. 8 ports. 21cm. (Veröffentlichungen der Henriette Becker - Stiftung) Jewish scientists and inventors. Arranged alphabetically by discipline; table of contents: p. 1-4.

12030   HUBERT, PAUL, ed.
Dictionnaire biographique des inventeurs, ingénieurs et constructeurs. Paris, Impr. de l'Armorial français, G. Colombier [1904] 131 p. illus. 29cm. [Collection des grands dictionnaires biographiques internationaux] At head of title: Société des grands dictionnaires biographiques. Biographical dictionary of inventors, engineers and builders.

12031   LAMI, EUGÈNE OSCAR
Dictionnaire encyclopédique et biographique de l'industrie et des arts industriels, par E. -O. Lami et A. Tharel. Paris, Lami, Tharel et Cie., 1881-88. 8 v. & supplement. illus. 4.º Encyclopedic and biographical dictionary of industry and the industrial arts.

12032   LIEBFELD, ALFRED
Polacy na szlakach techniki. Warszawa, Wydawnictwa Komunikacji i Lacznosci, 1966. 350 (ca.) p. ports. 20cm. A compilation of short biographies of Polish technologists—military engineers, civil engineers, geologists, chemical technologists, etc. Notices grouped by specialty and arranged chronologically thereunder.

12033   MATSCHOSS, CONRAD, 1871-1942, ed.
         Männer der Technik. Ein biographisches Handbuch, hrsg.
im Auftrag der Verein Deutsche Ingenieure. Berlin, VDI-Verlag,
1925. xi, 306 p. ports. 30cm. A biographical handbook for
engineers, technologists, etc.; over 850 biographical sketches.

12034   NOBLET, JOCELYN DE
         Design; introduction à l'histoire de l'évolution des formes
industrielles de 1820 à aujourd'hui [par] Jocelyn de Noblet avec
la collaboration de Catherine Bressy. [Paris] Stock-Chêne
[1974] 381 p. illus. 23cm. (Collection Eugène Clarence Braun-
Munk) An introduction to the history of the evolution of industrial design from 1820 to the present; pages 245-352 comprise a
dictionary of industrial designers and industrial design firms.

12035   REUTER, JONATAN
         Finlandssvenska tekniker. Biografiska anteckningar under
medverkan av flere författare. Helsingfors, Söderström, 1923-
25. 3 v. ports. 22cm. Biographical notices of Finno-Swedish
technicians. Edited by J. Reuter. Each volume is alphabetical,
A-O.

Agriculture

12036   AMERICAN MEN AND WOMEN OF SCIENCE:
         Agricultural, animal and veterinary sciences, 1974. Ed-
ited by the Jaques Cattell Press. New York, R. R. Bowker,
1974. xi, 832 p. 29cm. Ca. 14,200 biographies of persons in
disciplines related to food production and animal studies; selected from the 8-volume set of American men and women of
science, 12th ed.

12037   BHARAT KRISHAK SAMAJ.
         Yearbook. 1964-   New Delhi, Bharat Krishak Samaj.
         v. illus., ports. 24cm. Some issues include a 'who is who'
of outstanding Indian agricultural scientists. E.g., 1967 issue
(p. 689-716) has 105 biographical sketches.

12038   DANSK AGRONOMFORENING
         Biografisk leksikon over agronomer. [9. udg.] Udarbejdet
ved Alfred Larsen. Valby, Eksp.: Antoinettevej 5, 1967. 11,
471 p. illus. 26cm. Previously published by Foreningen af
danske landbrugskandidater under title: Danske landbrugskandidater. Biographical dictionary of Danish agriculturists.

12039   DANSKE FORSTKANDIDATERS FORENING.
         Danske forstkandidater; i anledning af skovbrugsundervis-
ningens 150 aars jubilaeum. København, 1936-56. 2 v. ports.
24cm. Vol. 2 has subtitle: I anledning af 150 aarsdagen for
Fredskovsforordningen af 27. september, 1805. Contents. --bd.

1. 1786-1936, ved C. Gandil.--bd. 2. 1890-1955, ved A. Thyssen. Danish foresters; portraits and biographical sketches.

12040　FERGUSON, JOHN, 1842-1913.
Pioneers of the planting enterprise in Ceylon (from 1830 [-1835] onwards); biographical notices and portraits (reprinted from the "Tropical agriculturist") Colombo, A. M. & J. Ferguson, 1894-1900. 3 v. illus., ports. 24cm.

12041　FORENINGEN AF DANSKE CIVILHORTONOMER.
Danske hortonomer 1970. Red. af J. H. Wanscher. Statistiske opstillinger udarb. af Svend Aa. Christensen. Valby, 1970. 233 p. illus. 22cm. Continuation of Danske havebrugs-kandidater, 1865-1946. Danish horticulturists flourishing as of 1970; a bio-bibliography.

12042　HELLENS, O　　VON
Suomen eläinlääkärien nimikirja vuosilta 1843-1942. Helsinki, Suomen Eläinlääkäriyhdistys, Finska Veterinärföreningen, 1942. 246 p. ports. 22cm. Register of Finnish veterinarians; biographical notices, p. 7-228; catalog of Finnish veterinarians from 1843 to 1938 (chronological, p. 235-246).

12043　JUGOSLOVENSKA POLJOPRIVREDA 1939-1969. Odgovorni urednik: Jordan Blaževski. Saradivali: Veljko Vidaković [i dr.] Na biografijama saradivali: Ranko Bonifačić [i dr.] Beograd, "Interpress"--Plasman, 1970. 624, [3] p. 29cm. Yugoslav agriculture, 1939-1969. Includes 2 biographical dictionaries (p. [151]-624) the first for agriculturists, the second for veterinarians.

12044　McDONALD, DONALD, 1857-
Agricultural writers from Sir Walter of Henley to Arthur Young, 1200-1800. Reproductions in facsim. and extracts from their actual writings, enl. and rev. from articles which have appared in "The Field" from 1903 to 1907, to which is added an exhaustive bibliography. New York, Burt Franklin [1968] 228 p. illus. 26cm. (Burt Franklin: Bibliography & reference series #217) Bio-bibliography of 46 early British writers on the agricultural arts. Reprint of the 1908 ed. (London, H. Cox)

12045　MAGNAN, JEAN CHARLES, 1891-
Le monde agricole. Montréal, Presses libres [1972] 263 p. illus., ports. Biographies of figures in agriculture in the province of Quebec with a few in world agriculture; differs somewhat from the author's Silhouettes; figures du terroir.

12046　MAGNAN, JEAN CHARLES
Silhouettes; figures du terroir. Montréal, Fides [1964,

c1963] 251 p. ports. 22cm. Biographical dictionary of Quebec's agronomists, professors of agronomy, leaders of agricultural associations, persons linked up with world agriculture.

12047 MEN OF AGRICULTURE & VETERINARY SCIENCES IN INDIA
(Distinguished who's who) 1st-   ed. : 1965/66-
New Delhi, Premier Publishers.   v. ports. 25cm. With
biographical sketches and portraits. Compiled 1965/66-
by C. L. Khosla.

12048 METCALF, HENRY HARRISON, 1841-
New Hampshire agriculture: personal and farm sketches.
Concord, N. H., Republican Press Association, 1897. 407 p.
illus., ports. 24cm. Biographical sketches and portraits of
124 prominent agriculturists from New Hampshire at the end of
the 19th century.

12049 MILLAK, KONRAD
Slownik polskich lekarzy weterynaryjnych biograficzno-
bibliograficzny 1394-1918. Lublin, Państwowe Wydawn. Rol-
nicze i Leśne, 1960/63. xx, 291 p. 30cm. Dictionary of Polish
veterinarians; a bio-bibliography, 1394-1918.

12050 NEUMANN, LOUIS GEORGES, 1846-1930.
Biographies vétérinaires. Avec 42 ports. dessinés par
l'auteur. Paris, Asselin et Houzeau, 1896. ix, 443 p. ports.
8.° A biobibliographical dictionary (767 entries) of veterinarians.

12051 NEWTON, JORGE
Diccionario biográfico del campo argentino. Buenos Aires,
1972. 436 p. 23cm. Biographical dictionary of Argentine agriculturists and farmers.

12052 NUMMELIN, CARL
Finska forststaten; biografiska anteckningar [1851-1904]
Helsingfors, Handelstryckeriet, 1906. xviii, 153 p. 22cm.
Finnish foresters, 1851-1904; biographical notes.

12053 ORTOLI, JEAN BAPTISTE FRÉDÉRIC, 1861-   ed.
Dictionnaire biographique des agriculteurs de France.
Fasc. 1. Paris, Impr. de l'Amorial français [1904] 83 p.
illus. 29cm. [Collection des grands dictionnaires biographiques
internationaux] At head of title: Société des grands dictionnaires
biographiques. Biographical dictionary of French agriculturists.
Only the first fascicle was published.

12054   PRESTWICH, ARTHUR ALFRED
        Who's who in aviculture. Southampton, Eng., Agricultural
        Book Co. [1929-   v. 8.º "Series 1" the only vol-
        ume published? Beekeepers of Great Britain.

12055   SCHAPSMEIER, EDWARD L
        Encyclopedia of American agricultural history, by Edward
        L. Schapsmeier [and] Frederick H. Schapsmeier. Westport,
        Conn., Greenwood Press, 1975. xii, 467 p. 25cm. Includes
        biographies of agriculturists.

12056   SMITH, Sir FREDERICK, 1857-1929.
        The early history of veterinary literature and its British
        development. London, Baillière, Tindall and Cox, 1919-33.
        4 v. illus. 25cm. A series of numerous bio-biographies of
        British veterinarians from 1700 to 1860. Each volume is sepa-
        rately indexed; no general index.

12057   VENEZUELA. MINISTERIO DE AGRICULTURA Y CRÍA.
        Galería del Ministerio de Agricultura y Cría. [Caracas?
        1966?] 111 p. ports. 23cm. Contains biographical data and
        portraits of officials of Venezuela's Ministry of Agriculture and
        Animal Husbandry.

12058   WHO'S WHO IN B. C. AGRICULTURE. Prepared jointly by
        the B. C. Dept. of Agriculture, University of British Co-
        lumbia [and] B. C. Institute of Agrologists. [Vancouver, n. d.
        (195- or 6-?)] 38 p. 28cm. Cover title. British Columbian
        agriculturists.

Aeronautics and Astronautics

12059   THE SOVIET ENCYCLOPEDIA OF SPACE FLIGHT. G. V.
        Petrovich, editor-in-chief. Translated from the Russian.
        Moscow, Mir Publishers, 1969. 619 p. illus., ports. 23cm.
        Translation of Kosmonavtika. A dictionary of astronautics
        which includes portraits and biographies of astronauts (Russian
        and American), pioneers in rocket research, etc.

12060   UNITED STATES. LIBRARY OF CONGRESS. SCIENCE POL-
        ICY RESEARCH DIVISION.
        Astronauts and cosmonauts biographical and statistical data;
        report prepared for the Committee on Science and Technology,
        U. S. House of Representatives, Ninety-fourth Congress, first
        session, by the Science Policy Research Division, Congressional
        Research Service, Library of Congress. [Prepared by Vikki A.
        Zegel and Marcia S. Smith] Washington, U. S. Govt. Print. Off.,
        1975. v, 179 p. ports. 24cm. At head of title: Committee

print. Includes biographical sketches and portraits of 94 American and 38 Russian astronauts and cosmonauts.

12061   WHO'S WHO IN AVIATION. 1973-   New York, Harwood
        & Charles Pub. Co.   v. 26cm.   A biographical directory intended to be biannual; includes aviators, astronauts, inventors, meteorologists, businessmen and scientists.

Engineering

12062   AMERICAN SOCIETY OF CIVIL ENGINEERS. COMMITTEE
        ON HISTORY AND HERITAGE OF AMERICAN CIVIL ENGI-
        NEERING.
        A biographical dictionary of American civil engineers.
        New York, 1972. x, 163 p. illus. 23cm. (ASCE historical
        publication, no. 2)

12063   BATEMAN, ALFREDO D   1909-
        Páginas para la historia de la ingenieria colombiana. Galería de ingenieria colombianos. Bogotá, Editorial Kelly, 1972.
        634 p. ports. 25cm. (Biblioteca de historia nacional, v. 114)
        The history of engineering in Colombia. The 'Gallery of Colombian engineers' (p. [173]-574) is a biographical dictionary (87 lives) Four additional biographies of foreign engineers who served in Colombia are included on p. [575]-616.

12064   DANSK INGENIØRFORENING.
        Dansk civil- og akademiingeniørstat 1971. Biografiske oplysninger om kandidater fra Danmarks tekniske højskole og Danmarks ingeniørakademi (1829-1968) samt 451 medlemmer af Dansk ingeniørforening, der ikke er udgået fra de naevnte laeranstalter. Udg. af Dansk ingeniørforening og Krak. [6. udg.] København, Eksp. Krak, 1971. 962 p. 26cm. 5th ed. published in 1956 under title: Dansk civilingeniørstat 1955. Biographical sketches of graduates of the Polytechnical College in Copenhagen (1829-1968) and the 451 members of the Danish Engineering Society.

12065   ENGINEERING ANNUAL OF PAKISTAN AND WHO'S WHO.
        1965-66--   Karachi, Engineering Annual of Pakistan.   v. ports. 22cm. Began 1965-66? "Annual edition of The Engineer." Vols. for 1965-66--   compiled by Rehman Akhtar. The who's who section of the 1965-66 ed. covers almost half of the volume. Advertising matter interspersed.

12066   ENGINEERS JOINT COUNCIL.
        Engineers of distinction, including scientists in related fields. 1st ed. New York, 1970. xx, 457 p. ports. 29cm.

A biographical dictionary of 4500 living American engineers; also includes a directory of American engineering societies. 2d ed. (q. v.) is listed under title.

12067 ENGINEERS OF DISTINCTION; a who's who in engineering. 2d ed. New York, Engineers Joint Council, 1973. vi, 401 p. ports. 29cm. Living American engineers. The 1st ed. (q. v.) is entered under: Engineers Joint Council.

12068 HO, JAMES K   K
Black engineers in the United States; a directory. James K. K. Ho, editor. Washington, D. C. , Howard University Press [1974] xix, 281 p. 24cm. A biographical dictionary containing 1, 511 names out of an estimated total of 7, 000 black engineers in the United States.

12069 PROMIS, CARLO, 1808-1872.
Gl'ingegneri militari che operarono o scrissero in Piemonte dall'anno MCCC all'anno MDCL; notizie raccolte da Carlo Promis. Bologna, Forni, 1973. 238 p. 22cm. (Italica gens; repertori di bio-bibliografia italiana, n. 47) Reprint of the 1871 ed. (Torino, Stamperia reale). Biographical notices of 74 military engineers who worked or wrote in the Italian Piedmont from 1400 to 1650; chronological arrangement with alphabetical approach through name index at end of volume.

12070 STRUNZ, HUGO, 1910-
Von der Bergakademie zur Technischen Universität Berlin. 1770-1970. [Hrsg.: Förderer der Berliner Fakultät für Bergbau und Hüttenwesen e. V. , Berlin. Essen, Verlag Glückauf in Kommission, 1970] 151 p. illus., ports. 31cm. A history of the Technical University of Berlin's Faculty for Mining and Metallurgy and its forerunner, the Mining Academy of Berlin. Includes 110 biographical sketches of earth scientists from the Faculty (p. 42-135) arranged by field of specialization. Dark printed page numbers in the name index refer to these biographical sketches.

12071 SUOMEN SÄHKÖINSINÖÖREJÄ. FINLANDS ELEKTROINGENJÖRER. [Mikkelissä, etc.] Suomen Sähköinsinööriliitto. v. ports. 22cm. Began publication with vol. for 1926-41. Title varies: Matrikkeli. Matrikel (cover title: Suomen sähköinsinööreja. Elektroingenjörer i Finland) A directory with portraits and biographical data for electric engineers in Finland.

12072 TARBÉ DE SAINT-HARDOUIN, FRANÇOIS PIERRE H
b. 1813?
Notices biographiques sur les ingénieurs des ponts et chaussées depuis la création du corps, en 1716, jusqu'à nos jours. Paris, Baudry, 1884. 276 p. 25cm. (Encyclopédie des travaux

publics) Biographical notices on civil engineers in France from
1716 to 1884.

12072a THACKERAY, Sir EDWARD TALBOT, comp.
Biographical notices of officers of the Royal (Bengal) Engineers. London, Smith, Elder, 1900. x, 276 p. front., port.
23cm.

Manufactures

(Including Instrument Makers)

12073 ANDRÉN, ERIK, 1904-
Snickare, schatullmakare och ebenister i Stockholm under
skråtiden. Stockholm, Nordiska museet, 1973. 185 p. illus.
22cm. (Nordiska museets handlingar, 81) Biographical dictionary of furniture workers in Stockholm, 1640-1850: p. 55-161.

12074 BASANTA CAMPOS, JOSÉ LUIS
Relojeros de España; diccionario bio-bibliográfico. Pontevedra, Tall. Gráf. E. Paredes, 1972. 151 p. illus. 17cm. At
head of title: Museo de Pontevedra. A bio-bibliographical dictionary of Spanish clock and watch makers.

12075 BERGH, EDVIND
Matrikel öfver handverks- och fabriksförhållendena;
Helsingfors samt redogörelse för handverks - och fabriks-
föreningens i Hesingfors versamhet under det senaste seklet, av
Edv. Bergh. Redigeringen efter dennes död slutförd of Eemil
Forsgren. Helsingfors, Handtverks- och fabriksföreningen,
1904. [4], ii, 300 p. illus. 22cm. Includes a register of artisans and industry in Helsingfors. Biographical notices on p.
241-296.

12076 BRITTEN, FREDERICK JAMES, 1843-1913.
Britten's old clocks and watches and their makers; a historical and descriptive account of the different styles of clocks
and watches of the past in England and abroad containing a list
of nearly fourteen thousand makers. 8th ed., by Cecil Clutton
and the late G. H. Baillie and C. A. Ilbert. Rev. and enl. by
Cecil Clutton, with diagrams by F. Janca and endpapers by L.
H. Cresswell. London, E. Methuen in association with E. & F.
Spon, 1973. xxii, 532 p. illus. 29cm. The listing of clock
and watch makers at the back of the volume does contain dates
and career material for some of the craftsmen. 1st ed. issued
in 1899; 2d (1904); 3d (1911); 4th (1920); 5th (1922); 6th (1933); 7th
(1956)

12077 BRYDEN, D. J.
Scottish scientific instrument-makers, 1600-1900. Edinburgh, Royal Scottish Museum, 1972. ix, 59 p. illus. 32cm.

(Royal Scottish Museum. Information series: Technology, 1)
An alphabetical listing on p. 43-59 yields names of individuals
or firms, dates when active and occasionally a descriptive
phrase or two, but primarily a listing with not much biographical data.

12078   DE DANSKE TRAEERHVERV. Faglig, biografisk håndbog for
de organiserede erhvervsdrivende inden for handel, hand-
vaerk og industri i trae- og tømmererhvervene i Danmark.
Udarb. i samråd med erhvervenes institutioner og organisa-
tioner. Faglig red.: Tage Uhrskov. Biografisk red.: Forlaget
Liber A/S. Ny udg. København, Forlaget Liber, 1970-
v. illus. 27cm. Includes biographical sketches of Danes
in the wood-using industries, lumber trade, carpentry, etc. 1st
ed. issued in 1958 (in 2 v.)

12079   DE VITA, CARLO
Armaioli romani. Dagli archivi dell'Università e della
Confraternità di Sant'Eligio dei ferrari in Roma. Roma, Marte,
1970. 244 p. illus. 25cm. Introduction also in English,
French and German. A biographical dictionary (biographical
notations are very brief) of gunsmiths in the City of Rome, 16th
to the beginning of the 19th century, with references to documents in the archives of the Arte de' ferrari and the Confraternità that contain information about the particular gunsmiths.

12080   DROST, WILLIAM E
Clocks and watches of New Jersey [by] William E. Drost.
Elizabeth, N. J., Engineering Publishers, c1966. xi, 291 p.
illus., ports. 27cm. "Clockmakers of New Jersey, 1710-1966"
(p. 13-239) is an alphabetical listing of individuals and firms with
biographical data when available.

12081   FOUCAUD, ÉDOUARD
Les artisans illustres, par Édouard Foucaud, sous la direction de Ch. Dupin et Blanqui aîné. Paris, Béthune et Plon, 1841.
643 p. illus., ports. 26cm. Famous artisans (with numerous
portraits); the work is divided into 4 historical periods: from the
Renaissance to 1789, 1789, 1804, & 1815-1840. Alphabetical index: p. 637-639.

12082   FOUCAUD, ÉDOUARD
The book of illustrious mechanics, of Europe and America.
Translated from the French of Edward Foucaud. New ed., with
a supplementary chapter on American mechanics and their inventions. Edited by John Frost. Hartford, Belknap and Ham-
ersley, 1849. 336 p. illus., ports. 21cm. Translation of Les
artisans illustres.

12083   GILL, HAROLD B
         The gunsmith in colonial Virginia, by Harold B. Gill, Jr.
Williamsburg, Va., Colonial Williamsburg Foundation; Char-
lottesville, Distributed by the University Press of Virginia
[1974] vii, 139 p. illus. 24cm. (Williamsburg research studies)
"Virginia gunsmiths, 1608-1800" (p. 69-108) yields brief biographical data in an alphabetical listing; also given are dates when
the particular gunsmiths flourished and references to printed or
manuscript sources which mention the gunsmiths.

12084   MALATESTA, ENZIO
         Armi ed armaioli. Milano, E. B. B. I., Istituto editoriale
italiano B. C. Tosi [1939] 435 p. illus., ports. 28cm. (Enciclopedia biografica e bibliografica 'Italiana,' ser. 50) A biographical dictionary of Italian armourers and gunsmiths.

12085   MASON, BERNARD, 1895-
         Clock and watchmaking in Colchester, England; a history of
provincial clockmaking from the fifteenth to the nineteenth centuries in the oldest recorded town in Great Britain. Feltham,
Country Life, 1969. 436 p. illus. 26cm. In large part a collection of biographical material, arranged chronologically; alphabetical approach thru' index.

12086   MAYER, LEO ARY, 1895-1959.
         Islamic armourers and their works. Geneva, A. Kundig,
1962. 128 p. 20 plates. 26cm. "Roll of swordsmiths" (p. [3]-
79) and "Roll of cannonmakers" (p. [80]-89) are biographical dictionaries.

12087   MAYER, LEO ARY, 1895-1959.
         Islamic metalworkers and their works. Geneva, A. Kundig,
1959. 126 p. illus. 27cm. "Roll of metalworkers" (p. [19]-
[92]) is a biographical dictionary.

12088   MORPURGO, ENRICO
         Nederlandse klokken- en horlogemakers vanaf 1300. Am-
sterdam, Scheltema & Holkema, 1970. vii, 152 p. illus. 26cm.
A biographical dictionary of Dutch clock and watch makers after
1300.

12089   ROBERTS, KENNETH D
         Planemakers and other edge tool enterprises in New York
State in the nineteenth century [by] Kenneth D. and Jane W.
Roberts. [Cooperstown, N. Y.] New York State Historical Association [1970, c1971] vii, 230 p. illus. 24cm. The "Checklist of New York State planemakers and dealers" (p. 144-190),
in dictionary format, yields biographical data for individuals
under personal names and company names.

12090   RUBTSOV, NIKOLAĬ NIKOLAEVICH, 1882-
        Slovar' russkikh liteĭshchikov XII-XVII vv. (In his: Istoriiá
        liteĭnogo proizvodstva v SSSR. Chast 1: IX-XVIII vv. Moskva,
        Mashgiz, 1947. 23cm. p. 188-244) Dictionary of Russian
        founders (casters).

12091   TARDY,
        Dictionnaire des horlogers français; documentation réunie
        par Tardy ... Avec l'apport des travaux de Paul Brateau ... et
        de Robert Ardignac. Paris, Tardy [1971-72] 2 v. in 1 (x, 760 p.)
        illus., ports. 24cm. (Collection Tardy, 125, 127) Contents. --
        1. ptie. A-K. --2. ptie. L-Z. A dictionary of French clock and
        watch makers.

Photography

12092   MATHEWS, OLIVER
        Early photographs and photographers; a survey in dictionary
        form. London, Reedminster Publications [1973] viii, 198 p.
        illus. 26cm. "Photographers and photographic inventors" (p.
        6-44) is a biographical dictionary.

12093   SAN FRANCISCO. MUSEUM OF ART.
        Women of photography; an historical survey. Organized by
        the San Francisco Museum of Art, April 18-June 15, 1975 ...
        Wellesley College Museum, April 12-May 23, 1976. [San Fran-
        cisco, San Francisco Museum of Art, c1975] 1 v. (unpaged)
        illus. 31cm. An exhibition catalog that consists of bio-biblio-
        graphies of 39 women photographers from Julia Margaret Cam-
        eron to Marcia Resnick (arrangement is chronological); the
        photographers are listed alphabetically in the section "Selected
        bibliography" at end of volume.

12094   TIME-LIFE BOOKS
        Great photographers, by the editors of Time-Life Books.
        New York [1971] 246 p. illus., ports. 27cm. (Life library of
        photography) Cover title: Great photographers: 1840-1960.
        Yields biographical data for 68 photographers.

AUTHOR INDEX

A. & A. Enterprise Incorpo-
rated, 9459

Aa, Abraham Jacob van der,
10959

Aagaard, Adolf, 9507

Åström, Paul, 12009

Abad, Rafael Gayano--SEE:
Gayano Abad, Rafael, 9690

al-Abbār, Muhammad ibn 'Abd
Allāh ibn--SEE: Ibn al-Abbār,
Muhammad ibn 'Abd Allāh,
9303-9304

'Abbās, Ihsān, 9310

'Abbās al-'Azzāwī--SEE: al-
'Azzāwī, 'Abbās, 9302

Abbaye de Notre-Dame de Port-
Royal des Champs--SEE:
Port-Royal des Champs (Ab-
bey of Cistercian nuns), 11761

Abbott, Frances Matilda, 9907

Abbott, Robert Tucker, 11894

'Abd al-'Azīz Mustafā al-Ma-
rāghi--SEE: al-Marāghi,
'Abd al-'Azīz Mustafā, 11323

'Abd al-Ghanī ibn 'Abd al-Wāhid
al-Jammā'ili--SEE: al-Jammā'ili, 'Abd al-Ghanī ibn
'Abd al-Wāhid, 11845

Abd al-Ghanī ibn Sa'īd al-Azdī--
SEE: al-Azdī (Abd al-Ghanī
ibn Sa'id ibn 'Alī ibn Sa'id),
11840

'Abd al-Hamid, Muhammad Muhyi al-Din--SEE: Muhammad
Muhyi al-Din 'Abd al-Hamid,
9320

'Abd al-Hayy ibn 'Abd al-Kabīr
al-Kattānī--SEE: al-Kattānī,
'Abd al-Hayy ibn 'Abd al-
Kabīr, 9319

Abd al-Janī ibn Sa'īd al-Azdī--
SEE: al-Azdi (Abd al-Ghanī
ibn Sa'id ibn 'Alī ibn Sa'id),
11840

'Abd al-Qadir ibn Muhammad ibn
Abī al-Wafā' al-Qurashi--SEE:
Ibn Abī al-Wafā' al-Qurashi,
'Abd al-Qadir ibn Muhammad,
11318

'Abd al-Qādir ibn Shaykh al-
'Aydarus--SEE: al-'Aydarus,
'Abd al-Qādir ibn Shaykh,
9296

'Abd al-Rahmān ibn Abī Bakr
(Jalāl al-Din) al-Suyūti--SEE:
al-Suyūti, 10846, 11854

'Abd al-Rahmān ibn Ahmad ibn
Rajab--SEE: Ibn Rajab, 'Abd
al-Rahmān ibn Ahmad, 11846

'Abd al-Rahmān ibn Muhammad
ibn 'Askar--SEE: Ibn 'Askar,
'Abd al-Rahmān ibn Muham-
mad, 9309

'Abd al-Razzāq Samsām al-
Daulah Shāh-navaz Khan,
9226

'Abd al-Wahhāb ibn Ahmad al-
Sha'rānī--SEE: al-Sha'rānī,
'Abd al-Wahhāb ibn Ahmad,
9330-9331

'Abd Allāh al-Jubūrī--SEE: al-
Jubūrī, 'Abd Allāh, 9292

'Abdulha'i ibn Fakhruddin al-
Hasani, 9227

'Abdu'l-Hayy ibn Fākhru'd-Din
al-Hasani--SEE: 'Abdul-
ha'i ibn Fakhruddin al-Hasani, 9227

Ábel, Péter, 10329

Abellán, Carmen Conde--SEE:
Conde Abellán, Carmen,
11252

Aberdeen University, 9632

Abeyesooriya, Samson, 9693

Abramov, Aleksei Sergeevich, 9612

Abū al-'Arab Muhammad ibn Ahmad al-Tamimi--SEE: al-Tamimi, Abū al-'Arab Muhammad ibn Ahmad, 10706

Abū al-Husayn Muhammad ibn Muhammad ibn Abī Ya'lā--SEE: Ibn Abī Ya'lā, Abū al-Husayn Muhammad ibn Muhammad, 11846

Abū al-Kasim Mir Kudrat Allah Kasim, 11286

Abū Bakr Ahmad ibn 'Alī al-Isbahānī--SEE: al-Isbahānī, Abū Bakr Ahmad ibn 'Alī, 11843

Abū Ja'far Ahmad ibn Ibrāhim ibn al-Zubayr--SEE: Ibn al-Zubayr, Abū Ja'far Ahmad ibn Ibrāhīm, 9308

Abū 'Ubaidallāh al-Marzubānī--SEE: al-Marzubānī, Muhammad ibn 'Imrān, 10843-10844

Abū 'Umar Muhammad ibn Yūsuf al-Kindī--SEE: al-Kindī, Abū 'Umar Muhammad ibn Yūsuf, 8841

Abū Ya'qūb Yūsuf ibn Yahyā al-Tādilī--SEE: al-Tādilī, Abū Ya'qūb Yūsuf ibn Yahyā, 11855

Abu Zakariyā Jahya al-Nawawī, Yahya ibn Sharaf--SEE: al-Nawawī, 9327

Abu'l Qasim Mir Qudratullah Qasim--SEE: Abū al-Kāsim Mir Kudrat Allah Kasim, 11286

Academia Salvadoreña de la Historia, San Salvador, 9627

Académie de médecine, Paris--SEE: Académie nationale de médecine, Paris, 11427

Académie des inscriptions et belles-lettres, Paris, 8949

Académie française, Paris, 8869

Académie nationale de médecine, Paris, 11427

Académie royale de langue et de littérature françaises, Brussels, 11009

Academy of Medicine of Cincinnati, 11515

Acadia University, Wolfville, N. S., 8632

Achard, Claude François, 9041

Achery, Luc d', 11634

Acosta C., Gustavo, 8688e

Acton, Jay, 9766

Actors' Union (Israel)--SEE: Igud ha-omanim, 10409

Adam, Gérard, 11942

Adam, Ingrid, 10792

Adam, Melchior, 11595

Adamec, Ludwig W., 8480

Adams, Russell L., 8305

Adams, Woodbury S., 9906

Addepalli Appala Narasimha Raju--SEE: Raju, Addepalli Appala Narasimha, 11278

Addison, Agnes--SEE: Gilchrist, Agnes Eleanor (Addison), 9762

Addison, William, 9184

Adelige Jomfrukloster, Odense, Denmark, 8820

Adelung, Friedrich von, 11993

Adelung, Nikolai Fedorovich, 11993

Adlerberth, Roland, 8272

Adling, Wilfried, 11061

Adloff, Richard, 8526, 8800

Adoff, Arnold, 10816

Afanasjeva, Rita, 10553

Affre, Henri, 8977

The African register, 9660

Agan, Patrick, 8412

Aggarwal, J. C., 10703

Aghababyan, Sowren, 10855

Aguilar, José I. Pinilla--SEE: Pinilla Aguilar, José I., 10099

Aguilera, Julián Marias--SEE: Marías Aguilera, Julián, 11253

Agulló y Cobo, Mercedes, 11481

Ahern, George, 11417

Ahern, Michael Joseph, 11417

Ahmad, Khwaja Jamil--SEE: Jamil Ahmad, Khwaja, 9316

Ahmad ibn Abd Allāh Khazrajī-- SEE: Khazrajī, Ahmad ibn Abd Allāh, 11847

Ahmad ibn al-Qādi--SEE: Ibn al-Qādi, Ahmad ibn Muhammad, 9307, 9485

Ahmad ibn al-Qāsim ibn Abī Usaybi'ah--SEE: Ibn Abī Usaybi'ah, Ahmad ibn al-Qāsim, 11411a

Ahmad ibn 'Alī, al-Najāshī, 11839

Ahmad ibn 'Alī ibn Hajar al- 'Asqalānī--SEE: Ibn Hajar al-Asqalānī, Ahmad ibn 'Alī, 11319, 11322

Ahmad ibn Muhammad al-Kalā- bādhī--SEE: al-Kalābādhī, Ahmad ibn Muhammad, 11843

Ahmad ibn Muhammad al-Kha- fājī--SEE: al-Khafājī, Ahmad ibn Muhammad, 10842

Ahmad ibn Muhammad ibn al- Qādī--SEE: Ibn al-Qādī, Ahmad ibn Muhammad, 9307, 9485

Ahmad 'Isā, 11411

Aichelburg, Errado di, 9338

Ajdukiewicz, Kazimierz, 11552

Ajia Kenkyūjo, Tokyo, 8709

Akademia Nauk Technicznych, Warsaw, 12024

Akademie der Wissenschaften, Munich. Historische Kom- mission, 9071

Akademiiā de Shtlintse a RSSM, 9484

Akademiiā khudozhesty. Nauch- no-issledovatel'skii institut teorii i istorii izobrazitel'- nykh iskusstv, 10206

Akademiiā nauk Kazakhskoi SSR, Alma-Ata, 9439

Akademiiā nauk SSSR, 12002

Akademiiā nauk SSSR. Institut filosofii, 11570

Akademiiā nauk SSSR. Institut geografii, 11992

Akademiiā nauk SSSR. Institut vostokovedeniiā, 11284

Akademiiā nauk SSSR. Otdele- nie ekonomii, 11943

al-Ālūsī, Jamāl al-Dīn, 9292

Alvarez, Paulino, 11635

Alvarez, Ramón, 11797

Álvarez-Sierra, José, 11482

Ambrogio a S. Teresa, 11636-11637

Ambrogio di S. Teresa--SEE: Ambrogio a S. Teresa, 11636-11637

Ambrosius a Sancta Theresia-- SEE: Ambrogio a S. Teresa, 11636-11637

American Association of University Women. Austin Branch, 9971

American Biographical Institute, 9778

American Biographical Publishing Company, 8674, 8682

American Chemical Society, 11907

American Contract Bridge League, 10614

American Council of Learned Societies Devoted to Humanistic Studies, 10729

American Council on Industrial Arts Teacher Education, 10736

American Express Company, 10231

American Express Pavilion, World's Fair, 1964-1965-- SEE: New York (City). World's Fair, 1964-1965. American Express Pavilion, 10231

American Gynecological Society, 11492

American Historical Society, 9950

American Osteopathic Assiciation, 11497

American Publishers' Company, 9930

American Society of Civil Engineers. Committee on History and Heritage of American Civil Engineering, 12062

Amezaza Aresti, Vicente de, 9989

Amico, Alicia d', 11155

Ammer, Christine, 10445

Amory, Cleveland, 8428

Amsterdam. Universiteit, 10713

Amtmann, Bernard, 10901

Anashkina, V. T., 11211

Anasyan, Hakob Sedrak'i, 8512

Andersen, Carl Christian, 8819

Andersky, Ed., 8551

Anderson, Albert, 11812

Anderson, Gerald H., 11609

Anderson, Hugh, 10859

Anderson, James, of Edinburgh, 9637

Anderson, Michael John, 10758

Anderson, William Pitcairn, 9633

Andhra Pradesh Akademi of Sciences, 11886

Andonie, George St., 11912-11913

Andrade, Cayetano, 11171

Andrade, Vicente de Paula, 11779

André, Louis, 8868

André, Valère, 10648, 10885

Andrea, Gioacchino d'--SEE:
D'Andrea, Gioacchino, 11772

Andrea, Valerius--SEE: André,
Valère, 10648, 10885

Andreini, Ivo, 10153

Andrén, Erik, 12073

Andreucci, Franco, 11977

Andrews, Ralph Warren, 9767

Andrieu, Jules, 8965

Ancrauds, Jānis, 11160

Angeles Caballero, César Augusto, 11185

Angelieva, Fani, 10745

Angelis, Luigi de, 11102

Anglade, Joseph, 11205

Anker, Carl Johan, 9506

Anne, Théodore, 8936

Anón Marco, Vicente, 9690

Anquetil, Louis Pierre, 8891

Ansell, Evelyn, 9146

Antezana, José, 9521

Anthon, Charles, 8392

Antropov, V. N., 11229

Anwar al-Jundī--SEE: al-Jundī,
Anwar, 9317

Anzu, Motohiko, 11867

Aparin, N. G., 9598

Apostólico Colegio de Nuestra
Señora de Guadelupe, 11802

Appleton, Marion Brymner, 9918

Arabantinos, Panagiōtēs, 10700

Arabinda Biswas--SEE: Biswas,
Arabinda, 10703

Aradi, Nóra, 11534

Araki, Tadashi, 10181

Arango Mejía, Gabriel, 8791

Arapova, N., 9606

Arata, Esther Spring, 10831

Arbellot, François, 9014

Arboleda, Gustavo, 8839

Archila, Ricardo, 11521-11522

Architect of the Capitol (United
States)--SEE: United States.
Architect of the Capitol, 9833

Archives nationales (France)--
SEE: France. Archives na-
tionales, 10115, 10127, 10380

Archivo General de la Nación,
Venezuela--SEE: Venezuela.
Archivo General de la Nación,
9997

Arco, Carlo d', conte, 10154

Arco, Manuel del, 9671

Ardashev, M. A., 9607

Ardignac, Robert, 12091

Arens, Fritz Viktor, 9115

Aresti, Vicente de Amezaza--
SEE: Amezaza Aresti,
Vicente de, 9989

Argegni, Corrado, 9339

Argenville, Antoine Nicolas De-
zallier d'Argenville, Antoine
Nicolas, 10264

Arguedas, Julio Díaz--SEE:
Díaz Arguedas, Julio, 8583-
8584

Ariel, Aharon, 8308

Arizona State University, Tempe.
Center for Latin American
Studies, 9453

Arnold, Bruno, 9206

Arnott, James Fullarton, 10397

Arras, France. Saint-Vaast
(Abbey), 11742

Arroyo, Leonardo, 8606

Art Gallery of Ontario--SEE:
Ontario. Art Gallery, 10090

Arte de' ferrari, Rome--SEE:
Rome (City). Arte de'
ferrari, 12079

Arteaga, Enrique Esperabé--
SEE: Esperabé Arteaga,
Enrique, 10721

Arthur Jensens forlag, Copen-
hagen--SEE: Jensens (Arthur)
forlag, Copenhagen, 8831

Arts Council of Great Britain,
10116, 10134

Aryal, Deepak Kumar, 9490

Arzumanian, A. A., 9828

Asahi jānaru, 11529

Asaoka, Okisada, 10182

Asatryan, Asatowr Avetisi,
10852

Ash, Brian, 10746

Asimov, Isaac, 11871

Aslan, Nicola, 8588

Aspara, K. E., 8853

al-Asqalāni, Ahmad ibn 'Ali ibn
Hajar--SEE: Ibn Hajar al-
'Asqalāni, Ahmad ibn 'Ali,
11319, 11322

Assiniwi, Bernard, 8492

Association for Asian Studies,
10649

Association for Asian Studies.
Ming Biographical History
Project Committee, 8710

Association for the Advancement
of Ukrainian Studies, 9831

Association française d'action
artistique, 10116

Association royale des demeures
historiques de Belgique, 8577

Astraudo, Amedeo Eugenio Pros-
pero Massimino, duca, 9628

'Ata'-Allah ibn Yahya, called
Nau'izada--SEE: Atāyi,
Ataullah Nev'izade, 9739

Ataian, R. A.--SEE: At'ayan,
Rhobert A., 10516

Atalay, Besim, 9738

Atanasova, Svetozara, 8623

Atāyi, Ataullah Nev'izade, 9739

Ataullah Nev'izade Atāyi--SEE:
Atāyi, Ataullah Nev'izade,
9739

At'ayan, Rhobert A., 10516

Atherton, William Henry, 8669

al-Athir, 'Izz al-Din ibn--SEE:
Ibn al-Athir, 'Izz al-Din,
9305

Atkinson, Frank, 10965

Atkinson, George Wesley, 9980

Atlantic Publishing and Engraving Company, 9863, 9911, 9945

Attar Singh--SEE: Singh, Attar, 9240

Aubert, Joachim, 9072

Audet, François Joseph, 8670, 11036

Audin, Marius, 9019

Auerbach, Ella F., 11516

Auerbach, Erich, 10446

Auffray, Jacqueline, 8863

al-'Aufi--SEE: 'Awfi, Muhammad, 11183

Augel, Johannes, 9125

Ault-Dumesnil, Édouard d', 8409

Aurenhammer, Hans, 11572

Auria, Vincenzo, 9388

Austen-Leigh, Richard Arthur, 9153

Australia. Parliament. Library, 8545

Austrian P. E. N. Club--SEE: P. E. N. Club, Austria, 10876

Avery, Catherine B., 9358, 10148

Avis-kronik-index, 8257

'Awfi, Muhammad, 11183

Awwad, Gurguis--SEE: 'Awwād, Kūrkīs, 11096

'Awwād, Kūrkīs, 11096

Axters, Stephanus Gérard, 11783

Ayala, Mariano d', 9340

al-'Aydarus, 'Abd al-Qādir ibn Shaykh, 9296

al-'Aydarūsi, Muhyī ad-Din 'Abd al Qadir ibn Sayh ibn 'Abd Allāh--SEE: al-'Aydarus, 'Abd al-Qādir ibn Shaykh, 9296

Ayeni, Peter M., 9501

al-Azdi (Abd al-Ghanī ibn Sa'īd ibn 'Alī ibn Sa'd), 11840

al-Azzāwi, 'Abbās, 9302

Baas, Johann Hermann, 11369

Babický, Oldřich, 11939

Baciu, Stafan, 11156

Backer, Cornelis Andries, 11895

Bacmeister, Walter, 9126

Baczko, Bronisław, 11535

Badauni, Nizami--SEE: Nizami Badauni, pseud., 11288

Bader, Gershom, 9057, 9420

Badlu Ram Gupta--SEE: Gupta, Badlu Ram, 11972

Bätzing, Gerhard, 11804

Bagalei, Dmitrii Ivanovich, 11325, 11474, 11928

al-Baghdadi, Ismail Pasha--SEE Ismail, pasa, 10840

Bagrow, Leo, 11994

Baguës, Ventura, 10612

Baguës Nasarre de Letosa, Ven tura--SEE: Baguës, Ventura, 10612

Bailey, Conrad, 9144

Bailey, Leaonead Pack, 10818

Baillie, Granville Hugh, 12076

Baini, Prashad--SEE: Prashad, Baini, 9226

Bair, Frank, 8423

Bajer, Jiří, 10563

Bajwa, Fauja Singh, 9274, 9276

Bakalowicz, Władysław, 9538

Bakeless, John Edwin, 9768

Bakeless, Katherine (Little), 9768

Balasubrahmanya Mudaliyar, M. --SEE: Mudaliyar, M. Balasubrahmanya, 11274

Balcar, Alexander J., 10315

Baldinucci, Filippo, 10155

Baldwin, William, 9160

Balkema, C. H., 10106

Ball, Robert, 11359

Balland, Joseph Antoine Félix, 11428

Ballester Escalas, Rafael, 8417

Baloch, Nabi Bakhsh, 11287

Balogh, Jolán, 10035

Baltische Historische Kommission, 8574

Baltzer, Ulrich, 9123

Balz, Hans Martin, 10501

Ban, Kōkei, 9399

Bandaranaike, S. W. R. D., 9698

Bandecchi, Pedro Brasil, 8598, 8606

Bandini Buti, Maria (Ferrari), 11103

Banerji, Sores Chandra, 11233

Banga, Jelle, 11463

Bankes, R. B., 11967

Bankinsurance news, 11980

Bannerman, Jean MacKay, 8634

Baptie, David, 10567

Baqir, Mohammed, 11184

Baraya, José María, 8792

Barba, Sharon, 10824

Barbacci, Rodolfo, 10557

Barbeau, Victor, 11037

Barbier, Antoine Alexandre, 8309

Barbieri, Alberto, 9382

Barboutau, Pierre, 10183

Bardong, Otto, 10686

Baril, Jacques, 10316

Barker, Eugene Campbell, 9969

Barker, William Pierson, 11573

Barksdale, Richard, 10819

Barnaul, Siberia. Altaĭskaiâ kraevaiâ biblioteka--SEE: Altaĭskaiâ kraevaiâ biblioteka, 11230a

Barnes, A. R., 8528

Barnes, Edwin Ninyon Chaloner, 10573

Barnes, Frederick Augustus, 9166

Barns, Florence Elberta, 10820

Barone, Michael, 9769-9770

Barot, Alexandre, 11896

Barr, E. Scott, 11869

Barr, George, 11574

Barrau, Hippolyte de, 9045

Barraud and Jerrard, photographers, London, 11370

Barré, Louis, 8310

Barreda, Rafael, 9662

Barreto, João Paulo de Mello, 8589

Barreto Villavisencio, Carlos A., 9520

Barriga López, Franklin, 10962

Barriga López, Leonardo, 10962

Barringer, Paul Brandon, 9974

Barrios, D. Walter, 9521

Barsacq, Léon, 10317

Barsukov, S. S., 9610

Bartelski, Lesław M., 11188

Barth, Bjarne Keyser, 9508

Barthélemy, Charles, 11743

Bartoš, Otakar, 11196

Bartsch, Adam von, 10125, 10194

Baruffaldi, Girolamo, 10156

Basan, Pierre François, 10046

Basanta Campos, José Luis, 12074

Baskin (O. L.) and Company, Chicago, 9861-9862

Baskin, Wade, 8311

Basovich, IA. I., 9604

Basso, Alberto, 10480

Bassotto, Camillo, 10358

Bateman, Alfredo D., 12063

Batterel, Louis, 11638

Batts, John Stuart, 9138

Baudot, Jules Léon, 11745

Bauer, Andrew, 10739

Baumann, Kurt, 9127

Baumeister, August, 9206

Baur, Frank, 11675

Baur, Samuel, 8418

Baussart, Laurent Deleville-- SEE: Deleville-Baussart, Laurent, 9492

Bautz, Friedrich Wilhelm, 11575

Bauzon, Louis Marie François, 11648

Bawden, Liz-Anne, 10344

Baxter, Clarice (Howard), 10575

Bayle, Louis, 11204

Bazala, Vladimir, 11422

Bazhan, Mykola Platonovych, 9746, 10228

B. C. Institute of Agrologists, 12058

Beach, Moses Yale, 11984

Beattie, Eleanor Gale, 10372

Beauregard, Gérard de, 8932

Beauvoir, Roger de, 8873

Beazley (Mitchell) Ltd.--SEE:
Mitchell Beazley, Ltd., 8386

Beck, Emily Morison, 8416

Beckwith, John, 10528

Becmann, Johann Christoph,
10687

Bedel, Charles, 11429

Bedeschi, D., 10546

Bedfordshire Historical Record
Society, 9179

Beĭsembaev, A. B., 9438

Belin, Jules Léonard, 8925

Belknap, Henry Wyckoff, 10232

Bell, Barbara L., 9748

Bell, S. Peter, 12022

Bellamy, Joyce M., 11966

Bellet, Benjamin Louis, 8918

Bellier de La Chavignerie,
Emile, 10111

Benavides, Ignacio Antonio da
Fonseca--SEE: Fonseca
Benavides, Ignacio Antonio
da, 11473

Bene, Lajos, 10702

Benedek, Marcell, 11083

Benedict, Clarence W., 11305

Benedict, George Grenville,
9972

Benedictines, 11639

Benedictines. Congrégation de
France (Solesmes), 11744,
11759

Benedictines. Congrégation de St.
Maur--SEE: Benedictines in
France. Congrégation de St.
Maur, 11634, 11753

Benedictines. Paris, 11745

Benedictines in France. Congrégation de St. Maur, 11634,
11753

Benedictines in France. Congrégation de Saint Vanne et Saint
Hidulphe, 11756

Benko, Nancy, 10071

Benmelekh, Avraham, 9336

Berenson, Bernhard, 10157

Berény, Robert, 11407

Berezhnoĭ, Aleksandr Feodoseevich, 9576

Berg, Alexander, 11377, 11443

Berger, Charles Victor, 11430

Berger, Paulo, 8590

Berger, Theodor, 8419

Bergeron, Arthur, 11719

Bergh, Edvind, 12075

Bergholm, Axel, 8848

Bergl, M., 10447

Bergsträsser, Gotthelf, 9306

Bergues La Garde, Joseph
Jacques Marie Casimir de,
8984

Beridze, Vakhtany Vukolovich,
9059

Berka, Hans, 11941

Berlin. Institut für Marxismus-
Leninismus--SEE: Institut für
Marxismus-Leninismus,
Berlin, 9091

Bielz, Julius, 9060

Biennale nazionale d'arte Città di Milano, 27th, 10158

Bierring, Walter Lawrence, 11498

Bihalji-Merin, Oto, 10016

Billings, Pat, 10424

Binani, G. D., 9249

Binder, Lucia, 10861

Bindi, Vincenzo, 10159

Birague, Aimé-Antoine de, 8414

Birkeli, Fridtjov, 11811

Birkelund, Palle, 8825

Birkerts, Pēteris, 10711

Birkner, Othmar, 10227

Birmingham, Cedric Osmond, 10402

Birt, Henry Norbert, 11768

Bishop, William John, 11372

Bisonó, Pedro R., 8835

Biswas, Arabinda, 10703

Bittencourt, Agnello, 8591

Bizzarro, Salvatore, 8688c

Björkbom, Carl, 9708

Bjurström, Per, 10223-10224

Black belt, 10634

Blackman, Lucy (Worthington), 9864

Blaeksprutten, 8822

Blair, David, 8529

Blair, Frank, 8423

Blakemore, Frances, 10184

Blakeney, Edward Henry, 8406

Blanc, Charles, 10047

Blanc, Élie, 11530

Blanchard, Pierre, 8314

Blanqui, Jérome Adolphe, 12081

Blanton, Wyndham Bolling, 11493

Blas, J. I. de, 10222

Błaszczyk, Leon Tadeusz, 10560

Blauveldt, Robert Brooks, 8673

Blayot, Louis, 8903

Blaževski, Jordan, 12043

Blech, Richard, 10319

Bleiberg, Germán, 11253

Blémur, Marie Jacqueline Bouette de, 11641

Bliss, Edward Munsell, 11590

Block, Eugene B., 9954

Blöss, Otto, 8808

Blom, Eric, 10449

Blondeau, Claude, 9020

Bluche, François, 11315

Blum, Daniel C., 10353

Blume, Clemens, 10472

Boalch, Doanld Howard, 10502

Bôas, Pedro Villas--SEE: Villas-Bôas, Pedro, 8615

Boase, T. S. R., 10140

Boatner, Mark Mayo, 9773

Bouchot, Henri François Xavier Marie, 8295

Boudin, Amédée, 8894

Bouette de Blémur, Marie Jacqueline--SEE: Blémur, Marie Jacqueline Bouette de, 11641

Bourde, Paul, 8880

Bourdeille Brantôme, Pierre de--SEE: Brantôme, Pierre de Bourdeille, seigneur de, 8426

Bourdin, Gustave, 8872

Bourg, Edme Théodore, known as Saint-Edme--SEE: Saint-Edme, Edme Théodore Bourg, known as, 8597

Bourgeois, Émile, 8868

Bourin, André, 11001

Bousquet, Jean Louis Etienne, 11747

Boutin, Leonidas, 8592

Bowdoin College. Museum of Art. Molinari Collection, 10305

Boyce, Katherine Randall, 9774

Boyce, Richard Fyfe, 9774

Boyens, A. J. H., 9658

Boyens, Adam Johannes, 9658

Boyer, Paul S., 9815

Bozhinova-Troianova, B., 11416

Bozhkova, Liuba Dimitrova-- SEE: Dimitrova-Bozhkova, Liuba, 11416

Bozzone, Antonio M., 11654

Bracco, Camillus Aloisius, 11704

Brachmer, Mieczysław, 11220

Bradbury, Malcolm, 10830

Bradfield, Robert, 10699

Bradford, Thomas Lindsley, 11373, 11494

Brambilla, Gian Alessandro, 11458

Branca, Vittore, 11115

Branco, Manoel Bernardes-- SEE: Portugal e os estrangeiros, 10748

Brankačk, A., 9464

Brant, Fuller, firm, Madison, Wis., 9981

Brantôme, Pierre de Bourdeille, seigneur de, 8426

Brasil Bandecchi, Pedro--SEE: Bandecchi, Pedro Brasil, 8598, 8606

Brassard, Gerard, 11799

Brateau, Paul, 12091

Brauer, Jerald C., 11622

Bravo Morata, Federico, 9666-9667

Brawley, Benjamin Griffith, 10821

Brazil. Congresso. Câmara dos Deputados. Biblioteca, 8593

Brazil. Ministério da Fazenda, 8594

Brazil. Ministério da Viação e Obras Públicas, 8595

Brazil. Ministério da Viação e Obras Públicas. Serviço de Documentação, 8596

Brazil. Ministério dos Transportes. Serviço de Documentação, 8596

Breban, Corrard de--SEE:
Corrard de Breban, 11336

Bréjon de Lavergnée, Arnauld,
10196

Bremen. Kunsthalle, 10048

Bremen. Staatsarchiv, 9109

Brenzoni, Raffaello, 10160

Bressy, Catherine, 12034

Bretos, Andreas Papadopoulos--
SEE: Vretos, Andreas
Papadopoulos, 11078

Brettauer, Josef, 11361

Breza, Eugen, Graf von, 9421

Bridger, Peter Anthony, 9557

Bridson, Gavin D. R., 11355

Briels, J. G. C. A., 11334

Briggs, Martin Shaw, 10262

Brigham, Johnson, 9880

Bright, Marion Converse, 9870

Brignano, Russell Carl, 9749

Brindeau, Serge, 11032

Briquet, John Isaac, 11897a

British Biographical Company,
9193

British Columbia. Dept. of Agriculture, 12058

British Columbia. University,
12058

British People Book Company,
9229

Britten, Frederick James, 12076

Brockmann, Henry Meyer--SEE:
Meyer-Brockmann, Henry,
10791

Brook, Donald, 10966

Brooklyn Institute of Arts and
Sciences. Museum, 10235

Brooklyn Museum--SEE: Brooklyn Institute of Arts and
Sciences. Museum, 10235

Brouette, Emile, 11654

Broughton, Carrie L., 9913

Broughton, Thomas Robert
Shannon, 9561

Brouka, Piatrus, 10005

Brown, Everit, 9775

Brown, John Buchanan--SEE:
Buchanan-Brown, John, 10751

Brown, Len, 10576-10577

Brown, Leonard Boardman, 9905

Brown, Peter Laurie, 8635

Brown, Sterling Allen, 10797

Brown, William Garrott, 8277

Browne, Edward Granville,
11183

Brownrigg, Ronald, 11577

Browtyan, Ts'its'ilia, 10517

Brož, Jaroslav, 10321-10322

Brož, Václav, 8807

Brtáň, Rudo, 11242

Bruckner, Albert Theophil,
11798

Bruel, F., 8881

Brüning, Eberhard, 10822

Brugos, Manuel García--SEE:
García Brugos, Manuel,
9451

Bruhat, Jean, 8882

Brunati, Giuseppe, 9392

Brune, Paul, 10112

Brunct, Gustave, 10750, 10753

Brunet, Jacques Charles, 10056

Brunn, Walter von, 11440

Bruns, Thomas Nelson Carter, Mrs., 9887

Brunschwig, Chantal, 10535

Brunswick (City). Herzog Anton-Ulrich-Museum, 10049

Brusali (i. e. Muhammad Tāhir ibn Rif'at--SEE: Muhammad Tāhir ibn Rif'at (Brusali), 11280

Brusendorff, Ove, 10323

Brusher, Joseph Stanislaus, 11642

Brutyan, Tsitsilia--SEE: Browtyan, Ts'its'ilia, 10517

Bruzelius, Anders Johan, 11489

Bry, Theodore de, 10749

Bryden, D. J., 12077

Brzozowska, Teresa, 11190

Buber, Salomon, 11859

Buch, Günther, 9099

Buchanan-Brown, John, 10751

Bucharest. Universitatea. Biblioteca Centrala. Sectorul de Documentare, 10718

Budapest. Magyar Nemzeti Galeria--SEE: Magyar Nemzeti Galeria, Budapest, 10149

Budovnits, Isaak Urielevich, 11213

Buenos Aires. Museo Nacional de Bellas Artes, 10275

Buess, Heinrich, 11490

Buffalo evening news, 9856

Bugge, Günther, 11908

Buhler, Kathryn C., 10289

Buitrago Trujillo, Rubén, 11735

Bulgari, Costantino G., 10284

Bŭlgarska akademiia na naukite, Sofia, 8618

Bŭlgarska akademiia na naukite, Sofia. Biblioteka, 10669

Bŭlgarska komunisticheska partiia. Okruzhen komitet (Kyustendil), 8622

Bŭlgarska komunisticheska partiia. Okruzhen komitet (Pernik), 8623

Bull, Storm, 10438

Bulletin de l'Afrique noire, 8487, 8489, 11953

Bulmer, Robert Harold, 9145

Bund der Vertriebenen, 9100

Bunten, Charles A., 10736

Bureau sinologique de Zi-ka-wei --SEE: Hsü-chia-hui ts'ang shu lou, Shanghai,

Burger, Combertus Pieter, 11347

Burgemeister, Ludwig, 10503

Burgess, Henry Thomas, 8530

al-Būrīnī, Hasan ibn Muhammad, 9297

Burke, William Jeremiah, 10823

Burma, 8625

Burmov, Aledsandŭr K., 10900

Burnham, Hampden, 8636

Burnham, J. Hampden--SEE:
Burnham, Hampden, 8636

Burnim, Kalman A., 10400

Burns, Netta Patricia, 8527

Burov, Abram Veniaminovich,
9611

Burrill, Bob, 10610

Burrows, Edmund H., 11479

Burt, A. R., 8727

Burton, E. Milby, 10285

Bury Classis (Presbyterian),
11822

Busch, Hermann J., 10503

Busch-Reisinger Museum of Germanic Culture--SEE: Harvard
University. Busch-Reisinger
Museum of Germanic Culture,
10130

Busić, Svetozar, 10599

Bustamante, Luis J., 8802

Busto Duthurburu, José Antonio
del, 9522

Buti, Maria Ferrari Bandini--
SEE; Bandini Buti, Maria
(Ferrari), 11103

Bux, Ernst, 8396

Bygdén, Anders Leonard, 11260

"C" Signo Editorial Argentino,
Buenos Aires, 8502

Caballero, César Augusto Ange-
les--SEE: Angeles Caballero,
César Augusto, 11185

Cabannes, Gabriel, 9011

Cabany, E. de Saint-Maurice--
SEE: Saint-Maurice Cabany,
E. de, 8910

Cabedo Torrents, Fernando, 9690

Cabo, Eusebio Castrillo de--SEE:
Castrillo de Cabo, Eusebio,
10606

Cabrera, Pablo, 8501

Caetani, Leone, principe di
Teano, 9298

Caetano de Sousa, Antonio--SEE:
Sousa, Antonio Caetano de,
11787

Caffaro Rossi, José María, 8498

Cagnacci, Fr., 11105

Caivano-Schipani, Felice, 9341

Calasibetta, Charlotte Mankey,
10286

Calcutta. University. Dept. of
Ancient Indian History and
Culture, 12017

Callejas, Jorge Posada--SEE:
Posada Callejas, Jorge, 8795

Calinau, L., 8883

Calvet, Louis-Jean, 10535

Calvi, Donato, 9368, 11106

Calvi, Girolamo Luigi, 10161

Calza, Raissa, 9562

Camard, Jean Pierre, 10110

Camariano-Cioran, Ariadna,
9569

Cambridge. University. King's
College, 9145

Cambridge. University. Peterhouse, 9146

Cameron, Elisabeth, 10425,
10425a

Cameron, Ian Alexander, 10425, 10425a

Cameroons, Southern. Parliament. House of Assembly, 8629

Campardon, Emile, 10378-10380

Campbell, Oscar James, 10324

Campbell, William Alec, 11909

Campeau, Fabien René Édouard, 8637

Campo Bello, Henrique Leite Pereira de Paiva de Faria Tavora e Cernache, conde de, 8597

Campos, José Luis Basanta-- SEE: Basanta Campos, José Luis, 12074

Campoy, Antonio Manuel, 10218

Canada. Public Archives, 8638, 10135

Canadian Biographies, Limited, 8675

Canadian Jewish Literary Foundation, 8648

Canadian Library Association, 10084

Canadian Music Centre, 10526, 10528

Canadian Press Syndicate, 8633, 8645

Canberra, Australia. National Library, 8545

Cândea, Sanda, 10718

Candler, Allen Daniel, 9869

Cankaya, Ali, 12021

Canniff, William, 11418

Canning, John, 8427

Cantalamessa-Carboni, Giacinto, 11107

Capasso, Gaetano, 11770

Capp, B. S., 9147

Cappellini, Antonio, 9373

Capponi, Vittorio, 9385

Caputo, Vincenzo, 9342

Caraffa, Pedro Isidro, 8499-8500

Carassiti, Rino, 11975

Carbone, Carlo, 11669

Carboni, Giacinto Cantalamessa --SEE: Cantalamessa-Carboni, Giacinto, 11107

Cárdenas y Espejo, Francisco de, 9669

Cardevacque, Adolphe de, 9037

Cardiff, Guillermo Furlong--SEE: Furlong Cardiff, Guillermo, 11710

Cardoso, George--SEE: Cardoso, Jorge, 11787

Cardoso, Jorge, 11787

Carey, Charles Henry, 9943

Çark, Y. G., 8514

Carnegie Mellon University. Hunt Institute for Botanical Documentation--SEE: Hunt Institute for Botanical Documentation, 11901

Carnegie Millon University. Rachel McMasters Miller Hunt Botanical Library--SEE: Hunt Botanical Library, 11901

Carneiro da Cunha Nóbrega, Apolonio--SEE: Nóbrega, Apolonio Carneiro da Cunha, 11718

Carneiro Giffoni, O.--SEE:
Giffoni, O. Carneiro, 11415

Carpelan, Tor Harald, 10681

Carr, James F., 10243

Carretero, José María, 9668

Carretero Novillo, José María--
SEE: Carretero, José María,
9668

Carriat, Amédée, 11001a

Carrillo, Pedro Emilio, 11523

Carrington, Evelyn M., 9971

Carter, Ernest Frank, 12026

Carter, George, 11834

Carteret, Léopold, 11002

Un Cartujo de Aula Dei, 11792

Casillas, Jose Gutiérrez--SEE:
Gutiérrez Casillas, Jose,
11780

Cassan, Stephen Hyde, 11624

Castagno, Margaret, 9655

Castellanos, Basilio Sebastián,
11576

Castillo, Ignacio B. del, 11167

Castillo, Julián N. Guerrero--
SEE: Guerrero Castillo,
Julián N., 8688a

Castle, Eduard, 10873

Castrillo de Cabo, Eusebio,
10606

Castro, Gloria Pachón--SEE:
Pachón Castro, Gloria, 8799

Castro, José de, 11788

Castro, José Ramón, 11250

Caswell, Edward Samuel, 10902

Catanzaro, Carlo, 11108

Gates, William Leist Readwin,
8359, 8390

Cathcart, William, 11628

Cavalcante de Albuquerque, Arcy
Tenório--SEE: Albuquerque,
Arcy Tenório Cavalcante de,
8307

Cavalcanti, Carlos, 10080

Caverley, Robert Boodey, 11967

Cavillier, François, 11897a

Cawkwell, Tim, 10325

Cazès, David, 11140

Cébeillac, Mireille, 9563

Ceccaroni, Agostino, 11647

Cederholm, Theresa Dickason,
10236

Ceillier, Remi, 11648

Cellius, Erhard, 10689

Center for the American Woman
and Politics--SEE: Rutgers
University, Brunswick, N. J.
Center for the American Woman and Politics, 9826

Central Intelligence Agency--
SEE: United States. Central
Intelligence Agency, 8803,
10001, 10719

Centre de création industrielle,
12027

Centro Regional de la Unesco
para el Fomento de la Ciencia
en América Latina--SEE:
United Nations Educational,
Scientific and Cultural Organization. Regional Center for
the Advancement of Science
in Latin America, 11906

Cereseto, Giovanni Battista,
9349

Ceretti, Felice, 9381

Cernache, Henrique Leite Pereira de Paiva de Faria Tavora e, conde de Campo Bello--SEE: Campo Bello, Henrique Leite Pereira de Paiva de Faria Tavora e Cernache, conde de, 8597

Černý, Annošt J., 10451

Cerri, Leopoldo, 11109

Československá akademie věd. Ústav pro českou literaturu, 10946

Ceylon. Jātika Rājya Sabhāva. Library--SEE: Ceylon. Jātika Rājya Sabhāva. Pustakālaya, 9694

Ceylon. Jātika Rājya Sabhāva. Pustakālaya, 9694

Ceylon. National State Assembly --SEE: Ceylon. Jātika Rājya Sabhāva, 9694

The Ceylon daily news, 9695-9697

Ceylon National Congress, 9698

Chabaneau, Camille, 11202, 11205

Chacón, Alfonso, 11670

Chajes, Saul, 11139

Chakŭrov, Nikola, 8620

Chalmers, Rob, 8550

Chamard, François, 11748

Chamberlain, Walter Max, 9497

Chambers, Frank M., 11203

Chamfort, Sébastien Roch Nicolas, called, 11017

Champeaux, Alfred de, 10287

Champsaur, Félicien, 8914

Chan, Tak-wan--SEE: Ch'ên, Tê-yün, 10920

Chandler, Sue P., 10832

Chandra Banerji, Sores--SEE: Banerji, Sores Chandra, 11233

Chang, Ch'ang, 8788

Ch'ang, Pi-tê, 8699

Chang, T'ai-ku, 10919

Chang, Ting, of Sung Dynasty, 8712

Chang, Ts'ai-t'ien, 8713

Chang, Wei-hsiang, 8789

Chang, Yüeh-ch'ing, 8714

Chaplin, Arnold, 9624, 11449

Chapuis, Monique, 11427

Charavay, Etienne, 8884

Charavay, Jacques, 8884

Charavay, Noël, 8885

Charbouclais, Louis Pierre François Adolphe, marquis de Chesnel de la--SEE: Chesnel de la Charbouclais, Louis Pierre François Adolphe, marquis de, 8316

Chase, Harold William, 11329

Chase, Joseph Cummings, 9776

Chaugy, François Madeleine de, 11649

Chaumeil, ------, abbé, 8975

Chaussin, Léon, 11745

Chavez, Angelico, 9908

Cogniat, Raymond, 10113

Cohane, Tim, 10617

Colegio Primitivo y Nacional de San Nicolás de Hidalgo, 11171

Coll, Edna, 11157

Collège de Saint-François-Xavier, Besançon, France, 11749

Collegium Carolinum, 8805

Collegium Politicum an der Universität Hamburg--SEE: Hamburg. Universität. Collegium Politicum, 12013

Collell Costa, Alberto, 11790

Collet de Messine, Jean Baptiste, 8908

Collin, Jean, 11750

Collin, Johan Gabriel, 9710

Collins, Herman LeRoy, 9947

Collins, Jimmie Lee, 10237

Colmenares, Diego de, 11251

Colmer, Montagu, 11331

Cologne. Wallraf-Richartz-Museum, 10050

Còlomo, Gavino, 11111-11112

Comanducci, Agostino Mario, 10163

Comay, Joan, 9422, 11581

Combs, Richard E., 10737

Comma, Carlton N., 9737

Commission des travaux historiques. Sous-Commission de recherches d'histoire municipale contemporaine, 9034

Commonwealth National Library --SEE: Canberra, Australia. National Library, 8545

Compère-Morel, Adéodat Constant Adolphe, 8429

Compton, Herbert Eastwick, 10401

Conde Abellán, Carmen, 11252

Confederazione generale dell'industria italiana, 11975

Confraternità di Sant'Eligio dei ferrari in Roma, 12079

Congrégation de St. Maur (Benedictines)--SEE: Benedictines in France. Congrégation de St. Maur, 11634, 11753

Congrégation du Saint-Esprit et du Sacre-Coeur de Marie--SEE: Holy Ghost Fathers, 11673

Congreso Internacional de Medicina--SEE: International Medical Congress, 11385

Coinsbee, Lewis Ralph, 9179

Conjeevaram Hayavadana Rao--SEE: Hayavadana Rao, Conjeevaram, 9241

Connolly, Margaret, 10699

Conrath, Marcel, 10999

Constable, William George, 8279

Constant, Alphonse Louis, 10755

Contee, Clarence Garner, 8280

Contemporary Art Society, Indianapolis, 10238

Conway Research, inc., Atlanta, 11946

Cooper, John Alexander, 8640, 11305

Cooper, Martin, 10452

Copenhagen. Garnisonsbibliothek, 8816

Cordell, Eugene Fauntleroy, 9894, 11495

Cordero y Torres, Enrique, 11172

Córdoba, Argentine Republic. Universidad Nacional, 8501

Corneau, Ernest N., 10427

Cornell University. Southeast Asia Program, 10726

Corps Suevia, Universität Tübingen--SEE: Tübingen. Universität. Corps Suevia, 9717

Corrard de Breban, 11336

Correa, Carlos René, 10909

Correa, Ramón C., 8794

Corrodi-Sulzer, Adrian, 9722

Cosma, Viorel, 10562

Cossío Salinas, Héctor, 10890

Costa, Alberto Collell--SEE: Collell Costa, Alberto, 11790

Costa, Marcelo Farias, 10370

Costa de la Torre, Arturo, 8582

Coste, Hilarion de, 11751

Coste, Jean François, 8892

Coste, Olivier de--SEE: Coste, Hilarion de, 11751

Coston, Henry, 8893, 11961

Couffon de Kerdellech, Alexandre François Marie, 8982

Couryel, Luis E. Páez--SEE: Páez Courvel, Luis E., 8797

Covarrubias, Manuel Moncloa y---SEE: Moncloa y Covarrubias, Manuel, 10414

Covarrubias, Ricardo, 9448

Cowen, David Laurence, 11496

Coysh, Arthur Wilfred, 10019

Cozens-Hardy, Basil, 9198

Craqéan, Qérovbē--SEE: Ch'rak'ian, K'erovbē, 10850

Crespi, Luigi, 10164

Crosby, Benjamin, 10398

Crosnier, Augustin, 11752

Cross, Frank Leslie, 11612

Crow, Carl, 8727

Cruikshank, Robert, 10399

Cruzat, Enrique Gajardo--SEE: Gajardo Cruzat, Enrique, 11412

Cubelić, Tvrtko, 10759

Cuéncar, Heriberto Zapata--SEE: Zapata Cuéncar, Heriberto, 10530-10531

Cummings, Paul, 10240

Cummings, Preston, 11829

Cunha Nóbrega, Apolonio Carneiro da--SEE: Nóbrega, Apolonio Carneiro da Cunha, 11718

Currier, Ernest M., 10289

Cutler, Harry Gardner, 9982

Cutter, Bob, 10602

Cuvier, Frédéric Georges, 11898

Czechoslovak National Council of America, 9819

Czechoslovak Republic. Komise pro knihopisný soupis českých a slovenských tisků až do konce XVIII. století, 10948

Czechoslovak Society of Arts and Sciences in America, 10734

Czerva, Rudolf von Granich-staedten--SEE: Granich-staedten-Czerva, Rudolf von, 11954

Czigány, Gyula, 10543

Czikann, Johann Jakob Heinrich, 8560

Dabrowski, Stanisław, 10417

Dacio, Juan, 11651

Dack, E. van 't, 8842

ad-Dahabi, Shams ad-Din Muham-mad--SEE: al-Dhahabi, Mu-hammad ibn Ahmad, 9299-9301

Dahl, Kai, 8824

Dahl, Willy, 11179

Dahlhaus, Carl, 10485

Dahlström, Lotten, 10680

Daiches, David, 10988

Daire, Louis François, 11005

Dairnvaell, Georges Marie Ma-thieu--SEE: Mathieu-Dairn-vaell, Georges Marie, 8934-8935

Dalmor, E. R., 11532

D'Amico, Alicia--SEE: Amico, Alicia d', 11155

Dampier, John Lucius Smith--SEE: Smith-Dampier, John Lucius, 9183

Danchov, Ivan Georgiev, 8617

Danchov, Nikola Georgiev, 8617

D'Andrea, Gioacchino, 11772

Dansk agronomforening, 12038

Dansk centralbibliotek for Sydslesvig, 10957

Dansk farmaceutforening, 11424

Dansk ingeniørforening, 12064

Dansk tandlaegeforening, 11524

Danske forstkandidators forening, 12039

Den Danske praesteforening, 11806, 11808

Danske sagførersamfund, 11308

Danske sprog- og litteratursel-skab, Copenhagen, 10760

Dantès, Alfred Langue, 8319

Danton, Henri, 9044

Da Ponte, Lorenzo L., 8397

D'Arco, Carlo, conte--SEE: Arco, Carlo d', conte, 10154

Daret, Pierre, 8431

D'Argenville, Antoine Nicolas Dé-zallier--SEE: Dézallier d'Ar-genville, Antoine Nicolas, 10264

Dasent, Arthur Irwin, 9149

Dass, Sita Ranjan, 10639

Dauer, Alfons M., 10476

Dautry, Jean, 8882

Davalillo, María, 10453

Davey, Frankland Wilmot, 10903

David de Penanrun, Louis Thé-rèse, 10263

Davies, J. K., 9207

Davila, Vicente, 9990, 9997

Davis, Ellis Arthur, 9859, 9888, 9909, 9966

Davis, Lenwood G., 9750

Davis, Mac, 10604

Davis, Robert Ralph, 9779

Davons, A., 8894

Dawdy, Doris Ostrander, 10241

Dawson, Thomas R. P., 10600

Day, Cedric, 10643

Day, Harvey, 11533

D'Ayala, Mariano--SEE: Ayala, Mariano d', 9340

De, Sushil Kumar, 9228

De Angelis, Luigi--SEE: Angelis, Luigi de,

Debiaggi, Casimiro, 10165

De Boni, Filippo--SEE: Boni, Filippo de, 10017

De Brune, Aidan, 8531

De Burgh, U. H. Hussey, 9293

Decalo, Samuel, 8814, 9735

De Carl, Lennard, 10433

Dedham Classis (Presbyterian), 11823

Deepak Kumar Aryal--SEE: Aryal, Deepak Kumar, 9490

Degen, Arsen Borisovich, 10420

Delaire, E., 10263

Del Castillo, Ignacio B--SEE: Castillo, Ignacio B. del, 11167

De Leo, Ernesto, 11113

De Leon-Paras, Corazon--SEE: Leon-Paras, Corazon de, 11324

Delepierre, Joseph Octave, 10077

Deleu, Jozef, 8861

Deleville-Baussart, Laurent, 9492

Dellagiacoma, Vittorino, 11709

Delmas, Juan Eustaquio, 9692

Delord, Taxile, 8920

Delpar, Helen, 9450

Del Vaux de Fouron, Henri Joseph Barthélemi, 8580

Dēmaras, Kōnstantinos, 10700

Dēmētrakopoulos, Andronikos K., 11074-11075, 11820

De Micheli, Mario--SEE: Micheli, Mario de, 10158, 10173

De Montalbo, Luigi, conte--SEE: Montalbo, Luigi de, conte, 9628

De Montreville, Doris, 10761

De Morgan, Augustus, 11920

Denina, Carlo, 11044

Denis, Auguste, 11006

Denmark. Kirkeministeriet, 11806

Dennis, Henry C., 9780

Dentu, Jean Gabriel, 8933

Déon, Léon Horsin--SEE: Horsin-Déon, Léon, 10120

Un Député, 8879

Derome, Louis Joseph Amédée, 8641

Desai, Ramnik Spripatray, 11080

Deseille, Ernest, 11007

Desmazières, Emile, 10078

Desrochers, Pierre Claude, 8895-8896

Detti, Tommaso, 11977

Deutsche Bibliothek, Frankfurt am Main--SEE: Frankfurt am Main. Deutsche Bibliothek, 11048

Deutscher Bühnenverein, 10392

Deutsches Institut für Wissenschaftliche Pädagogik, Münster, 10659

Devérité, Louis Alexandre, 9040

Devisme, Jacques François Laurent, 8968

De Vita, Carlo, 12079

Devoy, John, 9857, 9951-9952

Dewey, Langdon, 10357

DeWitt, William A., 8363

Dézallier d'Argenville, Antoine Nicolas, 10264

Dézsi, Lajos, 10762

al-Dhababī, Muhammad ibn Ahmad, 9299-9301, 11848

ad-Dhahabī, Shams ad-Dīn Muhammad ibn 'Utmān--SEE: al-Dhahabī, Muhammad ibn Ahmad, 9299-9301, 11847

Diachenko, IU. P., 10725

Di Aichelburg, Errado--SEE: Aichelburg, Errado di, 9338

Diamonstein, Barbaralee, 9781

Díaz, Carlos Morales--SEE: Morales Díaz, Carlos, 9476

Díaz, Esther M. Melón de--SEE: Melón de Díaz, Esther M., 9553, 9556

Díaz, Nicomedes Pastor, 9669

Díaz Arguedas, Julio, 8583-8584

Díaz de Escovar, Narciso, 9689

Dickie, John, 8485

Diem, Werner, 9321

Dienst, Rolf Gunter, 10128

Diezmann, August, 8362

Di Ferro, Giuseppe M.--SEE: Ferro, Giuseppe M. di, 9389

Digot, Paul, 9027

Di Lullo, Orestes--SEE: Lullo, Orestes di, 8509

Di Manzano, Francesco--SEE: Manzano, Francesco di, 11124

Dimberg, Ronald, 10651

Dimier, Anselme, 11654

Dimitriu-Pausesti, Alexandru, 11008

Dimitrova-Boshkova, Liuba, 11416

Dineschandra Sircar--SEE: Sircar, Dineschandra, 12017

Dion-Lévesque, Rosaire, pseud. --SEE: Lévesque, Léo Albert, 9805

Dionisotti, Carlo, 9393

Diugmedzhieva, Petia Trifonova, 10765

Diwald-Wilzer, Suzanne, 11842

Dlabac, Jan Bohumir, 10101

Documentación Española Contemporánea, 9679

Doderer, Klaus, 10783

Dodge, Bayard, 10839

Dodwell, Edward, 9151

Döring, Heinrich, 11583

Dolenz, Karl, 10665

Dolge, Alfred, 10504

Dolgov, Ivan Alekseevich, 9605

Dollar, George W., 11584

Dollinger, Hans, 8433

Dols, Jean Michel Emile, 11659

Domecq, Francisco Monte--SEE:
Monte Domecq, Francisco,
8510

Donaldson, Gordon, 9635

Doneaud, Alfred, 8929

Domini, Mauro, 10167

Doran, Genevieve C., 10243

Doria, Gino, 9346

Dornbusch, Charles Emil, 9751

Dornic, Francois, 8899

Doughty, Sir Arthur George,
8656

Douth, George, 9783

Downs, Winfield Scott, 8652

Doyé, Franz von Sales, 11660

Drachkovitch, Milorad M., 8448

Drenovac, Nikola, 11299

Dresden. Kupferstichkabinett,
10129

Dreux du Radier, Jean François,
8434, 9039

Dreves, Guido Maria, 10472

Drinker, Sophie Hutchinson, 9804

Driver, Arthur Harry, 11448

Drost, William E., 12080

Drugulin, W., Leipzig, 8281,
10439

Drugulin, Wilhelm Eduard, 8281

Drummond, Grace Julia, 8642

Duarte, Carlos F., 10259

Duarte de Almeida, A., 9541

Du Bose, Joel Campbell, 9851

Du Bose, John Witherspoon, 9855

Du Boys, Auguste, 9014

Duchesne, Louis Marie Olivier,
11682

Dudley, Donald Reynolds, 10937

Dützele, Gerhard Robert Walther
von Coeckelberghe--SEE:
Coeckelberghe-Dützele, Gerhard Robert Walther von, 8553

Dufäy, Charles Jules, 8966-8967

Duff, William Alexander, 9919

Duffield, Samuel Willoughby,
10540

Dufour, Antoine, 8327

Duisburg, Karl Ludwig von,
11366

Duke, Maurice, 10833

al Dūlābi, Muhammad ibn Ahmad, 11841

Duleau, Alphonse, 8900

Dulieu, Louis, 11432-11433

Dumas, Silvio, 8643

Dumay, Léon, 8901

Dumesnil, A. P. F. Robert--
SEE: Robert-Dumesnil, A.
P. F., 10125

Dumesnil, Édouard d'Ault--SEE:
Ault-Dumesnil, Édouard d',
8409

Dumesnil, René, 11396

Dupin, Charles, baron, 12081

Dupin, Louis Ellies, 10768,
11585-11586, 11597

Dupiney de Vorepierre, Jean
François Marie Bertet, 8328

Duplessis, Georges, 8293, 10125

Dupuy, Trevor Nevitt, 8452,
9784

Du Radier, Jean François
Dreux--SEE: Dreux du Ra-
dier, Jean François, 8434

Durai Raja Singam, S. --SEE:
Raja Singam, S   Durai,

Durivage, Francis Alexander,
8329

Durzak, Manfred, 11045

Dŭrzhavna biblioteka 'Vasil
Kolarov,' Sofia, 10900

Dŭrzhavne obedinenie Bŭlgarska
kniga, 10896

Duthurburu, José Antonio del
Busto--SEE: Busto Duthurburu,
José Antonio del, 9522

Dutuit, Auguste, 10193

Dutuit, Eugène, 10193

Duverrán, Carlos Rafael, 10942

Dwight, Henry Otis, 11590

Dyer, Gustavus Walker, 9962

Dzhangalin, M. O., 9438

D'znowni, Daniel, 8513

Dznuni, Daniél--SEE: D'znowni,
Daniel, 8513

Eagle, Dorothy, 10967

East Indies Institute of America,
New York, 10652

Eastern Nigeria. Ministry of Information, 9502

Easwaran Nampoothiry, E.,
11234

Ebeling, Friedrich Wilhelm,
11765

Éber, László, 10021

Ebert, John, 10242

Ebert, Katherine, 10242

Ebony, 9785, 9817

Echánove Trujillo, Carlos A.,
11936

Eck, Werner, 9565

Eckstein, Adolf, 8554

Ede, Harold Stanley, 10136

Edel, Leon, 10797

Eden, Peter, 11995

Edgar, Walter B., 9956

Edgett, Edwin Francis, 10426

Edib, Esref, 9314

Edições Melhoramentos. De-
partamento Editorial, 8598

Editorial Porrua, 9471

Edmar, 11099

Edmonds, Helen G., 9786

Eemans, Marc, 10079

Egge, Nils Martinsen, 9509

Egle, William Henry, 9944

Egli, Jean, 9721

Ehrlich, Sigmund, 10879

Eichbaum, Wilhelm Lange--SEE:
Lange, Wilhelm, 8352

Eisenstaedt, Alfred, 8435

Eisgruber, Heinz, 9077

Eka Venkata Subbarao--SEE:
Subbarao, Eka Venkata,
10590

Ekeland, Tønnes, 11812

Ekzempliarskiĭ, Aleksandr
Vasil'evich, 9579

Elam, Yigal, 9423

Elberling, Emil, 8826

Elberling, Victor Eugen, 8826

Elespuru, Juan Manuel Ugarte
--SEE: Ugarte Elespuru, Juan
Manuel, 10199

Elgar, Frank, 10113

Elk, Herb, 10631

El'konina, Faina Iosifovna,
11147

Ellinwood, Leonard Webster,
10580

Ellison, Rosemary, 10239

Ellmann, Richard, 10825

Elvert, Christian, Ritter d',
10555

Embid, Florentino Pérez--SEE:
Pérez Embid, Florentino,
8460

Emden, Alfred Brotherston,
9152

Encyclopaedia Britannica, 10654

Engelbarts, Rudolf, 9788

Engelbregt, L., 11675

Engelmüller, Karel, 10343

Engelstoft, Jesper, 10211

Engineers Joint Council, 12066-
12067

Englebert, Omer, 11663

Englund, Björn, 10569

Equipo Mundo, 9671

Ercole, Francisco, 9347

Erdinger, Anton, 11712

Eremian, Aram, 8515

Eriksen, Svend, 10290

Erkel Ferenc Múzeum, 10149

Errandonea, Ignacio, 8394

Esakoŭ, A., 11295

Escalas, Rafael Ballester--SEE:
Ballester Escalas, Rafael,
8417

Escher, Konrad, 9722

Escoyar, Narciso Díaz de--SEE:
Díaz de Escovar, Narciso,
9689

Eskelund, Lotte, 10740

Espejo, Francisco de Cárdenas
y--SEE: Cárdenas y Espejo,
Francisco de, 9669

Espejo, Juan Luis, 8688d

Esperabé Arteaga, Enrique,
10721

Espindola, Walter Hanisch--
SEE: Hanisch Espindola,
Walter, 11729

Espinosa, Luis María Fernán-
dez--SEE: Fernández Espi-
nosa, Luis María, 11665

Esposizione nazionale quadriennale d'arte, Rome--SEE:
Rome (City). Esposizione
nazionale quadriennale d'arte,
10257, 10280

Essen. Museum Folkwang,
10052-10053

Esteve, Juan Soriano--SEE:
Soriano Esteve, Juan, 9690

Esteves Pereira, João Manuel,
9542

Etelä-Pohjanmaan Maakuntaliitto, 8850

Ethridge, James M., 10756

Eton College, 9153

Etreillis, ------baron de,
10632

Ette, A. J. H. van, 9491

Eugster, Conrad Hans, 11889

Euler, Karl Philipp, 10637

Europa Publications, ltd., 8483

Evans, Clement Anselm, 9869

Evans, Edward, 9139

Evans, Webster, 10624

The Evening star, Washington,
D. C., 9789

Everts (H. L.), publisher,
Philadelphia, 9897

Evgenov, Semen Vladimirovich,
9583

Evstigneev, V. N., 9588

Ewen, David, 10458-10459,
10581-10582

Eyles, Allen, 10424

Fabretti, Ariodante, 9390

Fabritius, Albert, 8828, 8830,
10760

Fabroni, Angelo, 9348, 9384

Facal, Pedro A. Fontenla--SEE:
Fontenla Facal, Pedro A.,
8505

Facio, Sara, 11155

al-Fadl Ibrāhīm, Muhammad
Abū--SEE: Ibrāhīm, Muham-
mad Abū al-Fadl, 10845

Faerber, Meir, 9335

Faidherbe, Alexandre Joseph,
11414

Failor, Kenneth M., 9790

Fairfield, John Houghton,
10505

Fales, Martha Gandy, 10295

Falk, Byron A., 8282

Falk, Valerie R., 8282

Fallon, John P., 10291

Fang, Chao-ying, 8693, 8701,
8710

Fang, Hsüeh-ch'un, 8728

Fang, I., 8730

Fang, Joong, 11916

Farber, Eduard, 11910

Faria Tavora e Cernache, Henrique Leite Pereira de Pavia
de, conde de Campo Bello--
SEE: Campo Bello, Henrique
Leite Pereira de Paiva de
Faria Tavora e Cernache,
conde de, 8597

Farias Costa, Marcelo--SEE:
Costa, Marcelo Farias,
10370

Farmer, Edward L., 10651

Farr, Kenneth R., 9552

al-Fāsī, Taqī al-Dīn Muhammad ibn Ahmad, 9302

Fastenrath, Johannes, 9078

Fauja Singh--SEE: Bajwa,
Fauja Singh, 9274, 9276

Fauja Singh Bajwa--SEE: Bajwa.
Fauja Singh, 9274, 9276

Faure, Sébastien, 8436

Fauteux, Aegidius, 8646

Fedele, Benedetto, 11773

Feder, Lillian, 10935

Federal Writers' Project, 9793

Fedorowicz, Zygmunt, 11899

Fei, Shu, 8737

Feilden, Charles, 9229

Feillard, ----------, 8902

Fekete, Márton, 9220

Félibien, André, sieur des
Avaux et de Javercy, 10054

Fellmeth, Robert C., 9823

Fellowes, Edmund Horace,
11626

Fendell, Bob, 10602

Fendt, Tobias, 8438

Fère, François Fortuné Guyot
de--SEE: Guyot de Fère,
François Fortuné, 10109,
11011

Feret, Édouard, 8903, 9003

Ferguson, John, 12040

Ferluga, Jadran, 8844

Fernandes, Aparício, 10893

Fernandes, Nabor, 10894

Fernández, Juan Rómulo, 8504

Fernández, Salvador Aldana--
SEE: Aldana Fernandez,
Salvador, 10217

Fernández de los Ríos, Angel,
9673

Fernández Espinosa, Luis María, 11665

Fernández Guardia, Ricardo,
8801

Ferner, Helmut Richard, 11376

Ferrari, Enrique Lafuente--SEE:
Lafuente Ferrari, Enrique,
9546

Ferrarius, Philippus, 11774

Ferreira da Fonseca, Martinho
Augusto--SEE: Fonseca,
Martinho Augusto Ferreira da,
9544

Ferreira Martins, José Frederico,
9543

Ferro, Giuseppe M. di, 9389

Fess, Simeon Davidson, 9920

Feuchtersleben, Ernst,
Freiherr von, 8362

Feuilleret, Henri, 8991

Fevret de Fontette, Charles
Marie, 8866

Fevret de Saint-Mémin, Charles
Balthazar Julien, 9975

Fidalgo, Andrés, 10848

Fielding, Mantle, 10243

Fierville, Charles, 10684

Figueiredo, Pedro José de, 9549

Figueroa, Pedro Pablo, 10906

Figueroa, Ramón Rua--SEE: Rua Figueroa, Ramón, 11904

Filby, P. William, 9752

Film-Kurier, Berlin, 10330

Filonovich, T. S., 12002

Finden, William, 9154

Fines, John, 8410

Fink, Gary M., 11986

Finland. Puolustusministeriö. Sotahistoriallinen Toimisto, 8856

Finlands elektroingenjörsförbund --SEE: Suomen Sähköinsinö-öriliitto, 12071

Finotti, Joseph Maria, 10074

Firmo, João Sereno, 8605

Fischer, Albert Friedrich Wilhelm, 10538

Fischler, Shirley, 10626

Fischler, Stan, 10626

Fischlin, Ludwig Melchior, 11593

Fishbein, Morris, 11498

Fisher, Renee B., 10460

Fisher, Stanley W., 10137

Fitzgerald, Thomas W. H., 9294

Fitzpatrick, Horace, 10461

Fitzpatrick, Sheila, 9580

Flagg, Mildred (Buchanan), 10826

Flake, Lawrence R., 11819

Flandrin, Auguste, 8294

Flavius Philostratus--SEE: Philostratus, Flavius, 11549

Fleay, Frederick Gard, 10970

Fleischmann, Wolfgang Bernard 10771

Fleming, George Thornton, 9950

Fleming, John, 10265, 10270

Flemion, Philip F., 9625

Fletcher, Sir Banister Flight, 10273

Fletcher, William Younger, 11337

Fleury, Marie-Antoinette, 10115

Fleury, Victor, 8835

Florange, Charles, 11434

Floren Lazano, Luis, 10958

Florian, Theo H., 9651

Florida Historical Society, Jacksonville, 9865

Flügel, Gustav Leberecht, 11317, 11320

Flynt, Henry N., 10295

Föreningen Svenska tecknare, 10224

Fogarty (John E.) International Center for Advanced Study in the Health Sciences--SEE: John E. Fogarty International Center for Advanced Study in the Health Sciences, 11421, 11476

Fomin, Sergeĭ Vasil'evich, 11917

Fondation Paul Ricard, 10110

Fondo Colombiana de Investigaciones Científicas y Proyectos Especiales Francisco José de Caldas. Unidad de Recursos Humanos, 11879

Fonó, Györgyné, 9221

Fonseca, Martinho Augusto Ferreira da, 9544

Fonseca Benavides, Ignacio Antonio da, 11473

Font-Altaba, M., 11902

Fontenla Facal, Pedro A., 8505

Fontette, Charles Marie Fevret de--SEE: Fevret de Fontette, Charles Marie, 8866

Fonvieille, René, 10114

Foppa, Tito Livio, 10362

Ford, Charles, 10337

Foremost Americans Publishing Corporation, 9794

Foreningen af danske civilhortonomer, 12041

Foreningen af statsautoriserede revisorer, 10960

Forestier, Pierre, 11666

Forlaget Liber, Copenhagen, 8828, 8831

Formann, Wilhelm, 11046

Forschungsinstitut für Europäische Gegenwartskunde, 10784

Fortier, André, 11037

Fortunatus, pseud.--SEE: Mesure, Fortuné, 8937-8938

Foscarini, Amilcare, 11118

Foskett, Daphne, 10138

Foss, Gerald D., 9906

Fossari, Domingos, 8599

Fossel, Viktor, 11413

Foster, David William, 9453, 11158

Foster, Myles Birket, 10541

Foucaud, Édouard, 12081-12082

Fournié, H., 11435

Fournier, Alfred Fray--SEE: Fray Fournier, Alfred, 9013

Fouron, Henri Joseph Barthélemi del Vaux de--SEE: Del Vaux de Fouron, Henri Joseph Barthélemi, 8580

Fourquet, Émile, 9000

Fox, Charles Donald, 10333

Fox, Hugh, 10827

Fox, W. E., 11968

Frabša, František S., 10949

France. Archives nationales, 10115, 10127, 10380

France. Bibliothèque nationale, Paris--SEE: Paris. Bibliothèque nationale.

France. Conseil économique et social, 11962

France. Ministère d'Etat charge des affaires culturelles, 10278

France. Parlement (1946-). Assemblée nationale, 8904

France. Parlement (1946-   ).
Sénat. Secrétariat général de
la questure, 8905

Franciscans. Province of the
Most Holy Name of Jesus,
11644

Franck, -----------, 8924

Frank, Kaspar, 11594

Franco, Jean, 10830

Franco Preda, Artemio, 9517

Frank, Benis M., 9795

Frank, Louis Frederick, 11499

Frank, Mortimer, 11374

Franke, Konrad, 11047

Frankenstein, Alfred Victor,
10255

Frankfurt am Main. Deutsche
Bibliothek, 11048

Frankfurt am Main. Städelsches Kunstinstitut, 10055

Franz, Günther, 9094

Franzos, Karl Emil, 10862

Fratelli Treves, Milan, 9353-
9355

Frattarolo, Renzo, 11100

Fray-Fournier, Alfred, 9013

Frédéric, Louis--SEE: Louis-
Frédéric, pseud., 8523

Free Library of Norwich--SEE:
Norwich, Eng. Free Libra-
ry, 9194

Freeman, Sarah Elizabeth,
11386

Freimann, Arun, 11461

Freitas, Divaldo Gaspar de--SEE:
Freitas, Gaspar de, 8600

Freitas, Gaspar de, 8600

Freitas Lopes Gonçalves, Augusto
de--SEE: Gonçalves, Augusto
de Freitas Lopes, 10371

Fremantle,   Richard, 10168

Frémy, Jacques Marie Noël,
8333

Frenette, François Xavier Eugène, 11720

Freney, Giuseppe Vernaza, barone di--SEE: Vernazza, Giuseppe, barone di Freney,
11354

Frenz, Horst, 10797

Frère, Édouard Benjamin, 9030

Freund, Hugo, 11377

Frey, Karl, 10018

Frey, Richard L., 10614

Frey, Rudolf, 11441

Frida, Myrtil, 10321-10322

Fried, Frederick, 10292

Friedenwald, Harry, 11462

Friedman, Leon, 11330

Friedmann, Aron, 10548

Friedmann, Oscar, 8564

Friedrich, Gary, 10576-10577

Friedrich, Regine, 10883

Friedrich-Ebert-Stiftung. Forschungsinstitut, 8488

Friedrich Reinhold Kreutzwaldi
nimeline Eesti NSV Riiklik
Raamatukogu, 10996

Galle, Philippe, 10655

Gallego Morell, Antonio, 11255

Galleria La Gradiva, 10280

Gallery of Living Catholic Authors--SEE: Webster Groves, Mo. Gallery of Living Catholic Authors, 10811

Galletti, Angel Mancera--SEE: Mancera Galletti, Angel, 11291

Gallis, Joaquim Alfredo, 9545

Gallo Almeida, Luis, 10963

Galský, Besider, 8439

Gałuszka, Jerzy, 11123

Galván, José María Moreno--SEE: Moreno Galván, José María, 10220

Gamba, Bartolommeo, 11119

Gandil, Christian, 12039

Garaby, Malo Joseph de, 11754

Garcia Brugos, Manuel, 9451

García del Real, Eduardo, 11486

Garcin de Tassy, Joseph Héliodore Sagesse Vertu, 11094

Garga, Lakshmīnārāyana, 10544

Gargiulo, Bonaventura, 11667

Garland, Henry Burnand, 11049

Garland, Mary, 11049

Garlington, J. C., 9957

Garnett, James Mercer, 9974

Garnier, Joseph François, 8985

Garnisonsbibliotek, Copenhagen --SEE: Copenhagen. Garnisonsbibliothek, 8816

Garraty, John Arthur, 9796

Garrison, Fielding Hudson, 11360, 11374

Gartell, José Vives--SEE: Vives, José, 11791

Garton, Charles, 10418

Garzanti, firm, publishers, Milan, 10770

Gasiorowski, Ludwik, 11470

Gaskell, Ernest, 9182, 9191, 9195-9196, 9205

Gaskell, William, 9185, 9203

Gaspari, Gaetano, 10547

Gasparyan, Gaspar Karapeti, 10851

Gasser, Vinzenz, 10864

Gately, James J., 9797

Gathy, August, 10462

Gatti, Guido Maria, 10480

Gauss, Carl J., 11442

Gauthier, Henri, 11721

Gautier, Toussaint François Ange, 11010

Gavard, Charles, 8338

Gay, Jules, 8284

Gayano Abad, Rafael, 9690

Gažević, Nikola, 8384

Gazzetta per i lavoratori, 11975

Gazzino, Giuseppe, 9349

Gealy, Fred D., 10463

Geddes, John, 9636

Geffcken, Johannes, 8399

Geisler, Fridr. --SEE: Geissler, Friedrich, 10741

Geissler, Friedrich, 10741

Geldsetzer, Lutz, 11536

Gellért, Imre, 9798

Gelman, Steve, 10609

Genossenschaft Deutscher Bühnen-Angehöriger, 10392

Genthon, István, 10035

Genty, Geneviève Nicole--SEE: Nicole-Genty, Geneviève, 11427

Genty, Maurice, 11427

Geograficheskoe obshchestvo SSSR, 12002

Georgano, G. N., 10603

Georges, Henri, 8911

Georgiev, Vladimir Ivanov, 8618

Gerdts, William H., 10244

Gerkens, Gerhard, 10048

Gerlich, Fritz, 9071

Germany. Reichstag, 9081-9083

Germany. Reichstheaterkammer. Fachschaft Bühne, 10382

Germany (Federal Republic, 1949-   ). Bundesministerium der Verteidigung, 9101

Germany (Federal Republic, 1949-   ). Presse und Informationsdienst, 9102

Gerontological Society, 11379

Gerulewicz, Marisa Vannini de--SEE: Vannini de Gerulewicz, Marisa, 9995

Gesek, Ludwig, 10367

Gesellschaft für Freiheit der Kultur, 10880

Gesellschaft für Schleswig-Holsteinische Geschichte, 9131

Gesterkamp, Desiderius, 11766

Getz, Bernhard, 11466

Gewerbemuseum, Winterthur, Switzerland--SEE: Winterthur, Switzerland. Gewerbemuseum, 10227

Geysbeek, Pieter Gerardus Witsen, 10959

Gheno, Antonio, 9337

Giáp, Trân văn--SEE: Trân-văn-Giáp, 11293

Gibbens, Alvaro Franklin, 9980

Gibbney, Herbert James, 8527

Gibert, Lucien, 9468

Gibson, Arthur Hopkin, 10245

Giedroyć, Franciszek, 11471

Giffoni, O. Carneiro, 11415

Gilchrist, Agnes Eleanor (Addison), 9762

Gilibert, Françoise, 9723

Gill, Harold B., 12083

Gillie, Christopher, 10971

Gilman, Marcus Davis, 9972

Gilman, Susan, 9816

Ginanni, Pietro Paolo, 11120

Gini, Pietro, 11669

Giniiatullina, Asiia Kashafutdinovna, 11277

Gintl, Zdeněk, 8297

Giordani, Igino, 11668

Giordano, Alberto, 10551

Girindranath Mukhopadhyaya, 11456

Gironella, José María, 9674

Giuliari, Giovanni Battista Carlo, conte, 11101

Giuzelev, Vasil, 8616

Giving, Gerald, 11807

Gleeson, James, 10072

Glennon, James, 10518

Glenzdorf, Johann Casper, 9084

O Globo, Rio de Janeiro, 11935

Glorieux, Palémon, 11755

Głuszek, Zygmunt, 10594

Godbole, R. B., 9235

Godbout, Archange, 8647

Godefroy, Jean Ernest, 11756

Göttingen. Niedersächsische Staats- und Universitäts-bibliothek--SEE: Niedersächsische Staats- und Universitätsbibliothek, Göttingen, 9067

Gøtzsche, P. V., 8817

Gövsa, Ibrahim Alâettin, 8339, 9740

Goggioli, Giordano, 10593

Goil, Nand Kishore, 11093

Goldstein, Max Aaron, 11500

Golf magazine, 10625

Gołos, Jerzy, 10506

Golovshchikov, Konstantin Dmitrievich, 9623

Golubovich, Girolamo, 11785

Gombosi, György, 10021

Gómez, Ildefonso M., 11792

Gonçalves, Augusto de Freitas Lopes, 10371

Gonyea, Ramon, 10254

Goodenough, Caroline Louisa (Leonard), 10464

Goodrich, Luther Carrington, 8710

Goodspeed Publishing Company, 9902-9903, 9963

Goodwin, John, 11609

Gorina, Tat'iana Nikolaevna, 10206

Górnicki, Kazimierz, 9538

Gorostiaga, Manuel de Vizoso--SEE: Vizoso Gorostiaga, Manuel de, 8494

Gorovaia, Inna Georgievna, 9615

Goshen College, Goshen, Ind. Art Gallery, 10246

Gosudarstvennaia biblioteka Estonskoi SSR imeni Fr. R. Kreitsval'da--SEE: Friedrich Reinhold Kreutzwaldi nimeline Eesti NSV Riiklik Raamatukogu, 10996

Gosudarstvennaia biblioteka SSSR im. V. I. Lenina--SEE: Moscow. Publichnaia biblioteka, 9612, 10996, 11147, 11177, 11992

Gosudarstvennaia publichnaia istoricheskaia biblioteka RSFSR, 9575

Gosudarstvennaia respublikanskaia biblioteka MSSR--SEE:
Kishinev, Bessarabia. Gosudarstvennaia respublikanskaia
biblioteka MSSR, 11176-11177

Gosudarstvennaia respublikanskaia biblioteka Kazakhskoi
SSR, 11147

Goszczyńska, Maria, 11192

Gotev, Boris, 8623

Gotfredsen, Edvard, 11380

Gottesman, Eli, 8648

Gottlehrer, Barry, 10609

Gottlieb, Bernward Josef, 11443

Goudas, Anastasios N., 9212

Goujet, Claude Pierre, 10685,
11597, 11761

Goulin, Jean, 11381

Goyke, Ernst, 9103

Grabowska, Maria, 11192

Gräffer, Franz, 8560

Gräsbeck, Armas, 8852

Graham, Franklin, 10334

Grakanowt'yan Institowt, 10852

Grakanowt'yan Institowt. Sovetakan Grakanowt'yan Sektor,
10855

Grandjean, Louis E., 8830

Grandmaison, Charles L., 10117

Granges de Surgères, Anatole,
marquis de, 10118

Granholm, Åke, 10534

Granichstaedten-Czerva, Rudolf
von, 11954

Granjel, Luis S., 11480

Grant, Sir Francis James, 11326

Grant, John, historian, 9180-9181,
10003

Gratschoff, Louis, 11425

Gravel, Albert, 11722

Grāvītis, Olǵerts, 10553

Gray, Andy, 10542

Gray, Philip Howard, 10103

Great Britain. Diplomatic Service
Administration Office, 9150

Grečnerová, B., 10057

Greek Orthodox Church. Archdiocese of North and South America. Office of Education, 10728

Greene, Robert Ewell, 9799

Greenwood, Norman Neill, 11909

Grégoir, Edouard Georges
Jacques, 10507

Grigor'ev, Sergei Vladimirovich,
11900

Grigorov, Grigor, 10896

Grigson, Geoffrey, 10754

Grillet, Jean Louis, 9006

Grillet, Laurent, 10508

Grimschitz, Bruno, 10074

Grimwade, Arthur, 10294

Grinin, N. A., 9582

Grischow, Johann Heinrich,
10465

Grisolia, Luigi, 9370

Grlić, Danko, 11537

Gromyko, Andreĭ Andreevich, 8325

Groǹska, Maria, 10200

Grooten, Johan, 11538

Gross, Heinrich, 11050

Grossi, Carlo, 9391

Grossmann, Dieter, 10503

Grosul, IAkim Sergeevich, 9484

Grotpeter, John J., 9707

Groves, W. E., 10257

Gruppo Medaglie d'oro al Valor militare d'Italia, 9350

Gsteiger, Manfred, 11268

Gualdo, Girolamo, 10169

Guardia, Ricardo Fernández-- SEE: Fernández Guardia, Ricardo, 8801

Guarnacci, Mario, 11670

Gudgeon, Thomas Wayth, 9498

Gudrike, Biruta, 11162

Guérin, Bernard, 9004

Guérin, Jean, 9004

Guérin, Louis François, 11671

Guerra, Juan Néstor, 8506

Guerrero, Lola Soriano de--SEE: Soriano de Guerrero, Lola, 8688a

Guerro Castillo, Julián N., 8688a

Guest, Rhuvon, 8841

Guibert, Joseph, 8294

Guidicini, Giuseppe di Giovanni Battista, 9369

Guigard, Joannis, 8864

Guigonet, Jules, 8911

Guillmard, Désiré, 10027

Guimarães e Silva, Hugo Victor-- SEE: Silva, Hugo Victor Gui- marães e, 8610

Gujarat Vernacular Society, 11081

Gunadasa Liyanage--SEE: Liyanage, Gunadasa, 9701

al-Gundī, Anwar--SEE: al-Jundī, Anwar, 9317

Gunert, Johann, 10876

Guppenberger, Lambert, 11713

Gupta, A. K., 9248

Gupta, Badlu Ram, 11972

Gurguis Awwad--SEE: 'Awwād, Kūrkīs, 11096

Gurlitt, Willibald, 10485

Gurlt, Ernst Julius, 11382

Gurmukh Singh--SEE: Singh, Gurmukh, 9277

Gusin, Izrail' Lazarevich, 10497

Gussago, Germano Jacopo, 11121

Gustaw, Romuald, 11786

Guszczyǹska, Maria, 11192

Guthorn, Peter J., 11998

Gutiérrez Casillas, José, 11780

Guyot de Fère, François Fortuné, 10109, 11011

Guzmán, Augusto, 10891

Gyllenberg, Gideon, 11338

Gyula, Hungary. Erkel Ferenc Muzeum--SEE: Erkel Ferenc Muzeum, 10149

Haag, Herbert, 11598

Habig, Marion A., 11802

Habovstiakova, K., 11240

Hackmann, Heinrich Friedrich, 11560

Hadfield, Susan, 10858

Hadley, Ned, 10484

Hänsel, Willy, 10690

Haezrahi, Yehuda, 9336

al-Hafāji, Shihāb ad-Dīn Ahmad ibn Muhammad--SEE: al-Khafāji, Ahmad ibn Muhammad, 10842

Hafen, Le Roy Reuben, 9978

Hafenrichter, Wilhelm, 10368, 10521

al-Hāfiz al-Yaghmūrī, Yūsūf ibn Ahmad, 10843

Haga, Yaichi, 9402

Hagensick, A. Clarke, 9732

Haid, Johann Jacob, 10691

Haidacher, Anton, 11672

Hakhverdyan, Lewon, 10855

Hakim Abu'l Qasim Mir Qudratullah Qasim--SEE: Abū al-Kāsim Mir Kudrat Allah Kāsim, 11286

Hale, John Peter, 9981

Hall, Donald, 10992

Hall, James, 9800

Hall, Marshall, 10139

Hall of Fame at New York University--SEE: New York University. Hall of Fame, 9827

Hàm, Hồ Đắc--SEE: Hồ Đắc Hàm, 9999

al-Hamawī, Yāqūt ibn 'Abd Allāh --SEE: Yāqūt ibn 'Abd Allāh al Hamawi, 10847

Hamburg. Universität. Colegium Politicum, 12013

Hamburger, Ernst, 9085

Hambye, Edward Rene, 11833

Hamilton, Edward, 9140

Hamilton, Jack D., 10435

Hamma, Fridolin, 10509-10510

Hamma, Walter, 10510

Hammelmann, Hanns, 10140

Hammer-Purgstall, Joseph, Freiherr von, 8556

Hammerle, Alois Joseph, 8557

Hammerman, Gay M., 9784

Hammond, Nicholas Geoffrey Lemprière, 8402

Hamy, Alfred, 11757

Henderson, Henry Ebenezer, 11369

Handley-Taylor, Geoffrey, 10972-10980

Hanifi, Mohammed Jamil, 8481

Hanin, L., 11383

Hanisch Espíndola, Walter, 11729

Hanley, Reid M., 10647

Hanulak, Kazimierz, 10788

Harcourt, Louis, comte d', 8912

Hardie, Martin, 10141

Hardwick, John Michael Drinkrow, 10981

Hardwick, Michael--SEE: Hardwick, John Michael Drinkrow, 10981

Hardy, Basil Cozens--SEE: Cozens-Hardy, Basil, 9198

Hardzitski, Aliaksei, 11296

Harimohan Mukhopadhyay--SEE: Mukhopadhyay, Harimohan, 10888

al-Hārit ben Asad al-Hošani-- SEE: al-Khushani, Muhammad ibn Hārith, 10706

Harley, Sharon, 8280

Harling, Robert, 10297, 10310

Harmon, Noel Bailey, 11814

Harmon Foundation, inc., 10028

Harmonville, A. L. d', 8341

Harper, John Russell, 10086

Harrier, Richard C., 10340

Harrison, Brian Howard, 11937

Harte, Barbara, 10775

Hartman, Louis Francis, 11591

Harvard University. Busch-Reisinger Museum of Germanic Culture, 10130

Harvard-Yenching Institute--SEE: Yen-ching ta hsüeh, Peking.

Harvey, Sir Paul, 10967

Hasan, Mīr, 9253

Hasan ibn Hādī al-Sadr--SEE: al-Sadr, Hasan ibn Hādī, 11852

Hasan ibn Muhammad al-Būrīnī-- SEE: al-Būrīnī, Hasan ibn Muhammad, 9297

al-Hasanī, 'Abdulha'ī ibn Fakhruddīn--SEE: 'Abdulha'i ibn Fakhruddīn al-Hasani, 9227

Hāshimī Sandīlavī, Ahmad 'Alī Khān, 11184

Hass, Gerhart, 9074

Hassenberger, Eduard, 10866

Hastimalla, 11857

Hatfield, Edwin Francis, 10466

Hatje, Gerd, 10266-10267

Hauer, Johannes, 10867

Hauréau, Barthélemy, 11012, 11753

Havlice, Patricia Pate, 10014, 10738

Havránková, Zdenka, 11238

Hayavadana Rao, Conjeevaram, 9241

Hayden, Eleonora, 9790

Haydn, Joseph Timothy, 8382

Hayes, Charles W., 9868

Hayes, Grace P., 8452

Hayward, Elizabeth, 11628

Hayward Gallery, 10116

Hazan, Solomon, 11142

Hazlitt, William Carew, 11340

al-Hazraji, Ahmad ibn 'Abdallah --SEE: Khazrājī, Ahmad ibn Abd Allah, 11847

Hazzan, Shlomo--SEE: Hazan, Solomon, 11142

Heath, Dwight B., 8585

Hébert, ------, 10029

Hsiang, Ch'eng, 8744

Hsiang, To-nai, 8752

Hsiang, Tu-shou, 8745

Hsiao, T. C., 11922

Hsü, Ch'ien-hsüeh, 8746

Hsü, Hung, chin shih (1490),
8750

Hsu, Wan-ch'eng, 11956

Hsü-chia-hui ts'ang shu lou,
Shanghai, 11731

Hu, Cheng-chih, 8694

Hu, P'ü-yu, 8748

Hua, Chu, of Ch'ing Dynasty,
10672

Huang, Chi-lu, 8757

Huang, Chün-tung, 10926

Huang, Chung-chün, 8749

Huang, Hua, 10094

Huard, Pierre Alphonse, 11420

Huart, Louis, 8917

Hubbard, Frank McKinney, 9879

Hubbard, Robert Hamilton,
10087-10088

Hubert, Paul, 12030

Hudson, Noel Paul, 11510

Hürlimann, Martin, 9724

Huff, Edna Lenore (Webb), 9792

Huff, Warren, 9792

Hufnagel, Joseph, 9116

Huggett, Frank Edward, 9157a

Huguenin, Anne Marie (Gleason),
8649

Hui-chao, Shih. Kao sêng chuan,
11567

Hui-hung, 11562

Huitfeldt-Kaas, Henrik Jørgen,
9506

Hume, Edgar Erskine, 11491

Humm, Felix, 8441

Humphreys, Arthur Lee, 9202

Humphreys, Henry R. Morin,
8533

Humphries, Charles, 11341

Hung, William, 10093, 10911,
10916-10918

Hunt, Christopher John, 11342

Hunt Botanical Library, 11901

Hunt Institute for Botanical Documentation, 11901

Hurtaut, Pierre Thomas Nicolas,
9033

Hurzhii, Ivan Oleksandrovych,
12014

Husaini, Shāhid--SEE: Shāhid
Husaini, 9253

Husayn ibn Muhammad ibn Sukkarah al-Sadafi--SEE: Ibn
Sukkarah al-Sadafi, Husayn
ibn Muhammad, 9303

al-Hushanī, Muhammad ibn--SEE:
al-Khushanī, Muhammad ibn
Hārith, 10706

Huskisson, Yvonne, 10515

Huston, James, 11039

Hyams, Edward S., 8442

Hyderabad, India (State) Dept. of
Information and Public Relations, 9264

Iliopoulos, Nicholas D., 10728

Illescas, Francisco R., 11173

Illinois Biographical Association, 9875

The Illustrated American magazine, 10428

Imbert, Jean Baptiste Auguste, 8918

Imon, Hiroshi, 9404

Inamura, Tetsugen, 9404

'Inān, Muhammad 'Abd Allāh, 9312

India. Criminal Intelligence Office--SEE: India. Intelligence Bureau, 9236

India. Intelligence Bureau, 9236

India (Republic). Ministry of Information and Broadcasting, 9237

India (Republic). Parliament, 9238

India (Republic). Parliament. Council of States, 9239

India (Republic. Parliament. Rajya Sabha--SEE: India (Republic). Parliament. Council of States, 9239

Indian Arts and Crafts Board--SEE: United States. Indian Arts and Crafts Board, 10239, 10254

Indian National Science Academy, 11885

Indiana Biographical Association, 9879

Indianapolis Museum of Art, 10238, 10255

Indianapolis Sentinel Company, 9878

Indo-Burma Publishing Agency, 8628

Indonesia. Lembaga Pemilihan Umum, 9283

Indonesia. Pusat Sedjarah ABRI, 9284

Inglada, José María Milego--SEE: Milego e Inglada, José María, 9682

Iñigo, José María, 10456

Institucion 'Fernando el Católico,' 9683

Institut de recherches appliquées du Dahomey, 8815

Institut für Iberoamerika-Kunde, 11159

Institut für Marxismus-Leninismus, Berlin, 9091

Institut für Vergleichende Erziehungswissenschaft, Salzburg, Austria, 10659

Institut istorii partii, Makhach-Kala, Daghestan--SEE: Makhach-Kala, Daghestan. Institut istorii partii, 8813

Institut istorii partii, Moscow--SEE: Moscow. Institut istorii partii, 9612

Institut Néerlandais, Paris, 10107

Institut voennoĭ istorii, 9596

Institut zur Erforschung der UdSSR, 9584

Institute for the Study of the USSR--SEE: Institut zur Erforschung der UdSSR, 9584

Institute of Ecology, 11891

Institute of Historical Studies, 9252

Institute of International Relations, Taipei--SEE: Chunghua min kuo kuo chi kuan hsi yen chiu so, Taipei, 8729

Institute of Jamaica, Kingston. West India Reference Library, 9394

Institute of Sciences and Industrial Publications, 11973

Instituto Argentino de Ciencias Genealógicas, 8508

Instituto Historico e Geographico Brasileiro, Rio de Janeiro, 8601

Instituto Nacional de Cultura y Bellas Artes, 10258

Instituto Nacional del Libro Español, 11256

Institutul Romîn pentru Relatiile Culturale cu Străinatătea, 9572

Intendencia Municipal de Montevideo--SEE: Montevido. Intendencia Municipal, 9986

Intercontinental Press Service, 8845

International Association for Dental Research, 11525

International Chamber of Commerce. Sezione italiana, 11979

International Congress of Slavists, 6th, Prague, (1968), 11241

International Congress of Women, Berlin (1904), 8420

International Exhibitions Foundation, 10255

International Medical Congress, 14th, Madrid (1903), 11385

International Mineralogical Association, 11902

Internationaler Frauen-Kongress, Berlin, 1904--SEE: International Congress of Women, Berlin (1904), 8420

Inter-State Publishing Company, 9922

Ionkov, Khristo Markov, 8619

Iowa Press Association, 9881

Ireland, Norma (Olin), 8286

Iribarren, Manuel, 11257

Irick, Robert L., 10651

Irish Times, 9295

Irkutskaia oblastnaia biblioteka im. I. I. Molchanova-Sibirskogo, 11225

'Isā, Ahmad--SEE: Ahmad 'Isā, 11411

Isaacson, Ben, 9429

al-Isbahānī, Abū Bakr Ahmad ibn 'Alī, 11843

Iser, Carl, 9713

Ishida, Seitarō, 9405

Ishihama, Tomoyuki, 8786

Ishutinova, N., 11224

Isis. (Indexes), 11870

Isleido Susivientijimas Lietuviu Amerikoje--SEE: Lithuanian Alliance in America, 9806

Ismail, pasa, 10840

Israel, Fred L., 11330

Italy. Ministerio del commercio con l'estero, 11978

IUdin, Pavel Federovich, 11550-11551

IUr'ev, Mikhail Ivanovich,
10932-10933

Ivanenko, Viktor Trofimovich,
9609

Ivanov, Aleksandr Aleksandrovich, 11146

Ivanov, Stefan Krumov, 10765

Ivanova, Emiliía, 11944

Ivenskii, Semen Georgievich,
10205

Iwanek, Witold, 10212

'Iyād ibn Mūsá, 9315

'Izz al-Dīn Ahmad Mūsá--SEE:
Mūsá, 'Izz al-Dīn Ahmad,
9310

'Izz al-Dīn ibn al-Athīr--SEE:
Ibn al-Athīr, 'Izz al-Dīn,
9305

Jablonický, Jozef, 9652

Jackson, Arthur, 10436

Jackson, John Edward, 9204

Jackson, Margaret (Young), 9801

Jackson, Richard, 10574

Jackson, Russell Leigh, 11502

Jacob, Giles, 10983-10984

Jacobs, Arthur, 10471

Jacobs, Jay, 10031

Jacquemet, G., 11646

Jacquot, Albert, 10121, 10511

Jager, Cajetan, 11051

Jaencke, Johann David, 11600

Jagdish Saran Sharma--SEE:
Sharma, Jagdish Saran, 9254-
9255

Jahn, Janheinz, 10813

Jain, Sushil Kumar, 8630

Jakatdar, Shrikrishna Anant,
11540

Jalalu'ddin as-Suyuti--SEE: al-
Suyūtī, 10846, 10854

Jalard, Michel Claude, 10032

Jalovec, Karel, 10512

Jamāl al-Dīn al-Ālūsī--SEE: al-
Ālūsī, Jamāl al-Dīn, 9292

James, Edward T., 9815

James, Janet Wilson, 9815

Jamil Ahmad, Khwaja, 9316

al-Jammā'ilī, 'Abd al-Ghanī ibn
'Abd al-Wāhid, 11845

Janet et Cotelle, libraires,
Paris, 8891

Janicki, Stanisław, 10416

Janin Productions, 10373

Janneau, Guillaume, 10298

Janowski, Ludwik, 10716

Jansen, Evermode Joseph, 8580a

Jansen, J. E.--SEE: Jansen,
Evermode Joseph, 8580a

Jantzen, Hinrich, 9087

Japan. Gaimushō. Ajiakyoku,
8740, 8751

Japan. Gaimushō. Chōsakyoku,
8522

Jaqūt Ibn-'Abdallāh--SEE: Yāqūt
ibn 'Abd Allāh al Hamawi,
10847

Jaramillo, Miguel Angel, 10964

Jarnés, Benjamín, 10769

Jarnoux, Alphonse, 11758

Jarnut, Jörg, 9376

Javorsky, Friedrich, 8347

al-Jazarī, Muhammad ibn Muhammad ibn--SEE: Ibn al-Jazarī, Muhammad ibn Muhammad, 9306

Jean, Jean Pierre, 8919

Jeandet, Abel, 11881

Jeanne, René, 10337

Jeanneau, G., 8327

Jedding, Hermann, 10299

Jéhan, Louis François, 11541, 11601, 11874

Jehangir, Sorabji, 9243

Jenderko, Ingrid, 10050

Jensen, Hans Hald, 10679

Jensen, John Martin, 11805, 11807

Jensen, Theodor Andreas Topsoe--SEE: Topsoe-Jensen, Theodor Andreas, 8833

Jensens (Arthur) forlag, Copenhagen, 8831

Jericó, José, 11664

Jericó de la Concepción--SEE: Jericó, José, 11664

Jerrard and Barraud, photographers, London--SEE: Barrud and Jerrard, photographers, London, 11370

Jerusalem. Hebrew University--SEE: Hebrew University, Jerusalem,

Jerushalmi, Joseph, 11858

Jervise, Andrew, 9639

Jireček, Josef, 10950

Jirji Zaydan--SEE: Zaydan, Jirji, 9333

Jöcher, Christian Gottlieb, 10656

Jørgensen, John, 10479

Johannsen, Robert Walter, 9757

John E. Fogarty International Center for Advanced Study in the Health Sciences, 11421

John E. Fogarty International Center for Advanced Study in the Health Sciences. Geographic Health Studies Program, 11476

John Work Garrett Library--SEE: Johns Hopkins University. John Work Garrett Library, 11386

Johns Hopkins University. John Work Garrett Library, 11386

Johnson, Francis White, 9969

Johnson, J. Keith, 8638

Johnson, Robert Owen, 9754

Johnson, Selby, 8348

Johnson, Stanley Currie, 8348

Johnson and Johnson, inc. Ethicon Suture Division, 11503

Johnsson, Gunnar, 11426

Johnstad-Møller, Svend Erik, 8823

Joint Committee on the Foreign Area Fellowship Program, 10729

Joint Publications Research Service--SEE: United States. Joint Publications Research Service, 9557, 11914

Joksimović, Milan, 10011

Jón Borgfirðingur Jónsson--
SEE: Jónsson, Jón Borg-
firðingur, 11092

Jones, Anthony Mark, 10004

Jones, Arnold Hugh Martin,
9566

Jones, Charles Colcock, 9812

Jones (James O.) Company,
9959

Jones, John Andrews, 11602

Jones, Ken D., 10432

Jones, Martin J., 10605

Jonge, Johannes Cornelis de,
9492

Jónsson, Jón Borgfirðingur,
11092

Jordan, Weymouth T., 9914

Jordan, Wilfred, 9947

Joshi, Pralhāda Narahara--SEE:
Jósi, Pralhāda Narahara,
11875

Jósi, Pralhāda Narahara, 11875

Joubert, Léo, 8349

Jouin, Henri Auguste, 10108

Jourdan, Louis, 8920

Journal of dental research,
11525

Jovanovski, Meto, 11164

Jüan, Yüan, 11927

al-Jubūrī, 'Abd Allah, 9292

Jūdah, Hilāl, 11322

Judice, João Antonio de Mascarenhas, visconde de Lagoa--
SEE: Lagoa, João Antonio de
Mascarenhas Judice, vis-
conde de, 9547

Judson, Levi Carroll, 9802

Jünger, Harri, 10780-10781

Juncker, Christian, 9063

al-Jundī, Anwar, 9317

Jungmann, Josef Jakub, 10951

Jungstedt, Torsten, 10423

Juristforbundet, Copenhagen,
11309

Jurjī Zaidān--SEE: Zaydan,
Jirji, 9333

Justi, Ferdinand, 9289

Justice, Fred C., 10437

Justus, Wolfgang, 11387

Kaarsted, Tage, 10679

Kaas, Henrik Jørgen Huitfeldt--
SEE: Huitfeldt-Kaas, Henrik
Jørgen, 9506

Kaathoven, Cornelius Willem
Hendrik van, 11362

Kabadī, Vāmana P., 9242

Kadettikunta, 8853

Kagan, Solomon Robert, 11388,
11504

Kahhālah, 'Umar Ridā, 9318,
10841

Kaininš, Jānis, 11162

Kaiser, Ernest, 9822

Kaiser, Frances E., 10782

Kaji, Wataru, 8786

al-Kalābādhī, Ahmad ibn Muhammad, 11843

Káldor, Kálman, 9808

Kalić, Mita, 11236

Kalinin, Veniamin Vasil'evich,
9585

Kalinin, I. A., 9603

Kamelhar, Jekuthiel Aryeh,
11860

Kamínek, Karel, 10343

Kamp, Norbert, 11775

Kanapatippillai, Tenpulōliyur
M., 11272

Kandayya Pillai, N. C., 11273

Kangro, Bernard, 10995, 10998

Kansas City Press Club, Kansas City, Mo., 9885

Kantayya Pillai, N. C.--SEE:
Kandayya Pillai, N. C.,
11273

Kao, Yü-t'ai, 8753

Kapp, Ernst, 11052

Karataev, M. K., 9439

Karate illustrated, 10634

Kariher, Harry C., 10628

Karp, Theodore, 10473

Karst, Gene, 10605

Kasdaglēs, Emmanuel Ch.,
11076

Kāsim ibn Kutlūbūgha--SEE:
Ibn Qutlūbūgha, al-Qasim ibn
'Abd Allah, 11320

al-Kāsim Mir Kudrat Allah
Kāsim, Abū--SEE: Abū al-
Kāsim Mir Kudrat Allah
Kāsim, 11286

Kasumigaseikai, 8754

Kasumigaseki Kai, 8740

al-Kattānī, 'Abd al-Hayy ibn
'Abd al-Kabīr, 9319

Kauffmann, Claus Michael,
10067

Kaufman, Edmund George,
11813

Kawabe, Toshio, 8525

Kay, Ernest, 8453, 8472, 8486,
9449, 9631, 10030, 10078-
10079

Kayser, Carl Ludwig, 11549

Kayserling, Meyer, 9675

Kazankai, 8740

Kazeka, ÍAnka, 11295-11297

Kaznelson, Siegmund, 9088

Keene, Floyd Elwood, 11492

Kellen, Johan Philip van der,
10194

Kemp, Peter Kemp, 12005

Kemper, General William Harrison, 11505

Kempner, Benedicta Maria,
11603

Keng, Ting-hsiang, 8755

Kennedy, John Pendleton, 9973

Kennedy, Lawrence F., 9835

Kennedy, X. J., 10985

Kent, Ernest A., 9198

Kepeski, Petar, 11247

Keppen, Fedor Petrovich--SEE:
Köppen, Fedor Petrovich,
11903

Kerala, India (State). Legislative Assembly, 9266

Kerala Sangeetha Nataka
Akademy, Trichur, 10407

Kerbey, Janice, 9170

Kerdellech, Alexandre François
Marie Couffon de--SEE:
Couffon de Kerdellech,
Alexandre François Marie,
8982

Keresztury, Dezsö, 11088

Kerr, Laura J., 8287

Kerrigan, Evans E., 9803

Kerviler, Rene Pocard du
Cosquer de, 8983

Kesarioy ew Shrjakayits' Hayrenakts'akan Miowt'iwn.
Gahirēi Varch'owt'iwn, 8511

Kesten, Hermann, 11053

Kestner, Christian Wilhelm,
11389

Keyser, Eugénie de, 10276

al-Khafājī, Ahmad ibn Muhammad, 10842

Khaleyan, Ervand, 8516

Khalīl ibn Aybak al-Safadi--
SEE: al-Safadi, Khalīl ibn
Aybak, 9328, 9726

Khalilov, R., 10523

Khallikān, Ibn--SEE: Ibn Khallikān, 9310, 9320

Khanolkar, G. D., 11166

Kharkov. Universitet, 11325,
11477, 11928

Kharlamov, M. A., 9828

al-Khatīb, Ibn--SEE: Ibn al-
Khatīb, 10838

Khayr al Dīn al-Ziriklī--SEE:
al-Ziriklī, Khayr al-Dīn,
9334

Khazrajī, Ahmad ibn Abd Allāh,
11847

Khetsun Sangpo, 9734

Khosla, C. L., 12047

Khosla, R. K., 11346

Khosla, Raj J., 9251

Khovanskiĭ, Nikolaĭ Fedorovich, 9618

Khrusanova, Vesela, 10745

Khusainov, Gaisa Batyrgaleevich, 10884

al-Khushanī, Muhammad ibn
Hārith, 10706

Khwaja Jamil Ahmad--SEE:
Jamil Ahmad, Khwaja, 9316

al-Khwānsārī, Muhammad Bāqir ibn Zain al-'Abidin al-
Mūsawi--SEE: Muhammad
Bāqir ibn Zain al-'Abidīn,
al-Mūsawi al-Khwānsārī,
11848-11849

Kiêm, Thái Văn--SEE: Thái
Văn Kiêm, 9999

Kieniewiczowa, Grażyn, 9534

Kikuchi, Akishirō, 9406

Killian, Hans, 11390

Kin, Mong-p'il, 8376

Kim, Yŏng-yun, 10191

Kimber, Edward, 9158, 9640

al-Kindī, Abū 'Umar Muhammad ibn Yūsuf, 8841

Kindt, Werner, 9075

King's College Association (Cambridge University), 9145

Kingston, Jamaica. Institute of Jamaica--SEE: Institute of Jamaica, Kingston, 9394

Kinkle, Roger D., 10583

Kinnamon, Keneth, 10819

Kinney, Arthur F., 9159

Kinsky, George, 10474

Kirchhoff, Theodor, 11444

Kirchner, Johann Georg, 10465

Kirkpatrick, D. L., 10968

Kisch, Bruno, 11363

Kisei, Toraichi, 10098

Kishinev, Bessarabia. Gosudarstvennaia respublikanskaia biblioteka MSSR, 11176-11177

Kivell, Rex de C. Nan--SEE: Nan Kivell, Rex de C., 8544

Klang, Marcell, 8555

Klauser, Renate Neumüllers-- SEE: Neumüllers-Klauser, Renate, 9112

Klein, Anton, Edler von, 9089

Klein, Bernard, 9824

Klein, Donald W., 8756

Klein, Jean-Claude, 10535

Klepik, K. L., 9743

Klevenskiĭ, Mitrofan Mikhailovich, 9586

Klimesch, Karl, Ritter von, 8445

Klinger, Ruth, 10190

Klingspor, Carl Arvid, 9714

Klinkicht, Mor, 9090

Kloos, Rudolf, 9117

Kloot, M. van Rhede van der, 9285

Klose, Olaf, 9131

Knapp, Andrew, 9160

Knauer, Oswald, 8558

Knight, William Angus, 9641

Knobloch, Edward Joseph, 11054

Knüppeln, Julius Friedrich, 9107

Kobal, John, 10430

Kobro, Isak, 11465-11466

Koch, Charles Rudolph Edward, 11526

Koch, Peter, 11945

Kocourek, Vaclav, 11939

Koders, Roberts, 10554

Könnecke, Gustav, 11055-1055a

Köppen, Fedor Petrovich, 11903

Köppen, Friedrich Theodor-- SEE: Köppen, Fedor Petrovich, 11903

Kohl, Wilhelm, 12013a

Kohlmetz, Ernest, 9787

Kohn, David, 11861

Kokil, Prakash, 9245

Kokuritsu Kokkai Toshoken, Tokyo. Sanko Shoshibu, 9397

Kokuruyukai, 9408

Kokusho Kankokai, 9407

Kolinski, Charles J., 9518

Kolle, Kurt, 11391

Koller, Ludwig, Father, 8559

Komarov, N. G., 9607

Komise pro knihopisný soupis českých a slovenských tisků až do konce XVIII. stoleti-- SEE: Czechoslovak Republic. Komise pro knihopisný soupis českých a slovenských tisků až do konce XVIII. stoleti, 10948

Kommission zur Erforschung der Geschichte der Reformation und Gegenreformation, 9065

Kommunisticheskaia partiia Sovetskogo Soiuza. Permskii oblastnoi komitet. Partiinyi arkhiv, 9615

Kondaurov, Ivan Aleksandrovich, 9617

Kondō, Haruo, 10927

Konečná, Galina, 10207

Koninklijke Vereniging der Historische Woonsteden van Belgie--SEE: Association royale des demeures historiques de Belgique, 8577

Kononov, Andreĭ Nikolaevich, 11284

Konstantinov, Georgi, 10897-10898

Koontz, Paul Rodes, 11835

Kopáčová, Ludmila, 11090

Kopala, Barbara, 10756

Korea (Government-General of Chosen, 1910-1945). Chusuin, 9443

Koren, Nathan, 11460

Korneev, Stepan Gavrilovich, 11887

Kornilov, Petr Evgen'evich, 10208

Koromogawa, Isuyoshi, 8702

Kosel, Hermann Clemens, 11056

Koskinen, Eino Ilmari Lammin --SEE: Lammin-Koskinen, Eino Ilmari, 11313

Kostenkov, A., 9609

Kostić, Dušan, 10568

Kothari, Hemraj, 9244

Kotnik, Stanko, 11246

Kovács, Olga Székeley--SEE: Székely-Kovács, Olga, 11407

Kozák, Jan, 10532

Krämer, Georg, 11390

Kraft, Friedrich Karl, 8314

Krak, firm, publishers, Copenhagen, 8825

Kraks legat, Copenhagen, 12064

Krause, Walter, 10213

Kraushaar, Luise, 9091

Kravchenko, S. D., 9603

Kreiser, Klaus, 9321

Kremos, Geōrgios P., 11079

Kressel, Getzel, 9431

Krleža, Miroslav, 8366

Kroh, Paul, 10936

Krohn, Ernst Christopher, 10584

Kroll, Alex, 10297

Krollmann, Christian Anton Christoph, 9121

Kronenberger, Louis, 8416

Kronschwitz, Helmut, 11441

Krońska, Irena, 11552

Kropilák, Miroslav, 9652

Krug, Viktor, 11676

Krug, Wilhelm Traugott, 11542

Krul, R., 11464

Krupnik, Baruch, 10772

Krusenstjern, Georg von, 9463

Kryšpin, Vojtěch, 10952

Krzeminski, Stanisław, 11531

Krzyżanowski, Julian, 11190

Ku, Ssu-li, 8758

Kubiiovych, Volodomyr, 9744

Kudělka, Milan, 10676, 11240

Kudělka, Viktor, 11243

Kühn, Hugo Johann Wilhelm, 11057

Künstle, Karl, 11604

Kuev, Kuio M., 11241

Kuhn, Heinrich, 8808

Kuhn, Thomas S., 11932

Kuhn, Werner, 10693

Kuibyshevskaiā oblastnaiā biblioteka--SEE: Kuybyshevskaya oblastnaiā biblioteka, 11216

Kukuljević-Sakcinski, Ivan, 10260

Kuliczkowska, Krystyna, 10787

Kulju, Reino Ala--SEE: Ala-Kulju, Reino, 8850

Kulkarni, Sunita Vasant, 9245

Kulkarni, Vasant Sitaram, 9245

Kullnick, Heinz, 9108

Kumar, Virendra--SEE: Virendra Kumar, 11093

Kunc, Jaroslav, 10953-10954

Kunisch, Hermann, 11059

Kunitz, Stanley Jaspon. Twentieth century authors, 10808

Kunjukrishman, Pallipattu, 9246

Kunowski, Johannes von, 9092

Kunsthalle Bremen--SEE: Bremen, Kunsthalle, 10048

Kunsthalle Nürnberg--SEE: Nuremberg. Kunsthalle, 10060

Kunsthaus Chur--SEE: Chur, Switzerland. Kunsthaus, 8441

Kuo, T'ing-hsün, 8759

Lavergnée, Arnauld Bréjon de
--SEE: Bréjon de Lavergnée, Arnauld, 10196

Lavigne, Hubert, 10122

Lawlor, Hugh Jackson, 11627

Lazarova, Khristina, 11416

Lazić, Branko M., 8448

Leake, Chauncey Depew, 11392

Leal, Juan, 11678

Leão, Ermelino Agostinho de, 8602

Leardi, Peter, 11714

Learmonth, Agnes Moffat, 8535

Learmonth, Andrew Thomas Amos, 8535

Leavitt, Thaddeus, W. H., 8536

Lebed', Andreĭ, 9584

Lebedeva, E. I., 11216

Le Bihan, Alain, 8928

Le Blanc, Charles, 10056

Lecanu, Auguste, François, 11557

Lecestre, Léon, 8944

Lechner, Petrus, 11679

Leconte, Jacques Robert, 11605

Lecouvet, Ferdinand, 11151

Leer, Genrikh Antonovich, 8332

Le Fanu, William Richard, 11453

Lefebvre de Saint-Marc, Charles Hugues, 11761

Le Flâneur, Guillaume, pseud., 10383

Lefranc, Pierre, 8354

Lefrank, M., 9093

Legeay, Fortuné, 9048

Legrand, Émile Louis Jean, 11077

Lehmann, Einar Johannes, 8816

Lehrerverein, Pohorelice, Moravia, 10677

Lei, Li, 8760-8761

Lei, Yen-shou, 8696

Leigh, Richard Arthur Austen
--SEE: Austen-Leigh, Richard Arthur, 9153

Leimbach, Karl Ludwig, 11060

Leipziger Kunst-Comptoir, 8281

Leite Pereira de Paiva de Faria Tavora e Cernache, Henrique, conde de Campo Bello--SEE: Campo Bello, Henrique Leite Pereira de Paiva de Faria Tavora e Cernache, conde de, 8597

Leksikografski zavod FNRJ, Zagreb, 8366

Le Long, Jacques, 8866

Lembaga Pemilihan Umum--SEE: Indonesia. Lembaga Pemilihan Umum, 9283

Lembaga Sedjarah dan Antropologi, 9282

Le Mire, Aubert, 10886, 11690

Lemoisne, Paul André, 8293

Le Mond, Alan, 9766

Lempriere, John, 8397-8398

Liebfeld, Alfred, 12032

Liège. Université, 10668

Lietuvos TSR Mokslu Akademija, Vilna, 9462

Lieutaud, Soliman, 8988, 9015-9016

Lifschutz, E., 9755

Ligou, Daniel, 8450

Likhachev, Dmitrii Sergeevich, 11226

Liliencron, Rochus Wilhelm Traugott Heinrich Ferdinand, Freiherr von, 9071

Lin, Chi-k'ai, 10096

Lin, Chien-t'ung, 10096

Lin, Ssǔ-tê, 10912

Linden, Johannes Antonides van der, 11393

Linder, Carl E., 11807

Lindlar, Heinrich, 10486

Lindley, Harlow, 11510

Lindsay, William Bell, 10484

Lipomanus, Aloysius--SEE: Lippomano, Luigi, 11683, 11704

Lippert, Julius, 10705

Lippomano, Luigi, Bp., 11683, 11704

Liron, Jean, 8972, 11019-11020

Lissens, René Felix, 8862

List, Rudolf, 10075

Lithuanian Alliance in America, 9806

Liu, Ch'ang-hua, chu jên (1834), 8698

Liu, Chen, 8766

Liu, Pao, 8767

Liu, Ping-li, 8735

Liu, Tzu-ch'ing, 8768

Liverpool. Public Libraries and Art Gallery. Walker Art Gallery, 10116

Livingstone, E. A., 11612

Liyanage, Gunadasa, 9701

Llanas, Eduardo, 11664

Lloyd, David, 9162

Lo, Samuel E., 9807

Lobanov, Dmitrii Ivanovich, 9589

Lobies, Jean Pierre, 8285

Lobo, Jacobo de la Pezuela y--SEE: Pezuela y Lobo, Jacobo de la, 8804

Lockhart, James Marvin, 9523

Lohmann Villena, Guillermo, 9524

London. National Gallery, 10170

London. National Portrait Gallery, 9142, 9163

London. Royal College of Physicians--SEE: Royal College of Physicians of London, 11448-11450

Longeon, Claude, 11021

Longhurst, John Edward, 9676

Longstreet, Stephen, 10476

Loomis, Louis Ropes, 11681

Lopes Gonçalves, Augusto de Freitas--SEE: Gonçalves, Augusto de Freitas Lopes, 10371

López, Antonio Galdo--SEE: Galdó López, Antonio, 9682

López, Francisco Villa--SEE: Villa López, Francisco, 10941

López, Franklin Barriga--SEE: Barriga López, Franklin, 10962

López, Leonardo Barriga--SEE: Barriga López, Leonardo, 10962

López de Vega, Maximiliano, 11207

López Muñiz, Gregorio, 8355

Lothar, Rudolph, 10366, 10369

Loughridge, Adam, 11827

Louis-Frédéric, pseud., 8532

Louisiana Historical and Biographical Association, 9889

Louisiana Historical Bureau, 9888

Lourdoueix, Paul de, 8914

Loureiro de Souza, Antonio--SEE: Souza, Antonio Loureiro de, 8611

Lousse, Emile, 8432

Lowe, Robert William, 10397

Loyau, George E., 8538

Lozano, Luis Florén--SEE: Florén Lozano, Luis, 10958

Luca, Ignaz de, 10870

Luciani, France, 10171

Luciani, Lidia, 10171

Ludat, Herbert, 8844

Lübker, Friedrich Heinrich Christian, 8399

Lühe, Hans Eggert Willibald von der, 8356

Lührs, Wilhelm, 9109

Lueken, Wilhelm, 10477

Lueker, Erwin Louis, 11810

Luetenegger, Benedict, 11802

Lugt, Frits, 10033

Lukić, Sveta, 11302

Lullo, Orestes di, 8509

Lummis, William Murrell, 9164

Lund, Emil Ferdinand Svitzer, 8819

Lunel, Adolphe Benestor, 8422

Luniya, Bhanwarlal Nathuram, 12015

Lunn, Maurus, 11768

Lurbe, Gabriel de, 8973

Lutheran Church in America. South Carolina Synod. History of the Synod Committee, 11809

L'viv--SEE: Lvov.

Lvov. Universytet. Naukova biblioteka, 10720

Lynge, Gerhardt, 10533

Lyone, Harry, 8662, 8688

Lyonnet, Henry, 10385

Ma, Yung-i, 10921

Mabillon, Jean, 11634

McCallum, John Dennis, 10611

McClintock, John, 11606

McClure, Arthur F., 10432

MacColl, Dugald Sutherland, 10068

McCredie, Andrew D., 10519

McDonagh, Don, 10338

McDonald, Donald, 12044

MacDonald, Pirie, 9760

Macfarlane, Alastair D., 9642

Macfarlane, Margaret E., 9642

McGhan, Barry, 10742

McGill University, Montreal. Library. Reference Dept., 8631

Machado, José E., 11289

McHenry, Robert, 9839, 9842

Maciejewski, Jarosław, 11191

McIlwaine, Henry Read, 9973

MacInnes, John, 9643

Mackay, Donald Cameron, 10300

McKenney, Thomas Loraine, 9800

Mackenzie (Norman) Art Gallery --SEE: Norman Mackenzie Art Gallery, 10089

Mackey, Albert Gallatin, 8358

McLean, Janice W., 11988

McLoughlin, Denis, 9979

MacMillan, Keith, 10528

MacMurchy, Archibald, 10904

McPherson Library, University of Victoria--SEE: University of Victoria. McPherson Library,

Macqueron, Henri, 9051

McRaye, Walter, 8666

McWhirter, Norris Dewar, 10592

Madan, Ivan Konstantinovich, 11177

Madariaga, Luis, 10219

Mägi, Arvo, 10995

Maffei, Eugenio, 11904

Maffei, Francisco Scipione, marchese, 11122

Maftei, Ionel, 9570

Maggid, Hillel Noah, 9461a

Magill, Frank Northen, 10786

Magnan, Jean Charles, 12045-12046

Magnon, Antonio, 11723

Magyar Nemzeti Galéria, Budapest, 10149

Magyar Szocialista Munkáspart. Központi Bizottság. Párttörténeti Intézet, 11949

Magyarországi Kárpátegyesület, 9222

Mahalin, Paul, 10386

Mahon, A. Wylie, 10529

Mai, Chung-kuei, 11544

Mai, Ludwig H., 11947

Maier, Georg, 8837

Maignien, Edmond Auguste, 10123, 11344

Maillard, Robert, 10277

Mainardi, A., 9379

Maindron, Ernest, 11882

Maine Genealogical and Biographical Society, 9893

Mainiero, Lina, 10771

Maitron, Jean, 11948

Maity, Sachindra Kumar, 9269

Majer, Hans Georg, 9321

Majithia, Sudarshan, 9262

Majors, Monroe Alphus, 9809

Major, Ralph Hermon, 11394

Makarenko, L. G., 9585

Makhach-Kala, Daghestan. Institut istorii partii, 8813

Maksimtsov, Mikhail Danilovich, 9743

Malacarne, Vincenzo, 11477

Malatesta, Alberto, 8331, 9351

Malatesta, Enzio, 12084

Malawi. Dept. of Information, 9465

Mali, Matti, 11312

Malignon, Jean, 11022

Malkhasyan, Armo, 8517

Malkoff, Karl, 10829

Mallory, James, 8317-8318

Malmborg, Boo von, 9708

Mal'sagov, A. U., 11218

Malvasia, Carlo Cesare, conte, 10164, 10172

Manarin, Louis H., 9914

Mancera Galletti, Angel, 11291

Manchester Classis (Presbyterian), 11825

Manderscheid, Franz Joseph, Graf von Sternberg--SEE: Sternberg-Manderscheid, Franz Joseph, Graf von, 10101

Mandet, Francisque, 11021

Manen, Juan, 10478

Manet, François Gilles Pierre Barnabé, 9046

Manila. National Library. Bibliography Division, 9525a

Manitoba Library Association, 8667

Mann, Ernst, 10537

Manning, Eugène, 11654

Manno, Antonio, barone, 9352

Manriquez, Enrique Laval--SEE: Laval Manriquez, Enrique, 11419

Mansch, Anton, 8451, 11395

Mansell Information Publishing Company, 11883

Mansoor, Menahem, 9323

Mantinband, James H., 11072, 11150

Mantz, Paul, 10047

Manvell, Roger, 10335

Manwaring, George Ernest, 9165

Manzano, Francesco di, 11124

al-Maraghi, 'Abd al-Aziz Mustafa, 11323

Marcellino da Civezza, 11684

Marchmont, Frederick, 10789

Marco, Concha de, 9677

Marco, Vicente Añón--SEE:
Añón Marco, Vicente, 9690

Marcos, Miguel de la Plata y--
SEE: Plata y Marcos, Miguel
de la, 11487

Mardanas, 9282

Margoliouth, David Samuel, 10847

Margonari, Renzo, 10173

Mariacher, Bruno, 11345

Marías Aguilera, Julián, 11253

Mariel, Pierre, 11543

Marín Martínez, Tomás, 11791

Maring, Ester G., 8626, 9527

Maring, Joel M., 8626, 9527

Marinò, Angelo, 9380

Markotic, Vladimir, 9771

Marks, Henry S.,

Marquard, Emil, 8833

Marquardt, Dorothy A., 10069

Marques de Sousa Viterbo, Fran-
cisco--SEE: Sousa Viterbo,
Francisco Marques de, 10561

Marquez Montiel, Joaquín, 9474-
9475

Marquis Who's Who, inc., 8289,
9844, 11497, 11989

Marshall, Carrington Turner,
11332

Marsy, François Marie de, 10034

Martell, Paul, 8452

Martène, Edmond, 11685

Martin, Allan William, 8539

Martin, Antonio, 11793

Martin, Jules, 10124, 10387,
10389, 11025

Martin, Marcel, 10390

Martin, Michael Rheta, 10340

Martindale, John Robert, 9566

Martinek, Jan, 11153

Martínez, Rufino, 8836

Martínez, Tomás Marín--SEE:
Marín Martínez, Tomás,
11791

Martínez-Hidalgo, José Maria,
11996

Martínez-Hidalgo y Terán, José
Maria--SEE: Martínez-Hidalgo, José Maria, 11996

Martini, Pietro, 9387

Martins, José Frederico Ferreira
--SEE: Ferreira Martins, José
Frederico, 9543

Martins Zúquete, Afonso Eduardo
--SEE: Zúquete, Afonso Eduardo Martins, 9548, 9551

Martyn, John H., 9702

Maruyama, Makoto, 9404

Mary Joseph, Sister, 10811

Maryland. University. Art Gallery, 10251

al-Marzubānī, Muhammad ibn
'Imrān, 10843-10844

Mas, Manuel, 9691

Mascarenhas Judice, João Antonio de, visconde de Lagoa--
SEE: Lagoa, João Antonio de
Mascarenhas Judice, visconde
de, 9547

Mason, Anita, 10301

Mason, Bernard, 12085

Mason, Herbert B., 11997

Massachusetts Board of Certification in Psychology, 11545

Massachusetts Historical Society, Boston, 9896

Massey de Tyronne, Pierre François Marie, 8933

Mateu Sancho, Pedro, 11929

Matheson, Norman Murdoch, 11372

Mathews, Oliver, 12092

Mathieu-Dairnvaell, Georges Marie, 8934-8935

Matica slovenská Turčiansky sv. Martin, 11244

Matlaw, Myron, 10790

Matney, William C., 9846

Matoušek, Miloslav, 11423

Matschoss, Conrad, 12033

Matsudaira, Toshikazu, 9415

Matters, E., Mrs., 8540

Matthews, Douglas, 9769-9770

Matulis, Juozas, 9462

Matveeva, T. P., 12002

Mauer, Mare, 10996

Maulvault, Achille, 11631

Maunder, Samuel, 8359

Maung, G. Hla--SEE: Hla Maung, G., 10083

Maurer, Wilhelm, 9064

Maurin-Białostocka, Jolanta, 10202

Maximilian II, King of Bavaria, 9071

May, Denise Richter, 9026

May, Kenneth Ownsworth, 11911

Mayer, Leo Ary, 10302, 11930, 12086-12087

Mayr, Ambros, 10871

Mayröcker, Franz, 10667

Mazalic, Đoka, 10261

Mazarakēs, Anthimos, 9213

Mazas, Alexandre, 8936, 9324

Mazurin, Nikolaĭ Ivanovich, 9605

Mazzini, Franco, 10178

Mazzuchelli, Giovanni Maria, conte, 8283

Mead, C. H., 9898

Medical Society of the District of Columbia, 11507

Medina, José Toribio, 10907

Meer, Petrus Emmanuel van der, 11675

Mehlig, Johann Michael, 11607

Mehmed Süreyya, Bey, 9741

Mejía, Gabriel Arnago--SEE: Arango Mejía, Gabriel, 8791

Mejía, Geronimo, 10714

Mejía Robledo, Alfonso, 8796

Melchers, Erna, 11686

Melchers, Hans, 11686

Melik, Rouben, 10853

Mellado, Francisco de Paula, 8321

Mellin, Gustaf Henrik, 9715

Mello Barreto, João Paulo de--
SEE: Barreto, João Paulo de
Mello, 8589

Melloni, Giovambattistà, 11776

Mellor, Alec, 8360

Mellors, Robert, 9200

Melo, Veríssimo de, 8603

Melón, Esther M.--SEE: Melón
de Díaz, Esther, 9553, 9556

Melón de Díaz, Esther M., 9553,
9556

Melzi, Gian Battista, 8361

Menachery, George, 11833

Menchaca, José A., 11546

Mendell, Ronald L., 10608,
10618

Mendham, Roy, 8541

Mendonça, Rubens de, 8604

Mengod, Vicente, 10908

Mentsch, Josef, 11954

Mercati, Angelo, 11658

Mercer, James Kazerta, 9926-
9928

Mercklin, George Abraham,
11393

Merida, Venezuela (City). Universidad de los Andes--SEE:
Universidad de los Andes,
11290

Merin, Oto Bihalji--SEE: Bihalji-Merin, Oto, 10016

Merlet, Lucien Victor Claude,
8992, 11026

Merrill Library. Special Collections Dept., 11818

Merseburger, Carl Wilhelm,
10444

Meschinet de Richemond, Louis
Marie, 8991

Meschkowski, Herbert, 11919

Meshcherskii, Nikita Aleksandrovich, 11217

Messine, Jean Baptiste Collet
de--SEE: Collet de Messine,
Jean Baptiste, 8908

Městská knihovna, Prague--SEE:
Prague. Městská knihovna,
8297

Mesure, Fortuné, 8937-8938

Metcalf, Henry Harrison, 9907,
12048

Methodist Church (England).
Connexional Local Preachers'
Committee, 11816

Methodist Local Preachers'
Mutual Aid Association, 11816

Metodio da Nembro, Father,
11687

Metzger, Othman, 10050

Meursinge, Albert, 11854

Meusel, Johann Georg, 10656

Mexico. Secretaría de Hacienda.
Crédito Público y Comercio,
9481

Meyer, Antoine, 8970

Meyer, Conrad, 9725

Meyer, Hans, 11925

Meyer, Harvey Kessler, 9499

Meyer, Johann, 9725

Meyer-Brockmann, Henry, 10791

Mezö, Ferenc, 10596

Michaelis, Otto, 10477

Michaud, ----------, abbé, 8995

Michel, Louis Antoine, 9018

Micheli, Mario de, 10158, 10173

Mickelson, Arnold R., 11805

Middleton, Jesse Edgar, 8652

Mienicki, Ryszard, 10716

Miers, Horst E., 11547

Mihalić, Slavko, 10943

Mihelič, Stane, 11246

Mika, Helma, 8676

Mika, Nick, 8676

Mikadze, Givi, 11041

Mikhailov, Vasil, 8623

Mikkyō Daijiten Saikan Iinkai, 11563

Mikkyō Gakkai, 11563

Mikuma, Katen, 9399

Milego é Inglada, José María, 9682

Miles, Wyndham D., 11907

Milisavac, Živan, 11300

Milizia, Francesco, 10268

Millak, Konrad, 12049

Millar, Oliver, 9167

Millard's review, 8780

Miller, John Lane, 11608

Miller, Lillian B., 9814

Miller, Madeleine (Sweeny), 11608

Milojković, Mirko, 10012

Milska, Anna, 11193

Minckwitz, Johannes, 11062

Ming Biographical History Project Committee of the Association for Asian Studies--SEE: Association for Asian Studies. Ming Biographical History Project Committee, 8710, 10649

Ming-fu, 11564

Minkov, TSv., 10897

Minoccheri, Luigi, 11688

Miquet, François, 9008

Mīr Hasan--SEE: Hasan, Mīr, 9253

Mirecourt, Eugène de, 8454

Mirvish, Doreen Belle, 10216

Mishkov, Georgi, 8621

Missionary College of Zacatecas --SEE: Apostólico Colegio de Nuestra Señora de Guadelupe, 11802

Mitaritonna, Onofrio, 11459

Mitchell, C. H., 10186

Mitchell, Peter, 10058

Mitchell Beazley, Ltd., 8386

Mitev, Simon, 8616

Mitra, Shivratan, 10887

Mitra, Siva Ratan--SEE: Mitra, Shivratan, 10887

Mitrinović, Cedomil, 10013

Mitry, Jean, 10341

al-Mizzī, Yūsuf ibn al-Zakī 'Abd Rahmān, 11845

Modzalevskii, Lev Borisovich, 9591

Møller, Svend Erik Johnstad-- SEE: Johnstad-Møller, Svend Erik, 8823

Moenich, Károly, 11086

Moes, Ernst Wilhelm, 11347

Moidrey, Joseph Tarif de, 11732

Moisés, Massaud, 11201

Mojares, Resil B., 11187

Mokrousov, S., 9617

Molhuysen, Philip Christiaan, 9493

Molin, Gösta Gideon, 10722

Molina y Morales, Roberto, 9626

Molinari Collection--SEE: Bowdoin College. Museum of Art. Molinari Collection, 10305

Molineus, Werner, 11925

Molle, Paul van, 8581

Molossi, Giambattista, 9375

Moncloa y Covarrubias, Manuel, 10414

Monge Muley, Gerardo, 11485

Mongruel, L. P., 9356

Monoszon, I. I., 9607

Monro, Thomas Kirkpatrick, 11451

Monselet, Charles, 11027

Montalbo, Luigi de, conte, 9628

Monte Domecq, Francisco, 8510

Montenoy, Charles Palissot de-- SEE: Palissot de Montenoy, Charles, 11030

Montevideo. Biblioteca del Poder Legislativo. Sección Identificación de Autores, 9985

Montevideo. Intendencia Municipal, 9986

Montgomery, John Warwick, 10657

Montiel, Joaquín Marquez--SEE: Marquez Montiel, Joaquin, 9474-9475

Montreville, Doris de--SEE: De Montreville, Doris, 10761

Monville, Alexandre Bigot, baron de, 8907

Moonen, Francisco José, 9493

Moore, Daniel Decatur, 9889, 9959

Moore, Ernest Richard, 11154

Moore, Richard E., 9218

Moore, Walter Burritt, 9912

Moore's Who Is Who Publications, 9937

Morais, Henry Samuel, 9433

Morales, Roberto Molina y--SEE: Molina y Morales, Roberto, 9626

Morales Díaz, Carlos, 9476

Morata, Federico Bravo--SEE: Bravo Morata, Federico, 9666-9667

Mordovskaia respublikanskaia biblioteka, 11178

Moreau-Nélaton, Étienne, 8939-8940

Morel, Adéodat Constant Adolphe Compère--SEE: Compère-Morel, Adéodat Constant Adolphe, 8429

Morelia, Mexico. Colegio Primitivo y Nacional de San Nicolás de Hidalgo--SEE: Colegio Primitivo y Nacional de San Nicolás de Hidalgo, 11171

Morell, Antonio Gallego--SEE: Gallego Morell, Antonio, 11255

Moreno Galván, José María, 10220

Morgan, Henry James, 8651

Mori, Senzō, 9409

Moro, Tommaso, 11132

Morozova, M. N., 11992

Morpeth, Robert S., 9635

Morpurgo, Enrico, 12088

Morrill, Victor Eugene, 8683

Morris, Dan, 9810

Morris, Inez, 9810

Morris, J., 9566

Morris, Jeffrey Brandon, 9811

Morris, Kathleen, 10142

Morris, Peter, 10352

Morris, Richard Brandon, 9811

Morris, Sidney, 10142

Morrison, Arthur, 10187

Morrison, W. Frederic, 8542-8543

Moscow. Institut istorii partii, 9612

Moscow. Publichnaia biblioteka, 9612, 10996, 11147, 11177, 11992

Mosenthal, Salomon Hermann, Ritter von, 10872

Mosher, Frederic J., 10744

Moskovskoe matematicheskoe obshchestvo, 11917

Mostovets, N. V., 9828

Mottram, Eric, 10830

Moure, Jean Gabriel Emile, 11398

Moure, Nancy Dustin Wall, 10249

Mudaliar, A. Singervel--SEE: Singerval Mudaliar, A., 11276

Mudaliyar, M. Balasubrahmanya, 11274

Mülinen, Egbert Friedrich von, Graf, 12016

Müller, August, 10705

Müller, Emil, 11889

Münster, Ger. Deutsches Institut für Wissenschaftliche Pädagogik--SEE: Deutsches Institut für Wissenschaftliche Pädagogik, Münster, 10659

Münster, Ger. Provinzialinstitut für Westfälische Landes- und Volkskunde--SEE: Provinzialinstitut für Westfälische Landes-und Volkskunde, Münster, 9133

Muhammad 'Abd Allāh 'Inān--SEE: 'Inān, Muhammad 'Abd Allāh, 9312

Muhammad Abū al-Fadl Ibrāhīm --SEE: Ibrāhīm, Muhammad Abū al-Fadl, 10845

Muhammad Amin ibn Fadl Allāh
al-Muhibbi--SEE: al-Muhibbi,
Muhammad Amin ibn Fadl Allāh, 9325

Muhammad 'Awfi--SEE: 'Awfi,
Muhammad, 11183

Muhammad Bākir Khwānsāri--
SEE: Muhammad Bāqir ibn
Zain al-'Abidin, al-Musawi
al-Khwānsāri, 11848-11849

Muhammad Bāqir ibn Zain al-
'Abidin, al-Mūsawi al-Khwānsāri, 11848-11849

Muhammad Gamil as-Šatti--SEE:
al-Shatti, Muhammad Jamil,
9727-9728

Muhammad ibn 'Abd Allāh ibn al-
Abbār--SEE: Ibn al-Abbār,
Muhammad ibn 'Abd Allāh,
9303

Muhammad ibn 'Abd al-Rahmān
al-Sakhāwi--SEE: al-Sakhāwi,
Muhammad ibn 'Abd al-Rah-
mān, 11322

Muhammad ibn Ahmad al-Dhahabi
--SEE: al-Dhahabi, Muhammad
ibn Ahmad, 9299-9301, 11847

Muhammad ibn Ahmad al Dūlābi--
SEE: al Dūlābi, Muhammad
ibn Ahmad, 11841

Muhammad ibn al-Husayn al-Sula-
mi--SEE: al-Sulami, Muhammad ibn al-Husayn, 11853

Muhammad ibn al-Tayyib al-Qā-
diri--SEE: al-Qādiri, Muhammad ibn al-Tayyib, 8576

Muhammad ibn 'Ali-Shawkāni--
SEE: al-Shawkāni, Muhammad
ibn 'Ali, 9332

Muhammad ibn Hārith al-Khushani
--SEE: al-Khushani, Muhammad ibn Harith, 10706

Muhammad ibn 'Imrān al-Marzu-
bāni--SEE: al-Marzubāni, Muhammad ibn 'Imrān, 10843-
10844

Muhammad ibn Ishāq ibn al-Nadim
--SEE: Ibn al-Nadim, Muhammad ibn Ishāq, 10839

Muhammad ibn Khalaf Waki'--SEE:
Waki', Muhammad ibn Khalaf,
11323

Muhammad ibn Muhammad ibn al-
Jazari--SEE: Ibn al-Jazari,
Muhammad ibn Muhammad,
9306

Muhammad ibn Rāfi', Abu al-Ma'-
āli--SEE: al-Sallāmi, Muhammad ibn Rāfi, 9302

Muhammad ibn Shakir al-Kutubi--
SEE: al-Kutubi, Muhammad
ibn Shakir, 9320

Muhammad ibn Tāhir ibn al-Qay-
sarāni--SEE: Ibn al-Qaysa-
rāni, Muhammad ibn Tahir,
11843

Muhammad Jamil al-Shatti--SEE:
al-Shatti, Muhammad Jamil,
9727-9728

Muhammad Muhyi al-Din 'Abd al-
Hamid, 9320

Muhammad Tāhir ibn Rif'at
(Brusali), 11280

al-Muhibbi, Muhammad Amin ibn
Fadl Allāh, 9325

Mu'in al-Din Junaid al-Shirāzi,
11850

Mukařovský, Jan, 10946

Mukhopadhyay, Harimohan,
10888

Mukhopadhyaya, Girindranath--
SEE: Girindradranath Mukhopadhyaya, 11456

Mulas Pérez, I., 10613

Muley, Gerardo Monge--SEE:
Monge Muley, Gerardo,
11485

Mulk Raj Saraf--SEE: Saraf,
Mulk Raj, 9265

Mullo, I. M., 9582

al-Munajid, Salah al-Dīn, 9297

Muñiz, Gregorio López--SEE:
López Muñiz, Gregorio, 8355

Muñoz, Gustavo Otero--SEE:
Otero Muñoz, Gustavo, 10938,
11957

Muñoz Olave, Reinaldo, 11730

Muradian, Matevos Oganesovich,
10516

Murdoch, James, 10520

Murthy, K. R. Srikanta--SEE:
Srikanta Murthy, K. R.,
11457

Mūsá, 'Iyād ibn--SEE: 'Iyād ibn
Mūsá, 9315

Mūsá, 'Izz al-Dīn Ahmad, 9310

al-Musāwī al-Khwānsārī, Mu-
hammad Bāqir ibn Zain al-
'Abidīn--SEE: Muhammad
Bāqir ibn Zain al-'Abidīn, al-
Musāwī al-Khwānsārī, 11848-
11849

Musée de la monnaie, Paris,
10293

Musée Rodin, Paris, 10278

Museo civico, Biella, Italy,
10064

Museo Nacional de Bellas Artes,
Buenos Aires--SEE: Buenos
Aires. Museo Nacional de
Bellas Artes, 10275

Museum Folkwang, Essen--SEE:
Essen. Museum Folkwang,
10052-10053

Museum Galleries, London, 9156

Museum Historyczne, Warsaw,
9534

Museum of Fine Arts, Boston,
10230

Museum of Fine Arts, Boston.
School of the Museum of Fine
Arts, 10230

Museum of the Plains Indian,
Browning, Mont., 10254

Mushta, A. P., 9743

Mustafā ibn al-Husain al-Husaini
al-Tafrishi, 11851

Mutaliar, M. Balasubrahmanya
--SEE: Mudaliyar, M. Balasubrahmanya, 11274

Muteau, Charles François Thé-
rèse, 8985

Muzei na revoliutsionnoto dvizhenie v Bŭlgariia, 8624

Muzzi, Salvatore, 8383, 9357

Myers, Bernard Samuel, 10051

Myers, Carol Fairbanks, 10831

Myers, Robert Manson, 9812

Myers, Robin, 10987

Myint, U Sein--SEE: Sein Myint,
U., 8627

Mysore. Legislative Assembly--
SEE: Mysore. Legislature.
Legislative Assembly, 9271

Mysore. Legislative Council,
9270

Mysore. Legislature. Legislative Assembly, 9271

Mysore. Legislature. Legislative
Council--SEE: Mysore. Legislative Council, 9270

Nabi Bakhsh Baloch--SEE: Baloch, Nabi Bakhsh, 11287

Nader, Ralph, 9823

al-Nadīm, Muhammad ibn Ishāq ibn--SEE: Ibn al-Nadīm, Muhammad ibn Ishāq, 10839

Naftal, Abraham Moses, 11862

Nagaraj, M. N., 9248

Nagi, Mu'allim--SEE: Nājī, Mu'allim, 9326

Nagl, Johann Willibald, 10837

Nagoeva, T. B., 11223

Nagtglas, Frederik, 9494

Naĭdenov, Gr., 11410

al-Najāshī, Ahmad ibn 'Alī--SEE: Ahmad ibn 'Alī, al-Najāshī, 11839

Nājī, Mu'allim, 9326

Nakajima, Ichirō, 9406

Nakamura, Tadashi, 8525

Nakamura, Takeshi, 8350

Nakano, Miyoko, 10913

Names of Distinction, inc., 9916, 9977

Nampoothiry, E. Easwaran--SEE: Easwaran Nampoothiry, E., 11234

Nan Kivell, Rex de C., 8544

Nand Kishore Goil--SEE: Goil, Nand Kishore, 11093

Napier, Ronald, 10527

Narendra Bhanawat--SEE: Bhanawat, Narendra, 11857

Narodna biblioteka, Sofia--SEE: Sofia. Narodna biblioteka, 10765, 10900

Narodno pozorište Sarajevo, 10437a

Nasarre de Letosa, Ventura Baguës--SEE: Baguës, Ventura, 10612

Nash, Deanna, 9823

Nash, Jay Robert, 9813

Nataf, André, 11942

National Academy of Sciences, Washington, D. C., 11892

National Assembly of Thailand-- SEE: Thailand. Sathāban Bandit Phatthana Bōrihan Sāt. Samnak Wichai, 9732

National Association of Elementary School Principals (Founded 1970), 10735

National Book League, London, 10987

National Center of Afro-American Artists. Museum, 10230

National Central Library, Taipei --SEE: Chung yang t'u shu kuan, Taipei, 8692, 10925

National Gallery, London--SEE: London. National Gallery, 10170

National Gallery of Canada, 10087-10088

National Hockey League, 10629

National Institute of Child Health and Human Development, 11379

National Institutes of Health--SEE: United States. National Institutes of Health, 11476

National Library of Australia-- SEE: Canberra, Australia. National Library, 8545

National Library of Medicine (U.S.)--SEE: United States. National Library of Medicine, 11404

National Library of Nigeria, 9500

National Library of the Philippines--SEE: Manila. National Library, 9525a

National Portrait Gallery, London--SEE: London. National Portrait Gallery, 9142, 9163

National Portrait Gallery, Washington, D. C., 9756, 10255

National Portrait Gallery, Washington, D. C. Historian's Office, 9814

National Society of the Colonial Dames of America. Georgia. Historical Activities Committee, 9870

National Society of the Colonial Dames of America. Louisiana. Historical Activities Committee, 9887

Nationalmuseum, Stockholm-- SEE: Stockholm. Nationalmuseum, 10225

Nauchno-issledovatel'skii institut teorii i istorii izobrazitel' nykh iskusstv--SEE: Akademiiā khudozhesty. Nauchno-issledovatel'skii institut teorii i istorii izobrazitel'nykh iskusstv, 10206

Nau'izada, 'Ata'-Allah ibn Yahya, called--SEE: Atāyī, Atâullah Nev'izade, 9739

Nauman, St. Elmo, 11548

Navrátil, Michal, 11307

al-Nawawī, 9327

Nayral, Magloire, 8986

Neely, Ruth, 9940

Neill, Stephen Charles, Bp., 11609

Nélaton, Étienne Moreau--SEE: Moreau-Nélaton, Étienne, 8939-8940

Nembro, Metodio da-SEE: Metodio da Nembro, Father, 11687

Nemec, Jaroslav, 11404

Nemeskürthy, Istvan, 10329

Nencke, Carl Christoph, 9107

Nersisian Dprots', 8513

Nersisyants'ineri Avandakan Handipowmner Kazmakerpogh Handznazhogov, 8513

Nesbitt, Bruce, 10858

Nettleship, Henry, 8403

Neubauer, Paul, bookseller, Cologne, 8274

Neumann, Louis Georges, 12050

Neumann, Wilhelm, 10303

Neumüllers-Klauser, Renate, 9112

Neuner, Kassian, 11715

Nevin, Alfred, 11826

Nevins, Allan, 9757

Nev'izade, Atāyī Atâullah--SEE: Atāyī, Atâullah Nev'izade, 9739

New Mexico Historical Association, 9909

New York (City). World's Fair, 1964-1965. American Express Pavilion, 10231

New York Academy of Medicine, 11509

New York Historical Society, 9758-9760

New York Times, 8456

New York University. Hall of Fame, 9287

The New Yorker (New York, 1925-   ), 9754, 9764

New Zealand Library Association, 11358

Newby, Eric, 12003

Newerla, Gerhard J., 11399

Newton, Jorge, 12051

Niākhai, R., 11295

Nichols, John Benjamin, 11507

Nichols, William, 11595

Nicholson, Frank Walter, 9843

Nicolas, Michel, 11028

Nicolas, Sébastien Roch, called Chamfort--SEE: Chamfort, Sébastien Roch Nicolas, called, 11017

Nicole-Genty, Geneviève, 11427

Nicoloff, Assen, 10899

Nieciowa, Elzbieta Helena, 10717

Niedersächsische Staats- und Universitätsbibliothek, Göttingen, 9067

Nielsen, Henning Hjorth--SEE: Hjorth-Nielsen, Henning, 8823-8824, 11308

Nieto, A., 11793

Nieves, Cesáreo Rosa--SEE: Rosa-Nieves, Cesáreo, 9556

Nigeria. National Library--SEE: National Library of Nigeria, 9500

Nigg, Marianne, 10874

Nikhila Sarakāra--SEE: Sarakāra, Nikhila, 8465

Nikolaev, Valerii Alekseevich, 11348

Nirk, Endel, 10997

Nisenson, Samuel, 8363

Nissenbaum, Salmon Baruch, 9533

Niu, Hsien-ming, 8725

Nizami, Z. A., 9248

Nizami Badauni, pseud., 11288

Noblet, Jocelyn de, 12034

Nóbrega, Apolonio Carneiro da Cunha, 11718

Noël, Bernard, 8941

Nogueira, Octaciano, 8605

Nohra, Flor Romero de--SEE: Romero de Nohra, Flor, 8799

Nohrström, Kyllikki, 8290

Nordenstreng, Sigurd, 8854

Nordin-Pettersson, Brita Stina, 11888

Nordmann, Almut, 10813

Nordness, Lee, 10250, 10304

Norfleet, Fillmore, 9975

Norman Mackenzie Art Gallery, 10089

Norris, Andrea S., 10305

Norris, J. E., 9976

Norsk misjonsråd, 11811

Norske Nobelinstitutt--SEE: Oslo. Norske Nobelinstitutt, 9630

North Carolina. State Library,
Raleigh, 9913

North St. Louis Business Men's
Association, 9953

Norwegian Lutheran Church of
America. Board of Foreign
Missions, 11812

Norwich, Eng. Free Library,
9194

Nostredame, Jean de, 11205

Notre-Dame de Port-Royal des
Champs (Abbey of Cistercian
nuns)--SEE: Port-Royal des
Champs (Abbey of Cistercian
nuns), 11761

Novák, O., 11034

Novaka, Arna, 10995

Novillo, José María Carretero--
SEE: Carretero, José María,
9668

Novosibirsk. Oblastnaiâ biblioteka, 11221

Ntelopoulos, Kyriakos, 11073

Nürnberg--SEE: Nuremberg.

Nulman, Macy, 10549

Nummelin, Carl, 12052

Nuremberg. Kunsthalle, 10060

Nyiró, Jószef, 11534

Nykoruk, Barbara, 8423, 10747,
11985

Obermann, Karl, 9073

Obersteiner, Jakob, 11716

Oboishchikov, K., 9609

O'Brien, Thomas C., 11582

O'Clair, Robert, 10825

Odense, Denmark. Adelige Jom-
frukloster--SEE: Adelige Jomfrukloster, Odense, Denmark,
8820

Odieuvre, Michael, 8434

Oehlke, Waldemar, 11063

Österreichische Nationalbiblio-
thek--SEE: Vienna. Nationalbibliothek, 11339

Österreichischer P.E.N. Club--
SEE: P.E.N. Club, Austria,
10876

Özön, Nijat, 10345

Öztuna, T. Yilmaz, 10571

Ogawa, Tamaki, 10928

Ogilby, John David, 8397

Ohio. General Assembly, 9929

Ohio. State Library, Columbus,
9923

Ohio. State University, Columbus. College of Medicine,
11510

Ohio Newspaper Women's Association, 9940

Ojeda, Olivia, 9519

Okrŭzhen istoricheski muzeĭ,
Pernik, Bulgaria, 8623

Olave, Reinaldo Munoz--SEE:
Munoz Olave, Reinaldo, 11730

O'Leary, De Lacy Evans, 11610

Oliveira, Carolina Renno Ribeiro
de, 8607

Olivier, Paul, 11029

Olles, Helmut, 10793

Olshausen, Eckart, 8401

Olszewicz, Bolesław, 12004

Padāla Ramarāvu--SEE: Ramarāvu, Padāla, 9250

Páez Courvel, Luis E., 8797

Page (H. R.), Chicago, 9899

Page, Rosewell, 9974

Paischeff, Aleksander, 10104

Paiva de Faria Tavora e Cernache, Henrique Leite Pereira
de, conde de Campo Bello--
SEE: Campo Bello, Henrique
Leite Pereira de Paiva de
Faria Tavora e Cernache,
conde de, 8597

Pakistan, 9514

Pál, Ottó, 11087

Palais des beaux arts, Paris--
SEE: Paris. Palais des beaux-
arts, 10196

Páleniček, Ludvík, 8812

Palissot de Montenoy, Charles,
11030

Pallas, Gustav, 10794

Pallipattu Kunjukrishnan--SEE:
Kunjukrishnan, Pallipattu,
9246

Palm, Georg Friedrich, 8364

Pama, C., 9661

P'an, Hsing-nung, 8769

Pan, Xing-mong--SEE: P'an,
Hsing-nung, 8769

Pan'gong Todŏk Kyokuk Yŏn'-
guhoe, 8457

Pankratova, L. S., 11230a

Panneton, Georges, 11723

Pantzer, Gerhard von, 8575

Papadopoulos-Bretos, Andreas--
SEE: Vretos, Andreas Papadopoulos, 11078

Papenbroeck, Gerard van, 10713

Papillon de La Ferté, Denis
Pierre Jean, 10061

Paquet, René, 9025

Paras, Corazon de Leon--SEE:
Leon-Paras, Corazon de,
11324

Pardesi, Ram Gopal, 11095

Parent, Paul E., 8681

Paris. Académie des inscriptions
et belles-lettres--SEE: Académie des inscriptions et
belles-lettres, Paris, 8949

Paris. Académie française--SEE:
Academie française, Paris,
8869

Paris. Bibliothèque nationale.
Département des estampes,
8293-8295

Paris. Bibliothèque nationale.
Département des imprimés,
8867

Paris. Musée de la monnaie--SEE:
Musée de la monnaie, Paris,
10293

Paris. Musée Rodin--SEE: Musée
Rodin, Paris, 10278

Paris. Palais des beaux-arts,
10196

Parish, James Robert, 10433

Paroletti, Modesto, 9383

Parrinder, Edward Geoffrey,
11558

Pascoe, J. J., 8546

Polska Akademia Nauk. Instytut Filozofii i Socjologii, 11535

Polska Akademia Nauk. Institut Sztuki, 10202, 10417

Polurez, V. I., 10725

Ponsonailhe, Charles, 11691

Pontaut, Alain, 10374

Pontificia Universidad Eclesiástica, Salamanca--SEE: Salamanca. Pontificia Universidad Eclesiástica, 11795

Pontificio Ateneo antoniano, Rome--SEE: Rome (City). Pontificio Ateneo antoniano, 10710

Pontual, Roberto, 10081-10082

Popa, Marian, 11209

Popov, V. M., 10725

Popp, Georg, 8367, 11692

Porcel, Baltasar, 9678

Port-Royal des Champs (Abbey of Cistercian nuns), 11761

Porta, Frederico, 11349a

Portas, Rafael E., 10413

Porter, Hal, 10365

Portero, Antonio Sánchez--SEE: Sánchez Portero, Antonio, 11259

Porth, W., 8568

Portillo, Gregorio Vicent y--SEE: Vicent y Portillo, Gregorio, 9687

Posada, José Restrepo--SEE: Restrepo Posada, José, 11736

Posada Callejas, Jorge, 8795

Poulier, ------, 8883

Poussin, J. Clovis, 11596

Povijesni Muzej Hrvatske, 8688b

Powell, John Benjamin, 8727

Power, Sir D'Arcy, 11452

Pozsonyi, Gábor, 10329

Prabha Chopra--SEE: Chopra, Prabha, 9261

Pradier, ------, abbé, 11693

Prague. Městská knihovna, 8297

Prakash Kokil--SEE: Kokil, Prakash, 9245

Pralhāda Narahara Jośi--SEE: Jośi, Pralhāda Narahara, 11875

Pramathanātha Bhattacārya--SEE: Bhattacārya, Pramathanātha, 11836

Prashad, Baini, 9226

Prawer, Joshua, 8308

Pražák, František, 10678

Preda, Artemio Franco--SEE: Franco Preda, Artemio, 9517

Prem Narayan Tandon--SEE: Tandon, Prem Narayan, 11082

Press, Charles A. Manning, 9185

Preston, Rupert, 10197

Prestwich, Arthur Alfred, 12054

Pretzl, Otto, 9306

Preuss, Gisela, 10792

Priesdorff, Kurt von, 9124

Prigent, Simone, 8368

Prince, Lloyd N., 9882

Prinet, Max, 9036

Procházková, Marie, 10944

Promis, Carlo, 12069

Pronteau, Jeanne, 9034

Protod'iakonov, Vasilii Andreevich, 11298

Provençal, Evariste Levi--SEE:
Levi-Provençal, Evariste,
9308

Provinzalinstitut für Westfälische
Landes- und Volkskunde,
Münster. Historische Kommis-
sion, 9133

Provost, Joseph, 11694

Průšek, Jaroslav, 11180

Przymusiała, Andrzej, 11535

Pu, Yu-fu, 9729

Puaux, François, 11830

Public Archives of Canada--SEE:
Canada. Public Archives,
8638, 10135

Publichnaia biblioteka, Moscow--
SEE: Moscow. Publichnaia
biblioteka, 9612, 10996,
11147, 11177, 11992

Pudor, Fritz, 9126, 11964

Puerto Rico. Office of the Historical Index, 9554

Puerto Rico. Oficina del Historia-
dor Oficial--SEE: Puerto Rico.
Office of the Historical Index,
9554

Pulavar, Subramania Arittiru
Ramaswamy--SEE: Rama-
swamy Pulavar, Subramania
Arittiru, 11275

Punjab, India (State). Legislature.
Legislative Council, 9275

Punjabi University. Dept. of History and Punjab Historical
Studies, 9276

Purgstall, Joseph, Freiherr von
Hammer--SEE: Hammer-
Purgstall, Joseph, Freiherr
von, 8556

Pyke, E. J., 10279

al-Qādī, Ahmad ibn Muḥammad
ibn--SEE: Ibn al-Qādī, Ahmad
ibn Muhammad, 9307, 9485

al-Qadi, Wadād, 9310

al-Qādirī, Muhammad ibn al-
Tayyib, 8576

al-Qasīm ibn 'Abd Allah ibn Qut-
lūbūgha--SEE: Ibn Qutlūbūgha,
al-Qasīm ibn 'Abd Allah, 11320

Qasīm ibn Qutlūbūgha--SEE: Ibn
Qutlūbūgha, al-Qasīm ibn 'Abd
Allah, 11320

al-Qaysarānī, Muhammad ibn Tāhir ibn--SEE: Ibn al-Qaysarānī, Muhammad ibn Tāhir,
11843

al-Qiftī, 'Alī ibn Yūsuf, 10705,
10845

Quebbeman, Frances E., 11513

Quebec (Province). Dept. of
Cultural Affairs, 10278

Queen City Publishing Company,
Cincinnati, 9931, 9936

Quelqu'un, citoyen français, 8883

Quennell, Peter, 10989

Quépat, Nérée, pseud.--SEE:
Paquet, René, 9025

Quezon, Philippines. University
of the Philippines. Library,
10715

Quinn, Edward G., 10324

Quintero, Jorge Pacheco--SEE: Pacheco Quintero, Jorge, 10940

Quirielle, Roger de, 11033

Quirós, Juan, 10892

al-Qurashī, 'Abd al-Qadir ibn Muhammad ibn Abī al-Wafā'-- SEE: Ibn Abī al-Wafā' al-Qurashī, 'Abd al-Qadir ibn Muhammad, 11318

Qutlūbūgha, al-Qasīm ibn 'Abd Allah ibn--SEE: Ibn Qutlūbūgha, al-Qasīm ibn 'Abd Allah, 11320

Rachel McMasters Miller Hunt Botanical Library--SEE: Hunt Botanical Library, 11901

Rachewiltz, Igor de, 10913

Racic, Marko, 10599

Radice, Betty, 9209

Radier, Jean François Dreux du --SEE: Dreux du Radier, Jean François, 8434, 9039

Radisics, Elemér, 9223

Rader, Wilhelm, 11306

Rätisches Museum Chur, 8441

Ragut, Camille, 9047

Raillicourt, Dominique Labarre de--SEE: Labarre de Railli-court, Dominique, 8921

Raja Singam, S. Durai, 9703

Rajović, Radošin, 10011

Raju, Addepalli Appala Narasim-ha, 11278

Rake, Alan, 8485

Rákos, Petr, 11089

Ralph Nader Congress Project, 9823

Ram Gopal Pardesi--SEE: Par-desi, Ram Gopal, 11095

Ram Gupta, Badlu--SEE: Gupta, Badlu Ram, 11972

Rama Rao, T. V., 9249

Ramalakshmi, K., 11279

Ramarāvu, Padāla, 9250

Ramaswamy Pulavar, Subramania Arittiru, 11275

Ramnik Sripatray Desai--SEE: Desai, Ramnik Sripatray, 11080

Ranbir Publications, 9265

Randall Publishing Company, 10588

Rangel, Ricardo, 10413

Ranke, Kurt, 10773

Rao, Conjeevaram Hayavadana-- SEE: Hayavadana Rao, Con-jeevaram, 9241

Rao, T. V. Rama--SEE: Rama Rao, T. V., 9249

Rao, Tallak Subbanna Shama-- SEE: Shama Rao, Tallak Sub-banna, 11837

Raphael, Itzhak, 11863

Rapp, Alfred, 9105

Rasmussen, Bjørn, 10349

Rastawiecki, Edward, 10201

Raszewski, Zbigniew, 10417

Raumer, Kurt von, 9127

Raunié, Émile, 9036

Ravenel, Beatrice St. Julien, 10271

Reyna, Ferdinand, 10351

Reynolds, Sir Joshua, 9140

Rhede van der Kloot, M. A. van
--SEE: Klott, M. A. Rhede
van der, 9285

Rhoades, Elozabeth R., 9860

Rhodenizer, Vernon Blair, 10905

Riat, Georges, 8293

Ribas, Jaime Valero--SEE: Valero-Ribas, Jaime, 11375

Ribeiro de Oliveira, Carolina
Renno--SEE: Oliveira, Carolina Renno Ribeiro de, 8607

Ribes Tovar, Federico, 9555

Ribeyre, Félix, 8951-8953

Ricart, Gustavo, 8835

Richardson, Hubert N., 8954

Richemond, Louis Marie Meschinet de--SEE: Meschinet de
Richemond, Louis Marie, 8991

Richmond enquirer, 9973

Richmond Whig, 9973

Richter, Wilhelm Michael von,
11475

Rickwood, George, 9203

Riddell, Edwin, 9161

Rider, Fremont, 9748

Rieger, Heinrich, 11401

Riella, Amedeo Galati di, conte
--SEE: Galati di Riella,
Amedeo, conte, 9628

Riemann, Hugo, 10485

Riemens, Leo, 10475

Rife, Edward K., 9927

Rija. Politeknicheskiĭ institut--
SEE: Politechnicheskiĭ institut,
Riga, 12025

Rigler, Rudolf Richard, 8567

Rijksuniversiteit te Leiden--SEE:
Leyden. Rijksuniversiteit,
8288

Rikhter, Vil'gel'm Mikhaĭlovich
--SEE: Richter, Wilhelm
Michael von, 11475

Riksföreningen för svenskhetens
bevarande i utlandet, 9718

Riley, Carolyn, 10775

Riley, Carroll L., 9629

Ringheim, Tage, 10569

Rio de Janeiro. Instituto Historico
e Geographico Brasileiro--
SEE: Instituto Historico e Geographico Brasileiro, Rio de
Janeiro, 8601

Rion, Adolphe, 8955

Ríos, Angel Fernández de los--
SEE: Fernández de los Ríos,
Angel, 9673

Ríos Ruiz, Manuel, 11258

Rippa, B. K., 11478

Rippey, Joseph, 9825

Ristelhuber, Paul--SEE: Meyer,
Antoine, 8970

Ristikivi, Karl, 10995

Ritter, Wilhelm, 10394

Rivera, Bueno de, 8608

Riverain, Jean, 8369, 11402

Rivet, Antoine--SEE: Rivet de la
Grange, Antoine, 11761

Rivet de la Grange, Antoine,
11761

Ruiz, Manuel Ríos--SEE: Ríos Ruiz, Manuel, 11258

Rumiantsev, Aleksei Matveevich, 11943

Runes, Richard N., 8311

Runnquist, Åke, 11235, 11261

Ruoff, James E., 10990

Rush, Theressa Gunnels, 10831

Russo, Luigi, 11128

Rutgers University, New Brunswick, N. J. Center for the American Woman and Politics, 9826

Ryall, Henry Thomas, 9171

Ryan, Peter, 9516

Rybak, E. D., 9582

Rydon, Joan, 8547

Rye, Walter, 9194

Saarland. Landtag, 9128

Šabanović, Hazim, 11281

Sabatier, Agathon, 11763

Sabin, Robert, 10496

Sabor, Josefa Emilia, 8495

La Sabretache, 8930

Sabzwari, Ghaniul Akram, 11351

Sachaile, C., pseud.--SEE: Lachaise, Claude, 11436

Sachin Roy--SEE: Roy, Sachin, 12018

Sachindra Kumar Maity--SEE: Maity, Sachindra Kumar, 9269

Sacklén, Johan Frederic, 11489

al-Sadafī, Husayn ibn Muhammad ibn Sukkarah--SEE: Ibn Sukkarah al-Sadafī, Husayn ibn Muhammad, 9303

Sadoul, Georges, 10352

al-Sadr, Hasan ibn Hādī, 11852

al-Safadi, Khalil ibn Aybak, 9328, 9726

al-Safar, Muhammad Rashid, 9296

Saggi, Ludovico, 11699

St. Anthony's Guild, Paterson, N. J., 11644

St. Augustine's Abbey, Ramsgate, Eng., 11709

Saint-Edme, Edme Théodore Bourg, known as, 8957

Saint-Hardouin, François Pierre H. Tarbé de--SEE: Tarbé de Saint-Hardouin, François Pierre H., 12072

Saint-Hilaire, Amable Vilain de --SEE: Vilain de Saint-Hilaire, Amable, 10383

Saint-Hilaire, Émile Marc Hilaire, known as Marco de, 10383

Saint-Hilaire, Março de--SEE: Saint-Hilaire, Émile Marc Hilaire, known as Marco de, 10383

Saint-Jal, Alfred, vicomte de Lastic--SEE: Lastic Saint-Jal, Alfred, vicomte de, 9039

St. Louis. Public Library, 10229

Saint-Marc, Charles Hugues Lefebvre de--SEE: Lefebvre de Saint-Marc, Charles Hugues, 11761

Saint-Maurice Cabany, E. de, 8910

Saint-Mémin, Charles Balthazar Julien Fevret de--SEE: Fevret de Saint-Mémin, Charles Balthazar Julien, 9975

Saint-Pierre (Benedictine abbey), 11634

Saint-Vaast, Arras, France (Abbey)--SEE: Arras, France. Saint-Vaast (Abbey), 11742

Saint-Venant, Raoul, comte de, 9054

Sainte-Marie-de-Pontmain, Sister, 11725

Sainte-Marthe, Denis de, 11753

Sakamoto, Takeo, 9411

Sakcinski, Ivan Kukuljević--SEE: Kukuljević-Sakcinski, Ivan, 10260

al-Sakhāwī, Muhammad ibn 'Abd al-Rahmān, 11322

Salah al-Dīn al-Munajid--SEE: al-Munajid, Salah al-Dīn, 9297

Salakhiân, Akop Nishanovich, 11212

Salamanca. Pontificia Universidad Eclesiástica. Instituto de Historia de la Teología, 11795

Salcedo-Romero, Maria Corona --SEE: Romero, Maria Corona Salcedo, 11324

Salim, Efendi, 11282

Salinas, Héctor Cossío--SEE: Cossío Salinas, Héctor, 10890

al-Sallāmī, Muhammad ibn Rāfi', 9302

Salumbides, Vicente, 10415

Salvador. Ministerio de Educación, 9627

Salvat Editores, 11375

Salzburg, Austria. Institut für Vergleichende Erziehungswissenschaft--SEE: Institut für Vergleichende Erziehungswissenschaft, Salzburg, 10659

Samaganov, Dzhenbai, 11148

Sambucus, Johannes, 11403

Samec, Smiljan, 10421

Sammlung Dr. Josef Brettauer-- SEE: Vienna. Universität. Dr. Josef Brettauer-Stiftung, 11361

Samsons, Vilis, 9457

San Francisco. Museum of Art-- SEE: San Francisco Museum of Art, 12093

San Francisco Museum of Art, 12093

San Salvador--SEE: Salvador.

Sanabria G   , Floren, 8586

Sánchez, Agustin del Saz--SEE: Saz Sánchez, Agustín del, 11182

Sánchez de Valero, José Ramón de Lahoz y--SEE: Lahoz y Sánchez de Valero, José Ramón de, 9664

Sánchez Granjel, Luis--SEE: Granjel, Luis S., 11480

Sánchez Portero, Antonio, 11259

Sánchez Sarto, Luis, 10662

Sancho, Pedro Mateu--SEE: Mateu Sancho, Pedro, 11929

Sandberg, Willem, 10015

Sandberger, Frank, 8373

Sanders, Lloyd Charles, 8464

Sandīlavī, Ahmad 'Alī Khān
Hāshimī--SEE: Hāshimī
Sandīlavī, Ahmad 'Alī Khān,
11184

Sandys, Sir John Edwin, 8403

Sangali, Venkatesa, 11145

Sangeet Natak Akademi, 10545

Sangpo, Khetsun--SEE: Khetsun
Sangpo, 9734

Santamaría, Francisco Javier,
11174

Santander Rodríguez, María
Teresa, 11480

Santiago, Pedro A., 9994

Santiago de Chile. Biblioteca Nacional, 10910

Santini, Pier Carlo, 10065

Saraf, Mulk Raj, 9265

Saragossa, Spain. Institución
'Fernando el Católico'--SEE:
Institución 'Fernando el
Católico,' 9683

Sarakāra, Nikhila, 8465

Sarandev, Ivan Antonov, 10896

Saransk, Russia. Mordovskaiâ
respublikanskaiâ biblioteka--
SEE: Mordovskaiâ respublikanskaiâ biblioteka, 11178

Sarti, Telesforo, 9361-9362

Sarto, Luis Sánchez--SEE: Sánchez Sarto, Luis, 10662

Sas Orchassal, Andrés, 10559

Sashi Bhushan Vidyalankar--SEE:
Vidyalankar, Sashi Bhushan,
11838

Saska, Robert, 10488

Saskatchewan. Provincial Library. Bibliographic Service Division, 8299

Satan, pseud.--SEE: Mathieu-
Dairnvaell, Georges Marie,
8934-8935

Sathas, Kōnstantinos N., 11074-
11075

Satterthwaite, Gilbert Elliott,
11931

as-Šatti, Muhammad Ğamil--SEE:
al-Shatti, Muhammad Jamil,
9727-9728

Saupe, Emil, 10694

Saur, Karl Otto, 9104a

Savage, George, 8461

Savara, Sudershan K., 9240

Saville, John, 11966

Sawada, Akira, 10188

Saxon, Kurt, 11615

Saz Sánchez, Agustín del, 11182

Sbaraglia, Giovanni Giacinto,
11707

Schaal, Richard, 10441-10442

Schaller, Jaroslaus, 11739

Schang, F. C., 8466

Schapsmeier, Edward L., 12055

Schapsmeier, Frederick H.,
12055

Scharff, Robert, 10625

Scharping, Karl, 10598

Scheibert, Justus, 8568

Schelenz, Karl, 10598

Schellhorn, Rolf K. W., 9452

Schenck, Axel, 10042

Schepelern, H. D., 8820

Scherer, Georg, 11064

Scheyrer, Ludwig, 10877

Schiffmann, Genevieve, 11404

Schild, Ulla, 10813

Schipani, Felice Caivano--SEE:
Caivano-Schipani, Felice, 9341

Schleifer, Harold B., 11206

Schleman, Hilton R., 10489

Schleswig (City). Schleswig-Holsteinisches Landesmuseum,
9130

Schleswig-Holsteinisches Landes-
museum--SEE: Schleswig
(City). Schleswig-Holsteinisches Landesmuseum, 9130

Schlösser, Manfred, 11065

Schlossar, Anton, 10878

Schlosser, Katesa, 11559

Schmid, Bastian, 11897

Schmidt, Rudolf, 10076

Schmidt, Samuel Heinrich, 8419

Schmied, Wieland, 10133

Schneider, Marijana, 8688b

Schoeffler, O. E., 10309

Schöne, Wilhelm, 8396

Schöpflin, Aladár, 10339

Scholē Mōraitē. Hetaireia Spoudōn, 11076

Scholes, Percy Alfred, 10490

Scholz, Harry, 11446

School of the Museum of Fine
Arts, Boston--SEE: Museum
of Fine Arts, Boston. School
of the Museum of Fine Arts,
10230

Schottenloher, Karl, 9065

Schrey, Eero, 11313

Schröck, Daniel, 10741

Schröder, Anneliese, 10133

Schroeder, Felix von, 8843

Schuder, Werner, 11058

Schüssler, Wilhelm, 9076

Schulz, Heinrich E., 9584

Schuster, Mel, 10313-10314

Schwab, Gregor, 11700

Schwaiger, Georg, 11767

Schwartz, Hermann, 10663

Schwarz, Ernst, 10929

Schwarz, Holm-Dieter, 11439

Schwitzke, Heinz, 10798

Scot, Sir John, of Scotstarvet--
SEE: Scott, Sir John, Lord
Scotstarvet, 9647

Scotstarvet, Sir John Scott,
Lord--SEE: Scott, Sir John,
Lord Scotstarvet, 9647

Scott, Sir John, Lord Scotstarvet, 9647

Scullard, Howard Hayes, 8402

Sedeño, Juan, 8374

Sedgwick, Romney, 9172

Seeger, Horst, 10491

Seehusen, Sven, 8829

Shibata, Minoru, 8770

Shih, Tuan-chiao, 10930

Shihāb ad-Dīn Ahmad ibn Muhammad--SEE: al-Khafājī, Ahmad ibn Muhammad, 10842

Shilov, Georgii Evgen'evich, 11917

Shimoni, Yaacov, 9488

Shipley, Joseph Twadell, 10799

al-Shirāzī, Mu'in al-Din Junaid --SEE: Mu'in al-Din Junaid al-Shirāzī, 11850

Shisō Undō Kenkyūjo, 8771

Shivratan Mitra--SEE: Mitra, Shivratan, 10887

Shizuoka, Japan (Prefecture), 9412

Shlevko, Galina Mikhailovna, 9614

Shockley, Ann Allen, 10832

Shokina, N. A., 9575

Shorewood Publishers, inc., New York, 10044

Shortt, Adam, 8656

Shpak, Ivan Isaakovich, 11176-11177

Shreedharan, C. P. --SEE: Sreedharan, C. P., 11165

Shri Murari Sinha--SEE: Sinha, Shri Murari, 10800

Shrikrishna Anant Jakatdar-- SEE: Jakatdar, Shrikrishna Anant, 11540

Shtohryn, Dmytro M., 9831

Shu, Austin C. W., 10922

Shu-ho-tê, 8724

Shumakova, A. S., 11223

Shvedova, Ol'ga Ivanovna, 12019

Shvetsov, Stepan Dmitrievich, 9603

Shyamlal, 10408

Sianda, Giovanni, 11617

Siba Pada Sen--SEE: Sen, Siba Pada, 9252

Siddhesvara Shastri Chitrao-- SEE: Chitrav, Siddheshvar- shastri Vishnu, 9230-9231

Siddheshvarshastri Vishnu Chit- rav--SEE: Chitrav, Siddhesh- varshastri Vishnu, 9230-9231

Siddons, Joachim Hayward, 8378

Siebert, Karl, 9090

Siebs, Benno Eide, 9096

Siegmeister, Elie, 10492

Sierra, Carlos J., 9481

Sierra, José Álvarez--SEE: Ál- varez-Sierra, José, 11482

Sik, Casba, 11088

Sill, Howard, 10307

Silva, Hugo Victor Guimaraes e, 8610

Silva, Innocéncio Francisco da, 9544

Silva Pinto, Frederico da-SEE: Pinto, Frederico da Silva, 9486

Silva Rosa, Jacob S. da, 9675

Silver, Helene, 10814

Silver, Milton L., 10333

Silverman, Judith, 8300

Silverman, Morris, 9872

Sinard, André, 11726

Šimeček, Zdeněk, 10676

Simms, Rupert, 10991

Simon, Alfred, 10391

Simon, George Thomas, 10585

Simon, Gustave Clément--SEE:
Clément-Simon, Gustave, 11004

Simon, Matila, 10044

Simoni, Georges, 8368

Singam, S. Durai Raja--SEE:
Raja Singam, S. Durai, 9703

Singervel Mudaliar, A., 11276

Singh, Attar, 9240

Singh, Fauja--SEE: Bajwa,
Fauja Singh, 9274, 9276

Singh, Gurmukh, 9277

Sin'gu Munhwasa, Seoul, Korea,
9441-9442

Sinha, Shri Murari, 10800

Sinitsyn, A. M., 9588

Sir Banister Fletcher Library,
10273

Sirazi, Mu'in al-Din Junaid al-
--SEE: Mu'in al-Din Junaid
al-Shirāzi, 11850

Sircar, Dineschandra, 12017

Sita Ranjan Dass--SEE: Dass,
Sita Ranjan, 10639

Siva-Ratna Mitra--SEE: Mitra,
Shivratan, 10887

Sjöberg, Nils, 9716, 11488

Skaba, A. D., 9745

Skota, Mweli T. D., 9656, 9660

Skovran, Dušan, 10568

Skvortsov, Irinarkh Polikhron'-
evich, 11474

Slagmolen, Gerrit, 10493

Sliacky, Ondrej, 11245

Sliwinska, Irmina, 11195

Slonimsky, Nicolas, 10496,
10552

Słońska, Irena, 10787

Slušna, Ol'ga, 8807

Smirnov, Sergei Vasil'evich, 9576

Smith, David Eugene, 11920

Smith, Edward Francis, 11701

Smith, Sir Frederick, 12056

Smith, Helen Ainslie, 9827

Smith, Henry Perry, 9858

Smith, John Milton, 10325

Smith, Lyn Wall, 10249

Smith, Marcia S., 12060

Smith, Robert William Innes,
11453

Smith, Thomas M., 10614

Smith, Tom R., 10437

Smith, Sir William, 8406

Smith, William Charles, 11341

Smith and Deland, publishers,
Birmingham, Ala., 9852

Smith College, 9765

Smith-Dampier, John Lucius, 9183

Smithsonian Institution, 9776

Smolej, Viktor, 10422

Snow, Helen (Foster), 8772

Snow, Terence Benedict, 11768

Snyder, Louis Leo, 9097

Sobel, Robert, 9772

Soboleva, L. M., 11248

Socard, Émile, 8974

Social Science Research Council, 10729

Sociedad de Amigos del Libro Mexicano, 11175

Società di emigrati italiani, 9360

Una Società di letterati italiani, 12028

Société belge du librairie, 8579

Une Société de gens de lettres, 8335

Société de l'histoire de l'art français, 10122

Société des grands dictionnaires biographiques, 12053

Société nouvelle de publicité, 8660

Soderlund, Dorothy, 10729

Sørensen, Magnus, 8826

Soergel, Albert, 11067

Sofia. Dŭrzhavna biblioteka 'Vasil Kolarov'--SEE: Dŭrzhavna biblioteka 'Vasil Kolarov,' Sofia, 10900

Sofia. Muzeĭ na revoliutsionnoto dvizhenie v Bulgariia--SEE: Muzeĭ na revoliutsionnoto d- vizhenie v Bŭlgariia, 8624

Sofia. Narodna biblioteka, 10765, 10900

Sofia. Universitet, 10670

Sofia. Universitet. Biblioteka, 10745

Sofia. Universitet. Fakultet po slavianskoi filologii, 11241

Sōgensha, 8519

Sohn, Pow-key, 9440

Soiuz pisateleĭ Karel'skoĭ ASSR, 11146

Soiuz pisateleĭ SSSR. Kuybyshev- skoe otdelenie, 11216

Soiuz pisateleĭ Tadzhikistana, 11271

Sojutius--SEE: al-Suyūtī, 10846

Sokolov, Semion Dmitrievich, 11228

Sokolowska, Alina, 9534

Sola, Solmu Salomon, 10781

Solesmes, France. Saint-Pierre (Benedictine abbey)--SEE: Saint-Pierre (Benedictine ab- bey), 11634

Sollana, Emilio María de, 11796

Soni, B. M., 11973

Sons of the Revolution. Pennsyl- vania Society, 9829

Sorabji Jehangir--SEE: Jehangir, Sorabji, 9243

Sores Chandra Banerji--SEE: Banerji, Chandra Sores, 11233

Steiner, Gerhard, 10802-10803

Steiner, Robert, 10227

Steinmueller, John E., 11578

Steinschneider, Moritz, 11461

Stepanova, A. V., 11248

Stepanova, E. A., 11992

Stern, Julius, 10366, 10879

Sternberg-Manderscheid, Franz Joseph, Graf von, 10101

Sternfeld, Wilhelm, 11068

Sternstein, Jerome L., 9796

Sterry, Sir Wasey, 9153

Stettner, Béla, 10149

Stevens, Richard P., 8587

Stewart, John Craig, 9853

Steyning, June, 10318

Stiel, Beth, 10982

Stierneman, Anders Anton von--SEE: Stiernman, Anders Anton von, 11263

Stiernman, Anders Anton von, 11263

Still, Sir George Frederic, 11405

Stirling, William, 11406

Stock, Karl Franz, 10860

Stock, Marylène, 10860

Stockholm. Nationalmuseum, 10224

Stockholm. Nationalmuseum. Svenska porträttarkivet, 9709

Stocqueler, J. H., pseud.--SEE: Siddons, Joachim Hayward, 8387

Stoffel, Georges, 8971

Stoffel, Jean Georges--SEE: Stoffel, Georges, 8971

Stoĭanov, Man'o Manev, 10900

Stoĭanov, Stoĭan Ivanov, 11241

Stoicescu, Nicolae, 9574

Stoimenov, Stoĭan, 8624

Stojanović-Voks, Voja, 9650

Stopiti, Giacomo, 9363

Storer, Horatio Robinson, 11367

Storer, Malcolm, 11367

Storm, Kai, 11524

Storni, Giocondo, 11703

Story, Norah, 8657

Stowell, Ernest E., 11168

Strack, Joseph, 8569

Stratowa, Wulf, 10666, 10881

Stratton, Charles, 10633

Strauss, Albert, 9775

Strayer, Joseph Reese, 11316

Streeter, Edward Clark, 11374

Strelka, Joseph, 10882

Strel'nikova, N. T., 11224

Striker, Cecil, 11515

Strömbom, Sixten, 9709

Strong, James, 11606

Strunz, Hugo, 12070

Strutz, Edmund, 9135

Stüve, Johann Eberhard, 9120

Stupkiewicz, Stanisław, 11195

Stupnikov, Ivor Vasil'evich, 10420

Sturm, Heribert, 8805

Suárez, Victor M., 11169

Subbarao, Eka Vinkata, 10590

Subbarayan, B., 9258

Subh, Muhammad Mahmūd, 11322

Subramania Aritturu Ramaswamy Pulavar--SEE: Ramaswamy Pulavar, Subramania Arittiru, 11275

Suchaux, Louis, 9005

Sudarshan Majithia--SEE: Majithia, Sudarshan, 9262

Süreyya, Mehmed, Bey--SEE: Mehmed Süreyya, Bey, 9741

Suffridus, Petrus, 11040

al-Sulamī, Muhammad ibn al-Husayn, 11853

Sullivan, George, 10621

Sullivan, Kathryn, 11578

Sulzer, Adrian Corrodi--SEE: Corrodi-Sulzer, Adrian, 9722

Sun, Ch'eng-tse, 8773

Sun, Yü-hang, 10674

Sundman, Carl Eric, 10682

Sung, Lien. Yüan shih. (Indexes), 8703

Sunita Vasant Kulkarni--SEE: Kulkarni, Sunita Vasant, 9245

Suomen Matrikkeli, Kustannusliike, 8857

Suomen naisyhdistys, 8859

Suomen Sähköinsinööriliitto, 12071

Suomen Taiteilijaseura, 10104

Suppan, Wolfgang, 10494

Surgères, Anatole, marquis de Granges de--SEE: Granges de Surgères, Anatole, marquis de, 10118

Surius, Laurentius, 11704

Suryadinata, Leo, 9288

Sushil Kumar De--SEE: De, Sushil Kumar, 9228

Sushil Kumar Jain--SEE: Jain, Sushil Kumar, 8630

Sussel, Philippe, 8958

Suter, Heinrich, 11921

al-Suyūtī, 10846, 11854

Sužiedėlis, Simas, 9460

Švabinský, Max, 8812

Svenska läkaresällskapet, 11489

Svenska vetenskapsakademien, Stockholm, 11888

Svensson, Arne, 10412

Svoboda, Ludvík, 8393

Swettenham, John Alexander, 8658

Sychkov, N. E., 9602

Szana, Tamás, 10150

Székely-Kovács, Olga, 11407

Szemler, G. J., 11866

Szendrei, János, 10151

Szentiványi, Gyula, 10151

Szerdahelyi, István, 11534

Szigeti, Jószef, 11534

Szilágyi, Sándor, 9225

Szramkiewicz, Romuald, 11963

Szweykowski, Zygmunt, 11191

Szymanowski, Wojciech, 9538

Szymusiak, Jan Maria, 10804

Szyszkowitz, Gerald, 10883

Ta lu tsa chih she, 10671

Tagholt, Knud, 8832

Tabler, Edward C., 8491, 9559

al-Tādilī, Abū Ya'qūb Yūsuf ibn Yahyā, 11855

al-Tafrishī, Mustafā ibn al-Husain--SEE: Mustafā ibn al-Husain al-Husaini al-Tafrishī, 11851

Tagger, Nissim, 9600

al-Tahrānī, Aghā Buzurk, 11856

Tai-Shi Kōrōsha Denki Hensankai, 9413

Taiwan wen hua fu wu she, Taipei, 11982

Tajiri, Tasuku, 9414

Takagi, Sogo, 11138

Takayanagi, Mitsutoshi, 9415

Takeuchi, Rizō, 9416

Talbott, John Harold, 11408

al-Tālibī, Muhammad, 9315

Tallak Subbanna Shama Rao-- SEE: Shama Rao, Tallak Subbana, 11837

Tallinn, Estonia. Friedrich Reinhold Kreutzwaldi nimeline Eesti Riiklik Raamatukogu-- SEE: Friedrich Reinhold Kreutzwaldi nimeline Eesti NSV Riiklik Raamatukogu, 10996

Talphir, Gabriel, 10152

Tambs, Lewis A., 9453

Tamil Legislative Assembly--SEE: Tamil Nadu. Legislature. Legislative Assembly, 9278

Tamil Nadu. Legislature. Legislative Assembly, 9278

Tamil Nadu. Legislature. Legislative Council, 9279

al-Tamimi, Abū al-Arab Muhammad ibn Ahmad, 10706

Tamir, Nachman, 9419

Tandon, Prem Narayan, 11082

Taneri, Kemal Zülfü, 9742

Tanguay, Cyprien, 8647, 11727

Tani, Shin'ichi, 9417

Tao-hsüan, 11567

Taqi al-Dīn Muhammad ibn Ahmad al-Fāsī--SEE: al-Fāsī, Taqi al-Dīn Muhammad ibn Ahmad, 9302

Tarbé de Saint-Hardouin, François Pierre H., 12072

Tarbert, Gary C., 8276

Tardieu, Ambroise, 8959-8960, 8976, 8997, 9043, 11905

Tardy, 12091

Tashev, Todor, 11416

Tassé, Joseph, 8659

Tassi, Francesco Maria, 10178

Tassy, Joseph Héliodore Sagesse Vertu Garcin de--SEE:
Garcin de Tassy, Joseph
Héliodore Sagesse Vertu,
11094

Tatevosian, A. G., 10516

Taurisano, Innocenzo M., 11632

Tauro, Alberto, 11186

Tauš, Karel, 10945

Tavora e Cernache, Henrique
Leite Pereira de Paiva de
Faria, conde de Campo Bello
--SEE: Campo Bello, Hen-
rique Leite Pereira de Paiva
de Faria Tavora e Cernache,
conde de, 8597

Tayler, Alistair Norwich, 9649

Tayler, Helen Agnes Henrietta,
9649

Taylor, Alan John Percivale,
8323

Taylor, Archer, 10744

Taylor, Geoffrey Handley--SEE:
Handley-Taylor, Geoffrey,
10972-10980

Taylor, John Russell, 10436

Taylor, Welford Dunaway, 10833

Taylor, William Alexander,
9932

Taylor, William Cooke, 9173

al-Tayyib, Muhammad ibn, al-
Qādiri--SEE: al-Qādiri, Muhammad ibn al-Tayyib, 8576

Tcherpakoff, A. I.--SEE: Cherpakov, Avgust Ivanovich,
10753

Teichman, Josef, 10355

Teissier, Raoul, 9540

Tejera, Felipe, 11292

Tenório Cavalcante de Albuquerque, Arcy--SEE: Albuquerque,
Arcy Tenório Cavalcante de,
8307

Tenório d'Albuquerque, Arcy--
SEE: Albuquerque, Arcy Tenório Cavalcante de, 8307

T'ēoléolian, Minas, 10856

Terán, José María Martínez-Hidalgo y--SEE: Martínez-Hidalgo, José María, 11996

Tersen, Emile, 8882

Terziiski, Petŭr, 8620

Texas Historical Society, 9966

Thaarup, Frederik, 8827

Thackeray, Sir Edward Talbot,
12072a

Thái Văn Kiêm, 9999

Thailand. National Assembly--
SEE: Thailand. Sathāban Ban-
dit Phatthana Bǫrihān Sāt.
Samnak Wichai, 9732

Thailand. Sathāban Bandit Phatthana Bǫrihān Sāt. Samnak
Wichai, 9732

Tharel, A., 12031

Thelen, Fritz, 10494

Théoléoléan, Minas--SEE:
T'ēoléolian, Minas, 10856

Thesing, Curt Egon, 11897

Thiel, Pieter Jacobus Johannes
van, 10713

Thierman, Lois Mary, 10905

Thomas, Eugen A., 11889

Thōmopoulos, Sōz, 9214

Thompson, Donald Eugene, 10834

Thompson, Godfrey, 9175

Thompson, Kenneth, 10495

Thompson, Oscar, 10496

Thompson, Virginia McLean, 8526, 8800

Thoms, James R., 8672

Thomsen, Henrik, 11539

Thomson, David, 10356

Thomson, Kathleen, 8548

Thomson, Virgil, 10587

Thorlby, Anthony, 10795

Thorne, J. O., 8315

Thornton, John Leonard, 11368

Thornton, Lynne, 10110

Thorpe, Burton Lee, 11526

Thuile, Jean, 10311

Thuilier, René, 11764

Thuillier, René--SEE: Thuilier, René, 11764

Thyssen, Aksel, 12039

Tiedemann, Eva, 11068

Tiedemann, Manfred von, 9067

T'ien, Chi-tsung, 8700

Tiesler, Kurt, 9113

Time-Life Books, 12094

The Times, London, 8470, 9157

Times-Picayune, 9892

Ting, Fu-pao. Ch'üan Han San-kuo Chin Nan-pei ch'ao shih. (Indexes), 10914

Tirranen, Hertta, 10105

Tisseron, Louis, 8961-8963

Tiul'nikov, L. K., 9604

Tobolka, Zdeněk Václav, 10948

Todisco, Umberto, 8964

Toldy, Ferencz, 11091

Tolstoĭ, Ivan Ivanovich, 9579

Tomasini, Jacopo Filippo, 9364

Tomek, Vaclav Vladivoj, Ritter von, 10951

Tōō Nippō Sha, Aomori, Japan, 9398

Tooley, Ronald Vere, 12007

T'op'ch'yan, Ed., 10855

Toppin, Edgar Allan, 9830

Topsoe-Jensen, Theodor Andreas, 8833

Toradze, Gulbat Grigor'evich, 10536

Torbado, Jesús, 10456

Toriyama, Toyayasu, 8613

Torlopov, Georgiĭ Ivanovich, 11269

Toro Ruiz, I., 8839

Torre, Arturo Costa de la--SEE: Costa de la Torre, Arturo, 8582

Torrents, Fernando Cabedo--SEE: Cabedo Torrents, Fernando, 9690

Torres, Enrique Cordero y--SEE: Cordero y Torres, Enrique, 11172

T'o-t'o. Liao shih. (Indexes), 8703

Tovar, Federico Ribes--SEE: Ribes Tovar, Federico, 9555

Toye, William, 8657

Tracou, Jean, 8932

Trân-văn-Giáp, 11293

Treichel, Irena, 11352

Treichl, Fritz, 9084

Treves, firm, publishers, Milan--SEE: Fratelli Treves, Milan, 9353-9355

Trevisani, Carlo, 11130

Troeyer, Benjamin de, 11784

Trofimov, Ivan Trofimovich, 11230

Troiănova, B. Bozhinova--SEE: Bozhinova-Troiănova, B., 11416

Troisi, Luigi, 11131

Trojanowska, Izabella, 9535

Trudeau, Paul Albert, 11633

Truhlář, Antonín, 11153

Truitt, Evelyn Mack, 10357

Trujillo, Carlos A. Echánove--SEE: Echánove Trujillo, Carlos A., 11936

Trujillo, Rubén Buitrago--SEE: Buitrago Trujillo, Rubén, 11735

Truscott, Alan F., 10614

Ts'ai, Chin-chung, 10095, 10914

TSamerian, Ivan Petrovich, 11570

Tsan-ning. Sung kao sêng chuan, 11569

Tsêng, Chi-hung, 10931

Tsitselēs, Ēlias A., 9215

Tsitselis, Ilias A. --SEE: Tsitelēs, Ēlias A., 9215

Tsou, I, 8774

Tsung, Neng-cheng, 8775

Tu, Lien-chê, 8693, 8701

Tu, Ta-kuei, 8776-8777

Tu, Yüan-tsai, 8733

Tudeer, Lauri Oskar Theodor, 10681

Tübingen. Universität. Corps Suevia, 9717

Tumanov, G. M., 9601

Tumpić, Mihael, 11738

Tung, Ch'i-sheng, 10675

Tunney, Christopher, 8471

Tupper, Henry Allen, 11590

Turconi, Davide, 10358

Turcotte, Gustave, 8685

Turkaev, Kh. V., 11218

Turov, V., 10934

Tuvinskaiă respublikanskaiă biblioteka im. A. S. Pushkina, 11248

Tuvinskii nauchno-issledovatel'skii institut iăzyka, literatury i istorii, 11248

Tych, Feliks, 11981

Tyler, Albert Franklin, 11516

Tyronne, Pierre François Marie Massey de--SEE: Massey de Tyronne, Pierre François Marie, 8933

Ueda, Osamu, 10186

Ugarte Elespuru, Juan Manuel, 10199

Ughi, Luigi, 9372

Uhrskov, Tage, 12078

Uhse, Erdmann, 11619

Ujević, Mate, 8366

Ujifusa, Grant, 9769-9770

'Umar Ridā Kahhālah--SEE: Kahhālah, 'Umar Rida, 9318, 10841

Umeda, Yoshihiko, 11867

Umehara, Kaoru, 8702

Underwood, Felix Joel, 11517

Ungar, Frederick, 10771, 10865

Unger, Leonard, 10817

Union Research Institute, Kowloon--SEE: Yu lien yen chiu so, Kowloon, 8784

Union Saint-Jean-Baptiste d'Amérique, 9832

United Methodist Church. Commission on Archives and History, 11814

United Nations Educational, Scientific and Cultural Organization. Centro Regional para el Fomento de la Ciencia en América Latina--SEE: United Nations Educational, Scientific and Cultural Organization. Regional Center for the Advancement of Science in Latin America, 11906

United Nations Educational, Scientific and Cultural Organization. Regional Center for the Advancement of Science in Latin America, 11906

United States. Architect of the Capitol, 9833

United States. Central Intelligence Agency, 8803, 10001, 10719

United States. Civil Service Commission. Library, 9834

United States. Congress, 9835

United States. Congress. House. Committee on Science and Technology, 12060

United States. Congress. Senate. Committee on Veterans' Affairs, 9836

United States. Consulate General, Hongkong, 8778

United States. Dept. of State. Office of External Research, 10001

United States. Dept. of the Army. Chief of Military History, 8711

United States. Dept. of the Interior. Indian Arts and Crafts Board--SEE: United States. Indian Arts and Crafts Board, 10239, 10254

United States. Indian Arts and Crafts Board, 10239, 10254

United States. Joint Publications Research Service, 9477, 11914

United States. Library of Congress, 11421, 11476

United States. Library of Congress. Hispanic Foundation, 11940

Usaybi'ah, Ahmad ibn al-Qāsim ibn Abī--SEE: Ibn Abī Usaybi'ah, Ahmad ibn al-Qāsim, 11411a

Usher, Roland Greene, 11823

Usmani, M. Wasil, 11351

Uspenskiĭ, Aleksandr Ivanovich, 10210

Utlandssvenskarnas förening, 9718

Uzbekiston SSR fanlar akademiiāsi--SEE: Akademiiā nauk Uzbekskoĭ SSR, Tashkent, 9988

Vacca, Virginia, 9331

Vaičiulaitis, Antanas, 11163

Vaillancourt, Émile, 8686

Vainkop, IŪlian IĀkovlevich, 10497

Vaisse, Emilio, 10910

Valdizán, Hermilio, 11468

Valentini, Eugenio, 11705

Valero, José Ramón de Lahoz y Sánchez de--SEE: Lahoz y Sánchez de Valero, José Ramón de, 9664

Valero-Ribas, Jaime, 11375

Valko, William G., 8473

Valle, Rafael Heliodoro, 11781

Vallée, Louis, 11831

Valles, Roberto, 11170

Valori, Aldo, 9365

Valsecchi, Marco, 10066

Van Devanter, Ann C., 10255

Van Doren, Charles Lincoln, 9839, 9842

Vannini de Gerulewicz, Marisa, 9995

Vannucci, Atto, 9366

Van Tassel, Charles Sumner, 9930, 9933-9935

Vaquero, Quintín Aldea--SEE: Aldea Vaquero, Quintín, 11791

Varas, Carlos Poblete--SEE: Poblete Varas, Carlos, 10482

Verela Velásquez, Margarita, 11353

Vargas, Francisco Alejandro, 9996

Váross, Marian, 10214

Vasant Sitaram Kulkarni--SEE: Kulkarni, Vasant Sitaram, 9245

Vasconcellos, José Marcellino Pereira de, 8614

Vass, Henrik, 11949

Vaughn, Napoleon M., 9949

Vavroušek, Bohumil, 10955

Veats, Sydney H., 9558

Vecchietti, Filippo, 11132

Vega E, M., 8688g

Vega, Maximiliano López de--SEE: López de Vega, Maximiliano, 11207

Velasco, Alfonso Cobo--SEE: Cobo Velasco, Alfonso, 8793

Velásquez, Margarita Varela--SEE: Varela Velásquez, Margarita, 11353

Velikov, St., 10897

Venezuela. Archivo General de la Nación, 9997

Venezuela. Ministerio de Agricultura y Cría, 12057

Venkata Subbarao, Eka--SEE: Subbarao, Eka Venkata, 10590

Venkatesa Sangali--SEE: Sangali, Venkatesa, 11145

Venkov, Boris Stepanovich, 9597

Verein Deutscher Ingenieure, 12033

Vereinigung Österreichischer Bibliothekare, 11339

Verly, Hippolyte, 9012

Vernazza, Giuseppe, barone di Freney, 11354

Vernepliktige sjøofficerers forening, 9510

Versins, Pierre, 10805

Veselinov, G., 11241

Veselovskiĭ, Aleksandr, 9622

Veselovskiĭ, Aleksei, 9622

Vexler, Robert I., 9840

Vézina, Élie, 9832

Vezzosi, Antonio Francesco, 11706

Viazzi, Cesare, 9374

Vicens Vives, Jaime, 8381

Vicent y Portillo, Gregorio, •9687

Victoria, University of--SEE: University of Victoria, 10085

Victoria and Albert Museum, South Kensington, 10067

Vidal, Antoine, 10514

Vidyalankar, Sashi Bhushan, 11838

Vienna. Amt für Kultur, Volksbildung und Schulverwaltung, 10869

Vienna. Nationalbibliothek, 11339

Vienna. Universität. Dr. Josef Brettauer-Stiftung, 11361

Vier, Jacques, 11035

Vierordt, Hermann, 11409

Vigouroux, Fulcran Grégoire, 11620

Villain de Saint-Hilaire, Amable, 10383

Villa López, Francisco, 10941

Villas-Bôas, Pedro, 8615

Villavisencio, Carlos A. Barreto --SEE: Barreto Villavisencio, Carlos A., 9520

Villegas, Gonzalo Uribe--SEE: Uribe Villegas, Gonzalo, 11737

Villemessant, Jean Hippolyte Cartier de, 8872

Villena, Guillermo Lohmann-- SEE: Lohmann Villena, Guillermo, 9524

Villepelet, Ferdinand, 9038

Villiers, Christoffel Coetzee de, 9661

Vincent, Benjamin, 8382

Vinet, Bernard, 11036

Vinson, James, 10806-10807, 10968

Vinton, John, 10454

Virchow, Martin, 10395

Virendra Kumar, 11093

Virginia. State Library, Richmond, 9973

Virginia Association of Teachers of English, 10833

Virginia State Library--SEE: Virginia. State Library, Richmond, 9973

Virloys, Charles François Roland le--SEE: Roland le Virloys, Charles François, 10272

Vissh meditsinski institut I. P. Pavlov, 11416

Vita, Carlo de--SEE: De Vita, Carlo, 12079

Vitaitis, Stasys E., 9806

Viterbo, Francisco Marques de Sousa--SEE: Sousa Viterbo, Francisco Marques de, 10561

Vitolinš, Jēkabs, 10554

Vives, José, 11791

Vives, Jaime Vicens--SEE: Vicens Vives, Jaime, 8381

Vives Gartell, José--SEE: Vives, José, 11791

Vizoso Gorostiaga, Manuel de, 8494

Vlček, Jaroslav, 11244

Vocs, Voja Stojanović--SEE: Stojanović-Voks, Voja, 9650

Vodička, Felix, 11238

Voelkel, Titus, 11554

Vogl, Ferenc, 10406

Voigt, Mikuláš Adaukt, 8810

Voit, Max, 10695

Vokhrysheva, M. G., 11230a

Voks, Voja Stojanović--SEE: Stojanović-Voks, Voja, 9650

Volger, Bruno, 9129

Vollenweider, Marie Louise, 9567

Volta, Leopoldo Cammillo, 9379

Vol'tsenburg, Oskar Eduardovich, 10206

Vondruška, Isidor, 11740

Vorepierre, Jean François Marie Bertet Dupiney de--SEE: Dupiney de Vorepierre, Jean François Marie Bertet, 8328

Vormweg, Heinrich, 11047

Vorob'eva, T. A., 11221

Vretos, Andreas Papadopoulos, 11078

Vsesoiuznyi gosudarstvennyi fond kinofil'mov, 11229

Vučković, Mihajlo, 11991

Vuorisalo, K. K., 11310

Vutkovich, Sándor, 11086

Wachholtz, Florence, 9854

Wadād al-Qadī--SEE: al-Qadī, Wadād, 9310

Wadding, Luke, 11707

Waddy, Ruth G., 10248

Wageman, Thomas Charles, 10399

Wainwright, Nicholas B., 9820

Waite, Arthur Edward, 8474

Wakeman, Geoffrey, 11355

Wakeman, John, 10808

Waki', Muhammad ibn Khalaf, 11323

Wakimizu, Ken'ya, 11134

Walderkranz, Rune, 10360

Walden, Aaron, 9436

Walker Art Gallery, Liverpool --SEE: Liverpool. Public Libraries and Art Gallery. Walker Art Gallery, 10116

Wall, Alexander James, 9759

Wall, Bob, 10635

Wallace Collection, London, 10068

Wallraf-Richartz-Museum, Cologne--SEE: Cologne. Wallraf-Richartz-Museum, 10050

Walls, William Jacob, 11817

Walsh, James Joseph, 11518

Walsh, Thomas, 10809

Walter, Rudolf, 10503

Walters Art Gallery, Baltimore, 10180

Wandycz, Damian S., 9841

Wang, Chi-p'ei, 8703

Wang, Giuseppe, 11733

Wang, Hui-tsu, 8703

Wang, Kung-chi, 8736

Wang, Kuo-fan, 8790

Wang, Pao-hsien, 8704

Wang, Ping-hsieh, 8779

Wang, Tsu-i, 8705

Wanscher, Johan Henrik, 12041

Ward, Alfred Charles, 10810

Ward, John Owen, 10490

Ward, Martha Eads, 10069

Wardle, P., 8539

Waring, Joseph Ioor, 11519

Wark, K. R., 11769

Warner, Ezra J., 9960

Warrington, John, 8407

Warsaw. Akademia Nauk Technicznych--SEE: Akademia Nauk Technicznych, Warsaw, 12024

Warsaw. Museum Historyczne--SEE: Museum Historyczne, Warsaw, 9534

Washington, D. C. National Portrait Gallery--SEE: National Portrait Gallery, Washington, D. C., 9756, 10255

Washio, Junkei, 11568

Wasserberger, Igor, 10498

Wasserman, Paul, 11988

Waters, Clara Erskine Clement, 11621

Waters, Grant M., 10144

Waterson, Duncan Bruce, 8549

Watt, Donald Elmslie Robertson, 11789

Wattenbach, Wilhelm, 9069

Webb, Douglas, 8662, 8688

Webb, Edna Lenore--SEE: Huff, Edna Lenore (Webb), 9792

Webb, Mary Griffin, 9792

Webb, Emil, 8475

Weber, Ingrid, 10305

Weberstadt, Hans, 9098

Webster, Daisy de Jong, 8664

Webster Groves, Mo. Gallery
of Living Catholic Authors,
10811

Wegele, Franz Xaver von, 9071

Wegmann, Dietrich, 9132

Wehle, Harry Brandeis, 10256

Weinfeld, Eduardo, 9424

Weinschenk, Harry Erwin, 10396

Weisfert, Julius Nicolaus, 9114

Weiss, Anne, 10823

Weiss, Evelyn, 10050

Weiss, Irving, 10823

Weiss, Karl, 11069

Weissenbäck, Andreas, 10499

Weissman, Julia, 10247

Welding, Olaf, 8574

Weller, Allen Stuart, 10250

Wendell, Leslie, 10729

Wenz, Richard, 10696

Werner, Richard Maria, 10875

Wernicke, Rudolf, 8570

Wesleyan University, Middletown, Conn., 9843

Wessels, Cornelius, 11782

West India Reference Library--
SEE: Institute of Jamaica,
Kingston. West India Refer-
ence Library, 9394

Westergaard, Peder Basse
Christian, 8821

Westerlund, Adolf Wilhelm,
11313-11314

Western Historical Company,
Chicago, 9900

Western States Historical Publishers, 9904

Westphal, Margarethe, 9070

Westrup, Sir Jack Allan, 10449

Weszprémi, István, 11454

White, Frank F., 9895

Whitfield, Danny J., 10000

Whitfield, Richard Noble, 11517

Whitington, Don, 8550

Whitrow, Magda, 11870

Whittlesea, Michael, 9155

Who's Who in Mexico, 9483

Wichita Historical Museum Association, 9983

Wichmann, Christian August,
8387

Wickes, Stephen, 11520

Widmann, Horst, 10697

Widstrand, Axel, 11489

Wieczynski, Joseph L., 9590

Wiedemann, Erik, 10497

Wieger, Léon, 8782

Wien--SEE: Vienna.

Wiener Gesellschaft, 8552

Wood, John Clairmont, 10146

Woodcock, Percival George, 8408

Woodhouse, Charles Platten, 10147

Woodward, Bernard Boling-broke, 8390

Worcester Art Museum, 10070

The World (New York, 1860-1931), 10836

World Methodist Council, 11814

World's Fair, 1964-1965--SEE: New York (City). World's Fair, 1964-1965.

Wretholm, Eugen, 10226

Wright, Arnold, 9706

Wright, Brian, 10638

Wright, Frances Valentine, 10835

Wright, Frederick Adam, 8398

Wright, George Frederick, 9941

Wright, Philip, 9395

Wu, Hsiang-hsiang, 9730

Wüstenfeld, Heinrich Ferdinand, 9327, 10707

Wurzbach, Alfred Wolfgang, Ritter von Tannenberg, 8573

Wylie, Alexander, 11832

Wynn, Kenneth G., 9164

Wyoming Historical Institute, 9984

al-Yaghmūri, Yūsuf ibn Ahmad al-Hāfiz--SEE: al-Hāfiz al-Yaghmūri, Yūsuf ibn Ahmad, 10843

Yahni, Roberto, 10849

Yahya ibn Sharaf, Muhyi al-Dīn Abu Zakariyā, al-Nawawī--SEE: al-Nawawī, 9327

Yakutsk, Siberia. Respublikan-skaia biblioteka, 10006

Yale University. Library, 9748

Yamamoto, Teijirō, 10098

Yanai, Kenji, 8377

Yang, Chiao-lo, 8706

Yang, Lu-jung, 8783

Yāqūt ibn 'Abd Allāh al Hamawī, 10847

Yearns, Wilfred Buck, 9960

Yen, K'o-chün, 10911

Yen, K'o-chün. Ch'üan Shang ku San tai Ch'in Han San kuo Liu ch'ao wên. (Indexes), 10915

Yen-ching ta hsüeh, Peking, 10911

Yen-ching ta hsüeh, Peking. Yin tê pien tsuan ch'u, 8698, 8700-8701, 8707-8708, 8777, 10095, 10914, 10916-10918

Yi, Hong-jik, 9446

Yi, Hŭi-sŭng, 9441

Yi, Ka-wŏn, 9447

Yi, Sŏng-ho, 8391

Yi, Wŏn-gi, 10550

Ying, Wei-ch'ih, 9731

Yoell, John H., 10566

Yoshia, Teruji, 10189

Young, Henry, 8304

Young, William C., 10361

Young Men's Christian Association. Great Britain, 9178

Yü, Ch'ien, 11569

Yü, Min-chung, 8724

Yü-hsing. Ming kao sêng chuan,
11569

Yu lien yen chiu so, Kowloon,
8784

Yüan, Chih, 8785

Yüan, Yeong-jinn--SEE: Yüan,
Yung-chin, 10923

Yüan, Yung-chin, 10923

Yunesuko Higashi Ajia Bunka
Kenkyu Senta, Tokyo, 10664

Yūsūf ibn Aḥmad al-Ḥāfiz al-
Yaghmūri--SEE: al-Ḥāfiz al-
Yaghmūri, Yūsūf ibn Ahmad,
10843

Yūsuf ibn al-Zaki 'Abd Rahmān
al-Mizzī--SEE: al-Mizzī,
Yūsuf ibn al-Zaki 'Abd Rāh-
man, 11845

Zabārah, Muhammad ibn Muhammad, 10008

Zabiras, Geōrgios Ioannou,
10079

Zacatecas, Mexico (City). Apos-
tólico Colegio de Nuestro
Señora de Guadelupe--SEE:
Apostólico Colegio de Nuestra
Señora de Guadelupe, 11802

Zádor, Anna, 10035

Zagreb. Leksikografski zavod
FNRJ--SEE: Leksikografski
zavod FNRJ, Zagreb, 8366

Zahn, Peter, 9119

Zaidān, Jurjī--SEE: Zaydan,
Jirji, 9333

Žakovský, Richard, 8439

Zakrzewski, Zbigniew, 9539

Zand, Mikhail Isaakovich, 11271

Zannandreis, Diego, 10179

Zapata Cuéncar, Heriberto,
10530-10531

Zapriānov, N., 11410

Zarev, Pantalei, 10669

Zaverio, Francesco (de S. Lorenzo della Costa), 11777

Zaydan, Jirji, 9333

Zazo, Alfredo, 9386

Zdobnov, Nikolai Vasil'evich,
11231

Zeeuwsch Genootschap der Weten-
schappen, Middleburg, 9494

Zegel, Vikki A., 12060

Zeidler, Jakob, 10873

Zell, Hans M., 10814

Zeri, Frederico, 10180

Zernov, Nicolas, 11232

Zernov, Nikolai--SEE: Zernov,
Nicolas, 11232

Ziebarth, Erich Gustav Ludwig,
8399

Zieliński, Stanisław, 12008

Ziemke, Hans-Joachim, 10055

Zimmermann, Alfons M., 11708

Zimmermann, Paul, 10692

Zinglersen, Bent, 8834

TITLE INDEX

al-A'lām ... , 9334

A'lām an'nisā' fī ālamay al-'Arab wa al-Islām, 9318

Album Academiae Helmstadiensis, 10692

Album academicum des Polytechnikums zu Riga, 12025

Album-contemporain, 8924

Album de Boyacá, 8798

Album de la colonie française au Chili, 8688g

Album di 57 (cinquantasette) ritratti di scienziati, 11873

Album Lettonorum, 9456

Album musical, 10474

Album of biography and art, 8343

Album of Canadian mayors, 8633

Album of great outstanding and eminent personalities of Russia, 9595

Album of photographs of musicians, 10443

Album of the fellows of the American Gynecological Society, 11492

Album of the Michigan State officers and Legislature (1877-8), 9898

Album van Suid-Afrikaanse volksfigure, 9658

Album významných výročí a osobností ZSSR, 9593

Album zasłuźonych lekarzy polskich, 11469

The Aldine centennial history of New South Wales, 8542

The Aldine history of Queensland, 8543

Algunos seudónimos dominicanos, 10958

Alicantinos ilustres, 9682

Allgemeine deutsche Biographie, 9071

Allgemeines Gelehrten-Lexikon, 10656

Allgemeines Handwörterbuch der philosophischen Wissenschaften, 11542

The Almanac of American politics, 9769-9770

Almanach československých právníků, 11307

Almanakh na Sofiĭskiia universitet Sv. Kliment Okhridski, 10670

Alpes Maritimes (et principauté de Monaco), 8969

Alphabetarion, 11285

Alphabetical list of the Honourable East India Company's civil servants, 9151

Alphabetisches Verzeichnis zum Kao sêng ch'uan, 11560

Alt-Köln-Lexikon, 9110

Altösterreichische Unternehmer, 11954

Altpreussische Biographie, 9121

Die Altwiener Maler. English, 10074

Alumni record of Wesleyan University, 9843

Am Quell der Muttersprache, 10867

Amar jīvan, 9253

Annuaire bio-bibliographique
des jeunes écrivains de
France, 10999

Annuaire biographique (années
1830-1834), 8413

Annuaire biographique des artistes français, 10109

Annuaire biographique et descriptif de la France, 8870

Annuaire de l'Académie française, 8869

Annuaire des artistes français,
10109

Annuaire des états d'Afrique
Noire, 8484

Annuaire du spectacle, 10377

Annuaire du théâtre, musique,
radio, télévision, 10377

Annuaire général du spectacle
en France, 10377

Annuaire historique et biographique des souverains, 8414

Annuaire parlementaire des
états d'Afrique Noire, 8484a

Annuaire statistique des artistes
français, 10109

Annuaire suisse du monde et
des affaires, 9719

Annual directory of the psychic
register international, 11555

An Annual of new art and artists,
10015

Annuario svizzero del mondo e
degli affari, 9719

Año cristiano, 11678

Año seráfico, 11665

Gli Anonimi veronesi, 11101

Anónimos y seudónimos hispano-
americanos, 11154

'Anshe ha-'aliyah ha-sheniyah,
9419

Anshe shem ..., 11859

Ansiklopedik sinema sözlügö,
10345

Antecedentes biográficos santi-
agueños, 8509

Anthems and anthem composers,
10541

Anthropologists in India, 12018

The Antique buyer's dictionary
of names, 10019

Das Antlitz des germanischen
Aerztes in vier Jahrhunderten,
11443

Antología artística colombiana,
10099

Antología crítica de la poesía
colombiana, 10939

Antología de escritores nicolai-
tas, 11171

Antología de la poesía en Colombia, 10940

Antología de la poesía latino-
americana (1950-1970), 11156

Antología de poesía amorosa
contemporánea, 11252

Antología de poetas valencianos,
10894

Antologia dei poeti, narratori,
scrittori d'Italia (al 1971),
11113

Antología general de la poesía
panameña, 11182

Anuário artístico e literário de
Portugal, 11199

Bibliographie des Bénédictines de la Congrégation de France, 11744

Bibliographie des Clerus der Diöcese Linz, 11713

Bibliographie des Clerus der Diöcese St. Pölten, 11712

Bibliographie des Missionaires oblats de Marie Immaculée, 11640

Bibliographie des recueils biographiques de contemporains, 8863

Bibliographie des recueils collectifs de poésies publiés (de 1597 à 1700), 11015

Bibliographie des sciences médicales, 11365

Bibliographie générale de l'Agenais, 8965

Bibliographie générale du Perigord, 9038

Bibliographie hellénique, 11077

Bibliographie iconographique du Lyonnais, 9019

Bibliographie poitevine, 11014

Bibliographie tournaisienne, 10078

Bibliographie zur deutschen Geschichte im Zeitalter der Glaubensspaltung, 9065

Bibliographie zur Geschichte des deutschen Porträts, 9066

Bibliography and research manual on the history of mathematics, 11911

Bibliography of American and Canadian Jewish memoirs, 9755

A Bibliography of biographies and memoirs on Nigeria, 9500

A Bibliography of British naval history, 9165

Bibliography of persons and books in the Old Testament, 11858

A Bibliography of the Prairie Provinces (to 1953), 8678

The Bibliography of Vermont, 9972

Biblioteca Clarense, 11121

Biblioteca española-portugueza-judaica, 9675

Biblioteca hispano-chilena (1523-1817), 10907

Biblioteca histórica de Cartagena, 9687

Biblioteca Picena, 11132

Bibliotheca Belgica, 10885

Bibliotheca biographica, 8274

Bibliotheca Carpatica, 9222

Bibliotheca Cartvsiana, 11690

Bibliotheca chalcographica, 10749

Bibliotheca classica (Lempriere), 8397

Bibliotheca Dominicana Neerlandica manuscripta, 11783

Bibliotheca Staffordiensis, 10991

Bibliothèque chartraine (Liron), 11019-11020

Bibliothèque chartraine (Merlet), 8992

Bibliothèque d'Anjou, 8972

Biographical and heraldic dictionary of the Catholic bishops in America, 11799

Biographical appearance file of Chinese officials (1951-1967), 8778

A Biographical bibliography of electrical engineers and electrophysicists, 12023

A Biographical chronicle of the English drama (1559-1642), 10970

Biographical cyclopedia of the Catholic hierarchy of the United States (1784-1898), 11801

Biographical dictionaries master index, 8276

A Biographical dictionary of actors, actresses ... in London (1660-1800), 10400

A Biographical dictionary of American civil engineers, 12062

Biographical dictionary of American music, 10579

Biographical dictionary of botanists represented in the Hunt Institute portrait collection, 11901

A Biographical dictionary of film, 10356

The Biographical dictionary of illustrious men, chiefly at the beginning of Islamism, 9327

Biographical dictionary of Japanese literature, 11136

Biographical dictionary of Korean artists and calligraphers, 10191

A Biographical dictionary of leading computer professionals, 11923

A Biographical dictionary of scientists, 11878

A Biographical dictionary of the cinema, 10356

Biographical dictionary of the Comintern, 8448

Biographical dictionary of the Federal judiciary, 11329

Biographical dictionary of Tibet and Tibetan Buddhism, 9734

A Biographical dictionary of wax modellers, 10279

A Biographical dictionary of World War II, 8471

Biographical directory of American labor leaders, 11986

Biographical directory of Americans and Canadians of Croatian descent, 9771

Biographical directory of certified psychologists in Massachusetts, 11545

A Biographical directory of clergymen of the American Lutheran Church, 11805

Biographical directory of members of the International Association for Dental Research, 11525

Biographical directory of Negro ministers, 11623

A Biographical directory of pastors of the American Lutheran Church, 11805, 11807

Biographical directory of the American Congress (1774-1971), 9835

Biographical directory of the members of the Czechoslovak Society of Arts and Sciences in America, inc., 10734

Biographie complète des sénateurs (Clère), 8890

Biographie complète des 300
sénateurs, 8879

Biographie de la Charente-Inférieure (Aunis & Saintonge),
8991

Biographie des condamnés pour
délits politiques, 8918

Biographie des députés (Clère),
8889

Biographie des députés de la
Chambre septennale (de 1824
à 1830), 8933

Biographie des deputés (session
de 1828), 8927

Biographie des hommes illustres
de l'ancienne province du
Limousin, 9014

Biographie des hommes illustres
du départment de la Côte-
d'Or, 8995

Biographie des Malouins célèbres,
9046

Biographie des marins français
contemporains, 8895

Biographie des membres du
Gouvernement révolutionnaire
provisoire de la République
du Sud Viet Nam, 9998

Biographie des peintres flamands
et hollandais, 10106

Biographie des personnages de
Troyes, 8974

Biographie des personnages
notables du département de
l'Ain, 8966

Biographie des personnes remarquables de la Haute-
Auvergne, 8975

Biographie des représentants à
l'Assemblée nationale, 8951

Biographie des sénateurs et des
députés, 8952

Biographie historique et généalogique des hommes ... de Lorraine, 9018

Biographie maritime, 11999

Biographie montpelliéraine, 9023

Biographie nouvelle et complète
des pairs de France, 8955

Biographie rémoise, 9044

Biographie satirique de la nouvelle Chambre des députés,
8934

Biographie satirique des députés,
8935

Biographie universelle des contemporains, 8422

Biographie valenciennoise, 9052

Biographieen solcher Schriftsteller ... welche über die
Thierwelt ... gehandelt haben, 11903

Biographien denkwürdiger Steier-
märker, 8572

Biographien der österreichischen
Dichterinnen, 10874

Biographien und Leichensteinin-
schriften von Rabbinen [etc.],
11859

Biographies aghlabides, 9315

Biographies alsaciennes, 8970

Biographies de Rimouski, 8680

Biographies des artistes japonais,
10183

Biographies des botanistes à
Genève, 11897a

The Catholic encyclopedia (rev. ed.), 11579

The Catholic encyclopedia and its makers, 11645

The Catholic encyclopedia for school and home, 11580

Catholicisme, hier, aujourd'hui, demain, 11646

Cebuano literature, 11187

Celebrità argentine dell'epoca dell'independenza nazionale, 8499

Les Célébrités du jour, 8920

Celebrities of the century, 8464

Celebrity register, 8428

Cem benfeitores da humanidade, 8307

Cenni biografici dei letterati ed artisti friulani, 11124

100 (Cent) ans de chanson française, 10535

Cent ans de représentation bretonne, 8983

Cent poètes, 11029

Centennial history of New South Wales, 8542

Centum illustrium Poloniae scriptorum elogia et vitae, 11198

The Century Italian Renaissance encyclopedia, 9358

A Century of American illustration, 10235

A Century of Missouri music, 10584

Česká literární bibliografie (1945-1963), 10953

Česki spisovatelé dnešni doby, 10949

Československé práce o jazyce, dějinách a kultuře slovanských narodů (od r. 1760), 10676

Českoslovenští koncertni umělci a komorni soubory, 10532

Češti spisovatelé z přelomu 19. a 20. století, 10947

Ceylon State Council (1931), 9695

Chamber's biographical dictionary, 8315

Le Chambre de mil huit cent vingt, 8886

La Chambre de 1889, 8874

La Chambre des députés (1898-1902), 8875

La Chambre des représentants (1894-1895), 8579

Ch'an lin seng pao chuan, 11562

La Charente. Dictionaire biographique et album, 8989

A Chart of British artists, 10136

Chávash pisatelésem, 10932

Checklist of the permanent collection, National Portrait Gallery, Smithsonian Institution, 9756

Cher. Dictionnaire, annuaire et album, 8993

Cheshire, Derbyshire and Staffordshire authors today, 10794

Ch'i chen yeh sheng ch'u chi, 8774

Chi scrive, 11110

Chicorel index to biographies, 8278

Chung-hua chin tai ming jên chuan, 8727

Chung-hua li tai ming chiang chuan, 8748

Chung hua min kuo ming jên chuan chih (4), 11982

Chung-hua min kuo tang tai wên i tso chia ming lu, 10925

Chung i chi wên lu, 8715

Chung kung jên ming lu, 8728

Chung kung jên ming lu. English, 8723

Chung-kuo chin tai hsüeh jên hsiang chuan, 10671

Chung-kuo chin tai jên wu chuan chi tzŭ liao so yin, 8692

Chung-kuo ch'ing nien tang hsün kuo ssŭ nan chi i ku t'ung chih lüeh chuan, 8729

Chung-kuo chu tso chia tz'u tien, 10924

Chung-kuo Fo hsüeh jên ming tz'ŭ tien, 11564

Chung-kuo jen-min cheng-chih hsieh-shang hui-i jen-wu chih, 8781

Chung-kuo jên ming ta tzu tien, 8730

Chung-kuo li tai jên wu p'ing chuan, 8768

Chung-kuo li tai ming jên nien p'u mu lu, 8764

Chung-kuo li tai shu hua chuan ko chia tzŭ hao so yin, 10094

Chung-kuo li tai ti hou hsiang, 8734

Chung kuo li tai ti wang pu hsi hui pien, 8718

Chung-kuo mei shu nien piao, 10092

Chung-kuo ti hao piao t'i i lan, 8694

Chung wai jên ming tz'u tien, 8735

Chung wai jên wu chuan chi, 8736

Church of England year-book, 11625

Chuzhdestranni pisateli na bŭl-garski ezik, 10765

100 (Cien) biografías centro-americanas, 8688a

100 (i. e. Cien) biografías de puertorriqueños ilustres, 9555

Cien dominicanos célebres, 8835

100 (Cien) españoles y Dios, 9674

Las Cien mejores poesías boliv-ianas, 10892

Las Cien mejores poesías de Puerto Rico, 11207

Cien mexicanos y Dios, 9479

Cien músicos de América, 10551

101 (Ciento un) hijos ilustres del reino valenciano, 9690

50 (Cincuenta) semblanzas argen-tinas, 8498

Les 557 (Cinq cents cinquante-sept) députés et leurs pro-grammes électoraux (1881-1885), 8915

Citizens look at Congress, 9823

Civil War books; a critical bib-liography, 9757

Die Classen der hanefitischen Rechtsgelehrten, 11317

Die Deutschen Bischöfe bis zu Ende des 16. Jahrhunderts, 11765

Die Deutschen Dichter der Neuzeit und Gegenwart, 11060

Die Deutschen Geburtshelferschulen, 11442

Die Deutschen Kanzelredner, 11583

Deutscher Chirurgen-Kalender, 11440

Deutscher Dichterwald, 11064

Deutscher Literaturatlas, 11055a

Deutsches Bühnen-Jahrbuch, 10392

Deutsches Dichterbuch aus Oesterreich, 10862

Deutsches Soldatentum; 100 Lebensbilder, 9092

Deutschlands Geschichtsquellen im Mittelalter, 9069

Deutschlands Olympiakämpfer 1928 in Wort und Bild, 10598

Deutschlands, Österreich-Ungarns und der Schweiz Musiker in Wort und Bild, 10537

Deux-Sèvres. Dictionnaire biographique et album, 8999

Devon, Dorset and Somerset authors today, 10975

Devonshire leaders, 9182

al-Dhayl 'alā Raf' al-isr, 11322

Diarium patrum, fratrum et sororum ordinis Minimorum Provinciae Franciae, 11764

Diccionario bio-bibliográfico de filósofos, 11546

Diccionario biográfico (Buenos Aires), 8502

Diccionario biográfico brasileiro, 8592

Diccionario biográfico contemporáneo sud-americano, 9662

Diccionario biográfico de claros varones de Vizcaya, 9692

Diccionario biográfico de contemporáneos sud-americanos, 9663

Diccionario biográfico de Costa Rica, 8801

Diccionario biográfico de figuras contemporáneas, 9520

Diccionario biográfico de hombres ilustres, 8320

Diccionario biográfico de las artes plásticas en Venezuela, 10258

Diccionario biográfico de médicos venezolanos, 11521

Diccionario biográfico de México, 9470

Diccionario biográfico del campo argentino, 12051

Diccionario biográfico español contemporáneo, 9670

Diccionario biográfico-histórico dominicano, 8836

Diccionario biográfico médico mundial, 11485

Diccionario crítico del arte español contemporáneo, 10218

Diccionario de artes gráficas, 11349a

Diccionario de astronomía y astronáutica, 11929

Diccionario de autoridades médicas, 11482

Diccionario de boyacenses ilustres, 8794

Diccionario de celebridades musicales, 10478

Diccionario de escritores gaditanos, 11258

Diccionario de historia eclesiástica de España, 11791

Diccionario de la literatura ecuatoriana, 10962

Diccionario de la música, 10482

Diccionario de las artes plásticas en Venezuela, 10258

Diccionario de literatura española, 11253

Diccionario de los papas, 11651

Diccionario de medicina peruana, 11468

Diccionario de pedagogía, 10662

Diccionario de santos, 11652

Diccionario de seudónimos peruanos, 11185

Diccionario de sociología, 11936

Diccionario del hogar católico, 11653

Diccionario del mundo clásico, 8394

Diccionario enciclopédico de la guerra, 8355

Diccionario enciclopédico de las Américas, 8493

Diccionario enciclopédico regional del Estado de Coahuila, 9472

Diccionario general de la literatura venezolana, 11290

Diccionario geográfico, estadístico, histórico de la isla de Cuba, 8804

Diccionario histórico biográfico de los conquistadores del Perú, 9522

Diccionario histórico, biográfico, geográfico e industrial de la República (Mexico), 9480

Diccionario historico e geographico do Paraná, 8602

Diccionario histórico geográfico de Tacna, 9521

Diccionario historico, geographico e ethnographico do Brasil, 8601

Diccionario médico argentino, 11412

Diccionario Porrúa de historia, biografía y geografía de México, 9471

Diccionario taurino, 10613

Diccionario teatral del Perú, 10414

Diccionario teatral del Río de la Plata, 10362

Diccionario universal de historia y de geografía (Madrid), 8321

Diccionario universal de historia y de geografía (México), 8322

Diccionario y cronología histórica americana, 8494

Dichter aus Österreich, 10868

Dichter im deutschen Schulhaus, 10696

Dichter und Schriftsteller der Heimat, 11265

Dichtung und Dichter der Zeit, 11067

Dicionário amazonense de biografias, 8591

Dicionário bibliográfico portugues, Aditamentos ao, 9544

Dicionário bio-bibliográfico brasileiro de escritores médicos, 11415

Dicionário biográfico mato-grossense, 8604

Dicionário brasileiro de artistas plásticos, 10080

Dicionário das artes plásticas no Brasil, 10082

Dicionário de história do Brasil, 8598

Dicionário de história de Portugal, 9550

Dicionário de sociologia, 11935

Dicionário histórico das ruas do Rio de Janeiro, 8590

Dicionário histórico e literário do teatro do Brasil, 10371

Dictionar al literaturii franceze, 11008

Dictionar al marilor dregatori din Tara Româneasca si Moldova, 9574

Dictionarul contimporanilor din România (1800-1898), 9573

Dictionarul de literatura româna, 11209

Dictionary of African biography, 8486

A Dictionary of all the principal names and terms relating to the geography, topography, history ... of antiquity, 8397

Dictionary of American biography, 9782

Dictionary of American painters, sculptors and engravers, 10243

Dictionary of American philosophy, 11548

A Dictionary of American politics, 9775

A Dictionary of anonymous and pseudonymous Swedish literature, 11260

A Dictionary of architecture (Pevsner), 10270

A Dictionary of art and artists (Burma), 10083

Dictionary of art and artists in Southern California (before 1930), 10249

A Dictionary of artists of the English school from the Middle Ages to the nineteenth century, 10143

A Dictionary of Asia, 8523

The Dictionary of Australian bushrangers, 8541

A Dictionary of Australian history, 8528

A Dictionary of ballet (Wilson), 10360

A Dictionary of biography (Robinson), 8370

A Dictionary of biography, past and present (Vincent), 8382

Dictionary of Black culture, 8311

Dictionary of pseudonyms and pen names, 10965

Dictionary of pseudonyms in Indian literature, 11093

Dictionary of Scandinavian biography, 9631

A Dictionary of surrealism, 10039

A Dictionary of twentieth-century composers, 10495

Dictionary of Victorian painters, 10145

A Dictionary of watercolour painters, 10137

A Dictionary of world economists, past and present, 11947

Dictionary of world history, 8323

The Dictionary of world pottery and porcelain, 10282

Dictionnaire abrégé de peinture et d'architecture, 10034

Dictionnaire, annuaire et album de la Charente-Inférieure, 8990

Dictionnaire, annuaire et album des Bouches-du-Rhône, 8980

Dictionnaire bibliographique du Canada français, 11037

Dictionnaire bio-bibliographique des auteurs du pays creusois, 11001a

Dictionnaire bio-bibliographique du Dahomey, 8815

Dictionnaire biographique d'Alsace, 8971

Dictionnaire biographique de l'ancien département de la Moselle, 9025

Dictionnaire biographique de la province de Liège, 8580

Dictionnaire biographique des agriculteurs de France, 12053

Dictionnaire biographique des inventeurs, ingénieurs et constructeurs, 12030

Dictionnaire biographique des personnages notables du département de l'Ain, 8967

Dictionnaire biographique du département du Pas-de-Calais, 9037

Dictionnaire biographique du mouvement ouvrier international, 11948

Dictionnaire biographique et album de l'Isère, 9010

Dictionnaire biographique international des naturalistes, 11896

Dictionnaire critique du théâtre québécois, 10374

Dictionnaire d'architecture, 10272

Dictionnaire d'ascétisme, 11596

Dictionnaire de biographie générale (Joubert), 8349

Dictionnaire de danse, 10316

Dictionnaire de la Bible (Spol), 11618

Dictionnaire de la Bible (Vigouroux), 11620

Dictionnaire de la Commune, 8941

Dictionnaire de la Franc-maçonmerie et des Franc-maçons, 8360

Dictionnaire portatif des femmes célèbres, 8351

Dictionnaire portatif des prédicateurs français, 11741

Dictionnaire portatif historique et littéraire des théâtres, 10384

Dictionnaire topographique, historique, biographique ... du Vendômois, 9054

Dictionnaire universel de la franc-maçonnerie, 8450

Dictionnaire universel et classique d'histoire et de géographie, 8324

Les Dictionnaires départementaux, 8969, 8978-8980, 8989-8990, 8993, 8999, 9001-9002, 9007, 9009-9010, 9021-9022, 9024, 9028-9029, 9031-9032, 9042, 9049-9050, 9053, 9055

Die Israel führen, 9335

Le Diocèse de Trois-Rivières (1962), 11723

Dioceses e bispos do Brasil, 11718

Diócesis y obispos de la iglesia argentina, 11710

The Diplomatic Press Ghana trade directory, 9136

The Diplomatic Service list, 9150

Diplomaticheskii slovar', 8325

Directorio de científicos y profesionales en Colombia, 11879

Directorio de escritores mexicanos, 11175

Directorio latinoamericano de ciencias geológicas, 11906

Directory and who is who of Ghaziabad industries, 11973

Directory & who's who of homoeopathic practitioners, 11455

Directory: Foreign area fellows (1952-1972), 10729

Directory of American scholars, 10727

Directory of contemporary authors of the Republic of China, 10925

Directory of environmental life scientists, 11891

A Directory of Eskimo artists in sculpture and prints, 10103

Directory of fellowships and scholarships (1917-1970), 10661

Directory of Ghana, 9136

Directory of key personnel in public enterprises, 9233

Directory of osteopathic specialists, 11497

Directory of personalities of the Cuban Government, 8803

Directory of the psychic register international, 11555

Directory of the Republic of Ghana, 9136

Directory with Who's who in Liberia, 9459

Discovering music, 10468

I Disegni italiani del Seicento, 10176

Distinguished men of Philadelphia and of Pennsylvania, 9948

Distinguished men of the county (Kinross-shire), 9634

Les Écrivains foréziens du XVIe siècle, 11021

Edgelow's Who's who in British Columbia,

Eerdman's handbook to the Bible, 11587

Eesti kirjandus paguluses, 10995

Effigies virorum ac foeminarum illustrium, 9208

Effigies virorum eruditorum atque artificium Bohemiae et Moraviae, 8806

Ehrenbuch der Röntgenologen und Radiologen aller Nationen, 11925

Ehrentempel verdienter ungarischer Israeliten, 9224

Einführung in der Geschichte des freien Gedankens, 11554

Ekonomicheskaia entsiklopediia, 11943

Elämäkertoja ja muistelmia, 8290

Elef Yehudim ba-'et ha-hadashah, 9423

Eleh ezkerah ... , 11864

Elektroingenjörer i Finland, 12071

El Elemento vasco en el siglo XVIII venezolano, 9989

Les Élites africaines, 8487

Elizabethan recusancy in Cheshire, 11769

Elogia virorum literis & sapientia illustrium ad viuum expressis imaginibus exornata, 9364

L'Émigration militaire: campagne de 1792. Armée des princes, 8945

L'Émigration militaire: campagne de 1792. Armée royale, 8946

L'Émigration militaire; emigrés de Saintonge, 8947

Eminent educationists of India, 10704

Eminent freedom fighters of Punjab, 9274

Eminent Israelites of the nineteenth century, 9433

Eminent Orientalists, 10653

Empire State notables (1914), 9910

Enchiklopediia Sovetike Moldoveniaske, 9484

Enchiridion renatae poesis Latinae in Bohemia et Moravia cultae, 11153

Enciclopedia biográfica de la mujer, 8330

Enciclopedia biografica e bibliografica 'Italiana,' 12084

Enciclopedia cinematográfica mexicana, 10413

Enciclopedia de la Biblia, 11588

Enciclopedia de la literatura, 10769

Enciclopedia de la literatura argentina, 10849

Enciclopedia de la música pop, 10456

Enciclopedia de la religión cathólica, 11661

Enciclopedia dei liguri illustri, 9374

Enciclopedia del cattolico, 11662

Enciclopedia del cristianismo, 11589

Enciclopedia dell'architettura moderna, 10267

Enciclopedia dell'arte Garzanti, 10022

Enciclopedia della letteratura Garzanti, 10770

Enciclopedia della musica Garzanti, 10457

Enciclopedia dello sport, 10593

Enciclopedia Garzanti dell'arte, 10022

Enciclopedia Garzanti della letteratura, 10770

Enciclopedia Garzanti della musica, 10457

Enciclopedia general del mar, 11996

Enciclopedia general ilustrada del país vasco, 9685

Enciclopedia histórica de Portugal, 9541

Enciclopedia ilustrada del cine, 10328

Enciclopedia judaica castellana, 9424

Encyclopedia militare, 8331

Enciclopedia monografica della storia, 8379

Enciclopedia popular cubana, 8802

Enciclopedia regional ilustrada Coahuila, 9472

Enciclopedia Salvat de ciencias médicas, 11375

Enciclopedia universale SEDA dell'arte moderna, 10023

Los Encuentros, 9678

Encyclopedia Canadiana, 8644

Encyclopaedia Judaica, 9425

Encyclopedia Lituanica, 9460

Encyclopedia of American agricultural history, 12055

Encyclopedia of American biography, 9796

Encyclopedia of American history (Kohlmetz), 9787

Encyclopedia of American history (Morris), 9811

Encyclopedia of astronomy, 11931

Encyclopaedia of Australia, 8535

The Encyclopedia of auto racing greats, 10602

Encyclopedia of biography of Connecticut, 9863

An Encyclopedia of Canadian biography, 8645

The Encyclopaedia of Ceylon's prominent personalities, 9704

Encyclopedia of chronology, historical and biographical, 8390

Encyclopaedia of contemporary biography of New York, 9911

Encyclopedia of contemporary biography of Pennsylvania, 9945

The Encyclopedia of country and western music, 10576

Encyclopedia of English and American poets and poetry, 10992

Encyclopedia of espionage, 8468

Encyclopedia of Freemasonry, 8358

Encyclopedia of genealogy and biography of the State of Pennsylvania, 9946

Encyclopedia of golf (Evans), 10624

Encyclopedia of golf, Golf magazine's, 10625

Encyclopaedia of India's struggle for freedom, 9254

Encyclopedia of Latin America, 9450

Encyclopedia of literature (Shipley), 10799

The Encyclopaedia of missions, 11590

Encyclopedia of modern architecture, 10266

Encyclopedia of modern world literature, The Concise, 10754

The Encyclopedia of motor sport, 10603

Encyclopedia of mountaineering, 10636

Encyclopedia of mystery and detection, 10969

Encyclopedia of Ontario, 8676

Encyclopedia of painting, 10051

Encyclopaedia of Papua and New Guinea, 9516

Encyclopedia of pop, rock and soul, 10586

Encyclopedia of rock and roll, 10577

The Encyclopedia of Russian writers, 11214

Encyclopaedia of ship and shipping, 11997

Encyclopedia of Southern Baptists, 11629

Encyclopedia of swimming, 10645

The Encyclopedia of Texas, 9966

Encyclopedia of the American Revolution, 9773

Encyclopaedia of the history and geography of Andhra,

An Encyclopedia of the Old West, 9979

Encyclopedia of the opera (Ewen), 10459

Encyclopedia of the Philippines, 9526

The Encyclopaedia of the Presbyterian Church in the United States of America, 11826

Encyclopedia of the Third Reich, 9097

Encyclopedia of 20th century men's fashions, 10309

Encyclopedia of world biography, The McGraw-Hill, 8357

The Encyclopedia of world boxing championships, 10611

Encyclopedia of world drama, 10785

Encyclopedia of world literature in the 20th century, 10771

The Encyclopedia of world Methodism, 11814

Encyclopedia of Zionism and Israel, 9426

Encyclopaedia Rhodesia, 9557

Encyclopaedic dictionary and directory of education, 10703

Encyclopedic dictionary of Judaica, 9427

Encyclopedic dictionary of the Bible, 11591

Encyclopédie anarchiste, 8436

Gallerie der ausgezeichneten
Israeliten aller Jahrhunderten,
9421

Gallerie der Menschen nach alphabetischer Ordnung, 8306

Gallerie der Zeitgenossen, 9079

Gallerie merkwürdiger Männer
aus der älteren und neueren
Geschichte, 8337

Gallery of Hebrew poets, 11141

The Gallery of Living Catholic
Authors, 10811

The Gallery of one hundred famous portraits of great men
and women, 9156

Gallery of players, 10428

Gallery of plays and players from
the Illustrated American,
10428

Gallia Christiana, 11753

Galveston; history of the island
and the city, 9868

Gandhiji's early contemporaries
and companions, 9256

Gard. Dictionnaire biographique
et album, 9001

Garonne. Dictionnaire biographique et historique illustré,
9002

Gedenkhalle für die Gefallenen
des Dritten Reiches, 9098

Die Geistige Elite Österreichs,
8555

Geistliche Schriftsteller, Künstler und Forscher Österreichs,
8559

Die Gelehrtenbiographien des
Abū 'Ubaidallāh al-Marzubāni,
10843

Gelehrtes Baden, 11051

Gelehrtes Pommer-Land, 11600

Gem dictionary of biography, 8318

Die Gemälde des 19. Jahrhunderts,
10055

Gendai Chūgoku Chosen jimmei
kan, 8751

Gendai Chūgoku jimbutsu hyakusen,
8770

Gendai Chūgoku jimbutsu hyō,
8739

Gendai Chūgoku jimmei jiten,
8740, 8754

Gendai Chūgoku no sakka to saku-
hin, 10927

Gendai sakka jiten, 11135

Gendai Tōa jimmei kan, 8522

Genealogía [de los] hombres de
Mayo, 8508

Genealogías de Antioquia y Caldas,
8791

Genealogies of old South African
families, 9661

Genealogisches Taschenbuch der
Ritter- und Adelsgeschlechter,
9080

Genealogisches Taschenbücher
der adeligen Häuser, 9080

Genealogiske och biografiske
anteckningar hörande till Nor-
rköpings stads historia, 9713

La Generación liberal veracruzana, 9477

General Conference Mennonite
pioneers, 11813

Die Generale der österreichischen
Armee, 8569

Goldschmiedekunst in Königsberg, 10308

Golf magazine's encyclopedia of golf, 10625

Gospel song writers biography, 10575

Gothaer Bibliothekare, 11349

De Gouverneurs-Generaal en Commissarissen-Generaal van Nederlandsch-Indië, 9285

Governadores gerais e vice-reis do Brasil, 8597

The Governors and judges of Egypt, 8841

The Governors of Alabama, 9853

The Governors of Louisiana, 9890

The Governors of Maryland, 9895

Grabschriften Aller Friedhöfe von Grätz, 8567

Grabstätten berühmter Männer und Frauen, 8565

Grafique hongroise, 10149

Gran enciclopedia asturiana, 9684

Gran enciclopedia de la música pop, 10456

Gran enciclopedia de la región valenciana, 9691

Grand dictionnaire biographique des personnages historiques (Puy-de-Dôme), 9403

Grand dictionnaire historique, généalogique et biographique de la Haute-Marche, 8997

Grand dictionnaire socialiste, 8429

Grandes e humildes na epopeia portuguesa do Oriente, 9547

I Grandi convertiti, 11668

I Grandi del Cattolicesimo, 11669

Granth ane granthakar, 11081

Graphik der Welt, 10060

Graphik in der DDR, 10129

Les Graveurs d'acier et la médaille de l'antiquité à nos jours, 10293

Die Grazer Friedhöfe, 8566

Great flower painters, 10058

Great college football coaches of the Twenties and Thirties, 10617

The Great historical Indians, 9246

Great men and women from Britain's past, 9155

Great Negroes, past and present, 8305

Great photographers, 12094

Great pop stars, 10542

Great Scots, 9636

Das Grosse Bilderbuch des Films, 10330

Grosse Frauen der Weltgeschichte, 8340

Grosse Nervenärzte, 11391

Grosse Schweizer, 9724

Die Grossen der Kirche, 11692

Die Grossen Sänger und Dirigenten, 10483

Historia de la administración hacendaria en México, 9481

Historia de la insigne ciudad de Segovia, 11251

Historia de la literatura chilena, 10908

Historia de la medicina en España, 11486

Historia de los matadores de toros, 10612

Historia de los nombres de las calles de Barcelona, 9666

Historia do teatro cearense, 10370

Historia pragmática e interna de la Universidad de Salamanca, 10721

Historiae; seu, Vitae sanctorum, 11704

An Historical account of the lives and writings of our most considerable English poets, 10983

Historical and cultural dictionaries of Asia, 8481, 8626, 9247, 9489, 9527, 9629, 10000

Historical and cultural dictionary of Afghanistan, 8481

Historical and cultural dictionary of Burma, 8626

Historical and cultural dictionary of India, 9247

Historical and cultural dictionary of Nepal, 9489

Historical and cultural dictionary of Saudi Arabia, 9629

Historical and cultural dictionary of the Philippines, 9527

Historical and cultural dictionary of Vietnam, 10000

Historical and political who's who of Afghanistan, 8480

Historical biography of the United States, classified, 9825

Historical dictionary of Bolivia, 8585

Historical dictionary of Chile, 8688c

Historical dictionary of Dahomey, 8814

Historical dictionary of Ecuador, 8837

Historical dictionary of El Salvador, 9625

Historical dictionary of Guatemala, 9218

Historical dictionary of Nicaragua, 9499

Historical dictionary of Panama, 9515

Historical dictionary of Paraguay, 9518

Historical dictionary of Puerto Rico and the U. S. Virgin Islands, 9552

Historical dictionary of Somalia, 9655

Historical dictionary of Swaziland, 9707

Historical dictionary of the Gambia, 9058

Historical dictionary of the People's Republic of the Congo, 8800

Historical dictionary of the Republic of Botswana, 8587

Historical dictionary of Togo, 9735

Historical dictionary of Uruguay, 9987

History of services of officers holding gazetted appointments in the Government of Pakistan, 9514

History of southeastern Ohio and the Muskingum Valley, 9924

History of southwest Missouri, 9903

History of Tennessee from the earliest times to the present, 9963

A History of Texas and Texans, 9969

History of Texas ... Houston and Galveston, 9968

History of Texas ... Milan, Williamson [etc.] counties, 9967

A History of the American Medical Association, 11498

History of the Arkansas Valley, Colorado, 9862

A History of the Baptists of Louisiana, 11630

History of the bench and bar of Oregon, 11331

History of the bench and bar of Wisconsin, 11328

A History of the City of Buffalo, 9856

History of the City of Buffalo and Erie County, 9858

A History of the City of Buffalo and Niagara Falls, 9857

A History of the City of St. Louis and vicinity, 9952

History of the Connecticut Valley in Massachusetts, 9897

A History of the courts and lawyers of Ohio, 11332

History of the Great Kanawha Valley, 9981

History of the Lake Huron shore, 9899

History of the Lower Shenandoah Valley, 9976

A History of the Lutheran Church in South Carolina, 11809

History of the Medical Society of the District of Columbia, 11507

A History of the Methodist Church in Ceylon, 11815

History of the Ohio Falls cities and their counties, 9942

History of the Upper Peninsula of Michigan, 9900

History of the Western Reserve, 9982

A History of the Westminister Assembly of Divines, 11824

Histrionic Montreal, 10334

Hnit hna-ya Myanma naing-gan thamaing abidan, 8627

Hockey encyclopedia, Fischler's, 10626

Hojas militares, 9997

Holandeses no Brasil, 9493

Hollywood album, 10429

Hollywood glamor portraits, 10430

The Hollywood musical, 10436

Hollywood players: the Forties, 10433

Hollywood today, 10424

Imagines L (quinquaginta) doctorum virorum, 10655

Imena moskovskikh ulit̃s, 9583

The Immortal San Franciscans, 9954

Importantes personalidades del mundo, 9452

L'Impressionisme. English, 10113

L'Imprimerie, les imprimeurs et les libraires à Grenoble, 11344

In Köln verliebt, um Köln verdient, 9110

In memoriam; an obituary of Aberdeen and vicinity, 9638

In memoriam; or, Funeral records of Liverpool celebrities, 9192

Inbāh al-ruwāt 'alā anbāh al-nuhāt, 10845

Index alphabétique des biographies des profès et des novices décédés, 11633

Index bio-bibliographicus notorum hominum, 8285

Index biographique des membres ... de l'Académie de médecine, 11427

Index över svenska porträtt, 9709

Index of Pacific Northwest portraits, 9918

Index of portraits in books: physicians, surgeons, and others, maintained in the Library of the Royal College of Physicians, 11450

An Index of wind-instrument makers, 10513

Index to artistic biography, 10014

Index to authors in T'ang shih chi shih, 10917

An Index to biographical fragments in unspecialized scientific journals, 11869

Index to biographical material in Chin and Yüan literary works, 10913

Index to biographical materials of Sung figures, 8699

Index to biographies of contemporary composers, 10438

Index to biographies of Englishmen, 1000-1485, found in dissertations and theses, 9143

An Index to Black American artists, 10229

Index to Li tai t'ung hsing ming lu, 8698

Index to literary biography, 10738

Index to obituary notices in the Richmond enquirer, 9973

Index to 'Portraits' in West Africa (1948-1966), 8482

Index to profile sketches in New Yorker magazine, 9764

An Index to·profiles in The New Yorker, 9754

Index to short biographies, 8303

Index to the authors in Ch'üan Han San-kuo Chin Nan-pei ch'ao shih, 10914

Index to the authors in the Sung shih chi shih, 10916

Index to the authors in Yüan shih chi shih, 10918

Index to thirty-three collections of Ch'ing dynasty biographies, 8701

Leading personalities of Western Australia, 8534

Leben und Bildnisse grosser Deutschen, 9089

Lebendige Stadt, 10869

Lebens- u. Arbeitsbilder sudetendeutscher Lehrer, 10677

Lebensbeschreibungen und Charakterschilderungen berühmter Manner, 8364

Lebensbilder aus dem rheinischwestfälischen Industriegebiet, 11964

Lebensbilder berühmter Kantoren, 10548

Lebensbilder der Heiligen, 11702

Lebensbilder der Liederdichter und Melodien, 10477

Lebensbilder-Register, 9061

Lebensbilder von der Elb- und Wesermündung, 9096

Lebensläufe aus Franken, 9111

Lebensmittelarbeiter als berühmte Zeitgenossen, 11941

Lecturers on Southeast Asia, 10652

Lefnadsteckningar öfver de utmärktare personerna under kriget emot Ryssland, 9710

Légendaire d'Autun, 11760

La Législature de Québec, 8684

Der Lehrer als Dichter, 11056

Lehrer als Schriftsteller, 11057

Die Leitenden staatlichen Verwaltungsbeamten der Provinz Westfalen, 9132

Lekhsikon historii, 8308

Le-korot ha-Yehudim be-Lublin, 9533

Leksikon filozofa, 11537

Leksikon pisaca Jugoslavije, 11301

Leksikon umjetnika slikara, vajara ... , 10261

Levensberichten van Zeeuwen, 9494

Lexicon of Afro-American history, 9779

Lexicon polemicum, 11617

Lexikon aktueller Persönlichkeiten, 8433

Lexikon der Ägyptologie, 8840

Lexikon der antiken Autoren, 10936

Lexikon der christlichen Ikonographie, 11572

Lexikon der islamischen Welt, 9321

Lexikon der Jugendschriftsteller in deutscher Sprache, 10861

Lexikon der Kinder- und Jugendliteratur, 10783

Lexikon der klassischen Altertumskunde, 8403-8404

Lexikon der modernen Architektur, 10267

Lexikon der Pädagogik, 10659

Lexikon der vom Jahr 1750 bis 1800 verstorbenen teutschen Schriftsteller, 10656

Lexikon der Weltliteratur, 10803

Lexikon der Weltliteratur im 20. Jahrhundert, 10784

Maine genealogist and biographer, 9893

Die Mainzer Goldschmiedezunft, 10281

Les Maîtres ornemanistes, dessinateurs ... , 10027

Majmu'a-i-naghz, 11286

Makers of America, an historical and biographical work, 9865

Makers of modern India, 9248

Makers of the harpsichord and clavichord (1440-1840), 10502

Mal literaturen leksikon, 11164

Malá encyklopédia bádatel'ov a vynálezcov, 11872

Malá encyklopédia filmu, 10319

Ma-lai-ya Ch'ao ch'iao tung chien, 8769

Maler in Hamburg, 10131

Maleri nach 1945 in Deutschland, Österreich und der Schweiz, 10133

Malý biografický slovník československých lékařů, 11423

Malý slovník sovětských hudebniků, 10563

Malý slovník sovětských malířů, 10207

Malý slovník sovětských spisovatelů, 11219

Mały słownik kultury antycznej, 8400

Mały słownik kultury świata arabskiego, 9322

Mały słownik literatury dlia dzieci i młodzieży, 10787

Mały słownik pionerów polskich kolonjalnych i morskich, 12008

Mały słownik pisarzy angielskich i amerykańskich, 10986

Mały słownik pisarzy francuskich, belgijskich i prowansalskich, 11023

Mały słownik pisarzy narodów europejsich ZSRR, 11220

Mały słownik pisarzy polskich, 11192

Mały słownik pisarzy świata, 10788

Mały słownik pisarzy włoskich, 11123

Mały słownik pisarzy Zachodnio-słowiańskich i Południowo-słowianskich, 11239

Manuel de l'amateur d'estampes (Dutuit), 10193

Manuel de l'amateur d'estampes (Le Blanc), 10056

Manuel du bibliographe normand, 9030

Manuel historique du département de l'Aisne, 8968

Mar del Plata, sus calles, plazas y monumentos, 8506

Maréchaux de France, 8881

Marine Corps oral history collection catalog, 9795

Marks of early American silversmiths, 10289

Marks of London goldsmiths and silversmiths, 10291

Marne. Dictionnaire biographique et historique illustré, 9021

Mémoire historique et littéraire sur le Collège royal de France, 10685

Mémoires domestiques pour servir à l'histoire l'Oratoire, 11638

Mémoires littéraires, critiques, philologiques, biographiques et bibliographiques, 11381

Mémoires pour servir à l'histoire de notre littérature, 11030

Mémoires pour servir à l'histoire des hommes illustres de Lorraine, 9017

Memoirs and portraits of one hundred Glasgow men, 9644

Memoirs of 300 contemporary public characters, British and foreign, 8459

Memoria acerca del estado del Instituto Vizcaíno, 11254

Memoria intorno i letterati e gli artisti della città di Ascoli nel Piceno, 11107

Memoria theologorum Wirtembergensium ressuscitata, 11593

A Memorial and biographical record of Iowa, 9883

Mémorial des compagnons de la Libération, 8942

Mémorial universel des hommes du temps, 8469

Memorials of Protestant missionaries to the Chinese, 11832

Memorias biográficas de la Provincia de Nuestra Señora de la Candelaria de la Orden de Recoletos de San Agustín, 11735

Memorie d'alcuni uomini illustri della città di Lodi, 9375

Memorie degli architetti antichi e moderni. English, 10268

Memorie degli scrittori Cosentini, 11129

Memorie e documenti per la storia dell'Università di Pavia, 10709

Memorie per la storia letteraria di Piacenza, 11109

Memorie storiche de più uomini illustri pisani, 9384

Memorie storico-critiche degli scrittori ravennati, 11120

Men and ideas in economics, 11947

Men of achievement, 8453

Men of affairs in greater Kansas City (1912), 9885

Men of affairs of Houston and environs, 9873

Men of agriculture & veterinary sciences in India, 12047

The Men of Cajamarca, 9523

Men of Canada, 8640

Men of library science and libraries in India, 11346

Men of northwestern Ohio, 9934

Men of Nottingham and Nottinghamshire, 9200

Men of Ohio, 9925

Men of Tennessee, 9964

Men of the South, 9959

Men of the time in Australia, 8533

Men of the time; sketches of living notables, 9957

Men of today in the Eastern Townships, 8683

Men of Wood County and familiar faces of Ohio, 9933

Mennonite artists contemporary (1975), 10246

Menschen, die Geschichte machten, 8372

Merit's who's who among American high school students, 9845

Meshur adamlar hayatları, essleri, 8339

Messages; a thematic anthology of poetry, 10985

The Methodist local preachers' who's who, 11816

La Meuse. Dictionnaire, annuaire et album, 9022

Mexican writers and pseudonyms, 11168

Meyers Handbuch über die Literatur, 10792

Meyers Handbuch über die Musik, 10486

Micul dictionar enciclopedia, 9571

Midwestern Nigeria Legislature: Who's who (1964), 9501

Mighty men of Zion, 11819

Mikkyō Jiten Hensankai Mikkyō daijiten, 11563

Mil figuras de la historia, 8381

Militärisches Pantheon ... aller preussischen Helden, 9122

Militärisches Pantheon ... der K. K. Oesterreichischen Armee, 8551

Militair-Conversations-Lexikon, 8356

A Military and naval encyclopaedia, 8388

Military bibliography of the Civil War, 9751

The Military encyclopedia, 8378

1,508 (Mille cinquecento otto) deputati al Parlamento per la XXIII Legislatura, 9353

1,535 (Mille cinquecento trentacinque) deputati al Parlamento per la XXVI Legislatura, 9354

1,535 (Mille cinquecento trentacinque) deputati al Parlamento per la XXVII Legislatura, 9355

MDCCCLX (Mille huit cent soixante). Le Senat de l'Empire français, 8963

MDCCCLXII (Mille huit cent soixante-deux). Le Corps législatif et le Conseil d'Etat, 8962

1650 (Mille seicento cinquanta) Giardino di Chà Gualdo, 10169

Min ko pai jên chuan, 9730

Ming ch'ên pei chuan wan yan chi, 8776

A Ming directory (1968), 10651

Ming hsien shih tsu yen hsing lei kao, 8712

Ming ju yen hsing lu, 10673

Ming shih lieh chuan, 8746

Ming tai ming jen chuan, 8710

Miniaturen '70 (Siebzig) International, 10026

Ministri, deputati, senatori (dal 1848 al 1922), 9351

Ministros da Fazenda, 8594

Los Ministros de la Audiencia de Lima, 9524

Minutes of the Bury Presbyterian Classis, 11822

Minutes of the Manchester Presbyterian Classisis (1646-1660), 11825

Missionari francescani, 11773

Missouri music, 10584

Die Mitglieder der Historischen Kommission Westfalens, 12013a

Die Mitglieder des Ordens [pour le Merite für Wissenschaften und Künste], 11876

Modenesi da ricordare, 9382

Modern Chinese authors: a list of pseudonyms, 10922

The Modern encyclopedia of basketball, 10607

The Modern encyclopedia of Russian and Soviet history, 9590

Modern landscape painting, 10065

The Modern medical world, 11388

Modern world drama; an encyclopedia, 10790

Moderna nordiska författare, 11235

Moderna svenska författare, 11261

Moderna svenska konstnärer, 10226

Moldavskaiā literatura, 11177

Le Monde agricole, 12045

Montreal (1535-1914), 8669

Monument national. Portraits des députés ... , 8959

Monumenta sepulcrorum cum epigraphis, 8438

Monumental inscriptions of Jamaica, 9395

Morayshire M. P. s since the Act of Union, 9649

Morbihan. Dictionnaire, annuaire et album, 9024

More books by more people, 10828

More Mexican writers and pseudonyms, 11168

Mosaik Jazzlexikon, 10479

Motion picture directors, 10313

Motion picture performers, 10314

Motion pictures in the Philippines, 10415

The Mountain men and the fur trade of the Far West, 9978

Il Movimento operaio italiano, 11977

M. S. de Venezuela, la biografía del merito y el trabajo, 9991

Müveszeti lexikon (Éber), 10021

New Dictionary of modern sculpture, 10277

A New dictionary of music, 10471

A New encyclopaedia of Freemasonry, 8474

New encyclopedia of philosophy, 11538

The New encyclopedia of Texas, 9966

The New encyclopedia of the opera, 10459

The New extinct peerage (1884-1971), 9168

The New Frontiersmen, 9789

New Hampshire agriculture, 12048

New International illustrated encyclopedia of art, 10036

The New Jersey Pharmaceutical Association, 11496

New men in the Roman Senate, 9568

The New music lover's handbook, 10492

The New Newgate calendar, 9160

The New peerage (Kimber), 9158

The New Standard Jewish encyclopedia, 9434

New World companion to English and American literature, 10994

The New York times biographical edition, 8456

The New York times directory of the film, 10342

New York times index, Personal name index to the, 8282

Newfoundland and Labrador who's who, 8672

Newfoundland who's who, 8672

Newgate calendar, The new, 9160

The Newgate calendar improved, 9176

The Newspaper reference book of Canada, 8653

NHL action players (74/75), 10629

Nieuw biografiesch, anthologiesch en kritiesch woordenboek van Nederlandsche dichters, 10959

Nièvre. Dictionnaire, annuaire et album, 9028

Nihon bukke jimmei jisho, 11568

Nihon gaka jiten, 10188

Nihon jimbutsu bunken mokuroku, 9396

Nihon jimmei jiten, 9402

Nihon kodai jimmei jiten, 9416

Nihon no shisoka, 11529

Nihon rekishi jimmei jiten, 9403

Nihon sekai jimmei jiten, 8350

19th century Louisiana painters, 10257

90 (Nittio) grafiker, 10223

Nizkor; sefer zikaron le-talmidim, 9336

Nobel laureates of literature, 10800

Nobel Prize winners in chemistry, 11910

Die Nobelpreisträger der Medizin, 11384

Poketto Nihon sekai jimmei jiten, 8350

Polacy na szlakach techniki, 12032

Polish contribution to arts and sciences in Canada, 8661

Political and diplomatic history of the Arab world (1900-1967), 9323

Political dictionary of the Middle East in the 20th century, 9488

Political works of concealed authorship relating to the United States, 10815

Politico-criminal who's who (India), 9236

La Politique africaine (en 1969), 8489

Polscy Olimpijczycy, 10594

Polscy pisarze wspóloześni, 11188

Pomorska enciklopedija, 8366

Pontificium Athenaeum Antonianum, ab origine ad praesens, 10710

Popes through the ages, 11642

Popular American composers from Revolutionary times to the present, 10582

A Popular cyclopedia of history, ancient and modern, 8329

The Popular Jewish encyclopedia, 9429

Populární politický slovník, 11939

Porträtgallerie des steiermärkischen Adels, 8556

Die Porträtgemmen der römischen Republik, 9567

Porträtkatalog der Siebenburger Sachsen, 9060

Portraets der Zürcher Bürgermeister (von 1336), 9725

Portraetsamlingen i Odense adelige Jomfrukloster, 8820

Porträtt af svenska läkare och apotekare, 11488

Porträtt från den forna Åbo akademi, 10680

Le Portrait à la cour des Valois, 8940

Portraits; a catalog of the engravings, etchings ... and lithographs presented to the Stanford University Library, 8302

Les Portraits aux crayons des XVIe et XVIIe siècles, 8295

Portraits bretons des XVIIe et XVIIIe siècles, 8984

Portraits de femmes (Canada), 8649

Portraits de personnages remarquables dans touts les genres, 8333

Portraits des généraux français, 8960

Portraits des hommes et des femmes célèbres qui ont paru en France, 8908

Les Portraits des hommes illustres de la province du Maine, 9020

The Priests of the Roman Republic, 11866

Primer diccionario biográfico [argentino] contemporáneo ilustrado, 8505

Les Princes militaires de la maison de France, 8950

Prinzipale; zur Genealogie des deutschsprachigen Berufstheaters, 10348

Pro and senior hockey guide, 10631

Pro football A to Z, 10621

Próceres trujillanos, 9990

Le Procuste parlementaire, 8937

Professoren der Chirurgie unserer Zeit an den Universitatan von Oesterreich-Ungarn, Deutschland, Schweiz, Belgien, Holland, Dänemark, 11401

Die Professoren der Universität Rinteln, 10690

Profiles of New York authors, 10826

Profils parlementaires, 8922

Profily zahraničních režiseru, 10322

Prokuraattori, 11310

Prominent Hungarians: home and abroad, 9220

Prominent Indonesian Chinese in the twentieth century, 9288

Prominent men of West Virginia, 9980

Prominent people of the Province of Ontario, 8675

Prominenten-Almanach, 8564

Prontuario biografico dei più illustri musicisti italiani i stranieri, 10546

Proper names in the lyrics of the troubadours, 11203

Propheten in Afrika, 11559

Prosopographia merowingischer Amtsträger, 8411

Prosopographia Ptolemaica, 8842

Prosopographie der hellenistischen Königsgesandten, 8401

Prosopographie zur Geschichte des Pyrrhos, 8373

Prosopographische und sozialgeschichtliche Studien zum Langobardenreich in Italien, 9376

The Prosopography of the Later Roman Empire, 9566

Prosthēkai kai diorthōseis eis ten Neoelleniken filologian Konstantinou Satha, 11075

Province de Lyon (1582-1762), 11757

La Prusse littéraire sous Frédéric II, 11044

Prvo Jugoslovensko narodno pretstavnistvo izabrano 8 novembra 1931 godine, 10013

Pseudonimi di giuliani friulani i dalmati, 11099

Pseudónimos de escritores nacionales y extranjeros en la prensa nacional, 10960

Pseudónimos en la prensa del Ecuador, 10961

Pseudonymes canadiens, 10901

Pseudonymes québécois, 11036

Pseudonyms in Indian literature, 11093

A Reader's guide to African
literature, 10814

Reallexikon des klassischen
Altertums, 8399

Recentioris aevi numismata virorum de rebus medicis et
physicis meritorum memor-
iam servantia collegit et
recensuit, 11366

Recherches bibliographiques en
forme de dictionnaire sur les
auteurs, 11006

Recherches bio-bibliographiques
pour servir à l'histoire des
sciences naturelles en Bour-
gogne, 11881

Recherches sur la chevalerie du
duché de Bretagne, 8982

Recherches sur les personnages
nés en Champagne, 8988

Recherches sur l'établissement
et l'exercice de l'imprimerie
a Troyes, 11336

Reclams Hörspielführer, 10798

Reclams Jazzführer, 10450

Records of the graduates (Acadia
University, 1843-1926), 8632

Recueil de tous les membres
composant l'ordre royal et
militaire de Saint-Louis,
8916

Recueil des historiens de la
France, 8949

Les Recueils collectifs de
poésies libres et satiriques,
11016

Recuerdo del 14. Congreso Internacional de Medicina, Madrid,
abril (1903), 11385

Reference encyclopedia of the
American Indian, 9824

Reference guide of India (Who's
who), 9251

Les Régents et censeurs de la
Banque de France, 11963

A Register of admission to King's
College, Cambridge, 9145

Register of Polish American
scholars, scientists, writers
& artists, 9841

A Register of the governors of
the states of the United States
of America, 9797

Die Reichsrats-Abgeordneten des
allgemeinen Wahlrechtes,
8571

Reichstags-Handbuch, 9081-9083

Reihe aller bisherigen Erzbischöfe zu Salzburg, 11714

Rekidai meijin nempu, 8743

Rekidai meijin nempu mokuroku,
8695

Relojeros de España, 12074

Répertoire alphabétique des
personnes et des choses de
Port-Royal, 11631

Répertoire bibliographique des
travaux des médecins, 11430

Répertoire biographique des
Savoyards contemporains,
9008

Répertoire de maîtres en théologie de Paris au XIIIe siècle,
11755

Répertoire général des causes
célèbres anciennes et mo-
dernes, 8957

Répertoire générale du clergé
candadien per ordre chronologique, 11727

Senken meika betsugō beshō jiten, 11134

Septemvriiskoto vŭstanie (1923), 8621

Serbski biografski slownik, 9464

Serie cronologica dei reverendissimi superiori di Terra Sancta, 11785

Serie degli uomini i più illustri nella pittura, 10043

Serie di vite e ritratti de' famosi personaggi degli ultimi tempi, 8467

Sesenta escritores granadinos, 11255

Setnik pisarzów polskich albo pochwaɫy, 11197

Seudónimos de escritores colombianos, 10938

The Seventeenth and eighteenth century Italian schools, 10170

The Seventeenth century marine painters of the Netherlands, 10197

Seznam imen za slovenska biografski leksikon, 9654

Shadd al-izār fī haṭṭ al-awzār 'an zuwwār al-mazār, 11850

Shang-hai pai yeh jen ts'ai hsiao shih, 11956

Shem ha-gedolim he-hadash ... , 9436

Shên sêng chuan, 11566

Sheng kuo tsai fu lu, 8775

Shêng ming ti kuang hui, 8719

Shih fu pao chien, 8755

Shih pin lu, 10921

Shina mondai jiten, 8738

Shina shoga jimmei jisho, 10097

Shinshū sekai jimmei jiten, 8377

Shinto daijiten, 11868

Shintō jiten, 11867

Shizuoka-ken jimbutsu shi, 9412

The Shorewood art reference guide, 10044

Short biographical sketches of personalities mentioned in Vedas [etc.], 11838

A Short list of works relating to the biographies of Norfolk men and women, 9194

Shôzô senshû, 9417

Shu-ch'êng ch'i chiu lu, 8790

Siapa-apa (who's who) pedjabat teras HANKAM/ABRI, 9284

Sicill-i Osmanî, 9741

77 (Siebenundsiebzig) Porträtskizzen der Mitglieder des Burgtheaters, 10368

Le Siècle de Rembrandt, 10196

Signers of the Declaration [of Independence], 9768

Silat as-sila, 9308

Silences that speak, 9633

Silhouettes; figures du terroir, 12046

Silhouettes franco-américaines, 9805

Silversmiths and related craftsmen of the Atlantic provinces, 10300

Sindh men Urdū shā'irī, 11287

Słownik artystów polskich, 10202

Słownik bio-bibliograficzny dawnego Uniwersytetu Wileńskiego, 10716

Słownik biograficzny działaczy polskiego ruchu rabotniczego, 11981

Słownik biograficzny teatru polskiego (1765-1975), 10417

Słownik filosofów, 11552

Słownik historii Polski, 9537

Słownik polskich lekarzy weterynaryjnych biograficzno-bibliograficzny, 12049

Słownik pracowników ksiazki polskiej, 11352

Słownik rytowników polskich tudziez obcych w Polsce osiadłych lub czasowo w niej pracupacych, 10201

Słownik wczesnochrześcijańskiego piśmiennictwa, 10804

A Smaller classical dictionary, 8406

Smolandi Upsalienses, 10722

Snickare, schatullmakare och ebenister i Stockholm, 12073

Sō Gen Min Shin shoga meiken shoden, 10098

Social security beneficiaries who have lived to 100, 9839

Soedinennye Shtaty Ameriki; slovar-spravochnik, 9828

Soldatisches Führertum, 9124

Some apostles of physiology, 11406

Some founders of physiology, 11392

Some historians of medieval India, 12015

Some nineteenth century Scotsmen, 9641

Some Pennsylvania women during the War of the Revolution, 9944

Some portraits of geographers, 12007

The Somerset roll, 9202

Something about the author, 10801

Sophia Smith collection, Picture catalog of the, 9765

Sorok let ZhZL, 8301

Les Sources de l'histoire de France, 8868

Sources for history of quantum physics, 11932

South African artists (1900-1958), 10216

South Carolina silversmiths, 10285

Southern Cameroons House of Assembly: Who's who, 8629

Souverains et notabilités d'Indochine, 9281

Sovetahay grakanowt'yan patmowt'yown, 10855

Sovetakan Banaki hay gortsich'nerĕ, 8517

Sovetskaia voennaia entsiklopediia, 9596

Sovetskye uchenye, 11887

The Soviet encyclopedia of space flight, 12059

Soviet personalities in biomedicine, 11476

Ta'sīs al-Shi'ah li-'ulūm al-Islām, 11852

T'aterakan dēmk'er, 10363

Tazkirah-'i makhzan al-ghara'ib, 11184

Te vechno shte zhiveiãt, 8622

O Teatro no Brasil, 10895

Teikoku jimmei jiten, 9418

Tennessee lives, 9965

Teologisk stat, 11806

Tesauro de datos históricos, 9554

Texas writers of today, 10820

Tezkiri Salim, 11282

Tezkire-i Mesahir-i Osmaniyye'-nin, 9741

Theater in Ungarn (1945 bis 1965), 10406

Theatrical illustrations, Cumberland's, 10399

Theatrum pontificum, imperatorum, regum, ducum, principum, pace et bello illustrium, 8380

Thesaurus pseudonymorum quae in litteratura Hebraica et Judaeo-Germanica inveniuntur, 11139

These will I remember, 11864

They had faces then, 10435

They made history: great men and women from Britain's past, 9155

Third book of junior authors, 10761

1,000 successful Blacks, 9817

Three centuries of Freemasonry in New Hampshire, 9906

Three hundred years of Canadian art, 10088

Ti hou tang wu kung tso t'ung chih hsün nan shih lüeh hui pien, 8731

T'iflisi haykakan pant'eonnerowm, 8515

Tiroler Dichterbuch, 10871

Titled Elizabethans, 9159

Tōa senkaku shishi kiden, 9408

Tōdai no shijim ⟶ so no denki, 10928

Toldot ha mekubalim, ha-Shabeta'-im veha-Hasidim, 11861

Toldot Yehude Bukhara be-Bukhara uvi-Ysra'el, 9600

Die Tonkünstler-Porträts der Wiener Musiksammlung von Aloys Fuchs, 10442

Trade directory of the Republic of Ghana, 9136

Die Träger des Wiener Liedes, 10521

Translators and translations, 10782

Tratado de todos os vice-reis e governadores da Índia, 9551

Travaux scientifiques des pharmaciens militaires français, 11428

Le Trésor du bibliophile romantique et moderne, 11002

Trois cents ans d'art canadien, 10088

Trovadores do Brasil, 10893

Victorian painters, Dictionary of, 10145

The Victoriana collector's handbook, 10147

A Vida dos imigrantes japoneses pioneiros do Brasil, 8613

La Vie des Justes, 11685

Vie des saints de Franche-Comté, 11749

Vies des saints du sud marocain, 11855

La Vie des saints pour tous les jours de l'année, 11693

Vie politique de tous les députés à la Convention nationale, pendant et après la Révolution, 8956

Vienne. Dictionnaire biographique et album, 9055

Vierundsechzig Porträtzeichnungen, 8570

Vies des bienheureux et des saints de Bretagne, 11754

Vies des fameux architectes depuis la Renaissance des arts, 10264

Vies des fameux architectes et sculpteurs, 10264

Vies des fameux sculpteurs depuis la Renaissance des arts, 10264

Les Vies des femmes célèbres, 8327

Vies des hommes illustres et grands capitaines, 8426

Les Vies des plus célèbres et anciens poètes provençaux, 11205

Les Vies des saints de l'ordre de Saint Benoît, 11641

Vies des saints du diocèse de Beauvais, 11763

Vies des saints et des bienheureux, 11745

Les Vies des saints, patrons, martirs et évêques d'Autun, 11666

Les Vies des saints personnages de l'Anjou, 11748

Vies des saints pour tous les jours de l'année, 11696

Vietnam era Medal of Honor recipients, 9836

Viêt-Nam nhân-vât-chỉ vung biên, 9999

La Vieux Grenoble, ses artistes, 10114

Vilàgirodalmi lexikon, 10762

Vioi paralleloi tōn epi tēs anagenēseōs tēs Hellados diaprepsantōn andrōn, 9212

The Violin makers of Bohemia, 10152

De Viool, geschiedenis, bouw ... , 10467

Virginia authors, past and present, 10833

Virorum doctorum de disciplinis benemerentium effigies XLIII, 10655

Visage du Canada, 10135

Visiting cards of celebrities, 8466

A Visual dictionary of art, 10045

La Vita e le opere dei 360 più noti scrittori d'Italia, 11130

Vita e ritratti di sessanta Piemontesi illustri, 9383

Vitae, et res gestae Pontificum Romanorum et S. R. E. Cardinalium, 11670

Vitae Italorum doctrina excellentium, 9348

Vitae sophistarum, 11549

Vite de' pittori bolognesi non descritte nella Felsina pittrice, 10164

Vite de' pittori e scultori ferraresi, 10156

Vite de' pittori, scultori e architetti bergamaschi, 10178

Vite de' pittori, scultori ed architetti perugini, 10174

Vite degli italiani benemeriti della libertà, 9340

Le Vite dei pittori, scultori e architetti veronesi, 10179

Le Vite dei santi per tutti i giorno dell'anno, 11703

Vite d'Italiani illustri da Pitagora a Vittorio Emmanuele II, 9357

Vite e detti di santi musulmani, 9331

Le Vite e i film, 10358

Vite e ritratti degli uomini più celebri di tutti i tempi e di tutte le nazioni, 8383

Vite e ritratti di illustri italiani, 9367

Vlaamse tekeningen uit de zeventiende eeuw, 10107

Vocabulaire médical, 11383

Völkische und deutschnationale Führer, 9077

Vojna enciklopedija, 8384

Vologzhane-kraevedy, 9622

Von den Stillen im Lande; Pflichtschullehrer als Dichter ... , 10667

Von der Bergakademie zur Technischen Universität Berlin, 12070

Voorname Belgische toonkunstenaars, 10524

Vydaiushchiesia urozhentsy i deiateli Kirovskoi oblasti, 9608

Vydatni radians'ki istoryky, 12014

Vytoki pesni, 11297

Wafayāt al-a'yān wa-anbā' abnā' al-zamān, 9310

La Walhalla y las glorias de Alemania, 9078

Wallace Collection catalogues, 10068

Warwickshire leaders, 9203

Wasa Hofrätts presidenter, 11327

Water-colour painting in Britain, 10141

The wealthy citizens of New York, 11984

Webster's American biographies, 9839

Webster's biographical dictionary, 8385

Webster's guide to American history, 9842

Webster's New World companion to English and American literature, 10994

Wedgewood portrait medallions; an introduction, 8462

Wedgewood: the portrait medallions, 8461

Der Weg ins 20. Jahrhundert, 10227

Weimarer historisch-genealoges Taschenbuch des gesamten Adels jehudäischen Ursprunges, 9435

Wer is wer in der Schweiz?, 9719

Western movie stars, Hall of Fame of, 10427

The Western contribution to Buddhism, 11565

Westfälische Lebensbilder, 9133

The Westminster dictionary of church history, 11622

White unto harvest, 11812

White's conspectus of American biography, 9761

Who are they? A biographical reference book, 8348

Who counts in Western Australia, 8540

Who did what, 8386

Who is who (Andhra Pradesh Akademi of Sciences), 11886

Who is who in and from Ohio, 9936

Who is who in Ohio, 9937

Who is who: Nepal (1972-74), 9490

Who is who of Greek origin in institutions of higher learning in the United States & Canada, 10728

Who is who: Philippine guerrilla movement (1942-1945), 9528

Who is who (Tamil Legislative Council), 9279

Who was who in American history, arts and letters, 9844

Who was who in American politics, 9810

Who was who in American sports, 10595

Who was who in Florida, 9866

Who was who in the USSR, 9584

Who was who on the screen, 10357

Who's notable in Mexico, 9483

Who's where in books, 8287

Who's who among American high school students, 9845

Who's who among Black Americans, 9846

Who's who among elementary school principals, 10735

Who's who among innkeepers, 11987

Who's who among music students in American high schools, 10588

Who's who among Pacific Northwest authors, 10835

Who's who among students in American vocational and technical schools, 9847

Who's who in Africa, 8485

Who's who in African literature, 10813

Who's who in Alberta, 8662

Who's who in art and antiques, International, 10030

Who's who in Asian studies, International, 10658

Who's who in atoms, 11933

Who's who in — au Québec, 8687

Who's who in aviation, 12061

Who's who in aviculture, 12054

Who's who in basketball, 10608

Who's who in B. C. agriculture, 12058

Who's who in book manufacturing, 11356

Who's who in boxing, 10610

Who's who in Bristol?, 11968

Who's who in British Columbia, 8665

Who's who in British finance, 11969

Who's who in Burma, 8628

Who's who in Burns, 9646

Who's who in Canadian Jewry, 8648

Who's who in Canadian placement, 11955

Who's who in China (biographies of Chinese), 8780

Who's who in church history, 11573

Who's who in commerce and industry, 11989

Who's who in community service, International, 11938

Who's who in computer education and research, 11922

Who's who in computers and data processing, 11923

Who's who in consulting, 11988

Who's who in Cypriote archeology, 12009

Who's who in dancing, 10403

Who's who in education, 10699

Who's who in finance, 11969

Who's who in filmdom, 10318

Who's who in finance and industry, 11989

Who's who in Florida, 9867

Who's who in football (Barnes, Newberry & Co.), 10644

Who's who in football (Mendell), 10618

Who's who in football, The Clipper annual of, 10638

Who's who in Georgia, 9871

Who's who in German politics, 9104a

Who's who in government, 9848

Who's who in Greater Philadelphia in the Negro community, 9949

Who's who in Greater Wichita, 9983

Who's who in Guernsey, 9187

Who's who in hockey, 10628

Who's who (in India), 9257

Who's who in India (Kothari), 9244

Who's who in Indian radiology, 11934

Who's who in Indonesia, 9287

Who's who in industrial arts teacher education, 10736

Who's who in Iowa (Lake), 9882

Who's who in Iowa, The Iowa Press Association's, 9881

Who's who in Ipswich, 9189

Who's who in Italian economic life, 11978

Who's who in Jersey, 9190

Who's who in Jewish history, 9422

Who's who in Karnataka, 9272

Who's who in Kentucky, 9886

Who's who [in Kerala's Legislative Assembly], 9266

Who's who in labor, 11990

Who's who in Latin America, 9455

Who's who in Liberia, 9459

Who's who in librarianship and information science, 11357

Who's who in librarianship in Pakistan, 11351

Who's who in Louisiana, 9891

Who's who in Louisiana and Mississippi, 9892

The Who's who in Malaysia, 9466

Who's who in Malaysia and guide to Singapore, 9466

Who's who in medicine, 11447

Who's who in Michigan, 9901

Who's who in Midwestern Nigeria Legislature, 9501

Who's who in modern Japanese prints, 10184

Who's who in Mysore, 9272-9273

Who's who in national athletics high school football, 10622

Who's who in national high school football, 10623

Who's who in New Zealand libraries, 11358

Who's who in Nigeria, 9503

Who's who in North Carolina (Names of Distinction, inc.), 9916

Who's who in North Carolina (United States Public Relations Service), 9917

Who's who in North St. Louis, 9953

Who's who in North Vietnam, 10001

Who's who in Northampton, 9197

Who's who in Norwich, 9199

Who's who in Ohio, 9938

Who's who in Ontario art, 10091

Who's who in poetry, International, 10779

Who's who in professional baseball, 10605

Who's who in publishing, 11345

Who's who in railroading and rail transit, 11951

Who's who in railroading in North America, 11951

Who's who in railroading, United States, Canada, Mexico, Cuba, 11951

Who's who in Reading, 9201

Who's who in reigning royalty, 8473

Who's who in Saskatchewan, 8688

Who's who in science fiction, 10746

Who's who in science in Europe, 11877

Who's who in Scottish history, 9635

Who's who in soccer, 10641

Who's who in South Carolina, 9958

Who's who in Southeast Asia (August 1945-Dec. 1950), 8526

Who's who in sports in Malaysia and Singapore, 10600

Who's who in Texas, 9970

Who's who in Thailand, 9733

Who's who in the ancient world, 9209

Who's who in the Bible, 11574

Who's who in the Buckeye State, 9930

Who's who in the Chinese People's Political Consultative Conference, 8781

Who's who in the computer field, 11923

Who's who in the film world, 10437

Who's who in the Hyderabad Legislative Assembly, 9264

Who's who in the Italian economic life, 11979

Who's who in the Italian section of the I. C. C., 11979

Who's who in the martial arts and directory of black belts, 10635

Who's who in the Middle Ages, 8410

Who's who in the motor and commercial vehicle industries, 11970

Who's who in the motor industry, 11970

Who's who in the New Earth, 9766

Who's who in the New Testament,. 11577

Who's who in the Old Testament, 11581

Who's who in the psychic world, 11555

Who's who in the sporting world: Witwatersrand and Pretoria, 10601

Who's who in the United Nations and related agencies, 8476

Who's who in the world, 8477

Who's who in track and field, 10647

Who's who in Trinidad and Tobago, 9737

Who's who in Virginia, 9977

Who's who in Wizo, 9437

Who's who (Indian Parliament, 1950), 9238

Who's who (Indian Parliament Council of States), 9239

Who's who (Kerala Legislative Assembly), 9266

Who's who (Mysore Legislative Assembly), 9271

Who's who (Mysore Legislative Council), 9270

Who's who, Northern Region of Nigeria Legislature, 9504

Who's who of Afghanistan, 8480

Women of photography, 12093

The Women poets in English, 10993

Woordenboek der Vaderlandse geschiedenis, 9495

Worcestershire leaders, 9205

World atlas of exploration, 12003

World authors (1950-1970), 10808

The World biographical dictionary, 8376

World directory of mineralogists, 11902

The World encyclopedia of film, 10325

World military leaders, 8452

World's who's who in commerce and industry, 11989

World's who's who in finance and industry, 11989

The World Who's who of Women, 8478

World's great men of color, 8371

Writers' gallery, 10966

The Writers Workshop handbook of Assamese literature, 10857

Wu ch'ao Hsiang shih chia shih yung, 10931

Wu chung jen wu chih, 8788

Wu tu fa ch'eng, 11561

Wykaz polskich pracownikow na polu kartografii, 12004

Xalapeños distinguidos, 9478

Yeni Mülkiye târihi ve Mülki-yeliler, 12021

Yijo myŏngin yŏichŏn, 9447

Yin wan lu, 8783

20 (i. e. Yirminci) yuzyıl Türk musıkisi, 10572

Y. M. C. A. who's who and annual, 9178

Yorkshire authors today, 10980

Young American sculpture, East and West, 10231

Yüan ch'ao jen wu lüeh, 8773

Yüan shih chi shih chu chê yin tê, 10918

Yüan yen chi shan ts'un fu yin tê, 8777

The Yugoslav co-operative encyclopedia, 11991

Za vlast' Sovetov v IAkutii, 10007

The Zacatecan missionaries in Texas, 11802

Zadružni leksikon FNRJ, 11991

Zarys historii budowy organów w Polsce, 10506

Zasłużni sinovi, 9650

Zbiór poetów polskich XIX w., 11189

Zbiór wiadomósci do historyi sztuki lekarskiéj w Polsce, 11470

Die Zeitgenössischen Literaturen der Schweiz, 11268

Die Zeitgenossen Friedrichs des Grossen, 9093

Die Zeitlose Wort, 10882

Die Zentralbehörden des Herzogtums Württemberg, 9134

Zhizn' samechatel'nykh liudei. (Indexes), 8301

SUBJECT INDEX

Africa, Southern, 8490, 10515

Africa, Southwest, 8491

Africa, Sub-Saharan, 8483-8484a,
11953

Africa, West--Portraits--Cata-
logs, indexes, etc., 8482

African historical dictionaries,
8587, 8800, 8814, 9058,
9655, 9707, 9735

African Methodist Episcopal
Zion Church, 11817

Afro-American artists--SEE:
Artists, Afro-American,
10229-10230, 10236, 10248,
10821

Afro-American authors--SEE:
Authors, Afro-American,
10817-10819, 10821, 10831-
10832

Afro-American poets--SEE:
Poets, Afro-American,
10816

Afro-American women--SEE:
Women, Afro-American,
9809

Afro-Americans, 9748-9750,
9779, 9785-9786, 9793, 9799,
9801, 9809, 9817, 9822,
9830, 9846, 9944, 10229-
10230, 10236, 10248, 10817-
10819, 10821, 10831-10832,
11623, 11817
Philadelphia, 9944

Afro-Americans--Bibliography,
indexes, 9748-9750, 9801,
10229

Agarwals, 11972

Aged, 9838

Agenais, France, 8965

Aggarwals--SEE: Agarwals,
11972

Agriculturists, 12036-12038,
12040-12041, 12043-12048,
12051, 12053-12055, 12057-
12058
Argentine Republic, 12051
British Columbia, 12058
Canada, 12045-12046,
12058
Denmark, 12038
France, 12053
India, 12037, 12047
New Hampshire, 12048
Quebec, 12045-12046
Sri Lanka, 12040
United States, 12036, 12048
Venezuela, 12057
Yugoslavia, 12043

Ain, France (Dept.), 8966-8967

Aisne, France (Dept.), 8968

Akademia Nauk Technicznych,
Warsaw, 12024

Akademiia nauk SSSR. Institut
SShA i Kanada, 10719

Akademiia nauk URSR, Kiev,
10724

Alabama, 9851-9853, 9855

Alabama--Governors, 9853

Alberta, Can., 8662

Alicante, Spain (Province), 9682,
9691, 11796

Alpes-Maritimes, France (Dept.),
8969

Alsace, 8970-8971, 11746

Altayskiy Kray, Russia, 11230

Amazonas, Brazil, 8591

America, 8492-8494

American Gynecological Society,
11492

American Indian artists--SEE:
Artists, American Indian,
10239, 10254

American Lutheran Church
(1961-   ), 11805, 11807

American Medical Association,
11498

American poets--SEE: Poets,
American, 10816, 10824-
10825, 10827, 10829, 10837,
10968, 10985, 10992

Amiens, France, 11005

Amsterdam, 10288, 11347

Anarchists, 8436

Anatomists, 11376, 11458

Andalusia, 9308, 10838

Andhra Pradesh, India, 9258-
9259, 10590, 11886

Anesthesiologists, 11441

Anglican Church--SEE: Church
of England.

Animal painters, 10146

Anjou, France, 8972, 11748

Ankara. Üniversite. Siyasal
Bilgiler Fakültesi, 12021

Anonyms and pseudonyms,
10739-10744, 10789, 10803,
10815, 10858, 10901, 10919-
10923, 10938, 10944-10945,
10950, 10958, 10960-10961,
10965, 11036, 11041, 11043,
11073, 11093, 11099-11101,
11134, 11154, 11167-11170,
11185-11186, 11210, 11260,
11278, 11289
    American, 10815, 10965
    Australian, 10858
    Canadian, 10901

    Chinese, 10094, 10919-
    10923
    Colombian, 10938

Anonyms and pseudonyms (cont'd)
    Czech, 10944-10945,
    10950
    Dominican (Santo Domin-
    go), 10958
    Ecuadorian, 10960-10961
    English, 10965
    French-Canadian, 11036
    Georgian (Caucasus),
    11041
    German, 11043
    Greek (Modern), 11073
    Hebrew, 11139
    Indic, 11093
    Italian, 11099
    Japanese, 9402, 11134
    Jewish, 11139
    Mexican, 11167-11170
    Peruvian, 11185-11186
    Russian, 11210
    Spanish-American--Bibli-
    ography, indexes, etc.,
    11154
    Swedish, 11260
    Telugu, 11278
    Venezuelan, 11289
    Yiddish, 11139

Anonyms and pseudonyms--Bib-
liography, indexes, etc.,
11544

Anthropologists, 12012, 12018

Anti-Nazi movement, 9091

Antioquia, Colombia (Dept.),
8791, 8796, 10530

Aomori, Japan (Prefecture),
9398

Aquitaine, 8973

Arab countries, 9322-9323,
9334, 9487, 10838-10847

Arabia, 9629

Arabs in Spain, 9303-9304, 9308,
9311

Aragon, Spain, 9683, 11794

Archaeologists, 12009, 12011

Architects, 10034, 10036, 10262-
  10273, 10297
    Charleston, S. C., 10271
    France, 10263
    Great Britain, 10273
    South Carolina, 10271

Argentine Republic, 8495-8510,
  9664, 10362, 10848-10849,
  11412, 11710-11711, 12051

Argentine Republic--Bibliography,
  indexes, etc., 8495

Argentine Republic--Portraits,
  8497-8498

Arizona, 9854, 11513

Arkansas Valley, Colorado,
  9862

Armenia, 8511-8518, 10363,
  10516-10517, 10850-10856,
  11211, 12010

Armenians in Kayseri, Turkey
  (Province), 8511

Armenians in Turkey, 8511,
  8514

Armorers, 12084, 12086

Art collectors, 10033

Art dealers, 10033

Art nouveau, 10110, 10227

Artisans, 10151, 10154, 10169,
  10213, 10287, 10290, 10299,
  10304, 12075, 12081-12082
    Finland, 12075
    France, 10287, 10290
    Hungary, 10151
    Italy, 10154, 10169
    Silesia, Upper (Province),
      10213
    United States, 10304

Artists, 10014-10280, 10306,
  10310
    Abruzzi, 10159
    Afro-American--Bibliog-
      ography, indexes, etc.,
      10229

Artists (cont'd)
    American Indian, 10239,
      10254
    Australia, 10071-10073
    Austria, 8559, 10074-10076
    Belgium, 10077-10079
    Bergamo, 10178
    Black, 10028
    Bohemia, 10101-10102
    Brazil, 10080-10082
    Burma, 10083
    California, 10249
    Canada, 10084-10091
    China--Bibliography, in-
      dexes, etc., 10092-
      10095
    Croatia, 10100
    Czechoslovakia, 10101-
      10102

    Durham, Eng. (County),
      10139
    Eskimo, 10103
    Ferrara, 10156
    Finland, 10104-10105
    Flanders, 10106-10107
    France, 10108-10127,
      10290
    France
      Portraits--Catalogs,
        10107
    Friuli, 11124
    Georgia (Transcaucasia),
      9059
    Germany, 9107, 10128-
      10133
    Great Britain, 10134-10147
    Greece, Ancient, 10148
    Hungary, 10149-10151
    Israel, 10152
    Italy, 10018, 10153-10180,
      11108, 11111-11112
    Japan, 10181-10189
    Jewish, 10190
    Korea, 10182, 10191
    Lorraine, 10121
    Mantua, 10154
    Mennonite, 10246
    Michigan, 10245
    Milan, 10161
    Netherlands, 10192-10198
    Northumberland, Eng.,
      10139
    Ontario, 10091
    Padua, 10175
    Peru, 10199
    Perugia, 10174

Authors (cont'd)
  Polish, 11185-11186,
    11188-11198
  Portuguese, 11199-11201,
    11249
  Provençal, 11023, 11202-
    11205
  Provençal--Bibliography,
    indexes, etc., 11202
  Provençal (Modern), 11204
  Puerto Rican, 11206-11207
  Romanian, 11208-11209
  Russian, 11210-11232
    Altayskiy Kray,
      11230a
    Armenia, 11212
    Baikal Lake region
      11222
    Chechen-Ingush
      A.S.S.R., 11218
    Chuvashia, 10932-
      10933
    Kabardino-Balkar
      A.S.S.R., 11223
    Krasnoyarsk, 11215
    Kuybyshevskaya
      oblast', 11216
    Saratov, 11228
    Siberia, 11210-11211,
      11221-11222, 11225,
      11230-11231
    Smolensk (Province),
      11230
    Ural mountain region,
      11211
    Voronezh, 11224
  Sanskrit, 11233-11234
  Scandinavian, 11235
  Scottish, 10978
  Serbian, 11236-11237
  Slavic, 11238-11241
    SEE ALSO: Individual
      Slavic literatures.
  Slovak, 10948, 10955,
    11242-11245
  Slovenian, 11246-11247
  Soyot, 11248
  Spanish, 11249-11259,
    11487, 11790, 11792-
    11794, 11796
    Aragon, 11794
    Alicante (Province)
      11796
    Bilbilis, 11259
    Cadiz (Province),
      11258
    Cartagena, 11793

Authors (cont'd)
    Catalonia, 11790
    Granada, 11255
    Málaga (Province),
      9689
    Navarre, 11257
    Segovia, 11251
    Tudela, 11250
    Vizcaya, 11254
  Spanish American, 11154-
    11158
  Swedish, 11260-11263
  Swiss, 11034, 11264-11268
  Syryenian, 11269
  Tajik, 11270-11271
  Tamil, 11272-11276
  Tatar, 11277
  Telugu, 11278-11279
  Turkish, 11280-11282
  Turkoman, 11283
  Ukrainian, 11285
  Urdu, 11286-11288
  Venezuelan, 11289-11292,
    11522
  Vietnamese, 11293
  Welsh, 10972
  Wendic, 11294
  White Russian, 11295-11297
  Yakut, 11298
  Yugoslav, 11299-11302

Authors--Bibliography, indexes,
  etc., 10737-10738

Authors--Portraits, 10791

Authors, Women, 10824, 10874,
  11050, 11069, 11103, 11108,
  11279
  Austria, 10874
  Germany, 11050, 11069
  India, 11279
  Italy, 11103, 11108
  United States, 10824

Autographs, 8479, 8872, 11076

Autobiography--Bibliography, indexes, etc., 8299, 9070

Automobile industry and trade,
  11970

Automobile racing, 10602-10603

Autun, France (Diocese), 11666,
  11760

Berlin, 9107-9108

Berlin. Technische Universitat--
SEE: Technische Universitat
Berlin.

Bern, 11264-11266

Berner Schriftsteller-Verein,
11264-11266

Beuthen--SEE: Bytom, Poland
(City), 9536

Bible--Biography, 11574, 11578,
11587-11588, 11591, 11598-
11599, 11606, 11608, 11615,
11618, 11620

Bible. New Testament--Biogra-
phy, 11577

Bible. Old Testament--Biogra-
phy, 11581, 11865

Bible. Old Testament--Biogra-
phy--Bibliography, indexes,
11858

Bibliographers, 11348

Bibliography, indexes, portrait
catalogs (Universal), 8272-
8304
SEE ALSO: Bibliography, indexes, portrait catalogs
under certain subjects or
under countries, etc.; e.g.,
Performing arts--Bibli-
ography, indexes, portrait
catalogs; France-- Bibli-
ography, indexes, portrait
catalogs.

Bilbilis, Spain, 11259

Bio-bibliography--Bibliography,
indexes, 8285, 8304

Biochemists--Bibliography, indexes, etc., 11893

Biography, Universal, 8277,
8305-8479, 8506, 8584, 8735,
9448, 9476, 9666, 9680, 9742,
9821, 10766, 11876, 11942
Middle Ages, 8409-8411

Biography, Universal (cont'd)
16th century, 8421, 8426,
8431, 8438
17th century, 8431, 8462
18th century, 8418-8419,
8462, 8467
19th century, 8420, 8422,
8427, 8429, 8436, 8440,
8442, 8451, 8454-8455,
8458-8459-8460, 8463-
8464, 8466, 8469, 8870,
8896, 8924
19th century--Catalogs, indexes, etc., 8282
20th century, 8412, 8417,
8423-8425, 8427-8429,
8433, 8435-8436, 8439,
8442, 8446, 8448, 8451-
8453, 8456, 8458, 8460,
8465-8466, 8470-8473,
8476-8479, 9221
20th century--Bibliography,
indexes, 8280, 8282,
9754, 9764

Biography, Universal--Bibliogra-
phy, indexes, etc., 8272-8304,
8864, 9754, 9764

Biography, Universal--Juvenile
literature, 8305-8306, 8368

Biography, Universal--Juvenile
literature--Bibliography, indexes, 8287, 8300, 8303

Biography, Universal--Periodi-
cals, 8423, 8437

Biologists, 11897, 11903

Birmingham, Ala., 9855

Birmingham, Eng., 10142

Bishops, 11624, 11710-11711,
11714, 11716, 11718, 11736-
11737, 11765, 11775, 11788,
11799-11801, 11817
Argentine Republic, 11710-
11711
Austria, 11714, 11716
Brazil, 11718
Colombia, 11736-11737
England, 11624
Germany, 11765
Italy, 11775

Buckinghamshire, Eng., 9181

Budapest, 9219

Buddhist priests--SEE: Priests,
  Buddhist, 11561-11562,
  11566

Buddhists, 11560-11569
  China, 11560-11562, 11564,
    11566-11567, 11569
  China--Bibliography, in-
    dexes, etc., 11560
  Japan, 11568
  Tibet, 9734

Buenos Aires (Archdiocese),
  11711

Buffalo, N. Y., 9856-9858

Bukhara, Russia (Province),
  9600

Bukovina, 9597

Bulgaria, 8616-8624, 10669-
  10670, 10745, 10896-10900,
  11241, 11416

Bull-fighters, 10612-10613

Burgtheater, Vienna--SEE: Vienna. Burgtheater, 10366,
  10368-10369

Burgandy, 8985, 11881

Burma, 8625-8628, 10083

Business consultants, 11988

Businessmen, 9233, 11953-11954,
  11956, 11961, 11967-11976,
  11978-11980, 11982-11985,
  11988-11989
  Africa, 11953
  Austria, 11954
  Canada, 11989
  China--Portraits, 11956
  England, 11968
  France, 11961
  Germany, 11964
  Great Britain, 11968-11970
  India, 9233, 11971-11974
  Italy, 11975-11976, 11978-
    11979

Businessmen (cont'd)
  New York (City), 11984
  Pakistan, 11980
  Taiwan, 11982-11983
  United States, 11984-11985,
    11988-11989

Bytom, Poland (City), 9536

Cabala, 11861

Cabinet officers (Netherlands),
  9491

Cabinet officers (United States),
  9840

Cadiz, Spain (Province), 11258

Calabria, Italy, 9370

Calcutta. University, 12017

Caldas, Colombia (Dept.), 8791

California, 9859-9860, 9954-
  9955, 10250

California, Southern, 9860, 10250

Calligraphers, 10094-10095,
  10097-10098, 10181, 10191

Calligraphers--Bibliography, indexes, etc., 10094-10095

Cambridge. University. King's
  College, 9145

Cambridge. University. Peterhouse, 9146

Cameroons, Southern, 8629

Campines, Belgium, 8580a

Canada, 8630-8688, 9771, 9831,
  10084-10091, 10300, 10372-
  10374, 10526-10529, 10901-
  10905, 11036-11039, 11303-
  11305, 11417-11418, 11719-
  11727, 11955, 11989, 12045-
  12046, 12058

Canada--Armed Forces, 8658

Canada--Bibliography, indexes.
8276, 8630-8631, 10526-
10527

Canada--Portraits, 8640

Canada--Governors-general,
8641

Canada. Parliament, 8638-8639

Canadian Northwest--SEE: Northwest, Canadian, 8659

Cantabria, Spain, 9686

Cantal, France (Dept.), 8975

Cantors, 10548

Capuchins, 11687, 11715, 11771,
11777, 11796

Cardinals, 11670, 11718, 11762,
11788

Caribbean area, 9449, 10004

Carmelites, 11636-11637, 11699

Carpathian mountain region,
9222, 9597

Cartagena, Spain, 9687, 11793

Carthusians, 11680, 11690, 11792

Cartographers, 11994-11995,
11998, 12004, 12007

Cartographers--Portraits, 12007

Cartoonists, 10251-10252

Castellón, Spain (Province), 9691

Castrati, 10469

Castres, Frances, 8986

Catalonia, 11790

Catholic authors--SEE: Authors,
Catholic, 10572, 10774, 10809,
10811

Catholic Church, 11541, 11579-
11580, 11589, 11631, 11802

Catholic Church (cont'd)
  Argentine Republic, 11710-
    11711
  Austria, 11712-11716
  Bavaria, 11767
  Belgium, 11717
  Bohemia, 11739-11740
  Brazil, 11718
  Canada, 11719-11727
  Chile, 11728-11730
  China, 11731-11733
  Colombia, 11734-11737
  Croatia, 11738
  England, 11769
  France, 11666, 11741-11764
  Germany, 11765-11767
  Great Britain, 11768-11769
  Italy, 11770-11777
  Japan, 11778
  Mexico, 11779-11781
  Netherlands, 11783-11784
  Poland, 11786
  Portugal, 11787-11788
  Scotland, 11789
  Sicily, 11775
  Spain, 11790-11797
  Switzerland, 11798
  United States, 11799-11801

Catholic Church--Bibliography,
  indexes, etc., 11631-11633

Catholic converts--SEE: Converts,
  Catholic, 11650, 11668

Caucasus, 9601

Ceará, Brazil (State), 8610,
  10370

Central America, 8688a

Central Europe--Portraits--
  Catalogs, 8688b

Cephalonia, Greece (Island),
  9213, 9215

Československá akademie věd,
  11880

Ceylon. For works about this
  country see under its latest
  name: Sri Lanka.

Ceylon National Congress, 9698

Chalon-sur-Saone, France (Diocese), 11760

Chalons-sur-Marne, France, 8987

Champagne, France, 8988, 11006

Champagne, France--Portraits--Catalogs, 8988

Ch'ang-chou, China, 8789

Chaplains, Military, 11605

Charente, France (Dept.), 8989

Charente-Inférieure, France (Dept.), 8990-8991

Charleston, S. C., 10271

Chartres, France, 8992, 11019-11020

Chechen-Ingush A.S.S.R., 11218

Chemists, 11907-11910

Chemical engineers, 11907

Cher, France (Dept.), 8993

Cheshire, Eng., 10974, 11769

Chiari, Italy, 11121

Chicoutimi, Que. (Diocese), 11720, 11726

Chihuahua, Mexico (State), 9474

Children as musicians, 10460

Children's authors, 10761, 10783, 10787, 10801, 10828, 10859, 10861, 10956, 11245

Chile, 8688c-8688g, 10906-10910, 11419, 11728-11730

China, 8525, 8689-8790, 10092-10098, 10671-10675, 10911-10931, 11420-11421, 11560-11562, 11564, 11566-11567, 11569, 11731-11733, 11927, 11956

China--Armed Forces, 8720

China--Bibliography, indexes, 8689-8708, 10911-10918

China--Kings and rulers, 8713, 8718, 8734

China--Portraits, 8734

China (Republic of China), 9729-9731

Chinese Communist Party--SEE: Chung-kuo kung ch'an tang, 8722

Chinese in foreign countries, 8744, 8754

Chinese in Indonesia, 9288

Chinese in Malaysia, 8769

Chính-phu' Cách-mang Lâm-thoi' miền Nam Việt-Nam, 9998

Chios (Island), 9217

Choreographers, 10326

Chouans, 8943

Christian authors--SEE: Authors, Christian, 10755, 10804, etc.

Christian biography, 11570-11835

Ch'üan T'ang shih--Indexes, 10912

Chung-kuo ch'ing nien tang, 8729

Chung-kuo kung ch'an tang, 8722

Chung-kuo kung ch'an tang. Chung yang wei yüan hui, 8721

Church of England, 11624-11626

Church of Ireland, 11627

Church of Jesus Christ of Latter Saints--SEE: Mormons.

Church of Scotland, 9637

Chuvashia, 10932-10933

Cinema--SEE: Moving pictures.

Cistercian nuns, 11761

Cistercians, 11654

City planners, 9529

Civil engineers, 12062

Classical biography, 8373, 8392-
8408, 9206-9210

Clavichord makers, 10502

Clergy
  Afro-American, 11623
  Austria, 11712-11714,
    11716
  Canada, 11719-11720,
    11722-11723, 11726-
    11727
  Chile, 11728, 11730
  China, 11731-11733
  Colombia, 11734, 11736-
    11737
  Denmark, 11806, 11808
  France, 11741, 11747,
    11753, 11758, 11762
  Germany, 11603, 11804
  Great Britain, 11602,
    11624-11626, 11769,
    11822-11825, 11827-
    11828
  Hesse, 11804
  Ireland, 11627
  Italy, 11770
  London, 11602
  New England, 11829
  Quebec, 11719-11720,
    11722-11723, 11727
  Scotland, 11789, 11824,
    11828
  United States, 11623, 11799-
    11801, 11805, 11826,
    11829

Clock and watch makers, 12074,
  12076, 12080, 12085, 12088,
  12091

Coahuila, Mexico, 9472

Coimbra. Universidade, 8600

Colchester, Eng., 12085

Collège royal de France, 10685

College teachers
  Great Britain, 10698

Cologne, 9110

Colombia, 8791-8799, 10099,
  10530-10531, 10938-10941,
  10353, 11734-11737, 11879,
  11957, 12063

Colorado, 9861-9862

Comic strip artists--SEE: Cartoonists, 10251-10252

Comintern--SEE: Communist
  International, 8448

Commonwealth of Nations, 10988

Communist International, 8448

Communist Party of China--SEE:
  Chung-kuo kung ch'an tang,
  8722

Communists (General), 8448,
  8457, 11061, 11949
  Bulgaria, 8622-8624
  China, 8721-8723, 8728,
    8732, 8756, 8772, 8784

Composers, 10340, 10438, 10453-
  10454, 10458, 10473, 10477,
  10481, 10484, 10488, 10492,
  10495, 10497, 10515-10516,
  10519-10520, 10523, 10526-
  10528, 10530-10531, 10533,
  10535-10536, 10541, 10543,
  10556, 10562, 10566, 10568,
  10570, 10572, 10582, 10587
  Africa, Southern, 10515
  Armenia, 10516
  Australia, 10519-10520
  Austria, 10667
  Azerbaijan, 10523
  Canada, 10526-10528
  Denmark, 10533
  France, 10535
  Georgia (Transcaucasia),
    10536
  Great Britain, 10541
  Hungary, 10543

Composers (cont'd)
    Norway, 10556
    Romania, 10562
    Scandinavia, 10566
    Serbia, 10568
    Tajikistan, 10570
    Turkey, 10572
    United States, 10582, 10587

Composers--Bibliography, indexes, etc., 10438

Composers--Portraits, 10484

Computer operators, etc., 11922-11923

Concepción, Chile (Diocese), 11730

Conductors (Music), 10483, 10560

Confederate States of America. Congress, 9960

Congo (Brazzaville), 8800

Congrégation de Saint-Maur, ordre de Saint-Benoît en France--SEE: Benedictines. Congrégation de Saint-Maur, 11759

Congrégation du Saint-Esprit et du Sacre-Coeur de Marie-- SEE: Holy Ghost Fathers, 11673

Congressional Medal of Honor-- SEE: Medal of Honor, 9803, 9836

Connecticut, 9863, 9872

Connecticut Valley, Mass., 9897

Conseil d'État (France)--SEE: France. Conseil d'État, 8962

Conservationists, 9777

Conservative Party of Canada, 8635

Contract bridge, 10614

Converts, Catholic, 11650, 11668

Cooperation, 11991

Cooperative Commonwealth Federation. British Columbia, 8664

Copenhagen. Polyteknisk laereanstalt--SEE: Polyteknisk laereanstalt, Copenhagen, 12064

Copenhagen. Universitet, 10679, 11808

Córdoba, Argentine Republic, 8501

Córdoba, Argentine Republic. Universidad Nacional, 8501

Corinth, Greece, 9214

Cornell University. Southeast Asia Program, 10726

Corrèze, France (Dept.), 8994

Cortes Españolas--SEE: Spain. Cortes, 9679

Cosenza, Italy, 11129

Costa Rica, 8801, 10942

Côte d'Or, France (Dept.), 8995

Counter-culture (U. S.), 9766

Cour des comptes (France)--SEE: France. Cour des comptes, 8964

Courland, 11306

Cranks--SEE: Eccentrics, 9393, 10750, 10753

Cremona, Italy, 9371

Creuse, France (Dept.), 8997, 11001a

Cricket, 10615

Crime and criminals
    Australia, 8541

Crime and criminals (cont'd)
   France, 8957
   Great Britain, 9160, 9176
   United States, 9813

Crimean War (1853-1856), 9164

Critics, 10340

Croatia, 10100, 10943, 11422,
   11738

Croatians in Canada, 9771

Croatians in the United States,
   9771

Crusades--Biography, 8409

Cuba, 8802-8804

Current biography yearbook--
   Indexes, 8280

Custodia Terrae Sanctae (Franciscan mission), 11785

Cuyo, Argentine Republic (Province), 8500

Czechoslovak Society of Arts and
   Sciences in America, 10734

Czechoslovakia, 8805-8812, 10101-
   10102, 10375, 10532, 10676-
   10678, 10944-10955, 11240, ·
   11307, 11423, 11880

Czechs in the United States, 9819,
   10734

Daghestan, 8813

Dahomey, 8814-8815

Damascus, 9726-9728

Dancers, 10315-10316, 10326,
   10338, 10403, 10544
   SEE ALSO: Ballet.

Danmarks ingeniørakademi,
   12064

Danske folkekirke, 11806, 11808

Danske sprog- og litteraturselskab,
   Copenhagen, 10760

Data processing, 11922-11923

Dauphiné, France, 8998

Declaration of Independence (United States)--SEE: United States.
   Declaration of Independence.

Delhi, India, 9261

Denmark, 8816-8834, 10533,
   10679, 10956-10957, 11308-
   11309, 11424, 11524, 11806,
   11808, 11958-11960, 12038-
   12039, 12041, 12064, 12078

Denmark--Bibliography, indexes,
   etc., 8816-8821

Denmark--Portraits, 8819, 8830,
   10957

Denmark--Portraits--Catalogs,
   8816-8817, 8819-8821

Denmark. Flaade, 8824, 8833

Denmark. Haer, 8816, 8823

Denmark. Haer--Portraits, 8816

Denmark. Rigsdagen, 8826

Dentists, 11425, 11524-11528
   Denmark, 11524
   Finland, 11425
   Germany, 11527
   Sweden, 11528
   United States, 11525-11526

Derbyshire, Eng., 10974

Designers, 10155, 10297, 10306,
   10310

Detective and mystery story
   wroters. 10969, 10982

Deutsche Oper am Rhein, 10393

Deux-Sèvres, France (Dept.),
   8999

Devon, Eng., 9182, 10975

Devotio Moderna, 11659

Diplomats, 8325, 9150, 9774

Döblinger Friedhof, Vienna, 8561

Dominican Republic, 8835-8836, 10958

Dominicans, 11632, 11635, 11674, 11717, 11724, 11783, 11790, 11794

Dominicans--Bibliography, indexes, etc., 11632

Don Valley, Russia, 9602-9603

Dordogne, France (Dept.), 9038

Dorset, Eng., 10975

Dramatists, 10374, 10422, 10758, 10785, 10790, 10798, 10806, 10883, 10895, 10984, 11017-11018, 11025, 11090
    Austria, 10883
    Brazil, 10895
    Canada, 10374
    France, 11017-11018, 11025
    Great Britain, 10970, 10984
    Hungary, 11090
    Quebec, 10374
    Slovenia, 10422

Dublin. St. Patrick's Cathedral, 11627

Durham, Eng. (County), 10139, 11342

Dutch in Brazil, 9493

Dutch in Indonesia, 9285

Earth scientists, 12070

East (Far East), 8521-8522, 8524

East Anglia, 9183

East India Company (English), 9151

East Prussia (Province)--SEE: Prussia. East (Province), 9114, 9123

Eastern Europe--SEE: Europe, Eastern, 8843-8846, 10376

Eastern Nigeria. Legislature, 9502

Eastern Townships, Que., 8683

Eccentrics, 9393, 10750, 10753

Ecologists, 11891

Economic development planners, 11946

Economists, 11309, 11943-11944, 11947, 11950, 11959, 11962

Ecuador, 8837-8839, 10960-10964

Edinburgh, 9633

Edinburgh. Faculty of Advocates, 11326

Educators and scholars, 10648-10736, 11009, 11565, 11645
    Arabic, 10705, 10707
    Austria, 8559, 10665-10667, 10696-10697, 11056-11057
    Belgium, 10668
    Bulgaria, 10669-10670
    Canada, 10727-10728
    China, 8716, 10671-10675
    China--Bibliography, indexes, etc., 8689
    Czechoslovakia, 10676-10678
    Denmark, 10679
    Finland, 10680-10682
    France, 10683-10685
    Germany, 9107, 10686-10697, 11056-11057
    Great Britain, 10698-10699
    Greece, Medieval & modern, 10700-10701
    Hungary, 10702
    India, 10703-10704
    Islamic countries, 10705-10707, 11847, 11849, 11854

Educators and scholars (cont'd)
Italy, 10708-10710
Jewish, 9057
Latvia, 10711
Muslim, 10706, 11847,
11849, 11854
Netherlands, 10712-10713
Philippine Islands, 10714-
10715
Poland, 10716-10717
Romania, 9569, 10718
Russia, 10719-10720
Spain, 10721
Sweden, 10722
Switzerland, 10723
Turkey, 9739
Ukraine, 10724-10725
United States, 10726-10736

Educators and scholars--Bibli-
ography, indexes, etc., 11870

Educators and scholars--Por-
traits, 10650, 10654

Egypt (Ancient), 8840, 8842

Egypt (Medieval & Modern),
8841, 11319

Elbe Valley, Ger., 9096

Elberfeld, Ger., 9135

Electrical engineers, 12023,
12071

Electrical engineers--Bibliog-
raphy, indexes, etc., 12023

Elementary school principals
United States, 10735

Elginshire, Scot., 9649

Emigrés, 8945-8947

Engineers, 10272, 11879, 12022-
12023, 12030, 12033, 12062-
12072a
Afro-American, 12068
Colombia, 11879, 12063
Denmark, 12064
Finland, 12071
France, 12072
Great Britain--Bibliogra-
phy, indexes, etc.,
12022

Engineers (cont'd)
Pakistan, 12065
United States, 12062, 12066-
12068

England--SEE: Great Britain,
8470, 9138-9205, etc.

Engravers, 8284, 10046, 10056,
10060, 10064, 10086, 10125,
10129, 10149, 10187, 10193-
10194, 10200-10201, 10293
Canada, 10086
Flanders, 10193-10194
France, 10125
Germany, 10129
Hungary, 10149
Italy, 10163, 10166
Netherlands, 10193-10194
Poland, 10200-10201

Entertainers
Canada, 10373
France, 10380

Epirus, 8373

Epitaphs, 8438, 8750, 9036, 9112,
9115, 9119, 9395, 9639, 11859
China, 8750
France, 9036
Germany, 9112, 9115, 9119
Jamaica, 9395
Paris, 9036
Poland, 11859
Scotland, 9639

Eponyms, 8342

Erfurt, Ger., 11527

Eskimos, 10103

Espionage--SEE: Spies, 8468

Essex, Eng., 9184-9186

Estonia, 10995-10998

Etalä-Pohjanmaa, Finland (Province)--SEE: Österbotten,
Finland, 8850

Eton College, 9153

Europe, 8414, 8434, 8441, 8454, 8462, 8475, 9079, 9356, 10296, 11877

Europe, Central--SEE: Central Europe, 8688b

Europe, Eastern, 8843-8846, 10376

European War (1914-1918), 8458, 8930, 9632, 9850, 11605

European War (1914-1918)--Portraits, 8458, 8930

Explorers, 8686, 12000-12001, 12003, 12008, 12028

Faculty of Advocates, Edinburgh --SEE: Edinburgh. Faculty of Advocates, 11326

Fashion designers, 10286, 10309

Fathers of the Church, 11571, 11611, 11616, 11648

Ferrara, 9372, 10156

Fez, Morocco, 9485

Fifth Monarchy Men, 9147

Finland, 8847-8860, 9631, 10104-10105, 10283, 10534, 10680-10682, 11310-11314, 11338, 11425-11426, 12035, 12042, 12052, 12071, 12075

Finland--Armed Forces, 8853

Finland--Bibliography, indexes, etc., 10680

Finland--Portraits--Catalogs, 8847, 10680

Finland. Korkein Oikeus, 11312

Finland. Oikeuskansleri, 11310

Flanders, 8861-8862, 10106-10107, 10192-10195, 11414

Flemish Movement, 8861

Flintshire, Wales, 10003

Florence, Italy, 10168

Florida, 9864-9867

Flower painters, 10058

Folk painters, 10242

Food industry and trade--Biography, 11941

Football, 10616-10623

Football coaches, 10617

Foresters, 12039, 12052

Forez, France, 11021

Formosa--SEE: Taiwan, 8731, 8754, etc.

Founders (Metallurgy), 12090

France, 8454, 8863-9056, 10108-10127, 10263, 10287, 10290, 10298, 10311, 10377-10391, 10535, 10683-10685, 10999-11035, 11315-11316, 11336, 11427-11438, 11741-11764, 11830, 11881-11882, 11905, 11961-11963, 11999, 12027, 12053, 12072, 12091

France--Bibliography, indexes, etc., 8863-8868

France--Portraits, 8338, 8872, 8891, 8900, 8903-8906, 8908-8909, 8914, 8919, 8924, 8930, 8939-8940, 8948, 8959-8960

France--Portraits--Catalogs, 8293, 8865-8866, 10120

France--Revolution, 8883, 8899, 8909, 8954, 8956

France--Revolution--Portraits, 8909

France. Armée, 8873, 8881, 8892, 8912-8913, 8921, 8936, 8944-8947, 8966, 11428

France. Assemblée nationale
(1848-1852), 8878

France. Assemblée nationale
(1871-1942), 8951-8952

France. Assemblée nationale
(1871-1942). Chambre des
députés, 8874-8875, 8887-
8889, 8901, 8911, 8915, 8953

France. Assemblée nationale
(1871-1942). Sénat, 8876, 8879,
8890

France. Chambre des députés
(1814-1848), 8886, 8927,
8933-8935, 8937

France. Conseil d'État, 8962

France. Conseil économique et
social, 11962

France. Convention nationale
(1792-1795), 8956

France. Corps législatif (1852-
1870), 8922, 8961-8962

France. Cour des comptes, 8964

France. Marine, 8895, 8936,
11430

France. Parlement (1946-   ).
Assemblée nationale, 8904

France. Parlement (1946-   ).
Sénat, 8905

France. Parlement, Paris, 8900,
11315

France, Parlement, Rouen, 8907

France. Sénat (1852-1870), 8963

Franche-Comté, 9000, 10112,
11749

Franciscans, 11665, 11667, 11684,
11707, 11772-11773, 11784-
11785, 11793, 11802

Franco-Prussian War (1870-
1871), 9106

Franconia, 9111

Frankfurt an der Oder. Universität, 10686-10687

Free thought (Rationalists), 11554

Freemasons, 8358, 8360, 8450,
8474, 8588, 8852
    Brazil, 8588
    Finland, 8852
    France, 8928
    New Hampshire, 9906
    North Carolina, 9915

Freiburg im Breisgau, 11051

French-Canadians, 8646-8647,
8649-8650, 8654-8655, 8659-
8660, 10087, 10278, 10374,
11036-11039

French Canadians in the United
States, 8659, 8686

French in America, 9832

French in Chile, 8688g

French in the United States, 9805,
9832

French-speaking Equatorial Af-
rica--SEE: Africa, French-
speaking Equatorial, 8487

French-speaking West Africa--
SEE: Africa, French-speaking
West, 8487, 8489

Fribourg, Switzerland (Canton),
9720

Friedhof zu Sankt Marx, Vienna,
8562

Friends, Society of, 11803

Friesland, 11040

Friuli, Italy, 11124

Furniture makers, 10298, 12073

Gynecologists, 11492

Haarlem, Netherlands, 10198

Hadith--Authorities, 11840,
11843-11845

The Hague, 11464

Hahnemann Medical College and
Hospital, Philadelphia, 11494

Hainaut, Belgium (Province),
8578, 11151

Hall-marks, 10294

Hamburg, 10131

Hampshire, Eng., 10973

Hanafis, 11317-11318, 11320

Hanbalites, 11846

Hand-to-hand fighting, 10634-10635

Harpsichord makers, 10502

Hartford, Conn., 9872

Harvard University--Portraits,
8277

Haryana, India, 9263

Hasidism, 11860-11861, 11863

Haute-Marche, France (Region)
--SEE: Marche, Haute-,
France (Region), 8997

Haute-Saône, France (Dept.),
9005

Haute-Savoie, France (Dept.),
9006-9008

Hautes-Alpes, France (Dept.),
8981

Heidelberg, 9112

Helmstedt. Universität, 10692

Helsingfors--SEE: Helsinki.

Helsinki, 12075

Helsinki. Yliopisto, 8847, 10681

Helsinki. Yliopisto--Portraits--
Catalogs, 8847.

Hérault, France (Dept.), 9009

Herefordshire, Eng.--Portraits,
9188

Heretics, 11594, 11607, 11617

Hermits
China, 10672

Hermits of St. Paul, 11738

Hesse, 10501, 11804

High school students
United States, 9818, 9845,
10588

High school teachers
United States, 10733

Hindu saints--SEE: Saints,
Hindu, 11836

Hinduism, 11836-11838

Historians, 12010, 12013-12016,
12019-12020

Hockey, 10626-10631

Hoftheater, Vienna--SEE: Vienna.
Burgtheater, 10366, 10368-
10369

Holy Ghost Fathers, 11673

Homeopaths, 11373, 11455

Honan, China (Province), 8787

Hongkong, 8778

Horn-players, 10461

Horsemanship, 10632-10633

Horse-racing, 10632

Horticulturists, 12041

Hospitalers, 11700

Hotel managers, 11987

Houston, Tex., 9873

Huguenots, 11830

Hunan, China (Province),
10931

Hungarians in the United States,
9798, 9808

Hungarians in foreign countries,
9220

Hungary, 9219-9225, 10149-10151,
10406, 10470, 10543, 10596,
10702, 11083-11091, 11454

Hyderabad, India (State), 9264

Hyderabad, India (State). Legislature, 9264

Hymn writers, 10463-10466,
10472, 10477, 10529, 10538,
10540-10541, 10575, 10580

I͡Akutiia--SEE: Yakutia.

I͡Aroslavl', Russia (Province)--
SEE: Yaroslavl', Russia
(Province), 9623

Iceland, 11092

Illinois, 9874-9875

Illustrators, 10069, 10140, 10186,
10224, 10235, 10251, 10818,
10828, 10859, 11374

Illustrators, Medical, 11374

Impressionism (Art), 10113,
10126

India, 9226-9280, 9316, 10364,
10407-10408, 10544-10545,
10590, 10615, 10639, 10703-
10704, 11080-11082, 11093-
11095, 11144-11145, 11165-
11166, 11233-11234, 11272-

India (cont'd)
11276, 11278-11279, 11346,
11455-11457, 11540, 11833,
11836-11838, 11857, 11885-
11886, 11934, 11971-11974,
12015, 12017-12018, 12037,
12047

India (Republic). Lok Saba, 9238-
9239, 9245

India (Republic). Lok Saba. Council of States, 9238-9239

India (Republic). Parliament--
SEE: India (Republic). Lok
Saba, 9238-9239

Indian National Science Academy,
11885

Indiana, 9876-9879, 10834, 11505

Indians of North America, 8492,
9767, 9780, 9824, 10239,
10254

Indians of North America--Por-
traits, 9767, 9800

Indochina, 9281

Indonesia, 9282-9288

Indonesia. Departemen Pertahanan
Keamanan, 9284

Indonesia. Majelis Permusyawaratan Rakyat, 9283

Industrial arts, 10736, 12031,
12033, 12081-12082

Industrial designers, 12027, 12034

Innsbruck. Universität, 10666

Instrument-makers, 12077

Insurance--Biography, 11958,
11967, 11980

International agencies, 8476

Inventors, 11872, 12026, 12028,
12030, 12081-12082

Ionian Islands, 9211

Iowa, 9880-9883

Ipswich, Eng., 9189

Iran, 9289-9291, 11183-11184

Iran--Bibliography, indexes, etc.,
9289

Iran--Kings and rulers, 9291

Iraq, 9292, 11096

Ireland, 9293-9295, 11097-11098,
11627, 11827

Isère, France (Dept.), 9010

Islam, 9297, 9299, 9306-9307,
9311, 9313-9316, 9326, 9330-
9332, 11839-11856

Islam--Bibliography, indexes,
etc., 11841

Islamic countries, 9296-9334,
10705-10707, 11317-11323,
11921, 11930, 12086-12087

Islamic Empire, 9324, 9327

Israel, 9335-9336, 9426, 10152,
10409

Israel-Arab War (1967-   ),
9336

Italians in the Argentine Republic, 8503

Italians in the Rhine Valley, 9125

Italians in Venezuela, 9995

Italy, 9337-9393, 10153-10180,
10274-10275, 10280, 10284,
10410-10411, 10510, 10546-
10547, 10708-10710, 11099-
11132, 11485-11459, 11658,
11770-11777, 11975-11979,
12069, 12079, 12084

Italy--Bibliography, indexes,
etc., 9337

Italy. Esercito, 9339

Italy. Parlamento, 9343, 9351,
9353-9355, 9361-9362

Italy. Parlamento. Camera dei
deputati, 9353-9355

Italy, Southern, 11775

Jacobins, 8883

Jaffna, Sri Lanka, 9702

Jains, 11857

Jalapa, Mexico (City), 9478

Jamaica, 9394-9395

Jamaica. Assembly, 9394

Jammu and Kashmir, 9265

Jansenists--Bibliography, indexes, etc., 11631

Japan, 9396-9418, 10181-10189,
10412, 11134-11138, 11529,
11568, 11778, 11867-11868

Japan--Bibliography, indexes,
etc., 9396-9397

Japan--Portraits, 9417

Japanese in Brazil, 8613

Japanese in China, 9408, 9413

Japanese in Korea, 9408

Japanese in Mukden, 9406

Jazz musicians, 10450, 10476,
10479, 10498, 10534, 10578,
10583

Jersey, 9190

Jesuits, 11729, 11757, 11780-
11782

Jesuits in Chile, 11729

Jesuits in France, 11757

Jesuits in Mexico, 11780-11781

Jesuits in the Moluccas, 11782

Jewellers, 10301

Jewish authors--SEE: Authors,
Jewish, 9057, 9675, etc.

Jews, 8648, 8846, 9057, 9085,
9088, 9224, 9419-9437, 9461a,
9533, 9600, 9675, 9755, 9872,
10190, 10548-10549, 11460-
11462, 11505, 11858-11865,
12029

Jews--Bibliography, indexes,
etc., 11460-11461, 11858

Jews in Austria, 11143

Jews in Canada, 8648

Jews in Canada--Bibliography,
indexes, 9755

Jews in Eastern Europe, 8846

Jews in Galicia, 9057

Jews in Germany, 9085, 9088,
9435

Jews in Hungary, 9224

Jews in Lithuania, 9461a

Jews in Palestine, 9419

Jews in Poland, 9533, 11859

Jews in Portugal, 9675

Jews in Russia, 9600

Jews in Spain, 9675

Jews in the United States, 9755,
9872, 11504

Jews in the United States--Bibli-
ography, indexes, 9755

Jews in Tunisia, 11140

Journalists, 9576, 10836, 10879,
11237, 11242
    Austria, 10879
    Russia, 9576

Journalists (cont'd)
    Serbia, 11237
    Slovakia, 11242
    United States, 10836

Judaism, 11858-11865

Judaism--Bibliography, indexes,
etc., 11858

Judges
    Canada, 11304-11305
    Egypt (Medieval & Modern)
        8841, 11319
    Finland, 11310, 11312-
        11313
    France, 11315
    Islamic--SEE: Judges,
        Muslim, 11322-11323
    Muslim, 11322-11323
    Ohio, 11332
    Ontario, 11305
    Oregon, 11331
    Philippine Islands, 11324
    Quebec (Province), 11304
    Sweden, 11327
    United States, 11328-11332
    Wisconsin, 11328

Judo, 10635

Jujuy, Argentina (Province),
8496, 10848

Justice Party (Madras Presidency, India), 9268

Kabardia, 11223

Kalinin, Russia (Province),
9605-9606

Kanawha Valley, W. Va., 9981

Kandy, Sri Lanka, 9699

Kansas, 9983

Kansas City, Mo., 9884-9885

Kao seng ch'uan--Indexes, 11560

Karachayevo-Cherkesskaya
avtonomaya oblast', 10934

Karate, 10635

Mato Grosso, Brazil, 8604

Maumee Valley, Ohio, 9935, 9939

Mayors
Canada, 8633
Finland, 8849
Great Britain, 9166
Zürich, 9725

Medal of Honor, 9803, 9836

Medallists, 10305

Medical illustrators--SEE: Illustrators, Medical, 11374

Medical research--Biography, 11377

Medicine--Biography--SEE: Physicians, Surgeons, and similar headings.

Mennonites, 10246, 11813

Mercure de France--Indexes, 8864

Merovingians, 8411

Messin, France (Region)--Portraits--Catalogs, 9015

Metal-workers, 12087, 12090

Methodist Church, 11814-11817

Meuse, France (Dept.), 9202

Mexico, 8322, 9469-9483, 10413, 11167-11175, 11179-11781

Mexico--Bibliography, indexes, etc., 9469

Mexico. Secretaría de Hacienda, Crédito Público y Comercio, 9481

Mexico (City), 9476, 11779

Mexico (City). Catedral--SEE: Santa Iglesia Catedral de Mexico, 11779

Michigan, 9898-9901, 10245

Michigan. Legislature, 9898

Middle East--SEE: Near East.

Midlands, Eng., 10142

Midnapore, India (District), 9269

Midwestern Nigeria. Legislature, 9501

Milan, 10161

Military biography (Universal), 8316, 8331-8332, 8355-8356, 8378, 8384, 8388, 8452
Austria, 8551, 8568-8569
Canada, 8636
China, 8711, 8719-8720, 8748
Colombia, 8798
France, 8873, 8881, 8884, 8912-8913, 8921, 8932, 8936, 8944-8947, 8950, 8960, 8966
Germany, 8568, 9086, 9092, 9124
Great Britain, 9164
Italy, 9338-9340, 9350, 9365
Norway, 9508-9509, 9511-9512
Prussia, 9124
Russia, 8332, 9582, 9585, 9588, 9592, 9596-9597
Scotland, 9643
Spain, 9681
Sweden, 9710, 9712
United States, 9776, 9799, 9803, 9836, 9914
Venezuela, 9997

Military chaplains--SEE: Chaplains, Military, 11605

Military engineers, 12069, 12072a

Millenialists, 9147

Milwaukee, 11499

Minas Geraes, Brazil, 8608

Mineralogists, 11902

Miniature painters, 10138

Minims, 11764

Mirandola, Italy, 9381

Missionaries, 11590, 11609,
11614, 11637, 11640, 11677,
11782, 11811-11812, 11832

Mississippi, 9892, 11517

Missouri, 9884-9885, 9902-9903,
9952-9953, 10584, 11500

Młoda Polska, 11191

Modena, 9382

Moldavia, 9484, 11176-11177

Moluccas, 11782

Monaco, 8969

Monograms, 10441

Montana, 11512

Montevideo, 9986

Montpellier, France, 9023,
11432-11433

Montreal, 8669-8671

Montreuil, France, 9040

Moravia, 8806, 8810, 10512,
10555, 11153.

Morbihan, France (Dept.), 9024

Morelia, Mexico, 11171

Mormons, 11818-11819

Mormons--Bibliography, indexes, etc., 11818

Morocco, 9485

Moscow, 9612

Moselle, France (Dept.), 9025

Motel managers, 11987

Motion pictures--SEE:
Moving-pictures.

Mountaineering, 10636

Moving-picture actors and actresses, 10319-10320, 10323,
10331-10332, 10347, 10353,
10357, 10396, 10402, 10408,
10413, 10419, 10423, 10425-
10425a, 10427, 10430-10437
Australia, 10365
Great Britain, 10042
India, 10408
Mexico, 10413
Russia, 10419
Sweden, 10423
United States, 10402, 10425-
10425a, 10427, 10430-
10437

Moving-picture actors and act-
resses--Bibliography, indexes,
etc., 10314

Moving-picture producers and
directors, 10313, 10321-10322

Moving-picture producers and
directors--Bibliography, indexes, etc., 10313

Moving-pictures, 10317-10323,
10325, 10327-10333, 10335-
10337, 10341-10342, 10344-
10347, 10349-10350, 10352-
10353, 10356-10359, 10364-
10365, 10367, 10372-10373,
10375-10377, 10390, 10396,
10402, 10404, 10411-10413,
10415-10416, 10419, 10423-
10425a, 10427, 10429-10437
Asia, 10364
Austria, 10367
Canada, 10372-10373
Czechoslovakia, 10375
Europe, Eastern, 10376
France, 10390
Germany, 10396
Great Britain, 10402, 10404
India, 10364, 10408
Italy, 10411
Japan, 10412
Mexico, 10413
Philippine Islands, 10415
Poland, 10416
Russia, 10419
Sweden, 10423
United States, 10402, 10404,
10424-10425a, 10427,
10429-10437

Moving-pictures--Portraits,
10330-10332, 10342

Mozambique, 9486

Munchen--SEE: Munich, 9116-
9117

Mukden, 9406

Mulhouse, France, 9026

Munich, 9116-9117

Munich. Südlicher Friedhof--SEE:
Südlicher Friedhof, Munich,
9116

Music critics, 10564

Music printers, 11341

Music students, 10588

Musical instrument makers,
10501-10514

Musicians, 10394, 10438-10589
SEE ALSO: Composers, Jazz
musicians, Singers, etc.
Armenia, 10516-10517
Australia, 10518-10520
Austria, 10461, 10521-
10522, 10537
Azerbaijan, 10523
Belgium, 10524
Bohemia, 10461
Canada, 10526-10529, 10551
Colombia, 10530-10531
Czechoslovakia, 10461,
10532
Denmark, 10533
Finland, 10534
France, 10535, 11025
Germany, 10394, 10537-
10539
Great Britain, 10540-10542
Hungary, 10470, 10543
India, 10544-10545
Italy, 10546-10547
Jewish, 10190, 10548-
10549
Korea, 10550
Latin America, 10551-
10552
Latvia, 10553-10554
Missouri, 10584

Musicians (cont'd)
Moravia, 10555
Norway, 10556
Peru, 10557-10559
Poland, 10560
Portugal, 10561
Rhine Valley, 10539
Romania, 10562
Russia, 10563-10565
Scandinavia, 10566
Scotland, 10567
Serbia, 10568
Silesia, 10555
Sweden, 10569
Switzerland, 10537
Tajikistan, 10570
Turkey, 10571-10572
United States, 10551, 10573-
10588
United States--Bibliography,
indexes, 10573-10574
Vienna--Portraits, 10521
Women, 10443, 10573
Women--Bibliography, in-
dexes, etc., 10440

Musicians--Bibliography, indexes, etc., 10438, 10440-10441

Musicians--Portraits, 10442-
10443, 10446, 10474

Musicians--Portraits--Catalogs,
indexes, etc., 10439, 10442

Muskingum Valley, Ohio, 9924

Muslins in India, 9226-9227

Mutazilites, 11842

Mysore, 9270-9273

Mysore. Legislative Assembly--
SEE: Mysore. Legislature.
Legislative Assembly, 9271

Mysore. Legislative Council,
9270

Mysore. Legislature. Legislative Assembly, 9271

Mysore. Legislature. Legislative
Council--SEE: Mysore. Legislative Council, 9270

Mystery story writers--SEE:
Detective and mystery story
writers, 10969, 10982

Nancy, France, 9027

Nantes, France, 10118

Nantes, France (Diocese), 11758

Naples, 9346

Naples (Province), 11772

Napoleon Bonaparte--
Friends and associates, 8954

Nariño, Colombia (Dept.), 10531

Nassau (Duchy), 9118

Natal, 9659

National Hockey League, 10627

Nationalsozialistische Deutsche
Arbeiter-Partei, 9097-9098

Naturalists, 11896, 11898, 11900,
11905

Naval biography (Universal),
8316, 8332, 8366, 8369,
8388, 11996-11997, 11999,
12005
Finland, 8858
France, 8895, 8929, 8936,
11999
Great Britain, 9165
Norway, 9507-9508, 9510
Russia, 8332, 9596
United States, 9837
Venezuela, 9996

Navarre, Spain, 11257

Near East, 9316, 9487-9488

Nebraska, 11516

Negroes--SEE: Afro-Americans
(for Black people in the United
States); Blacks (for Black
people outside the United
States)

Negroes (Afro-Americans)--SEE:
Afro-Americans.

Nepal, 9489-9490

Nersisian·Dprots', 8513

Netherlands, 9491-9495, 10192-
10198, 10288, 10712-10713,
10959, 11152, 11334, 11347,
11463-11464, 11783-11784,
12088

Netherlands--Portraits, 8288,
10713

Netherlands Antilles, 9496

Neuchâtel, Switzerland (Canton)--
Bibliography, indexes, 9723

Neurologists, 11391, 11472

Nevada, 9904

Nevers, France (Diocese), 11752

New Democratic Party (Canada),
9664

New England, 9805, 10295, 11829

New France, 8655

New Guinea, 9516

New Hampshire, 9905-9907,
12048

New Jersey, 11496, 11520, 11803,
12080

New Jersey Pharmaceutical Association, 11496

New Mexico, 9908-9909

New Orleans, 9889

New South Wales, 8539, 8542

New South Wales--Bibliography,
indexes, 8527

New South Wales. Parliament.
Legislative Assembly, 8539

New York (City), 11984

New York (State), 9856-9858, 9910-9912, 9951, 9961, 10826, 11518, 11984, 12089

New York (State)--Portraits, 9857-9858, 9910

New Zealand, 9497-9498, 11358

New Zealand--Portraits, 8544

Newfoundland, 8672

Newgate Prison, London, 9160, 9176

Ngamiland, 8491

Niagara Falls, N. Y., 9857

Nicaragua, 9499

Nicknames, 10743

Nicolet, Quebec (Diocese), 11719

Nièvre, France (Dept.), 9028

Nigeria, 9500-9505

Nigeria--Bibliography, indexes, etc., 9500

Nigeria. House of Representatives, 9505

Nigeria, Midwestern--SEE: Midwestern Nigeria.

Nimes, France, 11028

Nivernais, France, 9028

Nobel Prize, 8425, 10800, 11384

Nobility, 8419, 8556, 8955, 9080, 9158-9159, 9168, 9407, 9435, 9548, 9574, 9640, 9664-9665, 9721
    Austria--Portraits, 8556
    France, 8955
    Germany, 9080, 9435
    Great Britain, 9158-9159, 9168
    Japan, 9407

Nobility (cont'd)
    Moldavia, 9574
    Portugal, 9548
    Romania, 9574
    Scotland, 9640
    Spain, 9664-9665
    Styria--Portraits, 8556
    Switzerland, 9721

Nord, France (Dept.), 9029

Norfolk, Eng., 9183, 9186, 9194-9195

Norfolk, Eng.--Bibliography, indexes, etc., 9194

Normandy, 9030, 11438

Normandy. Parlement--SEE: France. Parlement, Rouen, 8907

Norrköping, Sweden, 9713

North Africa--SEE: Africa, North, 9309

North Carolina, 9913-9917

North Carolina--Bibliography, indexes, etc., 9913

North Vietnam--SEE: Vietnam (Democratic Republic, 1946-), 10001

Northampton, Eng., 9197

Northamptonshire, Eng., 9196-9197

Northern Ireland, 11827

Northern Region of Nigeria, 9504

Northern Region of Nigeria. Legislature, 9504

Northumberland, Eng., 10139, 11342

Northwest, Canadian, 8659

Northwest, Pacific, 9918, 10835

Northwest, Pacific--Portraits--
Catalogs, indexes, 9918

Norway, 8833, 9506-9512, 10556,
11719, 11465-11467, 11811

Norway--Bibliography, indexes,
portrait catalogs, 9506

Norway--Portraits--Catalogs,
9506

Norway. Haeren, 9508-9509,
9511-9512

Norway. Marinen, 8833, 9507-
9508, 9510

Norwegian Lutheran Church of
America, 11812

Norwich, Eng., 9198-9199

Notre-Dame de Port-Royal des
Champs (Abbey of Cistercian
nuns)--SEE: Port-Royal des
Champs (Abbey of Cistercian
nuns), 11761

Nottingham, Eng., 9200

Nottinghamshire, Eng., 9200

Nova Scotia, 8632, 8673

Nürnberg--SEE: Nuremberg,
9119

Nuremberg, 9119

Obituaries (General), 8413, 8470
France, 8949
Germany--Bibliography,
indexes, etc., 9069
Japan, 9410
Virginia--Bibliography,
indexes, etc., 9973

Obituaries--Bibliography, indexes, etc., 9069, 9973

Oblates of Mary Immaculate,
11640

Oborishte, Bulgaria, 8619

Obstetricians, 11442

Occult sciences--Biography,
11532-11533, 11543, 11547,
11553

Oceanica, 8521

Odessa, 9613

Österbotten, Finland, 8850

Österreichischer P.E.N. Club--
SEE: P.E.N. Club. Austria,
10876

Ohio, 9919-9942, 9982, 11332,
11510, 11515

Ohio--Portraits, 9923, 9925

Ohio. General Assembly, 9929

Ohio. State University, Columbus. College of Medicine,
11510

Ohio Valley, 9942

Oise, France (Dept.), 9031

Olympic Games, 10591, 10594,
10596, 10598

Omsk, Siberia (City), 9614

Omsk, Siberia (Province), 9614

Ontario, 8647-8676, 10091, 11305

Oratoire de Jésus-Christ et de
Marie Immaculée, 11638

Orden pour le Merité für Wissenschaften und Künste, 11876

Ordre de Saint-Louis, 8916, 8936

Oregon, 9943, 11331, 11506

Organ-builders, 10501, 10503,
10506-10507

Organists, 10506-10507

Orientalists, 9334, 10649, 10651-
10653, 10658, 10664, 10726

Orientals in the United States, 9807

Orleans, France, 10119

Orne, France (Dept.), 9032

Orthodox Eastern Church, 11820-11821

Orthodox Eastern Church, Russian, 11232, 11821

Osaka, Japan, 9405

Osnabrück, 9120

Osteopaths, 11497

Otolaryngologists, 11398

Outlaws, 8541

Oxford. University, 9152

Oxfordshire, Eng., 9180

Pacific area--Portraits, 8544

Pacific Northwest--SEE: Northwest, Pacific, 9918, 10835

Padua, Italy, 10175

Painters, 10034, 10047-10055, 10057-10061, 10063, 10065-10068, 10070, 10072, 10074, 10078, 10083, 10086, 10093-10098, 10106-10107, 10110, 10116, 10120, 10126, 10130, 10133-10135, 10137, 10141-10142, 10145-10146, 10153, 10157, 10162-10164, 10166, 10168, 10170-10173, 10180, 10182, 10185, 10187, 10189, 10192, 10195-10197, 10199, 10207-10210, 10219-10220, 10222, 10231, 10234, 10238-10239, 10242, 10250, 10253, 10256-10257
    Australia, 10072
    Austria, 10074, 10133
    Basque Provinces, Spain, 10219
    Belgium, 10078
    Bologna, 10164, 10172
    Burma, 10083

Painters (cont'd)
    Canada, 10086-10087
    China, 10096-10098
    China--Bibliography, indexes, etc., 10093-10095
    England, 10139-10140, 10142-10143
    Flanders, 10106-10107, 10192, 10195
    Florence, 10168
    France, 10116, 10120, 10126
    French-Canadian, 10087
    Germany, 10130-10131, 10133
    Great Britain, 10134-10135, 10137-10138, 10141-10142, 10145-10146
    Italy, 10153, 10157, 10162-10164, 10166, 10168, 10170-10173, 10180
    Japan, 10182, 10185, 10187, 10189
    Korea, 10182
    Louisiana, 10257
    Netherlands, 10192, 10195-10197
    Peru, 10199
    Quebec, 10087
    Russia, 10207-10210
    Spain, 10219-10220, 10222
    Switzerland, 10133
    United States, 10231, 10234, 10238-10239, 10242, 10250, 10253, 10256-10257

Pakistan, 9232, 9513-9514, 11286-11288, 11351, 11980, 12065

Palatinate, Ger., 9127

Palestine, 11785

Panama, 9515, 11182

Papua-New Guinea (Territory), 9516

Paraguay, 9517-9518

Paraná, Brazil (State), 8602

Paris, 8880, 8882, 8941, 9033-9036, 11434-11436

Photographers, 12092-12094

Photographers, Women, 12093

Physical educationists, 10637

Physicians, 11359-11523
    Arabic, 11411-11411a
    Argentine Republic, 11412
    Arizona, 11513
    Austria, 11413
    Belgium, 11414
    Brazil, 11415
    Brittany, 11437
    Bulgaria, 11416
    Canada, 11417-11418
    Chile, 11419
    China, 11420-11421
    Croatia, 11422
    Czechoslovakia, 11423
    Finland, 11425-11426
    Flanders, 11414
    France, 8892, 11427-11438
    France--Portraits, 11434-
      11435
    Germany, 11440-11447
    Germany--Portraits, 11443-
      11445
    Great Britain, 11448-11453
    Great Britain--Portraits--
      Catalogs, indexes, etc.,
      11448-11450
    Hungary, 11454
    India, 11455-11457
    Indiana, 11505
    Italy, 11458-11459
    Italy--Bibliography, index-
      es, etc., 11459
    Jewish, 11460-11462
    Jewish--Bibliography, in-
      dexes, etc., 11460-
      11461, 11504
    Latin America, 11485
    Maryland, 11495
    Massachusetts, 11502
    Mississippi, 11517
    Missouri, 11500
    Montana, 11512
    Nebraska, 11516
    Netherlands, 11463-11464
    New Jersey, 11520
    New York (State), 11518
    Normandy, 11438
    Norway, 11465-11467
    Ohio, 11510-11515
    Oregon, 11506
    Paris, 11434-11436

Physicians (cont'd)
    Peru, 11468
    Poland, 11469-11472
    Portugal, 11473
    Prussia, 11446
    Russia, 11474-11476
    Savoy, 11477
    Slovakia, 11478
    South Africa, 11479
    South Carolina, 11519
    Spain, 11480-11487
    Spain--Bibliography, in-
      dexes, 11480
    Sweden, 11488-11489
    Sweden--Portraits, 11488
    Switzerland, 11490
    Texas, 11514
    Transylvania, 11454
    United States, 11491-11520
    United States--Portraits,
      11509, 11515
    United States--Portraits--
      Catalogs, 11491
    Venezuela, 11521-11523
    Virginia, 11493
    Washington, D. C., 11507
    Wisconsin, 11499

Physicians, Homeopathic--SEE:
    Homeopaths, 11373, 11455

Physicians--Bibliography, in-
    dexes, etc., 11359-11368

Physicians--Portraits, 11370,
    11378, 11385, 11388, 11395,
    11403, 11515

Physicians--Portraits--Catalogs,
    indexes, etc., 8273, 11359,
    11361-11364, 11366-11367,
    11386, 11448-11450

Physicists, 11924, 11926, 11928,
    11932-11933, 12023

Physicists--Bibliography, index-
    es, etc., 12023

Physicists--Portraits, 11924

Physiologists, 11384, 11392,
    11406, 11458

Piacenza, Italy, 11109

Piano makers, 10504

Piarists, 11664, 11739

Piceno, Italy, 11132

Piedmont, Italy, 9383, 11354, 12069

Pisa, 9384

Pistoia, Italy, 9385

Pittsburgh, 9950

Placement officers, 11955

Poets, 10776, 10779, 10816, 10824-10825, 10827, 10829, 10837-10838, 10842, 10844, 10853, 10862-10863, 10866-10867, 10871-10872, 10878, 10881-10882, 10890-10894, 10902, 10909, 10912, 10914, 10916, 10918, 10928-10931, 10939-10943, 10968, 10983-10985, 10992-10993, 11013, 11015-11016, 11026, 11029, 11032, 11035, 11060, 11064-11065, 11091, 11126, 11138, 11141, 11151, 11153, 11156, 11182-11184, 11190, 11202-11203, 11205, 11207, 11252, 11273-11275, 11283, 11286-11287, 11431
   Afro-American, 10816
   American, 10816, 10824-10825, 10827, 10829, 10837, 10968, 10985, 10992
   Arabic, 10838, 10842, 10844
   Armenian, 10853
   Austrian, 10862-10863, 10866-10867, 10871-10872, 10878, 10881-10882, 11064
      Tyrol, 10871
   Bolivian, 10890-10892
   Brazilian, 10893-10894

   Canadian (English), 10902
   Chilean, 10909
   Chinese, 10912, 10914, 10916, 10918, 10928-10931

Poets (cont'd)
   Chinese--Bibliography, indexes, 10912, 10914, 10916, 10918
   Colombian, 10939-10941
   Costa Rican, 10942
   Croatian, 10943
   Dutch, 10959

   English, 10968, 10983-10985, 10992-10993
   French, 11013, 11015-11016, 11026, 11029, 11032, 11035, 11431
   German, 11060, 11064-11065
   Hungarian, 11091
   Italian, 11126
   Japanese, 11138
   Jewish--Portraits, 11141
   Latin (Medieval and modern), 11151, 11153
   Latin American, 11156
   Muslim, 10838, 10842, 10844
   Panamanian, 11182
   Persian, 11183-11184
   Polish, 11189
   Provencal, 11202-11203, 11205
   Puerto Rican, 11207
   Spanish, 11252
   Spanish-American, 11156
   Tamil, 11273-11275
   Turkoman, 11283
   Urdu, 11286-11287
   Women, 10825, 10874, 10993

Poitou, France, 9039, 11014

Poland, 9529-9539, 10200-10203, 10416-10417, 10560, 10594, 10716-10717, 11188-11198, 11352, 11469-11472, 11531, 11535, 11786, 11899, 11981, 12004, 12008, 12024, 12032, 12049

Polish-Americans, 9841

Polish-Canadians, 8661

Politeknicheskii institut, Riga, 12025

Printers (cont'd)
    Austria, 11343
    Belgium, 11350   ]
    Bohemia, 11335
    France, 11336, 11344
    Great Britain, 11343, 11355
    Italy, 11354
    Netherlands, 11334, 11347
    Sardinia, 11354
    United States, 11356

Printmakers, 10184, 10223

Prophets, 11557, 11559

Protestant churches (General), 11829-11832

Protestants in France, 11830

Protestants in Spain, 9676

Provence, 9041, 11023, 11202-11205

Provence--Bibliography, indexes, etc., 11202

Provisional Revolutionary Government of the Republic of South Vietnam--SEE: Chinh-phu Cách-mang Lâm-thoi' miên Nam Viêt-Nam, 9998

Prussia, 9114, 9121-9124, 11446

Prussia. Armee, 9122

Prussia, East (Province), 9114, 9123

Psychiatrists, 11391, 11407 11444

Psychiatrists--Portraits, 11391, 11407

Psychical research, 11553, 11555

Psychologists, 11543, 11556

Public administrators, 11938

Publishers, 11345, 11350
    Belgium, 11350

Puebla, Mexico (State), 9475, 11127

Puerto Rico, 9552-9556, 11206-11207

Punjab, 9274-9277

Punjab, India (State). Legislature. Legislative Council, 9275

Pushkin, Aleksandr Sergeevich--Friends and associates, 9613

Puy-de-Dôme, France (Dept.), 9042-9043

Pyrrhus, King of Epirus--Friends and associates, 8373

Quakers--SEE: Friends, Society of, 11803

Quebec (City), 8679

Quebec (Province), 8680-8687, 10278, 11303, 12045-12046

Quebec (Province). Legislature, 8684

Quebec (Province). Legislature. Legislative Assembly, 8681

Quebec (Province). Legislature. Legislative Council, 8685

Queensland, Australia, 8532, 8543, 8549

Queensland, Australia--Bibliography, indexes, 8527

Queensland, Australia. Parliament, 8549

Quezon, Philippines. University of the Philippines, 10715

Quito, Ecuador, 8838

Rabbis, 8846, 9533, 11859-11860

Radio, 10373, 10405

Radiologists, 11925, 11934

Railroads, 11951

Ravenna, Italy, 11120

Reading, Eng., 9201

Reformation, 11595

Reformation--Bibliography, indexes, etc., 9064-9065

Reformed Presbyterian Church of Ireland, 11827

Reims, France, 9044

Religious biography, 11558

Revolutionists, 8442, 8757

Rheinische Friedrich-Wilhelms-Universität zu Bonn--SEE: Bonn. Universität.

Rhine Valley, 9125-9126, 10539, 11766

Rhodesia, 9557-9559

Rhodesia, Northern, 11614

Rhodesia, Southern, 9557

Rhodesia and Nyasaland, 9558

Riga, 9458

Riga. Politeknicheskii institut--SEE: Politeknicheskii Institut, Riga, 12025

Rijksuniversiteit te Leiden--SEE: Leyden. Rijksuniversiteit.

Rinteln. Universität, 10690

Rio Grande do Norte, Brazil (State), 8603

Rio Grande do Sul, Brazil (State), 8612, 8615

Rio Grande do Sul, Brazil (State)--Bibliography, indexes, etc., 8615

Rochester, N. Y., 9951

Rock musicians, 10589

Roman emperors, 9562

Roman Empire, 9208-9209, 9560-9568, 10418, 11866

Roman Empire--Portraits, 9208, 9562, 9567

Roman Empire. Senate, 9565, 9568

Roman priests--SEE: Priests, Roman, 11866

Romania, 9569-9574, 10562, 10718, 11208-11209, 11912-11913

Rome (i.e. the Roman Empire)--SEE: Roman Empire, 9208-9209, etc.

Rome (City), 12079

Rome (City). Pontificio Ateneo antoniano--SEE: Pontificio Ateneo antoniano, Rome, 10710

Rostov on the Don, Russia (Province), 9603

Rouergue, France, 9045, 11747

Royal College of Surgeons of England, 11452

Royal Society of London, 11884

Ruhr Valley, 11964

Rumania--SEE: Romania, 9569-9574, etc.

Russia, 8332, 9575-9623, 10205-10210, 10419-10420, 10563-10565, 10719-10720, 11210-11232, 11325, 11348, 11474-11476, 11887, 11900, 11914, 11917-11918, 11928, 11992, 12002, 12006, 12014, 12019, 12059-12060, 12090

Russia--Armed Forces, 9596

Russia--Bibliography, indexes, etc., 9575

Russia--Portraits, 9581, 9589, 9595

Russia--Revolution (1917-1921), 9576, 9578, 9612, 9615, 10007

Russia. Armiia͡--Portraits, 9581

Russia (1917-   R.S.F.R.). Armiia͡, 8517

Russia (1923-   U.S.S.R.). Armiia͡, 8517

Russia (1923-   U.S.S.R.). Narodnyĭ komissariat po prosveshcheniiu͡, 9580

Russian Orthodox Eastern Church --SEE: Orthodox Eastern Church, Russian, 11232, 11821

Russo-Swedish War (1808-1809), 9710

Ruthenia, 9653

Saar Valley, 9127-9128

Saarland, 9128

Saint-Flour, France (Diocese), 8975

St. Helena, 9624

St. Louis, Mo., 9952-9953

Saint Malo, France, 9046

St. Patrick's Cathedral, Dublin-- SEE: Dublin. St. Patrick's Cathedral, 11627

St. Thomas Christians, 11833

Saints, 11572, 11604, 11610, 11613, 11620-11621, 11634- 11635, 11641, 11652, 11657, 11660, 11663, 11676, 11678, 11683, 11686, 11688-11689, 11691-11696, 11698-11699, 11701-11704, 11709, 11740,

Saints (cont'd)
   11743, 11745-11746, 11748- 11750, 11752, 11754, 11760, 11763, 11767, 11774, 11778, 11786-11787, 11821
   Bavaria, 11767
   Bohemia, 11740
   Egypt, 11610
   France, 11743, 11745-11746, 11748-11750, 11752, 11754, 11760, 11763
   Hindu, 11836
   Italy, 11774
   Japan, 11778
   Muslim, 9330-9331, 11850
   Poland, 11786
   Portugal, 11787
   Russia, 11821

Salamanca. Universidad, 10721

Salentina Peninsula, Italy, 11118

Salesians, 11705

Salisbury, Eng. (Diocese), 11624

Salvador, 9625-9627

Salvador. Asamblea Nacional, 9626

Salzburg, Austria, 8557

San Francisco, 9954-9955

San Marino, 9628

San Salvador--SEE: Salvador, 9625-9627

Sandusky Valley, Ohio, 9939

Sankt Pölten, Austria (Diocese), 11712

Sannio, Italy, 9386

Santa Catarina, Brazil--Por- traits, 8599

Santa Iglesia Catedral de México. Capitulares, 11779

Santander, Colombia, 8797

Wales, 9166, 10003, 10972

Warsaw, 9530, 9534, 10203

Warsaw. Akademia Nauk Technicznych--SEE: Akademia Nauk Technicznych, Warsaw, 12024

Warwickshire, Eng., 9203

Washington, D. C., 11507

Water-color painters, 10137, 10141

Wax modellers, 10279

Weser Valley, Ger., 9096

Wesleyan University, Middletown, Conn., 9843

The West, 9978-9979

West Africa--SEE: Africa, West.

West Africa (Periodical)--Indexes, 8482

West Indies, 10004

West Pakistan, 9513

West Virginia, 9976, 9980-9981

Western Asia--SEE: Asia, Western, 9324

Western Australia, 8534, 8540

Western Reserve, 9982

Westminster Assembly of Divines, 11824

Westphalia, 9126, 9132-9133, 12013a

White Russia, 10005, 11295-11297

Wichita, Kan., 9983

Wiener Zentral-Friedhof, 8563

Williams College, 9850

Wilno--SEE: Vilna.

Wiltshire, Eng., 9204, 10973

Wind instrument makers, 10513

Wind instrument players, 10494, 10565

Wisconsin, 11499

Witwatersrand, 10601

Wolfhagen, Ger., 11804

Women (General), 8327, 8330, 8340, 8351, 8353, 8387, 8420, 8472, 8478, 10443, 10573, 10993
    Afro-American, 9809
    Afro-American--Bibliography, indexes, 9750
    Austria, 10874
    Canada, 8634, 8642-8643, 8649, 8651
    Colombia, 8799
    Finland, 8859
    Florida, 9864
    France, 8931
    Germany, 11050-11069
    Great Britain--Portraits, 9154
    India, 11279
    Italy, 9359, 11103
    Jewish, 9437
    Massachusetts--Portraits--Catalogs, 9896
    Mexico, 9482
    Muslim, 9318, 9329
    Ohio, 9940
    Pennsylvania, 9944
    Spain, 9677
    Texas, 9971
    United States, 9781, 9788, 9794, 9804, 9809, 9815-9816, 9826, 9849, 9864, 9896, 9940, 9944, 9971, 10237
    United States--Bibliography, indexes, etc., 9804, 10573
    United States--Portraits--Catalogs, 9765